CONCISE ENCYCLOPEDIA
OF PHILOSOPHY OF LANGUAGE

CONCISE ENCYCLOPEDIA
OF PHILOSOPHY OF LANGUAGE

Edited by

PETER V. LAMARQUE
University of Hull

Consulting Editor

R. E. ASHER
University of Edinburgh

PERGAMON

UK	Elsevier Science Ltd, The Boulevard, Langford Lane, Kidlington, Oxford OX5 1GB, UK
USA	Elsevier Science Inc, 655 Avenue of the Americas, New York, NY 10010, USA
JAPAN	Elsevier Science Japan, 9-15 Higashi-Azabu 1-chome, Minato-ku, Tokyo 106, Japan

Copyright © 1997 Elsevier Science Ltd

Library of Congress Cataloging in Publication Data
Concise encyclopedia of philosophy of language / edited by Peter V. Lamarque ; consulting editor, R. E. Asher.
    p.   cm.
  ISBN 0–08–042991–2 (hardcover)
  1. Language and languages—Philosophy—Encyclopedias.
I. Lamarque, Peter. II. Asher, R. E.
P106.C5946   1997
401—dc21   97–28781
                                                            CIP

British Library Cataloguing in Publication Data
A catalogue record for this book is available from the British Library.

ISBN 0–08–042991–2 (HC)

#3733l637

∞™ The paper used in this publication meets the minimum requirements of the American National Standard for Information Sciences—Permanence of Paper for Printed Library Materials, ANSI Z39.48–1984.

Printed and bound in Great Britain by BPC Wheatons Ltd, Exeter, UK.

Contents

Contents

Section III: Language and Mind

Section IV: Truth and Meaning

Contents

Section V: Reference

Section VI: Language and Logic

Section VII: Formal Semantics

Contents

Section VIII: Pragmatics and Speech Act Theory

b) 20th Century

Section X: Indexes

Editor's Foreword

At the core of this volume are 80 or so articles I commissioned in the late 1980s and early 1990s for the 10-volume *Encyclopedia of Language and Linguistics (ELL)*, edited by Ron E. Asher (Pergamon, 1994), for which I was the philosophy Subject Editor. These articles were almost exclusively written by professional philosophers and a high proportion by philosophers who are pre-eminent in the subject about which they write. It would be hard to think of better qualified authors than, for example, Tom Baldwin on theories of meaning, Andrew Brennan on identity, Jonathan Cohen on linguistic philosophy, John Cottingham on rationalism, Mark Crimmins on propositions, Martin Davies on modal logic, Alec Fisher on reasoning, Graeme Forbes on necessity, Elizabeth Fricker on Davidson's philosophy, Sam Guttenplan on the history of logic, Susan Haack on deviant logics, Christopher Hookway on Peirce and Quine, Paul Horwich on truth, Jonathan Lowe on universals, Stephen Read on relevant logic, Mark Sainsbury on Russell, Kim Sterelny on reference, Charles Travis on Wittgenstein, Alan Weir on realism, Tim Williamson on vagueness, Andrew Woodfield on intentionality, and many more besides. This broad spread of expertise gave the philosophy entries in *ELL* a well-grounded authority in this area, no doubt contributing to the high respect accorded to the work as a whole.

When I was invited to edit this *Concise Encyclopedia of Philosophy of Language*, drawing on articles from the original encyclopedia, I had a substantial and impressive core to build on. From there it was a matter of scouring the immense resources of *ELL* to supplement the core subject; I was confronted with an *embarras des richesses*. In *ELL*, I had worked closely with the two semantics Subject Editors, Pieter Seuren and Östen Dahl (whose advice and help I take this opportunity to acknowledge with gratitude) and I have helped myself to many of the articles they commissioned, including their own contributions.

However, one serious issue of principle inevitably arose in my process of selection for the *Concise Encyclopedia of Philosophy of Language*: it concerned how narrowly I was to conceive the range of the subject. Even turning to the semantics topics, commissioned by Seuren and Dahl, I found I was for the most part looking at work, not by philosophers as such, but by theoretical linguists. Of course philosophy of language is not the unique preserve of professional philosophers, so that in itself produced no difficulties in principle. In fact, it became increasingly clear to me that there is no sharp line between work done by theoretical linguists and philosophers of language. All share a common interest in foundational questions about meaning, reference, the semantics of natural language, the nature of signs, the distinction between sense and nonsense, the characterization of logical forms, and so on. However, as I expanded my search there was no doubt that I was being tempted beyond even the loose boundary between philosophy of language and other approaches.

I make no apology for succumbing to this temptation. Certainly I have included articles mostly, but not exclusively, of an empirical nature, which would not normally count as contributions to the philosophy of language: for example, the articles on Apes and Language, Pragmatics, Language Acquisition in the Child, Negation, and some of the articles on logical topics. My belief is that these strengthen the volume, not only because they are likely to be of interest to philosophers who are not familiar with such work, but because they open up the wider context within which issues of a more strictly philosophical character are debated. Thus it is that I have included work by psychologists, literary critics, formal logicians, empirical linguists, as well as theoretical linguists and philosophers. Within the constraints of the project I have also attempted to spread the net wider than the confines of so-called analytical philosophy; the inclusion of the fascinating article on Indian Theories of Meaning introduces a different cultural perspective and the articles on Deconstruction and Literary Structuralism reveal different intellectual currents within the Western tradition.

One slight—I think harmless—anomaly in the collection, which directly reflects its origins in a work devoted to language and linguistics, is what might be seen as an imbalance, at times, in favor of linguistics over philosophy. An example of this is in Section IX: **Key Figures**, where philosophers might be surprised to find entries on Noam Chomsky and Ferdinand de Saussure considerably more substantial than those on, for example, Donald Davidson or Saul Kripke. Of course, comparisons of influence are notoriously hard to make and there is no doubt that Chomsky and Saussure are important figures in philosophy of language; but arguably the influence of Davidson and Kripke is as great, if not more so. However, I was not inclined to tinker with the original contributions, certainly not just for the sake of appearance of parity and not if it meant trimming down valuable articles. The articles on Chomsky and Saussure give an immense amount of illuminating detail which directly engages central issues in philosophy of language and the work of Davidson and Kripke (taking only those two examples) is covered elsewhere in the volume.

The fundamental aim of any encyclopedia is to give the readers ready access to basic information on key topics likely to be of interest to them. But there are different kinds of information and different forms of presentation. In this work, articles take different forms and are presented at different levels of technicality, therefore a word about the underlying rationale might be helpful.

First of all, the articles are not merely listed in alphabetical order, but are grouped into sections covering major divisions of the subject: **Language, Metaphysics, and Ontology**; **Language and Mind**; **Truth and Meaning**; **Reference**; **Language and Logic**; **Formal Semantics**; **Pragmatics and Speech Act Theory**; and **Key Figures**. Within each section the articles are arranged alphabetically and there are often cross-references to other items in the section (or elsewhere), perhaps showing where ideas are further expanded. It is hoped that this division will make this encyclopedia easier to use by highlighting clusters of topics and giving some structure to the whole. Needless to say the divisions are not hard and fast and items could often appear under different headings.

Some articles are concerned with particular ideas or specialist terms: for example, A Priori, Category-mistake, Sortal Terms, Analyticity, Holism, Language Game, Entailment, Intentionality, Intuitionism, Ontological Commitment, Verificationism, Radical Interpretation, Type/Token Distinction, De Dicto/De Re, Denotation, and so on. The purpose of these entries is, in a relatively concise way, to explain the meanings of the terms and their place in philosophical debates. The information conveyed is of a straightforward explanatory kind, of especial help to those unfamiliar with this basic philosophical terminology.

Other articles take the form of surveys of an intellectual territory: for example, Meaning: Philosophical Theories, Indian Theories of Meaning, Semiotics, Literary Structuralism and Semiotics, Logic: Historical Survey, Pragmatics, Speech Act Theory, and the introductory article itself on Philosophy of Language. The point of these is to sketch out an area of enquiry, drawing a map on which specific debates are located and contextualized. The articles often involve accounting for the historical development of ideas.

Another kind of survey article tracks, not historically but intellectually, a particular area of contention, perhaps around a problematic concept or hypothesis, perhaps connected to a particular school of thought: for example Deconstruction, Sapir–Whorf Hypothesis, Hermeneutics, Semantic Paradoxes, Metaphor, Metaphor in Literature, Rules, Truth, Deviant Logics, Presupposition, and Semantics vs Syntax. These articles are much more likely to contain polemical discussion, assessing rival positions and staking out a point of view of their own. It is worth drawing attention here to the cluster of articles on Speech Act Theory, written by Keith Allan. Together these provide a comprehensive account of the ideas, debates, and controversies in this important branch of the philosophy of language. The divisions into separate articles are largely for ease of access, although anyone who is unfamiliar with the topic could profitably begin with Speech Act Theory: Overview.

There can be no denying that some articles are technically demanding and will not be readily accessible to those without an adequate background in philosophy and/or symbolic logic. Although for the most part the articles in Section IV: **Language and Logic** do not give particular prominence to technical symbolism, many from Section VII: **Formal Semantics** do. The simple fact is that formal semantics is "formal" in the sense that it uses the vocabulary and methodology of logic to attempt a rigorous characterization of selected features of natural language. The survey article on Formal Semantics gives a general overview of the central aims of this approach, although here too, some technical language is used. Much philosophy of language draws on work in logic. Indeed this is a feature of analytical philosophy in general, of which philosophy of language has been a core component.

Given the presence of these relatively technical articles, it is clear that the intended readership of the volume is diverse, including those already knowledgeable about the subject, seeking to consolidate or build on their knowledge, as well as those looking for basic information or just starting out. Such is the way with most encyclopedias. It is my hope that this work will be useful to a wide range of readers at all levels of expertise. It aims to be as comprehensive as possible in covering the main issues and concepts in the philosophy of language of the 1990s, to be a resource as a reference work, and also a volume to dip into for the intrinsic interest of the subject matter. The extensive bibliographies on each topic point to sources for further research.

As stated previously, earlier versions of all the articles (with the exception of the short article on H.P. Grice) first appeared in the *Encyclopedia of Language and Linguistics*. The contributors were invited to modify, update, and edit their articles and many have produced significant changes, not least to their bibliographies. I would like to thank all the contributors for the speed and efficiency with which they cooperated in this process. I would also like to thank the editorial team at Elsevier, in particular Chris Pringle and Janine Smith, for the considerable time and effort they have put into the project, and the constant support and advice they have given me.

Peter Lamarque
University of Hull
September 1997

SECTION I

Introduction

Philosophy of Language

P. V. Lamarque

Although some of the topics debated within the philosophy of language can be traced back to classical Greek philosophy and the refinements of medieval logic (see Section IX), in fact the label 'philosophy of language' for a distinct branch of the subject did not gain currency until after World War II. Long before then, in the early years of the twentieth century, there had been a clear shift of emphasis in philosophy toward linguistic analysis, which gave a prominence to language within philosophy unprecedented in the eighteenth and nineteenth centuries, but it was not until later that philosophers turned their attention to a systematic study of natural language itself and its foundations. This new inquiry focused on fundamental questions about the nature of meaning, truth, and reference. A convergence of interest developed with theoretical linguistics, spurred on by increasingly sophisticated methods in logic, and the twin areas of semantics and pragmatics came to constitute a central core of analytical philosophy for roughly two decades (the early 1960s to the early 1980s). Since then, to some extent influenced by problems arising from the philosophy of language (on intentionality, propositional attitudes, mental content, thought), there has been a further shift at the center of philosophy toward philosophy of mind, though debate continues on all disputed issues, especially relating to truth and meaning. The main purpose of this introduction is to identify some of the basic areas of contention within philosophy of language and point to the relevant entries in the encyclopedia where they are taken up.

1. The Twentieth-century Origins of Philosophy of Language

Not just any connection between philosophy and language constitutes the subject matter of the philosophy of language. Philosophy in one form or another has always had things to say about language. For example, language (with a sufficiently complex syntactic and generative structure) has been thought to be the distinguishing feature of human beings, a

mark of human rationality; without language there would be no possibility of abstract thought or even perhaps self-reflection. The seventeenth-century philosopher René Descartes emphasized the connection between language and the human intellect. But these general observations about language and human nature to a large extent presuppose the distinctive qualities of language. The philosophy of language, as a more narrowly conceived inquiry, seeks to identify and define precisely what qualities these are, what it is for something to be a language in the first place. Significantly, Noam Chomsky's work on syntactic structures in the 1950s and 1960s led him to reexamine traditional philosophical debates about the 'species-specific' nature of language and the way that language learning has a bearing on fundamental disputes in epistemology. The articles on *Chomsky*, *Rationalism* and *Innate Ideas* follow up that debate. For the historical background of philosophical concerns with language, see the first part of Section IX; several articles in Section II explore the metaphysical and methodological background.

1.1 Philosophy of Language and Linguistic Philosophy

As late as 1969, with the publication of *Speech Acts: An Essay in the Philosophy of Language*, John Searle felt the need to emphasize the difference between the philosophy of language and 'linguistic philosophy,' under the assumption that the latter was much more familiar to his readers. In the 1990s, with linguistic philosophy no longer preeminent, probably the opposite assumption might more reasonably be made; but the fact remains that the two are distinct in important ways. Linguistic philosophy, which had its origins in the logical analysis of Gottlob Frege, Bertrand Russell, Ludwig Wittgenstein, and G. E. Moore at the beginning of the twentieth century, was largely a revolution in *method*, allied to a view about the nature of philosophy. A powerful underlying thought was that philosophical problems—even those of the most traditional kind, about knowledge, ontology, morality, metaphysics—are at a deep level really problems

1

about language and thus that the best way to approach those problems is to analyze the meanings of relevant concepts and propositions; these analyses, so it was claimed, are likely to show either that the problems are spurious or that they can be illuminated by revealing otherwise unnoticed logical or conceptual relations. In contrast to this, philosophy of language is not a kind of method but a kind of *subject matter* (i.e., focusing on language and meaning themselves). Nor does it rest on any polemical view about the nature of philosophical problems. For a closer look at the characteristics of linguistic philosophy, see *Linguistic Philosophy*.

1.2 Logical Analysis and Philosophy of Language

Although philosophy of language is distinct from linguistic philosophy, there is no doubt that many of the problems addressed by philosophers of language can be traced back to problems connected to logical analysis. Indeed Frege, whose principal work was in the foundations of mathematics and in the development of first-order logic, is widely regarded as the father figure of modern philosophy of language. Frege's new logical symbolism for representing different kinds of judgments—universal and existence statements, identities, conditional statements, and so forth—and his adaptation of the mathematical notation of functions, quantifiers, and variables to sentences of natural languages not only revolutionized the representation of logical patterns of inference but made it possible for the first time to provide a truly perspicuous representation of a sentence's *logical form* as distinct from its surface *grammatical form*. At the heart of logical analysis was the search for logical forms. Many of the areas to which the new logic was applied—anaphora, tense, adverbial modification, identity, definite description, propositional attitude verbs, indexicality, modality—and where logical form was a central analytical tool subsequently developed into specialist studies in the philosophy of language. An even more direct link with philosophy of language comes from Frege's work in semantics, which arose out of his more strictly logical studies, in particular his distinctions between sense and reference and between concept and object (Frege, 1952); his conception of thoughts or propositions has also been of seminal importance (a penetrating study of Frege's contribution to philosophy of language is in Dummett, 1973). For further discussion of the philosophical aspects of logical analysis, see *Concepts*; *Entailment*; *Identity*; *Linguistic Philosophy*; *Logic: Historical Survey*; *Logical Form*; *Proposition*; *Singular/General Proposition*.

1.3 Verificationism

Other developments in analytical philosophy also became assimilated into the subject matter of philosophy of language. One of these was the veri-

ficationism connected with logical positivism in the 1930s and 1940s. The 'verification principle' was offered as a criterion of meaningfulness or cognitive significance: only propositions that were empirically testable or analytic were deemed meaningful, the rest (which included large tracts of metaphysics, theology, and ethics) being either purely of 'emotive' value or downright nonsense. Although the aims of the verification principle were basically epistemological (logical positivism was conceived as a linguistic version of classical empiricism), the principle itself clearly embodied a view about meaning.

Versions of verificationism have survived the demise of logical positivism and have reappeared in verificationist (or 'antirealist') semantics. Roughly, the idea is to equate the meaning of a statement not with the conditions under which it would be true, but with the conditions under which it could justifiably be asserted. Michael Dummett is a principal exponent of this doctrine, but his concern is not so much to demarcate the meaningful from the meaningless as to relate meaning to learnability. Understanding, or knowledge, of a language, he argues, must be grounded in linguistic practices, including the making of assertions and denials, without relying on a ('realist') conception of truth which might outrun human recognitional capacities. If this view is right, then philosophy of language must draw significantly on epistemology. Verificationist semantics also has implications for logic itself, involving a rejection of the classical law of excluded middle and the semantic principle of bivalence, which holds that every statement is either true or false. Intuitionistic logic grew up on this basis.

See also Intuitionism; Deviant Logics; Realism; Verificationism.

1.4 Ordinary Language Philosophy

Another offshoot of linguistic philosophy was 'ordinary language philosophy', which flourished for a relatively short period after World War II, principally in Oxford, and under the leadership of J. L. Austin. Again ordinary language philosophy was characterized both by its methodology—a close attention to the nuances and fine distinctions in ordinary usage—and its view of philosophy. But the emphasis that it gave to natural languages, rather than the artificial languages studied by formal logicians, and its rejection of the program of logical analysis (along with notions like 'logical form,' 'canonical notation,' 'regimentation') became a powerful influence in the development of speech act theory, as well as theories of communicative intention, speaker's meaning, implicatures, and so forth, which were at the heart of philosophically inspired pragmatics. Indeed the leading figure in both enterprises—ordinary language philosophy and speech act theory—was Austin himself. A distinctive approach to philosophy of language, characterized by the work of Austin (1962), Strawson (1971), Searle (1969), and perhaps to a lesser degree Grice (1989) (see Sects. 2.2, 2.3 and 2.4 below) developed in Oxford alongside and largely under the influence of ordinary language philosophy. See *Austin, J. L.* and *Ordinary Language Philosophy* for more details.

1.5 The Importance of Wittgenstein

It would be impossible to survey the origins of modern philosophy of language without mentioning Ludwig Wittgenstein. Yet, in spite of being arguably the most important philosopher of the twentieth century to write about language, his influence on leading theories in semantics and pragmatics is comparatively slight. His early work, which culminated in the *Tractatus Logico–Philosophicus* (1921), was closely connected to the program of logical analysis associated with Russell and Frege. Like them he rejected psychologism in logic and sought to establish the fundamental conditions under which a signifying system could represent states of affairs. One of his principal concerns in that work—a concern common also to his later work—was how to draw the boundary between sense and nonsense. He advanced the thesis that is so-called atomic propositions, constituted by simple names whose meanings are logical atoms in the world, *picture* possible or actual states of affairs; all genuinely meaningful complex propositions, he argued, had to be truth-functions of these elementary propositions. Clearly the account is highly idealized and, from the point of view of ordinary applications, puts intolerably severe constraints on meaningfulness.

In his later work, Wittgenstein turned his attention more to natural nonidealized languages and emphasized their 'multiplicity.' Disarmingly, in the *Philosophical Investigations* (1953), he insisted that it was not the job of philosophers to offer *theories* of any kind, and thus not theories of meaning, though his famous dictum 'the meaning of a word is its use in the language,' along with his other often highly complex observations about the foundations of language, have led commentators to try to reconstruct a theory of meaning from his writings (Kripke 1982; McGinn 1984; Travis 1989). Much attention has focused on his discussion of rule-following, particularly as it bears on arguments against the possibility of private language, and the postulation, in the later work, of 'language-games' as determiners of sense. Also of importance is his rejection of the idea that general terms must be defined through necessary and sufficient conditions, a criticism embodied in the idea of 'family resemblance.' Detailed examinations of Wittgenstein's views on language can be found in different articles, notably *Wittgenstein, Ludwig*; *Picture Theory of Meaning*; *Language Game*; *Family Resemblance*; *Private Language*; *Rules*.

2. Meaning

If Wittgenstein's ideas have not fed directly into contemporary semantics, it might be partly due to his antipathy to theory and his disinclination to generalize from his observations about language. No such disinclination has constrained other theorists of meaning. Broadly speaking, it is possible to discern two kinds of approaches taken by philosophers to the analysis of meaning: one takes *truth* to be fundamental, including the conditions under which a sentence is true or false, the other takes *intention* to be fundamental, giving priority to the role of communication. The issue of controversy lies not in the choice between truth-conditions or communicative-intentions in an account of meaning, for it is far from clear that they are in opposition; rather it is the claim that one is more fundamental than the other. A compromise suggestion (though not one that would be universally accepted) might be that the emphasis on truth highlights the *semantic* aspects of language, viewed as those aspects concerned with the representation of (states of) the world; while the emphasis on intention highlights *pragmatic* aspects, viewed as those concerned with communicative exchanges in context. The question of the priority, or basicness, of one with regard to the other was raised in P. F. Strawson's inaugural lecture at Oxford 'Meaning and Truth' (in Strawson 1971); Strawson argued that the notion of truth-conditions cannot be explained without reference to the function of communication, so the latter is more fundamental. (For an analytic account of different theories of meaning in the philosophical tradition see *Meaning: Philosophical Theories*.) It is instructive to compare these approaches with those of a different cultural tradition, cf. *Indian Theories of Meaning* and a different intellectual tradition, cf. *Deconstruction*.

2.1 Meaning and Truth-conditions

Truth-conditional theories of meaning draw partly on the intuition that the meaningfulness of language resides in its ability to represent how things are in the world and partly on advances in logic in describing the semantics of formal or artificial languages. From the latter came the thought that an ideal semantic theory is one that specifies the meaning (i.e., truth-conditions) of every sentence of a language as a theorem derived from a formal axiomatized theory, where the axioms of the theory assign semantic properties to the component expressions of those sentences.

Donald Davidson (1984) pioneered this approach in application to the semantics of natural languages, explicitly drawing on the formal work of Tarski (1956). Rejecting the format *sentence s means that p* for the theorems of the semantic theory, Davidson argues instead for the Tarskian formula *sentence s is true if and only if p*. However, it would be wrong to suppose that Davidson simply defines meaning as truth-conditions and leaves it at that. The interest of his account lies in the way he applies the insights of the idealized semantics (of artificial languages) to actual languages. Sentences of actual languages, unlike those of artificial languages, already have applications to objects and states of affairs in the world and this imposes an empirical constraint on the acceptability of the theorems of the semantic theory.

To develop this idea Davidson follows Quine (1960) in postulating a fictional situation of an interpreter attempting to translate a native language totally unknown to him, spoken by people about whom he knows nothing. This is the situation of 'radical interpretation.' The radical interpreter's task is to assign truth-conditions to native sentences without presupposing an understanding of them. This can only be done by observing the linguistic and other behavior of the native people and attempting to correlate sentences (utterances) with salient features of the occasions of their utterance. The overall aim is to be in a position to issue reliable formulas of the kind *sentence s is true if and only if p*. Of course several assumptions are required for this: one is that speakers intend to speak the truth and believe that what they say is true, another is that their sentences actually are true, for the most part. The former is a general assumption of rationality, the latter a 'principle of charity,' as Davidson describes it. These assumptions play a profound role in Davidson's epistemology and philosophy of mind and have been widely debated (e.g., Grandy 1973; Evans and McDowell 1976). For Davidson, attributing beliefs to speakers and meanings to the sentences they utter are closely interconnected. Although he holds that sentence meaning cannot be reduced to nonsemantic concepts (like belief or intention) he does suggest that the constraints on radical interpretation provide the best available philosophical elucidation of meaning.

One of Davidson's initial principles in developing a theory of meaning is the innocuous sounding dictum that 'the meanings of sentences depend upon the meanings of words.' The principle is important for a number of reasons. If a language is to be learnable, the stock of words in the language—its vocabulary—must be finite; thus there can only be a finite number of axioms specifying the meanings of these basic components. Also, the principle articulates what many have seen as a fundamental premise in semantics, the compositionality of meaning, which has been more precisely formulated as follows: 'The meaning of a compound expression is a function of the meanings of its parts and of the syntactic rules by which they are combined' (see *Compositionality of Meaning*). The compositionality principle lies at the foundation of attempts to provide a formal semantics (see *Formal Semantics*) for natural language and is especially prominent in the work of Richard Montague (see

Montague Grammar). However, it is by no means unproblematic; semantic primitives have to be identified and classified, they have to be assigned meanings, which must not be dependent on the meanings of whole sentences, combinatorial rules have to be defined, and so on. The idealized artificial languages of logic hold out a tempting model for how this might be achieved, and how it might look, but in application even to fragments of natural language the difficulties are formidable.

One issue that has been much debated in the context of Davidson's semantic theory concerns the implications for what a competent speaker knows in knowing a language. In principle such a speaker knows the meaning of any given sentence from a potentially infinite set which can be generated by the language. As we have seen, Davidson takes it as a constraint on the learnability of a language that a 'theory of meaning,' in his sense, be finitely axiomatized, though that has been challenged by Schiffer (1987). The question remains as to the explanatory value of a semantic theory of which competent speakers have no conscious knowledge (the same problem arises for syntactic theories (Chomsky 1986)). One suggestion is that the knowledge is *tacit* (Evans 1985), another that semantic theories are *rational reconstructions* (Wright 1986).

2.2 Meaning and Communicative Intention

The question of what speakers know who know a language invites a deeper inquiry into the very basis of linguistic meaning. While formal semantic theories—at least those of a broadly *compositional* nature—attempt to assign meanings to sentences on the basis of the meanings of their component parts, a rather different philosophical enterprise is to try to explain what kind of fact it is, about people's behavior, mental states, the life of a community, etc., that makes it true that a word or expression or sentence has the meaning it does, or indeed has any meaning at all. It is questions of this kind that concerned Wittgenstein and also Quine, the latter developing an essentially skeptical view, on a behavioristic base, to the effect that what facts there are radically underdetermine hypotheses about meaning (see *Indeterminacy of Translation*).

Perhaps the most systematic attempt to explain meaning in nonsemantic terms comes from the program of H. P. Grice (1957, 1968, 1969; and others collected in 1989), developed by Schiffer (1972), Bennett (1973, 1976), Strawson (1964), and Searle (1969, 1983). Grice began by distinguishing 'nonnatural meaning' from 'natural meaning,' the latter, which he identifies only to set aside, being of the kind *Those clouds mean rain*. Linguistic meaning, Grice argues, belongs in the genus of nonnatural meaning which includes a wide range of communicative behavior. The bedrock for Grice's account of nonnatural meaning is an analysis of the conditions which make it true that a person *means something by an utterance* (where 'utterance' covers signs, gestures, marks, or spoken sounds). What is involved, according to Grice, is a complex intention, directed toward an audience, that the utterance *bring about a certain response in the audience by means of the recognition of that intention*. A great deal of subtle revision and qualification has ensued, mostly about the nature of the intended response (usually explained in terms of belief) and the need for further audience-directed intentions, but the basic analysis remains. Grice's project is to move from an analysis of *Someone meant something by uttering X* to *X meant something* to *X means (in a language) that p*. The idea, in short, is to ground semantics in psychological states such as intention (and belief).

The program faces considerable difficulties. How can the full complexities of linguistic meaning be explained on so slender a basis? One obvious problem concerns the role of *convention*. Standardly, so it would seem, the recognition of a speaker's meaning-intention is at least partly based on recognition of the conventional meaning of the sentence uttered by the speaker. But that threatens circularity in the Gricean account. However, David Lewis (1969) has presented an analysis of convention which, at least by not presupposing linguistic meaning, offers an important supplement to the intentionalist analysis. Lewis explains convention in terms of a regularity of behavior in a group to which members of the group conform so as to bring about a coordination equilibrium, based on the common knowledge that everyone prefers to conform on condition that the others do. Much ingenuity has been exercised (Lewis 1969; Bennett 1976; Blackburn 1984) in trying to apply this kind of convention to linguistic meaning, for example by postulating conventional correlations between utterances or utterance-types and specific beliefs and intentions. However, persistent objections center on the difficulty for this view in accounting for the compositionality of semantics and the fact that natural languages can generate an infinity of unuttered sentences. An early exponent of Grice's theory believes (Schiffer 1987) that the whole program is doomed to failure, though that can hardly be claimed as the last word on the matter. For more details, see *Grice, H. P.*; *Convention*; *Meaning: Philosophical Theories*.

Pursuing the enquiry into conditions of communication, philosophers of language came to examine those aspects of meaning which go beyond semantic content encoded in sentences. This has issued in two important developments: speech act theory and the theory of implicature, both of which are commonly located within the pragmatics of language. (For a comprehensive general survey of the scope of pragmatics, from the point of view of linguistics as well as philosophy, see *Pragmatics*.)

2.3 Speech Acts

Speech act theory originated with J. L. Austin's analysis of performative utterances—such as *I promise to pay, I pronounce you man and wife*—the assessment of which, he proposed, should be determined not by truth-conditions but by felicity-conditions (appropriateness, sincerity, background context, intention, etc.). Austin (1962) came to see, though, that even statements, the paradigm truth bearers, could be assessed in terms other than just their truth: in particular as *actions* of a certain kind. He introduced a threefold distinction among speech acts: locutionary acts (acts *of* saying something, with a sense and reference), illocutionary acts (such as stating, promising, warning, performed *in* saying something), and perlocutionary acts (such as persuading, convincing, annoying, amusing, performed *by* saying something). Austin's early death meant that he was not able to refine the theory in detail, though he did offer a rudimentary taxonomy of illocutionary acts. The theory was, however, developed by, among others, Searle (1969, 1979), Strawson (1964), who attempted to assimilate speech acts into Grice's analysis of speaker's meaning, and Holdcroft (1978).

The relation between meaning and speech acts (especially illocutionary acts) has never been clear or uncontroversial. At the extreme, some (e.g., Cohen 1964) have dismissed 'illocutionary force' altogether, incorporating the idea of 'force' into a wider theory of semantic content. Others, following an initial insight from Frege about assertion, have wanted a clear demarcation between the *force* of an utterance and its *content* or thought expressed. Yet others, like Searle (1969), propose to explain meaning, and ultimately language itself, in terms of speech acts. Searle introduces the 'propositional acts' of referring and predicating, thereby extending the theory into the heart of traditionally conceived semantics. He sees as a fundamental task for the philosopher of language the elucidation of *constitutive rules* governing the full range of speech acts.

The encyclopedia contains extensive coverage of all aspects of speech act theory (in Section VIII); see *Speech Act Theory: Overview*; *Speech Act Classification*; *Speech Act Hierarchy*; *Speech Acts and Grammar*; *Speech Acts: Literal and Non-Literal*; *Felicity Conditions*; *Indirect Speech Acts*; *Performative Clauses*.

2.4 Implicatures

A general problem for any philosophical theory of meaning is how to account for those instances of communication where more than, or something different from, the information semantically encoded in a sentence is conveyed. Irony, figuration, and hyperbole are familiar examples and meaning shifts associated with intonational contour, stress pattern, and so forth, are well charted. But it was not until Grice's theory of conversational implicatures, developed in his William James Lectures of 1967, that any systematic attempt was made to identify principles underlying the whole class of phenomena of this supposedly nonsemantic kind.

Grice (1989) proposes a distinction between (a) *what is said* in an utterance, as determined by the semantic properties of the words uttered, (b) *what is conventionally implicated*, those implications which although not strictly semantic can nevertheless be drawn from the conventional meanings of the words, and (c) *what is conversationally implicated*, those implications which arise not from conventional meaning but from certain general features of discourse.

Imagine the following exchange, drawn from Grice's discussion:

A. I am out of petrol.
B. There is a garage round the corner.

According to Grice, there is a conversational implicature in B's reply that B thinks the garage has petrol, is open, etc., even though that is not strictly part of what B said, nor a consequence of the meanings of the words. Grice suggests that such implicatures arise from a tacitly accepted 'cooperative principle' governing conversation, in conjunction with conversational maxims of the kind *be as informative as is required, say only what you take to be true, be relevant, be perspicuous*. Conversational implicatures characteristically arise where these maxims appear to have been flouted but have not in fact been flouted; on the basis of that assumption a hearer is forced to construe the utterance (what the speaker intended) such that it conforms to the cooperative principle.

Two prominent applications for the idea of conversational implicatures have been to the meaning of logical connectives and to presuppositions. Grice (1989) seeks to explain the apparent divergences between the truth-functional definitions of the logical particles (&, $\vee$, $\supset$, $\sim$) and the meanings of *and, or, if ... then,* and *not* by appeal to implicatures. His general strategy is to relocate the distinctive features of the natural language particles from semantic content to pragmatic conditions of context-based speech. Thus, for example, the temporal connotation of *and* (with the implication *and then*) is not, he argues, part of the semantics of *and* but arises from the orderliness of discourse. The second application, to presupposition theory, is associated with a more general program to define presuppositions independently of truth-conditions. A standard account of presupposition is that if *p* presupposes *q* then *q* is a necessary condition for the truth-or-falsity of *p* and the negation of *p* also presupposes *q*. A radical proposal is to supplant this conception and explain the phenomena to which it is standardly applied with the twin notions of logical entailment and conversational implicature (see Kempson 1975). This serves, as in the

case of the logical particles, to sustain a relatively uncomplicated truth-conditional semantics. Needless to say, these proposals remain highly controversial and face serious difficulties in their implementation. For an indication of some of the difficulties and further applications, see Davis (1991).

Philosophers of language have explored other linguistic phenomena whose location within the pragmatics/semantics axis is problematic. One such is *metaphor* (see *Metaphor*), which has been the subject of more or less every standard approach, from truth-conditional semantics to speech acts to pragmatic implicatures (Ortony 1979). Another is *fictionality*, which can be viewed either as a kind of utterance, subject to speech act conditions (Searle 1979), or as a degenerate case of reference (Donnellan 1974), or indeed in other ways besides.

For more detail on Grice's theory of implicature, see *Grice, H. P.*; *Conversational Maxims*; *Cooperative Principle*. On presupposition theory, see *Presupposition* and *Presupposition, Pragmatic*. Also *Metaphor*; *Fiction, Logic of*.

3. Reference

The final major area of concern within philosophy of language is *reference* in its many forms. One issue which reflects, though is not entirely coincident with, the debate between semantics and pragmatics is whether reference is best understood as a relation between symbols and objects or between speakers, objects, and hearers. According to the latter view, it is speakers who refer to things, while in the former it is expressions in a language which refer (or denote).

3.1 Definite Descriptions

This issue is most famously associated in philosophy of language with the debate over Russell's Theory of Definite Descriptions. According to Russell, definite descriptions of the kind *the father of Charles II* or *the fastest man on earth* should not be treated logically as naming expressions but rather as 'incomplete symbols,' which acquire meaning only in the context of a proposition and can be contextually paraphrased such that in a fully analyzed sentence they give way to quantifiers and predicates. Thus the sentence *The father of Charles II was executed* analyzes into *There is one and only one person who begot Charles II and that person was executed*. Russell's account was praised as a 'paradigm of logical analysis' and indeed it neatly solved several problems for the formal representation of referring expressions, not least by showing how meaningfulness could be retained for sentences containing definite descriptions which failed to refer (*the present King of France*, and so on). However, it came under attack, notably by P. F. Strawson (see essays in Strawson 1971), for treating reference as a property of expressions rather than as something that speakers perform in an utterance characteristically for the purpose of identifying an object. For Strawson, when a definite description fails to apply to anything a basic *presupposition* for successful communication has failed and no truth-value can be assigned to the resulting assertion (Russell had given the value *false* to sentences with failed references). Strawson's analysis was contributory to the enormous subsequent interest in presupposition. Donnellan (1966), pursuing the idea of reference as grounded in contexts of utterance, argued that there are at least two fundamental uses of definite descriptions which he called *referential* and *attributive*, the latter being somewhat akin to Strawson's conception, but the former, controversially, giving definite descriptions a role more like that of proper names. (For an account of this highly influential theory, and its ramifications, see *Names and Descriptions*; *Russell, Bertrand*; *Identity*.)

3.2 Proper Names

Russell and Wittgenstein (in his early work) developed the idea of a 'genuine' or 'logically' proper name the sole function of which is to denote a single and simple object, such that the object itself constitutes the meaning of the name (if there were no such object the name would be meaningless). Both were constrained by the search for an ideal logical language. In contrast, Frege argued that even in an ideal language denotation by means of a proper name must be mediated by something he called *Sinn* (sense). Philosophers of language have long debated the merits of these opposing views, and versions of them have proliferated. Even Russell admitted that his conception of a logically proper name did not fit ordinary proper names in natural languages (*Socrates*, *London*, etc.), which he took to be 'truncated descriptions' analyzable according to the Theory of Descriptions. However, Saul Kripke (1972) and others have attempted to revive something like the pure denotation view applied to ordinary proper names, rejecting both Fregean *Sinn* and Russell's 'descriptivism.' This has led to so-called 'causal theories' of names, where what determines the reference of a name is not the 'mode of presentation' embodied in the name's sense or whatever object satisfies an implied description but rather a direct causal link back to the object initially 'baptized' with the name (see Devitt and Sterelny 1987). In Kripke's terminology names are 'rigid designators,' in the sense that they designate the same object in all possible worlds where the object exists. Definite descriptions do not designate rigidly because in different possible worlds different objects will satisfy the descriptions. Versions of causal theories are probably in the ascendancy, though increasingly sophisticated accounts attempt to reassimilate something like Fregean sense (see Moore, 1993). Searle (1983) presents a powerful case against causal theories, locating reference in the philosophy of mind and arguing for the central place of *intentionality* in an account of language (see *Intentionality*).

3.3 Indexicals

One particularly perplexing class of referential devices are indexical expressions (e.g., *I*, *here*, *now*, *this*, etc.) whose reference or extension is determined by context of utterance. The reference of 'I' changes from person to person, *It is late now* changes truth-value when uttered at different times, and so forth. Once again it was Frege who set up the modern debate by proposing that sentences containing indexicals do not express a 'complete thought' until supplemented by indications of time, place, and other contextual determinants; while sentences contain indexical terms, thoughts (i.e., propositions) do not, for thoughts, if true, are timelessly true. Other philosophers have attempted by different strategies to eliminate indexicals. Perhaps the most systematic and widely regarded modern treatment is by David Kaplan (1989). An important distinction drawn by Kaplan, which has applications and consequences elsewhere in philosophy of language, is between two aspects of sense: 'content' and 'character.' The character of an expression such as 'I' is most naturally associated with its 'meaning,' conceived as a rule which roughly identifies the use of 'I' to refer to the speaker. Its content is given only relative to a context of use and is associated with *what is said* in that context: for Kaplan, when two people use the sentence *I am tired* in different contexts not only will the truth-value be affected but the content will differ also. Kaplan's conception of indexicals as 'directly referential,' not mediated by Fregean sense, places him broadly in the same camp as the 'causal theorists' of reference. The article *Indexicals* explores philosophical approaches (notably Kaplan's), while *Deixis* presents the issues from the perspective of theoretical linguistics.

3.4 Natural Kind Terms

There is one further area where the distinction between sense and reference has come under pressure and where debate closely parallels that between descriptivists and causal theorists: this concerns the meaning of certain kinds of general terms, such as *lemon*, *tiger*, *gold*, *water*, which, reviving scholastic vocabulary, are said to stand for 'natural kinds'. On one view, stemming from Locke, the meaning of such terms is given by specifying salient properties of the natural kinds in question: 'a yellow citrus fruit with a bitter taste...,' and so on. This meaning will then determine the reference (extension) of the term, in the sense that the term will have in its extension, by definition, all those things which satisfy the description. However, the very foundations of this view have come under attack, principally by Hilary Putnam and Kripke. Putnam (1975) argues that natural kind terms should be treated as rigid designators whose extension is determined not by clusters of descriptions but by the very structure of nature, as investigated by science. The initial application of a term—parallelling the initial 'baptism' of an object by a proper name, on Kripke's account—is done by 'ostension' (or deixis): names are attached to stereotypical samples which are pointed at or have their reference fixed by a small set of experiential properties. But the observed properties of the stereotype are not incorporated into the *meaning* of the term, indeed it might turn out that the natural kind has none of the properties *essentially* that are experienced in the stereotype (science might reveal that it is not essential to being a lemon that it is either yellow or bitter). In this way Putnam's theory is *realist* (see *Realism*) and *antiverificationist*, in that the existence of natural kinds is independent of the experiences on which humans base their claims about them. Although Putnam has significantly modified his realist theory, his work has been enormously influential in philosophy of language, especially among those who pursue naturalized accounts of meaning and who seek to extend the underlying insights of causal theories of reference (e.g., Devitt and Sterelny, 1987). For a detailed account of naturalized semantics and causal theories of natural kind terms, see *Reference, Philosophical Issues*.

3.5 Truth

The concept of truth underlies nearly all investigations in philosophy of language, certainly those concerned with both meaning and reference. Section 2.1 showed how meaning is sometimes elucidated through appeal to truth-conditions. Within Fregean semantics truth-values stand to sentences rather as objects stand to names; just as the sense of a name determines its reference so the thought a sentence expresses determines its truth-value. But when the focus turns on truth itself, philosophers of language have a number of principal interests: the first is to account for the meaning of the truth predicate 'is true,' another is to identify appropriate truth-bearers, and a third addresses the paradoxes associated with truth.

One longstanding debate about the meaning of 'is true' centers on whether the predicate is logically *redundant*: an influential view is that *the statement that snow is white is true* is identical to *the statement that snow is white*. Various 'minimalist' theories of truth—theories that reject as unnecessary such substantive elucidations as given in traditional 'correspondence' or 'coherence' accounts—have been at the forefront of debate in the 1990s (Horwich 1990) though they are by no means unchallenged (Blackburn 1984). The debate is outlined in *Truth*.

What are the appropriate subjects of the truth-predicate? Many candidates have been offered, and not only linguistic ones: beliefs, thoughts, and judgments have all been designated truth-bearers. So also have sentences, statements, and propositions. Most sentences—for example, all those containing indexical expressions—can be assigned truth-values only relative to contexts. Statements are contenders for truth-

assessment precisely when viewed as contextualized uses of sentences, though an ambiguity in the term *statement* makes it unclear whether an *act* of stating can be true or false or only *what is stated* (the content) (Strawson 1971). Finally, the most traditional truth-bearer is thought to be a *proposition*, considered as an abstract, even timeless, entity expressed by sentences and corresponding roughly to the meaning of a sentence in context. A great deal of controversy surrounds the idea of a proposition and different conceptions have been developed with more or less commitment to abstract entities (see the discussion in *Proposition*; also *Singular/General Proposition*).

Semantic paradoxes (see *Paradoxes, Semantic*) have long been associated with truth, the oldest being the liar paradox which, in its standard version, asks for the truth-value of *This sentence is false*: seemingly, if the sentence is true, then it must be false, if false, then it must be true. Within philosophy of language the problem has been addressed both in connection with formalized languages (Tarski 1956) but also within the semantics of natural language. (Different strategies are outlined in *Paradoxes, Semantic* and *Truth and Paradox*; see also *Formal Semantics*; *Metalanguage versus Object Language*; *Deviant Logics*.)

4. Conclusion

This article has addressed only a selection of topics within the philosophy of language centered on the key areas of meaning and reference, broadly conceived, along with certain issues on the relationship between semantics and pragmatics. Each of the topics has its own subtle ramifications and developments, and there are many more topics besides which philosophers would want to classify within this important branch of the subject; see, for example, *Analyticity*; *Concepts*; *Emotive Meaning*; *Identity*; *Innate Ideas*; *Intensionality*; *Natural Deduction*; *Ontological Commitment*; *Private Language*; *Vagueness*. While it is common to think of philosophy as dealing with *conceptual* or *a priori* questions, in contrast to linguistics conceived as an *empirical* inquiry, in fact that distinction between the disciplines is by no means clear-cut. For one thing, philosophers are increasingly sensitive to work in related empirical fields and draw on it substantially (philosophers, of course, like other students of language, also draw on their own linguistic intuitions), but within theoretical linguistics work is sustained at no less a conceptual level than found in philosophy. There is no doubt that in some areas—formal semantics, the theory of implicature, quantification theory, indexicality, anaphora, and so forth—there is commonality of approach between philosophers and theoretical linguists. But in other areas—perhaps in the theory of reference or in approaches to truth or questions of intentionality and propositional attitudes—philosophers do have a distinct contribution, at a foundational level, to an understanding of natural language. Undoubtedly, quite remarkable advances have been made since Frege took the first significant steps in modern philosophy of language in the late nineteenth century.

Bibliography

Austin J L 1962 *How to Do Things with Words*. Clarendon Press, Oxford

Bennett J 1973 The meaning-nominalist strategy. *Foundations of Language* 10: 141–68

Bennett J 1976 *Linguistic Behaviour*. Cambridge University Press, Cambridge

Blackburn S 1984 *Spreading the Word: Groundings in the Philosophy of Language*. Clarendon Press, Oxford

Chomsky N 1986 *Knowledge of Language: Its Nature, Origin and Use*. Praeger, New York

Cohen L J 1964 Do illocutionary forces exist? *Philosophical Quarterly* 14: 118–37

Davidson D 1984 *Inquiries into Truth and Interpretation*. Clarendon Press, Oxford

Davis S (ed.) 1991 *Pragmatics: A Reader*. Oxford University Press, Oxford

Devitt M, Sterelny K 1987 *Language and Reality: an Introduction to the Philosophy of Language*. Basil Blackwell, Oxford

Donnellan K 1966 Reference and definite descriptions. *Philosophical Review* 75: 281–304

Donnellan K 1974 Speaking of Nothing. *Philosophical Review* 83: 3–32

Dummett M 1973 *Frege: Philosophy of Language*. Duckworth, London

Dummett M 1978 *Truth and Other Enigmas*. Clarendon Press, Oxford

Evans G 1985 Semantic theory and tacit knowledge. In: Evans G *Collected Papers*. Oxford University Press, Oxford

Evans G, McDowell J 1976 *Truth and Meaning: Essays in Semantics*. Clarendon Press, Oxford

Frege G 1952 *Translations from the Philosophical Writings of Gottlob Frege*. Basil Blackwell, Oxford

Grandy R 1973 Reference, meaning and belief. *Journal of Philosophy* 70: 439–52

Grice H P 1957 Meaning. *Philosophical Review* 66: 377–88

Grice H P 1968 Utterer's meaning and intentions. *Philosophical Review* 78: 147–77

Grice H P 1969 Utterer's meaning, sentence-meaning and word-meaning. *Foundations of Language* 4: 1–18

Grice H P 1989 *Studies in the Way of Words*. Harvard University Press, Cambridge, MA

Hacking I 1975 *Why Does Language Matter to Philosophy?* Cambridge University Press, Cambridge

Holdcroft D 1978 *Words and Deeds*. Clarendon Press, Oxford

Horwich P G 1990 *Truth*. Basil Blackwell, Oxford

Kaplan D 1989 Demonstratives: an essay on the semantics, logic, metaphysics, and epistemology of demonstratives and other indexicals. In: Almog J, Perry J, Wettstein H (eds.) *Themes From Kaplan*. Oxford University Press, Oxford

Kempson R 1975 *Presupposition and the Delimitation of Semantics*. Cambridge University Press, Cambridge

Kripke S 1972 Naming and necessity. In: Davidson D, Harman G (eds.) *Semantics of Natural Language*. Reidel, Dordrecht

Kripke S 1982 *Wittgenstein on Rules and Private Language*. Basil Blackwell, Oxford

Lewis D 1969 *Convention*. Harvard University Press, Cambridge, MA

Martinich A P (ed.) 1990 *The Philosophy of Language*. Oxford University Press, New York

McGinn C 1984 *Wittgenstein on Meaning*. Basil Blackwell, Oxford

Moore A W (ed.) 1993 *Meaning and Reference*. Oxford University Press, Oxford

Neale S 1990 *Descriptions*. MIT Press, Cambridge, MA

Ortony A 1979 *Metaphor and Thought*. Cambridge University Press, Cambridge

Putnam H 1975 *Mind, Language and Reality: Philosophical Papers*, vol. 2. Cambridge University Press, Cambridge

Quine W V O 1960 *Word and Object*. MIT Press, Cambridge, MA

Russell B 1905 On Denoting. *Mind* 14: 479–93

Russell B 1919 *Introduction to Mathematical Philosophy*. George Allen and Unwin Ltd, London

Searle J R 1969 *Speech Acts: An Introduction to the Philosophy of Language*. Cambridge University Press, Cambridge

Searle J R 1979 *Expression and Meaning*. Cambridge University Press, Cambridge

Searle J R 1983 *Intentionality*. Cambridge University Press, Cambridge

Schiffer S 1972 *Meaning*. Oxford University Press, Oxford

Schiffer S 1987 *The Remnants of Meaning*. MIT Press, Cambridge, MA

Strawson P F 1964 Intention and convention in speech acts. *Philosophical Review* 73: 439–60

Strawson P F 1971 *Logico-Linguistic Papers*. Methuen, London

Tarski A 1956 The concept of truth in formalized languages. In: *Logic, Semantics, Metamathematics*. Clarendon Press, Oxford

Travis C 1989 *The Uses of Sense*. Clarendon Press, Oxford

Wittgenstein L 1953 *Philosophical Investigations*. Basil Blackwell, Oxford

Wittgenstein L 1961 (transl. Pears D, McGuinness B) *Tractatus Logico-Philosophicus*. Routledge and Kegan Paul, London

Wright C 1986 *Realism, Meaning and Truth*. Basil Blackwell, Oxford

Wright C, Hale R (eds.) 1997 *A Companion to the Philosophy of Language*. Blackwell, Oxford

SECTION II
Language, Metaphysics, and Ontology

A Priori

E. J. Lowe

The notion of the 'a priori' has its primary application in the field of epistemology, where it is standardly used to characterize a species of propositional knowledge (knowledge that p, where p is a proposition) and, derivatively, a class of propositions or truths, namely, those that are knowable a priori (though strictly this way of classifying propositions should be relativized to a type of knowing subject, the usual presumption being that human subjects are in question). In a related usage, certain concepts are sometimes classified as a priori, namely, those that figure as substantive constituents of a priori truths.

1. A Priori Knowledge

Knowledge is said to be a priori (literally: prior to experience) when it is knowledge which does not depend for its authority upon the evidence of experience. This is not the same as saying that it is knowledge which is acquired independently of experience, whether because it is innate knowledge or because it is knowledge learned without the substantive contribution of experience (for instance, knowledge learned through the exercise of pure reason). How knowledge is acquired and how knowledge claims are justified are quite distinct, albeit related, matters. The converse of a priori knowledge is 'a posteriori' knowledge. The history of the a priori/a posteriori distinction may ultimately be traced back to Aristotle, but modern usage owes much to the influence of Immanuel Kant. Until the twentieth century, the distinction was viewed with increasing skepticism by epistemologists, but interest in and respect for it have been revived.

2. A Priori and Innateness

Although the notion of a priori knowledge and the notion of innate knowledge are quite distinct, historically philosophers have tended to run them together by confusing questions of justification with questions of acquisition. Mathematical knowledge is usually held up as the paradigm of a priori knowledge and certainly it is true that mathematical knowledge claims, unlike the claims of physical science, do not normally depend for their justification or confirmation upon observational or experimental evidence (an exception being claims based on the results of electronic computation rather than on direct mathematical proof). Few would think it appropriate to test the truth of the arithmetical proposition $7 + 5 = 12$ empirically, by repeatedly conjoining and counting sets of seven and five objects. (Unusually amongst major philosophers, however, John Stuart Mill did believe that mathematics rested ultimately upon induction from experience.) But even accepting the a priori status of mathematical knowledge, it is quite another matter to hold (as Plato did) that mathematical knowledge is innate (though this in turn is not to deny that experience may be needed to 'trigger' such latent knowledge, as happens in Plato's account of the slave boy in the *Meno*). Conversely, contemporary linguists like Noam Chomsky and philosophical psychologists like Jerry Fodor, who notoriously hold that much of our knowledge of language is innate, do not therefore wish to claim for (say) principles of universal grammar the same epistemological status as mathematical truths as far as their justification is concerned: linguistics, unlike mathematics, is an empirical science, answerable to observational evidence.

3. A Priori and Analyticity

'Empiricist' philosophers have traditionally held that all a priori knowledge is of necessary, analytic propositions, and conversely that all a posteriori knowledge is of contingent, synthetic propositions. David Hume, for instance, is standardly interpreted as adopting this view. Kant, however, famously held that we have some a priori knowledge of certain very general synthetic propositions (such as the proposition that every event has a cause), though he too believed that all a priori knowledge could only be of necessary truths. However, in his highly influential onslaught upon the 'dogmas of empiricism,' W. V. O. Quine was to argue that none of these distinctions could be defined without implicit circularity of a sort which condemned them as useless for the purposes of a scientifically minded philosophy of language and knowledge. Only during the course of the twentieth century have philosophers been prepared once more to use these terms with confidence, thanks largely to the work of the modal logician and essentialist metaphysician Saul A. Kripke. Kripke points out that while the a priori/a posteriori distinction is an epistemological one, the analytic/synthetic distinction is a semantic one and the necessary/contingent distinction is, as he terms it, metaphysical in character. Accordingly he holds that in principle the three distinctions may cut quite across one another, and indeed Kripke has famously argued that there are both necessary a posteriori truths (such as that water is H_2O) and contingent a priori truths (such as that the standard meter bar is one meter in length).

See also: Analyticity; Necessity.

Bibliography

Moser P K (ed.) 1987 *A Priori Knowledge*. Oxford University Press, Oxford
Stich S P (ed.) 1975 *Innate Ideas*. University of California Press, Berkeley, CA

Abstract Ideas

E. J. Lowe

The doctrine of 'abstract ideas' is most closely associated, historically, with John Locke's theory of language, where they are invoked to explain the function of general terms. Locke's explanation is constrained by his commitment to nominalism, empiricism, and an ideational theory of thought and language. His nominalism and empiricism induce him to deny that general terms designate real extramental universals and to hold that an understanding of the meaning of general terms must somehow arise from experience of particulars, while his ideationism leads him to suppose that general terms must signify general ideas in the minds of those who use them. He postulates the process of abstraction as the mechanism whereby the mind generates the significata of general terms from its experience of particulars.

1. The Process of Abstraction

The process of abstraction supposedly consists in comparing various particulars which are encountered in experience, noting their similarities and differences, ignoring the latter and retaining the former in mind as a sort of pattern or template which can be employed in classifying further particulars that are met. These mental patterns or templates are the abstract general ideas. Locke illustrates the process by an example of how a child supposedly acquires the abstract general idea of a human being from its diverse experiences of the various individual people it encounters—its mother, father, and so on.

2. Criticisms of Abstraction

Locke's doctrine has been subjected to severe criticism, notably at the hands of his contemporary George Berkeley, and until the late twentieth century many philosophers considered it unworthy of serious consideration. First, there is the problem of indeterminacy: if, for example, the abstract idea of a man leaves out differences of stature and coloration, one is left with the idea of a man who has no definite height or color, and this (Berkeley holds) is absurd. To this it may be replied that the abstract idea of a man is, rather, just an idea of a man which leaves the question of his height and color undetermined, and that this is perfectly intelligible if one does not (as Locke arguably did not) adopt an imagistic conception of ideas (as Berkeley himself did).

Second, there is the problem of individuation: Locke's account of abstraction fails to accommodate the fact that particular objects of experience are only individuable as objects *of some sort*, and hence as falling already under some scheme of classification. But this does not show that humans do not have abstract general ideas, only that at least some of them would have to be innate (contrary to Locke's empiricist assumptions).

Third, there are problems with the role that similarity or resemblance plays in the theory: for instance, it is said that similarity must always be similarity in some (general) respect, which threatens to reintroduce the reference to universals which Locke is attempting to eliminate; again, it is pointed out that in principle anything is similar to and different from anything else in infinitely many ways, so that it is necessary to distinguish important or salient dimensions of similarity from others, and this once more indicates the operation of innate cognitive constraints in human thought and experience.

Fourth, there is the problem of classification: Locke supposes that when a newly encountered particular is classified, it is done so by 'matching' it with an abstract general idea—but abstract ideas are themselves (mental) particulars, by Locke's own principles, so the question arises as to how a particular idea is classified as being, for example, an abstract general idea of a man. A vicious regress is clearly threatened. A possible answer is to say that the original process of classifying by matching does not require an active search through the stock of mental patterns or templates as one might search through a wallpaper pattern-book, and hence does not demand an ability to classify one's own ideas: rather, the process can be thought of as more or less automatic, perhaps by analogy with the way in which a confectionery machine dispenses a bar of chocolate upon receiving a coin of the right denomination.

3. Renewed Interest in Abstract Ideas

The intuitive appeal of Locke's doctrine, and the fact that none of the objections standardly raised against it is conclusive, help to explain its staying power, especially outside the realms of professional philosophy. Indeed, in the late twentieth century views recognizably akin to it (though often shorn of Locke's extreme nominalist and empiricist assumptions) have again become popular with many psychologists and philosophers interested in the mental aspects of language use, though now under the guise of talk about 'prototypes' (Eleanor Rosch) or 'stereotypes' (Hilary Putnam). An important difference, however, is that stereotypes are not, unlike Lockean abstract ideas, thought of as rigidly determining the extensions of the general terms with which they are associated.

See also: Natural Kinds; Sortal Terms.

Bibliography

Locke J 1975 [1690] *An Essay Concerning Human Understanding*, Nidditch P H (ed.). Clarendon Press, Oxford
Lowe E J 1995 *Locke on Human Understanding*. Routledge, London
Putnam H 1975 The meaning of 'meaning.' In: Putnam H *Mind, Language and Reality*. Cambridge University Press, Cambridge

Category-mistake

P. V. Lamarque

Within philosophy, the *locus classicus* for discussion of 'category-mistakes' is Gilbert Ryle's influential work *The Concept of Mind* (1949: ch. 1) where he argues that the traditional dualist (Cartesian) view of the mind as a separate substance, or 'ghost in the machine,' falsely 'represents the facts of mental life as if they belonged to one logical type or category... when they actually belong to another' (Ryle 1949: 16). In at least his early writings in philosophy Ryle believed that philosophical problems themselves were characteristically 'category-problems' and that philosophical mistakes were more often than not grounded in confusions about logical categories.

1. Identifying Category-mistakes

Category-mistakes arise, according to Ryle, not only in philosophy but in quite ordinary contexts of thinking or speaking. He gives the example of a foreigner being shown round Oxford or Cambridge who, having seen the colleges, libraries, playing fields, museums, scientific departments and administrative offices, then asks where the university is, 'as if "the university" stood for an extra member of the class of which these other units are members,' rather than being a term which describes 'the way in which all that he has already seen is organized.' Category-mistakes of this kind occur when speakers misunderstand concepts (in this case, the concept 'university').

But they can also arise where no such conceptual ignorance exists. Ryle illustrates this with the example of a student of politics who is aware of the differences between the British and, say, the American constitutions (the former not being embodied in any single document) but who becomes confused when trying to discuss the relations between the Church of England, the Home Office, and the British Constitution.

Because these names do not attach to entities of the same logical type no straightforward comparison can be made between the entities as different kinds of institutions. Confusion on this point can lead, so Ryle believed, to describing the British Constitution as 'a mysteriously occult institution,' just as the person who thinks of the Average Taxpayer as a fellow-citizen might suppose him to be 'an elusive insubstantial man, a ghost who is everywhere but nowhere.'

On Ryle's view, it is precisely a mistake of the latter kind that Descartes, and subsequent Cartesian dualists, made in proposing that the mind is a non-material substance existing in parallel to material substance and defined for the most part negatively in contrast to it: not in space, not in motion, not accessible to public observation, etc.; 'minds are not bits of clockwork, they are just bits of notclockwork,' as Ryle mockingly puts it. On his own theory, Ryle develops the idea that terms applied to mental life ('knowing,' 'willing,' 'feeling,' 'imagining,' and so forth) do not describe mysterious inner occurrences or processes but rather dispositions in a physically observable person. Mental terms are thus restored to their proper logical category.

2. Categories and Category-differences

Whatever the merits of Ryle's concept of the mind, there is no doubt that his conception of a category-mistake enjoyed considerable influence among philosophers, particularly in the movement known as 'ordinary language philosophy.' However, the value and clarity of the conception depended in the end on the precision that could be attached to the idea of a category and it was probably on this point that Ryle's conception ultimately foundered. Everyone can recognize intuitively striking differences between kinds of entities—trees, Wednesdays, the number seven, a musical note, the Battle of Hastings. Such differences can readily be labeled 'category-differences.' Likewise, certain kinds of sentences seem to involve not just factual errors but something more fundamental which could be called 'category-mismatch': 'The number five is blue,' 'Wednesdays are in B minor,' 'The Battle of Hastings fitted into his pocket,' and so forth. Theories of metaphor sometimes make use of such an idea of category-mismatch. However, when an attempt is made to state precisely what makes an entity belong to one category or another difficulties abound. Yet if no such account is forthcoming then more controversial applications—like the idea that minds and bodies belong in different categories—can only rest on vague intuitions.

In an early and important paper on categories (Ryle 1938), Ryle did attempt to give some precision to the concept, though without following either Aristotle or Kant in supposing there is some fixed number of categories into which all human thought must fall. He offered the following definition:

Two proposition-factors are of different categories or types, if there are sentence-frames which are such that when the expressions for those factors are imported as alternative complements to the same gap-signs, the resultant sentences are significant in the one case and absurd in the other.

(Ryle 1938: 203)

The problem with this criterion is that it relies on a unexplained notion of 'absurdity.' P. F. Strawson (1971) has shown that as it stands Ryle's criterion produces anomalous results: '[o]ne should try importing first "27" and then "37" as complements to the gap-sign in "She is over … and under 33 years old"; or first "mother" and then "father" into "It's not your … but your father"; or first "Green" and then "Red" into "… is a more restful color than red"' (Strawson 1971: 187). Clearly only a special kind of absurdity—indeed a category-absurdity—is presupposed in Ryle's definition but one has not advanced very far if to explain category-differences one must appeal to category-absurdity. Another suggestion might be that category-absurdity is a species of analytic falsity, that is, falsity determined by meanings alone, but the sentence 'Some bachelors are married' while analytically false does not seem to involve any category-mismatch. Thus it remains to be said what kind of analytic falsity underlies category-mismatch.

3. Category-mistakes and Philosophical Method

Although Ryle gave prominence to the idea of a category-mistake in *The Concept of Mind*, even suggesting that '[p]hilosophy is the replacement of category-habits by category-disciplines' (Ryle 1949: 8), he came to think that no precise definition can be given to the concept of a category, which consequently can never be used as a 'skeleton-key' which will 'turn all our locks for us' (Ryle 1954: 9). Nevertheless, the idea that philosophy is centrally concerned with identifying the logical categories of its key terms—where necessary exposing category-mistakes—and undertaking what Ryle called 'logical geography' to find the proper location for problematic concepts was a powerful driving-force in conceptual analysis and produced some of the most valuable work of the 'ordinary language philosophers.'

See also: Ordinary Language Philosophy.

Bibliography

Ryle G 1938 Categories. *Proceedings of the Aristotelian Society* **38**: 189–206
Ryle G 1949 *The Concept of Mind*. Hutchinson, London
Ryle G 1954 *Dilemmas*. Cambridge University Press, Cambridge
Sommers F 1963 Types and Ontology. *Philosophical Review* **72**: 327–63
Strawson P F 1971 Categories. In: Wood O P, Pitcher G (eds.) *Ryle*. Macmillan, London

Deconstruction

E. Crasnow

Deconstruction is the name of a kind of writing and a kind of thinking that symptomatically resists formulation. It is associated with the work of the French philosopher Jacques Derrida; but Derrida's own explosively various publications from the late 1960s onwards was accompanied by a dissemination of deconstruction, notably but not exclusively in the USA, where it was initially pursued by lettrists rather than philosophers, and played a key role in the rise of interest in literary theory, prompting continued debate in the humanities. Rather than attempting to cover all this activity, the present article will concentrate on Derrida's own work; but even this concentration does not offer a single identity. In terms of nationality, for instance, Derrida has pointed out the sense in which he is 'not French': 'I come from Algeria. I have therefore still another relation to the French tongue.' The sense of 'another relation,' of otherness, is pervasive.

Deconstruction is not an autonomous discourse; it exists in relation to other texts, in a reading of what Derrida calls 'loving jealousy' which displays the alterity in the texts' identity, the indigestible element in their system. This in turn gives a certain textual specificity to deconstructive writing, which is all too easily lost in a general discussion. This article therefore includes an extended consideration of one recent text.

1. Philosophy and Literature

The sense of otherness also affects the question of a single discipline. Derrida is a philosopher by training and occupation, but his books are often denounced as alien to their apparent discipline, and he can describe himself as other than a philosopher:

> I ask questions of philosophy, and naturally this supposes a certain identification, a certain translation of myself into the body of a philosopher. But I don't feel that that's where I'm situated.
>
> (Derrida 1985: 140)

In a 1981 interview he speaks of 'my attempt to discover the non-place or *non-lieu* which would be the "other" of philosophy. This is the task of deconstruction.' The interviewer asks 'Can literary and poetic language provide this *non-lieu* or *u-topos*?' and Derrida replies:

> I think so: but when I speak of literature it is not with a capital L; it is rather an allusion to certain movements which have worked around the limits of our logical concepts, certain texts which make the limits of our language tremble, exposing them as divisible and questionable.
>
> (Derrida 1984: 112)

This is an instructive passage in several ways. It presents the ambition to transcend a (philosophical) discourse, to get outside or beyond it into a metalanguage. But here as elsewhere, the transcendent gesture is ultimately impossible. On another occasion Derrida asks skeptically:

> Can one, strictly speaking, determine a nonphilosophical place, a place of exteriority or alterity from which one might still treat *of philosophy*?
>
> (Derrida 1982: xii)

The implied answer is no: one must differ from within. Deconstruction must use the very tools it seeks to question.

Another instructive aspect of the interview is its offer of literature as an alternative to philosophy, to replace it. Philosophy and literature are now in opposition, and such binary pairs are a frequent object of deconstructive analysis. These pairings are commonly marked by the speaker's preference. Thus from a philosopher's point of view the opposition between philosophy and literature might appear as the opposition between rigor and frivolity, and the advocate of literature would attempt to reverse this valuation. Deconstruction, however, specifically avoids a symmetrical reversal. Derrida will therefore not substitute Literature with a capital L for Philosophy with a capital P. Neither of these capitalized monoliths attracts him. For it is precisely the monolith, the self-identical structure, that provokes deconstruction, which in turn displays the monolith as already fissured, discovering the otherness in its apparent sameness; as in the discovery that an apparently rigorous nonliterary discourse is already tainted by the figuration that it would seek to exclude. For example, Thomas Sprat's 1667 *History of the Royal Society* celebrates the scientific ambitions of the body which he helped to found, and rails against the unscientific 'beautiful deceit' of 'fine speaking,' against 'specious *Tropes* and *Figures*.' The Society's members have resolved, he writes:

> to reject all amplifications, digressions, and swellings of style; to return back to the primitive purity and shortness, when *men* deliver'd so many *things* almost in an equal number of *words*. They have exacted from all their members a close, naked, natural way of speaking...
>
> (Sprat 1667)

The metaphoricity of this diatribe against metaphor, this impure argument for purity, needs no emphasis. The metaphors link to form an implicit sequence: 'to return back ... primitive purity ... natural.' The opposition between pure and impure, between nature and artifice, is bolstered by a myth of origin which privileges the first term of each of these pairs. Sprat also privileges 'a natural way of speaking' as against the 'swellings of style.' Here style appears as unnaturally evident; and, through the Latin *stilus* (a pointed instrument for use with a wax tablet), it recalls the artifice of inscription, a writing as opposed to a speech.

2. Speech and Writing

To examine the implications of this ranking of 'speech' over 'writing' has been a recurrent task for Derrida. He traces it in Saussure, in Lévi-Strauss, in Rousseau, and in the *locus classicus*: Plato's *Phaedrus*. Socrates, in this dialogue, tells of the Egyptian god Thoth, who invented writing and offered it to the king with 'a paternal love,' but found his gift refused; the parent is not always the best judge of children. The figure of parenthood is developed as Socrates describes the fate of speeches when transferred to writing: tumbled about anywhere with no parent to protect them, and unable to reply for themselves. As opposed to these abandoned children, however, there is 'a son of the same family, but lawfully begotten... the intelligent word graven in the soul of the learner, which can defend itself, and knows when to speak and when to be silent.' This is 'the living word of knowledge... of which the written word is properly no more than an image.' Plato's idealism is evident; the written word, depreciated as it is, functions in the same way as the image of the bed in the *Republic*. Yet the intelligent word is 'graven,' inscribed, in the soul: the rejected image of writing somehow taints the site from which it is excluded.

The written word, for Plato, suffers an absence; there is no parent to speak up for it; it lacks the principle of reason which, by contrast, is present to the lawful son, the intelligent word graven in the soul. The intelligent word and the soul are both principles of reason; that is, reason is here present to itself and confirms itself. This self-presence is for Derrida characteristic of western metaphysics, whose various systems are organized around self-present, self-confirming centers which control and legitimate their surrounding structures.

3. Logocentrism

Building on the Greek *logos*, which can mean both 'word' and 'rational principle,' Derrida calls this Western tradition 'logocentrism.' It is apparent in Western religions, most obviously in the Fourth Gospel, which appropriates the pagan *logos* for Christian divinity:

> In the beginning was the Word, and the Word was with God, and the Word was God.
>
> (John 1: 1)

And, even earlier, the 'I am that I am' of Exodus 3: 14 is an example of presence confirmed by reflexive self-definition. But the practice is not exclusively religious;

on the contrary, logocentrism can be entirely secular, as in Husserl's phenomenology, where the self-presence of consciousness, purified by a process of bracketing or reduction, attains what he calls a 'realm of essential structures of transcendental subjectivity immediately transparent to the mind.'

These logocentrisms go beyond the world of physical fact. In their organizing mastery, they transcend the physical: they are metaphysical. Deconstruction engages in a questioning of metaphysics, insofar as metaphysics provides a repertoire of logocentric master terms: foundation, origin, end, essence. And the counterclaim is: 'There will be no unique name, even if it were the name of Being.' So deconstruction, in dealing with binary pairs, does not simply reverse the direction of dominance and privilege the under-privileged. This would be to exchange the rule of centrism for another, the principle of mastery remaining intact. It has been shown how Derrida's attempt to discover the 'other' of philosophy entailed not an opposing recourse to literature, but rather 'an allusion to certain movements which have worked around the limits of our logical concepts.' These disruptive movements are what forestall a symmetrical reversal, and naming them is doubly problematic. In the first place is the risk of producing yet another master term, another 'unique name.' Second, to name and codify the deconstructive operation is to make it available for appropriation and vulgarization, particularly at a time when theories are fashionably marketable. As Adorno wrote, 'No theory today escapes the marketplace. Each one is offered as a possibility among competing opinions; they are all put up for choice; all are swallowed.' Once packaged for consumption, deconstruction is easily domesticated, its disruptive potential dissipated. It is for this reason that Derrida denies that deconstruction is a method or even a critique. But appropriations of one sort or another are unavoidable. American deconstructors, in particular, have been driven to definitions, which include Paul de Man's equation of the deconstructive potential of language with literature itself—a privileged role not envisaged by Derrida. Again, as de Man says:

> I have a tendency to put upon texts an inherent authority, which is stronger, I think than Derrida is willing to put upon them. I assume, as a working hypothesis (as a working hypothesis, because I know better than that), that the text *knows* in an absolute way what it's doing.
>
> (de Man 1986: 118)

In fact the hypothetical nature of de Man's assumption is not always evident in his more apodictic statements. But, flirtations with literariness aside, deconstruction's influence on literary theory and criticism has been marked, not least because of its attention to the preconditions of discourse; to what goes into (and what is kept out of) the constitution of an identity, be it a discipline, a genre, a system, an institutional practice; and how identity may be opened up to alterity, to a 'contamination of genres.' J. Hillis Miller, another American deconstructor long resident at Yale, has listed some of the assumptions of traditional literary studies that deconstruction has challenged. They include accounting for a literary work by reference to the writer; arranging literary history in an organic development of definable periods; holding that a good work should have a definable, unified meaning; that language is primarily referential, and that figurative language is 'an adventitious flourish added to a literal base' (Miller 1991: 335). The list is apposite; its final point about figurative language has already been demonstrated with reference to Sprat. But it is in some ways deceptive. What it claims as deconstructive is not exclusively so; reference to the writer in interpreting the work, for example, is not questioned by deconstruction alone. Moreover, a list inevitably omits the point that, in Derrida and in some of his followers, it is the very language of deconstruction, its presentation and terminology, that constitutes the primary challenge. Derrida's own style varies according to its occasion; but it is commonly obtrusive, often obscure, elliptical, wittily performative. Its challenge proves rebarbative for some readers; for others it shapes the exhilarating experience of deconstruction as a kind of writing. In part, it shares with the differing idioms of Lacan or Althusser the desire to resist facile assimilation. Yet presentation in itself is no defense; there will always be popularizations, of which this is one. And terminology, however resistant, is open to appropriation. None of Derrida's coinages, no matter how neologistic or bizarre, has escaped. They have multiplied as if to prevent the emergence of a unique name, and in response to the readings of particular texts. He calls them 'undecidables'; and they take the risk, already mentioned, of naming those 'movements which have worked around the limits of our logical concepts,' and which are to be set to work in the text at hand.

4. Differance

One of the most wide-ranging of these undecidables is the famous 'differance.' The usual 'e' is replaced by an 'a,' and the replacement is inaudible—an effect of writing rather than speech. Differance retains some of the usual connotations of difference; deconstruction reads with difference insofar as it reads against sameness, the noncontradictory, the homogeneous. It builds on Saussure's claim that 'in language there are only differences without positive terms.' This is not to claim that Saussure is a deconstructionist avant la lettre. His preference for speech over writing is at times logocentric, as Derrida points out; and his positive view of the combination between signifier and signified is replaced in deconstruction by a regressive series of significations, each signified always in the position of another signifier, a process whose closure

could only come about through the imposition of what Derrida calls a 'transcendental signified' to curb the play of semiotic slippage, which ultimately cannot be curbed and which produces the 'indeterminacy' of deconstruction. From this point of view, Saussure is not differential enough. But difference is not the only concern. The French verb *différer* indicates not only differing but also deferring or delaying; it can thus be read as displacing the moment of self-presence in logocentrism, 'spacing and temporalizing' as Derrida puts it. All these functions of difference and deferment are combined in the neologism 'differance': 'the movement that structures every dissociation... what in classical languages would be called the origin or production of differences.' And despite various disclaimers—'Differance is neither a word nor a concept'—it remains, as Derrida acknowledges, a metaphysical name. Indeed, it is a name for something that has been unnameable within the logocentrism of Western culture (though it appears 'almost by name' in the work of radical thinkers like Heidegger, Nietzsche, Freud). With this series of denials the discussion begins to sound very much like negative theology, but with a difference:

> This unnameable is not an ineffable Being which no name could approach: God, for example... there never has been, never will be, a unique word, a master-name.
> (Derrida 1991: 76)

For all that, within eight years of the French publication of 'Différance' in 1968, it was possible for Gayatri Chakravorty Spivak, the translator of *Of Grammatology*, to describe it as 'close to becoming Derrida's master concept.' Whatever disclaimers are offered, the forces of appropriation will seek mastery, even negative mastery. One possible reaction is to seek safety in numbers by multiplying the undecidables. In Derrida's later work, however, there seems to be at least a partial despecialization of terminology, with an increasing concentration on topics like translation, or names and naming: topics which work without recourse to neologism. On the contrary, they signal a continuum with others' analyses, as in Derrida's repeated readings of Benjamin on translation.

5. Puncepts

A further aspect of deconstructive terminology or indeterminology is its use of wordplay and the compound pun. Gregory Ulmer has offered the term 'puncept' for this habit; a mutation that recalls the derivation of 'concept' from the Latin *conceptus*, a participle of the verb *concipio*, itself formed from *com* ('with, together') and *capio* ('to take hold of, to grasp'). That is to say, the term 'concept' has a centrist etymology; to replace it with the pun or puncept is a decentering move. Puns disrupt the propriety of language, but they need not be unmotivated, and Derridean wordplay is functional. For example, one of his discussions of translation is called '*Des Tours de Babel*' (1980). In this title, the biblical tower of Babel is pluralized into a symptom rather than an event. *Des* can be read as 'of the' or 'about the'—here, as in the later *Of Spirit*, there is an echo of the diction of an academic monograph; but we can also read *Des* as the casual 'some,' which undermines formal diction. One cannot tell from *Des Tours* whether *tour* is feminine, which would make it a tower; or masculine, which would make it a turn, a twist, a trope: varieties of indirection that the essay will apply to translation as such and to language in general. This indirection is emphasized by punning on *Des Tours* and *détour*; detour, like delay is an aspect of differance. Accordingly, the failed structure of Babel becomes a deconstruction:

> The 'tower of Babel' does not figure merely the irreducible multiplicity of tongues; it exhibits an incompletion, the impossibility of finishing, of totalizing, of saturating, of completing something on the order of edification, architectural construction, system and architectonics.
>
> (Derrida 1991: 244)

'Improper' procedures like the pun are deliberately courted as a means of interrogating propriety, property, and the proper. In 1975 Derrida gave a lecture, later expanded into a book, on the poet Francis Ponge. The title seems innocuous; *SignéPonge*, perhaps 'Signed Ponge,' as if inscribed below a Ponge text. Lurking within this sober compound, however, is a sign of the drunken *éponge*: a 'soak,' or an amorphous 'sponge.' *Passer l'éponge sur* is to blot out or obliterate; thus *l'éponge éponge, l'éponge est* Ponge: 'the sponge expunges, the sponge is Ponge' . . . The sponge becomes a deconstructive operator with which to interrogate the notion of signature as the identifying mark of the proper name; and this is carried out in and through the outrageous wordplay and the readings of Ponge's texts.

6. Inside and Outside

A milder but notorious piece of wordplay comes from *Of Grammatology*, one of three books published in 1967. During a discussion of Rousseau, Derrida turns, as he so often does, to the question of reading, and produces the sentence *Il n'y a pas de hors-texte*. This saying raises crucial questions and has become a rallying cry against deconstruction. Rendered as 'there is nothing outside the text' it is used to accuse deconstruction of a narrowly text-based reading practice; or, more generally, of a nihilistic indifference to context and history. But there are other readings. A small slippage produces *Il n'y a pas dehors-texte*: there is no outside of or to the text (recall the earlier question of whether there was a place outside philosophy). If the text (whatever that turns out to be) has no outside, it seems boundless; rather than narrowing the field, this opens it widely. Then again, *hors-texte* seems to echo

other *hors*-compounds; for example, *hors concours*. A picture at an exhibition is *hors concours* if it is above its class, out of competition. Perhaps to be *hors-texte* is to be out-of-text in the sense that one is out of the game, out of play. But this is a negative sentence, so that the possibility of being out of play is precisely what it denies. These readings suggest the impossibility of an appeal to:

> a signified outside of the text whose content . . . could have taken place outside of language, that is to say, in the sense that we give here to that word, outside of writing in general.
>
> (Derrida 1976: 158)

An outside in this sense is strictly utopian, the u-topos or non-lieu already described. A problematics of outside and inside develops in deconstruction; leading, for example, to the question of what is formally outside a text—preface, afterword, footnote, commentary—and the presumption of priority or authority that such elements may claim. This in turn produces a recurrent questioning of boundaries, margins, and frames, and in some cases the disruption of the printed page as a visual unit; *Glas* (1974) is printed in two columns which deal with Hegel and Genet, the proper and the improper; but which are multifariously interrupted, not only by other discourses but also by typographical intrusions, inset blocks of print which give the page the appearance of a collage.

7. Ethics and Politics

The problem of inside and outside has further implications which lead into ethics and politics. They can be approached through the notion of context as an outside, and the indifference to context which has been read into *Il n'y a pas de hor-texte*. This may imply an extension of textuality rather than an encapsulation of the text. Derrida refers to this extension as the 'general text,' as in these comments during a controversy that followed the publication of some of his anti-apartheid writing:

> That's why South Africa and apartheid are, like you and me, part of this general text, which is not to say that it can be read the way one reads a book. That's why the text is always a field of forces: differential, heterogeneous, open and so on. That's why deconstructive readings and writings are concerned not only with library books, with discourses, with conceptual and semantic contents . . . They are also effective or active (as one says) interventions, in particular political and institutional interventions that transform contexts . . . .
>
> (*Critical Inquiry* **13**: 167–68)

In this and in other passages there appears to be a convergence between general text and context, as an open field of forces which is subject to intervention, but which, through its very openness, cannot be determinately specified—as in the gesture of specifying a context that will determine the meaning of a text. The context is never 'saturated.' Thus Derrida can include Freud's personal history in a discussion of *Beyond the Pleasure Principle*, but cannot claim any psycho-biographical authority; his title is '"*Spéculer*"—*sur Freud*,' and he considers how even an auto-biography might speculate.

The larger question of a deconstructive politics has been widely debated. Barbara Johnson, one of the shrewdest American deconstructors, says:

> There's no political program, but I think there's a pol-itical attitude, which is to examine authority in language, and the pronouncements of any self-constituted authority for what it is repressing or what it is not saying.

Johnson's attitude is antidogmatic; political dogma itself, as it asserts a party line, can become one of those monolithic structures which deconstruction views as always already fissured by otherness. And the positive, indeed affirmative role claimed by deconstruction has increasingly focused on its response to the other and to otherness, to the alterity that self-identity tries to exclude: 'every culture is haunted by its other.' Decon-struction can then claim to contribute to a necessary cultural self-interrogation whose range is potentially vast: Derrida, describing 'the violent relationship of the whole of the West to its other,' invokes ethno-logical, economic, political, and military relation-ships, besides the linguistic and philosophical relationships which form his usual approach (Derrida 1982: 134–35). His work on denegation, marginal-ization, violent suppression, and exclusion during the 1980s concentrated on Nazism. There are several reasons for this concentration. No doubt it owes something to Derrida's own experiences as a Jewish child in colonial Algeria after the fall of France (Wood and Bernasconi 1985: 113). More recently, violent debates followed the discovery that Paul de Man—a personal friend—had during World War II produced a body of journalism in occupied Belgium that included some collaborationist and anti-Semitic sen-timents (Miller 1991: 359–84). Most particularly, per-haps, it stemmed from the wish not to suppress awkward facts about philosophers whose work had been important to him. Thus it was necessary not to avoid the specific Nazi involvement of Martin Hei-degger during the 1930s, and his silence about sub-sequent events.

8. Derrida on Heidegger

Derrida was one of several writers (including Lacoué-Labarthe and Lyotard) to reopen Heidegger's case. His book *Of Spirit: Heidegger and the Question* appeared in French in 1987; the title's strategy recalls '*Des Tours de Babel*'; and on this occasion, the reader is specifically reminded of how *De l'esprit* invoked a tradition of the learned treatise; the overlap of French and Latin *de* lends it classical authority. But the title

also echoes 'a scandalous book' of the same name: Helvétius's *De l'esprit*, proscribed and burned in 1759. This too is conveyed to the reader, in a mysteriously proleptic footnote which begins 'Since the whole of this discourse will be surrounded by fire...'; it goes on to describe the burning of other heretical books, and indeed the burning of a heretic. Already, with this apparent digression, Ciceronian learned solemnity is wearing thin; a different interest appears through the opposition of dogma and heresy, the deconstructive interest in exclusion and repression. The notion of system or structure as that which perpetuates the same at the expense of the other is acted out here through disruptions at various levels of the text. Thus, what seems to be on offer is a formal scheme, an analytic narrative about Heidegger's use of a certain set of terms between 1927 and 1953; but its methodical sequence is constantly interrupted by retrospect and anticipation: 'Twenty years later, Heidegger will have to suggest....' And, as in the Helvétius footnote, a digressive tendency, a substitution for the apparent topic, is constantly suggested by initially obscure interventions:

> I shall speak of ghost [*revenant*], of flame, and of ashes. And of what, for Heidegger, *avoiding* means.

These are the opening sentences; with hindsight, they are purposefully ambiguous. In one sense, their con-cerns are all present in the narrative; in another they are largely absent, excluded, 'avoided' in their his-torical aspect—which is nevertheless invoked through passages like the Helvétius footnote, which with its burning of books and bodies can hardly fail to recall Nazi incinerations. The rare direct references are powerfully understated: 'this was not just any quarter century.' Through such reticence the text mimes Hei-degger's attempted avoidance of an historical referent in the postwar period; and, at another level, the Nazi attempt to efface the Final Solution.

8.1 Language and Nationalism

Another way of putting this would be to describe the return of the repressed. What returns, in French, is a *revenant*, a ghost; and a ghost in German is *der Geist*; but *Geist* is also spirit—*Geist* and its compounds are what *Of Spirit* is 'about.' In its oscillation between concept and context the book works like a huge and tragic pun. This pun is also an oscillation between languages, and questions of translation recur through-out. And unlike the treatment of translation in '*Des Tours de Babel*,' where it serves as what Derrida calls a 'conceptual generality,' translation in this text is particularized: 'What I am aiming at here is, obviously enough, anything but abstract.' One particular field of translation concerns philosophical nationality and nationalism; not only in the linguistic problems revealed by translating *Geist* into the languages of its European neighbors, but also in the massive ideological implications of this move: a translation, as Derrida puts it, of discourse into history. The extreme privilege that Heidegger grants to German, or German-and-Greek, is well known; 'horribly dangerous and wildly funny,' says Derrida. Heidegger's geo-politics forms a sort of selective Eurocentrism with the Greek *pneuma*, the Latin *spiritus*, and the German *Geist* inscribed in what Derrida calls a 'linguistico-historical triad' of spirit. German is still privileged here because it depends on what Heidegger claims is an 'ordinary meaning.' The whole situation should by now be familiar: maintenance of the same by exclusion of the other, endorsement of the same by a myth of origin.

Deconstructive analysis intervenes by showing the other as already inscribed within the same, and under-mines the myth by showing the origin as already het-erogeneous and hence not a pure identity. The stages are no longer spelt out as they were in previous works, but the strategy survives. In a piquant move, the tri-adic foreclosure of spirit is opened up to include the Hebrew *ruah*, with as good a claim to origin as any other term for spirit; it is 'what Greek and the Latin *had* to translate by *pneuma* and *spiritus*.' Moreover, *ruah* is shown as linked with *pneuma* through the Gos-pels, and as containing both good and evil in the manner that Heidegger ascribes to *Geist*. What was avoided has been included, from the outset.

8.2 Heidegger's Deconstruction

Geist is itself, to an extent, avoided by Heidegger. It never receives the interrogation afforded to terms like *Dasein* or *Denken*—this despite *Geist*'s importance in the nineteenth century, not only as an index of national culture, but also as a focus for philosophical enquiry, as in Hegel's *Phenomenology of Spirit*. It is part of Heidegger's great work of 1927, *Being and Time*, to question this importance and this focus, inso-far as *Geist* follows a Cartesian emphasis on sub-jectivity that for Heidegger marks a wrong turning in philosophy. As he recounts this questioning, Derrida is in fact describing a *Heideggerian* deconstruction, which will expose the apparent autonomy of *cogito ergo sum* as fissured by the ignoring or avoiding of *sum*; emphasis is all on the *cogito*, which leads to a subsequent 'neglect of being,' a failure to investigate existence, in the 'Cartesian–Hegelian' tradition. *Being and Time* attempts a reorientation: 'the "substance" of man is not spirit as a synthesis of the soul and the body but *existence*.' The suspect term 'spirit' is commonly placed between quotation marks in *Being and Time*—a typographical warning which, like Hei-degger's crossings-out, has had its own influence on Derrida—who, after all, derives 'deconstruction' itself from Heidegger's *Destruktion* and *Abbau*. He could easily have used *Destruktion* for Heidegger's ques-tioning at this point; instead, he uses his own word and invokes his own practice, as if to emphasize that

deconstruction is no absolute safeguard against the snares of thought. For there is a drastic change to come.

8.3 Heidegger's Logocentrism

The 'tortuous prudence' of *Being and Time* is aban-doned in 1933, when Heidegger, as the newly-appointed rector of the University of Freiburg, gives an address on the self-assertion of the German uni-versities. The prophylactic quotation marks are deleted as he offers a 'spiritual world' which 'guaran-tees the people its grandeur,' and which is not the people's culture or knowledge but 'the deepest power of conservation of its forces of earth and blood.' The exaltation of will, order, and destiny, the rejection of academic freedom, are unmistakably Fascist. 'One could say,' writes Derrida, 'that he spiritualizes National Socialism.' But in doing so Heidegger goes back on his own deconstruction, at least insofar as the 'massive voluntarism' of the address, its will to power, is a return to the subjectivity which he had been at pains to question.

Of Spirit follows the fortunes of Heidegger's *Geist* through the various stages of its 'inflammation and inflation'—terms that turn out to be more than meta-phorical. The book is described as surrounded by fire; its climax comes in Heidegger's comments on the poet Trakl, where the inflammation is actual. Here, '*Der Geist ist das Flammende*' and '*Der Geist ist Flamme*'; spirit is a 'flame which inflames, or which inflames *itself*'; it 'can devour tirelessly and consume everything up to and including the white of the ash.' As he has done before, Derrida shows how what had been excluded returns in Heidegger's discourse; and here he invokes Hegel whose determination of spirit had previously called for deconstruction. Now Derrida points the reader towards the treatment of Hegel in *Glas*; and, turning to that text, he quotes Hegel's description of spirit as luminous essence, in terms that sound very like Heidegger's spirit-in-flames:

> Pure and figureless, this light burns all. It burns itself in the all-burning it is; leaves, of itself or anything, no trace, no mark, no sign of passage.
>
> (Derrida 1986: 238)

Heidegger has rejoined Hegel and the logocentric tra-dition. The purity of this self-consuming, figureless figure recalls 'I am that I am' (and perhaps the burning bush) in its reflexive autonomy, free of difference, free of the other as residue. Again, Derrida does not spell out the deconstructive response to all this. Rather, he invokes the inevitable return of the other, the haunting revenant in its full range of implications from semantic difference to social difference. Some of this range is suggested in *Glas* when Hegel's pure light is described as a kind of offering or sacrifice, but Derrida imposes another term:

> ... the word *holocaust* that happens to translate *Opfer* is

more appropriate to the text than the word of Hegel himself. In this sacrifice, all (*holos*) is burned (*caustos*)...
(Derrida 1986: 241)

—another total figure that leaves no trace. *Glas* uses its two-column layout to juxtapose this point with a scene in an Algerian synagogue. *Of Spirit*, as we know, is more reticent. The Holocaust is never named, but it is implicitly suggested and deconstructed, both as a conceptual and as an historical totality: the Solution that was not Final, the ash that was not consumed.

9. Conclusion

It should by now be apparent that the very appearance of deconstruction in the context of an encyclopedia is paradoxical. An encyclopedia surveys established knowledge in a necessarily dogmatic fashion, while deconstruction seeks precisely to question the dogmatic and the established. Yet, as already shown, it has to differ from within; and this not only justifies its placing in reference books but, in a larger sense, gives it its cultural role.

Bibliography

Davis R C, Schleifer R (eds.) 1985 *Rhetoric and Form: Deconstruction at Yale*. University of Oklahoma Press, Norman, OK

Derrida J 1976 (trans. Spivak G C) *Of Grammatology*. Johns Hopkins University Press, Baltimore, MA

Derrida J 1982 (trans. Bass A) *Margins of Philosophy*. The Harvester Press, Brighton

Derrida J 1984 Dialogue with Jacques Derrida. In: Kearney R (ed.) *Dialogues with Contemporary Continental Thinkers: The Phenomenological Heritage*. Manchester University Press, Manchester

Derrida J 1985 (trans. Kamuf P) *The Ear of the Other: Otobiography, Transference, Translation*. Schocken Books, New York

Derrida J 1986 (trans. Leavey J P Jr, Rand R) *Glas*. University of Nebraska Press, Lincoln, NB

Derrida J 1989 (trans. Bennington G, Bowlby R) *Of Spirit: Heidegger and the Question*. University of Chicago Press, Chicago, IL

Derrida J 1991 *A Derrida Reader: Between the Blinds*. Harvester Wheatsheaf, New York

Man P de 1986 *The Resistance to Theory*. University of Minnesota Press, Minneapolis, MN

Miller J H 1991 *Theory Now and Then*. Harvester Wheatsheaf, New York

Norris C 1991 *Deconstruction: Theory and Practice*, rev. edn. Routledge, London

Wood D, Bernasconi R (eds.) 1985 *Derrida and Differance*. Parousia Press, Coventry

Essentialism

T. R. Baldwin

Several twentieth-century philosophers of language have argued that the semantic properties of language have important essentialist implications. Essentialism is, however, a vague doctrine, and before examining its modern manifestations it is helpful to look briefly at its historical origins.

1. Aristotelian Essentialism

There is a manifest difference between those properties which objects possess only at some times and those which they possess throughout their existence. If this distinction is extended to embrace possible changes as well as actual ones, one arrives at one conception of an object's 'essential' (as opposed to its accidental) properties, namely those properties which it cannot fail to possess. Aristotle held that in identifying that essential property of an object which identifies what kind of thing it is—its essence—the means is provided for an understanding of all the object's properties, since all explanations rest upon 'first principles' which concern these essences. This thesis was enormously influential, and is the basis of traditional essentialism. Descartes shows its influence when he discusses the essences of mind (thought) and matter (extension), and constructs his psychology and physics upon these identifications. But the essentialist tradition became problematic as new sciences developed without reference to traditional essences. Locke shows well the resulting situation: he acknowledged the traditional doctrine in his theory of 'real essences,' but, doubting people's ability to know anything of them, he held that the classifications employed in the new sciences are only 'nominal essences,' that is, not really essential properties at all.

In Kant's works essentialism returns, but now as a doctrine about the essential features of objective experience, and thus only indirectly as a doctrine about essential features of the world. Nonetheless, Kant's doctrines provided the stimulus for an idealist essentialism according to which all aspects of the world are essentially related. Since the analytic program in philosophy arose as a reaction against the excesses of this idealist essentialism, for the first half of the twentieth century there was little interest in essentialist doctrines (with the notable exception of Wittgenstein's *Tractatus*). Indeed W. V. O. Quine famously argued that essentialism is incoherent (Linsky 1971). Within the phenomenological movement, by contrast, essentialist doctrines flourished, though in the writings of Heidegger and his disciples the use of essentialist terminology is problematic.

2. Modern Essentialism

Since the development of possible world semantics for modal logic in the 1960s, however, essentialist doctrines have become fashionable within analytic philosophy. Quine's arguments against the very idea of essentialism were decisively refuted by Kripke (Kripke 1980), and some philosophers have sought to revive Aristotelian doctrines (Putnam 1975). What remains wide open to argument, however, is the extent of a defensible essentialism.

A modest position draws on familiar necessary truths (e.g., that 5 is less than 7) and argues that these can be reinterpreted as identifying essential properties of the objects referred to (i.e., that it is an essential property of 5 that it is less than 7). Where this modest essentialism concerns abstract objects, such as numbers, it suggests that these are just nodes within a network of internal relations. More ambitious essentialist positions concern concrete objects and, drawing on the thesis that an object's identity is essential to it, argue that its essential properties include its causal origin, its material constitution, and its kind (the traditional Aristotelian essence); it is even urged that each object has a distinctive essential property (its haeccity) which sustains its identity through different possible situations.

Kripke and others have argued that the initial thesis here is a logical consequence of the necessary reflexiveness of identity, and although this argument is not persuasive, the thesis itself seems integral to the concept of identity (though some theorists reject it—cf. David Lewis 1986). But whether this thesis has significant implications is much disputed. Critics argue that since possible situations can be specified by permutations of the properties of actual objects there is no need for the hypothesis of 'haeccities.' Furthermore, it is argued (Mellor 1977), essentialists misrepresent natural necessity: the genetic dependence of children upon their parents should not be regarded as embodying a special 'metaphysical' necessity. Similarly, natural kinds should not be represented as Aristotelian essences, since the existence of generalizations about a kind at one level of explanation is compatible with a diversity of structures at a deeper level; thus water is a natural kind even though D_2O as well as H_2O is water. The only defensible essentialism in the natural sciences appears to be one which invokes only Locke's nominal essences.

See also: Analyticity; Concepts; Natural Kinds; Necessity.

Bibliography

Kripke S A 1980 *Naming and Necessity*. Blackwell, Oxford
Lewis D 1986 *On the Plurality of Worlds*. Blackwell, Oxford
Linsky L (ed.) 1971 *Reference and Modality*. Oxford University Press, Oxford
Mellor D H 1977 Natural kinds. *British Journal of the Philosophy of Science* **28**: 299–311
Putnam H 1975 The meaning of 'meaning.' In: Putnam H *Mind, Language and Reality*. Cambridge University Press, Cambridge

Falsificationism

A. A. Brennan

Verificationist theories of meaning are concerned with cognitive significance. Their intention is to separate sentences into two distinct classes, namely those that have cognitive significance, or empirical meaning, on the one hand, and those that are meaningless on the other. However, in his *Logic of Scientific Discovery* Karl Popper argued that a criterion for demarcating the scientific from the nonscientific could be based not on how a claim, hypothesis, or theory is verified but rather on whether it is capable of falsification.

Universal statements such as 'All ravens are black' are not completely verifiable, since it would require examination of an infinite number of cases to establish their truth. However, one counter example alone is sufficient to establish the falsity of such a statement. If a clear (but nowadays controversial) distinction is made between theory and observation, then theories could be divided into those which are open to falsification (hence, for Popper, having empirical content) and those which are not. Theories which are vulnerable to empirical refutation and which withstand it are, he claimed, thereby confirmed to some degree. Science makes progress, he suggested, by scientists making conjectures and then looking to see if nature refutes them.

Popper's work is based on a number of doubtful commitments. These include recognizing a clear theory–observation distinction, maintaining a realistic conception of the objects of scientific study, and also holding that the sciences have a hypothetico-deductive structure in terms of which notions like confirmation and testability can be explicated. Under the impact of Thomas Kuhn's sociological approach to the sciences, and of serious qualms about the viability of realism in metaphysics, theory of meaning, and the sciences, many contemporary philosophers of science would be reluctant to endorse Popper's image of an objective science being driven forward by the method of conjecture and refutation. This is not to deny that scientists make conjectures and test them: but this is only part of a range of activities in which they engage and may play a relatively minor role in determining which portions of current theories are rejected and which retained.

See also: Verificationism.

Bibliography

Hacking I 1983 *Representing and Intervening*. Cambridge University Press, Cambridge
Kuhn T S 1970 *The Structure of Scientific Revolutions*, 2nd edn. University of Chicago Press, Chicago, IL
Popper K R 1968 *The Logic of Scientific Discovery*, rev. edn. Hutchinson, London

Foundations of Linguistics

F. D'Agostino

Questions about foundations of (or for) linguistics might be either 'ontological,' 'epistemological,' or 'theoretical.'

1. Ontological Foundations

Foundations for linguistics in the ontological sense are established through identifying and describing the ultimate constituents or aspects of reality which linguistic theories seek to refer to and to characterize. (Similar questions arise in relation to other disciplines. Are social facts really, ultimately, facts about individual human beings? This is a question about ontological foundations for the social sciences.) Theorists concerned with this issue have formulated distinct accounts of the ontological foundations of linguistics.

According to 'psychologism,' linguistic theories are meant to characterize the psychological states of language users and, in particular, their competence to employ their language (see Chomsky 1986: ch. 1).

According to Platonism, the objects which linguistic theories are meant to characterize (namely, sentences) are purely abstract in the same way as are the objects of mathematical theorizing—they have, in other words, no material existence or embodiment per se (though they might be 'represented' by given material objects or events) (see Katz 1981).

According to 'behaviorism,' linguistic theories seek to characterize the actually occurring speech behavior of individual language users and to identify the stimulus circumstances and patterns of conditioning which give rise to it (see Skinner 1957).

According to 'conventionalism,' linguistic theories aim at characterizing the socially constituted conventions which regulate individuals' speech behavior (see, for instance, Bennett 1976).

'Instrumentalism' is a radical alternative to these more committed positions on ontological foundations, according to which it is unnecessary, when theorizing about linguistic phenomena, to provide any account of deeper realities which might be manifested in these phenomena; linguistic theories, on this account, need only provide a basis for the prediction of phenomena. (Instrumentalism, less fashionable in the early 1990s than previously, was perhaps most appealing in relation to quantum mechanics, where it is notoriously difficult to give, within the framework of classical physical theories and of commonsense concepts, a coherent interpretation of underlying realities.)

2. Epistemological Foundations

Foundations for linguistics in the epistemological sense are established when a category of claims is identified with respect to which all other claims are to be justified. (Foundationalism in this sense is no longer as reputable, in the general philosophical context, as it certainly once was. According to contemporary thinking, epistemic justification is provided not by establishing links between foundational claims and those which are to be justified, but, instead, by exhibiting the 'coherence' of the claims which are to be justified with other claims already, though only defeasibly, assumed to be justified.)

According to some, it is native speakers' 'intuitions' about grammaticality, synonymity, etc., that are to be used to test linguistic hypotheses. (This position is associated with the program initiated by Chomsky.) Others reject this approach on the grounds that such intuitions do not provide a suitably intersubjective basis for testing linguistic claims. (How are cases in which some speakers claim grammaticality and other speakers deny it to be understood? For critical discussion of this approach, see Sampson 1975: ch. 4.)

Alternatives (or supplements) to such intuitionism include psycholinguistic investigation of speech production and comprehension, and corpus-based investigation of distributional structure.

Those who seek psycholinguistic foundations demand, for the justification of some claim, that it be supported by evidence about the psychological states of language users. That the sentences *Alf persuaded Beth to leave* and *Alf expected Beth to leave* have different 'deep structural' analyses has its epistemic grounding, on this account, in facts, revealed in 'click paradigm' experiments, about language users' perceptual images of these sentences (Fodor et al. 1974: ch. 6).

Corpus-based investigations, by contrast, take as epistemically primitive observations of the distribution, in an attested corpus of utterances, of various subsentential elements (for an influential account, see Harris 1964).

3. Relations Between Ontological and Epistemological Foundations

There is no straightforward relation between positions on questions about ontological and epistemological foundations. Someone who accepts a psychologistic account might but need not be an intuitionist; s/he might reject intuitionism in favor of a psycholinguistic approach. Perhaps more surprisingly, a Platonist might adopt the same intuitionistic approach to epistemological foundations as a rival psychologistic theorist. Of course, in treating users' intuitions as authoritatively justificatory, these rival theorists will interpret them differently—the 'psychologist' will interpret them as evidence about competence, whereas the Platonist will interpret them as evidence (on the

model of perceptual evidence) about structures which exist independently of human psychological states.

4. Theoretical Foundations

Another approach to linguistic foundations is embodied in attempts to articulate the findings of linguistics with those of other sciences. Those involved in the neurolinguistic enterprise are plausibly represented as seeking to discover the bases or foundations, in the architecture and functioning of the brain, of human linguistic capacities and performances. In a distinct but related way, comparative ethologists might try to discover the precursors of human language capacities and performances in the capacities and performances of nonhuman species (see Lieberman 1984).

Articulation of mathematical models for linguistic structure provides another example of theoretical foundationalism. Investigations of the properties of mathematical systems might even be thought to bear on the adequacy of devices of grammatical representation. (For some applications of mathematical techniques to the understanding of language acquisition, see Wexler and Culicover 1980.)

Bibliography

Bennett J 1976 *Linguistic Behaviour.* Cambridge University Press, Cambridge
Chomsky N 1986 *Knowledge of Language: Its Nature, Origin, and Use.* Praeger, New York
Fodor J A, Bever J G, Garrett M F 1974 *The Psychology of Language.* McGraw-Hill, New York
Harris Z 1964 Distributional structure. In: Fodor J A, Katz J J (eds.) *The Structure of Language.* Prentice-Hall, Englewood Cliffs, NJ
Katz J J 1981 *Language and Other Abstract Objects.* Blackwell, Oxford
Lieberman P 1984 *The Biology and Evolution of Language.* Harvard University Press, Cambridge, MA
Sampson G 1975 *The Form of Language.* Weidenfeld and Nicolson, London
Skinner B F 1957 *Verbal Behavior.* Appleton-Century-Crofts, New York
Wexler K, Culicover P W 1980 *Formal Principles of Language Acquisition.* MIT Press, Cambridge, MA

Instrumentalism

P. Carr

The term 'instrumentalism' is used in the philosophy of science to describe a particular way of interpreting scientific theories, and the terms embedded in those

theories. Instrumentalism is usually defined in contradistinction to 'realism.' Realist philosophies of science claim that scientific theories describe a reality over and above observable events, a reality which may not be directly observable, but which causes those events to occur. A realist, for instance, would interpret the term 'gravitational force' as describing a physical reality which brings about certain observable events, such as objects falling to earth and airplanes remaining within the earth's orbit. It may not be possible to observe gravitational force directly, but its existence is postulated as a causal factor in bringing about a wide range of events which *are* observable. The instrumentalist claims that such an interpretation of theoretical constructs is unwarranted, and all that can be justifiably asserted about terms like 'gravitational force' is that they permit a certain measure of success in predicting and ordering the events in question. The instrumentalist's objection is to the idea of a nonobservable reality 'hidden,' as it were, behind observable events. The emphasis, for the instrumentalist, is on science as being concerned with that which is strictly observable.

A case of conflict between realist and instrumentalist views of science, which is often cited, concerns the realist interpretation given by Galileo of the heliocentric theory concerning the Earth and the sun. The objection raised by the Catholic Church was not to the theory *per se*, but to Galileo's realist interpretation of it, under which it was held to describe a physical reality (the earth's solar system). The Church was prepared to accept only an instrumentalist interpretation of the theory, under which it was seen merely as a useful means of predicting movements of heavenly bodies.

Instrumentalist views of science have been common throughout the history of science (for an introduction to the issues, set in a historical perspective, see Popper 1963). In the twentieth century, when the theory of the atom first began to be developed, many physicists wished to deny the reality of atoms, and to accept an instrumentalist interpretation of atomic theory. Instrumentalist interpretations of science were common among the group of philosophers, active in the 1930s, known as the Vienna Circle. Their philo-

sophical position, known as logical positivism, influenced work done in linguistics in America at the time; and this is said to be evident in the work of the Post-Bloomfieldians (see, for instance, Twaddell 1957 for an instrumentalist interpretation of phonological constructs).

For the Post-Bloomfieldians, if linguistics were to be scientific, it must concern itself with observable events, and not with, for instance, unobservable 'mental states.' Chomsky is said to have rejected such instrumentalism in favor of a realist interpretation of linguistic theory, under which theoretical terms refer to unobservable linguistic realities which lie behind observable linguistic behavior. For Chomsky, these are mental states (see Chomsky 1986).

Although Chomsky's realist interpretation of linguistic theory is widely accepted within generative linguistics, it is common to find generative linguists withholding any bold claims as to the reality of the objects, structures, and relations they postulate. In one generative theory of syntax which emerged in the 1980s, there was an explicit denial as to the psychological reality of the objects and structures postulated. However, to deny that one's theory characterizes a psychological reality need not commit one to instrumentalism. A realist interpretation could be supplied for those objects which is not psychological in nature. (For a fuller account of instrumentalism in linguistics, cf. Carr 1990: ch. 3.)

See also: Realism.

Bibliography

Carr P 1990 *Linguistic Realities*. Cambridge University Press, Cambridge
Chomsky N 1986 *Knowledge of Language: Its Nature, Origin, and Use*. Praeger, New York
Popper K 1963 Three views concerning human knowledge. In: *Conjectures and Refutations: The Growth of Scientific Knowledge*. Routledge and Kegan Paul, London
Twaddell W F 1957 On defining the phoneme. In: Joos M B (ed.) *Readings in Linguistics*, vol. 1. University of Chicago Press, Chicago, IL

Linguistic Philosophy
L. J. Cohen

'Linguistic philosophy' is the name often given to the conception of philosophical problems as problems about meaning or meanings. Until the twentieth century, no important philosopher held *all* philo-

sophical problems to be of this nature. For example, Hobbes (1651) thought that truth consists in 'the right ordering of names in our affirmations,' and asked whether, in a language in which predication was expressed by the adjunction of subject and predicate rather than by a copula, there would be any terms equivalent to 'entity,' 'essence,' or 'essentiality.' But Hobbes's account of political obligation was not linguistic: a citizen's obligation to obey the law, he thought, arises out of the social contract that all citizens make with one another to obey a sovereign who will protect them. However, in the first half of the twentieth century, a more comprehensively linguistic approach to philosophy was encouraged or developed, along at least seven different, though interrelated, lines.

1. Linguistic Approaches to Philosophy

1.1 Frege's (1893) and Russell's (1903) Project for the Reduction of Mathematics to Logic

In this project, all arithmetical concepts were to be defined in terms of logical ones and all arithmetical truths were to be shown provable from logical ones. Thus the correct philosophy of mathematics was to be rigorously and conclusively demonstrated. The project itself encountered a number of deep-seated difficulties; but it nevertheless inspired many philosophers to think it worthwhile exploring the possibilities of exact formal–logical analysis in regard to other areas of language use. Among such searches for logically ideal languages or language fragments, one could list Carnap's (1951) work on the measurement of inductive support, von Wright's (1951) on the logic of obligation, Hempel's on the structure of scientific explanation, Hintikka's (1962) on the relations between knowledge and belief, Prior's (1957) on the role of verb tense in statements about past, present, and future, Plantinga's (1974) on the nature of necessity, and so on. Not all these writers have confined themselves to the linguistic method of philosophizing; but they all contributed towards exploring its possibilities.

1.2 Moore's Minute Analysis of His Contemporaries' Writings (e.g., Bradley, Russell, Stout)

By exposing layer after layer of ambiguity in another philosopher's statements, G. E. Moore (1922) dissected the apparently tenable from the apparently untenable in ways that seldom failed to leave his mark on the problem. He thus introduced strikingly higher levels of rigor into the discussion of important questions in epistemology and metaphysics, such as issues about sense data or other minds, where formal–logical techniques of analysis, like those practiced by Frege and Russell on mathematical issues, are inappropriate or unproductive. And, as his work demonstrated the value of discussing philosophical issues in a more precise linguistic style, it was natural to believe that a certain type of philosophical analysis consisted in just such discussion. Indeed, where it turns out that the only justifiable conclusions about these issues are of relatively little interest, the achievement of precision, rather than the truth of what is made precise, becomes

the principal objective in view. So, among many who attended Moore's lectures at Cambridge, or read his articles, philosophy became the critique of language. But Moore himself never explicitly endorsed such a conception of philosophy, and he was quite ready on occasion to philosophize in a nonlinguistic mode, as when he argued that the most valuable things imaginable are the pleasures of personal affection and the enjoyment of beautiful objects (1903). He also (1942: 660–67) explicitly rejected the view that philosophy should be concerned with the meanings of verbal expressions as distinct from the analysis of concepts or propositions.

1.3 Wittgenstein's Claim (1922) that the Purpose of Philosophy is the Logical Clarification of Thoughts

Philosophy, on this view, is not a theory but an activity, and the result of philosophy is not a number of philosophical propositions but just to make propositions clear. In his later work (1953), Wittgenstein retained his opposition to philosophical 'theories' while stressing the enormous variety of ways in which language functions and the role which it plays in creating philosophical puzzlement. Legitimate progress is then to be made only by assembling detailed examples, without making any generalizations. Such a view of philosophy, however, also cuts itself off from the right to articulate the professed conception of philosophy in general terms. As a consequence, Wittgenstein's approach to philosophy is more easily seen to promote discussion of Wittgenstein's own intentions and achievements than to encourage imitation. However, Schlick (1930); Waismann (1965); Malcolm (1972), and others have acknowledged their debt to his conception of philosophy, and the details of his arguments on particular issues have been widely influential.

1.4 A View of the Characteristic Task of Philosophy

Ayer (1936), Ryle (1949), Hare (1952), and others held the view that philosophy has as its characteristic task the explicit analysis of conceptual thought. Philosophy, so conceived, differs on the one side from the study of the facts about which people think and on the other from the psychological study of the processes of thinking. Its distinctive objects are best seen as the meanings of the words, phrases, or sentences that express the thoughts to be analyzed. It is often occupied with mismatches between the superficial grammatical appearance of a sentence and its underlying logical form or conceptual structure. Thus Ryle (1949), for example, argued that those who ask how a person's mind is related to his body are making what he called a 'category-mistake': they are treating the word 'mind' as if it belongs to the same, locatable-entity category as the word 'body'; they are treating the word 'vanity' as if it belongs to the same category as 'feeling'; and so on. Similarly, legitimate areas of philosophical puzzlement about knowledge, say, or moral duties, or political activity, were held by many to be confined to issues discussable in linguistic terms. Examples were, respectively, the determination of necessary and sufficient conditions for predicating 'He knows that...' of someone, the definition of 'duty' in terms of universal imperatives, and examination of the vocabulary of political dialogue.

1.5 Philosophical Concern about How Language Itself Functions

The concept of meaning has been much discussed, and attention has been particularly focused on the role played by truth-conditions (Davidson 1984), verifiability (Ayer 1936), social conventions (Lewis 1969), or psychological factors (Grice 1957) in an adequate theory of meaning. A connected topic is the theory of reference, including questions about what the world has to be like for reference to be possible (Strawson 1959).

1.6 Quine's Holism

W. V. O. Quine (1953) argued that linguistic philosophers like Ayer (1936) are wrong to suppose that sentences expressing beliefs can be divided into two fundamentally different groups—those that are thought acceptable in virtue of empirically detectable facts, and those that are thought true solely in virtue of their meanings, such as *My brother is in London* and *My brother is my sibling*, respectively. Instead, all beliefs are at risk before the tribunal of experience, though each individual may be more reluctant to change some than others. Nevertheless, Quine (1960) endorsed the methodological strategy of what he calls 'semantic assent.' By semantic assent, speakers may, according to Quine, avoid difficulties that arise in talking about the existence or nature of certain alleged things, events, or processes: they are to talk instead about the contexts in which it is appropriate to use those things' names. Correspondingly, the underlying structure of mathematical and scientific theories is best disclosed by regimenting them into a logically more perspicuous notation.

1.7 Ordinary Language Philosophy

This is the philosophical perspective principally associated with J. L. Austin and his followers, as articulated in Austin's seminal paper (Austin 1957) and discussed in more detail in the article *Ordinary Language Philosophy*. The idea is that, by attention to the fine nuances of actual linguistic usage, a philosopher can notice important conceptual distinctions and relations which might provide new insights into traditional philosophical problems, including those of knowledge, ethics, and mind.

2. Linguistic Philosophy in the 1990s

In the first half of the twentieth century, analytical philosophy was describable as comprehensively 'linguistic,' sometimes because of the problems with which it dealt (Sects. 1.4, 1.5), sometimes because of the methods that it adopted (Sects. 1.1, 1.2, 1.6), and sometimes because of the claims that it asserted (Sects. 1.3, 1.7). Since about 1960, however, analytical philosophers have progressively tended to take up less doctrinaire positions. For example, it is generally seen as a legitimate philosophical enterprise to discuss the rival merits of appealing to a presumptive social contract, or to the maximization of human happiness, for the foundations of justice (rather than merely focusing on the meanings of the terms used or the status of the speech acts involved). Substantive ethical issues about abortion, euthanasia, reverse discrimination, etc., are also thought legitimate subjects of philosophical debate. The results of psychological experiments are no longer regarded as being outside the domain of philosophical interest, since they may affect issues about memory, belief, rationality, etc. Nor is the nature of time, or of matter, thought a suitable topic for discussion by philosophers unacquainted with relevant areas of theoretical physics. Those who still assert a comprehensively linguistic conception of philosophy, such as Dummett (1978: 458), have become rather rare.

Bibliography

Austin J L 1957 A plea for excuses. *Proceedings of the Aristotelian Society* (reprinted in Austin J L 1961)
Austin J L 1961 *Philosophical Papers*. Clarendon Press, Oxford
Ayer A J 1936 *Language, Truth and Logic*. Gollancz, London
Carnap R 1951 *Logical Foundations of Probability*. Routledge and Kegan Paul, London
Davidson D 1984 *Inquiries into Truth and Interpretation*. Clarendon Press, Oxford
Dummett M A E 1978 *Truth and Other Enigmas*. Duckworth, London
Frege G 1893 *Grundgesetze der Arithmetik, begriffschriftlich abgeleitet*. H Pohle, Jena
Grice H P 1957 Meaning. *The Philosophical Review* 66: 377–88
Hare R M 1952 *The Language of Morals*. Clarendon Press, Oxford
Hintikka J 1962 *Knowledge and Belief*. Cornell University Press, Ithaca, New York
Hobbes T 1651 *Leviathan*. J. M. Dent and Sons, London
Lewis D K 1969 *Convention: A Philosophical Study*. Harvard University Press, Cambridge, MA
Malcolm N 1972 *Problems of Mind: Descartes to Wittgenstein*. Allen and Unwin, London
Moore G E 1922 *Philosophical Studies*. Kegan Paul, London
Moore G E 1942 A reply to my critics. In: Schilpp P A (ed.) *The Philosophy of G E Moore*. Northwestern University, Evanston, Chicago, IL
Plantinga A 1974 *The Nature of Necessity*. Clarendon Press, Oxford
Prior A N 1957 *Time and Modality*. Clarendon Press, Oxford
Quine W V O 1953 *From a Logical Point of View*. Harvard University Press, Cambridge, MA
Quine W V O 1960 *Word and Object*. Technology Press, Cambridge, MA

Russell B 1903 *The Principles of Mathematics*. Allen and Unwin, London
Ryle G 1949 *The Concept of Mind*. Hutchinson, London
Schlick M 1930 The future of philosophy. In: Mulder H L, Velde-Schlick B F B van de (eds.) 1979 *Moritz Schlick Philosophical Papers*, vol. 2. Reidel, Dordrecht
Strawson P F 1959 *Individuals: An Essay in Descriptive Metaphysics*. Methuen, London

Waismann F 1965 *The Principles of Linguistic Philosophy*. Macmillan, London
Wittgenstein L 1922 *Tractatus Logico–Philosophicus*. Kegan Paul, London
Wittgenstein L 1953 *Philosophical Investigations*. Basil Blackwell, Oxford
Wright H G von 1951 Deontic logic. *Mind* **60**: 1–15

Logical Positivism

D. Bell

Logical positivism—known also as scientific or logical empiricism—was a movement that flourished in Vienna during the early decades of the twentieth century. The overall aim of its members was to make philosophy 'scientific.' They took this to mean, in general terms, that the concepts, the methods, and the language used by philosophers should be made more rigorous and exact, and that philosophers should be induced to eschew all forms of vague, untestable, or transcendental speculation. More specifically, a central tenet of logical positivism was the thesis that any significant discourse must comprise either substantive, empirically testable claims about the world, or merely formal, analytical propositions that do no more than record the adoption of certain conventions governing the use of signs. Logical positivism thus attempted to combine the radical empiricism of Hume and Mach with the conventionalism of Poincaré and the new logic of Frege and Russell. The claims made by traditional metaphysicians were stigmatized by the Vienna positivists as 'unscientific,' that is, as incomprehensible 'pseudo-claims' lacking all cognitive content.

1. Historical Origins

As early as 1907 a group of Viennese scientists had begun meeting regularly to discuss the philosophical problems which arose in the foundations of their various disciplines. They included Philipp Frank, a physicist, Hans Hahn, a mathematician, and Otto Neurath, a sociologist, economist, and polymath. The dominant influence on this group was Ernst Mach, who had held the newly created Chair of History and Philosophy of the Inductive Sciences in the University of Vienna, 1895–1901. It was not, however, until 1922, when Moritz Schlick came to Vienna to occupy that chair, that the Vienna Circle was properly constituted.

To begin with, the Circle was merely an informal group of like-minded thinkers who met in Schlick's house on Thursday evenings to discuss philosophical problems. By 1928, however, they had founded the Ernst Mach Society, and their manifesto, aptly titled *Wissenschaftliche Weltauffassung: Der Wiener Kreis* (*The Scientific Conception of the World: The Vienna Circle*), was published a year later. From 1928 to 1938 the Circle published a substantial number of monographs on logic, language, mathematics, science, and theory of knowledge.

The list of philosophers and scientists who were members of the Circle is distinguished. In addition to Schlick and the others already mentioned, it includes Gustav Bergmann, Rudolf Carnap, Herbert Feigl, Felix Kaufmann, Kurt Gödel, Victor Kraft, Karl Menger, Béla von Juhos, and Friedrich Waismann. Other philosophers and scientists, although not strictly a part of the Circle, were in close and sympathetic contact with its members for some or all of this period. They include, amongst others, Kazimierz Ajdukiewicz, A. J. Ayer, Kurt Grelling, Albert Einstein, Carl Hempel, Stanisław Leśniewski, Jan Lukasiewicz, Arne Naess, Karl Popper, W. V. O. Quine, Hans Reichenbach, Alfred Tarski, Richard von Mises, and Ludwig Wittgenstein.

The Circle continued, under Schlick's leadership, as a coherent group for nearly 15 years, until the rise of National Socialism and the *Anschluss* forced its members to disperse.

2. Empiricism and Semantics

Central to logical positivism is the goal of establishing the limits and structure of meaningful discourse; and central to the achievement of this goal is the formulation of a criterion of factual meaningfulness or cognitive significance. 'The purpose of this criterion is to delimit the type of expression which has possible reference to fact, from the other types which do not have this kind of significance: the emotive, the logico-mathematical, the merely formal' (Feigl 1943). The criterion itself is empirical: 'there is no way to understand any [factual] meaning without reference to "experience" or "possibility of verification".' (Schlick 1936.) To be intelligible, it was claimed, genuine proper names must stand for objects with which we are acquainted; predicates must stand for observable properties; and sentences must in principle be verifiable in experience.

3. Syntax, Logic, and Mathematics

According to the logical positivists, if a true, scientifically useful sentence is not synthetic, verifiable, and knowable only a posteriori, then it must be analytic, tautologous, empty of empirical content, and knowable a priori. Analytic assertions, they believed, are 'linguistic' in the sense that they merely express arbitrary conventions governing the use of signs. The discipline Carnap called the 'logical syntax of language' was intended to investigate the formal properties of different sets of linguistic conventions, both natural and artificial; and his principle of tolerance denied that any such set was intrinsically more accurate or basic than any other: 'it is not our business to set up prohibitions, but to arrive at conventions.' Both formal logic and number theory, it was claimed, consist of conventionally true analytic statements.

4. Pseudo-problems and the Language of Metaphysics

One consequence of verificationism eagerly embraced by the positivists was this: many sentences of traditional metaphysics are mere pseudo-sentences, and many traditional problems in philosophy are merely pseudo-problems. Unverifiable statements about the ultimate nature of reality, say, or about God, the soul, moral goodness, or beauty were dismissed as empty and meaningless. In this connection Carnap distinguished between 'internal' and 'external' questions. The former are questions concerning the existence or nature of certain objects that can be answered by meaningful sentences belonging to a particular language. The latter are pseudo-questions which attempt to raise issues independently of the power of any language to answer them. If, for example, a language is constructed whose primitive terms refer to physical objects (or sense data, or numbers), then within this language it will make sense to ask whether there exist such things as physical objects (sense data, or numbers). But if one tries to ask, in general, whether physical objects *really* exist, say, or whether numbers are parts of the ultimate furniture of the world, then the questions lack content. Problems can only be posed, and solved, within some particular, conventional language; and outside language there is simply nothing to be said.

See also: Analyticity; Verificationism.

Bibliography

Ayer A J (ed.) 1959 *Logical Positivism*. Free Press, New York
Ayer A J 1971 *Language, Truth and Logic*. Penguin, Harmondsworth
Bergmann G 1954 *The Metaphysics of Logical Positivism*. Longmans, Green, New York
Carnap R 1928 *Der logische Aufbau der Welt*. Weltkreis-Verlag, Berlin (1967 *The Logical Structure of the World and Pseudoproblems in Philosophy*. Routledge & Kegan Paul, London)
Carnap R 1934 *Logische Syntax der Sprache*. Springer, Vienna (1937 *The Logical Syntax of Language*. Kegan Paul, London)
Feigl H 1943 Logical empiricism. In: Runes D D (ed.) *Twentieth Century Philosophy*. Philosophical Library, New York
Gower B (ed.) 1987 *Logical Positivism in Perspective*. Croom Helm, London
Kraft V 1950 *Der Wiener Kreis. Der Ursprung des Neopositivismus*. Springer, Vienna (1953 *The Vienna Circle. The Origins of Neo-positivism*. Philosophical Library, New York)
Reichenbach H 1951 *The Rise of Scientific Philosophy*. University of California Press, Berkeley, CA
Schlick M 1936 Meaning and verification. *The Philosophical Review* **45**: 339–69

Methodological Solipsism

A. Woodfield

Solipsism is the metaphysical doctrine that nothing exists except one's self or mind. Methodological solipsism, in contrast, is a regulative principle prescribing how psychological states (one's own or anyone else's) should be individuated. Its advocates, far from being solipsists, are usually realists about the physical environment and the organisms that live within it. They argue that the principle is a legitimate and necessary constraint upon any scientific investigation into how a mind works. The principle has linguistic implications. Crudely, it recommends that one should construe propositional attitude sentences *opaquely*, by ignoring the referential semantic properties of their embedded 'that' clauses.

1. Defining Methodological Solipsism (MS)

Though the term is found in Kant, methodological solipsism in its late-twentieth-century sense was defined by Putnam (1975: 220) as 'the assumption that no psychological state, properly so called, presupposes the existence of any individual other than the subject to whom that state is ascribed.' Davidson (1987), criticizing this definition, pointed out that describers or descriptions presuppose things; psychological states do not. To sidestep this, it would be possible to substitute 'constitutively requires' for 'presupposes.' Fodor (1987: 42) defines MS as 'the doctrine that psychological states are individuated without respect to their semantic evaluation.'

2. Identifying Psychological States

Mary's *knowing that Paris is full of tourists* is not a pure psychological state because she cannot be in that state unless Paris is indeed full of tourists, which requires that Paris exists and a lot of tourists exist. 'Know,' and many other psychological verbs, are factives. But Mary's *believing that there is a beautiful city full of tourists*, on the other hand, *is* a state that could obtain even if there were no city and no tourists. It appears, then, to be a psychological state properly so called.

It seems commonsensical to ignore whether an agent's beliefs are true or false when explaining behavior. The majority of philosophers and psychologists have always accepted this. Suppose that two 'green' individuals, A and B, share many attitudes and aspirations. Each believes that his local atmosphere is dangerously polluted. Because of that belief, each decides not to buy a car. A lives in Mexico City, which is dangerously polluted, while B lives in Copenhagen, which is not. The fact that A's belief is true while B's is false is irrelevant to the fact that their beliefs have the same cognitive role and the same effect. Psychology should try to build upon generalizations of this sort, abstracting from the fact that people inhabit numerically distinct local environments.

3. Psychological States and the Explanation of Action

Not all explanations abstract from the agent's embeddedness in a particular environment, nor is the truth of a belief always irrelevant to the explanation. It depends on how the behavior is described, and on the type of explanation. Suppose that A and B are motivated to sell their old cars. If A's action is described as 'selling A's car,' then B's act is not of *that* type. This merely shows that actions, too, should be individuated according to the MS principle. Suppose

that the act being explained is a success whose achievement depended upon a belief's being true. Defenders of MS reply that such explanations are *hybrids* in which contextual truths and relationships are 'woven in' to the description of the agent's mental states and actions. To maximize one's chances of picking up significant generalizations, one should prise off the explanation's external component and then try to describe the agent's mind and behavior in a pre-suppositionless way.

Some rationales for MS rely on strong philosophical assumptions about the nature of the mind. Stich (1983) defends a principle of the autonomy of psychological states: 'the states and processes that ought to be of concern to the psychologist are those that supervene on the current, internal, physical state of the organism.' Any scientific inquiry into how a system works must define the boundary between the system and what lies outside it. Psychology is concerned to discover how the mind works, and the mind is a system that depends on the brain. So, if two people had physically and functionally identical brains, their psychological states ought to be counted as the same. The fact that they have different histories and are in different environments is irrelevant, unless and until such differences cause the two people's current inner states to diverge.

4. Inner States and Cognitive Processes

Fodor (1980) assumes that cognitive processes are computational manipulations of internal symbolic representations. Such operations, in both animals and machines, are purely *formal* or *syntactic*. 'Formal operations,' says Fodor, 'are the ones that are specified without reference to such semantic properties of representations as, for example, truth, reference, and meaning.' But, as Stich (1983) is quick to point out, the formality assumption threatens all content-based classifications of psychological states, because content per se is a kind of meaning. Having a *sense* is a semantic property. If all semantic properties are explanatorily irrelevant, then cognitive science must become entirely syntactic (as Stich recommends).

The assumptions made by Stich and Fodor entail conclusions that are stronger than the doctrine of MS defined by Putnam. It is one thing to ignore a belief's truth-value, quite another to refuse to look at the conditions under which it *would be* true. If MS is interpreted in the latter way, as enjoining that psychological states should not be individuated by their truth-conditional contents, then psychological states will be far removed from mental states as normally conceived. Even then, though, MS does not undercut all talk of content in cognitive science. 'Two-factor' theorists such as Schiffer (1981), McGinn (1982), and Block (1986), hold that a *part* of a belief's content is its *conceptual role*, and that this component is 'narrow,' just as MS requires. The article on *Intentionality* discusses some of these issues more fully.

Bibliography

Block N 1986 Advertisement for a semantics for psychology. In: French P A, Uehling T E, Wettstein H K (eds.) *Midwest Studies in Philosophy*, vol. 10. University of Minnesota Press, Minneapolis, MN

Davidson D 1987 Knowing one's own mind. *Proceedings and Addresses of the American Philosophical Association* **60(3)**: 441–58

Fodor J A 1980 Methodological solipsism considered as a research strategy in cognitive psychology. *Behavioral and Brain Sciences* **3**: 63–109

Fodor J A 1987 *Psychosemantics*. MIT Press, Cambridge, MA

McGinn C 1982 The structure of content. In: Woodfield A (ed.)

Putnam H 1975 The meaning of 'meaning.' In: *Mind, Language and Reality: Philosophical Papers*, vol. 2. Cambridge University Press, Cambridge

Schiffer S 1981 Truth and the theory of content. In: Parret H, Bouveresse J (eds.) *Meaning and Understanding*. de Gruyter, Berlin

Stich S 1983 *From Folk Psychology to Cognitive Science*. MIT Press, Cambridge, MA

Woodfield A (ed.) 1982 *Thought and Object*. Clarendon Press, Oxford

Natural Kinds

E. J. Lowe

There is less agreement on what 'natural kinds' themselves are than on what natural kind 'terms' are. The latter are a species of general term and fall into two classes, sortal terms and mass terms, though not all terms in these two classes are natural kind terms. Examples falling into the first class are *tiger* and *lemon* while examples falling into the second are *water* and *gold*. Natural kind terms are often contrasted with terms for artefactual kinds, like *pencil* and *yacht*, one important distinguishing feature being that the former but not the latter typically feature in statements of natural scientific law.

1. The Semantics of Natural Kind Terms

According to philosophers like Saul Kripke and Hilary Putnam, whose work in this area has been most influential, natural kind terms have a number of distinctive semantic characteristics which set them apart from other general terms. In particular, Kripke holds that natural kind terms are, like proper names, rigid designators and accordingly that they are not definable in terms of complex descriptions in the way that empiricist philosophers like John Locke had supposed. Locke believed that a general term like *water* signified an abstract idea composed of the ideas of various observable properties which the user of that term took to be the essential or defining characteristics of a certain kind of substance. This abstract idea constituted the 'nominal essence' of water for that speaker, to be distinguished from water's 'real essence,' which Locke took to be its (then unknown) internal physico–chemical constitution and which

modern science has since identified as its molecular structure, H_2O. In Locke's view it is a purely contingent fact that *water*, as ordinary English speakers understand that term, designates H_2O. Kripke, by contrast, holds that *water* rigidly designates H_2O and consequently that *water is H_2O* is a necessary truth, albeit not an a priori truth.

Putnam has argued that the rigidity of natural kind terms follows from their having a quasi-indexical semantic status, deriving from the role that demonstrated specimens play in the identification of the referents of such terms. For Putnam, *gold*, for example, refers to any metal which is relevantly similar in its internal physico–chemical structure to the samples which competent users of the term in a specific linguistic community would characterize by saying *This is gold*. He points out too that one would defer to the opinion of experts when in doubt as to whether something is gold and consequently that the use of such natural kind terms is subject to what he calls a 'division of linguistic labor.' Finally, Putnam contends that although natural kind terms are associated in speakers' minds with 'stereotypes' (for instance, the stereotypical tiger is striped and four-legged), these stereotypes do not, unlike Lockean abstract ideas, determine logically necessary and sufficient conditions for membership of the associated natural kinds.

2. The Ontology of Natural Kinds

As to what natural kinds *are*, ontologically speaking, no consensus presently exists. Some metaphysicians hold a species, like the tiger, to be a set or class of individual animals (or, more sophisticatedly, a function assigning to each possible world a set of individual animals existing in that world). Others regard the species itself as a sprawling, scattered individual of which individual tigers are constituent parts or members, while yet others hold it to be a universal wholly present in each of its individual instances.

Bibliography

Schwartz S P (ed.) 1977 *Naming, Necessity, and Natural Kinds*. Cornell University Press, Ithaca, NY

Nominalism

D. Bell

Strictly interpreted, nominalism is an ontological theory according to which reality is composed entirely and exclusively of particular items. It entails a denial, that is, of the existence of any intrinsically nonparticular or general entities—for example, properties, relations, species, universals, types, or common characteristics. The mistaken belief that there are such things as these is then diagnosed as resulting from a misconstruction of the way in which common names and general terms function.

1. Strong and Weak Versions

On the most austere version of this view, for example, there is nothing whatsoever that all trees (or chisels, or red things) have in common—except for the fact that the term *tree* (or *chisel*, or *red*) is applied to them. Few philosophers have embraced so extreme a view—though Thomas Hobbes came close:

> 'every [common name], though one name, is nevertheless the name of diverse particular things; in respect of all of which together it is called a universal; there being nothing in the world universal but names, for the things named are every one of them individual and singular'
> (Hobbes 1651: ch. IV)

Less strictly interpreted, nominalism is the name of a tendency, in the sense that a theory is nominalistic to the extent that it successfully restricts assignment of explanatory role to things that are either concrete, or individual, or both. Nominalism, in other words, requires at the very least that one eschew reference either: (a) to abstract objects like sets, numbers, propositions, facts, and truth-values, or (b) to nonparticular, 'predicative' entities like properties, relations, functions, and universals.

2. Issues Relating to Nominalism

As this last claim indicates, however, there are in fact two quite separate issues to be considered here.

2.1 Universals

The first has its origins in ancient debates concerning universals and particulars, the one and the many. In this connection there arise the ontological, logical, linguistic, and epistemological problems to do with the distinction between single, individual items, on the one hand, and, on the other, the shareable attributes or general characteristics they have in common. Nominalism of this sort first emerged in the thought of Roscelin, Abelard, and William of Ockham as a rejection of the Platonic doctrine that universals enjoy real, objective existence. The impetus towards nominalism of this kind has a number of sources. One is perhaps a straightforward ontological intuition, to the effect that reality just is particular, and that there is something fishy about the very idea of a general or universal entity. Many nominalists were motivated, for instance, by their failure to see how a universal could be simultaneously and wholly present in a number of different objects, without becoming divided in the process. Another historically important impetus came with the emergence in the Middle Ages of radical empiricism; for if all knowledge and understanding originates in sensory experience, and if such experience only ever provides data that are irreducibly particular, then the claim that we possess any knowledge or understanding of things that are nonparticular can appear highly problematic. Finally, for those who accept the desirability of ontological parsimony—as formulated for instance in the principle known as Ockham's Razor ('entities should not be multiplied beyond necessity')—there is a requirement that universals be dispensed with, if this can be done coherently.

2.2 Abstract Objects

The second issue associated with the topic of nominalism has a shorter history than the first, having received clear formulation only in works of post-Fregean philosophy. The issue concerns the existence of, and the indispensability of our reference to, abstract objects. An abstract object (a proposition, say, or a set) is a particular object, but one that possesses neither spatio-temporal characteristics nor causal powers. This is a different issue from the first, because abstract objects are themselves particular individuals: they do not have instances; they do not inhere in substances; and so the problems concerning the nature of universals, and the relation of universals to the particulars that instantiate them have no special pertinence with respect to them.

See also: Ontological Commitment; Ontology; Universals.

Bibliography

Carré M H 1946 *Realists and Nominalists*. Oxford University Press, London
Field H H 1980 *Science without Numbers. A Defense of Nominalism*. Blackwell, Oxford
Goodman N 1956 *A World of Individuals. The Problem of Universals*. University of Notre Dame Press, Notre Dame, IN
Goodman N, Quine W V O 1947 Steps towards a constructive nominalism. *Journal of Symbolic Logic* 12: 105–22
Hobbes T 1962 *Leviathan* Collins/Fontana, London
Loux M J (ed.) 1970 *Universals and Particulars: Readings in Ontology*. Anchor Books, New York

Ontological Commitment

C. J. Hookway

The world appears to contain many different things: mountains, people, neutrons, battles, numbers, sets, and so on; and both the variety of these objects and their properties can be investigated. However, lists of these different sorts of things are always controversial: nominalists dispute the claim that there are really abstract objects such as sets and numbers; some positivists refuse to countenance theoretical entities such as neutrons; and other philosophers insist on listing events, such as battles, alongside other objects. Somebody is *ontologically committed* to objects of a certain kind if such objects must exist for their beliefs about the world to be true. It is often thought that standards of simplicity should oblige people to keep their ontological commitments to a minimum; but it is unclear what criteria should be employed in settling whether objects of some kind exist.

1. Criteria of Ontological Commitment

It can often be difficult to identify someone's ontological commitments. A sentence which appears on the surface to involve reference to objects of a certain kind may be paraphrased in a way that shows this to be misleading. 'The lost city of the Incas did not exist' appears to involve reference to a (nonexistent) lost city; the paraphrase 'It is not the case that there was a lost city of the Incas' removes this appearance. Many philosophical 'analyses' offer paraphrases which reduce persons' ontological commitments: analyzing numbers as sets or inscriptions, social institutions as sets of people, and so on. And it is sometimes argued that sentences carry ontological commitments which

are not apparent from the surface. Donald Davidson has argued, controversially, that asserting 'Shem killed Shaun with a knife' refers not only to Shem, Shaun, and the knife but also makes a covert reference to an event of killing (Davidson 1980: ch. 6). So a rule or criterion is needed which, applied to a set of sentences expressing a theory or corpus of beliefs, determines what the ontological commitments of one who accepts those sentences would be. Quine's paper 'On what there is' (1953: ch. 1) is an early attempt to find such a criterion.

Ideally a criterion of ontological commitment would point to a syntactic feature of natural language sentences which always signals acceptance of the existence of objects of a certain kind. Use of singular terms will not provide such a criterion: names of nonexistent things are used; definite descriptions do not always have a referring function; and many things exist which cannot be named or described. Quine proposed that ontological commitments are most explicitly signaled by the existential quantifier: I display my commitment to the existence of neutrons by saying 'There are neutrons.' Quine has acknowledged the 'triviality' of this view. In fact it can still mislead: there are locutions in ordinary language which appear to have this form but which probably do not carry ontological commitments. Thus application of the criterion requires that sentences first be paraphrased into First Order Logic, the Predicate Calculus. A body of sentences carries ontological commitment to objects of a certain kind if its paraphrase into First Order Logic involves quantification over objects of just that kind.

Some philosophers influenced by Meinong, insist that people can talk and think about nonexistent objects; fictional characters might be examples. If one can quantify over nonexistent things, Quine is wrong to believe that existence is what is expressed by the 'existential quantifier.' Others question his reliance upon extensional First Order Logic, claiming that other logics are better equipped for displaying the contents of thoughts. Yet others object than an adequate semantic account of First Order Logic shows that ontological commitments can be carried by expressions other than quantifiers.

2. Ontological Relativity

If Quine's thesis of the indeterminacy of translation is correct, there are implications for his account of ontological commitment. The indeterminacy of reference, a corollary of the more general indeterminacy thesis, suggests that there is no fact of the matter as to what the general terms of a language apply to. By systematically adjusting the translations of other expressions, one could interpret the same native predicate as applying to rabbits, to stages in the history of rabbits, to areas of space one mile to the north of rabbits, and so on. Any translation, that might be found, would be compatible with all the relevant evidence. According to the translation manual used in formalizing the native language and applying Quine's criterion, commitment to an ontology of rabbits, rabbit stages, or areas of space, and so on will be found. At best one can state the ontological commitments of a theory or theorist relative to a manual for translating his speech into our own. Other than relative to a translation manual, there is no fact of the matter as to what the ontological commitments of sentence or theory are (Quine 1969: ch. 2). This is Quine's thesis of 'ontological relativity,' a doctrine he describes as a mere corollary of the indeterminacy or inscrutability of reference. Ontology may be less important than often supposed.

This does not mean that the criterion is without value. When one examines one's own ontological commitments, these relativities are disguised since one uses the 'identity transformation' as the translation manual: one translates 'rabbit' as 'rabbit,' and so on. Reliance on such a translation manual is deeply embedded in the practice of reflecting on thoughts and commitments. But it simply disguises the relativity; according to Quine, it does not eliminate it.

See also: Indeterminacy of Translation; Ontology; Universals.

Bibliography

Alston W P 1958 Ontological commitment 25. *Philosophical Studies* **6**: 8–16
Church A 1958 Ontological commitment. *Journal of Philosophy* **55**: 1008–14
Davidson D 1980 *Essays on Actions and Events*. Clarendon Press, Oxford
Meinong A 1960 The theory of objects. In: Chisholm R M (ed.) *Realism and the Background of Phenomenology*. The Free Press, Glencoe, IL
Quine W V O 1953 *From a Logical Point of View*. Harvard University Press, Cambridge, MA
Quine W V O 1969 *Ontological Relativity and Other Essays*. Columbia University Press, New York
Quine W V O 1990 *The Pursuit of Truth*. Harvard University Press, Cambridge, MA

Ontology

A. D. Oliver

Ontology is the branch of metaphysics which aims to discover what entities exist and attempts to sort these entities into categories. Examples of such categories are: individuals, events, processes, properties, relations, facts, numbers, classes. Other attempts to categorize the contents of the world lead to cross-classification. For example, entities may be abstract or concrete, actual or merely possible. In constructing metaphysical theories, philosophers are guided by Ockham's razor: 'entities are not to be multiplied beyond necessity.' Other things being equal, a theory is to be preferred if it posits the least number of categories of entity.

1. Quine's Criterion of Ontological Commitment

How do we tell what a theory says there is? We might claim that to each name of the theory's language there corresponds an entity named. But in ordinary discourse we use names of nonexistent objects such as 'Pegasus.' Are we to suppose that Pegasus has a mysterious grade of existence inferior to that of ordinary real objects?

W. V. O. Quine avoids this mystery by taking the vehicles of ontological commitment to be existential quantifiers rather than names. He suggests the following criterion of ontological commitment: 'we are convicted of a particular ontological presupposition if, and only if, the alleged presuppositum has to be reckoned among the entities over which our variables range in order to render one of our affirmations true' (Quine 1980: 13). Or, more tersely, to be is to be the value of a variable. So, for example, mathematics includes the sentence 'there is a prime number which is greater than 1,000.' The existential quantifier in this sentence ranges over prime numbers which must be assumed to exist if this sentence is to be true.

2. What Are Numbers?

The diverse pressures facing an ontology are well illustrated by the plethora of accounts of number. For example, the goal of Frege's logicist project was to supply an epistemologically secure foundation for arithmetic. Thus Frege attempted to prove arithmetical truths from logic alone by reducing the category of natural numbers to a category of logical objects: classes. Statements quantifying over numbers were viewed as abbreviating statements quantifying over classes.

But the commitment to classes is epistemologically problematic. In particular, classes, standardly conceived, have neither causes nor effects. Yet knowledge seems to require some causal commerce with the objects known.

Those who cut their ontology to suit their epistemology will supply different accounts of number. For instance, formalists and intuitionists identify numbers with inscriptions and mental constructs, respectively. But these categories of objects cannot supply enough objects to be numbers. Further, numbers look to be necessary existents whereas both inscriptions and mental constructs are contingent existents.

A more radical response to the epistemological problems is to deny the existence of numbers. Given Quine's criterion, to deny the existence of numbers is to deny the literal truth of sentences purporting to quantify over numbers. On such a view, arithmetical sentences are useful fictions that make for smoother science but are, in principle, dispensable. This claim of dispensability must be justified by showing how scientific theories can be expressed without reference to numbers.

3. Respect for Ordinary Discourse

Quine's criterion tells us what a theory says there is. To tell what there is we must also know which theories are true. A wide range of methodological and evidential criteria have been proposed as guides to the truth of a theory. It is a vexed question whether these criteria will vindicate the theories implicit in ordinary discourse.

A semantics for natural language will inevitably commit the users of that language to various categories of entity. For example, verbs of action might be best characterized as referring to events and modal operators best characterized as quantifiers over possible worlds. Moreover, some have thought syntactic and semantic characteristics of language determine the nature of the entities referred to. For example, Frege took the incompleteness of predicates to indicate an incompleteness of the properties to which the predicates refer. Similarly, some have argued from the vagueness of language to the existence of vague objects in the world. But many metaphysicians have less respect for ordinary language, diagnosing the apparent ontological commitments of our everyday discourse as the result of distinctively human interests and limitations which should not be taken as a guide to what there is.

Bibliography

Quine W V O 1980 On what there is. In: *From A Logical Point of View*, 2nd edn, revised. Harvard University Press, Cambridge, MA

Ordinary Language Philosophy

L. J. Cohen

'Ordinary Language Philosophy' is the title sometimes given to the views developed at Oxford by J. L. Austin and those influenced by him, or associated with him, in the period 1936–60.

1. The Debt to J. L. Austin

Austin (1957) recommended English-speaking philosophers to study the meanings and uses of English words on the grounds that the ordinary language of the English speech community embodies 'the inherited experience and acumen of many generations of men.' By finding out what distinctions are implicitly present in the English vocabulary of some nontechnical activity, such as that of making excuses, one is sure, he said, to discover something worth knowing, however much one may also need to study the relevant technical requirements of jurisprudence or psychology. Hence, one would do well to begin by consulting some fairly concise English dictionary, so as to make a complete list of the terms relevant to the chosen topic. In this way, one may perhaps come across such facts as that a high percentage of the terms connected with excuses prove to be adverbs (as if most excuses depend not on what has been done but on the manner, state of mind, etc., in which it was done). In pursuit of such an inquiry, one may also expect 'the fun of discovery, the pleasures of cooperation, and the satisfaction of reaching agreement.'

Austin (1962) applied this conception of philosophy to important issues in pragmatics as well as in semantics. He distinguished the locutionary act of saying something (e.g., *It's cold*), the illocutionary act performed in saying it (e.g., requesting the hearer to close the window), and the perlocutionary act achieved by saying it (e.g., persuading the hearer to close the window). This aspect of his work was further developed after Austin's early death by J. R. Searle (1969) and others.

It should be noticed, however, that ordinary language philosophy, in Austin's style, need not be confined to problems about the terminology and structure of everyday, nontechnical speech. Achinstein (1968; 1983) showed how it can be usefully applied also to certain problems in the philosophy of science. He contrasted what he called the 'positivist' approach to these problems with his own. Positivists, such as Quine (1960) and Hempel (1965), wanted to replace the actual linguistic procedures of science by supposedly superior ones—procedures that are logically perspicuous. But Achinstein himself wanted to characterize them as they are. So, on his view, explanation, for example, was to be analyzed as a certain kind of illocutionary act, and not as a locutionary act that asserts, say, a covering law, as Hempel's model proposes.

2. The Limits of Ordinary Language Philosophy

The expression 'ordinary language' is therefore to be understood in this context as meaning *normal* language, whether technical or nontechnical. But neither Austin nor his followers would have agreed with Naess (1947) that the proper way for philosophers to pursue their inquiries into ordinary language is by using the techniques of opinion-polling and statistical data collection that have been developed in sociology and social psychology. In this respect, the Austinians' attitude toward semantics and pragmatics may be compared with Chomsky's attitude toward syntax. Like Chomsky, they sought, in effect, to characterize competence, not performance. They aimed at constructing a consistent and coherent idealization of ordinary usage, not a tabulation of its actual practice that includes all the malapropisms, solecisms, and other anomalies that in fact occur. They were therefore responsive to the intuitions of language-speakers, rather than to the statistics of people's linguistic practices, as their basic source of relevant information.

Ordinary language philosophy has sometimes been called 'Oxford Philosophy'; but this is a misnomer. Several prominent Austinians lived in Oxford for only a few years, mainly as students (such as Searle and Achinstein), and developed their philosophical ideas subsequently in the USA, while Austin himself had several prominent colleagues at Oxford who were not converted to his way of doing philosophy (such as Ryle, Kneale, Strawson, Dummett, and Williams).

Wittgenstein's later philosophy (1953; 1956, etc.) is sometimes regarded as a form of ordinary language philosophy; but this too is a mistake. Wittgenstein's views were certainly not influenced by Austin, since they began to develop several years earlier; and Berlin (1973: 11) states that Wittgenstein's views had little effect on Austin's circle. Moreover, there were also important differences between the two philosophical methodologies. Wittgenstein did not regard his philosophical thoughts as being relevant to a particular natural language, and from the start they were published in both English and German versions. But Austin explicitly professed to occupy himself with English, even if many of his remarks about English could have been matched by corresponding remarks about other natural languages. Wittgenstein thought of all philosophical theories as arising from the bewitchment of human intelligence by language, and he certainly rejected the idea that he himself was advocating any kind of philosophical theory or generalization. But Austin thought that some philosophical theories—mainly his own—were correct. Wittgenstein's recommendation to ask for the use of a word, not its meaning, tended to blur the difference between semantic and pragmatic issues, whereas Austin sought to show the importance of that difference.

3. Achievements

Ordinary language philosophy had two principal achievements. First, it forced all those who entered into any kind of dialogue with its supporters to keep a sharp eye open for fine nuances and subtleties of linguistic usage, which they might otherwise have neglected, in the exposition or criticism of philosophical arguments. Second, it provided the first fruitful system of ideas for the foundations of pragmatics. However, it began to lose its cutting edge in the 1960s, along with other doctrinaire forms of linguistic philosophy.

Bibliography

Achinstein P 1968 *Concepts of Science: A Philosophical Analysis*. Johns Hopkins Press, Baltimore, MD
Achinstein P 1983 *The Nature of Explanation*. Oxford University Press, New York
Austin J L 1957 A plea for excuses. *Proceedings of the Aristotelian Society* **57**: 1–30
Austin J L 1961 *Philosophical Papers*. Clarendon Press, Oxford
Austin J L 1962 *How to Do Things with Words*. Clarendon Press, Oxford
Berlin I 1973 Austin and the early beginnings of Oxford philosophy. In: Warnock G J (ed.) *Essays on J L Austin*. Clarendon Press, Oxford
Hempel C G 1965 *Aspects of Scientific Explanation and Other Essays in the Philosophy of Science*. The Free Press, New York
Naess A 1947 *Interpretation and Preciseness*. Universitets Studentkontor, Oslo
Quine W V O 1960 *Word and Object*. Technology Press, Cambridge, MA
Searle J R 1969 *Speech Acts: An Essay in the Philosophy of Language*. Cambridge University Press, London
Wittgenstein L 1953 *Philosophical Investigations*. Basil Blackwell, Oxford
Wittgenstein L 1956 *Remarks on the Foundations of Mathematics*. Basil Blackwell, Oxford

Philosophy of Linguistics and of Science

P. Carr

The philosophy of science asks what counts as evidence in science, how theories are tested, what the nature of scientific knowledge is, and indeed whether there are any clear senses in which scientific knowledge can be distinguished from non-scientific knowledge. Similarly, the philosophy of mathematics asks what the nature of mathematical inquiry is, and the philosophy of the social sciences asks to what extent the social sciences are distinct from the natural sciences. The philosophy of linguistics is parallel to these endeavors: it asks what the nature of linguistic inquiry is; what the object of inquiry is; what counts as evidence in linguistics; how theories are tested; to what extent the methods adopted in the various branches of linguistics are parallel to those of the natural sciences.

The philosophy of linguistics is often referred to by other names. One of these is 'foundations of linguistics.' Because these questions concern the nature of theorizing in linguistics, i.e., have theories themselves as their object of inquiry, the endeavor is often referred to as metatheory (theory about theories). Another term used is 'methodology,' since the questions crucially concern the nature of linguistic method (although the term 'methodology' is also used in a more specific way, when discussing, for instance, the way in which a particular investigation is carried out). Here, potentially misleading terminological matters will be dealt with, which will provide a little more detail about the sorts of problem which arise in the philosophy of linguistics.

1. Philosophy of Linguistics and of Language

The terms 'philosophy of linguistics,' 'philosophy of language,' and 'linguistic philosophy' are not synonyms, even though there are questions which they share. The philosophy of language (see Devitt and Sterelny 1987) is a branch of philosophy which deals with the relationship between language, knowledge, and reality. It asks, for instance, whether it is possible to make a systematic distinction between these three domains, whether and to what extent 'reality' is language-dependent. To consider the relationship between language, reality, and knowledge is to consider the nature of linguistic meaning. Because of this, there is no clear dividing line between semantic theory and the philosophy of language.

Linguistic philosophy denotes an approach to philosophy which has emerged in the evolution of twentieth-century philosophy, especially in the English-speaking world. It seeks to address traditional philosophical questions in a new way, by asking about philosophical terms themselves and the way they are used. Thus, with classical problems like 'the mind/body problem,' it is held that much of what was taken to constitute the problem arose from the very terms used; if philosophers examined the terms themselves, it is claimed, problems like this might well simply dissolve. The 'linguistic turn' in philosophy put the philosophy of language much more at the center of philosophy than it had been previously.

A central figure in linguistic philosophy is Ludwig

Wittgenstein. His ideas on, for instance, what it is to follow a rule of a language (see Wittgenstein 1958, Kripke 1982), are equally well described as belonging to any of the three fields that have been defined. Some scholars, such as Baker and Hacker (1984) have attempted to use the work of Wittgenstein to show that theoretical linguistics simply has no object of inquiry. Others, such as Itkonen (1978) have used Wittgenstein to support the view that theoretical linguistics not only has an object of inquiry, but is autonomous with respect to neighboring disciplines. Wittgenstein sought to show that the notion of private language was incoherent, that the notion of a rule of language can be given a coherent interpretation only if the individual speaker is not considered in isolation from his speech community. This is the argument against 'private language.' Itkonen has tried to show that Chomsky's conception of linguistic reality is tantamount to the claim that there may be private rules of language, and is therefore incoherent. Chomsky (1986) has replied that Wittgensteinian skepticism about rules as speaker-internal states is simply a version of the refusal to postulate underlying realities for observed behavior.

2. Philosophies of Linguistics

As in most areas of philosophy, 'isms' abound in the 'philosophy of linguistics.' (The entry *Foundations of Linguistics* describes five of these: psychologism, Platonism, behaviorism, conventionalism, and instrumentalism.) Katz (1981) outlines three main positions in the philosophy of linguistics: realism, nominalism, and conceptualism. Some commentary on the relationship between these terms, and extent to which they overlap, is therefore necessary.

One can align Katz's terms with those cited in the *Foundations of Linguistics* entry. For Katz (1981), 'realism' means Platonic realism. This is therefore not entirely equivalent to realism in the philosophy of science. There, realist interpretations of theoretical constructs assume that they correspond to extra-theoretical entities. Thus, Chomsky is a realist in the latter sense, but not in the Platonic sense: he takes linguistic theories to refer to extra-theoretical states (mental states), but not to *Platonic* states of affairs. The term 'realism' in the philosophy of language has a somewhat wider sense than the same term in the philosophy of science: while realism in the philosophy of language concerns terms in general, scientific realism concerns scientific terms.

Nominalism denies that there are linguistic realities over and above the observable, strictly physical, marks on paper and noises in the air which many linguists take to be *manifestations* of language, rather than language per se. It is, therefore, an instrumentalist position. Closely related to this position are empiricism and the version of empiricism known as behaviorism; they share the view that it is the observ-able phenomena themselves which constitute the object of inquiry in linguistics. Chomsky is not an empiricist in this sense, because he denies that observable behavior constitutes the object of linguistic inquiry.

The term 'conceptualism' as used by Katz (1981), is equivalent to the term 'psychologism' (as described in *Foundations of Linguistics*. It denotes a position which claims that linguistic objects are speaker-internal states of affairs (i.e., mental states).

Chomsky (1995) is the best known advocate of this position. His is an internalist philosopher of linguistics, in that the object of linguistic inquiry is, for him, strictly mind-internal in a special sense: it is a specifically linguistic cognitive state which contains an 'austere' computational procedure, austere in the sense of having very limited access to perceptual systems of behavior. The objects of inquiry are a genetically-encoded, specifically linguistic initial cognitive state and the individual 'final states' (referred to informally as 'knowing a language') which are said to be manifestations of that initial state. Despite his avowed internalism, Chomsky appears to allow that observable behavior may be said to be linguistic since it is exposure to 'linguistic experience' ('primary linguistic data') which is said to trigger the transition from initial to final state. The relation between internal linguistic cognitive states and observable external behavior is, for Chomsky, one of internalization/externalization. It is arguable that this conception of the relation undermines any attempt at radical internalism, since, in allowing that language may be internalized one is, arguably, conceding that it may be mind-external. An alternative conception of the relation between radically internal language and the observable products of speakers' behavior is given by Burton-Roberts (1994), who claims that the latter are produced in aid of physically representing the former, without themselves being linguistic. Hence the relation is conventional.

Bibliography

Baker G, Hacker P 1984 *Language, Sense, and Nonsense.* Blackwell, Oxford
Burton-Roberts N 1994 Ambiguity, sentence and utterance: a representational approach. *Transactions of the Philological Society* **92**: 179–212
Chomsky N 1986 *Knowledge of Language: Its Nature, Origin and Use.* Praeger, New York
Chomsky N 1995 Language and nature. *Mind* **104**: 1–61
Devitt M, Sterelny K 1987 *Language and Reality: an Introduction to the Philosophy of Language.* Blackwell, Oxford
Hkonen E 1978 *Grammatical Theory and Metascience.* Benjamins, Amsterdam
Katz J J 1981 *Language and Other Abstract Objects.* Blackwell, Oxford
Kripke S A 1982 *Wittgenstein on Rules and Private Language: An Elementary Exposition.* Blackwell, Oxford
Wittgenstein L 1958 *Philosophical Investigations.* Blackwell, Oxford

Rationalism

J. Cottingham

The term 'rationalism' is standardly used in histories of philosophy to contrast with 'empiricism.' Rationalists (from the Latin *ratio* 'reason') are said to maintain that knowledge can be arrived at by reason alone, independently of the senses, while empiricists (Greek *empeiria* 'experience') take it that there can be no knowledge which is not ultimately derived from sensory inputs. The classification is perhaps most familiar in textbooks of seventeenth- and eighteenth-century philosophy, where the 'British empiricists,' Locke, Berkeley, and Hume, are routinely contrasted with the 'continental rationalists,' Descartes, Spinoza, and Leibniz. But this blunt and schematic contrast is in many respects misleading; the 'rationalist' Descartes, for example, insists on the vital importance of sensory observation in testing scientific theories, while the 'empiricist' Locke, though asserting that 'all our knowledge is founded in experience,' nonetheless stresses the crucial role played, in the development of knowledge, by the mind's own active faculties for combining, comparing, and abstracting from sensory data.

1. Innate Ideas

Despite its problems, the rationalist/empiricist distinction does provide a useful focus for a number of central issues in the philosophy of language. The most important of these is the issue of 'innateness'. Rationalists like Descartes, following a tradition that goes back as far as Plato, maintained that the human mind at birth is already imprinted with certain innate 'ideas'—a term which covered both concepts (such as the concept of God or of triangularity) and also propositions or principles (such as the principle of noncontradiction in logic). This implies, in effect, that there is a kind of innate language—a language of thought—which all human beings are born knowing. The term 'knowing' is a slippery one in this context, since it is clear that young children, for example, do not possess any *explicit* awareness of principles like the law of noncontradiction; and this led Locke and others to dismiss the whole notion of innate ideas. To this innatists replied that the knowledge in question might be present *implicitly*; in a suggestive analogy used by Leibniz in his *New Essays on Human Understanding* (ca. 1704), the human mind at birth is likened to a block of marble—not a uniform block indifferently suited to receive any shape the sculptor may choose to impose on it, but one already veined in a certain pattern. In this metaphor, the blows of the sculptor's hammer are likened to sensory inputs: without them there could be no sculpture, just as without

sensory inputs there could be no knowledge. But though the hammer blows are necessary, the internal veining is also necessary to explain the final shape. And similarly, a crude empiricism that appeals to sensory input alone is insufficient to explain knowledge of certain fundamental and universal principles of logic and mathematics; an innate prestructuring of the human mind must also be invoked.

2. A Universal Language of Thought

There is some similarity between the issues addressed in these early debates and the linguistic controversy over Noam Chomsky's notion of a 'universal grammar.' Just as Chomsky argues that the mind must be endowed from birth with certain deep structural principles which enable the young child to learn any language on the basis of very meager and defective linguistic data, so the earlier 'rationalists' argued for the theory of innate ideas by citing human ability to perceive and acknowledge fundamental conceptual and logical truths, whose validity is recognized as extending far beyond those cases which have actually been perceived by the senses. In both cases, what makes the argument persuasive, or at the very least challenging, is its insistence on the need to explain the gap between the limited actual empirical input in early life and the richness and scope of the eventual abilities (whether logical or linguistic) which all human beings normally develop.

The idea of a universal language of human thought is a pervasive one in rationalist philosophy, and is not confined to discussions of the innateness question. In the seventeenth century, the notion is often connected with a belief in a divine creator who has illuminated our minds with (at least some of) the fundamental principles which govern the universe as a whole. In a famous pronouncement, Galileo declared in *Il Saggiatore* (1623) that 'The great book of the universe cannot be understood unless one can read the language in which it is written—the language of mathematics.' Some years later, Descartes announced his revolutionary program for the mathematicization of physics in closely similar terms. The qualitative language of earlier scholastic philosophy was resolutely to be avoided; all scientific explanations were to be couched in quantitative terms. 'I recognize no matter in corporeal objects,' wrote Descartes, 'apart from what the geometers call quantity . . . i.e., that to which every kind of division, shape and motion is applicable' (*Principles of Philosophy* 1644). Part of what this new program involved was a rejection of the ordinary language of the senses, with its supposedly 'commonsense' vocabulary of terms like 'warm,' 'wet,' 'hard,' 'heavy,' 'bitter,' 'smooth.' Such terms may be applied on the basis of sensory experiences which are vivid enough, yet the rationalists argued that they lacked the transparency and precision of mathematical terms. 'Sensible properties are in fact occult properties,' wrote Leibniz later in the seventeenth century, 'and there must be others more manifest which could render them more understandable.'

3. *Characteristica Universalis*

A recurring dream of rationalism was that of a *characteristica universalis*—a clear, precise, and universal symbolic alphabet in terms of which the whole of human knowledge might be represented. It is probably fair to say that the philosophical consensus nowadays is that any such aspiration is radically misconceived. Briefly, there seem to be two major obstacles in its way. The first is the problem of 'commensurability': it is hard to see how the languages of different branches of science (and perhaps even of different theories within the same branch) can be readily inter-translatable, or reducible to a common currency of 'neutral' or universal symbols. And the second is the problem of 'justification': it is hard to see how traditional rationalism could defend its claim to have discovered the master vocabulary or canonical language which describes the universe 'as it really is.' Many of the issues involved here are complex and still unresolved. What is clear is the enduring importance of the rationalist tradition in philosophy, if only because so much contemporary philosophy of language and theory of meaning defines itself by its opposition to that tradition.

See also: A Priori; Chomsky, Noam; Innate Ideas.

Bibliography

Cottingham J 1984 *Rationalism*. Paladin Books, London
Chomsky N 1966 *Cartesian Linguistics: A Chapter in The History of Rationalist Thought*. Harper and Row, New York

Realism

A. Weir

Dictionaries of philosophy tend to define the philosophical doctrine of realism along the following lines: realism is the view that the entities one takes to exist, do so independently of our minds and mental powers. Realism thus explicated is then contrasted with idealism, which holds that the items of everyday experience or scientific investigation are in some sense mental constructs.

1. Historical Context

Historically two specific forms of realism are often distinguished: (a) medieval realism regarding the existence of properties; (b) the dispute between direct realists on the one hand and phenomenalists and representationalists on the other. In the first dispute, realists argued that predicates such as 'is wise' stand for mind-independent correlates—here the property of wisdom, just as names such as 'Socrates' stand for independently existing objects. Their opponents argued that 'is wise' can apply meaningfully and truly to mind-independent objects without it being the case that it too stood for some mind-independent entity.

Insofar as predicates designate anything at all, they designate mind-dependent entities such as concepts.

Direct realists in perception argued for a distinction between first the act of perceiving, second its content—e.g., that a tree is in front of me—and finally the object of perception. The latter, where it exists, is a mind-independent entity, the direct realist maintains, whereas the act of perceiving and its content are clearly mind-dependent. Opponents of direct realism reject the distinction between act, content, and object in perception and hence maintain that the immediate objects of perception are mind-dependent entities—ideas, sense data, and so forth. Both disputes, then, exemplify the general pattern—realism affirms mind-independence for some sort of entity, idealism or anti-realism denies it.

2. 'Realism' in Philosophy

In analytical philosophy 'realism versus antirealism' seems to be used to cover two somewhat different sets of problems. The first concerns scientific realism which is usually contrasted with forms of instrumentalism.

The instrumentalist distinguishes between observational and theoretical sectors of language and maintains that only sentences of the former sector are objectively true or false. Theoretical sentences are instrumentalistically useful to the extent that their observational consequences turn out to be true but truth for the theoretical sector consists in nothing more than such predictive utility. For the scientific realist, by contrast, even if one can draw a significant distinction between observational and theoretical sectors, which some doubt, there is no difference in respect of truth: sentences from either sector are rendered true or false by a mind-independent world. Scientific realism is also often taken to include the antiskeptical view that science inevitably progresses, if correctly pursued, closer and closer to the truth, and that the theoretical terms of current science are not empty but refer to mind-independent entities with natures of roughly the same type as we ascribe to them.

The extreme instrumentalist denial that the concept of truth applies to scientific theory (found in some logical positivists) did not survive Tarski's demonstration of the definability of truth for certain formal languages. But instrumentalistic views are common amongst philosophers influenced by the positivists or by pragmatism. W. V. O. Quine, for instance, draws a fairly sharp observation/theory distinction and denies there is any mind and theory-independent distinction of fact not reflected in a difference in observational data. His views incline towards a relativism regarding truth for those theories compatible with, but transcending, the empirical facts. Similarly relativistic views on scientific truth can be found in many other influential philosophers (in the early writings of T. S. Kuhn, for instance) and are incompatible with the realist view of a mind-independent realm of facts against which theories can be measured absolutely for truth or falsity.

As well as scientific realism, 'realism' is also currently used as a name for certain fallibilistic doctrines. The fallibilist about a certain class of beliefs holds that such beliefs, even if arrived at in optimal conditions for belief formation, can be wholly false. The linguistic turn of modern philosophy has led to fallibilism being interpreted as a semantic doctrine: that truth for sentences transcends the evidence for them. A tension thus emerges between the skepticism of fallibilism and the antiskepticism of the scientific realists (who often claim the semantic doctrine of fallibilism has little to do with traditional realism). Nonetheless the idea of mind-independence needs explicating—antirealists agree the world is independent of, for example, the will—and fallibilism offers one fairly clear way of doing so. On the other hand, traditional realism did not involve radical skepticism towards sentences such as 'there are physical objects,' the very reverse in fact. Even if the fallibilist evinces no actual doubt regarding this sentence but holds merely that our opinions and the truth on this matter might have come apart, realists with a naturalistic approach to cognition might demur. Conversely one might take a fallibilist view towards, say, mathematics while denying that it deals with mind-independent entities. A compromise is to characterize realism towards a class of entities as the view that some beliefs (typically linguistically expressed) *about* them are fallible. Antirealist fallibilism in mathematics then consists in denying that mathematics is about anything. Explicating just what 'aboutness' comes to, is the major difficulty with this proposal.

Fallibilism is taken to be the key realist notion by philosophers skeptical of its truth such as Hilary Putnam and Michael Dummett. They agree of course that one is often wrong; that, for example, the objects one applies terms to in actual linguistic practice are often not those one ought to apply them to if one is to respect the objective content of the expression. But they insist objective content is rooted in our linguistic practices too. Empiricist views of sentence meaning— the meanings transmitted and learnt in language-learning cannot transcend the empirical circumstances of the learning—then lead them to suggest the notion of truth is identified or replaced with epistemic notions such as verifiability or justified assertibility and to deny that beliefs arrived at in optimal circumstances can be false. Thus metaphysical doctrines such as realism are held to depend on theories from the philosophy of language.

Critics of such views counter that they rest on poor epistemology. Skeptics about the notion of non-deductive justification will find the notion of justified assertibility dubious. And Chomskyans will charge the antifallibilists with a crude empiricist theory of the acquisition and transmission of linguistic meaning, holding by contrast that the empirical circumstances of language learning may act only as a catalyst activating a largely innate cognitive state of understanding which can transcend its experiential inputs. Even if the general negative arguments against realism fail, however, the task of establishing it as correct for particular cases, for example, for microphysical objects, quantum mechanical states, abstract objects, and so forth, is still a substantial and unrealized one.

See also: Instrumentalism.

Bibliography

Devitt M 1991 *Realism and Truth*. Blackwell, Oxford
Dummett M 1978 *Truth and Other Enigmas*. Duckworth, London
Kuhn T S 1970 *The Structure of Scientific Revolutions*. University of Chicago Press, Chicago, IL
Putnam H 1978 *Meaning and the Moral Sciences*. Routledge and Kegan Paul, London
Quine W V O 1992 *The Pursuit of Truth*. Harvard University Press, Cambridge, MA

Sortal Terms

E. J. Lowe

'Sortal terms' are a species of general term falling within the grammatical category of common or count nouns (or, more generally, count noun phrases). The adjective 'sortal' was apparently coined by John Locke, who used it to describe names for sorts or species of individual substances, and modern usage more or less agrees with this. Typical examples of sortal terms in English are *horse, tree,* and *clock.* Some sortal terms, like *horse,* denote natural kinds and others, like *clock,* denote artefactual kinds. Yet others denote abstract kinds, for example, the logico–mathematical sortal terms *set* and *number.*

1. The Semantics of Sortal Terms

A distinguishing semantic feature of sortal terms is that the application of any such term is typically governed by criteria of individuation and identity—principles determining the individuation and identity-conditions of the particular items characterizable by that term. Thus a full grasp of the meaning of the term *horse* will involve an understanding of what makes for the individuality of any particular horse (how, for instance, the horse as a whole is related to its parts) and what defines the persistence of an individual horse over time. Possession of such an understanding is a necessary condition of a speaker's being able to identify, distinguish, and hence count individual horses. The question of *how many* individual items characterizable by a given sortal term exist subject to some further condition (for instance, how many horses exist in the UK today) is one which always makes sense, even if it cannot always be answered. It should be noted, however, that not all count nouns (nouns which form plurals and admit numerical adjectives) satisfy this condition, and hence that not all count nouns qualify as sortal terms. It makes no determinate sense, for instance, to ask how many *things* exist in a given room at a certain time, because the noun *thing* is not governed by any distinct criterion of identity. Such nouns are sometimes called 'dummy sortals.' It is important to realize too that not all sortal terms are governed by the same criterion of identity, a fact which Locke himself clearly appreciated. (Locke argues at length that the sortal terms *man* and *person* convey different identity conditions.) However, where the sorts denoted by two sortal terms are related as species to genus (as, for example, with *horse* and *mammal*), the terms in question must indeed be governed by the same criterion of identity, for one and the same individual may be characterizable by both such terms and such an individual cannot be subject to two

different sets of identity-conditions, on pain of contradiction.

2. Classifications of Sortal Terms

Sortal terms may be further subclassified in various ways. So far only syntactically simple sortal terms have been mentioned, but there are also syntactically complex ones, exemplified by such count noun phrases as *white horse* and *tree which sheds its leaves in winter.* Some sortal terms which are syntactically simple appear nonetheless to be semantically complex: for instance, *mathematician* is arguably semantically equivalent to something like *person who studies mathematics,* and is therefore governed by the same criterion of identity as governs the unqualified sortal term *person* (though whether or not the latter is in turn semantically complex is a matter for debate). Sortal terms like *boy* and *tadpole* are examples of what David Wiggins has called 'phased sortals,' because they characterize the items to which they apply only during one phase of their existence. It appears that many but not all phased sortals which are syntactically simple are semantically complex. For instance, *boy* is arguably analyzable as meaning *young male human being* but it is debatable whether *tadpole* is synonymous with *immature frog with gills and a tail,* for even if the latter two terms are necessarily coextensive this is not obviously something of which competent speakers of English have a priori knowledge.

Sortal terms bear certain close affinities to mass terms like *water* and *gold.* Many terms in both classes are alike in designating natural kinds. But mass terms are unlike sortal terms in being dissective (gold is divisible into parts which are themselves gold, but the parts of a horse are not themselves horses) and in not supplying principles of enumeration for their instances. Thus, whereas it makes sense to ask how *many* horses, say, exist in a given region, it only makes sense to ask how *much* water or gold does. Even so, a mass term like *gold* clearly does have a criterion of identity governing its application, for it makes sense to ask whether the gold existing in a region at one time is the *same* gold as that existing there or elsewhere at another time. Where mass terms crucially differ from sortal terms, then, is in lacking criteria of individuation governing their application. There are however standard ways of creating complex sortal terms out of simple mass terms: for instance, *drop of water* and *nugget of gold.* It should also be noted that some general terms are ambiguous in that they admit both a sortal term and a mass term interpretation, as is illustrated by the ambiguity of the sentence *Mary had a little lamb*.

Bibliography

Lowe E J 1989 *Kinds of Being: A Study of Individuation, Identity and the Logic of Sortal Terms*. Basil Blackwell, Oxford
Pelletier F J (ed.) 1979 *Mass Terms: Some Philosophical Problems*. Reidel, Dordrecht
Wiggins D 1980 *Sameness and Substance*. Basil Blackwell, Oxford

Universals

A. D. Oliver

It is an undisputed fact that particulars have properties and stand in relations to other particulars. Those who believe in universals, the realists, analyze this fact by supposing that particulars are related to a distinct category of entity, universals, which are identified with properties and relations. Philosophers have suggested that universals offer solutions to a variety of linguistic and nonlinguistic problems. Historically, the primary problem is to give an account of the objective resemblances of particulars (the so-called 'problem of universals' or 'problem of the one over the many'). In metaphysical terms, how is it that distinct particulars can be of the same type? In linguistic terms, how is it that distinct particulars can be characterized by the same predicate? Realists explain sameness of type as the sharing of a universal by the particulars. Nominalists reject universals and so reject this explanation of sameness of type.

1. Realist Theories

Realist theories differ along two dimensions. First, universals can be either transcendent or immanent (the scholastic distinction between *universalia ante res* and *universalia in rebus*). For example, Plato's Forms are often interpreted as transcendent universals. They inhabit a puzzling platonic heaven separate from the particulars that imitate or participate in them. Aristotle brought universals down to earth by denying that they can exist separately from and independently of the particulars that are related to them—universals are 'in' particulars. D. M. Armstrong (1989) has tried to cash out the metaphor of immanence. He argues that a 'thin' particular, say Socrates, is related to a universal, say wisdom, by a primitive relation of instantiation. The 'thick' particular, consisting of Socrates instantiating all his nonrelational universals, actually contains those universals. Universals are located in space and time but, mysteriously, they are wholly present wherever they are instantiated.

The second dimension of difference between realist theories concerns the abundance of universals. At the abundant extreme, a universal corresponds to each predicate. At the sparse extreme, universals are only admitted if they are required to characterize the objective resemblances and causal powers of particulars. On the sparse view, the relationship between predicates and universals is more complex. As Armstrong says, 'given a predicate, there may be none, one or many universals in virtue of which the predicate applies. Given a universal, there may be none, one or many predicates which apply in virtue of that universal' (Armstrong 1978, vol. 2: 9). Armstrong's sparse and immanent theory of universals is motivated by empiricism. Universals exist in our space–time world and, by examining this world, science determines *a posteriori* what universals there are.

2. What Work Will Universals Do?

In thought and language we pick out particulars and ascribe properties to them and relations between them. A realist theory of universals gives the ontological ground for this activity of predication. For example, the predicate 'is wise' applies to Socrates because he instantiates the universal wisdom. The predication relation is explained via the primitive relation of instantiation. One predicate can apply to many different particulars because each particular instantiates the universal that is the ontological correlate of the predicate. Socrates and Plato are both wise because each instantiates wisdom. So universals solve the linguistic form of the 'one over many' problem.

But a sparse theory of universals cannot offer this solution because there is no guarantee that our predicates pick out the objective resemblances among particulars that science will discover—there might be no universal wisdom. Hence, Armstrong offers his sparse theory as a solution to the metaphysical version of the 'one over many' problem. The objective resemblances between particulars (which may or may not be picked out by our ordinary language predicates) sort them into types. Particulars of the same type, say being 1 kilogram in mass, literally have something in common, the universal 1 kilogram in mass, which grounds the resemblance.

3. A Nominalist Response

David Lewis (1983) rejects Armstrong's universals. Lewis suggests that properties are classes of actual and possible particulars. Predication is analyzed by the primitive relation of class-membership—to have a property is just to be a member of a class. Since every class of particulars is a property, properties are even more abundant than predicates. Such indiscriminate properties cannot ground the objective resemblances of particulars. But Lewis suggests classes can be ordered on a scale of naturalness. The perfectly natural classes are those which contain particulars of the same type. Unlike Armstrong, Lewis does not attempt to analyze the facts of resemblance but rather takes these facts as primitive.

So Armstrong and Lewis both do justice to the facts of resemblance by having a sparse conception of properties. But because Armstrong does not tie universals to language, he cannot easily employ universals in giving that language a semantics. Lewis, on the other hand, also has an abundant conception of properties that can supply ready-made semantic values for predicates—to each predicate there corresponds the class of actual and possible particulars that satisfy the predicate. Indeed, such classes can function as the semantic values for other linguistic categories as well. For example, *red is a color* employs 'red' as an abstract singular term. It is extremely difficult to paraphrase this sentence so that the apparent reference to a property disappears. But it is also implausible to suppose that 'red' stands for a universal (on Armstrong's sparse theory). So Lewis suggests that 'red' stands for the class of red particulars. Such classes also prove to be the best candidates for the values of the variables of second-order quantifiers as in *some zoological species are cross-fertile*.

4. Future Work

There can be no doubt that both sparse and abundant conceptions of properties and relations are required. A semantics for natural language will require an abundant conception, whereas work in metaphysics suggests that the sparse conception can do much more besides accounting for sameness of type among particulars. The compulsory and widely contested question is how one should characterize these two conceptions and their relationship to one another. It should be mentioned that a theory of tropes, or abstract particulars, is receiving increasing attention as a viable alternative to both Armstrong's realism and Lewis's class-nominalism.

See also: Nominalism; Ontology; Realism.

Bibliography

Armstrong D M 1978 *Universals and Scientific Realism*, 2 vols. Cambridge University Press, Cambridge
Armstrong D M 1989 *Universals: An Opinionated Introduction*. Westview Press, Boulder, CO
Campbell K 1990 *Abstract Particulars*. Blackwell, Oxford
Lewis D K 1983 New work for a theory of universals. *Australasian Journal of Philosophy* **61**: 343–77
Loux M J 1976 The existence of universals. In: Loux M J (ed.) *Universals and Particulars: Readings in Ontology*, rev. edn. University of Notre Dame Press, Notre Dame, IN
Mellor D H Oliver A D (eds.) 1997 *Properties*. Oxford University Press, Oxford
Oliver A D 1996 The metaphysics of properties. *Mind* **105**: 1–8.

Verificationism

S. Shalkowski

Verificationism is the latter-day incarnation of classical empiricism. In keeping with the classical empiricist tradition formulated by Locke, Berkeley, and Hume, verificationists give a preeminent place to experience in the acquisition of knowledge. During the nineteenth century, while idealism was prevalent in Germany and Britain, Vienna became a center for European empiricism. This Viennese tradition continued into the twentieth century and took a very clear and influential form in the 1920s with the formation of the Vienna Circle and the development of the set of philosophical ideas that became known as 'logical positivism.' Influenced by the anti-metaphysical positions of the scientifically inclined Ernst Mach and Henri Poincaré, the Vienna Circle opposed the apparently extravagant metaphysical claims of German and British idealism which seemed to be based on an allegedly supra-scientific access to truth. Thinkers in the Vienna Circle rejected both idealist metaphysics and the possibility of any nonscientific method for acquiring knowledge, making a sharp distinction between metaphysics and science.

1. Cognitive Significance

The fundamental problem for these opponents of idealism was how to separate assertions that are worthy of our attention from those that are not. What principled basis could they give for declaring 'Jupiter has natural satellites' acceptable, but 'The Absolute is active' not? They sought the answer to this question by focusing on the general problem of meaning or cognitive significance. The question of how to separate science from unacceptable metaphysics depended on an answer to the question of when a statement is meaningful or cognitively significant.

In his *Tractatus Logico–Philosophicus*, Wittgenstein maintained that the claims of metaphysics are nonsense and that the only propositions which are sayable are those of natural science. Subsequently, empiricists tried to identify two different ways in which cognitive significance can be attained. Analytic statements are meaningful because their truth depends on the accepted conventions about how to use words. So 'All bachelors are unmarried' was said to be meaningful because it is true in virtue of the way words like 'bachelor' and 'unmarried' are used in English. Analytic truths can be thought of as following from the truths of logic together with certain linguistic conventions (what Carnap called 'meaning postulates'). If all of mathematics could be reduced to logic, its truths, central as they are to the sciences, would belong to the category of the meaningful. All other statements are meaningful, according to the 'verifiability principle,' only insofar as they are in principle capable of being verified by (actual or possible) experience. The trouble with 'The Absolute is active' is that there is no set of observations that could, even in principle, establish its truth.

2. The Verifiability Principle

The verifiability principle provided verificationism with both a theory of meaning and a solution to what Karl Popper called the 'problem of demarcation,' the problem of how to separate science from nonscience. For verificationists, the separation of science from nonscience coincided with the separation of sense from nonsense. As well as metaphysics, much of what had traditionally been part of epistemology, ethics, and other branches of philosophy, was now said to consist of nonscientific, meaningless claims. Constructions like 'Murder is wrong,' may have an emotive content, but are, at best, pseudostatements devoid of factual meaning.

Early formulations of the verifiability principle restricted meaningfulness to statements capable of conclusive verification. Under this formulation, the principle entails that a nonanalytic statement is meaningful if and only if some set of basic observation statements entail (and are entailed by) the statement in question. This formulation of the principle, however, was too restrictive to serve the verificationists' purposes. In particular, this formulation renders all universal laws of science nonscientific and meaningless. No unrestricted universal statement can be conclusively established on the basis of a limited number of observations alone. Since verifiability was intended to legitimize science, as well as condemn metaphysics, emasculating science by declaring all scientific laws to be nonsense was unacceptable. In *Language, Truth and Logic*, A. J. Ayer weakened the principle to make verifiability equivalent to confirmability. This meant that a nonanalytic statement is meaningful just in case it is possible that there be some evidence that counts in favor of the truth of that statement. On Ayer's account, an empirically meaningful statement is one that can be conjoined with suitable auxiliary hypotheses to derive observational consequences that are not derivable from the auxiliary hypotheses alone.

While this weaker criterion of empirical meaning gives the verdict that scientific laws are empirically meaningful, it also gives the verdict that 'The Absolute is active' is meaningful because we can take 'If the Absolute is active, then Rover is brown' as an auxiliary hypothesis and with the two of these statements derive 'Rover is brown,' which is entailed by neither the statement in question nor the auxiliary hypothesis alone. A further attempt was to suggest that all empirically meaningful statements can be reduced to statements in a suitably restricted language whose primitive predicates all designate only characteristics of immediate experience. Other variations on the theme of formulating an acceptable criterion of meaningfulness in terms of verifiability were proposed, but each had the weakness of either excluding too much or too little from the realm of the meaningful.

3. Falsifiability

According to Karl Popper, theories like astrology are defective not because they are not amenable to confirmation but because they are too confirmable. No matter what happens, pseudoscientific claims are compatible with the outcome. Astrology is pseudoscientific precisely because it is confirmed by everything and falsifiable by nothing. In contrast, Einstein's theory of relativity makes risky predictions that could turn out to be incorrect. Thus, Popper suggested that the hallmark of science is not any form of verifiability, but *falsifiability*. For him, the issue of separating science from pseudoscience and the issue of separating sense from nonsense were independent issues, the former being a genuine philosophical problem while the latter is a typical philosophical pseudoproblem. Popper was concerned only with the line of demarcation between science and pseudoscience. His critiques of the general confirmationist or inductivist approaches to science were misconstrued as alternative proposals about meaning and many of his criticisms were unheeded for several decades.

4. Verificationism and Semantic Theory

Verificationism is still a prevalent doctrine in semantic theory. Verificationism in semantic theory is the doctrine that the meaning of a statement is at least partially a function of the evidence one has for that statement. Michael Dummett's verificationist semantics, sometimes called semantic antirealism, claims that the meaning of a statement is the conditions under which a speaker has sufficient justification for asserting it. However, Dummett's project is not to distinguish science from pseudoscience or sense from nonsense. Rather, it is to account for linguistic knowledge. If language is to be learnable, he argues, meanings are things to which speakers will have sufficient access in order to associate those meanings with the appropriate statements. By contrast, truth-conditional semantics allows that statements may be true (or false) even though those who understand them may be in principle incapable of recognizing this. Thus, contemporary verificationists explicate semantic properties in terms of epistemological properties. For them, the theory of meaning is just the theory of linguistic understanding; and meanings are not entities, but structured practices of competent speakers of a language.

In ways that earlier verificationists did not fully appreciate, verificationist (antirealist) semantics has implications for the proper form of logical theory, and for acceptable metaphysical theses. If statements do not have truth conditions that transcend verification, then to assert a statement is equivalent not to the assertion that the statement is true, but to the assertion that the statement is justified. The assertion that p is equivalent to the assertion that 'p' is justified. It follows that the assertion that ~p is equivalent to the assertion that '~p' is justified. Consider now the classical law of excluded middle, which says that every instance of 'p ∨ ~p' is true. If verificationist semantics is adopted, this reduces to the claim that it is always true that either 'p' is justified or else '~p' is justified. But, there are many statements we have neither sufficient reason to assert nor sufficient reason to deny. For them, the proper action is refusal either to assert or deny. Accordingly, excluded middle is rejected by contemporary antirealists along with the classical logic in which this law is embedded.

It is widely recognized that a thoroughgoing empiricist semantics requires a radical rethinking of the nature of valid inference. If truth is thought to be closely associated with warranted assertibility, then the semantic principle of bivalence, that every statement is either true or false, must also be rejected by the verificationist for parallel reasons.

Verificationism has parallel consequences for metaphysics. If some statements are neither true nor false, and truth requires metaphysical truthmakers (be they cognizer-independent facts or cognizer-dependent epistemic conditions), then—as it were—the world has metaphysical gaps. Suppose 'p' is such a statement. There is no truthmaker for 'p' and there is no truthmaker for '~p' (there is no fact of the matter). Far from verificationism laying all metaphysical claims to rest, it appears to carry with it its own metaphysical commitments.

See also: Analyticity; Meaning Postulate; Falsificationism; Intuitionism; Logical Positivism; Realism.

Bibliography

Ayer A J 1936 *Language, Truth and Logic*. Gollancz, London
Ayer A J (ed.) 1959 *Logical Positivism*. Free Press, Glencoe
Carnap R 1967 (trans. George R A) *The Logical Structure of the World [and] Pseudoproblems in Philosophy*, 2nd edn. Routledge and Kegan Paul, London
Dummett M 1978 *Truth and Other Enigmas*. Harvard University Press, Cambridge, MA
Hempel C 1950 Problems and changes in the empiricist criterion of meaning. *Revue Internationale de Philosophie* **4**: 41–63
Popper K 1959 (trans. Popper K) *The Logic of Scientific Discovery*. Hutchinson, London
Quine W V O 1951 Two dogmas of empiricism. *Philosophical Review* **60**: 20–43

SECTION III
Language and Mind

Apes and Language
S. L. Williams, E. S. Savage-Rumbaugh, D. M. Rumbaugh

The second half of the twentieth century has seen a great surge of interest both in *language* and in *apes*. With regard to language, the questions have been focused upon the pattern and process whereby it is acquired by children and whether its roots are in genetics or in learning. With regard to apes, the questions focused upon evolution and the genetic relatedness of apes to the early hominoids and humans. The intensity of debates on both topics has been substantial and sustained. It should come as no surprise, then, that the question, 'Can apes acquire language?' also gives rise to great controversy. After all, to answer that question presumes that one can define 'language.' Language, along with all other similar concepts, can be defined—but not to everyone's satisfaction. Is speech, for example, a requisite to language? What constitutes a *natural*, versus an artificial language? Also, one might even object to that question by declaring, 'If, as many hold to be the case, language is a distinguishing attribute of our species, apes cannot possibly acquire it!' Nevertheless, within this confusion matrix, a number of investigators did launch research programs to answer the question, 'Can apes acquire language?'

Why might the ape be expected to acquire language? The answer is, of course, that they are very closely related to us. Chimpanzees, for example, are more closely related to us than they are to gorillas. Humans share 99 percent of genetic material with these apes (Andrews and Martin 1987), and human lineage diverged from theirs only 4–6 million years ago (Sibley and Ahlquist 1984).

1. Early Attempts to Teach Language

Since neural limitations and the anatomy of the vocal tract prevent the ape from producing sounds necessary for human speech (Lieberman 1968), alternative modes for communication have been sought.

The 1960s witnessed the beginnings of two important chimpanzee projects, each with a unique approach to communication: one by Beatrix and Alan Gardner of the University of Nevada and another by David Premack at the University of California, Santa Barbara. The Gardners used a manual sign language, the American Sign Language for the Deaf, as their medium for establishing 'two-way communication' with a chimpanzee. They believed that their chimpanzee (*Pan troglodytes*), Washoe, would be competent to make such signs and that she would be acquiring a 'natural' language as she did so. Premack used plastic tokens to stand for words with his chimpanzee, Sarah. His method employed an artificial language system. Despite different methods and goals, both Washoe and Sarah learned to use their signs and tokens and impressed many with their accomplishments.

The 1970s saw the launching of the LANA Project by Rumbaugh and his associates of Georgia State University, the University of Georgia, and the Yerkes Primate Center of Emory University. Unique to the LANA Project was the introduction of a computer-monitored keyboard, with each key having a distinctive geometric pattern called a 'lexigram.' Instead of letters, each lexigram key on the chimpanzee Lana's keyboard was meant to serve as a whole word. The priority goal of the LANA Project was to determine whether a computer-controlled language-training system might be perfected to advance research where learning and language abilities were limited, either due to genetics (i.e., apes, whose brains are one-third the size of the human brain) or brain damage (i.e., children with mental retardation). Development of the computer-controlled system succeeded beyond expectations. That system also was a prototype for portable language-communication keyboards that are now commercially manufactured and in wide use by children with mental retardation (Romski and Sevcik 1992). Through such keyboards, many retarded children are able to communicate and thus participate in the world as they have not been able to in the past.

The 1970s also saw Terrace's Project Nim (Nim was a chimpanzee) launched at Columbia University and Miles's Project Chantek (Chantek was an orangutan, of the genus *Pongo*) at the University of Tennessee, Chattanooga. Also, Fouts led his own project, first at the University of Oklahoma and then at Central Washington College. All three of these projects used manual signing based on the American Sign Language for the Deaf. Primarily through use of various modes of trial-and-error teaching methods entailing molding of the ape's hand, young chimpanzees learned at least *when* to make a given manual sign or gesture in relation to each of a variety of exemplars and events (Fouts 1972). Whether the apes *knew* what they were signing was, at that time, not recognized as a central question. The emphasis was upon production, i.e., the use of signs by the apes.

In retrospect, all of the foregoing projects shared a common error. All project leaders naively assumed that, if an ape appropriately produce a sign, that it would also comprehend or understand that sign when used by other social agents. Since 1980, however, it has been learned that the skills of production do *not* by themselves warrant the conclusion that understanding, by the user, is in place. In 1992 data and arguments also strongly support the conclusion that it is comprehension or understanding that is the critical ingredient for language, not the ability to produce signs, or to make specific sounds.

As discussed below, language understanding can be instated in chimpanzees by rearing them from birth much as human children are reared—in an environment where language is used to announce and to coordinate social activities (Savage-Rumbaugh, et al. 1993).

A review of research, enabled by the computer-monitored lexigram keyboard that has led to our present-day understanding of language and the processes whereby apes can acquire it, is in order.

1.2 The LANA Project

Research with Lana was designed so that she could exercise substantial control over her environment and life through use of her keyboard. On that keyboard, each key was embossed with a distinctive geometric symbol, called a lexigram. Each lexigram was intended to function as a word, just as words generally do in our vocabularies. The first symbolic communications learned by Lana were 'stock' sentences, i.e., they were specific sentences which had to be used by her in order to activate a variety of devices controlled by the computer. The software program in the computer specified certain relationships between words that had to be honored if Lana's multilexigram productions were to have any effect. Examples of stock sentences were, 'Please machine give milk,' 'Please machine make window open,' 'Please machine give piece of apple (or bread, banana, etc.),' and so on. Lana's use of stock sentences availed to her a variety of foods and drinks, music, slides, movies, a view out of the window, and so on. In addition, two-way symbolic communication between Lana and her caretakers became possible at least to the extent that specific

kinds of tests could be conducted to determine her skills of naming objects and their colors (e.g., 'What name-of this that's blue [or red, orange, green, black, etc.]?,' 'What color of this box [or ball, cup, shoe, etc.?]').

Lana demonstrated that an ape could learn to use more than 200 lexigram symbols, either singly or in stock sentences, with relatively high levels of accuracy. Lana also made interesting modifications in several portions of her stock sentences and phrases in a manner that suggested insight on her part that such could be used to achieve special purposes. For example, a cucumber was asked for as 'the banana which is green,' an orange-colored commercial soft drink was asked for as the 'Coke which is orange,' and a whole orange (i.e., fruit) was called the 'apple which is orange (color)' and the 'ball which is orange.' She also modified several stock sentences (Rumbaugh 1977) so as to achieve unique communications with caretakers. For example, Lana readily modified her stock sentence, 'Please machine give coffee,' to 'You give coffee to Lana,' and 'You give this which is black,' in contexts where the well-mastered stock sentence, for various reasons, failed to net her a cup of coffee (e.g., where people, and not the machine, had the coffee).

Lana also learned to differentiate valid versus invalid stems or beginnings of stock sentences that were up to five lexigrams long. Given a valid stem, constructed by the experimenter, she would complete it appropriately. For example, if the experimenter gave Lana the sentence stem, 'Please machine . . . ,' Lana could add, ' . . . give Coke,' ' . . . give piece of banana,' and so on. Given an *in*valid stem, such as 'Machine please . . . ,' or 'Please give machine of piece . . . ,' rather than 'Please machine,' or 'Please machine give piece of . . . ,' she would erase it rather than waste effort with it. (She erased it through use of the 'period' key, which served to clear the incorrect stem from the keyboard. She learned early on, and by herself, to use the period key to erase her own errors of production.) In this and other ways, Lana exhibited competence with the grammar of her language system, a grammar which had to be complied with if her requests were to be 'honored' by the computer that monitored her productions and that controlled the activation of the incentive-vending devices of her room.

After five years of training, Lana could produce sentences with up to 11 lexigrams in length. However, in the final analysis, Lana failed to show skills of comprehension that one would expect of her, given her impressive skills of 'production.' Simply learning associations between lexigrams and exemplars and learning rudimentary rules of grammar were not sufficient to produce a competence commensurate with a young child's language development, which reflects a far greater degree of understanding language. Consequently, an additional program of research that focused upon pragmatics and semantics or language understanding was begun.

1.3 Sherman and Austin

Beginning in 1975, two other chimpanzees, Sherman and Austin, were taught to use the lexigram keyboard in settings that emphasized communication between them. A clear requisite for competent communication between Sherman and Austin to be achieved was the ability to comprehend the meanings of lexigrams.

To cultivate comprehension, the chimpanzees learned that they both had to share specific information and to act upon that information. For example, prized foods and drinks (e.g., referents of lexigrams) were placed in sealed containers, hence not necessarily immediately present and directly observable. Because, on any given trial, only one of the two chimpanzees saw, and hence knew, the *specific* food or drink that was placed in the container and because neither could receive the food unless both asked for it properly, the onus was upon the first chimpanzee to communicate the contents of the container to the second one. If the second chimpanzee comprehended the communication and properly requested the item which it had not seen, the food was shared between them. Otherwise, the palatable incentive was withheld. Thus, the need to communicate was instated. More importantly, when their keyboard was taken away, the chimpanzees demonstrated that they had learned the importance of communication as well as how representational symbol systems work. This they demonstrated by inventing their own symbol system. With no lexigrams available, they used manufacturers' brand names and labels (M & M, Coke, etc.) to tell one another the identity of the hidden food.

In these and a variety of other contexts, experiences served to encourage learning that the use of symbols enabled communication 'about' things, rather than that their use was just a ritual of responses necessary to access 'things.' Through many other additional communication paradigms that stressed the use of symbols to refer to things removed in space and time, Sherman and Austin became highly competent in labeling (i.e., naming) items, requesting items, complying with the requests of others, and most importantly in understanding language symbols (see Savage-Rumbaugh 1986).

The communicative value of language for Sherman and Austin served to cultivate comprehension and generated other untaught, unanticipated uses of their word lexigrams. Sherman and Austin became the first chimpanzees to systematically communicate their wishes and desires to one another through the use of printed symbols. They learned to take turns, to exchange roles as speaker and listener, and to coordinate their communicating activities. Once they had learned the referential value of symbols, they began to use the keyboard to *announce* their intended actions: what it was they were going to do (e.g., tickle, chase, play-bite, or to set about getting a specific food or drink from a refrigerator in another room).

Sherman and Austin also demonstrated impressive symbol-based, cross-modal matching abilities (e.g., to equate the 'feel' of objects via touch to lexigrams and vice versa). Without specific training to do so, they were able to look at a lexigram symbol and then reach into a covered box and select the appropriate object on the basis of tactual cues alone. They could also feel or palpate an object not in view, and state the name of that object.

The most important demonstration that lexigrams were *meaningful* symbols to Sherman and Austin was achieved in a study where they, first, learned about the *categories* of 'food' and 'tool,' and then, second, appropriately classified lexigrams of their vocabularies using those categories.

Initially, only three foods and three tools were used to introduce the concept of 'categories' to them. Each chimpanzee was taught to label three edible items as 'foods' and three implements as 'tools.' They were then shown other food and implements to see if they could generalize the categorical concepts to things that had not been used during training. They could. Then they were shown the word-lexigram symbols for a variety of foods and implements and asked whether or not each word symbol (e.g., banana, straw, cheese, magnet, corn chips, etc.) stood for a food or a tool. They were able to label these word lexigrams as food-words or tool-words the *first* time they were asked and did so without specific training. Thus, they revealed an understanding of the fact that word symbols stood for things. They also knew the specific things each symbol stood for—otherwise they could not have called the word lexigram for 'corn,' a food and the word lexigram for '(drinking) straw,' a tool; for it was not the word lexigrams *themselves* that were food or tools, but rather the things they stood for that enabled them to categorize them correctly. Such skills left little doubt but that for Sherman and Austin their lexigrams served as representations of things not necessarily present and that they had mastered the essence of *semantics* (e.g., symbol or word meaning).

2. Later Studies with *Pan paniscus*

All of the chimpanzees discussed to this point were so-called 'common' chimpanzees of the genus and species, *Pan troglodytes*. There is a second major species of chimpanzee that has been erroneously called the 'pygmy' chimpanzee. It is now clear that this second species is *not* a pygmoid version of another form, and it is now by preference called the bonobo (*Pan paniscus*).

Bonobos are even rarer and more endangered than the common chimpanzee and they more closely resemble humans. Bonobos frequently walk upright more readily and competently than *P. troglodytes*. Also, they use eye contact to initiate joint attention, iconic gestures to entice others to assume physical orientations and actions, and use vocal communication with greater frequency than does the common chimpanzee. They also tend to be more affiliative. Both the bonobo and common chimpanzee maintain strong social, though somewhat unique, bonds within their group.

Matata, a wild-born female that dwelled in the forest until an estimated age of six years, was the first bonobo introduced to the lexigram system. Methods that had proved successful with both Sherman and Austin in the majority failed with Matata. At best, Matata learned only eight lexigrams and, then, only how to use them to request that things be given to her. Even after years of effort, Matata failed to use even these few lexigrams reliably and gave no evidence that any of them functioned as symbolic representations of their individual referents. Nevertheless, Matata otherwise appeared to be a very bright chimpanzee.

During her lexigram training, Matata had her adopted son, Kanzi, with her. No systematic effort was made to teach Kanzi lexigrams while work with Matata was underway. He was always present, however, whenever Matata was worked with. Consequently, he always had the unintended opportunity to *observe* her training.

When Kanzi was two and a half years old, he was separated from Matata when she was taken to another site to be bred. Only then did it become obvious that something unexpected had happened. Kanzi had learned the symbols that experimenters had been attempting to teach Matata. He needed no special training to use symbols to request that things be given to him, to name things, or even to announce what he was about to do.

As a consequence, a significant change was made in research tactics. Structured training protocols were terminated, and Kanzi was introduced to a life in which throughout his waking hours he was part of a social scene. People talked in English to Kanzi and touched the appropriate lexigrams on his keyboard whenever they coincided with words of spoken utterances. Through continued observation of others' use of language Kanzi also learned language and its functions in the real world. Kanzi was encouraged to listen to speech and to observe others; however, he was never denied objects or participation in activities if he did not use his keyboard. Caregivers used the keyboard to comment on events (present, future, and past), to communicate with each other concerning their intentions or needs, and, in particular, to talk about any thing that appeared to be of interest to Kanzi.

Kanzi quickly learned to ask to travel to several of the named sites throughout 55 acres of forested land that surrounds the laboratory. He learned to ask to play a number of games, to visit other chimps, to get and/or prepare and even cook any number of specific foods, and to watch television. Kanzi's lexigram vocabulary increased to 149 words by the time he was

five and a half years old. It was only a short time before it was also noted that, in contrast to Lana, Sherman, Austin, and Matata, Kanzi appeared to be comprehending human speech—not just single words, but sentences as well.

As a consequence, an experiment was undertaken to assess Kanzi's speech comprehension and to compare it with that of a human child, Alia (Savage-Rumbaugh, et al. 1993). Under controlled conditions, designed to preclude inadvertent cueing as to what should be done, both Kanzi and Alia were given 660 novel sentences which requested them to do a variety of unusual things. For example, they were asked to take a specific object to a stated location or person ('Take the gorilla [doll] to the bedroom'; 'Give Rose a carrot'), to do something to an object ('Hammer the snake!'), to do something with a specific object relative to another object ('Put a rubber band on your ball'), to go somewhere and retrieve a specific object ('Get the telephone that's outdoors'), and so on.

An everchanging and wide variety of objects was present, and the subjects were asked to act upon members of each array in a variety of ways. This practice ensured that 'compliance with a request' was *not* simply a result of a given subject doing whatever was obvious on a given trial. Thus, when asked to 'Get the melon that's in the potty,' a second melon was on the floor—even in Kanzi's path to the potty; and when asked to 'Get the lettuce that's in the microwave (oven),' Kanzi found not only lettuce, but a variety of other things in the oven as well.

At the time of the study, Alia was two and a half years old and Kanzi was about nine years old. Interestingly, Kanzi's comprehension of novel spoken sentences was quite comparable to Alia's. Both subjects were about 70 percent correct in carrying out the sentences of novel requests on their first presentation.

By the time Kanzi was eight years old, his productive competence of lexigrams with gestures was comparable to an 18-month-old child. His lexigram vocabulary consisted of well over 250; his comprehension of spoken English was commensurate with that of a two and a half-year-old child.

Kanzi was the first ape that had acquired language skills *without* formal training programs. He developed language by observing and by living. The pattern whereby he did so paralleled that of the normal human child who, first, comes to comprehend the speech of others and then subsequently talks.

Was Kanzi an exceptional bonobo? Or, could his skills of comprehension be replicated with other chimpanzees?

To answer this question, Kanzi's younger sister, Mulika, was exposed to the same kind of linguistic environment that Kanzi had, but was introduced to it at a much earlier age. She, too, first developed comprehension of spoken English and lexigrams as used by others and then began to use them productively.

At the age of about 18 months, although Mulika could use only seven or eight lexigrams with competence, tests revealed that she understood 70 others!

2.2 Interspecies Comparisons

Was the ability to comprehend spoken English a particular characteristic of bonobos or, given rearing from birth in a language-saturated environment, would the common chimpanzee exhibit similar competency? An answer to this important question was sought in a study that involved corearing the two species of *Pan*, *P. paniscus* and *P. troglodytes*, so as to give them the same early exposure to spoken English and social communicative use of the lexigram keyboard. The two subjects selected were Panbanisha, a bonobo, and Panzee, a common chimpanzee. Their ages differed by only six weeks at the beginning of the study. From shortly after their births, for the next four years these two chimpanzees were uniformly provided with an enriched environment that emphasized communication as did Kanzi's.

The experimenters expected that, under the conditions of their rearing that lacked all formal training, only the bonobo would come to comprehend English and use the keyboard. Initial results, up until the subjects were about two years old, supported that expectation. Notwithstanding, the common chimpanzee also evidenced significant, though lesser competence in both speech comprehension and in the spontaneous learning of the lexigrams and their meanings. She understood words and used her keyboard to communicate, thus revealing that *environment* was *the critical ingredient* in the spontaneous emergence of language skills in the chimpanzee as well as in the bonobo. On the other hand, the bonobo infant, Panbanisha, was substantially ahead of the common chimpanzee infant, Panzee, in all criteria. This observation, coupled with the extraordinarily limited speech comprehension skills of our four other common chimpanzees, discussed above, strongly suggests that the bonobo has a unique proclivity for benefiting in language acquisition if reared from birth in a language-saturated environment.

3. Important Factors in Language Acquisition—What Can be Concluded from these Studies?

Kanzi, Mulika, Panbanisha, and Panzee learned language without the typical trial-based learning paradigm involving reward-based contingencies. Given the appropriate environment from shortly after birth and continuing for several years, an ape can acquire linguistic skills without contingent reinforcement in formal trial-by-trial training. (All other apes before them—Sherman, Austin, and Lana—required formal training designed to cultivate various language functions.) Normal human children do not require formal training to learn language. Most certainly, the fact that most children experience a communicative environment from the moment they are born is critical to the acquisition of language.

Research with apes supports the view that a sensitive period exists for language acquisition (Greenough, et al. 1987): exposure to language during this period is necessary for the activation and further development of cognitive structures supported by specific brain circuitry. Kanzi's mother, Matata, was an adolescent when first given language training, training from which she could not significantly benefit. Her language competence was negligible when compared to that of Kanzi and Panbanisha's who were given very rich language environments within which to develop from shortly after birth. Similarly, Lana, Sherman, and Austin were between 18 months and two years old when their language training began. They were, by comparison, minimally able to comprehend human speech or to learn the meanings of lexigrams spontaneously. These observations suggest that it is during the first few months of life that exposure to language, including speech, is important if the continued development of language is to be optimal.

Germane to the support of this point are observations on Tamuli, another bonobo; at the age of three years she was given the same experiences as Kanzi and Panbanisha's for seven months to see if she could acquire a vocabulary of lexigrams and come to comprehend spoken English. Tamuli failed to benefit other than minimally from that experience. Her lack of progress is consistent with the view that it is early within the first year of life that the sensitive time occurs for exposure to language to impact optimally upon brain and cognitive structures. The competence for language is laid postnatally, if not prenatally, and during early infancy—not in the school's classroom.

If exposure to language is sufficiently early, no training is needed for chimpanzees and bonobos to begin to understand speech and that symbols represent things and ideas. They will spontaneously begin to communicate under these conditions if provided with a keyboard. If exposure to language occurs after infancy, once the apes have already reached the juvenile period, language skills can be inculcated through training but they do not appear spontaneously. In addition, even with training, the speech comprehension skills of such apes remain extremely limited.

If exposure to language occurs at adolescence or later, even training appears to be insufficient to inculcate functional, representational language skills in the ape. Of course, better training techniques could be discovered in the future which would make it possible even for these apes to learn language.

In humans, and now in apes as well, language acquisition entails, first, comprehension. Comprehension develops long before the speech musculature has matured enough for vocal control permitting language production in the child (Golinkoff, et al. 1987).

It is now known that human children, raised from birth with the keyboards, use the lexigrams both to communicate their needs and to name things long before they can speak the words. Such prespeech use of lexigrams can begin as early as seven and a half months and offers an early and highly unique access to the child's language and cognitive development.

4. What Have Lexigrams Done to Aid Language Development?

The lexigram keyboard appears to help structure the linguistic information as it is presented. Because the ape's attention is brought to the lexigram symbol simultaneously as it hears the spoken word, it appears to be better able to parse out spoken words from the soundstream that otherwise characterizes the hearing of a spoken sentence. In turn, this parsing probably serves to enhance the learning of individual word meanings. Speech coupled with corresponding use of lexigrams appears to facilitate the encoding of words and word meaning.

As children with severe language deficiencies acquire competence in the use of these keyboards, they become more sociable at home and in the school and enjoy enhancement of interactions with normal peers. Their competence in using their boards extends to the real world, as per ordering food in restaurants and in work. Use of the keyboards also serves to stimulate the children's effort to speak, apparently in response to hearing the speech sounds which are under their control when the keyboard is used.

5. Summary

By studying apes, a great deal has been learned about language and how early environment serves from birth to support its acquisition. The work has enabled symbolic language skills to be acquired by children with language deficits due to mental retardation. In due course, studies of language acquisition will help us to understand better how language evolved and how our early ancestors may have used it to communicate.

Bibliography

Andrews P, Martin L 1987 Cladistic relationships of extant and fossil hominoids. *Journal of Human Evolution* **16**: 101–08

Fouts R 1972 Use of guidance in teaching sign language to a chimpanzee (*Pan*). *Journal of Comparative Psychology* **80**: 515–22

Gardner R A, Gardner B T 1969 Teaching sign language to a chimpanzee. *Science* **165**: 664–72

Golinkoff R M, Hirsh-Pasek K, Cauley K M, Gordon L 1987 The eyes have it: Lexical and syntactic comprehension in a new paradigm. *Journal of Child Language* **14**: 23–45

Greenough W T, Black J E, Wallace C S 1987 Experience and brain development. *Child Development* **58**: 539–59

Lieberman P 1968 Primate vocalizations and human linguistic ability. *Journal of the Acoustical Society of America* **44**: 1157–64

Miles L 1978 Language acquisition in apes and children. In: Peng F C C (ed.) *Sign Language and Language Acquisition in Man and Ape*. Westview Press, Boulder, CO

Premack D 1970 A functional analysis of language. *Journal of the Experimental Analysis of Behavior* **14**: 107–25

Romski M A, Sevcik R A 1992 Patterns of language learning by instruction: Evidence from nonspeaking persons with mental retardation. In: Krasnegor N A, Rumbaugh D M, Schiefelbusch R L, Studdert-Kennedy M (eds.) *Biological and Behavioral Determinants of Language Development*. Erlbaum, Hillsdale, NJ

Rumbaugh D M (ed.) 1977 *Language Learning by a Chimpanzee: The LANA Project*. Academic Press, New York

Savage-Rumbaugh E S 1986 *Ape Language: From Conditioned Response to Symbol*. Columbia University Press, New York

Savage-Rumbaugh E S, Brakke K, Hutchins S 1992 Linguistic development: Contrasts between co-reared *Pan troglodytes* and *Pan paniscus*. In: Nishida T (ed.) *Proceedings of the 13th International Congress of Primatology*. University of Tokyo Press, Tokyo

Savage-Rumbaugh E S, McDonald K, Sevcik R A, Hopkins W D, Rubert E 1986 Spontaneous symbol acquisition and communicative use by pygmy chimpanzees (*Pan paniscus*). *Journal of Experimental Psychology: General* **115(3)**: 211–35

Savage-Rumbaugh E S, Murphy J, Sevcik R A, Williams S, Brakke K, Rumbaugh D M 1993 Language comprehension in ape and child. *Monographs of the Society for Research in Child Development*, Nos. 2 & 3

Sibley C G, Ahlquist J E 1984 The phylogeny of hominoid primates as indicated by DNA-DMA hybridization. *Journal of Molecular Evolution* **20**: 2–15

Terrace H S 1979 *Nim: A Chimpanzee Who Learned Sign Language*. Knopf, New York

Innate Ideas

C. Travis

The ancient idea of innate ideas was later given new life and substance first by Descartes, then by Leibniz. Since Leibniz, innate ideas have come in two strengths. Some are ideas or concepts that could not have been acquired through experience, or simply were not so acquired. This is the weaker strength. The others, more potent ideas, are innate because, were they not already in place, experience would have nothing to teach us, or there would be nothing that we could learn, at least within some wide domain. For example, Leibniz thought that certain logical ideas—in effect, those of truth and identity—were of this type.

1. The Traditional Problems: Descartes and Leibniz

Descartes's appeal to innate ideas stemmed from the following kinds of considerations. No-one has ever drawn or seen a perfect triangle. Rather, what we confront are at best only approximations to that ideal, which raises the question of why we detect that particular pattern in the samples where we do, or why we view them as approximations to that ideal or indeed to anything. Experience does not teach us to choose that ideal, so the idea of a triangle is not acquired, which means it must be innate (weaker strength). Moreover, it takes the right constitution to see triangles where something quite nontriangular occurs in the brain.

By contrast, Leibniz's problems were of this nature: 'If I do not know already that no contradiction is true, then how can experience teach me, say, that a hawk is not a handsaw?' Granted, hawks fly, and handsaws do not. But perhaps that just means: hawks/handsaws fly and do not. If Leibniz is right about the problem and its solution, then there are innate ideas in the stronger sense.

Leibniz and his main opponent, Locke, agreed that the key issue was not over innate ideas, but rather over innate principles, i.e., *knowledge that* such-and-such. What one needed to know to learn about hawks and handsaws was that no contradiction is true. But Leibniz and Locke also agreed that there can be no *knowledge that* without the conceptual resources for formulating it. To know that no contradiction is true, one needs the idea of truth. Perhaps in having the latter, one just does know the former.

Innate ideas thus played a role in a theory of innate logical competence, which was their most important application from the seventeenth to the twentieth centuries. Some have thought logical competence, in Leibniz's sense, bogus. Their idea, in brief, is that the reason why any rational animal knows that no contradictions are true is that we could not recognize any animal as rational without crediting it with that knowledge. In seeing someone as rational, we must do him the further courtesy of seeing him as logical to that extent. We are forced so to interpret him. The 'competence' is thus all in the eye of the beholder; it points to no specific psychological real internal organization. Even if this view were plausible (i.e., the logically competent reliably perform in quite concrete ways, which leaves room for that performance to be explained by something), it just pushes the problem to a new domain. We are forced to see rational animals

in 'such-and-such' a way. Again, one answer to what forces us is supplied by innate ideas.

2. Chomsky's Conception of Innate Ideas

The idea of innate ideas has been used in the twentieth century by Noam Chomsky. Like Leibniz, his main concern is with a specific competence; in Chomsky's case a linguistic, or syntactic, one. The idea is that one could not learn a language without being innately constituted to learn (by natural means) a specific type of language as opposed to others. The type is characterized by a certain set of principles, which, since they fix what humans are constituted to learn, are universal in human languages. At least for a time, Chomsky characterized this innate constitution, in one way among others, by ascribing knowledge of these principles to the language learner. By the Locke–Leibniz principle, knowledge of principles requires the conceptual resources for formulating them. Hence, Chomsky concluded, we have innate grammatical ideas.

Chomskyan innate ideas may be seen as modified Leibnizian ones—modified enough to make their existence a partly empirical question. It is not that the particular innate grammatical ideas that he would posit could not conceivably have been acquired, as with the ideas of truth and identity. Those grammatical ideas could have been acquired, had we had suitable others to start with. But we must start somewhere, with some innate ideas. The form of the claim is: in fact, we started *here*. Similarly, it is not inconceivable that we should have learned some language without the specific grammatical principles that we are supposed to know innately. We might have had innate knowledge of different principles. We would then have learned languages of different forms—different, that is, from those that are humanly possible. What is not an empirical thesis is that learning language requires innate knowledge of grammatical principles. What is empirical is that we satisfy that requirement by knowing thus and so innately.

3. The Idea of 'Idea'

The 'innate ideas' debate in the seventeenth and eighteenth centuries was deformed through entanglement with the 'idea' idea, from which it has not yet completely disentangled itself. With that thesis, having an idea or a concept (of, say, licorice or a pentagon) consists in having a representation accessible to direct conscious inspection, and exhaustively specified by what one thus inspects; one starts having an idea simultaneously with the onset of this awareness. To Locke, that notion made it seem much easier than it in fact is to show that there are no innate ideas: for every such representation, there must be an onset of awareness of it. If not, then we do not inspect it 'in consciousness,' so it does not determine the having of an idea at all.

This 'idea' idea is another legacy of Descartes, who presents it in virtually the same place where he offers a better idea of ideas. In the third *Meditation*, he says:

> if I hear some sound, if I see the sun, or feel heat, I have hitherto judged that these sensations proceeded from certain things that exist outside of me . . . .
> And my principal task in this place is to consider, in respect to those ideas which appear to me to proceed from certain objects that are outside of me, what are the reasons which cause me to think them similar to these objects.
>
> (Descartes 1641)

Here, ideas are equated with representations, the conscious having of which is indistinguishable from such things as the experience of seeing, or seeming to see, thus and so. That is the 'idea' idea which moved Locke and others. But immediately before that remark, Descartes says:

> for, as I have the power of understanding what is called a thing, or a truth, or a thought, it appears to me that I hold this power from no other source than my own nature.
>
> (Descartes 1641)

Here, Descartes equates having an idea, or concept, with a specific 'power' or capacity. That is Descartes's better idea. Leibniz took the better idea, rejecting the 'idea' idea, which is why he wrote, for example:

> And, in effect, our soul always has within it the quality of representing to itself whatever form or nature, when the occasion arises for thinking about it. And I hold that this quality of our soul, inasmuch as it expresses some nature, form, or essence, is properly the idea of the thing.
>
> (Leibniz 1686)

Such differing conceptions of having an idea or concept have often led to mutual incomprehension in 'innate ideas' debates.

4. From Particular to General: A Further Application

Locke's case against a Leibnizian account does not just rest on the 'idea' idea. Locke also had the plausible intuition that, for example, where inference or proof is concerned, we proceed from the particular to the general case. First, we learn that such-and-such a specific argument is a good or a bad one. When we have learned many specific facts of this sort, acquiring along the way an ability to go on to novel cases in particular ways, the character of our final state may be described correctly by saying that we know such-and-such general principles. (This is to model knowledge of good argument on knowledge of furniture—we first see specific sofas, then later get the general idea.) The notion that an idea of great subtlety and complexity, about whose general features there is much to say (e.g., an idea of oneself, of a proposition, of knowledge) may arise out of many special-case, small-time rules and facts, all of which hold for one

and the same idea simply because they are to be taken to do just that, was developed in some detail by Wittgenstein in his later philosophy, which suggests something that might be made of the Lockean intuition.

One could never proceed very far along the Lockean path from particular to general without being innately constituted to go on in certain ways as opposed to others. Here, too, Wittgenstein has much to say. He recognizes that the intricate sorts of judgments we often make, e.g., a specific judgment that Pia knows where Hugo is tonight, rest on a background of shared 'natural reactions.' However, construing these reactions in terms of innate ideas often fails to serve the required purpose in describing our cognitive transactions.

The ideas of a progression from particular to general, and of systems of natural reactions, need not be incompatible with the idea of innate ideas. However, these Lockean ideas, given fresh life by Wittgenstein, run counter to some Leibnizian arguments for innate ideas. In Wittgensteinian terms, where we work out, say, that wormwood is not sugarplums, Leibniz illegitimately sees us as 'operating with a calculus according to definite rules' (Wittgenstein 1958: Sect. 81). These ideas may harbor an alternative picture of logical competence, though this but gestures at as yet unexplored territory.

See also: A Priori; Chomsky, Noam; Concepts.

Bibliography

Chomsky N 1966 *Cartesian Linguistics*. Harper and Row, New York
Chomsky N 1972 *Language and Mind*. Harcourt Brace Jovanovich, New York
Chomsky N 1975 *Reflections on Language*. Pantheon, New York
Descartes R 1641 *Meditationes de Prima Philosophiae*. Paris [see especially Meditation III]
Descartes R 1641 *Author's Replies to the Fifth Set of Objections*. English translation in: Cottingham J, Stoothoff R, Murdoch D (transl.) 1984 *The Philosophical Writings of Descartes*, vol. II. Cambridge University Press, Cambridge
Descartes R 1648 *Notae in Progamma quoddam*. Translated as *Comments on a Certain Broadsheet*. In: Cottingham J, Stoothoff R, Murdoch D (trans.) 1985 *The Philosophical Writings of Descartes*, vol. I. Cambridge University Press, Cambridge
Leibniz G 1686 *Discours de Métaphysique*
Leibniz G 1705 *Nouveaux Essais sur l'Entendement Humain*
Locke J 1690 *An Essay Concerning Human Understanding*
Putnam H 1967 'The Innateness Hypothesis' and explanatory models in linguistics. *Synthese* **17**: 12–22
Stich S (ed.) 1975 *Innate Ideas*. University of California Press, Berkeley, CA
Wittgenstein L 1958 *Philosophical Investigations*. Basil Blackwell, Oxford

Intentionality

A. Woodfield

The term 'intentionality' derives from Scholastic philosophers' use of 'intentional' to mean *mental* or *existing in or for the mind* or *having an essence consisting in appearance*. Franz Brentano, who revived the term in his *Psychologie vom empirischen Standpunkt* (1874), characterized intentionality somewhat unclearly as a property, possessed by mental phenomena, of having 'reference to a content, a direction upon an object (by which we are not to understand a reality in this case).' Given the parenthesis, it seems that Brentano meant to exclude the property of direction upon a real object. In recent philosophy, intentionality has been seen as a family of properties distinctive of representations in general, that is, of public representations (words, pictures, diagrams, sculptures, as well as mental phenomena (perceptions, judgments, beliefs). Modern usage treats intentionality as *representationality*. This wide category includes mental and linguistic semantic properties such as reference, sense, and intension. The topic is intimately connected with recent theories of language; if there is a 'language of thought,' then the tools developed for studying natural languages will surely help to shed light upon its properties.

1. Aboutness

There are several senses in which a representation may be said to be 'about' an object. If a person visually hallucinates a pink elephant, or judges that there is a pink elephant in front of him, his visual experience or judgment is in a sense directed upon a pink elephant, even if no pink elephant is present. This 'subjective aboutness' was probably Brentano's main concern, and it has also been much studied within the tradition of phenomenology. The ability to represent nonexistent things is also possessed by pictures and sentences; it is not unique to mental phenomena.

If a subject correctly perceives or judges that there is an apple in front of him, his mental act is directed upon a real apple. Real aboutness is also not unique to mental phenomena. In such cases, it may be suggested that the representation has two objects, a real object and an intentional object. If the perception or judgment had not been veridical, it would have lacked a real object but it still would have been subjectively about an apple. This insight lies behind all attempts to study pure intentionality without looking at the external world.

Another distinction exists between a representation's being *of* a particular and a representation's being *about* any member of a class. The sentence 'Tom thinks that a man is in the kitchen' could be interpreted as meaning that there is a particular man, say Jim, whom Tom thinks is in the kitchen, or as meaning that Tom thinks that some man or other is in the kitchen. In fact, the idea of 'direction upon an object' runs together a host of issues that modern theories of reference try to separate.

2. Content

Representations of all sorts also have content, sense, or meaning. A perception or a judgment, but equally a sentence, a picture or a diagram, can represent an object as having a property, or as being of a certain kind. Some, but not all representations have propositional contents: they represent *that* something is the case. Having a content is, perhaps, more essential than having an object. Some representations (e.g., the belief that it is raining) are not 'directed upon an object,' yet they have contents. However, recent work in the philosophy of mind has unearthed many kinds of content, and several distinct notions of it. Here too, the topic of intentionality fragments.

Many philosophers accept that mental intentionality has primacy. The meaningfulness of pictures and words depends upon their being interpreted as meaningful by their producers and consumers, whereas mental states have contents for their possessors regardless of whether anyone actually ascribes contents to them. The central problem of intentionality is to explain *mental* content and *mental* aboutness. Other items derive their content and aboutness from the original mental intentionality of their human makers and users.

3. Intentionality and Intensionality

A caveat must be issued concerning *intensionality*. This term refers to a cluster of semantic peculiarities exhibited by certain types of sentences, including sentences with modal operators, sentences used to state causal and other explanations, and sentences used to report propositional attitudes. Such sentences are concerned to get across information about attributes, aspects, or points of view. The rationale for construing propositional attitude reports intensionally is connected to the fact that such reports are second-order representations. They *are* linguistic representations, they *have* propositional contents, but they are *about* mental representations which have contents in their own right. The report must not be confused with that which is reported. The mental state ascribed by an intensional sentence is not itself intensional.

This article is not concerned with the semantics of propositional attitude sentences. It is hard to theorize about the mind without theorizing about talk about the mind, but on the other hand it is important to avoid intellectualist or sentientialist fallacies. It would be clearly fallacious to infer, from the fact that a true ascription of a thought was in English, the conclusion that the thought itself was in English. Equally, one cannot argue that the content of a person's perception was conceptualized by that person, simply from the fact that an ascriber conceptualizes the perception when he reports it. Yet it is sometimes legitimate to base a hypothesis about a mental representation upon facts and intuitions about the correctness or incorrectness of certain ways of reporting it or talking about it. Many of the arguments employed by philosophers in the late twentieth century have attempted to do just this.

4. Contemporary Philosophical Background

Discussion has been strongly influenced by scientific naturalism, and by the idea that mental discourse is a 'folk theory.'

4.1 Science and Mental Phenomena

The natural sciences constitute our most successful and systematic body of knowledge. The scientific world view eschews supernatural entities and forces. Intentional phenomena have not yet been fully explained by science, but it is desirable that psychology be integrated eventually with biology and physics. If this cannot be done, something will have to give, and naturalists fear that the likely loser will be our current conception of the mind. Philosophers have seen their task as that of investigating, in cooperation with the sciences, whether the mind can in principle be naturalized, and if so, how.

4.2 Folk Psychology

The terms and generalizations that ordinary people use to describe the mind (in particular concerning beliefs and desires) constitute a theory, so it is said, because the terms purport to denote states which are hidden inside the person, and the generalizations yield predictions and explanations by adverting to interactions among such states. It is a *folk* theory, because it is taken for granted by everybody in the culture and is unreflectively transmitted by one generation to the next. From the ordinary person's point of view, it does not seem to be a theory at all. Philosophers, distancing themselves from the mental 'language game,' have sought to evaluate folk psychology by the same criteria they use to assess empirical theories in the philosophy of science. Are the theoretical terms to be construed in a realist or an instrumentalist way? If realist, do the terms in fact refer to real states and properties, and are the generalizations true? If there are such states and properties, are they reducible to the states and properties recognized by other branches of science? If they are not reducible, are they ground-

able? In the space of possible answers, almost every position has been occupied by someone or other (for surveys, see Fodor 1985; Dennett 1987).

There exist, of course, professionals concerned with mental states; academic and clinical psychologists borrow these popular constructs. The question is whether this is good policy. The rise of interdisciplinary cognitive science has inspired searching critical reflection upon the very idea of mental representations. Probably the dominant view has been that although folk psychology is flawed in some ways, much of it seems sound. Is it possible, permissible, or necessary to individuate psychological states by their intentional contents? Eliminativists say it is retrograde (Churchland 1981) and observer-relative (Stich 1983), but their censures have not persuaded many to drop the habit. What criteria of individuation should cognitive science use? Should it be methodologically solipsist? At what processing levels (personal and subpersonal) should contentful states be postulated?

Prescriptions for science are not the same as descriptions of folk psychology as it is. It seems sensible to get clear about the principles of classification which people actually use before passing judgment upon them. Many important discoveries about content-taxonomies were made in the 1980s.

4.3 Semantic Information Theory

Philosophers have also drawn upon the resources of a content-based theory that is distinct from folk psychology, namely, semantic information theory. Dretske (1981) has shown how to analyze the intentionality of natural information bearers (signals) in a wholly physicalist way. There can be no objection to employing this notion in science. Questions do arise, however, concerning its relation to the notion of mental intentionality. Some theorists hope that the notion of information will open the door to a reductive analysis, while others hold the two notions to be mutually irreducible.

4.4 Causal Efficacy of Content

Why does mental intentionality have question marks hanging over it? One reason is the suspicion that it is a mere epiphenomenon. Folk psychology treats the contents of mental states as causally relevant. When a desire and a belief jointly produce an action, their combined contents jointly determine which type of action is produced. But many theorists doubt whether contents can be causally efficacious; the popular assumption may be a myth. Their doubts spring from reflection upon the Hobbesian idea, exploited in Artificial Intelligence, that ratiocination equals computation. A digital computer is useful precisely because its internal states can be assigned external semantic values. The computer is programmed to juggle its internal states according to rules and thereby to model real-world operations upon the entities that are the states' semantic values. But the fact that the computer models reality is not relevant to how it works. The transitions from one state to another are determined by the physical structure of the machine and its program, interacting causally with the physical aspects of the states. These processes would be exactly the same even if the states had not been assigned any 'meanings.' Computers are physical engines that realize syntactic engines. They *seem* to be semantic engines but really are not; for their semantic properties do no causal work (Searle 1980; Dennett 1982). If the intentionality of a mental state is like the semanticity of a computational state, it too is causally irrelevant to the production of subsequent mental states and bodily movements. Contents ride along on top of the physical properties which 'encode' them.

This powerful line of argument relies on quite a few assumptions. Reactions to it take two main forms. One is to query the analogy between computer semantics and mental semantics. After all, mental phenomena are not assigned meanings, they have meanings intrinsically (but see Dennett 1987 for a dissenting opinion). The second reaction has been a revival of interest in how reason-giving explanations work, and in the notions of causal efficacy, causal relevance, and explanatory relevance.

5. Varieties of Intentional Contents

5.1 Information Content

The distinction between information content and mental content parallels Grice's distinction between natural meaning ('indicating') and non-natural meaning. A natural sign (the signal) carries information about another event or state in virtue of a nomic dependence of the former upon the latter (Dretske 1981: 198–99). For example, the firing of a neural unit in the frog's brain indicates that there is a bug in the frog's visual field if, and only if, under normal conditions the unit fires just when a bug flies in front of the frog. Dretske (1988) has refined the basic notion of 'indicating' in a number of ways. He constructs the notion of 'functional meaning' out of the idea of a structure's acquiring the biological *function* of indicating something. He thereby gives sense to the idea that a structure can mean that *p* on occasions when, because *p* is false, the structure fails to indicate that *p*. By this move Dretske diminishes the conceptual distance between the naturalistic notion and the mentalistic notion, for it is a key feature of judgments and beliefs that they can misrepresent as well as correctly represent. Many philosophers join with Dretske in hoping that the marriage of information theory with biological teleology will help to explicate mental intentionality. However, there is nothing psychological about the basic notion of information; a footprint in the sand can carry information. Even if there is an organism for whom an internal state is supposed to indicate that *p*, it is not necessary that the whole organism be capable of cognizing that *p*. Subpersonal states do carry information, so this kind of intentionality may legitimately figure in theorizing about how the brain processes information, but some writers have doubted that the notion of mental content can be fully analyzed in informational terms. The sheer range of types of mental contents makes the reductive task a daunting one.

5.2 Mental Content

Mental contents are multifaceted. They have semantic properties (truth-conditions or satisfaction conditions, reference, truth-values); explanatory roles; internal structures (concepts and other content-elements are combined in various ways); and they are integrally related to other contents in networks governed by minimal rationality constraints. It is not surprising, therefore, that they can be typed according to various principles. The main ways of classifying, expanded upon below, are by manner of presentation, by Fregean modes of presentation contained within them, and by real-world referents.

5.2.1 Manner of Presentation

Seeing that there is an apple in front of you is a different experience from thinking (without seeing) that there is an apple in front of you, even when the object is the same. Not only are seeing and thinking different attitudes, but also the contents are different. Whether an object is presented perceptually or conceptually (or perhaps volitionally) makes a difference to how the content is individuated. Peacocke (1986a) has argued that certain perceptual contents, which he calls 'analogue contents,' cannot be adequately individuated by the rules for individuating conceptual modes of presentation.

5.2.2 Modes of Presentation

Some thought-contents are purely descriptive; they involve the exercise of general concepts only. On the other hand, singular thoughts may incorporate either an individual concept or 'mental name' of an individual thing, or they may contain indexical elements: the subject thinks about an object demonstratively as 'this' or 'that,' or thinks about a place as 'here' or 'there,' or about a time as 'now' or 'then'. Also some thoughts are anaphoric. These are completed by being thought against the background of other thoughts and memories to which they hark back. Frege called these various ways of thinking 'modes of presentation.'

Content-classification must take account of modes of presentation in order to capture the roles that thoughts play in rational inferences and in the control of behavior. Frege's 'intuitive criterion of difference for thoughts' (Evans 1982) is that if a rational person judges an object to have property *P* and at the same time judges it not to have property *P*, it must be the case that he conceives the object under distinct modes of presentation in the two judgments. If not, the person is inconsistent. Also the mode of presentation employed will determine the thought's explanatory role. For example, the indexical 'self' mode of presentation and demonstrative modes of presentation of objects link in special ways to agency.

5.2.3 Real-world Referents

Thoughts about objects, kinds, and properties can be classified in a way that is sensitive to the entities that they represent. If the thought's identity is made to depend upon its worldly object, then its content is likewise world-dependent or 'externalist.' Evans (1982) defines a 'Russellian singular thought' to be one whose object is literally a constituent of it. Without the object, there would be no genuine thought. Similar accounts have been given of thoughts about natural kinds. Putnam (1975) showed that the meanings of natural-kind words are not fully encoded in the heads of speakers or hearers; the actual referent of 'water' helps to fix its meaning. The same could go for natural-kind *concepts*. Perhaps the actual referent of the concept *water* helps to individuate that concept. A different referent would make a different concept even if the two concepts seemed subjectively the same.

The distinctions already made between Fregean modes of presentation can be grafted onto the referent-sensitive typology to yield a set of fine-grained modes of presentation individuated jointly by cognitive role *and* by real-world referent.

6. Is Intentionality in the Head?

How one classifies a person's mental state depends on one's interests, and there seem to be plenty of ways to choose from. But can these crosscutting taxonomies really coexist peacefully? Is there not a 'right' one, or one that is 'best for scientific purposes'? A full treatment of the many arguments cannot be given here. A central issue concerns the location of contents: are they wholly in the head? It is useful to look first at singular thoughts, then at general thoughts.

It would be hard to deny that Evans-style singular thoughts, if they exist, are object-involving, and folk psychology certainly makes heavy use of indexical thoughts whose referents are contextually fixed. If such thoughts are individuated by their truth conditions, they are not wholly in the thinker's head. Yet two-factor theorists claim that such thoughts can be dissected into an in-the-head component, and a external component (see Loar 1981; McGinn 1982; Block 1986). The inner component is said to have 'narrow content.' Narrow contents cannot be specified by 'that' clauses, but they can be got at indirectly by subtracting the contribution made by the subject's context to the determination of the object of thought. Fodor, in *Psychosemantics* (1987), holds that the narrow content of an indexical type is a function from contexts and mental episodes onto truth conditions.

Fodor is not an eliminativist about intentionality; the representational folk theory can be salvaged for science provided the representations are suitably trimmed. The trouble with singular thoughts, in his view, is that they crosscut the scientific classification. A content-based taxonomy should facilitate causal generalizations about types of thought, and this means abstracting from the contexts in which thought tokens occur. The causal interactions between thoughts inside the head must hold in virtue of their narrow contents. This is the traditional view. Note, however, that if narrow contents were causally epiphenomenal, computational psychology would not need them any more than it would need wide, world-involving contents. All its causal generalizations would be over neural states typed physically or syntactically (Stich 1983).

Turning now to general thoughts which are not directed upon particular objects, if content-externalism says that contents are world-involving, can it possibly apply to these? McGinn (1989) distinguishes two versions: weak externalism holds that a given content requires the mere existence of an object or property in the world at large, while strong externalism insists that real relations (e.g., a causal relation) must be instantiated between the subject and worldly items. The strong version seems appropriate for, say, demonstrative thoughts; the subject must be in the context of the object at the time of thinking the demonstrative thought about it. But perhaps some thoughts require that there should have been causal interactions between the subject and things *in the past*, that is, that S's life-historical environment had to be a certain way. The intuition here is that S's concept *water* (say), exercised at time t, had to develop out of S's earlier experiences. If the formative experiences prior to t had not been interactions with genuine H^2O samples, the concept exercised at t would not have been the concept *water*. And perhaps the same goes for concepts for simple qualities: past experience of genuine instances of quality Q is necessary in order for the current concept to count as concept Q. So externalism has some plausibility for general thoughts. The subject has indeed strayed a long way away from Brentano.

7. Normative Aspects of Intentionality

According to Peacocke (1986b), the nature of concepts and contents can be illuminated by investigating what it is for a person to *possess* concepts. His approach immediately brings normative considerations to the fore, since possessing a concept involves knowing how to employ it correctly.

Frege took concepts to be abstract entities, graspable by many minds but not dependent for their existence upon minds. Wittgenstein said that mastery of a concept was an ability to follow a rule. Both emphasized that, because a concept can be exercised either correctly or incorrectly, the yardstick of correctness must lie outside the set of actual performances. Norms governing proper use fix *which* competence a person has.

One lively area of late-twentieth-century work seeks to uncover the *sources* of the norms that regulate concept-use. The source of these norms affects the ontological status of concepts and the nature of the folk theory which is committed to them. If the norms are social, then concepts are socially constituted. If the norms are Platonic, then so are concepts; in which case they are presumably not in the domain of natural science. If the source of the norms lies within the individual, the theory of content can be individualistic. If the norms are biological in origin, then the theory of content can be naturalistic.

See also: Language of Thought; Representation, Mental.

Bibliography

Block N 1986 Advertisement for a semantics for psychology. In: French P A, Uehling T E, Wettstein H W (eds.) *Midwest Studies in Philosophy*, vol. 10. University of Minnesota Press, Minneapolis, MN

Churchland P M 1981 Eliminative materialism and the propositional attitudes. *Journal of Philosophy* **78**: 67–90

Dennett D C 1982 Beyond belief. In: Woodfield A (ed.)

Dennett D C 1987 *The Intentional Stance*. MIT Press, Cambridge, MA

Dretske F I 1981 *Knowledge and the Flow of Information*. Basil Blackwell, Oxford

Dretske F I 1988 *Explaining Behavior*. MIT Press, Cambridge, MA

Evans G 1982 *The Varieties of Reference*. Clarendon Press, Oxford

Fodor J 1985 Fodor's guide to mental representation. *Mind* **XCIV**: 76–100

Fodor J 1987 *Psychosemantics*. MIT Press, Cambridge, MA

Loar B 1981 *Mind and Meaning*. Cambridge University Press, Cambridge

McGinn C 1982 The structure of content. In: Woodfield A (ed.) *Thought and Object*. Clarendon Press, Oxford

McGinn C 1989 *Mental Content*. Basil Blackwell, Oxford

Peacocke C 1986a Analogue content. *Proc. Aristotelian Society Supp. vol. LX*

Peacocke C 1986b *Thoughts: An Essay On Content*. Basil Blackwell, Oxford

Putnam H 1975 The meaning of 'meaning.' In: *Mind, Language and Reality: Philosophical Papers*, vol. 2. Cambridge University Press, Cambridge

Searle J 1980 Minds, brains and programs. *Behavioral and Brain Sciences* **3**: 417–24

Searle J 1983 *Intentionality*. Cambridge University Press, Cambridge

Stich S 1983 *From Folk Psychology to Cognitive Science*. MIT Press, Cambridge, MA

Woodfield A (ed.) 1982 *Thought and Object*. Clarendon Press, Oxford

Language Acquisition: Categorization and Early Concepts

R. N. Campbell

To characterize the structure of language adequately, linguists require a considerable array of concepts, many of them quite abstract, corresponding to classes of the 'clause,' the 'phrase,' the 'word,' etc. To characterize the content of linguistic expressions a further array of concepts is required, corresponding to the types of 'objects' and 'properties' denoted, of 'propositions' expressed, of 'modes of expression' and so forth. Thus, in order to give an adequate account of how any utterance functions, it is necessary to deploy this army of concepts. Yet young children, 4 or 5 years of age, use and understand the simpler structures of their native language fluently, without benefit of any special instruction and often despite quite unhelpful-looking regimes of child-rearing. In order to do so, it seems as if children must employ mental structures homologous to the linguists' concepts. But it is known

from other work that children's ability to construct concepts of arbitrary categories is initially very weak and develops slowly.

1. Approaches to the Problem

This paradoxical observation has one well-known resolution, namely that the necessary concepts do not have to be constructed by children; instead, they are innately specified. In addition it is often proposed that the mental apparatus needed to speak and understand language is encapsulated and isolated from other cognitive resources, that it constitutes a 'mental module.' This module has several parameters, initially set to default values. In the course of development, exposure to the language around them 'triggers' the values of these parameters to appropriate settings, perhaps according to some maturational schedule also regulated by inherited material.

Another route towards a resolution involves a number of linked ideas:

(a) that to characterize children's early language adequately a much reduced and simpler set of concepts is required;

(b) that children are more adept at constructing concepts than hitherto supposed;

(c) that to employ a concept explicitly, as a linguist does, is a very different thing from employing it tacitly, as a speaker does;

(d) that the contribution of genetic material to the process of acquisition is much more general, thus not encapsulated, or perhaps confined to some specific aspect of language, for instance to production and reception of speech.

The general theory of acquisition attempting this sort of resolution is known as 'semantic bootstrapping.' It has been explored by Pinker (1984).

So knowledge of children's categorization abilities, of the sorts of concept they are able to construct and of the innate resources that these abilities imply, is needed in order to make an adequate assessment of the plausibility of the program just outlined. Also, whatever theory of first language acquisition is proposed, such knowledge is needed in order to set upper limits to the possible content of children's utterances. The thought expressed may only partially reflect the thought that prompted expression, but it is surely absurd to propose that the former exceeds the latter in complexity of content. These two relationships are very programmatic and it cannot be claimed that much progress has been made with either of them. Thus far the most profitable relationship between children's categorization and first language has been the converse one; namely, that study of early language can reveal facts about early categorization (Vygotsky 1962), although here—by the same reasoning—conclusions about the content of early language can only set lower limits to categorization abilities.

The reader should perhaps be warned that there is no clear consensus amongst scholars about either cognitive or linguistic development during this period of childhood: in both fields a range of well-supported views is encountered spanning the two positions sketched above (Ingram 1989 provides a balanced review; Piattelli-Palmirini 1980 records a famous and instructive dispute). As noted above, there are even those who deny that the two fields of development are in any way connected.

2. Categorization

From a psychological perspective, categorization is involved whenever an individual treats distinct phenomena as if they were the same recurrent phenomenon. This arises in at least three different ways: (a) because the individual is biologically disposed to treat the phenomena in this way—these may be called 'constitutional categories'; (b) because the phenomena form a natural cluster, isolated from other such clusters—'environmental categories'; or (c) because, arising from some purpose of the individual, it makes sense to treat the phenomena in this way—'constructed categories.' Examples of constitutional categories might be certain regions of the color solid or certain classes of auditory event; a case has been made that some natural kinds such as lions and zebras are environmental categories (Mervis and Rosch 1981), although not all natural kinds are. It may be that artefactual kinds like *fork* or *spoon* provide purer cases of isolated clusters than do natural kinds. The best examples of categories that are clearly constructed are perhaps those categories of number, quantity, relation, etc. whose development was investigated by Piaget (1952). The term 'kind' is used as shorthand for what are sometimes called 'sortal categories'—categories whose members are readily individuated and, say, counted. Thus, *dog* denotes a sortal category. *How many dogs are here?* deserves an answer, and gets one. But *How many red things are here?* does not. For example, if there is a red handkerchief, should we count each thread, or molecule, etc.? The categories defined by qualities such as colors, shapes, etc. are thus clearly not kinds. This distinction is ancient, sortals corresponding to Aristotle's *substantia secunda*.

Mervis and Rosch's influential review (1981) presented evidence that a particular level within natural kind hierarchies was psychologically privileged. Categories at this level, called 'basic-level categories,' are environmental categories inasmuch as within-category similarity is maximal relative to between-category similarity at this level. They argued that this level is the point of entry to the hierarchy for children, pursuing an older insight of Brown (1958), and the level of category most easily manipulated by adults in a range of experimental tasks. For biological hierarchies, this level falls roughly at the level of the genus (e.g., *tiger*, as opposed to *Felid*, or *Siberian tiger*).

Whereas constitutional categorization is presumably automatic, and environmental categorization may come about as the outcome of simple perceptual processes that detect some invariant property that distinguishes the isolated clusters with reasonable reliability or by other simple methods, constructive categorization is presumed to involve mental effort, at least in early stages of the categorization process. The operation of these processes by no means always progresses from the particular to the general, nor does it follow the same pathways in different communities. To illustrate, initial stop consonants may be allocated to numerically distinguished constructed categories of voice onset time (with the aid of suitable instruments). These categories are of course finer grained than the categories detected by unaided listeners, and these latter environmental categories are different in different speech communities, say Spanish and English. Moreover, although it is unclear whether children form relevant constitutional categories, their discrimination of stops varying in voice onset time is certainly sharpest around environmental category boundaries. So one may say that the environmental categories formed have an established constitutional basis, at least.

3. Concepts

It is essential to distinguish between the mental structure which represents a category and the category itself. Within psychological discussions, these mental structures corresponding to and representing categories have been called 'concepts.' (This usage is different from that found in most philosophical discussions, following Fregean practice, in which concepts are taken to be abstract entities specifying the intension of a category.) Two important varieties of concept are, or ought to be, distinguished: 'individual-concepts' and 'type-concepts.' Concepts may represent categories in different psychological functions. Perhaps the simplest such function is 'recognition.' Preliminary definitions would then be:

(a) An individual-concept is a mental structure that enables recognition of the same individual, encountered at different times and places;

(b) A type-concept is a mental structure enabling recognition of different individuals as being of the same type (i.e., belonging to the same category).

In the late twentieth century, most psychologists outside the behaviorist and some cognitive-science traditions insist on rather more by way of definition than what is offered above. The definitions given above are minimal in several senses. For instance, recognition can be based on a very partial specification of the recognized individual or type, provided individuals and types are well-separated in the world in question. To take an example from Dennett (1987: 290), in a particular country, a coin-operated device may distinguish the desired type of coin from others on the basis of a partial specification of weight and shape, ignoring, say, embossed or engraved marks and inscriptions. As an instantiated type-concept such a device is very defective, though it may work well enough, since the objects inserted form well-separated clusters. If the device were improved in conceivable ways, then the danger would arise of its rejecting perfectly good coins because of surface imperfections, etc., so it may be seen that attainment of a fully effective instantiated type-concept is a difficult goal. In fact, it is an impossible requirement. A fully effective type-concept for a given coin specifies a history for the coin—that it was minted in a particular place by certain machines. Exactly the same conclusion follows for individual-concepts: ideal individual-concepts will

distinguish 'indiscernible' individuals (pennies, twins) and will not be diverted by 'disguise' changes. Ideal individual-concepts will therefore require the specification of a history as well. Though such ideal concepts perhaps cannot be attained, it is a common enough notion that concepts should not be ascribed to creatures or devices, unless they can pick out something like the correct category in most circumstances. This requirement of additional functionality may be characterized as a demand that concepts should be 'computationally effective.'

A second notion of desired functionality, additional to that specified in definitions (a) and (b), is that concepts should be 'representationally effective': they should allow their possessors to hold the target individual/type in mind when it is absent or competing for attention with other categories. This notion of concept coincides more or less with Piaget's.

A third suggestion for additional functionality is that concepts should be susceptible to combination, so that novel properties, relations, and relational properties may be constructed from familiar concepts. There is no doubt that this sort of additional functionality is highly desirable: the creative and imaginative capacities of individuals depend on the possession of such 'productively effective' concepts.

These three different characterizations of the additional functionality required need not lead to three different theories of concepts. Instead, it may be reasonable to attempt a theory of concepts that satisfies all three requirements simultaneously. After all, the requirements answer to capacities that work together developmentally. Individuals become creatures that (a) are not easily fooled (concepts become computationally effective), (b) can think about remote objects, etc. (concepts become representationally effective), and (c) show some capacity for representational novelty (concepts become productively effective).

Only the nature and origins of representationally effective concepts are discussed here. However, as noted, it is hoped that attainment of such concepts is at least associated with the other two sorts of additional functionality.

The definitions (a) and (b) above clearly do not define concepts in any of the senses just described, but they are useful notions nonetheless. The structures defined there will be referred to instead as 'individual-' and 'type-detectors.'

3.1 Formation of Early Concepts

Traditionally, following Vygotsky (1962) and Inhelder and Piaget (1964), it has been assumed that the free-sorting task, in which children form a large collection of diverse objects into groups that share a similar property, depends upon the ability to hold the shared property in mind across the several sorting operations and despite constant change in the other properties.

Typically, these tasks involve objects characterized by variation in size, shape, color, or similar simple properties, usually denoted by adjectives—qualities, in a word. So, on the basis of the well-known studies mentioned above the following research findings may be identified:

> *Finding* (1): Children in the age range 3–6 years can hold a quality in mind so as to organize free-sorting performance, but cannot readily switch to a different principle of organization, nor coordinate two such principles in multiplicative fashion.

Such children then, according to the criterion of representational effectiveness, possess concepts of these qualities, although there are still some limitations to the flexibility with which they are employed. Younger children, although unable to form concepts of these properties, can execute simpler versions of the free-sorting task. Ricciuti (1965) showed that if the set of objects to be sorted consists of subsets of objects belonging to different simple kinds, such as dolls and boats, and if one requires only that the subjects should touch or handle these subsets successively (rather than form them into spatial groups), then even 1-year olds show some ability and 2-year olds can carry out the task, thus redefined. These findings have been confirmed by Sugarman (1983), who also showed that 2-year olds will treat locally well-separated categories (for example, a set of green cylinders and a set of red circles) as if they were kinds. So, taking Ricciuti's and Sugarman's results together one arrives at the second research finding:

> *Finding* (2): Children in the age range 1–3 years can hold some sortal categories in mind so as to organize their free-sorting performance.

Such children can therefore form concepts of some kinds, but cannot form concepts of qualities. These sortals cover roughly the same ontological ground as Mervis and Rosch's notion of basic-level category. Also, the timing of this achievement, beginning around 18 months, coincides with Stage 6 of 'object permanence' (Piaget 1954). If this latter achievement is taken as marking the first construction of representationally effective individual concepts, then it would seem that the formation of concepts of simple individuals and concepts of basic-level categories are developmentally simultaneous. This is perhaps not surprising, in view of the next finding, after Mervis and Rosch, that individuals play an important role in the formation of such concepts:

> *Finding* (3): Basic-level concepts are resemblance structures. For any such concept and the population that employs it, some objects (stereotypes or prototypes) are better examples of the target category than others. Judged membership of such categories depends on similarity to the prototypes rather than on some (set of) common attribute(s).

Readers with philosophical backgrounds will be reminded of similar discussions in traditional metaphysics, notably in connection with the problem of universals (see Armstrong 1980). In that context (sometimes called 'first philosophy') the problem is to characterize the notions of object and property (by means of the metaphysical notions of particular and universal—or not, as the case may be)—so as to give a satisfactory account of what things there are. The psychological context is different: it is to characterize a variety of mental representations—concepts—so as to give a satisfactory account of how we come to know whatever things there are. However, as noted, there are many affinities between the two sorts of investigation. In metaphysical discussions, whether realist or nominalist in tendency, such resemblance structures have often been proposed as characterizations of properties. In *realist* analyses, beginning with Plato, there is a single external target against which resemblance is measured, a pure or Ideal Form: in *nominalist* analyses, for example, the well-known discussion of games by Wittgenstein (1951), there is an endless chain of global resemblance. However, as has often been pointed out, one is left minimally with the universal properties (relations) of resemblance and with the task of characterizing these. Similarly, in the account of concepts given in finding (3), one is led to wonder on what fundamental capacities the judgment of similarity to prototype depends. Substantial help is provided here by study of the ranges of application of children's first names for basic-level categories. Studies by Clark (1973) and especially Bowerman (1978) make it quite evident that judged similarity is by no means global but, rather, sharply structured by attributes, features, and qualities of shape, color, texture, etc. Although the theory of the development of word meaning proposed by Clark has now been discarded, it is sometimes forgotten that the data persist, and that these data show clearly that children's apprehension of similarity is strongly structured by these qualities. Hence the finding:

> *Finding* (4): Children younger than 2 years form concepts with pronounced resemblance structure. However, similarity to prototype clearly depends on formation of concepts of attributes, features, and qualities.

4. Paradoxes of Early Concept Formation

The findings (1) to (4) just described generate two formidable developmental paradoxes:

> *Paradox* (1): Whereas studies of object sorting and handling suggest that children younger than 3 years cannot yet form concepts of qualities, the studies of early word use suggest that they must have done so.

The distinction between minimal type-detectors (definition (a) above) and representationally effective type-concepts may be effective in resolving this puzzle. Or, conversely, this puzzle makes it evident that the distinction is necessary. Whereas findings (1) and (2) pertain to representationally effective quality concepts, the bases of similarity in findings (3) and (4) are not quality concepts but quality detectors.

A closely similar puzzle arises when one considers how individuals are recognized. To be sure, an individual concept must be essentially historical. Stage 6 of object permanence is only attained when the infant can construct a history for an individual as it is moved from place to place invisibly. Likewise, Piaget's story (1952: 225) of his daughter Jacqueline's mistaken recognition of the slug encountered when leaving the house and some hundreds of yards further off suggests a failure to construct such a history. However, it must be presumed that recognition of individuals is often merely heuristic and depends not upon construction of a space–time trajectory but on the detected recurrence of a particular cluster of attributes and qualities. At any rate, under this presumption individual detectors consist of just such cluster-specifications. But this leads to:

> *Paradox* (2): The formation of a type-detector depends on apprehension of the world as consisting of distinct individuals, rather than of a single recurring individual. This in turn depends upon the formation of individual-detectors which define unit categories. But such detectors can only be aggregates of perceived attributes, features and qualities, in other words of type-detectors, completing a vicious circle.

Paradox (2) is surely sensibly resolved by supposing that certain type-detectors of attributes, features, and qualities are genetically transmitted. Even the parsimonious philosopher Quine (e.g., 1969) allows some such innate quality 'space' as a cognitive given. These innate type-detectors will then bootstrap the process of acquisition of individual-detectors and then of novel type-detectors, breaking the vicious circle.

5. First Language and First Concepts

According to the previous section, 18-month-old children can form concepts of individuals and of certain environmental categories such as basic-level categories. But they cannot yet form concepts of qualities such as shapes or colors. These early concepts are underpinned by individual- and type-detectors, some of which detect constitutional categories and are therefore innately specified.

Studies of early vocabulary broadly confirm these conclusions. Eighteen-month-old vocabulary contains many proper names and pronominal expressions denoting individuals, and nominal expressions denoting basic-level categories. Moreover, Katz, et al. (1974) showed that very young children, presented with the contrasting ostensions *This is X* and *This is an X* are apt to take X to denote an individual in the former case and a basic-level category in the latter.

Expressions denoting qualities are slow to appear in early language, with color adjectives, for example, not well established until the fourth year. Early adjectives appear to denote instead temporary, undesirable properties such as *hot*, *wet*, *dirty*, and *broken* (Nelson 1976). These extrinsic properties are psychologically salient and command attention, whereas intrinsic properties of shape, color, etc., are always in competition for attention. It may be that the psychological prominence of these extrinsic properties makes it easier for children to form concepts of them.

The prospects for establishing alignments between the developing conceptual apparatus of children and the structures of early language are therefore reasonably promising, and such alignments should assist the development of theory in both domains of development. Besides the obvious need for examination of other sorts of early concept than those so far explored, notably of concepts of action, study of the issues considered here is badly hampered by the lack of suitable metalanguage for describing the content of expressions (meaning) and the thoughts that prompt such expressions.

See also: Language Acquisition in the Child; Thought and Language.

Bibliography

Armstrong D M 1980 *On Universals* (2 vols.). Cambridge University Press, Cambridge
Bowerman M 1978 The acquisition of word meaning: An investigation of some current conflicts. In: Waterson N, Snow C (eds.) *The Development of Communication*. Wiley, New York
Brown R 1958 How shall a thing be called? *Psychological Review* **65**: 14-21
Clark E V 1973 What's in a word? In: Moore T E (ed.) *Cognitive Development and the Acquisition of Language*. Academic Press, New York
Dennett D C 1987 *The Intentional Stance*. Bradford Books, MIT Press, Cambridge, MA
Ingram D 1989 *First Language Acquisition*. Cambridge University Press, Cambridge
Inhelder B, Piaget J 1964 *The Early Growth of Logic*. Routledge and Kegan Paul, London
Katz N, Baker E, Macnamara J 1974 What's in a name? *Child Development* **45**: 469–73
Mervis C B, Rosch E 1981 Categorization of natural objects. *Annual Review of Psychology* **32**: 89–115
Nelson K 1976 Some attributes of adjectives used by young children. *Cognition* **4**: 13–30
Piaget J 1952 *The Child's Concept of Number*. Routledge and Kegan Paul, London
Piaget J 1954 *The Construction of Reality by the Child*. Basic Books, New York
Piattelli-Palmirini M 1980 *Language and Learning: The Debate between Jean Piaget and Noam Chomsky*. Harvard University Press, Cambridge, MA
Pinker S 1984 *Language Learnability and Language Development*. Harvard University Press, Cambridge, MA
Quine W V O 1969 The nature of knowledge. In: Guttenplan S (ed.) *Mind and Language*. Oxford University Press, Oxford
Ricciuti H N 1965 Object grouping and selective ordering

behavior in infants 12–24 months old. *Merrill-Palmer Quarterly* **11**: 129–48

Sugarman S 1983 *Children's Early Thought.* Cambridge University Press, Cambridge

Vygotsky L S 1962 *Thought and Language.* MIT Press, Cambridge, MA

Wittgenstein L 1951 *Philosophical Investigations.* Blackwell, Oxford

Language Acquisition in the Child

P. Fletcher

The major thrust of studies of children's language development from the perspective of linguistics has involved the *grammatical* analysis of spontaneous speech samples obtained from the child's conversations with their mothers and other interlocutors. Phonological, lexical and discourse issues have also been pursued, but it is at the grammatical level that much of the research energy has been directed, in the main because it is here that links between linguistic theory and language acquisition are most directly made. Also, spontaneous speech from children is relatively easy to collect, and furnishes extensive corpora of utterances in naturalistic settings. These samples are used to estimate a child's grammatical status at successive stages of the developmental process. Certain utterances by the child have proved of particular importance for researchers. These are often referred to as 'errors.' More accurately, they are non-adult forms which the child produces, and they often provide a window into the child's construction of grammar which would not otherwise be available. The most frequently cited example of this in English is over-regularization of past tense. Productions by the child of forms like <u>comed</u>, <u>hitted</u>, and <u>buyed</u>, in place of the irregular forms *came, hit,* and $\overline{bought}$ are evidence of grammatical immaturity, certainly, but they also indicate clearly that the child has mastered the rule for regular past tense formation. While the focus of enquiry has not changed over the 30 years or so of linguistic studies of language acquisition, methodological advances and theoretical reformulations have had significant effects on the field. The following sections will concentrate on the major trends in the methodology and theory of child language studies, so far as they relate to grammatical development.

1. Methodology and Theory: The First Phase

The modern history of the study of children's language development begins in the early 1960s. Not surprisingly, for any branch of linguistic research in the second half of this century, Noam Chomsky was a formative, though initially indirect, influence. The first research project of the modern era was planned and directed by Roger Brown at Harvard University from 1962, following a five-year period Brown had spent at the Massachusetts Institute of Technology. The project, written up in Brown (1973) and numerous theses and research papers, was designed to determine the stages of grammatical acquisition in English-speaking children. In its concentration on the child's construction of grammar, independently of the context in which it was acquired, using as a database longitudinal samples of children's speech over the whole of the preschool period, Brown's project is a model which other researchers in the field have copied, modified or reacted against. This section therefore begins by looking in more detail at the methodology of this important study, as a starting-point for a more general consideration of methodological and theoretical issues in the field.

1.1 Sampling the Data

The study of children's development over time (hence 'longitudinal') was not new with Brown. The late nineteenth and early twentieth century saw a number of 'diary studies' on the acquisition of various languages (see Ingram 1989: 7ff for a review). Typically an interested parent would note the child's utterances, from the emergence of recognizable words onward, and provide a commentary on what appeared to him/her to be interesting features. The frequency of entries, the timespan of the child's development covered, and the features of interest noted, were somewhat unpredictable from diarist to diarist. A major handicap for the diarist, and later researchers who wanted to use the information contained in them, was the inevitable selectivity imposed by the method of handwritten records of increasing quantities of speech once the child passed the second birthday.

In his study, which examines the preschool development of three children (code-named Adam, Eve, and Sarah) Brown had the inestimable advantage over his diarist predecessors of being able to tape-record spontaneous speech samples from his subjects. This technological advance made a major difference to the data available to researchers. A permanent record of what the child and his interlocutors said was now available, which could be used to provide reliable written records of conversations involving the child. Investigators were no longer limited by their own immediate memory of what the child said, but could collect lengthy samples, at regular sampling intervals, which could then be transcribed and analyzed at their convenience. Brown and his co-workers selected a sampling interval of one month for two of their subjects, and collected fortnightly samples for the third. It should be emphasized that the new methodology imposed costs. It has been estimated that one hour of conversation between mother and child can take up to 10 hours simply to transcribe. Adding in time for analysis, and remembering that monthly sampling intervals will provide over 40 samples for a typical monitoring of a child's language development between 18 months and five years of age, it will be obvious that this type of research is extremely labor-intensive. This tends to lead, as seen in other studies, to a trade-off between number of subjects and sampling interval. The most important longitudinal study of the 1970s, by Gordon Wells in Bristol (Wells 1985), involved 64 children from 15 months to five years of age, but selected a sampling interval of three months, and each sample was limited in time to about 25 minutes. The advantage of Brown's study, and others like it, with a comparatively large amount of data on each child, at frequent sampling intervals, is that it is feasible to observe the organic growth of grammatical systems and subsystems. The large subject sample with correspondingly less data on each child may lack for some linguistic detail. It does, however, permit the investigation of the relationship between independent variables such as age, sex, social class, interaction, style, etc. on the dependent variable, language development. The Brown and Wells studies, a decade apart in the planning, were also distinct in their data collection procedures. The differences are instructive in what they reveal of shifts in thinking within the child language research community as the initially close relationship between linguistic theory and language acquisition study cooled. Brown collected his data in the child's living room, with the tape-recorder on show and at least one observer present to make notes on the conversation that mother and child engaged in. Wells, sensitized to the possible effects of the social context on language, and more particularly, of the importance of 'naturalistic' observation of the language used not only by the child, but by the mother to the child, removed observers from the sampling situation. Children in the study wore a wireless microphone, which transmitted to a remote tape-recorder which switched on and off, on each day of recording, according to a predetermined program, of which the family were not aware.

1.2 Innateness and Environment

The first influential statement of this linkage between language acquisition and linguistic theory came in Chomsky (1965), where his so-called 'innateness' hypothesis drew a parallel between the task of the linguist in characterizing a new language, and the child in learning the grammar of the language of his surroundings. Noting that an infant is biologically ready to learn any language, Chomsky exploited the ambiguity of the term 'grammar,' as both the product of the linguist's explicit *description* of the language he is describing, and the implicit *mental representation* that the child establishes as the basis for his speech and understanding. Chomsky's hypothesis was that the child came to the language acquisition task with essentially the same equipment that the linguist brought to his work, i.e., a 'generative grammar.' In more recent terminology, the human infant is 'hard-wired' for the acquisition task with prior expectations, in terms of linguistic universals about the language he will be exposed to. Given the obvious surface differences between languages, even those as closely related as, say, English and Dutch, such expectations will be at a rather abstract level of generality, e.g., the availability of an autonomous syntax, categories such as Noun, Verb, and the form of rule statements within the syntax. This specification of the formal apparatus available to the child was accompanied by assertions concerning the speed with which the child accomplished the acquisition task, and the defective nature of the data with which the child was presented for language learning. It was difficult to see, Chomsky argued, how the child could learn language in the face of these disadvantages without an extensive 'pre-programming' for language learning.

The initial Chomskyan hypothesis suffered under two handicaps. First, toward the end of the 1960s, linguistic theory became somewhat less monolithic, and so the exact nature of the formal apparatus assumed to be available to the language learner became rather uncertain. Second, and more seriously, it was not at all clear how to address data from children's language learning to the innateness hypothesis. Brown, himself no formalist, was concentrating in his project on topics such as semantic relations in early grammar, and the order of acquisition of grammatical morphemes. Neither of these appeared directly relevant to the theoretical issues. A third problem was that one of Chomsky's buttressing arguments for the innateness hypothesis, the assumption of defective input, was becoming increasingly untenable.

In its own version of the nature–nurture debate, language acquisition studies now polarized around a (temporarily) less influential Chomskyan view, and a body of research designed to characterize the input to children (child-directed speech or CDS), and (much more difficult) to test its role in the acquisition process (an overview of this work appears in Gallaway and Richards 1994).

It had long been known that in the *absence* of input, children do not develop a language. Accounts of feral children—historical oddities such as *The Wild Boy of Aveyron* and others, who have been restored to normal human contact after a period of living wild—attest to this obvious point (Brown 1958: 189). But the character of input language to children, and its role, had not been extensively studied. It quickly became clear that CDS, at least among middle-class English-speaking mothers, the usual subjects of enquiry, constitutes an identifiable language variety. It has phonological modifications, nonsegmental and segmental, and specific grammatical characteristics. So, for example, fundamental frequency is higher than comparable speech to adults, and pitch range wider. Pronunciation is said to be more careful and precise than is usual in adult-to-adult conversation. Adults speak to children in short, grammatical sentences. It would be plausible to assume that such modifications would assist the child in the language learning task. It would be equally plausible, however, to interpret the modifications as ways adults have (or learn) to make themselves comprehensible to small children with limited language capacity. Studies which have attempted to resolve this issue by correlating the effects of variation in syntactic input on development, have had mixed success. One result which has been replicated, originally established by Newport, et al. (1977), concerns the effect of utterance–initial auxiliaries on the child's development of this category. There does appear to be a positive correlation. The more a mother uses auxiliaries like *can*, *will*, *shall*, in her utterances to her 18-month-old child, the more likely she is to hear them from the child six months later. While similar examples of established effects of syntactic variation in CDS on language growth in the child are few, research on the effect of discourse modifications—expansions or extensions by the interlocutor which pick up on the child's topic and expand or extend it—suggests that these strategies by mothers may be effective in facilitating language development. What is not clear is how any feature of CDS which turns out to be facilitative in language development actually achieves its effect. It is still necessary to hypothesize a learning mechanism, or a component of it, which can use the relevant input to advance its learning.

2. Methodology and Theory: The Current Phase

The recording technology of the late 1950s allowed Brown to make permanent records of the speech of the children he was investigating. Apart from the major study by Wells that followed a decade after Brown, there have been dozens of other studies, initially on English and then on other languages, which have used tape-recorded language samples as the basis for the investigation of grammar construction. Some of these studies involve *longitudinal* sampling, where the same children serve as subjects at all stages of the research. Other studies have involved *cross-sectional* simulations of language development:

groups of different children at different ages (e.g., a group of three-year olds, one of five-year olds, and a third of seven-year olds) provide the language samples. It is assumed that the linguistic changes one finds between, say, the members of the three- and five-year-old group are similar to those one would find if the same children were sampled at three and again two years later.

2.1 Data Archiving and Theoretical Debates

By the end of the 1970s the field of child language was served by two academic journals, the *Journal of Child Language* and *First Language*, entirely devoted to research in the area. It was (see below) about to resume its close relationship with linguistic theory. It was in one sense rich in data, with nearly 20 years of data collection behind it. Data was not, however, readily accessible to researchers other than those associated with the particular project that had generated it, and there seemed no obvious way of aggregating data from different projects. At this point, in a project funded by the MacArthur Foundation, Catharine Snow and Brian MacWhinney founded the Child Language Data Exchange System (MacWhinney and Snow 1985; MacWhinney 1995). This is a computer archive of child language transcript data, with material from more than 20 projects on English (including the Brown and Wells data), and data in addition from Afrikaans, Danish, Dutch, French, German, Hebrew, Hungarian, Spanish, Tamil, and Turkish. The archive is available on request to any researcher and affords a facility to test hypotheses systematically against large bodies of quantitative data. This methodological advance leads to new theoretical insights. So, for example, Marcus, et al. (1992) were able to assess the validity of the assumption that the child's overregularization of past tense represents 'U-shaped' development. The reference is to learning which proceeds from initial correct forms (irregular pasts such as *came*, *sang*, *hit*) to a period in which, because of the acquisition of the regular past tense rule, the irregular past forms are substituted for by regularized forms (*comed*, *singed*, *hitted*). After this period of uncertainty, the child establishes essentially the adult system, with regulars and irregulars correctly differentiated. Marcus, et al. review an extensive range of data from the CHILDES database, and establish that, while overregularization rates do vary across children, these forms are in a relatively small minority—usually under 10 percent of all forms. So in reality there is no period of marked U-shaped development. (The U is to be imagined as a graph, with the first tail representing correct performance on irregulars, the trough representing a large number of errors, and then the second tail showing the child's recovery to correct performance on both regulars and irregulars). Marcus, et al. interpret the new data as indicating a process of development which advances from rote learning to the discovery of the regular rule. Once the regular rule is discovered, it applies to all verbs unless there is an irregular past tense form available in the child's lexicon, causing blocking of the general rule. Overregularization is attributed to a lack of memory strength for a 'blocking' irregular form. When an irregular form is unavailable, the regular past tense rule is applied to the irregular stem as a default.

The Marcus, et al. study is a contribution to the debate about the acquisition of morphology, and ultimately about acquisition generally. It represents a perspective on learning which, in common with the majority of studies, assumes that the child's language development depends on the organization and reorganization of rules and representations. The alternative view, often referred to as 'connectionism,' sees statements such as the rule for past tense formation as merely descriptions of features of the language. The connectionist view sets out to demonstrate how a model of language acquisition could avoid reliance on mechanisms using rules that manipulate discrete symbols, but still account for what happens in the child's language learning. The battleground for the competing theories has been past tense formation in English, and the connectionists' hypothesis testing has implemented computer simulations of learning, using parallel distributed processing (PDP) models (Rumelhart and McLelland 1986; Plunkett and Marchman 1991). Such models are constructed in the form of networks (claimed to be analogous to neural networks) which are 'trained' on sets of past tense forms from the language, and which 'learn' from successive sweeps through the input. Successive outputs from the network can then be checked for their approximation to what is known of successive stages of the child's development. In the rather restricted area of the development of past tense, the simulations have been relatively successful, though they are still the subject of extensive debate.

2.2 Linguistic Theory and Language Acquisition

As seen above, linguistic theory was a major influence on language acquisition studies at the outset. After a period of estrangement, the relationship was renewed during the 1980s as the reformulation of Chomskyan theory (which is referred to as 'Principles and Parameters Theory'—PPT) offered the prospect of testing predictions against language acquisition data, in a way that had not been possible before. It is obviously not feasible to deal with the full complexity of PPT here (see Atkinson 1992 for a book-length treatment). However, one of its crucial dimensions, parameterization, can be introduced via a specific example.

The original linkage between linguistic theory and language acquisition depended on commonalities between languages at a rather abstract level. PPT maintains this view that there are universal features of language but also acknowledges cross-linguistic differences by specifying, within modules of the grammar, 'parameters'—dimensions of variation from which languages select possible values. The most widely discussed such dimension in the child language literature is the 'null subject parameter.' One of the differences between English and a Romance language like Italian is that in the latter subjects of sentences do not need to be explicitly realized by a noun phrase or a pronoun, as verb paradigms are inflected for person and number, as well as indicating tense. So an Italian hearing a sentence which consists only of a verb and an object noun will be able to identify the subject of the sentence from the verb form. In English, by contrast, subjects must be expressed. There are exceptions to this rule, but they are limited to certain well-defined contexts such as responses to questions, e.g.,

Q. what did you do?
A. finished my drink and left.

Faced with the problem of learning their language, Italian and English children have to determine which way the null subject parameter is set, on the basis of the input evidence they hear. More generally, for each parameter that is made available within the theory to account for linguistic variation, the child has to determine which setting his particular language selects. The PPT theory is still very much an innateness hypothesis. As before, the child is seen as coming to the task of acquisition 'hard-wired' with the principles of the theory, and with the parameters. Input (earlier called CDS) is more significant, in this view of the linguistic theory–language acquisition relationship, but only to provide just enough evidence to set the relevant parameters. And input to the child is restricted to what is called 'positive evidence.' An important part of the argumentation for the new innateness hypothesis is that the child does not receive any overt evidence about the structure of the language. In particular, he receives no 'negative evidence' when he makes errors (such as overregularizations). This view does seem to be borne out by studies of CDS, at least so far as clearly explicit parental correction of syntactic or morphological error is concerned. Mothers and fathers do not generally take any notice of grammatical errors on the part of their preschool children. They seem to regard them, rightly, as a normal part of development, which the child will grow out of. Furthermore, even if an adult does try to correct overtly a child's error, the attempt is unlikely to be successful, unless the child is ready to make the change to the more adult-like form. As a consequence, any incorrect hypotheses about the structure of the language which are made by the child have to be eliminated by his own efforts, without any direct intervention by adults. This can only be achieved, it is argued, if the 'hypothesis space' for language learning is heavily constrained from the outset. The principles and parameters of linguistic theory are offered as the constraining influences. The child has certain degrees of freedom available, in making suppositions about the constituent structure of his language, but these are limited by the potential allowed by the parameters and the settings which they specify.

How does this new version of the innateness hypothesis fare when subjected to empirical test? Hyams (1992) uses data from the CHILDES database to explore a child's setting of the null subject parameter for English. It is assumed that the child's original setting will be null. If the language he hears fails to have morphological paradigms of the Italian type, and has a high proportion of expressed subjects, this will trigger the resetting of the parameter to non-null. Hyams finds a rapid increase in the realization of subjects (from 10 to 70%) in a five-month period from 2 years 7 months to 3 years, and interprets this as the child realizing that English is not a null subject language. Not surprisingly the opening up of the innateness hypothesis to empirical test has led to attempts to provide alternative explanations of language development. Bloom (1990), for example, presents data to buttress his view that children acquiring English represent the correct grammars from the start, on the basis of input data, but omit subjects because of performance factors.

3. Conclusion

The exploration of the alternative models for language learning afforded by linguistic theory and connectionism will be central to research. Important information for both frameworks will be provided by *cross-linguistic* studies. A major program of research on the acquisition of languages other than English has been coordinated by Dan Slobin at the University of California, Berkeley for over 20 years (see Slobin 1985; 1992). Some of these languages, e.g., Hungarian, K'iche' Mayan (Guatemala), Walpiri (Australia), Western Samoan, are typologically very different from English (and each other). They provide new testing grounds for hypotheses concerning language acquisition. They may also, in turn, cause researchers to look afresh at the acquisition of English.

See also: Language Acquisition: Categorization and Early Concepts.

Bibliography

Atkinson M 1992 *Children's Syntax: An Introduction to Principles and Parameters Theory*. Blackwell, Oxford.

Bloom P 1990 Subjectless sentences in child language. *Linguistic Inquiry* **21**: 491–504

Brown R 1958 *Words and Things*. Free Press, New York

Brown R 1973 *A First Language: The Early Stages*. Allen and Unwin, London

Chomsky N 1965 *Aspects of the Theory of Syntax*. MIT Press, Cambridge, MA

Gallaway C, Richards B 1994 *Input and Interaction in Language Acquisition*. Cambridge University Press, Cambridge.

Hyams N 1992 A reanalysis of null subjects. In: Weissenborn J, Goodluck H, Roeper T (eds) *Theoretical Issues in Language Acquisition: Continuity and Change in Development*. Lawrence Erlbaum, Hillsdale, NJ

Ingram D 1989 *First Language Acquisition: Method, Description and Explanation*. Cambridge University Press, Cambridge

MacWhinney B 1995 *The CHILDES Project: Computational Tools for Analyzing Talk*, 2nd edn. Lawrence Erlbaum, Hillsdale, NJ

MacWhinney B, Snow C 1985 The child language data exchange system. *Journal of Child Language* **12**: 271–96

Marcus G F, Pinker S, Ullman M, Hollander M, Rosen T J, Xu F 1992 Overregularization in language acquisition. *Monographs of the Society for Research in Child Language Development*, Stanford, CA

Newport E, Gleitman H, Gleitman L 1977 Mother, I'd rather do it myself: Some effects and non-effects of maternal speech style. In: Snow C, Ferguson C (eds.) *Talking to Children: Language Input and Acquisition*. Cambridge University Press, Cambridge

Plunkett K, Marchman V 1991 U-shaped learning and frequency effects in a multi-layered perceptron: Implications for child language acquisition. *Cognition* **38**: 43–102

Rumelhart D E, McLelland J L 1986 Learning the past tense of English verbs: Implicit rules or parallel distributed processing. In: MacWhinney B (ed.) *Mechanisms of Language Acquisition*. Lawrence Erlbaum, Hillsdale, NJ

Slobin D (ed.) 1985 *The Cross-linguistic Study of language Acquisition*, vols. 1 and 2. Lawrence Erlbaum, Hillsdale, NJ

Slobin D (ed.) 1992 *The Cross-linguistic Study of Language Acquisition*, vol. 3. Lawrence Erlbaum, Hillsdale, NJ

Wells C G 1985 *Language Development in the Pre-school Years*. Cambridge University Press, Cambridge

Language of Thought

R. Carston

The idea that there is a language of thought (LOT) amounts to this: having a thought with a particular content is a matter of being related in a certain way to a sentence in an innately given mental language. The sentences or formulas in this language (mentalese) are like the sentences of public natural languages

(Japanese, Urdu, English, etc.) in that they have syntactic and semantic properties. That is, they are composed of constituents in particular structural configurations and their semantics is a function of the semantics of their basic elements and their syntactic structure. The grammar of mentalese may, however, differ quite radically from the grammar of any natural language. The basic elements (concepts, perhaps) denote entities and properties in the world. The full formulas are truth-conditional, so have truth-values as determined by the way the world is, and they bear logical relations to each other, such as entailment.

The following discussion is confined to descriptive thoughts (thoughts about states of affairs), but it should be noted that there are also what are called interpretive (or metarepresentational) thoughts (see Sperber and Wilson 1995). These are thoughts which represent other representations (such as thoughts or utterances); their relation with that which they represent is not one of truth/falsity but of propositional resemblance (which is a matter of degree). The language of thought hypothesis is just as relevant to them as it is to truth-based descriptive thoughts, but they introduce considerable additional complexity.

1. The Representational Theory of Mind

The relevant notion of a thought here is that of an 'intentional' state of mind, where intentional mental states are those that have the property of being representational, that is, of being about the world. Beliefs, desires, intentions, hopes, and fears are different types of intentional mental states. They are sometimes called propositional attitudes since they involve the having of an attitude to a content or proposition, for example, having the belief attitude to the 'Mrs Thatcher has resigned' content. These intentional mental states play a central role in cognitive psychology in the explanation of human intentional behavior. For example, it is because Jane wants to drink some cola and she believes that there is some cola in the refrigerator that she goes to the refrigerator and reaches inside it. On the LOT view, having a belief or a desire, etc., with a certain content entails being in a relation to an internally represented sentence with that content, so the explanation of Jane's refrigerator-oriented behavior will include a specification of the interaction of the sentences which represent the content of her relevant beliefs and desires.

The LOT hypothesis arises then in the context of the current computational model of the mind, whereby mental processes, such as reasoning, are sequences of mental states and the transitions between states are effected computationally. Conceiving of these computations as formal/syntactic operations defined over mental representations gives a mechanical explanation for mental processes. That is, they operate on symbols in virtue of the form of the symbol, not in virtue of any semantic property of the symbol, just

like the operations performed by a computer or the transitions from line to line in a logic proof. This approach to the causal explanation of mental processes is known as 'methodological solipsism' (see Fodor 1981; Lycan 1990). It follows that as far as our cognitive life is concerned two beliefs or desires are distinct if and only if the representations of their contents are formally distinct. For example, the desire to meet the husband of Janet Fodor and the desire to meet the staunchest advocate of the language of thought hypothesis are identical in their truth-conditional content (given that the definite description in each case picks out the same individual in the world, namely Jerry Fodor). However, so far as cognitive activity is concerned these are quite distinct types of desire as they may be the effects of different sequences of thought and each may cause further different thoughts. Furthermore, they may issue in quite distinct behaviors: in the first case one might telephone Janet Fodor to ask her and her husband for dinner, in the second one might seek out conferences on the philosophy of mind. The crucial point here is that thoughts have their causal roles as a function of their formal properties. Semantic properties are respected only insofar as they are mimicked by formal properties, which of course they are to at least some extent since deductive reasoning, which preserves truth, plays a major role in human thought.

2. Why Should Thoughts Have Syntactic Structure?

One could be an 'intentional realist,' that is, one could accept (a) that beliefs and desires really exist, (b) that they are physically instantiated in the brain, and (c) that they play a causal role in sequences of thought and in overt behavior, without positing a 'language' of thought in which the objects of attitudes are couched. What is crucial about language is constituent structure, that is, that a sentence is made up of parts and these same parts can occur in a range of different sentences. So what distinguishes the LOT view from other intentionally realist views is that it entails that belief/desire states are structured states. Fodor (1975) claimed that the language of thought was implicit in the computational approach to psychological explanation since computation presupposes a medium in which to compute. However, the emergence of an alternative computational approach, 'new connectionism' (see Sterelny 1990 for an introduction), indicates that more in the way of arguments for structured thought is required, since according to connectionism the mental causes of intelligent behavior can be modeled by patterns of activation across networks of nodes and connections, involving no level of symbolic representation. One of Fodor's arguments for syntactic thought (Fodor 1987a) involves an appeal to the 'productivity' and 'systematicity' of thought. The set of thoughts is potentially infinite and the ability to think any particular thought is intrinsically connected to the ability to think various other thoughts. So, for example, anyone who can form the thought 'the ruthless spy has seen the desperate terrorist' can also form the thoughts 'the desperate terrorist has seen the ruthless spy' and 'the desperate spy has seen the ruthless terrorist,' etc. The parallel with natural language is obvious and the explanation for the productivity and systematicity of natural language is its combinatorial syntax and semantics, so it is natural to assume that thought too has combinatorial structure. However, see Clark (1994) and Maloney (1994) for a range of objections to the LOT thesis.

3. The Relation between Thought and Public Language

Fodor believes that the semanticity of natural language, that is, the capacity of natural language symbols to be about the world, is dependent on the representationality of thought. So the answer to the question 'How is it that the sentence, *Mrs Thatcher has resigned* is about Margaret Thatcher?' is something like: 'Because that sentence is a vehicle for expressing a thought about Margaret Thatcher.' On this view an account of the semanticity of natural language will follow from an account of how it is that thoughts refer to the world. Attempts are being made to develop this logically prior theory of 'psychosemantics' (see, for example, Millikan 1984, Fodor 1987b, and Fodor 1990), though they are as yet embryonic.

See also: Intentionality.

Bibliography

Clark A 1994 Language of thought (2). In: Guttenplan S (ed.) *A Companion to the Philosophy of Mind*. Blackwell, Oxford
Fodor J 1975 *The Language of Thought*. Harvester Press, Sussex
Fodor J 1981 *Representations*. MIT Press, Cambridge, MA
Fodor J 1987a Why there still has to be a language of thought. In: Fodor J *Psychosemantics*. MIT Press, Cambridge, MA
Fodor J 1987b *Psychosemantics*. MIT Press, Cambridge, MA
Fodor J 1990 *A Theory of Content*. MIT Press, Cambridge, MA
Lycan W G 1990 The language of thought hypothesis. In: Lycan W G (ed.) *Mind and Cognition: A Reader*. Blackwell, Oxford
Maloney J C 1994 Language of thought (1). In: Guttenplan S (ed.) *A Companion to the Philosophy of Mind*. Blackwell, Oxford
Millikan R 1984 *Language, Thought and Other Biological Categories*. MIT Press, Cambridge, MA
Sperber D, Wilson D 1995 *Relevance: Communication and Cognition*, 2nd edn. Blackwell, Oxford
Sterelney K 1990 *The Representational Theory of Mind*. Blackwell, Oxford

Private Language

C. Travis

The term 'private language' has several customary uses. For example, sometimes it refers to the phenomenon of children talking to themselves. Or it might refer to codes or idiosyncratic sign systems formulated for particular purposes, perhaps for private communication within a group. This article will discuss a special notion of private language which stems from Ludwig Wittgenstein, and is related to what has become known as 'the private language argument' (i.e., Wittgenstein's argument against private language). This conception and the problems related to it concern foundational issues in the philosophy of mind and the philosophy of language. The questions to be addressed are: What is a private language in this sense? Why should Wittgenstein (or anyone) bother with it? What might an argument against it be? What is Wittgenstein's argument? (By way of proviso, it should be noted that there is a conception of Wittgenstein's later philosophy according to which his purpose is not to argue against positions, but to present alternative pictures, so as to show a picture not to be compulsory. On that view, Wittgenstein has no 'private language argument.' This view of Wittgenstein is largely neglected in what follows. But it should be borne in mind.)

1. Preliminaries on Privacy

Wittgenstein introduces the notion of a private language in *Philosophical Investigations* Sect. 243:

> But is a language conceivable in which one could record, or articulate, his inner experiences—his feelings, moods, etc.—for his own use?—Can't we do that in our usual language?—But I don't mean it like that. The words of this language would apply to what only its speaker can know; to his direct, private, experiences. So another cannot understand this language.

(The term 'private language' does not occur before Sect. 256, where it appears in quotation marks.)

Privacy may come in various strengths, according to what makes language private. Private language might just be language spoken by only one person. In that case, Robinson Crusoe, alone on his island, spoke a private language, especially if he invented his own terms for the strange flora and fauna he met there. So would the last surviving speaker of a vanishing Amerindian language. Most—though certainly not all—commentators agree that this is not what Wittgenstein had in mind, as the (unquoted) first half of Sect. 243 makes clear. If we came to rescue Crusoe, we would have no trouble seeing what his neologisms meant, nor do field linguists face special in-principle problems if they can find only one informant. In rescuing Crusoe, we do not rescue his language from privacy; it faced no such danger. That remark imposes a dual constraint: whatever the private language argument is, it should leave Crusoe untouched; whatever about our usual language lets it escape the argument should not vanish for one-speaker languages.

Crispin Wright (1986) and Margaret Gilbert (1983) have each suggested, independently, two relevantly different notions of privacy. On one notion, words are private if their semantics, or content, or proper understanding, is available only to their speaker: only that person could produce words with that semantics, or understand/take words as having it. On the other notion, though two people, Pia and Pol, may each attach the same semantics, Pia to her words W, and Pol to his, W*, they could never have good reason to believe that that is what they were doing. These are certainly two ways of being unable to understand another's words. Whether the distinction matters depends on what the case against private language is.

2. Private Language and Mental Life

Why is private language worth thinking about? Partly because of its relation to our picture of mental life, or that part we care enough to have words for. Since a large stretch of the *Philosophical Investigations* before the private language discussion (from Sect. 138), and a large stretch after it, are concerned with questions about mental life, the conclusion that this is one of the points of the discussion seems inescapable. (Before Sect. 243, the concern is to attain 'greater clarity about the concepts of understanding, meaning, and thinking'; during and for a stretch after, the concern is primarily with sensations, notably pain.)

The picture of the mind a private language discussion would target derives from Descartes. Notoriously, such a view weaves problems of mind into problems of knowledge. On this view, mental life consists, for the most part, of a series of events or experiences, which form, as it were, a stream of consciousness. Elements in this stream, since they are the subject's experiences, are directly accessible to his inspection, but not available for inspection by anyone else. So the subject can know what the elements are in a way in which no one else can. Moreover, they are independent of things outside our skins. While some

of them may represent such things as being thus and so (these, according to Descartes, are ideas), none requires anything of the 'external' world for its being the element it is. It cannot be essential to any of these experiences, for example, that it is an experience of seeing a cow; for then it could not occur without the cow. The actual elements of the scheme, on Descartes's view, are what might be in common to cases of seeing a cow and cases of only seeming to. Some would embroider this picture as follows: what I judge in judging my stream now to have a certain character (to contain elements of this or that type) is incorrigible; I could not, in principle, be wrong about it. The embroidery is not needed for a private language argument to get a grip. Note too that Wittgenstein concentrates on experiences, like pain, which are world-independent in the required Cartesian sense. So it does not matter much for this discussion if there is no experience common to seeing a cow and only seeming to.

I know what my mental life is, according to this picture, by observing its elements and seeing of each I observe that it is thus and so. That is to say, I may just see of an element that it is of a certain sort or type. I may observe it to be, roughly, a pain in the foot, or an intention to go sailing, etc. That is rough. But more precisely, of what type might I observe such an element to be? Thinking on the model of observable features of objects—colors, say—the feature or type in question would be fixed in this way: it is that feature observably exemplified by such and such elements in streams—the elements that exhibit such and such a pattern. That it is the one so exemplified is essential to identifying which feature it is. But the only elements I can observe, in principle, are ones in my own stream. So the feature I have in mind when I take one of my current elements to be thus and so must be fixed as the one exemplified by such and such (prior) elements in my stream; that is essential to its being the one I am thinking of. But now, what decides whether my current element is of that type? Only I could be in a position to judge that. My thought about my current element, in identifying it as such and such, is thus, in a clear sense, a unit of a private language.

3. Criticisms of Private Language Based on the Cartesian View of Mind

Insofar as the private language discussion is directed against this picture, the first point is this. It is simply not possible that only I can be in a position to see what is exemplified (by seeing what exemplifies it), consequently to judge whether an item has the character that there gets exemplified. A language that worked in such a way would be incoherent. It would have neither correct nor incorrect applications, to elements of a stream of consciousness or to anything else; there could be no standard of correctness for it. Conversely, any language, public or private, which does say something about our mental lives must have a publicly accessible semantics: anything which fixes in what way it says things, or a thing, to be—any facts relevant to determining whether it says things to be this way or that, or whether this or that would count as being as they are said to be—must be facts a multitude might, in principle, recognize to hold, and on which they might base their judgments. Crudely put, if words (about X's mental life) say X to be F, there must be a publicly observable, or specifiable, state of affairs of which one could truly say, 'This is (what we call) (X's) being F.' (This point is as much about thought as about language. To some, it has smacked of behaviorism. Whether it is that depends on what one allows to fall within the range of the observable. For Wittgenstein, it certainly was not that.)

The general problem about our mental lives is this. There is a familiar system of concepts under which aspects of our mental lives fall. For each of us, there is also our own stream of consciousness—all those experiences we are aware of by, or in, having them. What is the relation between the two? Different things in different cases, no doubt. The private language discussion, viewed as aimed at this problem, shows one thing the relation could not be. To fit one of those concepts could not be for an element, or several, in one's stream to be thus and so, where what counts as being thus and so is only fixed given other facts about that stream which only its subject could see to hold.

4. Language and a Background of Shared Reactions

The private language discussion does not only address the problem of mental life. It has a longer reach. Note that Sect. 243 is preceded by a brief discussion of language and thought in general. The point is that intelligible language or thought rests on a certain background of agreement in judgment. (Elsewhere Wittgenstein refers to systems of natural reactions.) The kind of dependence involved is illustrated in Sect. 142: 'The procedure of putting a lump of cheese on a balance and fixing the price by the turn of the scale would lose its point if it frequently happened for such lumps to suddenly grow or shrink for no obvious reason.' Similarly, the procedure of saying something to be thus and so—to fit, or not, a given concept, or to be, or not, as it is said to be in given words— would lose its point if there were no regularity in our reactions in taking things to be that way or not; if we could not rely on what informed and reasonable people would do when called upon to judge such matters. Were 'reasonable' people as mercurial in their reactions in, say, taking things to be red or not, as Wittgenstein's cheeses, we would lose a range of facts as to where things are reasonably taken to be red, and with that, the point of speaking of things as red or not. (Saying that a cheese weighs a kilo is not saying that it will not grow or shrink. Nor is calling something red saying that most people would say so.)

Given philosophy's penchant for making one thing out to be another, this idea that an activity makes sense only against some backgrounds—so that only against a certain background does it make sense to suppose given words to say anything at all—has suggested to some that the upshot of the private language discussion is a 'community view' of how (public) language is possible: for words W to have been spoken correctly, so for them to have said things to be as they are, is for their speaker to be in step with what the rest of his linguistic community would say. He says that his car is red; so would they. Speaking correctly just means not falling out of line with the community. However, that is the wrong way to see a background as functioning. It serves its purpose only if it remains in the background.

5. Formulating a Private Language Argument

The question, then, is whether some broader and more original point about language is made by the private language discussion. One way to press this question is by pressing on features of private language that have seemed to play a role thus far. For example, in the Cartesian model, private words applied to types or classes of private 'objects'—the elements of one person's stream. Must there be private objects for private language? Consider the made-up word *gronch*. It applies, let us suppose, to some vases, doorknobs, drapes, and turtles, but not to others. Only I, though, am able to discern what something's being gronch requires. In principle, only I am ever in a position to make fully informed and authoritative judgments on such matters. Is that private language? Or suppose a 'private' language did not belong to just one person, but, say, to 10. Might that still be private language? Textual evidence suggests a 'Yes' answer both times (see, e.g., Sect. 207 and Sect. 237).

To press further, ask what a private language argument might be. Here is the first of two suggestions. The private linguist, Pol, examines some thing or situation, and judges that 'F' is true of it, F being some private term. (It matters not in the least whether the examined thing is private.) But how does Pol know he has not made a mistake? Perhaps he misremembers what is involved in being F, or he is just bad at distinguishing Fs from Gs. If what it is to be F is anything one could remember, then this seems a possibility. But if it is, Pol cannot check that he has not made such an error, except in ways that let just the same sort of doubt creep in again. So, since there are always doubts he cannot settle, it seems that he cannot ever know whether F is true of a thing or not. But if he cannot know this, no one can, F being private. Language no one could ever know to apply to anything is no real language at all. So there can be no private language. (What is important here is the unavailability to others of at least some of the facts which determine how F is to be used—its actual semantics. Private objects play no role.)

Here is a second argument. Let Pol judge, 'A is F.' Now ask: in principle, might Pol be wrong in judging this? Might he have mistaken what his own 'is F' required for truth of A, or whether that requirement was satisfied? If not, then his words are reduced to the level of an inarticulate cry. For they must be governed by the rule: they were spoken correctly exactly wherever Pol felt inclined (enough) to speak them. If so, then suppose his words said of A that which is true of A. What might such a fact consist in? Not in Pol's reactions to the words, as exhibited in his judgment. But then, evidently, in nothing else either. (This being private language, only his reactions matter.)

Neither of these arguments, one might object, is available to Wittgenstein. Each depends on a principle he explicitly rejects—the first on a rejected epistemology (see, for example Sect. 84); the second on the rejected idea that facts of some genre, to be such, need to consist in anything else. (See, for example, Sects. 135–37.) The objection vanishes, though, when we ask what entitles Wittgenstein to reject these principles. In the first case, for instance, there is normally a distinction between real doubts, which might show you do not know, and merely imaginable doubts, which show nothing. Where such a distinction is drawable, the mere possibility of misremembering what a word means cannot show someone not to know that it has been used correctly. But that distinction rests on a background 'system of natural reactions': we take certain doubts seriously, others not, given which there are facts as to some doubts being real, others not. That background is unavailable in the case of private language. So there can be no appeal there to such a distinction; no such thing as 'the reasonable way of drawing it.' Given such lacunas in the private case, the private linguist lacks the means for resisting either of the otherwise noncompelling arguments.

We normally suppose, rightly, that we can tell a hawk from a handsaw; further that if in some case we have failed to, there will be something to show either that we missed some pertinent fact, or that we judged unreasonably. The above argument shows the importance of both suppositions. Without room for something to override our judgments, there would be no judgment. The second supposition is safe just where there are means for drawing a distinction between what is the reasonable view of, or reaction to, a situation, and what is not. A private linguist may seem to have semantic reactions; to take his private language to have one semantics rather than another. Without the resources to distinguish reasonable understandings of it from others, he can in fact be doing no such thing; nor could his language have a semantics, except perhaps that of an inarticulate cry. Those appear to be resources he would lack.

Frege encouraged the view that if we could just get words to have the right properties—e.g., to have a proper and univocal sense—then their doing that would settle, effectively, all questions as to how and where the words apply correctly. Such a perfect language, like a perfect machine, would run on forever under its own power; facts as to what bits of it were true would depend in no way on our, or on any, reactions to those bits; the language would have sufficient resources in itself to generate those facts on its own. The illusion that there might be private language rests on the idea of language functioning that way: whether a private word is true of an item depends not at all on anyone else's reactions, and, if the private linguist might be mistaken in such matters, not on his reactions either. Rather, properties intrinsic to the language are conceived as carrying all the weight in determining that the facts about its application are thus. Wittgenstein shows this Fregean ideal for language to be a chimera; no words could have that property. That would be enough to show up private language as an illusion. Conversely, dealing directly with private language is a way of showing why Frege's conception could not be right.

6. Private Language and Rules

Wittgenstein first makes the crucial point about this chimera in his discussion of rules and their requirements (see Sects. 84–7). For any rule, there are various conflicting things, each of which would count as following it correctly, if only this or that understanding of the rule were the right one—the one it in fact bore. We are often capable of seeing what following a rule in a specific case requires. The fact that the rule does require that is not independent of our seeing this. For that fact depends on that understanding of it being the most reasonable one. But in matters of reasonableness, we, or beings like us, must be the ultimate arbiters. It is no good appealing to anything like a rule to fill the gap we would leave at that point. For a word to have properties which, all on their own, decide that it applies correctly to (in) exactly these cases and no others is for it to be governed by a rule that requires it to be applied exactly there. But Wittgenstein's point is that no rule, in isolation, can do that job. For it does that only given sufficient facts as to its proper understanding; but there are no such facts without a background of natural reactions to the rule, by reasonable beings, for those facts to rest on. One way to see the point is to consider language with all such background cut away. Private language is such language. It fails to be genuine language precisely because it lacks such a background. The conception of semantic properties which Wittgenstein's discussion of rules supports thus becomes compulsory. Language in need of no one (for the standards of its correct use) is language for no one.

See also: Family Resemblance; Rules; Wittgenstein, Ludwig.

Bibliography

Blackburn S 1984 The individual strikes back. *Synthese* **58**: 281–301
Gilbert M 1983 On the question whether language has a social nature. *Synthese* **56**: 301–18
Kripke S 1982 *Wittgenstein on Rules and Private Language.* Harvard University Press, Cambridge, MA
McDowell J 1984 Wittgenstein on following a rule. *Synthese* **58**: 325–63
Pitcher G (ed.) 1966 *Wittgenstein: The Philosophical Investigations.* Macmillan, London
Travis C 1989 *The Uses of Sense.* Oxford University Press, Oxford
Wittgenstein L 1967 (trans. Anscombe G E M) *Philosophical Investigations*, 2nd edn. Basil Blackwell, Oxford
Wright C 1986 Does *Philosophical Investigations* I.258–60 suggest a cogent argument against private language? In: McDowell J, Pettit P (eds.) *Subject, Thought and Context.* Oxford University Press, Oxford

Representation, Mental

A. Garnham

The notion of representation is a familiar, if philosophically problematic, one. It becomes more problematic, and less familiar, when modified with the epithet 'mental.' Nevertheless, the notion of mental representation is crucial both in cognitive psychology and cognitive science. It is also crucial in linguistics itself, at least for those who accept Chomsky's views that grammars describe part of the contents of the minds of language users, and that linguistics is correctly construed as part of cognitive psychology.

1. Representation and Mental Representation

It is a fundamental assumption of cognitive psychology and cognitive science that explanations of behavior make reference not only to inputs and outputs but to information encoded in the mind. In order to provide an information processing account of a particular ability it is necessary, therefore, to describe how inputs, outputs, and stored information are internally encoded. It is natural to think of these encodings as depending on a mental representation scheme or language. Following Jerry Fodor (1975) this language is usually referred to as the language of thought, though different mental faculties may use different representational schemes. Although this view of mental processing is widely accepted, it raises a very difficult question: what is a mental representation?

One can make a start on answering this question by considering everyday types of representation that are easier to understand. A simple two-dimensional town map represents space spatially. In general, however, there need be no such direct correspondence between what is represented and how it is represented. British Ordnance Survey maps represent the third spatial dimension using contour lines, and they represent things in the landscape by symbols that may (church with a tower) or may not (coach station) resemble what they represent. In such a representational scheme, the correspondence between what is represented and the elements of the scheme must play a role in both the production and the use of particular representations—only in aberrant cases will it not do so. In particular, resemblance is not sufficient for representation, as a consideration of portraits, particularly those of identical twins, shows. Causation is crucial in determining what something represents. Indeed, some philosophers (e.g., Fodor 1990) have suggested purely causal theories of how a mental state comes to represent something in the world.

There is little difficulty understanding how maps work. But maps require people to create and interpret them. We, as mapmakers, create the representational schemes that allow us to make particular maps and, thus, to achieve our navigatory goals. And we, as map users, have the goals that make maps useful. Mental representations differ from maps in both respects. First, the meanings of the elements of a system of mental representation are not arbitrarily stipulated. They arise from natural effects that the environment has on people or animals. However, not every effect that the world has on an animal gives rise to a mental representation. For an effect to be a representation, it must have the function of providing information about what it represents. Second, although natural effects can have representational functions imposed upon them, mental representations typically have functions that derive from the natural goals of people or animals. Furthermore, an account of mental representations cannot be based on the idea of a person inside the head setting them up and using them—homunculus theories cannot explain cognition.

If the job of cognitive scientists is to discover the representational schemes used by the mind, that job is very different from a mapmaker's. Mapmakers decide what to represent, taking into account how their maps will be used, and they stipulate a representational scheme to encode the relevant information. Depending on the mapmaker's skill, the map may or may not be easy to use. Cognitive scientists have to assess the purpose of a piece of mental apparatus, to postulate a representational scheme that, together with processes to operate on it, satisfies that purpose. Then they must try to find evidence that that scheme is used. This process is a complex one, not only because cognitive scientists cannot look and see what the elements of the representational scheme are, but also because they have to make inferences about processes as well as representations. The representational scheme needed to perform a task depends on what processes act upon the representations allowed by the scheme.

The philosopher Fred Dretske (1988) contrasts mental representations with maps by classifying them as a type, indeed the most important type, of natural representation system. He claims that natural representation systems are the source of intentionality in the world. Intentionality is the 'aboutness' which philosophers take to be a defining characteristic of mental phenomena. A map is 'about' the terrain it represents, but only derivatively. Its aboutness derives from the fact that people interpret it as being about a certain part of the world. The aboutness of mental representations is not derivative, and it is for this reason that mental representations are so important and so difficult to understand. It is also for this reason that the study of maps can only take us so far in understanding the concept of mental representation.

Dretske analyzes the notion of representation in terms of indication. One thing indicates another if its occurrence provides information about what it indicates. Because of the rich correlational structure of the world, there are many instances of indication. A bear's paw prints in the snow indicate that a bear has passed this way. The ringing of a door bell indicates that someone is at the door (and also, for example, that current is flowing in the door bell's electric circuit). Certain patterns of activity in a person's visual cortex indicate that they have seen a chair (to anyone or anything that can register them). For Dretske, there is no misindication. If signs are misinterpreted, they are being used as representations.

An indicator becomes a representation if it is given the function of indicating the state of something else. Now misrepresentation is possible. If a car's fuel gauge jams, it does not really indicate that the tank is full. But since it has been given the function of indicating how much fuel is in the tank, it misrepresents how full it is. Misrepresentation can be a nuisance, or worse. However, the possibility of misrepresentation goes hand in hand with a very useful property of representational schemes: their elements can be recombined at will. Maps of imaginary countries can be drawn. I can mentally represent not only what the world is like, but how I want it to be, how I think you

falsely believe it to be, and so on. Thus, although natural systems of representation derive from natural indicators of things in the real world, particular representations can be decoupled from the world. They need not be caused by what they represent.

2. Neural Substrates and Connectionism

Cognitive scientists assume that the mind is a mechanism, in the very general Turing machine sense, and that its physical substrate is the brain. Thus, every mental state is associated with a corresponding brain state. If that mental state is a complex representational one, each element of the representation is associated with some aspect of that brain state. For most of our cognitive abilities, no more can be said at present. It is not even known whether equivalent mental states are always associated with the same brain state. And even when a good deal is known about the underlying neural substrate—as in the case of low-level visual processing, for example—it has been argued (e.g., by David Marr 1982) that questions about representational schemes and the processes that act on them can often be addressed independently of questions about neural substrates, via an information processing analysis of the relevant ability.

It is, of course, possible to take a purely functionalist approach to cognition in general and to mental representations in particular. Functionalism holds that the correct, or best, theory of a particular mental ability is the one that best explains the psychological data. The mental representations people use are the ones postulated in that theory. On one interpretation this view is vacuous, because the decision about which explanation is best may be influenced by non-psychological factors, such as compatibility with what is known about brain structure. On another interpretation functionalism is a substantive, though almost certainly false, doctrine. On this interpretation, considerations about brain structure are irrelevant to choosing the best psychological theory.

Since about 1980 the substantive version of functionalism has been challenged by people working in the parallel distributed processing (PDP) or connectionist framework. Connectionists attempt to reproduce human behavior using networks of simple processing elements whose properties resemble those of brain cells or clusters of them. The behavior of a connectionist machine may suggest that it is following a set of rules (couched in a language of thought). However, nothing in the machine corresponds to the rules in the way that a piece of code in a traditional computer model of the mind does.

The correct interpretation of connectionist models has been a matter of intense debate. It is known that connectionist machines can simulate traditional serial computers (von Neumann machines), just as von Neumann machines can simulate connectionist machines. However, connectionist machines as they are used in cognitive modeling do not perform such simulations. How should such machines be described? On one view they do not contain representations of the rules they appear to be following. Rules are traditionally represented symbolically, and connectionism has been described as a subsymbolic approach to cognition. A contrasting view is that connectionist machines represent rules indirectly, and usually in a distributed fashion. Trying to decide which account is correct is complicated by the fact that many connectionist machines do not exactly follow the rules that their designers wanted them to, so it is not surprising that they do not represent those rules. In one famous example, a network was trained to produce the past tenses of English verbs from their stem forms (Rumelhart and McClelland 1986). However, a detailed analysis of the performance of the machine (Pinker and Prince 1988) showed its knowledge to be lacking in many respects. In particular, it had not encoded the fact there are no phonological conditions on whether the regular (*-ed*) rule can be applied. Some connectionist systems do follow (usually much simpler) sets of rules exactly, and properties of their (matrix algebra) descriptions may correspond to information that one would intuitively want to say is represented in the system. However, this representation is not so obvious as a traditional symbolic one. So connectionist machines raise in an acute form the question of when information is represented explicitly and when implicitly.

The contrast between implicit and explicit representation can be illustrated with a simple example from semantic memory. Sparrows are represented as a subclass of birds. Birds are represented as being able to fly, unless there is specific information to the contrary. There is no specific information that sparrows cannot fly. From the explicitly encoded information it can, therefore, be inferred that sparrows can fly—that information is implicitly represented. Whether information is encoded explicitly or implicitly determines how easily a particular task can be performed. Implicit information should take longer to compute than explicit information takes to retrieve. It may appear from this example that the contrast

between explicit and implicit representation is a clear one. However, it is not, as the questions raised by representation in connectionist networks show. Indeed, although the contrast between implicit and explicit representation has become increasingly important recently, it remains unclear whether there is one distinction or several.

Although connectionist machines raise important questions about how mechanisms encode rules and follow them, their existence in no way bears upon the very difficult philosophical questions about rule following raised by Wittgenstein (1953), which have sometimes been taken to challenge Chomsky's (e.g., 1972) idea of linguistic rules in the mind. The description of a connection machine (or, for that matter, a von Neumann machine) as following a rule is part of a description of its behavior by us. Wittgenstein's questions about how people follow rules turn into questions about what we, as cognitive scientists expect of a machine that we describe as following a certain set of rules. It does not matter whether those rules are encoded explicitly, or only implicitly.

See also: Intentionality.

Bibliography

Chomsky N 1972 *Language and Mind*. Harcourt Brace Jovanovich, New York
Dretske F 1988 *Explaining Behavior: Reasons in a World of Causes*. MIT Press, Cambridge, MA
Fodor J A 1975 *The Language of Thought*. Crowell, New York
Fodor J A 1990 *A Theory of Content and Other Essays*. MIT Press/Bradford Books, Cambridge, MA
Marr D 1982 *Vision: A Computational Investigation into the Human Representation and Processing of Visual Information*. Freeman, San Francisco, CA
Pinker S, Prince A 1988 On language and connectionism: Analysis of a parallel distributed processing model of language acquisition. *Cognition* **28**: 73–193
Rumelhart D E, McClelland J L 1986 On learning the past tenses of English verbs. In: McClelland J L, Rumelhart D E, et al. *Parallel Distributed Processing: Explorations in the Microstructure of Cognition. Vol. 2: Psychological and Biological Models*. MIT Press, Cambridge, MA
Wittgenstein L 1953 *Philosophical Investigations* (trans. Anscombe G E M). Blackwell, Oxford

Sapir–Whorf Hypothesis

O. Werner

1. Statement of the Hypothesis

The relationship between language and culture, or language and world view, has been noted at least since Wilhelm von Humboldt (1836). But discussion

remained relatively dormant until the 'Golden Age of Native American Indian Linguistics' in the first half of the twentieth century.

Although everyone calls it the Sapir–Whorf hypothesis, its most persistent proponent was Whorf (Carroll 1956). And yet, perhaps surprisingly, the most popular formulation comes from Sapir.

1.1 Sapir's, or the Lexical, Version

Sapir never sought the interface between language and culture anywhere but in the lexicon. The quote below is used most commonly to characterize the Sapir–Whorf hypothesis:

> Human beings do not live in the objective world alone . . . but are very much at the mercy of the particular language which has become the medium of expression for their society. The worlds in which different societies live are distinct worlds, not merely the same world with different *labels* attached.
>
> (Sapir in Mandelbaum 1963: 162, emphasis added)

A similar statement stressing the classificatory or categorizing nature of language is expressed in even stronger terms by Whorf (though this quote is seldom used to characterize the hypothesis):

> We dissect nature along lines laid down by our native languages. The categories and types that we isolate from the world of phenomena we do not find there because they stare every observer in the face. . .
>
> (Whorf in Carroll 1956: 213)

Both quotes emphasize the words or lexical resources of a language. That is, both stress that while nature is continuous human beings cut nature into discrete categories and each culture does this cutting somewhat differently. People make up words or concepts in order to talk about their world or cultural universe.

This version of the Sapir–Whorf hypothesis is one of two alternatives. It is called the lexical version in this article.

While one could ascribe the 'anomaly' that the hypothesis is usually characterized by the first, or Sapir's, quote to some historical accident, there seem to exist deeper reasons that will soon become apparent.

1.2 Whorf's, or the Grammatical, Version

The view expressed by Whorf in the second quote (above) is relatively unusual. He searched for the interface between language and culture beyond the vocabulary (or the lexicon) and sought to discover the roots of cultural regularities in a language's grammar:

> . . . the grammar of Hopi bore a relation to Hopi culture, and the grammar of European tongues to our own 'Western' or 'European' culture.
>
> (Whorf 1939: 73)

(The Hopi Indians live in villages in Arizona and speak a language of the Uto–Aztecan language family), and:

> By 'habitual thought' and 'thought world' I mean more

than simply language, i.e., than the language patterns themselves.

> (Whorf in Carroll 1956: 147)

(following the usage of the times one can equate 'language patterns' with grammar), and again:

> . . . the background linguistic system (in other words the grammar) of each language is not merely a reproducing instrument for voicing ideas but rather is itself the shaper of ideas, the program and guide for the individual's mental activity, for his analysis of impression, for his synthesis of his mental stock in trade.
>
> (Whorf in Carroll 1956: 212)

Finally, in the statements in which Whorf gives the Sapir–Whorf hypothesis its alternate name, he again sees the relationship of language and culture in grammar:

> . . . the 'linguistic relativity principle,' which means, in informal terms, that users of markedly different grammars are pointed in different evaluations of externally similar acts of observations, and hence are not equivalent as observers but must arrive at somewhat different views of the world.
>
> (Whorf in Carroll 1956: 221)

These quotes represent the second way of interpreting the Sapir–Whorf hypothesis—the grammatical version.

1.3 Discussion

The two versions of the Sapir–Whorf hypothesis, or the 'linguistic relativity principle,' namely, the lexical version, espoused by Edward Sapir, and the grammatical, the predominant view of Benjamin Lee Whorf, have created considerable mischief in the profession. The reasons for the confusion lie in the different definitions of language used by anthropologists and linguists.

To anthropologists it was self-evident that the lexical resources of a language are part of that language. Therefore, the anthropological definition of language, at least implicitly, consists of phonology, grammar (syntax), *and* the lexicon.

The definition of language used by linguists explicitly excludes the lexicon. To this day linguists tend to give the lexicon short shrift. The science of linguistics considers only the structured parts of language amenable to analysis. One can easily detect pattern (i.e., structure) in phonology and in grammar (syntax). The lexicon was perceived as a 'collection of idiosyncratic features' (Gleason 1962), therefore not amenable to scientific analysis, and in the end, outside of what linguists considered to be language (perhaps best stated as 'language is what linguists do'). H. A. Gleason summarizes this view: 'lexicography is something that cannot be done but must be done.'

Several conferences about the hypothesis in the 1950s (Hoijer 1954; Hymes 1960; McQuown 1960) remained strangely inconclusive, largely because participating anthropologists and linguists operated with a basic misunderstanding about the nature of language. These conferences demonstrated vividly Kuhn's (1970) notion that discussions between members subscribing to two different scientific paradigms (views of the world) are always inconclusive. The irony of these discussions is that they are about language and world view, though Kuhn (ibid.) demonstrates that all world view disputes are hampered by the same sounding words used with different senses (e.g., 'language' as used by linguists versus anthropologists).

The Sapirean formulation of the hypothesis gained wide acceptance. The influence of grammar on world view was difficult to demonstrate. Whorf's exotic interpretations of Hopi thought were often attributed to his imaginative native consultant (Carl F. Voegelin, personal communication). (Most of Voegelin's later work, with Florence M. Voegelin, dealt with the Hopi Indian language and culture, e.g., Voegelin and Voegelin 1957.)

Meanwhile the basic linguistic attitude changed from an orientation that 'every language must be described in its own terms' (the structuralist paradigm) to a preoccupation with language universals ushered in by Chomsky's transformational/generative revolution in linguistics. Suddenly all languages looked very similar.

Many more or less serious statements were made to this effect. Robert E. Lees is credited with asserting that 'all languages are dialects of English.' A few years later James McCauley 'corrected' Lees's assertion by declaring that 'all languages are dialects of Japanese.' McCauley's remark was prompted by the surface structure of Japanese which appeared to be very close to a universal, hypothetical deep structure valid for all languages.

The interdependence of a culture and the lexicon that speakers associate with that culture to talk about their experiences seems almost obvious—especially to anthropologists. The validity of the hypothesis was, of course, of much greater interest to anthropologists than to linguists and found, concurrent with the Chomskyan revolution but independent of it, expression in the New Ethnography (Sect. 3).

In 1970 Oswald Werner demonstrated that the contribution of grammar to world view can only take place through grammatical categories. However, grammatical categories are, in the prevailing theories of linguistics, inherently part of the lexicon—specifically of lexical entries. In transformationalist theories of language these lexical entries are in the semantic component of the grammar of specific languages. Each entry of the form (C, P) has a conceptual part C—a representation of the 'meaning'—and a phonological part P—representing directions for pronouncing the entry. Therefore, the 'linguistic relativity principle' becomes an investigation of the relationship between a culture and its associated lexicon—including grammatical categories.

It may be useful to recapitulate briefly Werner's argument. His demonstration starts with the Chomskyan assumption that the parts of a grammar are known and can be represented by the formula (1):

$$G\,(\#, \frown, \rightarrow, S, V_{nt}, V_t) \tag{1}$$

where the $\#$ symbol represents the boundary conditions of a sentence (or utterance). This is the silence (absence of speech) that precedes and follows every sentence. The $\frown$ symbol stands for the operation of concatenation. The rewrite symbol $\rightarrow$ (right arrow) stands for the rewrite operation that specifies structure, for example, the formula (2):

$$S \rightarrow NP \frown VP \tag{2}$$

(read: 'rewrite sentence as consisting of a noun phrase followed by a verb phrase') specifies the structure of S, the sentence, that consists of a noun phrase followed by a verb phrase. Thus, S in (1) stands for sentence, V_{nt} for the nonterminal vocabulary of the grammar, such as NP and VP in (2), and V_t for the terminal vocabulary. These lowest level units of a grammar or grammatical categories have no further structure (no rewrite rules can be applied and therefore these symbols never appear on the left side of any rewrite rules). In the process of sentence generation or production, actual lexical entries replace terminal vocabulary items in each language in question. (For details on the rules governing lexical insertion into terminal grammatical categories see the publications of Noam Chomsky.) Typical terminal categories are 'mass noun,' 'count noun,' 'performative verb,' 'manner adverbial,' 'definite article,' etc.

Obviously, $\#$, $\frown$, and $\rightarrow$ are part of the formalism of all grammars, hence language universals, and cannot therefore contribute to meaning and world view.

The high level nonterminal vocabulary V_{nt} are assumed by linguists to be also universal, that is, they occur in every language and cannot therefore influence language specific world views. Languages such as Nootka (one of a large number of languages spoken on the northwest coast of the USA) which consists almost entirely of verbs, and Sierra Miwok (one of a large number of languages spoken in the state of California), which consists almost entirely of nouns, can be made to conform naturally to the structure of noun phrases and verb phrases. In Nootka nouns are formed by nominalizing verbs (English analogue: to walk—to take a walk) and in Sierra Miwok verbs are formed by verbalizing nouns (English analogue: table—to table, e.g., a motion).

The above argument leaves only the low level nonterminal (V_{nt}) and the terminal (V_t)—the lowest level of grammatical categories of a given language—as potential contributors to language specific aspects of world view.

If M. A. K. Halliday's principle of 'delicacy' is now added, that states that when the limit of linguistic analysis (the ultimate delicacy) is reached, then every lexical item in every language represents its very own unique grammatical category.

The parts of grammar that could contribute to world view are therefore the low level nonterminal and the terminal grammatical categories. But since these are part of the lexicon, in any language, the interaction of language and culture must be seen as firmly rooted in the lexicon.

Ultimately, therefore, the Sapirean definitions and the definition of the hypothesis in Whorf's first quote of this article prevail. In the other, the Whorfian formulation, every time he mentions 'grammar,' or 'pattern,' these terms should be read as standing for 'low level grammatical categories,' or 'language specific grammatical categories.'

2. The Contribution of Grammatical and Lexical Categories

Before examining the issue of how these language specific categories contribute to world view, two additional notions require discussion: the strong version of the Sapir–Whorf hypothesis, according to which language *determines* thought, and the weak version, which asserts that language has a tendency to influence thought. Whorf is often viewed as representing the strong version. However, a review of his quotes (for example, in Sect. 1.2) reveals that he always qualifies his assertions.

While Whorf does say that speakers of different languages 'must arrive' at different interpretations of the world, these interpretations are not totally different only 'somewhat different' (Whorf in Carroll 1956: 221). Hopi grammar does not determine Hopi culture only 'bore a relation to [it]' (Whorf 1939: 73). And the 'background linguistic system' is not a determiner of ideas but merely a 'shaper of ideas.' He talks about 'habitual thought' rather than thought fully determined by the language of the speakers. It is thus difficult to find representatives of the strong version of the hypothesis.

All other points of view, including Whorf's, represent relatively stronger or relatively weaker versions of the weak version of the cultural relativity principle. The Sapir–Whorf hypothesis can therefore be paraphrased as follows:

> The categorial system of every language, including lower level grammatical and all lexical categories, points its speakers toward somewhat different evaluations of externally similar observations. Hence speakers of different languages have somewhat different views of the world, somewhat different habitual thought, and consequently their language and cultural knowledge are in a somewhat different relationship to each other. They don't live in the same world with different labels attached but in somewhat different worlds. The more dissimilar two languages

are, in their lexicon—that is, in conceptual and grammatical categories—the greater their tendency to embody different world views.

Finally, Whorf's search for traces of world view in grammar, or in grammatical categories, is not without merit considering that different parts of language tend to change at different rates. Thus lexical items referring to objects change fastest as technology and customs change. For example, in Anglo–American culture new words like 'jeep,' 'radar,' 'laser,' 'napalm,' 'frozen yogurt,' 'yuppie,' and many others are quickly adopted into everyday use.

Verbs change more slowly. For example, until 1957 only planets, comets, and meteorites could orbit. Since Sputnik, the Soviet Union's first artificial satellite, an assortment of objects propelled into space are in orbit. A few years ago a telescope could not be thought of as orbiting. However, with the Hubble Deep Space Telescope in orbit, the range of the verb has been extended even to human beings. For example almost everyone understands the sentence *The astronauts are orbiting the earth.* There are other verbs introduced or extended by the rapid changes in Anglo–American culture. For example, *I word processed all morning*; *This program is good at error trapping*, etc. Not too surprisingly, new verbs are harder to think of than new nouns.

Still rarer are examples of changes in low level grammatical categories. These aspects of language change slowest and have therefore a much more lasting influence on 'habitual thought.'

In the following sections the amended definition of the Sapir–Whorf hypothesis (above) is used to explain a number of anomalies in the relationship between language and culture.

2.1 The Role of Different Symbol Systems

This amended definition still contains some mystification, for example, the dilemma of how it is that different categorial systems, that is, different languages, lead to somewhat different world views.

The insight that the choice of a symbol system is crucial to the solution of a mathematical problem is attributed to the Hungarian mathematician George Polya. A solution may be easy, difficult, or impossible depending on how a problem solver symbolizes the problem. Though mathematical problems are hardly identical with human problems for which language may provide a symbolization, mathematical problems display many similarities to such problems. Language provides human beings with categories of thought (see Lucy and Shweder 1979, below); these may or may not facilitate thinking in a given cultural domain.

It is clear from the Ethnoscience movement of the 1960s and 70s that speakers of different languages often do classify things very differently. For example, the Navajo Indians classify the plant world as in Fig. 1.

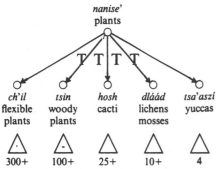

Figure 1. Navajo classification of plants. The T's symbolize the taxonomic relationship, e.g., *hosh nanise' át'é*, or 'A cactus is a (kind of) plant.'

It is clear from Fig. 1 that Navajos use different criteria for classifying plants than do speakers of English. Strangely, in Navajo—with about 500 named plants—no further subdivisions of even the largest class of flexible plants seem to exist.

However, alternate classifications do exist. One Navajo medicine man classified all plants according to their use. The surprise was a subclass of dangerous plants that were poisonous. However an even greater surprise was that each dangerous plant has an antidote plant that can undo the effect of the poison.

One more unusual example showing that a language can facilitate talk (and solutions?) on some topics: the Navajo language has a rich vocabulary for describing the 'behavior' of lines. I list half a dozen examples from a growing corpus of about one hundred:

dzígai	a white line running off into distance (infinity)
adziisgai	a group of parallel white lines running off into distance
hadziisgai	a white line running vertically upward from the bottom to the top of an object
ahééhesgai	more than two white lines form concentric circles
ałch'inidzígai	two white lines coming together to a point
áłnánágah	a white line zigzagging back and forth

The ease with which Navajos talk about the behavior of white and other colored lines is amazing. This facility with 'geometry' is perhaps explainable by Navajo names or descriptions of features of the landscape that rarely utilize similarities to everyday objects (e.g., Hat Rock). Instead Navajos use geometrical description of verticals, horizontals, lines, and points. For example, a rock formation near Tuba City, Arizona, called by Navajos *Tsé Áhé'ii'áhá*, 'two rocks standing vertically parallel in a reciprocal relationship to each other' was named by English speakers 'Elephant's Feet.'

2.2 Language and Culture do not Covary

The *perfect* correlation of different cultures speaking different languages was an artifact of the biases of early cultural anthropology. In the formative years of the profession each ethnographer selected his or her own tribe with a distinct language. Nevertheless, anomalies to language/culture homogeneity were soon noted.

Three small tribes in Northern California represent the paradigm case. The Yurok, Karok, and Hupa Indians (the Yurok language is distantly related to the Algonquian, Karok to the Siouxan, and Hupa to the Na-Dene (Athabascan) language family) in the Klamath and Trinity river valleys near the California–Oregon border speak three different languages belonging to three different language families, yet their cultures are almost identical.

The linguistic record is incomplete, but there is evidence that many lexical categories (and possibly grammatical categories) were converging in the three languages. For example, all three use the phrase 'fish eater' for naming the sea otter.

There is growing evidence that extensive language and cultural leveling appears in areas where speakers of very different languages live in close proximity and in intimate contact with each other. For example, on the border of the Indo-European and Dravidian languages of India there are communities where vocabulary and grammar of the two languages (Marathi, Indo-European and Kannada, Dravidian) converge to such a high degree that people do seem to live in an almost identical world with different labels attached (Gumperz 1971).

In other words, very different languages can, over time, under the influence of their converging cultures, level many of their differences, while similar languages may diverge over time if their cultures are developing in different directions.

Examples of the latter case are the Apachean languages of the southwest USA. The Navajo Indian language, in the Apachean group, accommodates a culture that incorporates many Puebloan traits into its world view. None of the Apachean-speaking tribes live in villages. The Puebloan villagers have relatively homogeneous cultures but speak a diversity of languages. The other Apacheans did not assimilate Puebloan elements into their culture. Navajo and the other Apachean languages do remain similar, but the Navajos use extensive specialized vocabularies (and folk theories) appropriate to their world view that is alien to the other Apacheans.

2.3 Language Mixing

Bilinguals when in each other's company tend to mix languages. The reasons seem obvious. There are many things that can be said better, more efficiently, in an aesthetically more pleasing manner, in one language than in another. Language purity is usually maintained only in the presence of (especially) high status monolinguals who would consider mixing the discourse with an unknown language offensive.

Language mixing, a universal occurrence when bilinguals converse, provides a good indicator of the utility of the idioms or technical vocabulary of one language over another. That is, different languages offer different (more or less elegant?) solutions to speech about the same or similar 'cultural things.'

2.4 Language Acquisition

Since all definitions of culture stress that culture includes all things '. . . acquired [learned] by man as a member of society' (Tylor 1958), any language learned by children belongs therefore within culture. This fact underlies the formulation of the relationship as 'language *in* culture.'

However, many scholars became concerned that language is not just 'in culture' or 'part of culture,' but is also the major vehicle for the acquisition of culture. The confusion of culture with its chief vehicle of transmission proved troublesome, particularly since language is held responsible for the cumulativeness of culture. That is, language makes possible not only the transmission of culture, but also the increase of culture from generation to generation. This cumulativeness through language is the major mechanism of cultural evolution.

The solution, while 'obvious' in light of the developments of cognitive anthropology (Ethnoscience and New Ethnography are near synonyms) was nevertheless never clearly formulated.

Only one additional assumption need be made: the acquisition of language by a child has a natural history and in the course of this development language changes its function. At first the child learns its native language 'as a member of society' and therefore following the standard definitions of culture, language is part of culture.

However, there is more to it. Language acquisition specialists agree that language learning is complete by the age of 4–6 years. Formal education, the institutionalized commencement of the acquisition of culture through language, begins after the child fully masters its native language. This happens universally at the age of 5 or 6 years. The child has now completed learning those aspects of culture that do not require language and begins to learn the accumulated wisdom and technology of the social group in which it is growing up, and that is encoded in language. Through language the child learns the verbalizable aspects of his or her culture. The function of language has shifted, now culture is in language, or it is acquired through language.

3. Cognitive Anthropology and the Sapir–Whorf Hypothesis

The New Ethnography or Ethnoscience entered anthropology with two papers published in *Language* by Floyd Lounsbury (1956) and his student Ward Goodenough (1956). The topic was a componential analysis of the Pawnee (which belongs to the Cadoan language family and was spoken in the southern Great Plains) and the Trukese (Austronesian-speaking Micronesians) kinship systems.

The point of componential analysis, in the context of the Sapir–Whorf hypothesis, is that kinship terminology or the kinship lexicon of every language/culture combination views the same kinship space, but tends to subdivide it differently. The examples of kinship terminologies confirm the 'linguistic relativity principle.' Speakers of languages in different cultures experience the same 'objective reality' but assign different terminology to it. The speakers of different languages lexicalize (set to words) the universal kinship space very differently.

For example, the Yankee kinship system used by English-speaking North Americans merges all cousins: most Americans no longer fully understand the terminology that classifies cousins by degree (first, second, . . . cousin) based on the distance from a common ancestor (first cousin = two generations, i.e., shared grandparents, etc.) and by generational distance (once, twice, . . . removed).

For example, Tagalog, the main language of the Philippines, makes no distinction between grandparents and grandparents' brothers and sisters. Crow and Omaha, both Siouxan languages spoken in the Great Plains, merge some of the terms for cousins with certain aunts or uncles. Since the Crow reckon descent through the maternal line (they are matrilineal) and the Omaha through the paternal line (they are patrilineal) the two systems are mirror images of each other. Navajo and Hungarian, a Finno–Ugric language of central Europe, on the other hand, make a careful distinction between the relative age of brothers and sisters. The list of culturally prescribed differences in kinship terminologies is virtually endless.

Componential analysis was soon followed by the discovery of folk taxonomies. Folk classifications had been noted before (e.g., Mauss 1964) but this was the first time that anthropologists/ethnographers collected folk taxonomies systematically. The seminal monograph was Conklin's *Hanuno'o Agriculture* (1954; the Hanuno'o are Austronesian speakers living on the island of Mindanao in the Philippines). A flurry of activity followed taxonomizing everything from ethno-anatomies to folk zoologies. Werner, et al. (1983) even presented the taxonomic aspects of the entire traditional Navajo universe.

In this lively debate the Sapir–Whorf hypothesis was mentioned only rarely and often outside the context of the New Ethnography. The participants in this ferment tacitly assumed that componential analysis and folk taxonomies clearly demonstrate the weak lexical version of the hypothesis.

Out of these developments arose cognitive anthro-

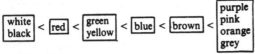

Figure 2. The cultural evolution of color terminology. If a language has the term 'red,' then it also has 'black' and 'white'; if a language has the term 'green' and 'yellow,' then it also has 'red,' 'white,' and 'black,' etc. The more technologically developed a given culture, the more of the 11 basic color terms are in use. (In the third box either order of [green < yellow] or [yellow < green] is possible).

pology that took as its goal the investigation of human cognition, especially cultural knowledge. It soon developed two branches. One is ethnoscience ethnography, which tacitly assumes the validity of the weak lexical form of linguistic relativity but does not elaborate this link to the past. The more pressing task is seen as the perfection and systematization of ethnography.

The second branch moved closer to cognitive psychology and by that route to cognitive science. Berlin and Kay (1969) soon emerged as the leaders in this field with their work on color terminology. That different language/culture groups have different color terminologies was considered in the debates of the 1950s and early 1960s the prime example of the lexical version of the Sapir–Whorf hypothesis. Obviously, the color spectrum is a continuum of colors from red to purple, but human beings in different parts of the world partition this continuum differently.

Berlin and Kay's first important discovery was that the color spectrum is not a good example for the hypothesis. '[C]olor categorization is not random and the foci of basic color terms are similar in all languages' (Berlin and Kay 1969: 10) and '... the eleven (see Fig. 2) basic color categories are panhuman perceptual universals' (Berlin and Kay 1969: 109).

However, Berlin and Kay (1969: 160 n.2) stress that their work should not be confused with a thorough study of the ethnographic ramifications of color terminology. That is, '... to appreciate the full cultural significance of color words it is necessary to appreciate the full range of meanings, both referential and connotative ...' or the lexical/semantic fields in which individual color terms are embedded.

Their second discovery was that color terminology evolves in a very lawful sequence. Although their formula has been 'fine tuned' following new cross-cultural data, it can be represented as shown in Figure 2 (their original formulation, 1969: 4).

Lucy and Shweder (1979) revived the controversy by showing in several well-designed experiments that color memory is highly sensitive to the lexical resources of a language and culture. They conclude that the universality of color categories is overstated

by Berlin and Kay and that the weak Sapir–Whorfian lexical formulation corresponds more closely to the facts.

Willet Kempton extended the methodology of cognitive anthropology to the shapes of objects, thus exploring the boundary between categories. Cecil Brown applied the evolutionary idea in Fig. 2 to other aspects of human vocabularies, especially botanical and zoological terminologies.

Ethnographers soon expanded their view beyond componential analysis after it was shown by a number of anthropologists and linguists that components are also lexical items and hence most often language specific rather than universal. John Lyons's critique of componential analysis as a universal theory for cultural knowledge (and semantics) is devastating. Nevertheless, componential analysis remains a superb tool for understanding exotic kinship terminologies.

In 1970 Casagrande and Hale, who had collected a large number of folk definitions in Papago (an Uto–Aztecan language of southern Arizona) published 13 lexical/semantic relations. They failed to find examples of a postulated 14th, the part/whole relation. A close analysis of their data shows that the part/whole relation did appear in its inverse form: that is, instead of 'A is a part of B' they found and classified as a spatial relation the inverse 'B has an A.'

Casagrande and Hale's work was seminal for a number of researchers (see the summary in Evens, et al. 1980). Through these scholars their work was linked to the cognitive sciences. However, this link did not develop into strong ties.

The major insight of field theory can again be framed in terms of the linguistic relativity principle: the weak lexical version is accepted as self-evident. The lexical/semantic fields of the languages used in different cultural contexts look very different. However, there is unity because the lexical/semantic fields are held together by *universal* lexical/semantic relations.

Unfortunately there is no agreement on the basic set of lexical/semantic relations which range from Werner's (Werner and Schoepfle 1987) two to the over 50 lexical relations of Apresyian, et al. (1970). Werner's two relations are 'taxonomy' and 'modification' plus several derived complex relations, a relation for sequential phenomena, and logical relations, including modal logic. Apresyian, et al.'s relations are derived from practical lexicography or the construction of more systematic dictionaries. For example, their relation EQUIP is the relation in 'ship' EQUIP 'crew' ('A crew operates a ship'). The folk taxonomic model can be applied to whole cultures. Closely related encyclopedic works display the lexical and cultural knowledge dimensions of a culture. That is, a background document fully exploring the lexical resources of a language represents an important aspect of the culture as a whole.

Ethnography is seen by many scholars as translation *par excellence*. Ethnographic translation fundamentally encourages translator's notes (definitions), which explain cultural ramifications of lexical items (or phrases) in native texts. Therefore, a carefully documented encyclopedic lexicon may represent an extensive set of translator's notes prepared in advance of the analysis of any future ethnographic texts.

An extension of these ideas is the recent focus on cultural schemata (Casson 1983). Schemata, recast into the lexical version of the Sapir–Whorf hypothesis, are folk theories often labeled by words (especially verbs) or phrases that usually require complex (e.g., up to monograph length and beyond) explanations or folk definitions.

4. Summary and Conclusions

The choice of the symbol system (e.g., language) affects the ease or difficulty with which one can talk about particular domains of cultural reality and solve problems in them. Thus the lexicon of language does provide a loosely laced straitjacket for thinking because it limits individuals to customary categories of thought. Only in this sense does it constrain thought.

At the same time language allows the inventive human mind to create alternative categorizations for solving new problems. The history of science and the rich diversity of thousands of human languages and cultures attests to the inventiveness of the human spirit.

True, the combinatorial possibilities in human language are enormous. Thus the very use of language results in a drift of meanings and with it inadvertent changes in world view. This process is analogous to genetic drift. But in addition there are analogues and historical examples of meaning mutations: conceptual revolutions and conversions.

However, these escapes from the mold of one's habitual language patterns are never easy—'... anomaly is recognized only with difficulty' (Kuhn 1970). It usually takes genius to show the rest of humanity how to see the world in a new light, that is in new categories. In such conversion experiences the language is affected 'to the core' (Kuhn 1970)—specifically, most grammatical categories remain the same but geniuses revamp lexical categories in ways that facilitate new thought which the rest of humanity may in time follow.

See also: Thought and Language.

Bibliography

Apresyian Y D, Mel'čuk I A, Žolkovsky A K 1970 Semantics and lexicography: Toward a new type of unilingual dictionary. In: Kiefer F (ed.) *Studies in Syntax and Semantics*. Reidel, Dordrecht

Berlin B, Kay P 1969 *Basic Color Terms: Their Universality and Evolution*. University of California Press, Berkeley, CA

Carroll J B (ed.) 1956 *Language, Thought, and Reality: Selected Writings of Benjamin Lee Whorf*. MIT, New York

Casagrande J B, Hale K L 1967 Semantic relationships in Papago folk definitions. In: Hymes D H, Bittle W E (eds.) *Studies in Southwestern Ethnolinguistics*. Mouton, The Hague

Casson R 1983 Schemata in cognitive anthropology. *Annual Review of Anthropology*: 429-62

Conklin H C 1954 The relation of Hanuno'o culture to the plant world (Doctoral dissertation, Yale University)

Evens M W, Litowitz B E, Markowitz J A, Smith R N, Werner O 1980 *Lexical/Semantic Relations: A Comparative Survey*. Linguistic Research, Edmonton

Gleason H A 1962 The relation of lexicon and grammar. In: Householder F W, Saporta S (eds.) *Problems in Lexicography*. Indiana Research Center in Anthropology, Bloomington, IN

Goodenough W H 1956 Componential analysis and the study of meaning. *Lg* 32: 195–216

Gumperz J J 1971 Dialect differences and social stratification in a North Indian village. In: Gumperz J J, Dill A (eds.) *Language in Social Groups*. Stanford University Press, Stanford, CA

Hoijer H (ed.) 1954 *Language in Culture*. University of Chicago Press, Chicago, IL

Humboldt W von 1836 (1960) *Über die Verschiedenheit des menschlichen Sprachbaues*. Dümmler, Bonn

Hymes D H 1960 Discussion of the symposium on the translation between language and culture. *AnL* 2(2): 81–84

Kuhn T S 1970 *The Structure of Scientific Revolutions*, 2nd edn. University of Chicago Press, Chicago, IL

Lounsbury F G 1956 A semantic analysis of the Pawnee kinship usage. *Lg* 32: 158–94

Lucy A J, Shweder R A 1979 Whorf and his critics: Linguistic and nonlinguistic influences on color memory. *AmA* 81: 581–615

Mandelbaum D G (ed.) 1963 *Selected Writings of Edward Sapir in Language, Culture, and Personality*. University of California Press, Berkeley, CA

Mauss M 1964 On language and primitive forms of classification. In Hymes E (ed.) *Language in Culture and Society*. Harper Row, New York

McQuown N A 1960 Discussion of the symposium on the translation between language and culture. *AnL* 2(2): 79–80

Tylor E B 1958 *Primitive Culture*, new edn. Harper, New York

Voegelin C F, Voegelin F M 1957 Hopi domains: A lexical approach to the problem of selection. *IJAL* 23(2)1: Memoir 14

Werner O, Manning A, Begishe K Y 1983 A taxonomic view of the traditional Navajo universe. In: Sturdevant W C, Ortiz A (eds.) *Handbook of North American Indians. Vol. 10: Southwest*. Smithsonian Institution, Washington, DC

Werner O, Schoepfle G M 1987 *Systematic Fieldwork, Vol. 1: Foundations of Ethnography and Interviewing, Vol. 2: Ethnographic Analysis and Data Management*. Sage Publications, London

Whorf B L 1939 The relation of habitual thought and behavior to language. In: Spier L (ed.) *Language, Culture, and Personality*. Sapir Memorial Publication Fund, Menasha, WI

Shared Knowledge

J. K. Gundel

'Shared knowledge' is one of a number of different terms (such as presupposition, given information, background information, common ground) which have been used to refer to the knowledge, beliefs, and/or discourse entities common to both speaker and addressee. Shared knowledge may be based on general cultural knowledge shared by all members of the same speech community or on more specific experiences shared by speech participants, including information derived from the immediate physical environment and preceding utterances in the discourse. While there is some question as to whether 'shared knowledge' is the most appropriate term for describing the phenomenon at issue here, or indeed whether there is a unitary phenomenon involved here at all, it is clear that assumptions about what is shared by the speaker and addressee in a discourse are involved in both the production and interpretation of natural language utterances. Shared knowledge plays a crucial role in resolving ambiguity, in the appropriate use of specific linguistic constructions, and in defining general conditions for successful communication (e.g., knowledge of the language itself and of appropriateness conditions for the performance of various illocutionary acts such as requesting or promising).

1. What is Shared—Knowledge or Beliefs, Propositions or Entities?

The term 'knowledge' implies knowledge of some fact. As a condition for successful communication, however, what is crucial is not whether a particular proposition actually is true, but whether it is believed to be true by the participants in a discourse. This suggests that shared knowledge is a pragmatic relation holding between language users and their beliefs about the world. Sperber and Wilson (1995) define an even weaker notion of 'mutual manifestness' which includes not only what speech participants believe, but what they are capable of believing. Others have argued that truth is not a factor here at all, since what is shared is not a proposition, but rather familiarity with some entity (cf. Prince 1981). A number of problems associated with the notion of shared knowledge disappear on this latter view. These include the fact that something can be assumed for the purpose of conversation even though none of the speech participants believes it to be true, as well as the fact that shared knowledge is not necessarily associated with certain constructions in all contexts (see Gundel 1985).

2. How is Knowledge Shared? The Problem of Infinite Regress

It has been suggested that in order for speaker and hearer to know which assumptions they share, they must make higher order assumptions about these assumptions. Thus, in order for successful communication to take place, it is not only necessary that both speaker and hearer know some proposition (p), but that each knows that the other knows that p and that each knows that the other knows that he/she knows that p, and so on ad infinitum. Shared knowledge of this infinitely regressive sort was termed 'mutual knowledge' by Schiffer (1972). Since the mutual knowledge requirement is unrealistic from a processing point of view, Clark and Marshall (1981) propose that such knowledge is not a reality but 'an ideal people strive for because they will want to avoid misunderstanding whenever possible' (p. 27). Speech participants will thus behave as if they have mutual knowledge, even though they cannot conclusively establish its existence. Sperber and Wilson (1995) argue, on the other hand, that 'there is no indication that any particular striving after mutual knowledge goes on' (p. 19) and that 'mutual knowledge is a philosopher's construct with no close counterpart in reality' (p. 38). They propose that their own concept of 'mutual manifestness' is not open to the same psychological objections as mutual knowledge, since a claim that an assumption is mutually manifest is not a claim about actual mental states or processes.

3. Degrees of Shared Knowledge: One Phenomenon or Many?

The concept of shared knowledge is crucial in describing appropriateness conditions for a number of constructions across languages. These include definite reference, focus and topic constructions, cleft sentences, contrastive stress, and pronominal forms. The type or degree of shared knowledge which is required, however, may differ from one construction to another. For example, the demonstrative determiner *that* in *That cake we had was good* is appropriate only if the referent of the noun phrase which contains it is familiar to both speaker and addressee. On the other hand, appropriate use of a demonstrative pronoun like *that* in *That was good* requires not only that the referent be known or familiar, but that it be present in the immediate linguistic or extralinguistic context. And the referent of an unstressed personal pronoun like *it* in *It was good* requires that the speaker's attention actually be focused on the referent at the current point in the discourse. In order to account for such facts, it is necessary to distinguish different ways in which knowledge can be shared. Much of the current research on shared knowledge is devoted to the question of how many different degrees of knowledge need to be distinguished and what particular constructions are correlated with these different degrees across languages (see Gundel, et al. 1993).

See also: Pragmatics; Relevance.

Bibliography

Clark H H, Marshall C R 1981 Definite reference and mutual knowledge. In: Joshi A K, Webber B L, Sag I A (eds.) *Elements of Discourse Understanding*. Cambridge University Press, Cambridge
Gundel J K 1985 'Shared knowledge' and topicality. *J Prag* **9**: 83–107 (issue devoted to Shared Knowledge)
Gundel J K, Hedberg N, Zacharski R 1993 Cognitive status and the form of referring expressions in discourse. *Language* **69**: 274–307
Kreckel M 1981 *Communicative Acts and Shared Knowledge in Natural Discourse*. Academic Press, London
Prince E 1981 Towards a taxonomy of given-new information. In: Cole P (ed.) *Radical Pragmatics*. Academic Press, New York
Schiffer S R 1972 *Meaning*. Clarendon Press, Oxford
Smith N (ed.) 1982 *Mutual Knowledge*. Academic Press, London
Sperber D, Wilson D 1995 *Relevance: Communication and Cognition*, 2nd edn. Blackwell, Oxford

Thought and Language

P. T. Smith

There are two themes to this article. First, that thinking involves mental operations or 'representations.' Representations may be of the real world—how to tie a shoelace, the layout of a supermarket, Chomsky's current views on transformations—or of fictional or hypothetical worlds—Hedda Gabler's motivations; what I would do if I were Prime Minister. Successful thinking involves manipulating these representations: planning an efficient route round the supermarket; deciding who would be Chancellor of the Exchequer in my hypothetical government. It should be clear from these examples that representations are necessary: without them we would live in a here-and-now world with an overlay of habits derived from past experience, where no planning is possible beyond overt trial and error. It should also be clear that by no means all representations are readily described by language, spatial representations being an obvious example. The success of preverbal human infants and nonverbal animals in solving spatial problems is a straightforward indication that thought can exist without language. Nonetheless language is a very powerful and flexible medium for creating representations, and this is where one should look for its influence on thought.

The second theme is that there is a progression from immediate reactions to the world (catching a ball that has been thrown towards one) to reflections about the world (remembering catching a ball yesterday, coaching someone in catching balls, writing a treatise on ballistics). The more immediate the task the more likely it is that the representations will be determined by external nonlinguistic factors (space, gravity); the more reflective tasks will show greater propensity for

language to play an important role in the representation. These points may seem obvious, but in the history of discussions about language and thought they have often been ignored.

1. History

The prime difficulty in discussing the relationship between language and thought is being forced to use language to describe this relationship: in particular, by attempting to summarize thoughts in some form of words it is but a short (and erroneous) step to assuming that a thought and a verbal summary of it are the same thing. This tendency pervades European thought of the last few centuries. Thus the influential *Port Royal* grammar of 1660 examines different mental operations and identifies them with different grammatical devices: propositional judgments with the subject–predicate structure of simple sentences; interrogation with the various syntactic devices for asking questions, etc. (see Chomsky 1966).

From a more general perspective, Jenisch, in a prizewinning essay of 1796 (cited in Jespersen 1922), identifies national stereotypes and their language:

> In language the whole intellectual and moral essence of a man is to some extent revealed... As the Greek was subtle in thought and sensuously refined in feeling, as the Roman was serious and practical rather than speculative, as the Frenchman is popular and sociable, as the Briton is profound and the German philosophic, so are also the languages of each of these nations.
>
> (Jespersen 1922: 30)

Sentiments such as these are part of a tradition developed in the nineteenth century by Wilhelm von

Humboldt and in the twentieth century by Edward Sapir, greatly influenced by the study of non-European languages, and culminating in the work of Benjamin Lee Whorf: this viewpoint has been called 'linguistic relativity'. In Whorf's words:

> We cut nature up, organize it into concepts, and ascribe significances as we do, largely because we are parties to an agreement to organize it in this way—an agreement that holds throughout our speech community and is codified in the patterns of our language.
>
> (Whorf 1956: 213)

Whorf gave lexical examples (the familiar assertion that American Eskimoes have more words than Europeans for snow) and syntactic examples of the differences between languages which he claimed reflected differences in thought. Thus the Hopi, lacking in their language a system of tenses similar to English past, present, and future, would also lack English notions of time and velocity. For Whorf, similarities of grammatical structure necessarily led to similarities of conceptual structure:

> The English sentences 'I push his head back' [in Shawnee *ni-kwaskwi-tepe-n-a*] and 'I drop it in water and it floats' [Shawnee *ni-kwask-ho-to*] are unlike. But in Shawnee the corresponding statements are closely similar, emphasizing the fact that analysis of nature and classification of events as like or in the same category (logic) are governed by grammar.
>
> (Whorf 1956: 235)

What all these examples, from Port Royal to Whorf, lack is any assessment of thought processes independent of their expression in language. How does one know that the propositions used in judgment correspond to the subject–predicate linguistic structure, that one has assessed the 'profundity' of the British and their language separately, that Shawnee conceptual categories correspond to Shawnee grammatical categories? Listeners are notoriously bad at keeping the ideas expressed in a linguistic message separate from superficial features of the message. Thus the same message, expressed in identical words by speakers with different dialects, is often less favorably evaluated when spoken in a socially less prestigious dialect, e.g., Quebec French. This is not an example of Whorfian linguistic relativity (the words and the grammar are the same), merely a demonstration that it is no trivial matter to assess such things as Jenisch's 'moral essence' and language separately.

2. Experimental Tests of the Whorfian Hypothesis

It is unfortunate that the largest research effort related to the Whorfian hypothesis has involved rote learning of simple colored stimuli. The idea seems appealing: choose a dimension for which we can be sure the sensory information is processed similarly the world over, but where different languages code this sensory information in reliably different ways. However, color is too tightly related to the physics and physiology of vision, and rote learning is too modest an exemplar of what could be regarded as thought for significant interactions between language and thought to be apparent.

Initial investigations, however, were promising. A study by Brown and Lenneberg (1954) assessed the linguistic 'codability' of colors and showed this was related to the colors' discriminability and memorability. Codability was assessed by a number of measures of length and speed of response and intersubject and intrasubject consistency: a color which was given a short response (e.g., *red*), and which subjects produced rapidly and consistently on repeated presentations of the color was regarded as highly codable; a color that might be described *reddish purple*, which was produced more hesitantly and with less consistency would be regarded as less codable. Examples of these colors were briefly presented to American college students (first language English) and after delays ranging from seven seconds to three minutes they were required to point to them on a large chart of possible colors. There were positive correlations between codability and memory performance, and these correlations were larger the greater the delay. A study of Zuni Indians, using similar materials, showed that there was not a complete correspondence between the codability of colors for English speakers and Zuni speakers. In particular, the Zuni do not have a label to distinguish between orange and yellow, and this was related to the Zuni speakers' memory performance, where they frequently confused orange and yellow stimuli.

The notion of codability, which proves to be a useful concept, shall be returned to, but first it must be pointed out that crosslinguistic studies with color have proved to be more difficult to interpret than was first thought. Rosch's work was prominent in the 1970s. Rosch's starting point was the work of Berlin and Kay in 1969, who had established that color terminology was not arbitrary across languages and, despite disagreements between speakers about where the boundaries between various color terms should be placed, there was good agreement, even across languages, about the identities of certain basic color terms, which Berlin and Kay termed 'focal' colors. Rosch studied the Dani, an agricultural people of West Irian, who have only two color terms. For them, focal colors were not more codable than other colors, but they were more memorable (tested by recognition after 30 seconds) and they were more learnable (tested by pairing colors and arbitrary names and testing learning over several days). This suggests that an important influence on performance on these tasks is the precise location of the color in a psychological representation, which is determined by innate and universal properties of the color-vision system, not by language-specific labels.

Further work, however, has suggested that the effects of the innate differential discriminability of colors can be partialed out in appropriately designed experiments. A measure of 'communication accuracy' (how well a speaker can describe a color to enable it to be identified by a listener) then proves an effective predictor of memory performance. So effects of language on memory for colors are demonstrable, but they are effects of some subtlety, and are not the most direct examples of language influencing thought. A succinct review of this work is provided by D'Andrade (1989).

3. Codability

Codability is a concept that has appealed to many experimental psychologists working on short-term memory: the quantity of material individuals are capable of retaining accurately in short-term memory is limited, and different encodings of the same information can differ in how readily they can be 'squeezed in.' An early demonstration of this was by S. Smith (cited in Miller 1956), who trained subjects to recode a list of binary digits (0s and 1s) into octal (the digits 0 to 7), so 000 is recoded as 0, 001 as 1, 010 as 2, etc. Subjects so trained were able to recall accurately much longer sequences of binary digits than subjects who had not received this training.

Such a result points to one important general function of language in thought: recoding material in a compact form enables us to retain more of it in short-term memory, and any thought processes that depend on manipulation of such material should benefit. The details of this idea have been worked out more fully recently: 'working memory' is the preferred term for manipulations of material on a short-term basis, and it has been established that immediate recall of verbal material is heavily dependent on the operations of an 'articulatory loop' in working memory, whose capacity is limited by how much the subject can *say* in 1.5–2 seconds. If the material takes longer than 2 seconds to say (because it contains many syllables or because the subject is not an agile articulator) then it will not always be accurately recalled (for a good review, see Baddeley 1986).

This property of the human memory system has curious implications for crosscultural intelligence testing. Many tests of intelligence include as a component a test of 'digit span' or some similar measure of immediate recall of unrelated words. Digit span (how many digits one can reliably recall immediately after one has heard them) depends on how fast they can be said. Compared with a monosyllabic digit speaker, subjects who speak languages with polysyllabic digits will be able to say fewer digits in two seconds and thus remember fewer of them. If this is not taken into account in comparing raw intelligence test scores across languages, the polysyllabic speaker will seem less intelligent. This effect was first demonstrated for

Welsh and English by Ellis and Hennelley in 1980, and confirmed in a study of English, Spanish, Hebrew, and Arabic by Naveh-Benjamin and Ayres (1986). The results are quite substantial, with English speakers (mean number of syllables per digit 1.0, the digit 7 being excluded from the Naveh-Benjamin and Ayres study) having a mean span of 7.21 digits, and Arabic speakers (mean number of syllables per digit 2.25) having a mean span of 5.77. Whether this early bottleneck in processing has any implications for more complex thought processes is not clear: there are no reports of speakers of a particular language being particularly disadvantaged in calculation, and it would be fanciful to suppose that the Arabs developed algebra because they were having such difficulties with arithmetic. Perhaps the effects of the bottleneck exist, but are too subtle to have been recognized so far.

The value of labeling in some problem-solving tasks has been demonstrated. Rommetveit (in Campbell and Smith 1978) asked 8-year old Norwegian children to solve a number of problems appearing in one of two linguistic forms: either they had to select an object with respect to two adjectival properties (e.g., in an array of circles of different colors and sizes, they were asked to select the second largest white circle), or one of the adjectives was combined with the noun into a single label (the phrase *white circle* was replaced by *snowball*). The children performed better on the second version of the task.

Examples of language as a coding device are not restricted to material that is already in a verbal form. Labeling of nonverbal material (e.g., pictures) is a useful mnemonic strategy, particularly because words are more easily rehearsed than visual images—use of this strategy does not appear in children until they are of school age. But labels simplify or even distort the information they are summarizing. A study by Carmichael, et al. (1932) presented subjects with ambiguous figures (e.g., a crescent shape) for which different subjects were given different labels (*crescent moon* or *Letter C*). In reproducing these figures later, subjects made systematic distortions of the original figure in the direction of the label they had heard (the crescent was more moon-like or more C-like).

A further example of the way language can distort nonverbal memory is provided in a study by Loftus and Palmer (1974). They showed subjects a film of a car crash and afterwards asked them how fast the cars were traveling when the collision occurred. If the word *smashed* was used in the question, estimates for speed were higher than if the more neutral word *hit* was used. Moreover, when questioned later, subjects who had previously received the *smashed* question were more likely to report (erroneously) the presence of broken glass.

4. Presuppositions and Prejudice

The examples in Sect. 3 are small-scale and short-term: labeling may effect memory for isolated patterns for a few minutes, but are there more long-term influences of language on significant areas of our cognitions? One fruitful source of evidence is in the presuppositions people bring to the interpretation of utterances. If this author talks of a *surgeon* many listeners in his culture will assume he is referring to a man, even though this is not explicitly stated, nor is it necessarily true. If he says *Jeff is a worse player than George* he is suggesting that both Jeff and George are bad players, otherwise he would have used the more neutral *George is a better player than Jeff*. Disentangling the distinctive contribution of language is tricky: in the author's culture most surgeons are male, and this is a fact about the culture, not about language, so it is not easy to tell whether language is relevant here.

One approach is to use problems which are neutral with respect to culture. Noordman (1978) gave Dutch students problems such as *A is the father of B, A is the grandfather of C, B is not the father of C, What relation could B be to C?* The students gave predominantly male answers, and in particular they more often chose the correct answer *uncle* (50 percent of choices) than the correct answer *mother* (20 percent of choices). The pattern changed when *mother* and *grandmother* replaced *father* and *grandfather* in the problem: here there was a bias to give female answers, though it was not so strong as the male bias in the male version of the problem, and in particular the correct answer *father* (38 percent) was chosen more often than the correct answer *aunt* (30 percent). These results show that problem solvers use the language of the problem to create a representation which may be incomplete: a problem in which only one gender is referred to may lead to a representation in which all the possible solutions may have the same gender. However, the greater bias exhibited when all the terms are male than when they are all female may have cultural, not linguistic, roots (one is more used to reading examination problems which refer to *he* than *she*).

Gender biases could be viewed as an example of the more general phenomenon of 'markedness.' Here bipolar adjectival pairs such as *good/bad, tall/short, fast/slow* are not considered to be symmetrical, but the preferred 'unmarked' member of the pair does double duty, both indicating a particular pole and naming the entire dimension (this 'neutral' aspect of the unmarked adjective can be seen in such phrases as *six feet tall* and *How fast is your typing?*). Clark (1969) showed that problems involving unmarked adjectives are easier than their marked-adjective counter parts (*If John is better than Pete, and Pete is better than Dick, then who is best?* is solved faster than *If John is worse than Pete, and Pete is worse than Dick, then who is worst?*). A full interpretation of this result is controversial, since it is not known whether it derives from some fundamental property of linguistic structure or from the more mundane observation that marked adjectives have greater general frequency of usage in the language than unmarked adjectives; nonetheless Clark's results show that problem solvers prefer to create representations based on one set of linguistic labels rather than another.

A further example of the influence of labels on thought is the phenomenon of 'functional fixedness.' Subjects generally find it difficult to solve problems requiring them to use objects in novel ways, such as using a spanner to complete an electrical circuit: the normal function of the object appears 'fixed.' This phenomenon is enhanced if the experimenter uses the label *spanner* in presenting the problem: the label appears to encourage subjects to create an inappropriate representation for the problem.

The most contentious area concerned with the effects of labeling on thought is that of prejudice. There is a choice of labels to refer to an individual (*nigger/negro/colored/black/Afro-Caribbean; queer/ poof/gay/homosexual; chick/crumpet/date/escort/girl-friend*). The label chosen undoubtedly reflects some of the attitudes of the speaker, but one can also ask whether use of a label can shape attitudes—does referring to a person who presides over a committee as a *chairman* lead one to expect that this person should be a man? In this author's culture, a 25-year old woman is often referred to as a *girl*, whereas the corresponding term *boy* is much less frequently used of a 25-year old man—does this influence attitudes to people referred to in this way? The evidence suggests that such influences exist. For example, subjects who were asked to describe the images suggested by chapter headings in a sociological text were more likely to report images containing only males when headings used generic man (*Industrial Man*) than when gender was not mentioned (*Industrial Society*). Kitto (1989) composed short references for hypothetical applicants for jobs. All the applicants were females aged 25. Subjects (mainly university students) preferred applicants whose reference referred to them as *girl* for the low-status job of waitress, but they preferred applicants referred to as *woman* for the higher-status job of personal assistant. Subjects commented that the persons described in the *girl* references were livelier but less reliable or competent than the persons referred to in the *woman* references: this was true even for subjects who appeared unaware that their attitudes were being manipulated by the presence of *girl* or *woman*. One way of looking at these results is that *girl* elicits many presuppositions including those associated with the 'proper' use of the term to refer to a female of school age—such females are typically livelier but less competent than their adult counterparts. Society will not change overnight by banning the use of words like *girl* (when applied to an adult) and *chairman*, but it is important to realize how these terms may provoke prejudices which are all the more insidious for our not always being aware of them.

5. Representations

The term 'representation' has been used throughout this article without giving a precise account of what a representation is. Behaviorist psychologists have often criticized cognitive psychologists for using such hypothetical constructs without precision, and hence without explanatory power. The problem is not easy, and it is not made any easier by the need to consider how much of a subject's performance is to be ascribed to mental representations per se, and how much can be accounted for by the mental processes used to access these representations.

Occasionally psychologists have produced theories where the representations have been specified very precisely. For example, Johnson-Laird's theory of syllogistic reasoning proposes that propositions such as *All A are B* or *Some B are not C* are encoded by subjects into a 'mental model,' and the form of encoding for each proposition, and how the subject combines propositions, are fully specified. The theory is very successful at predicting the relative difficulty of different syllogisms.

A rather different approach to representations is to ask subjects to make judgments about some domain (perceptual, such as the similarity of rectangles of different heights and widths; or conceptual, like the similarity of various animals) and then use mathematical and statistical techniques to infer the structure of the subjects' underlying representations (for an authoritative but difficult review, see Suppes, et al. 1989: ch. 14). A general summary of this work is that perceptual judgments can often be successfully characterized by representations with spatial properties (with percepts corresponding to points in a space, and the dissimilarity of two percepts corresponding to distance apart of the corresponding points in the space). However, categories with verbal labels, such as animals or countries, are often better described by tree structures or (equivalently) by collections of features. Here, dissimilarity can be characterized by distance apart in a tree, where each concept corresponds to a terminal node of the tree (end of a branch) and distance is measured by distance between the branches.

Features have the advantage of providing a richer description of the relation between two concepts: in particular, the features can be parceled into three sets (what features concept A has that concept B does not, what features concept B has that concept A does not, and what features they have in common). With such a characterization, judgmental asymmetries and the effects of context can be neatly handled. For example, it has been shown that subjects' judgments of the similarity of North Korea to China (concentrating on features that North Korea has but China does not) exceeded their judgments of the similarity of China to North Korea (concentrating on features that China has but North Korea does not). Also, when asked to make judgments about *similarity*, subjects put greater emphasis on common features than when asked to make judgments of *dissimilarity*: this explains why one group of subjects rated the former West and East Germany as more similar than Sri Lanka and Nepal, but a different group of subjects also rated the former West and East Germany as more dissimilar than Sri Lanka and Nepal.

The implication of this work for the relation between language and thought is that concepts, at least those that can be readily labeled, seem to be characterized largely with features, and features also play an important role in linguists' characterization of language. Thus, one important common ground between thought representations and linguistic descriptions is at the feature level. Note, however, that such a statement stops well short of Whorf's claim that linguistic features *determine* conceptual features.

6. Inner Speech

The final area of interaction to be considered in this survey concerns the supervisory role of language in monitoring complex tasks. Vygotsky is prominent among psychologists who have suggested that talking to ourselves is an important aspect of problem solving. In the course of cognitive development overt use of speech when thinking gives way to what Vygotsky called 'inner speech,' but such activity retains all the grammatical and semantic properties of overt speech. By talking to ourselves we can bring together in working memory strands of ideas which might otherwise be kept separate in different modules of our cognitive system. This is much the same function as has been suggested for consciousness itself (see Oatley 1988 for a discussion of 'Vygotskyan consciousness') though consciousness would embrace more than inner speech.

Linking speech with consciousness should suggest that speech is not always advantageous for efficient cognitive functioning. It can readily be shown that on occasion conscious processes interfere with an activity: describing what we are doing while we are tying a shoelace or riding a bicycle disrupts performance. Formal demonstration of this point is provided, for example, by Hayes and Broadbent (1988). They asked subjects to interact with a computer so as to control the computer output. The output was determined by one of two equations linking the subject's input and the computer's present or previous output. Hayes and Broadbent discriminated two forms of learning: S-mode (selective) learning, which is explicit and reportable; and U-mode (unselective) learning, which is implicit and not readily reportable. They were able to show that one of the equations in the computer-control task led to most subjects using S-mode learning, while the other led to U-mode learning. (This is based on the amount of material that needs to be held in working memory: if the capacity of working memory is exceeded, only implicit U-mode learning is possible.) Hayes and Broadbent (1988) trained subjects on these tasks and then unexpectedly changed the equations determining the computer's output. Subjects who had learnt in S-mode coped with the transfer better than subjects who had learnt in U-mode. The experiment was repeated with different subjects who in addition were required to generate a 'random' sequence of digits while carrying out the interaction with the computer. In this experiment U-mode subjects adjusted better to the unexpected change in the equation than did S-mode subjects.

The relevance for the present discussion is as follows. S-mode learning involves the use of 'inner speech' in working memory; disrupt the speech by a task involving a verbal component, such as random digit generation, and the learning is disrupted. U-mode learning does not rely on inner speech, and indeed when an unexpected problem is met, such as the change in equation in the computer task, attempts to use inner speech interfere with efficient performance; irrelevant concurrent verbal activity actually helps, because this stops interference from inner speech.

Extending the idea of inner speech to nonhumans has obvious risks, but the success of training apes to use language-like symbol systems (sign language, manipulation of plastic tokens) suggests looking at the cognitive benefits such animals derive from language training. On the whole, evidence for language training benefiting ape cognition is slight. In particular, it is difficult to demonstrate differences in cognitive abilities before and after training. However, one clear example does exist: Premack (1988) reports an experiment in which chimpanzees derived significant benefit from language training when they attempted an analogy task. The key element of the language training was the acquisition of the plastic symbols for 'same' and 'different.' It is tempting to see these same/different elements as forming a crucial part of ape inner speech which is used to operate on the analogy problem.

7. Conclusion

Successful demonstrations of the influence of language on thought have been confined largely to the lexicon: information is more successfully retained and manipulated in working memory if it is in an articulatorily compact, and linguistically unmarked, lexical form, and particular lexical items can influence our memories and lead us to make possibly erroneous presuppositions in problem solving and in making judgments. Several of these demonstrations are purely quantitative, for example, the limited capacity of the articulatory loop, and whether the subject is articulating or not when attempting a problem. Qualitative aspects beyond the lexicon, in particular whether grammar influences thought, have not been addressed. An analogy with mathematical thinking

may help: rather than say *The area of a square is equal to the length of one of its sides multiplied by itself,* significant compression can be achieved by using the algebraic expression $A = s2$. If this was all that could be achieved with algebraic notation, a modest quantitative improvement in notation would have been made. But mathematicians have used this notation to extend knowledge, for example, in expressions for the volume of a cube ($V = s3$), and even for the volume of an unvisualizable *n*-dimensional hypercube ($V = sn$). The notation can also be used to manipulate existing knowledge, for example to derive the length of side of a square of known area ($s = A1/2$). So the important property of this algebraic notation is not simply that it compresses the represented information, but that it offers ways to operate on and extend this information. The same is undoubtedly true for the relation between language and thought. However, current work has stopped largely at the level of language as a compressing device, and understanding of the richness of language as a representational medium for thought (alluded to by Whorf, but certainly not established by him) remains as yet beyond our grasp.

See also: Concepts; Sapir–Whorf Hypothesis.

Bibliography

Baddeley A D 1986 *Working Memory.* Clarendon Press, Oxford

Brown R W, Lenneberg E H 1954 A study in language and cognition. *Journal of Abnormal and Social Psychology* **49**: 454–62

Campbell R N, Smith P T (eds.) 1978 *Recent Advances in the Psychology of Language*, 2 vols. Plenum Press, New York

Carmichael L, Hogan H P, Walter A A 1932 An experimental study of the effect of language on the reproduction of visually perceived form. *Journal of Experimental Psychology* **15**: 73–86

Chomsky N 1966 *Cartesian Linguistics.* Harper and Row, New York

Clark H H 1969 Linguistic processes in deductive reasoning. *Psychological Review* **76**: 387–404

D'Andrade R G 1989 Cultural cognition. In: Posner M I (ed.) *Foundations of Cognitive Science.* MIT Press, Cambridge, MA

Hayes N A, Broadbent D E 1988 Two modes of learning for interactive tasks. *Cognition* **28**: 249–76

Humboldt W von 1971 *Linguistic Variability and Intellectual Development.* University of Miami Press, Coral Gables, FL

Jespersen O 1922 *Language: Its Nature, Development and Origin.* George Allen and Unwin, London

Johnson-Laird P N 1983 *Mental Models.* Cambridge University Press, Cambridge

Kitto J 1989 Gender reference terms: separating the women from girls. *British Journal of Social Psychology* **28**: 185–87

Loftus E F, Palmer J P 1974 Reconstruction of automobile destruction: An example of the interaction between language and memory. *Journal of Verbal Learning and Verbal Behavior* **13**: 585–89

Miller G A 1956 The magical number seven, plus or minus

two: Some limits on our capacity for processing information. *Psychological Review* **63**: 81–96

Naveh-Benjamin M, Ayres T J 1986 Digit span, reading rate, and linguistic relativity. *Quarterly Journal of Experimental Psychology* **38(A)**: 739–51

Noordman L G M 1978 Foreground and background information in reasoning. In: Campbell R N, Smith P T (eds.)

Oatley K 1988 On changing one's mind: A possible function of consciousness. In: Marcel A J, Bisiach E (eds.) *Consciousness in Contemporary Science*. Clarendon Press, Oxford

Premack D 1988 Minds with and without language. In: Weiskrantz L (ed.) *Thought Without Language*. Clarendon Press, Oxford

Rosch E 1974 Linguistic relativity. In: Silverstein A (ed.) *Human Communication: Theoretical Perspectives.* Erlbaum, Hillsdale, NJ

Sapir E 1912 Language and environment. *AmA* **14**: 226–42

Suppes P, Krantz D H, Luce R D, Tversky A 1971–1990 *Foundations of Measurement*, vol. 2. Academic Press, New York.

Vygotsky L S 1978 Tool and symbol in children's development. In: Cole M, John-Steiner V, Scribner S, Souberman E (eds.) *Mind and Society*. Harvard University Press, Cambridge, MA

Whorf B L 1956 *Language, Thought and Reality*. MIT Press, Cambridge, MA

Truth and Meaning

Analyticity

A. Millar

On what may be called the traditional view, a statement is analytic if it is true solely in virtue of the meanings of the expressions it contains. For example, *A triangle is a three-sided figure* is analytic because true in virtue of the meanings of the expressions *triangle* and *three-sided figure*. Much controversy, however, surrounds the concept of analyticity, which has had a prominent role in philosophy since the time of Kant, particularly in connection with topics in the theory of knowledge and the theory of meaning. This article deals first with the traditional view and its ramifications and then considers criticisms of the notion of analyticity deriving from the work of W. V. O. Quine.

1. The Traditional View

The familiar way of defining analyticity given above raises a question about the bearers of truth-values. In the sense intended here statements are declarative sentences in a particular language. It may be wondered whether statements as opposed to what they express are properly regarded as being either true or false. Even so, it is clear that statements may express truths. The statement *A triangle is a three-sided figure* may count as analytic insofar as the meanings of its constituent expressions guarantee that it expresses a truth. By contrast, *Tom drew a triangle on a sheet of paper* is not analytic (following Kantian terminology it would be called a synthetic statement) because the meanings of its constituent expressions do not guarantee that it expresses a truth. Whether the statement is true or not depends upon what Tom did and not just on the meanings of the relevant expressions. Thus far analyticity has been taken to apply to statements conceived as a kind of sentence. Yet the term may also be used of what statements express. The analytic statement *A garage is a place for storing or repairing motor vehicles* is a sentence of the English language expressing the proposition that a garage is a place for storing or repairing motor vehicles. This same proposition may be expressed in languages other than English provided they have expressions which express the

same concepts and thus have the same meanings as the expressions of which the English sentence is composed. Moreover, the proposition in question may be said to be analytic in that it is true in virtue of its constituent concepts, these being the concepts expressed by the English expressions *garage* and *place for storing or repairing motor vehicles*.

In the light of the preceeding account it comes as no surprise that analyticity, conceived as truth in virtue of meanings, should be thought to explicate the concept of necessity, conceived as truth in all possible worlds. Suppose that the statement *A triangle is a three-sided figure* expresses a truth (a true proposition) in virtue of the meanings of the relevant constituent expressions. Then the truth of the proposition expressed is in no way dependent on facts about the actual world. No matter what the world is or might have been the proposition in question would remain true and that is what is captured by the claim that it is true in all possible worlds.

2. The Philosophical Significance of the Traditional View

The concept of analyticity offers a solution to a difficulty in empiricist theory of knowledge. In its classical version empiricism holds that all knowledge in some sense derives from experience. However, it is plausible to suppose that we know some things a priori, that is to say, independently of experience. At any rate it seems that we can know that a triangle is a three-sided figure or even that the angles of a triangle add up to 180° without having empirical grounds for accepting these propositions. In the first of these cases it is tempting to regard the proposition in question as self-evident—we just see that it is true. In the second case it seems that we can prove that the proposition is true from propositions which are self-evident.

The traditional view yields an account of how we can have a priori knowledge. The propositions which we can know a priori are analytic. If a proposition is self-evident the knowledge that it is true is guaranteed by a grasp of its constituent concepts. If we fail to see that a bachelor is an unmarried man then we lack a grasp of the concept of a bachelor. There are other analytic propositions which, though not self-evident, we know a priori because there is proof of them from self-evident premises which we know a priori. The ability to appreciate the validity of such proofs is to be explained in terms of abilities which constitute a grasp of the relevant concepts. Having these conceptual abilities will not guarantee that we can produce proofs on demand. But the account has it that recognition that a proof is valid is explained by the interlocking exercise of conceptual abilities.

This application of the traditional view has the virtue of making a priori knowledge seem unmysterious. If it is along the right lines then it can be explained how we know some things to be true independently of experience, that is, in the absence of empirical grounds for believing that they are true. However, the account has to be supplemented if it is to show how a priori knowledge can be squared with classical empiricism. What is missing is an explanation of how it can be that we have a priori knowledge if all knowledge is in some sense derived from experience. In classical empiricism the required supplement is provided by a theory of concepts. The theory has it that no concept is innate and that all concepts are acquired via the impact of experience. So, for example, we would acquire the concept of redness by a process of abstraction from properties of the visual experiences we have as we look at red things. Thus even a priori knowledge would be derived from experience insofar as concepts are derived from experience.

3. Analyticity and Semantics

The concept of analyticity is of interest aside from its links with the empiricist doctrines outlined above for it has a place within a broad conception of what is involved in understanding the meanings of expressions in natural languages. There is some plausibility in the idea that if one understands the English term *garage* then one has a mastery of certain rules or conventions governing the use of the term. For example, there might be rules which require that if *garage* applies to something then *place for storing or repairing motor vehicles* also applies to it, and vice versa. The totality of rules governing a given term would determine its meaning and thus what concept it expresses. This conception can be extended to cover logical expressions like *and, either ... or ...* , and the logical concepts linked with these expressions. In the case of *and* there might be a rule which requires that if you take a conjunction of the form *P and Q* to express a truth then you must take *P* to express a truth and *Q* to express a truth. An analytic statement would be a statement the rules for whose constituent expressions are such that anyone who has a mastery of these rules, and thus understands the expressions

involved, would be committed to taking the statement to express a truth.

4. The Attack on Analyticity

In a classic article entitled 'Two dogmas of empiricism' (in Quine 1961) W. V. O. Quine argues that the concept of analyticity is irredeemably obscure. The discussion assumes a distinction between analytic statements which are logical truths like

No unmarried man is married   (1)

and analytic statements which are not logical truths like

No bachelor is married   (2)

Logical truths are statements which are true and remain true under all interpretations of their nonlogical vocabulary. Nonlogical analytic statements can be turned into logical truths by substituting synonyms for synonyms. So (2) can be turned into (1) by substituting *unmarried man* for *bachelor*. Much of the discussion of 'Two dogmas' focuses on the idea of nonlogical analyticity. A major theme is that concepts commonly used to explain this notion are no clearer than what they are meant to explain, and further, that when one tries to elucidate them one finds oneself in turn falling back on the notion of analyticity. For example, the notion of synonymy just used to account for the analyticity of (2) is, according to Quine, obscure and its obscurity is not removed by accounting for the synonymy of *bachelor* and *unmarried man* in terms of the analyticity of *All and only bachelors are unmarried men*. (This line of thought is submitted to close scrutiny in Grice and Strawson 1956.)

Quine is equally pessimistic about the idea of deploying the concept of a semantic rule to account for analyticity. Here the main target is work of Carnap on artificial languages (Carnap 1956). Carnap devised for artificial languages of a certain type a system of semantic rules which, roughly speaking, combine to fix the truth conditions for the sentences of these languages. It turns out that there are certain sentences whose truth is guaranteed by the relevant semantic rules. These are the 'L-true sentences.' Quine argues that L-truth fails to provide the required elucidation for analyticity since, among other things, a satisfying theory of semantic rules is not available. J. J. Katz has developed an account of analyticity within the context of a general semantic theory which represents the meanings of lexical items in terms of semantic markers denoting conceptual constituents of meanings (see Katz 1972 for discussion and further references). From Quine's standpoint, however, an account is still needed of what determines which conceptual constituents should be assigned to a given lexical item.

In writings subsequent to 'Two dogmas' Quine attempts to make sense of analyticity in behavioral terms. A sentence is said to be stimulus analytic if it commands assent no matter what sensory stimulations the subject is undergoing. As Quine recognizes, this only roughly approximates to the traditional notion since it fails to discriminate between sentences of the kind *No bachelor is married* and cases like *There have been black dogs.*

In 'Two dogmas' Quine takes the concept of logical truth to be relatively unproblematic, though he implies that nothing is gained by regarding logical truths as analytic. He assumes that the explication of logical truth does not require the notion of analyticity or any of the other problematic notions with which it is linked. P. F. Strawson has argued that this assumption is false (Strawson 1957). The statement *No un-illuminated book is illuminated* is true, and indeed logically true, on readings which take the two occurrences of *illuminated* to have the same meaning. But it does not remain true on a reading which gives the first occurrence the sense of *lit* and the second the sense of *decorated*. So it does not remain true under all interpretations of its nonlogical vocabulary, but only on those interpretations which give the same meaning to all occurrences of its nonlogical vocabulary. Strawson's point is that Quine cannot after all dispense with the notion of sameness of meaning even at the level of logical truths.

Work by Hilary Putnam and Saul Kripke on theoretical terms in science and on natural-kind terms casts doubt on the idea that the meanings of such terms are captured by analytic statements. Their discussions point to the deeper issue of whether the use of terms like these is governed by the sort of rules which would generate analytic truths. Among other important issues also discussed by Putnam and Kripke is whether all necessary truths are analytic truths and whether only analytic truths can be known a priori. Scepticism about analyticity is widespread, but for a more optimistic review of the issues, see Boghossian 1997.

See also: A Priori; Concepts; Meaning: Philosophical Theories; Natural Kinds; Necessity.

Bibliography

Ayer A J 1946 *Language, Truth and Logic*, 2nd edn. Gollancz, London
Boghossian P A 1997 Analyticity. In: Hale B, Wright C (eds) *A Companion to the Philosophy of Language*. Blackwell, Oxford
Carnap R 1956 *Meaning and Necessity*, 2nd edn. University of Chicago Press, Chicago, IL
Grice H P, Strawson P F 1956 In defense of a dogma. *The Philosophical Review* **65**: 141–58
Katz J J 1972 *Semantic Theory*. Harper and Row, New York
Kitcher P 1984 *The Nature of Mathematical Knowledge*. Oxford University Press, New York
Kripke S A 1980 *Naming and Necessity*. Blackwell, Oxford
Putnam H 1975 *Mind, Language and Reality* Philosophical Papers, vol. 2. Cambridge University Press, Cambridge
Quine W V O 1960 *Word and Object*. MIT Press, Cambridge, MA
Quine W V O 1961 *From a Logical Point of View*, 2nd edn. Harvard University Press, Cambridge, MA
Strawson P F 1957 Propositions, concepts and logical truths. *The Philosophical Quarterly* **7**: 15–25; repr. in Strawson (1971)
Strawson P F 1971 *Logico–Linguistic Papers*. Methuen, London

Communication

K. L. Berge

The content and use of the term 'communication' is even by humanistic standards extremely ambiguous, and it has therefore often been difficult to use in practical, empirical work. The most exact use of the term has been standardized in Shannon and Weaver's information theory. Within the tradition of semiotics, the value of communication as a term has been questioned, and in linguistics the term has sometimes been used as a synonym or part-synonym with more exactly defined terms such as use, parole, text, behavior, and performance. In spite of this, certain theorists—often those with a background in cybernetics—have used 'communication' as a generic term for all theories about man, in the same way as semioticians have defined the domain of semiotics.

A very simple and general, but neither unproblematic nor uncontroversial, way of defining communication is to view it as an information process going on between at least two human communicators (not necessarily two persons as long as one can communicate with oneself) embedded in a context, and a situation. More specifically, communication can be defined as a generic term covering all messages uttered in different contexts and situations.

A message can be divided into sign-vehicle and meaning. The sign-vehicle then covers all possible variants on the expression plane of linguistic utterances, and meaning covers all possible variants on what is called, in the glossematic school, the content plane. In this way, communication is used as a sociological term, and language is viewed as a primarily social fact.

Furthermore, communication can also be conceived of as inherent in the linguistic message. The situation, the context, and the communicators involved in communication make their mark on the content and expression planes of the message. This definition is neutral with regard to the different traditions in linguistics which divide language for instance into 'langue' or 'system' on the one hand, and 'parole' or 'behavior' on the other.

1. 'Communication': Different Models and Metaphors

One possible way of bringing order into the rather chaotic world of the different approaches to the study of communication in linguistics, is to differentiate between the various trends in communication-relevant research. These trends can be classified according to the basic models of communication they have adopted. Or rather, according to the different metaphors that linguists use in order to try to illustrate or make explicit the phenomenon of communication.

1.1 The Linear, Conduit Model

The simplest model of communication has been called the conduit model (Reddy 1979) because of its underlying assumption that language functions as a sort of channel, or tool for transferring a linguistic message from a source (or sender) to a destination (or hearer). This idea of communication has some of its roots in information theory. To separate what they call information from communication, certain philosophers of language (e.g., Grice) have advocated the idea that communication proper is characterized by intentional communication, or what Grice calls 'non-natural meaning.' The idea is that the addresser ('sender') intends that the message (or utterance) will cause what is called an effect in the addressee ('receiver'). The only necessary condition is that the addressee recognize this intention. In spite of the differences between these approaches, they are basically teleological models of communication, and this makes them closely related to perhaps the oldest theory of communication, namely that of classical rhetoric. Rhetoric can be defined as a theory of communication that seeks to find the quality which makes it possible for an addresser to persuade or convince his addressee about something.

The most problematic aspects in these models are the notion of effect, or perlocution on the addressee's side, and the notion of intention on the addresser's side. How are we to build a theory of communication on such vague terms, and how are we to find out what is/was the intention in a message and how are we to distinguish between the different effects? Other problematic aspects are the basically individualistic and monological views of communication that advocates of such models implicitly accept. Such views are seriously challenged in the three following communication models.

1.2 The Circular, Dialogic Model

The basic idea in what is here called the circular or dialogic model, is that for communication to take place, it is not sufficient that an addresser manifests his intention in a message which results in an effect in the addressee. It is also necessary to give the addressee a more active role in communication.

First, this active part is the more or less conscious interpretation process that the addressee must be involved in for the intended message to get through.

Second, a more or less expressed manifestation of the intended effect in the form of a response, answer, action, etc. from the addressee is necessary for the addresser to understand that his message has been received—in fact, *is* a message. Without a response of some sort, the addresser would be left in a situation where he is at best talking to himself, at worst is indulging in a monologue more typical of madness. Thus, the interpretation requirement is not restricted to the addressee alone. The addresser, too, has to identify some sort of signal in the addressee's message which can be interpreted as a response or reaction to the intended message.

In this way, communication can be seen as a system of questions and answers, or as a sort of cooperation where the communicators are actively organized in the construction of the message. It is not necessary that the addresser's intended meaning is identically reproduced by the addressee. If such an interpretation is at all possible, it is certainly limited to extremely restricted contexts, e.g., when certain logicians communicate solely with the help of logical formulas. The prototypical communication between humans is in fact characterized by the opposite: a partial, or limited understanding, or even misunderstanding, on the part of the addressee, which has to be clarified by further messages. Communication is not only the transfer of intentions with language as its tool. It is a constructive process going on in time. The message is constructed through the mutual activity of the actors. In this way, communication is a creative dynamic process. In fact, if communication did not have these qualities, a great deal of quite normal linguistic activity, like small talk during a lunch break, would be meaningless.

What is retained in this model from the conduit communication model, is the notion of intention. For dialogue to take place, it is necessary that the communicators intend to take part in the conversation, that they accept some sort of honesty principle, etc. Such principles are described in theories of conversational implicatures or of pragmatic universals.

1.3 The Feedback, Interaction Model

The third model of communication distinguishes itself from the dialogical model by doing away with the notion of intention altogether. In this model, communication is viewed in a much more general way than in the two previous ones. Communication would include all those processes by which human beings influence one another. In its most extreme form, this model entails that all behavior can be said to be communicative. The interaction of human beings is characterized by the necessity to communicate; this necessity is superior to the notion of intention, which is based not only on the will to communicate, but also the will to interpret. Communication is thus part of perception; attention to and interpretation of communication are part of the process of perceiving.

What remains in this model are the principles of mutuality and reciprocity as basic requirements for communication to take place. However, those principles are not governed by normatively colored principles, such as Grice's conversational implicatures and Habermas's universal pragmatic consensus principles. In those frameworks, communication is a certain mutual tuning which necessarily must involve a certain moral commitment, that one believes what one says to be true, that one intends that which one says, and that the addressee necessarily takes for granted that the addresser follows these and similar principles. Communication, in the feedback model, is not characterized by a search for what could be called mutual knowledge, consensus, or intersubjective understanding. Rather, the opposite is the case, namely that to communicate is to experience such principles as ideal goals: one cannot share other people's experiences or mental worlds, or truly understand the intentions of other communicators. The reason is that these principles of general reciprocity and mutuality are subject to societal power relations. Such relations are neither intended to be recognized in the message, nor perhaps even intended to be a part of the meaning of the message at all. But as sociologists insist on telling the naive linguist, power relations are inherent in every communicated message. There is no society in existence without social hierarchies of some sort; a powerless utopia is at best a pastoral idyll, at worst a totalitarian goal.

The basic problem in the feedback model is how to distinguish communication from information. As long as neither the addresser's nor the addressee's intentions are preconditions to communication, how are we to discriminate between all the incoming information, both on the content and expression planes of a message—an amount of information which, according to certain theorists, is infinite? It seems that this problem can be solved only by defining communication as involving both information (in the sense of information theory), the conveyed message, and the understanding of the message. Advocates of this model focus on the temporal nature of communication; communication is viewed as an enduring process which imposes meaning upon disturbances and noise, through the selective processes of information, message conveyance and understanding. Such a selection process is, of course, determined by the internalized language of the communicators, and is governed by other semiotic systems as well.

1.4 The Self-regulatory (Autopoesis) Model

The autopoesis model appears to be a radicalized version of the feedback model, in the sense that the model seems to have done away with what have been called the principles of reciprocity and mutuality. The autopoesis model is therefore something as seemingly paradoxical as a solipsistic model of communication. In this model, the communicators (or as they are called, the 'emitters' and 'receivers') do not communicate in order to transfer and create a message (as in the conduit and dialogue models), or even to create some information, a conveyed message, and an understanding, but simply to integrate elements from the communicative situation (the environment) which can contribute to the communicators' so-called self-regulation and self-creation (hence the term 'autopoetic'). This self-regulation and self-creation is an individual, idiosyncratic version of an interaction input. A basic goal of this self-regulation or autopoesis is to create a difference with respect to all other (real or potential) communicators. In this sense, communication is necessary for the individual in order to be constituted as an individual. The communicators are seen as closed systems, insofar as nothing can be integrated which is not specified in the system's own structure. It is important to note that the system is not a static structure, but rather a process. Communication is self-reflection, characterized as an unceasing search for functional substitutes.

Interestingly enough, this model allows for another, more advanced view of linguistic messages, such as written texts, than is normal in the linguistic tradition. Instead of being viewed as inferior reproductions of the prototypical or even 'natural' linguistic communication, namely verbal conversation, written messages are viewed as more communicative and creative, in that they not only allow for a finer distinction between the individual communicator and his communicative environment, but also for more permanent self-referential and autopoetic activity on the part of the individual communicator. Oral dialogue is thus reduced to one type of communication among others.

2. The Relation Between Communication and 'Language'

So far, the fundamental problem of the relation between communication and language has not even been superficially touched upon. Language is what most linguists recognize as the one and only object of linguistics; however, its relation to communication is a matter of continuous controversy: in fact, it is not even clear that the phenomenon of communication is at all relevant for the study of languages, and of language as such (see Sect. 3, below).

Still, most linguists are willing to accept a division of the phenomenon of language. On the one hand, it is seen as a kind of stable, over-individual structure, or type-schema, which for the sake of simplicity may be called a 'signification system.' On the other hand, it can be viewed as a set of tokens somehow belonging to such a schema, these may be called 'utterances.' This opposition between a system of signification and its associated utterances has many names, e.g., langue–parole (Saussure), schema–usage (Hjelmslev), code–behavior (Halliday), competence–performance (Chomsky), to name just a few of the most influential. The status of communication varies depending on, first, which opposition one considers most relevant, and second, which element in the opposition one chooses as most fundamental for the study of language.

The latter alternative allows us to distinguish between what the Soviet philosopher of language V. N. Voloshinov called 'abstract objectivists' on the one hand, and on the other, a heterogeneous group (consisting of behaviorists, empiricists, nominalists, 'socio'–linguists, processualists, etc.) called 'skepticists.' These groups will be dealt with in the following.

2.1 The Abstract Objectivist View

The abstract objectivist view can, in the light of the history of modern linguistics, be considered the traditional way of seeing things. The prototypical abstract objectivist sees language as a relatively stable, finite, and invariant system of signification, that is either as a unifunctional, adult-type system which is the goal of socialization, or as a social institution (Saussure's 'langue'), or as a universal innate mental grammar (Chomsky's 'competence'), or even as a pure form (Hjelmslev's 'schema'). The relation between signification system and utterances is seen as an either–or opposition: either one studies language systematically (i.e., as a signification system), or one doesn't study it at all. In this view, language is then something which precedes communication.

It does this in two different ways: First, as a generic term for language utterances, and therefore as a synonym of performance, behavior, usage, and parole. Second, communication can be viewed as the context where language is used between communicators uttering tokens belonging to the signification schema, i.e., the language system.

In both these views, language is seen as a precondition to communication, either as a structuring grammar of utterance tokens, or as a common code of some sort, defining the difference between what has meaning and what is meaningless. The code is necessary for communicators transferring a message, as in the conduit model (see above, Sect. 1.1),

accomplishing a dialogue, as in the circular model (see Sect. 1.2), interacting with one another, as in the feedback model (see Sect. 1.3), or reaching a state of autopoesis, as in the self-regulatory model (see Sect. 1.4).

2.2 The Skepticist View

Common to the skepticist view is the radical critique of the abstract objectivist opposition between the system of signification and the utterances derived from the system.

The skepticists challenge this opposition in three different and not necessarily compatible ways. In all three, communication plays a more important role in research and reflection on language than in the abstract objectivist tradition.

2.2.1 Language as Communicative Behavior

The skepticists' first option is to get rid of the opposition altogether. Language as a signification system is viewed as a mentalistic abstraction from a heterogeneous mass of data. This mentalistic abstraction is considered a type–schema product created by the analyst. Language is, then, a generic term for communicative behavior. This view is typical of the nominalist and the radical descriptivist. A prominent group of philosophers of language embracing these ideas are the so-called 'analytic philosophers' in the Anglo–American tradition (e.g., the later Wittgenstein, Strawson, Grice, Quine, Goodman). Meaning of linguistic messages in communication can only be said to belong to a signification system as an arbitrary classification of intentional (or habitual) acts having some sort of common similarity, the so-called 'family concepts'. An abstract objectivist theory of meaning, such as the (Saussurean) structuralist theory of semantic components and fields is in principle impossible, since in any case, message meaning is determined by an infinite number of components in a steadily changing communication situation, where intention, contextual setting, contextual restriction and other situational components play a major role.

2.2.2 Communication as Determining Language

The second option turns the abstract objectivist view upside down. It claims that communication (as a set of messages, not utterances) precedes, and is a precondition of, the signification system, not the other way round. Communication is viewed as determining language. Language is a message structure (Rommetveit) embedded in time, which at the same time structures, constructs, and creates meaning as the result of an ongoing dialogic process. This view of language is closely related to the circular communication model (see above, Sect. 1.2), but it can also be seen as related to the non-intentional search for a common code which makes communication work in the interaction model (see Sect. 1.3), and to the notion of consensual domains as prerequisite for the process of communication in the autopoesis model (see Sect. 1.4).

Many linguists involved in a sociological description of language choose this option. Approaching language from the corpus of messages, and not from a hypothetical, abstract system, one is struck by the heterogeneity of the data. Not only is communication a multi-dimensional semiotic, where verbal and written language play a subordinate role (as in phenomena of the 'double bind' type), but communicators may use different signification systems simultaneously, or even systematically break such systems' unconscious normative rules. This heterogeneity in communicative activity could be interpreted as a process of signification whose variation is an index of the conflicts between different, incompatible signification schemes.

An example of how such a linguistic heterogeneity and flexibility in verbal communication can be legalized as the norm of a national written language is furnished by the two standards of written Norwegian. These standards represent two languages, in fact two competing conceptions of what constitutes 'Norwegian.' Since these conceptions are socio–culturally determined, the languages could be called written sociolects. In each language, a great number of morphemic and lexemic variants are admitted. For instance, the following are all possible determiners of the singular substantive *bok* 'book': *bok-en*, *bok-a*, *bok-i* 'the book.' On the lexical level, variation is allowed, where other written languages normally would have only one lexeme. For instance, two variants for the lexeme 'language' are possible: *sprog*, *språk*. Morphological variants such as these have different social, political, stylistic, regional, etc. meanings dependent on context and genre; these different meanings are familiar to every relatively language-competent Norwegian. For a descriptive, synchronic grammar of written Norwegian which pretends to be exhaustive, it is thus necessary to allow for situational rules, sociological parameters, and the like. It is not in principle possible to reduce the morphemes *-en*, *-a*, *-i* to a single abstract archimorpheme, or the lexemes *sprog*, *språk* to one and only one invariant ideal. In fact, the history of written Norwegian in the twentieth century is characterized by a willingness on the part of the language planners to accept a great many variants, because of these variants' different meanings in different contexts and situations. Interestingly enough, this sociologically determined multi-dimensionality seems to be one of the crucial factors that explains why Norwegians generally are much better at understanding their closely related neighbors, the Swedes and the Danes (who use written codes of the more uni-functional type), than the other way round.

2.2.3 *Communication and Language as Complementary Phenomena*

The third alternative to the abstract objectivist view of language and communication is to claim that the elements in the opposition are complementary to each other. Language is *both* a signification system *and* communication (understood as a set of messages); this relation cannot be understood as an either–or. Therefore, language phenomena are conceived of as a process (i.e., communication of messages) and a product (i.e., a signification system), both at the same time. Which aspect one focuses upon is determined by one's theoretical model and one's more or less explicit interests in the study of verbal messages.

As a signification system, language is viewed as an open system or semiosis. The system is not finite, but as a social reality, it is open for modifications of different kinds, such as restructuring and creativity during communication. The signification system thus has the form of a variation grammar, a system of multifunctional potentialities, allowing for orderly variation and flexible regularities. These regularities can be described not in the form of abstract 'rules,' 'principles,' and the like, but as social norms or even potential 'resources,' i.e., arbitrary conventions grounded in communication. More specifically, grammar is conceived of as a network of relations: a systemic network, not a system of rules.

From the communication angle, language can be viewed as some socially controllable elaboration and/or modification of an earlier established reality, i.e., an already internalized system. But communication-as-language can also be conceived of as the creation of such a system. One consequence of this language conception is seen in our understanding of the language acquisition process. In this process, the child is not interpreted as a passive agent, but as an active and meaning-seeking organism trying to adapt itself during either the dialogue, interaction, or self-regulation process, towards an environment and other communicators in the environment.

Furthermore, this conception neutralizes one of the classical oppositions in the abstract, objectivist conception of language, namely that between diachronic and synchronic. As a communication process, language seeks a stability that can never be achieved. Diachronicity is an inherent quality of language; the synchronic is merely a fixation of this diachronic quality, necessitated uniquely by the conscious rationalization of a supposed mutual intelligibility, by the need for an abstract, objectivist description of language, or by the language planner's urge for codification; for all of these, translating process to product is an essential demand.

3. Linguistics and Communication

The phenomena of communication have often been thought of as peripheral in linguistic research. This view is a result of the strong hold the abstract objectivist language conception has had on modern linguistic thought. Most workers in this tradition share (implicitly or explicitly) the idea that the essence of language is to represent some intellectual structure; thus, they reduce communication to a subordinate place amongst the possible functions of language.

Some linguistic schools have advocated a more communication-relevant approach to language; here, one could name the Prague School, and different versions of linguistic functionalism. This low status attributed to communication is similarly challenged by different pragmatic approaches to language, as well as by language-relevant research in related disciplines such as sociology, poetics, psychology, or anthropology. Only some of the more important and coherent attempts of such communication-relevant approaches to language will be mentioned here.

3.1 Soviet Semiotic Dialogism

In the pre-Stalin era of Soviet intellectual life, a group of scholars emerged with a more or less common view of language, cognition, and communication; the language philosopher V. N. Voloshinov, the psychologist L. S. Vygotsky, and the literary critic M. M. Bakhtin. All these scholars launched an attack on the basic ideas of abstract objectivism. For political reasons, it took a long time before their ideas reached the western world, but since the late 1960s, their approach to humanistic studies has come to play an increasingly important role in a great number of humanistic disciplines such as psychology, sociology, poetics, philosophy, semiotics, and linguistics.

The basic idea of these scholars is that language is essentially dialogic. This dialogicity is not to be mistaken for a possible external, instrumental use of language; it is dialogic in its most radical sense, i.e., that of the inner dialectic quality of the language sign. The addresser and the addressee are integrated as part of the nature of language. Language never exists as a uni-functional, closed system: rather, it is a process of communication. This process is furthermore characterized by the notions of multiaccentuality, heterogeneity, polyphony, intertextuality, and in particular 'voicing', all referring to the social nature of language. In communication, language never appears as single-voiced: the situation, the tradition, the power relations between the communicators, and so on, all place their mark in the message. Thus, language really is this multivoiced message or speech process.

The Soviet dialogists see the nature of language as fundamentally social. The study of the content plane of linguistic messages becomes part of the study of ideology, whereas the object of study of the expression plane are the so-called speech genres. Consequently, even cognition is interpreted as a communication process, or, as it is called: 'inner speech.' Cognition or 'thought' is only possible through language; language is this multiaccentuated interaction process.

It remains to be seen whether the ideas of the Soviet dialogists can stimulate the traditional study of languages and language in the same way as they have influenced psychology and text linguistics. But one linguistic theory has emerged which partly seems to have been inspired by this school: namely the theory of enunciation and polyphony, developed above all by the French linguist Oswald Ducrot. This theory not only focuses on the self-referential aspects of language, such as deictic elements and shifters, but also on the fact that each message may have more than one source, and therefore may represent several points of view. These qualities are grammaticalized in language, for instance in the system of modalities. One consequence of the theory is that the monolithic notion of the addresser's integrity is suspended.

3.2 The Prague School and Functionalism

The Prague School was a linguistic school which did not limit its study of language to isolated utterances in so-called 'normal' situations. Quite the contrary: its focus was on a number of different types of human communication where language was used as a tool, such as literature and film. The school's basic relevance for the study of communication lies in the Prague linguists' development of a process theory of syntax, based on the notions of *theme* and *rheme*. Theme and rheme refer to the different linguistic qualities in the message which, in the communication process, signal already given meaning as 'theme,' and introduce new meaning as 'rheme.'

An even more important contribution to a communicative approach to language study is the Prague School's development of different taxonomies of so-called communicative functions. These taxonomies play an important role in Trubetzkoy's phonological theory. Another linguist (who is often associated with the Prague school), André Martinet, also challenges the traditional view of the basic function of language as representation. To Martinet, language is an instrument for communication. Martinet's stance appears to stem (at least in part) from his view on language as serving the need for mutual understanding. This 'sociological' attitude may also be prompted by Martinet's interest in what he calls the 'vocal basis' of language and by his studies in diachronic phonology. This basic communicative function of language could, e.g., explain why certain phonemes do not merge, and why the distinctive values of a language system are retained, even though its substance is fundamentally changed.

Like the Soviet dialogists, but perhaps in a less radical fashion, the Praguians refuse to reduce the essence of language's functions to intellectual representation. To them, language is a polyfunctional potential: its different functions are grammaticalized at different strata in the language system. Moreover, each individual utterance of a language is seen as a potential which in the interpretation process is reduced and given a coherent structure. Interpretation thus happens according to a more or less conscious choice of what is called a 'dominant': among the possible functions of an utterance in a specific communicative situation, the one is picked that is felt to be the most important for the message. It was in this way that Roman Jakobson explained the poetic quality of language: not as something extrinsic, but as an inherent quality.

3.3 Rommetveit's Message Structure Theory

The Norwegian psycholinguist Ragnar Rommetveit developed his theory of message structure over the years 1968–90, often in opposition to dominant paradigms in American linguistic research, such as Generative Grammar and Montague Grammar. The theoretical basis for his theory is a combination of experimental psychology (e.g., experiments with word associations), G. H. Mead's symbolic interactionism, and the European hermeneutic tradition. In fact, Rommetveit has made a point of being a methodical pluralist.

Rommetveit's basic idea is that language is embedded in a social matrix or context. Language can never be studied in isolation from the interaction of context. The analysis of interaction and communication is then related to the actual needs, feelings, intentions, and understanding of the subjects involved and their life worlds. Therefore, meaning is necessarily bound to context. Rommetveit attacks all ideas about 'literal' meaning, minimal semantic universals, etc., as fantasies based on theories of language that are in reality theories of written, formal language. On the content plane, messages are considered to be so-called 'meaning potentials.' Rommetveit, without being a nihilist, advocates a theory of perspectival relativity, in keeping with the sociological perspective of his theory. The social nature of language is guaranteed by so-called 'drafts of contracts.'

Contracts are seen as a process of negotiating tacit agreement and a shared world of discourse; the process is characterized by the notion of *message structure*. In the process of structuring a message, the communicators try to build a temporarily shared social reality. The message structure consists of cyclic patterns of nesting new (or, as it is called, 'free') information into given (or 'bound') information.

To the theoretical-oriented linguist, Rommetveit's theory appears to be somewhat limited, as it seldom focuses on what the theory means in terms of the grammar. It is basically an interaction theory which focuses on the content plane of messages, not on the structure of the sign vehicles.

3.4 Halliday's Socio–semiotic Theory of Language

As a student of the English linguist J. R. Firth , M. A. K. Halliday was also influenced (albeit indirectly) by the anthropologist Malinowski. Consequently, he has referred to his theory as an 'ethnographic or descriptive grammar.' Language, or as it is called, the combination of a 'semantic,' a 'lexico–grammatical,' and a 'phonological system,' is studied as the product of a social process, a *social reality* is schematized (or 'encoded') as a semantic system. However, among the systems that construct culture (the *semiotic* systems, as they are called), language is just one, even though it has a privileged place: most other semiotic systems are obligatorily mediated through language and its system. The product of the social process is the 'code'; human behavior is essential for its explanation. In Halliday's words the 'system is determined by the process.'

Typical of Halliday, then, is the endeavor to explain the structure of language as a consequence of social dialogue, of which it is in some way an abstraction. As this dialogic process is determined by the exchange of commodities, language is both determined by the nature of the commodity (such as 'goods and services' versus 'information'), and by the rules defined for the commodity exchange (such as 'giving' and 'demanding'). However, this is not a monolithic process: language develops characteristic realizations at its different levels in accordance with what Halliday calls 'congruence patterns.'

Thus, Halliday's theory of language is structured as a system network, where the expression plane is conceived of as manifestations of meanings chosen from a semantic system (the encoded social reality). While the notion of 'choice' is central to Halliday, it should not be mistaken for a conscious act of choosing, but understood as a term referring to the processual nature of the socio–semiotic system of language.

4. Future Work

A great deal of what has been discussed above is often classified as belonging to the domain of 'pragmatics' in linguistics. But if pragmatics is conceived as a superficial attribution to, or even as a 'waste-basket' for the more systematic, and therefore more prestigious, studies of syntax and semantics, this is a misrepresentation. Among the fundamentally radical views that some of the most important communication-oriented linguists share, not least the four 'schools' explicitly mentioned here have inspired, or are still systematically searching for, such an alternative. For the linguist who is skeptical about most of the traditional conceptions in linguistics associated with what has been referred to here as 'abstract objectivism,' there exist several research alternatives.

Bibliography

Bakhtin M M 1981 *The Dialogic Imagination*. University of Texas Press, Austin, TX

Bourdieu P 1982 *Ce que parler veut dire*. Libraire Arthème

Fayard, Paris (1991 *Language and Symbolic Power*. Polity Press, Cambridge)

Ducrot O 1984 *Le dire et le dit*. Les Editions de Minuit, Paris

Habermas J 1984–87 *The Theory of Communicative Action*. Vol. 1. Beacon Press, Boston, MA. Vol. 2. Polity Press, Cambridge

Halliday M A K 1993 Language as cultural dynamic. *Cultural Dynamics* **VI**: 1–2

Halliday M A K 1994 *An Introduction to Functional Grammar*. Edward Arnold, London

Heen Wold A (ed.) 1992 *The Dialogical Alternative. Towards a Theory of Language and Mind*. Scandinavian University Press, Oslo

Köck W K 1980 Autopoesis and communication. In: Benseler F, Heilj P M, Köck W K (eds.) *Autopoesis, Communication and Society*. Campus, Frankfurt

Martinet A 1964 (trans. Palmer E) *Elements of General Linguistics*. Faber and Faber, London

Reddy M J 1979 The conduit metaphor—A case of frame conflict in our language about language. In: Ortony A (ed.) *Metaphor and Thought*. Cambridge University Press, Cambridge

Rommetveit R 1974 *On Message Structure*. Wiley, London

Steiner P (ed.) 1982 *The Prague School. Selected Writings, 1929–46*. University of Texas Press, Austin, TX

Todorov T 1984 (trans. Godzich W) *Mikhail Bakhtin: The Dialogical Principle*. University of Minnesota Press, Minneapolis, MN

Vachek J (ed.) 1964 *A Prague School Reader in Linguistics*. Indiana University Press, Bloomington, IN

van Dijk T (ed.) 1997 *Discourse Studies. A Multidisciplinary Introduction. Volume 1: Discourse as Structure and Process. Volume 2: Discourse as Social Interaction*. Sage Publications, London

Voloshinov V N 1986 *Marxism and the Philosophy of Language*. Harvard University Press, Cambridge, MA

Wertsch J V 1991 *Voices of the Mind*. Harvard University Press, Cambridge, MA

Compositionality of Meaning

T. M. V. Janssen

A simple formulation of the principle of compositionality one often encounters is:

> The meaning of a compound expression is a function of the meanings of its parts.

Thus formulated, the principle is immediately appealing and widely accepted. It may well be that much of its attraction derives from the fact that this formulation contains certain terms which call for a specific interpretation, such as *meanings*, *parts*, and *function*.

In theories of natural language that primarily deal with syntax this principle does not play an important role. Moreover, there is much research in the semantics of natural language that focuses on the semantic aspects, and where natural language is treated as a source of problems, but where the principle is not part of the descriptive aims (e.g., when designing a model for tense in natural language). The principle is, however, important in theories where meaning is investigated in its relation to syntax. It is, for instance, the fundamental principle of Montague Grammar (see Montague 1970). There the principle of compositionality of meaning is given a precise interpretation, which has led to interesting discussions with practitioners of other theories of grammar. In this article, the important features of this interpretation are discussed and some of the issues raised in the discussions are mentioned. For a more extensive discussion see Janssen 1997.

1. Theoretical Preliminaries

If one considers natural language, it becomes immediately clear that knowing the meanings of the parts is not sufficient for determining the meaning of the complete sentence. Parts may form several sentences with differences in meaning. An example is *Suzy married, thereafter Suzy got a baby* versus *Suzy got a baby, thereafter Suzy married*. One has to know how the parts fit together. The notion 'parts' is, therefore, always interpreted as including the information in which way they are parts. Since the syntactic rules give information on how the expressions are formed, a connection with syntax seems obvious. Several authors make this explicit in their formulation of the principle. One formulation expressing this is:

> The meaning of a compound expression is a function of the meanings of its parts and of the syntactic rule by which they are combined.
>
> (Partee, et al. 1990: 318)

In this formulation some theoretical assumptions are implicit. The formulation assumes that a distinction is made between two aspects of sentences, i.e., the way in which the expressions are generated in the syntax, and their meanings. The principle is necessarily at odds with any theory not distinguishing these two. The formulation also assumes that the syntactic rules determine what the parts are, whereas the first formulation only assumes structures, no matter how they are given. The formulation regards the syntax as the input for meaning assignment, and the principle then describes how the meanings are projected from this input.

It is instructive to look at these assumptions in the light of a grammatical theory like generative semantics. This theory distinguishes two structural levels, one called 'semantic' and the other 'surface.' The grammar or syntax consists of formation rules for the semantic structures and a gradual transformational mapping procedure between semantic and surface structures. Here the syntactic form is projected from the meanings, and the semantic structures provide the compositional framework for a calculus producing meanings. Under certain assumptions this process is in accordance with the first formulation of the principle of compositionality of meaning, but not with the formulation given in this section.

2. Interpretation of Compositionality

The interpretation of the principle of compositionality provided in Montague Grammar (and in other forms of logical grammar as well) is an application of the essential methods of formal logic to the study of natural language semantics (for a more extensive discussion, see Gamut 1991; Janssen 1997). The main features are the following.

2.1 Rule-to-rule Correspondence

The syntax contains several rules and thus provides several ways to form a compound from parts. Each of these possibilities may have its own semantic effect. Therefore, for each syntactic rule there is a corresponding semantic function expressing the semantic effect of that rule, i.e., for each syntactic rule there is a corresponding semantic rule. This is known as the rule-to-rule correspondence. This correspondence asks for a uniform method to obtain the meaning of the resulting expression. It does not, however, imply that each syntactic rule should produce a change in meaning: the semantic rule corresponding with a syntactic rule can be the semantic identity function. Neither does it imply that every detail of a syntactic rule has a semantic counterpart. For instance, in English, the rule for yes–no question formation as well as certain other constructs involves Subject–Aux inversion. This inversion occurs in some rules of syntax, yet it does not seem to have any semantic effects. One might use a terminology in which such operations are called 'subroutines' of rules.

2.2 'Part' is a Theoretical Concept

The principle of compositionality speaks about the parts of an expression, which implies that it has to be determined somehow what these parts are. As it is

the syntax which provides the rules for the formal construction of expressions we shall let the syntax determine what the parts of an expression are. Different syntactic theories may assign different structures. Consider, for example, the English sentence *Mary does not cry*. A grammar might distinguish the main constituents *Mary* and *does not cry*, but it may also impose a tripartite structure consisting of *Mary*, *does not* and *cry*. A theory might also neglect constituents, focusing on logical aspects, and have a negation rule that takes the positive sentence *Mary cries* as its one-part input. This means that 'part' is a technical notion, that only coincides with intuitions for certain kinds of rules, to which one may wish to restrict the theory.

Parts of sentences may have parts themselves, and so on. Usually this analysis stops at the level of words or word stems. In logical grammar, lexical words such as *love* or *know* are left unanalyzed and considered to correspond with semantic primitives. Words like *all* and *only*, on the other hand, are analyzed further in the semantics with the help of logical tools.

2.3 Parts Have Meanings

The principle presupposes that parts have meanings. This excludes approaches in which only complete sentences can be semantically interpreted. More to the point, the principle requires that all expressions arising as structural parts have an independently given meaning. For some structural parts it is easy to imagine intuitively what their meaning specification should be. A verb phrase like *loves Mary*, for example, is immediately interpretable on an intuitive level. Not all parts, however, have a semantic interpretation that is readily supported by intuition. Constituents like *only Mary*, for example, in the sentence *John loves only Mary*, or *whether John comes* in *Mary knows whether John comes*, seem less readily interpretable on purely intuitive grounds. But compositionality requires that we choose a meaning. The criterion for such a choice is then whether the meaning is a suitable ingredient for building the meaning of the whole expression.

2.4 The Role of Derivational History

The meaning of an expression is determined by the way in which it is formed from parts. The derivational history of an expression is, therefore, the input to the process of determining its meaning. Since the compositionality principle, based on such part–whole relations, is taken to give a complete characterization of how the meaning of an expression is computed, there is no other input to the process of meaning assignment than the derivational history of the sentence in question. No outside factors are allowed to have an effect on the meaning of a sentence. This applies for instance to contextual factors: the Montagovian perspective does not allow for any kind of 'discourse' input to the compositional calculus determining the meaning of an expression. The most it allows for in this respect is an admission of ambiguity of the expression involved. If one wishes discourse factors to contribute to meaning, the notion of meaning must be enriched in order to incorporate such factors (see Sect. 3 below).

2.5 Ambiguities are Lexical or Derivational

Ambiguities may simply be lexical. If they are not, the principle of compositionality of meaning as applied in Montague Grammar allows for only one alternative source: a difference in the derivational history. This has certain consequences for the theory. Suppose, for example, that one takes the sentence, 'Every Belgian speaks two languages.' to be ambiguous between a reading in which there are two languages that are spoken by every Belgian, and one in which, merely, every Belgian is bilingual. The Montagovian compositionality principle now requires that the ambiguity resides either in the words or in the derivational history of this sentence. The former option being less likely, the syntax will have to be such as to reflect at least two different derivational histories of this sentence. Semantic decisions are thus seen to impose conditions on the syntax. In Montague Grammar, syntax and semantics, though distinct, are thus forced to remain in step with each other.

3. Representations of Meanings

Meanings are, in Montague Grammar and in almost all semantic theories, considered to be model-theoretic entities, such as truth values, sets of a certain kind, or functions of a certain type. Usually these abstract entities are represented by means of an expression in some logical language (e.g., $\forall x[man(x) \rightarrow mortal(x)]$). These representations are not themselves meanings, and should not be confused with them. Differences in representation do not always constitute a difference in meaning: $\psi \wedge \varphi$ and $\varphi \wedge \psi$ express the same meaning. And logically equivalent expressions are equally good as representations for some meaning. A semantic theory cannot be based on accidental properties of meaning representations, since then it would be a theory about representations and not the meanings themselves.

As has been shown above, there is for each syntactic rule a corresponding semantic rule that says how the meaning of the compound expression depends on the meanings of the parts. Since these meanings are represented by logical expressions, it seems natural to represent such functions by means of an operation on logical expressions. This operation has to represent an operation on meanings and therefore it should not make use of accidental properties of the meaning representation. For instance, the operation 'enclose the formula between brackets and write a negation sign in front of it' is acceptable since it corresponds with the semantic operation of negation. But the operation 'negate the second conjunct of the formula' is not

acceptable since it does not correspond with an operation on meanings. This is evident from the fact that it has different effects on the two equivalent meaning representations $\varphi \wedge \psi$ and $\psi \wedge \varphi$.

The above discussion, however, only makes sense if one takes meanings to be abstract entities. In some theories such as discourse representation theory (Kamp 1981, henceforth DRT) meaning representations are an essential ingredient of the semantic theory. This claim of DRT is linked with the postulation of the psychological relevance of their representations. In such a theory, operations on representations of meaning are, of course, acceptable. For such operations the issue of compositionality can be raised as well, but it becomes a different issue.

Thus two extremes have been met: no use of representations and total dependency on them. There are also theories that lie somewhere in between; for instance, some theories for anaphora essentially use the indices of variables (for a discussion see Landman and Moerdijk 1983).

4. The Status of Compositionality

The principle of compositionality implies no restrictions on the rules of syntax. We know that a rich variety of rules is needed. A rule is needed, for example, to introduce the verb *do* in the negative sentence *Mary does not cry*, and one to ensure the correct morphological form *does*, or *cries* in *Mary cries*. In general, rules may perform permutations, insertions and deletions, and have therefore the same power as Turing machines or Chomsky type-0 grammars. The principle implies no restrictions either on the nature of meanings or on the operations that can be performed on them. It can be proven that, in such a system, any sentence can be assigned any meaning in a compositional way (see Janssen 1986a; 1997). Compositionality, therefore, implies no restriction on the final results that can be obtained. Without additional empirical constraints compositionality has no empirical content. For this reason the principle of compositionality in Montague Grammar is not considered to be a claim about natural language, but merely a methodological or heuristic principle, i.e., a criterion for evaluating theories (not all theories that have been proposed are compositional).

As such it has proved its value. Proposals that do not satisfy the compositionality criterion often turn out to be inadequate precisely at the points where they infringe the principle. Janssen (1986b; 1997) discusses several proposals from the literature that do not obey compositionality, in the sense sketched in Sect. 3. It is shown that those proposals have unacceptable logical consequences, and that by reformulating the underlying ideas in a compositional way, they gain in generality and empirical adequacy.

Now a more elaborated illustration of the heuristic value of the principle will be considered. It has to do with discourse pronouns. Let us consider first the relevant phenomena on the basis of the following two discourses:

A man walks in the park. He whistles. (1)

Not all men do not walk in the park. He whistles. (2)

In (1), the pronoun *he* in the second sentence is interpreted as anaphorically linked to the term *a man* in the first sentence. This is not possible in (2), where *he* has to refer to a third party. The meanings of (1) and (2) are, therefore, different. And since the second sentences of (1) and (2) are identical, we must look to the first sentence to find the meaning difference:

A man walks in the park. (3)

Not all men do not walk in the park. (4)

These two sentences are logically equivalent. If meaning is taken to be identical to truth-conditions, as is customary, then (3) and (4) have the same meaning. But so do the second sentences of (1) and (2). Therefore, if the meaning of each discourse, (1) and (2), were a function of the meaning of the constituent sentences, (1) and (2) would have identical meanings, which is contrary to fact. This phenomenon thus seems to provide an argument against the assumption of compositionality in discourses.

In discourse representation theory, meaning representations constitute an essential level. There, (3) and (4) are assigned different representations. The two negation signs in the representation of (4) trigger different interpretation strategies for the discourse. This is one of the ways in which the difference between DRT and compositional grammars becomes evident.

Nevertheless, a compositional treatment for this kind of phenomenon is quite feasible and, in fact, the principle itself points to a solution. Since the two discourses (1) and (2) have different meanings, and their second sentences are identical, the difference must reside in their first sentences, i.e., (3) and (4). And since (3) and (4) have identical truth-conditions, a richer notion of meaning is required if the principle of compositionality is to be saved for discourses. Truth-conditions of sentences (which involve possible worlds and assignments to free variables) are just one aspect of meaning. Another aspect is that the preceding discourse has a bearing on the interpretation of a sentence (and especially of the so-called discourse pronouns). Moreover the sentence itself extends this discourse and thus has a bearing on sentences that follow it. Thus a notion of meaning is required which takes into account the semantic contribution that a sentence makes to a discourse. Sentences (3) and (4) make different contributions to the meaning of the discourse, especially concerning the interpretation of later discourse pronouns. These ideas have led to dynamic predicate logic and dynamic Montague Grammar, a compositional theory that accounts not only for the phenomena that are treated in DRT, but for other phenomena as well (see Groenendijk and Stokhof 1991). Thus it is seen that the attempt to stay compositional led in a certain direction. Since this approach has its intrinsic value, it is not surprising that, independently of any compositionality requirement, it is proposed by other authors as well, e.g., Seuren 1985. For more discussion, see van Eyck and Kamp 1997.

5. Formalization of the Principle

As the rules of grammar specify the structural parts of an expression, they can be regarded as operators taking input expressions and delivering output expressions. Mathematically speaking, this means that they are considered operators in an algebra of expressions, turning the grammar into an algebra. The notion 'part of an expression' is defined as 'being the input to a rule forming that expression.' As has been shown above, the meaning of an expression is determined by its derivational history. This means, mathematically speaking, that meaning assignment is a function that is defined on the elements of the term algebra over the grammar for the source language.

The principle of compositionality also describes the character of meaning assignment. Suppose an expression is obtained by application of operation f to arguments $a_1, \ldots, a_n$, hence with the derivational history $f(a_1, \ldots, a_n)$. Then the meaning in a model should be obtained from the meanings of its parts, hence by application of an operator g (corresponding with f) to the meanings of $T(f(a_1, \ldots, a_n))$. If T denotes the meaning function, then:

$$T(f(a_1, \ldots, a_n)) = g(T(a_1), \ldots, T(a_n))$$

The meaning assignment is thus seen to be a homomorphism.

These considerations produce the following formalization of the principle: *A compositional meaning assignment of language A is obtained by designing an algebra $\langle A, F \rangle$ as syntax for A, an algebra $\langle B, G \rangle$ as a semantic model, and by letting the meaning assignment be a homomorphism from the term algebra over A to $\langle B, G \rangle$.*

Since there is no restriction on the operators, any language that can be generated by some algorithm (i.e., any recursively enumerable language) can be described by a compositional grammar. Furthermore, it can be shown that every meaning assignment to sentences can be put in the form of a homomorphism. If some logic is used to represent meanings, $\langle A, F \rangle$ is in fact translated into expressions from a logical algebra $\langle C, H \rangle$. This algebra is then homomorphically interpreted in the semantic algebra $\langle B, G \rangle$. The requirement that meaning assignment be compositional is guaranteed if one translates into polynomials over $\langle C, H \rangle$. This model is introduced in Montague (1970). For an introduction see Halvorsen and Ladusaw (1979), and Janssen (1986a) for a detailed description of the mathematical model.

6. Objections Against Compositionality

Several objections have been raised against compositionality. Some authors, investigating phenomena that seem to call for a noncompositional solution, argue that natural language is not compositional at all. But often a non-compositional proposal can be replaced by a compositional one, which then not only turns out to solve the original problem but also has a wider area of application. Partee (1984) considers many phenomena where context seems to play a role, e.g., the different interpretations of the subjects in 'the horse is widespread' versus 'the horse is in the barn.' She refers in some cases to proposals in the literature where a satisfactory and compositional solution is given, but other phenomena remain a challenge.

Not all phenomena of natural language have (yet) found a compositional solution. And those solutions that have been or can be proposed are of course always open to further debate. In all cases, however, the right question to ask is not whether a compositional treatment is in principle possible (it always is), but what price has to be paid, or what the reward of a compositional solution is.

A different objection, of a more methodological nature, concerns the various kinds of meanings used in Montague Grammar. If meanings are built from meanings of structural parts, then meanings of parts tend to become highly abstract. One kind of meaning which has proved to be of great use is the type of term phrases, which led to the theory of generalized quantifiers. But other kinds seem to be motivated only by the wish to keep the system compositional. Montague Grammar has been criticized for its apparent willingness to accept any kind of abstract entity in the semantic domain. And indeed, if one expects of a semantic theory that it not only accounts for the semantic phenomena of language but, in addition, does so under certain philosophical constraints, such as maximal simplicity of the used elements, then there can be a problem.

Compositionality is not an empirically verifiable property of natural language. Compositional rules, powerful as they are, can seem quite counter intuitive. There are authors who reject compositionality for this reason, or replace it by a more restrictive version. One may propose to restrict it to grammars in which the derivations are closer to the surface form. However, if restricted too much, the principle may no longer be applicable to natural language, and its advantages will be lost. Several proposals for restrictions have been put forward. Partee (1979) proposed to use only a few basic syntactic operations. Generalized phrase structure grammar (Gazdar, et al. 1985) can be seen as a form of Montague Grammar in which only context-free rules are used, and categorial grammar can be

seen as an even more restricted form. Hausser (1984) aims at what he calls 'surface compositional grammars.'

An argument against compositionality sometimes raised by grammarians in the Chomsky tradition has to do with the position of syntax in a compositional grammar. They defend the principle of the autonomy of syntax, which is meant to specify the well-formedness conditions of sentences on syntactic grounds only. As has been shown in Sect. 2.5, a compositional grammar, being homomorphically connected with the semantics (so that every non-lexical ambiguity is syntax-based), allows for semantic considerations to have relevance for the selection and formulation of the rules of syntax. The very notion of autonomous syntax thus implies a rejection of such semantic considerations in syntax. But, as Gamut (1991: 148) says, 'It remains an open question whether this potential transgression of the autonomy of syntax by semantics will be encountered in reality, that is, in the actual description of some natural language.'

7. Why Compositionality?

An interpretation of the principle of compositionality of meaning has been discussed here, and somewhat implicitly, the argument has been in favor of it. A theoretical argument is that compositionality makes for an attractive framework in which semantic problems are dealt with as locally as possible, the various solutions being combined into larger wholes. Compositionality thus provides a strategy for dealing with the complexities of language. A practical argument is that experience has taught us that observance of compositionality usually leads to better solutions, which makes it a useful and attractive heuristic device.

See also: Montague Grammar.

Bibliography

Gamut L T F 1991 *Logic, Language and Meaning. Vol. II: Intensional Logic and Logical Grammar*. University of Chicago Press, Chicago

Gazdar G, Klein E, Pullum G, Sag I 1985 *Generalized Phrase Structure Grammar*. Basil Blackwell, Oxford

Groenendijk J, Stokhof M 1991 Dynamic predicate logic. *Linguistics and Philosophy* 14: 39–100

Halvorsen P K, Ladusaw W A 1979 Montague's 'Universal Grammar.' An introduction for the linguist. *Linguistics and Philosophy* 3: 185–223

Hausser R 1984 *Surface Compositional Grammar*. W. Fink, Munich

Janssen T M V 1986a *Foundations and Applications of Montague Grammar. Part 1: Foundations, Logic, Computer Science*. CWI Tract 19. Center for Mathematics and Computer Science, Amsterdam

Janssen T M V 1986b *Foundations and Applications of Montague Grammar. Part 2: Applications to Natural Language*. CWI Tract 28. Center for Mathematics and Computer Science, Amsterdam

Janssen T M V 1996 Compositionality. In: van Benthem J, ter Meulen A (eds.) *Handbook of Logic and Language*. Elsevier, Amsterdam/MIT Press Cambridge, MA

Kamp H 1981 A theory of truth and semantic representation. In: Groenendijk J, Janssen T, Stokhof M (eds.) *Formal Methods in the Study of Language*. Mathematical Centre, Amsterdam

Landman F, Moerdijk I 1983 Compositionality and the analysis of anaphora. *Linguistics and Philosophy* **6**: 89–114

Montague R 1970 Universal grammar. *Theoria* **36**: 373–98

Partee B H 1979 Montague grammar and the well-formedness constraint. In: Heny F, Schnelle H S (eds.) *Selections from the Third Groningen Round Table*. Syntax and Semantics **10**. Academic Press, New York

Partee B H 1984 Compositionality. In: Landman F, Veltman F (eds.) *Varieties of Formal Semantics*. Grass 3. Foris, Dordrecht

Partee B H, ter Meulen A, Wall R E 1990 *Mathematical Methods in Linguistics*. Kluwer, Dordrecht

Seuren P 1985 *Discourse Semantics*. Basil Blackwell, Oxford

van Eyck J, Kamp H 1996 Representing discourse in context. In: van Benthem J, ter Meulen A (eds.) *Handbook of Logic and Language*. Elsevier, Amsterdam/MIT Press, Cambridge, MA

Concepts

A. Millar

A rough idea of what concepts are can be gleaned from the statement that to possess the concept of an F (say, an uncle) is to know what it is for something to be an F (an uncle). Evidently there is a close relationship between knowing the meaning of a word and possessing the concept expressed by that word. If you know the meaning of *uncle* then you will possess the concept of an uncle. However, the converse does not hold. You may possess the concept of an uncle yet not know the meaning of the English word *uncle*. This article focuses on concepts rather than their expression in any particular language, but the issues raised clearly have a bearing on the theoretical representation of word meanings.

1. Concepts and Propositional Attitudes

What is a concept? Abstractly considered a concept is an ingredient of the content of a propositional attitude. If you believe that interest rates are too high the content of your belief is given by the proposition that interest rates are too high. The concept of interest rates and the concept of what it is for such rates to be too high are ingredients of that proposition. What is it to possess a concept? A plausible, if minimal, answer is that to possess a concept is to possess abilities which are exercised in the management of propositional attitudes whose contents contain the concept as an ingredient. Suppose that you believe that Bill is kind. Then you have an attitude to the proposition that Bill is kind, namely, the attitude of taking the proposition to be true. Now if you are capable of forming such an attitude you will also be capable of forming an indefinite number of similar attitudes to the effect that such-and-such a person is kind, for example, the beliefs that Mary is kind, that John is kind, that Zelda

is kind, etc. So it seems natural to think of the abilities in which possessing the concept of being kind consists as including the ability to form beliefs of this type. Similarly, if you want Bill to be kind then, arguably, you have an attitude to the proposition that Bill is kind, this time the attitude of wanting it to be true. Abilities associated with the concept of being kind would be exercised in the formation of such desires.

The concept of being kind is predicative insofar as it is expressible by means of a predicate. Not all concepts are of this predicative type. Suppose you believe that if interest rates stay high then the government will lose the election. One may think of the formation of that belief as involving the exercise of abilities which in English are associated with the conditional *If— then—*. These abilities could be exercised in relation to an indefinite number of other beliefs having the same conditional form. By analogy with descriptive concepts they may be taken to be at least partially constitutive of what it is to possess the logical concept expressible by *If—then—*. Among examples of other logical concepts are those expressible by *and*, *not*, and *either—or—*.

The approach just outlined might be thought to apply also to proper names like *John* and *Fido*. After all, if you believe that John is bald then you are exercising abilities which may also be exercised in the formation of other beliefs to the effect that John is such-and-such. Why not regard such abilities as constitutive of possession of a concept associated with the proper name *John*? If this terminology is adopted great care must be taken in spelling out precisely what such abilities amount to. There are well-known difficulties in equating the concept associated with a proper name with the concept expressed by some singular description which applies to the bearer of the name.

2. Conceptual Abilities

If the approach proposed above is along the right lines then a major task for a theory of concepts is to specify the structures of diverse conceptual abilities (see Peacocke 1992). Granted that conceptual abilities are implicated in the management of beliefs one needs to know what form these abilities take.

Clearly, conceptual abilities are exercised when beliefs are formed on the basis of other beliefs. For example, if you come to believe that interest rates will remain high and you already believe that if interest rates remain high then the government will lose the election then you may, on the basis of these beliefs, form the belief that the government will lose the election. It would be a mistake, however, to suppose that whenever you possess the concept of the conditional *If—then—* , and believe a particular proposition of the form *If p then q*, you will form the belief that *q* provided that you come to believe that *p*. People do not routinely believe even the obvious implications of what they already believe. Much depends on their current interests and on the extent to which the current beliefs are liable to become activated.

Often when one forms a belief that *p* on the basis of beliefs that *q, r, . . .* one does so unreflectively. Think of seeing bottles of milk outside a neighbor's apartment and coming to believe that the neighbor is still in bed. In these circumstances one would probably not spell out to oneself the relevant premises nor any inference from these premises yielding the relevant conclusion. One would simply come to have a belief in response to the interaction between a perception-based belief and various stored beliefs. But people do sometimes reason in a manner which involves explicitly taking account of inferential links between propositions. Such reasoning brings into play the ability to discriminate between valid and invalid inferences and that ability is arguably a further aspect of what is involved in possessing the relevant concepts. So, for example, possessing the concept of the *If—then—* conditional would bring with it the ability to recognize as valid inferences which instantiate the pattern modus ponens: *If p then q. p. Therefore q.*

3. Concepts and 'Family Resemblance'

Some predicative concepts have definitions spelling out characteristics, possession of which is necessary and sufficient for something to be an instance of the concept. This is true, for example, of kinship concepts like those of an uncle, father, mother, brother, etc. It is widely recognized that not all concepts have definitions in this sense and consequently that mastery of such concepts cannot be represented solely in terms of the ability to employ such definitions. Much of the discussion of this matter by psychologists and theoretical linguists, as well as philosophers, takes off from Wittgenstein's remarks about games (Wittgenstein 1958). Wittgenstein suggested that it is misguided to look for defining characteristics which are common to everything we regard as a game. Games are related by overlapping family resemblances. Each game shares some features with some other games though there may be no features which all games share. The idea of a family resemblance concept does not preclude the possibility of there being some features shared by all instances. But such features are not required and even when present are not definitive of the concept. Note that the application of family resemblance concepts has no clear boundaries since there is no determinate yes or no answer to the question whether putative new cases resemble agreed cases in appropriate ways.

Where a concept is a family resemblance concept the abilities constitutive of its possession cannot plausibly be explicated in terms of a grasp of deductive inferential links between propositions to the effect that the concept applies to some thing and propositions ascribing defining characteristics to that thing. This may also be true of natural kind concepts (whether or not they are family resemblance concepts). It is certainly relevant to the mastery of the concept of a lemon that typical ripe lemons are seen as being yellow. Yet we seem to allow for the possibility that a thing may be a ripe lemon though not yellow. If this is so then being yellow when ripe cannot be a defining characteristic of lemons. Putnam has argued (Putnam 1975: ch. 8) that it may be wrong even to think that *typical* ripe lemons are yellow. Whether or not this is so, some account is required of the role in our thinking of those characteristics which are associated with what are regarded as typical instances of certain concepts, even if they are not defining characteristics for the concept.

Further complications emerge when one takes into account the fact that many concepts can be applied on the basis of perception. One comes to have beliefs not only via other beliefs but also via current sensory experiences. On touching your cup of coffee you may come to believe that it is hot. It is arguable that mastery of the concept of being hot which most normal people employ essentially involves an ability to make such transitions from experiences to beliefs (Millar 1991).

4. The Normative Dimension of Concepts

According to the approach sketched above the notion of a concept is helpful in describing certain types of ability which are exercised in thinking and, consequently, also in the use of language. Concepts have an explanatory role in that they enter into explanations of, among other things, the formation, maintenance, and abandonment of beliefs. An important feature of concepts is that they also have a normative dimension (see Brandom 1994). Concepts may be mistakenly or correctly employed and any abstract representation of what concepts are must illuminate what is involved in their correct employment. As suggested above, part of the story must have to do with inference. It may be that logical concepts are entirely individuated by means of patterns of legitimate (in this case deductively valid) inference. It seems plausible that many predicative concepts will be implicated in inferential links of some kind or other. Some such concepts will in addition embody standards for legitimate transitions from perception to belief.

5. Topics of Concern in the 1990s

Concepts form a focal point for overlapping theoretical concerns of linguists, psychologists, and philosophers. A very basic topic for further enquiry concerns the abstract representation of concepts and the characterization of conceptual abilities in terms of these representations. Such enquiries will have to take account of empirical work by psychologists on predicative concepts indicating that many concepts are associated with typicality effects. (Rosch and Mervis 1975; Rosch 1978 are classic papers. For useful surveys, see Roth and Frisby 1986; Smith 1988.) In the case of a concept like that of furniture, for example, subjects will regularly count chairs as more typical instances than radios. It seems also that instances of a given sort are regarded as typical in proportion to the extent to which they have family resemblances to instances of other sorts. Further, some concepts relate to categories which are basic in that there is a high level of family resemblance between the diverse sorts of instances which they include. How precisely these findings bear on the theoretical representation of concepts remains to be seen.

A cardinal tenet of traditional empiricism is that all concepts are acquired. Fodor (1975) has argued that the very idea of acquiring a concept is paradoxical (see also Woodfield 1987). Certainly, one learns to associate concepts with linguistic expressions but, Fodor thinks, the most plausible account of how one does so assumes that one already possesses the concepts in question. This is one of the considerations which leads Fodor to posit a language of thought. The hypothesis of a language of thought is itself a matter of lively debate stimulated by the development of connectionist models of the mind (see Cussins 1990).

The development of conceptual abilities in children is an area of fruitful interaction between psychologists and philosophers (see, for example, Carey 1985 and Keil 1989).

For further reviews of current issues, see numbers 1 and 2 of the journal *Mind and Language*, 4 (1989). These contain articles on concepts by psychologists, theoretical linguists, and philosophers.

See also: Analyticity; Family Resemblance.

Bibliography

Brandom R B 1994 *Making It Explicit*. Harvard University Press, Cambridge, MA
Carey S 1985 *Conceptual Change in Childhood*. MIT Press, Cambridge, MA
Cussins A 1990 The connectionist construction of concepts. In: Boden M A *The Philosophy of Artificial Intelligence*. Oxford University Press, Oxford
Fodor J A 1975 *The Language of Thought*. Crowell, New York
Keil F C 1989 *Concepts, Kinds, and Cognitive Development*. MIT Press, Cambridge, MA
Lakoff G 1987 *Women, Fire and Dangerous Things*. University of Chicago Press, Chicago, IL
Millar A 1991 *Reasons and Experience*. Clarendon Press, Oxford
Peacocke C 1992 *A Study of Concepts*. MIT Press, Cambridge, MA
Putnam H 1975 *Mind, Language and Reality. Philosophical Papers*, vol. 2. Cambridge University Press, Cambridge
Rosch E 1978 Principles of categorization. In: Rosch E, Lloyd B B (eds.) *Cognition and Categorization*. Erblaum, Hillsdale, NJ
Rosch E, Mervis C B 1975 Family resemblances: Studies in the internal structure of categories. *Cognitive Psychology* 7: 573–605
Roth I, Frisby J 1986 *Perception and Representation: A Cognitive Approach*. Open University Press, Milton Keynes
Smith E E 1988 Concepts and thought. In: Sternberg R J, Smith E E (eds.) *The Psychology of Human Thought*. Cambridge University Press, Cambridge
Wittgenstein L 1958 (trans. Anscombe G E M) *Philosophical Investigations*, 2nd edn. Blackwell, Oxford
Woodfield A 1987 On the very idea of acquiring a concept. In: Russell J (ed.) *Philosophical Perspectives on Developmental Psychology*. Blackwell, Oxford

Convention

P. Pagin

While it might seem obvious to many that language is *in some way or other* conventional, or based on 'conventions,' the notion is remarkably difficult to make precise and remains a matter of considerable controversy concerning, for example, the nature of linguistic conventions, how they arise in the first place, and by what means they are enforced. The most systematic, and widely debated, attempt to explain the concept of a convention comes from the philosopher David Lewis and it is his account that will provide the principal focus for this article. But the grounds on which some philosophers reject a convention-based account of language altogether will also be investigated. (For a fuller discussion of the related notion of a 'rule' applied to language see *Rules*.)

1. David Lewis's Account of the Concept of a Convention

The idea that languages are conventional, that the meaning of a word is a matter of convention, is frequently entertained, though rarely with any accompanying conception of what a convention is. One cannot just adopt the familiar view of a convention as an explicit verbal agreement, since then the account becomes circular: conventions are needed for language and language is needed for conventions. It was not until David Lewis's work on the concept (Lewis 1969) that a fully developed alternative was available. Lewis built upon earlier work by T. C. Schelling on game theory (Schelling 1960) and by David Shwayder (1965) on the concept of a rule.

The basic ideas are as follows. Conventions are regularities in action. Conventions are social, they concern interaction between members of a community, or population. Conventions coordinate actions of different members in particular types of situation. Conventions tend to perpetuate themselves since the existence of a convention in a population gives the members reasons of self-interest to conform to it. Conventions are arbitrary; where there is a convention to act in a certain way there are also other ways of acting that would achieve coordination equally well. A regularity in action is conventional only if there is, in a sense, knowledge in the population that the regularity is conventional; more precisely, members must know that other members conform for the same reason as they do themselves.

One of Lewis's prime examples is the convention to drive on the right hand side of the road. This achieves coordination since there is a common interest of avoiding head-on collision. It is arbitrary, since keeping to the left would serve this interest equally well. Drivers prefer to keep to the right only insofar as they expect other drivers to keep to the right and they expect other drivers to prefer keeping to the right for the same reason.

The final definition, (in Lewis 1969), runs as follows:

> A regularity R in the behavior of members of a population P when they are agents in a recurrent situation S is a *convention* if and only if it is true that, and it is common knowledge in P that, in almost any instance of S among members of P:
> (a) almost everyone conforms to R

> (b) almost everyone expects almost everyone else to conform to R
> (c) almost everyone has approximately the same preferences regarding all possible combinations of actions
> (d) almost everyone prefers that any one more conform to R, on condition that almost everyone conforms to R
> (e) almost everyone would prefer that any one more conform to R', on condition that almost everyone conform to R'
> where R' is some possible regularity in the behavior of members of P in S, such that almost noone in almost any instance of S among members of P could conform both to R' and to R.

The notion of common knowledge, although defined differently by Lewis (1969), is roughly this: common knowledge in P that p means that almost everyone in P knows that p, and almost everyone in P knows that almost everyone in P knows that p, and almost everyone in P knows that almost everyone in P knows that almost everyone in P knows that p, and so on. The common knowledge condition in the definition is to ensure that members know that other members have the same reasons for conforming as they have themselves. Keeping to the right would not, according to Lewis, be a convention if everyone believed that everyone else kept to the right by sheer habit.

2. Criticism of Lewis's Account

Lewis's account has been widely appreciated and it undoubtedly captures important aspects of many social phenomena. It has also, however, been heavily criticized, mostly for being too strict in a number of ways, that is, for imposing conditions that are not necessary for something to be a convention.

One such objection is that a convention need not be a regularity in action. It is perfectly possible, by means of explicit agreement, to create a convention for one particular occasion, e.g., a particular sign. Moreover, there may be social conventions which are not generally conformed to, not even in the majority of cases.

There may well be conventions which create conformity even in the absence of any preference for conformity per se. Fashion in mode of dressing may simply influence people's tastes, but should be regarded as conventional nonetheless.

A language is conventional even if speakers of the language are not aware of the possibility of alternative languages. It is, moreover, conventional even if the speakers deny that the meanings of its words are arbitrary. So the common knowledge requirement is too strong.

These objections suggest that Lewis has over-rationalized conventions. On the other hand, however, Lewis has also been criticized for not succeeding in making conformity fully rational. The reason for failure in this respect is that common knowledge of conditional preferences (that is, preference for conformity given that most others conform) does not yield a sufficient reason for believing that others will in fact conform, and hence not a sufficient reason for conformity on one's own part.

3. Lewis on Language Conventions

On Lewis's conception, a possible language is an abstract entity, roughly an infinite set of sentences together with meanings and grammatical moods (this is more precisely specified in terms of functions, utterance occasions, and possible-worlds semantics). The notion of a convention enters the picture when it comes to explaining what makes a possible language the actual language of a population. The idea is that a possible language *L* is the actual language of a population *P* in case there is a convention, among members of *P*, of truthfulness in *L*. In conforming to such a convention, a member of *P* assertively utters a sentence of *L* only if that sentence is true (with respect to the utterance occasion), given the interpretation of that sentence as a sentence of *L*.

In a later paper, (Lewis 1975), with a slightly different definition of the concept of a convention, the convention of truthfulness in *L* is replaced by a convention of truthfulness and trust in *L*. In either case it is intended that Grice's analysis of communication intentions shall result as a special case of conformity to a convention.

To this proposal it is, inter alia, objected that either it presupposes that members of *P* can already think, independently of their capacity to speak *L*, or else the general convention reduces to a convention of truthfulness and trust simpliciter, which, if a convention at all, belongs to the moral rather than to the linguistic order.

4. Is Language Conventional?

Lewis has claimed that the view that there are conventions of language is a platitude, something only a philosopher would dream of denying. It has, indeed, been denied by philosophers, but the more interesting kind of dissent has the form of denying that any fundamental properties of languages, or linguistic practices, can be acceptably explained by appeal to conventions, or rules.

4.1 Quine on Conventions and Semantic Rules

As early as the mid-1930s, W. V. O. Quine attacked the view of the logical positivists that logical truth is conventional. The idea was that a logically true sentence, or rather a logically valid sentence schema, is true (valid) either directly in virtue of a convention, which holds of axioms, or indirectly, in virtue of consequences of conventions, which holds of theorems. The conventions in question govern the use of, and thus determine the meaning of, logical expressions such as *and* and *if–then*, or their symbolic counterparts. The first part of Quine's main objection (Quine 1976) was this: in order to arrive at the logical validity of the theorems, from the statements of the conventions, one must make inferences, and in those inferences one must already make use of logical properties of expressions occurring in those statements, particularly *if–then*. Since logical properties of expressions are determined by conventions it seems that a further convention is required, and so on. To this it may be replied that the problem arises only under the assumption that a convention must be formulated in advance of being adhered to, and that this assumption is false. Quine agrees that this reply is reasonable, but the second part of his objection is that appeal to unstated conventions runs the risk of reducing the notion of a convention to an empty label. This argument has been very influential. However, it has been objected against Quine that conventions governing the use of logical expressions should not have the form of *if–then* sentences but, for example, of deduction-rule schemata of other kinds. This reply is to some extent effective against the first part of Quine's argument, but not at all against the second.

The empty-label theme was further pursued. Quine (1980) has inveighed against Carnap and others that notions such as synonymy, analytic truth, and necessary truth cannot be explained by appeal to semantic rules, simply for the reason that the notion of a semantic rule is as much in need of explanation as the other notions. Without such an explanation no more is known than that a semantic rule is something stated on a page under the heading 'semantic rules'.

It might be said that what characterizes definitions, logical and mathematical truths, and other statements thought of as expressions of rules, or of consequences of rules, is that they are immune to revision; no observation, come what may, can render them false. Quine has stressed, however, that when the need to revise a theory arises because of new observations, then any part of that theory can be dropped, including statements that were once adopted as definitions; no statement is ultimately immune to revision. Moreover, there is no difference in principle between, say, a revision of logic and a revision of quantum theory, no acceptable reason for saying that the one is a change of rules and the other a change of theory.

Quine has expressed appreciation of Lewis's analysis of the notion of a convention (in the foreword to Lewis 1969), but the problems of synonymy and related notions are not eliminated, since such notions are already made use of in Lewis's semantics of possible languages.

4.2 *Davidson on the Appeal to Meaning Conventions*

Davidson (1984) has provided a different argument. Even if the notion of a semantic rule, or meaning convention, is tolerably clear, it does not have any explanatory value. A shared meaning convention is not necessary—by adherence to which we all mean the same with our linguistic expressions—in order to communicate, simply for the reason that we do not have to mean the same. It suffices that I know what you mean and you know what I mean. Neither do I need any convention in order to know what you mean. We can indeed be said to have, within a community, the convention of interpreting each other as meaning the same, even though from time to time, the assumption of sameness of meaning, mostly concerning individual words, must be revised. Without that convention, linguistic communication would be cumbersome. Conventions could be essential only if I needed to know, before your utterance, what you *would* mean by the sentence you uttered. But, according to Davidson, it suffices for communication that I can find out afterwards, drawing on all kinds of contextual clues. I could, in fact, start from scratch, without any assumptions about or any knowledge of the meaning of your words, and, in a process of what Davidson calls 'radical interpretation,' acquire that knowledge. There are principles governing radical interpretation, principles which rule out unacceptable interpretations, and although these principles are normative, in Davidson's view, they are not conventions but well-motivated methodological principles. Since the concept of meaning is to be explained, to the extent that it can be, by appeal to the principles of radical interpretation, the notion of convention is not needed in such an explanation. It is not necessary to make any assumption about a speaker's knowledge of linguistic rules or conventions, only find out what he means.

Michael Dummett (1986; 1991; 1994) has objected to Davidson's criticism of the conventionality of language. According to Dummett, the notion of a common language, a language shared by a speech community, is conceptually prior to that of an idiolect, i.e. the language, or ways of speaking, of the individual speaker. One of his arguments is based on the observation that speakers hold themselves responsible to socially accepted ways of speaking. On Dummett's view, the goal of successful communication requires adherence to the socially accepted ways, and because of this, that responsibility is essential to the speaker's linguistic practice. Davidson acknowledges that such adherence does further successful communication, but denies that responsibility adds anything of theoretical interest to the adherence itself.

Dummett also argues, in a Wittgensteinian manner, that meaningful speech requires the speaker to be a member of a speech community. This, too, is accepted by Davidson, but he denies that it requires the existence of a common language in the community. And indeed, the idea of the priority of the common language is hard to make good theoretical sense of, unless the conventionality, or normativity, of the common language is assumed at the outset.

In Davidson's mind the appeal to conventions is misguided for a further reason. One cannot attribute the observing of conventions to creatures to whom one cannot attribute beliefs and desires, and one cannot attribute beliefs and desires to creatures to whom one cannot attribute a language. Thus, having a language is a precondition of having a convention, but, as the earlier argument shows, not vice–versa.

See also: Analyticity; Meaning: Philosophical Theories; Radical Interpretation; Rules.

Bibliography

Burge T 1975 On knowledge and convention. *Philosophical Review* **84**: 249–55
Davidson D 1984 Communication and convention. In: *Inquiries into Truth and Interpretation.* Clarendon Press, Oxford
Davidson D 1986 A nice derangement of epitaphs. In: LePore (ed.) *Truth and Interpretation. Perspectives of the Philosophy of Donald Davidson.* Basil Blackwell, Oxford
Davidson D 1994 The social aspect of language. In: McGuinness, Oliveri (eds.) *The Philosophy of Michael Dummett.* Kluwer, Dordrecht
Dummett M 1986 A nice derangement of epitaphs: Some comments on Davidson and Hacking. In LePore (ed.) *Truth and Interpretation. Perspectives of the Philosophy of Donald Davidson.* Basil Blackwell, Oxford
Dummett M 1991 *The Logical Basis of Metaphysics.* Duckworth, London
Dummett M 1994 Reply to Davidson. In: Mcguinness, Oliveri (eds.) *The Philosophy of Michael Dummett.* Kluwer, Dordrecht
Gilbert M 1983 Agreements, conventions and language. *Synthese* **54**: 375–407
Lewis D K 1969 *Convention: A Philosophical Study.* Harvard University Press, Cambridge, MA
Lewis D K 1975 Languages and language. In: Gunderson K (ed.) *Language, Mind and Knowledge.* University of Minnesota Press, Minneapolis, MN
Quine W V O 1976 Truth by convention. In: *The Ways of Paradox and Other Essays,* 2nd edn. Harvard University Press, Cambridge, MA
Quine W V O 1980 Two dogmas of empiricism. In: *From a Logical Point of View,* 2nd edn. Harvard University Press, Cambridge, MA
Schelling T C 1960 *The Strategy of Conflict.* Harvard University Press, Cambridge, MA
Shwayder D 1965 *The Stratification of Behavior.* Humanities Press, New York
Ullman-Margalit E 1977 *The Emergence of Norms.* Clarendon Press, Oxford

Emotive Meaning

O. M. Meidner

'Emotive meaning' is the charge of feeling carried by a particular word in a given utterance or 'text.' It should be distinguished from feeling conveyed more directly by speech gestures and vocal behavior (which are aspects of speech rather than language). There are brief utterances having purely emotive meaning (e.g., exclamations of surprise, anger, pleasure) which nevertheless use words and thus are part of language. Far more commonly, words combine emotive meaning with cognitive or 'referential' meaning. Essentially the feeling expressed in a particular word is simple, being either a positive or a negative attitude of the speaker towards his subject matter or his addressee, and varying only in degree, as Hayakawa saw when he wrote of 'purr' words and 'snarl' words (Hayakawa 1964: 44–45).

Native speakers' intuitive expertise in 'expressing themselves' in dual-function words, and in responding to others' expressions, can readily be applied to making a conscious distinction between the emotive and the cognitive components of meaning in a given utterance. To do so it is necessary first to grasp what appears to be the overall import and then to focus on individual words. Usually some relevant alternative words must be brought into consideration, that might have been used instead. This can be illustrated by the joke: 'I am firm. You are obstinate! He is pig-headed!' (attributed to Bertrand Russell; see Hayakawa 1964: 95). Here the cognitive content common to all three judgments is clear, while the emotive meanings of the adjectives are so different (or the range of feeling so wide) as to produce ironic humor.

The term 'emotive' owes its currency to the writings of Ogden and Richards in the 1920s. They always used the phrase 'emotive language,' not 'emotive meaning,' and distinguished two contrasting uses of language, the emotive and the referential (or 'scientific'). They tended to ridicule emotive language, and so far as they hoped to oust it from certain kinds of texts, the growth of the social sciences since their time has largely produced that result. Nevertheless, no matter how strong the tendency of formal education to promote objective use of language, emotive meaning retains a place: e.g., in the language of public rituals as in churches and law courts; and also wherever personal opinions are acceptable, whether they directly express their feelings (as in personal relations), or record impressions and perceptions (as by a travel writer or a critic of the arts), or express judgments leading to joint action (as in 'political' activity in its widest sense).

Richards (1924) believed that poetry is justifiably emotive language but that literary criticism is not. In the context of this view and of related theories of meaning current before World War II, techniques of 'close reading' were developed. Students of the humanities were taught to scan each word or phrase in a given text (literary or not) to account fully for its contribution, including emotive meaning, to its present context by reference both to elements surrounding it in the given text and also to connotations acquired from its past applications. Such 'semantic' analysis is different from 'semantics' as a division of linguistics, which marshals the meaning components of given words apart from any actual text or utterance. Semantic analysis may produce results akin to deconstruction, though resting on a different view of language and of literature. Close reading is indispensable to both, and also to the assessment of emotive meaning.

Bibliography

Hayakawa S I 1964 *Language in Thought and Action*, 2nd edn. Allen & Unwin, London
Ogden C K, Richards I A 1923 *The Meaning of Meaning*. Kegan Paul, London
Richards I A 1924 *Principles of Literary Criticism*. Kegan Paul, London

Family Resemblance

C. Travis

'Family resemblance' is an expression used by Ludwig Wittgenstein in *Philosophical Investigations* (1958) during a discussion of meaning, particularly concerning the ways that words and concepts apply. While it is doubtful that Wittgenstein saw himself as presenting a general theory based on the notion of family resemblance or that he intended to introduce a new technical term into philosophy or linguistics, nevertheless his discussion—along with the expression 'family resemblance' itself—has generated a great deal of interest in the philosophy of language and elsewhere.

1. Family Resemblance, Definition, and Counter-examples

Wittgenstein's discussion of family resemblance (1958: Sects. 65–ca. 92) begins with captivating imagery, in response to the question of whether games have something in common in virtue of which they are games:

> Don't say: 'there *must* be something in common, or they would not be called "games"'—but *look and see* whether there is anything common to all.—For if you look at them you will not see something that is common to *all*, but similarities, relationships, and a whole series of them at that. To repeat: don't think, but look!... And the result of this examination is: we see a complicated network of similarities overlapping and criss-crossing: sometimes overall similarities, sometimes similarities of detail. (Sect. 66)

> I can characterize these similarities in no better way than by the expression 'family resemblance'; for the various resemblances between members of a family overlap and criss-cross in just that way: build, features, color of hair, gait, temperament, etc.... (Sect. 67)

Some take the imagery to exhaust the point, which they then see as tied to either or both of these theses: first, there is no feature (other than family resemblance) shared by all items to which concept X (e.g., the concept 'game') applies; second, a weakening of the first, no feature (other than family resemblance) shared by all items to which concept X applies is absent from all items to which X fails to apply. Either thesis might be taken to apply only to certain concepts, which would then be of a special type, viz. family resemblance concepts; or to apply to all concepts, in which case family resemblance is a feature essential to concepts, at least human ones. In either case, the theses are generally taken to rule out defining a concept, at least by stating 'necessary and sufficient' conditions—that is, definitions of the kind 'an item fits the concept "chair" just in case it is $F_1 \ldots F_n$.' For, according to this view, it is always possible to find a counterexample to any purported definition of this sort, at least where family resemblance holds.

It should be noted, however, that a sufficiently narrow notion of feature might rule out a definition of the above form while there were still statable necessary and sufficient conditions for the concept to apply, e.g., disjunctive ones. Wittgenstein considers and rejects this as a possible way round his point. This rules out any reading of the point on which it is specifiable which features make for relevant resemblance.

If this is the idea of family resemblance, it seems questionable. In fact, many have questioned it. Any

philosopher nowadays is reasonably skillful at the counterexample game. ('Suppose Martians had crystalline brains and wheels. Couldn't one of them, though conscious, actually function as a tram? And then couldn't a tram intentionally run over someone?') However, suppose one wanted to construct an adequate semantic theory of English. In dealing with the lexicon, should just any such counterexample be taken into account? If not, then it might be argued—and some have done—that Wittgenstein is in fact wrong about most of the lexicon. (Incidentally, Wittgenstein places no weight in the discussion on a distinction between, say, concepts and predicates. This is in line with his general eschewing of technical distinctions between types of items, such as sentences and propositions. Here it is worth keeping track of his use of 'Satz' and of its standard translations into English.) Moreover, there are those who hold that, while 'tin,' for example, might have turned out to be something other than it did, it could not have *been* anything else, which seems to make the concept 'tin' definable by necessary and sufficient conditions.

2. Rules and the Application of Concepts

Perhaps, though, family resemblance concerns a deeper point. Grant that family resemblance is, at least in part, a principle about all cases of what a concept would apply to. There is still the problem of what it is for a concept to apply to something, and of what sort of case would be a case of that; indeed there is still the problem of just which phenomenon Wittgenstein has in mind. Some features of the text may point to the answer.

2.1 Rules

One remarkable fact is that Wittgenstein's famous discussion of rules is entirely contained within the family resemblance discussion—insofar as it is purely concerned with problems of how a rule could, in fact, require such-and-such in a specific case. (The discussion occurs in Sects. 84–7.) One point of the discussion is: for any rule, and any occasion for applying it, there are mutually inconsistent courses of action (applications of it) such that, for each, one can conceive of it being in fact what that rule requires. The rule might be: place a marble in the left basket just in case it is blue, otherwise place it in the right basket. Now choose your marble. There is a way of conceiving (understanding) the rule in which following it means putting that marble in the left basket; and another way in which following it means placing that marble in the right basket. For each candidate way of following the rule in this particular case, there is a way of understanding the rule which is a possible understanding of that rule, on which that is what following the rule requires. For each such understanding, it is conceivable that that should be the right understanding of the rule.

However, Sects. 84–7 contain a very carefully structured discussion. Each paragraph with a remark tending in the above direction contains a counterbalancing remark to block any skeptical interpretation of the point. For example, in Sect. 84, 'Can't we imagine a rule determining the application of a rule, and a doubt which *it* removes—and so on?' is balanced by 'But that is not to say that we are in doubt because it is possible for us to *imagine* a doubt.' People are generally capable of perceiving what rules, or at least familiar ones, require at this or that point. That people are—and there is no reasonable doubt that that is what they are doing—is sufficient guarantee that there are facts as to what rules require; all the guarantee one should expect. Very roughly, those facts are what we perceive them to be, except where the rational course, for a specific, special reason, is to take us to be misperceiving. If facts about what rules require need to be constituted by anything, then it is by our natural reactions, plus the surroundings in which we have them—those in which the rule might require this or that.

2.2 Fitting Concepts to Objects

It is remarkable that all these points are made within and in aid of the family resemblance discussion. With that in mind, return to the problem. Pick a concept and an object. For the object to fit the concept is for it to satisfy the rule: count an object as fitting that concept just in case such-and-such, where that 'such-and-such' would obtain just where an object did fit the concept. But now, independent of the question of what such a rule might be—how the dummy 'such-and-such' might be filled in—one may question what it would be for it to be a fact that thus and so was in conformity, or not, with such a rule. This question now directs attention, in seeking the core point of family resemblance, away from the form that some definition might take to a more fundamental level concerning the application of concepts in conformity with rules.

2.3 Explanations of Meaning

Before attempting an answer, some more features of the text should be noted. Another point that Wittgenstein emphasizes here is that what we know about what words mean, or which concept any given one is, and (so?) what words do mean, and which properties concepts have, is actually stated, with no inexpressible residue, in those explanations of meaning that we can and do give (see Sects. 69, 71, 75). Wittgenstein concentrates on cases where we explain meanings in terms of examples. But the point is: such explanations are as good as explanations by general formulae (e.g., those providing necessary and sufficient conditions). Either style of explanation is equally, and just as fully and explicitly, an actual explanation of what the relevant words mean. Whatever shortcomings beset

explanation by example also beset explanation by formula, and vice versa. Either sort of explanation might be adequate; but there is no point in saying this if one has a proof that explanations of the latter sort could not be correct, as per the initial imagery-driven reading (in Sect. 1 above).

2.4 Family Resemblance and Proper Names

In Sect. 79, Wittgenstein makes a crucial application of the idea of family resemblance to the case of proper names, or individual concepts, primarily to the Biblical name 'Moses.' On one interpretation, suggested by Kripke (1980), and perhaps due to John Searle, the application consists in a 'loose-backing-of-descriptions' theory of names. On such a theory, a name, in a particular use, is to be understood in terms of a specific, though perhaps loosely bounded, set of descriptions, or general properties. Their function is this: the name, so used, refers to that unique individual, if there is exactly one, of whom most of those descriptions are true. Wittgenstein does consider such a theory in the first sentence of the second paragraph of Sect. 79, but immediately rejects it. It occurs as one of a series of trial balloons he punctures en route to his goal.

The remarkable features of Sect. 79 lie elsewhere. The simplest is that in the course of that section he applies the idea of family resemblance to concepts of all types ('The fluctuation of scientific definitions'), including cases where he obviously recognizes that one can give definitions in terms of general formulae. So the 'impossibility' of doing that cannot be the message of family resemblance.

Second, the initial imagery limps badly and obviously when applied to proper names. General concepts, simply conceived, as per the initial picture, have extensions which, as a rule, contain multitudes, at least in principle. Overlapping similarities between cases may then be overlapping similarities between items in the extension. Here, we at least know where we stand. However, 'Moses' applies to, if anything, only one thing. If there are overlapping similarities, it is not clear between which items they hold.

'Moses' refocuses attention away from objects that are to fit a concept or not, towards the surroundings in which they are to do so. There are different circumstances in which one may be confronted with a person who either is or is not Moses (the bearer of that name). In such different circumstances, different things will count as required for being that referent—so says Sect. 79. (This, incidentally, provides an alternative treatment of all the phenomena that led Kripke and others to apply a notion of 'direct reference' to names.) Note that this is not the 'loose-backing-of-descriptions' view. There is no fixed stock of descriptions, the majority of which must fit a referent. Requirements on a referent merely vary. It would be equally out of step with Sect. 79 to see a general concept such as *chair*, *game*, or *number*, as tied to a fixed stock of features, such that 'overlapping similarities' between items in the extension consisted in overlapping subsets of that stock which the various items possessed.

2.5 Rules, Concepts, and the Importance of Surroundings

With an eye on surroundings, we can return to the fundamental question. Though any rule admits of various understandings, we often see what rules require in specific cases. Another understanding would have been the right one if it were one that a reasonable person would have. But it is not. Sometimes, though, what we see is that one would say different things about what a rule requires, depending on the surroundings in which we are to say them. The variations in understanding that some being might have are sometimes variations in the understanding that we would have under varying circumstances. We pick up a marble, but it is a cat's eye: the part that is colored is blue (for the most part), but much of it is clear. Into which basket must it go according to the rule? Into the left one, if it is a blue marble. But is it? We have various ways of classifying things as blue or not, and accept different ways for different purposes. In some surroundings, placing the marble in the left basket would be correctly perceived as just what the rule requires. In others, it would not. Nor need that mean that we confront a different rule each time.

The phenomenon of an object fitting a concept takes shape from the family resemblance discussion: it is a view of the object counting as doing that in given surroundings where it is to count as doing so or not. Changing the surroundings may change whether it so counts. In different surroundings, what is required for *then* fitting the concept may differ. Looking at the various surroundings in which an object may be judged to fit a concept, and what would be required, in each, for doing so, one may perceive in these fluctuating requirements networks of 'overlapping and criss-crossing similarities.' That point is completely orthogonal to the question of whether words can be defined by general formulae—an orthogonality that Wittgenstein emphasizes.

3. Family Resemblance and the 'Essence of Language'

The family resemblance discussion begins and ends with a reference to 'the essence of language.' In Sect. 65, the point is that Wittgenstein will supply no essence; family resemblance explains why not. In Sects. 91–2, the points are at least twofold. First, though it may be useful to analyze words in one way or another for some purposes, there is no such thing as the way in which they really are to be analyzed, no unique logical form. For the lexicon, there is no purpose-independent fact as to whether a word is really to be defined via a formula or in some other way. An analysis draws a comparison between words and one picture of how to do or say things; one which may be useful, but which reveals no unsuspected essence of the words in question.

Second, one might think of an essence of words, or language, as something which determines just how and where they are correctly applied, of what spoken truly; some property of the words which is what really confers on them all the facts of this sort. In that sense, words have no essence. There is certainly none contained in what they mean. (The point of the rule-following discussion is to show that there could not be such an essence and to show how we may live, and think, quite well without any.) What facts there are of the correct use of words come from the constantly shifting surroundings of their use. The idea of family resemblance aims to get us to the point of seeing that.

See also: Concepts; Names and Descriptions; Private Language; Rules; Wittgenstein, Ludwig.

Bibliography

Cavell S 1979 *The Claim of Reason*. Oxford University Press, Oxford

Kripke S 1980 *Naming and Necessity*. Basil Blackwell, Oxford

Travis C 1989 *The Uses of Sense*. Oxford University Press, Oxford

Wittgenstein L 1958 *Philosophical Investigations*. Basil Blackwell, Oxford

Hermeneutics

E. Itkonen

'Hermeneutics' is a Continental, mainly German, philosophical tradition whose originators include Friedrich Schleiermacher (d. 1834) and Wilhelm Dilthey (d. 1911). The former based text interpretation on the interaction between 'grammatical understanding' (of what a sentence means) and 'psychological understanding' (of what the writer means by a sentence). The latter emphasized the difference between the natural sciences and the human sciences (*Geisteswissenschaften*). Karl-Otto Apel may be mentioned as a modern representative of hermeneutics. Relying in part on work by Peter Winch, he has shown close similarities between many traditional hermeneutic themes and Wittgenstein's later philosophy.

Hermeneutics is naturally opposed to 'methodological monism' (also called 'positivism'). According to this philosophical doctrine, there exists only one scientific method which applies equally well to all types of phenomena. Yet it is precisely within physics that this method has been most fully developed, with the consequence that all other sciences are supposed to imitate the example of physics in every respect.

As against this standpoint, hermeneutics adduces several nonmonistic arguments. First, while the causal relation between two physical events can only be externally observed, it may be claimed that in the 'causation of human actions' the causal tie between reasons and actions is experienced directly, and that understanding actions by others is based on this kind of experience. This is the famous distinction between observation and understanding (= *Verstehen*, also called 're-enactment' by R. G. Collingwood). This distinction goes back to the ancient distinction between 'observer's knowledge' and 'agent's knowledge' already employed by Plato and Aristotle.

Second, it is evident that the human world contains entities that are absent from the inanimate world, most notably 'norms.' And since norms, although directly known by intuition, are not reducible to the physical space and time, it follows that those sciences which analyze norms must remain qualitatively different from physics. This seems to be the case not just for grammatical theory (also called 'autonomous linguistics'), but also both for (formal) philosophy and for (philosophical) logic (see Itkonen 1978).

Third, the study of the social world may give rise to a (scientific) 'critique' of this very world. Again, this dimension is necessarily absent from (the study of) the inanimate world.

After stating (some of) the differences between the natural sciences and the human sciences, it is good to point out that there are similarities as well. In fact, the issue of 'similarity vs. difference' is relative to the level of abstraction: the higher the level of abstraction, the more similarities emerge between the sciences. At the highest level, all sciences (or 'academic disciplines') are similar insofar as they yield theoretical descriptions which are evaluated and ranked on the basis of (more or less) intersubjective criteria.

On a more purely philosophical level, hermeneutics continues the tradition of transcendental philosophy insofar as, rather than analyzing that which is known, it tries to explicate that which makes knowledge possible in the first place. It rejects, however, the Kantian approach, which assumes the existence of some timeless and intraindividual framework. Instead, the historical and social (= interindividual) preconditions of knowledge are emphasized. As a consequence, hermeneutics is much concerned with the issue of 'relativism vs. universalism.' This also shows the connection with Husserl's notion of *Lebenswelt*, and with Wittgenstein's notion of 'form of life.'

See also: Husserl, Edmund.

Bibliography

Apel K-O 1973 *Transformation der Philosophie*. Suhrkamp, Frankfurt
Collingwood R G 1946 *The Idea of History*. Clarendon Press, Oxford
Itkonen E 1978 *Grammatical Theory and Metascience*. Benjamins, Amsterdam
Winch P 1958 *The Idea of a Social Science*. Routledge and Kegan Paul, London

Holism

A. Weir

Holism, in the philosophy of language, is an approach which emphasizes the mutual interdependence of all the items of linguistic knowledge so that, for example, understanding the meaning of a given expression is said to require understanding the meaning of the sentences of a large sector of the rest of one's language (perhaps the entire language). Often such linguistic holism derives from a more general holism with regard to the mind and its cognitive states.

1. Arguments for Linguistic Holism

One argument in favor of linguistic holism proceeds from a nativist account of language learning in conjunction with a form of holism in the philosophy of science known as the Quine/Duhem thesis. The nativist account of learning one's first language sees such acquisition as a process of unconscious scientific theorizing about the interpretation of the public language of one's adult teachers, the theorizing carried out in an innate language of thought, a 'machine code' in the brain. The Quine/Duhem thesis holds that only fairly comprehensive bodies of theoretical beliefs— hypotheses plus auxiliary hypotheses, plus data about boundary conditions etc.—entail empirical consequences. Applying such holism to linguistics, one might conclude that only interpretations of large fragments of a person's language have testable consequences. Hence only such comprehensive theories can be justified; only such theories could be known to be true. The nativist then concludes that only when the language learner has unconsciously formed an interpretative theory of most or all of the public language, does he or she have knowledge of that language.

A second, rather negative argument, is the antinaturalist one: intentional, outward-directed psychological states are fundamentally different from natural phenomena. In particular, humans, unlike stars or atomic particles, are rational agents, and this means explanation in the human sciences must be of a wholly different character from that in the natural: to do with empathetic understanding and interpretation rather than with capturing the phenomena in mathematical equations. According to Donald Davidson, the role of rationality in understanding agents necessitates an holistic account of mind and language (see *Davidson, D.*).

A third argument in favor of holism is also a negative one: the alternatives to holism are unacceptable. Often the only alternative is thought to be an atomistic approach to mind and language, as found in behaviorists such as Skinner. Holists have convincingly argued that cognitive states issue forth in behavior only as mediated by further states and this point demolishes any attempt to identify pieces of linguistic knowledge one-by-one with disconnected behavioral dispositions and, more generally, any view on language which does not take account of the interconnectedness of language understanding.

2. Counterarguments against Holism

The first argument for holism will carry little weight with those who find implausible the idea of an innate language of thought, or of young children engaging, even 'tacitly,' in complex linguistic theorizing. More generally, it will be dismissed by those who deny that knowledge of meaning is an example of knowledge that some proposition is correct. Similarly the second argument will be unpersuasive to anyone of a naturalistic bent unless it can be shown that a natural scientific explanation of agents is blocked by their purported rationality. The third argument has been

interpreted as providing an impossibility proof of this type. However, antinaturalist holism is not the only alternative to atomism. Many views on language and mind can be described as 'molecularistic.' On this approach, the mind is an hierarchically organized system of behavioral dispositions, with an extremely rich structure—perhaps too rich to be fully comprehended by the mind itself. The more complex elements of the hierarchy are dependent on some or all of the simpler, down to a bedrock of minimally complex proto-cognitive states whose nature is much as the behaviorist supposed all mental states were.

One example of a molecularist approach in the philosophy of language is Michael Dummett's according to which sentences stand in a hierarchy of complexity with grasp of all but the simplest sentences requiring grasp of others lower down in the hierarchy. For the holist, though, molecularism does not do sufficient justice to the interconnectedness of the items of our linguistic knowledge. Consider semantic fields, such as the system of color concepts. It looks as if grasp of one requires grasp of all the others, so one gets a circle of interdependencies with no winding down to a common primitive base.

3. Conclusion

Success in accounting for semantic fields, then, is one crucial test area where an adjudication between the molecular and holist approach to language may be found. Another might lie in compatibility with generally accepted scientific approaches to mind. Molecularism, for instance, fits well with an information-processing approach to mind, whereas holism does not: e.g., if there is a circle of interdependencies in semantic fields then it looks as if the program which models our understanding of the elements of the field will loop, and so never issue in output to other parts of the system.

Failure to connect with a natural science approach is not, of course, a vice for militant antinaturalists. Even Davidson, however, feels the need to introduce rigorous theory into the interpretation of language via Tarski's method for defining truth for certain formal languages, a definition which incorporates an explanation of the truth conditions of complex sentences in terms of simpler. The Davidsonians seek to generalize this method to natural language and use it to generate, for each sentence of the language under study, a specification of a state of affairs which we then interpret as the content of utterances of the sentence by the language users. This forms part of an overall attempt to make rational sense of their behavior and the linguistic interpretation is successful insofar as the overall attempt is (if the latter is not, one has, in accordance with the Quine/Duhem thesis, a choice of where to pin the blame). The suspicion arises, however, that this rigorous Tarskian theory is an idle cog in the holist interpretive exercise. Any old method for assigning sentences of the interpreter's language to those of the subject language will do, it seems, as a means of generating linguistic interpretations to be tested as part of the overall psychology. One might ask more of the truth theory—that it be 'internalized' by the subject language speakers, for instance. This, however, is a problematic notion; Gareth Evans attempted to make sense of it in terms of correspondence between dependencies of understanding—what sentences would one lose understanding of if one forgot the meaning of *s* etc.—and derivability relations in different candidate truth theories. But the danger for the holist is that such an approach might presuppose molecularism. The fate of holism, then, is likely to hinge on how well it can be integrated with successful programs in cognitive psychology.

Bibliography

Davidson D 1980 Mental events. In: *Essays on Actions and Events*. Clarendon Press, Oxford
Davidson D 1984 *Inquiries into Truth and Interpretation*. Clarendon Press, Oxford
Dummett M A E 1976 What is a theory of meaning? (II) In: Evans G, McDowell J (eds.) *Truth and Meaning*. Clarendon Press, Oxford
Evans G 1985 Semantic theory and tacit knowledge. In: *Collected Papers*. Clarendon Press, Oxford
Fodor J, Lepore E 1992 *Holism: A Shopper's Guide*. Blackwell, Oxford

Indeterminacy of Translation

C. J. Hookway

The indeterminacy of translation was defended by W. V. O. Quine in his *Word and Object* (1960). Suppose one is translating another language into English. Quine holds that alternative translations could be constructed differing in their translations of individual sentences but all fitting the speech dispositions of native speakers of the language. There is no fact of the matter which is correct; indeed, all are. One may be more useful than another, perhaps allowing one to interpret the aliens as agreeing with one's own view of the world. But this does not mean that the preferred translation manual is true or correct.

1. Quine's Argument

According to Quine:

> Two translators might develop independent manuals of translation, both of them compatible with all speech behavior, and yet one manual would offer translations that the other translator would reject. My position was that either manual could be useful, but as to which was right and which wrong there was no fact of the matter.
> (1979: 167)

If correct, the thesis undermines the objectivity of talk of meaning and synonymy.

Quine's argument for his thesis focuses on the nature of 'radical' translation: the attempt to understand a wholly alien language unaided by knowledge of related tongues and without the help of bilinguals, etc. This makes the evidential basis for translation as clear as possible. Both in learning language and in translation, he urges, 'we depend strictly on overt behavior in observable situations' (Quine 1990: 38). Since he is concerned with 'cognitive' meaning, his view of which 'speech dispositions' are relevant is quite restricted: we attend to the circumstances in which speakers assent to different sentences.

'Observation sentences' are reliably correlated with distinctive sorts of sensory stimuli: these provide a bridgehead for translation; one seeks to translate them by sentences assented to in the same sensory conditions. But other occasion sentences, whose application depends upon supplementary information about the context, and all standing sentences cannot be correlated with sensory stimuli. Once a speaker accepts a standing sentence, his disposition to assent to it is not correlated to distinctive current sensory stimulation. The indeterminacy of translation then rests on the possibility that translation manuals may offer contrasting translations of standing sentences and some occasion sentences while agreeing in their predictions about the empirical circumstances in which observation sentences will be accepted. Quine defends a form of holism: one makes experiential predictions on the basis of one's beliefs only with the aid of a mass of background theory and assumptions, so there are no precise entailments between particular standing sentences and observation sentences. This introduces a 'looseness of fit' between 'theory' and observation which makes room for indeterminacy.

A form of indeterminacy is defended even for observation sentences: the indeterminacy of reference. Suppose that an alien sentence is uttered only in the

119

presence of rabbits or rabbit traces. Translations of this sentence as 'A rabbit is nearby,' 'Rabbithood is instantiated locally,' 'There is an undetached part of a rabbit nearby,' and so on, would all fit the evidence. Quine therefore suggests that alternative translation manuals may differ in their translation of words occurring in observation sentences while still fitting all the appropriate evidence.

2. The Importance of the Indeterminacy of Translation

Quine's thesis would show that there is no objective notion of synonymy: words and sentences are 'synonymous' only relative to a translation manual. This challenges the intelligibility of a number of concepts depending upon meaning or synonymy: the distinction between analytic sentences (those which are true by virtue of meaning) and synthetic sentences would be untenable; no sense would attach to analyzing the meaning of words or concepts; the notion of a proposition, something expressed by any of a class of synonymous sentences, would have to be abandoned. So the thesis threatens ideas which are central to traditional ideas of philosophical analysis.

Our ordinary conception of mind regards people as possessing 'propositional attitudes,' states like belief having a content given by a 'that-clause': for example, the belief that snow is white; the hope that it will not rain at the weekend, and so on. Any indeterminacy in the meanings of one's utterances will infect one's propositional attitudes. Thus a further consequence of Quine's thesis is lack of an objective basis for propositional attitude psychology: there is no fact of the matter concerning what one believes, other than relative to a manual of translation or interpretation.

Finally the indeterminacy of reference introduces indeterminacy into our ontological commitments: according to the translation manual one adopts, someone may be speaking of rabbits, of rabbithood, or of undetached rabbit parts: this is Quine's doctrine of ontological relativity.

3. Responses to Quine's Thesis

Although Quine has not displayed in detail how alternative translations could fit all his 'evidence,' few have doubted the possibility. Critics have generally noted how restricted is the evidence which Quine allows the translator and argued that one can also observe when aliens find utterances inappropriate, or when they find the denial of a claim absurd rather than merely eccentric. Moreover an adequate translation attributes to the aliens an intelligible set of beliefs and desires as well as standards of plausibility and methods of inquiry which one can understand. And there may be restrictions on the kinds of grammar which must be read into a language.

Such suggestions may merely lessen the degree of indeterminacy without refuting the doctrine. Quine may respond that while such criteria influence which translation one uses, they are irrelevant to the question of 'correctness.' But many philosophers would reject the naturalistic empiricism grounding his position.

See also: Holism; Occasion Sentences and Eternal Sentences; Ontological Commitment; Radical Interpretation.

Bibliography

Davidson D 1984 *Inquiries into Truth and Interpretation*. Clarendon Press, Oxford

Quine W V O 1960 *Word and Object*. Technology Press of the MIT, Cambridge, MA

Quine W V O 1979 Facts of the matter. In: Shahan R W, Swoyer C (eds.) *Essays on the Philosophy of W. V. Quine*. Harvester, Hassocks

Quine W V O 1990 *Pursuit of Truth*. Harvard University Press, Cambridge, MA

Rorty R 1972 Indeterminacy of translation and of truth. *Synthese* **23**: 443–62

Indian Theories of Meaning

F. Staal

Unlike some Western theories, Indian theories of meaning, though often logical or philosophical in character, are based upon a sound empirical foundation because their proponents were familiar with the techniques and results of the Indian grammatical tradition. It may be noted, furthermore, that Sanskrit terms for 'meaning' are, in general, used only of words, sentences, and other elements of language. There are no Sanskrit expressions corresponding to English 'the meaning of existence' or 'the meaning of life,' expressions that have caused much trouble in the West not only in popular speculation but also in philosophy.

1. Early Efforts

Theories of meaning arise only after centuries of effort at interpretation, and to this generalization India is no exception. The earliest Indian efforts are found in a class of prose works, the Brāhmaṇas, which from the beginning of the first millenium BC were attached to each of the Vedic schools and which interpreted not so much difficult phrases in the Vedic corpus as ill-understood points of ritual described there. A typical Brāhmaṇa passage explains why a particular rite is performed and why a particular Vedic phrase or *mantra* is recited at that time. When elucidating the mantras themselves, paraphrases are given and identities between entities are postulated, as in the following example in which the phrases from the Veda that are interpreted are given within single quotes, and in which reference is made to the deities Prajāpati, Savitṛ, and Agni:

> He offers with 'Harnessing the mind,'—Prajāpati, assuredly, is he that harnesses, he harnessed the mind for that holy work; and because he harnessed the mind for that holy work, therefore he is the harnessing one.
> 'Savitṛ stretching out the thoughts,'—for Savitṛ is the mind, and the thoughts are the vital airs;—'gazing reverently at Agni's light,' that is, having seen Agni's light;—'bore up from the earth'; for upwards from the earth he indeed bears this (offering).
> (*Śatapatha Brāhmaṇa* 6.3.1.12–13; transl. J. Eggeling.)

Like modern hermeneutics, to which it is by nature related, the Brāhmaṇas abound in interpretations that are empty, obvious, or arbitrary.

An effort at more systematic etymological interpretations of a portion of the vocabulary of the Ṛgveda was given in the *Nirukta,* Yāska's commentary on the *Nighaṇṭu* which consisted of lists of Vedic words, often arranged in groups that cover a semantic field. In the first section of the *Nighaṇṭu* there are, for example, 23 words for 'night.' There are also sections dealing with ambiguous words, that is, words that have two or more distinct meanings; in such cases, the *Nirukta* provides different etymologies, often fanciful, for each of these meanings. There are also general discussions on the parts of speech and their general meanings, for example: 'verbs express "becoming" and nouns, "being".' The *Nirukta* seems to belong to approximately the fifth century BC, the same period as the grammar of Pāṇini (most scholars have treated the *Nirukta* as preceding Pāṇini because of the undoubted priority of the Vedic to the grammatical tradition; according to Paul Thieme, however, Pāṇini is earlier than the *Nirukta*).

2. The Grammatical Tradition

The grammatical tradition started as an ancillary science to the Vedas, but it was different from the other ancillary sciences in that it neither restricted itself to a particular school nor provided separate grammars for each of the schools (like the *Prātiśākhyas* did for phonology). It pertained to all the schools. Linguistics attained full independence from the Vedas when Pāṇini shifted attention to the ordinary, daily speech of his contemporaries. Among the early grammarians, Patañjali (150 BC) is most explicit, when he states that ordinary speech is the empirical material or means of knowledge upon which the study of grammar is based:

> A man who wants to use a pot, goes to the house of a potter and says: 'Make a pot, I want to use it.' But a man who wants to use words does not go to the house of a grammarian and say 'make words, I want to use them.' When he wants to express a meaning he uses the appropriate words.
>
> (*Mahābhāṣya* 1.1.1)

Grammar includes the study of regional usage, e.g., 'Southerners are fond of *taddhita* suffixes,' and deals with special cases such as shouting from afar or the idiom of gamblers.

The grammar of Pāṇini (ca. 500 BC) seems, at first sight, to refer to the meanings of words only haphazardly. Accordingly, it has long been held that Pāṇini dealt almost exclusively with phonology and morphology and neglected not only syntax but also semantics. This view, however, cannot be maintained. Pāṇini's grammar deals with both the meaning of words and the meaning of sentences. The latter analysis is naturally based on his treatment of syntax, which is not only insightful but also extensive. The extent to which his syntactical theories capture the entire domain of Sanskrit syntax remains a subject of discussion.

2.1 Word Meaning

Pāṇini's grammar refers to the meaning of words in two distinct cases:

(a) In the grammar itself if meanings determine form, as in: *khaṭvā kṣepe* (2.1.26), '*khaṭvā* "bed" is compounded in the Accusative in a Tatpuruṣa compound when an insult is implied.' Example: *khaṭvārūḍha* 'lying on the bed' which means: 'rude, of bad behaviour.'

(b) In a list of about 2,000 verbal roots, the *Dhātupāṭha,* in which the verbs are classified in accordance with the 10 classes of verbs distinguished by Pāṇini in his grammar. Some scholars have doubted that the earliest *Dhātupāṭha* known was composed by Pāṇini but, whatever is the case, there is little doubt that a *Dhātupāṭha* with a similar structure and methodology, adapted to the structure of the grammar, was used by him. Following the eleventh-century grammarian Kayaṭa, others have argued that the meaning entries were added later, but there is no reason to accept this view (Bronkhorst 1981).

In the *Dhātupāṭha,* each verbal root is indicated by a metalinguistic marker and followed by its meaning, expressed by a noun in the locative case, that is, in the form 'root X in the meaning of Y.' The roots with their markers are treated like nouns: for example, a root with suffix *-i* is declined like a noun ending in *-i,* and *sandhi* rules apply to its combination with the following word. Some of the meanings are given in terms of nouns derived from the same verbal root so that the information is circular and uninformative. When there are several meanings, these are distinguished and different metalinguistic elements are used to distinguish the roots from each other. The following are examples from the fourth and seventh classes:

> iv, 68   *yuja samādhau* 'the root *yuj-* in the meaning of concentration'
> vii, 7   *yujir yoge* 'the root *yuj-* in the meaning of conjunction.'

Like Pāṇini's grammar itself, the *Dhātupāṭha* is part of the Indian scholarly tradition and its traditional curriculum that characterizes the Indian *paideia* of a classical education. Throughout the centuries, Sanskrit authors have referred to it whenever meanings are discussed. For example, the main commentary on the *Yogasūtra,* the *Yogasūtrabhāṣya* attributed to Veda Vyāsa of the seventh or eighth century AD, says in commenting on the first *sūtra:*

> Doubt as to the actual thing (*yoga*) is occasioned by doubt as to the meaning of the word. This doubt is removed by stating that in the language of the *sūtra, yoga* is etymologically derived from the root *yuja* in the sense of concentration and not from the root *yuji* in the sense of conjunction. [This comment shows, incidentally, that most contemporary interpretations of *yoga* in terms of 'union' are mistaken.]

2.2 Sentence Meaning

Sentence meanings are derived with the help of the *kāraka* theory. *Kāraka* relations, like 'deep structures,' occupy a level between semantic interpretations and surface structures. This level of linguistic analysis was intentionally added; it does not depend on historical accident and has little to do with 'mismatch' or 'tension,' terms used by Deshpande (1991) in an otherwise interesting hypothesis about its ritual backgrounds. There is need for such a level because there is no one-to-one correspondence between the levels, as illustrated by the following example (see Kiparsky and Staal 1969: 85). The sentence *akṣair dīvyati* (he plays (with) dice) has as part of its semantic interpretation the information that the dice stand to the action of playing in the instrument relation which is expressed by the instrument (*karaṇa*) *kāraka,* realized on the surface level by the suffix *-bhis* which becomes *-ais* yielding:

> **akṣais dīvyati*

which subsequently, because of a *sandhi* rule, turns into:

> *akṣair dīvyati* 'he plays with dice.'

But the semantic interpretation of this sentence also contains the information that dice stand to the action of playing in the *object* relation which is expressed by the object (*karman*) *kāraka,* realized on the surface level by the suffix *-ān* yielding:

> *akṣān dīvyati* 'he plays dice'

Pāṇini distinguishes seven *kāraka* relations characterized in semantic terms as follows:

> (a) *apadāna* 'the fixed point from which something recedes' (1.4.24);
> (b) *sampradāna* 'indirect object' (1.4.32);
> (c) *karaṇa* 'the most effective means' (1.4.42);
> (d) *adhikaraṇa* 'locus' (1.4.45);
> (e) *karman* 'what is primary desired by the subject' (1.4.49);
> (f) *kartṛ* 'what is independent' (1.4.54);
> (g) *hetu* 'what prompts the *kartṛ'* (1.4.55).

This system accounts for the meaning of sentences and complex meaning relationships between sentences by using mechanisms such as illustrated in the dice-playing example, that is, by systems of rules that operate between the different levels and that are carefully ordered and related to each other. The resulting derivations account for equivalencies like those between the Active and the Passive. Other illustrations are discussed in Kiparsky and Staal (1969) including the causative relations that make use of the *hetu kāraka,* which accounts for meaning relationships between sentences such as *The elephant-driver mounts the elephant* and *The elephant allows itself to be mounted by the elephant-driver,* or *The pupil learns grammar from the teacher* and *The teacher teaches grammar to the pupil.* Such meaning relationships, then, are treated by the grammar and not relegated to a dictionary.

The *kāraka* system also accounts for the the meanings of nominal compounds and various other nominal forms that are related to simple sentences, for example, *maker of pots, pot-maker = potter,* in addition to: *he makes pots, pots are made by him,* etc.

In the realm of theoretical semantics, Pāṇini made an important discovery (Brough 1951): the distinction between 'use' and 'mention.' In ordinary Sanskrit, a 'mentioned' or 'quoted' expression is indicated by the particle *iti* which follows it, that is, English *a* corresponds to Sanskrit *a-iti.* Since grammar deals in the majority of cases with the form of expressions and not with their meaning or use, the grammar would be riddled with such *iti's.* Grammarians have accordingly restricted ordinary usage, and expressions without *iti* refer to their *form.*

The underlying distinction between language and metalanguage is explicit in Pāṇini, the latter being referred to as *upadeśa* (literally, 'teaching'). Metalinguistic elements like the suffix -*i* attached to verbal roots are called *anubandha* ('marker'). They do not belong to the language that is the object of the description, i.e., Sanskrit. For example, the Sanskrit root referred to is *yuj*, not *yuji* or *yuja*. In the finally derived surface forms, the *anubandha* marker has to be removed. Patañjali explains how this is similar to ordinary usage—a crow that sits on the roof of a house, for example, may be utilized to identify the house: '"Which of these two is Devadatta's house?" "That where the crow sits." When the crow flies away and the house is no longer marked, one knows in consequence which house was indicated' (*Mahābhāsya,* ed. Kielhorn 84.21–85.3). Similarly, English grammar has to account formally for the fact that the past tense of 'drive' is 'drove,' not 'drive + *ed*' or 'drive + *past suffix -ed.*'

The *sūtras* or rules of grammatical description belong to the metalanguage of grammar. But there is a higher, meta-metalevel to which the metarules (*paribhāsā*) of grammatical description belong. The most famous of these is a rule that safeguards the consistency of at least part of the grammar by eliminating contradictions: *vipratisedhe param kāryam* 'in case of contradiction, the latter (rule) prevails (over the former)' (1.4.2).

In order for this rule to apply, the rules were listed in a specific order. The discovery of rule order is therefore closely related to that of metalanguage. The use made of metarule 1.4.2 proves, incidentally, that the Sanskrit grammarians recognized and utilized the principle of noncontradiction. This principle was formulated and adhered to at the same time or earlier in the ritual manuals, and subsequently in Indian logic and in most of the philosophical systems.

3. Philosophical Theories of Meaning

The following three sections include only a sample of Indian theories of meaning, excluding much that is of later date and all the Jaina and Buddhist contributions.

3.1 *Mīmāmsā Theories*

The Mīmāmsā (short for Pūrva- or Karma-Mīmāmsā) is a system of ritual philosophy that provides a particular interpretation of the Vedas. It is similar to the Brāhmanas in this respect, but it has incorporated the methodology of the ritual and grammatical *sūtras* and is therefore more principled and systematic. According to the Mīmāmsā, the core of the Veda consists of 'injunctions' (*vidhi*). The logical and semantical analysis of these is of special interest from a comparative point of view because it complements the prevailing paradigm of sentence interpretation in Western logic and philosophy, which have long looked upon sentences as if they were primarily statements. The excessive preoccupation of the Mīmāmsā with the optative

corresponds to the Western obsession with the indicative.

The stock example of *vidhi* is the injunction expressed by *yajeta* 'he shall sacrifice.' According to the grammatical analysis which the Mīmāmsā accepts, this expression consists of the verbal root, *yaji* (where -*i* is the indicatory element) and the optative ending -*eta*. According to the Mīmāmsā philosophers, the principal semantic feature of this composite expression is not the root but the ending, because it is through the ending that a word is brought in relation to other words. The ending in turn expresses two elements: 'general verbality' (*ākhyātatva*) and 'optativeness' (*liṅtva*). Of these two, the latter is again the marked feature, for every verb denotes an action but only the optative force is prompted by the Vedic injunctions. This optative force is 'the ultimate of ultimates, the peg on which the whole system of Vedic duty hangs' (Edgerton 1928: 176).

The grammarians had already characterized the sentence in terms of its final verb. The Prabhākara Guru school of Mīmāmsā extended the analysis of Vedic injunctions in a similar spirit to the more general semantic theory of *anvitābhidhāna*, according to which the meaning (*abhidhāna*) of a sentence is a single entity that depends on the *combined* meanings of its constituent elements (*anvita*). The other Mīmāmsā school, that of Kumārila Bhatta, was satisfied with the apparently simpler and more commonsensical theory, that the meaning of a sentence arises from *abhihitānvaya*, a stringing together or collection (*anvaya*) of the meanings of its constituent elements (*abhihita*). The former theory is closely related not only to the analysis of Vedic injunctions but also to a logical or syntactic analysis in which sentences (not necessarily statements) are the main units of discourse. The latter theory is more easily related to a dictionary-oriented semantics.

The theory that sentence meaning depends on word meaning is especially unsatisfactory when trying to account for logical connectives such as negation and other syncategoremata. This problem is not solved by introducing dictionary entries such as 'Neg,' for '*not-A* is not a function of *not* and *A,* but a recursively defined expression.' Thus, *He did not do it* is analyzed as 'it is not the case that he did it.' This goes back, in historical terms, to the Aristotelian insight that 'the negation of the sentence is the negation of the predicate,' which is reflected in turn by the logical symbolism F(a), formed so that the negation of *F(a)* is $\sim F(a)$, or, more explicitly (as in the *Principia Mathematica*):

$$(F(a)) \leftrightarrow ((\sim F)(a)).$$

That the meaning of not-A is not a function of the meanings of not and A was obvious to the followers of the *anvitābhidhāna* theory. But they went further and constructed a theory of negation which is richer than most Western theories because it includes injunctions. This theory may be expressed with the help of symbols that directly translate the basic Mīmāṃsā concepts. Let sentences be expressed as functions with two functors, A (*ākhyātatva*, 'verbality') and L (*liṅtva*, 'optativeness'), for example:

L(A(k)), 'the knot (k) should be (L) tied (A).'

Now, if one expresses negation again by ∼, there are two possible negations:

∼L(A(k)), 'the knot should not be tied'

and:

L∼(A(k)), 'the knot should be untied.'

The Mīmāṃsā took another step and introduced the negation of terms, which the above formalism in fact suggests, but which is not used in Western logic (where the equivalent is expressed in the theory of classes by means of complementation):

L(A(∼x)), 'the not-knot should be tied.'

This is interpreted as: 'another knot should be tied.' These types of negation were arrived at because of the existence of traditional injunctions such as *ananuyājeṣu yeyajāmahaṃ kuryāt* ('at the not-after-rites he should say "Ye-Yajāmahe"') which is not interpreted as: 'at the after-rites he should *not* say "Ye-Yajamahe"' but as: 'at rites *other than* the after-rites he should say "Ye-Yajāmahe".'

The correctness of the *anvitābhidhāna* theory was also argued from learning theory. A child who hears his father use the sentences *gāmānaya* and *aśvamānaya* first understands the meanings of the entire expression from the context or situation: in the first instance, he sees someone go and return with a cow; in the second, with a horse. The child concludes that the two sentences mean: 'bring a cow' and 'bring a horse,' respectively. Then, by analysis of identity and difference or a substitution procedure, he arrives at the word meanings and concludes that *gām* means 'cow,' *aśvam* 'horse,' and *ānaya* 'bring.' Only later will he discover that endings such as *-m* are suffixes which express the relation of the words to each other. This process of analysis, called *anvayavyatireka*, was mentioned, probably for the first time, by Kātyāyana in a *vārtikkā* (*Mahābhāṣya* 1.2.2) and was widely used by the grammarians.

The Mīmāṃsā made several other contributions to the theory of meaning. The Wittgensteinian slogan that the meaning of a word lies in its use was not only known much earlier in the West by Latin schoolmasters as *verba valent usu*, but also in India by the followers of the Mīmāṃsā and other theorists who accepted the principle that *rūdhi*, the conventional meaning, established by usage, is stronger than *yoga*, the meaning arrived at by etymological derivation. Thus for example, *dvirepha* (etymologically 'two (*dvi*)

r's (*repha*)') does not mean 'two r's' but 'bee.' (The reason is that another word for 'bee,' *bhramara*, has two r's.) The Mīmāṃsā analysis went further by distinguishing four classes of words:

(a) *rūḍha*, 'conventional,' e.g., *dvirepha*
(b) *yaugika*, 'derivative,' e.g., *pācaka* 'cook' from *pac-* 'to cook'
(c) *yogarūḍha*, 'both derivative and conventional'; e.g., *paṅkaja* 'anything that grows in mud' (*paṅka*), but also more specifically 'lotus' (which does grow in the mud)
(d) *yaugikarūḍha*, 'either derivative or conventional,' e.g., *aśvagandhā* which can mean either 'smelling like a horse' (*aśva*) or refer to a particular plant (which does not smell like a horse).

3.2 Bhartṛhari

Bhartṛhari, a fifth-century philosopher from Kashmir, northwest India, influenced by Vedāntic and Buddhist ideas, erected in his *Vākyapadīya* a metaphysical superstructure on the traditional semantics with which he was intimately familiar (he wrote a subcommentary on Patañjali's commentary on Pāṇini). In this metaphysics, the principle of the universe is a 'language principle' (*śabdatattva;* sometimes translated as 'speech essence'), unchanging and without beginning or end. It introduces time, that is, past, present, and future, into the world of names and forms (*nāmarūpa*).

The principle of the universe may be grasped by a timeless, unitary flash of experience which Bhartṛhari called *pratibhā* (intuition). But the meaning of a sentence is also grasped by *pratibhā;* in fact, it *is pratibhā*. This doctrine reacts to the theory of sentence perception of Nyāya logicians and others, according to which the process of understanding follows the hearing of the sentence that is being uttered in time, from beginning to end; when the last word is perceived, the meaning is finally grasped. Bhartṛhari's doctrine adds innate order and syntax to one's understanding and thereby changes the philosophic perspective: instead of a barren empiricism he offers an insight into the deep structure of language.

According to Mark Sideritis (1985: 137), this theory 'would have us believe that the notion of word meaning is the product of a misleading analysis of linguistic phenomena,' which is counterintuitive and conflicts with the work of lexicographers. This is almost true. According to both Bhartṛhari and the Mīmāṃsā *anvitābhidhāna* theory, word meaning is arrived at by abstraction and *anvayavyatireka*, that is, by comparing forms that are partly identical and partly different—for example *gāmānaya* (bring-the-cow) and *aśvamānaya* (bring-the-horse); see above—but it is not therefore 'misleading.' From a historical point of view, these sentence-centered theories reflect the development of the Indian tradition of language analysis which started with the cutting up of the continuous flow of sounds of the Vedic Saṃhitā into the word-for-word representation of the Padapāṭha.

Bhartṛhari's view that the relation between words and meanings is based upon *samaya* (convention), has caused confusion (as have Saussure's and Carnap's quite dissimilar contentions), but it has recently been shown that Bhartṛhari's term denotes 'established usage' where 'established' implies a tradition of elders (Houben 1992). The question as to whether the first establishment was arbitrary does not arise, since Sanskrit is held to be eternal.

Most publications on the *Vākyapadīya* confine themselves either to philology or to the metaphysics of its early parts. The semantico-philosophical speculations, especially of the third part, still await a thorough investigation from a linguistic point of view.

3.3 Later Doctrines

From the insights of the Mīmāṃsā and the gradually improving logical analysis of the Nyāya, semantic theories of great richness and depth developed and were adapted by most of the later philosophical schools. They were also put into practice by the literary critics of Indian poetics and aesthetics (*Alaṃkāraśāstra*). The latter tradition had been inspired by one of the classics of Sanskrit literature, Bharata's *Nāṭyaśāstra* (seventh century AD?), which dealt primarily with dramaturgy, dance, and music. This tradition was developed especially in Kashmir, the home not only of Bhartṛhari but also of Kashmir Śaivism and Tantrism. A good idea of the insights and subtleties of the resulting scholarship can be obtained by immersing oneself in the recent translation of Ānandavardhana's *Dhvanyāloka* ('Light on (the Doctrine of) Suggestion'), with its commentary *Locana* ('the Eye') by the critic, philosopher, and Śaiva mystic Abhinavagupta (Ingalls, et al. 1989). This article can do no more than list the elements of such treatises and the traditions they represent.

Indian theorists were familiar with many problems of word meaning, but the idea of sentence meaning occupied the central place in Indian semantics. The early grammarians had evolved the doctrine that a sentence is 'what possesses a finite verb,' a step beyond the naive idea that it was simply 'a collection of words.' The Mīmāṃsā developed the theory of *ākāṅkṣā* or 'mutual (syntactic) expectancy' as an additional criterion required for full sentencehood. They argued that a sentence is neither a collection of words such as *cow horse man elephant*, nor one that possesses a finite verb such as *cow irrigates man elephant*. *He irrigates with water*, however, is a sentence because there is a mutual syntactic connection, *ākāṅkṣā*, between all its constituent words.

Such an *ākāṅkṣā* also exists between the words of *he irrigates it with fire*, and yet this is not a sentence. One says that such a sentence is 'syntactically' but not 'semantically' well formed. According to the Indian theorists, another criterion must be fulfilled: a sentence must possess *yogyatā* (semantic compatibility). This is present in *he irrigates it with water* and absent from *he irrigates it with fire*, and also from such expressions as:

> There goes the barren woman's son with a chaplet of sky-flowers on his head. He has bathed himself in the waters of a mirage and is holding a bow of rabbit's horn.
>
> (Bhattacharya 1962: 141)

As a further condition, *āsatti* or *saṃnidhi* (contiguity) is required; it eliminates the case of words that are separated by other words or uttered at long intervals (we would regard this requirement as pertaining to performance, not competence). The final requirement is *tātparya* (speaker's intention), a controversial and much debated concept that reminds us of some of the work of Paul Grice. There are Buddhist parallels (for example *ābhiprāyika;* see Ruegg 1985, 1988). The underlying idea of *tātparya* is that the denotative power of words is fixed, but when constructing and uttering a sentence, the intended meaning that is conveyed may depend on the 'speaker's intention' (*vaktrabhiprāya*).

The intended meaning need not be individual; it can be part of the culture. This is reflected by a similar concept, *vyañjanā* (suggestion), that was developed by the literary critics of the Alaṃkāra school. When a poet refers to *gaṅgā* (the river Ganges), this carries the suggestion of coolness and purity. Not necessarily, however, for that suggestion is absent in the bare statement 'there are many fish in the Ganges' (quoted by Ingalls, et al. 1989: 579).

The metaphorical use of language was invoked in philosophical contexts, for example, by the followers of the Advaita Vedānta. In 'great statements' such as the Upaniṣadic *tat tvam asi,* traditionally (but erroneously: see Breloer 1986) interpreted as 'thou art that,' the reference to the Absolute is not through the primary meaning of the word, but through its secondary meaning (*lakṣaṇā*). Secondary meaning may exclude primary meaning (*jahallakṣaṇā*), include it (*ajahallakṣaṇā*), or both include and exclude it (*jahalajahallakṣaṇā*). An example has already been cited of the first: *dvirepha* ('with two r's') which denotes 'bee,' but bees do not possess r's. An example of the second is *kuntāḥ praviśanti*, literally, 'the lances enter,' which refers to the men who carry lances but also to the lances themselves. An example of the third is the *tvam* ('thou') of the Upaniṣadic statement *tat tvam asi:* this does not refer to the person in the dialogue, namely, Śvetaketu son of Uddālaka, but denotes his universal self, stripped of all individual attributes such as limited intelligence.

According to the later logicians, when a sentence, thus characterized as a string of words with *ākāṅkṣā*, *yogyatā*, and *āsatti*, is uttered, it generates in the hearer a cognition of its meaning (*śabdabodha*). This cognition is a single entity, but since it may be complex, it is analyzed in terms of recursively applied expressions of the form *X which is qualified by Y,'* that is 'X which is qualified by (Y which is qualified by Z...),' etc. This analysis in terms of nominal expressions conflicts with the grammarians' analysis that presents a sentence as a verbal form with nominal (and other) adjuncts. The meaning cognition of *Hari sees a bird,* for example, is analyzed by the logicians as: 'the operation generating the activity of seeing which has a bird as object is qualified by Hari as its doer.' Such an analysis is not merely 'artificial'; it is an expression of an artificial language which is well formed in accordance with the principles of its construction. Attempts at formalization have accordingly been made, by Matilal and others (see Matilal 1968; 1988; Staal 1988: 249–55).

Bibliography

Even confined to publications in English, the literature on Indian theories of meaning is extensive. The present article is based on various sources referred to, along with many others, in Staal (1988). The most useful general introduction remains Kunjunni Raja (1963).

Bhattacharya B 1962 *A Study in Language and Meaning: A Critical Examination of Some Aspects of Indian Semantics.* University of Calcutta, Calcutta

Brereton J P 1986 'Tat Tvam Asi' in Context. *Zeitschrift der deutschen morgenländischen Gesellschaft* **136**: 98–109

Bronkhorst J 1981 Meaning entries in Pāṇini's *Dhātupāṭha. Journal of Indian Philosophy* **9**: 335–57

Brough J 1951 Theories of general linguistics in the Sanskrit grammarians. *TPhS* 27–46

Cardona G 1975 Paraphrase and sentence analysis: Some Indian views. *Journal of Indian Philosophy* **3**: 259–81

Deshpande M M 1991 Prototypes in Pāṇinian syntax. *JAOS* **111**: 465–80

Houben J E M 1992 Bhartṛhari's *Samaya*/Helarāja's *Saṃketa. Journal of Indian Philosophy* **20**: 219–42

Ingalls D H H, Masson J M, Patwardhan M V (trans.) 1989 *The* Dhvanyāloka *of* Ānandavardhana *with the* Locana *of Abhinavagupta.* Harvard University Press, Cambridge, MA

Kiparsky P, Staal F 1969 Syntactic and semantic relations in Pāṇini. *Foundations of Language* **5**: 83–117

Kunjunni Raja K 1963 *Indian Theories of Meaning.* The Adyar Library and Research Centre, Adyar, Madras

Matilal B K 1968 *The Navyanyāya Doctrine of Negation. The Semantics and Ontology of Negative Statements in Navyanyāya Philosophy.* Harvard University Press, Cambridge, MA

Matilal B K 1988 Śabdabodha and the problem of knowledge-representation in Sanskrit. *Journal of Indian Philosophy* **16**: 107–22

Ruegg D S 1985 Purport, implicature and presupposition: Sanskrit *abhiprāya* and Tibetan *dgoṅs pa*/*dgoṅs gži* as hermeneutical concepts. *Journal of Indian Philosophy* **13**: 309–25

Ruegg D S 1988 An Indian source for the Tibetan hermeneutical term *dgoṅs gži* 'intentional ground.' *Journal of Indian Philosophy* **16**: 1–4

Sideritis M 1985 Word meaning, sentence meaning and *apoha. Journal of Indian Philosophy* **13**: 133–51

Staal F 1988 *Universals: Studies in Indian Logic and Linguistics.* University of Chicago Press, Chicago, IL

Tabler J A 1989 The theory of the sentence in *Pūrva Mīmāṃsā* and Western philosophy. *Journal of Indian Philosophy* **17**: 407–30

Tarkatirtha Pandit V 1992 The *Nyāya* on the meaning of some words. *Journal of Indian Philosophy* **20**: 41–88

Tola F, Dragonetti C 1990 Some remarks on Bhartṛhari's concept of *pratibhā* . *Journal of Indian Philosophy* **18**: 95–112

Language Game

M. W. Rowe

'If I had to say what is the main mistake made by philosophers of the present generation...,' remarked Wittgenstein, 'I would say that it is when language is looked at, what is looked at is a form of words and not the use made of the form of words' (1966: 2). The idea of a language game, which is central to Wittgenstein's later conception of philosophy, is expressly designed to combat this mistake. The core notion of a language game, which can be found throughout his later work, consists of examples of simple language use, together with enough background information about the speakers and context to render the purposes of the utterances intelligible. The context can either be natural or invented, and the overall aim is to shed philosophical light on the concepts and issues involved.

1. What a Language Game Is

Although the phrase 'language game' is used in the *Philosophical Grammar* (PG), the concept makes its first mature appearance in *The Blue Book* (Bl.B) dictated to pupils in 1933–34:

I shall in the future again and again draw your attention to what I shall call language games. These are ways of using signs simpler than those in which we use the signs of our highly complicated everyday language. Language games are the forms of language with which a child begins to make use of words. The study of language games is the study of primitive forms of language or primitive languages. If we want to study the problems of truth and falsehood, or of the agreement and disagreement of propositions with reality, of the nature of assertion, assumption, and question, we shall with great advantage look at primitive forms of language in which these forms of thinking appear without the confusing background of highly complicated processes of thought. When we look at such simple forms of language the mental mist which seems to enshroud our ordinary use of language disappears. We see activities, reactions, which are clear-cut and transparent. On the other hand we recognize in these simple processes forms of language not separated by a break from our more complicated ones. We see that we can build up the complicated forms from the primitive ones by gradually adding new forms.

(Bl.B: 17)

Oddly, the notion is not mentioned again in *The Blue Book*, and he does not illustrate it with a single explicitly signalled example. However, in *The Brown Book* (Br.B) of 1934–35 virtually every page provides a case. Here are two:

Imagine this language:- ...Its function is the communication between a builder A and his man B. B has to reach A building stones. There are cubes, bricks, slabs, beams, columns. The language consists of the words 'cube,' 'brick,' 'slab,' 'column.' A calls out one of these words, upon which B brings a stone of a certain shape. Let us imagine a society in which this is the only system of language.

(Br.B: 77)

The men of a tribe are subjected to a kind of medical examination before going into war. The examiner puts the men through a set of standardized tests. He lets them lift certain weights, swing their arms, skip, etc. The examiner then gives his verdict in the form 'So-and-so can throw a spear' or 'can throw a boomerang' or 'is fit to pursue the enemy,' etc. There are no special expressions in the language of this tribe for the activities performed in the tests; but these are referred to only as the tests for certain activities in warfare.

(Br.B: 102)

By the time the reader reaches Wittgenstein's late masterpiece, *Philosophical Investigations* (PI), published posthumously in 1953, the notion of a language game has broadened significantly. At § 23 he gives his most extensive list of examples: giving and obeying orders; describing the appearance of an object or giving its measurements; constructing an object from a description (a drawing); reporting an event; speculating about an event; forming and testing a hypothesis; presenting the results of an experiment in tables and diagrams; making up a story and reading it; play acting; singing catches; guessing riddles; making a joke, telling a joke; solving a problem in practical arithmetic; translating

from one language to another; asking, thanking, cursing, greeting, praying. This is a deliberately chaotic list, explicitly designed to elude capture by any single classificatory scheme. It is clear, however, that 'language game' no longer simply refers to the kind of simple, artificially constructed examples found in Br.B (although there are plenty of those in PI as well), or to 'the forms of language with which a child begins to make use of words' mentioned in Bl.B; 'language game' in PI can frequently mean any isolated aspect of the whole practical, social, and intellectual background against which language is used.

2. The Purposes of the Game Analogy

A central purpose is to break the hold of a very tempting philosophical theory. This says that people give their words meaning by privately matching them with objects—either physical objects or properties, Platonic objects or mental concepts—and that the way these words are actually employed in sentences and speech acts is something secondary, derivative, and inessential. The analogy is intended to show that the speaking of a language is something people *do*, part of a communal, social, activity. Words only have meaning through being used in sentences, and sentences only have a meaning through being used in speech-acts. Speech-acts themselves are only to be understood through understanding the needs, values, and social practices of the society that uses them—a complex which Wittgenstein calls a 'form of life' (PI: § 23). What might be called the contingently private uses of language—thinking to oneself, making entries in a diary—are parasitic on language's more public forms:

How should we counter someone who told us that with *him* understanding was an inner process?—How should we counter him if he said that with him knowing how to play chess was an inner process?—We should say that when we want to know if he can play chess we aren't interested in anything that goes on inside him.—And if he replies that this is in fact just what we are interested in, that is, we are interested in whether he can play chess— then we shall have to draw his attention to the criteria which would demonstrate his capacity, and on the other hand to the criteria for the 'inner states.'

(PI: 181)

A major advantage of a philosophy of language that gives *use* (PI: 43) priority over denotation or meaning is that it helps end the tyranny of declarative sentences and propositions. There is more temptation to think that declarative sentences have their meaning conferred by private acts of ostensive definition than orders, questions, and requests which seem intrinsically more other-directed. There are very few declarative sentences which would naturally prompt a specific, expected reaction, but the repertoire of natural responses to orders etc. is invariably both more limited and closer to the occasion of prompting.

Nondeclarative uses of sentences are therefore more important for children learning their first language and also anthropologists learning the languages of alien societies. It is no accident that the language-game that begins both PI and the Br.B is concerned with builders telling assistants what materials must be fetched. In addition, the game analogy helps end the obsession of philosophers with nouns and substantives (*man, sugar, today* (Br.B: 77)) and encourages attention to be focused for once on all the other parts of speech (*but, not, perhaps* (Br.B: 77)) which, for obvious reasons, the denotative or matching model tends to overlook.

Wittgenstein's earliest interest (June 1930) in the games analogy came from noting that the rules of a game offered a way of understanding how ink marks or sounds could acquire significance without linking them to occult entities:

> The truth in [mathematical] formalism is that every syntax can be regarded as a system of rules for a game.... I was asked in Cambridge whether I think that mathematics concerns ink marks on paper. I reply: in just the same sense in which chess concerns wooden figures. Chess, I mean, does not consist in my pushing wooden figures around a board. If I say 'Now I will make myself a queen with very frightening eyes; she will drive everyone off the board' you will laugh. It does not matter what a pawn looks like. What is much rather the case is that the totality of rules determines the logical place of a pawn. A pawn is a variable, like 'x' in logic....
>
> (quoted in Waismann 1967: 104)

For a time Wittgenstein continued to think of language as a rule-governed calculus, or series of calculi, but he soon grew disenchanted with the notion. The Italian economist Piero Sraffa is usually credited with breaking the hold this idea had on him. Wittgenstein was explaining that a proposition must have the same logical form as what it describes. Sraffa listened, made the Neapolitan gesture of brushing his chin with his fingertips, and then asked, 'What is the logical form of that?' In the following passage from PG (1933–34) he can not only be seen moving away from the more formal, logical area of language but simultaneously realizing the limitations of the chess analogy:

> I said that the meaning of a word is the role which it plays in the calculus of language. (I compared it to a piece in chess.)... But let us think also of the meaning of the word 'oh!' If we were asked about it, we would probably say, 'oh!' is a sigh; we say, for instance, 'Oh, it is raining again already' and similar things. In that way we would have described the use of the word. But now what corresponds to the calculus, to the complicated game which we play with other words? In the use of the words 'oh' or 'hurrah' or 'hm' there is nothing comparable.
>
> (PG: 67)

By the time he came to write PI he had grown profoundly skeptical about the explanatory power of rules. In one of the earlier sections he begins to doubt

that any game can be said to be wholly rule-governed: 'I said that the application of a word is not everywhere bounded by rules. But what does a game look like that is everywhere bounded by rules? whose rules never let a doubt creep in, but stop up all the cracks where it might?—Can't we imagine a rule determining the application of a rule, and a doubt which *it* removes—and so on?' (PI: §84). Eventually, in §§143–242, the whole notion of rule-following is placed under intense scrutiny. Basically, Wittgenstein's argument is that no occurrent mental event or disposition (including grasp of a formula) can explain why an individual follows a rule correctly. Correctness is determined by whether an individual follows a rule in the same way as all the other members of his society, and this depends on nothing more (but nothing less) than a shared sense of value, importance, similarity, and appropriateness. So-called logical necessity is a special case of psychological necessity. In PI it is less the rule-governedness of certain games than the sheer multiplicity of games as a whole that makes them such a compelling analogy for linguistic practices. At Sect. 65 of PI he considers an objection to his views:

> 'You take the easy way out! You talk about all sorts of language-games, but have nowhere said what the essence of a language-game, and hence of language, is: what is common to all these activities, and what makes them into language or parts of language.'

He replies:

> Consider for example the proceedings that we call 'games.' I mean board-games, card-games, ball-games, Olympic games, and so on. What is common to them all?—Don't say: 'There *must* be something common, or they would not be called "games" '—but *look and see* whether there is anything common to all.—For if you look at them you will not see something that is common to *all*, but similarities, relationships, and a whole series of them at that.
>
> (PI: §66)

'Language game' is not a technical term with a strict definition, but a phrase intended to prompt the reader into seeing an analogy. This is important because there are aspects of games which are clearly not present in linguistic practices, and which are not, for the most part, of interest to Wittgenstein. Games are, in a sense, insulated from real life, whereas Wittgenstein would be the first to insist that language is very much part of it; most games—like rugby and cricket—do not develop and do not interact with one another, yet Wittgenstein clearly thought that language games do overlap, develop, and interact; finally, 'game' suggests something frivolous, a pastime, whereas most language-use is perfectly serious (although Wittgenstein does say at one point that even the amusingness of children's language games may be relevant to the concept he develops (Br.B: 81)). To keep the analogy in perspective it must be considered alongside two others, namely, tools (PI: § 11) and money (PI: § 120). The analogy between language and tools captures the idea of seriousness, variety, and engagement with everyday practical life, but it loses the social and conventional element in language; the analogy with money captures the idea of serious engagement with practical life and conventionality, but loses the aspect of variety.

3. Language Games and Philosophical Method

An understanding of language games is vital for understanding Wittgenstein's later conception of philosophy and philosophical method. Language games are 'the primary thing' (PI: § 656): it is only in the context of such games that language has meaning, significance, and point. Philosophical problems arise because philosophers have a false picture of how certain complex words (e.g., *knowledge, being, object* (PI: § 116)) function. This invariably arises either because the use of a word in one language game is confused with its use in another (e.g., the use of measurement in the language game of temporal measurement is confused with its use in the language game of spatial measurement (Bl.B: 26–7)), or because a term is considered 'outside language-games,' in abstraction from the context in which it has its life or meaning (PI: § 47). In the latter case Wittgenstein says that language is 'idling ' (PI: § 132), and has gone 'on holiday' (PI: § 38). This leads to perplexity, muddle, and confusion, and, in extreme cases, to the erection of grandiose and often paradoxical metaphysical theories which seem profound, but which are really no more than the magnified products of linguistic error.

Traditional philosophy, on Wittgenstein's conception, is an 'illness' (PI: § 255) which can only be cured by the quiet weighing of linguistic facts. He regarded his central task as one of bringing 'words back from their metaphysical to their everyday use' (PI: § 116). His method consists in 'assembling reminders' (PI: § 127) as to how words are actually used. This involves describing and noting the language games in which they have a role. Although new language games can develop and old ones disappear, they are not the kinds of things which can ultimately be explained or justified. If asked to justify the use of a certain word in a certain context, the only reply may be: 'This language-game is played' (PI: § 654). Philosophy no longer puts forward theses, or attempts to explain: it clears up linguistic confusions (PI: § 128).

For example, there is the traditional problem of other minds: I can know that *I* think, have pains, feel emotions but I can never know if this is true of others; the most I can know in these cases is that they exhibit (for example) pain-behavior. It is quite possible, therefore, that I always have been and always will be surrounded by automata. Wittgenstein thinks this chilling, metaphysical vision arises through misunderstanding, having a false picture of the language game we play with 'know' and 'believe' when used in conjunction with psychological words:

> I can know what someone else is thinking, not what I am thinking.
> It is correct to say 'I know what you are thinking,' and wrong to say 'I know what I am thinking.'
> (A whole cloud of philosophy condensed into a drop of grammar.)
>
> (PI: § 222)

See also: Family Resemblance; Private Language; Wittgenstein, Ludwig.

Bibliography

Baker G P, Hacker P M S 1983 *Wittgenstein: Meaning and Understanding*. Blackwell, Oxford
Hilmy S S 1987 *The Later Wittgenstein*. Blackwell, Oxford
Hinttikka M B, Hintikka J 1986 *Investigating Wittgenstein*. Blackwell, Oxford
Kenny A 1976 *Wittgenstein*. Penguin Books, Harmondsworth
Waismann F 1967 *Ludwig Wittgenstein und der Weiner Kreis*. Blackwell, Oxford
Wittgenstein L 1958 *The Blue and Brown Books*. Blackwell, Oxford
Wittgenstein L 1958 (trans. Anscombe G E M) *Philosophical Investigations*, 2nd. edn. Blackwell, Oxford
Wittgenstein L 1966 *Lectures and Conversations on Aesthetics, Psychology and Religious Belief*. Blackwell, Oxford
Wittgenstein L 1969 *Philosophische Grammatik*. Blackwell, Oxford

Literary Structuralism and Semiotics

T. Threadgold

Literary structuralism and semiotics has been and is a complex and constantly changing phenomenon. Its various forms and practices in the twentieth century constitute the most explicit poetics that Western literary, linguistic, and critical theories have been able to offer. It is however difficult to provide a neat developmental outline. The practices involved have been chronologically disrupted and disruptive. The major figures have migrated from school to school, country to country, crossing political and ideological boundaries. As a consequence, theories developed in one political context become transformed and recontextualized in another where they function as different technologies for understanding the literary. There are many disjunctive traditions involved, deriving from different cultural sources and influences. These spring up in different places and apparently in isolation from each other. They are chronologically overlapping and separate rather than neatly sequential, and they frequently arrive at similar conclusions from different perspectives.

The plurality which characterizes the history of twentieth-century literary structuralism and semiotics now constitutes its present. The state of the art at the end of that century is its own disjunctive history. This article attempts to produce an archaeology, in Foucault's sense (see Foucault 1972), rather than a history, to map the terrain, to identify the major continuities and discontinuities, and to argue for some rereadings of the taken-for-granted arguments about what literary structuralism and semiotics are supposed to be.

The first section provides a kind of history, arriving at some general statements about the current state of the art. The second gives a brief overview and set of preliminary definitions. It also attempts to signpost some major theoretical shifts in position. The third looks at matters of theory and methodology, and provides an archaeology of the terminology which derives from structuralism and semiotics and is still used in poststructuralism, deconstruction, and feminism.

1. The Complex Evolution of the Field

The twentieth-century field of literary studies has become accustomed to a narrative chronology which locates structuralism as prior to, and later developed by, a semiotics which is in turn superceded by a number of new movements all generally characterized as being 'post-' both structuralism and semiotics. This chronology (Culler 1975) ignores many of the complexities of early formalist work in Russia in the 1920s, and of the Prague School in the 1920s and 1930s, each of which was properly both structuralist and semiotic, but historically preceded what is usually identified as 'structuralist' and located in New York in the 1940s and then in Paris from 1950 to 1970 (O'Toole and Shukman 1975–83).

This order of events is further complicated by the ubiquitous presence of Roman Jakobson (1971, 1981) in all these places and movements, by the movement of Claude Lévi-Strauss (1963) from Czechoslovakia to the United States in 1941, and then to Paris in 1950; and by the effects of the uncertain authorship and

delayed translation of the ideas of Mikhail Bakhtin, Voloshinov, and Medvedev (Voloshinov 1973; Bakhtin 1981, 1984, 1986), whose work in Russia in the 1920s and later, known to the Prague School in the 1930s and 1940s, did not have its effect on Paris structuralism and semiotics until it was taken up by Tzvetan Todorov (1984) and Julia Kristeva (1980) in the late 1960s.

In Russia, the inheritance of the formalists (Matejka and Pomorska 1971; Steiner 1984), of Prague School semiotics (Mukařovský 1977; Matejka and Titunik 1976), and of Bakhtin himself (who continued working in Russia until he died in 1975) has been the Tartu school of semiotics, illustrated in the work of its leader, Yuri Lotman (1977). In Paris a very influential group led by A. J. Greimas developed into a Paris School semiotics (Greimas 1987; Perron and Collins 1989) which in many ways has stood outside the more poststructuralist and postmodern aspects of French literary theory, and derives from different traditions from the Barthes–Kristeva kinds of semiotics. Both traditions are the products of early formalism, but Barthes and Kristeva take from such work as Jakobson's (1960: 18–51) on the poetic function, Tynjanov's (see Matejka and Pomorska 1971) on literary evolution, Bakhtin's on genre, dialogue, and dialogism, while the Greimas group have been much more strongly influenced by works like Eichenbaum, *The Theory of the Formal Method* (see Matejka and Pomorska 1971), Propp, *Morphology of the Folktale* (1958), and by Lévi-Strauss's (1963) crucial work on myth. Greimassian semiotics has been primarily a narrative and cognitive semiotics (Greimas 1987). It has preserved the scientificity of an earlier formalism in ways which run counter to contemporary tendencies to critique such scientism (Grosz and de Lepervanche 1988). At the same time it has explored areas that are central to quite different kinds of semiotics and poststructuralism: the production of meaning, the recognition that the apparent presence of meaning in a text is always an illusion, that 'Meaning, in the sense of the forming of meaning, can thus be defined as the possibility of the transformation of meaning' (Jameson, in Greimas 1987: 10). Central to it has been Greimas's rewriting of Propp as the famous semiotic square (Greimas 1987), a powerful heuristic and mediating device which can 'reduce' a narrative to a series of 'cognitive' or ideological positions, or can rewrite a cognitive/scientific or literary text into a narrative process in which contradictory terms attempt a synthesis. Later (Perron and Collins 1989) the work also became much more self-reflexive. In all of these areas, it is impossible to characterize it as structuralist or semiotic without recognizing the links it has with many aspects of poststructuralism as well.

The writings of Bakhtin and Voloshinov were translated (Kristeva 1969) and took effect in Paris in the late 1960s, and this coincided with the point at which Paris structuralism moved in the direction of post-structuralism, a body of theory which still belongs within the ambit of what is here being called literary structuralism and semiotics. Bakhtin's ideas were particularly 'readable' in a context where many of the basic tenets of earlier structuralist and semiotic paradigms were being questioned and rethought. The seminal texts of this new poststructuralist moment would include: those of Bakhtin himself; Roland Barthes, *Elements of Semiology* (1967b); *S/Z* (1974); Julia Kristeva, *Revolution in Poetic Language* (1984); Jacques Derrida, *Of Grammatology* (1976); Michel Foucault, *The Order of Things* (1974), *The Archaeology of Knowledge* (1972), and *The History of Sexuality* (1984). The standard chronology of these events belies the similarities between what was done in the name of formalism, semiotics, and structuralism and what counts as 'post-' both structuralism and semiotics—such literary/linguistic or poetics enterprises as are characterized by the names poststructuralism, deconstruction, and feminism.

The above account of the provenance of literary structuralism and semiotics ignores a number of important schools and traditions which have contributed to the analysis and understanding of structuralist poetics and semiotics of the literary. Four should be mentioned. All are related to the traditions discussed above, and to the work of Jakobson and Eco which are treated below.

1.1 The United States and Canada

The traditions of North American semiotics associated with Thomas Sebeok and Paul Bouissac came to semiotics from quite different directions, although they share a background in the history that runs from formalism to Paris structuralism and beyond. The differences have been in the influence of C. S. Peirce (1986) and A. J. Greimas. Sebeok's (1979) work, and semiotics in the US in general, have been strongly influenced by a Peircean pragmatism which does not mesh easily with the European and French traditions. The work is characterized by the contributions to the journal *Semiotica*. This school has not been primarily interested in literary structuralism and semiotics, and is therefore not treated in depth here.

In Canada, the Greimas school, and links with other French theory and poststructuralism as well as feminism, British Marxist stylistics and cultural studies, and linguistic pragmatics and discourse analysis, have produced a semiotics which differs from both its US and European counterparts, and which has found the scientific pretensions of the US version problematic (Bouissac 1981). The work is illustrated by the predominantly text-based, literary theoretical, and semiotic orientations of the publications in the journal of the Toronto Semiotic Association, *RSSI: Recherches Sémiotiques/Semiotic Inquiry*.

1.2 Roman Jakobson

Jakobson provided the impetus for a different development in stylistics in 1958, when, at the conference whose proceedings were later published as *Style in Language* (Sebeok 1979), he presented the 'concluding statement' paper. This paper contained his arguments about the poetic function of language, arguments which revitalized many aspects of his and others' earlier work (in Russia and Prague in the 1920s and 1930s) on literary language and the poetics of literature. This work was functionalist, structuralist–semiotic, and essentially Marxist in its orientations. It was Marxist in the sense that, despite the debates in Russia in the 1920s about the excesses of 'vulgar' sociological Marxism in literary studies, it involved literary analysis which related literary texts to the social and cultural conditions of their production, and to the material bases of the societies which produced them. In Jakobson's 1958 paper, the relation of the functions of language to a contextualized theory of the communication situation, the concern with the relations of the word to the world, and the location of a poetics which deals with verbal structure within the realm of general semiotics, are all issues that are implicitly materialist and sociological.

Jakobson was influenced by Husserl's phenomenology as well as by Saussure's focus on the system that was language, and was interested in the first instance in what it was that constituted 'literariness.' He was interested in literature only insofar as it constituted another kind of evolving and changing system, like language (Steiner 1984). In a paper first published in Czech in 1933–34 and in English in 1976, Jakobson responded to criticisms of formalism that it 'fails to grasp the relationship of art to real life,' that it calls for an 'art for art's sake approach,' that 'it is following in the footsteps of Kantian aesthetics' (1981: 749). His response is worth quoting in full here:

> Neither Tynjanov nor Mukařovský nor Sklovskij nor I—none of us has ever proclaimed the self-sufficiency of art. What we have been trying to show is that art is an integral part of the social structure, a component that interacts with all the others and is itself mutable since both the domain of art and its relationship to the other constituents of the social structure are in constant dialectical flux. What we stand for is not the separatism of art but the autonomy of the aesthetic function.
> (Jakobson 1981: 749–50)

Jakobson's literary work was very different in its implications from the largely unpoliticized and decontextualized work of Chomsky, and from the generative linguistics which was his other main area of influence and interest in the US at the time of the 1958 paper on the poetic function of language. However, his work on the literariness of the literary was coopted in unpredictable ways, in this new historical context, in both America and Britain, by a very different aesthetic that derived from new criticism and other text-based approaches to the literary (e.g., Richards 1929). This was specifically middle-class and individualistic. It found the emphasis on form in Jakobson's poetics compatible with its own tendency to treat the aesthetic text in isolation from questions of social or historical context.

The 1958 conference also connected with different developments in North American semiotics, and marked a period of high enthusiasm for a new kind of interdisciplinarity in the humanities which drew on linguistics, literary theory, psychology, and cultural anthropology.

1.3 British Stylistics

In the 1960s, transformational linguistics began to have an influence in Britain. But it was the theories of the British linguist Michael Halliday (1978, 1985), theories that are functionalist, systemic, Marxist, and semiotic in orientation and belong to the Neo-Firthian tradition in linguistics and anthropology, which became the dominant linguistic force in British Stylistics. Halliday's was a fundamentally structuralist approach to the linguistic analysis of literary texts (Halliday 1980). This approach was, however, mediated by versions of Halliday's theory of language as social semiotic. This is a constructivist theory which sees language as constructing the social, rather than simply representing a social order that pre-exists language. It is associated with a theory of the semiotics of context which theorizes the ways in which texts are both realizations of their producing contexts and constructive of the speaking subjects and the social realities that constitute those contexts. In this intellectual environment, Jakobson's and other formalist and Prague school analyses of the literary were appropriate and compatible influences, and were not subject to the recontextualizations that affected them elsewhere. British stylistics has always been underpinned by a specific concern with the semiotics of text–context relations, as well as with the structural analysis of texts themselves.

British stylistics and linguistic criticism reached its most influential point at the end of the 1970s, with the publication of Kress and Hodge, *Language as Ideology* (1979), Fowler, et al. *Language and Control* (1979), Aers, et al. *Literature, Language and Society in England 1580–1680* (1981). All three books used both transformational and systemic linguistics, and an overtly structuralist and Marxist theoretical approach to the analysis of literary texts. All three were also more concerned with locating literature in a wider social context, and in its relations to other texts, to institutions and power, than had ever been the case in early or even later structuralist work on the literary within this context (Hasan 1985).

1.4 Social Semiotics in Britain and Australia

One book stands out as signaling new directions in British stylistics, and marking its transition to something that might properly be called 'social semiotics.' Its difference was in its preparedness to deal with French theory, and in the important new directions that made possible. The book is Roger Fowler's *Literature as Social Discourse: The Practice of Linguistic Criticism* (1981). Its most important contribution is its bringing together of the British work outlined above with that of Roland Barthes, Bakhtin, and others from the European traditions. This made possible an explicitly theorized move from an intrinsic structuralist linguistic criticism which focused on the production or writing of the text, and on its formal linguistic properties, to a literary and textual semiotics which foregrounded the role of the socially and linguistically constructed reading subject, and allowed an account of that reader's ability to decode (in Barthes' sense of code as used in *S/Z*, or Eco's 1977 use of the term) the patterns such an intrinsic criticism might discover. The decoding was theorized as a form of intertextuality: the reader was making sense of this text in terms of codes that were familiar from other texts.

This marked the beginnings of many attempts under the heading of 'social semiotics' to bring French and poststructuralist theoretical positions into contact with the British stylistics and Hallidayan traditions (see, for example, Birch and O'Toole 1988).

There was also a new interest in British stylistics in the 1970s, in the larger structures of texts, and in the networks of relations within which they circulate. Theories of discourse analysis, sociolinguistics, and pragmatics were used to relate the form of a text to its patterns of use, and to the social contexts in which it operates. Much of this work has recourse to Hallidayan linguistics, and to register and genre theory as adumbrated within that tradition and others. Ronald Carter's (1982) and Roger Fowler's (1986) work is typical. The continued vitality of this work in the 1990s was marked by the appearance of two new journals: *Language and Literature*, which appeared in Britain in 1992, and *Social Semiotics*, first published in Australia in 1991.

1.5 Umberto Eco and Italian Semiotics

All the traditions discussed so far derive linguistically from Saussure in Geneva at the beginning of this century. Nearly all were further influenced by the Prague Linguistic Circle, particularly Jakobson and Trubetskoy. The Danish linguist Hjelmslev (1961) surfaced as an important influence at about the same time in the semiotics of Roland Barthes (1974) and Eco (1977). There are many other kinds of linguistics which have served as models or metaphors for the literary text, or as actual methods of doing the analysis.

In his *Theory of Semiotics* (1977), Eco brings all of these and the work of C. S. Peirce into a coherent relationship. His rewriting of Saussurean linguistics in

Hjelmslevian and Peircean terms is significant. He accomplished a bringing together of structuralist methodology with semiotic and poststructuralist insights into the relations of texts to other texts. Eco provided, in his use of Hjelmslev, Jakobson, and Peirce, a detailed semiotically based account of the pragmatics and practical textual functioning of the constant 'deferral,' to use a Derridean deconstructive term, which is meaning. Using Hjelmslev's (1961) concept of 'connotative semiotic' and Peirce's articulation of the 'interpretant' (1986), Eco (1981a: 261 ff.) developed the theory of 'infinite semiosis' and of the 'open' text in ways which used and supplemented Jakobson's structuralist/semiotic understandings of the nature of the literary text. Eco brings together many traditions to focus on writing, reading, and textuality. His theory is profoundly linguistic and philosophical, and yet transcends both in its concern with general semiotics. It has much wider implications than the literary, but offers crucial insights into the structures and semiotics of literary texts.

In *A Theory of Semiotics* (1977) Eco challenges the directions of Julia Kristeva's semiotics. She was the only other semiotician, in the 1970s, to be working as broadly as Eco himself, but her work had taken on psychoanalysis by this time (1984) and she had begun to insist on the semiotics of subjectivity, and on the subjectivity of the reading/writing subject as the means by which intertextuality interacts with the structures of texts. Eco's theory of codes remains in the arena of the social and the linguistic and he refuses both Kristeva's psychoanalytical move and the focus on subjectivity.

1.6 Semiotics in the 1990s

Semiotics has come to deal with the ways in which meanings are made in social systems and within cultures, and with the complex ways in which this social making of meanings in turn constructs the social and the cultural. Semiosis is seen, as predicted by Saussure, to operate not only through language and in forms mediated by language (e.g., literature and myth, history, science, and practices of educational transmission), but in and through other media (e.g., the built environment, architecture, art, fashion, music, gesture, film, the body). To study semiotics in the 1990s is to learn to read and write the world as text.

Historically, both structuralism and semiotics came to be identified with a primary concern with language and the literary, with what it was that constituted the literary as opposed to other kinds of verbal texts, with issues of reading the literary. This was always an important issue, but only one of many areas of inquiry that occupied the Russian formalists, and the Prague School semioticians. In Russia in the 1920s, there was already a trenchant critique of the dominant literary establishment. The aim to provide a 'scientific'

account of literature, within a Marxist framework, was intended to empower the proletariat and subvert the literary institution. That literary structuralism and semiotics became almost solely identified with the description and analysis of the aesthetic in later accounts has to do with the contexts into which the early work was received when it was translated and popularized by Jakobson and Lévi-Strauss in the US in the 1940s. Their work was appropriated by the humanist traditions of literary study in the universities, traditions which fostered the notion of a purely aesthetic realm where the literary, literary texts, and authors of great works are self-evident, given objects that do not become implicated in the 'other' realms of politics, economics, and ideology.

On the other hand, literary structuralism and semiotics were frequently rejected outright by these same institutions, identified as linguistic and 'scientific,' and seen as inherently antagonistic toward the privileged realm of the private, the subjective, and the creative, which was the aesthetic. The language/literature debates of the post-World War I years in Cambridge, for example, saw the separation within English of traditions of language study derived from Germanic philology from a new focus on literary response brought about by close, but nonsystematic, and certainly nonlinguistic, reading. What became linguistic stylistics and literary structuralism in the 1950s and 1960s could often only be located in the language sections of English departments, and thus became institutionally isolated from the literary which was their primary concern. These processes were repeated in the 1960s and 1970s with the second wave of influence of these ideas (see Sect. 1.3 above). These debates and anomalies have continued in English studies in British universities. They are now complicated by further controversies about the role of theory, particularly poststructuralist theory, and the relation of literary studies to more broadly based cultural studies (derived from semiotics) which would look at cultural artefacts and processes of all kinds, including the literary, as texts (film, the visual, popular culture forms like television and media, performance, and theatre).

It has in fact been the very ecumenical nature of semiotics that has slowly changed and rewritten both of these entrenched literary positions. As literary structuralism and semiotics have evolved alongside poststructuralist theory, it has come to be recognized that literary texts do not operate in isolation from social processes, the socializing practices, the disciplines, or the institutional relations of power which affect all textual production, and within which subjects and their practices are constituted. Literary texts, like all other texts, are forms of social discourse, in which meanings, often conflicting and contradictory meanings, are negotiated in an ongoing and productive dialogue with changing contexts and with other institutionally produced forms of social discourse (the law, economics, medicine, etc.).

The next sections of this article trace the essential terms of structuralist and semiotic metalanguages, as these were derived from linguistics, and suggest that later poststructuralism is still very much indebted to these metalanguages.

2. Structuralism, Stylistics, and the Linguistic Metaphor

Twentieth-century linguistics has had a number of different kinds of influence on literary studies. Structuralism has primarily been concerned with the structures of literary artefacts, specifically with the systematic nature of those structures. This systematicity is seen to be what constructs them as literary, rather than as some other kind of text. At one level then literary structuralism uses linguistics, specifically Saussurean linguistics, as a metaphor or model for thinking about the structures of literary texts as autonomous systems. The literary system which is a poem, for example, functions like the synchronic linguistic system which Saussure described for language.

Structuralism has been concerned with understanding the 'grammars' or 'codes' which provide the resources, and the rules for the putting together of those resources, that enable the users of such grammars or codes to produce cultural phenomena such as myths, narratives, music, ritual, visual art, architecture, and literary texts. In many kinds of structuralism, the use of linguistics remains largely metaphorical; nevertheless, a detailed structuralist analysis of a literary text also draws on the analyst's knowledge of the grammar of the language, and thus always involves some grammatical or linguistic theory which functions as a metalanguage for identifying and categorizing the linguistic patterns in the text. If one is going to identify patterns of verbs and nouns in a text, or patterns of stress and intonation, one first needs a grammar which identifies, and thus enables one to label, those categories.

There is a distinction to be drawn here between structuralism and stylistics or linguistic criticism. Stylistics or critical linguistics takes some linguistic theory, and uses its categories to analyze a literary text as a piece of, an instance of, language. There need not be any presupposition that the text being analyzed functions like a language. That presupposition is, however, a usual aspect of the use of the linguistic metaphor in structuralism. A stylistician or critical linguist may be interested in the use of nominalizations in Hemingway's prose, or in the systematic patterns of ungrammaticality in E. E. Cummings's verse. He will tend to make sense of these in relation to the linguistic theory he is working with, using it as a metalanguage to decode the text, and

accepting the meanings it attributes to the categories he is identifying. A transformationalist will read nominalizations as transformations of simpler deep structures. A Hallidayan systemic linguist will read them as grammatical metaphors, requiring 'unpacking' to reveal the ideologies their compact grammatical form conceals.

Where the linguistic theories concerned are discourse analysis, sociolinguistics or pragmatics, or a functional theory of language as social semiotic like Halliday's (1978), the analysis also involves another level, which roughly parallels, but is very different to, the level of language as metaphor in structuralism. In general, all these theories relate the patterns of language produced by linguistic analysis to the social contexts of the text's use. Consistent patterns of agentless passives may thus be identified as marking the text's provenance as a scientific text. In a literary analysis from a feminist perspective, the fact that the female participant is never the subject of active verbs, or that what is attributed to her adjectivally is consistently attributed by a male who is always the subject of the verbs of knowing, may be read as indicating the text's provenance within a patriarchal order.

At stake here is the ability of the analyst first to identify, in terms of some linguistic metalanguage, and then to 'decode' in terms of the same metalanguage, the patterns of language identified in the text. The decoding is a form of interpretation which depends on a theory of context and of text–context relationships, and which involves identifying parts or all of this text as being like other texts in the culture. Such analysis is frequently associated with analytical categories like register, genre, and ideology, or discourse, so that the patterns of language that constitute a text are identified as being those that characterize a particular register or genre, or that are characteristic of a particular set of beliefs or ideas (ideology or discourse of patriarchy, of science, of the child etc.). Much of this work also takes the next step and moves one level higher, to locate the registers, genres, ideologies, and discourses within institutional structures and in relation to power and issues like race, age, and gender. That is, such 'stylistic' work has become a 'critical linguistics' or 'social semiotics,' appropriating the rudiments of social and political theory in order to make sense of linguistic structures and the way they function in literary and other texts. In this respect it agrees with earlier forms of literary formalism or structuralism/semiotics, and has parallels with later versions of literary semiotics and poststructuralism.

The point of difference between the older and newer theoretical positions is the initial use of the Saussurean linguistic system as a metaphor for understanding the literary, and use of any linguistic theory as a metalanguage to establish, in an apparently objective manner, the patterns and the meanings that constitute a text. The Saussurean system used as metaphor is inadequate to deal with all the complex contextual matters outlined above. What Saussure excluded from the linguistic system as parole (i.e., all the social and contextual factors to do with language use) was precisely what critical linguistics, social semiotics, and poststructuralism have later wanted to deal with.

Most forms of linguistics, even those that concern themselves explicitly with questions of context, maintain a version of the Saussurean system as the basis for their analysis of texts. They have maintained a belief in the concept of linguistic value as Saussure formulated it, arguing that linguistic elements have an intrinsic value or meaning that derives from their relationships of similarity and opposition to other elements within the linguistic system (see Sect. 3.1 below). They believe that the linguistic system they construct as linguists provides an objective metalanguage for establishing the intrinsic value or meaning of linguistic elements in texts. But for poststructuralism and many kinds of semiotics, all metalanguages, languages about language, theories of language, including the linguistic, are themselves texts. Poststructuralists therefore argue that grammars or linguistic systems, like other texts, are always an interpretation from someone's perspective. As such they cannot be any more objective than contextual criticism, which in its most recent forms includes the subjectivity of the interpreter as an essential part of understanding the analytic and interpretive process. On these grounds, they refuse the distinction between intrinsic and extrinsic value or meaning, and even go so far as to argue that there is no meaning in texts, only meaning that results from the interaction between texts and the speaking subjects (subjectivities) who read and write them, and in so doing provide the links with contexts that quite literally 'make meanings.' Poststructuralists therefore relocate value or meaning in the social processes in which texts are made, and deny the reality of the abstract linguistic system, which they see as a theoretical fiction.

2.1 Reading as Rewriting

In critical linguistic and poststructuralist readings, the reader maps from the language of the text being analyzed to other interpreting codes or texts (metalanguages). There is no qualitative difference between the linguistic and the other practices. The linguistic theory is just another code. The authority it carries however means that its effects in interpretive contexts cannot be discounted. That was one of the things Barthes (1974) was saying in *S/Z* in his rereading of Hjelmslev and his refusal of the then normal modes of linguistic analysis. His approach was to take chunks of Balzac's text, explore his own techniques of making sense of them, and then categorize his responses as involving five specific codes, or theories of the world; 'grammars,' that gave him the resources

to 'make meanings' with this text, to make sense of bits of it by relating them to bits of other codes/texts with which he was familiar. In *S/Z* all 'decoding' became not only connotative, but inherently subjective in that it was always mediated by the subjectivity, the socially constructed and positioned subjectivity, of the reader.

So 'analysis' became a productive reading process, in which reading involved rewriting. The recognition that reading is a rewriting, and that linguistic readings are also rewritings, went along with the deconstruction of the opposition between denotation and connotation, and the theorizing of the openness of texts to new interactions with their environments. It was one of the first performances of what it was to rewrite a story and tell it differently as a form of literary and cultural criticism.

As such, it has important links with research that was going on elsewhere on the essential narrativity of all texts (the Greimas school in Paris: Greimas 1987); on the binary structures that characterize and structure all narratives (Propp 1958; Lévi-Strauss 1963); on the relationships between narrative, poetry, and myth (Jakobson and Lévi-Strauss 1962), on the constitutive nature of metaphor and metonymy in all types of discourse (Jakobson 1971); on the fact that not only the text-types (genres) that constitute a culture, but also its larger discursive formations and institutions, are constituted of narrativity and binarisms (Foucault 1972; Derrida 1976; Kristeva 1984, 1980). These connections linked the denial of the possibility of denotative meaning in Barthes (1974) to what eventually appeared to be a quintessentially poststructuralist discovery of the narrativity, metaphoricity, and fictionality of all texts.

The work of Jean-François Lyotard (1984) is exemplary here. Its consequences for literary work were the interesting extension of theories and models developed for the analysis of the literary into the analysis of the social sciences generally, on the assumption that all texts are stories, written from some position, and for some specific purpose; that they are therefore in a very real sense fictions, and can be expected to be analyzable like other fictions such as myths or literature. So the theories and practices of a modernist literary institution—literary structuralism and semiotics—were appropriated by the practices and theories of poststructuralism.

Poststructuralists have not, by and large, 'used' linguistics as a tool of analysis. Reoriented by the work of Hjelmslev, Barthes, Foucault, Derrida, and Kristeva, who can be located respectively within structuralism, poststructuralism, deconstruction, semiotics, and feminism, they read and rewrite, they perform their texts, remaking meanings in and through the doing of language. Poststructuralist practice has reconstructed the reader as empowered to rewrite the primary text from the intertextual resources of her own subjectivity and experience. The text itself, its linguistic and semiotic stuff, is not irrelevant to this enterprise. It is however theorized differently. It becomes the trace of a writing which can be remade, rewritten as the processes of semiosis begin again with the interaction of the language traces of this text with those of the embodied, sexed, speaking subject/text who is its reader. Reading and writing cease to be qualitatively different processes. There is also an important difference, effected through the work of Michel Foucault, in the position of the intellectual/cultural critic. The author has lost her institutional authority. The intellectual/critic can no longer be an objective observer. She is now in the middle of her own textual productions. There is no outside of ideology, and therefore only a practice, a doing, and never a mode of analysis, is actually possible.

That is the textual politics of poststructuralist critique: to subvert and remake, from some position other than the dominant one, the hegemonic and socially ratified versions of the world which are the culture and the social narrativized. The whole enterprise is, if not profoundly linguistic, at least profoundly semiotic; nor are its politics so different from those of a critical linguistics or a social semiotics.

3. Archaeology of a Metalanguage: Continuities and Discontinuities

This section focuses on particular texts and writers in order to trace the patterns of continuity and discontinuity that characterize the apparent 'evolution' of the metalanguages of literary structuralism and semiotics into the metalanguages of poststructuralism.

3.1 The Heritage of Saussure

Saussure's (1960) formulation of synchronic linguistics as constituting an important part of a semiology which would study the life of signs in a society provided the basic concepts for the twentieth century's early structuralist/semiotic inquiry. His theory of language provided the terminology and, indeed, the methodology. The specific aspects of Saussure's linguistics which were borrowed as a model/metaphor for analyzing systems of meaning analogous to language, including the structure of literary texts and the nature of literariness, were small in number but have remained central to most literary and textual analysis.

3.1.1 *Language as Synchronic System: Uses and Rewritings*

The concept of language as a synchronic system and the notion of linguistic opposition (the patterns of similarity and difference which determine the value of individual elements within the system) were among the most important ideas borrowed from Saussure. The related dichotomy langue/parole, which functioned in Saussure to exclude from the domain of linguistics what people actually did with language, in favor of an attempt to construct the abstract system which made that activity possible, has been a source of constant controversy. This dichotomy also involved the exclusion of the diachronic or the historical from the description of the synchronic or current state of a linguistic system.

The notions of system and value have come in for much criticism in poststructuralist circles, and were already criticized by the Bakhtin Circle in Russia in the 1920s (Voloshinov 1973). Both concepts have to be seen in the context which produced both Saussure's linguistics and the early formalist work for which it became a model. The central tenets of both enterprises were in keeping with the latest ideas in the philosophy of science at the time, in particular Husserl's phenomenology and its links with and critique of nineteenth-century positivism. The crucial aspect of this philosophy for both Saussure and the formalists was its emphasis not on the sensory experience of 'facts' as in positivism but on the role of intuition in enabling 'the direct grasp of the essences underlying the phenomenal world which provide it with its categorial identity' (Steiner 1984: 255).

This was the basis for Saussure's proposing a strict separation of what is linguistically phenomenal, individual, and accidental from what is essential, social, and rule-governed: *langue* (potential linguistic system) versus *parole* (actual speech). Langue would be the sole object of linguistics. In this, Saussure's *Course in General Linguistics* provided the young formalists with a program for what they wanted to achieve in literary studies: a science generated intrinsically on the basis of its own subject matter. Like language, literature is a social institution, a system governed by its own regularity and more or less independent of contiguous fields of culture. This was a conception of literature that informed Tynjanov's notion of literary history, Jakobson's poetics, and Tomashevsky's metrics (Steiner 1984: 175–85).

Even within formalism, there was much variation in the way these ideas were used. The semiotic concept underlying Husserl's or Saussure's expressionist model is absolutely antidialogic. The identity of intrinsic linguistic meaning can only be preserved within the linguistic system, the potential that underlies linguistic activity: Saussurean linguistics is monologic. Even though the *Course* begins with a discussion of a dialogue between two disembodied heads, these heads are two identical instances of the same social consciousness: they are two terminals whose semiotic input and output are one, monologic. In these heads is langue, the set of all linguistic elements internalized by the linguistic community at any one time. All minds have the same content. These are the aspects of Saussurean linguistics which prompted Voloshinov's critique of the notion of intrinsic meaning and the linguistic system (1973: 67ff).

3.1.2 *Jakobson and the Linguistic System*

Jakobson's concept of the linguistic system deconstructed many of the classic Saussurean dichotomies. Saussure claimed that the causes of linguistic change (diachrony) are extrasystemic, accidental, and to be excluded from synchronic description. Jakobson's linguistics was profoundly dialectic, and this made any separation of the system from its history impossible. For him, linguistic change is triggered by contradictions within language itself, and is subject to the rules of the system. The axis of succession (see below for a discussion of syntagm in Saussure), the present synchronic moment of the linguistic signifier, is always impregnated with history. At the same time, the axis of simultaneity or choice (see 'paradigm' below), the potential that is the system in Saussure, consists in Jakobson of several simultaneous and overlapping systems, not one. These are the functions of language made famous in his 1960 paper, and the several systems of functional registers they give rise to. The system for him is a complex field of synchronic and diachronic elements, revolutionary and conservative forces, and it is in a constant state of disjunctive equilibriums and disequilibriums. It is both a state and a process of change.

This rewriting of the linguistic system in Jakobson derives from and is produced in interaction with his work on the literary system. It is linked with the concept of defamiliarization in his discussions of the evolution of verbal art. The oscillation between the old, which has become automatized, and the new, which defamiliarizes, is never conceived of as a linear progression in which each new state of the literary system simply leaves the last one 'automatized': the interaction of old and new which produces defamiliarization in art is an essentially dialogic phenomenon—and dialogism here takes on in Jakobson's work many of the characteristics Bakhtin (1986) will be attributed with having discovered. The system is an ongoing struggle between antithetical tendencies and heterogeneous elements, and it is not internalized, as in Saussure, uniformly and totally by every speaking subject. This difference allows change, but preserves the system.

Jakobson's expressionist debt to Husserl, which preserved his belief in the system which underpinned the potential subversiveness of dialogism, and his interest in the dialogic, began to become incompatible. The problem of the literary and its relation to the system was central. How far apart can a writer and his readers be before they cease to share anything? What are the limits of the system? The problem of writing became crucial, because writing makes it possible for a literary work to transcend the moment of its production and become available to a distant readership, which will project it against a poetic system different from the one that produced it. High literature was identified by Jakobson and Bogatyrev as distinct from folklore on the basis of its production and reception. The immediacy of the oral performance of popular culture, its closeness to speech, and to the demands of its conditions of production, made it a fact of langue. If it was to be successfully received it had to correspond to the normative structure of a system and fulfill its collective demands. Literature was more like parole, dialogic and able to interact with many contexts (quoted in Steiner 1984: 228). This statement would seem to be at odds with Jakobson's notion of verbal art as a social institution, like language and like Saussure's system.

The starting point of Jakobson's poetics was the concept of the expression, a sign which referred only to itself. The poetic function of language involved a focus on the message for its own sake, and was the centerpiece of a theory of the autonomy of the aesthetic. The problem arose when Jakobson conceived of the semiotic identity of this sign in terms of a Saussurean social and rule-governed system (which would preserve its identity) but then relativized this system by rewriting langue as a series of historically changing functional varieties. Poetic language, driven by its need for incessant defamiliarization, exhibited the highest degree of change, and was thus, paradoxically, the least reliable function in terms of long-term semiotic identity (or intrinsic meaning, to use the terminology used above).

This was the basis for the linguistic principle of Jakobson's poetics. It is related to the issues that became popularized as the differences between 'ordinary' and 'poetic' language in the Prague School (Mukařovský 1977). In Jakobson the literary work is always perceived against the basis of contemporary 'ordinary' language. Poetic language is a superstructure built upon that system, and the aesthetic functioning of the literary text depends upon that system. The same metaphor is in Eco's (1977) much later formulation of the overcoding and extracoding that are required to make sense (a) of the literary conventions, the literary systems that constrain the production of literary texts, and (b) the hypothesizing and Peircean abduction that is necessary to make sense of the aesthetic text as invention, its radical 'deautomatizing' moments. What preserves the possibility of interpretation is the linguistic moment, the shared code of the common linguistic system. For Jakobson and Eco, the writer and reader cannot be totally isolated from each other as long as they share a language. The literary text will make sense as an utterance in that language, even projected against a set of poetic norms or an aesthetic code that is alien to it. The interpretation of any literary text, for Jakobson, will therefore always involve meanings that are intrinsic to it by virtue of its participation in the system that is language.

3.1.3 *The System and the Poetic Function of Language*

One of the major tenets of Jakobson (1960) was that language was functionally differentiated in relation to the significant elements of the communication situation. These he formulated as shown in (1):

$$\text{CONTEXT} \quad (1)$$
$$\text{ADDRESSER} \quad \text{MESSAGE} \quad \text{ADDRESSEE}$$
$$\text{CONTACT}$$
$$\text{CODE}$$

The elements are related to six functions, one corresponding to each of the factors in the communication situation as shown in (2):

$$\text{REFERENTIAL} \quad (2)$$
$$\text{EMOTIVE} \quad \text{POETIC} \quad \text{CONATIVE}$$
$$\text{PHATIC}$$
$$\text{METALINGUAL}$$

All messages were characterized by more than one function, and the dominant function (Jakobson 'The dominant' 1935) in any one message specified it as belonging to one functional variety rather than another.

The referential function, oriented towards the context, the so-called 'denotative' function of language, which 'refers' to the extralinguistic, is often regarded as the predominant linguistic function. But Jakobson demonstrated that every message also involves a number of other functions, and that many messages foreground functions other than the referential. The emotive function focuses on the addresser, offering a direct expression of the speaker's attitude to what he is speaking about. The conative function involves an orientation toward the addressee, and finds its clearest grammatical expression in the vocative and imperative. The phatic function is oriented towards contact, and functions primarily to establish and maintain communication. The metalingual function is focused on the code itself, but not only in scientific or theoretical modes of talking about language. Whenever speakers use language to check up on whether they are using the same code to explain meanings or to quote or refer to other language, they are using it metalingually.

The function of language which focuses on the message for its own sake is the poetic function of language: this is the dominant function in verbal art. In all other functions it acts as a subsidiary constituent. On the other hand all the other functions also participate in verbal art: one cannot specify the particularities of different poetic genres 'without specifying the differently ranked participation of the other functions alongside the poetic function' (Jakobson 1981: 26). Epic poetry (third person) involves the ref-

erential function of language, lyric poetry (first person) is intimately linked with the emotive function, and second-person poetry is linked to the conative (see Sect. 3.3 below).

For Jakobson, the problem of the relativity of literary interpretation was solved by this bond between functional varieties. The fact that even the poetic function always involved the referential actually limited the spatiotemporal dislocation which might threaten the identity of the literary work. The conservative system of 'ordinary' language was common to succeeding and different literary canons and sets of poetic norms. Although Jakobson claimed that 'every word of poetic language is in essence phonically and semantically deformed vis-à-vis practical language,' and that the aesthetic function is a specific variety 'governed by its own immanent laws,' he concluded that 'a poetic form cannot distort its material to such a degree that it loses its linguistic nature' (Steiner 1984: 231).

3.1.4 *Phonology and the Problem of Poetic Violence*

The structure that underpins all functional varieties is the phonological system of a given language. It was phonology that Jakobson chose as the key to the identity of the literary sign, even as he argued that it was phonological parallelism and repetition that produced semantic polysemy, ambiguity, and heterogeneity in the literary artefact. Phonology was an important element of Saussure's system. The focus on phonology, and the idea that the spoken is the original, authentic form of language, constituted what Derrida (1976) would call phonocentrism in Saussure. For Saussure and Jakobson, phonology controls the infinite semiosis that is a consequence of written language, the result of the process of spatiotemporal dislocation which relativizes the identity of the written sign. If writing is made secondary to an originary speech, merely a representation of it, then the cause of the semiotic slippage, written language, is eliminated. Saussure's contradictory and violent narrative, structured around the speech/writing binarism, of the violence done to speech by writing (1960: ch. 6), was the text Derrida chose for his deconstruction of the intrinsic meaning arguments in linguistics (1976). The intrinsic value of the verbal sign is guaranteed only while it remains within the synchronic system of langue, written as the science of the phone, the latter's amorphous multiplicity reduced to a limited inventory of elements and incorporated into the relational grid of similarities and differences that constitute that system.

The voice in Saussure is logocentric, the voice of reason. The phoneme, the minimal unit of the signifier, is defined through its relationship to the signified, in terms of the rational differentiations in meaning that it enables within the system. Phonology offered Jakobson the solution to both his problems. As a mere secondary representation of sound, the written text must always be able to be read in relation to voice, the primary substance, and the basic structure of that substance is provided by the phonological structure of a given language. Phonology also solves the problem of the second cause of semiotic slippage, the distance between the participants in the literary process. Of all the systems of norms and stratal levels of organization that constitute language, the phonological system is the one that interlocutors must share if any dialogue is to take place. This postulate derives from the Saussurean concept of the double articulation of language. This says that all linguistic signifiers that carry meaning are made up of smaller elements that do not signify in themselves but function to differentiate meanings. These meaning-differentiating elements are the phonemes that constitute the most elementary linguistic system, and are indispensable to the semiotic functioning of language.

Poetic violence cannot deform this system, or verbal art would lose its linguistic nature: thus the identity of the literary text is preserved from the relativism inherent in its dialogic interaction with different contexts by the stability of the phonological system and its insistence on intrinsic meaning. On the other hand, the poetic function in Jakobson's formulation foregrounds the phonological. What functions in ordinary language as a means to a communicative end, serves to defamiliarize the verbal medium in verbal art, and makes the structure of the verbal sign the focus of attention. As in the system itself, repetitions of sound in verbal art produce meaning: but here the repetitions are not constrained by the system, for the paradigmatic has already projected itself into the syntagm, and revolution is imminent.

The issues raised by these incompatible tendencies in Jakobson's work surface in Julia Kristeva's work on revolution in poetic language. Her arguments for the aesthetic as a place of revolution are not the same as Jakobson's, to which she is greatly indebted in all other respects. While he saw phonology as the means of containing 'poetic violence,' she transforms his understanding of the role of phonology in poetry, reading only its revolutionary poetic aspects in Jakobson, its extrasystemic, transgressive potential. As she rewrites the linguistic metaphors with metaphors from psychoanalysis, phonology becomes the link with the body and the unconscious, and then with the repressed feminine and a rewritten semiotic. She refuses to identify the phonological with that aspect of the linguistic system which is beyond deformation, what she calls the symbolic and identifies as the patriarchal order of language. For her the phonological becomes the semiotic, the excess which is responsible for disruption of the fixity and rationality of the symbolic, the patriarchal system of language. Poetic violence she takes from Jakobson, but the nature of her revolution is very different from his. The difference comes from the

psychoanalytic move which relates the Freudian or Lacanian conscious/unconscious binarism to her own symbolic/semiotic, the linguistic system/process, syntagm/paradigm, syntax/phonology binarisms and the cultural binarisms masculine/feminine, rational/irrational, mind/body. In this scheme of things the unconscious is the place of the semiotic and all the repressed connections between the body and phonology. Phonology is the bodily source of, and not the rational and systemic constraint on, revolution.

3.1.5 *Challenge and Deconstruction: Bakhtin and Prague School Positions*

The phonocentrism and logocentrism of Saussure were the subject of critique and deconstruction long before Derrida. The Bakhtin Circle in Russia in the 1920s offered a trenchant critique of Saussurean linguistics, and thoroughly rewrote formalist theories of language and the literary. For Voloshinov (1973) every sign was an ideological phenomenon, a reality standing for some other reality. For Medvedev (1978) the literary was an ideological phenomenon, a system of metasigns which 'refract what lies outside them,' that is, nonartistic, ideological phenomena.

From a linguistic point of view, a sign that reflects another sign is exactly like an utterance that comments on, or replies to, or quotes another utterance. The process is inherently dialogic, and dialogue became a dominant metaphor in the semiotics of Bakhtin and Prague School members. Voloshinov argued that the formalists remained concerned with what he called the centripetal forces in language, the elements that make it systemic and monologic. The Bakhtin Circle was interested in the opposite tendencies: language as process, as an ongoing struggle between different points of view, different ideologies, a dialogue with other texts, and other voices; the heterogeneity of language. They took as their main target the formalist vision of a literary system independent of all other cultural domains. Bakhtin's late essays 'The Problem of the Text' and 'The Problem of Speech Genres' (1986) provide an overview of many of these concerns.

The Prague School also rejected this view of literature as autonomous system. They argued that the poetic function never operated in isolation from the other contiguous structures with which it changed in time (the political, economic, ideological). Mukařovský insisted on the semiotic point of view which would enable the theorist to recognize the existence and dynamism of the literary system, and to understand its development as a movement in constant dialectic with the development of other spheres of culture. Prague School aesthetics reveals its debts to both formalism and the Bakhtin School.

3.2 *Signifier and Signified: Contrastive Meaning*

The arbitrary nature of the linguistic sign was essential to Saussurean linguistics. Arbitrariness was closely related to Saussure's rewriting of the sign (often previously read as simply the name for a thing) as the *union* of a concept (signified) and a sound image (signifier). This union, the relationship of sound and meaning, is arbitrary; the actual value or meaning of the sign depends on its relations of differential opposition with other signs within a system or code. The signifier is not a 'thing,' but part of a relational structure, and the signified is defined through relations of opposition, and not through being related to non-semiotic entities or the 'world.' The fact that the concept 'tree' is related to different sound images in different languages, for example, *arbre* (French), *Baum* (German), and *tree* (English), is adduced as evidence for the arbitrary nature of the sound-/meaning relationship that constitutes the unity of signified and signifier as sign. The fact that the sign for tree in English has the value it has, is due to its relationship to other signs that may share some aspects of its value or meaning but are significantly different from it: *bush, vine, shrub, forest, fern, conifer,* etc. *Tree* means what it does because these other signs exist to restrict its meaning: the distinctive feature of being a tree is constituted by what they are not. A sign acquires its value within a code or system which is a set of formally structured oppositions and differences. This is the source of the notion of intrinsic linguistic meaning discussed in Sect. 3.1.4.

3.2.1 *Phonological Opposition and Binarism*

Jakobson and Trubetskoy, in the area of phonology, considerably developed the idea of language as a system of conventional oppositions or differences, when they analyzed the system of sound contrasts in language. If one begins otherwise similar words with distinctively different sounds, one will produce distinctively different words, different in meaning: for example, *sin, din, tin*. In other words, the contrasts between these sounds in English are functional. Such functionally different sounds are what Saussure, Jakobson, and Trubetskoy called phonemes. A central property of phonemes is that when one is substituted for another one gets contrasts in meaning. They are the contrastive and meaningful units of sound that constitute any particular linguistic system, distinguished from one another by two-way or binary contrasts, like voiced/unvoiced (*s, t* versus *d*), fricative and nonfricative (*s* versus *t, d*), etc.

This binary organization of the phonological system in Jakobson and Trubetskoy is a theoretical instance of what became a much more widely adopted principle in the structuralism of the 1940s and 1950s, associated with Jakobson and Lévi-Strauss in New York and Paris. Structuralist analyses of anything from language to culture were characterized by this underlying principle of definition by contrast, so that the elements of a culture might be said to include such 'basic oppositions' as: male/female, culture/nature,

rational/irrational, right/left, reason/madness, and so on. The narrative or ritual or mythic practices of a culture, including verbal art, were seen as functioning to resolve or synthesize, or otherwise make sense of, these binarisms that were inherent to their structure.

There is a connection between this structuralist use of binarisms and narrative analysis, and later deconstructive methods and strategies developed by Jacques Derrida, and appropriated for feminism by Luce Irigaray (1985). Structuralism accepted the binarisms as objective structuring principles, and used binary analysis as a methodology for understanding the nature and function of cultural objects and narrative processes. Deconstruction sees binarisms as culturally biased and contingent ways of constructing what appear to be observed data. It points to the oppositional value systems that are built into binary structures: one term is defined in terms of the other (female is defined as what is not male); one term is positively valued and the other negatively. In the series above, in this culture, male, culture, rational, right, and reason would be valued positively against the elements that constitute the other sides of the pairs. Binarisms and narrative structures remain closely linked in deconstructive critique. Once these binarisms become constitutive of a culture and its texts, only certain narratives, plot structures, heroes, and denouements are possible. The focus of deconstructive work in later critical cultural and semiotic analysis has been to unsettle the taken-for-granted nature of these binarisms and the narratives they structure. The aim is not simply to reverse the value systems, nor to resolve the differences, as in structuralist methodology, but rather to question the very existence of the binary opposition itself as a structuring principle, and to attempt to show that the members of a binary pair are unique in their differences and not definable in terms of one another. Derrida's rewriting of Saussure, and Luce Irigaray's rewriting of Freud, are two typical examples of this deconstructive methodology. It is arguable that without structuralism's prior investigations of these issues they might not have been so early on the deconstructive and feminist agendas.

3.3 *Syntagm and Paradigm: Versions of the Poetic Function*

The syntagm/paradigm opposition in Saussure is concerned with relations of combination (one thing after another, the linearity of the signifier) and of choice (one thing instead of another at a particular point in the signifying chain). The horizontal axis of language, its chain relationships, is the syntagm. The vertical axis, the sets of choices which are available to fill particular slots in the chain, are called paradigms. The system consists of a set of paradigms or choices, and a set of rules which enable elements of these sets to be combined to form chains of signifying elements:

The cattle drink from the creek (3)
Those mice meet near those bushes
    Cats sleep on every branch
All felines frolic

In the examples in (3), the horizontal sequences are formed grammatically, according to rule, by choosing from the paradigms of elements which form the system, which can be identified with the vertical columns. *The, those,* and *all* are all choices of the same kind, which can fill the first slot in this kind of sequence: similarly *cattle, mice, cats,* and *felines,* and so on.

This concept of language as system is based on the idea that what is paradigmatic, the alternative sets of equivalent choices available within the system, is never constitutive of the syntagm, which is by definition characterized by difference not similarity, by the combination of significantly different elements. It is difference that constitutes value or meaning at the level of the syntagm, just as it is at the basic level of the phoneme. When Jakobson (1960: 27) defined the poetic function of language as projecting 'the principle of equivalence from the axis of selection into the axis of combination,' he argued that in verbal art, in contradistinction to the normal state of affairs in language, '*equivalence becomes the constitutive device of the sequence*' (italics added). Parallelism at all levels of phonological structure, from stress, alliteration, and rhyme to intonation constitutes the poetic syntagm. The phonological structure is built around patterns of binary oppositions, stress/unstress, sameness of sound, and difference in meaning (e.g., rhyme), rising and falling tones or beats, and the parallelisms that arise from recurrent metrical, stanzaic, and other generic forms such as the sonnet.

Jakobson showed that within the system which is the poetic text, 'equivalence in sound, projected into the sequence as its constitutive principle, inevitably involves semantic equivalence' (1960: 40). Words similar in sound are drawn together in meaning. Phonological parallelism is frequently accompanied by grammatical parallelism which serves to increase the ambiguity and semantic richness of the 'double-sensed message' (1960) and 'The supremacy of the poetic function over the referential function does not obliterate the reference but makes it ambiguous' (1960: 42).

The split reference of the double-voiced message finds its correspondence in a split addresser and a split addressee. Hence Jakobson's enduring interest in linguistic shifters, particularly pronouns, and in the issue of a subjectivity constructed in language. Shifters were of interest to him, as they were to Benveniste (1986), because they are distinguished from all other constituents in the linguistic code by their compulsory reference to the message and its context. They are a complex category where code (*langue*) and message (*parole*) overlap, where meaning cannot be established

without reference to the context. They therefore offer another instance, like the poetic function of language, where the strict separation of langue and parole will not work (1957a: 132). Jakobson's analysis of split subjectivity was of particular interest to later structuralists and semioticians in the 1960s and 1970s, as subjectivity, and the construction and positioning of the subject in language, became issues for a semiotics and poststructuralism that were rethinking the humanist subject in the light of linguistic, semiotic, discursive, narrative, and psychoanalytic theories.

3.4 Jakobson and Lévi-Strauss: Textual Analysis

Jakobson's analysis of the poetic text as system, and of the poetic function of language, inevitably questioned the Saussurean notion of system, particularly if it is remembered that the poetic function is *constitutive of* but *not limited to* poetic texts. The emphasis on the sound/meaning nexus in poetry meant that the 'arbitrariness' of the linguistic sign had to be questioned and rewritten. The projection of the paradigmatic into the syntagmatic meant that the text as utterance contained the system, was indeed the only place where the system could be. The text became both product and process, and this weakened the opposition between langue and parole. These were the subversive elements in Jakobson that Julia Kristeva, Umberto Eco, and Jacques Derrida would find most compatible with their own poststructuralist enterprises. For Kristeva they were elements that also connected with her discovery of Bakhtin, whose work in these areas was in fact much earlier than Jakobson's.

These ideas were expressed by Jakobson quite late, much later than his work with the formalists. For him these were the characteristics of the poetic function of language, not of all functions and, as suggested above, he sought to contain the subversiveness of these elements (see Sect. 3.1.4 above). The relevant analyses are (with L. G. Jones) 'Shakespeare's Verbal Art in "Th'Expense of Spirit"' and (with Claude Lévi-Strauss) '"Les Chats" de Charles Baudelaire.' They are among many such analyses published in various languages in Volume III of Jakobson's *Selected Writings* (1981), but they are the two best known in the English-speaking context. Both are typical examples of the binary structuralist methodology, relying on the patterns of variables that constitute the texts to provide meanings intrinsic to the texts as systems. The paper on 'Les Chats' describes the poetic text in ways which anticipate Barthes' later 'discovery' of 'readerly' (closed) and 'writerly' (open) texts (1967a). The position taken by Jakobson and Lévi-Strauss anticipates by some considerable time later versions of the 'open' text. These derive variously from linguistics-based structuralism, from the revival of Bakhtinian carnival in Kristeva's work, or from the insertion into the reading process of the psychoanalytic unconscious and of pleasure, drives, and the body in the later Barthes and Kristeva (Barthes 1975; Kristeva 1984). Eco's differently derived but related Peircean and Hjelmslevian construct of the open text was formulated considerably later.

As Jakobson and Lévi-Strauss explain in the paper on 'Les Chats' (1962: 385–86), the poetic text is described first, as consisting of patterns of variables (or paradigms) which exist 'on a number of superimposed levels: phonological, phonetic, syntactic, prosodic, semantic etc.,' and then as consisting of 'systems of equivalences which fit inside one another and which offer, in their totality, the appearance of a closed system.' This is what gives the poem 'the value of an absolute object.' And yet there is another way of looking at it 'whereby the poem takes on the appearance of an open system in dynamic progression from beginning to end.'

The progress from the structuralism of Saussure is very considerable. The extension of these principles to other kinds of texts, to nonpoetic texts, is also immanent in this analysis. Referring to his own earlier use of Jakobson's work in his analysis of myth (1963), Lévi-Strauss speaks of the opposition that he set up between poetry and myth. He argues that the difference between poetry and myth is that the poetic text contains the system of variables which are the multiple levels of the paradigmatic projected into the syntagm, while the mythic text lacks this principle of equivalence. It can be interpreted only on the semantic level, and the system of variables which constitute it can only be established outside the text, in the multiplicity of versions of the same myth. What is important however is that the system is to be found in texts, that is, in instances of parole, and that it is constituted by patterns of repetition. There is a version of the ordinary/poetic language binarism at work in the qualitative difference that is perceived to distinguish the language of poetry and myth, but even that is questioned when Lévi-Strauss acknowledges that the methods of analysis of poetry and myth 'in the final analysis, can be substituted for one another' (1963: 373). In 1963 he had argued that:

> Among all social phenomena language alone has thus far been studied in a manner which permits it to serve as the object of truly scientific analysis, allowing us to understand its formative process and to predict its mode of change. This results from modern researches into the problems of phonemics . . . The question which now arises is this: is it possible to effect a similar reduction in the analysis of other forms of social phenomena?

This was the question that 'The Structural Analysis of Myth' set out to answer, and answered in the affirmative:

> Myth is language . . . myth like the rest of language is made up of constituent units . . . The true constituent units of myth are not the isolated relations but *bundles*

> *of such relations*, and it is only as bundles that these relations can be put to use and combined so as to produce meaning.
>
> (Lévi-Strauss 1963: 58–59, 210–11)

The analysis showed that the syntagm of any single version of a myth was a selection of choices from the bundles of paradigmatic relations that constituted the system of that myth as a whole in the form of its many different textual realizations.

These poststructuralist moments in classic structuralist texts had a number of consequences. They finally put paid to the old distinction between ordinary and poetic language, as structuralist semioticians extended the use of the structuralist methodology beyond the analysis of the literary to the analysis of cultural texts of all kinds, in not only verbal media, and took up the agendas of the Bakthin and Prague Schools to explore the relations of the literary as semiotic system to other semiotic systems and institutional practices. This agenda became a particularly urgent one as poststructuralist theory—this time in the form of Foucault's work on discourse, power, subjectivity, and institutions—set out to explore some of the same questions from a perspective that polemically rejected linguistics, structuralism, and semiotics, but remained in many ways structuralist–functionalist and constructivist in its major premises.

Another major consequence was the result of the correlation in Lévi-Strauss's (1963) work of the poetic, the mythic, and the scientific. This correlation, summarized in his statement that 'logic in mythical thought is as rigorous as that of modern science' (1963: 230) had important ramifications in the deconstruction of a number of structuralist binarisms. The primitive/cultured opposition is the first to be at risk, but the prose/poetry, fact/fiction oppositions cannot be far behind in this context. Thus, paradoxically, while structuralist/semiotic research, following these early leads in Jakobson, Lévi-Strauss, and elsewhere, took up the challenge of studying the literary as social institution in its relations of specificity and difference to other social institutions such as the law, religion, science, economics, specifying the register and genre of texts produced in and through these institutional practices, the very same classic structuralist texts also contributed to the poststructuralist deconstruction of the boundaries and framing procedures that would be so established.

The 'poststructuralist' effort, which is never entirely separate from the semiotics that is contemporary with it in the 1960s and 1970s, set about establishing the essentially fictional, metaphoric, and constructed nature of all language and of all texts and genres. It was not concerned, as Lévi-Strauss was, with demonstrating the scientific nature of myth and poetry, but rather the poetic and mythical nature of science. The links had been made, and they were not insignificant in the later poststructuralist and feminist work on the literary (narrative and metaphoric) qualities of all texts.

Despite all these anticipations of later literary structuralism and semiotics, the structuralist work of Jakobson and Lévi-Strauss remained an intrinsic structuralism, which did not theorize the reading or writing subject, and which did not theorize the relations of texts to their contexts, nor move beyond the denotative level of linguistic analysis. The function of connotative semiotics in making sense of myth or poetry as explored later by Barthes in *S/Z*, for example, was not even considered. Nor was what Barthes would later call the *myth* of the denotative level itself ever raised in this context: 'denotation is not the first meaning, but pretends to be so ... the superior myth by which the text pretends to return to the nature of language, to language as nature' (1974: 9). The reader was assumed to know what Lévi-Strauss and Jakobson knew: structuralist facts were transparent and the same for everyone. Lévi-Strauss could confidently say: 'We shall use the Oedipus myth, which is well known to everyone' (1963: 213). And his readings of the bundles of relations he finds in the system of that myth, presented as if they were intrinsic to the text and the system, are of course connotative readings, structured by binarisms, and produced in relation to cultural and hermeneutic codes that only a reader constructed and positioned as a highly trained and educated structural anthropologist would produce.

3.5 Metaphor and Metonymy

Jakobson linked the principles of similarity and parallelism that constituted the code or the paradigm, and metaphor, which always involves saying one thing in terms of another. These similarity relations were particularly in evidence in the case of the metalinguistic function and its focus on the code through paraphrase, and in the poetic function with its focus on the message. On the other hand, he connected the constitutive role of difference in the syntagm, its patterns of contiguity which always involved relations of parts to wholes in the context of the linearity of the signifier, to metonymy.

As so often with Jakobson, the insights come from phonology. Speaking of the exchange between the cat and Alice in Lewis Carroll's *Alice in Wonderland*: '"Did you say *pig* or *fig*?" said the Cat. "I said *pig*," replied Alice'—he points out that in her response Alice makes a choice between 'the distinctive feature stop versus continuant,' and combines this choice with certain other features combined into a bundle of distinctive features, called the phoneme, in this case the phoneme /p/. This is then followed by the phonemes /i/ and /g/, themselves bundles of distinctive features. 'Hence the concurrence of simultaneous entities and the concatenation of successive entities are the two ways in which we speakers combine linguistic constituents' (Jakobson 1957b: 242). Here in fact is what

he would define as the poetic function established as a constitutive feature of all language.

He speaks (Jakobson 1957b: 243) in the same context of the 'ascending scale of freedom' with which the speaker operates as he moves from the phonemic level, where choices are fully established by the code, to the levels of word, sentence, or utterance where 'the freedom of any individual speaker to create novel utterances increases substantially.' Every sign is made up however of constituent signs and occurs in combination with other signs. This means that every linguistic unit is simultaneously a context for simpler units and has its own context in a more complex unit. 'Combination and contexture are two faces of the same operation.' This leads him to a critique of Saussure's concepts of the operation of syntagm and paradigm, as mutually exclusive, and of the linearity of the sign. He argues that Saussure recognized only the temporal sequence, and not the two varieties of concatenation and concurrence in the linguistic signifier: he 'succumbed to the traditional belief in the linear character of language "*qui exclut la possibilité de prononcer deux éléments à la fois*".' According to Jakobson, the constituents of a context are in a state of contiguity (metonymy), while the elements of a substitution set are linked by various degrees of similarity (metaphor). It is these two operations which provide every linguistic sign with two interpretants (he quotes Peirce's use of this term), one which links the sign internally to the code and the other which links it externally to the context. Every sign has a meaning that derives from the code, and meanings derived from its contextual relations with other signs in a sequence. It is the first that for Jakobson ensures the transmission of the message between addresser and addressee.

The context he was talking about was *internal* to the linguistic system. Halliday has used the same insights to explore the internal semiotics of texts, the metonymic and metaphoric relations between clause and text grammars (1980), and his concept of grammatical metaphor also works to explore metaphoric and metonymic relations internal to the linguistic system (1985: ch. 10). His textual function of language however and his theory of the relations between texts and the semiotic constructs that are their contexts (a realizational relation) begins to provide a linguistic account of similar relations that are *external* to the system. Jakobson's important insights about the simultaneity of metaphor and metonymy to every linguistic sign could easily have been extended to describe the metonymic and metaphoric relations with contexts external to the text that are the stuff of Hjelmslev's connotative semiotics, and at issue in Lévi-Strauss's reading of the Oedipus myth. Nevertheless, once it was recognized that the paradigmatic was always constitutive of the syntagmatic, of textuality, as discussed above, the recognition of the essential metaphorcity of all language was an inevitable consequence of Jakobson's position. This helped to break down the dichotomy Saussure's work had set up, and provided one of those crucial insights that would go on taking effect as the critical perspectives of poststructuralist theory developed to thinking about all texts and genres as essentially fictional in the sense of being always metaphors.

Jakobson made it clear that the denotative level of meaning, which was theorized as intrinsic to the linguistic system, actually operated connotatively, as Barthes argued, on the basis of metaphor (similarity and paraphrase relations), metonymy (part/whole relations), and indexicality (pointing relations involving the overlap of code and message and again part/whole relations).

It was not so clear what would make connotative semiotics (which would relate the patterns in a text by way of the subjectivity of its readers, to contexts extrinsic to it) any different. Such relations involve paradigmatic relations of similarity which enable a reader to 'gloss' metalinguistically the fact that this word or larger chunk of text is similar to that one, to read this as a metaphor for that. They involve metonymy, relations of contiguity with contexts that are recognized as part/whole relations: this chunk of text is part of that whole context and can be made sense of accordingly. And they involve indexicality. These ideas were the basis for Barthes' later turning to this kind of semiotic, instead of the intrinsically linguistic, to decode or 'read' *Sarrasine*. The concepts are already theorized but never realized in Jakobson or in the structuralist textual work of Halliday. Missing from both is the role of the reader (Eco 1981b).

These were the connections that Eco made when he used metaphor as an illustration of the process of unlimited semiosis. Metaphor as resemblance is only definable through the metonymic chains of association in which it is imbedded. These chains of association are, in effect, an infinite chain of interpretants, a network of culturally agreed metonymies, contiguities between signifiers and signifieds, in the code, in the co-text, and in the referent. The entire 'global semantic space,' to use Eco's formulation, becomes a network of metaphors built on contiguity.

Here, in essence, are the concepts that would lead to the radical unsettling of the order of things in literary structuralism and semiotics referred to in the previous section. This is the moment when literary theories, theories of what it is to be literature, are suddenly recontextualized and used as technologies for rewriting the rules of what it is to be not literature. What was ordinary or practical language in formalist, Prague School, and structuralist work suddenly becomes the focus of a new kind of literary activity. If everything is metaphor, or narrative, or myth, if everything is discursively constructed, if genres can be rewritten, then there has been a very considerable deconstruction of the fact/fiction, primitive/cultured, feminine/masculine, rational/irrational dichotomies. Contemporary French culture is rewritten as myth (Barthes 1983). Eco defines semiosis as everything that can be used to tell a lie, and rewrites presidential speeches as narrative strategies of lying (Eco 1985); history and anthropology are rewritten as literature, fiction (White 1978; Clifford and Marcus 1986). Ethnography is relocated with 'us' not 'them' (Pratt 1986). The categories that emerge from all this structuralist, semiotic, and poststructuralist literary activity are reappropriated from poststructuralism as a metalanguage for exploring the social semiotics of the metaphors and metonymies of text/reader/context interactions (Kress and Threadgold 1988) and this social semiotic and poststructuralist work negotiates and makes use of strategies of analysis that have a long and complex archaeology in structuralist texts which it is supposed to have moved beyond, and which continue to coexist alongside it in discontinuous and overlapping series.

Poststructuralism, feminism, deconstruction, literary structuralism, and semiotics continue to coexist as never quite separable phenomena, characterized by discontinuities and incompatibilities that belie the usual stories of measured and logical evolution from literary structuralism and semiotics to its feminist, psychoanalytic, Foucauldian, and deconstructive 'posts.' That heterogeneity and difference are what characterize literary structuralism and semiotics today.

Bibliography

Aers D, Hodge B, Kress G 1981 *Literature, Language and Society in England 1580–1680*. Gill and Macmillan, Dublin

Bakhtin M M, Holquist M (eds.) 1981 (trans. Emerson C, Holquist M) *The Dialogic Imagination*. University of Texas Press, Austin, TX

Bakhtin M M, Emerson C (eds., trans.) 1984 *Problems of Dostoevsky's Poetics*. Manchester University Press, Manchester

Bakhtin M M, Emerson C, Holquist M (eds.) 1986 The problem of speech genres: The problem of the text. In: (trans. McGee V) *Speech Genres and Other Late Essays*. University of Texas Press, Austin, TX

Barthes R 1967a (trans. Lavers A, Smith C) *Writing Degree Zero*. Hill and Wang, New York

Barthes R 1967b (trans. Lavers A, Smith C) *Elements of Semiology*. Hill and Wang, New York

Barthes R 1974 (trans. Miller R) *S/Z*. Hill and Wang, New York

Barthes R 1975 (trans. Miller R) *The Pleasure of the Text*. Hill and Wang, New York

Barthes R 1983 Myth today. In: (trans. Lavers A) *Mythologies*. Jonathan Cape, London

Benveniste E 1986 The semiology of language. In: Innis R E (ed.) *Semiotics: An Introductory Reader*. Hutchinson, London

Birch D, O'Toole M (eds.) 1988 *Functions of Style*. Pinter, London

Bouissac P 1981 Figurative versus objective semiotics: An epistemological crossroads. In: Deely J N, Lenhart M D (eds.) *Semiotics 1981*. Plenum Press, New York

Carter R (ed.) 1982 *Language and Literature: An Introductory Reader in Stylistics*. Allen and Unwin, London

Clifford J, Marcus G E (eds.) 1986 *Writing Culture: The Poetics and Politics of Ethnography*. University of California Press, Berkeley, CA

Culler J 1975 *Structuralist Poetics: Structuralism, Linguistics and the Study of Literature*. Routledge and Kegan Paul, London

Derrida J 1976 (trans. Spivak G) Linguistics and grammatology. In: *Of Grammatology*. Johns Hopkins University Press, Baltimore, MD

Eco U 1977 *A Theory of Semiotics*. Macmillan, London

Eco U 1981a Peirce and the semiotic foundations of openness: Signs as texts and texts as signs. In: Eco U 1981b

Eco U 1981b *The Role of the Reader: Explorations in the Semiotics of Texts*. Hutchinson, London

Eco U 1985 Strategies of Lying. In: Blonsky M (ed.) *On Signs*. Basil Blackwell, Oxford

Foucault M 1972 (trans. Smith A S) *The Archaeology of Knowledge*. Tavistock, London

Foucault M 1974 *The Order of Things: An Archaeology of the Human Sciences*. Tavistock, London

Foucault M 1984 (trans. Hurley R) *The History of Sexuality. Vol. 1: An Introduction*. Penguin, London

Fowler R 1981 *Literature as Social Discourse: The Practice of Linguistic Criticism*. Batsford Academic, London

Fowler R 1986 *Linguistic Criticism*. Oxford University Press, Oxford

Fowler R, Hodge R, Kress G, Trew T 1979 *Language and Control*. Routledge and Kegan Paul, London

Greimas A J 1987 (trans. Perron P J, Collins F H) *On Meaning: Selected Writings in Semiotic Theory*. Pinter, London

Grosz E A, de Lepervanche M 1988 Feminism and science. In: Caine B, Grosz E A, de Lepervanche M (eds.) *Crossing Boundaries: Feminisms and the Critique of Knowledges*, Allen and Unwin, Sydney

Halliday M A K 1978 *Language as Social Semiotic: The Social Interpretation of Language and Meaning*. Edward Arnold, London

Halliday M A K 1980 Text semantics and clause grammar: Some patterns of realization. In: Copeland J E, Davis P W (eds.) *The Seventh LACUS Forum*. Hornbeam Press, Columbia

Halliday M A K 1985 *An Introduction to Functional Grammar*. Edward Arnold, London

Hasan R 1985 *Linguistics, Language and Verbal Art*. Deakin University Press, Geelong, Victoria

Hjelmslev L 1961 (trans. Whitfield F J) *Prolegomena to a Theory of Language*, rev. edn. University of Wisconsin Press, Madison, WI

Irigaray L 1985 (trans. Gill G C) *Speculum of the Other Woman*. Cornell University Press, Ithaca, New York

Jakobson R 1935 The dominant. In: Jakobson R 1981

Jakobson R 1957a Shifters, verbal categories and the Russian verb. In: Jakobson R 1971

Jakobson R 1957b Two aspects of language and two types of aphasic disturbances. In: Jakobson R 1971

Jakobson R 1960 Linguistics and poetics. In: Jakobson R 1981

Jakobson R 1971 *Selected Writings. Vol. II: Word and Language*. Mouton, The Hague

Jakobson R 1981 *Selected Writings. Vol. III: Poetry of Grammar and Grammar of Poetry*. Mouton, The Hague

Jakobson R, Lévi-Strauss C 1962 'Les Chats' de Charles Baudelaire. In: Jakobson R 1981

Jakobson R, Bogatyrev P 1978 On the boundary between studies of folklore and literature. In: Matejka L, Pomorska K (eds.) *Readings in Russian Poetics*. MIT Press, Cambridge, MA

Jakobson R, Jones L G 1981 Shakespeare's verbal art in 'Th'Expense of Spirit'. In: Jakobson R 1981

Kress G, Hodge R 1979 *Language as Ideology*. Routledge and Kegan Paul, London

Kress G, Threadgold T 1988 Toward a social theory of genre. *Southern Review (Adelaide)* 21(3): 215–43

Kristeva J 1969 Word, dialogue and novel. In: Kristeva J 1980

Kristeva J 1980 *Desire in Language: A Semiotic Approach to Literature and Art*. Columbia University Press, New York

Kristeva J 1984 (trans. Waller M) *Revolution in Poetic Language*. Columbia University Press, New York

Lévi-Strauss C 1963 The structural study of myth. In: *Structural Anthropology*. Basic Books, New York

Lotman Y 1977 (trans. Vroon R, Vroon G) *The Structure of the Artistic Text*. University of Michigan, Ann Arbor, MI

Lyotard J F 1984 (trans. Bennington G, Massumi B) *The Postmodern Condition: A Report on Knowledge*. Manchester University Press, Manchester

Martin J R 1991 Intrinsic functionality: Implications for contextual theory. *Social Semiotics* 1: 99–162

Matejka L, Pomorska K (eds.) 1971 *Readings in Russian Poetics: Formalist and Structuralist Views*. MIT Press, Cambridge, MA

Matejka L, Titunik I R (eds.) 1976 *Semiotics of Art: Prague School Contributions*. MIT Press, Cambridge, MA

Medvedev P N 1978 (trans. Bakhtin M M, Wehrle A J) *The Formal Method in Literary Scholarship: A Critical Introduction to Sociological Poetics*. The Johns Hopkins University Press, Baltimore, MD

Mukařovský J 1977 (trans. Burbank J, Steiner P) *The Word and Verbal Art: Selected Essays*. Yale University Press, New Haven, CN

O'Toole L M, Shukman A (eds.) 1975–83 *Russian Poetics in Translation*. University of Essex, Colchester

Peirce C S 1986 Logic as semiotic: The theory of signs. In: Innis R E (ed.) *Semiotics: An Introductory Reader*. Hutchinson, London

Perron P, Collins F (eds.) 1989 *Paris School Semiotics. Vol. I: Theory; Practice*. John Benjamins, Amsterdam

Pratt M L 1986 Fieldwork in common places. In: Clifford J, Marcus G E (eds.) *Writing Culture*. University of California Press, Berkeley, CA

Propp V 1958 (trans. Scott L) *Morphology of the Folktale*. Indiana University Research Centre in Anthropology, Bloomington, IA

Richards I A 1929 *Practical Criticism: A Study of Literary Judgement*. Kegan Paul, Trench, Trubner, London

Sebeok T A 1979 *The Sign and its Masters*. University of Texas Press, Austin, TX

Saussure F de 1960 (trans. Baskin W) *Course in General Linguistics*. Peter Owen, London

Steiner P 1984 *Russian Formalism: A Metapoetics*. Cornell University Press, Ithaca, NY

Threadgold T 1997 *Feminist Poetics: Poiesis, Performance, Histories*. Routledge, London

Todorov T 1984 (trans. Godzich V) *Mikhail Bakhtin: The Dialogic Principle*. Manchester University Press, Manchester

Voloshinov V N 1973 (trans. Bakhtin M M, Matejka L, Titunik I R) *Marxism and the Philosophy of Language*. Seminar Press, New York

White H 1978 The historical text as literary artefact. In: *Tropics of Discourse: Essays in Cultural Criticism*, The Johns Hopkins University Press, Baltimore, MD

Meaning: Philosophical Theories

T. R. Baldwin

Philosophical reflection on meaning is as old as philosophy. Plato, confronted by the sophists, found that he needed to theorize about language and its meaning in order to escape from his opponents' sophistry (cf. *Euthydemus, Sophist*); and he went on to open the debate concerning the extent to which language is conventional (cf. *Cratylus*). Aristotle took matters much further: in *De Interpretatione*, he introduced a subject–predicate analysis of sentences, and in his logical writings this analysis is developed into a theory about the semantic roles of the terms that occur in sentences. The resulting theory provided the framework for most subsequent writing on the subject at least until the end of the medieval period. This included a great deal of sophisticated work on logic and the semantic roles (*suppositio, appellatio*) of terms. Many of the issues raised in these early investigations have remained in contention, but the focus for this article will be the subtle and varied developments in theories of meaning in postmedieval philosophy.

1. Ideas and Meanings

A central issue in philosophical debates about meaning concerns the relationship between semantics and psychology. One can obtain a route into these debates by pursuing the fate of the characteristic thesis of early modern philosophy–that, as Locke put it, 'Words in their primary or immediate Signification, stand for nothing, but the *Ideas* in the Mind of him that uses them' (Locke 1698: 3.2.2). The presumption here was that the relationship between ideas and the world is straightforward, at least in the case of certain simple ideas; and that the relationship between language and the world should be explicated in terms of the former relationship. Thus, on this view, semantics is reduced to psychology.

One objection, stressed by Hegel, concentrates on the role of language in providing the essential means for the articulation of complex thoughts; Hegel had poetry primarily in mind, but one can equally think of scientific speculation. Since these thoughts are dependent upon language, it is argued, the reduction of semantics to psychology cannot be carried out. But this objection is not decisive: even Locke held that certain complex ideas were only held together by the common use of language. He could allow this role to language because of his distinction between simple and complex ideas, and this exemplifies the route standardly employed in responding to the objection: upholders of a psychologistic position argue that one can have simple thoughts without language, and that a language introduced on their basis then provides the means for the more complex thoughts which are language-dependent.

A different objection concerns the anxiety that, if meanings are merely 'ideas in the mind of him that uses them,' then they are subjective and perhaps idiosyncratic; the very idea of communication becomes problematic. Again, Locke anticipated this objection; but here his response is problematic. He suggests that as long as people agree in paradigmatic situations about the application of names for simple ideas, communication can proceed successfully even if individuals' ideas are in fact quite different. This only provides a general solution to the problem if the identity of all ideas is fixed via that of the simple ones; Locke took this view, though it commits him to a deeply implausible empiricist reductionism. But what is more worrying is that if he allows that communication can succeed despite differences in the ideas signified for speakers by words, it seems to follow that the theory of ideas does not have a central role in the theory of communication.

Locke's difficulty here is connected with a general difficulty that his approach faces, namely that of clarifying what a simple idea is an idea of. Locke suggests that simple ideas are abstracted from sense-experiences in a way which implies that they have qualitative features which makes their content immediately available to introspection. But this conception of ideas as, in effect, mental images is untenable. Complex thoughts are certainly not just complicated images; indeed, the details of imagery are usually irrelevant to a thought's identity. Furthermore, as Berkeley observed, one cannot abstract from one's perceptions of triangles a single image which will fit all triangles. Finally, as Wittgenstein showed (Wittgenstein 1934), tempting though it is to say that what makes an image an image of red is that it is itself red, in truth the subjectively manifest qualities of an image do not determine which objective qualities it is an image of. Given different contexts or causal histories, images with the same subjective qualities can be images of different things.

It is clear from all this that improved versions of the psychologistic thesis will not rely on introspective psychology and will need to provide an account of communication which explains more clearly than Locke does why meaning is fundamentally psychological. However, before looking at proposals to this effect, alternative approaches to the concept of meaning need to be considered.

2. Gottlob Frege

The characteristic feature of Frege's approach is his concept of 'sense' (*Sinn*). He distinguished the sense of an expression from its 'reference' (*Bedeutung*), the object or property which it would normally be taken to stand for, in order to account for differences of meaning among expressions with the same reference—for example, different names of the same planet (Frege 1892). Since Frege also held, most emphatically, that senses are not in any way psychological, he concluded that senses belong to an abstract, but objective, 'third realm' (Frege 1918): they are depsychologized ideas and thoughts, abstract representations whose association with a linguistic expression determines that expression's reference. Among senses, the senses of sentences are fundamental; words have sense only insofar as they contribute to the sense of sentences in which they occur. This thesis of Frege's contrasts with the priority assigned by Locke to names of simple ideas and with the autonomous significance of terms within Aristotelian semantics. Yet Frege also recognized that people understand a sentence by understanding its constituent phrases—this is his *compositionality* thesis. This does not conflict with the priority of sentence meaning; for in understanding a phrase, one grasps in abstraction its contribution to the sense of sentences in which it occurs.

Frege's sense/reference distinction, his compositionality thesis, and his emphasis on the semantic priority of sentences are fundamental advances in our understanding of meaning. But many philosophers disliked the 'Platonism' of his abstract conception of sense. In some cases, the proposed cure was worse than the disease. Russell, who was as hostile to psychologism as Frege, rejected Frege's sense/reference

distinction and tried to base a conception of meaning upon reference to the objects of immediate experience. Quite apart from the difficulties in explaining how shared meaning is possible if meaning is founded only upon reference to objects of immediate experience, Russell discovered that without a sense/reference distinction he could not give a satisfactory account of the possibility of meaningful, but false, sentences. What was needed was not a repudiation of Frege's categories, but a way of fitting them into a broader framework that harmonized with a tenable philosophy of mind. Wittgenstein seemed to offer a way forward here: rejecting as illusory the Fregean thesis that 'what must be added to the dead signs in order to make a live proposition is something immaterial,' he proposed that 'if we had to name anything which is the life of the sign, we should have to say that it was its *use*' (Wittgenstein 1934: 4).

3. Meaning and Use

The question is then how the injunction to ground an account of the meaning of language on its use is to be developed. Empiricists interpreted it in the light of their emphasis on ostensive definitions. As mentioned in connection with Locke, this approach provides a way in which attributions of meaning can be rendered public, by defining meanings in terms of the types of evidence which would verify or falsify sentences. Yet this seems to imply that the meaning of all sentences, however theoretical, should be definable in terms of observable evidence alone; and though some logical positivists embraced this conclusion, its reductionist conclusions were recognized as unacceptable—for example, that the meaning of sentences concerning the past or the future should be given in terms of present evidence for their truth or falsehood.

This, however, is not the end for empiricist conceptions of meaning. Quine argued that reductionist implications can be avoided by taking account of the holistic structure of evidence (the 'Duhem–Quine thesis') and incorporating this into a holistic conception of meaning (Quine 1960). Quine's position rests on an empiricist, indeed behaviorist, insistence that attributions of meaning be grounded on the dispositions of speakers to assent or dissent to stimuli; but although he allows that the meaning of 'observation-sentences' can be thus defined, he denies that this is generally the case, since for most sentences, there is no determinate package of stimuli that determines assent or dissent. The dispositions of speakers depend upon their other beliefs, and one can indefinitely permute attributions of meaning and ascriptions of belief while remaining faithful to all the behavioral evidence. However Quine does not then hold that it makes no sense to attribute meaning to individual sentences (other than observation sentences); his position is articulated through the fiction of the radical translator, the ideal anthropologist who aims to translate native talk solely on the basis of his observations of native assent and dissent to stimuli. Quine's claim is that the behavioral evidence, however extended, underdetermines the translation of individual sentences, and, since this evidence is all there is to attributions of meaning, their translation is radically indeterminate. Nonetheless, relative to one of the empirically acceptable schemes of translation of the native language, translation of single sentences can be achieved.

Quine's conclusion seems no less problematic than the reductionist one that he sought to avoid. For the indeterminacy thesis cannot be restricted to alien languages: it must begin at home, if at all. Yet, one cannot easily acknowledge that the meanings of one's own utterances, including those in which the indeterminacy thesis itself is formulated, are radically indeterminate. To avoid this conclusion, Dummett has argued that Quine's semantic holism should be rejected in favor of a 'molecular' conception of meaning according to which meaning is given by a determinate specification of the kinds of evidence relevant to the assertion or denial of sentences of various types. This position implies that one can give a nonholistic account of the evidence which warrants the assertion of sentences containing theoretical terms; not surprisingly, this denial of the Duhem–Quine thesis is much contested. But a more pressing question is whether Dummett avoids the reductionism that Quine's holism enables him to escape.

Dummett's answer, which he connects with Wittgenstein's thesis that meaning is use, is that the link between meaning and evidence concerns the 'assertibility-conditions' of sentences rather than their truth-conditions (Dummett 1978). One side of this is straightforward: assuming that there is an intrinsic link between meaning and truth-conditions (a point which is revisited below), the characterization of the existence of some type of evidence as the truth-condition of a sentence implies that the sentence merely means that there is evidence of that kind. What is less clear is how it helps to describe the evidence as the sentence's assertibility-condition. The explanation suggested by Dummett's self-description as 'anti-realist' is that meaning is fundamentally an epistemic matter, so that an account of the meaning of a sentence is based upon an account of the types of evidence which warrant its assertion or denial. As long as it is then held that such an account is not an account of its truth-condition, the reductionist conclusion is avoided. But there still remains the question of how its truth-condition is determined. One alternative (advocated more clearly by Peacocke (1986) than by Dummett himself) is that these types of evidence suffice to identify a distinct possible state of affairs as the sentence's truth-condition. Another, more radical, alternative is just to deny that an account of meaning should yield an account of truth-conditions. On this

view meaning, as traditionally conceived, is a 'realist' illusion.

This radical alternative is one which Saul Kripke has suggested should be embraced anyway in the light of Wittgenstein's 'rule-following' argument (Kripke 1982). As reconstructed by Kripke, this argument starts from the thesis that there is nothing in a speaker's use of language, in either past practice or linguistic dispositions, which determines how words used by that speaker should be applied to future cases: even if there is a natural rule of projection ('green' has previously been applied only to green things, so on the next occasion it will be correct to describe something as 'green' just in case it is green), there is nothing in principle to rule out a deviant rule ('green' has previously been applied only to green things, but on the next occasion it will be correct to describe a thing as 'green' just in case it is blue). Yet, the argument continues, the traditional concept of meaning implies that the assignment to a sentence (e.g., 'grass is green') of a definite meaning (that grass is green) prescribes in advance under what conditions the sentence is true (namely, when grass is green). Hence, Kripke concludes, since this traditional concept cannot be grounded in the use of language by speakers, it should be rejected as illusory, and instead one should embrace the antirealist account which limits itself to an external description of the practices of speakers, including their practices of correcting each other.

It will be obvious that this 'skeptical' conclusion is even more paradoxical than that of Quine, which it extends. In Wittgenstein's writings, the rule-following considerations are associated with his criticisms of any Lockean approach which attempts to ground meaning on introspective psychology; hence Wittgenstein emphasizes the importance of 'blind' rule-following, assertion unguided by introspective directions (Wittgenstein 1953). One can accept this, but question Kripke's extension of the argument in one of two ways, depending on one's attitude to the relation between psychology and semantics. Those who hold that semantic facts are irreducible to psychological ones welcome Kripke's negative argument, but hold that it does not follow that meaning is an abstract illusion; instead, they hold, people's lives—their reasonings and actions—are permeated by an involvement with meanings which does not need to be grounded in anything else. By contrast, those who accept the reducibility of semantics to psychology hold that once a description of the use of language includes both its social context and the underlying causal facts concerning human psychology, it is possible to understand how meaning does not transcend physical fact.

4. Truth-conditions and Meaning

Donald Davidson's position exemplifies the first alternative (Davidson 1984). Like Quine and Dummett,

Davidson starts from an empiricist constraint, that all facts about meaning must be manifest somehow in the use of language, and he puts this constraint to work in the importance which he assigns to the fiction of radical interpretation—his variant of Quine's fiction of radical translation. The shift from 'translation' to 'interpretation' represents Davidson's rejection of Quine's behaviorist conception of meaning in favor of an approach based upon an account of the truth-conditions of sentences.

It seems at first that the concept of truth-conditions is too weak to capture that of meaning, since it is entirely extensional (so that all true sentences have the same truth-conditions). But Davidson's insight was to propose that an account of the meaning of a sentence is provided by that account of its truth-conditions which is generated by a theory which (a) assigns correct truth-conditions to the sentences of the speaker's language on the basis of assignments of contributory roles to the phrases of the language and to their manners of combination (the *holistic* condition) and (b) yields an interpretation of the language which can be integrated into a satisfactory understanding of the linguistic and other acts of the speakers (the *empirical* condition). So, Davidson does not simply identify meaning with truth-conditions; rather, for him, the meaning of a sentence is that account of its truth-conditions which explains its role within the language and its use by speakers.

Davidson's approach implies that a radical interpreter is able to assign truth-conditions to native sentences without a prior understanding of them. He maintains that the interpreter can legitimately achieve this by observing the distinctive conditions under which the natives hold various sentences to be true, and then assuming that these conditions are, for the most part, truth-conditions for these sentences. This assumption of truth for the most part (the *principle of charity*) is justified by Davidson by means of an externalist theory of psychological content, that, by and large, beliefs are about their external causes. But Davidson stresses that this assumption of truth brings with it an assumption of widespread agreement; for, of course, all interpreters take their own beliefs to be true. Thus, for Davidson, the radical interpreter initially projects onto the natives the interpreter's own beliefs and preferences in assigning truth-conditions to native utterances and uses these as the defeasible basis for a rational understanding of action, including speech acts. This presumption of agreement is a key component of Davidson's nonreductive approach; one can interpret others on the basis of their observed behavior only because one brings to that interpretation one's own understanding of the world and oneself.

Critics have urged that this presumption is both parochial and insecure. It is parochial because it implies that one's own beliefs and preferences set the limits of intelligibility. It is insecure since Davidson's own theory threatens self-understanding. The threat arises from the possibility of replicating Quine's indeterminacy thesis within Davidson's conception of radical interpretation: as Davidson has sometimes seemed ready to acknowledge, his conception does not incorporate any guarantee that a unique interpretation will emerge. But if more than one interpretation is held to be possible, and one then recognizes that it applies to oneself, it threatens one's own self-understanding and equally the significance of the procedures of radical interpretation.

5. Psychology and Meaning

These difficulties in Davidson's position make it all the more important to consider the alternative which reduces semantics to psychology. This has two parts: an account of meaning in terms of psychological and social facts (beliefs, intentions, and conventions), and an account of these facts which shows that they are not dependent upon semantic facts. The first part draws on the work of H. P. Grice and David Lewis; the second part looks to cognitive science. Grice proposed the following account of *speaker-meaning* (Grice 1957): a speaker S means that p by a declarative utterance of x to an audience A if and only if (a) S intends that A should come to believe that p; (b) S intends that A should recognize that S uttered x with intention (a); and (c) S intends that this recognition (b) should be among A's reasons for coming to believe that p. Subsequent discussion showed that a further condition is required: (d) S does not have any further intentions in uttering x of which A is unaware. Although further refinements have been proposed, there is a broad consensus that conditions (a–d) are at least sufficient for speaker-meaning. But two issues now arise: what is required in supposing that conditions (a–d) are satisfied; and how one is to move on from an account of speaker-meaning to an account of the meaning of sentences. One can try to solve the first problem for a few cases by thinking of S making appropriate iconic gestures and noises; but this is clearly very limited and offers no route to a solution of the second problem. Of course, if one could already rely on a solution to the second problem, then that would bring a solution to the first one; but that would subvert the strategy of basing an account of sentence-meaning upon that of speaker-meaning.

Lewis's account of conventions offers a way forward here (Lewis 1969). Lewis argued on general grounds that conventions, such as driving on the left, are regularities which coordinate the behavior of agents with interests which will be satisfied if and only if almost everyone abides by the same regularity; the need for a convention arises where it is not obvious in advance which regularity others will adhere to. Hence, Lewis claimed, a convention exists where there is a regularity for which it is common knowledge that everyone else's conformity gives each person a good reason for conforming themselves. It turns out to follow from this that, where a system of signals is employed as a conventional means of coordinating signals and beliefs, those who produce the signals satisfy Grice's conditions for speaker-meaning; so the thesis that sentence *s* means that *p* just where there is a convention that *s* is used to signal that *p* is a natural development of Grice's proposal. It does not follow from this, however, that human language is a system of Lewis-type conventions; and, indeed, the thesis that it is has been criticized by Davidson on the grounds that human uses of language are too varied and trivial to meet Lewis's requirements. But Lewis allows that basic communicative conventions can be qualified by higher-order conventions that permit violations of the original convention, so Davidson's point is not fatal. Yet, more needs to be said, in response to the above question of what is required in supposing that conditions (a–d) are satisfied, as to how a radical interpreter could verify that native linguistic behavior is conventional. Nonetheless, it does not seem unreasonable to suppose that an infant learning a language is, among other things, being inducted into a system of communicative conventions.

The Grice–Lewis account of meaning will only deliver a reduction of semantics if it is supplemented by an account of the nature of psychological states (such as the Gricean conditions (a–d)) which does not draw on semantic facts. There are two approaches to this: one aims to articulate and justify a physicalist theory which can be applied directly to all relevant psychological states; the other allows that sophisticated beliefs and intentions presuppose semantic facts, but aims to provide a noncircular developmental account (both for the species and the individual) based on a physicalist account of simple beliefs and intentions. Even this latter enterprise is contentious, although, unreflectively, people seem content to ascribe quite complex beliefs and intentions to higher mammals without reference to language. But issues here remain cloudy because of difficulties in finding satisfactory accounts of the content of even simple psychological states. Most theorists favor an approach which takes account both of the causation

and of the functional role of such states, and many will add that mental representation requires a 'language of thought'—a system of physical structures in the subject which somehow matches the content of the subject's thoughts (Fodor 1987). However, it is not yet possible to present any consensus on these issues, and to that extent philosophical debates concerning meaning remain inconclusive. Nonetheless, the importance of the debate shows that an adequate understanding of the concept of meaning is of absolutely fundamental importance not only for theorizing about language but also for an understanding of human beings and their place in nature.

See also: Convention; Holism; Indeterminacy of Translation; Radical Interpretation.

Bibliography

Bennett J 1976 *Linguistic Behaviour*. Cambridge University Press, Cambridge
Blackburn S W 1984 *Spreading the Word: Groundings in the Philosophy of Language*. Clarendon Press, Oxford
Davidson D 1984 *Inquiries into Truth and Interpretation*. Oxford University Press, Oxford
Dummett M A E 1978 *Truth and Other Enigmas*. Duckworth, London
Fodor J 1987 *Psychosemantics*. MIT Press, Cambridge, MA
Frege G 1892 On sense and reference. In: Geach P, Black M (transl.) 1970 *Translations from the Philosophical Writings of Gottlob Frege*. Basil Blackwell, Oxford
Frege G 1918 The thought: A logical inquiry. In: Strawson P (ed.) 1967 *Philosophical Logic*. Oxford University Press, Oxford
Grice H P 1957 Meaning. *Philosophical Review* **66**: 377–88
Kripke S A 1982 *Wittgenstein on Rules and Private Language*. Basil Blackwell, Oxford
Lewis D 1969 *Convention*. Harvard University Press, Cambridge, MA
Locke J 1698 *An Essay Concerning Human Understanding*. Nidditch P (ed.) 1975, Clarendon Press, Oxford
Peacocke C 1986 *Thoughts: An Essay on Content*. Basil Blackwell, Oxford
Quine W V O 1960 *Word and Object*. MIT Press, Cambridge, MA
Wittgenstein L 1934 Blue book. In: Rhees R (ed.) 1958 *The Blue and Brown Books*. Basil Blackwell, Oxford
Wittgenstein L 1953 *Philosophical Investigations*. Basil Blackwell, Oxford

Meaning Postulate

T. M. V. Janssen

Meaning postulates provide a method used in model-theoretic semantics to restrict the possible interpretations of an object language L by describing lexical meanings in terms of analytically true sentences in L. The method was formulated by Carnap (1947: 222–29) and is called for as lexical meanings tend to escape the powers of logical analysis. By applying the method of meaning postulates one is able to regiment lexical meanings to a much greater extent in terms of logical analysis and modeltheoretic interpretation.

A model is constructed from basic sets using standard constructions such as powerset formation. In the interpretation of a language L the basic elements of L are assigned an extension for each possible world and each moment of time. In some cases, in particular for logical elements, this interpretation is very specific and easily definable for all possible worlds and moments of time. For example, the negation sign of logic is interpreted as a function from truth-values to truth-values assigning *true* to *false* and *false* to *true*. In other cases, however, the interpretation remains less specific. If L contains the English predicate 'walk,' for example, the predicate will be assigned a set of individuals for each possible world and each moment of time, but the interpretation is unable to specify the individuals that may be said to walk in each case. The reason for this difference is, in Carnap's words (1947: 222), that 'the truth of some statements is logical, necessary, based upon meaning, while that of other statements is empirical, contingent, dependent upon the facts of the world.' By introducing meaning postulates one is able to make certain contingent truths dependent on others, thus restricting the total number of possible interpretations for the language L as a whole.

Meaning postulates are statements (postulates) formulated in the object language L, the language under interpretation. These statements must be analytically true, i.e., true in virtue of meaning, in all models considered. One may, if one wishes, subdivide meaning postulates into a number of distinct classes. For example, predicates denoting binary relations may be said to be reflexive, symmetrical, transitive, irreflexive, etc., as the case may be (Carnap 1947: 226–28). The predicate W (warmer than), for example, may be said to be transitive and irreflexive (and hence asymmetrical) by stipulating that:

if '$W(\alpha, \beta)$' and '$W(\beta, \gamma)$,' then '$W(\alpha, \gamma)$' (1a)
(where α, β, and γ are names for individuals)

$\neg W(\alpha, \alpha)$ (1b)

Or one can define one predicate's meaning in terms of the meanings of other predicates, as in:

if 'seek(α, β)' then 'try$(\alpha, \text{find}(\alpha, \beta))$,' and vice versa (2)

Or entailment relations, such as equivalence, can be expressed for combinations of individual predicates:

if 'necessarily(always (ϕ))' then 'always(necessarily(ϕ)),' and vice versa (where ϕ is a sentence) (3)

Likewise, entailment relations with respect to one or more terms can be expressed, as in:

if 'cause(α, ϕ)' then 'ϕ' (4)

If one wishes to be strict, one may consider the possibility of formulating a meaning postulate as a criterion of formal adequacy for dictionary definitions.

See also: Analyticity; Montague Grammar; Possible Worlds.

Bibliography

Carnap R 1947 *Meaning and Necessity. A Study in Semantics and Modal Logic*, 2nd edn. University of Chicago Press, Chicago, IL
Gamut L T F 1991 *Logic, Language and Meaning. Vol. II: Intensional Logic and Logical Grammar*. University of Chicago Press, Chicago, IL

Metaphor

E. Steinhart and E. F. Kittay

Metaphor, a trope in which one thing is spoken of as if it were some other thing, is a ubiquitous feature of natural language. While the ability to understand metaphors and use them is characteristic of mature linguistic competence, the ability to use metaphors well was considered by Aristotle a 'mark of genius' and remains today a feature of intelligence tests and assessments of creativity. In literature, in professional discourses (e.g., theology, philosophy, and law), in scientific language, and in daily discourse, metaphors provide expression for experiences and concepts for which literal language seems insufficient, thereby increasing the range of articulation possible within the language.

What is called a 'metaphor' spans the fresh and startling use of language (illustrated by Melville's metaphor '[He] slept off the fumes of vanity'), the frequently used and barely noticed conventional metaphors, (exemplified in using terms of light to refer to knowledge e.g., 'I see'), and the entirely familiar, even 'dead metaphor' (employed, for instance, by the aquatic term 'current' used to speak of electricity). Whether occupied with metaphors novel or commonplace, theorists of language and of cognition have come to recognize that no understanding of language and linguistic capacities is complete without an adequate account of metaphor.

Studied in many disciplines and from many perspectives, metaphors, as seen by linguists and other students of language, are primarily linguistic utterances, produced by speakers and processed by listeners. In analyzing metaphors as linguistic phenomena, investigators want to understand the structure of metaphorical utterances, the features that distinguish them from both literal utterances and other figurative speech, and their truth and meaning; they study how metaphors are used in communication insofar as what is intended to be understood is different than what is literally said; and they try to answer why people so often resort to metaphor to communicate and stretch the cognitive and expressive capacities of language.

1. Theories of Metaphor

1.1 Historical Background to Contemporary Theories

The first systematic treatment is found in the Poetics, where Aristotle asserts that a metaphor 'is the application to something of a name belonging to something else, either from the genus to the species, or from the species to the genus, or from a species to another species, or according to analogy.' In the Rhetoric, Aristotle articulates the Elliptical Simile theory of metaphor, in which a metaphor is taken as being a comparison abbreviated by dropping the word 'like.' The metaphor 'Man is a wolf,' for example, would be an ellipsis derived from the comparison 'Man is like a wolf.'

Aristotle's treatment of metaphor, dominant until very recently, set the tone for Classical and Renaissance texts. The view that metaphor was a decorative use of language prevailed first amongst the proponents of metaphor's virtues and later amongst its detractors. According to Cicero, metaphor first arises from the limitations of the impoverished vocabulary of a new language. But as a language matures and acquires an enhanced vocabulary, metaphor enriches a language by providing its speakers with more dignified and delightful ways of expressing themselves. The rhetorical force that so charmed and impressed Cicero, however, was the same characteristic which dismayed thinkers from Locke to Bachelard. The decorative was for these writers a mere distraction which, in Bachelard's phrase, 'seduces the Reason.'

The creative feature of metaphor stirred the interest of the Romantics, from Rousseau to Coleridge and Croce, and of Nietzsche, whose perspectivalism was especially compatible with giving metaphor pride of place. For these theorists, metaphor was thought to be not something added on and dispensible, but generative, even originative of linguistic meaning.

The twentieth century has witnessed an explosion of theories of metaphor. I. A. Richards (1936), a scholar of Coleridge, raises the Romantic interest in metaphor to a new level of rigor. First he introduces the idea that metaphor is composed of two components which he calls 'vehicle' and 'tenor.' The vehicle of the metaphor (now also called the 'source,' or 'base') is the idea conveyed by the literal meaning of the words used metaphorically. The tenor (now called 'topic' or 'target') is the idea conveyed by the metaphor. In the metaphor 'a seed of hope' the vehicle is 'the seed'; the tenor is hope. Second, Richard contends, a metaphor not only consists of the words used, but is a 'transaction between the contexts' provided by both vehicle and tenor.

Max Black (1962), building on Richard's work, insists that a metaphor is not an isolated word. Veering away from the rhetorical view of metaphor as novel name, Black takes metaphor as a predication whose expression is a sentence: metaphors do not just rename an entity, they make a statement. This shift brings metaphor into the purview of cognitively significant discourse. In contrast to both Substitution theories (wherein metaphors are decorative substitutes for mundane terms where a heightened rhetorical or aesthetic effect is desired, but without cognitive import) and Comparison theories (which are associated with the elliptical simile theory attributed to Aristotle, according to which metaphors are implicit comparisons that can generally be made explicit through a simile, again with no cognitive gain), Black proposes an Interaction theory, stressing the conceptual role of metaphor. Metaphor's cognitive contribution to language and thought results from an interaction of 'the Principal Subject,' (roughly Richard's tenor) and 'the Subsidiary Subject' along with its system of associated commonplaces (roughly Richard's vehicle). In 'Man is a wolf,' the system of associations of the subsidiary subject, 'wolf' (e.g., a wolf is fierce, is brutally competitive, and so on) is used as a 'lens' or 'filter' through which the principal subject 'man' is understood. The wolf-system *highlights* implications shared by the commonplaces (which need not by true, only commonly believed) of the subjects (such as ferocity), and *downplays* implications not shared (such as wolves' den habitation), thereby reshaping our understanding of man, and even of wolves. Nelson Goodman (1968) underscored the systematicity of metaphor. Attention to metaphor by such rigorous students of language as Black and Goodman expanded the interest in metaphor from literary theory and rhetoric to philosophy of language and scientific investigation of natural language.

1.2 The Legacy of and Reaction against Interaction Theories

Among those who have exploited the potential of the Interaction theories have been philosophers of science interested in the role of metaphor in scientific language and theory, and cognitive psychologists interested in building models of mind which account for the role of metaphors in cognition. Mary Hesse (1966) develops the understanding of metaphors as 'systematic analogies' with a strong affinity to scientific models, arguing that they are not only heuristically valuable but are irreducible in explanation and prediction. Dedre Gentner (1982) proposes evaluative procedures by which to determine what makes some metaphors better than others in serving cognitive ends. The Experientialist Theory of Metaphor of Lakoff and Johnson (1981) stresses the systematic coherence of metaphor and its role in grounding the human conceptual system in lived experience. The Semantic Field Theory of Metaphor (Kittay 1987) employs the linguistic tools of semantic field theory to develop the work of Black and Goodman by showing how metaphor transfers the semantic structures and relations from the semantic domain of the source to that of the topic, thus inducing a new structure in the topic field.

In reaction to the predominance of interactionist-inspired theories, Donald Davidson (1978) and others reconsider the view that metaphors are implicit comparisons. Although these theories have been quite influential amongst philosophers, they have not attracted scholars interested in developing formal approaches to natural language sufficient to the challenges and opportunities provided by computational technologies. Because of the availability and promise of these technologies, metaphor research has become an area of concern for computer scientists and artificial intelligence researchers attempting to enable computers to understand natural language. These researchers have developed theories using the formal tools of contemporary linguistics, such as componential analysis, fuzzy logic, model-theoretic semantics, and semantic networks. A variety of computational approaches both to the generation and comprehension of metaphor are now available (Indurkhya 1986; Chandler 1991).

2. Figurative Language, Literal Truth, and Metaphor

An adequate theory for the identification of metaphors must first distinguish figurative from literal language, then distinguish metaphors from other figures. Figurative utterances somehow breach the norms of literal language and yet are understood as meaningful utterances. Rules governing literal language include syntactic, semantic, and pragmatic constraints. Figurative utterances generally obey syntactic rules, sometimes flout semantic rules, and most often violate pragmatic constraints. The flouting of these rules results in sentences which are either obviously not true or are clearly inappropriate if understood literally. Since metaphor, although occasionally identified with figurative language in general, is more precisely a par-

ticular trope, it is to be contrasted with other tropes such as irony, hyperbole, metonymy, and synecdoche. Metaphors are characteristically identifiable by the form of the semantic and pragmatic violation.

2.1 Semantic Deviance

An utterance may fail to be literally true either because it is empirically false or because it cannot be assigned any literal truth-value. An utterance cannot be assigned any literal truth-value if the terms to which its predicates are applied fail to satisfy 'selectional restriction' conditions—rules restricting the categories to which the predicate can be literally applied. For instance, the predicate 'drinks' requires something animate in the thematic role, 'agent,' and something liquid in the role, 'patient.' Sentences employing synecdoche, metonymy, and often metaphor fail to be literally true because they contain predications violating selectional restrictions. While the violation of selection restriction is often a mark of these types of figuration, synecdoche and metonymy violate these conditions differently than does metaphor. Consider the synecdoche 'A hundred feet marched up the hill.' Although one can say that it is feet that march, it is more accurate to say that one marches *with* feet. That is, the selection restriction rules on 'march' call for the restriction [human] on the agent role, and for [means of mobility] on the thematic role of instrument. 'Feet' should occupy the thematic role of instrument; instead it occupies the thematic role of agent. While it is not literally correct to speak of feet marching, however, 'feet' are not conceptually unrelated to 'march.' This sort of deviance is also characteristic of metonymy, but different from what occurs in the case of metaphor. In the metonymic sentence, 'The White House issued a statement affirming the right of gays and lesbians to serve in the military,' the predicate 'issues a statement' has [human] as a selection restriction on the agent role. 'The White House,' however, is where the statement is issued and so fills the thematic role of location.

In the case of metaphors, however, the violation of selection restrictions results from the importation of a term from a distant semantic domain, rather than the term's deviant occupation of a particular thematic role. For instance, Socrates explains the distress of his student, Theaetetus, by declaring that the young man is 'giving birth to an idea.' The difficulty in giving 'Theaetetus is giving birth,' a literal reading is because the procreative domain encompassing the activity of giving birth is not appropriately inclusive of human males. It is not because 'Theaetetus' occupies an inappropriate thematic role, agent; Theaetetus is the agent under consideration.

2.2 Pragmatic Constraints

Philosopher H. P. Grice provides a 'logic of conversation' consisting of maxims obeyed by speakers adhering to a Cooperative Principle of Conversation, the principle by which the intention to engage in meaningful conversation is indicated. He suggests that when a maxim is flouted and yet the speaker appears to otherwise adhere to the cooperative principle, then one must ask what is implicated by the utterance. Such implicature has been taken as a condition for figurative language. Figures such as irony, hyperbole, synecdoche, metonymy, and metaphor in general violate the conversational maxim of Quality: 'Try to make your contribution one that is true.' Metaphors, when true, typically violate the conversational maxim of Relevance. Mao was reputed to have said 'A revolution is not a dinner party.' Such violations of conversational maxims cause the listener to attempt a figurative interpretation.

The way in which a listener will bring the obviously false or inappropriate sentence into conformity with the Co-operative Principle will be determined by the nature of the figurative language used. An ironical sentence, for example, fails to be true because it states the contrary of what the speaker takes to be true, and so the listener will reverse the sense of the predication. When a metaphorical sentence fails to be true, the listener will seek an interpretation of those parts of the sentence or the utterance which are *conceptually* incongruous in the context of the discourse.

2.3 Metaphor and Conceptual Incongruity

The claim that metaphors are false when read literally has been stressed by Beardsley's Controversion Theory of Metaphor. The violation of selectional restrictions by metaphors is the source of the incongruity emphasized by the Semantic Deviance Theory of metaphor. Joseph Stern (1985) and others have pointed out that the semantic deviance theory fails to be an adequate account of metaphor since some metaphorical sentences violate no selection restrictions: Mao's statement, and idioms such as 'He's up against the wall' may be both literally and figuratively true. Stern adopts the view that metaphors are a sort of demonstrative, which he dubs 'M-that' on analogy with philosopher David Kaplan's treatment of the demonstrative 'D-that.' On Stern's account, metaphors are ways of pointing ('metaphorically that') to some referent and at the same time 'characterizing' the referent in terms of the semantic content of the metaphorically used term. On this account, appeal to the semantic deviance of a metaphor is unnecessary.

Others have argued that even where there is no falsity or semantic deviance in the sentence containing the metaphorically used terms, metaphors depend on a conceptual incongruity which is evident, if not within the metaphorical sentence, then between the sentence and a larger discursive context. They have argued that this conceptual incongruity is essential for the conceptual inventiveness of metaphors, an inventiveness that is part of their cognitive effectiveness. It

is the conceptual incongruity characterized by speaking of one thing in terms of another that is an important differentia between metaphor and other figurative speech.

3. Interpretation of Metaphor

3.1 Meaning of Metaphors

Two opposing positions have been staked out concerning the interpretation of metaphoric utterances. The first holds that metaphoric utterances have one and only one meaning, the literal meaning. The second view maintains that there is in addition to the literal meaning, a meaning distinctive to the metaphor and which is the outcome of an interpretive process unique to metaphors.

According to the first position, the interpretation of metaphor is a matter of pragmatics. In this school of thought, the older convictions held that metaphors are, at best, decorative, and at worst, the vehicles by which we 'insinuate wrong ideas, move the passions, and thereby mislead the judgment' (Locke, *An Essay on Human Understanding*, Bk 3: ch. 10). More recently writers have acknowledged the importance of metaphor for cognitive concerns, but have argued that the cognitive contribution is made not by virtue of an unparaphraseable metaphorical meaning but because metaphors play a causal role in some other cognitive activity. Davidson (1978), the chief proponent of this position, writes that metaphors 'intimate similarities' and so cause the speaker to make the comparison that the metaphor intimates. A related causal contribution is to create an intimacy between the speaker and hearer that joins them in the search for similarity (Cohen 1978; Cooper 1986).

Black took it to be a feature of the interaction theory that when a metaphor is interpreted, it is given a distinct unparaphraseable meaning. The interaction of the two subjects of the metaphor renders an irreducible cognitive meaning. A number of more recent writings have suggested that the interpretation of a metaphor proceeds by a function applied to the literal meaning of the constituent terms and so yields a distinct metaphoric meaning. Proposals include a possible world or game theoretic analysis (Bergman 1982; Hintikka and Sandu 1990), a mapping of a sentence meaning to a speaker meaning (Searle 1979), and an analogical mapping from the domain of the vehicle to that of the topic (Gentner 1983; Kittay 1987).

3.2 Paraphrasing Metaphor

The task of interpreting metaphors has sometimes been taken to mean providing the metaphor with a paraphrase. The most troubling question concerning the assignment of a paraphrase is whether or not it is possible to supply an 'exact literal' paraphrase for each metaphor, or whether any literal paraphrase is at best only approximate. On the one hand, it has been argued that no literal utterance or set of literal utterances can fully capture the meaning of a metaphor, and that, furthermore, the paraphrases that seem most natural are often metaphorical themselves. For instance, although 'Theaetetus gives birth to an idea' approximately metaphorically means that Theaetetus painfully expresses an idea, the paraphrase means that neither exactly, nor exhaustively, nor entirely literally (since *express* may be thought a metaphorical predication as well). In this regard it is sometimes suggested that the metaphorical meaning of a metaphor is another metaphor, or set of metaphors. For instance, 'Juliet is the sun' metaphorically means that Romeo's world *revolves* around Juliet.

The thesis of Lakoff and his associates is that certain metaphors belong to the basic conceptual schemes by which understanding of the world is organized and which guide action, and so admit of no literal paraphrase. These conceptual metaphors generate the large number of the metaphors found in ordinary language, metaphors such as 'Life is a journey,' 'Up is good,' 'Anger is heat,' 'The mind is a container,' and so forth. A metaphorical sentence such as 'She lost her cool' is interpreted as easily and as quickly as it is because it is generated from a basic conceptual understanding of anger as heat and the mind as a container, a conceptual understanding shared by speaker and hearer.

3.3 Rules for Interpreting Metaphors

Along with the question of whether interpreting metaphors is a matter of providing a distinctive meaning which is not a literal paraphrase, comes the question of whether such interpretation is rule-governed. Those who maintain that there is no metaphoric meaning generally hold that there are no rules for providing the metaphorical interpretation—that the interpretation depends on an intuitive grasp of the contextual factors, along with a general ability to make similarity judgments. Those who propound the view that metaphors have meaning look for the rules by which such meaning may be derived from the utterance (and sometimes its context).

Most metaphor theorists, especially those working on formal or computational models of metaphor, have opted for the second claim and have sought to provide such rules. The debate that ensues amongst these rule-based theories is whether an interpretation requires a one-stage or a two-stage process. One-stage theorists maintain some version of the claim that the metaphorical is essentially continuous with the literal, a case of a polysemy where the metaphorical meanings are the furthest removed from the term's prototypical meaning. Two-stage theories assume that metaphorical meaning is some function of the literal meaning, and that there is some discontinuity between the literal and the metaphorical.

Metaphorical interpretation can follow one of several routes:

(a) According to the Elliptical Simile Theory and most, but not all Comparison Theories, 'S is P' metaphorically means S is like P. (Some comparison theories deny the existence of metaphorical meaning as such.) Some have argued that such interpretations are ill-suited to other grammatical forms of metaphor (Tirrell 1991).

(b) According to the Abstraction Theory, metaphorical meaning is obtained by raising metaphorical predicates to a more abstract level at which there is no semantic incongruity. Feature Transfer Theories (Levin 1977) adopt this strategy. Thus 'Theaetetus gave birth to an idea' metaphorically means that Theaetetus produced an idea, since 'produced' is an abstract version of 'gave birth' that is not semantically incongruous.

(c) According to Analogy Theory, offshoots of an interactionist view of metaphor, 'S is P' metaphorically means S is analogous to P. Interpreting metaphors requires specifying analogous domains and the homomorphisms between the domains. One advantage of this theory is that it is best suited to capture the ways in which metaphors are extended, that is, how terms are used from the semantic domain of the vehicle to elaborate aspects of the topic.

The Analogy Theory is the favored approach by those searching for computationally tractable theories of metaphor.

See also: Metaphor in Literature.

Bibliography

Bergman M 1982 Metaphorical assertions. *Philosophical Review* **91**: 229–45
Black M 1962 Metaphor. In: Black M (ed.) *Models and Metaphors*. Cornell University Press, Ithaca, NY
Brooke-Rose C 1970 *A Grammar of Metaphor*. Seeker and Warburg, London
Chandler S R 1991 Metaphor comprehension: A connectionist approach to implications for the mental lexicon. *Metaphor and Symbolic Activity* **6**: 227–58
Cohen T 1978 Metaphor and the cultivation of intimacy. *Critical Inquiry* **5**: 3–12
Cooper D 1986 *Metaphor*. Blackwell, Oxford
Davidson D 1978 What metaphors mean. In: Sacks S (ed.) *On Metaphor*. University of Chicago Press, Chicago, IL
Gentner D 1982 Are scientific analogies metaphors? In: Miall D S (ed.) *Metaphor: Problems and Perspectives*. Humanities Press, New York
Gentner D 1983 Structure-mapping: A theoretical framework for analogy. *Cognitive Science* **7**: 155–70
Goodman N 1968 *Languages of Art*. Bobbs-Merrill, Indianapolis, IN
Hesse M 1966 *Models and Analogies in Science*. Sheed and Ward, London
Hintikka J, Sandu G 1990 Metaphor and the varieties of lexical meaning. *Dialectica* **44**: 57–78
Indurkhya B 1986 Constrained semantic transference: A formal theory of metaphors. *Synthese* **68**: 445–80

Johnson M (ed.) 1981 *Philosophical Perspectives on Metaphor*. University of Minnesota Press, Minneapolis, MN

Kittay E F 1987 *Metaphor: Its Cognitive Force and Linguistic Structure*. Oxford University Press, New York

Lakoff G, Johnson M 1980 *Metaphors We Live By*. University of Chicago Press, Chicago, IL

Levin S R 1977 *The Semantics of Metaphor*. Johns Hopkins University Press, Baltimore, MD

MacCormac E R 1985 *A Cognitive Theory of Metaphor*. MIT Press, Cambridge, MA

Miller G A 1979 Images and models, similes and metaphors. In: Ortony A (ed.)

Ortony A (ed.) 1979 *Metaphor and Thought*. Cambridge University Press, New York

Richards I A 1936 *The Philosophy of Rhetoric*. Oxford University Press, Oxford

Searle J 1979 Metaphor. In: Ortony A (ed.)

Stern J 1985 Metaphor as demonstrative. *Journal of Philosophy* **82**: 667–710

Tirrell L 1991 Reductive and nonreductive simile theories of metaphor. *Journal of Philosophy* **88**: 337–58

Metaphor in Literature

V. R. L. Sage

Metaphor (from the ancient Greek verb *metapherein*, to 'carry over, transfer') means 'to speak about X in terms of Y'—e.g., 'The moon is a sickle.' Aristotle (384–322 BC) defines it in his *Poetics* (ca. 339 BC) thus:

> Metaphor consists in applying to a thing a word that belongs to something else; the transference being either from genus to species or from species to genus or from species to species or on grounds of analogy.
>
> (1965: 61)

Aristotle's distinction between 'simple replacement' and 'analogy' governs, effectively, the difference between simple and complex 'metaphor.' Discussion of metaphor varies along an axis of assumptions about what Aristotle terms here 'analogy' as to whether it is conceived of as including the mental act of perceiving analogy—the idea-content—or whether it is a strictly and exclusively linguistic operation—the language level. Writers vary significantly, but most—though certainly not all—lie between these two extremes. Thus puzzles about metaphor may, at the one end of the scale, raise problems in psychology and philosophy and, at the other, problems in the study of language. In between these extremes lie the problems the subject raises for literary criticism, both traditional and modern. Metaphor is also an index of the power relations between literary genres and what is said about metaphor often indicates what the assumptions of a period or a critic are about these matters: what is sayable microcosmically about metaphor is often sayable macrocosmically about literature.

1. The Classical View: Aristotle

Metaphor is treated by Classical writers as a desirable rhetorical means, not an end in itself. This does not mean, however, as is often assumed, that it is treated as a simple ornament.

Most rhetorics of the ancient world contain an account of metaphor which places it firmly as a figure of speech (trope, paradigmatic) rather than a figure of thought (schema, syntagmatic). The strongest version of this distinction is Quintilian's in the *Institutio Oratoria* (ca. 75 AD) but he derives it from Greek sources. However, most rhetorical treatises are written not about poetry and poetics, but about speaking and prose writing. They are a set of written instructions, to train the reader in the art of persuasion, either forensically—as was first the case with Corax of Syracuse (467 AD)—or epideictically (decoratively, publicly in a more general sense than simply advocacy). Aristotle's is the only *Poetics* surviving from the ancient world, even including Longinus' treatise *On The Sublime* of the second century AD, which is a general rhetorical manual. It is characteristic of this split between the genres that Aristotle should separate his remarks about poetry from his other discussion of metaphor in the *Rhetoric* (337 BC). Thus the use of metaphor in poetry and in prose is formally separated, though it is noticeable that Aristotle and Quintilian both choose their examples of metaphor from poetry—the former from Hesiod, Homer, and the dramatists, and the latter from Virgil and Ovid.

The development from fifth-century Greece to Augustan Rome seems to be that of a progressive pragmatism. Aristotle always takes an empirical approach, but he believes rhetoric to be an art of the possible whereas for Quintilian it is a set of exercises to commit to memory. For Aristotle in the *Rhetoric*, metaphor is a part of the larger topic of the enthymeme (from Greek *en themon* 'in the mind'), a kind of rhetorical syllogism, looser than the strictly logical forms but vital to the art of manipulating the 'probable.' For both of them, metaphor gives *energeia* which means 'force, vigor,' or, as the Loeb edition interestingly translates it, 'actuality.' But Aristotle makes an important distinction between metaphor and simile:

> For the simile, as we have said, is a metaphor differing only by the addition of a word, wherefore it is less pleasant because it is longer, it does not say this *is* that, *so that the mind does not even examine this.*
>
> [Author's italics]

It follows that the characteristic compression and enigma of metaphor makes the mind of the beholder entertain something not immediately understandable and thus 'a kind of knowledge (*oion mathesis*) results.' Metaphor, says Aristotle, is proportionate or analogical (*kat'analogian*), and sets things 'before the eyes.' But he insists that the analogy should be between things that are unlike or resistant to an extent, 'just as, for instance, in philosophy it needs sagacity to grasp the similarity in things that are apart...' And he goes on to link this *energeia* to the defeat of expectations:

> Most smart sayings are derived from metaphor, and also from misleading the hearer beforehand. For it becomes evident to him that he has learnt something, when the conclusion turns out contrary to his expectation, and the mind seems to say, 'How true it is! but I missed it.'

Metaphors are like jokes and philosophical paradoxes. This is not an assimilation of metaphor to simile, nor is it a simple view of metaphor as comparison. Aristotle's more famous structural insistence in the *Poetics* on the analogical proportion idea in metaphor—B is to A as D is to C—needs to be put in the context of the above remarks because they show that analogy has plenty of room to include the idea of implicit meaning (the distance of the elements one from another and the suppressed aspects of analogy) and is a source of wit, or a contrast between appearance and reality. This is a more mentalistic view of metaphor than the Roman Quintilian's recipe-book approach to the store of ornamental figures.

2. The Platonic Tradition: Metaphor and the Paradox of Representation

Plato (429–347 BC) does not have a 'view' of metaphor stated in any one place like Aristotle. Nevertheless his dialogues abound in examples and ideas about the significance of metaphor and figurative language which—deeply ambiguous as they are—have proved enormously influential, especially on the practice of poetry. There are two lines of thought in Plato, both of which are sometimes found within the same dialogue. One is that all language originates in metaphor and figuration. The *Cratylus*, for example, represents an often playful and obscure enquiry into the origins

of language in which Socrates mounts a critique of representation—the names for abstractions like 'truth' and 'necessity' are broken down into their earlier elements which point (figuratively) towards the 'true' elements (by metaphor) of our current speech, which we have forgotten—hence the word for 'truth,' for example, i.e., *aletheia*, 'really' means 'a divine wandering' because it is made up of the elements *ale* and *theia*, or necessity means 'walking through a ravine' because 'necessary' (*anangkaion*) is made up of *an angke ion* meaning literally 'going through a ravine.' In this way, argues Socrates, perhaps abstract language itself—and therefore the very language of definition—contains hidden figuration and is an extended metaphor whose origins perpetually threaten its ability to represent abstractly.

However, metaphor reveals the traces of its divine origin, for 'speech' says Socrates, punning on the Greek words for 'they speak' and 'everything' (*pan*), 'signifies all things':

> *Socrates* You are aware that speech signifies all things (*pan*) and is always turning them round and round, and has two forms, true and false.
> *Hermogenes* Certainly.
> *Socrates* Is not the truth that is in him the smooth or sacred form which dwells above among the Gods, whereas falsehood dwells among men below, and is rough like the goat of tragedy, for tales and falsehoods have generally to do with the tragic or goatish life, and tragedy is the place of them?
> *Hermogenes* Very true.
> *Socrates* Then surely, Pan, who is the declarer of all things (*pan*) and the perpetual mover (*aei polon*) of all things, is rightly called *aipolos* (goatherd), he being the two-formed son of Hermes, smooth in his upper part, and rough and goat-like in his lower regions. And, as the son of Hermes, he is speech or the brother of speech, and that brother should be like brother is no marvel.

Language is portrayed, metaphorically, as a satyr: through a grasp of its perpetually dual form—i.e., analogy—one can get glimpses of the truth it can offer. The other view playfully expressed here is that language is perpetually unstable, untrustworthy, and quite unsatisfactory for reasoning with, because it can never identify absolutely with what it seeks to picture and therefore can only be, at best, an approximation to an inner truth. Skepticism about representation in language is thus inseparable from a self-consciousness about the figurative. But Plato, the enemy of poets in the *Republic*, gives the grounds here for a profound defense of metaphor as a positive instrument of thought.

Later, in the Medieval and Renaissance periods, Nature becomes a book written by God, and, in a common extension of the metaphor, language is again thought of as a repository of hidden analogies and correspondences which form—to use the usual sub- or associated metaphor—the signatures or traces of God's presence. This view also uses the technique of 'poetic etymology' which purports to uncover the original metaphors of language itself. So Sir Philip Sidney (1554–86), who claimed in his *Apologie For Poetrie* (1595) that only the poets can recreate the 'golden world,' is borrowing the technique of Socrates in the *Cratylus*.

This self-conscious view of the conceptual paradox posed by metaphor in representation was systematized by one continental eighteenth-century philosopher. One can see the Platonist influence in the *The New Science* (1725) of the Italian protostructuralist thinker, Vico (1668–1744)—particularly in the important place given to metaphor in Vico's inquiries into the origin of languages. Vico proposes a universal fourfold development for every national culture; and to every phase he gives a rhetorical master trope, beginning with the original of all perception: 'metaphor.' Then follow 'metonymy,' 'synecdoche,' 'irony.' Language originates in metaphor in this tradition; and culture, in epic.

3. Empiricism

In the latter half of the seventeenth century, a new hostility to metaphor emerged. The English empiricist Thomas Hobbes (1588–1679) in his treatise *Leviathan* (1651), classified metaphor as an 'abuse of speech': '... when they [men] use words metaphorically; that is, in other sense than they are ordained for; and thereby deceive others' (1651: 102). Hobbes conceives of language as a kind of 'naming' and the problem he seeks, as a result, to solve is the problem of 'inconstant signification':

> For one man calleth Wisdome, what another calleth *feare*; and one *cruelty*, what another *justice*; one *gravity*, what another *stupidity*, etc ... And therefore such names can never be true grounds of any ratiocination. No more can metaphors, and tropes of speech: but these are less dangerous, because they profess their inconstancy; which the other do not.

Here one sees graphically the decline of rhetoric: Hobbes has a profound distrust of metaphor, but his 'realism' contradicts what Aristotle has to say by suggesting that metaphor always declares itself as deceptive. This view initiated the cult of the plain style.

Later, John Locke (1632–1704), in his *Essay Concerning Human Understanding* (1690), also tackled the problem of the 'unsteady uses of words.' He regards language as a process of labeling, and the 'reform of language'—i.e., the precedence of the 'literal' over all figuration is explicitly a part of the age's antirhetorical project. Like the Puritan side of Plato, Locke is deeply suspicious of abstractions but also equally so of metaphor and simile. Metaphor is thus not distinguished from any other form of figuration—all of which for Locke are ruled by one prior law; the association of ideas. The satire of Laurence Sterne (1713–68) in *Tristram Shandy* (1760–67) employs metaphor

directly at the expense of Locke's association of ideas principle, obeying it and yet triumphantly violating it at the same moment:

> —My young Master in London is dead! said Obadiah.
> —A green satin night-gown of my mother's, which had been twice scoured, was the first idea which Obadiah's exclamation brought into Susannah's head.—Well might Locke write a chapter upon the imperfections of words.—
> —Then, quoth Susannah, we must all go into mourning—But note a second time: the word *mourning* notwithstanding Susannah made use of it herself—failed also of doing its office; it excited not one single idea, tinged either with grey or black,—all was green,—The green satin night-gown *hung there* still.
>
> [Author's italics]

This passage is a perfect illustration of Locke's theory that thought and language are ruled by the association of ideas, except that the association is not the conventional one between mourning and black which it should universally be, according to Locke, but a private one, based on a combination of desire and habit which is so dominant that Susannah's mind is transformed, comically, by metaphor, into a wardrobe. The separation, vital for Locke's whole theory, between the idea in the mind and the thing being thought of, is eroded. It is Sterne's metaphor 'hung there' which creates this satirical refutation: this metaphor will not unpack properly into idea and thing, and therefore is not replaceable by a 'concrete,' 'simple,' or 'literal' paraphrase without loss of significance.

4. Neoclassicism

'As to metaphorical expression,' said Samuel Johnson (1709–84), 'that is a great excellence in style, when it is used with propriety, for it gives you two ideas for one.' Neoclassical attitudes to metaphor are founded on the linguistic pragmatism of the Roman, as opposed to the psychological subtlety of the Greek writers. Horace's (65–8 BC) highly pragmatic update of parts of Aristotle's thinking in the *Ars Poetica* (ca. 17 BC) is mainly concerned with such things as appropriateness, decorum, and consistency: significantly, it does not mention metaphor.

An example of what Johnson means is in his famous emendation of the speech of Shakespeare's Macbeth at v, iii, 27–8; 'My way of life/Is fall'n into the sere, the yellow Leafe,' which Johnson amended to 'My May of Life' on the grounds of metaphorical propriety. The result, which reveals the prejudices of the age, is a rococo prettification, in the name of consistency, of something that strikes the ear as massive and rugged. It is likely that Shakespeare felt 'way of life' to be a metaphorical expression, but if Johnson thought of it as a metaphor at all, then it was an inconsistent one which made the whole line metaphorically mixed. He reconstructed the phrase on the assumption of a compositor's error, thus restoring the stylistic consistency which he felt that Shakespeare would not have missed.

It is from this strain of thought that the familiar idea of the inappropriateness of mixed metaphor, which survived until the Edwardian period in manuals of composition, is derived.

5. The Romantic View

In the Romantic period, poetry gained a new ascendancy as the paradigm of literature itself. The Romantics, reacting against the rhetoric of Augustan Rome and reaching back to Aristotle and Plato, as Vico had done, gave an enormous impetus to metaphor as the dynamic founding trope of poetry and literary culture.

Two views are to be distinguished here, which ultimately influence the modern tradition in different ways; the Organicism of Samuel Taylor Coleridge (1772–1834) and the Romantic Platonism of Percy Bysshe Shelley (1792–1822), both of which make equally far-reaching claims for metaphor but by different routes.

Metaphor for Coleridge is part of the 'inter-inanimation of words' and his view is neither that of 'simple replacement' nor 'substitution' nor 'comparison,' but of 'organic unity.' In his 'Lectures on Shakespeare' (1808, publ. 1836), Coleridge closely analyzes how metaphors reveal an inexhaustible mutual reactiveness amongst their elements, which creates an unparaphraseable richness of meaning. This approach depends on Coleridge's notion of the 'imagination' as a separate and dynamic faculty. Coleridge's view of metaphor is deeply antiempiricist. A metaphor has the form of a duality but is always surmounted by a unity in the mind of the perceiver. Coleridge's main distinction is to have isolated and stressed this drive towards unity-in-difference in metaphor.

Shelley's *Defence Of Poetry* (1821) again uses the argument from the origins of language, but gives it a new, optimistic twist. Language, it is argued, was in its beginning not a set of atomic labels, of names, as the empiricists would argue, but 'the chaos of a cyclic poem'; and 'In the infancy of society every author is necessarily a poet, because language itself is poetry...' A defense of poetry amounts to a defense of metaphor, which is the agent by which language produces new meaning. 'Their language [i.e., the poets'] is vitally metaphorical; it marks the before unapprehended relations of things...' Metaphor, for Shelley, is the Ur-perception of analogy and hence the governing trope of language and poetic art. 'Language,' he claims in the *Defence*, 'is arbitrarily produced by the imagination, and has relation to thoughts alone.' Shelley's poetic practice is ruled by perpetually dispensible analogy, as in his triply metaphorical description of Plato as '*kindling harmony* in thoughts *divested* of shape and action'—a phrase in which the reader is required to shift lightly from music, to fire, to clothing, without pausing or isolating these single

elements, in order to apprehend fully Shelley's notion of the entirely conceptual nature of Plato's art.

6. Post-Romantic Views

Coleridge's view of 'organic form' has been heavily influential in the modern period, developed, transformed, and hardened into the loose collection of doctrines known as Anglo–American Formalism. This movement is a continuation of the Romantic opposition between Poetry and Science, which crystallizes in the early statements of I. A. Richards (1893–1975). In 'Science and Poetry' (1926), Richards proposed to reduce meaning to two types—the 'emotive' and the 'referential,' in which metaphor belongs to the former not the latter category. There is a residue of 'empiricism' and utilitarianism in the early Richards which he later came to change.

The notion that a metaphor is a vital part of language's power to generate new meanings, is an assumption which underlies three or four different movements in poetry and criticism in the modern period, and in this tradition the romantic view of metaphor is preserved but renamed and assimilated into certain related terms, for example, 'image' and 'symbol,' which seem to many writers in this period exclusive features of lyric poetry itself, not of discourse in general, but which can be regarded as reducible to metaphors with one term suppressed, and which no longer display explicitly their analogical character.

There is a general movement in both theory and practice towards the autonomy of figurative language. Poetic theory, in Symbolist France and Imagist England up to the 1920s, turns inward. Despite the rise of the novel, the ascendancy of lyric poetry—and the corresponding demand for a theory of the lyric moment in language—is unbroken from the Romantic to the Modern Periods and the modulation from high Romanticism into Symbolism which has been exhaustively documented, yields a high concentration on the autonomy of symbolic—in reality, metaphoric—language as part of the general conception of what Eliot called the 'autotelic' nature of poetic language.

This attitude is reified in the obsession with 'imagery' in the Anglo–American criticism of the postwar period, which began in Shakespeare criticism and spread into general critical vocabulary under this rather misleading name, and which later writers, notably P. N. Furbank, in his book *Reflections on the Word 'Image'* (1970), have again reduced to metaphor. I. A. Richards, however, shifted his viewpoint radically and went on to write one of the most influential modern accounts of how metaphor works based on a significant re-reading of Coleridge, which pushes him much more towards the anti-Empiricist and Platonist tradition—the so-called Interaction theory of metaphor. In his later book *The Philosophy of Rhetoric* (1930) Richards attacks the empiricist account of metaphor quite explicitly as 'The Proper Meaning

Superstition' and calls for a new rhetoric which can clarify the confusion inherited from the Lockeian tradition. Richards identifies the confusion as lying in the distinction between the 'metaphorical' and the 'literal' meaning of expressions and demonstrates convincingly that the so-called literal meaning is not equivalent to the meaning of the whole expression. Instead, he invents the terms 'tenor' and 'vehicle' for the two parts of a metaphor—which correspond, in empiricist language, to the 'literal' and the 'figurative' parts—e.g., in the 'moon is a sickle,' the tenor is the 'moon' and the vehicle is the 'sickle'—and he then shows how in complex metaphors the tenor and the vehicle can change places—for example he quotes the Sufi apothegm: 'I am the child whose father is his son and the vine whose wine is its jar' and asks his reader to entertain the deliberate chain of exchanges, designed, for the purposes of spiritual meditation, to defeat a 'literal' paraphrase.

Richards' theory is a modified, nonmystical version of the interaction view of metaphor which resists the tautology involved in supposing that there is such a thing as the 'literal meaning' which can replace the 'metaphorical meaning.' A development of this attitude can be found in William Empson's theory of Mutual Comparison elaborated in *Some Versions of Pastoral* (1936). Another effective analysis of metaphor in this tradition is W. Nowottny's *The Language Poets Use* (1962).

7. Structuralism

The most persuasive and influential Structuralist account of metaphor is contained in Roman Jakobson's classic essay, 'Two Types of Aphasia' (1956). In this essay, Jakobson examines the evidence from the records of the speech of aphasics, and from this evidence he classifies speech defects into two types—failures of vocabulary (lexis, paradigmatic axis of selection) and failures of grammar (syntagmatic axis of combination). From there he goes on to show that both types of patients make substitutions which correspond to metaphor and metonymy. He then maps this point on to the Saussurean binary distinctions between linguistic axes. The two tropes then become, in his classic 'Closing Statement: Linguistics and Poetics' (1960), the master tropes governing different literary genres, and this can yield a complete definition of what poetry characteristically does.

This view of the relations between the tropes explicitly changes again the center of gravity for the literary genres. Metaphor is firmly and explicitly consigned to the paradigmatic axis of discourse and associated with poetry, and opposed in a binary fashion to the trope of metonymy, which becomes syntagmatic, and which generates prose narrative. The account is in some ways reductive—metaphor is a form of substitution of in absentia particles of lexis from the paradigm (selection axis), and there is no way in this account for metaphor

to enter the syntagm and become a combinative factor. By definition it is held in a certain position by its mutual opposition with metonymy's chain of linear substitutions.

In some ways this idea ought to be merely a relativistic instrument of analysis: both poetry and prose narrative may contain both metaphor and metonymy. On the macrolevel, genre and form are generated by the extent to which each text foregrounds metaphor or metonymy: a text which is all metaphor will be a lyric poem and one which is all metonymy will be a realistic novel. (However, Jakobson does suggest that metonymy, not metaphor, is the method of surrealism, which is sometimes conveniently forgotten.)

In Jakobson's own critical practice, however, the oppositional method works to minimize the cognitive content of metaphor and yield a formalist analysis of poetry. In general, the structuralist analysis of poetry, compared with its insights into prose narrative, has been disappointing—precisely because of the reductive account of metaphor which its taxonomic grid relies upon.

The structuralist account has the advantage of getting rid at a stroke of the old-fashioned and rather Cartesian confusion between 'figures of thought' and 'figures of speech'—metaphors can coexist on the linguistic and the conceptual levels without any problem; but it does not add to the traditional understanding of metaphor (as opposed to metonymy which becomes a more important concept than ever before), except in rearranging its relations with other tropes.

However, the very stabilizing of this taxonomic grid itself presents further difficult problems in relation to the concept of metaphor.

8. Poststructuralism

Nietzsche's remarks about metaphor in his 1873 essay *Über Wahrheit und Lüge im außermoralischen Sinn* ('On truth and falsity in their ultramoral sense'), form an important reference point for the poststructuralist account of metaphor. Nietzsche argues, in a hostile, but also dependent, parody of Socrates, that we necessarily and often unknowingly use metaphors when we discuss the question of truth, taking them to be the original things themselves:

> When we talk about trees, colors, snow, and flowers, we believe we know something about the things themselves, and yet we only possess metaphors of the things, and these metaphors do not in the least correspond to the original essentials.

This is another version of the argument-from-origins, used to attack the worn-out humanist tradition. Nietzsche attacks our confidence in our own representations, arguing that language itself is metaphorical and that when we seek definitions of things, we deceive ourselves unknowingly and take for truths those things which are merely our own anthropomorphic fictions:

> What therefore is truth? A mobile army of metaphors, metonymies, anthropomorphisms: in short a sum of human relations which became poetically and rhetorically intensified, metamorphosed, adorned, and after long usage seem to a nation fixed, canonic and binding . . .

In a manner reminiscent of the Socrates of the *Cratylus*, he self-consciously uses the metaphor, for our notions of truth, of coins whose obverses have become effaced, and which have lost their value as a result. Perception of nature can only be, originally, metaphorical but man, argues Nietzsche, 'forgets that the original metaphors of perception *are* metaphors, and takes them for things themselves.'

There are two main areas in which this argument has been influential.

First, some of the most eloquent writing about literature in the immediate postwar period takes up this antihumanist posture and attacks anthropomorphic fictions in literary language. This leads to experiments in a new form of writing in the Paris-based group, the Nouveau Roman, led by Alain Robbe-Grillet. Robbe-Grillet's explicit hostility to figurative language, including metaphor in particular, as a literary 'consolation,' is recorded in a number of brilliant essays, of which perhaps the most notable is 'Nature, humanism and tragedy' (1958) which uses the same argument as seen in Nietzsche (i.e., that 'nature knows no forms') to make a plea for a new kind of literature which will not 'take refuge' in tropes. Robbe-Grillet himself experiments in writing which agonizingly prolongs the act of meticulous description without figuration, notably in the opening of his novel *Le Voyeur* (1958). This posture is echoed in the early critical work of Roland Barthes, particularly in *Writing Degree Zero* (1953, transl. 1967) which argues for a neutral 'zero' style in prose fiction which rejects the bourgeois compromise of 'style.'

Second, explicitly indebted to Nietzsche for its central metaphor of worn-out coins, stands the elaborate discussion of metaphor by Jacques Derrida, 'White mythology' (1974). The basic point which Derrida seeks to demonstrate is that it is impossible to arrive at a 'metaphorology' because metaphor cannot be eradicated from any metalanguage which would stabilize itself as non-metaphorical. This is because the nature of metaphor is such that it leaves its mark upon concepts—in a passage of almost Socratic bravura, Derrida reveals the metaphorical element in the Greek term 'trope' which means 'a turning,' and which is used, as shown above, as a stable instrument of taxonomy, to confine metaphor to a linguistic level only and remove it from the domain of the conceptual. Thus he argues that anything that claimed to be a metalanguage would have to have a meta-metalanguage which would 'lead to classifying metaphors by their source'; but the self-defeating nature of such a tropology is obvious:

> If we wanted to conceive and classify all the metaphorical possibilities of philosophy, there would always be at least one metaphor which would be extended and remain outside the system: that one, at least, which was needed to construct the concept of metaphor or, . . . the metaphor of metaphor.

Thus metaphor is assimilated to *aporia* and *mis-en-abyme* and made the instrument of an infinite regress at the heart of any empirical effort to separate the defining from the defined.

Paradoxically, in the realm of literary criticism, metaphor has once again assumed a position of tremendous power and is cultivated, by the Yale group of poststructuralists who follow Derrida, in particular Paul de Man and Hillis Miller, as a critical instrument for revealing the *aporia* of largely romantic, lyric poetry. Deconstruction, as it has come to be known, is in practice a secondary wave of Anglo–American formalism, using self-conscious metaphors of infinite regress to draw a charmed circle around literariness, largely in the genre of lyric poetry. Deconstruction—because of its obsession with the 'tropical'—is not a method which can be readily used in the discussion of extended narrative or prose fiction.

However, the discussion of metaphor has recently begun to use more representational assumptions. These are even evident in the earlier Derrida of *Dissemination* (transl. 1972). The tour de force of this volume is the essay called 'Plato's *Pharmakon*' in which, drawing on the work of J. P. Vernant, he exposes the complexities of hidden metaphor in the Greek text of Plato's *Phaedrus*, using the technique triumphantly to draw attention to the metaphor used by Socrates, at the climactic point of his exposition, in claiming that truth is 'written upon the soul' and thus ostensibly to defeat his argument that 'writing,' and indeed rhetoric, is logically secondary to the spoken dialectic. The claim that Socrates is contradicting himself rests upon the presence of what Derrida takes to be unacknowledged metaphor in this text.

The implication here is that the use of a metaphor for Derrida, is not only conceptual, but also representational: the metaphor can drag along with it, it is implied, the whole of a belief system:

> But it is not any less remarkable here that the so-called living discourse should suddenly be described by a 'metaphor' borrowed from the order of the very thing one is trying to exclude from it, the order of its simulacrum. *Yet this borrowing is rendered necessary by that which structurally links the intelligible to its copy*, and the language describing dialectics cannot fail to call upon it. [Author's italics]

Derrida is using, ironically, against Plato, the Platonic argument of the *Cratylus*. But: 'that which *structurally* links the intelligible to its copy,' is in fact an old argument about metaphors in some sense representing domains of thought, or *topoi*.

However, a more pragmatic version of this representational notion of metaphor, which locates its source in a whole ideological complex of often unconscious beliefs, forms an important part of the more mainstream contemporary analysis of metaphor in discourse. It is consistent, of course, with the Freudian analysis of metaphor as a revelation of unconscious meaning. A version of it is also employed in more eclectic linguistic analyses of discourse such as the influential *Metaphors We Live By* (1980) by George Lakoff and Mark Johnson. Political analysis of the racist and feminist bias in much contemporary rhetoric uses this assumption about metaphor—i.e., that it has a mimetic or representational relationship to the subconscious or, more often, unconscious beliefs of a speaker or writer, or a society. The metaphors it uses are symptomatic of the state of a culture. For example, the recent writings of Susan Sontag—e.g., *Illness as Metaphor* (1978) and *AIDS and its Metaphors* (1989)—tend to use similar assumptions.

Bibliography

Aristotle 1926 (337 BC) (trans. Treece H) *The Art of Rhetoric*. Loeb Classical Library, Cambridge, MA

Aristotle 1965 *Poetics*. In: Dorsch T R (ed. and trans.) *Classical Literary Criticism*. Penguin, Harmondsworth

Barthes R 1988 The old rhetoric: An aide-memoire. In: Barthes R *The Semiotic Adventure*. Basil Blackwell, Oxford

Booth W C 1978 Metaphor as rhetoric. *Critical Inquiry* 5: 49–72

Brooke-Rose C 1958 *A Grammar of Metaphor*. Secker and Warburg, London

Burke K 1941 Four master tropes. *Kenyon Review* 3: 421–38

Derrida J 1972 Johnson B (ed.) *Dissemination*. University of Chicago Press, Chicago, IL

Derrida J 1974 White mythology: Metaphor in the text of philosophy. *New Literary History* 6: 5–74

Furbank P N 1970 *Reflections On The Word 'Image'*. Secker and Warburg, London

Hawkes T 1972 *Metaphor*. Methuen, London

Jakobson R 1956 Two types of aphasic disturbance. In: Jakobson R, Halle M 1956 *Fundamentals of Language*. Mouton, The Hague

Jakobson R 1960 Closing statement: Linguistics and poetics. In: Sebeok T A (ed.) *Style in Language*. MIT Press, Cambridge, MA

Lakoff G, Johnson M 1980 *Metaphors We Live By*. University of Chicago Press, Chicago, IL

Lodge D 1970 *The Modes of Modern Writing*. Edward Arnold, London

Nowottny W 1962 *The Language Poets Use*. Athlone Press, London

Ong W J Metaphor and the twinned vision. *The Sewanee Review* 63: 193–201

Quintilian M F 1920–2 (ca. 75 AD) (trans. Butter H E) *Institutio Oratoria*. Heinemann, London

Richards I A 1965 (orig. 1936) *The Philosophy of Rhetoric*. Oxford University Press, London

Ricoeur P 1977 *The Rule of Metaphor*. Routledge & Kegan Paul, London

Shelley P B 1953 (orig. 1821) Brett-Smith (ed.) *The Defence of Poetry*. Oxford University Press, London

Sontag S 1978 *Illness as Metaphor*. Farrar, Strauss and Giroux, New York

Sontag S 1989 *AIDS and Its Metaphors*. Farrar, Strauss and Giroux, New York

Vico G 1984 (orig. 1725) *The New Science*. Cornell University Press, Ithaca, NY

Paradoxes, Semantic

R. C. Koons

The semantic paradoxes are a family of arguments or proofs. A 'paradox' or 'antinomy' is an argument in which a contradiction is logically derived from apparently unassailable and fundamental principles. A 'semantic' paradox is a proof of the logical inconsistency of certain laws governing such semantic notions as 'truth,' 'denotation,' or 'definition.' A central task for anyone constructing a semantic theory relying upon any of these notions must be devising some way of averting the semantic paradoxes.

1. History of the Semantic Paradoxes

The oldest of the semantic paradoxes is the so-called 'Paradox of the Liar,' which is attributed to Eubulides of the Megaran school (fourth century BC): 'A man says that he is lying. Is what he says true or false?' Extensive medieval study of the problem referred to the paradoxical statement by the apostle Paul in Titus 1: 12. Paul quotes approvingly the statement, by a Cretan poet, that all Cretans are liars. The *Sophismata* of Jean Buridan (1295–1356) provide the most sophisticated medieval treatment of the problem (see Moody 1953).

The development of mathematical logic and the renewal of interest in the philosophy of language led to the re-emergence of semantic paradoxes as objects of study early in the twentieth century. In 1905, Jules Richard (1906) used a Cantorian diagonal argument to 'define' a real number which is distinct from every 'definable' real number. Berry's paradox (see Russell 1908) used the definition: 'the least integer not nameable in fewer than nineteen syllables,' a definition which itself contains only eighteen syllables. Kurt Grelling created the paradox of heterologicality: he defined a 'heterological' predicate as a one-place predicate which is not true of itself (e.g., the predicate 'is long' is heterological, since 'is long' is not long). Grelling then raised the paradoxical problem: is 'is heterological' a heterological predicate? Finally, in 1932, Tarski modified Gödel's 1931 proof of the incompleteness theorem (which was itself inspired by Richard's paradox) to create a formal version of Eubulides' Liar Paradox, which Tarski used to prove the undefinability of 'truth'. Tarski introduced a schema, called Convention T, which constitutes a necessary condition of adequacy for any purported definition of truth: *s* is true if and only if *s* (e.g., an instance of this schema would be: 'snow is white' is true if and only if snow is white). Tarski demonstrated that no language can contain a predicate 'true' which makes every instance of convention T true. He did this by constructing a Liar sentence L which says, in effect, that L is false. Convention T then implies that L is true if and only if L is false.

2. The Semantic Paradoxes as Diagonal Arguments

In 1891, Cantor developed an argument known as the diagonal argument. The argument includes a method for constructing, given an infinite list of infinite sequences, an infinite sequence which does not belong to the list. The two-dimensional array which results from arranging the infinite sequences one after the other is examined below. Then the diagonal of this array is looked at, and a sequence is constructed which differs from the diagonal at every step. The resulting sequence will be different from every sequence on the original list, since it will differ with each such sequence at at least one point: the point at which the diagonal crosses the sequence. The relevance of this construction to the semantic paradoxes can be illustrated by means of Grelling's heterological paradox. First, all of the one-place predicates expressible in English are placed in some fixed order. The predicates are then arranged both along the top and the left-hand side of a two-dimensional array. At each point in the array, a T is placed if the predicate of the row is true of the predicate of the column, otherwise an F is inserted. The predicate 'is heterological' can now be defined by reference to the diagonal of the array: if the nth row has a T in the nth column, then the nth predicate is not heterological, so the predicate 'is heterological' gets an F in the nth column. Similarly, if the nth row has an F in the nth column, then 'is heterological' gets a T in the nth column. By Cantor's argument, 'is heterological' cannot appear in the list of predicates, that is, it is not a predicate expressible in English. Yet,

this cannot be, since we have in fact so expressed it (see Simmons 1990).

3. Avoiding the Paradoxes in Formal Languages: Type Theory

Both Bertrand Russell and Tarski recommended that mathematicians work in a rigidly typed formal language which avoids the semantical paradoxes. Russell called his language the language of 'ramified type theory'. Tarski proposed the distinction between 'object language' and 'meta language'. Alonzo Church (1979) demonstrated that Tarski's distinction is implied by Russell's type theory. According to Tarski, the semantic theory for a language *L* (the object language) must be carried out in a distinct language *L'* (the metalanguage). Thus, the predicates 'is a true sentence of *L*' or 'is a heterological predicate of *L*' cannot be expressed in *L* itself but only in a distinct metalanguage for *L*. If one wishes to develop a semantic theory for the metalanguage *L'*, one must do this in yet another language *L⟩*, the meta-metalanguage. This series of increasingly powerful languages, each with the capacity for expressing the semantic theories of its predecessors, is known as 'the Tarskian hierarchy'.

4. Semantic Paradox in Natural Language: Soluble or Insoluble?

Tarski characterized natural languages as inconsistent, since they plainly violate his principle of the distinctness of object language and metalanguage. According to Tarski, natural languages purport to be universal, to be able to express anything which can be expressed. Tarski believed that the semantic paradoxes demonstrate that no language can in fact be universal. Consequently, formal semantics cannot be carried out in a natural language like English, for if it could, then the semantics for any language (including English itself) could be carried out in English, causing us to run afoul of the semantic paradoxes. Furthermore, no fully satisfactory semantics for English as a whole can be given (in any language), since the semantic rules for words like 'true' or 'definable' implicit in ordinary practice are logically inconsistent. Thus, Tarski held that the semantic paradoxes constitute an insoluble problem for the semantics of natural language. Defenders of this view in the 1980s and 1990s, such as Anil Gupta and Stephen Yablo, study the semantic paradoxes in order to describe mathematically the incoherences and instabilities of natural language, and to diagnose exactly how natural language goes wrong (see Gupta 1982; Yablo 1985).

Beginning in the 1970s, a number of proposals have been made to solve the semantic paradoxes in natural languages. According to these proposals, it is possible to consistently assign semantic values of some kind to the sentences of natural language, including instances of paradoxes like the Liar. It is claimed that properly understood, the semantic rules implicit in ordinary linguistic practice, or very close approximations to these, are coherent and defensible.

5. Contemporary Diagnoses of the Paradoxes as Insoluble

Gupta (1982) has urged that any attempt to assign stable semantic values to paradoxical sentences in natural language be abandoned. He suggests that there is no semantic rule of application associated with the predicate 'is true' in English (no assignment of a set of things of which the predicate is true). Instead, there is only a rule of revision which tells us, given a putative interpretation of 'is true,' how to make marginal improvements. According to Gupta, the interpretation of 'is true' oscillates as more and more improvements are made, until a stabilization point is reached, at which every sentence which will ever stabilize has already stabilized. Paradoxical sentences like the Liar never stabilize: instead, they oscillate endlessly between truth and falsity. Yablo (1985) has developed a similar construction in which better and better approximations to the ideal represented by Tarski's convention T are achieved at each stage. Gupta's construction has the advantage that it makes all theorems of logic stably true, for example, 'the Liar sentence is true or it's not true' becomes stably true on his account. On Yablo's account, not all such theorems of logic come out as definitely and uniquely true, but his account instead respects an intuition about the 'groundedness' of truth: a disjunction should not count as true unless one of its disjuncts does; a conjunction should not count as false unless one of its conjuncts does, etc.

The principal drawback to approaches such as Gupta's and Yablo's is that any attempt to say anything definite about the paradoxical sentences of natural language runs afoul of another paradoxical diagonal argument. For instance, Gupta's theory leads one to divide the sentences of a natural language like English into three categories: stably true, stably false, and paradoxical. Since Gupta's theory is presented in English, it would seem that English has the capacity of expressing these concepts. Therefore, it should be possible to express the concept of 'super-heterologicality': a predicate of English is super-heterological if and only if it is either false of itself, or results in a paradoxical sentence when applied to itself. On Gupta's account, the predicate 'is super-heterological' results in a paradoxical sentence when applied to itself. But this means that, by definition, 'is superheterological' is superheterological, and so it should result in a true sentence when applied to itself. Gupta's diagnostic theory about semantic paradox is subject to the very same sort of paradox.

Anyone who is really convinced that the semantic paradoxes are insoluble must follow Wittgenstein's dictum from the *Tractatus Logico–Philosophicus*:

'whereof we cannot speak, thereof must we remain silent.' Semantic theory on this conception must remain radically incomplete: it may assert that certain sentences are true and others false, but it must not try to introduce any *tertium quid*. Any attempt to distinguish the paradoxical as a separate semantic category will simply reintroduce paradoxicality into one's semantic theory itself.

6. Proposed Solutions to the Liar Paradox in Natural Language

6.1 Blocking Self-Reference: The Redundancy Theory of Truth

Frank Ramsey in 1927 proposed the redundancy theory of truth as a way of averting the semantic paradoxes in natural language. Ramsey denied that 'is true' is a predicate at all. Instead, 'is true' is simply a redundant operator: to say ' "snow is white" is true' is simply a long-winded way of saying 'snow is white.' A Liar sentence, like 'this sentence is not true,' is simple nonsense. Unfortunately, this theory cannot account for sentences in which the place of the truth-bearer is replaced by a variable of quantification, as in: 'whatever the Pope says is true,' or 'I hope that what Jones says is true'.

6.2 Denying the Universality of Pretheoretical Natural Language

Saul Kripke (1975) developed an inductive construction in which the extension (the set of sentences of which the predicate is true), and the anti-extension (the set of sentences of which it is false) of the predicate 'is true' are gradually increased, beginning with an empty interpretation, in which both extension and anti-extension are empty, and ending with some sort of fixed point, at which Tarski's Convention T is at least approximated. Kripke's work inspired similar constructions by Gupta (1982), Burge (1979), Herzberger (1982), and Yablo (1985). At one of Kripke's fixed points, some sentences are true, some are false, and some (like the Liar sentence) have a truth-value 'gap.'

In order to avoid being liable to semantic paradox himself, Kripke distinguishes between pretheoretical natural language, which, he claims, lacks the conceptual resources needed to express the trichotomy true/false/neither, and the theoretical metalanguage in which he expresses his theory. Kripke, as well as Herzberger (1982), denies that the claim to universality is essential to natural language. In some sense, Kripke would admit, his theory is expressed in natural language, but it is in natural language at a different stage of conceptual development from the natural language which is its object of investigation. In effect, Kripke introduces a Tarskian hierarchy of languages by suggesting a theory of the dynamics of language change. In fact, however, ordinary English does seem to have the capacity of expressing the concept 'neither true nor false,' since this is a phenomenon which occurs in other contexts, as in the case of presupposition failure (e.g., 'the present king of France is bald'). In any case, the transition from metalanguage to metametalanguage does not seem to require any further 'conceptual' change.

6.3 Separating Assertibility and Deniability from Truth and Falsity

By means of the diagonal argument, it is possible to construct a Liar sentence L which says: L is not true (either false, or neither-true-nor-false, or paradoxical, or whatever). Clearly, one cannot truthfully assign the value 'true' to L, since this quickly leads to a contradiction. So, if the semantic theory says anything at all about L, it must say that L is not true (because paradoxical, or whatever). But this means that the theory will include a statement which is equivalent in meaning to the paradoxical sentence L. This is known as the problem of the Strengthened or Extended Liar. (The problem of superheterologicality above is an example of this phenomenon.) In the 1980s, two novel solutions to this problem were proposed. T. Parsons (1984) has suggested that we *deny* that L is true without *asserting* the paradoxical claim that L is not true. Feferman (1984) has proposed that it should be asserted that L is not true without claiming that what has been asserted (which amounts to L itself) is true. Thus, either deniability is distinguished from the assertibility of the negation, or assertibility is distinguished from truth. Both involve quite radical departures from ordinary practice.

6.4 Accepting Some Contradictions as True

An even more radical departure from ordinary practice was suggested by Graham Priest (1984). He recommends accepting as true the claim: 'the Liar sentence is both true and false.' Priest does not propose the development of a consistent theory (in some metalanguage) about an inconsistent semantic theory (expressed in the object language); such a proposal would be a variant of Kripke's (see Sect. 6.2 above). Instead, Priest rejects the object/metalanguage distinction and knowingly embraces an inconsistent theory about the paradoxical. This necessitates the development of a 'paraconsistent logic' in which, unlike classical logic, not everything follows from a contradiction. Unfortunately, such logic turns out to be quite weak, lacking such rules as modus ponens and the disjunctive syllogism.

6.5 Context-Dependent Type Theory

The semantic paradoxes can be averted and the universality of natural language preserved if a natural language is identified with a transfinite Tarskian hierarchy of formal languages. Unfortunately, there are several obvious objections to such an identification. First, there is nothing in the syntax of natural language to suggest the existence of Tarskian type restrictions. Second, paradoxical statements like the Liar do not seem to be ungrammatical. Third, when making some claim about all or some sentences of a certain kind, such as 'All of Nixon's utterances about Watergate are false,' the speaker typically has no way of knowing the Tarskian levels of Nixon's relevant statements, and so has no idea of the appropriate level to attach to his own use of 'false.' Fourth, as Kripke (1975) and Prior (1961) have pointed out, the paradoxicality of some statements depends on contingent, empirical facts. Paradoxicality does not seem to be an intrinsic feature of the meaning or logical form of a sentence. For example, the sentence 'the sentence written on the blackboard in Waggener Hall 321 on June 12, 1990 at noon is false' is paradoxical if that very sentence is in fact on that blackboard at that time, a fact which cannot be ascertained simply by inspecting the sentence itself.

All of these objections can be met if the relativity to a Tarskian level is a pragmatic, context-dependent feature of a sentence token. This idea was first proposed by Ushenko (1957) and Donnellan (1957), and developed by Charles Parsons (1974), Burge (1979), Gaifman (1988), and Barwise and Etchemendy (1987). Burge combined the Tarskian hierarchy idea with Kripke's truth-value gap theory, stipulating that sentence tokens which are interpreted as containing an inappropriately low level of 'is true' are not to be categorized as ungrammatical or meaningless (as in Russell's or Tarski's type theory). Each level of truth is semantically incomplete: for each level α, some tokens are neither $true_\alpha$ nor $false_\alpha$. Each level of truth incorporates all of the semantic information about lower levels. Burge's account of the Strengthened Liar goes as follows. The Liar token $L = L$ *is not true* is assigned the level 0. So, $L = L$ *is not $true_0$*. The token L is not in fact $true_0$, since $truth_0$ cannot include any evaluation of $paradoxical_0$ tokens like L (a consequence of the diagonal argument). Since L correctly states that it is not $true_0$, L is $true_1$. $Truth_1$ can incorporate the information about L's $nontruth_0$. It is not in fact contradictory to conclude 'L is not true and L is true,' since the interpretation of the predicate 'is true' has shifted between the first and second conjunct, for context-dependent reasons.

Barwise and Etchemendy (1987) have developed a similar account using what is known as 'situation theory,' combining non-well-founded set theory with a realist theory about such entities as properties, relations, and propositions. Gaifman (1988) and Koons (1990) have developed algorithms for assigning Tarski/Burge levels to occurrences of 'is true' in concrete networks of tokens. A difficulty which remains to be overcome is the development of an account of how the theory itself can be stated with sufficient generality, given the restriction that every occurrence of 'is true' must be assigned to some definite level

165

in the Tarskian hierarchy. In response to the same problem in connection with ramified type theory, Russell introduced the idea of 'typical ambiguity.' As an alternative, Barwise and Etchemendy have suggested that some occurrences of 'is true' be interpreted as transcending the Tarskian hierarchy altogether. Paradoxes can be avoided by denying such transcendent status to the relevant occurrences of 'is true' in paradoxical statements.

McGee (1991) offers a suggestion along these lines inspired by Carnap's idea of the partial definition of theoretical predicates. McGee distinguishes between *truth* and *definite truth*: the Liar may be either true or false (we cannot say which), but it is neither definitely true nor definitely not true. McGee agrees with Tarski that natural language is inconsistent, since the ordinary notion of truth carries with it Tarski's T schema, which leads to inconsistency. McGee urges that we replace this ordinary concept with a scientifically respectable but only partially defined predicate. We should no longer assert the Tarski biconditionals, although we can continue to use the corresponding inference rules (from 'p' to infer 'True(p)', and vice versa) outside hypothetical contexts. We cannot assert that the Liar (and other pathological propositions) are not true, but we can assert that they are not definitely true. McGee avoids a paradox involving definite truth ('This sentence is not definitely true') by denying that we can assert all instances of the schema DT: if 'p' is definitely true, then p. The set of definite truths may be inconsistent, if the meaning postulates embedded in our current scientific language are (unbeknownst to us) inconsistent.

See also: Categories and Types; Formal Semantics; Metalanguage versus Object Language; Presupposition; Truth and Paradox.

Bibliography

Barwise J, Etchemendy J 1987 *The Liar: An Essay on Truth and Circularity*. Oxford University Press, New York
Burge T 1979 Semantical paradox. *Journal of Philosophy* 76: 169–98
Church A 1979 A comparison of Russell's resolution of the semantical antinomies with that of Tarski. *Journal of Symbolic Logic* 41: 747–60
Donnellan K 1957 A note on the liar paradox. *The Philosophical Review* 65: 394–97
Feferman S 1984 Toward useful type-free theories, I. *Journal of Symbolic Logic* 49: 75–111
Gaifman H 1988 Operational pointer semantics: Solution to the self-referential puzzles, I. In: Vardi M (ed.) *Proceedings of the Second Conference on Theoretical Aspects of Reasoning About Knowledge*. Morgan Kaufman, Los Altos, CA
Grelling K, Nelson L 1908 Bemerkungen zu den Paradoxien von Russell und Burali-Forti. *Abhandlungen der Friesischen Schule* 2: 301–34
Gupta A 1982 Truth and paradox. *Journal of Philosophical Logic* 11: 61–102
Herzberger H G 1982 Notes on naive semantics. *Journal of Philosophical Logic* 11: 1–60
Koons R 1990 Three solutions to the liar paradox. In: Cooper R, Mukai K, Perry P (eds.) *Situation Theory and Its Applications*. Center for the Study of Language and Information, Stanford, CA
Koons R 1992 *Paradoxes of Belief and Strategic Rationality*. Cambridge University Press, New York
Kripke S 1975 Outline of a theory of truth. *Journal of Philosophy* 72: 690–716
Martin R L (ed.) 1984 *Recent Essays on Truth and the Liar Paradox*. Clarendon Press, Oxford
McGee V 1991 *Truth, Vagueness and Paradox*. Hackett Publishing Company, Indianapolis, IN
Moody E A 1953 *Truth and Consequence in Medieval Logic*. North Holland, Amsterdam
Parsons C 1974 The liar paradox. *Journal of Philosophical Logic* 3: 381–412
Parsons T 1984 Assertion, denial and the liar paradox. *Journal of Philosophical Logic* 13: 137–52
Priest G 1984 Logic of paradox revisited. *Journal of Philosophical Logic* 13: 153–79
Prior A N 1961 On a family of paradoxes. *Notre Dame Journal of Formal Logic* 2: 16–32
Richard J 1906 Les Principes des mathématiques et le problème des ensembles. *Acta Mathematica* 30: 295–96
Russell B 1908 Mathematical logic as based on the theory of types. *American Journal of Mathematics* 30: 222–62
Simmons K 1990 The diagonal argument and the liar. *Journal of Philosophical Logic* 19: 277–304
Ushenko 1957 An addendum to the note on the liar paradox. *The Philosophical Review* 65: 394–97
Yablo S 1985 Truth and reflection. *Journal of Philosophical Logic* 14: 297–349

Picture Theory of Meaning

D. E. B. Pollard

The term 'meaning' is susceptible of many different and sometimes conflicting characterizations. The term 'picture,' by contrast, seems more intuitively accessible, and naturally suggests something visible. The term 'picture theory of meaning,' therefore, signals an analogy if not a metaphor which purports to elucidate something fundamental about the way language works and fulfills its communicative function.

1. Preliminary Considerations

Among the most general if simple-minded questions one can ask about language is: how is it that a sequence or combination of words can be used to represent things in the world? Another question is: how is it that we can understand sentences composed of familiar words but which we have never heard before? Questions such as these raise a more general issue, namely, what (if any) are the most general and abstract constraints on what and how language can be said to represent? The idea that language has a representational function is probably as common as it is ancient. Indeed, the notion of representation itself carries with it the suggestion of some sort of matching or correlation of language with what lies beyond it. Thus sentences (and the words of which they consist) get their meaning, if not their truth and reference, by virtue of such a relation. Where truth is concerned, the traditional notion has been that of correspondence. A sentence, or rather the proposition it expresses, is said to be true if it corresponds to reality. The exact nature of this correspondence has proved difficult to articulate, but some recent theories of meaning have taken the notion of truth as central to the project of explaining meaning and understanding. According to this kind of approach, understanding a sentence is knowing the conditions for it to be true. The attractiveness of the picture theory of meaning is that it promises to deliver a detailed account of this representational relationship between language and the world.

2. Elements of a Theory

The most comprehensive and sustained articulation of a picture theory of meaning is undoubtedly that due to the philosopher Ludwig Wittgenstein. In his famous early work, the *Tractatus Logico–Philosophicus*, he speaks of sentences or propositions as pictures. For him, the essence of representation is description, and a proposition represents what he calls a possible 'state of affairs.' By itself, a proposition neither asserts or denies anything. Crucial to Wittgenstein's account are two theses: (a) isomorphism, i.e., there must be a one-to-one correspondence between the elements of a proposition and the elements of the state of affairs it represents. In other words, it must have the same structure and number of elements as the reality it portrays; (b) atomism, i.e., every proposition is a function of its constituent expressions, and in the case of the most basic or elementary propositions, these constituent expressions must be simple names, expressions which are not further analyzable and which appropriately and uniquely identify individual basic objects—the most fundamental constituents of reality. These simple names have reference only; their role or meaning resides solely in their hav-

ing such unique reference. The picturing relationship, therefore, depends ultimately upon this basic relation between names and objects. More complex propositions are functions of such elementary propositions, that is to say, they are truth-functional compounds generated by means of logical constants or operators such as 'not,' 'and,' 'or,' etc.. The truth status (truth-value) of such compounds depends entirely on the truth possibilities assigned to the constituent propositions. Thus in the case of negation, for example, the proposition *It is not the case that it is snowing* is false if it is in fact snowing and true if it is not snowing. Any logic satisfying this compositional feature is usually described as 'extensional', and where just the two truth values 'true' and 'false' are operative, the logic is generally also called 'classical.' An important characteristic of the elementary propositions which distinguishes them from all the others, is that they are independent of one another: no one of them depends for its truth (or comprehension) on any other elementary proposition. As to the logical constants themselves, their function is not representational: they merely signify the operations by which the compound propositions are generated.

3. Problems and Criticisms

Some problems are specific to Wittgenstein's own version of the theory, and they have produced a considerable secondary literature of exegesis and interpretation. Among these problems are the notion of 'logical form' (the form elementary propositions are supposed to share with the corresponding state of affairs) and the fact that the 'basic' objects are not explicitly characterized. In this latter respect, the account differs from the theory of logical atomism put forward by Bertrand Russell. However, there are more general difficulties. First of all, there is a problem with any austerely extensional treatment of language. There are a number of constructions which are not readily or immediately accommodated within such a scheme, e.g., modal contexts of the form 'Necessarily *p*' or 'Possibly *p*,' and statements of 'propositional attitude' like *Joan believes (hopes, fears) that p*, which at least prima facie look like logical functions of the constituent proposition *p*. However, in neither of these cases does the truth-value of the constituent proposition totally determine the truth-value of the compound. For example, it could be true that Joan believes that the Earth is flat regardless of whether the proposition that the Earth is flat is true or false. Second, there is a wide variety of propositions for which the pictorial analogy seems counterintuitive or implausible. Examples of these include not only those mentioned above, but also the highly abstract propositions of mathematics, the general or law-like statements of the kind typical of scientific theory and physics in particular, and those propositions which conspicuously exhibit the feature commonly termed 'egocentricity' or 'deixis,' like *I shall see you there tomorrow*. Ultimately, however, even the most banal examples seem to point up the salient differences between linguistic and pictorial modes of representation. If one takes the hackneyed example *The cat sat on the mat*, then a drawing of the relevant state of affairs would show the representation of a cat and the representation of a mat, but no obvious element answering to the linguistic element 'sat on.' Yet despite this difference, there is a sense in which it would be perfectly legitimate to claim that the same state of affairs has been communicated by both the drawing and the proposition.

4. The Aftermath of the Theory

Despite the general consensus that the picture theory is fatally flawed, some of its traits have proved remarkably tenacious. For at least some theorists, there remains a serious question of whether an atomistic metaphysics can be made to serve the project of constructing a theory of meaning for a formalized language, i.e., a rigorous technical idiom sufficiently sophisticated to render explicitly the subtleties and more contextually bound features of natural language. Additionally, many of the prominent logico–semantic theories are compositional, if not simply truth-functional in complexion, and usually appeal to some distinction between fundamental and derived semantic categories. Thus, for example, in some such schemes, sentences and (simple) nouns or nominals are taken as basic, while predicate and functional expressions are taken as belonging to a derived category of expressions which make sentences out of nouns or out of other sentences. So a predicate like ' ... is sitting' would combine with the noun 'Socrates' to yield the sentence *Socrates is sitting*.

However, the demise of the original theory has also had its more skeptical consequences. The difficulty of constructing a plausible account of the central notion of isomorphism has raised doubts about the very feasibility of systematic attempts to 'match words to the world.' In the spirit of Wittgenstein's own later work,

it has been argued in some quarters that the notion of such an isomorphism of language and world is itself an artefact of language, 'a shadow cast by grammar.' The natural corollary of this view is that reality (or one's conception of it) is if anything constituted by language. In its most extreme form, this latter position implies that different languages embody 'distinct realities'. Interestingly, this issue of relativism in linguistic theory has an echo in discussions of artistic representation: if there are different conventions of pictorial representation rendering nugatory any claims to the effect that one kind of picture is any more 'objective' than any other, then it might be argued that this undermines the very metaphor or analogy on which the picture theory depends. Whether this point has negative implications for representational accounts of language in general remains an open question.

See also: Wittgenstein, Ludwig.

Bibliography

Ayer A J 1986 *Ludwig Wittgenstein*. Penguin Books, Harmondsworth
Anscombe G E M 1967 *An Introduction To Wittgenstein's Tractatus*. Hutchinson, London
Copi I M, Beard R W (eds.) 1966 *Essays on Wittgenstein's Tractatus*. Routledge & Kegan Paul, London
Hacker P M S 1981 The rise and fall of the picture theory. In: Block I (ed.) *Perspectives on the Philosophy of Wittgenstein*. Blackwell, Oxford
Pears D F 1971 *Wittgenstein*. Fontana, London
Russell B A W 1956 The philosophy of logical atomism. In: Marsh R C (ed.) *Logic and Knowledge*. Allen and Unwin, London
Urmson J O 1956 *Philosophical Analysis: Its Development Between the Two World Wars*. Clarendon Press, Oxford
Waismann F 1965 *Principles of Linguistic Philosophy*. Harre R (ed.) Macmillan, London
Wisdom J 1969 *Logical Constructions*. Random House, New York
Wittgenstein L 1953 (trans. Anscombe G E M) *Philosophical Investigations*. Blackwell, Oxford
Wittgenstein L 1961 (trans. Pears D F, McGuiness B F) *Tractatus Logico–Philosophicus*. Routledge & Kegan Paul, London

Radical Interpretation

E. M. Fricker

The scenario of 'radical interpretation' is that of an individual—perhaps a field linguist—who finds herself amongst a people with which her own culture has had no previous contact, and who must try to come to understand them and their language. Philosophers in what may be called the 'interpretationist' school in analytic philosophy have thought that, by considering how she might proceed with her task, light may be thrown on the nature of mental and semantic concepts. The tactic has a broadly verificationist inspiration: their idea is that one can find out what meaning and the mind are, by seeing how one detects them in others.

1. W. V. O. Quine

Use of the scenario for this purpose first came to prominence with the publication in 1960 of Quine's *Word and Object*. The discussion in ch. 2 of 'radical translation' is a landmark in the philosophy of language, and all debate about the nature of meaning since is necessarily informed by, even if it rejects, Quine's approach. Quine subscribed to behaviorism about meaning, holding that, insofar as it is fixed at all, 'meaning is a property of behavior.' Accordingly, he set out to consider how much of ordinary semantic notions can be constructed from a basis of purely physical facts about the 'natives' disposition to verbal behavior. His true concern was thus not so much epistemic as metaphysical: not to see how we might in practice seek to determine the meanings of native sentences, but rather to explore how, as David Lewis has put it, 'the facts (about behavior) determine the facts (about meaning).' Quine used the scenario as a heuristic device to explore this latter question; although his verificationist leanings mean that for him the metaphysical question of if and how the facts are fixed becomes one with the question of how they might, at least in principle, be verified. Quine considered how a translator might arrive at a correct 'translation manual' from the natives' language into her own. He concluded, notoriously, that the data of natives' dispositions to verbal behavior does not suffice to narrow the choice down to just one: all the constraints available on the translator's task leave many manuals equally acceptable. The most disturbing element in this thesis of the 'indeterminacy of translation' was Quine's claim of the 'inscrutability of reference': there is no basis to discriminate between alternative 'analytical hypotheses' about sentences which assign different references to terms and predicates, where these yield logically equivalent translations for whole sentences. So, in Quine's example, it is indeterminate whether native talk is about rabbits, rabbit parts, or rabbit time-slices. This thesis about reference has been convincingly argued against by Evans, but it is now generally recognized that some considerable indeterminacy in translation exists.

2. Donald Davidson

Quine was concerned solely with how the meaning of native sentences might be discovered by a translator. But it is now generally recognized that this task can be accomplished only simultaneously with another: the 'interpretation' of the speakers of the language to be translated—that is, the ascription to them of beliefs, desires, and other mental states. The impossi-

bility demonstrated by Quine of constructing sentence meanings from facts about speakers' dispositions to verbal behavior is part of the more general falsity of behaviorism. Behaviorism is false because there is no simple, one-by-one relation of the mental states of persons to their observable behavior: what a person does in response to a given stimulus depends not just on what she believes, but also on what she wants, and there is no principled limit on the further mental states which may crucially affect her response. Similarly, what the sentences of a subject's language mean has no implications for her behavior except as mediated by her mental states. Thus Davidson, continuing the investigation of mental and semantic concepts by means of the radical interpretation scenario, noticed how meaning and belief 'conspire' together to determine which sentences a subject holds true (and hence which she will assent to). In Davidson's work the primary focus switches to the mental: his concern is with how a 'radical interpreter' might ascribe mental states to the natives. He holds that the essential nature of the mind can be illuminated by this method. He uses it to argue, for example, that beliefs are by nature mainly true. One must, he claims, use a principle of 'charity' in interpreting others—that is, ascribe to them mainly true beliefs; and he makes a characteristic interpretationist move from this claim about the inevitable method of interpretation, to a conclusion about the nature of belief itself. The product of a successful interpretation exercise will be both an ascription of beliefs, etc., to the natives, and a theory of meaning for their language. Davidson argues that, while explicit reduction of sentence meaning to non-semantic notions is impossible, by giving an account of how such an interpretation of a community can be achieved, one gives all that is needed by way of philosophical explanation of the nature of meaning. He holds that a theory of truth can serve as a theory of meaning, and has suggested that telling the radical interpretation story can also serve as all that is needed by way of philosophical explanation of what truth is. It has, however, been questioned whether the same story can illuminate both truth and meaning.

3. State of the Art

That meanings cannot be constructed from speakers' dispositions, as Quine showed, is now generally recognized. But while Quine drew the moral that ordinary semantic notions are not scientifically respectable, most nowadays would conclude instead that his standard for respectability was too severe. But the appeal to radical interpretation in the philosophical elucidation of the mental and semantic remains much in evidence. Doubts about Davidson's work focus on two main issues. It is uncontroversial that an interpretation must 'make sense' of the individual(s) to be interpreted, and that this requires seeing a certain pattern in the interrelations amongst their mental states, and in how these states relate to the meanings of sentences of their language. But whether this requires the dominant role for 'charity' urged by Davidson, or exactly what this comes to, has been contested. More radically, the methodology behind the radical interpretation approach to meaning and the mind may be questioned. It assumes that an account of what mental states and meanings are is to be extracted from an account of how one goes about ascribing them to others; but the true relation of priority may be the reverse: it is not until there is a philosophical account of the nature of the mind, that it will be possible to determine how, if at all, one can come to know the mental states of others.

See also: Indeterminacy of Translation.

Bibliography

Blackburn S 1984 *Spreading the Word*. Clarendon Press, Oxford
Davidson D 1984 *Inquiries into Truth and Interpretation*. Clarendon Press, Oxford
Evans G 1975 Identity and predication. *Journal of Philosophy* **72**: 343–63
Goldman A 1989 Interpretation psychologized. *Mind and Language* **4**: 161–85
LePore E (ed.) 1986 *Truth and Interpretation: Perspectives on the Philosophy of Donald Davidson*. Blackwell, Oxford
Lewis D 1974 Radical interpretation. *Synthese* **27**: 331–44
McGinn C 1977 Charity, interpretation and belief. *Journal of Philosophy* **74**: 521–35
Quine W V O 1960 *Word and Object*. MIT Press, Cambridge, MA

Rules

P. Pagin

The idea that linguistic practice is essentially rule-governed has found widespread acceptance, especially among those engaged in constructive work in grammar or semantics, and has been regarded by some as almost self-evident. Nonetheless it is highly controversial within the philosophy of language. Proponents have suggested a great number of kinds of linguistic rule, and serious attempts at demarcating and explicating the concept of a rule have been made, whereas opponents have concentrated on more general epistemological issues particularly regarding what it is to know a language and the place that rules might have in such knowledge. (For further discussion, see *Convention*.)

1. The Concept of a Rule

1.1 General Characterization

The term 'rule' belongs to a group of terms, including 'norm,' 'convention,' 'standard,' 'regulation,' 'directive,' 'instruction,' 'law' (in the prescriptive sense), many of which frequently occur together in dictionary explanations, sometimes presented as synonyms. Ordinary linguistic usage does not provide clear-cut distinctions and no taxonomic consensus has been established among theorists.

Nevertheless, there are differences between the use of the term 'rule' and uses of its cognates which to some degree explain why it is often preferred in theories of language.

(a) 'Rule' is less tied to the notion of an authority, for example with power to issue rules, than 'law' and 'regulation.'

(b) 'Rule' is more closely tied to the notion of guiding persons in action than are 'norm' and 'standard.'

(c) 'Rule' is more closely tied to the notion of evaluating actions as right or wrong than, for example, 'convention' and 'direction.'

(d) 'Rule' is more closely tied (than, for example, 'norm' and 'standard') to direct evaluation of action as opposed to indirect evaluation, in which someone is judged responsible for defects in a product. There is, however, a traditional distinction between on the one hand so-called rules of action, or ought-to-do rules (Tunsollen) and on the other hand so-called ideal rules, or ought-to-be rules (Seinsollen), such as standards for chemicals.

(e) 'Rule' has a stronger suggestion of arbitrariness than, for instance, 'norm.' It often refers to items that can be introduced, adopted, and replaced by decision, whereas 'norm' is typically used for standards perceived as not being subject to choice. Connected with this is the tendency, again marking a difference, to use 'norm' so that being in force, in a community, say, is built into the concept of being a norm.

(f) 'Rule,' more than related terms, is used with respect to special procedures (rules of inference) and institutionally created activities, such as games. The modern tradition distinguishes between regulative rules, serving to regulate preexisting activities (traffic regulations), and so-called constitutive rules, which define institutions and create new types of action (like checkmating).

(g) 'Rule' is tied to a notion of generality in a way which, for instance, 'instruction' is not and which is often taken to exclude overlap with the use of 'command.' Two kinds of generality are usually seen as characteristic of rules. On the one hand a rule concerns a type of action; it can be violated or complied with indefinitely many times. On the other hand it concerns agents generally, or agents in a type of situation; it can be violated or complied with by an indefinite number of people. Although this characterization is not without problems it points at a feature which can be claimed to be essential to the concept.

(h) There is a use of 'rule,' as in 'strategic rule' and 'rule of thumb,' such that an item of this more factual kind (sometimes called technical) is subject to direct justification: does complying with it generally lead to desired results? It is essential here that what counts as a desired result is well-determined; stating the purpose may be part of stating the rule (If you want to...) or else the purpose may be clear from the area of application of the rule (as in strategic rules of chess). This double usage is convenient, since something may be called a rule whether it imposes or just registers a regularity (such as a grammatical one).

In explicating the concept of a rule some writers are content to elaborate on features such as those already listed. Some proceed to analyze the structure of rules. Von Wright (1963), by using 'norm' as the most general term, distinguishes between 'character' (obligation, permission, prohibition), 'content' (type of action or activity; that which is obligatory, permitted, prohibited) and 'condition of application' (a condition that is met in a situation where someone can act in accordance with or against the rule). He also distinguishes between categorical and conditional rules, and between positive, negative, and mixed rules, depending on whether the content is a type of doing something, forbearing to do something, or a mixed complex of these. This analysis is then fitted into a so-called deontic logic, that is, a logic of rules (norms, or better, norm-statements).

Explications or analyses more or less similar to that of von Wright have been given within ethics and philosophy of law. What is generally missing in such treatments are distinctions between kinds of correctness: an utterance may be semantically correct and yet a violation of etiquette. That is, the particular respect in which actions are evaluated with respect to a rule is not perceived as corresponding to an ingredient in the rule itself.

1.2 What Rules Are

The question of what rules really are has received much less attention. It is common to think of rules as abstract entities. Some, however, take them to be linguistic, while others take them to be nonlinguistic. Ross, for instance (1968), takes rules to be a species of directives, themselves intrinsically normative entities that are meanings of prescriptive sentences, like propositions are of descriptive sentences. Although rules have even been thought to be particular inscriptions of rule-sentences, the concept of a rule is normally distinguished from that of a formulation of a rule, as described by Max Black (1962). Black, however, denies that rule-formulations designate, describe, or even express rules (as their meanings). Instead, to understand what a rule is we must look to the use of rule-formulations. This is in line with Wittgenstein's later philosophy.

To Wittgenstein (1958) the concept of a rule is a family resemblance concept: members of the family of rules have various features in common with other members, but it is misguided to look for any defining feature common to all members, an essence of rules. To understand the concept of a rule, consideration should be given not only to what is called a rule, but also to all that is involved in a rule-following practice, including training, explaining (how to proceed), justification (and limits thereof), and evaluation of actions by means of reference to rules.

Many other theorists insist on social function or social acceptance as part of what it is to be a rule. Ross, for instance (1968), takes a rule to be a rule of some community, a (general) directive corresponding to social facts, being generally complied with in the community. Bartsch (1987) characterizes norms, social rules, as the social reality of correctness notions. This feature is particularly prominent in Shwayder's attempt at a truly informative explication (Shwayder 1965). Roughly, a rule (in the primary, communal sense) is a system of expectations in a community concerning behavior of its members, such that (a) members believe other members to have the same expectation, (b) the expectations of others constitute the reason for a member to act in accordance with them, and (c) members expect that other members conform for this reason. This idea has been developed and refined by David Lewis for the notion of a convention (regarded by Lewis as a kind of rule) and has, via Lewis, given rise to a whole tradition of varieties of the approach.

2. Linguistic Rules

The notion of a linguistic rule is perhaps most immediately associated with very general rules of traditional school grammars; rules of spelling (e.g., *nn* never occurs before *t*), phonological rules (e.g., voiced endings turning voiceless in certain contexts), morphological rules (e.g., endings of regular verbs in various tenses), and simple syntactic rules (e.g., noun and verb must agree in number). Rules of this kind are explicitly stated, used in language teaching, applied as standards of correct linguistic usage, and, usually in contradistinction to much else included in grammars, called rules.

What should properly be called a linguistic rule, however, is another matter. To the extent that the required generality of a rule concerns its relation to behavior, the statement that *killed* is the past tense form of the verb *kill* is a statement of a rule, since it is general with respect to agents and highly general with respect to particular speech acts governed by it. Seen in this light the general rule about past tense forms of regular verbs appears to be a more factual or technical rule, a general guide or recipe for speaking in accordance with the more particular rules (governing individual verbs) that may be regarded as normative. In this way normativity, or the degree thereof, may be inversely related to the degree of generality.

Stating that in English *gold* is a noun, or a mass noun, is not generally considered as stating a rule, but rather as stating a fact. To the extent that the property of being a mass noun in English is a conventional one, however, this is a fact about a convention, and the statement may then also be regarded as a statement of the convention, or rule, itself. Together with, say, the rule that mass nouns do not take the indefinite article, the rule (about *gold*) so stated also has a share in syntactic standards of linguistic behavior. Indeed, from a formal point of view it may be regarded as a rule of higher order, implicitly laying down what other (lower order) rules apply to *gold* (namely the rules governing mass nouns).

On the other hand, however, the statement that *gold* is a mass noun may also be regarded in a number of other ways. The situation is quite unlike that with respect to formal languages. The class of sentences of a language for predicate logic is determined by a few simple clauses, stating on the one hand the basic vocabulary of signs of various categories, and on the other hand the formation rules, which comprise rules for forming atomic sentences (by way of joining terms and predicate letters) and for forming complex sentences out of these and the logical symbols (for example, if *A* and *B* are sentences, then *A&B* is a sentence). These rules are easily stated, and learned, and define the language in question.

2.1 Syntactic Rules in Generative Grammar

Specifying the class of sentences of a natural language, like English, on the other hand, is the task of modern generative grammars. The syntactic part of such a grammar may consist of a set of phrase structure rules, a set of lexical insertion rules, and a set of transformation rules. Rules of the first kind produce so-called deep structures of sentences (the most basic being S → NP VP, which, roughly stated, produces the category structure NOUN PHRASE–VERB PHRASE out of the category SENTENCE). Rules of the second kind provide for inserting linguistic expressions (lexical items) into structures, at appropriate places, depending on their respective categories (such as NOUN). Rules of the third kind are rules for transforming results of applying rules of the former kinds by way of operations such as reordering and deletion (as with the rule of equi NP deletion, for removing a repeated occurrence of a particular noun phrase).

Such systems are readily understood as systems of rules for producing sentences. They are stated and can be followed. It is another question in what sense, if any, they are rules of a particular natural language. On the one hand the grammar may be incorrect in the sense of producing sentences which are not recognized as well-formed by speakers of the language. Even if correct its rules are clearly not, in any strict sense, followed by the speakers. Neither is it generally claimed by linguists that such rules are subconsciously operative in actual practice. It is, on the other hand, claimed, for example, by Chomsky (1976, 1980), that a grammar which is adequate in a stronger sense represents the linguistic competence of the speakers, their knowledge of the language. If this claim is good there is a sense in which the rules of such a grammar are rules of the language, but in that sense they can hardly be said to define it.

2.2 Semantic Rules

With respect to formal languages semantic rules, concerning meaning, can be stated and regarded as just as normative/defining as formation rules. Carnap (1956) distinguishes between rules of designation for simple expressions (predicates—'H' designates Human—and individual constants—'s' designates Walter Scott) and rules of truth (e.g., *A&B* is true if and only if *A* is true and *B* is true). In addition to rules of this kind he also proposes so-called meaning postulates, such as a rule to the effect that the formal counterpart of *Bachelors are not married* is true, in order to capture nonlogical conceptual (analytical) truths. In Montague semantics (Montague and Thomason 1974) there are meaning postulates as well as semantic rules corresponding to Carnap's rules of truth (and also for other operators and functions of higher types), but they belong to a grammar for (a fragment of) natural English. Thus, they are presented as in some sense being rules of English.

So-called truth theories of natural languages, according to Davidson's conception (1984), are to contain statements of virtually the same kind as Carnap's statements of rules of designation and rules of truth. However, to the extent that they are rule statements the rules are just rules of the theory; the claim that they govern the practice of the speakers is not part of the theory and it is also rejected by Davidson. In the conception of Lewis, on the other hand, the connection between a set of abstract syntactic and semantic rules, thought of as defining a particular natural language, itself regarded as an abstract entity, is forged by means of a highly general rule, or convention (in Lewis's sense), which the speakers actually follow.

2.3 Semantic Rules in Generative Grammar

In a grammar of modern linguistic theory the semantic component may look like this: on the one hand there is a so-called dictionary, the entries of which consist of lexical rules for primitive expressions, providing meaning (where possible by means of verbal meaning explanations) and grammatical category. On the other hand there are so-called projection rules for arriving at the meaning of complex expressions, and ultimately sentences, by way of selecting the readings of ambiguous simpler expressions that fit together within the more complex ones. In grammars of other kinds, however, what are thought of as semantic structures (doubling as phrase structures) are generated directly, providing the basis for transformations and insertion of lexical items. Such generating rules are not semantic in the sense of (directly and overtly) providing interpretations of linguistic expressions. Within modern linguistic theory the notion of a syntactic rule is clearer than that of a semantic rule, but for several reasons, in part connected with the existence of various constraints imposed on syntax by semantics or vice versa, the two notions are not sharply separated.

2.4 Semantic Rules and Language-games

In Hintikka's game-theoretic semantics (Hintikka and Kulas 1983;), developed for both formal and natural languages, a different conception of semantic rules concerning truth can be found. A sentence *S* is true in case there is a winning strategy, for the player Myself against the player Nature, in the semantical game associated with *S*. Such a game is defined by a number of rules, such as: the first move in a game associated with a conjunction *A&B* is Nature's choice of either *A* or *B*, whereupon the rest of the game is that associated with Nature's choice (that is, *A* or *B*; since Nature makes the choice, Myself must have a winning strategy for *A* as well as for *B*). Hintikka connects this approach with Wittgenstein's notion of a language-game, claiming that a speaker's understanding of a sentence actually consists of his mastery of the rules associated with it and that semantic (word–world) relations are established in linguistic activity as governed by such rules.

In Sellars's writings (1963, 1974) a more abstract conception of the nature of semantic rules can be found. Sellars, too, employs the notion of a language-game, and makes the analogy with (some) ordinary games rather close. In using a linguistic expression one takes a position in the language-game. A move in the game is a transition from one position to another.

Rules of inference, material as well as formal (logical), govern such moves. One example (material) is the move from calling something *red* to calling it *extended* (the rule of which corresponds to a meaning postulate in Carnap's sense). Other rules, however, govern transitions which are not moves proper but transitions into (language entry) and out of (language departure) the game. The transition from observing a red patch to calling it *red* is of the former kind, and the transition from uttering *I am going out* to going out is of the latter kind. Rules of these three kinds determine the meaning of expressions, but for epistemological reasons (compare Sect. 3) they are primarily to be thought of as ought-to-be rules, that is, as rules providing standards for linguistic behavior, not as rules to be directly obeyed. Corresponding to these rules, however, there are ought-to-do rules for mature language users, requiring them to see to it that those standards are met, by training, teaching, and criticism (including self-criticism). Sellars's picture of linguistic practice as rule-governed is, of course, highly speculative, and it is doubtful that it can be borne out by more detailed considerations.

The notion of a language-game is originally Wittgenstein's (1958). The analogy with games strongly suggests a view of linguistic practice as rule-governed, and although it often arises in connection with other points, Wittgenstein repeatedly speaks of rules of language-games. It is open to debate, however, to what extent he acknowledges the existence of semantic rules as determining the meaning of linguistic expressions.

On the one hand there are in Wittgenstein references to grammatical rules, though 'grammar' is not here used in the ordinary sense but rather in the sense of a set of standards of description, which themselves give rise to rules of inference. Such standards can be expressed in so-called grammatical statements, such as *White is lighter than black*, or *An order orders its own execution*. These rules provide for inferences from *A is white* and *B is black* to *A is lighter than B*, and from *A was ordered to V* and *A didn't V* to *A didn't execute the order*. They also exclude descriptions which are inconsistent with such inferences as nonsensical, counter to grammar. These grammatical statements are normative; they do not flow from the meanings of the words involved but are part of the determination of meaning.

On the other hand it is not fully clear whether Wittgenstein's view was that there is, for example, a meaning-determining rule governing the use of *red*, or just something closely analogous, namely (institutional) standards of correctness of that use. The difference, if there is one, would be that if there were such a rule, then that rule would concern a certain transition, namely that from recognizing something as red to calling it *red*, and at least, so Wittgenstein argues, there is no rule of that kind. It may be, however, that the point is not to insist on a distinction, but to correct an erroneous conception of (semantic) rules. This is suggested in other passages, where it is stressed that the determination of the use of a word by rules is not complete; new situations can always arise which are not covered by the rules (so-called open-texture).

2.5 Pragmatic Rules

The notion of pragmatic rules is one of rules governing linguistic activity in respects other than those of syntax and semantics, in respects peculiar to communication. This is an area where it is difficult to distinguish features characteristic of linguistic practice as such from other factors, such as (everyday) human psychology, cultural or social norms, and contexts; indeed the desirability of employing that distinction is also questionable. Nonetheless, elaborate pragmatic analyses in terms of linguistic rules have been carried out, above all concerning individual speech acts and features of conversational interaction.

J. L. Austin (1976) introduced the notion of illocutionary acts, speech acts such as asserting, promising, commanding, congratulating. A speech act belongs to one of these categories by virtue of intrinsic properties, as opposed to properties depending on further reactions of the hearer, by virtue of which the act can be characterized as an act of scaring, amusing, or persuading. In contradistinction to acts of these kinds, called perlocutionary, illocutionary acts were held by Austin to involve conventions, but he did not develop this idea. It was later developed by Searle (1969), who extracted a number of rules for various kinds of illocutionary act. As regards promising, Searle's main example, there are five rules, understood as governing the use of expressions such as *I promise* and other linguistic devices indicating the illocutionary type of promising (and in virtue of this Searle characterizes these rules as semantic). The first of these requires that such an expression be uttered only in the context of predicating a future action of the speaker (the propositional content rule), the second that it be uttered only if the hearer prefers performance of that action to nonperformance and the speaker also believes this of the hearer, the third that it be uttered only if that action would not obviously be performed anyway (preparatory rules), the fourth that it be uttered only if the speaker intends to perform the action (the sincerity rule). These four rules are held to regulate the practice of promising. The fifth, on the other hand, the so-called essential rule, is seen by Searle as constitutive of that practice, as a rule which makes promising possible. This is the rule which (provided that the requirements of the first three rules are met) holds that such an utterance counts as undertaking an obligation to perform the action in question. These rule statements no doubt capture standard features of promisory utterances, even though Searle's

conception of the rules themselves, especially the fifth, has been subject to discussion.

A different kind of pragmatic rule is the one which Grice (1989) has labeled conversational maxims. It includes rules such as: Make your contribution as informative as required (for the current purposes of the exchange)! Do not say that for which you lack adequate evidence! Be relevant! By means of reference to such rules Grice explains varieties of so-called conversational implicature, as in the phenomenon of deliberately conveying or implying something else than one is literally saying.

3. Is Linguistic Practice Rule-governed?

The idea that linguistic practice is essentially rule-governed, that the meaning of linguistic expressions is determined by rules, is intimately connected with a conception of linguistic capacity as a kind of knowledge. On this conception a speaker stands in a cognitive relation to his own mother tongue; his ability to use it is a way of knowing the meaning of its expressions. Given the further idea that the meaning of a linguistic expression is arbitrary, the speaker's knowledge must be a knowledge of rules. These two tenets, about determination of meaning by rules and about knowledge of one's language, are almost invariably discussed together.

3.1 Language as Conventional

The most basic conception of meaning as determined by rules is that of meaning as conventional. One argument against this (Davidson 1984) is that we can give an account of what a speaker means by his words without requiring that the speaker *knows* the meaning of his words, and hence without requiring that he knows conventions. The basic point of another well-known argument (Quine 1976) is that, since proponents of the view must ultimately appeal to *unstated* conventions, the claim that speakers go by conventions runs the risk of becoming empty (for more on this, see *Convention*).

Sellars, too (1974), stresses that only antecedently stated rules can be said to be obeyed. His conclusion, however, is that for this reason rules which determine meaning must be so-called ought-to-be rules (compare Sect. 2.4). In this way Sellars hopes to avoid a regress: knowledge of language requires knowledge of rules, which is knowledge of rule formulations, which in turn requires knowledge of language, and so on. However, since just conforming to ought-to-be linguistic rules, in Sellars's view, falls short of constituting understanding, it is not clear that the regress is really avoided.

3.2 Wittgenstein on Normative Linguistic Practice

In Wittgenstein's view (1958) there are other ways of stating rules than that of providing full-fledged verbal formulations. The word *elephant* can be explained (partially, at least) by pointing at one, saying that that is an elephant. The point is that in doing so it is not just giving one example of how the word is applied, not just giving a hint for guessing at how to apply it in other cases. It is an explanation in its own right, a way of specifying the standards governing the use of the word, a way of expressing a rule. The tendency to think otherwise, that is, to think that no number of mere examples of using a word, or applying a rule, could determine future applications, presupposes that understanding of an expression, grasp of a rule, is something essentially private, something which cannot be fully conveyed to others. But, so Wittgenstein argues, nothing mental could determine the correctness or incorrectness of future applications, since anything mental could at most be contingently related to them. Hence, understanding cannot be essentially private, a hidden mental phenomenon; if a word is understood, then it can also be explained to others.

Wittgenstein's point of departure is the practice of speaking a common language. Such a practice stands out as normative, involving training, explaining, and correcting. Accordingly, a speaker taking part in the practice is pictured as one who has acquired knowledge of the practice, a great number of interrelated abilities. Such an ability is not only in conformance with communal standards, but is an ability to specify and independently apply those standards.

Only within such a practice does a rule-formulation have meaning. The rule, however, is no more precise than the interpretation of the expression of the rule. Therefore, what is determined by, or is a consequence of, a rule, is nothing other than that which is determined within the practice of applying that rule (and related rules). This has consequences within the philosophy of mathematics (Wittgenstein 1978). It is a necessary outcome of rules of mathematics that $2 + 3 = 5$ only insofar as this is regarded as a necessary outcome within mathematical practice. Saying that it is a necessary outcome is a legitimate way of expressing a normative attitude, the attitude of treating $2 + 3 = 5$ as unshakable, immune to revision, as a rule of grammar, in Wittgenstein's sense, but humans are inclined to misconceive themselves as having observed a logical or metaphysical fact, independent of any human activity, as if the rules could grind out consequences on their own.

On Wittgenstein's view there must be something intermediary between finding out the consequences of a rule and just adding to the explanation, or definition, of the rule itself. The notion of such an intermediary is, however, problematic.

Following the publication of Kripke's seminal interpretation of Wittgenstein in Kripke (1982), much interest has been devoted to questions of rule following, normativity of language and the role of speech communities. For an overview, see Boghossian (1989).

3.3 Deep Linguistic Competence

In Chomsky's view (1976, 1980, 1986), if there are two grammars for a given language, both of which correctly specify the class of sentences of that language, then there is a basis for claiming that only one of them is the correct one, that it specifies the class of sentences in the right way.

What the right way is depends on the linguistic knowledge of the speakers. That knowledge is knowledge of the rules of the language. It is not knowledge of any ordinary kind, but a special kind of competence, consisting in having the rules of the language internally represented, in the mind, or in the brain. That grammar is correct which provides the rules which are so represented. This conception is shared by many other linguists. Linguistics is, accordingly, regarded as a branch of psychology.

According to Chomsky, the correct grammar is the one which conforms to general grammatical principles, together making out the so-called 'universal grammar.' These principles are common to all humanly possible languages. On the one hand these principles specify grammatical categories and category structures, like the noun phrase–verb phrase structure, which are common to all possible languages, and on the other hand they impose restrictions on further rules; some transformations, for instance, are acceptable, while others are not.

The universal grammar is thought by Chomsky to play the decisive role in the explanation of language acquisition. The problem is to explain how the child, being exposed to only a comparatively small number of grammatically well-formed sentences, can develop the competence to produce an indefinite number of well-formed sentences himself. The reason why this is a problem is that the fragment of sentence examples which the child has encountered can be described by infinitely many different grammars, most of which do not correctly describe the whole language. Somehow the child learns to conform to rules that are correct, not only for the initial fragment, but for the entire language.

This is explained as follows. Given a sufficiently large and diverse finite set of sentences of a language, the universal grammar, in virtue of the restrictions it imposes on acceptable rules, selects the correct grammar of the language. Assuming that the child's development is somehow guided, or determined, by the principles of the universal grammar, the set of sentence examples which the child encounters will yield internal representations of the rules of the correct grammar. Thus, the acquisition of linguistic competence can be explained by assuming that the universal grammar, or knowledge of it, is innate, perhaps in virtue of the structure of the brain.

3.4 Criticism of the Idea of Deep Linguistic Competence

This theory has met with much criticism, only some of which, however, focuses on the nature of rules. Quine (1976) has rejected the idea that there is anything intermediary between, on the one hand, merely conforming to rules and and, on the other hand, being guided by explicitly stated rules. You can learn a foreign language by way of learning to follow rules, as explicitly stated, but you do not learn your mother tongue that way. Since there is nothing intermediary, learning a mother tongue is not a matter of acquiring rules at all. Consequently there is no basis for claiming that a grammar which correctly specifies the class of sentences of a language may still be incorrect. The student can only choose between equally good grammars on the basis of preference for elegance and simplicity.

An extensive criticism, based on interpretation of Wittgenstein, directed at Chomsky and other linguists as well as at several modern philosophers of language, has been provided by Baker and Hacker (1984). First of all, they stress that to the extent that there are rules of a language, these rules have normative force. Only rules which speakers of the language in fact express, apply, and appeal to in teaching, justification, and criticism can have normative force. Rules which are only discovered by the linguist and thought to operate unconsciously, by way of being internally represented, cannot have any normative force and are not, therefore, rules which govern the linguistic practice. This issue, however, runs the risk of reducing to a terminological one about the word *rule*, and it is treated as such in Chomsky (1986).

Another, even more basic, point concerns the very notion of a set of rules which determine the whole class of well-formed, meaningful sentences, and also provide interpretations of them. According to Baker and Hacker, this conception belongs to the mistaken picture of rules grinding out consequences on their own. The correct view is that the meaning of an expression is determined by nothing else than its actual use. This holds for complex expressions as much as for individual words. It is a mistake to think that the meaning of a sentence is determined in advance. It is again a mistake to think that a line can be drawn, once and for all, between what is a sentence and what is not a sentence, and between expressions that make sense and expressions that do not. Something which does not make sense in one context of use may make perfectly good sense in another.

Above all, so Baker and Hacker claim, it is a mistake to think that there is any particular problem about producing and understanding new sentences, something which needs to be explained and which is to be explained by appeal to rules. Only if it is assumed that the meaning of a new sentence is determined in advance does the question arise as to how one can know what it is. Against this, however, it can be said that what needs to be explained is just the fact that speakers do understand new sentences in the same way, regardless of whether the meanings of those sentences are determined in advance. It seems plausible that an appeal to rules is part of a good explanation of this fact. It is another question whether the normative aspect of rules has a role to play in such an explanation.

3.5 Concluding Remarks

A person can be said to have an ability only if what counts as success, in exercising that ability, is sufficiently well determined. In the case of linguistic abilities, however, it can only be speakers of the language who decide what is to count as success. So it seems that what counts as successful exercise of linguistic abilities is determined precisely by exercise of linguistic abilities. This makes the notion of rules of language problematic.

On the other hand, if we want to retain the idea of a common language as something which all members in a speech community *know*, something which is more than just similarities in the ways speakers talk and interpret each other, then it seems that the notion of normative rules of language is required, for without this notion it remains unclear what a common language, so conceived, would be.

See also: Analyticity; Convention; Conversational Maxims; Game Theoretical Semantics; Language Game; Montague Grammar; Private Language.

Bibliography

Austin J L 1976 *How to Do Things with Words*, 2nd edn. Oxford University Press, Oxford
Baker G P, Hacker P M S 1984 *Language, Sense & Nonsense*. Basil Blackwell, Oxford
Baker G P, Hacker P M S 1985 *Wittgenstein, Rules, Grammar and Necessity*. Basil Blackwell, Oxford
Bartsch R 1987 *Norms of Language*. Longman, London
Black M 1962 The analysis of rules. In: *Models and Metaphors*. Cornell University Press, Ithaca, NY
Boghossian P 1989 The rule following considerations. *Mind* **98**: 507–549
Carnap R 1956 *Meaning and Necessity*, 2nd edn. University of Chicago Press, Chicago, IL
Chomsky N 1976 *Reflections on Language*. Temple Smith, London
Chomsky N 1980 *Rules and Representations*. Basil Blackwell, Oxford
Chomsky N 1986 *Knowledge of Language: Its Nature, Origin and Use*. Praeger, New York
Davidson D 1984 *Inquiries into Truth and Interpretation*. Clarendon Press, Oxford
Grice P 1989 *Studies in the Ways of Words*. Harvard University Press, Cambridge, MA
Gumb R D 1972 *Rule-governed Linguistic Behavior*. Mouton, The Hague
Hintikka J, Kulas J 1983 *The Game of Language*. Reidel, Dordrecht

Kripke S A 1982 *Wittgenstein on Rules and Private Language*. Basil Blackwell, Oxford

Lewis D K 1969 *Convention A Philosophical Study*. Harvard University Press, Cambridge, MA

Montague R, Thomason R H (eds.) 1974 *Formal Philosophy*. Yale University Press, New Haven, CT

Quine W V O 1976 *The Ways of Paradox and Other Essays*, 2nd edn. Harvard University Press, Cambridge, MA

Ross A 1968 *Directives and Norms*. Routledge and Kegan Paul, London

Searle J 1969 *Speech Acts*. Cambridge University Press, London

Sellars W 1963 Some reflections on language games. In: *Science, Perception and Reality*. Routledge and Kegan Paul, London

Sellars W 1974 Language as thought and as communication. In: *Essays in Philosophy and its History*. Reidel, Dordrecht

Shwayder D 1965 *The Stratification of Behavior*. Routledge and Kegan Paul, London

Wright G H von 1963 *Norm and Action*. Routledge and Kegan Paul, London

Wittgenstein L 1958 *Philosophical Investigations*, 2nd edn. Basil Blackwell, Oxford

Wittgenstein L 1978 *Remarks on the Foundations of Mathematics*, 3rd edn. Basil Blackwell, Oxford

Semiotics

S. E. Larsen

As human beings, we may decide not to eat or drink, not to talk or communicate, or perhaps not even to live, but as long as we do live we cannot choose not to convey 'meaning' to the surrounding world. 'Semiotics,' in the broadest sense, is the study of the basic human activity of creating meaning. 'Signs' are all types of elements—verbal, nonverbal, natural, artificial, etc.—which carry meaning. Thus, semiotics is the study of sign structures and sign processes. In certain research traditions, the name of this study has been 'semiology'; the distinction between semiology and semiotics has often been interpreted conceptually, and not just terminologically, whereas today this superficial distinction has been abandoned: 'semiotics' is the generally accepted ecumenical term, which will also be adopted here.

As a specific discipline, semiotics is most developed as the study of the signs which function in the world of human activity. Here, semiotics investigates three fundamental problems. First, how the world which surrounds us is 'constituted' as a human environment because of our perception and apprehension of it through signs; second, how this world is coded and decoded, and thus made into a 'specific cultural domain' consisting of networks of signs; third, how we 'communicate' and 'act' through signs in order to make this domain a collectively shared cultural universe.

Semiotics may deal with the basic and general aspects of such a study; in this case neighboring areas, covered by specialized disciplines such as linguistics, psychology, anthropology, sociology, or aesthetics, will to a certain extent be subsumed by semiotics.

Semiotics also carries out investigations of concrete sign processes. In this case, semiotics will have to take into account signs of different 'types' which are simultaneously engaged in the process, such as signals, multileveled meaning structures, unintended manifestations of meaning, etc., and their different systems of expression or 'media' (visual, verbal, gestural, tactile, etc.).

As a discipline in its own right, albeit a not too sharply delimited one, or as an integrated part of other disciplines, semiotics is involved whenever the production and exchange of information and meaning is studied. Such studies range from animal communication, through stimulus and response processes occurring throughout the biosphere, to the processing of information in machines. In these contexts, while semiotics does not define the fundamental research questions, it contributes methodologically or conceptually to the actual investigations.

1. Basic Semiotic Notions

The key notions of semiotics are generated in a variety of disciplines, and semiotic research is carried out by different semiotic schools. This situation produces a different terminology and different specific research interests inside the entire field of semiotics, but five notions are recurrent 'attractors' for the semiotic enterprise through the modern history of semiotics to the late-twentieth-century state of affairs, and will remain so in the future of semiotics. These five notions are 'code,' 'structure,' 'sign,' 'discourse,' and 'text.'

The following presentation of the notions opens with the most abstract ones, 'code' and 'structure.' They are modified by semiotics in order to serve its purpose: the study of the production of 'meaning.'

The following notions, 'sign' and 'discourse,' bring out the increasing complexity of the process of creating meaning. The final notion 'text,' encompasses the whole field of semiotics.

1.1 Code

Imagine a painter at work. He chooses different colors at the palette, mixes them, and, through repeated strokes of the brush, he combines the colors on the canvas. When he is finished, he adds his signature. A process of selection and combination of colors and letters has taken place, and a complex cultural sign, a work of art, has come into being.

This process is a rule-governed activity. The rules governing the combination and selection are called codes. Not all the coding mechanisms involved in the process are semiotically relevant, and the study of codes in general is broader than semiotics. From a simple definition of code, the discussion now moves to a more complex one of genuine semiotic character.

Assume that there are two elements which can be distinguished from each other. If a rule for their interrelation can be set up, the minimal requirement for the existence of a code will be fulfilled. The rule is a code. If the elements are characterized by one feature, say a straight line and a curved line, and if the rule dictates size, distance, iteration, vertical and horizontal order, it would be possible to produce most of the letters of the Latin alphabet through a coded process of 'combination' of the elements according to the rule. That is what the painter actually did when he signed the painting with his name.

If the elements are characterized by more than one feature, for instance if color is added to the straightness and curvedness of the lines, the rule must also be capable of 'selecting' among the different features, for instance shape 'or' color, or shape *and* color, in order to convey a 'specific identity' to the element in relation to other elements. Thus, the relevance of the selected features, and hence the identity of the element, is context-dependent, i.e., dependent on the context in which the rule-governed combination is to be realized.

If color and not shape is selected as the relevant feature, the rule of combination may produce an aesthetic object and not the letters. The elements are placed in an aesthetic context. If color is irrelevant and only shape is relevant, letters may be produced. One's signature on a contract is valid whether it is signed with blue, black, or green ink. But the two features, color and shape, may interact, as is most often the case, and create the signature of a painter on canvas, for example.

So far no specific semiotic codes, but only the code in general, has been dealt with: a rule for the selection and combination of relevant features in given elements. But when the painter has finished his picture through the coded combinations of (at least) color and shape, ending with a signature, an object with a content has emerged. The codes have been creating 'meaning.' Only codes such as these are 'semiotic codes.'

The minimal requirements for the existence of semiotic codes and of the process they initiate are more complex than for the code in general. In semiotics, two elements and a combination rule will not suffice: the elements 0 and 1 combined through a rule creating the series 0101010101 ... do not necessarily produce meaning. At least two sets of elements are required, each of them combined by using one or more rules according to selected features, e.g., clothing as fashion as one set and a more or less closed system of perceptual categories or social values as another. If one then has a rule for the combination of the two systems, so that one system can refer to or represent the other, it can be said that 'meaning' is produced.

In semiotics two levels of coding are at work simultaneously: at one level a code unites a set of elements as a well-defined, but not necessarily closed system, and at another a code combines at least two such systems. Here it can be said that the code transforms or translates one system into the other.

In agreement with Umberto Eco (1984: 164–88), the codes working at the first level could be called code systems or 's-codes,' and the codes working at the second level could be called transformation codes or simply codes. In language for example, the s-codes organize the semantic system and the expression system, while the codes bring about the combination of these systems into meaningful language signs. Semiotics works on the assumption that s-coded systems from which features relevant for the production of meaning can be selected already exist. The way these systems are built up in detail is not the subject of semiotics (but may be an area for linguistics, perceptual psychology, etc.).

When the painter puts his name on the canvas, the s-coded expression system of colored letters and the s-coded system of the more or less institutionalized social activity of creating art are combined through the coded process of signing, and the meaning 'Picasso did this painting' occurs.

If a more complex case like a theater performance is looked into, then a whole series of s-coded systems is met (dress, verbal dialog, hairdo, body movements, lighting, etc.) and a tight network of codes combining them in different ways and perhaps ways which change during the performance. The result is a highly complex and often, as in most works of art, ambiguous meaning. The two-level semiotic coding process does not normally give rise to propositions which are clearly true or false as in logic, but to a complex meaning which functions on all levels of our culture.

1.2 Structure

Semiotics has often been seen as totally absorbed by the structuralist wave. According to structuralist thought, the structure is an immanent relational network of elements constituting an object. The network is the specific identity of the object. So, the notion of structure and the notion of s-code is the same. As the s-code is only of semiotic interest when connected with the code proper, it is necessary to modify the general and rigid definition of the structure, in order to make it a semiotic prerequisite for the understanding of the occurrence of signs. However, the notion of structure has played an important role in semiotics as an 'epistemological' and 'methodological' entity.

In an epistemological perspective, the focus is on the ontological status of a structure. A structure is considered either as an immanent constitutive organization of the object itself, or as a theoretical construct. According to the first conception, the structure is the 'idea' of the object, a structure *an sich* which defines the object as a whole. The second interpretation results in considering a structure as a construction, based on specific aspects of a given object and in accordance with explicit theoretical criteria. The structure has to be related to a set of methodological procedures so that the constructed structure can be tested in relation to the object.

Raymond Boudon (1968) characterizes the first conception as an 'intentional' context for a definition of structure, the second as an 'effective' context. The basic presupposition in the first case is this: any object has an essential form which can be revealed. In the second case the assumption is weaker: there are phenomena which, to a certain extent, contain aspects which can be systematized. A 'structure' is one of several possible 'specifications' of this generally presupposed structurability which Boudon calls the 'object-system.' Although both conceptions have been part of semiotics, the latter is the more predominant.

In the effective context, four different types of object-systems can be specified as structures. First, there are systems constituted by interrelated elements with finite definitions, such as the elements of the Indo-European vowel system, or of the system of possible marriages in a South American Indian tribe, depending on kinship relations. The construction of a specific structure of vowels or of marriages can be tested directly or empirically in the linguistic and social reality.

A second type of object-system contains elements defined by an infinite number of features only delimited ad hoc. This is the case when, for example, a structure is ascribed to a population in an opinion poll during an election campaign, or to the semantic reservoir of a language. But still the structure can be empirically tested.

The traditional literary genres exemplify a third type of object-system. Like the first type, this one has a finite number of distinctive features according to specific literary theories. However, a structure of genres in a given historical period will be subject to

an indirect test, because the absence of a given genre or subgenre or the occurrence of literary works which do not belong to any genre, will not falsify the structural analysis, which is concerned with the predominant tendency or possible trends of literature.

Finally, if the psychoanalytical specification of the structure of associative networks in the human mind is taken into account, for example, we will meet the result of an analysis of a fourth type of object-system. It is defined by an infinite number of distinctive features and is only liable to indirect proof.

The classical notion of structure as a closed network of interdependent elements only covers the first type, and cannot, in semiotics, be identified with structure as such. However, it has been the basis of a widespread 'methodological' approach in semiotics: given one basic semiotic system, e.g., verbal language, others, like film, kinship relations, architecture, etc., will be conceived of as being 'analogous' to this system. This analogy permits the methods of structural linguistics in particular to be applied directly to the other systems in question.

However, when semiotics investigates all four types of object-systems, it cuts across epistemological as well as methodological borderlines. With the existence of an object-system, and thus of an s-coded phenomenon, as a basic assumption for the construction of structural specifications, semiotics is based on a 'soft' epistemology: semiotics argues neither for a pure nominalism (there is a radically arbitrary relation between structure and object), nor for a pure realism (the identity of the structure is derived from the identity of the object); neither does semiotics adopt a purely extensional view of the object (through the structure the object is identified as a member of a class of objects, the extension of the structure), nor a purely intensional view (the structure characterizes the object through the organization of its supposedly relevant features). Semiotics will assume a *predominantly* realistic and intensional attitude, because certain properties are presupposed as real, and because they are taken to be relevant for the production of meaning.

With regard to methods, semiotics often has to face objects which manifest several of the four types of object-systems at the same time, e.g., a theater performance or aspects of urban culture. Hence, semiotics will have to work with a plurality of methods in an interdisciplinary perspective without giving absolute priority to one single semiotic system as a master system or to the methods connected with that system. On the other hand, structures in which the 'sign' is essential will play the leading role.

1.3 Sign

According to the Scholastic definition of the sign, a sign occurs when *aliquid stat pro aliquo*. This statement was valid before the Middle Ages and it still is in the late twentieth century (Rey 1973: 76): a sign is any object which represents another object. Meaning is the representation of an object in or by another object. The sign or the representing object can have any material manifestation as long as it can fulfill the representational function: a word, a novel, a gesture, a reaction in the brain, a city, etc. On the status of the represented object nothing is made explicit by this definition. It may be material or mental, fictitious or factual, fantasized or real, natural or artificial. From this it follows that something which is a sign in one context may be an object in another and vice versa. Signs do not constitute a class of objects. A sign is a 'functional' unit.

Consequently, no object can be pointed out as a sign unless it is integrated in a concrete process, in which more than the sign itself will have to be included in order to actually produce meaning. Only here a concrete distinction and relation between sign and object is established. So, a sign in itself is a 'virtual' unit which is 'realized' in a process creating meaning. This *real* and coded process is called a 'semiosis.'

In a semiosis, one infers something from a phenomenon one thus considers as a sign, concerning something else, the object. Through this inference, the relation between sign and object is specified according to a code on the basis of certain presuppositions. Some of these presuppositions are derived from the notions of code and structure: there must be distinguishable elements at hand which show systematically organized features. Semiotics never starts *ab nihilo*, but from already existing experience, investigating how it works and how it can be reworked through semiosis. Here the inferential specification manifests itself in new signs, referring to already existing sign–object relations. The semiosis is a continuous process of sign production.

In the history of semiotics, two strategies have been followed in order to define this process. In agreement with the first one, the representational relation is conceived of as secondary to the sign itself. This is the *formal* tradition which emphasizes the role of the formal properties of the sign itself. In this tradition, the main purpose is to produce an immanent analysis of the manifestations of specific sign systems, e.g., verbal texts, in an attempt to *generalize* the formal properties of the particular sign system to be valid for semiotic structures as such.

The second strategy, in contrast to the formal one, stresses the representational function as constitutive for the sign. This is the *pragmatic* tradition which focuses on the sign–object relation without paying much attention to the specificity of particular sign systems. Here the semiotic theory is a 'general' theory of signs, trying to reach an understanding of the concrete functioning of any particular sign system.

1.3.1 *The Formal Tradition*

The origin of the formal tradition is, first of all, structural linguistics, especially as laid out by Ferdinand de Saussure (1857–1913) in particular. Here the linguistic sign is the point of departure for the semiotic generalization. The basic quality of a sign as a semiotic entity is its relative autonomy or arbitrariness vis-à-vis the object and the immanent dichotomization of the sign in expression and content. Each of the two sign components is built up by clusters of features, through the combination of which the phonetic and the semantic units respectively are coded as formal units. The identity of the units of the expression component is exclusively defined by the mutual relations between them. The specific totality of these relations is the structure of the component. The same goes for the identity of the units and for the structure of the content component. A sign is created through the relation between the two components.

According to this definition, a chess piece which is only used in order to play chess is not a sign, because there is no difference between expression and content: the content is the coded moves and the expression is the same coded moves. According to André Martinet (1908–) such an element is said to have only one articulation. A linguistic sign, however, has a double articulation: in a chain of signs there is a first articulation to articulate them according to their content; the separate signs have a second articulation according to the specific system of expression used. In a semiotic perspective, any sign is defined, totally or partially, through a double articulation which produces an asymmetry between the two levels of articulation. A one-to-one relation between all units of the two components, as with the chess piece, will never occur.

Following the formal tradition it is the double articulation that gives rise to representation. The chess piece, in the context referred to above, does not represent anything except itself. In a genuine sign, however, the double articulation forces us to unite expression and content through a specific mental act, an inference or interpretation, by Saussure called an association. As the associative inference cannot be located exclusively in the expression or in the content, representation is a derived effect of the double articulation of the sign which *creates* an object relation. Meaning is the representational effect produced and conditioned exclusively by the immanent properties of the sign. The order of things and the structure of experience is an effect of the sign structure.

The claim of this tradition is that the s-codes and the codes of the immanent structure of the sign are generally valid irrespective of the specific system of expression used. When two components are united through a double articulation, that is a sign which may be manifested in any medium such as the visual, the gestural, or the architectonic. The analysis of such sign systems that are formally identical with verbal language is carried out using the same methods as are applied in linguistics. Thus, the strategy for the semiotic generalization of the properties of the basic sign system is a methodological analogy.

1.3.2 *The Pragmatic Tradition*

In contrast to this tradition, the 'pragmatic' tradition is not concerned with the internal structure of the sign itself, and is therefore indifferent as to the specific medium of the sign. The sign is never seen in abstraction from the sign–object relation which is assumed to constitute the sign. In the pragmatic perspective, the main focus of interest is the way this relation is incorporated into the semiosis. The theoretical background of this tradition is, first and foremost, philosophy and logic with Charles Sanders Peirce (1839–1914) in particular, but also Karl Bühler (1879–1963) among the leading figures.

For pragmatic semioticians, the formal properties of the sign will not suffice to define it. The definition of the sign must include elements necessary to explain the *use* of the sign with regard to the object: the status of the object will have to be taken into account (real, fictitious, etc.) as well as the purposiveness of the sign process; the assumed properties of the sign in relation to the object (similarity, copresence, difference, etc.) as well as the types of code involved (mental, material, strategical, etc.) must be dealt with.

From the pragmatic point of view, the semiosis is the 'integration' of an object into a sign process in such a way that new knowledge concerning the object can be manifested in a new sign, which may be a word, an act, an image, etc. In the formal tradition the goal is different. Here the construction of an autonomous sign or structure of signs conveys an 'arbitrary layout' to the object.

If the object is the history of Europe, a sign may be a book, an exhibition, or a movie giving a specific version of this history which, in turn, makes us produce a new sign, e.g., the participation in a peace demonstration, the writing of a new book, the establishing of a new political party or just a psychological reaction of joy or frustration. As an effect of the first sign, each of these new signs establishes a relation to the same object on a new basis.

From a formal point of view the most important question which arises from this example is how the structure of the original sign, as it occurs in a specific system or systems of expression, creates a specific object. If any new sign is produced, the next question will be how the structure of this sign, related to its system of expression, forms an object. The pragmatic approach, on the other hand, looks for how the new sign comes into being as an effect of the manifestation of the first one. Here the transformation or translation between signs and sign systems, irrespective of their material specificity, is the pivotal point of the analysis. Meaning in the pragmatic context is this effect as embedded in a continuous sign production creating new object relations.

The two traditions have different problems to face in an application outside linguistics and philosophy, but they both attempt to cooperate with other disciplines. The formal tradition is anchored in the analysis of a specific sign system and thus it possesses strong methodological and applicative resources, which in fact have given this tradition a great deal of impact. But the strategy of seeing other sign systems as analogous to verbal language may underestimate the particular semiotic capacities of nonverbal sign systems.

Guided by the pragmatic tradition, the overall general logic of the semiosis forces us to concentrate on how different sign systems work together. This interest has broadened the scope of semiotics. But being neutral to the specific medium of the sign, this tradition sees no necessary link between the general structure of semiosis and the particular sign systems engaged in the semiosis. Hence, there are no precise analytical tools left for the understanding of specific sign processes.

A common focal point for the two traditions is the conception of the semiotic inference from sign to object or from expression to content as more comprehensive than logical inference. The goal of any semiotic process is meaning and not logical truth value, which is only one specific type of meaning, integrated in more important and multidimensional effects of meaning produced by the semiotic activity of everyday life. This being the case, the inferential process can never be reduced to a formal structure alone, but contains necessarily nonformal elements which define it as a 'discourse.'

1.4 *Discourse*

Through the notion of discourse, the semiotic inference is comprehended as an act, implying first of all a specific 'orientation' and a mark of 'subjectivity.'

'Intentionality' in general is defined by phenomenology as the capacity of any consciousness to be a consciousness about something. The mind is constituted by its always being oriented towards an object, which is totally unspecified except for being positioned in relation to the mind. In the discourse, consciousness, abstractly comprehended as intentionality, is embedded in a concrete sign process which is the starting point for the semiotic analysis of intentionality.

In order to be realized as a unity creating meaning, any sign has to be a link in a chain of signs, organized in an irreversible order which is oriented toward an object. From a semiotic point of view, even an anaphoric reference to a previous sign in a syntagmatic chain will contribute to the general irreversibility of the chain, because the anaphora takes place as a production of a new sign, thus basically a movement ahead. This irreversible intentional order is the discourse.

In this perspective, intentionality acquires a more differentiated definition than in philosophy or in descriptions of explicitly purposive instrumental acts. First, there is the 'general' intentionality, because any process of creating meaning is directed towards an object in order to be meaning productive at all. This goes for animals and machines as well as for human beings. Second, there is the 'subjective' intentionality, giving the fact that there is consciousness or human subjectivity involved. Third, we orient ourselves in accordance with the 'ontological' status of the object, the specific type of reality it presumably belongs to (dream, reality, etc.). Fourth, we have a 'specifying' intentionality which is inherent in the fact that a semiosis is aiming at identifying or giving a specific meaning to the intended object, e.g., in the semantic structure of a given sign system. Fifth, a discourse carries an instrumental purposiveness, a 'strategic' intentionality. In the discourse, all these types of intentionality work together so that virtual signs are realized in an 'act.'

The turning point is subjectivity. In the discourse the communicating subject is located in relation to other subjects and in relation to the referential dimension. This situating function is brought about by specific elements in the sign system which carry out this situational function, viz. the 'deictic' elements. Through these elements, e.g., a blast of a horn, a twitch of the eye, subjects and objects are located in time and space in relation to the semiosis. In verbal language, for example, pronouns, certain adverbs, forms of conjugation, are deictic elements; in a film, camera angle or perspective may carry this function; in gestural language, nodding and pointing may exercise deictic functions, etc. No system of elements can be a sign system without deictic elements, and each system is characterized by its particular deictic devices. Systems without deictic elements, like a set of chess pieces, will have to be embedded into semiotic sign systems, like language or gestures, in order to function in a process which creates meaning, e.g., a game one practices to win.

In this way the discourse is framed by a 'discursive universe' for the semiosis. The discursive universe is the set of 'presuppositions' which situates the semiosis in relation to subjects and objects in such a way that a semiosis can take place 'concerning these subjects and objects.' To put it in a less abstract way: the discursive universe is a shared cultural knowledge and experience which is involved in the semiosis, but which we do not need to make explicit. It is the context necessary for the understanding of the outcome of a semiosis.

All the five aspects of intentionality are not listed explicitly when signs are used in a discursive process. But whenever one says 'Look!,' any understanding of this utterance implies that we agree that we have an object outside the speaker; that we communicate to other subjects; that we are looking for something real we want to identify, unless we are explicitly informed

otherwise. On the basis of these presuppositions we may want to make certain intentional aspects explicit, e.g., the purpose for the outcry, and ask 'Why?'

The discursive universe is a 'shared' and thus social universe of already existing and accepted knowledge about what we consider a 'possible' world which we make 'real' in producing 'collective' or 'intersubjectively' 'valid' signs about it. The discourse makes the semiosis a 'communicative' act: the semiosis becomes a sign process between subjects about their world. This act is realized in 'texts'.

1.5 Text

The compound of actually realized signs, filtered through the discursive logic of intentionality, is a 'text.' The text might seem the most self-evident of the semiotic key notions: the material manifestation of signs, especially verbal signs. But it has in fact received different definitions and has been used on different levels of argumentation.

In Louis Hjelmslev's (1899–1965) linguistic version of the formal tradition, the text is the infinite chain of realized signs. The signs themselves are entities defined by elements in finite structures which are realized in the text. From the point of view of text 'production,' the text is the result of a code engendering an endless number of sign combinations based on a selection among a limited repertoire of sign components. From the 'reception' perspective, the text requires segmentation in delimited individual texts, according to certain methodological criteria which can separate textual features which are pertinent for the sign system in itself, from other features, e.g., genres or rhetorical elements. In this perspective, the discursive intentionality and the problem of contextualization are not taken into account. But on the other hand, the sign system as a stock of possibilities for an infinite sign production is important for semiotics.

When this conception is generalized in semiotics, other sign systems are dealt with as analogous with language. This means that other semiotic systems produce an endless text in the same material space as language, and that they have to be *received* according to the same analytical linguistic procedures. In this way, the entire world of human activity is turned into one global text or intertextual compound of texts. The globalization of the text removes it from the position as a material object which is accessible through specific methods, and turns it into a general notion concerning the status of objects in the world of human activity: they are all texts. Hence, on the methodological level the formal tradition can only make prescientific distinctions between texts according to the immediately perceived differences between expression systems: visual texts, verbal texts, gestural texts, etc.

The pragmatic tradition, too, also has its problems with the apparently simple notion of text. Here the notion of sign is not bound to a specific system of expression, so there is no distinction between sign and text on the empirical level: a book can be a sign in itself or be looked upon as being built by signs; a city can be regarded as one single sign or it can be seen as a text constituted by a complex networks of signs. So, in this tradition distinctions also have to be made ad hoc between signs and texts and between texts according to the context and to the goal of the analysis.

But as signs in the pragmatic tradition are defined according to the inferential semiotic process, the whole range of discursive elements are also part of the sign definition. So, we will have at our disposal concepts outside the sign system, but inside the semiosis, to operate a distinction between texts.

Seen in this light, everything is a possible text or sign, but not everything has the status of text or sign at the same time, i.e., not everything serves the concrete production of meaning in the actual semiosis. In any concrete semiosis we have a text: a delimited material manifestation of signs containing elements (a) which are necessary to operate a distinction between text and nontext, and (b) which are necessary to draw the line between presupposed elements and explicit elements in the text in order to produce an understanding of its meaning.

In a theater performance, everything on stage is part of a text in a complex network of individual sign systems. In everyday communication, words, gestures, facial expression, etc. as a whole make up a text. In both cases we have neutral elements which do not partake in the semiosis: they are not coded by the s-codes involved in the text in question. The architectural construction of the room or the clothing worn during the communication is irrelevant to the text, not because they do not belong to the sign systems in question, as a partisan of the formal tradition would have stated, but because they do not contribute to the semiosis. On the other hand, they *can* be integrated in the semiosis: the director can use the auditorium as part of the theatrical space of the performance and the limits between text and nontext may even change during the performance; the interlocutors can dress in a way which improves or deliberately interrupts the communication.

Certain elements *can never* be part of the text: parts of the body of the actor will never be coded as signs (illness, sexual dispositions, etc.) and will impose definite limits on the text; during the conversation the telephone may ring or a third person may turn on the radio so that the interlocutors cannot hear one word. These are all elements which are not part of the text as an 'intentional discursive phenomenon,' but they may be components of other texts, and they definitely mark the limits of a text.

No text can ever be infinite from this point of view, but the text itself will contain a level of presupposed elements which are necessary for the existence of the text as a discursive phenomenon. The presupposed elements which can be made explicit by the text, belong to the text, e.g., a theatrical metafiction with an autoreferential dimension may integrate auditorium, audience, technical staff, etc. in the text. Other presupposed aspects, like the actors' salaries, the state of the buildings, the budget of the house, etc. belong to other texts. This means that no text is self-sufficient in a kind of immanent infinity. When one cannot express oneself well enough in an oral verbal text, one can use gestures to compensate. This new verbal–gestural text as a whole now produces one meaning in an inter-semiotic textual totality.

In this way, signs and texts necessarily partake in a continuous semiosis through which the limits between texts and between presupposed and explicit elements are constantly moving. Signs are always meant to be transformed into other signs of similar or different types. The text is the materialization of this transformation.

2. Semiotic Schools

Semiotics has been institutionalized worldwide in many national associations, which communicate in journals and newsletters of more or less limited distribution. All of them are united under the umbrella of the International Association of Semiotic Studies, with *Semiotica* as its official journal. There are a number of centers and departments at institutions of higher education around the world offering semiotics programs on all levels, mostly integrated in more extensive programs. Apart from this administrative institutionalization, semiotics is guided by the concepts and ideas developed in four major schools.

2.1 Structuralist Semiotics

Structuralist semiotics was inaugurated by Ferdinand de Saussure's *Cours de linguistique générale* (1916) and further developed especially by Louis Hjelmslev's glossematic theory and Algirdas Julien Greimas's (1917–1992) structural semantics in particular.

Saussure sets out to define linguistics as a specific science by assigning a specific object to it, the particular aspect of language which can only be dealt with by linguistics. The genuine object of linguistics is the language 'system,' the closely interrelated structure of elements that are different from the individual *use* of language, which it determines in such a way that it becomes an understandable chain of meaning carrying verbal unities, signs, and not just a series of sound waves. Although they are parts of language as a global phenomenon, the sociological, physiological, psychological, or aesthetic aspects of language can be left to other disciplines: they are not the *differentia specifica* of verbal production of meaning.

The aim of this project is not to isolate linguistics from other sciences and its object from other sign systems, but to give a precise outline of linguistics and its object in such a way that, from the particularity of language and linguistics, the general aspects of sign systems and the general guidelines for the study of such systems can be developed. Language has to be seen as a particular sign system and linguistics has to be seen as a branch of semiotics, which Saussure himself calls 'semiology.'

With the notion of sign as the heart of linguistics, and with 'dichotomization' as the basic analytical device, Saussure sorts out the conceptual framework of linguistics in order to make the semiotic perspective possible. In a series of dichotomies, the opposition between *system* and *use* being the basic one, he defines a number of dimensions and elements of the language system, so that its internal structure of elements is constitutive for the sign. From a semiotic point of view, the most important among these dichotomies are those immediately connected with the sign, i.e., the distinction between the sign components, 'signifier' and 'signified,' the sign levels, 'form' and 'substance,' the distinction between the principles for the linkage of signs, 'paradigmatic' and 'syntagmatic' order, and, finally, the opposition between the two methodological viewpoints, 'synchrony' and 'diachrony.'

The identity of a signifier or of a signified is its relation, i.e., its simultaneous difference and similarity, to other signifiers and signifieds. This relational identity is the 'value' of the signifying and signified unit. The identity of the signifiers is not bound to the material character of the expression, and the identity of the signifieds does not depend on the quality of the signified objects. Through the value of the sign components, a sign as a whole is then defined as a 'formal' and not as a 'substantial' entity: its identity depends on its relation to other signs in the same system of expression. Thus, a radical or epistemological arbitrariness between sign and object is manifested in the sign as an internal arbitrariness between signifier and signified.

There are two kinds of arbitrariness working in cooperation in the sign system according to two rules of combination. A combination of signs or sign components can be 'syntagmatic,' i.e., bound to a sequential determination or relative arbitrariness, e.g., *str-* at the beginning of an English syllable must be followed by a vowel. If the combination of signs or sign components indicates simultaneous but alternating possibilities (as does the nominal case system), we have a 'paradigmatic' organization, based upon absolute arbitrariness.

Any system built upon arbitrarily combined signs or sign components can be studied from two viewpoints, the historical or 'diachronical,' or the 'synchronical,' i.e., that of a certain frozen situation.

With the notion of value as the key to the whole theory as a semiotic theory, Saussure succeeds in defining language both as a specific structure in its own right, depending on the specificity of the relations involved, and as an example of a general sign structure. This is due to the fact that value is a formal notion, indifferent to how it is materialized and to the character of the objects it represents, so that any system that acts like language in any medium and referring to any object, can be studied as a quasi-linguistic sign system.

With an extension of one of Saussure's own examples: the 8.45 pm train from Paris to Geneva is defined in relation to other trains as listed in the timetable, not with regard to the specific carriages used at any specific moment. The timetable is the paradigmatic order, the organization of carriages with the engine in front is the syntagmatic chain. Changes in the timetable or in the position of the engine, depending on technological developments for example, will be a diachronical study of the Paris–Geneva transportation system, while the analysis of what is going on with regard to rail traffic between the two cities in the 1970s will constitute a synchronical investigation.

In Louis Hjelmslev's glossematics, the semiotic key notions are 'form' and 'hierarchy.' Saussure regards form, *grosso modo*, as equivalent to independence of substance, while Hjelmslev takes form to mean what can be formalized according to formal logic. Formal elements are elements which are exclusively defined by their reciprocal or unilateral relation to other elements. The sign is also a type of reciprocal relation, called the 'sign function,' between two units, the 'expression plane' and the 'content plane.' Elements which are related by concurrence alone have no formal definition. In this way, the formal structure is defined only by these two types of formal relation.

This formalistic or algebraic interpretation of Saussure puts further constraints on the basic analytical principle of dichotomization, in order to set up the final object description. The analysis is carried out as a division of the object in units which can be related and thus defined and only defined by the formal relations. This will lead to a noncontradictory object description. The analysis is exhaustive when all elements which are only characterized as concurrent are left out. They do not belong to the formal description even if they can be repeated, e.g., the quality of Humphrey Bogart's voice, which is always concurrent with the verbal signs he utters. If more than one exhaustive description is possible, the simplest is to be preferred. With this notion of form, Hjelmslev has contributed considerably to the methodological development of semiotics.

Even if the concurrent elements are excluded from one sign system, they may acquire a formal definition by the description of another sign system. Thus, the rigid formalism opens a hierarchy of interrelated semiotic levels. Hjelmslev's vision is a complete structure of sign systems referring to each other in order to create form out of substance on a global scale.

The basic molecule of the hierarchy consists of several sign systems: first, we have a 'denotative' language, constituted by the sign function and thus having an expression plane and a content plane, e.g., the language used by Humphrey Bogart when he orders a scotch on the rocks in a bar. Second, we have a 'metalanguage' which contains an exhaustive formal description of this language as English, thus having the entire denotative language as its content plane and the glossematic description as the expression plane. Also, glossematics will contain nonformal elements, i.e., certain indefinable elements which can be integrated in a 'meta-metalanguage' and there be given a formal definition, i.e., in a nonlinguistic science (philosophy, logic, mathematics, etc.). This language will constitute a third step.

Now, if the metalanguage has left out what is only concurrent in the denotative language, there will be the possibility that another type of metalanguage, called the 'connotative' language, will deal with those formal leftovers. Such a language will have the entire denotative language as its expression plane and also comprise, for example, the quality of Humphrey Bogart's almost mythological voice as a condition for a specific content which is more comprehensive than the whisky as such ordered by the movie star, it is the-scotch-ordered-by-Humphrey-Bogart. This additional creation of meaning can roughly be characterized as 'symbolic' and allows for a new metalanguage that can provide us with a formal description *ad modum glossematicum* of this enlarged meaning, i.e., an analysis of aesthetic, ideological, or mythological effects. The connotative language is parallel to the metalanguage. The hierarchical relation between the denotative language, the metalanguage, and the connotative language with its progress to higher levels has enlarged the possibilities in structural semiotics to take into account a multileveled production of meaning.

After the publication of A. J. Greimas's *Sémantique structurale* (1966), the ideas of structuralist semiotics have had an impact on a variety of subdisciplines of semiotics: literary studies, film studies, anthropology, art history, architecture, etc. Especially in France, Denmark, Spain, Italy, Canada, Brazil (and now also in the USA), an ongoing application and reworking of notions are taking place.

2.2 Phenomenological Semiotics

Semioticians inspired by phenomenology can hardly be said to form a school. What they have in common is the application of notions and ideas from Edmund Husserl's (1859–1938) phenomenology, particularly as expounded in his *Logische Untersuchungen* (1900–01). They belong to a great variety of disciplines, and except for the activities of the Prague School between the two wars, they never formed a group. In the Prague group, influential personalities were Jan Mukařovský (1891–1975), Karl Bühler (1879–1963) and Roman Jakobson (1896–1982).

Husserl himself was not primarily preoccupied with semiotic questions, but with the traditional philosophical problem of how to obtain true knowledge. In order to reach that goal, we have to direct our consciousness toward the objects; we have to express this relation in signs; and, finally, we have to acknowledge that objectivity is based on certain structural principles. This argument leads to the introduction of three semiotically relevant key notions: 'intentionality,' 'sign,' and 'foundation.'

Husserl wants to use these notions to go beyond the realm of the sign to the truth of the object. The purpose of semiotics, on the other hand, is to study the domain of the sign with the sign as its object, to see how the sign is founded, and to see how intentionality works in a sign process to create meaning. As this endeavor is only an intermediary step in Husserl's research, the reference to Husserl in phenomenological semiotics is always selective and often indirect. He indicates a horizon for the semiotic research interest.

Husserl introduces two types of signs: first, the 'indication,' which is a sign that points to a *de facto* presence of the object, without attributing any content to it—the noise from an unidentified thing approaching you; second, the 'expression' in which a mind makes clear that it has been oriented towards an object—a shout like 'Watch out!' accompanied by a nodding head and a pointing finger. Here, the sign–object relation is rooted in a subjectivity, or to put it less phenomenologically: somebody wants to say something to somebody.

Now, the point is that this combination of sign and intentionality as a communicative intersubjectivity is not in the first place an act of deliberate will. It is made possible by the fact that the sign is 'founded,' i.e., it belongs to a structure of relations, called a pure logical grammar, through which it is constituted as a specific type of object, namely as capable of carrying intentionality in intersubjective communication. The notion of foundation is adapted by the Prague School as the notion of structure.

When Husserl's discussion of the sign is transferred to linguistics or other disciplines with a semiotic perspective, it is obvious that a sign structure can never be interpreted as an immanent formal structure. In the structure, the sign occupies the position of an intermediary instance in a communicative and referential structure, and the grammar of any sign system will have to pay special attention to elements which articulate the communicative functions, such as deictic elements.

This is what happens in Karl Bühler's so-called organon model (*Sprachtheorie* 1934). Here the sign is the 'organon' or medium through which an expressive relation to the sender, an appellative relation to the receiver, and a representative relation to an object are present 'simultaneously' in order to create meaning.

The precondition for the transformation of a material object into a sign is the 'abstractive relevance': Any sign–object, e.g., a gesture, has to be structured in such a way that we are able to retain only the features that are relevant for its meaning-creating function. This capacity of the subject and these objectively manifested features must be part of a collectively shared consensus, i.e., be founded in a formal grammar. From this argument Bühler is led to the seminal idea of phonology as an independent study of the structure of such features, which are formal in the sense that they are conditions for the function of sounds as differentiating meaning, but which are not formalistic in the sense that they are defined only through their internal organization.

Roman Jakobson develops Bühler's simple, phenomenologically based communication model into a more differentiated structure with more than three functional relations. One of these relations is of special semiotic interest: the so-called 'poetic' function. This is the function through which the sign is related to itself, the sign represents itself as an object within the communicative structure as a whole. In verbal language, this function can be specified as a transformation of syntagmatic relations into paradigmatic ones. As soon as a work of art is apprehended, it is in a way frozen as one set of simultaneously interrelated elements, in spite of the fact that it is perceived as a sequential order. In a novel the beginning and the end are directly connected once the reading is over.

This idea emerged among the Russian formalists, a group of linguists, literary scholars, poets, and artists, who worked together just before World War I. Parallel to Saussure, they tried to define the study of art as a specific scholarly activity based on the specific artistic character of its object, especially its 'literarity.' This phenomenon was seen as the specific set of devices (rhyme, narrative structure, genre structures, etc.) through which the material aspect of the artistic object is given its specific artistic character as opposed to the ordinary use of the same material, e.g., artistic language as opposed to everyday language. Hence, taken as art, a given object becomes autoreferential. Because the same material is also used outside the artistic context, the effect of the autoreferentiality is not an isolation of the arts, but it is a way of introducing new meaning in the ordinary context. The artistic function always works together with other communicative functions and with other sign systems. The specificity of the artistic object, and of any other object as a sign, is the devices it provides us with to carry out this intersemiotic relation.

This conception of aesthetics was taken up in Prague by Mukařovský, among others, and a semiotics of the arts (literature, theater, folklore, film, etc.)

was created with ideas which are still active in semiotics. Jakobson's contribution was to combine the ideas of Russian formalism and the Prague School with essential aspects of structuralist semiotics, without being taken in by its hard-core formalism.

Another link between phenomenology and structural semiotics is established on a philosophical level in the grammatological analysis of the sign as inaugurated by Jacques Derrida (1930–) in his *De la grammatologie* (1967) and in the hermeneutics of Paul Ricœur (1913–) in *Le Conflit des Interprétations* (1969).

Ricœur criticizes the rigid notion of structure behind the structuralist sign notion. It produces a biased view on the concrete sign process, which in his work is seen as a concrete event where several interpretations of the world meet, e.g., in metaphors and symbols, and not simply as a manifestation of a transindividual structure.

Derrida is more oriented toward the epistemological aspects of the structuralist sign notion: according to him, this notion implies the existence of a transcendental meaning that can be reached through the sign which is regarded as transparent vis-à-vis the virtual structure. But he also points out that this transcendental meaning has to be expressed in signs. The only mode of existence of what is beyond the sign, is the signs in which this beyond is expressed. This paradox is the creative dynamics of all texts. No text will ever express a conclusive meaning, but will always produce a continuous dissolution or 'deconstruction' of stable meanings.

While Ricœur anchors structuralist semiotics in the hermeneutical tradition, Derrida's work has inspired a philosophical relativism characterized as postmodern, deconstructionist, or poststructuralist. But as a whole, phenomenological semiotics is a broadly and *culturally* oriented movement which is still developing and focusing on how human beings are determined by signs.

2.3 American Semiotics

North American semiotics as a school is identical with Peircean semiotics, rooted in the works of Charles Sanders Peirce. Other types of semiotic activities in the USA are of non-American origin, being of structuralist or postmodern inspiration.

Peirce is a polyhistorian with logic as the center of his thought; logic considered as the way of reasoning about the world through the manipulation of signs which represent this world. So, for Peirce, logic is semiotics. Like Husserl, he is inspired by the medieval schoolmen and he adopts a phenomenological point of departure for his semiotics.

In Peirce, the core of semiotics is the 'semiosis' or the structured process in which the 'sign' imposes a 'coded relation' to an 'object' on a mind. Behind this triadic notion of semiosis are three basic phenomenologically conceived 'modes of being' of objects in relation to the mind. There is the mode of 'firstness,' the object as it is in itself as a virtuality; there is the mode of 'secondness' or the actually existing object as different from and opposed to the mind and to other objects; finally, there is the mode of 'thirdness' where the object is presented according to a law which makes it accessible to recognition. Semiosis is the process governed by thirdness.

The constitutive triad of the semiosis is the sign, the 'interpretant' or the coded relation, and the object. So, all signs are objects which function as instances of thirdness; they are liable to abstractive relevance, as Bühler would say.

The particularity of the sign in the semiosis depends on the sign–object relation inside the triadic relation. If this relation is based on 'similarity' between sign and object, i.e., expresses firstness, we have an 'iconic' sign. As the sign is part of a triadic structure, the similarity is not immediate, but coded as a specific similarity (spatial, oral, visual, olfactory, etc.). When the foundation of a sign–object relation is 'copresence,' the sign manifests 'secondness' and is called an 'indexical' sign (a pointing finger, the smoke of a fire, an outcry caused by pain, etc.). Finally, a sign–object relation may be established according to 'convention' and thus express 'thirdness,' which produces a 'symbolic' sign (a linguistic sign, gestures of politeness, etc.). Being an instance of thirdness in the semiosis, which is thirdness as a process, the symbolic sign is the most complete sign of the three types of signs.

The symbolic sign is similar to the arbitrary sign in Saussure and is also bound to a collectively shared structure of understanding. But it can never be isolated in the semiosis from manifestations of the other types of sign. Any semiosis is a compound of iconic, indexical, and symbolic signs: the indexical sign aspects establish a relation to an object, the iconic sign aspects open for analogies which are essential to our everyday behavior when we imitate former experience, and the symbolic sign aspects produce coded knowledge on which we can agree or disagree and reach new knowledge. No sign aspects can be disposed of. So, Peirce's semiotics is close to the phenomenological insistance on the whole dialogical structure of semiosis.

In being object-related, Peirce's sign is also close to the expression in Husserl's theory. Like Husserl, Peirce introduces a differentiation of 'objects': first, the 'dynamical' object, which is the object outside the semiosis towards which this process is directed, posed by the semiosis as its goal, but neither formed nor determined by it. Second, the 'immediate' object which is the object as represented in the semiosis, e.g., as expressed in the semantic structure of a language. The demarcation line between the two dimensions of the object is the result of the semiosis and it is constantly replaced by the semiotic activity when knowledge is created.

The 'interpretant' is the cornerstone of Peirce's semiotics. It is the code or law through which sign and object are related so that an effect of the semiosis can occur. It is not an imitation of an immanent structure of the sign or of the object, and it is not an arbitrary structure imposed on the object from the outside. The interpretant is the law which is made necessary by the sign–object relation in order to give this relation a generally valid character. The interpretant is an 'effect' of the sign–object relation, determined by it and, in turn, specifying it. That the relation is generally valid means that it can be subsumed under a law which can be agreed upon and repeated. So, the mode of being of an interpretant will be the 'habits' according to which we actually deal with the object. These habits will be manifested as signs in other semioses and reinterpreted and perhaps changed. The interpretant creates new signs and thus a continuous semiosis.

The interpretant as an effect has three aspects: the 'immediate' interpretant is the presupposed organized character of the object which make the application of a law possible, what Boudon calls the object-system. The 'dynamical' interpretant is the delimited effect, a concrete physical or mental act performed by somebody or something as the result of the sign–object relation. The 'final' interpretant will be this act regarded as the general truth about the object, such as a law which is a universally valid guideline for a habitual act, i.e., a way of reasoning in mathematics, independently of any individual subject. The connection between semiosis and habits made Peirce call his semiotics 'pragmatism.'

The dynamical interpretant is of particular semiotic interest, because it is this effect which is the motor of the semiosis. If a driver is waiting in a lane in front of a traffic light, ready to continue when the light is green, the traffic light will be the sign and the traffic the dynamical object. The immediate object will be the representation of the traffic in the sign systems known by the driver (urban phenomenon, regulated by law, dangerous, etc.). The rules which regulate the traffic through the traffic light (stop, go, wait, etc.) will be the interpretant. The object has presumably a certain order which makes it reasonable to learn and to obey the traffic light. This preconception of the object as structurable will be the immediate interpretant. The final interpretant, i.e., the ideal and universal organization of traffic is of mainly theoretical interest, but it is a working concept in functionalist urban planning, for example.

From this perspective, the dynamical interpretant will be the act which incorporates the code: as soon as the light turns green, the driver manipulates his car and off he goes. This interpretant is manifested in the semiosis as a new sign, the moving car, which in turn may be interpreted in relation to the same object by the drivers further down the lane who cannot see the traffic light: they turn on their engines, ready to go. If a driver had started while the light was red, his act would still have been a dynamical interpretant, but a police officer might have stopped him, taking it as a sign related to the same dynamical object but representing another immediate object. In this case, the traffic would no longer be a practical affair but a legal complex.

Because of the generality of Peirce's thought and its comprehensive character, bridging the gap between profound epistemological viewpoints, cultural and historical problems, and particular types of signs and sign processes in different disciplines, it has had an immense influence in all semiotic domains.

The tripartition of signs has been the emblem of his semiotics and has been used to characterize sign processes of all types and in all kinds of expression systems. And his emphasis on the dialogical structure of the semiosis and of the shared knowledge presupposed by the semiosis, has led to penetrating studies in philosophical and literary hermeneutics or in anthropology and the social sciences (e.g., Singer 1984). But in most cases the generality also means a lack of specific analytical devices, so that the application of Peirce's notions is normally integrated as specifying guidelines for a methodological pluralism. In this capacity, Peirce's semiotics has a global influence as well as a growing one.

2.4 The Moscow–Tartu School

With the Moscow–Tartu School, a school in the literal sense of the word was established. Founded in 1962, it continues the cooperation between the Slavic countries and the other countries on the European continent which dates back to Saussure and his foundation of structural linguistics, to Russian formalism, and to the Prague School. Among the leading figures are Jurij Lotman (1922–1993) from Tartu and Vjaceslav Ivanov (1929–1993) from Moscow.

Although the activities of the school have several sources of inspiration, structuralist semiotics is the most decisive: the Saussurean sign and the Hjelmslevian hierarchy (see Grzybek 1989). On the basis of these fundamentals, the ambition is to focus on more complex sign structures than verbal language and to transform the basic notions and methods of the linguistically based structural semiotics beyond a mere analogy. Hence, the main interest of the school is the study of 'culture' as a semiotic system. The basic notions are 'text' and 'model.'

Culture is based on a process of creation, exchange, and storage of information, and the specific 'unity' of this process is the object of cultural semiotics. The material for this study is the 'text' in which this process materializes, and the 'invariants' which can be found in the texts constitute the ultimate object of cultural semiotics. The text is a megasign, as it were, and is built up of binary signs. In the structuralist sign conception, the invariants are the relationally defined elements which constitute the signifier-component and the signified-component. But in the cultural flow of information, the invariants are neither located in the sign itself nor in the text in itself. Therefore, the signifier of the sign is seen as a material unit, not as a formal unit. Furthermore, when the text is seen in analogy with the sign, it is regarded as any delimited material unit with a content that can be divided in smaller units of the same kind.

Following this idea, the formal definition of the invariants requires another notion, the notion of 'model.' First of all, the notion of model implies a 'hierarchy' between two levels, a model being a model of something. The invariants are the elements which remain stable when meaning from one level in a hierarchy is transformed to another. Second, the notion of model is necessarily linked to the assumption of a basic 'code' or structure which reworks an object, duplicating or replacing it by a model. In culture the basic object is always a text, dealing with our world of experience, e.g., a linguistic or visual text. The model is another text which uses the first one as expression and which contains the rules by which this expression takes place. This is an application of the connotative hierarchy in Hjelmslev.

The point is that any text, also the basic one, in order to be text must be placed in a modeling hierarchy, either as the so-called 'primary modeling system,' e.g., the verbal text which functions as a model of our experience of the world, or as a 'secondary modeling system' which reconstructs the first modeling system's way of systematizing our experience. So, a 'model' is a text considered as an organizing system in relation to another text.

From this point of view, the cultural invariants are attached to the text-as-model, functioning in an irreducible double structure consisting of at least two modeling systems. The two systems will never be identical, neither by being identical repetitions nor by being infinite, because texts as models impose limits on the infinite flow of information from the surrounding world. They will be different and often in opposition.

The advantage of this approach is that the basic text, the primary modeling system, will be delimited according to the purpose of the analysis, i.e., the relation to another modeling system. Furthermore, in a cultural perspective the text is always linked to a hierarchy which cannot be reduced to a homogeneous whole where the two modeling systems function as one. Thus, culture is always seen as a dynamic intersection or a continuous process of unifying heterogeneous texts.

In an analogy to the notion of biosphere, this cultural space is called the 'semiosphere' by Jurij Lotman. With this notion he wants to draw our attention to the fact that the domain of texts, in order to be texts, is always opposed to a domain of phenomena which are not texts. The heterogeneous character of the semiosphere is a result of the continuous replacement of its limits by the production of texts confronting the nontextual sphere in a ongoing cultural attempt to integrate it into the world of human activity, producing an interior reorganization of this world of activity.

3. Semiotic Domains

A survey of the different fields of research in semiotics is given in the general semiotic encyclopedias (Nöth 1985; Sebeok (ed.) 1986; Posner (ed.) 1997). Contributions from the humanities (literary studies, epistemology, logic, hermeneutics, aesthetics, architecture, design, linguistics, film studies, musicology, theater studies) are abundant, but the social sciences (mass media studies, communication studies, studies of urban culture and popular culture, cultural anthropology, ideology studies, women's studies, pedagogics, marketing) and psychology (psychoanalysis, cognitive science) are also richly represented, as are theology and law. Less numerous are works in the sciences and medicine (animal communication studies, biology, computer sciences, pathological studies of body signs), but a growing interest is shown in these fields. Many of the separate domains organize the research in special associations with journals and congress activities.

4. Future of Semiotics

The late-twentieth-century activities of semiotics in an international perspective indicate at least four main roads for the future progress of semiotics, which will run parallel to a continuous activity in the particular fields of research.

4.1 Cooperation of Schools

The historical differences between two basic traditions and between the main semiotic schools will tend to disappear in the years to come: the formal tradition needs the global perspective of the pragmatic tradition which will, in turn, need the detailed knowledge of specific sign systems presented by the formal tradition. The turning point will be the elements in the specific sign systems, which define their particular pragmatic capacity, namely the elements through which any sign system is anchored in a discursive process in relation to other sign systems and to situational conditions. These are the elements carrying the 'indexical or deictic functions,' which will attract increasing attention also inside the specific branches of semiotics.

4.2 Cultural Semiotics

There is a growing interest in 'cultural semiotics.' This will encompass the study of whole cultures, such as European culture, or larger segments of culture, like youth culture, as complex sign systems, with a special emphasis on the intercultural dynamic exchange of signs. The endeavor of this study is to cover all cultural activities, from the basic establishment of time and space relations and structures of subjectivity to specific cultural phenomena such as political rhetoric or the arrangement of pedestrian zones, seen in the perspective of meaning production through signs. In this way, semiotics tries to integrate the more specific semiotic studies from recent years in a global perspective. But in the field of cultural studies, semiotics is at the same time constantly confronted with nonsemiotic approaches which are necessary to delimit the texts to be investigated, so that semiotics has now been forced into an open interdisciplinarity, breaking down the walls around semiotics itself.

4.3 Human and Nonhuman Signs

Another trend will be the 'combination of human and nonhuman sign production,' be it animal communication or the computerized processing of information. This orientation leads to a reevaluation of the notion of sign and will focus on other types of units which create meaning, like signals, units with one articulation, etc., and it will open to a stronger interest in communicative and informational acts which are not, like the more traditionally conceived interpretation, exclusively bound to doubly articulated signs and complex sign systems. Here an interest in studying the cooperation between signs and nonsigns will emerge.

4.4 Possible Worlds

An important aspect of our modern culture which has been permeated by the effects of computer technology, is the way the logical problem of 'possible worlds,' dating back to Leibniz, becomes part of the meaning production, not only in different types of fiction or of logical constructs, but in the process of the planning of the future. We have to be able to construct scenarios for the long-term consequences of things such as the depositing of nuclear waste, of huge climatic changes, of computerized communication processes and their influence on local cultures, etc. We are able to construct such scenarios in great detail, but none of us will live long enough to see if they will ever be real or true.

But despite the fact that these possible worlds (or virtual realities) only exist in sign systems, we have, nevertheless, to respond to them in terms of practical actions here and now, and in doing so we inevitably take a stand as to their reality. Semiotics will be of increasing importance in the construction of possible futures as cultural and not only technological universes.

See also: Literary Structuralism and Semiotics; Pragmatics.

Bibliography

Boudon R 1968 *A quoi sert la notion de structure?* Gallimard, Paris

Bühler K 1982 *Sprachtheorie*. Fischer, Stuttgart

Eco U 1984 *Semiotics and the Philosophy of Language*. Indiana University Press, Bloomington, IN

Greimas A J 1966 *Sémantique structurale*. Larousse, Paris

Greimas A J, Courtés J 1979–86 *Sémiotique: Dictionnaire raisonné de la théorie du langage*, 2 vols. Hachette, Paris

Grzybek P 1989 *Studien zum Zeichenbegriff der sowjetischen Semiotik*. Brockmeyer, Bochum

Hjelmslev L 1969 *Prolegomena to a Theory of Language*. University of Wisconsin Press, Madison, WI

Husserl E 1968 *Logische Untersuchungen*. Niemeyer, Tübingen

Innis R E 1985 *Semiotics: An Introductory Anthology*. Hutchinson, London

Lotman I U M 1990 *Universe of the Mind: A Semiotic Theory of Culture*. Tauris, London

Nöth W 1985 *Handbuch der Semiotik*. Metzler, Stuttgart

Peirce C S 1958 *Collected Papers*, 8 vols. Harvard University Press, Cambridge, MA

Posner R, et al. 1997 *Semiotik: Ein Handbuch zu den zeichentheoretischen Grundlagen von Natur und Kultur*. Walter de Gruyter, Berlin and New York

Rey A 1973 *Théories du signe et du sens*, 2 vols. Klincksieck, Paris

Saussure F de 1972 *Cours de linguistique générale*. Payot, Paris

Sebeok T A, et al. 1986 *Encyclopedic Dictionary of Semiotics*, 3 vols. Mouton de Gruyter, Berlin and New York

Singer M 1984 *Man's Glassy Essence*. Indiana University Press, Bloomington, IN

Tobin Y (ed.) 1988 *The Prague School and Its Legacy in Linguistics, Literature, Semiotics, Folklore and the Arts*. John Benjamins, Amsterdam

Sense

M. Crimmins

There is a perfectly ordinary use of 'sense' which is roughly equivalent to 'meaning' and opposed to 'nonsense.' We say that a sentence is true 'in a sense,' that we 'grasp its sense,' that a word 'has two senses,' and so on. One might hope that we could detail a single notion of the meaning of an expression that would unite these nontechnical uses of 'sense': meaningful expressions have 'meanings,' ambiguous expressions have multiple meanings, the meanings of sentences are things that can be true, that can be grasped, believed, and so on.

1. The Complexity of Meaning

However, Gottlob Frege argued persuasively that no single notion of meaning can play all these roles in a coherent theory. Frege held that an adequate theory of meaning must distinguish two aspects of the meaning of an expression. On the one hand there is the expression's 'referent' (*Bedeutung*), the entity the expression stands for. On the other there is the expression's 'sense' (*Sinn*), the way the expression presents the referent, or the aspect of the referent captured by the expression. Variants of this distinction have proved popular in philosophy of language, but have all been quite controversial.

2. Sense and Reference

The distinction is easiest to make with respect to singular terms (expressions designating objects). The two expressions 'the morning star' and 'the evening star' both stand for the planet Venus (so they have the same referent), but the first picks out Venus as the brightest star in the morning, while the second picks it out as the brightest star in the evening (so the expressions have different senses). According to Frege (though this interpretation of him is controversial; see Dummett 1981), the sense of an expression *determines* its referent, in that its referent is simply whatever entity has the features constituting its sense. This helps explain the fact that 'the morning star is the evening star' can be found informative, and is not a trivial truth concerning Venus's self-identity; the explanation is that informativeness is a matter of sense, not reference. The distinction also helps explain how someone might believe that the morning star is visible in the morning, without believing that the evening star is visible in the morning. Statements like these ascribe senses, not merely referents, as the objects of belief.

Frege's distinction forms the centerpiece of his two-level, doubly compositional semantics. The referent of a complex expression (truth value in the case of a sentence, (roughly) a set in the case of a predicate) is determined by only the referents of its component expressions, and the sense of a complex expression (an abstract 'thought' in the case of a sentence) is determined by only the senses of its parts. The truth values of 'propositional attitude' statements like belief reports depend on the senses and not on the referents of the embedded sentences. This forms no exception to the compositionality of reference, since on Frege's view the referents of embedded sentences in such statements are what normally would be their senses. However, this is an exception to the rule that the referent of an expression is determined independently of facts about which other expressions surround it.

The resulting systematic semantics is impressively powerful and strikes many as intuitively plausible. Unfortunately, the key notion of sense was left obscure by Frege, and later attempts to fill in the details have met with trouble.

3. Troubles with Sense

One difficulty facing accounts of sense with respect to proper names, is that it seems unlikely that there is a single definite aspect, feature, or group of features of an object universally associated with a given name for it. Frege mentioned that it is a defect of actual languages that the sense of a name can vary from person to person. As one of his chief concerns was with designing a formal language, the tactic of chiding natural language may have seemed adequate, but if Fregean semantics is to be seriously directed at natural languages, the interpersonal variation of sense presents an imposing obstacle. If different persons assign different senses to an expression, it is difficult to explain in what sense they can understand each other's statements. Similarly, it is difficult to explain (what ought to be easy on a Fregean account) how one person can report what another believes or says. This is not only because the two can assign different senses to the same words, but in some cases also because the two might not speak the same language, and so would not attach the same sense to any expression whatever.

Even if the difficulties about interpersonal differences can be handled, there remains a deeper problem. The notion that the referent of a term is whatever entity has the features constituting its sense (for a given person), has met with serious, possibly unanswerable challenges from several philosophers, notably Saul Kripke. Kripke argues that which individual one refers to with the name 'Einstein' does not hinge on what prominent features one attaches to the bearer of the name. If the only feature you attach to 'Einstein' is that he invented the light bulb, then your belief is about *Einstein*, and you have a false belief about him, not a true belief about Edison (the actual inventor of the light bulb). Your use of 'Einstein' refers to Einstein, Kripke proposes, because of the causal chain leading to your acquisition of the name: you got the name from someone who got the name from someone else who got the name, ultimately, from someone who dubbed Einstein with it. The features you attach to 'Einstein' do not come into determining reference.

In the face of these difficulties, some philosophers have recently pursued amended versions of Fregean semantics. These views give up one or another of the central features of traditional Fregeanism, such as that sense determines reference, or that sense is given by the important features one believes an object to possess (see Peacocke 1983; Forbes 1990).

See also: Frege, Gottlob; Names and Descriptions; Proposition; Reference: Philosophical Issues.

Bibliography

Dummett M 1981 *The Interpretation of Frege's Philosophy.* Duckworth, London
Forbes G 1990 The indispensibility of *sinn. Philosophical Review* **99**
Frege G 1952 *Translations from the Philosophical Writings of Gottlob Frege.* Basil Blackwell, Oxford
Kripke S A 1980 *Naming and Necessity.* Blackwell, Oxford
Peacocke C 1983 *Sense and Content.* Clarendon Press, Oxford

Topic and Comment

J. van Kuppevelt

Substantial topic–comment research started in the second half of the nineteenth century. Since German linguists, in particular Von der Gabelentz (1868), introduced this notional pair, it has become a fundamental part of linguistic theory and analysis. Besides linguists, however, philosophers, (formal) semanticists, cognitive scientists and (experimental) psychologists have also studied this subject, mainly from the perspective of the discipline concerned. The notions 'topic' and 'comment' are generally understood in the following way. The notions presuppose that a discourse unit U, a sentence or (part of) a discourse, has the property of being, in some sense, directed at a restricted set of entities and not at all entities that have come up in U. This restricted set of entities is what U 'is about' and constitutes the topic of U. The complementary notion 'comment' refers to what is newly asserted of the topic. The notion 'topic' is thus related both to sentences (utterances) and larger discourse units, resulting sometimes in an explicit formulation of a distinction between sentence topics and discourse topics. On the whole, however, research has restricted itself to an analysis of sentence topics.

1. Terminology

Topic–comment research is, unfortunately, characterized by the absence of uniformity in terminology. First, different terms are used in the literature to refer to the notion of 'topic.' There is the term 'topic' (e.g., Chomsky 1965; Hockett 1958; Hornby 1971; Lyons 1968; Reinhart 1981; Schank 1977; Sgall, et al. 1973; Strawson 1971, to mention just a few of the earlier approaches), but one also finds the term 'theme' (e.g., Daneš 1974; Firbas 1966; Halliday 1967; Kuno 1980 and many others after them) and, now slightly out of use, 'psychological subject' (e.g., Von der Gabelentz 1868; Hornby 1972; Paul 1880).

A second point is a difference often found in what may be called the 'categoriality' of the terms for 'topic' and 'comment.' Often, the second term is meant to refer to something which is categorically different from what is denoted by the first. Thus one finds a bicategorial pair *topic-focus* in, for example, Dik (1978) and Sgall (1979). The first term of this pair is usually formally defined in terms of 'aboutness,' the second in terms of 'informational status' such as *new* or *most prominent information* in a sentence.

The last point concerns structural, notional and/or ontological differences in term designation. Not all authors use the same term to refer to topics of structurally different levels. Some reserve different terms from the set of terms available to refer to different kinds of topic, for example, the term *topic* to denote a sentence topic and the term *theme* to denote the topic of a paragraph (Givón 1983: 7–8).

Some authors use terms like 'topic' and 'theme' to refer to notions that differ categorically from the 'topic' or 'aboutness' notion. Chafe, for example, reserves the term for 'the frame within which the sentence holds' (1976: 51). The topic 'sets a spatial, temporal or individual framework within which the main predication holds' (1976: 50). Chafe applies the term topic primarily to specific structural phenomena in so-called topic-prominent languages. But also temporal adverbia, which occur in English in sentence-initial position, are considered to be equivalent manifestations to which this term applies. Thus, in the English sentence 'Tuesday I went to the dentist,' the adverb *Tuesday* is 'topic' (1976: 51). The grammatical subject *I*, on the other hand, is identified with what the sentence is about: 'the subject is what we are talking about' (1976: 43). Similar uses of either the term 'topic' or the term 'theme' are found in Dik (1978) and Li and Thompson (1981).

Definitions of the notion 'sentence topic' show that terms like 'topic' and 'theme' are applied to entities which differ essentially in ontological status. The terms are applied not only to entities on the level of semantic extension, that is, the referents of linguistic expressions, but also to the linguistic elements themselves. In the first case, the topic of a sentence is formally defined as an entity in the world (or an n-tuple of such entities) that the sentence is about (e.g., Lyons 1968, Wason and Johnson-Laird 1972). Sentence 'aboutness' is thus assumed to be a two-place relation between a sentence S and an entity e that sentence S is about. Here terms like 'topic' and 'theme' are applied to e.

The application of these terms to linguistic entities may differ according to the 'aboutness' relation that is assumed. First, there are authors who define a sentence topic as a sentence part that refers to an entity in the world the sentence is about (Dahl 1969; Hornby 1971). Sentence 'aboutness' is here assumed to be a two-place relation between a sentence S and the extension $|s|$ of a structural element s in S. Terms like 'topic' and 'theme' apply to s. Second there are authors who, surprisingly, define a sentence topic as a sentence part the sentence is about (Davison 1984; Ryle 1933). In this case, sentence 'aboutness' is characterized as a two-place relation not between a sentence S and the extension $|s|$ of a structural element s in S but between a sentence S and the structure element s itself. In both cases the term used does not apply to entities in the world but to linguistic expressions which designate such entities.

2. The Kind of Phenomena Explained

The notions 'sentence topic' and 'discourse topic' are considered to function as explanatory principles for particular linguistic phenomena. The former often functions as an explanatory principle for specific, often assumed to be nontruthconditional differences in sentence (utterance) meaning. Many authors assume that these meaning differences are caused by differences in topic–comment modulation of the sentences in question. The following three sentences illustrate the differences in sentence meaning these authors wish to account for. The differences are marked by the position of the primary sentence accent which is rendered notationally by the use of capitals:

(a) (Who hit Bill?)   (1)
JOHN hit Bill.
(b) (What did John do to Bill?)
John HIT Bill.
(c) (Who did John hit?)
John hit BILL.

The explanation proposed is, in general terms, that the constituents which belong to the topic part of the (question-answering) sentence remain unaccented. Therefore, the accented constituents can have no topic function. The authors who give such an explication (e.g., Hornby 1971) identify the notions 'topic' and 'comment' operationally with the notions 'given/old information' and 'new information,' respectively. Topic-constituents are considered to be the representation of given, contextually bound information that is already stored in discourse. Because of their 'given' status they are, other than constituents which represent new information, no candidates for accent assignment.

Though an explication of meaning differences as in (1) is mostly given in terms of the 'topic' or 'aboutness' notion, no general consensus exists about the explanation of these phenomena. Some authors refrain from an explanation in terms of the topic–comment distinction. They exploit either the distinction between 'given/old' and 'new information' in the sentence (Halliday 1967; Kuno 1972) or a formally and operationally similar distinction between 'presupposition' and 'focus' (Chomsky 1971; Jackendoff 1972). When, besides a given-new (presupposition-focus) distinction, also a topic notion is assumed, this is not, as in the previous case, operationally identified with the notion 'given' or 'presupposed information.' Halliday (1967), for example, explains meaning differences like those between the sentences in (1) in terms of the given-new distinction, although according to his definition of topic ('theme') all these sentences are about John. Thus Halliday observes: 'Basically, the theme is what comes first in the clause.... The theme is what is being talked about, the point of departure for the clause as a message' (Halliday 1967: 212).

A similar view also implying a categorical distinction between what Halliday calls theme (topic) and given information is present in various, mainly so-called 'structured meaning' approaches that provide a syntactically oriented (formal) semantic representation of the focus structures (e.g., Jackendoff 1972; Jacobs 1983; Krifka 1991; Von Stechow 1981, 1989). A similar view is also present in some of the pragmatic accounts (e.g., Vallduví 1992, 1993). Contrary to these views, Steedman (1991) proposes an isomorphism between syntactic, informational and intonational structure based on Combinatory Categorial Grammar in which he adopts the same idea of two independent notional pairs but does not define the topic ('theme') of a sentence in terms of word order, that is, as the sentence-initial element.

From the beginning, the notion 'discourse topic' plays an important role in many, in particular, computational and (psycho)linguistic, theories and views about discourse coherence, either explicitly or implicitly (e.g., Grimes 1975; Hobbs 1982; Johnson-Laird 1983; Reichman 1978; Schank 1977). Especially in discourse (text) grammars (e.g., Van Dijk 1977) the notion often functions as the explanatory principle for the structural coherence underlying a well-formed discourse. In general it is assumed that a coherent discourse is composed of a set of hierarchically organ-ized discourse segments under one discourse topic. The overall discourse topic associated with the discourse as a whole and comprising all smaller discourse segments constitutes the superordinate discourse topic. Under this common superordinate discourse topic, the discourse topics of the subsegments are ordered paratactically or hypotactically, depending on whether there are inclusion relations between the subsegments. Although it is often claimed that structural coherence phenomena in discourse are 'explained' in terms of the notion 'topic,' these explanations are generally intuitive and fail to achieve formal precision due, mainly, to the absence of an empirically and operationally adequate definition of discourse topic and an unclarity with respect to the relation between discourse and sentence topics or between discourse topics themselves.

3. Topic Identification

In the topic–comment literature several tests and also several operational characterizations are presented to identify sentence topics. The tests and the characterizations will be dealt with below in separate sections. In the most satisfactory cases the proposed tests are meant to take as input a topic-bearing sentence and to give as output a specification of the topic of that sentence. In many cases, however, the test is only meant to determine whether some sentence element has topic function, indicating that this element is part of the topic constituent of the sentence. A characteristic of all tests, as opposed to characterizations, is the fact that the actual discourse context in which the topic-bearing sentence occurs is not a part of the test itself. The operational characterizations proposed in the literature can be classified into context-dependent and context-independent characterizations, as is clarified in Sect. 3.2.

3.1 Tests for Topic-hood

Well-known tests for topic identification are the fronting test (e.g., Kuno 1972; Lakoff 1971), the 'about'-context test (Reinhart 1981), the 'about'-question test (Gundel 1977), and a test which is commonly known as the question test (e.g., Sgall, et al. 1973, 1986). The first three tests are fundamentally restricted to the identification of noun phrase (NP) topics.

The fronting test is based on the assumption, not commonly accepted, that NPs which are fronted by, for example, a left-dislocation operation structurally mark topic-hood. This test implies that if a structurally unmarked sentence containing an NP_i ($S_{\langle NP_i \rangle}$) can be acceptably paraphrased according to the scheme *As for/Concerning/About NP_1, $S_{\langle NP_1 \rangle}$*, NP_1 represents the topic of the original sentence. In Reinhart (1981: 64–65) it is pointed out that the application of this test is restricted to sentences which introduce a new topic or lack a specific or generic indefinite topic–NP.

According to the 'about'-context test, a structurally unmarked sentence $S_{\langle NP_1 \rangle}$ is paraphrased by extending the sentence in agreement with a scheme like *He said about/of NP_1 that $S_{\langle NP_1 \rangle}$*. Properly speaking, the extended sentence is not an adequate paraphrase of the original sentence. The added part forces the original sentence to be about what is represented by NP_1 or, perhaps more precisely, what the person in question says about it. Without this addition, the original sentence may be about a different topic, depending on the preceding context.

In the case of the 'about'-question test the topic-bearing sentence $S_{\langle NP_1 \rangle}$ is not paraphrased but is placed in a context of a specific question *What about NP_1?* The test is based on the assumption that if sentence $S_{\langle NP_1 \rangle}$ is about NP_1, $S_{\langle NP_1 \rangle}$ is an acceptable answer to the 'about'-question. According to this test accented and clefted NPs have no topic function since the sentences which contain them constitute no acceptable answer to the 'about'-question. Like all other tests, this test does not make manifest how sentence topics affect discourse coherence. The coherence in discourse does not become apparent either when every topic-bearing sentence is preceded by an 'about'-question, or when every topic-bearing sentence is replaced by one of the proposed paraphrases.

Of all identification tests that have been proposed the question test is probably the best known. This test has many variants, the most comprehensive of which is presented in Sgall, et al. (1986). According to this test the division of a topic-bearing sentence in a topic and a comment (focus) part is determined by the set of *wh*-questions to which the sentence is an appropriate direct answer, both informationally and intonationally. Constituents of the sentence which appear in every question belong to the topic part and constituents which appear in no question belong to the comment part. The test fails to specify the status of the constituents that appear in only *some* of the questions.

When the question test is applied to, for example, the sentence *John hit BILL*, it determines that the constituents *John* and *Bill* belong to the topic and comment part respectively. Since the sentence constitutes an appropriate direct answer to both *What did John do?* and *Who did John hit?* the test leaves the status of the verb undecided. Although this sentence is also an appropriate answer to questions like *What happened?* and *What's new?*, these questions are excluded from the set. It is assumed that sentences in discourse which answer such general questions are topicless (1986: 212). A characteristic of this test is that different questions can determine the same topic–comment modulation, despite the fact that they may arise in different appropriate contexts. In addition to this test, an algorithm for topic-focus identification has been developed (Hajičová et al 1995).

3.2 Classification of Operational Characterizations

Context-independent operational characterizations of sentence topics can be divided into two types: either in terms of just *a specific syntactic category* (Chafe 1976) or in terms of *word order* (e.g., Chomsky 1965; Halliday 1967), with or without the requirement of a specific category. According to the former, the topic of a sentence is identified with the grammatical subject of the sentence. According to the latter, the topic (theme) of a sentence is, in principle, identified with the element in sentence-initial position. In Halliday (1967), which comes into the word order category, this characterization is meant to apply without any restriction as to the syntactic category of the sentence-initial element. Chomsky (1965) on the other hand (also of the word order class) explicitly states that sentence topics must have NP-status. The author characterizes a sentence topic as the leftmost NP immediately dominated by S in the surface structure.

Characterizations in terms of word order prevail. Three specific consequences of this type can be mentioned. The first consequence (which is not generally accepted) is that a topic is defined for every sentence, and that, moreover, this is always linguistically expressed. The second consequence is that the same topic is defined for succeeding utterances which have the same constituent in first position. Creider (1979) demonstrates that this is not always correct. He shows that especially a left-dislocated constituent cannot also serve as the topic of a succeeding utterance. The third consequence has to do with topic–comment phenomena that are related to question–answer pairs. Characterizations in terms of word order have as a consequence that the results of topic identification are inconsistent with the widely accepted assumption that one single topic is defined for question–answer pairs. This assumption implies that in question–answer pairs the topic is constituted by the question, so that, in the answer, the topic constituent always represents given information. According to word-order type characterizations, the topic constituent in the answer can also have new status. This is typically the case when the sentence element in sentence initial position receives the primary accent, for example, the constituent *Harry* in 'Who has been arrested?—Harry has been arrested.'

As has been said, some characterizations of sentence topics are context-dependent. These can be divided into three types: characterizations in terms of *informational status* (Bolinger 1977; Hornby 1970; Sgall, et al. 1973 and many others), sometimes involving the extra requirement of a status of contextually determined preference as is characteristic for the computational approach of Centering Theory (e.g., Grosz, et al. 1986, 1995; Joshi and Weinstein 1981; Walker, et al. 1997); characterizations in terms of *alternatives* as is suggested by the formal semantic approach known as Alternative Semantics (in particular Rooth

1985, 1992); and characterizations in terms of *questions* (e.g., Bartsch 1976; Keenan and Schieffelin 1976; Klein and Von Stutterheim 1987; Van Kuppevelt 1991; Stout 1896; Strawson 1971; Vennemann 1975).

Regarding the first type, the topic of a sentence is identified with the given/old or contextually bound information in the sentence. The identification of sentence topics is thus reduced to the identification of given information. A direct consequence of this approach is that sentences that only represent new information are topicless. Therefore, the criterion for sentence topics is that a given-new modulation is defined for it. Apart from the problem of how a sentence's given information can be identified, a more fundamental problem is whether givenness is a necessary and/or sufficient condition for topic-hood. In, for example, Reinhart (1981) it is argued that topics can also have new status and that given information need not be part of the topic. (On the given-new distinction see, for example, Chafe 1976; Clark and Haviland 1977; Halliday 1967; Prince 1981.)

In Centering Theory the notion of sentence topic is expressed by what is called the Backward-looking Center Cb of an utterance U_i ($Cb(U_i)$). $Cb(U_i)$ is a discourse entity evoked by U_i that is both contextually given and contextually preferred, implying that this entity was already introduced in the preceding utterance U_{i-1} and predicted to be the one U_i would be 'about.' As is the case with every utterance U_i, the set of discourse entities associated with U_{i-1}, called the set of Forward-looking Centers of that utterance ($Cf(U_{i-1})$), is a (partially) ordered set the ordering of which is language-specific, determined by various formal (syntactic, prosodic, etc.) characteristics of U_{i-1}. The highest-ranked element of this set is called the Preferred Center Cp of U_{i-1} ($Cp(U_{i-1})$), which expresses a preference with respect to the topic of the next utterance U_i. As mentioned, the full set of factors responsible for such an ordering is still to be determined. Backward-looking center and Forward-looking center correspond to Sidner's (1979) notion of current discourse focus and potential focus, respectively.

Although not explicitly part of the theory, the Alternative Semantics approach suggests that the topic of a sentence is the set of alternatives induced by the focus part of that sentence. The alternatives are defined as propositions obtained by that which in the given context can be inserted into the associated focus frame. As others have noted too (see, in particular, Partee 1991 and Rooth 1992), there is a non-trivial (and probably fruitful) relation between the alternative set associated with a sentence and Hamblin's (1973) notion of question meaning, formally analyzed as the set of propositions expressed by possible, direct answers to the question.

Characterizations in terms of questions identify the topic which is related to a question-answering sentence with a variety of things. In one approach (Bartsch 1976; Collingwood 1940; Vennemann 1975), the topic is identified with (one of) the presupposition(s) defined by the question. Others directly define the notion of topic in terms of questions and the set of possible ('alternative') answers they give rise to. This view is already central in the works of the British philosopher and (theoretical) psychologist G. F. Stout (e.g., Stout 1896, 1932): 'Questioning involves the thought of a set of incompatible alternatives. In asking a question we know what it is that we want to know in knowing that one or other of these alternatives is the right answer. But we do not know and have not decided, rightly or wrongly, which it is' (1932: 301). The set of incompatible alternatives is taken to be the topic ('psychological subject') of the question-answering sentence. More recently, in the mid-1980s, Carlson (1985), in the tradition of Hamblin (1973), identifies a topic with question meaning, whereas Klein and Von Stutterheim (1987: 164) take as topic what they call the 'alternative,' which they define as 'the choice between two or more possibilities' as an answer to the question posed. Still others (Van Kuppevelt 1991) identify the topic of a sentence with that which is questioned, i.e. an underdetermined singular or plural discourse entity that needs further specification. This underdeterminedness is then expressed in terms of the corresponding (actual) topic range specifying the (remaining) set of possible extensional counterparts. For all the approaches in terms of questions, the criterion for a sentence to have a topic is that it answers a question. In this respect it is assumed that sentences in discourse can also answer 'implicit,' that is not explicitly formulated, questions. However, when a sentence answers an implicit question, topic identification requires a reconstruction of the implicit question. To date, no fully satisfactory algorithm has been proposed that yields an unambiguous identification of implicit questions in discourse.

4. The Relation Between Sentence Topics and Discourse Topics

Finally, attention is paid to the relation between sentence topics and discourse topics, thereby refraining from other relevant subjects in this area of research, such as the important question of whether the topic–comment distinction is a syntactic, semantic and/or pragmatic phenomenon and the discussion on focus-sensitive operators.

Those (relatively few) authors who distinguish sentence topics from discourse topics do not agree with regard to the question of the distinctness versus the continuity of the notions 'sentence topic' and 'discourse topic.' In the context of discourse grammar, Van Dijk (1977), for example, assumes two notions which he defines in such a way that they are conceptually unrelated. A sentence topic is identified with an individual entity (or a set of entities or an ordered *n*-tuple of entities) about which new information is provided in the sentence. A discourse topic, on the other hand, is defined in terms of the entailments of the set of propositions expressed by the discourse (segment).

A uniform conception of sentence topics and discourse topics is assumed in certain other (formal) variants of discourse grammar (e.g., Polanyi and Scha 1984), in Asher's (1993) theory, which accounts for discourse structure in Discourse Representation Theory (Kamp 1981), as well as in theories of discourse central to which is the structuring function of (implicit) higher- and lower-order topic-forming questions (e.g., Carlson 1985; Klein and Von Stutterheim 1987; Van Kuppevelt 1991). In all these theories only one topic notion is assumed which covers both the notion of sentence topic and that of topic of larger discourse units. Contrary to the discourse theories in terms of questions, the first two approaches do not give a uniform topical account of discourse structure, as would appear from their assumption that not all discourse relations are topic-based. In Carlson's (1985) and Klein and Von Stutterheim's (1987) question theories, for example, hierarchical discourse structure is uniformly determined by topic-forming questions. However, the assigned structures are restricted because only subquestions of the quantitative type are presupposed: common topics defined by higher-order questions are modularly split up into more specific (entailed) subtopics defined by quantitative subquestions. The theory of Van Kuppevelt (1991 and other publications), on the other hand, provides a uniform, unrestricted topic notion. This notion is central in the explanation of hierarchical discourse structure in general, which is considered to be the result of the dynamics of contextually induced explicit and implicit (sub)topic-forming (sub)questions, thereby also providing a semantic, topical basis for pragmatic inferences known as Gricean conversational implicatures (Grice 1989). Besides the above-mentioned approaches, new dynamic approaches in terms of topics and questions have recently been proposed within formal semantics (e.g., Ginzburg 1996; Groenendijk and Stokhof 1993; Groenendijk, et al 1996; Roberts 1996; Zeevat 1994).

Bibliography

Asher N 1993 *Reference to Abstract Objects in Discourse.* Kluwer, Dordrecht

Bartsch R 1976 Topik-Fokus-Struktur und kategoriale Syntax. In: Ehrich V, Finke P (eds.) *Grammatik und Pragmatik.* Scriptor Verlag, Kronberg

Bolinger D 1977 Intonation across languages. In: Greenberg J (ed.) *Universals of Human Language.* Stanford University Press, Stanford, CA

Carlson L 1985 *Dialogue Games: An Approach to Discourse Analysis.* Reidel, Dordrecht

Chafe W L 1976 Givenness, contrastiveness, definiteness, subjects, topics, and point of view. In: Li C N (ed.) *Subject and Topic.* Academic Press, New York

Chomsky N 1965 *Aspects of the Theory of Syntax.* MIT Press, Cambridge, MA

Chomsky N 1971 Deep structure, surface structure, and semantic interpretation. In: Steinberg D D, Jakobovits L A (eds.) *Semantics. A Interdisciplinary Reader in Philosophy, Linguistics and Psychology.* Cambridge University Press, Cambridge

Clark H H, Haviland S E 1977 Comprehension and the given-new contract. In: Freedle R O (ed.) *Discourse Production and Comprehension.* Ablex, Norwood, NJ

Collingwood R G 1940 On presupposing. In: Collingwood R G *An Essay on Metaphysics.* Oxford University Press, Oxford

Creider C A 1979 On the explanation of transformations. In: Givón T (ed.) *Syntax and Semantics. Vol.* $_{12}$ *Discourse and Syntax.* Academic Press, New York

Dahl Ö 1969 *Topic and Comment. A Study in Russian and General Transformational Grammar.* Almqvist and Wiksell, Stockholm

Daneš F 1974 Functional sentence perspective and the organization of the text. In: Daneš F (ed.) *Papers on Functional Sentence Perspective.* Mouton, The Hague

Davison A 1984 Syntactic markedness and the definition of sentence topic. *Lg* **60**: 797–846

Dijk T A van 1977 *Text and Context. Explorations in the Semantics and Pragmatics of Discourse.* Longman, London

Dik S C 1978 *Functional Grammar.* North Holland, Amsterdam

Firbas J 1966 Non-thematic subjects in contemporary English. *Travaux Linguistiques de Prague* **2**: 239–56

Gabelentz G von der 1868 Ideen zur einer vergleichenden Syntax: Wort-und Satzstellung. *Zeitschrift für Völkerpsychologie und Sprachwissenschaft* **6**: 376–84

Ginzburg J 1996 Interrogatives: questions, facts and dialogue. In: Lappin S *The Handbook of Contemporary Semantic Theory.* Blackwell, Oxford

Givón T 1983 *Topic Continuity in Discourse. A Quantitative Cross-Language Study.* Benjamins, Amsterdam

Grice H P 1989 *Studies in the Way of Words.* Harvard University Press, Cambridge, MA

Grimes J E 1975 *The Thread of Discourse.* Mouton, The Hague

Groenendijk J, Stokhof M 1993 Interrogatives and adverbs of quantification. In: Bimbo K, Mate A (eds.) *Proceedings of the 4th Symposium on Logic and Language.* Budapest

Groenendijk J, Stokhof M, Veltman F 1996 Coreference and modality. In: Lappin S *The Handbook of Contemporary Semantic Theory.* Blackwell, Oxford

Grosz B J, Joshi A K, Weinstein S 1986 Towards a computational theory of discourse interpretation. (Unpublished manuscript)

Grosz B J, Joshi A K, Weinstein S 1995 Centering: a framework for modeling the local coherence of discourse. *Computational Linguistics* **21**: 203–25

Gundel J K 1977 *Role of Topic and Comment in Linguistic Theory.* IULC, Bloomington, IN

Hajičová E, Sgall P, Skoumalová H 1995 An automatic procedure for topic-focus identification. *Computational Linguistics* **21**: 81–94

Halliday M A K 1967 Notes on transitivity and theme in English. Part 2. *JL* **3**: 199–244

Hamblin C L 1973 Questions in Montague grammar. In: Partee B (ed.) *Montague Grammar*. Academic Press, New York

Haviland S E, Clark H H 1974 What's new? Acquiring new information as a process in comprehension. *Journal of Verbal Learning and Verbal Behavior* **13**: 512–21

Hobbs J R 1982 Towards an understanding of coherence in discourse. In: Lehnert W G, Ringle M H (eds.) *Strategies for Natural Language Processing*. Erlbaum, Hillsdale, NJ

Hockett C F 1958 *A Course in Modern Linguistics*. Macmillan, New York

Hornby P A 1970 A developmental analysis of the 'psychological' subject and predicate of the sentence. *L&S* **13**: 182–93

Hornby P A 1971 Surface structure and the topic–comment distinction: A developmental study. *Child Development* **42**: 1975–88

Hornby P A 1972 The psychological subject and predicate. *Cognitive Psychology* **3**: 632–42

Jackendoff R S 1972 *Semantic Interpretation in Generative Grammar*. MIT Press, Cambridge, MA

Jacobs J 1983 *Fokus und Skalen: Zur Syntax und Semantik von Gradpartikeln im Deutschen*. Niemeyer, Tübingen

Johnson-Laird P N 1983 *Mental Models. Towards a Cognitive Science of Language, Inference and Consciousness*. Cambridge University Press, Cambridge

Joshi A K, Weinstein S 1981 Control of inference: Role of some aspects of discourse structure-centering. *Proceedings of the International Joint Conference on Artificial Intelligence*.

Kamp H 1981 A theory of truth and semantic representation. In: Groenendijk J, Janssen T M V, Stokhof M (eds.) *Formal Methods in the Study of Language: Part 1*. Mathematical Centre Tracts 135, Amsterdam (Reprinted in: Groenendijk J, Janssen T M V, Stokhof M (eds.) 1984 *Truth, Interpretation and Information*. Foris, Dordrecht)

Keenan E O, Schieffelin B B 1976 Topic as a discourse notion: A study of topic in the conversations of children and adults. In: Li C N (ed.) *Subject and Topic*. Academic Press, New York

Klein W, Stutterheim C von 1987 Quaestio und referentielle Bewegung in Erzählungen. *Linguistische Berichte* **109**: 163–83

Krifka M 1991 A compositional semantics for multiple focus constructions. In: Moore S, Wyner A (eds.) *Proceedings of SALT I*. Cornell University, Ithaca

Kuno S 1972 Functional sentence perspective: A case study from Japanese and English. *Lln* **3**: 269–320

Kuno S 1980 Functional syntax. In: Moravcsik E A, Wirth J R (eds.) *Syntax and Semantics 12: Current Approaches to Syntax*. Academic Press, New York

Kuppevelt J van 1991 *Topic en Comment. Expliciete en Impliciete Vraagstelling in Discourse*. (Doctoral dissertation, Nijmegen)

Kuppevelt J van 1995 Discourse structure, topicality and questioning. *JL* **31**: 109–47

Kuppevelt J van 1996 Inferring from topics. Scalar implicatures as topic-dependent inferences. *Linguistics and Philosophy* **19**: 393–443

Lakoff G 1971 On generative semantics. In: Steinberg D D, Jakobovits L A (eds.) *Semantics. An Interdisciplinary Reader in Philosophy, Linguistics and Psychology*. Cambridge University Press, Cambridge

Li C N, Thompson S A 1981 *Mandarin Chinese. A Functional Reference Grammar*. University of California Press, Berkeley, CA

Lyons J 1968 *Introduction to Theoretical Linguistics*. Cambridge University Press, Cambridge

Partee B H 1991 Topic, focus and quantification. In: Moore S, Wyner A (eds.) *Proceedings of SALT I*. Cornell University, Ithaca

Paul H 1880 *Prinzipien der Sprachgeschichte*. Niemeyer, Tübingen (8th edn., 1970)

Polanyi L, Scha R 1984 A syntactic approach to discourse semantics. In: *Proceedings of the International Conference on Computational Linguistics*. Stanford University, Stanford, CA

Prince E F 1981 Towards a taxonomy of given-new information. In: Cole P (ed.) *Radical Pragmatics*. Academic Press, New York

Reichman R 1978 Conversational coherency. *Cognitive Science* **2**: 283–327

Reinhart T 1981 Pragmatics and linguistics: An analysis of sentence topics. *Philosophica* **27**: 53–94

Roberts C 1996 Information structure in discourse: towards an integrated formal theory of pragmatics. (Unpublished manuscript)

Rooth M 1985 *Association with Focus*. (Doctoral dissertation, Amherst, MA)

Rooth M 1992 A theory of focus interpretation. *Natural Language Semantics* **1**: 75–116

Ryle G 1933 About. *Analysis* **1**: 10–12

Schank R C 1977 Rules and topics in conversation. *Cognitive Science* **1**: 421–41

Sgall P 1979 Towards a definition of focus and topic, part I. *Prague Bulletin of Mathematical Linguistics* **31**: 3–25

Sgall P E, Hajičová E, Benešová E 1973 *Topic, Focus and Generative Semantics*. Scriptor Verlag, Kronberg

Sgall P E, Hajičová E, Panevová J 1986 *The Meaning of the Sentence in its Semantic and Pragmatic Aspects*. Reidel, Dordrecht

Sidner C L 1979 *Towards a Computational Theory of Definite Anaphora Comprehension in English Discourse*. (Doctoral dissertation, MIT, Cambridge, MA)

Stechow A von 1981 Topic, focus and local relevance. In: Klein W, Levelt W (eds.) *Crossing the Boundaries in Linguistics: Studies Presented to Manfred Bierwisch*. Reidel, Dordrecht

Stechow A von 1989 *Focusing and Backgrounding Operators*. Universität Konstanz, Arbeitspapier Nr. 6, Konstanz

Steedman M 1991 Structure and intonation. *Language* **67**: 260–96

Stout G F 1896 *Analytic Psychology*. Sonnenschein, Macmillan, London

Stout G F 1932 Truth and falsity. *Mind* **41**: 297–310

Strawson P F 1971 Identifying reference and truth-values. In: Steinberg D D, Jakobovits L A (eds.) *Semantics: An Interdisciplinary Reader in Philosophy, Linguistics and Psychology*. Cambridge University Press, Cambridge

Vallduví E 1992 *The Informational Component*. Garland, New York

Vallduví E 1993 Information packaging: a survey. (Unpublished manuscript)

Vennemann T 1975 Topics, sentence accent, ellipsis: A proposal for their formal treatment. In: Keenan E L (ed.) *Formal Semantics of Natural Language*. Cambridge University Press, Cambridge

Walker M, Joshi A K, Prince E 1997 *Centering Theory in Discourse*. Oxford University Press, Oxford

Wason P C, Johnson-Laird P N 1972 *Psychology of Reasoning: Structure and Content*. Batsford, London

Zeevat H 1994 Questions and exhaustivity in update seman-

tics. In: Bunt H, Muskens R, Reiner G (eds.) In: *Proceedings of the International Workshop on Computational Semantics*. ITK, Tilburg

Truth

P. G. Horwich

The notion of truth plays a major role in our reflections on language, thought, and action. We may be inclined to suppose, for example, that 'truth' is the proper aim of scientific inquiry, that true beliefs are conducive to getting what we want, that the meaning of a sentence is the condition for its truth, that reliable preservation of truth as one argues from premises to a conclusion is the mark of valid reasoning, that moral pronouncements should not be regarded as objectively true, and so on. In order to assess the plausibility of such theses, and in order to refine them and to explain why they hold, there is a need for some view of what truth is—a theory that would explain its relations to other matters. Thus there can be little prospect of understanding our most important intellectual capacities in the absence of a good theory of truth. Such a thing, however, has been notoriously elusive. The ancient view that truth is some sort of 'correspondence with reality' has still never been articulated satisfactorily: the nature of the alleged 'correspondence' and the alleged 'reality' remain objectionably obscure. Yet the familiar alternative suggestions—that true beliefs are those that are 'mutually coherent,' or 'pragmatically useful,' or 'verifiable in suitable conditions'—have each been confronted with persuasive counterexamples. A twentieth-century departure from these traditional analyses is the view that being true is not a property at all—that the syntactic form of the predicate, 'is true,' hides its real semantic character, which is not to describe propositions but to endorse them. But this radical approach is also faced with difficulties and suggests, somewhat counterintuitively, that truth cannot have the vital theoretical role in semantics and elsewhere that we are naturally inclined to give it. Thus truth remains one of the most enigmatic of notions: an explicit account of it can appear to be essential yet beyond our reach. However, research in the late 1980s and early 1990s has provided some grounds for optimism.

1. Traditional Theories

The belief that snow is white owes its truth to a certain feature of the external world: namely, to the fact that snow is white. Similarly, the belief that dogs bark is true because of the fact that dogs bark. This sort of trivial observation leads to what is perhaps the most natural and popular account of truth, the correspondence theory, according to which a belief (statement, sentence, proposition, etc.) is true just in case there exists a fact corresponding to it (Austin 1950). This thesis is unexceptionable in itself. However, if it is to provide a substantial and complete theory of truth—if it is to be more than merely a picturesque way of asserting all equivalences of the form:

$$\text{The proposition } that\ p \text{ is true} \leftrightarrow p \qquad (1)$$

—then it must be supplemented with accounts of what facts are, and what it is for a belief to correspond to a fact; and these are the problems on which the correspondence theory of truth has foundered. For one thing, it is far from clear that any significant gain in understanding is achieved by reducing 'the proposition that snow is white is true' to 'the fact that snow is white exists'; for these expressions seem equally resistant to analysis and too close in meaning for one to provide an illuminating account of the other. In addition, the general relationship that holds between the belief that snow is white and the fact that snow is white, between the belief that dogs bark and the fact that dogs bark, and so on, is very hard to identify. The best attempt to date is Wittgenstein's (1922) so-called 'picture theory', whereby a proposition is a logical configuration of terms, a fact is a logical configuration of objects, and a fact corresponds to a proposition when their configurations are identical and when the terms in the proposition refer to the similarly placed objects in the fact. However, even if this account is correct as far as it goes, it would need to be completed with plausible theories of 'logical configuration' and of 'reference,' neither of which is easy to come by.

A central characteristic of truth—one that any adequate theory must explain—is that when a proposition satisfies its so-called 'conditions of proof (or verification),' then it is regarded as true. To the extent that the property of corresponding with reality is mysterious, it will be found impossible to see why what is taken to verify a proposition should indicate the possession of that property. Therefore a tempting alternative to the correspondence theory—an alternative which eschews obscure, metaphysical concepts and which explains quite straightforwardly why verifiability implies truth—is simply to identify truth with verifiability (Peirce 1932). This idea can take on various forms. One version involves the further assumption that verification is holistic—namely, that a belief is justified (i.e., verified) when it is part of an entire system of beliefs that are consistent and harmonize with one another (Bradley 1914; Hempel 1935; Blanshard 1939). This is known as the coherence theory of truth. Another version involves the assumption that there is, associated with each proposition, some specific procedure for finding out whether one should believe it or not. On this account, to say that a proposition is true is to say that it would be verified by the appropriate procedure (Dummett 1978; Putnam 1981). In the context of mathematics, this amounts to the identification of truth with provability.

The attractions of the verificationist account of truth are that it is refreshingly clear compared with the correspondence theory, and that it succeeds in connecting truth with verification. The trouble is that the bond which it postulates between these notions is implausibly strong. We do indeed take verification to indicate truth. But also we recognize the possibility that a proposition may be false even though there is perfectly good reason to believe it, and that a proposition may be true even though we are unable to discover that it is. Verifiability and truth are no doubt highly correlated; but they do not appear to be the same thing.

A third well-known account of truth is known as pragmatism (James 1909; Dewey 1938; Rorty 1982; Papineau 1987). As mentioned above, the verificationist selects a prominent property of truth and considers it to be the essence of truth. Similarly, the pragmatist focuses on another important characteristic—namely, that true beliefs are a good basis for action—and takes this to be the very nature of truth. True assumptions are said to be, by definition, those which provoke actions with desirable results. Again, this is an account with a single attractive explanatory feature. But again the central objection is that the relationship which it postulates between truth and its alleged analysis—in this case, utility—is implausibly close. Granted, true beliefs tend to foster success; but it can easily happen that an action based on true beliefs leads to disaster, and that, by a stroke of good luck, a false assumption produces wonderful results.

2. Deflationary Theories

One of the few uncontroversial facts about truth is that the proposition that snow is white is true if and only if snow is white, the proposition that lying is wrong is true if and only if lying is wrong, and so on. Traditional theories acknowledge this fact but regard it as insufficient and, as described above, inflate it with some further principle of the form 'X is true if and only if X has property P' (such as, corresponding to reality, verifiability, or being suitable as a basis for action), which is supposed to specify what truth is. A radical alternative to the traditional theories results from denying the need for any such further specification and taking the theory of truth to be nothing more than all equivalences of the form 'The proposition *that p* is true if and only if p' (Ramsey 1927; Wittgenstein 1953; Leeds 1978; Horwich 1990).

This proposal is best presented in conjunction with an account of the raison d'être of the notion of truth: namely, that it enables us to express attitudes towards those propositions we can designate but not explicitly formulate. Suppose, for example, you are told that Einstein's last words expressed a claim about physics, an area in which you think he was very reliable. Suppose that, unknown to you, his claim was the proposition that quantum mechanics is wrong. What conclusion can you draw? Exactly which proposition becomes the appropriate object of your belief? Surely not that quantum mechanics is wrong, because you are not aware that that is what he said. What is needed is a proposition, K, with the following properties: that from K and any further premise of the form 'Einstein's claim was the proposition that p' you can infer 'p,' whatever it is. Now suppose that, as the deflationist claims, our understanding of the truth predicate consists in the stipulation that any instance of the following schema, 'The proposition *that p* is true if and only if p,' must be accepted. Then your problem is solved. For if K is the proposition 'Einstein's claim is true,' it will have precisely the inferential power that is needed. From it and 'Einstein's claim is the proposition that quantum mechanics is wrong,' you can infer 'The proposition that quantum mechanics is wrong is true,' which, given the relevant axiom of the deflationary theory, allows you to derive 'Quantum mechanics is wrong.' Thus one point in favor of the deflationary theory is that it squares with a plausible story about the function of our notion of truth: its axioms explain that function without the need for any further analysis of 'what truth is.'

Not all variants of deflationism have this virtue. According to the redundancy/performative theory of truth, the following pair of sentences, 'The proposition that p is true' and plain 'p,' have exactly the same meaning and express the same statement as one another; so it is a syntactic illusion to think that 'is true' attributes any sort of property to a proposition (Ayer 1935; Strawson 1950). But in that case it becomes hard to explain why we are entitled to infer 'The proposition that p is true' from 'Einstein's claim is the proposition that p' and 'Einstein's claim is true.' For if truth is not a property, then we can no longer account for the inference by invoking the principle that if X is identical with Y then any property of X is a property of Y and vice versa. Thus the redundancy/performative theory, by identifying rather than merely correlating the contents of 'The proposition that p is true' and 'p,' precludes the prospect of a good explanation of one of truth's most significant and useful characteristics. So it is better to restrict our claim to the weak, equivalence schema: The proposition *that p* is true if and only if p.

Support for deflationism depends upon the possibility of showing that its axioms—instances of the equivalence schema—unsupplemented by any further analysis, will suffice to explain all the central facts about truth; for example, that the verification of a proposition indicates its truth, and that true beliefs have a practical value. The first of these facts follows trivially from the deflationary axioms. For given our a priori knowledge of the equivalence of 'p' and 'The proposition *that p* is true,' any reason to believe 'that p' becomes an equally good reason to believe that the proposition *that p* is true. The second fact can also be explained in terms of the deflationary axioms, but not quite so easily. Consider, to begin with, beliefs of the form:

If I perform act A, then S will happen. (2)

The psychological effect of such a belief is, roughly, to cause the performance of A if S is desired. That is:

If S is desired, then A is performed.

Also, when the belief is true, then, given the deflationary axioms, the performance of A will in fact be followed by S. That is:

If (2) is true, then if A is performed, S will happen.

Therefore:

If (2) is true and if S is desired, then S will happen.

In other words, when the belief is true, then the agent will get S if he or she wants it. So it is quite reasonable to value the truth of beliefs of that form. But such beliefs are derived by inference from other beliefs and can be expected to be true if those other beliefs are true. So it is reasonable to value the truth of any belief that might be used in such an inference.

To the extent that such accounts can be given of all the facts involving truth, then the explanatory demands on a theory of truth will be met by the collection of all statements like 'The proposition that snow is white is true if and only if snow is white,' and the idea that some deep analysis of truth is needed will be diminished.

However, there are several strongly felt objections to deflationism. One reason for dissatisfaction is that

the theory has an infinite number of axioms, and therefore cannot be completely written down. This alleged defect has led some philosophers to develop theories which show, first, how the truth of any proposition derives from the referential properties of its constituents; and, second, how the referential properties of primitive constituents are determined (Tarski 1943; Davidson 1969). However, it remains controversial to assume that all propositions—including belief attributions, laws of nature, and counterfactual conditionals—depend for their truth values on what their constituents refer to. And there is no immediate prospect of a decent, finite theory of reference. So it is far from clear that the infinite, list-like character of deflationism can be avoided.

Another source of dissatisfaction with this theory is that certain instances of the schema are clearly false. Consider (3) below:

THE PROPOSITION EXPRESSED BY THE SENTENCE IN (3)
SMALL CAPITALS IS NOT TRUE.

Substituting this into the deflationary schema, one obtains a version of the 'liar' paradox, namely:

The proposition *that the proposition expressed by the* (4) *sentence in small capitals is not true* is true if and only if the proposition expressed by the sentence in small capitals is not true.

from which a contradiction is easily derivable. (Given (4), the supposition that (3) is true implies that (3) is not true, and the supposition that it is not true implies that it is.) Consequently, not every instance of the equivalence schema can be included in our theory of truth; but it is no simple matter to specify the ones to be excluded (see Kripke 1975; Gupta 1982).

A third objection to the deflationary theory concerns its reliance on propositions as the basic vehicles of truth. It is widely felt that the notion of proposition is defective and that it should not be employed in semantics. If this is accepted, then the natural deflationary reaction is to attempt a reformulation that would appeal only to sentences: for example:

'p' is true if and only if p.

But this so-called 'disquotational theory of truth' comes to grief over indexicals, demonstratives, and other terms whose reference varies with the context of use. It is not the case, for example, that every instance of *I am hungry* is true if and only if I am hungry. And there is no obvious way of modifying the deflationary schema for sentences to accommodate this problem (see, however, Horwich 1990; Quine 1990).

3. The Role of Truth in Semantics

It is commonly assumed, following Davidson (1967), that a sentence is given meaning by associating it with a condition for being true. For example, our understanding of the sentence *Snow is white* would consist in our commitment to the proposition *that 'Snow is white' is true if and only if snow is white.* One frequently cited virtue of this so-called 'truth-conditional theory' is that it eliminates problematic notions such as 'means that' in favor of the relatively clear ideas, 'refers to' and 'is true.' Another alleged virtue is that it shows how the meanings of composite expressions depend on the meanings of their parts, and therefore how it is possible for us, with our finite minds, to understand a potential infinity of compound expressions. For example, if our knowledge of the meanings of sentences 'A' and 'B' consists in knowing that:

'A' is true if and only if snow is white.

and that:

'B' is true if and only if dogs bark.

then we can deduce that:

'A' is true and 'B' is true
if and only if snow is white and dogs bark.

But our understanding of 'and' tells us that:

'A and B' is true
if and only if 'A' is true and 'B' is true.

So we can conclude that:

'A and B' is true
if and only if snow is white and dogs bark.

thereby deriving the truth condition (i.e., the meaning) of the compound expression from our knowledge of the meanings of its parts.

Criticism of the truth-conditional theory of meaning comes from several directions. First, it can be argued that understanding an expression consists merely in associating it with a meaning and need not involve any knowledge of that association. Such knowledge—e.g., that 'A' means that snow is white, or that 'A' is true if and only if snow is white—would require possession of the concepts 'means that' or 'true'; yet it would seem that one might understand words like 'snow' without yet having acquired those sophisticated semantic concepts.

Second, the fact that a sentence, 'A,' is true if and only if snow is white does not entail that 'A' expresses the proposition that snow is white. It entails merely that 'A' and *snow is white* are either both true or both false. This difficulty may be mitigated by taking the words 'if and only if' in the statement of truth conditions to convey a sufficiently strong relation of equivalence between *A is true* and *Snow is white*. However, it is unclear that anything weaker than synonymy will do, in which case the initial promise to have dispensed with the obscure notion of 'meaning' will not be fulfilled.

A third criticism of the truth-conditional theory accuses it of being not so much false as unhelpful—of explaining facts that are easy to explain without it, yet having nothing to say about the features of meaning that are most in need of illumination (Dummett 1975, 1976). According to this critique, the compositionality of meaning follows trivially from the fact that the meaning of an expression is a compound entity whose constituents are the meanings of the constituents of the expression and whose structure is determined by the expression's syntactic form. This shows, without the need for a truth-conditional analysis, how we are able to figure out the meanings of complex expressions from the meanings of their parts. Moreover, the criticism continues, the most puzzling properties of meaning are not addressed at all by the truth-conditional approach. For example, in virtue of which facts about the mind or linguistic behavior does a sentence come to have the particular meaning it has? It is all very well to cite our committing ourselves to some proposition of the form 'A is true if and only if p'; but this is empty in the absence of some indication of what state of mind such a commitment consists in. Another important fact about meaning is that, if someone knows the meaning of a sentence, then he knows something about what counts as evidence for and against its being true. Again, an interesting account of what it is to know the meaning of a sentence would shed light on this fact, but the truth-conditional analysis leaves it in the dark. Perhaps the analysis can be supplemented with further theory and thereby explain these matters (see Davidson 1990). However, questions will remain as to whether the truth-conditional analysis is itself doing any explanatory work. Insofar as the supplementary theory does not deal separately with the elements of the analysans—notably, 'true,' and the above-mentioned, strong notion of 'if and only if'—but rather concerns the analysans taken as a whole, then it would be more straightforward to take the theory as a direct account of meaning, bypassing the truth-conditional analysis.

4. Falsity

The simplest plausible account of falsity is that a proposition is false just in case it is not true. An alternative formulation of this idea—one that parallels the equivalence schema for truth—is given by (5) below:

The proposition *that p* is false if and only if $-p$. (5)

These two formulations are equivalent, because the logical expression, '$-p$,' is shorthand for 'It is not the case that p.' But there is no reason to distinguish the concepts 'being true' and 'being the case.' So '$-p$' means nothing more or less than 'It is not true that p,' which is presumably synonymous with 'The proposition *that p* is not true.'

From this natural account of falsity, it follows that every proposition has a truth value; for to say of some proposition that it is neither true nor false would be to imply that it is both not true and not not true, which is a contradiction. This result has important ramifications in semantics, where it has often been found tempting to mark out certain 'odd' propositions as having no truth value.

One of the areas in which it has been popular to invoke truth-value gaps is in the treatment of vagueness. It is often said, for example, that if John is a borderline case of baldness, then the proposition that John is bald is neither true nor false. But this approach leads to the contradiction just mentioned. An alternative strategy is to draw a distinction between truth and determinate truth (in terms of the idea that the latter, but not the former, implies the possibility of conclusive verification). One can then characterize what is special about vague propositions, without running afoul of the above theory of falsity, by saying that, although true or false, they lack determinate truth values.

A second type of proposition to which the 'no-truth-value' strategy has been applied are those, such as *Santa drives a sledge*, which contain nonreferring constituents. Again, there is an alternative policy; namely, to regard such propositions as false. This can be sustained by converting names into predicates as proposed by Quine, giving, in this example:

> The unique possessor of the property of 'being Santa' drives a sledge.

and then employing Russell's theory of definite descriptions to obtain:

> There is exactly one thing possessing the property of 'being Santa,' and it drives a sledge.

which is uncontroversially false.

Finally, there is a famous 'emotivist' account of ethics according to which, appearances to the contrary, moral pronouncements purport not to assert facts but, rather, to express the feelings of the speaker, and therefore should not be regarded as true or false. However, there is no need to link the two components of this view. One might well agree that the peculiarity of ethical claims is that they are justified when the speaker has certain feelings. But this does not require the statement that they are neither true nor false—which, as shown above, is a position best avoided. Therefore, once again, no theoretical reason has been found to depart from the simple account of falsity as absence of truth.

See also: Deviant Logics; Paradoxes, Semantic; Reference: Philosophical Issues; Truth and Paradox; Truth Conditions; Vagueness.

Bibliography

Austin J L 1950 Truth. *Proceedings of the Aristotelian Society*, Supplementary vol. **24**: 111–28
Ayer A J 1935 The criterion of truth. *Analysis 3*
Blanshard B 1939 *The Nature of Thought*, vol. 2. Allen and Unwin, London
Bradley F H 1914 *Essays on Truth and Reality*. Clarendon Press, Oxford
Davidson D 1967 Truth and meaning. *Synthese* 17: 304–23
Davidson D 1969 True to the facts. *Journal of Philosophy* 66: 748–64
Davidson D 1990 The structure and content of truth. *Journal of Philosophy* 87: 279–328
Dewey J 1916 *Essays in Experimental Logic*. Henry Holt and Co., Chicago, IL
Dummett M 1975 What is a theory of meaning?, Part I. In: Guttenplan S (ed.) *Mind and Language*. Clarendon Press, Oxford
Dummett M 1976 What is a theory of meaning?, Part II. In: Evans G, McDowell J (eds.) *Truth and Meaning: Essays in Semantics*. Clarendon Press, Oxford
Dummett M 1978 *Truth and Other Enigmas*. Clarendon Press, Oxford
Gupta A 1982 Truth and paradox. *Journal of Philosophical Logic* **11**: 61–102
Hempel C 1935 On the logical positivist's theory of truth. *Analysis* **2**: 49–59
Horwich P G 1990 *Truth*. Basil Blackwell, Oxford
James W 1909 *The Meaning of Truth*. Longmans Green, New York
Kripke S 1975 Outline of a theory of truth. *Journal of Philosophy* **72**: 690–716
Leeds S 1978 Theories of reference and truth. *Erkenntnis* **13**: 111–29
Papineau D 1987 *Reality and Representation*. Basil Blackwell, Oxford
Peirce C S 1932 *Collected Papers*, vols. 2–4. Harvard University Press, Cambridge, MA
Pitcher G (ed.) 1964 *Truth*. Prentice-Hall, Englewood Cliffs, NJ
Putnam H 1981 *Reason, Truth and History*. Cambridge University Press, Cambridge
Quine W V 1990 *Pursuit of Truth*. Harvard University Press, Cambridge, MA
Ramsey F 1927 Facts and propositions. *Proceedings of the Aristotelean Society*, Supplementary vol. **7**: 153–70
Rorty R 1982 *Consequences of Pragmatism*. Minnesota University Press, MN
Strawson P 1950 Truth. *Proceedings of the Aristotelean Society*, Supplementary vol. **24**: 128–56
Tarski A 1943 The semantic conception of truth. *Philosophy and Phenomenological Research* **4**: 341–75
Wittgenstein L 1922 *Tractatus Logico-philosophicus*. Routledge and Kegan Paul, London
Wittgenstein L 1953 *Philosophical Investigations*. Oxford University Press, Oxford

Truth Conditions

S. Shalkowski

A semantic theory, whether for a natural language or for a formal language artificially constructed for specific clearly defined purposes, is a theory of what makes language (or some uses of it) meaningful. One familiar theory of the meaningfulness of language is that the meaning of a declarative sentence is its truth conditions, i.e., those conditions which render the sentence true. Thus, the meaning of *Snow is white* is explained in terms of what it is for that sentence to be true, captured by:

(T) *Snow is white* is true if and only if snow is white.

If truth conditions are the basis of meaning, the theorems of a fully developed truth-conditional theory of meaning will be statements of the form:

(M) *Snow is white* means that snow is white.

1. Semantics and Truth Conditions

Classical logic tacitly presents a partially truth-conditional semantics for formal systems. The semantics for sentential logic begins with the possible distributions of truth values over the atomic sentences. The interpretation of compound statements is then given solely on the basis of the truth conditions of their components, as given by the truth tables for the sentential connectives. Thus, according to classical semantic structures, logically equivalent sentences are semantically equivalent. The semantics for quantificational and intensional logics are truth conditional to the extent that they rely on the classical semantics for the sentential connectives.

2. Truth Conditions and the Nature of Truth

The precise nature of meaning is incompletely specified by the simple statement that meanings are truth conditions. If truth is correspondence with reality, then truth-conditional semantics is the doctrine that meanings are objective metaphysical structures of the world, structures that are not wholly a function of what language users believe or have good reason to believe. If truth is the coherence of the elements in a system of belief, or the tendency to satisfy goals and purposes in a noteworthy manner, or the support by a sufficient amount of evidence, then the truth conditions that constitute the meanings of statements are at least partly a function of the theoretical, pragmatic, or assertibility conditions in which speakers find themselves.

Truth-conditional semantics was proposed by Ludwig Wittgenstein in the *Tractatus Logico–Philosophicus* where he claims that a true statement pictures or depicts a state of affairs. Components of the sentence structure contribute to the meaning of the whole by referring to components of the depicted fact. J. L. Austin, Alfred Tarski, and Donald Davidson define truth as correspondence with reality by defining truth in terms of reference and the satisfaction of a predicate without relying on structured facts. These accounts provide a general basis for the semantics of classical logic. If statement meanings are truth conditions that obtain regardless of a speaker's knowledge that they obtain, then statements of the form:

$$p \vee \sim p$$
$$\forall x(Fx \vee \sim Fx)$$

are necessarily true.

Strict empiricists found this metaphysical account of truth conditions objectionable and gave an alternative semantics for logic and natural language. It is a mere terminological issue whether to describe them as rejecting truth-conditional semantics or as merely rejecting a specific formulation of the proper theory of truth. Mathematical intuitionists maintain that the truth of a mathematical statement is parasitic upon the conditions of proof of that statement and that the meaning of the logical operators is given by the conditions of constructing a proof of compound statements containing those operators. Thus, logical truth is identified with provability and, more generally, the meanings of statements are the conditions of their warranted assertibility. Disjunctions are accepted as true only when there is a proof of one of the disjuncts. For this reason, instances of excluded middle are not intuitionistically valid, since there may be proofs of neither disjunct. Standard *reductio ad absurdum* proofs are intuitionistically acceptable, however, so long as they do not involve the use of the double negation elimination rule.

See also: Intuitionism.

Bibliography

Austin J L 1950 Truth. *Proceedings of the Aristotelian Society* **24**: 111–28
Davidson D 1984 *Inquiries into Truth and Interpretation*. Clarendon Press, Oxford
Dummett M 1978 *Truth and Other Enigmas*. Harvard University Press, Cambridge, MA
Heyting A 1956 *Intuitionism: An Introduction*. North-Holland, Amsterdam
Tarski A 1943/44 The semantic conception of truth. *Philosophy and Phenomenological Research* **4**: 341–75
Tarski A 1958 The concept of truth in formalized languages. In: *Logic, Semantics, Metamathematics: Papers from 1923 to 1938*. Oxford University Press, Oxford
Wittgenstein L 1961 (trans. Pears D F, McGuinness B F) *Tractatus Logico–Philosophicus*. Routledge and Kegan Paul, London

Vagueness

T. Williamson

An expression or concept is vague if it has borderline cases, where it neither definitely applies nor definitely fails to apply. For example, *tall* is vague because some people are neither definitely tall nor definitely not tall. If a term is not vague, it is precise. Vagueness is one source of logical paradoxes. It constitutes a major challenge to the attempt to describe natural languages by means of formal semantics.

1. Kinds of Vagueness

Vagueness must be distinguished from ambiguity, unspecificity, and context-dependence. Competent speakers associate an ambiguous term with at least two separate meanings, each of which may be precise; a vague term may be associated with just one meaning, a vague one. The vagueness of *tall* is not ambiguity; the ambiguity of *bank* is not vagueness. An unspecific term covers a wide range of cases, but is not vague unless its boundary is blurred. Although *acute* [angle] is unspecific, it is not vague. A context-dependent term draws different boundaries in different contexts; this too is not a matter of blurriness. That 'less than 97 miles away' applies to Glasgow if said in Edinburgh and not if said in London does not make the phrase vague; equally, 'not far away' may be vague even as said by a particular speaker in a particular place with a particular purpose in mind.

A term is extensionally vague if it has borderline cases. It is intensionally vague if it could have such cases. Borderlines are of different kinds. Consider the word *lake*: a certain body of water may be neither definitely a lake nor definitely not a lake; a given lake may neither definitely contain nor definitely not contain a certain drop of water. Borderline cases give a term first-order vagueness. If some cases are neither definitely borderline cases nor definitely not borderline cases, the term has second-order vagueness. Higher orders of vagueness are defined similarly.

Almost any word in natural language is at least slightly vague in some respect. Used as a technical term, 'vague' is not pejorative. Indeed, vagueness is a desirable feature of natural languages. Vague words often suffice for the purpose in hand, and too much precision can lead to time-wasting and inflexibility. Although specific words need to be made less vague for specific purposes, there is no question of making one's whole language perfectly precise. Any linguistic stipulations intended to introduce such precision would themselves have to be couched in one's pre-existing vague language.

Attempts have been made to measure vagueness experimentally, by gathering statistics about variation between speakers in their application of terms and variation over time or indecision at a time in given speakers. However, such effects would be expected even for precise terms, owing to ignorance, error, or confusion. In the absence of a filter for these extraneous effects, the statistics do not cast much light on vagueness.

2. Paradoxes of Vagueness

Vagueness provokes paradoxes. The best-known is attributed to Eubulides, a contemporary of Aristotle. The removal of one grain from a heap apparently still leaves a heap; thus if grains are removed one by one from a heap of 10,000 grains, at each stage there should still be a heap; yet eventually no heap is left. Similar paradoxes can be constructed for most vague terms. They are known as 'sorites' (from Greek *sōros* 'heap').

A sorites paradox may be conceived as an argument with an apparently true major premise (e.g., *For every positive number n, if n grains made a heap then n−1 grains made a heap*), an apparently true minor premise (e.g., *Ten thousand grains made a heap*) and an apparently false conclusion (e.g., *One grain made a heap*). Yet the argument apparently consists of a series of valid steps of elementary logic (from the major premise and *n grains made a heap* to *n−1 grains made a heap*), and should therefore preserve truth from premises to conclusion. A major test of a theory of vagueness is its ability to diagnose sorites paradoxes. Which appearance is misleading and why? Is one of the premises false, or the conclusion true, or the argument invalid?

The obvious solution is to deny the major premise. However, this commits one by standard logic to asserting that for some n, n grains made a heap and n−1 did not. Given the vagueness of 'heap,' how can one grain make such a difference?

3. Theories of Vagueness

It is often assumed that vague statements are neither true nor false in borderline cases. If so, they are counterexamples to the principle of bivalence, according to which every statement is either true or false. Since the best-developed attempts to give formal semantics for natural languages assume bivalence, they are challenged by the phenomenon of vagueness.

Commitment to bivalence has led some philosophers, notably Frege, to deny coherent meaning to vague terms. Thus systematic semantic descriptions can be given only of ideally precise, and therefore artificial, languages. However, most theories of vagueness have been advanced in attempts to accommodate vagueness within systematic semantic descriptions of natural languages. Most modify bivalence. Many replace the dichotomy between truth and falsity by a continuum of degrees of truth.

Degrees of truth are often associated with many-valued or fuzzy logics. Such logics treat the degree of truth of a complex statement as determined by the degrees of truth of its components; this generalizes the bivalent notion of truth-functionality. 'A and B' is usually assigned the lower of the degrees of truth of 'A' and 'B,' 'A or B' the higher. The associated diagnosis of sorites paradoxes is that their major premises are less than perfectly true; the degree of truth of *n grains made a heap* gradually decreases as n decreases. However, generalized truth-functionality has implausible consequences. If Tweedledum and Tweedledee are exactly the same height, it seems completely false to say that *Tweedledum is tall and Tweedledee is not tall;* but if it is half true that Tweedledum is tall, generalized truth-functionality makes it half true to say that *Tweedledum is tall and Tweedledee is not tall.* Another problem is higher-order vagueness; the assignment of degrees of truth to vague statements seems to be as arbitrary as the assignment of bivalent truth-values.

Rejection of bivalence does not require acceptance of generalized truth-functionality. An alternative is the theory of supervaluations. On this view, a vague language permits a range of bivalent interpretations, called 'sharpenings.' A statement is true if all sharpenings make it true, false if all sharpenings make it false, and neither true nor false otherwise (this assignment is the supervaluation; degrees of truth may also be accommodated, if a statement's degree of truth is measured by the proportion of sharpenings that make it true). The failure of truth-functionality is a consequence of this view. As for sorites paradoxes, their major premises are false, for every sharpening has a cut-off point somewhere. Thus *For some n, n grains made a heap and n − 1 did not* is true. However, for no n is *n grains made a heap and n − 1 did not* true, for different sharpenings have cut-off points in different places. This result is sometimes found puzzling. Another problem is that supervaluations do not satisfy a plausible constraint derived from Tarski's work on truth, that 'n grains made a heap' should be true if and only if n grains made a heap. This might be an acceptable price for a precise concept of truth, but the occurrence of higher-order vagueness means that supervaluationist truth is not precise.

A quite different approach is the epistemic theory of vagueness. On this view, vague terms have cut-off points whose location is unknown. Bivalence is preserved, and vagueness is a kind of ignorance. For some n, n grains made a heap and n − 1 did not, but speakers cannot tell which number n is. The semantic boundaries of 'heap' are not settled by nature or explicit convention; to trace them one would need exact knowledge of both the use of 'heap' and the general principles by which use determines semantic boundaries. Even if one had such knowledge of use, one would still lack it of the general principles, according to the epistemic theorist. Controversial issues about speakers' semantic knowledge are raised by the claim that they understand vague terms without being able to trace the semantic boundaries which those terms have.

See also: Deviant Logics; Formal Semantics.

Bibliography

Barnes J 1982 Medicine, experience and logic. In: Barnes J, Brunschwig J, Burnyeat M F, Schofield M (eds.) *Science and Speculation.* Cambridge University Press, Cambridge

Dummett M A E 1975 Wang's paradox. *Synthese* **30**: 301–24

Fine K 1975 Vagueness, truth and logic. *Synthese* **30**: 265–300

Horgan T (ed.) 1995 Vagueness. Southern Journal of Philosophy 33: Suppl.

Keefe R, Smith P (eds.) 1997 *Vagueness: A Reader.* MIT Press, Cambridge, MA

Lakoff G 1973 Hedges: A study in meaning criteria and the logic of fuzzy concepts. *Journal of Philosophical Logic* **2**: 458–508

Sorensen R A 1988 *Blindspots.* Clarendon Press, Oxford

Sperber D, Wilson D 1985/6 Loose talk. *Proceedings of the Aristotelian Society* **86**: 153–71

Williamson T 1994 *Vagueness.* Routledge, London

Williamson T (ed.) 1998 Vagueness. *Monist* **81**(2)

SECTION V

Reference

Anaphora

P. Sells and T. Wasow

The term 'anaphora,' as it has come to be used in modern grammatical theory, encompasses the phenomena of pronominal reference and various kinds of ellipsis. What these have in common is that an element or construction is dependent for its interpretation on being associated with something else in the context. Developing an understanding of these phenomena has become an area of intense activity among linguists, although many major questions remain unsolved.

A few examples of different types of anaphora are given in (1). The underlined portions of these examples are anaphoric elements; the italicized expressions are referred to as their 'antecedents.'

(a) *The children* love <u>their</u> parents. (1)
(b) *The children* love <u>themselves</u>.
(c) *The children* love <u>each other</u>.
(d) The young *children* love the older <u>ones</u>.
(e) This dress has three *large holes* and that shirt has two ___.
(f) Children will *break the law* if adults <u>do it</u>.
(g) Children will *break the law* if adults do ___.
(h) Some people who *break the law* <u>do so</u> repeatedly.

There are a variety of issues relating to anaphora that have been extensively investigated. They can be divided roughly into three categories: syntactic, semantic, and pragmatic. The central syntactic problem in anaphora is determining what will serve as an antecedent for each type of anaphoric element. Subsumed under this general problem are such questions as whether antecedents must be grammatical constituents and, if so, of what type; what relative positions in a sentence anaphoric elements and their antecedents may be in; and whether a given choice of antecedent is optional or obligatory. The central semantic issue is how the interpretation of an anaphoric element is related to the interpretation of its antecedent. Investigations of this issue have raised many difficult theoretical questions regarding the nature of meaning and semantic representation. The central pragmatic question is what factors determine which antecedent is chosen for a given anaphoric element, when more than one is syntactically and semantically permissible. There has been substantial work on this subject (especially in the computational linguistics literature), but it will not be reviewed here (see Grosz, et al. 1989, and references cited there).

1. Syntax

1.1 Pronominal Anaphora

By far the most widely studied anaphoric elements are third person pronouns (both reflexive and nonreflexive) with noun phrase (NP) antecedents. (Traditional grammar holds that the antecedent of a pronoun is a noun; however, it is clear that the antecedent is really a noun phrase.) The most basic observations about these elements that any analysis must capture include the following: (a) a reflexive pronoun must have an antecedent nearby; (b) the antecedent of a nonreflexive pronoun cannot be too nearby; and (c) the antecedent of a pronoun cannot be in a position that is subordinate to it. These generalizations are illustrated in (2), using the notation of 'coindexing' (i.e., assigning identical subscripts) to indicate anaphoric relations. (Thus examples (2c) and (2e) are ungrammatical (only) under the interpretation indicated.)

(a) The children$_i$ entertained themselves$_i$. (2)
(b) *The children$_i$ remember that we entertained themselves$_i$.
(c) *The children$_i$ entertained them$_i$.
(d) The children$_i$ remember that we entertained them$_i$.
(e) *They$_i$ remember that we entertained the children$_i$.

The most influential account of these observations, known as the 'Binding Theory' (henceforth BT), was put forward by Chomsky (1981), building on much earlier work. BT consists of three principles, corresponding to the three observations made above.

Before presenting them, however, it is necessary to offer some definitions.

(a) Node A *c-commands* node B if every   (3)
branching node dominating A dominates B.
(b) A node is *bound* if it is coindexed with a c-commanding
node.
(c) A node is *free* if it is not bound.

These definitions are formulated in terms of standard phrase structure trees. It is assumed that readers are familiar with this type of representation and with terms like 'node' and 'dominate.' The intuitive notion behind the formal notion of c-command is something like being higher in the tree or being superordinate. To test whether A c-commands B, trace up the tree from A until a branching node is encountered and then seek a path down the tree to B. Other definitions of c-command have been proposed in the literature, replacing the criterion of 'branching' with a different one.

The principles of BT can now be presented although a few key technical terms will be left undefined for the moment:

(a) Principle A: An anaphor must be bound by   (4)
an antecedent in its governing category.
(b) Principle B: A pronominal must be free in
its governing category.
(c) Principle C: An R-expression must be free.

The term anaphor here is used to cover reflexive pronouns and reciprocal expressions (e.g., *each other;* replacing *themselves* by *each other* in (2) does not alter the pattern of grammaticality). The term 'pronominal' covers nonreflexive pronouns. 'R-expressions' are noun phrases that are not pronouns (i.e., names and descriptions). The phrase 'in its governing category' in the principles corresponds to the word 'nearby' in the informal statement of the observations above. Extensive discussion has gone into giving the phrase a precise definition, and a number of candidates have been proposed, each of which has many other implications for the theory of grammar. For present purposes, we will simplify considerably and say that the governing category of an element is usually the minimal NP or S properly containing it. (There are cases in which this simplification is inadequate, including those with anaphors in the subject position of nonfinite clauses, which sometimes has no governing category, and positions internal to certain NPs, where the governing category is not the minimal dominating NP. Some such cases will be discussed below.)

Returning to the simple cases, Principle A of BT says that reflexives and reciprocals must c-commanding antecedents in the same clause (as in (2a)) or minimal NP (as in *Mary$_i$'s picture of herself$_i$*). Principle B says that nonreflexive pronouns cannot have c-commanding antecedents in the same clause (2c) or minimal NP (*Mary$_i$'s picture of her$_i$*). Principle C entails that neither kind of pronoun may c-command its antecedent (2e). It also says that even those R-expressions

that may take antecedents can never be c-commanded by their antecedents; this is illustrated by (5).

(a) When John$_i$ arrived, the idiot$_i$ sat in the   (5)
wrong chair.
(b) *John$_i$ regretted that the idiot$_i$ sat in the
wrong chair.

The brevity and relative simplicity of BT is deceptive: it represents the culmination of many years of research into these topics, and it embodies a number of important insights that emerged during those years. Hence, a few comments are in order.

First, BT does not actually say which elements may be the antecedents of which others. Rather, it gives the conditions under which pronouns may or must be bound. While the data on which BT is based are intuitions of antecedence, those intuitions do not necessarily coincide with binding relations. In particular, the reference of a pronoun may be understood to be the same as that of another NP that does not c-command it, as in (6); but it is built into the definition of binding that only c-commanding NPs may bind a pronoun.

(a) John$_i$'s mother loves him$_i$.   (6)
(b) The fact that we teased the children$_i$ upset
them$_i$.

Notice, however, that nothing in BT prohibits co-indexing in these cases. Indeed. BT says nothing about which NPs pronominals may be coindexed with; neither (6) nor (7) is explicitly covered by the principles.

John$_i$ thinks everyone loves him$_i$.   (7)

BT only says that there are certain NPs which pronominals must not be coindexed with. This is because, quite generally, nonreflexive pronouns need not have antecedents in the same sentence. For that matter, they need not have linguistic antecedents at all—that is, they can refer to salient entities that are not mentioned in the discourse. Hence BT, unlike most earlier work, does not pair nonreflexive pronouns with antecedents. But it permits coindexing in just those environments where speakers find coreferential interpretations possible.

Second, BT has no asymmetry based on linear precedence. That is, it permits pronouns to be bound by elements that follow them. Initially, this may seem counterintuitive, for it is natural to think of anaphoric elements as deriving their interpretations from something previously mentioned. But there are cases of 'backwards anaphora' (or 'cataphora,' as it is sometimes called), such as (8).

If he$_i$ is lucky, John$_i$ will win.   (8)

While there have been a number of proposals that do include linear precedence as one factor governing anaphoric binding, BT follows Reinhart in claiming that the relevant structural factors are hierarchical.

To the extent that there appears to be a left–right asymmetry, it is because English is predominantly right branching, according to this view.

Third, Principles A and B are not limited to third person pronouns. Facts like the following are subsumed under the principles, even though first and second person pronouns are not really anaphoric, at least as anaphora are characterized here.

(a) *I$_i$ think that nobody listens to myself$_i$.　　(9)
(b) *You$_i$ amuse you$_i$.

Fourth, BT says nothing about the fact that anaphoric elements and their antecedents usually must agree in person, number, and gender. A reasonable first approximation is to say that coindexed NPs must agree in these features. There are, however, cases like (10) where pronouns do not agree with their apparent antecedents, suggesting that such agreement is actually a function of the semantics.

I bought a Veg-o-matic$_i$ after I saw them$_i$　　(10)
　　advertized on TV.

1.2 The Binding Theory and Empty Categories

Government and Binding theory (GB) posits several kinds of empty categories—that is, elements that are not pronounced, but play a role in the syntax and/or semantics of sentences. The application of BT to these elements plays a central role in accounting for a variety of syntactic facts within this theory (though not in others). In this section, a few of the most important uses of BT in connection with empty categories in GB will be summarized.

The trace left behind by NP movement (in constructions like the passive) is treated as an anaphor, and hence is subject to Principle A. This accounts for distinctions like the following (where t represents a trace):

(a) Pat$_i$ was told t$_i$ that I saw Chris.　　(11)
(b) *Chris$_i$ was told Pat that I saw t$_i$.
(c) Pat$_i$ is believed t$_i$ to be dangerous.
(d) *Pat$_i$ is believed t$_i$ is dangerous.

This pattern parallels the distribution of overt anaphors, as Principle A predicts:

(a) They$_i$ told each other$_i$ that I saw Chris.　　(12)
(b) *They$_i$ told Pat that I saw each other$_i$.
(c) John$_i$ believes himself$_i$ to be dangerous.
(d) *John$_i$ believes himself$_i$ is dangerous.

The traces of wh-movement are treated as R-expressions, and hence subject to Principle C. This accounts for a phenomenon known as 'strong crossover,' exemplified in example (13):

(a) Which linguist$_i$ did you say t$_i$ thought I had　　(13)
　　insulted him$_i$?
(b) *Which linguist$_i$ did you say he$_i$ thought I
　　had insulted t$_i$?

In such sentences, the relative positions of the pronoun and the wh-phrase provide no basis for predicting whether an anaphoric relationship is possible, but the relative positions of the pronoun and the trace permit them to be differentiated. More generally, treating wh-traces as R-expressions predicts that examples involving wh-movement will behave with respect to anaphora as if the wh-phrases had not been moved. Sentences like the following, exemplifying what is known as 'weak crossover,' provide some support for this prediction: in general, the pattern of grammaticality between a pronoun and an NP that the pronoun does not c-command is preserved if the NP is moved away, leaving a trace. The use of '%' indicates that only some speakers accept the examples. The difference in acceptability in the examples in (14) raises many issues of analysis, which will not be detailed here. For most speakers, anaphora to a kind-denoting term like *bulldogs* is easier than to the quantificational *certain breeds:* nonrestrictive relative clauses typically allow the anaphora, restrictive relative clauses are harder, and interrogatives the hardest (see Wasow 1979).

(a) Only people who own them$_i$ could love　　(14)
　　bulldogs$_i$.
(b) He breeds bulldogs$_i$ which$_i$ only people who
　　own them$_i$ could love t$_i$.
(c) %People who own them$_i$ love certain
　　breeds$_i$.
(d) %Which breeds$_i$ do people who own them$_i$
　　love t$_i$?

A third type of empty category in GB is PRO, which appears in the subject position of most infinitives. PRO is analyzed as a pronominal anaphor—that is, as an element subject to both Principle A and Principle B of BT. This entails, paradoxically, it would seem, that PRO must be both bound and free in its governing category. The contradiction is only apparent, however, because not every element has a governing category. In particular, the subject position of some nonfinite clauses has no governing category. Evidently, the distribution of PRO is crucially dependent on the definition of governing category, and hence linked to claims about the binding of pronouns. This connection and its derivation from BT are referred to as 'the PRO theorem.'

Notice that the PRO theorem depends crucially on the domain of Principles A and B being the same, for this was the basis of the apparent contradiction. But the identity of the two domains has another consequence: it implies that anaphors and pronominals will be in complementary distribution wherever there is a governing category. For overt anaphors and pronominals, this consequence turns out to be a good first approximation, but not a reliable generalization. For example:

(a) The children$_i$ love their$_{i/}$each other$_i$'s (15)
   parents.
(b) John$_i$ expected that a picture of him$_i$/himself$_i$
   would be in today's newspaper.

Such deviations from fully complementary distribution of anaphors and pronominals can be accounted for either by permitting the domains of Principles A and B to be different, or by exempting certain pronouns from the principles. Both strategies have been explored in the literature; the issue remains an active topic of research. The complexity of the problem is compounded in languages like Norwegian which have possessive forms of reflexive pronouns, as seen in (16).

Jon$_i$ beundrer sin$_{i/}$*hans$_i$ mor. (16)
John admires self's/*his mother

In this case, it seems that the obligatory use of the possessive reflexive blocks a similar interpretation for the possessive pronoun, even though in other cases, such as (17) below, an alternation like that seen in (15) is more readily available.

Jon$_i$ gjorde oss glad i huset sitt$_i$/hans$_i$. (17)
John made us fond of house self's/his

The idea that pronouns may be exempt from normal binding conditions in certain positions is supported by the existence of certain cases where anaphors are coreferential with antecedents which do not c-command them (18).

John$_i$'s most prized possession is the picture of (18)
   himself$_i$ hanging in the living room.

By definition, such an anaphor is not bound; hence, no modification of the characterization of the domains of the binding principles can cover such examples. Rather, they seem to be subject to a different set of constraints (see Sect. 1.4 for discussion of a related phenomenon).

1.3 Choice of Antecedents

In Sect. 1.2, the question of determining the domain in which antecedents are found has been treated. However, there are other constraints on the choice of antecedent even within the specified domain. For example, in many languages, but not English, only subject NPs can be antecedents for reflexive pronouns.

Norwegian is such a language. It has four anaphoric (sets of) forms, excluding the reciprocal. The pronoun *ham* is just like English *him*, and must be free in its clause, so both (19c) and (19d) are acceptable.

(a) *Ola$_i$ snakket om ham$_i$. (19)
   Ola talked about him
(b) *Vi fortalte Ola$_i$ om ham$_i$.
   We told Ola about him
(c) Ola$_i$ vet at vi snakket om ham$_i$.
   Ola knows that we talked about him
   'Ola knows that we talked about him.'

Another form is *ham selv* (lit. 'him self'), and this must be bound to a nonsubject within its clause. Unlike English, then, (20a) is ungrammatical.

(a) *Ola$_i$ snakket om ham selv$_i$. (20)
   Ola talked about himself
(b) Vi fortalte Ola$_i$ om ham selv$_i$.
   We told Ola about himself
   'We told Ola about himself.'
(c) *Ola$_i$ vet at vi snakket om ham selv$_i$.
   Ola knows that we talked about himself

The form *seg* is one that must take a subject antecedent. That antecedent must lie within the local tensed domain, but outside of the most local clause. This distinguishes examples (21c) and (21d). Hence, *seg* will only appear inside of infinitival clauses, and may in principle be arbitrarily far away from its antecedent, so long as only nonfinite clauses intervene.

(a) *Ola$_i$ snakket om seg$_i$. (21)
   Ola talked about self
(b) *Vi fortalte Ola$_i$ om seg$_i$.
   We told Ola about self
(c) *Ola$_i$ vet at vi snakket om seg$_i$
   Ola knows that we talked about self
(d) Ola$_i$ bad oss snakke om seg$_i$.
   Ola asked us to-talk about self
   'Ola asked us to talk about him.'

In (21c) *seg* is bound by a subject outside of its minimal tensed domain, and so the example is bad. In (21d) the embedded clause is nonfinite, and this allows *seg* to take the matrix subject as antecedent.

Finally, the form *seg selv* must be bound to a subject within its clause.

(a) Ola$_i$ snakket om seg selv$_i$. (22)
   Ola talked about self
   'Ola talked about himself.'
(b) *Vi fortalte Ola$_i$ om seg selv$_i$.
   We told Ola about self
(c) *Ola$_i$ vet at vi snakket om seg selv$_i$.
   Ola knows that we talked about self

Subject-orientation of anaphors (those forms which must be bound, in some domain) is very common. Interestingly, reciprocals typically do not show such subject-orientation. For example, the Russian reflexive *sebja* must be bound to a subject, while the reciprocal *drug druga* can be bound to nonsubjects.

Another not uncommon choice for antecedent is the 'logical subject,' intuitively, the agent of the action. Compare the Norwegian examples in (23) with the Marathi examples in (24).

(a) *En politimann$_i$ arresterte Jon$_j$ i sin$_{ij/*j}$ (23)
                                      kjøkkenhave.
   A policeman$_i$ arrested John$_j$ in self$_{ij/*j}$'s
                                      kitchen-garden.
(b) Jon$_j$ ble arrestert av en politimann$_i$ i sin$_{*i/j}$
                                      kjøkkenhave.
   John$_j$ was arrested by a policeman$_i$ in self$_{*i/j}$'s
                                      kitchen-garden.

(a) Jon$_i$-nii bil$_j$-laa aaplyaa$_i$ gharaat maarle.   (24)
John$_i$-ERG Bill$_j$-ACC self$_i$'s house-in hit
'John$_i$ hit Bill$_j$ in self$_{i/*j}$'s house.'

(b) Bil$_j$-laa jon$_i$-kaduun aaplyaa$_i$ gharaat maarle gele.
Bill$_j$-ACC John$_i$-by self$_i$'s house-in hit was
'Bill$_j$ was hit by John$_i$ in self$_{i/*j}$'s house.'

In Norwegian, the antecedent of the reflexive *sin* is the grammatical subject, and hence changes under passivization. (Some speakers allow both indexed NPs in (23b) to antecede *sin*.) In contrast in Marathi, the antecedent is always the one performing the action, the logical subject, and cannot be the surface subject in a passive example like (24b).

Above, it was remarked that Principles A and B of the Binding Theory are (supposed to be) complementary in English. Generally, complementarity between anaphors and pronouns does not hold. For example, English allows many cases of overlap.

John$_i$ thinks that these pictures of him$_i$/himself$_i$ are   (25)
not very flattering.

In Marathi, a different situation obtains: there are two reflexive forms, *aapaN*, which is bound to logical subjects, and *swataah*, which is bound to surface subjects. However, the pronoun, *to*, is like English *him*, free from all coarguments within its minimal clause.

As the data in this section indicate, there is significant variation across languages in the principles determining binding of anaphors. Determining the precise parameters and range of variation that is possible is a topic of considerable research in the late twentieth century.

1.4 Logophors

In some anaphoric systems, the choice of antecedent is not determined syntactically. Pronouns with this property are known as 'logophors'—the ones which are 'bearer of the word.' In the words of G. N. Clements, the antecedent of a logophoric pronoun must be the one 'whose speech, thoughts, feelings, or general state of consciousness are reported.'

In the West-African language Ewe, a special set of pronouns has logophoric uses. Here *yè* is a logophoric pronoun, and *e* is nonlogophoric.

(a) Kofi be yè-dzo.   (26)
Kofi say LOG-leave
'Kofi$_i$ said that he$_i$ left.'

(b) Kofi be e-dzo.
Kofi say PRO-leave
'Kofi$_i$ said that he$_j$ left.'

In other languages, the reflexive pronoun takes on a logophoric function. The examples in (27) are from Icelandic, and (28) are Japanese. In each case, the example is well-formed only if the antecedent of the reflexive was the source of some communication.

(a) Hann$_i$ sagði að sig$_i$ vantaði hæfileika.   (27)
He$_i$ said that self$_i$ lacked ability
'He$_i$ said that he$_i$ lacked ability.'

(b) *Honum$_i$ var sagt að sig$_i$ vantaði hæfileika.
He$_i$ was told that self$_i$ lacked ability
'He$_i$ was told that he$_i$ lacked ability.'

(a) *Yamada ga Hanako$_i$ ni zibun$_i$ no   (28)
Yamada NOM Hanako$_i$ DAT self$_i$ GEN
ie de atatakaku motenasareta
house at warmly was-treated
'Yamada was warmly entertained by Hanako$_i$ at her$_i$ house.'

(b) Yamada ga Hanako$_i$ ni zibun$_i$ no
Yamada NOM Hanako$_i$ DAT self$_i$ GEN
ie ni kuru yoo ni tanomareta.
house to come COMP was-asked
'Yamada was asked by Hanako$_i$ to come to her$_i$ house.'

Such phenomena are far from rare. Languages on every continent show some logophoric-type behavior. Even English reflexive pronouns show such sensitivity when they fall outside of the binding theory, as exemplified in (29).

John$_i$ was very angry, Those pictures of himself$_i$ (29)
in the hot tub had been taken illegally.

One senses that the second sentence here is a reflection of John's thoughts. It is possible that this logophoric binding is also at work in examples like (18).

1.5 Other Kinds of Anaphora

The discussion thus far has been limited to pronouns that take NP antecedents. As noted in the opening paragraph, however, there are other kinds of anaphora. Some involve pronouns or other overt elements that take something other than NPs as antecedents. Others involve ellipsis—that is, a construction in which something seems to be missing, but can be understood from the context. Two issues have been the focus of attention regarding the syntax of these types of anaphoric elements: what are their possible antecedents; and whether an optimal analysis involves positing some sort of deletion of an identical 'copy' of the missing material.

It is shown in (30) that backwards anaphora is not limited to pronouns, and (31) shows that an analogue to Principle C is operative in these cases, as well. (Coindexing will be used to indicate antecedence, even though BT is not applicable.)

(a) Anyone who wants to ___$_i$ can   (30)
[learn to lambada]$_i$.

(b) Anyone who wants one$_i$ can buy a gun$_i$.

(a) *Pat did ___$_i$ after Chris [learned to   (31)
lambada]$_i$.

(b) *One$_i$ can be bought by anyone who wants
to buy a gun$_i$.

Thus, the structural relations that may obtain between anaphoric elements and their antecedents appear to be the same for a variety of types of anaphora.

In contrast, the types of antecedents seem to vary.

In (30) it is shown that the appropriate elements can take VP (*learn to lambada)* or N′ (*gun)* antecedents; (32) is an example with S serving as an antecedent; and (33) shows that, in some cases, nonconstituents (in this case, *make...wash the floors)* may serve as antecedents.

> I know that [Pat was here]$_i$, but I don't know when ___$_i$. (32)

> They may make Pat wash the floors, but they wouldn't do it to Chris. (33)

Hankamer and Sag (1976) distinguished two classes of anaphoric elements. Anaphoric elements of the first class, exemplified by ordinary third-person pronouns, can derive their interpretations from anything that is semantically appropriate and contextually salient. The others, exemplified by VP ellipsis, require a linguistic antecedent of a certain syntactic type. They called these 'deep' and 'surface' anaphora, respectively. The following examples provide a minimal contrast between the two types:

> [Pat tries to jump over a fence and trips] (34)

> (a) Chris: I'll bet I could do it.
> (b) *Chris: I'll bet I could ___.

Likewise, surface anaphora requires a greater degree of syntactic parallelism between anaphoric element and antecedent than is required for deep anaphora:

> (a) Pat's phone was tapped by the FBI, though they claim they didn't do it. (35)
> (b) ?*Pat's phone was tapped by the FBI, though they claim they didn't ___.

Hankamer and Sag argue that surface anaphora is the result of deletion under identity, but that deep anaphoric elements are base generated. There are a number of other arguments supporting a deletion analysis of surface anaphora. For example, the case marking in (36) depends on structure that can be missing on the surface.

> (a) Someone helped Pat, but I don't know who/*whom (helped Pat). (36)
> (b) Pat helped someone, but I don't know who/whom (Pat helped).

This argument is even clearer in a language like German, where idiosyncratic case (such as the dative marking on the object of *helfen)* must be preserved.

> Pat hat jemand   geholfen, aber ich weiß (37a)
> Pat has someone helped,   but I   know
>   nicht wem/*wen
>   not   who-DAT/*who-ACC
> (Pat geholfen hat).
> (Pat helped   has)

> Pat hat jemand   gesehen, aber ich weiß (37b)
> Pat has someone seen,   but I   know
>   nicht wen/*wem
>   not   who-ACC/*who-DAT
> (Pat gesehen hat).
> (Pat seen   has)

However, examples like (38) pose a problem for deletion analyses, because the would-be deletion site is inside its antecedent, so that trying to reconstruct the predeletion structure leads to an infinite regress. This problem is not insurmountable, provided that the notion of 'deletion under identity' is formalized with appropriate care, but there is considerable controversy regarding how best to handle such phenomena. (The problem presented by such 'antecedent contained deletions' is reminiscent of a celebrated argument known as 'the Bach–Peters Paradox.' Examples like (i), it was claimed, show that pronouns cannot be transformationally derived from full copies of their antecedents, without positing infinite underlying structures. (i) [The pilot who shot at it$_i$]$_j$ hit [the MIG that chased him$_j$]$_i$.)

> Pat [reads everything Chris does ___$_j$]$_i$. (38)

Though the literature on these other types of anaphora is rich, there is no treatment of them that enjoys the same sort of currency as the Binding Theory for pronouns with pronominal antecedents.

2. Semantics

The nature of 'identity' which anaphora is supposed to represent has also been the subject of much research. For example, the VP-ellipsis examples in (39) show that strict (syntactic) identity is not at the basis of such constructions.

> A: Do you think they'll [like me]$_i$? (39)
> B: I'm sure they will ___$_j$.
> = 'like you'
> ≠ 'like me'

As indicated, what is reconstructed is not the form *like me,* but rather some semantic unit 'like x,' where x is anchored to the speaker for the first sentence (and hence would be referred to as *you* by B).

2.1 Coreference

The usual idea about pronominal anaphora is that the pronoun refers to the same individual as the antecedent—thus, the two corefer. An example like (40a) then, would be interpreted as in (40b).

> (a) John$_i$ read his$_i$ mail. (40)
> (b) John$_i$ read John$_i$'s mail.

However, coreference is just one semantic relation between a pronoun and its antecedent.

2.2 Bound Variables

If the interpretation of anaphora just involved coreference, then an example like (41) would mean that Max read John's mail, for the reconstructed VP would be 'read John's mail.'

John*i* read his*i* mail and Max did too.　　(41)

However, this sentence clearly has another interpretation, under which Max read his own mail. This is even clearer in (42). (Note that the concern here is only with the set of possible interpretations; the issue is not about preferences for a particular interpretation on a particular occasion of utterance.)

John*i* read his*i* mail before Max did.　　(42)

Here, the content of the VP that is being reconstructed and predicated of Max seems not to be what is paraphrased in (43a), but (43b).

(a) An x such that x read John's mail.　　(43)
(b) An x such that x read x's mail.

The second 'x' corresponds to the pronoun, and indicates that the pronoun is being interpreted like a variable (say, a variable in first-order logic); its *reference* varies with whatever value is assigned to x. Hence, this is known as the 'bound variable' interpretation of a pronoun.

Following the interpretation of a variable in logic, it can be shown that reference is not relevant at all for the bound variable interpretation of a pronoun. In (44), the existence of any relevant individuals is denied, but the pronoun still may take the NP *no manager* as its antecedent, and receives a bound variable interpretation—whichever manager one chooses, it is not the case that he read his mail on Friday.

No manager*i* read his*i* mail on Friday.　　(44)

Additionally, a pronoun may only be bound as a variable by a quantifier which has scope over it. Consequently, while anaphora is possible in (45a), it is blocked in (45b).

(a) Each guest*i* brought a present which she*i* had　　(45)
picked out at Macy's.
(b) Each guest*i* brought a present. *She*i* had
picked it out at Macy's.

Even though the coreferential and bound variable uses of pronouns are distinct, they both obey the Binding Theory: in (46) below, the quantified NP *every ballerina* may (logically) take scope over the rest of the sentence, but nevertheless the anaphora indicated is not possible. This is because the syntactic configuration violates Principle C of BT.

*She*i* danced on every ballerina*i*'s toes.　　(46)

These observations indicate that the coindexing that BT refers to may not have a uniform semantic interpretation: sometimes it may represent coreference, and sometimes the binding of a variable (see Evans 1980, Reinhart 1983).

2.3 E-type Pronouns

Examples like the following have been claimed to show that other interpretations of anaphora are possible.

Farmer Jones owns some sheep*i*. The village vet　　(47)
examines them*i* every spring.

The reasoning is as follows: the antecedent *some sheep* does not really refer to a particular group of sheep, but rather just asserts the existence of some such group. Hence it would be odd to think of the pronoun *them* as coreferring. Yet, if the pronoun were interpreted in the other way, as a variable, then (47) should have an exact paraphrase in (48) (a relative pronoun always gets the variable interpretation).

Farmer Jones owns some sheep*i* which*i* the village　　(48)
vet examines every spring.

However, the two do not seem to mean the same thing; (47) seems to say that the vet examines all of Jones's sheep, while (48) seems to say that the vet only examines some of them. Hence, the pronoun is not receiving the variable interpretation, either. This new interpretation is known as the 'E-type reading' (after G. Evans).

In other examples, the pronoun is clearly neither coreferential with its antecedent, nor a bound variable.

The man who gave his paycheck*i* to his wife is wiser　　(49)
than the one who gave it*i* to his mistress.

Here, the pronoun seems to be functioning simply as a shorthand for a repetition of its antecedent (*his paycheck*).

3. Conclusion

The period since the mid-1960s has seen significant progress in the understanding of the range and complexity of anaphoric types, the most prominent of which have been surveyed here. However, many important aspects of analysis still remain to be discovered, for example for the 'paycheck' sentence just mentioned, or the *weak crossover* structures in (14). The bibliography cites works which have been influential in setting out problems and/or suggesting approaches for their solution.

Bibliography

Chomsky N 1981 *Lectures on Government and Binding*. Foris, Dordrecht
Evans G 1980 Pronouns. *LIn* **11**: 337–62
Faltz L M 1985 *Reflexivization. A Study in Universal Syntax*. Garland Publishing, New York

Grosz B J, Pollack M E, Sidner C L 1989 Discourse. In: Posner M I (ed.) *Foundations of Cognitive Science*. MIT Press, Cambridge, MA

Hankamer J, Sag I 1976 Deep and surface anaphora. *LIn* 7: 391–428

Heim I A 1988 *The Semantics of Definite and Indefinite Noun Phrases*. Garland Publishing, New York

Karttunen L 1976 Discourse referents. In: McCawley J D (ed.) *Syntax and Semantics 7: Notes from the Linguistic Underground*. Academic Press, New York

Lasnik H 1989 *Essays on Anaphora*. Kluwer, Dordrecht

Reinhart T 1983 *Anaphora and Semantic Interpretation*. Croom Helm, London

Sells P 1987 Aspects of logophoricity. *LIn* 18: 445–79

Wasow T 1979 *Anaphora in Generative Grammar*. E. Story-Scientia, Ghent

Definite Expressions

F. Zwarts

The term 'definite expression' is used to describe a class of words and phrases whose semantical behavior resembles that of multiplicative expressions. Typical examples are proper names and noun phrases of the forms *the n N* (where *n* is a numeral), *the N*, singular or plural, as the case may be, *this N, that N, these N, those N*, and *both (N)*. Although there is no watertight test for membership in this class, definite expressions characteristically do not occur in existential statements of the form *There is/are NP (X)*, as shown by the ill-formed sentences **There are the three students sick* and **There are both children*, which contrast sharply with *There are three students sick* and *There are two children*. In addition, only definite expressions can appear as part of a partitive noun phrase. Thus, the occurrence of *the sheriffs* in the expression *some of the sheriffs* is completely acceptable, whereas the indefinite noun phrase *many sheriffs* immediately causes ungrammaticality (cf. **some of many sheriffs*).

Besides being multiplicative, definite expressions also behave in a semantically uniform way when combined with a negated verb phrase. The resulting sentence of the form NP (NEG VP) invariably entails one of the form NEG (NP VP). For this reason, definite noun phrases are said to validate the conditional schema NP (NEG VP) → NEG (NP VP). As a consequence, the sentence *Both feet are not ulcerated* logically implies *It is not the case that both feet are ulcerated*. Noun phrases which exhibit this type of behavior are said to be consistent in that they exclude that two sentences of the form NP VP and NP (NEG VP) are both accepted as true or both as false. In practice, what this amounts to is that with a definite noun phrase as subject the use of predicate negation invariably implies sentence negation. The class of definite expressions so defined appears to have a negative counterpart and is therefore more accurately referred to as the class of *positive* definite expressions. To be sure, *negative* definite expressions are also consistent in nature, but they form a subset of the class of antiadditive expressions. Typical examples are *neither (N)*, *none of the n N* (where *n* is a numeral), and *none of her N* (where *N* is plural), none of which can occur in an existential statement of the form *There is/are NP (X)*. It should be noted that, according to the definitions given above, homomorphic and antimorphic expressions are definite as well; the former being positive definite, the latter, negative definite. Consequently, reflexive pronouns, transitive verbs, and intransitive verbs must all be regarded as belonging to the class of positive definite expressions. The negative adverb *not* and the negative auxiliary *didn't*, on the other hand, are properly treated as members of the class of negative definite expressions.

Bibliography

Barwise J, Cooper R 1981 Generalized quantifiers and natural language. *Linguistics and Philosophy* 4: 159–219

Deixis

S. Levinson

The term 'deixis,' from the Greek word for pointing, refers to a particular way in which the interpretation of certain linguistic expressions ('deictics' or 'indexicals') is dependent on the context in which they are produced or interpreted. For example, *I* refers to the person currently speaking, *you* to the intended recipients or addressees, *now* to the time of speaking, *here* to the place of speaking, *this finger* to the currently indicated finger, and so on. These deictic expressions introduce a fundamental relativity of interpretation: uttering *I am here now* will express quite different propositions on each occasion of use. This relativity makes clear the importance of the distinction between sentence-meaning and utterance-meaning or interpretation: in large part because of deixis, one cannot talk about sentences expressing propositions—only the use of an affirmative sentence in a context expresses a determinate proposition. For this reason, some philosophers (e.g., Montague 1974) equate the semantics vs. pragmatics distinction with, respectively, the description of (artificial) languages without indexicals vs. (natural) languages with them, but the distinction then serves no linguistic purpose as all natural languages would then be 'pragmatic' (see Levinson 1983: ch. 2).

The contextual dependency introduced by deixis is quite pervasive; for example, it inheres in tense, and nearly every English sentence is tensed, so that *The capital of the USSR was Moscow* makes a claim only of a time prior to the time of speaking. Yet such relativity of interpretation seems to inhere only in certain expressions, not for example in proper names like *The Parthenon* or descriptive phrases like *the tallest building in the world*. Most semantic theories have been primarily fashioned to handle the latter kind of expression, and it is controversial whether such theories can simply be extended (as opposed to fundamentally recast) to handle deixis adequately.

The phenomenon of deixis has been of considerable interest to philosophers, linguists, and psychologists. It raises a great number of puzzles about the proper way to think about the semantics of natural languages, and about the relation of semantics and pragmatics. It also reminds us that natural languages have evolved for primary use in face-to-face interaction, and are designed in important ways to exploit that circumstance. As people take turns talking, the referents of *I, you, here, there, this, that*, etc. systematically switch too; children find this quite hard to learn (Wales 1986), but the penalties of such a system far outweigh the advantages of, e.g., substituting unique proper names (if indeed such a system could even in principle operate in a full language, see Lyons 1977: 639ff).

1. Philosophical Puzzles

Philosophers often call deictic expressions 'indexicals,' and the corresponding contextual dependency of interpretation 'indexicality.' C. S. Peirce, who introduced these terms, considered indexicals to form a special class of signs characterized by an existential relation between sign and referent; however, his notion was broader than that commonly found today in analytic philosophy or linguistics (but see, e.g., Hanks 1990).

The phenomenon raises a number of fundamental philosophical puzzles about the nature of meaning in natural language (see Yourgrau 1990). On the face of it, a central 'design feature' of language is its context-independence: the truth of *The atomic weight of gold is 196.967.* does not depend on who says it where and when (otherwise science could hardly progress). It is the constancy of lexical meanings, together with invariant rules of sentential composition, that are normally taken to be the principles that allow us to generate unlimited sentences and yet still understand the associated meanings. Hence in formal semantics, it is normally held that the 'intensions' (or senses) of expressions determine the corresponding 'extensions' (or referents) in every 'possible world' (any set of circumstances). The phenomenon of deixis shows that this is, at best, an oversimplification: the extension of deictic expressions depends not only on the described circumstances (if any), but also on who says them, to whom, where, and when.

One influential modern treatment (due to Montague 1968) is to let the intension of an expression only determine the extensions relative to a set of contextual indices (e.g., speaker, addressee, time, and place of utterance). Another rather more interesting approach (due to Kaplan 1989) is to distinguish between two aspects of meaning: one aspect, the 'character,' concerns how the context determines the content or intensions, the other, the 'content,' concerns how intensions determine extensions in different circumstances (or possible worlds). On this account, nondeictic expressions have invariant, vacuous character and invariant intensions, picking out variable extensions in varying circumstances (or different possible worlds). But deictic expressions have potentially variable character, and vacuous or variable content, picking out different extensions in different contexts. (Kaplan 1989 himself holds that indexicals are directly referential and have no intension, but contribute to the intensions of the containing expressions; but others have found fruitful the idea that the character of indexicals determines variable intensions.)

Kaplan's scheme raises the query: to what extent are deictic expressions really exceptional, and to what extent is *character* quite generally determinative of meaning throughout natural language lexicons? The suspicion that much of the vocabulary may really be quasi-indexical is raised, first, by noticing that there are many kinds of deictics easily overlooked, like *ago* or *local*. Second, many expressions have a wide latitude of interpretation like *near* which specifies very different kinds of proximity in the phrases *near the kidneys* vs. *near the North Pole*, given an understanding of the likely contexts of use. Just as *today* is a word containing a deictic parameter (it might be glossed as that diurnal span including the time of speaking), so perhaps *near* contains a parameter fixed contextually. Third, even expressions that look least

215

like indexicals in fact require contextual information for interpretation: thus definite descriptions presuppose a circumscribed domain in which they pick out unique referents (*the white dog* will not do in a situation with more than one), and quantifiers presuppose a domain of discourse (*All the boys ran away* quantifies over a contextually given set of boys). These suspicions have given rise to various fundamental reorganizations of formal semantics, notably Situation Semantics (Barwise and Perry 1983) designed to capture what is taken to be the partially deictic character of most linguistic expressions.

Another philosophical puzzle is posed by deictic expressions. There is a quite widely entertained idea that there is, as it were, a 'language of thought' (to use the phrase popularized by Fodor), structurally close to, or even identical with, the semantical system in which propositional content is represented. How can the content of indexical expressions be represented (e.g., for memory and recall) in such a language, which must itself be nonindexical? It is tempting to think that all one would need is the content, the extensions determined by the context and circumstances. But if I am lost, I can say or think *I'll never find my way out of here* without knowing where *here* refers to, and replacing *here* with, e.g., *Sherwood forest* may not be recognizable as my thought. It would seem that indexical or deictic expressions cannot easily be reduced by translation into a nonindexical language.

There are further puzzles. For example, 'demonstratives' like *this* and *that* which sometimes only succeed in referring by virtue of an accompanying gesture, seem a fundamental, primitive kind of referring expression, and are sometimes held (e.g., by Lyons 1975) to be the ontogenetic origin of referring in general. But as Wittgenstein, Quine, and others have pointed out, pointing itself depends on prior understandings: otherwise, how does the recipient know when I point at a flying bird whether I am referring to a particular part, the colour, or the event? The success of pointing would seem to rely on complex assumptions about mutual salience and identification, and on examination ostension is anything but self-explanatory.

2. Frameworks for the Linguistic Description of Deixis

Linguists normally think of deixis as organized around a 'deictic center,' constituted by the speaker and his or her location in space and time at the time of speaking. This is an oversimplification because the identity and location of the addressee are also normally presumed, forming a two-centered system. A further normal assumption is that where linguistic expressions exhibit both deictic and nondeictic uses, the deictic ones are basic, and the nondeictic ones derived (or transposed, as Bühler put it). Thus *here* and *now* normally refer to the place and time of speak-

ing, but in *What should he do here now, Harry wondered?*, the deictic center has been shifted or transposed from the writer to the protagonist, *Harry*.

Further distinctions between kinds of usage of deictic expressions are necessary (Fillmore 1975). A fundamental distinction is between gestural and nongestural usages: *this finger* requires a demonstration indicating which finger is being referred to, *this afternoon* requires no such gestural demonstration. Many expressions that would normally be used nongesturally, like *you* or *we*, may be used gesturally to pick out a subset of possible referents (*you, not you*, or *we but not you*). Other expressions, like *here*, are used equally either way (*We like it here in Holland* vs. *Place the chairs here and here*). Yet other expressions that would not normally be deictic in character (e.g., *the man wearing the hat* or *him* in *Look at him!*) can be converted into deictics, as it were, by gestural specification. Many languages have deictic elements that (in their deictic uses) may only be used gesturally, e.g., presentatives like French *voici*, or the English demonstrative pronoun *that* as in *Who is that?* Where gestural specification is required, it raises very interesting problems for semantic theory (Kaplan 1989). When deictic expressions are used nondeictically, one needs to distinguish anaphoric usages (*We saw Macbeth. We enjoyed that.*) from nonanaphoric ones (*Over the weekend, I just did this and that.*).

It then becomes an empirical matter to try to establish the kinds of contextual parameter that are encoded in deictic linguistic expressions in the languages of the world. A number of surveys are available (see Anderson and Keenan 1985; Fillmore 1975; Levinson 1983: ch. 3; Weissenborn and Klein 1982), and the following sections, organized around the primary deictic parameters, summarize some of this work.

2.1 Person Deixis

The traditional grammatical category of person, as reflected, e.g., in pronouns and verb agreements, involves the most basic deictic notions. First person, for example, encodes the participation of the speaker, and temporal and spatial deixis are organized primarily around the location of the speaker at the time of speaking. The traditional paradigm of first, second, and third persons is captured by the two semantic features of speaker inclusion (S) and addressee inclusion (A): first person ($+S$), second person ($+A$), and third person ($-S$, $-A$), which is therefore a residual, nondeictic category. As far as is known all languages have first and second person pronouns (though sometimes, as in Japanese, these may derive from third person titles), but not all have third person pronouns. The traditional notion of 'plural' (likewise 'dual' and so on) as applied to the person system nearly always needs reanalysis (e.g., *We* does not mean more than one speaker); in some pronominal systems 'plural' can be neatly analyzed as augmenting a minimal deictic specification with 'plus one or more additional individuals' (AUG). Thus the distinction between *I* and *We* might be analyzed as (+S, −AUG), (+S, +AUG). Many languages distinguish 'inclusive we' from 'exclusive we,' i.e., (+S, +A) from (+S, −A, +AUG).

More sustained analysis will show that it is necessary to distinguish between various finer-grained kinds of participation in the speech event: e.g., to 'decompose' the role of speaker into source of the message vs. transmitter, and addressee into recipient vs. overhearer, and so on, simply in order to describe grammatical distinctions in various languages (see Levinson 1988).

Many other features are often encoded in person systems, whether in pronominal paradigms or predicate agreements, including gender (e.g., masculine, feminine, neuter, or further classes) and honorific distinctions (which are intrinsically deictic on a separate deictic parameter, see below). In languages with predicate agreement, most sentences will obligatorily carry person deictic specification, ensuring the prominence of this deictic parameter.

2.2 Time Deixis

As mentioned, the deictic center is normally taken to be the speaker's location at the time of the utterance. Hence *now* means some span of time including the moment of utterance, *tomorrow* means that diurnal span succeeding the diurnal (or nocturnal) span including the time of utterance, and one reckons *ten years ago* by counting backwards from the year including the speaking time. In written or recorded uses of language, one may need to distinguish 'coding time' from 'receiving time,' and in particular languages there are often conventions about whether one writes *I am writing this today so you will receive it tomorrow* or something more like *I have written this yesterday so that you receive it today*.

Most languages exhibit a complex interaction between systems of time measurement, e.g., calendrical units, and deictic anchorage through, e.g., demonstratives. In English, units of time measurement may either be fixed by reference to the calendar, or not: thus *I'll do it this week* is ambiguous between guaranteeing achievement within seven days from utterance time, or within the calendar unit beginning on Sunday (or Monday) including utterance time. *This year* means the calendar year including the time of utterance (or in some circumstances the 365 day unit beginning at the time of utterance), but *this November* means the next monthly unit so named (usually, the November of this year), while *this morning* refers to the first half of the diurnal unit including coding time, even if that is in the afternoon (see Fillmore 1975).

But the most pervasive aspect of temporal deixis is 'tense.' The grammatical categories called tenses usually encode a mixture of deictic time distinctions and aspectual distinctions, often hard to distinguish. Analysts tend to set up a series of pure temporal distinctions that roughly correspond to the temporal aspects of natural language tenses, and then note discrepancies. For example, one might gloss the English present tense as specifying that the state or event holds or is occurring during a temporal span including utterance-time; the past as specifying that the relevant span held before utterance-time; the future as specifying that the relevant span succeeds utterance-time; the pluperfect as specifying that the past tense relation held at a point in time preceding utterance-time; and so on. Obviously, such a system fails to capture much English usage (*The summit meeting is tomorrow; I have hereby warned you; John will be eating right now*, etc.), but equally it is clear that there is a deictic temporal element in most of the grammatical distinctions linguists call tenses.

Although tense is an obligatory deictic category for nearly all sentences in English and many other languages, firmly anchoring interpretation to context, it is as well to remember that there are many languages (like Chinese or Malay) that have no tenses.

2.3. Space Deixis

Deictic adverbs like *here* and *there* are perhaps the most direct examples of spatial deixis. As a first approximation, *here* denotes a region including the speaker, *there* a distal region more remote from the speaker. This suggests a distinction between proximal and distal regions concentric around the speaker, and indeed as a first approximation the demonstrative pronouns *this* and *that* contrast in the same way. Many languages seem to make a similar three-way distinction (*here, there, yonder*) or even, allegedly in the case of Malagasy adverbs, a seven-way distinction. But caution is in order, as the distal categories are often in fact organized around the addressee or other participants, as in Latin *hic* 'close to speaker,' *iste* 'close to addressee,' *ille* 'remote from both speaker and addressee' (see Anderson and Keenan 1985). Further, careful analysis of actual examples of use shows a much more complex pattern, where, e.g., proximal and distal deictics may be used to refer to things at an equal physical but different social distance (Hanks 1990).

Demonstratives often occur in large paradigms, with distinctions of relative distance from speaker or proximity to addressee crosscut by other deictic distinctions, for example visibility to participants. It is tempting, but incorrect, to assimilate the visibility dimension to spatial deixis: many languages (e.g., North West Coast Native American ones) show a systematic sensitivity to mode of apprehension of referents, and some require obligatory marking of noun phrases for this dimension. Further spatial distinctions found in demonstrative systems (in, for example, some Austronesian and Australian languages) include 'upriver/downriver from speaker,' 'above/below speaker,' 'north/south/east/west from speaker,' and so on. Such dimensions import absolute, fixed angles into spatial deixis, contrasting greatly with more familiar systems of relative spatial organization. Finally, it should be noted that there are close diachronic and semantic links between demonstratives and definite articles; some analysts (e.g., Lyons 1977) suggest that English *the*, for example, is simply a demonstrative determiner contrasting with *this* and *that* by being unmarked on the proximal/distal dimension, thereby suggesting a fundamental link between the concept of definiteness and deixis.

Spatial deixis is also frequently encoded in verbal roots or affixes, with a typical basic distinction between 'motion towards speaker' (cf. English *come* in some uses) and 'motion away from speaker' (cf. English *go*). Some languages, like the Mayan ones, have a set of a dozen or so motion verbs, encoding distinctions like 'arrive here' vs. 'arrive there.' Sometimes, the basic distinction is between 'motion towards speaker' vs. 'motion towards addressee' (rather than 'motion away from speaker'), or 'motion towards vs. away from speaker's home base.' English *come* in fact exhibits a complex set of such conditions, as shown by examples like *I'm coming to you* vs. *Come home with me*. Parallel notions are often encoded in adverbial or question particles like (archaic) English *hither*, *thither*, *whence?*, *whither?*

Just as the interpretation of *this year* rests on a complex interaction between calendrical units and deictic anchorage, so the interpretation of *on this side of the table* relies on a complex interaction between deixis and nondeictic spatial descriptions, wherein sides, fronts, backs, insides, etc. are assigned to objects. As frequently noted, *The cat is in front of the truck* is ambiguous between the cat being at the intrinsic front of the truck (as determined by direction of canonical motion), and the cat being between the truck and the speaker. *The cat is in front of the tree* can only have the latter kind of interpretation, because trees are not assigned intrinsic facets in English (as reportedly they are in some cultures). This kind of interpretation is curious because there is no overt deictic element: the tree is assigned a front as if it were an interlocutor facing the speaker. In Hausa, a sentence glossing 'The cat is in front of the tree' would be interpreted to mean the cat is behind the tree, as if the tree was an interlocutor facing away from the speaker. Similarly, English *The cat is to the left of the tree* is taken to have implicit deictic specification (left in the speaker's visual field). These examples point to the fundamentally deictic nature of spatial organization in many languages (but not all: some languages, for example, some Australian ones, have no relative spatial notions like 'left of'/'right of,' employing absolute, cardinal point-like, notions instead).

2.4 Discourse Deixis

In a spoken or written discourse, there is frequently occasion to refer to earlier or forthcoming segments of the discourse (as in *in the previous/next paragraph*, or *Have you heard this joke?*). Since a discourse unfolds in time, it is natural to use temporal deictic terms (like *next*) to indicate the relation of the referred-to segment to the temporal location of the present utterance in the discourse. But spatial terms are also often employed, as in *in this chapter*.

Reference to parts of a discourse which can only be interpreted by knowing where the current coding or receiving point is, are clearly deictic in character. Less clear is the status of anaphora in general, wherein extratextual entities are referred to, but often through a device (as in the legal use of *the afore-mentioned party*) which likewise relies on knowing where one is in a discourse. Analysts tend to make a practical distinction between anaphora (taken to be nondeictic) and textual deixis, while noting that the phenomena grade into one another, and in any case that anaphora is ultimately perhaps deictic in nature (Lyons 1977). Anaphora is fundamental to much syntactic structure, and once again deixis can be shown to be connected to the heart of linguistic organization.

2.5 Social Deixis

Honorifics are frequently encountered in the languages of the world, drawing on recurrent metaphors of plurality, height, distance, and so on (see Brown and Levinson 1987 for references). They are often thought of as an aspect of person deixis, but although organized around the deictic center like space and time deixis, honorifics involve a separate dimension of social deixis. Honorifics encode the speaker's social relationship to another party, frequently but not always the addressee, on a dimension of rank. There are two main kinds: referent honorifics, where the honored party is referred to, and non-referent addressee honorifics, where respect is signaled without referring to the addressee. The familiar pronouns of respect, like French *vous* to a singular addressee, are referent honorifics (which happen to refer to the addressee). But in Korean, Japanese, Javanese, and many other languages it is also possible to describe any situation (e.g., the meal is ready) and signal a particular degree of respect to the addressee by a choice between alternate lexical and grammatical items. In such languages, it is difficult to say almost anything without encoding the relative status of speaker to addressee, and no treatment of the lexicon is complete without such specifications. The so-called 'speech levels' of the southeast Asian languages are usually customary collocations of both referent and addressee honorifics, forming locally recognized degrees of politeness (see, for example, Errington 1988 on Javanese).

There are other aspects of social deixis, for example,

similar linguistic devices may be used to encode specific kinship relations, as in some Australian languages, rather than disparities in social rank. Perhaps all languages have distinguishable formality levels or genres that serve in a Peircean sense to index the social gravity of the context of utterance; but some languages have discrete, grammaticalized levels of this kind, for example the diglossic levels of Tamil encoded especially in distinct morphology.

There are many sociological aspects of other deictic dimensions, e.g., whether to describe some space as 'here' vs. 'there' may depend on whether one thinks of it as near 'us' or near 'them,' this being sociologically defined (for an exemplary study, see Hanks 1990).

3. Conclusions

Some languages require all (or nearly all) sentences to be tensed; others require all noun phrases to be marked with spatially deictic information; and others require a specification of honorific level. As a result, most sentences in most natural languages are deictically anchored, that is, they contain linguistic expressions with inbuilt contextual parameters whose interpretation is relative to the context of utterance.

Bibliography

Almog J, Perry J, Wettstein H (eds.) 1989 *Themes from Kaplan*. Oxford University Press, Oxford
Anderson S R, Keenan E 1985 Deixis. In: Shopen T (ed.) *Language Typology and Syntactic Description. Vol. 3: Grammatical Categories and the Lexicon*. Cambridge University Press, Cambridge
Barwise J, Perry J 1983 *Situations and Attitudes*. MIT Press, Cambridge, MA
Brown P, Levinson S 1987 *Politeness*. Cambridge University Press, Cambridge
Bühler K 1982 The deictic field of language and deictic words. In: Jarvella R J, Klein W (eds.)
Errington J 1988 *Structure and Style in Javanese*. University of Pennsylvania Press, Philadelphia, PA
Fillmore C 1975 *Santa Cruz Lectures on Deixis*. Indiana University Linguistics Club, Bloomington, IN
Hanks W 1990 *Referential Practice: Language and Lived Space in a Maya Community*. University of Chicago Press, Chicago, IL
Jarvella R J, Klein W (eds.) 1982 *Speech, Place and Action: Studies of Deixis and Related Topics*. Wiley, New York
Kaplan D 1989 Demonstratives. In: Almog J, Perry J, Wettstein H (eds.)
Levinson S 1983 *Pragmatics*. Cambridge University Press, Cambridge
Levinson S 1988 Putting linguistics on a proper footing. In: Drew P, Wootton A (eds.) *Erving Goffman*. Polity Press, Cambridge
Lyons J 1975 Deixis as the source of reference. In: Keenan E (ed.) *Formal Semantics of Natural Language*. Cambridge University Press, Cambridge
Lyons J 1977 *Semantics*, 2 vols. Cambridge University Press, Cambridge
Montague R 1974 Pragmatics. In: Thomason R H (ed.) *Formal Philosophy*. Yale University Press, New Haven, CT
Peirce C S 1955 *Philosophical Writings of Peirce: Selected Writings*. Dover, New York
Wales R 1986 Deixis. In: Fletcher P, Garman M (eds.) *Language Acquisition*, 2nd edn. Cambridge University Press, Cambridge
Weissenborn J, Klein W 1982 *Here and There: Cross-linguistic Studies on Deixis and Demonstration*. Benjamins, Amsterdam
Wittgenstein L 1958 *Philosophical Investigations*. Blackwell, Oxford
Yourgrau P (ed.) 1990 *Demonstratives*. Oxford University Press, Oxford

Denotation

J. van Eijck

The denotation of a phrase of some (formal or natural) language in a model is the thing or set of things in the model that the phrase is taken to refer to. If the model under consideration is (some suitable part of) the real world, denotations of phrases are the things in the real world that the phrases are about. The denotation of a phrase in a model is also called its 'interpretation' in the model.

The nature of the denotation of a phrase depends on its syntactic category. In the simplest possible setup, denotations for various kinds of phrases take the following shapes. Denotations of proper names are individuals; the denotation of *Mary* is the thing in the model that the name refers to. Denotations of verb phrases (*is a doctor*) and nouns (*doctor*) are sets of individuals: the individuals in the model satisfying the verb phrase or the noun. Denotations of noun phrases consisting of a determiner and a noun (*every doctor*) are sets of sets of individuals: *every doctor* denotes the set of predicate extensions satisfied by every doctor in the model. Denotations of transitive verbs (*love*) are sets of pairs of individuals: *love* denotes the pairs in the model of which the first element loves the second. Finally, denotations of sentences (*It rained, John is a doctor, Mary loved John*) are truth and falsity: sen-

tences are things that are true in a model if the model supports them, false if the model does not support them.

See also: Formal Semantics; Names and Descriptions.

Donkey Sentences
P. A. M. Seuren

The problem of 'donkey sentences' occupies a prominent place in the logical analysis of natural language sentences. The purpose of logical analysis in the study of language is to assign to sentences a structure suitable for logical calculus (i.e., the formally defined preservation of truth through a series of sentences). Such structure assignments usually take the form of a 'translation' of sentence structures into propositions in some accepted variety of predicate calculus or quantification theory.

Modern predicate calculus or quantification theory, insofar as it remains purely extensional, is such that a term in a proposition that has a truth-value in some world W must either be an expression referring to an individual (or set of individuals) that really exists when W really exists, or else be a bound variable. Modern predicate calculus leaves no other choice. (A propositional language is 'extensional' just in case it allows in all cases for substitution of co-extensional constituents *salva veritate*.) Russell (1905) proposed his theory of descriptions precisely in order to get rid of the logical problems arising as a result of natural language expressions that have the appearance of referring expressions but fail to refer (as in his famous example 'The present king of France is bald'). It now appears that the very same problem still rears its head: there are natural language sentences whose logical analysis is considered to result in purely extensional propositions but which can be true or false in W even though they contain one or more terms that neither refer to an existing individual nor allow for an analysis as bound variable. Natural language thus seems to resist analysis in terms of modern predicate calculus or quantification theory.

It was the British philosopher Peter Thomas Geach who first adumbrated this problem, without, however, getting it into sharp focus. He deals with it for the first time in his book *Reference and Generality* (1962), in the context of the question of how to translate pronouns into a properly regimented logical language. In dealing with this problem he typically uses as examples

sentences containing mention of a donkey. Hence the name donkey sentences. If, he says (1962: 116–18), the subject expressions in sentences like (1) and (2):

Any man who owns a donkey beats it. (1)

Some man who owns a donkey does not beat it. (2)

are taken to be structural constituents in logical analysis, the pronoun *it* 'is deprived of an antecedent.' A solution, he says (p. 118), might be found in rewording these sentences as, respectively (3) and (4):

Any man, if he owns a donkey, beats it. (3)

Some man owns a donkey and he does not beat it. (4)

where *it* allows for a translation as a bound variable. But now there is a translation problem, since 'now the ostensible complex term has upon analysis quite disappeared.' (Apparently, Geach sets greater store by the structural properties of natural language sentences than Russell did.) The problem crops up again on pp. 128–30, again in the context of logical translation. Here he gives the sentences (5)–(7):

If any man owns a donkey, he beats it. (5)

If Smith owns a donkey, he beats it. (6)

Either Smith does not own a donkey or he beats it. (7)

Again, a solution would seem to require a thorough restructuring of the problematic sentences, creating the artificial predicate 'either-does-not-own-or-beats any donkey,' whose subject can then be *any man* or *Smith*. All this, however, is still more or less beating about the bush.

The real problem comes to a head in the example sentences (6) and (7) just given. Both these sentences should translate as strictly extensional propositions (they contain no nonextensional elements). In the standard logical analysis of the truth-functions *if* and *or* they come out as true if Smith owns no donkey. Now, *it* cannot be translated as a referring expression *(the donkey)* as it lacks a referent. It should therefore be translatable as a bound variable. But then, too, there are severe and probably insurmountable problems.

One obvious thought (Geach 1962: 17) is to apply an extended analysis to (6) and (7), which would then be rephrased as (8) and (9), respectively:

If Smith owns a donkey, he owns a donkey (8)
and beats it.

Either Smith does not own a donkey or (9)
he owns a donkey and beats it.

In *Logic Matters* (1972: 115–27) Geach argues that a sentence of the form *Smith owns a donkey and he beats it* should not be translated as a conjunction of two propositions, i.e., as the form $A \wedge B$, but rather as, using restricted quantification, $(\exists x)$ donkey $[\text{Own}(\text{Smith}, x) \wedge \text{Beat}(\text{Smith}, x)]$, i.e., as a quantified construction, with *it* translated as a bound variable. This, however, cannot be a solution, as this analysis makes (8) and (9) true if Smith owns two donkeys and beats only one of them, whereas (6) and (7), in their normal interpretation, must be considered false in such a case (Geach 1962: 117–8). Examples (8) and (9) are thus not equivalent with (6) and (7). Moreover, as was pointed out in Seuren (1977), the analysis itself as proposed in Geach (1972) lacks generality in view of such cases as (10):

It's a good thing that Smith owns a donkey, (10)
but it's a bad thing that he beats it.

where treatment of *it* as a bound variable leads to insurmountable scope problems. This particular approach should therefore be considered unsuccessful.

Another obvious thought is to translate *a donkey* in (6) and (7) as a universally quantified constituent, leading to, respectively (11) and (12):

$$\forall x[\text{Donkey}(x) \wedge \text{Own}(\text{Smith}, x) \rightarrow \text{Beat}(\text{Smith}, x)]. \quad (11)$$

$$\forall x[\text{Donkey}(x) \rightarrow [\neg\text{Own}(\text{Smith}, x) \vee \text{Beat}(\text{Smith}, x)]]. \quad (12)$$

This, however, is ad hoc and thus inevitably leads to a lack of generality in the translation procedure, as appears from cases like (13) and (14), which, again, lead to insurmountable scope problems under this analysis:

If it's a good thing that Smith owns a donkey, (13)
it's a bad thing that he beats it.

Either Smith no longer owns a donkey or he still (14)
beats it.

It thus seems that, even if radical restructuring is allowed in logical translations, there is a hard core of extensional sentences, such as (6) and (7), that resist semantically equivalent translation into any accepted variety of modern predicate calculus. These sentences contain definite expressions, preferably pronouns, which are neither referring expressions nor bound variables.

It must be noted, in this connection, that the grammatical behavior of these pronouns is that of anaphoric pronouns: referring expressions anaphorically linked up with an antecedent, and not that of bound variable pronouns (or of reflexive pronouns, which are not at issue here). These two categories differ, among other things, in that the former allow for substitution by a lexical noun phrase, whereas the latter do not. Thus, *it* in (15), (16), and (17) can be replaced by, for example, *the animal*, without any change in meaning, but *it* in (18) does not allow for such substitution (15)–(18):

Smith owns a donkey and he beats it/the animal. (15)

If Smith owns a donkey he beats it/the animal. (16)

Either Smith does not own a donkey or he (17)
beats it/the animal.

Every donkey owned by Smith fears that Smith (18)
will beat it/*the animal.

The difference is that *it* in (18) functions as a bound variable, whereas in (15)–(17) it does not.

The problematic pronouns thus behave like referring expressions even though they cannot be, and their analysis as bound variables meets with systematic failure. Kamp (1981) recognized the fundamental nature of this problem and proposed a radical departure from standard notions and techniques of semantic interpretation. He defends an analysis whereby the donkey pronouns and other definite expressions in extensional sentences do not 'refer' directly to real entities in the world at hand, but instead 'denote' mental representations of possibly real world entities. In this theory, known as discourse representation theory, the mechanism of reference is mediated by a cognitive system of mental representations, whose relation to any actual world is a matter of independent concern. The insertion of this halfway station of mental representations creates some extra room for a semantic account of donkey sentences. Even so, however, it must be recognized that standard logical analyses are inadequate for natural language. What logic will do better justice to the facts of language is therefore still an open question. Groenendijk and Stokhof (1991) is an attempt at answering it.

See also: Anaphora; Formal Semantics; Reference: Philosophical Issues.

Bibliography

Geach P T 1962 *Reference and Generality: An Examination of Some Medieval and Modern Theories.* Cornell University Press, Ithaca, NY
Geach P T 1972 *Logic Matters.* Blackwell, Oxford
Groenendijk J, Stokhof M 1991 Dynamic predicate logic. *LaPh* **14**: 39–100

Kamp H 1981 A theory of truth and semantic representation. In: Groenendijk J, Janssen T, Stokhof M (eds.) *Formal Methods in the Study of Language,* vol. 1. Mathematisch Centrum, Amsterdam

Russell B 1905 On denoting. *Mind* **14**: 479–93
Seuren P A M 1977 Forme logique et forme sémantique: Un argument contre M. Geach. *Logique et Analyse* **20**: 338–47

Indexicals

M. Leezenberg

Indexicals, expressions the interpretation of which depends on the occasion on which they are uttered (e.g., *I, here, today, this*...), are one of the major and most pervasive means to enhance the efficiency of natural language. However, they have posed particular challenges to all semantic theories of the twentieth century. If, for example, indexicals do not function either as referring or as describing terms, how do they fit into a general theory of meaning? Do they have a fixed, unchanging meaning apart from their ever-changing reference, and if so, what is it? At one time their status was even considered so problematic that attempts were made to eliminate them altogether; but these have not been successful. In this article only the philosophical, semantic aspects will be treated. (For an overview of more descriptively oriented approaches, see e.g., chapter 2 of Levinson 1983.) Terminology tends to be confusing: instead of 'indexicals' (this term, coined by Peirce, will be used generically here), one may encounter terms like 'deictic expressions' (preferred by the more pragmatics-oriented authors), 'egocentric particulars' (Russell), 'token-reflexive expressions' (Reichenbach), 'demonstratives' (Perry), etc., all of which deal with roughly the same phenomenon.

1. Frege

The first important treatment of indexicals in modern philosophy of language was given by Gottlob Frege, who distinguished the 'reference' of linguistic expressions from their 'sense,' i.e., their descriptive content (what he calls a 'manner of presentation'). Sense determines reference, Frege holds, but not vice versa. This explains how identity statements involving names can be informative: in $a = b$, 'a' and 'b' have the same referent which is presented in two different manners, unlike in $a = a$. Sentences, whose referent is a truth value, have for their sense a 'thought,' which for Frege is not a private representation but an unchanging, Platonic entity, so that different people can grasp the same thought. The sense of a sentence is determined by the sense of its parts, so if one term

lacks sense, then the whole sentence will have no sense either.

Now how can sentences containing indexical expressions like *today,* whose referent changes with the occasion of utterance, express unchanging thoughts? In his essay 'Der Gedanke' (1918; translated as 'Thoughts' 1984), Frege tackles this problem by stating, first, that a sentence containing an indexical does not yet express a 'complete thought' by itself, but requires a specification of the time of utterance to determine its truth value (in other words, an incomplete thought is not a thought at all, as it cannot yet be said to be either true or false); therefore, the time of speaking is also part of the expression of the thought. Second, Frege claims that an indexical sentence, once it is supplemented with an indication of utterance time and other necessary contextual elements, and thus expresses a complete thought, has an unchanging truth value. If a (complete) thought is true, it is always true. In other words, sentences may contain indexical terms, but thoughts never do so.

In 'Frege on Demonstratives' (1977; repr. in Yourgrau 1990), John Perry has argued against this Fregean treatment of indexicals. The unchanging meaning of 'today' in (1):

> Russia and Canada quarrelled today (1)

is what he calls a 'role,' a function that takes us from the context of utterance to a day, but this is not a Fregean sense and therefore cannot complete the thought. Senses do not carry us from context to the referent (as we would want for indexicals), but directly to the referent, regardless of the context. In this case, the referent, i.e., the day of utterance, cannot complete the sense of (1) either, for an infinite number of senses corresponds to each referent; for Frege, there is no road back from reference to sense.

So, Perry claims, one cannot, using Frege's apparatus, get from an incomplete thought, as expressed by *Russia and Canada quarrelled,* an indexical like *today,* and a context of utterance, to a complete thought. Frege may have noticed this difficulty: in fact, he nowhere discusses what could be the sense of an indexical. As an alternative, Perry suggests treating senses as roles, and thoughts as information expressed; so that (1) expresses different thoughts on different occasions, although its role remains constant. We can thus no longer equate thoughts with senses as Frege wanted to.

2. Russell and Reichenbach: Can Indexicals be Eliminated?

In the wake of logical empiricism, several philosophers have attempted to reduce the importance of indexical expressions in natural language, or even to eliminate them altogether by translating indexical sentences into supposedly equivalent nonindexical or 'eternal' ones. In *An Inquiry into Meaning and Truth* (1940) Bertrand Russell sets out to reduce all indexicals or, as he calls them, 'egocentric particulars' (defined as terms whose denotation is relative to the speaker) to nonindexical terms plus the one indexical *this*; so *I* means 'the biography to whom this belongs,' *now* means 'the time of this,' etc. But this leaves the problem of their status: what is the constant meaning that they have? Unlike names (with which they appear to share a lack of descriptive content), they refer to different objects on different occasions without being ambiguous; unlike descriptions, they always apply to one thing at a time only, and not to everything that is ever a 'this'; and unlike general concepts, any instances they may have are an instance only at that particular moment. To get rid of this embarrassment, Russell tries to eliminate this single remaining indexical element by defining it in terms of so-called 'minimal causal chains' between a nonverbal stimulus and a verbal response. But if an expression like *this* is really to apply to something we directly experience, it cannot refer to an object in the outer world, but only to our own percepts. In other words, its designation is a sense datum (1940: 114). However, as sense data are private phenomena, this analysis makes communication between two individuals, or even within one individual at different points in time, impossible.

In his *Elements of Symbolic Logic* (1947), Hans Reichenbach treats indexicals in a manner similar to Russell's; but with him, they do not refer to sense data but to the act of speaking itself. He calls them 'token-reflexive,' because they refer to the particular token of their type used on the occasion of utterance. Therefore, he holds, they can also be *defined* in terms of the phrase 'this token,' so e.g., *I* means the same as 'the person who utters this token,' *now* the same as 'the time at which this token is uttered,' etc.

Reichenbach states that the symbol 'this token' is not really a phrase but an operator; it is not a term with a fixed meaning, as its different tokens will not be equisignificant to one another. He therefore calls it a 'pseudo-phrase,' an operator the meaning of which can only be formulated in the metalanguage; in other words, all token-reflexive words are pseudo-words that can be eliminated. Thus, like Russell, Reichenbach first reduces all indexicals to one kind, which he then attempts to eliminate from the object language. We will see whether this treatment is feasible in the discussion of Kaplan below (Sect. 3.2).

Reichenbach's application of these ideas to one particular class of indexicals, viz. the tenses of verbs, in which he postulated the need for distinguishing several different contextual factors, has exerted a considerable influence on many linguistic theories of tense, and on Hans Kamp's theory of double indexing discussed below (Sect. 3.1).

3. Model-theoretic Semantics

For a variety of reasons, in natural language semantics verb tenses have received the most attention of all kinds of indexicality, especially through A.N. Prior's work in tense logic. Prior rejected Reichenbach's treatment, which he thought would lead to an undesirable proliferation of reference points for the more complex tenses; in his own approach, these could be easily treated by the repeated application of a small number of tense-logical operators. Richard Montague applied these ideas to natural language semantics.

3.1 Montagovian Pragmatics; Index Theory

Richard Montague defined pragmatics as the study of indexicals, and proposed it should study the notion of truth, not only in a model or under an interpretation as in semantics, but also with respect to a context of use. Sentences of a pragmatic language should be interpreted with respect to an *index* or point of reference, instead of merely at a world-time pair. An index $i = \langle s, w, t \rangle$ is a complex of all relevant aspects of the context: the speaker s, the world w, the time t, etc. An index is *proper* if s exists at t in w. Logical validity can now be defined as truth on every proper index in every structure. This gives a unified account of meaning for indexicals and nonindexicals alike by extending the semantic notion of world-time to that of context of use.

The standard treatment involved a single index for the time of utterance; however, Kamp (1971) showed that a *double* indexing was required. A proper account of sentences that combine temporal indexicals with tense-logical operators must distinguish the *context of utterance* (i.e., the time of speaking) from the *circumstance of evaluation* (the time determined by the tense operators). In sentences without both indexicals and tense operators, context and circumstance coincide, but in (2) they do not:

One day you will be grateful for what I do now. (2)

In purely tense-logical terms, (2) would be true at time t_0 if *you are grateful for what I do now* is true at some later time t_1, i.e., if the hearer is grateful at t_1 for what the speaker does at t^1. But obviously, *now* should refer not to t_1 (the circumstance of evaluation) but to t_0, the context of utterance. In other words, the indexical takes wide scope over the operator. The realization of this point was an essential ingredient of Kaplan's Logic of Demonstratives formulated soon after.

The standard model-theoretic treatment of indexicals was not without its critics; for example, Cresswell (1973) argued against the parametrization of contextual features. He holds that an indefinite number of contextual aspects can be relevant, and that we cannot tell in advance precisely which one will be needed: should we postulate a 'previous drink parameter' for sentences like 'Just fetch your Jim another quart'? Instead of postulating a fixed list of contextual parameters beforehand, we should speak in terms of the properties a context may have or not have; for example, a context may have the property that John is a speaker there. This, he claims, allows for a more flexible and natural treatment of context-dependence.

3.2 Kaplan's Theory of Direct Reference

David Kaplan's theory (most fully stated in the seminal 'Demonstratives: an essay on the semantics, logic, metaphysics, and epistemology of demonstratives and other indexicals' 1977, published in Almog, et al. 1989) is widely accepted as the standard treatment; it also stands at the basis of several important new treatments of related problems.

3.2.1 Basic Notions

The single most important aspect of Kaplan's theory, which also distinguishes him from all his predecessors, is that he calls all indexicals *directly referential*. By this he means that the linguistic rules for indexicals directly provide us with a referent for each context of utterance (e.g., the time of speaking), without the mediation of a Fregean sense: they do not yield an intension that still needs to be evaluated at a circumstance (i.e., a possible world–time pair) in order to yield an extension.

The term 'direct reference' is likely to cause confusion. First, it does not mean that indexicals do not have a conventional meaning or a descriptive content. The conventional meaning of *I* gives us the speaker for every context; but as Kaplan stresses, its extension is not something to be settled by the circumstances of evaluation: rather, given a context of use, a directly referential term will have its content determined by that context, whatever the circumstances may be. Secondly, it does not mean that the referent (a physical object) is part of the abstract proposition, but only that the object referred to determines what the proposition expressed is, rather than the other way round; put differently (and against Frege), there is a road back from reference to sense. Thirdly, it does not imply that we must know the referent of an indexical for it to refer directly. In his work 'The logic of demonstratives' (1979), however,

Kaplan formally treats indexicals as expressions with a constant intension, which implies that there is an individual concept (albeit a stable one) involved instead of an individual; but he really intends them to be simply independent of circumstances (cf. Almog, et al. 1989: 497, 507).

Kaplan distinguishes two aspects of meaning for indexicals: *character* and *content*. Content corresponds to Montague's intension: it is a function from circumstances to extensions. A content is *fixed* or *stable* if it is a constant function: for example, proper names have a stable content. Character (which resembles Perry's notion of 'role') is the function that determines the content in different contexts of utterance; it captures what we informally call the 'meaning' of indexicals (in fact, in Kaplan's logic, sameness of character is the closest approximation of true synonymy, i.e., sameness of meaning). Nonindexical terms have a stable character, but their content may vary; indexicals have a nonstable character, but a stable content: given a context of use, they refer to the same individual in every circumstance.

Reichenbach and Russell, he claims, did not acknowledge the directly referential character of indexicals, and therefore mistakenly think that the rule identifying *I* and 'the person uttering this token' captures the *meaning* of the indexical, whereas in fact the description merely fixes the *referent* of the directly referential term. Descriptions depend on circumstances for their interpretation and are therefore not directly referential. Against Russell, Kaplan also argues that we cannot completely eliminate indexicals, because we will never have enough names available to refer to every possible object under the right character.

Kaplan also distinguishes *pure indexicals*, i.e., expressions such as *I* or *now*, the referent of which is entirely determined by linguistic rules, from demonstratives proper, expressions that require an act of—usually nonlinguistic—demonstration, like pointing, in order to determine their referent or demonstratum. One object can be demonstrated in different manners, so a demonstration may, in Fregean terms, be seen as a manner of presenting a demonstratum.

Kaplan criticizes Montague's treatment, which conflates context and circumstance into a single index, and thus blurs the distinction between context-dependent and context-free expressions. This approach, he holds, cannot adequately deal with

$$\text{I am here now.} \tag{3}$$

This is true, but not necessarily true: in other circumstances, I could have been elsewhere. However, in a sense, (3) cannot be uttered falsely. We cannot adequately account for this unless we strictly separate context and circumstance, and add the rule that indexicals refer directly. (Here, Kaplan does not do full justice to Montague (cf. Bennett 1978: 3): the latter would not accept *if p is logically valid, then so is*

Necessarily p, because logical truth applies only to all *proper* points of reference, and he also allows for structures with improper points of reference).

In an early paper, 'Dthat' (1970, repr. in Yourgrau 1990), Kaplan recognized a *demonstrative use* of definite descriptions following Donnellan's distinction between referential and attributive use, and introduced a special demonstrative *dthat* to capture this use. This operator turns a description (or an arbitrary singular term) into a directly referring expression. The singular term then functions as the demonstration of the demonstrative *dthat*, so that its demonstratum is the denotation of that singular term in that context. This makes $a = dthat$ [a] logically true for any singular term *a*, but not *Necessarily* ($a = dthat$ [a]), for given a context, descriptive terms may under different circumstances refer to different objects, while the referent of *dthat [a]* remains fixed. We can think of *dthat* as an intensional operator, one that rigidifies any singular term, or alternatively as an incomplete demonstrative, whose associated demonstration is not itself part of the content. Kaplan allows for intensional operators, which operate on content, but not for terms that operate on character (such terms, which could easily be introduced into his logic, he calls 'monsters'); for otherwise, a sentence like (4)

In some contexts it is true that I am not tired now (4)

would be true in a context c_0 if some speaker is not tired in some context c_1. But then *I* in (4) has nothing to do with me, the speaker in c_0, which violates its directly referential character. According to Kaplan, the only way to control the character of a term is to use quotation marks.

3.2.2 *Applications: Problems and Prospects*

Kaplan's theory has interesting epistemological consequences. First, we can now distinguish *logical truth* (or truth in all contexts of utterance, which is a matter of character) from *necessary truth*, which is truth in all circumstances and thus a matter of content. 'I am here now' is analytically true as I could not have uttered it falsely, but not necessarily true: at this moment, I might just as well have been somewhere else.

Further, Kaplan identifies content with the object of thought (what Frege called the thought expressed), and character with cognitive significance. Therefore, identity claims such as $dthat[a] = dthat$ [a] and $dthat$ $[a] = dthat[b]$ may express the same thought, whereas their cognitive significance differs. People may believe the former without therefore being committed to accept the latter as well. Character may be seen as a manner of presenting a content, but unlike a Fregean sense, the same manner of presentation associated with *I* will usually present different contents to different persons, namely themselves. This implies that cognitive states are *context-sensitive*: we may hold

different propositional attitudes to the same content if it is presented under different characters. Again, however, this distinction cannot formally be made in Kaplan's logic (see also the papers by Salmon and Soames in Almog, et al. 1989; see Recanati (1993) for an application of the theory of direct reference to the problem of *de re* thoughts; for Fregean criticism of Perry and Kaplan, see Gareth Evans in Yourgrau 1990).

Another area where Kaplan's ideas can be fruitfully applied is that of figurative language (see Leezenberg (1995) for an extensive treatment along Kaplanian lines). Josef Stern has claimed that metaphors are context-dependent in a way similar to indexicals. He postulates a 'metaphorical operator' *Mthat* analogous to Kaplan's *dthat*, which converts any literal expression p into a 'metaphorical expression' *Mthat* [p] of nonstable character, sensitive to a 'metaphorically relevant feature of the context' (Stern 1985: 695). Thus, Stern treats metaphor as the *destabilization of character*. However, for him, neither *Mthat* nor *dthat* is an intensional operator: they do not work on content, but on character and are thus, in Kaplan's vocabulary, 'monsters.'

The same applies to analyses of context-dependent expressions other than those referring to individuals (be those individuals persons or places). Kaplan does not treat demonstratives involving properties or plural referents, like *these books*, *this big*, and *thus*; but other expressions are even more problematic. Bartsch (1987) calls attention to the context-dependence of property expressions like *good*. She calls these *thematically weakly determined*: they require a knowledge of the 'thematic dimension' of the context, i.e., the kind of property an utterance is about: in saying *John is good*, do we speak of his moral qualities, his tennis skill or something else? This analysis also allows for monsters: for one can supply a thematic dimension for *John is good* by adding a predicate-limiting adverbial like *with respect to tennis playing* or *morally*. Such adverbials, however, may shift the contextually given dimension, and thus are monstrous operators in Kaplan's sense. So apparently, we should distinguish between those context-dependent expressions that are directly referential and those that are not. Kaplan's analysis still holds for indexicals like *I*, *here*, and *this*, but it does not apply to the latter ones, so perhaps we had better not call them 'indexicals' after all.

See also: Montague Grammar; Names and Descriptions; Reference: Philosophical Issues.

Bibliography

Almog J, Perry J, Wettstein H (eds.) 1989 *Themes from Kaplan*. Oxford University Press, Oxford
Bartsch R 1987 Context-dependent interpretations of lexical items. In: Groenendijk J, De Jongh D, Stokhof M (eds.)

Foundations of Pragmatics and Lexical Semantics. Foris Publications, Dordrecht

Bennett M 1978 Demonstratives and indexicals in Montague grammar. *Synthese* **39**: 1–80

Cresswell M 1973 *Logics and Languages*. Methuen, London

Frege G 1918 Der Gedanke (transl. as 'Thoughts'). In: McGuinness B (ed.) 1984 *Gottlob Frege: Collected Papers*. Blackwell, Oxford

Kamp H 1971 Formal properties of 'now.' *Theoria* **31**: 227–73

Levinson S C 1983 *Pragmatics*. Cambridge University Press, Cambridge

Leezenberg M M 1995 *Contexts of Metaphor: Semantic and Conceptual Aspects of Figurative Language Interpretation*. ILLC, Amsterdam

Recanati F 1993 *Direct Reference: From Language to Thought*. Blackwell, Oxford

Stern J 1985 Metaphor as demonstrative. *Journal of Philosophy* **82**: 681–710

Names and Descriptions

P. V. Lamarque

The relation between a name and what it names has long been viewed as fundamental in semantics, though exactly what that relation is has been a matter of considerable controversy. Within philosophy of language there is a longstanding debate, highlighted in the work of Frege, Russell, and Wittgenstein from the early years of analytic philosophy, as to how words or symbols attach to objects. One focus for this debate has been the question whether a name secures its reference through a direct, albeit conventional, association with its object or in virtue of an implied conceptual content or sense. This article explores the main lines of this debate and should be read in conjunction with the articles on *Reference: Philosophical Issues* and *Indexicals*.

1. Denotation and Connotation

The starting point for modern discussions of names is usually taken to be John Stuart Mill's account in *A System Of Logic* (published 1867). According to Mill, '[p]roper names are not connotative: they denote the individuals who are called by them; but they do not indicate or imply any attributes as belonging to those individuals' (Mill 1970: 20). The contrast here is with connotative terms which do 'imply an attribute'; they convey information and they have meaning. A proper name, on Mill's view, is an 'unmeaning mark.' Mill believed there to be a fundamental difference between proper names such as *Dartmouth, Socrates, John*, and general terms like *white, long*, and *virtuous*. Although he thought the latter do have denotation—they denote all white things, all long things, and so forth—they also imply or connote attributes: whiteness, length, virtue. He acknowledges that in various ways proper names can be associated with attributes; but such associations are never essential to the functioning of

the name itself. For example, speakers often have a reason for giving an object one name rather than another: the town Dartmouth was so named for being situated at the mouth of the River Dart. But if, perhaps through geological movement, that association between town and river ceased to hold, the name could still be used: '[p]roper names are attached to the objects themselves, and are not dependent on the continuance of any attribute of the object.'

Mill's view of proper names conforms to several commonplace assumptions about names. Proper names seem quite arbitrarily connected to objects: no doubt there are social conventions governing the *kinds* of names (words) appropriate for different kinds of objects (people, places, pets, pop groups, etc.), but a proper name is not determined for an object by any properties of the object. Nor is a name naturally thought of as having a conceptual content in the way that a descriptive phrase has. An important consequence of Mill's theory is a sharp distinction between proper names and what subsequently became known as 'definite descriptions,' that is, descriptions involving the definite article, such as *the first man on the moon*, or *the father of Socrates*. For Mill, although these descriptive phrases serve, like proper names, to pick out just a single individual, they are nevertheless, unlike proper names, connotative terms: they connote properties, as well as denoting individuals. One difference can be illustrated by those cases of definite descriptions which fossilize into proper names, for in just such cases the connoted properties cease to be an integral part of the denotation. Thus New College in Oxford was originally so described in virtue of being new; but what was once a description became in time a name and the connotation of newness dropped away. Significantly, while there is a contradiction in the statement *The new college in Oxford is not new*, there is no contradiction in the statement *New College is not new*; in the former the description 'new college' is active semantically, bringing the attribute of newness into the truth-conditions, while in the latter the descriptive content in 'New College,' used as a proper name, is semantically inert. The phenomenon seems to confirm Mill's basic intuition that proper names have a different semantic role from definite descriptions.

2. Problems for the Pure Denotation View of Proper Names

However, Mill's view, as applied to ordinary proper names, faces a number of serious difficulties. The first, originating from Frege (1892), concerns identity statements. Consider the two statements:

Dr Jekyll is Dr Jekyll. (1a)

Dr Jekyll is Mr Hyde. (1b)

Ignoring the fictional nature of the example, it seems clear that the statements have different 'cognitive value,' to use Frege's term; the first is trivially true, while the second conveys significant information. Yet if Mill is right that the sole function of a proper name is to denote an object, and if the names 'Dr Jekyll' and 'Mr Hyde' do denote the same object, then there could be no difference of meaning between the statements. Nor does it seem satisfactory to claim that such identity statements are really about names themselves, not about the objects denoted. Perhaps the statement *New York is The Big Apple* might be construed as about the name 'The Big Apple' (i.e., stating that New York is also called 'The Big Apple') but there are other cases, like *Shakespeare is Bacon*, where attention is clearly directed to the identity of a person, not to either of the names per se; furthermore, the reader is being told something other than just that Shakespeare is identical to himself.

A second problem concerns existence attributions. It is common to raise existence questions or make existence claims using proper names: *Did Homer exist?*, *Jonah did not exist*, *Carlos the Terrorist did exist*, and so on. But on the view that the sole function of a proper name is to denote an object, it is hard to see what sense could be attached to such attributions. All negative existence statements using proper names would be at best self-contradictory, at worst completely meaningless, yet as the examples suggest they need be neither. All positive existence statements using proper names would, again contrary to the evidence, become tautological, and questions about existence answered trivially. This strongly suggests that there is more to the meaning of proper names than just denotation. Perhaps, in defense of Mill, the statement *Jonah did not exist* should be construed as being a metastatement, not about the man but about the name, i.e., as stating that the name 'Jonah' denotes

nothing. However, what if the name 'Jonah' does denote someone, a barkeeper, say, in Cleveland, Ohio: does that make it false that *Jonah did not exist*? The obvious response is that it is not *that* Jonah who is being referred to. But in determining *which* Jonah is the relevant one some kind of connotation or conceptual content seems to be required for the name.

Another related problem comes from the use of proper names in fiction or mythology. Speakers seem to have no difficulty using names which have no actual denotation: *Pegasus is the winged horse of Greek mythology*, *Sherlock Holmes is the famous detective*, etc. These sentences are readily comprehensible. An unsatisfactory solution is to postulate a special class of objects—fictional objects—as the referents of such names; apart from the suspect ontological implications, this move is in danger of trivializing Mill's theory, in stipulating an arbitrary denotation for every problematic name. Another move might be to suggest that fictional names denote objects in the mind. But that threatens to produce counterintuitive truth assessments: the seemingly true statement *Pegasus does not exist* would become false if 'Pegasus' refers to something real—an idea—in the mind and *Sherlock Holmes is a detective*, which seems to have some truth, would also turn out false because being a detective could not be true of anything mental. These common uses of proper names do not fit the model of naming as pure denotation and demand careful logical analysis.

A fourth and final problem for Mill's theory, which like the first emanates from Frege, centers on the use of proper names in nonextensional contexts. So-called 'propositional attitude' verbs—hope, believe, fear, think, dream, etc.—are thought to generate such contexts. So, to use a standard example, consider the statements:

John believes that Cicero denounced Catiline. (2a)

Cicero is Tully. (2b)

If both are true, it would seem on the pure denotation view that (2c) could be inferred without further ado:

John believes that Tully denounced Catiline. (2c)

In other words if the name 'Cicero' in the first statement has only the semantic role of denoting Cicero then any other name with an identical role, like 'Tully,' should be substitutable without affecting the truth-value of the whole. The trouble is the inference does not seem to go through; it seems quite conceivable that the last statement might be false—where John has never heard the name 'Tully'—even though the first two are true. If that is so, then denotation cannot exhaust the semantic role of the name 'Cicero' in this context.

3. Frege on the Sense and Reference of Proper Names

What these problem cases suggest is that something more is needed than just denotation to account for the functioning of proper names. Frege's (1892) solution is to introduce the idea of 'sense' to supplement that of reference. The sense of a proper name, he argued, contains the 'mode of presentation' of the referent; the reference of a name is the object it denotes. Thus two different names might refer to the same object but possess different senses, i.e., present the object in different ways. That, Frege claims, is precisely what accounts for the 'cognitive' difference between identity statements of the kind *Dr Jekyll is Dr Jekyll* and *Dr Jekyll is Mr Hyde*.

The introduction of sense as well as reference provides a potential solution also to the problem of fictional names: these are names with sense but no reference. Although Frege appears to endorse that solution in Frege (1892), it is a matter of controversy whether it is consistent with his wider semantic theory (Evans 1982: ch. 1).

Perhaps the most elegant application of the distinction comes in Frege's treatment of reported speech and the contexts of propositional attitude verbs. Frege's simple but important observation is that speakers do not always use names (or signs in general) to speak of their 'customary reference,' i.e., the objects they standardly refer to. Sometimes indeed they use them to talk about the names themselves: in the sentence *'Frege' contains five letters* the name 'Frege' is not being used to refer to Frege the man. Sometimes names are used to refer to their 'senses,' not to their customary objects of reference. In reported speech the aim is to capture the sense of another person's remarks. Thus when someone reports *John said that Frege was clever* the name 'Frege' is being used not with its customary reference (i.e., Frege the man) but with an 'indirect reference' (i.e., the customary sense of the name 'Frege'). Likewise when someone reports what John believed or thought, the names within the context of the attitude verbs lose their customary reference and acquire their indirect reference. This account neatly explains why names with the same denotation cannot always be substituted—'Tully' and 'Cicero,' for example—in all contexts and truth-value preserved. The names 'Tully' and 'Cicero' have different senses and in those contexts where the senses are being referred to, substitutions would be expected to make some difference.

One difficulty with Frege's theory is stating more precisely what the sense of a proper name is supposed to be. Frege offers only general remarks about the notion. An important feature is that sense is objective—it is public, graspable by different speakers, and does not reside merely in an individual's mind. In this it contrasts with subjective 'ideas' associated with names. How can the sense of a name be specified? One way—though it is far from clear that Frege thinks this is the only way—is to provide a definite description which indicates the means by which the reference is identified. It might be, he suggests, that different

people attach different senses—thus different descriptions—to the names they use. His own example is *Aristotle* which might have the sense of *the pupil of Plato and teacher of Alexander the Great* or *the teacher of Alexander the Great who was born in Stagira* or some other descriptive content. Frege thought it was an imperfection of natural languages that single names should have such variations of sense. Nevertheless, his account of the sense of ordinary proper names (like *Aristotle*) has been the basis for a tradition of 'descriptivist' theories of names, which is returned to in Sect. 7.

4. Russell on 'Logically Proper Names'

Curiously, although Bertrand Russell (1905) rejected Frege's account of sense and reference, he ended up with a theory of ordinary proper names which also belongs in the 'descriptivist' tradition. In many ways Russell is closer to Mill than to Frege. He took over several of Mill's central ideas about names but dropped Mill's terminology—'connotative terms,' 'implying attributes,' etc.—and revolutionized the subject matter by bringing to bear the apparatus of logical analysis. Like Mill, and unlike Frege, Russell postulated a fundamental distinction between proper names and definite descriptions and held that proper names have a purely denotative function. Unlike Mill, though, he argued that ordinary proper names—*Aristotle, Dartmouth, New College*—are not genuine proper names at all but 'disguised descriptions'; and he provided a logical account of definite descriptions, which became a paradigm of logical analysis, precisely to show how they differed from genuine names.

According to Russell, a genuine or 'logically' proper name has the most direct possible relation with the object that it names. He called such names 'simple symbols,' in the sense that they could not be defined, and their sole semantic role was to denote or stand for some unique, and simple, object. The very *meaning* of a logically proper name, on this conception, is the object it denotes, such that should it turn out there is no such object then the name would be meaningless. Russell's austere conception of a logically proper name was partly motivated by the constraints of an ideal or 'logically perfect' language and partly by an epistemological distinction between knowledge by 'acquaintance' and knowledge by 'description.' (A similar view of names is found in Wittgenstein 1961, though without the epistemological element.) Humans are acquainted, Russell believed, only with the immediate objects of awareness: individual sense-data principally, but perhaps also certain universals, and the self. These alone can be the referents of logically proper names. Knowledge of other things—all complex objects—like portions of matter, persons, other minds, is knowledge by description. Clearly, then, such objects as Aristotle or Dartmouth, being complex, can be known only by description not by acquaintance and cannot be directly named. The nearest in English speakers can get to logically proper names are the indexicals *this* and *that*, as used in a limited range of contexts (e.g., to refer to individual sense data).

5. Russell's Theory of Definite Descriptions

Russell severely restricts the list of potential 'logically proper names' partly in recognition of the kinds of problems that were identified for Mill's theory in Sect. 2. In particular, he produced strong reasons for denying the status of 'genuine' names to definite descriptions. The conclusion is important for it shows, among other things, that there are significantly different ways in which objects can be 'denoted' linguistically. The fact that proper names and definite descriptions both perform the role of 'standing for' a unique object turns out to be less important, if Russell and Mill are right, than the fact that they do so in logically different ways. The point relates more generally to one of the insights from logical analysis, namely that syntactic form is not always a good guide to logical form. The prime example of this, for the purposes of this article, is the distinction between subject and predicate as applied in grammar and in logic.

There is a long tradition within philosophy which takes the syntactic division of sentences into subjects and predicates to reflect a fundamental division in the world between particular things and their properties (sometimes called universals). Thus in the sentence *Socrates is wise* the grammatical subject-term 'Socrates' stands for a particular man, Socrates, while the predicative expression 'is wise' picks out a property, wisdom, which is ascribed to the subject. The sentence is true just in case the man possesses that property. Russell believed the principle itself to be sound—subjects denote individuals, predicates characterize those individuals—but thought that very often the grammatical subject of a sentence was not its true, or logical, subject; and furthermore that not all sentences, after logical analysis, would prove to be of the subject/predicate form. In this he disagreed, for example, with Alexius Meinong who was prepared to let grammar determine denotation and was led to postulate different 'realms' of objects corresponding to different subject terms.

In his famous Theory of Descriptions, Russell (1905, 1919) argued that sentences containing definite descriptions have a different logical form from sentences containing (logically) proper names. He gives the example:

Scott is Scotch. (3a)

The author of *Waverley* is Scotch. (3b)

While grammar suggests that these are similar in form, logic dictates, according to Russell, that the latter is not a subject/predicate proposition and should be analyzed as a complex conjunction of three propositions:

At least one person wrote *Waverley*. (3c)
At most one person wrote *Waverley*.
Whoever wrote *Waverley* was Scotch.

Taken together this conjunction yields an existentially quantified statement *There is one and only one person who wrote Waverley and that person is Scotch*; the apparent naming expression 'the author of *Waverley*' has been replaced, contextually paraphrased into a predicative expression. The sharpest distinction is now evident between logically proper names and definite descriptions, on Russell's analysis: the latter are 'incomplete symbols,' which get their meaning only in the context of a complete proposition; they do not correspond to any component of a fact, they are complex symbols and can have a meaning whether or not they denote anything.

Several benefits flow from this analysis, some of which recall the problems for Mill's pure denotation view of proper names. The first is that sentences containing definite descriptions which fail to denote anything—*the present King of France*, *the golden mountain*, etc.—can be shown to be meaningful, albeit false. If taken to express a genuine subject/predicate proposition, the statement:

The present King of France is bald. (4)

invites a gratuitous search for something for it to be 'about.' For Russell, the sentence, properly analyzed, loses the misleading grammatical subject and can be seen to advance the false but meaningful claim *There is a unique person who is currently King of France and is bald*. Russell went on to argue that there are two ways of negating this sentence, depending on the scope of the negation: either, on the narrow scope, *There is a unique person who is currently King of France and is not bald*, which like the sentence it negates is also false, given the falsity of the existential content, or *It is not the case that there is a unique person who is currently King of France and is bald*, which turns out true. Thus on the latter, wide-scope, construal of the negation, bivalence is preserved.

Suppose someone wants to deny the existence of the present King of France. For those who hold that subject terms must denote, there is a troubling paradox in any sentence of the form:

The present King of France does not exist. (5a)

Yet Russell's analysis entirely removes any apparent contradiction. For the content of the sentence is equivalent to:

It is not the case that there is some unique person (5b)
currently King of France.

This in turn yields a formula which allows Russell to cope with existential statements involving all ordinary proper names: *Homer existed, Pegasus did not exist,* etc. The apparent names cannot be logically proper names—pure denoting symbols—so must be treated as abbreviated descriptions. The first step is to find some description that the name abbreviates: perhaps *Homer, the author of the Iliad and the Odyssey.* Then the statement that Homer exists can be analyzed as:

> There is one and only one person who wrote the   (6)
> *Iliad* and the *Odyssey.*

W. V. O. Quine has developed this analysis by suggesting that if no appropriate definite description can be found with which to replace the proper name, it is possible, from a technical point of view, simply to turn the name directly into a predicate. In his example, the existence of Pegasus can be denied by denying the existence of anything which 'pegasizes' (Quine 1953).

Another advantage of the Theory of Descriptions concerns identity statements. The sentence *Scott is the author of Waverley* clearly has a different cognitive value' from *Scott is Scott,* implying that the expression 'the author of *Waverley*' has a semantic role over and above that of denotation. Russell maintains that the sentence's true logical form is: *There is one and only one person who wrote Waverley and that person is identical with Scott.* If someone holds that *Tully is Cicero* is something more than a tautology, he must be using one or more of the names as disguised descriptions, in which case again he must follow the two-step process of substituting descriptions for the names and then analyzing the descriptions accordingly.

6. Criticisms of Russell on Descriptions

Amongst the vast literature of commentary on Russell's Theory of Descriptions one general kind of criticism has been prominent, and is relevant to the debate about the relations between names and descriptions. This is the criticism that Russell's theory fails to account for the purposes for which people use 'referring expressions' in their ordinary speech. The most influential attack along these lines was made by P. F. Strawson (1950) who charged that Russell failed to distinguish a sentence or expression from its 'use on a particular occasion.' The very idea of a 'logically proper name' is flawed, Strawson thinks, through a confusion of what an expression 'means' and what it is being used to 'refer' to on an occasion; and likewise not any use of a sentence containing a definite description should be assumed to involve a true or false assertion. There might be occasions where, even though the sentence is perfectly meaningful, nothing true or false has been said. The existential implication that Russell took to be part of the 'content' of a sentence with a definite description is, according to Strawson, merely a 'presupposition' for saying something true or false by means of the sentence. By seeing reference as something that speakers do, on an occasion of utterance, rather than something that

expressions in a language do, Strawson radically altered the perspective for talking about names and descriptions.

Pursuing a critique along similar lines, Keith Donnellan (1966) has argued that there are at least two distinct uses of definite descriptions, which he called 'referential' and 'attributive' uses. He gives the example of the sentence *Smith's murderer is insane.* In a context where several people believe (perhaps quite wrongly) that a certain individual (Jones) murdered Smith, then the sentence could be used to make the statement that Jones is insane. This referential use of the definite description, 'Smith's murderer,' does not require for its success that it be true that Jones murdered Smith, or even that Smith was murdered; it is true just in case Jones is insane. By contrast, a speaker using the description attributively to claim that 'whoever murdered Smith is insane' cannot be making a true assertion, according to Donnellan, if it turns out that Smith has not been murdered at all. Donnellan suggests that Russell's theory gives at best an account of the attributive use of definite descriptions. Part of the interest of Donnellan's work is that he identifies a use of definite descriptions which make them look far more like proper names, conforming indeed to something approaching Mill's account, in that 'referential' uses do not rely essentially on their descriptive ('connotative,' in Mill's terms) content (for refinements and problems, see Kripke 1977; Searle 1979).

7. Description Theories of Proper Names

Returning to proper names, it was noticed that both Frege and Russell arrive at a similar account of ordinary proper names, though through different routes. For Frege, names like *Aristotle* have a sense which might be specified by definite descriptions of the kind *The teacher of Alexander the Great ...*; for Russell, proper names of that kind are really 'truncated descriptions' and should be treated, within a full logical analysis, as definite descriptions in the manner of the Theory of Descriptions. The common, 'descriptivist,' element, which some philosophers view as amounting to a theory of proper names, has several advantages: it meets the difficulties confronting Mill's account; it explains how names become attached to particular objects (the related descriptions are true of those objects); it offers a straightforward way of determining which objects the names refer to and indeed whether they refer to anything at all.

There are problems, though, with the Frege/Russell version of the description theory. One is that it leaves unclear exactly which descriptions are supposed to be connected to which names. Is there some *principal* description attached to each name such that if it fails to apply, the name itself fails? But one could not expect agreement in particular cases as to what that description should be. A deeper problem is that it seems to generate unwanted necessary truths: if the principal description for Aristotle was 'the teacher of Alexander' then the statement *Aristotle was the teacher of Alexander* acquires a kind of necessity or analyticity. Yet this relation between Aristotle and Alexander seems paradigmatically a contingent matter.

Strawson, and others following him, refined the description theory by emphasizing the idea of a speaker's 'using' a proper name to 'make an identifying reference' (for a hearer); reference, by means of proper names or other devices, was seen as a kind of communication. The question then became what knowledge a speaker needed, and what assumptions were needed about a hearer, for a successful reference by means of a proper name. Strawson and his followers, notably J. R. Searle (1958), argued only that *some* identifying knowledge (characteristically, though not essentially, in the form of definite descriptions) about the object of reference was presupposed in the use of a proper name but that this was not part of the meaning or content of the name itself.

8. Kripke's Objections to Description Theories

The Strawson/Searle view of proper names remained the orthodoxy until Saul Kripke published his highly influential critique in 1972. Kripke's objections revolve round two features of descriptivist theories: the role of identifying knowledge and the modal implications.

8.1 Identifying Knowledge

Kripke offers a series of examples aimed at showing that it is neither necessary nor sufficient for a successful (referring) use of a proper name that a speaker should have available identifying knowledge of the object referred to. Against the necessity of such knowledge, he points out that people commonly use names of famous figures—*Socrates, Cicero, Einstein*—with only the most meagre background knowledge about the persons concerned: *a famous philosopher, a Roman orator, the man who discovered the Theory of Relativity*, etc. Such knowledge as they have is often not 'identifying' knowledge (i.e., it is true of more than one person); it is often 'circular' (i.e., the knowledge presupposes the referent, in the sense that the Theory of Relativity might be identifiable only as 'Einstein's theory'); and it is often not even knowledge at all but 'false belief' (e.g., Columbus was almost certainly not the first European to discover North America, though that might be all that people 'know' about him).

Kripke uses other examples to challenge the sufficiency of identifying knowledge. Among mathematical logicians, Gödel is known as the man who discovered the incompleteness of arithmetic. But, Kripke hypothesizes, suppose he did not do this and the proof was really the work of one Schmidt, from whom Gödel stole the result. Would it follow that those logicians whose 'backing description' for the name 'Gödel' was 'the discoverer of incompleteness,' would in fact be referring to Schmidt whenever they used the name 'Gödel'? That would appear to be a consequence of the descriptivist theory. But Kripke believes it to be quite counterintuitive. They are referring to Gödel, he insists, but just have false beliefs about him.

8.2 Modal Implications

According to description theories, speakers cannot have many false beliefs about the objects they name, for the identifying descriptions (or at least a core of them) that they connect with the name, determine what the name stands for. As Searle puts it: 'it is a necessary fact that Aristotle has the logical sum, inclusive disjunction, of properties commonly attributed to him: any individual not having some of these properties could not be Aristotle' (Searle 1958: 160). Kripke rejects this modal implication of description theories. He holds that in principle none of the commonly held beliefs associated with a proper name might be true of any individual, yet still the name could refer to someone. This is particularly true of semi-legendary, e.g., biblical, figures like Jonah: perhaps the biblical stories built round Jonah are all fabrications or exaggerations but it does not follow that 'Jonah' is an empty name. There could be some actual person who is the basis of the stories.

Kripke seeks to capture the modal intuitions, e.g., that Aristotle 'might have been different in many respects' (might not even have been a philosopher), by saying that the name 'Aristotle,' and every other ordinary proper name, is a 'rigid designator'. Something is a rigid designator if in every possible world where it has a designation it designates the same object. There is a possible world in which (i.e., it might have been the case that) Aristotle was not a philosopher, never taught Alexander the Great, never wrote *The Nicomachean Ethics*, etc. Yet in all such worlds it is still Aristotle that the name designates. Here then is a sharp distinction, on Kripke's account, between proper names and definite descriptions, for the latter are not rigid designators. Take *the teacher of Alexander*; that description designates different people in different possible worlds, indeed it designates whoever in each possible world satisfies the description. (Note the assumption here that the definite description is being used attributively in Donnellan's sense.)

9. Causal Theories of Proper Names

Kripke insists that he is not offering a theory of proper names, only an alternative 'picture' to that of description theories. His followers, though, have tried to construct a theory (commonly called a 'causal' theory) on the basis of his observations about how proper names function. Kripke's picture seems to point back to Mill and pure denotation views. What determines the reference of a name is not an implied descriptive content but an appropriate relation between users of the name and some individual to whom the name was originally given. So the account essentially has two components: the first postulating an initial 'baptism' of an individual with a name, the second explaining how the name gets transmitted through a community and across time. On the first, Kripke holds that an object may be named ('baptized') either by ostension or by the use of a description (e.g., *the first puppy to be born will be called X*); but 'fixing the reference' by means of a description is not equivalent to 'giving the meaning' of the name (one thinks here of Mill's example of Dartmouth). As for transmitting the name from person to person, all that is required, at least on Kripke's account, is an intention on the part of users to refer to the same object as the person they learnt the name from. Thus a 'chain' is set up that links users of the name with the object originally named. That chain determines what is referred to.

Of course, as described, the chain is by no means merely a sequence of external causal relations, independent of human thought processes. Among those who have developed causal theories there are those, like Kripke and Evans (1973), who acknowledge a role at least for 'intention' in the transmission of names, and those, like Devitt (1981), Devitt and Sterelny (1987), and in a qualified manner Donnellan (1966), who seek a 'purer' or more external form of causal linkage. J. R. Searle (1983) has objected that causal theories, especially those of Kripke and Donnellan, turn out to be just variants of descriptivist theories in that they presuppose an essential role for intentional contents both in reference fixing and in transmission. Searle, in defending descriptivism, argues that in practice names become associated with richer kinds of intentional content than merely 'parasitic' kinds like 'the same object as so-and-so referred to.'

Although strict causal theorists like Devitt and Sterelny see themselves following in the footsteps of Mill, they acknowledge that there is more to the meaning of a name than just its denotative role. By a curious replay of history, they reintroduce the idea of 'sense' as well as reference, albeit not quite as Frege described it. Sense now becomes a 'designating chain' making up a 'network' connected with each name. The informativeness of identity statements like *Dr Jekyll is Mr Hyde* is explained in terms of the distinct causal networks underlying the two names. Significantly, several other philosophers (McDowell 1984; Forbes 1990) have sought to defend neo-Fregean accounts of sense, as applied to proper names, within a broadly causal framework.

10. Conclusion

The debate between descriptivist and causal theories of names has not been finally resolved, though there might be some convergence as implied by the revised versions of sense theories. Certainly the issues are clearer now than in the work of Mill and even Russell. Furthermore, Kripke's work, and also Putnam's (1975), has shown how questions about proper names can be extended to other terms in language, particularly natural-kind terms, where causal theories have led to a radical reappraisal of ancient debates about essentialism.

See also: Indexicals; Reference: Philosophical Issues; Russell, Bertrand.

Bibliography

Devitt M 1981 *Designation*. University of Chicago Press, Chicago, IL
Devitt M, Sterelny K 1987 *Language and Reality: An Introduction to the Philosophy of Language*. Basil Blackwell, Oxford
Donnellan K 1966 Reference and definite descriptions. *Philosophical Review* **75**: 281–304
Evans G 1973 The causal theory of names. *Proceedings of the Aristotelian Society* suppl. vol. **47**: 187–208
Evans G 1982 *The Varieties of Reference*. Oxford University Press, Oxford
Forbes G 1990 The indispensability of *Sinn*. *Philosophical Review* **99**: 535–63
Frege G 1892 On the sense and reference. In: Geach P, Black M (eds.) 1952 *Translations from the Philosophical Writings of Gottlob Frege*. Basil Blackwell, Oxford
Irvine A, Wedeking G A 1993 (eds.) *Russell and Analytic Philosophy*. University of Toronto Press, Toronto
Kripke S 1972 Naming and necessity. In: Davidson D, Harman G (eds.) *Semantics of Natural Language*. Reidel, Dordrecht
Kripke S 1977 Speaker's reference and semantic reference. In: French P, Uehling T, Wettstein H (eds.) *Contemporary Perspectives in the Philosophy of Language*. University of Minnesota Press, Minneapolis, MN
McDowell J 1984 *De Re* senses. *Philosophical Quarterly* **35**: 98–109
Mill J S 1970 *A System of Logic*. Longman, London
Neale S 1990 *Descriptions*. MIT Press, Cambridge, MA
Putnam H 1975 *Mind, Language and Reality: Philosophical Papers*, vol. 2. Cambridge University Press, Cambridge
Quine W V O 1953 *From a Logical Point of View*. Harvard University Press, Cambridge, MA
Russell B 1905 On denoting. *Mind* **14**: 479–93
Russell B 1919 *Introduction to Mathematical Philosophy*. Allen and Unwin, London
Searle J R 1958 Proper names. *Mind* **67**: 166–73
Searle J R 1979 Attributive and referential. In: *Expression and Meaning*. Cambridge University Press, Cambridge
Searle J R 1983 *Intentionality*. Cambridge University Press, Cambridge
Strawson P F 1950 On referring. *Mind* **59**: 320–44
Strawson P F 1974 *Subject and Predicate in Logic and Grammar*. Methuen, London
Wittgenstein L 1961 (transl. Pears D, McGuinness B) *Tractatus Logico-Philosophicus*. Routledge and Kegan Paul, London

Pictorial Representation

N. Wolterstorff

Not until the latter part of the twentieth century have there been what could be called 'theories' of pictorial representation. There have been comments and observations about pictorial representation, claims and counterclaims, ever since Plato's charge that because the painter composes an imitation ('mimesis') of an appearance of a physical object, this latter in turn being an imitation of a Form, the painter's composition is 'at the third remove' from reality. But not until the late twentieth century have there been well-developed theoretical accounts of what pictorial representation *is*. Three quite different accounts are available: that by Nelson Goodman, that by Nicholas Wolterstorff, and that by Kendall Walton. All three are subtle and highly qualified; here most of those complexities will have to be bypassed, as will the polemics between and among the theories.

1. Goodman's Account

Goodman's account was first on the scene, appearing in his 1968 book, *The Languages of Art*. His account is a 'symbol' theory of pictorial representation, its fundamental thesis being that a picture is a character in a representational symbol system. The unpacking of this formula is begun with that last concept, the concept of a 'symbol system.' 'A symbol system,' says Goodman, 'consists of a symbol scheme correlated with a field of reference' (1968: 143). In turn, a symbol scheme 'consists of characters, usually with modes of combining them to form others. Characters are certain classes of utterances or inscriptions or marks' (1968: 131). A symbol 'system' is then an ordered pair whose first member is a set of characters, that is, a symbol scheme, and whose second member is a function which assigns sets of entities to the characters in the scheme, the members of a set being the 'extension' of the character to which the set is assigned. For a set to be assigned to a character, the character must 'refer' to members of the set; 'reference' is the central unexplained concept in Goodman's conceptual framework.

As to what makes a symbol system 'representational,' Goodman's thesis is that this happens just in case the system is syntactically and semantically dense, and has a relatively replete symbol scheme. 'A scheme is syntactically dense if it provides for infinitely many characters so ordered that between each two there is a third' (1968: 136); and a 'system' is 'semantically' dense if it provides for a set of extensions so ordered that between each two there is a third. Thus, for example, the scheme of arabic-fraction characters is syntactically dense, and the system of arabic frac-

tions is semantically dense. But arabic-fraction characters are obviously not pictures. That is because all that differentiates one character in the scheme from another is the shape; size, color, texture, none of those make any difference. By contrast, in a representational system, differences with respect to any of a rather large number of properties function to differentiate one character from another.

What is striking about Goodman's view is that, though a character is never a picture *as such*, but is a picture only *as* a character in a symbol system of a certain sort, namely, a representational system, nonetheless a character's functioning as a picture has nothing to do with any relation between its look and the look of what it represents; Goodman's theory is resolutely anti-iconic.

2. Wolterstorff's Account

By contrast, Wolterstorff's theory, presented in his 1980 book, *Works and Worlds of Art*, is an iconic theory. An even more fundamental difference between the two theories, however, is that Wolterstorff's theory is an 'agent–action' theory of representation. In Wolterstorff's theory, the fundamental reality is not that of some symbol being a representation of something, but that of someone performing the action of representing something by means of doing something with some design. The phenomenon of an object's, or a design's, representing something is treated as parasitic on the phenomenon of a person's representing something with that object or design.

J. L. Austin's concept of 'illocutionary' actions, in distinction from 'locutionary' and 'perlocutionary' actions, is by now well known; examples are asserting, asking, and commanding. An important feature of illocutionary actions is that, though they can indeed be performed *by* performing locutionary actions—that is how Austin introduced them—nonetheless they can be performed in other ways as well. Rather than issuing a command by uttering words, one can do so by presenting a picture. A fundamental thesis of Wolterstorff's theory is then that in representing something, one performs an illocutionary action. More specifically, one takes up an illocutionary stance toward some state of affairs (proposition); in picturing a man on a horse one introduces, and takes up an illocutionary stance toward, the state of affairs of 'there being a man on a horse.'

What remains is to pick out that particular species of illocutionary action which consists of representing something. It is at this point that Wolterstorff introduces iconicity. To pictorially represent a man on a horse, one must make or otherwise present a visual design which can (by the relevant person(s)) 'be seen as a man on a horse.' And further, to eliminate cases of sheer coincidence, the agent must 'intend' that it be *by* his composition or presentation of this iconic design that he perform the action of indicating the state of affairs of a man's riding a horse.

3. Walton's Account

Walton's account, presented in his 1990 book, *Mimesis as Make-Believe*, is a 'social practice' theory of representation. The theory makes essential use of the concept of 'imagining.' Walton first articulates a theory of mimesis, or representation, in general. His claim is that something is a representation in case its function is to serve as a prop in games of make-believe authorized for it. Games of make-believe are 'games' whose rules specify that so-and-so is to be imagined. And an object is a 'prop' in a game of make-believe if, in that game, it plays an essential role in bringing it about that such-and-such imaginings are mandated for the players of the game. Often an object will have the 'function' of serving as a prop in some game of mandated imagining rather than just doing so in ad hoc fashion; one may then speak of the game as 'authorized' for that object.

What remains is to specify which, of all the objects that are representations by the above account, are 'pictorial' representations. The core of Walton's answer is this: an object is a pictorial representation of something, say, of a man riding a horse, just in case, if one looks at it, one is mandated to imagine that one's perceptual act of looking at it is one's seeing a man riding a horse.

A symbol theory of representation, an agent–action theory, and a social practice theory—those are the main contenders on the scene in the 1990s. No consensus has emerged as to which approach is the most promising. But in the articulation of these theories, and in their polemics with each other, the nature of pictorial representation has been probed much more profoundly than ever before; and consensus has at least emerged on certain of the data which any theory must recognize and give an account of if it is to be satisfactory—for example, that one can represent, or compose a representation of, something without there existing something which one has represented or of which a representation has been composed.

Bibliography

Austin J L 1962 *How to Do Things with Words*. Oxford University Press, Oxford
Goodman N 1968 *Languages of Art: An Approach to a Theory of Symbols*. Bobbs-Merrill, Indianapolis, IN
Walton K 1974 Are representations symbols? *The Monist* **58**: 236–54
Walton K 1990 *Mimesis as Make-Believe*. Harvard University Press, Cambridge, MA
Wolterstorff N 1980 *Works and Worlds of Art*. Clarendon Press, Oxford

Reference: Philosophical Issues

K. Sterelny

The problem of reference—in the broadest terms, that of how words relate to the world—is fundamental in semantics and the philosophy of language. Analytic philosophy, particularly in the pioneering work of Gottlob Frege, Bertrand Russell, and Ludwig Wittgenstein, places reference and truth at the center of philosophical analyses of language, treating as semantic or meaning paradigms, on the one hand, the relation between a name and an object and, on the other, the relation between a sentence and a state of the world. In theoretical linguistics problems about reference, naming, and truth have figured both in the development of semantic theory and in pragmatic theories of speech acts. This article, which presents central philosophical issues concerning reference through the perspective of a certain broad-based pro-

gram in the philosophy of language, should be read in conjunction with the articles on *Names and Descriptions* and *Indexicals*, which complement the treatment here by focusing on specific modes of reference.

1. Philosophical Theories of Language

We talk and think about the world, or so it seems. Whole utterances tell us how a speaker believes, or wants, the world to be. They represent some state or aspect of the world; in the favored jargon, whole sentences specify 'states of affairs.' Thus, if Max says *Times are tough* he speaks the truth only if the economic life of his society is in recession. But it is not just whole sentences that are about the world; parts of sentences also have representational functions. Those chunks from which utterances are built refer to individuals and kinds in the world. Reference is a relation between an expression and an object or kind. Paradigms of 'singular reference' are proper names, demonstratives, and definite descriptions; 'singular' because a name—'Chomsky,' for example—refers in a particular use, if it refers at all, to just one object. 'General terms,' 'table,' 'electron,' and the like, refer not to particular objects but to kinds or (as some prefer to think of it) to the properties that all tables or electrons share.

Little in the philosophy of language is uncontroversial, and the theory of reference is no exception. In a provocatively sceptical work, Stephen Schiffer (1987) has reminded us that the problems with which philosophers have struggled may be artifacts of their conception of language. He thinks that all that is bedrock is:

> we humans have noise and mark making proclivities, and, like earthworms and flounders, we survive for some finite period of time in the environments into which we are born.
>
> (Schiffer 1987: 1)

The rest is philosophers' theory which, in Schiffer's view, is mostly pretty bad theory. Schiffer is right at least to the extent that we cannot take talk of meaning, or truth, or reference for granted. The ideas that 'Kripke' is the name of Kripke, that 'tiger' refers to tigers, that the sentence *the moon is made of green cheese* is false, despite their commonsense appearance, involve theoretical ideas about language. So they must be judged by the usual standards (inchoate though they be) that apply to all theories. Because humans have been immersed in language so long, philosophical reflection on language must take its point of departure from human responses to this long experience, to what is called 'folk theory.' Philosophers' theories of language are mostly rival attempts to systematize, debug, and extend this folk theory. We should not too prematurely follow Schiffer and resign ourselves to the failure of all these attempts.

As a species we have invested a huge chunk of our cognitive resources in language. Learning a language is probably the most intensive and the most critical achievement of any child, and no child comes empty minded to the job; the human larynx certainly, and the human brain most probably, are adapted to that task. So it seems reasonable to conclude that our noise and marking activities are adaptive, and are so in virtue of some feature(s) of the marks and noises so produced. It is of course a further step to the idea that the function of language is to represent our physical and social world. But we need a theory of those features that make our investment in language pay, and our only starting point is the theory we have, a theory in which reference and truth play a central role in capturing the relations between language and the world.

2. The Theory of Reference: An Outline of an Ambitious Program

What is reference, and what is its place in an overall account of the nature of language? These questions are best answered by articulating and evaluating an ambitious semantic program, namely one which aims to explain meaning via reference and sentence structure, and then to give an account of reference that appeals to nothing semantic. The ultimate aim of this theory of reference is to explain the relationship between linguistic representation and the world represented. That requires that it rely on no semantic notions, else it presupposes the very relationship to be explained. This program (hereafter the ambitious program) has four enabling assumptions; those who think it *too* ambitious take it that at least one of these is false.

2.1 The Need for a Theory of Meaning

The first assumption is that what is needed, and can legitimately be looked for, is a theory of meaning. General truths about the nature and organization of language are to be discovered. Thus what is needed, in some broad sense, is a theory. Looking for a theory of *meaning* makes the working assumption that the folk-theoretic notion of meaning—that notion which informs our unreflective modes of speaking about meaning—is not hopelessly compromised. Thus defenders of the ambitious program suppose that our intuitive notions of meaning will need to be clarified and revised rather than abandoned in favor of something completely different. Neither part of this assumption is uncontroversial. Schiffer, for example, challenges the need for theory, and Quine, among others, is sceptical of the prospects of finding a definition of meaning which is not either vacuous or circular.

2.2 Meaning and Truth-conditions

The second assumption is that one fundamental element of sentence meaning is a sentence's truth-conditions. A minimum condition of successful translation, for example, is that the translating sentence have the same truth-conditions as the sentence translated. Moreover, if the point of language is to enable us to represent our physical and social world, and if truth is our fundamental mode of evaluating representation, then two sentences sharing truth-conditions share a very significant property. They will be true and false in just the same circumstances. An explanation of a sentence's truth-conditions does not tell us all we need to know about a sentence's meaning. There is some interesting difference between *Edward is not very clever* and *Edward is a dork* but both sentences share something very important. The idea that sentence meaning is captured through a theory of truth-conditions is not quite as coarse grained as might seem. Even if *Cordates are vertebrates* and *Renates are vertebrates* have the same truth-conditions in virtue of the fact that all and only renates are cordates, it by no means follows that the explanation of the two sentences having that truth-condition is the same. So a theory of meaning focused on truth-conditions need not count the two sentences as semantically equivalent.

Of course, this assumption rests on fallible and controversial ideas. It is by no means universally agreed that a basic function of language is the representation of the speaker's world, nor that representation is best understood by appeal to truth. It is quite widely argued that an epistemic notion, verification, is the central element of sentence meaning. The logical positivists thought that the meaning of a sentence is determined by its method of verification, that is by the conditions under which it would be rational to accept the sentence into one's belief system, and sophisticated versions of this view are still extant.

2.3 Decompositional and Atomic Theories of Meaning

The ambitious program develops a 'decompositional' theory of meaning, a theory that explains a sentence's meaning by appeal to the semantics of the words it contains and its structure. The argument for a decompositional theory is simple and strong. Natural languages are productive, that is, they are unbounded. There is no longest sentence of English. We can add to any sentence without turning the meaningful into the meaningless. Of course, as sentences get longer, they become harder to keep track of both in production and comprehension. So they become less communicatively salient. But there is a slow fade out of intelligibility, not a line between sense and nonsense. Moreover, languages are systematic. We do not learn to speak a language sentence by sentence. To acquire a new word is to acquire the capacity to speak and understand a range of new sentences; the same is true of mastering a new syntactic construction. In learning a language we learn words one by one together with techniques for combining them into more complex constructions. These facts suggest that a theory of meaning should consist of three parts. One is a theory of word meaning; on this view word meaning is the most fundamental semantic property. A second is a theory of sentence structure; syntax tells us how words are organized into phrases, and phrases into sentences. The third part is a theory of 'projection rules.' These tell us how the meanings of the words of a constituent and its structure explain that constituent's meaning.

A theory of meaning conforming to this pattern is an 'atomic' theory; a theory which takes the reference of a term to be its key semantic property is 'referential atomism.' Most agree that languages are productive and systematic (though some of those developing 'connectionist' models of human cognitive architecture deny this), but many deny that a theory of meaning should be atomic. Defenders of molecular

theories of meaning, for example, take the sentence to be fundamental. Theorists as different as Davidson, Dummett, and Grice have resisted the inference from productivity to atomism. They do not deny that words have meaning. Instead they take the meaning of a word to be derived from the meaning of sentences in which it appears (though it has proven difficult to give an explicit account of this derivation). Word meaning does not explain sentence meaning but is derived from it. This approach is supported by the fact that the most interesting semantic properties are properties of sentences. The units of linguistic communication and representation seem to be sentences. Even one word utterances like *Idiot!* are best construed as sentences, not bare words; they seem to have truth values.

It may well be true, as Davidson, Quine, and Dummett in their differing ways have argued, that sentence meaning is more evidentially basic than word meaning. Davidson, following Quine, has urged that confronted with the speakers of an untranslated language, we have some reasonable hopes of determining which sentences they assent to, which sentences they 'hold true,' and that this is the empirical basis of a theory of meaning. One could quarrel with the conception of Quine and others concerning the evidential resources for the semantic theory. But more importantly, the atomists' case is that word meaning is explanatorily fundamental, not that it is evidentially fundamental. There is no doubt that the physical behavior of macroscopic objects has been, and is, evidentially fundamental in the development of physical theory, but talk of middle-size objects traveling slowly is not the most fundamental level of explanation in physical theory. Similarly, the evidential primacy of facts about sentences establishes nothing about explanation. A semantic theory which reduces all other semantic notions to word meaning may get its crucial confirmation from facts about sentences.

2.4 Naturalized Semantics

The final enabling assumption of the ambitious program is that we should look not just for a semantic theory but for a naturalized semantic theory. The 'naturalist' demand derives from an epistemic idea and a metaphysical idea. The epistemic idea is that philosophical theories enjoy no special status. They differ from the theories of the natural sciences in important ways; for example, they are less precisely formulated and much harder to bring into contact with data. But they share with the sciences their fallible and provisional character. So semantic theory is empirical and provisional. The idea is that semantic theory is a protoscience that will one day jettison its prefix. The further commitment is that semantic theory be physicalist. It is notoriously difficult to formulate precisely the requirements of a physicalist ontology, and its bearing on the 'special sciences' (the social sciences, psychology, linguistics, and biology).

236

But the intuitive idea is that the properties, mechanisms, and processes posited in the special sciences must be explicable by more fundamental ones, and, while it is hard to come up with a general formula, particular cases are often clear enough. If cognitive psychologists posit, for example, a capacity to access a special pictorial memory, they owe an explanation of the mechanism of access, an explanation appealing to simpler psychological or neural mechanisms. So the ambitious program is committed to giving an account of the relation between words and the world, not just taking that relation as primitive. It is most plausible to suppose that the semantic can be explained by the psychological. So naturalist programs have reductive intentions towards semantics.

There is a lot of scepticism about the prospects for naturalizing semantics. Both Kripke and Putnam argue that the reductive intent is unnecessary and incapable of fulfillment. It is just a mistake to think of the human sciences in general, and semantics in particular, as protosciences. For one thing, that is to miss the normative element of a theory of meaning. No regularity of behavior, or psychological disposition underlying that regularity, can give sense to the notion of a term being misapplied. Suppose that some benighted tourist points at a wallaroo and says *Lo! A kangaroo*. They have said something false. But that is so only if their tokens of 'kangaroo' apply to all and only kangaroos, not to kangaroos *and* wallaroos. But they have just demonstrated that their 'kangaroo'-using disposition is the disposition to apply the term to both varieties of macropod. Since such dispositions and their ilk are, in his view, about the only facts the naturalist has to trade in, Kripke is decidedly sceptical about the prospects for an account of reference in naturalistic terms with sufficient resources to give a robust account of misrepresentation.

So defenders of the ambitious program propose to develop a theory of meaning with reference as its core semantic notion, deriving a theory of sentence meaning from that core. But they do not take referential relations to be primitive; on the contrary, these are to be explained by appeal to more fundamental facts.

3. Description Theories and Causal Theories

Traditional theories of reference, concerning either singular or general terms, were not naturalist theories. Consider, for example, the theories that have been offered for general terms, such as *photon* and *tiger*. These are both examples of natural kind terms, one theoretical, the other observational.

3.1 Theoretical and Observational Terms

Theoretical terms have been the focus of intense debate in philosophy of science. In the heyday of logical empiricism, the idea was to explain the semantics of 'photon' and kindred terms by reducing their semantics to the semantics of the observation language; perhaps by direct definition, perhaps more subtly. Not just evidence but also meaning depended on observation; hence the 'logical' in 'logical empiricist.' But attempts to explain the meaning of theoretical terms by appeal to observational ones simply have not succeeded. So it has been supposed that the semantics of theoretical terms is derived from the role they play in the theories that contain them. The term 'species,' for example, derives its semantic properties from its role in the theories of evolution, ecology, and population genetics, the theories that essentially appeal to that notion. So 'species' means something like 'evolving interbreeding ecologically coherent populations,' for that is how these theories characterize species. The idea was originally proposed as a theory of the meaning of theoretical terms, but unless a term's meaning is to be completely decoupled from its reference, we can take it to be a theory of reference as well: the term refers to all and only those biological entities that (perhaps only approximately) fit that characterization.

This conception of the semantics of theoretical terms faces serious problems, for it follows that the semantics of a term change not just when the theory undergoes revolutionary restructuring, but whenever the theory is significantly modified. Though a number of philosophers have embraced some version of the idea that theory-change entails meaning-change, it has implausible consequences. It becomes difficult to explain how even those who accept differing versions of the same basic theory routinely succeed in communicating with each other, and still more difficult to explain the successful communication between those whose views are very far apart. But Darwin and Owen, for example, despite their very different views on the nature of species, understood each other perfectly well; understanding was a precondition of their deep disagreement. Moreover, this view of the semantics of theoretical terms makes it difficult to give an account of the cumulative aspects of scientific change.

So these theories of the semantics of theoretical terms may not work on their own lights, but even were they to work, they are inadequate by the atomist's lights. For term meaning is explained by appeal to other semantic facts. Logical empiricists attempted to reduce the meaning of 'photon' and its ilk to the semantics of observation terms. The defenders of 'theoretical role' semantics explained term meaning by appeal to the meaning of the sentences that jointly make up a theory. We have here no explanation of representation by a more fundamental class of fact.

3.2 Componential Analysis

'Theoretical role' semantics at best explains some semantic facts by appeal to others; the same might well be said of many theories of the meaning of words like 'tiger' or 'sloop.' These terms have received less explicit attention in the philosophical literature, but there has been a substantial theory of word meaning developed in linguistics and related disciplines, a theory known as 'componential analysis'. The idea is simple, and is also common in philosophy: these terms acquire their meaning from definitions. 'Tiger' means 'large, carnivorous, striped Asian feline'; 'Sloop' means 'a one-masted cutter with a fixed bowsprit.' Once more, this idea is naturally seen both as a theory of meaning and as a theory of reference; the term refers to those entities which fit the definition. As a general view of the semantics of natural kind or artifact terms, this story has problems. Putnam has pointed out that *tigers are carnivores* is very different from the genuinely definitional *triangles are three-sided,* for it is both contingent and empirically corrigible. Fodor (1981) has pointed out that it is in fact extremely difficult to construct extensionally correct definitions in which the defining terms are more conceptually basic than the defined term.

There is a deeper problem for componential analysis. Definitions do not yield an explanation of the relationship between language and the world. Rather, in Devitt's felicitous phrase, they 'pass the semantic buck'; they explain the meaning, and hence the reference, of the term defined, only insofar as some further adequate explanation can be given of the semantics of the defining terms. 'Passing the buck' is not pointless if it is passed to terms that are in some way special; terms whose semantic properties can be explained, not just presupposed. Logical empiricists thought that observation terms were special, but the official 'anti-psychologism' of that movement, the ban on appeal to psychological process, prevented them from giving any explanation of the semantics of observation terms. Many contemporary semantic theories are far from being anti-psychologistic. But the clear failure to reduce theoretical language to observation language, and the difficulty of reducing quite ordinary terms to a reasonably small set of more basic ones, threatens our ability to profitably 'pass the buck.'

3.3 Singular Terms

Kripke has constructed a similar argument about names. He has argued that names cannot be abbreviated descriptions because a name has the same bearer, or none, in every possible world. In his terminology, names are referentially 'rigid.' But the reference of a description, or even a cluster of them, can vary from possible world to possible world. Hence there can be no semantic equivalence between names and descriptions. In some respects then, Kripke supports John Stuart Mill's view of names, namely, that while names, like other terms, might have connotations, those connotations do not determine the reference of the name; 'Kripke' does not refer to Kripke in virtue of any connotation of 'Kripke.' Proponents of 'direct ref-

erence' theories of names have taken his arguments to support the stronger thesis that there is nothing to the semantics of names but their denotation; more about this in Sect. 4.

Kripke's provocative metaphysical views have aroused much debate, but Devitt has pointed out that his arguments 'from ignorance and error' are clearer and more convincing, for they do not rest on corrigible metaphysical intuitions. Kripke points out that 'descriptivist' theories of names imply that we can use a name to designate its bearer only if we can identify that bearer, if not in a police lineup then at least in knowing some unique characteristic of the bearer. He goes on to illustrate the implausibility of this view. Human language (unlike many animal systems of communication) is not stimulus bound. We can speak of the elsewhere and elsewhen. Given our cognitive limitations, and the stimulus freedom of language, referring to Einstein had better not closely depend on knowing about Einstein. Putnam has made much the same kind of point about general terms. But the most critical point against the description theory of names is not that it forges too close a link between referring and knowing, for no doubt suitably cunning amendments to the theory might be able to finesse that problem. Rather, it is a buck-passing theory.

3.4 Causal Chains

So what kind of theory might avoid buck-passing? Since the early 1970s or so, causal hypotheses about reference have been explored (see Field 1972; Devitt 1981; Devitt and Sterelny 1987). The central idea is that the referential relation is constituted by a causal chain between a term token, and its reference. Let us follow Putnam in imagining how this might go for natural kind terms. Joseph Banks disembarks at Botany Bay, and is confronted by the first kangaroo anyone in his speech community has seen. There is causal commerce between him and the roo, as a result of which Banks says 'We will call these animals "kangaroos".' There is a causal chain between the term token and its bearer in virtue of which the term refers to kangaroos. Others hear him talk of kangaroos, or read his letters about them, and acquire a causal connection to kangaroos indirectly, via Banks's linguistic behavior. They 'borrow' their reference from his.

Naturally, this sketch is oversimplified. The introduction of a natural kind term involves not just an ostensive but also a structural component. A term is introduced into the language by perceptual contact with samples of the kind. But the extension of the term goes beyond these samples, concerning all those objects having the same nature as the samples. In a first approximation, the nature of kinds is determined by internal structure. So the term 'kangaroo' applies to all animals having the same internal structure as that of the samples; the term 'plutonium' to that stuff having the same internal structure of the samples produced through the Manhattan Project. Having the same nature, then, is a matter of scientific discovery; internal structure is discovered only through empirical investigation. The link between referring and knowing is cut, for the introduction of the term does not depend on the term's coiner knowing the nature of this structure, and hence the nature of the 'same kind as' relation. It follows that the users of a natural kind term need not, and often do not, know necessary and sufficient conditions for membership of the kind. Indeed they may not just be ignorant, they may be quite mistaken without prejudice to their capacity to use the name to refer to a kind. We have here not just an account of how kangaroos got their (English) name; it is an account of what reference is. On this view, the referential relation is just an appropriate type of causal chain between represented and representation.

4. Causal Theories and Semantic Data

Causal theories of reference are partly motivated by the problems of semantic buck-passing. But they also help to meet problems for theoretical role views of reference. Reference often seems to be stable over major scientific change; Cuvier and Huxley both used 'species' to refer to species despite their work at opposite sides of a great scientific divide. However, because nothing fits the characterization that Cuvier gave of species—for example, he thought they were immutable—that poses a problem for theoretical role views and other related views of reference. We want to say that Cuvier was wrong in what he wrote about species, not that he wrote about, literally, nothing. Putnam's theory, in cutting the link between the capacity to refer and the capacity to characterize a kind correctly, explains how reference can be stable over theory change. Kripke took the rigidity of names, and the fact that our capacity to use a name is insensitive to our epistemic grip on its bearer, to count against description theories and in favor of causal ones. But Field and Devitt have emphasized the fact that causal theories might be ultimate theories of reference. For causal relations between the speaking mind and bespoken world are physical facts.

4.1 Fregean Problems and Description Theories

The ambitious program confronts two distinct classes of problem. It faces the naturalization problem; the fundamental semantic notion must be explicable non-semantically, otherwise there is an unexplained relation at the root of the theory (see Sect. 5). Further, though, and simultaneously, the theory must do justice to the semantic phenomena. In the literature on names that has dominated discussions of reference, the semantic agenda has been developed around problems associated with Frege. A theory of names, the idea has been, must do justice to the following facts:

(a) The sentence *Mount Egmont = Mount Taranaki* differs in some very important way from *Mount Egmont = Mount Egmont* even though Mount Egmont is Mount Taranaki.

(b) The sentence *Alfred believes that Mount Egmont is the highest mountain in New Zealand's north island* differs in some important way from *Alfred believes that Mount Taranaki is the highest mountain in New Zealand's north island*, again, despite the identity.

(c) The sentence *Vulcan is the closest planet to the sun* is meaningful even though 'Vulcan' is an empty name.

Though they have received less attention, similar phenomena arise for general terms. Consider, for example, empty terms. Piltdown man was a fraud, hence the species *Dawsoni* never existed; still *Eoanthropus Dawsoni was the precursor to homo sapiens* is meaningful, though false.

Description theories of names and general terms have many problems. It was on semantic grounds that Putnam rejected abbreviation accounts of general terms and Kripke descriptivist theories of names. But whatever their other troubles, description theories do justice to these problems. If names are abbreviated descriptions, it is no surprise that distinct but coreferential names are not semantically equivalent. If names are abbreviated descriptions, then a name is meaningful but empty if its associated description fails uniquely to designate some object. Russell's theory of descriptions thus solves the problem of the meaningfulness of empty names, granted an account of general terms.

The problem of belief contexts is tougher, but a common idea is that in such contexts it is not merely the reference of the name that is relevant to the truth-conditions of the belief sentences in which it appears; the mechanism of reference is also relevant. Frege christened mechanisms of reference 'sense'. Though 'Mount Egmont' and 'Mount Taranaki' refer to the same mountain, their mechanisms of reference, the descriptions associated with them, are not the same; hence the two belief sentences have distinct meanings.

Some at least of this machinery can be applied to general terms. These too have a mechanism of reference of some kind. Though Weismann believed that the germ plasm was responsible for inherited similarities between organisms, he did not believe that DNA was responsible for those similarities, unaware as he was of the identity of germ plasm and DNA. Perhaps we can appeal to distinct mechanisms of reference to explain the differences between these belief sentences, and the apparently related difference between *Germ plasm is germ plasm* and *Germ plasm is DNA*. Of course, within buck-passing semantics, this idea is of restricted utility; for it cannot be deployed for those general terms to whom the referential buck is ultimately passed. A logical empiricist might argue that meaningful observational predicates are never empty, and that coextensive observational terms are semantically interchangeable, but this position is very difficult to defend for those who admit a wider range of undefinable general terms.

4.2 Causal Theories and the Fregean Problems

Causal theories of reference may well be able to meet the Fregean problems in the same way that description theories do, by holding that a term's mechanism of reference is semantically relevant. The mechanism of reference, on the causal account, is not a description but a causal network linking term token to reference (see Devitt and Sterelny 1987). Distinct causal networks link tokens of 'Mount Taranaki' and 'Mount Egmont' to Mount Taranaki, one network ultimately deriving from the linguistic behavior of Maori-speaking New Zealanders and the other, English-speaking New Zealanders. Because the two tokens refer in virtue of their linkage to distinct networks, *Egmont is Taranaki* differs in meaning from *Egmont is Egmont*.

For the same reason, belief sentences differing only in the substitution of one name for the other differ in meaning. A name can be meaningful but empty through being associated with a causal network similar to that of standard names, but which is not grounded in any object. The substitution of causal networks for descriptions in this revised approach to Frege's problem has the advantage of being extendable to the parallel problems with general terms, and without the restriction implicit in buck-passing theories.

The idea of deploying causal theories to reconstruct the notion of sense is very controversial; most see the causal theory as a theory of 'direct reference,' a theory that dispenses with Frege's notion of sense and his agenda of problems for the semantics of singular terms (see Wettstein 1986; Almog, et al. 1989). Proponents of 'direct reference' do not of course deny that there is some interesting difference between *Alphonse believes that Samuel Clement wrote Huckleberry Finn* and *Alphonse believes that Mark Twain wrote Huckleberry Finn*; they just deny that there is a semantic difference between them, for there is just one proposition—the set of worlds in which Twain wrote the book—for Alphonse to be related to. Explaining the difference between the sentences is a job for pragmatics or psychology or both, but not for semantics, the proper role of which is an explanation of the information load of linguistic representation (see Almog, et al. 1989). This division of labor may be appropriate, though troubles plague it. Direct reference theorists have mostly concentrated on singular reference, yet Fregean problems seem to arise for general terms as well. Even within singular reference, most attention is paid to identity and opacity. It is hard to see what account of the meaningfulness of sentences essentially containing an empty name can be given by those who abjure any surrogate for the notion of sense.

4.3 Other Problems for Causal Theories

However the Byzantine disputes between different factions of causal theorists might resolve themselves, causal theories can probably handle Frege's problems. But they face some of their own. The causal theory, like the description theory, is not fully general. There are a raft of examples that do not fit it. Some natural kind terms have been introduced not by encounter with samples but by prediction; 'neutrino' and 'black hole' are famous examples. The same can be true of names; 'Nemesis' has been introduced as the name for a hypothesized companion of the sun that disturbs the Oort cloud every 26 million years. Rather more prosaically, architects sometimes name their buildings, and parents their children, before these have progressed beyond planning. At the time of their introduction, these terms do not depend for their semantic properties on a causal chain between term and thing. There is within language some passing of the semantic buck, and the causal theorist must accommodate that.

Moreover the causal theories seems to deem impossible something that clearly is possible: reference change. Simple versions of the theory imply that the reference of a term is fixed by the acts that introduce that term into the language; all future use depends on those introducing uses. Yet reference clearly can change; 'Aotearoa' is now widely used in New Zealand as an alternative name for New Zealand, but it originally named only the north island. The same is true of general terms. We use 'consumption' as a Victorian synonym of TB, but they used it for a much wider range of respiratory complaints. 'Gay' is another general term that has shifted reference vigorously in recent times. Clearly, causal theorists need a more complex account in which an expression's reference will depend not just on the introducing use but also on the ongoing uses; on not just their initial 'grounding' on their bearers but on re-encounters, 'regroundings' on them. Empty names and general terms are also trouble. The introduction of a term always has some cause, yet some are empty. 'Phlogiston' does not designate oxygen even though oxygen was the usual salient cause of the experimental results culminating in the introduction of 'phlogiston.' 'Santa Claus' is empty despite a connection with a real historical figure and its 'regrounding' on assorted impostors.

No consensus has emerged; there is even debate about just what the phenomena are, let alone which theory best handles them. The most devoted defender of causal semantics could not claim that they offer a complete and satisfactory account of the phenomena in their domain. Still, sophisticated causal theories do a fairly good job with the most pressing items on their semantic agenda. The story is much less cheerful when the reduction of the semantic to the nonsemantic is considered.

5. Naturalizing Reference

The ambitious program is in trouble if reference turns out to be inexplicable. Quine, as noted earlier, has long been sceptical that any account of meaning can be had. In arguing against the analytic/synthetic distinction he claimed that sameness of meaning, hence meaning, can be explained only by other semantic notions. There is no escape from the circle of semantic concepts. So these notions have no place in real science, however attractive they may be. Quine is right in demanding that semantic properties be explained or abandoned; defenders of causal theories hope however to show he is too pessimistic about the prospects of explaining meaning.

The reductive task is formidable. Late-twentieth-century attempts rely on the notion that representation is a causal relation. As we have seen, the root idea is that the 'tiger'–tiger connection depends in some way on the causal connections between 'tigers' and tigers. But the causal relations in question are crucially ambiguous. Consider the relations between Max's uses of 'tiger' and that set of tigers Max has encountered. His 'tiger's, surely, apply to these tigers and to all the others. But how could that be so? He has no causal connection with the rest. Somehow the term's range of application must be generalized beyond the grounding set, and by just the right amount. It must apply to all tigers, but not more: not to all large carnivores, all felines, all tigerish looking things, or to everything that is either a tiger or will be born next year. It must include all tigers; not all except those born in the New York Zoo. Even the notion of the grounding set itself is problematic. For consider the causal chain. It goes via the sensory impressions of tigers, tiger surfaces, tigers, the causal history of there being tigers near Max. So why aren't Max's uses of 'tiger' about tigerish retinal projections or tiger surfaces rather than tigers? Ambiguity problems seem to arise in one way or another for all attempts to explain representation.

5.1 The Appeal to Psychology

The natural way to resolve these indeterminacies is to appeal to the psychology of the language speaker, to what the speaker intended or believed. Max refers to tigers, not their characteristic retinal projections, because he intends to speak of a kind of animal. Responses along these lines threaten naturalistic semantics with circularity. For the response seems to be presupposing just the same capacities in thought that are to be explained in talk; causal theories of reference totter on the edge of being buck-passing theories after all. Psychological processes can appropriately be appealed to in giving a theory of meaning for natural language. But it is not much of an advance to presuppose the very properties of mental representation that are to be explained in linguistic representation. Moreover, in appealing to a speaker's knowledge, a

more cognitive theory threatens to return causal theories to the descriptive theories from which they were in flight.

Names pose the same problem. On the Kripkean view, names are introduced into the language in formal or informal naming ceremonies. Max acquires a jet black kitten with fierce yellow eyes and proposes to his friends that they call her 'Satan.' Thus Satan is named, a name for the cat, not a cat surface or a temporal slice of a cat. Those present, in virtue of their interaction with the cat and the name, acquire the semantic ability to designate that cat by that name. This story is plausible, but it clearly presupposes that sophisticated perceptual, intentional, and linguistic capacities are already in place.

Naturalist semantics thus faces a dilemma. Representation seems to be a species of causal relation. Yet causal relations do not seem sufficiently determinate. They leave too many candidates as the content of any given term. Winnowing these candidates requires one to move back inside the mind. In turn, this threatens the project with circularity.

5.2 'Semantic Bootstrapping'

There is a natural strategy for escaping this dilemma, which might be called 'semantic bootstrapping.' Perhaps there is a hierarchy of terms: from pure causal terms through descriptive–causal terms to descriptive terms. A pure causal term is one for which no descriptive knowledge of the referent is required. It can be acquired atomically, hence no threat of circularity arises. This base could play a role in the explanation of the reference of some nonbasic ones, names, perhaps, or natural kind terms. The descriptive knowledge required for their acquisition might require only base level concepts. This larger class could then play a role in our story for others, and so on. Successful bootstrapping would simultaneously explain both the nature of the referential relation, and explain how terms with those referential properties could be acquired.

Tough problems confront this proposal. Can the less basic be explained by the more basic in some way that does not presuppose that nonbasic terms are defined? There is very good reason to deny that many concepts are definable. So descriptive elements must be built into a causal theory of reference in ways compatible with its original demonstration that our capacity to refer to the world's furniture does not in general depend on identifying knowledge of that to which we refer.

Still more serious is the problem of actually finding basic terms. Sensory terms at first sight seem candidates, but even for them the ambiguity problem arises. Does 'red' (when first acquired by some child) name a color or a shade of that color, or even an intensity level of light? Concepts for which no problem of ambiguity arise look decidedly thin on the ground. So our basis for bootstrapping our way to the rest of our conceptual equipment may not be available.

6. Linguistic Representation and Mental Representation

This problem suggests that the Kripkean story may not be the right story of primitive content, but rather plays a role in the explanation of more cognitively sophisticated linguistic and mental representation, representations whose content presupposes a conceptual backdrop. Causal semantics then is faced with the problem that the cognitive capacities it relies on in explaining reference seem to presuppose the representational capacities that we most want explained. Trading in the problems of linguistic representation on the problem of mental representation might be progress. For one thing, there is that latter problem anyway. For another, it might be that the psychological problem is more tractable than the linguistic one, even though the trade-in constrains the solution. If we psychologize semantics, we can hardly explain mental representation by appeal to linguistic representation, as some have hoped.

How then might we hope to explain the mental capacities on which causal semantics depend? There seem to be only three options in the literature: reliable correlation, or indication; biological function; and functional role. All have problems.

6.1 Indication

The essential intuition behind indication theories is that representation is reliable correlation; a concept is a tiger concept just when its tokening covaries with the presence of tigers in the vicinity. Concept tokens are counterfactually dependent on their object; Max would not produce 'tiger' tokens unless confronted with tiger instances. Indication seems best suited to explain perception; it is obviously hard to extend indicator theories to mental representation in general, and from concepts for ostensively definable kinds to other concepts. Yet it seems that the causal semantics of names and natural kind terms require an account of the 'aboutness' of intentions and beliefs, not just perceptions. But the most severe problem for indication is misrepresentation. Leopards, practical jokes, noises in the undergrowth can all cause Max nervously to token 'tiger,' yet that concept is not the concept of tigers and anything else that goes grunt in the night. No-one tokens the tiger-concept only when tigers are present. Moreover, indication does not seem to deliver an account of the representational properties of even basic concepts, for indication is a relation not between a representation and an object or kind of object, but a relation between a representation and a state of affairs, the state of affairs of there being a tiger here now. For a defense of indication theories, see Dretske (1981, 1988) and Stampe (1986).

6.2 Teleology

One popular response to the problems of historical causal theories and of indication is to appeal to the biological function of a representation-forming mechanism. A mechanism has its biological function in virtue of its evolutionary history, so this appeal is uncontroversially naturalistic. Further, it seems to have the potential to solve the problem of misrepresentation. Robins feed their chicks when they gape and screech. But robins are vulnerable to cuckoos. In feeding a young cuckoo, the robin represents it, indeed misrepresents it, as her chick. For the biological function of the representation is to direct the robins in feeding their chicks, not to direct them in feeding their chicks or cuckoos, nor to feed retinal images or chick surfaces. That mechanism evolved because it led to robin ancestors feeding robin chicks, and despite the fact that it sometimes led them to feed cuckoos.

The proposal to add teleological elements to the causal story seems very attractive. For an appeal to the biological function of a representation is thoroughly naturalistic, yet does give more discriminatory machinery. We can specify the circumstances in which a mental state represents rather than misrepresents: it represents when the token is caused by circumstances of the same kind as those selectively responsible for the existence of the type. Beavers have the cognitive capacity to have tokens that represent the immediate presence of a wolf, because wolf-here-now circumstances were critical to the evolution of that capacity. So a beaver represents when she tokens that thought when confronted with a wolf, misrepresents when she tokens it in other circumstances. The appeal to teleology allows to specify the circumstances in which representation is veridical in a nonintentional, nonarbitrary way.

Teleological theory looks to be a very plausible account of the semantics of innate structures, and it may well be that there will be an important teleological element in our total theory of mental representation. But the attempt to extend the teleological story to the human propositional attitudes, and hence to the cognitive capacities that causal theories of names and general terms presuppose, faces great difficulties. Human beliefs do not have evolutionary histories. Very few human beliefs have been available to the ancestral population long enough to be the subjects of an evolutionary history. Moreover, the representational structures that are the standard examples of teleological semantics are fixed, isolated, innate. Beavers' representations of danger, ducklings' mother-thoughts, and frogs' musings on flies seem likely to be unstructured; they don't have component representations. Human intentions and beliefs, representations that are implicit in causal theories of reference, are complex. For creatures whose representational systems are languages of thought, the fundamental relationship is not between some way the world is and a sentence in the language of thought. It is rather between elements of the world—individuals and kinds—and concepts. A teleological semantics needs to be recast as a theory of reference.

It is at best an open question whether teleological theories explain enough of our capacities for mental representation to get causal theories of reference off the ground. Millikan (1984) and Papineau (1987) have both defended ambitious teleological programs, but have yet to win many converts.

6.3 Functional Role

Can the representational capacities implicit in causal theories of reference be explained by looking upstream from the formation of the concept rather than, or as well as, downstream to its causes? There is some plausibility in the idea that a concept is a cow concept rather than a cow-appearance concept or a cow-or-thin-buffalo concept because of the way it is used in the cognitive system. 'Two factor' theories of content have been quite popular in the literature on the mind (see Field 1978; Lycan 1988). They take content to be fixed by some combination of causal relations between mind and world, and functional relations within the mind. Unfortunately there are important problems in recruiting two factor theories to the problem of explaining the nature of primitive referential relations.

First, in their normal formulation two factor theories presuppose a solution to referential semantics, taking their problem to be accounting for an extra dimension of content, a functional notion that explains the differences between referentially identical representation. Field (1978) and Lycan (1988) take referential semantics and functional role to be independent vectors; if so, functional role is no use in eliminating indeterminacies of reference.

Second, functional role theories concentrate on inference, but an appeal to inference seems unlikely to explain the reference of concepts. For concepts do not have inferential roles. Only sentences, or sentence-like representations, do. Moreover, an inferential role theory of content may leave us with a holistic theory of content. For the inferential productivity of a representation depends on the other intentional states of the system. The belief that wallaroos are edible prompts the belief that the moon is full if you happen also to believe that wallaroos are edible when the moon is full. Holistic theories of representation are problematic in making representation idiosyncratic; people never act the same way because they mean the same thing, because they never do mean the same thing.

7. Conclusion

The ambitious program is ambitious, but it is a worthy ambition. It deserves pursuit, for success would enable us to integrate our folk and scientific conceptions of ourselves qua language users. A failure (in the absence of an alternative route for the reduction of the semantic to the more fundamental) would force us either into the wholesale rejection of our folk theory of ourselves as thinkers and talkers or into dividing our self conception into two incommensurable chunks, a scientific and a folk image. The relation between these chunks would be obscure, and their joint truth would be still more so. The ambitious program is not yet triumphant, but neither has it failed.

See also: Indexicals; Meaning: Philosophical Theories; Names and Descriptions; Sense.

Bibliography

Almog J, Perry J, Wettstein H (eds.) 1989 *Themes From Kaplan*. Oxford University Press, Oxford
Davidson D 1984 *Inquiries into Truth and Interpretation*. Clarendon Press, Oxford
Devitt M 1981 *Designation*. Columbia University Press, New York
Devitt M, Sterelny K 1987 *Language & Reality*. Blackwell/MIT Press, Oxford
Dretske F 1981 *Knowledge and the Flow of Information*. Basil Blackwell, Oxford
Dretske F 1988 *Explaining Behavior: Reasons in a World of Causes*. Bradford/MIT Press, Cambridge, MA
Dummett M 1975 What is a theory of meaning, vol. 1. In: Guttenplan S (ed.) *Mind and Language*. Clarendon Press, Oxford
Dummett M 1976 What is a theory of meaning, vol. 2. In: Evans G, McDowell J (eds.) *Truth and Meaning*. Clarendon Press, Oxford
Field H 1972 Tarski's theory of truth. *Journal of Philosophy* **69**: 347–75
Field H 1978 Mental representations. *Erkenntnis* **13**: 9–61
Fodor J 1981 *Representations*. Bradford/MIT Press, Cambridge, MA
Kripke S 1980 *Naming and Necessity*. Harvard University Press, Cambridge, MA
Kripke S 1982 *Wittgenstein on Rules and Private Language*. Harvard University Press, Cambridge, MA
Lycan W 1988 *Judgement and Justification*. Cambridge University Press, Cambridge
Millikan R G 1984 *Language, Thought and Other Biological Categories*. Bradford/MIT Press, Cambridge, MA
Papineau D 1987 *Reality and Representation*. Basil Blackwell, Oxford
Putnam H 1975 *Mind, Language and Reality: Philosophical Papers*, vol. 2. Cambridge University Press, Cambridge
Putnam H 1981 *Reason, Truth and History*. Cambridge University Press, Cambridge
Quine W V O 1960 *Word and Object*. MIT Press, Cambridge, MA
Schiffer S 1987 *Remnants of Meaning*. Bradford/MIT Press, Cambridge, MA
Stampe D 1986 Verification and a causal account of meaning. *Synthese* **69**: 107–37
Wettstein H 1986 Has semantics rested on a mistake? *Journal of Philosophy* **83**: 185–209

Sign

P. A. M. Seuren

Although there is a general if only implicit agreement in modern linguistics that natural languages are a specific kind of sign system, there is hardly any mention of the notion of 'sign' in contemporary theoretical and philosophical linguistic literature. It is absent from modern grammatical and phonological theory, even from semantics. Saussure represented an old tradition in saying that 'Language is a system of signs expressing ideas' (1922: 33). He even invisaged a universal theory of the use of signs in societies, a 'semiology,' of which linguistics would be a part. But linguistics, as it subsequently developed, did not become a branch of such a semiology. On the contrary, the sign was quietly dropped from linguistic theory. Only in the collection of approaches falling under the name of semiotics was Saussure's suggestion of a universal semiology followed up. But semiotics, it is fair to say, falls outside linguistics proper, having a literary rather than a linguistic orientation. Given the central importance of the notion of sign in earlier linguistic theorizing, its eclipse in twentieth-century linguistics calls for an explanation. A closer look at the history of the philosophy of signs and the definitional and notional problems involved will reveal why modern linguistics, in particular formal semantics, feels ill at ease with this notion. It will also show that there is a price to pay for its neglect.

From classical antiquity till quite recently, the notion of sign played an important role in both religious and philosophical thinking. In philosophy, two main traditions can be distinguished in the way this notion has been approached through the centuries. The first, which here is termed the 'associative tradition,' goes back to Aristotle and takes the defining characteristic of a sign to be its property of 'standing' for something else. The second has its origins in ancient Stoic thinking and sees a sign primarily as a perceptible object or event from which something else can be 'inferred' in virtue of the perceiver's inductive, empirical world knowledge. This is termed the 'inferential tradition.' These two traditions were, though clearly distinct, not totally separated: they kept influencing each other through the ages.

The former, associative, tradition led to a concept of sign that was so general as to lose relevance, while the latter, though relevant and specific, involved notions and perspectives that found no place in the intellectual climate of either behaviorist linguistics or model-theoretic semantics. One would expect the cognitive turn taken in psychology after 1960 to have made at least the inferential tradition respectable again, but, in spite of the psychologists' beckoning, theoretical linguistics became increasingly formalistic

and inward-looking, while formal semantics simply remained uninterested in the cognitive dimension of language.

1. The Associative Tradition

The associative tradition originates with Aristotle, who says:

> Sounds are tokens ('sýmbola') of the experiences of the soul, and so are letters of sounds. And just as not everybody uses the same letters, sounds are also used differently. However, what those are primarily signs ('sēmeîa') of are the same experiences of the soul for everybody, and the things ('prágmata') of which these are likenesses ('homoiṓmata') are likewise the same for all.
>
> (*De Interpretatione*: 1, 16a4)

Thus, sounds 'symbolize' thoughts and graphemes 'symbolize' sounds; both 'signify' thoughts and concepts, which in turn 'represent' the objectual world; sounds and graphemes vary cross-linguistically, but thoughts and objects do not.

It is important to realize that Aristotle had to improvise terminologically. The terms *sýmbolon, sēmeîon,* and *homóiōma* still lacked any standardized philosophical meanings. Accordingly, it was necessary to improvise likewise in the English translation, choosing the approximate equivalents 'token,' 'sign,' and 'likeness,' respectively. In any case, Aristotle's followers and interpreters have tended to take these terms as largely synonymous, the common denominator being the relation of *standing for.* Ockham, commenting on this Aristotelian passage, uses one pair of terms only, 'signum' and 'signify,' and, no doubt correctly, extends Aristotle's analysis with an element of 'subordination':

> I shall not speak of the sign in such a general way. We say that sounds are signs that are subordinated to intentional concepts, not because the sounds primarily signify, in the proper sense of the word 'signum', the concepts, but because sounds are used to signify precisely those things which are signified by the mental concepts.
>
> (*Summa Totius Logicae*: I, 1 ,4)

Locke in his *Essay Concerning Human Understanding* elaborates Ockham's idea further:

> The use, then, of words, is to be sensible marks of ideas; and the ideas they stand for are their proper and immediate signification.... Words, in their primary or immediate signification, stand for nothing but *the ideas in the mind of him that uses them*, how imperfectly soever or carelessly those ideas are collected from the things which they are supposed to represent.... But though words, as they are used by men, can properly and immediately signify nothing but the ideas that are in the mind of the speaker;

yet they in their thoughts give them a secret reference to two other things. First, *They suppose their words to be marks of the ideas in the minds also of other men, with whom they communicate:* for else they should talk in vain, and could not be understood.... Secondly, Because men would not be thought to talk barely of their own imagination, but of things as really they are; therefore they often suppose the *words to stand also for the reality of things.* (italics original)

(*Essay Concerning Human Understanding,*
Book III: ch. 2)

Locke's terminology is clear and virtually modern. Words are perceptible forms that 'stand for' or are 'marks of' ideas and nothing but ideas, i.e., concepts and propositions, which are nonperceptible. These in turn may stand for whatever is in the real world, and the latter property is often functionally primary. What the relation of standing for amounts to is largely left open.

C. S. Peirce carries this through to its logical conclusion. Taking over Locke's lack of specificity regarding the relation of standing for, Peirce presents the following definition, or description, of what constitutes a sign:

A sign, or *representamen*, is something which stands to somebody for something in some respect or capacity. It addresses somebody, that is, creates in the mind of that person an equivalent sign, or perhaps a more developed sign. That sign which it creates I call the *interpretant* of the first sign. The sign stands for something, its *object*. It stands for that object not in all respects, but in reference to a sort of idea, which I have sometimes called the *ground* of the representamen. 'Idea' is here to be understood in a sort of Platonic sense, very familiar in everyday talk. (italics original)

(Hartshorne and Weiss 1931, vol. II: 135)

In his article 'Sign' in *The Encyclopedia of Philosophy* (1967), Alston comments (p. 438) that Peirce's definition can be summarized as '*x* stands for *y* (for a person *P*).' This, he says, can be taken in an 'ideational sense': 'When *P* becomes aware of *x*, it calls *y* to mind,' or in a 'behavioral sense': 'When *P* perceives *x*, he is led to make some behavioral response appropriate to *y*.' Both interpretations are associative: no notion of rule-governed inference is involved. The latter interpretation is obviously behaviorist, well-known, for example, from chapter 2 in Bloomfield's *Language* (1933). The former interpretation, in terms of associative psychology, is found in the famous triangle (Fig. 1) presented by Ogden and Richards (1923: 11), which is, in principle, a summing up of Locke's analysis.

On both interpretations, however, Alston observes (p. 438), 'there are grave difficulties.' The ideational account is so general that it risks being weakened 'to the point that anything becomes a sign of anything.' The behavioral account is, says Alston, even less adequate. For example, 'It would be very odd for one to respond to a diagram of a high compression engine

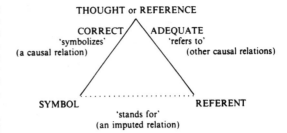

Figure 1.

in anything like the way he responds to the engine itself,' though, clearly, the diagram *stands for* the engine. One is thus led 'to ask whether there is any interesting single sense in which one thing stands for another,' which makes it doubtful whether any useful notion of sign will come about when this associative line of analysis is pursued. Alston, who rests heavily on Peirce's approach, thus appears to admit to some skepticism about the usefulness of a notion of sign thus explicated.

2. The Inferential Tradition

Perhaps surprisingly, however, Alston fails to mention the inferential tradition in the philosophy of signs, which started with the Stoics. The crucial difference with the associative tradition is that the relation of standing for is replaced, and thereby specified, by the relation of 'providing knowledge of the reality of.' On this account, a sign is a perceptible form or event *S* whose perception enables the perceiver *P* to make a reliable inference about some nonperceptible state of affairs or event *N* in the actual world beyond the immediate inference of the reality of *S*. *N* here is perceived as the 'significate' of *S* (more or less the 'signifié' in Saussure's definition of the linguistic sign). The 'meaning' of S is its property of allowing for the reliable inference of the reality of the significate.

P's inference is justified by his inductively acquired knowledge of systematic co-occurrences, in particular causes and effects, in the world. The theory of signs is thus part of epistemology. When the inference to *N* is certain, there is then a sign in the full sense. When the inference is merely probabilistic and needs further confirmation (for example when S is part of a syndrome), there is a 'symptom.'

As Kneale and Kneale report (1962: 140–41), the Stoics developed their notion of sign in connection with their investigations into the nature of the logical form of the conditional: 'if A then B.' In normal usage, conditionals involve an element of epistemic necessity in that the consequent is taken to be somehow necessitated by, or follow from, its antecedent. Suppose there is a sound conditional, i.e., a conditional grounded in sound induction. Let the antecedent A describe a perceptible and the consequent B a nonperceptible state of affairs or event. Then, if A is true, B follows, and one can say that A describes a sign *S* and B its significate *N*. Clearly, the inference is made, i.e., the sign is interpreted, only if *P* recognizes the conditional as sound. If *P* lacks the knowledge required for the inference from *S* to its significate, he will fail to understand *S*. The logical form of the epistemically grounded conditional thus describes the nature and the functioning of the sign.

A conditional like 'If it is day it is light' therefore cannot describe the working of a sign since the consequent clause describes a state of affairs which is necessarily perceptible whenever the state of affairs described by the antecedent clause is (Kneale and Kneale 1962). But a conditional like 'If he shouts he is angry' will, if sound, describe a sign whenever the antecedent is perceptibly true, since though the consequent will also be true it will not be true in virtue of direct perception.

The significate, moreover, must be part of present reality. That is, it must be a fact of the present or the past. Whenever the significate's description refers to a future fact, the significate must be taken to be a present state of affairs that will inevitably lead to the effect described. For example, when a cloud is correctly interpreted as a sign of impending rain, the significate must be taken to be the present state of the atmosphere, which is such that rain will inevitably follow, even though the conditional is of the form 'If there is a cloud it will rain.'

The main propagator of the Stoic analysis of the sign has been St Augustine, in whose theology signs were a central element. The definition and analysis of this notion is a recurrent theme in his numerous writings, for example, 'A sign is something which shows itself to the senses and beyond itself something else to the knowing mind' (*Dialectica*: ch. 5).

It may be observed, at this point, that Augustine's analysis of the sign, like that developed in the Stoa (in so far as it can be reconstructed from the mainly secondary sources), does not distinguish between cases where the nonperceptible fact, the 'something else,' causes (or motivates) the perceptible fact and those where the perceptible fact causes the nonperceptible 'something else.' When the former relation holds it is perfectly natural to speak of the perceptible element as a sign. But when the perceptible fact is itself the cause of the something else, so that perception of the cause induces certain knowledge (prediction) of the effect to come, it seems less natural to speak of a sign, even though the Stoic-Augustinian analysis allows for it. For example, on seeing a man jump from the roof of a tall building, one knows that he will die. Yet, it seems inappropriate, or anyway less appropriate, to say that the man's jump is a sign of his imminent death. It is, therefore, perhaps useful to add the following criterion to the analysis of the sign: if a

causal relation is involved between a perceptible and a nonperceptible fact, then, for the perceptible fact to function as a sign it must be caused by the imperceptible fact, and not vice versa. Mere systematic co-occurrence seems insufficient as a criterion.

3. Signs: Natural and Conventional

Augustine amply discusses the Stoic distinction between *natural* and *conventional signs* (e.g., in *De Doctrina Christiana*, Book II: chs. 1–4). It is mainly through the enormous influence of his writings that this distinction became commonplace through the ages. It amounts to the following. Natural signs result from world knowledge. They need not be learned separately, as signs: factual knowledge suffices. For anyone who knows that smoke cannot come about unless as a result of combustion, smoke is a sign of (signifies) fire. Analogously, footprints signify the past passing of an animal or person, and the distant hum of aircraft may, in certain contexts, be a sign of a state of affairs that will soon lead to bombing. Or the presence of a limousine adorned with white flowers signifies, in certain cultures, that a wedding is being celebrated.

A conventional sign, on the other hand, results from a convention to produce a given form with the intention of making it known to an informed perceiver that the producer takes a particular stance with regard to a particular thought. Thus, the producer of a conventional sign can make it known that he commits himself to the truth of the thought expressed, or wishes it to be made true, or wants to be informed about its truth-value, etc. Emotions usually find a natural, nonconventional expression, but articulated, i.e., propositional, thoughts cannot, on the whole, be read off the body of the person thinking. Since it is often important that others know of a person that he entertains a particular thought in a particular mode (as an assertion, a wish, an order, a question, etc.), communities select certain forms that cannot easily occur unless as a result of a conscious decision to produce them. These forms are then assigned to certain thoughts, including their mode of entertainment, so that the members of the community in question know with reasonable certainty that when someone produces a form S, he entertains the thought T conventionally associated with S. The inference is certain to the extent that it is certain that S cannot have been produced other than by conscious decision, barring possible errors or random processes.

4. A Language as a Conventional Sign System

Comprehension of a conventional sign S consists in the reconstruction of S's significate, the underlying thought, by the perceiver. A system of forms allowing for structural articulations that map onto articulated, propositional thoughts in regular ways is a (natural or artificial) language. For a language to bring about a regular correspondence between forms and thoughts it must have well-defined 'building blocks' (lexical words, that is), which can be combined into full signs (sentences) and correspond regularly with structural parts of thoughts, in particular 'predicates' (in the sense of bundles of satisfaction conditions). It is customary to speak of conventional signs not only when referring to full sentences but also in the case of lexical words.

To be able to interpret a conventional sign one must know the convention according to which its mental significate, whether full thought or predicate, has been fixed. In the case of a language, this 'convention' consists of a rule system or 'grammar' mapping sentences and thought schemata onto each other, in combination with a 'lexicon,' which lists the words to be used in the sentences of the language. Although it is widely accepted nowadays that world knowledge is a necessary prerequisite for the adequate comprehension of sentences, there still is a fundamental difference between world knowledge and linguistic knowledge. The former is about facts irrespective of conventional sign systems. The latter is specifically about conventional linguistic sign systems.

5. The Referential Aspect

Thoughts are by their very nature intentional, i.e., about something. This may be termed their 'referential aspect.' It follows that the reconstruction of a given thought by a perceiving subject necessarily involves a copying of its referential aspect. In fact, in most speech situations the perceiver will not be primarily interested in the speaker's thought but rather in what the thought is about, i.e., its referential aspect. The transfer of thought is often only a means towards the end of organizing the actual world. This is what made Ockham introduce his notion of subordination, the fact that, as Locke said, men 'often suppose the words to stand also for the reality of things,' as seen above. The referential aspect, though primarily a property of thoughts (and their predicates), thus automatically carries over to sentences and words. But it must be remembered, as Locke keeps stressing, that linguistic forms possess their referential aspect only as a derived property, mediated by the thoughts and their predicates (ideas), which carry the referential aspect as their primary property.

An adequate analysis of the notion of sign helps to see language and language use in their proper ecological setting. When language is used the listener (reader) makes a mental reconstruction of the thought process expressed by the speaker (writer), including the latter's commitment or stance ('mode of entertainment') with regard to what is referred to. In principle, the certainty systematically induced by the occurrence of a linguistic sign in virtue of the conventional sign system at hand extends primarily only to the presence of the thought process concerned. Any relation to the real world is mediated by the thought processes, and any certainty about real world conditions induced by a linguistic message depends on external factors such as the speaker's reliability, not on the linguistic system in terms of which the message is presented.

6. The Price for Neglecting the Notion of Sign

This obvious and important fact has, however, not always been recognized. There is a tradition, which originated with Descartes and has had something of a career in the philosophy of perception, where conventional linguistic signs are taken as prototypical of, or at least parallel to, the physical sense data impinging on the senses. At the beginning of his essay 'The world, or essay on light,' Descartes argues, in the wider context of his rationalist theory of innate ideas, that physical sense data have nothing in common with the mental sensations or ideas evoked by them. Hence, he concludes, the mental sensations must have an independent source, besides the physical stimuli, which determines their qualities. This independent source is a set of innate principles and ideas. In setting up his argument he draws a parallel with words:

> You know well that words, which bear no resemblance to the things they signify, nevertheless succeed in making us aware of them, often even without our paying attention to the sounds or syllables. Whence it may happen that having heard a stretch of speech whose meaning we understood full well, we cannot say in what language it was pronounced. Now, if words, which signify nothing except by human convention, suffice to make us aware of things to which they bear no resemblance, why could not Nature also have established a certain sign that makes us have the sensation of light even though this sign has nothing in itself resembling this sensation? Is this not also how she has established laughs and tears, to let us read joy and sadness on the faces of men? (author's translation)
> (Adam and Tannery, vol. xi: 4)

This parallel between linguistic signs on the one hand and sense data on the other is, of course, entirely spurious and confused. Descartes himself seems somewhat unconvinced by it as well. He continues to say that some might object that in the case of speech sounds the parallel is not the awareness of things but rather the 'acoustic image' that corresponds to the sound. Even so, he says, it all happens in the mind, and he cuts the argument short not wishing 'to lose time over this point.'

Nevertheless, 'this analogy will make quite a career in seventeenth and eighteenth century theories of perception (e.g., those of Berkeley and Reid) and, with new theoretical implications, it will also figure prominently in Helmholtz's cognitive theory of perception' (Meijering 1981: 113). Quite recently it was seen cropping up again in Fodor's book *The Modularity of Mind*:

> Now about language: Just as patterns of visual energy arriving at the retina are correlated, in a complicated but

regular way, with certain properties of distal layouts, so too are the patterns of auditory energy that excite the tympanic membrane in speech exchanges. With, of course, this vital difference: What underwrites the correlation between visual stimulations and distal layouts are (roughly) the laws of light reflectance. Whereas, what underwrites the correlation between token utterances and distal layouts is (roughly) a convention of truth-telling. ... Because that convention holds, it is possible to infer from what one hears said to the way the world is.

(1983: 45)

This analogy is clearly misguided. It rests on the false parallel between 'distal layouts' in the case of visual perception and the things, states of affairs, or events talked about in the use of language. What underwrites the correlation between token utterances and distal layouts is the laws of propagation and impingement of sound. In the auditory case the 'distal layouts' are nothing but the organisms or mechanisms through or with which the sounds in question are produced, not the reference objects, states of affairs, or events referred to (cp. Seuren 1985: 53–54). While Descartes confused world facts with mental representations, Fodor confuses them, more in the behaviorist vein, with the physical source of sense data. Closer reflection on the nature of the sign would have kept these authors from such aberrations.

It would also have had a beneficial effect on formal semantics and philosophy of language as these disciplines have been practiced over the past decades. There, full attention is paid to the referential aspect of linguistic forms, at the expense of their status as signs. The vast bulk of all efforts at formalization has concentrated on model theory, the formal, and definitely not causal, relation between linguistic struc-

tures and their possible denotations in some real or hypothetical world. All of formal semantics consists of a calculus of 'extensions' in possible worlds. Very little effort has gone into the formalization of the sign process, the way uttered sentences are reconstructed by hearers, to be integrated into any available long-term fund or store of 'encyclopedic' world knowledge on the one hand, and short-term knowledge of what has been built up in preceding discourse on the other. It is only in recent developments of discourse semantics that attempts are being made at developing formal theories of these cognitive interpretative processes.

Bibliography

Adam C, Tannery P (eds.) 1909 *Œuvres de Descartes*, vol. xi. Léopold Cerf, Paris
Alston W P 1967 Sign and symbol. In: Edwards P (ed.) *The Encyclopedia of Philosophy*, vol. vii, pp. 437–41. Macmillan, New York/London
Bloomfield L 1933 *Language*. Holt, New York
Fodor J A 1983 *The Modularity of Mind: An Essay on Faculty Psychology*. MIT Press, Cambridge, MA
Hartshorne C, Weiss P 1931 *Collected Papers of Charles Sanders Peirce*, 2 vols. Harvard University Press, Cambridge, MA
Kneale W, Kneale M 1962 *The Development of Logic*. Clarendon Press, Oxford
Meijering T C 1981 Naturalistic epistemology: Helmholtz and the rise of a cognitive theory of perception (Doctoral dissertation, University of California)
Ogden C K, Richards I A 1923 *The Meaning of Meaning: A Study of the Influence of Language upon Thought and of the Science of Symbolism*. Kegan Paul, London
Saussure F de 1922 *Cours de linguistique générale*, 2nd edn. Payot, Paris
Seuren P A M 1985 *Discourse Semantics*. Blackwell, Oxford

Language and Logic

Arbitrary Objects

W. P. M. Meyer Viol

In informal mathematics, to have shown of an arbitrary triangle that its interior angles add up to 180° is to establish that all triangles have interior angles adding up to 180°. This was once commonly held to show that in addition to individual triangles, there are 'arbitrary' triangles. In traditional logic, there was a time when the grammatical similarity between sentences like 'John owns a donkey' and 'every farmer owns a donkey' was taken to show that the phrase 'every farmer' denotes an entity called the 'arbitrary farmer.' This view entailed that, in addition to individual objects, there are arbitrary objects. By the principle of 'generic attribution,' an arbitrary object has those properties common to the individual objects in its range. (For an overview of the history of arbitrary objects see Barth 1974.)

1. Generic Attribution

The notion of an arbitrary object has fallen into total disrepute, because of fundamental problems concerning the principle of generic attribution. In its informal formulation, the principle of generic attribution leads in a straightforward way to contradictions for 'complex properties.' Take an arbitrary triangle. Then it is oblique or right-angled, since each individual triangle is either right-angled or oblique. But it is not oblique, since some individual triangle is not oblique; and it is not right-angled since some individual triangle is not right-angled. Therefore it is oblique or right-angled, yet not right-angled and not oblique. A contradiction. These problems have brought many logicians to the conclusion that arbitrary objects belong to the 'dark ages of logic' (Lewis 1972).

2. Fine's Theory

In a series of articles resulting in the book *Reasoning with Arbitrary Objects*, K. Fine (1985b) has set out to reinstate arbitrary objects, by formulating a coherent account of the principle of generic attribution, and constructing formal models for interpreting languages with constants denoting arbitrary objects. Fine argues convincingly that there are various areas of research where the introduction of arbitrary objects is well motivated. In linguistics, for instance, there are cases where reference to arbitrary objects seems most natural. Consider the following text:

Every farmer owns a donkey. He beats it regularly.　(1)

In Discourse Representation Theory, pronouns are taken to refer to objects that have in some sense been introduced by the previous text. But admitting only individuals in our ontology, this leads to problems; for to what individual farmer and individual donkey can the pronouns 'he' and 'it' be said to refer? It seems natural to have them refer respectively to the arbitrary farmer and the arbitrary donkey he owns.

The heart of Fine's theory of arbitrary objects consists of a reformulation of the principle of generic attribution. According to Fine, the argument showing that the notion of an arbitrary object leads to contradictions for complex properties, depends upon the failure to distinguish two basically different formulations of this principle: one is merely a rule of *equivalence* and is stated in the material mode; the other is a rule of *truth* and is stated in the formal mode.

To formulate the two versions of the principle, let a be the name of an arbitrary object a; and let i be a variable that ranges over the individuals in the range of a. The equivalence formulation of the principle of generic attribution then takes the form: $\phi(a) \equiv \forall i \phi(i)$. Given this formulation, contradictions can be derived. For, let $R(i)$ $(O(i))$ be the statement that triangle i is rectangle (oblique). Because $\forall i (R(i) \lor O(i))$ it follows that $R(a) \lor O(a)$ for arbitrary triangle a. But because $\neg \forall i R(i)$ and $\neg \forall i O(i)$ it follows that $\neg R(a) \land \neg O(a)$, and we have arrived at a contradiction. The truth formulation of the principle takes the form: *The sentence $\phi(a)$ is true if the sentence $\forall i \phi(i)$ is true*. In this version of the principle, the argumentation leading to a contradiction is blocked, and a coherent formulation is reached. But there is a price to pay; in general, formulas containing names for arbitrary objects don't decompose truth-functionally.

3. Further Connections

Although Fine does not develop in any depth the implications of his theory for the semantics of natural language, there are interesting connections with the disciplines working in the tradition of R. Montague (1973). In the Theory of Generalized Quantifiers, the phrase 'every farmer' is interpreted as the set of all properties satisfied by all and only all farmers. Now, a uniform semantic interpretation of noun phrases is achieved by identifying an individual with the set of all its properties, thus assimilating proper names to the semantic category of quantifier phrases. The theory of arbitrary objects suggests the opposite identification. Here the quantifier phrase 'every farmer' is assimilated to the semantic category of proper names, i.e., the category of entities, albeit arbitrary ones.

Bibliography

Barth E M 1974 *The Logic of Articles in Traditional Philosophy*. Reidel, Dordrecht
Fine K 1985a Natural deduction and arbitrary objects. *Journal of Philosophical Logic* **14**: 57–107
Fine K 1985b *Reasoning with Arbitrary Objects*. Blackwell, Oxford
Lewis D 1972 General semantics. In: Davidson D, Harman G (eds.) *Semantics of Natural Language*. Reidel, Dordrecht
Montague R 1973 The proper treatment of quantification in ordinary English. In: Hintikka K J J, Moravcsik J M E, Suppes P (eds.) *Approaches to Natural Language*. Reidel, Dordrecht

Aristotle and Logic

V. Sánchez Valencia

This article gives an account of Aristotle's contribution to logic. Although Aristotle did not use the word 'logic' in the modern sense, the scope of the study of logic was determined by the *Organon*—the collection of his logical treatises. This collection comprises: *The Categories, De Interpretatione*, the *Prior Analytics*, the *Topics*, the *De Sophisticis Elenchis*, and the *Posterior Analytics*. This article examines the first three treatises.

1. *The Categories*

Since antiquity it has been suggested that in this work Aristotle classifies types of things by using language as a clue to the differences between them. Aristotle argues that expressions are simple or compound. Every simple expression corresponds to a category. Compound expressions are the bearers of truth values. Aristotle gives a list of 10 categories: 'substance' (man, horse); 'quantity' (two cubits long); 'quality' (white); 'relation' (greater); 'place' (in the Lyceum); 'time' (last year); 'situation' (lies); 'state' (is armed); 'action' (cuts); 'passion' (is cut).

Among substances Aristotle distinguishes primary and secondary substances. Primary substances correspond to individual objects like Socrates. Primary substances are not predicative in that they are not asserted of a subject. They are the ultimate subject of predication. Secondary substances are the genera and the species which include primary substances. They are predicative in that they might be asserted of the subject. For Aristotle primary substances are the most real things. He makes clear that sentences involving secondary substances are dependent on sentences involving primary substances. For instance, he explains universal predication in terms of singular propositions. He says that a term *A* is predicate of all of another term *B* when no instance of *B* can be found of which *A* cannot be predicated. Similarly, he says that the sentence *No A is B* is equivalent to *No B is A*, because if *A* were predicated of an object *c* to which *B* is applied, it would no longer be true that *B* is not applied to any object to which *A* is applied, because *c* would be one of the *A*'s.

In spite of this predicative dependence, Aristotle's logic concerns primarily secondary substances. The reason behind this approach seems to be that Aristotle considered that there cannot be a science of primary substances.

2. *De Interpretatione*

Aristotle begins his analysis of categorical (assertive) sentences with definitions of the expressions 'noun,' 'verb.' Nouns and verbs in themselves are significative, but they lack a truth value. Aristotle holds that a noun is a sound with conventional meaning, without time reference and whose parts lack independent meaning. A verb is like a noun except that it has time reference and that it indicates predication. Among sentences Aristotle distinguishes the categorical sentences as the only bearers of truth value and as such they are distinct from other meaningful composite expressions like prayers, commands, etc. Aristotle divides categorical sentences into affirmative and negative. Each affirmative sentence has its own opposite negative, and each negative has its affirmative opposite. Every such pair of sentences is called contradictory—assuming that the terms involved are the same and used in the same sense. In *De Interpretatione* the division between primary and secondary substances is reflected in the division between universal and individual terms. Universal terms correspond to secondary substances, individual terms correspond to primary substances. A sentence is called universal when it has the form *Every A is B* or *No A is B* (or, equivalently, *Every A is not B*). A sentence is called particular when it has the form *Some A is B, Not every A is B* (or, equivalently, *Some A is not B*).

The combination of universal and affirmative sentences yields the well-known opposition schema:

(a) A pair of affirmative and negative universal sentences, involving the same terms used in the same way, is called contrary. Contraries cannot both be true at one time, but they can both be false.

(b) Pairs consisting of a universal affirmative sentence and a particular negative sentence or of a universal negative sentence and a particular affirmative sentence, involving the same terms used in the same way, are called contradictories. Contradictory sentences cannot both be true at one time, nor can they both be false at the same time.

3. The *Prior Analytics* and the Theory of Syllogisms

Initially, Aristotle did not restrict the term 'syllogism' to arguments having only two premises and three terms. He defines a syllogism as a discourse in which certain things being posited, something other than what is posited follows of necessity from their being so. However, the core of the *Prior Analytics* consists of an analysis of arguments with two premises relating three terms. Aristotle argues that every argument can be expressed as a series of syllogistic inferences. This is the so-called 'syllogistic thesis': every argument is a syllogism. The point is that Aristotle assumes that the conclusion of every nonformal deductive argument is a categorical sentence. He then argues that the only way such a conclusion can be derived is through premises which link the terms of the conclusion through a middle term relating them.

Aristotle's strategy in treating syllogistic consequence is the following. He considers 48 possible pairs of premises. Besides the so-called perfect syllogisms, Aristotle is able to eliminate by counterexample all but 10 other pairs of premises as having no syllogistic consequences. The remaining syllogisms are perfected (reduced) to first-figure syllogisms by using deductions. His method is this. He selects a few valid infer-

ence patterns and justifies the remaining valid patterns by showing that they are a conservative extension of the original core: one can move from the premises to the conclusion without them. The invalid inference patterns are rejected by using counterexamples. The traditional practices of using a formal deduction to show that an inference pattern is valid and using a counterexample to show that it is not are both introduced by Aristotle. The valid inference patterns which Aristotle employs are:

(a) The rules of conversion.
(b) The *reductio ad absurdum*.
(c) The perfect syllogisms.

The conversion rules are inference patterns based on special properties of the expressions *Some* and *No: Some A is B* entails *Some B is A* and *No A is B* entails *No B is A*.

The *reductio ad absurdum* is, in Aristotle's system, a kind of indirect proof: if from a set of assumptions S and a sentence P a contradiction follows, then one can derive the contradictory of P.

Aristotle divides syllogisms into perfect and imperfect ones. A perfect syllogism is a trustworthy principle of inference in that it needs nothing to prove that the conclusion follows from the premises: it can be seen directly that this is the case. These syllogisms have the following form (their traditional names are used here):

Barbara:	Every A B,	Every C A	$\Rightarrow$	Every C B.
Darii:	Every A B,	Some C A	$\Rightarrow$	Some C B.
Celarent:	No A B,	Every C A	$\Rightarrow$	No C B.
Ferio:	No A B,	Some C A	$\Rightarrow$	Not all C B.

A syllogism is imperfect if it needs additional discourse in order to prove that the conclusion follows from the premises. Central to Aristotle's logical program is the proof that all the valid imperfect syllogisms are perfectible. The perfection of an imperfect syllogism consists in showing how one can move from the premises to the conclusion by using the rules of conversion, the *reductio* rule, and the perfect syllogisms. This means that Aristotle has to prove in the evident part of his system that each argument that uses nonevident syllogistic principles to prove a certain conclusion *C* can be replaced by a proof of *C* that uses only the evident principles. This goal is achieved by Aristotle in the *Prior Analytics,* which made him the founder of logic and metalogic at the same time.

4. Conclusion

The modern interpretation and assessment of Aristotle's logical theory started with Łukasiewicz (1957) in which Aristotle's method of perfecting syllogisms is cast in axiomatic form. According to Łukasiewicz, Aristotle used but did not develop a logic of propositions.

A more accurate interpretation of Aristotle's strategy was offered by Corcoran (1974). In this work

Aristotle's method is cast in the form of a natural deduction system. Corcoran convincingly shows that Aristotle's proofs can be read as objects generated by an underlying logical calculus which does not presuppose propositional logic.

An insightful logical assessment of Aristotle's achievements and program is embodied in Lear (1980), while Westerståhl (1990) offers an analysis of Aristotle's theories from the point of view of the generalized quantifier analysis of natural language quantification.

See also: Aristotle and the Stoics.

Bibliography

Aristotle 1928 *The Works of Aristotle Translated into English*, Ross W D (ed.), vol. 1. Oxford University Press, Oxford

Corcoran J 1974 Aristotle's natural deduction system. In: Corcoran J (ed.) *Ancient Logic and its Modern Interpretations*. Reidel, Dordrecht

Lear J 1980 *Aristotle and Logical Theory*. Cambridge University Press, Cambridge

Łukasiewicz J 1957 *Aristotle's Syllogistic*, 2nd edn. Oxford University Press, Oxford

Westerstavhl D 1990 Aristotelian syllogisms and generalized quantification. *Studia Logica* XLVIII

Conditionals
F. Veltman

In making plans, in evaluating actions, in justifying beliefs as well as in theorizing, hypothetical situations or deliberate counterfactual possibilities are frequently considered. Conditionals directly reflect this ability to reason about alternative situations. They consist of two constituents, the first of which is called the 'protasis' or 'antecedent' and the second the 'apodosis' or 'consequent.' The antecedent expresses what is hypothetically (counterfactually, possibly, ...) so, while the consequent states what, given this condition, will be (would have been, might be, ...) the case. See examples (1–2):

> If Shakespeare didn't write Hamlet, someone else did. (1)

> If Shakespeare hadn't written Hamlet, someone else would have. (2)

This pair of examples illustrates the contrast between indicative conditionals and counterfactuals. The first conditional (1) is obviously true. Given that the play Hamlet does in fact exist, and given the way plays come into existence, somebody must have written it. If not Shakespeare—and the use of the indicative suggests that we have to reckon with this possibility—it must have been somebody else. The use of the pluperfect in (2), however, strongly suggests that Shakespeare did in fact write Hamlet. And it is very difficult to give up this idea, as the antecedent of this counterfactual invites one to do, without giving up the idea that it was written at all. So, (2) seems downright false. This article is confined to general properties of conditional sentences and theories of indicative conditionals, and mentions counterfactuals only occasionally.

1. Conditional Markers

Every language has some way of forming conditional sentences. Descriptive studies of the range of forms used by native speakers to express conditionals show that these forms can be substantially different from the *if–then* construction, which is prototypical for English. There are even languages in which there is no clear prototypical construction at all. In Chinese, for example, most conditional sentences have the form of a conjunction, and their conditionality has to be read off from the context. In Latin, by contrast, the *si* unambiguously marks conditionality. In Classical Arabic there are two prototypes: *in* for expressing indicative conditionals, and *law* for counterfactual conditionals. A still more elaborate system can be found in Classical Greek in which even the degree of hypotheticality is sharply characterized. Although in English the *if–then* is the clear-cut mark of conditionality, neither the *if*, nor the *then* is necessary; *Tell him a joke, and he will laugh* expresses the same conditional as does *If you tell him a joke, he will laugh*. And in the sentence *No cure, no pay* mere juxtaposition suffices to enforce a conditional reading.

On the other hand, the occurrence of syntactic markers of conditionality is not a sufficient reason for conditionality either. A sentence like *I paid you back, if you remember* is generally considered not to be a real conditional sentence; for here the speaker is committed to asserting the consequent outright—not *if* something else is so.

The question as to the various means by which native speakers express conditionals is of considerable interest not only to the descriptive, but also to the historical studies of conditionals. In the latter tradition the main objective is to gain insight into the processes by which conditionals come to be expressed in new ways and how they come to express new functions. Traugott (1985) suggests the following set of nonconditional sources of conditional markers: (a) modals of possibility, doubt, and wish; (b) interrogatives; (c) copulas, typically of the existential kind; (d) topic markers and demonstratives; and (e) temporals. How could the change from any of these sources to conditionals take place? As already indicated above, the antecedent of a conditional raises the possibility of some alternative situation, which is subsequently treated as a conditional constraint on the consequent. It seems plausible that such alternative situations were originally indicated by the diacritics listed above, which then came to be the conventional means for expressing the fact that a conditional constraint was posited.

2. Truth Conditional Semantics

In the logical-philosophical tradition the problem of conditionals is addressed by abstracting away from the way conditionals are expressed in everyday language. Here the aim is to give a systematic account of their logical properties.

2.1 Material Implication

The oldest theory of conditionals states that *if . . . then* is just the so-called material implication. According to this theory, first proposed by the Megarian Philo (fourth century BC), a conditional sentence is true if and only if its antecedent is false or its consequent is true:

> *If p then q* is true if and only if *p* is false or *q* is true. (3)

In introductory logic courses this truth condition is usually motivated by pointing out that classical logic leaves one with no alternative. Given that the language of classical logic is truth-functional, and that within this framework every sentence has exactly one of the truth values 'true' and 'false,' there is just no room for *if . . . then* to mean anything else than (3) says.

This motivation will only appeal to those who, for some reason or other, believe that classical logic is the only correct logic. Others might prefer the conclusion that natural language conditionals cannot properly be analyzed within the framework of classical logic. There are strong arguments in favor of this position. For example, within classical logic the propositions $\neg(p \rightarrow q)$ and $(p \wedge \neg q)$ are equivalent. But the following two sentences clearly are not:

> It is not true that if you study hard, you will pass your exam. (4)

> You will study hard, and you will not pass your exam. (5)

Sentence (4) does not say that it is in fact the case that the antecedent of the conditional is true and its conse-

quent false (as (5) wants to have it), but at best that this is possibly so.

2.2 Strict Implication

Examples like the above naturally lead to the idea that the *if . . . then* of natural language is a strict implication rather than the material one. The example suggests that a conditional sentence is false if it is *possible* for its antecedent to be true while its consequent is false. By adding to this that it is true otherwise one gets:

> *If p then q* is true iff it is necessarily so that *p* is false or *q* is true. (6)

Restated in the language of possible worlds semantics (see *Intension*), this becomes (7):

> *If p then q* is true if *q* is true in every possible world in which *p* is true. (7)

There are various ways to make this truth definition more precise, depending on how one interprets 'possible.' But whatever interpretation one prefers—logically possible, or physically possible, or whatever else—difficulties arise. The theory of strict implication runs into similar problems as the theory of material implication by validating patterns of inference of which it is not immediately evident that they accord with the actual use of conditionals. One such pattern is the principle of 'strengthening the antecedent.' As a counterexample against the latter, one could suggest that from (8):

> If I put sugar in my coffee, it will taste better. (8)

it does not follow that (9):

> If I put sugar and diesel oil in my coffee, it will taste better. (9)

An analysis of this example along the lines suggested by (7) yields, however, that this argument is valid. Hence (7) calls for refinement.

2.3 Variable Strict Implication

The next truth condition was first proposed in the late 1960s by Robert Stalnaker (10):

> *If p then q* is true if *q* is true in every possible world in which (i) *p* is true, and which (ii) otherwise differs minimally from the actual world. (10)

It is easy to see how this amendment to (7) blocks the inference from *If p, then r* to *If p and q, then r*. Consider the set *S* of worlds in which (i) *p* is true and which (ii) in other respects differ minimally from the actual world. It could very well be that *q* is false in all these worlds. If so, the set *T* of worlds in which (i) both *p* and *q* are true, but which (ii) in other respects differ minimally from the actual world will not be a subset of *S*. So, *r* could be true in every world in *S*, but false in some of the worlds in *T*.

Definition (10) is the heart of what is the most

popular theory of conditionals. But it is not generally accepted. Not impressed by the examples cited above (which are due to Stalnaker), many logicians still believe that at least indicative conditionals can be properly interpreted as material or as strict implications. For example, a defender of the idea that indicative conditionals are strict implications will argue that the oddity of the diesel oil example is easy to explain away using Grice's theory of conversation. (Roughly: It is a conversational implicature of the conclusion that the coffee may well contain diesel oil. But given this possibility, the premise is false. Hence, the argument in question is pragmatically unsound.) And not only pragmatic arguments are invoked; people resort to syntactic arguments, too. For instance, a defender of the material implication might argue that negations of whole conditional statements, being rare in English, have an idiosyncratic interpretation: it is not a real negation, but something weaker than that. Therefore, it is wrong to translate (1) with a formula of the form $\neg (p \to q)$.

3. Other Approaches

It is typical for the field of conditional logic that there is no consensus as to what form a semantic theory should take. The theories mentioned so far all supply truth conditions, and, according to the majority of logicians, who take the classical standard of logical validity—preservation of truth—as the starting point of their investigations, that is what a semantic theory should do. But according to the relevance logicians (see Anderson and Belnap 1975) truth preservation is at best a necessary condition for the logical validity of an argument, but it is by no means sufficient. The premises of the argument must in addition be relevant to the conclusion. According to Adams (1975) the proper explanation of validity is to be given in terms of probability rather than truth.

The epistemic turn in semantics during the early 1990s has given rise to yet another notion of validity. On the dynamic view, knowing the meaning of a sentence is knowing the change it brings about in the information state of anyone who wants to incorporate the news conveyed by it. What matters is not so much what a sentence says about the world, but how it affects the information an agent has about the world. Accordingly, attention has shifted from 'truth' simpliciter to 'truth on the basis of the information available.'

As for conditionals, the main advantage of this approach is that more justice can be done to their highly context-dependent nature. They express constraints on how information states can grow. By accepting an indicative conditional *If p, then q*, the possibility is excluded that one's information state may develop into a state in which *p* is true on the basis of the available information but *q* is false. Unlike purely descriptive sentences indicative conditionals are not 'stable' under growth of information: *If p, then q* may be false on the basis of limited information (simply because it is not yet possible to rule out the possibility that *p* will turn out true while *q* will turn out false), and become true when more information comes at hand. Many of the logical peculiarities of conditional sentences are directly related to this instability.

See also: Counterfactuals.

Bibliography

Adams E 1975 *The Logic of Conditionals*. Reidel, Dordrecht
Anderson A R, Belnap N D 1975 *Entailment*. Princeton University Press, Princeton, NJ
Edgington D 1995 On Conditionals. *Mind* 104: 235–329
Harper W L, Stalnaker R, Pearce, G (eds.) 1981 *IFS: Conditionals, Belief, Decision, Chance, and Time*. Reidel, Dordrecht
Stalnaker R 1968 A theory of conditionals. In: *Studies in Logical Theory, American Philosophical Quarterly*. Monograph Series, 2. Basil Blackwell, Oxford
Traugott E C 1985 Conditional markers. In: Haiman J (ed.) *Iconicity in Syntax*. Benjamins, Amsterdam
Traugott E C, Meulen A T, Reilly J, Ferguson C (eds.) 1986 *On Conditionals*. Cambridge University Press, Cambridge

Counterfactuals

F. Veltman

Like most proverbs, the proverb 'If ifs and ans were pots and pans, there would be no need for tinkers,' suggests a moral. Surely, when some practical decisions have to be made here and now, there is no use in pondering how beautiful things would have been if only this or that had been the case. Still, the proverb does not do justice to our otherwise rather complicated relation to the past. Sometimes it *is* appropriate to utter a sentence of the form *If it had been the case that .... then it would have been the case that* ..., Could a decision ever be regretted if one had no reason to believe that it would indeed have made a difference if it had been decided otherwise? And would it ever be justified to call someone to account for his deeds, if everything would be exactly the same as it is now no matter what had been done by whom? Clearly, one does often reason about unactualized possibilities, thereby employing so-called counterfactual conditionals:

> If she had asked me, I would have danced with her. (1)

Counterfactuals are typically uttered in contexts where the antecedent is known to be false. Therefore, unlike indicative conditionals, they cannot possibly be analyzed as material implications. Material implications with a false antecedent are true no matter what the truth value of the consequent is. But one does not want to be forced to call both sentences (1) and (2) true:

> If she had asked me, I would not have danced (2)
> with her.

1. The Metalinguistic Approach

Taken at face value, counterfactuals refer to unactualized possibilities—a kind of entities that philosophers, in particular those standing in the empiricist tradition, look upon with suspicion. Accordingly, several attempts have been made to show that counterfactuals are only apparently about unactualized possibilities, and to give a logical analysis of their meaning in which no recourse to such entities is made. The *locus classicus* here is Goodman 1947. On Goodman's account a counterfactual *If A had been the case, C would have been the case* can best be thought of as a metalinguistic statement expressing that the antecedent A together with some suitable further premises $B1, \ldots, Bn$, logically implies the consequent C.

Which further premises $B1, \ldots, B$ are suitable to be used with a given antecedent? Obvious candidates to consider are sentences that express causal connections or other lawlike relationships between matters spoken of in the antecedent and matters spoken of in the consequent. We believe that John would have fallen to the ground, if he had jumped out of the window, and we appeal to a very simple form of the laws of motion to prove our point.

Natural laws are not the only further premises one needs. There are no natural laws establishing a connection between the antecedent and consequent of the next sentence:

> If I had looked in my wallet, I would have (3)
> found a penny.

This statement may very well be true just because there happened to be a penny in my wallet at the occasion I am referring to. Hence, in addition to natural laws also accidental truths have to be allowed as further premises.

The obvious next question is which accidental truths can serve as further premises and which cannot. Not everything goes. For one thing, we wouldn't want to allow the negation of the antecedent as a further premise even though the antecedent, together with its negation, implies the consequent. But where do we have to draw the line? The only natural answer to this question seems to be this: those accidental truths B for which the sentence *If A had been the case, B still would have been the case* is true. But as Goodman acknowledged, this answer turns the analysis into a circular one.

2. Minimal Change Theories

In 1968 Robert Stalnaker proposed an account of counterfactuals in which no attempt was made to explain away the reference to unactualized possibilities. Starting point for his analysis was a test for evaluating the acceptability of conditionals originally devised by Frank Ramsey. It can be summed up as follows:

> First, hypothetically, make the minimal revision of your stock of beliefs required to assume the antecedent. Then, evaluate the acceptability of the consequent on the basis of this revised body of beliefs.

Ramsey's original suggestion only covered the case in which the antecedent is consistent with the agent's stock of beliefs. In that case, which is typical of indicative conditionals, no adjustments are required. Following an idea of Rescher 1964, Stalnaker generalizes this to the case in which the antecedent cannot simply be added to the agent's stock of beliefs without introducing a contradiction. In this case, which is typical of counterfactuals, adjustments are required.

In effect what Stalnaker does is reconstruct the above belief conditions as truth conditions. He thinks that truth may not be allowed to depend on beliefs, that you have to appeal to the facts. So, in his rebuilt version the *actual world* plays the role that the agent's stock of beliefs plays in Ramsey's. And the minimal revision of the agent's stock of beliefs required to assume the antecedent is taken up as that possible world at which, (a) the antecedent is true and which (b) in all other respects differs minimally from the actual world.

This proposal raises an immediate question: Which of the conceivably many possible worlds at which the antecedent is true will be the world most similar to the actual world? According to Stalnaker, this is in essence a pragmatic question which has little to do with the semantic problem he is concerned with. He is ready to admit that contextual features may make a difference to the particular world which has the property concerned. But how these contextual features make that difference is less important, the only thing that matters is that there is an outcome.

Note that Stalnaker assumes that there will always

be one unique antecedent world most resembling the actual world. But can we really be sure of this? Will there always be, for any antecedent A at most one A-world most resembling the actual world? Couldn't there be cases where we have several such A-worlds, all equally close to the actual world and all closer to the actual world than any other world? In Lewis 1973 the following examples are given to show that such cases really do exist:

If Bizet and Verdi had been compatriots, Bizet (4) would have been Italian.

If Bizet and Verdi had been compatriots, Verdi (5) would have been French.

Because of the uniqueness assumption, Stalnaker's theory does not admit a situation in which both (4) and (5) are false while (6) is true:

If Bizet and Verdi had been compatriots, either (6) Verdi would have been French or Bizet would have been Italian.

According to Lewis one can accept (6) without having to accept (4) or (5), and so he rejects the uniqueness assumption. There are more variants of Stalnaker's theory on the market. They differ from each other mainly in assigning slightly different properties to the underlying comparative similarity relation of worlds, thus giving rise to slightly different conditional logics.

In Tichy 1976 an objection is raised against Stalnaker's theory which applies to other versions of the 'minimal change' paradigm as well. The argument runs as follows: 'Consider a man—call him Jones—who is possessed of the following dispositions as regards wearing his hat. Bad weather invariably induces him to wear a hat. Fine weather on the other hand, affects him neither way: on fine days he puts his hat on or leaves it on the peg, completely at random. Suppose moreover that actually the weather is bad,

so Jones is wearing his hat . . .' What is the truth value of the following counterfactual?:

If the weather were fine, Jones would be (7) wearing his hat.

Intuitively, this sentence is false—if the weather were fine, Jones might very well not be wearing his hat. But according to the theories mentioned above it is true. After all, it would seem that worlds where Jones keeps his hat on are at least in one respect more like the actual world than worlds were he takes it off.

The advocates of the minimal change approach are of course not ready to admit this. According to them the example shows at best that not all characteristics of the actual world are relevant in assessing which worlds resemble it more than which other worlds. The obvious next question—which characteristics are relevant and which are not?—is usually delegated to pragmatics.

See also: Conditionals.

Bibliography

Edgington D 1995 On Conditionals. *Mind* 104: 235–329
Goodman N 1946 The problem of counterfactual conditionals. *Journal of Philosophy* 44: 113–28
Harper W L, Stalnaker R, Pearce G (eds.) 1981 *IFS Conditionals, Belief, Decision, Chance, and Time*. Reidel, Dordrecht
Lewis D 1973 *Counterfactuals*. Basil Blackwell, Oxford
Ramsey F P 1931 General propositions and causality. In: Ramsey F P *Foundations: Essays in Philosophy, Logic, Mathematics and Economics*. Routledge and Kegan Paul, London
Rescher N 1964 *Hypothetical Reasoning*. North-Holland, Amsterdam
Stalnaker R 1968 A theory of conditionals. In: *Studies in Logical Theory, American Philosophical Quarterly*. Monograph Series, No. 2. Basil Blackwell, Oxford
Tichy P 1976 A counterexample to the Stalnaker–Lewis analysis of counterfactuals. *Philosophical Studies* 29: 271–73

Deviant Logics

S. Haack

'Logic' is not so well-defined a term, nor logic so tidy or static a discipline, as the popular conception of the logician as a paradigmatically convergent thinker minding his ps and qs might lead one to suppose. In the context of this article, 'logic' will be used in quite a narrow sense: to refer only to *deductive logic* (not

to inductive logic or other considerations of a more methodological stripe) and only to *formal* logic (not to theories of truth or reference or analyses of the proposition or other considerations of a more philosophical stripe). Even within logic thus narrowly conceived, however, a profusion of formal deductive systems has grown up, with the hegemony of 'classical' or 'standard' systems challenged by a variety of 'non-classical' or 'nonstandard' logics.

1. Scope and Background

'Classical logic' refers, not, as 'classical' might suggest, to Aristotelian syllogistic logic, but to a class of systems of modern deductive logic: two-valued propositional calculus and first-order predicate calculus with identity. There are many different formulations of classical logic; the term refers, not to a particular set of axioms and/or rules of inference expressed in terms of a particular primitive vocabulary and represented in a particular notation, but to a class of equivalent systems: those which, differences of notation, primitive vocabulary, axioms and/or rules aside, license a certain set of theorems and inferences. Systems which license different theorems and/or inferences are 'nonclassical' or 'nonstandard.'

The convenient dichotomy of 'classical' versus 'non-classical' logics should not be allowed to suggest too simple a historical picture. Though many nonstandard systems were developed, after the 'classical' logical apparatus had been formulated, by logicians who believed that that apparatus was inadequate or incorrect, the ideas motivating what are now called 'nonclassical' logics have a long history. Some of the key ideas that were to motivate modal and many-valued logics, for example, were explored by Aristotle. And nonstandard systems developed alongside the formulation of the now standard apparatus: in 1908, two years before the publication of Russell and Whitehead's *Principia Mathematica*, Hugh MacColl was recalling in the pages of *Mind* that for nearly thirty years he had been arguing the inadequacy of (what is now called) material implication, and, besides offering a definition of (what is now called) strict implication, arguing the merits of a 'logic of three dimensions'; in 1909 C. S. Peirce, recognized as a pioneer of quantification theory and the logic of relations, and the originator of truth-table semantics, gave truth-tables for a 'triadic' logic which, he claimed, is 'universally true.' What is known as 'classical logic' is simply that class of systems which emerged as the dominant, standard approach.

Its critics see classical logic as inadequate, as failing to license theorems or inferences which ought to be licensed, or as incorrect, as licensing theorems or inferences which ought not to be licensed—or, sometimes, as defective in both these ways. Correspondingly, nonstandard systems may extend classical logic, by adding new vocabulary and licensing additional theorems and/or inferences essentially involving that vocabulary ('extended logics'), or restrict it, by repudiating classical theorems and/or inferences ('deviant logics'), or both. This distinction is however somewhat rough and ready, because the apparently simple contrast between adding new theorems or inferences and repudiating old ones turns out (Sect. 4 below) to be less straightforward than it may appear.

There are many different nonstandard logics: modal logic, epistemic logic, tense logic, many-valued logic, intuitionist logic, relevance logic, quantum logic, free logic, fuzzy logic, etc. In fact there are many different non-standard systems within each of these categories: a multiplicity of modal logics, many many-valued logics, rival relevance logics, more than one family of fuzzy logic, etc. And the plethora of motivations offered for this plurality of nonstandard systems resists any simple classification, for different systems are offered for the same purpose, and the same system is put to different purposes. Comprehensiveness is obviously impossible; in what follows, therefore, after a preliminary survey focusing primarily on deviant systems, the emphasis will be on those challenges to the correctness of classical logic which arise in one way or another from considerations of language.

2. Survey and Glossary

2.1 Modal, etc., Logics

C. I. Lewis, the originator of modern modal systems, was primarily concerned to correct what he saw as the unacceptable weakness of the classical notion of implication. It is now more usual for modal logics to be presented simply as extending classical logic by adjoining the operators 'L' or '□,' meaning 'necessarily,' 'M' or '◇,' meaning 'possibly' (and definable as 'not necessarily not'), and '-ɜ,' representing strict implication (defined as necessity of material implication); and as licensing new, nonclassical theorems and inferences essentially involving this modal vocabulary.

Closely modeled after modal logics are epistemic logics (which introduce 'Kap,' meaning 'a knows that p,' and 'Bap,' meaning 'a believes that p'); deontic logics (which introduce 'Op,' meaning 'it is obligatory that p' and 'Pp,' meaning 'it is permitted that p'); and tense logics (which, first, construe the sentence letters of classical propositional calculus, not, as they are ordinarily construed, as tenseless, but as present-tensed, and then introduce 'Pp,' meaning 'it was the case that p,' and 'Fp,' meaning 'it will be the case that p').

2.2 Many-valued Logics

Classical propositional calculus has a two-valued characteristic matrix, i.e., truth-tables can be given in terms of the two truth-values 'true' and 'false' such that all and only the theorems of classical propositional calculus uniformly take the value 'true,' and all and only the inferences valid in classical propositional calculus are invariably truth-preserving, on those truth-tables. 'Many-valued logic' refers to propositional calculi matrices which require three or more values; in these systems some classical principles fail.

Among the best-known many-valued logics are Łukasiewicz's, Post's, Bochvar's, and Kleene's.

In Łukasiewicz's 3-valued logic (motivated by the idea, already suggested by Aristotle in *de Interpretatione* ix, that future contingent sentences are neither true nor false but 'indeterminate') both the Law of the Excluded Middle ('LEM'; 'p or not p') and the Law of Non-Contradiction ('LNC'; 'not both p and not-p') fail, taking the intermediate value when 'p' does. But the Principle of Identity ('if p then p') holds, since the matrices assign 'true' to a conditional when both antecedent and consequent are assigned 'intermediate.' Generalization yields 4- and more-valued logics.

Post (motivated by the mathematical interest of generalizing the method of truth-tables) developed a class of many-valued systems notable for an unusual, cyclic negation: in the 3-valued case, the negation of a true sentence is assigned the intermediate value, the negation of an intermediate sentence, 'false,' and the negation of a false sentence, 'true.' LEM, LNC and the Principle of Identity all fail.

Bochvar (motivated by the idea that semantic paradoxes such as the liar—'This sentence is false'—can be resolved by acknowledging that such sentences are neither true nor false) developed a 3-valued logic in which any sentence compounded by means of his 'primary' connectives of which any component is assigned 'paradoxical,' is itself assigned 'paradoxical'. Hence no classical theorems, expressed in terms of the primary connectives, are uniformly assigned 'true.' Bochvar also introduces an assertion operator, read 'it is true that,' which leaves a true sentence true and a false sentence false, but makes a paradoxical sentence false; and the classical theorems are restored in terms of 'secondary' or 'external' connectives, defined via the primary connectives and the assertion operator, which are 2-valued.

In Kleene's 3-valued system (in which the third value is to be read either 'undefined' or 'unknown, value immaterial') the matrices of the 'weak' connectives are like those for Bochvar's primary connectives. The matrices for Kleene's 'strong' connectives are constructed on the principle that a compound sentence with an undefined or unknown component or components should be assigned 'true' ['false'] just in case the assignments to the other components would be sufficient to determine the compound as true [false], whether the undefined or unknown component were true *or* false. So not only LEM and LNC, but also the Principle of Identity, fail; for 'if p then q' is assigned '*u*' if both 'p' and 'q' are assigned '*u*,' so 'if p then p' takes '*u*' when 'p' does.

2.3 Fuzzy Logic

In Zadeh's deviant set theory, intended to represent the extensions of vague as well as precise predicates, membership comes in degrees, the degree of membership of an object in a fuzzy set being represented by some real number between 0 and 1. 'Fuzzy logic' sometimes refers to the family of indenumerably-many-valued systems that results from using fuzzy set theory in a semantic characterization in which sentence connectives are associated in the usual way with set-theoretical operations (negation with complementation, implication with inclusion, etc.), but sentence letters can take any of the indenumerably many values of the interval [0,1]. But Zadeh himself reserves the term 'fuzzy logic' for the result of a second stage of 'fuzzification,' motivated by the idea that the metalinguistic predicates 'true' and 'false' are themselves vague. In this sense, 'fuzzy logic' refers to a family of systems in which the indenumerably many values of the base logic (Zadeh favors the indenumerably-many-valued extension of Łukasiewicz's 3-valued logic) are superseded by denumerably many fuzzy truth-values, fuzzy sub-sets of the set of values of the base logic, characterized linguistically as '*true, false, not true, very true, not very true, ...*,' etc. In fuzzy logic, according to Zadeh, such traditional concerns as axiomatization, proof procedures, etc., are 'peripheral'; for fuzzy logic is, he suggests, not just a logic of fuzzy concepts, but a logic which is itself fuzzy (for a further discussion, see Sect. 3.2 below).

2.4 Quantum Logic

It has sometimes been thought that certain peculiarities—'causal anomalies' in Reichenbach's phrase—of quantum mechanics can be accommodated only by a restriction of the logical apparatus representing quantum mechanical reasoning. The 'quantum logic' proposed by Reichenbach is Łukasiewicz's 3-valued system extended by new forms of negation, implication, and equivalence, and Destouches-Février's is also many-valued; but 'quantum logic' more often refers to the nontruth-functional system of Birkhoff and von Neumann, in which LEM and LNC hold, but the Distributive Laws (the principles that from '(A or B) and (A or C)' one may infer 'A or (B and C),' and from '(A or B) and C' one may infer '(A and C) or (B and C)') fail.

2.5 Intuitionist Logic

Intuitionism is a school in the philosophy of mathematics founded by L. E. J. Brouwer, who held that mathematical entities are mental constructions, and that logic is secondary to mathematics. These ideas motivate, first, a restricted mathematics in which nonconstructive existence proofs are not permitted, and, second, a restricted logic in which neither LEM nor the Principle of Double Negation ('DN'; 'if not-not-p then p') hold. There are rival systems of intuitionist logic, the best-known being Heyting's; others are more restricted yet.

2.6 *Relevance Logic (also called 'Relevant Logic')*

According to the classical conception an argument is valid just in case it is impossible for its premises to be true and its conclusion false; relevance logicians (Parry, Anderson, Belnap, Routley, etc.) hold that this is too weak, that it is also required that the premises be relevant to the conclusion. There are rival systems of relevance logic, the best known being Anderson and Belnap's system, R, the system of 'relevant implication,' and E, the combination of R with the modal system S4 to represent entailment. Relevance logics extend but also restrict classical logic; in virtue of their stronger conception of validity Anderson and Belnap disallow the classical principle of inference, *modus ponens* ('MPP'; from 'if A then B' and 'A' to infer 'B') for material implication.

2.7 *Paraconsistent Logic*

As a limit case, the classical conception admits as valid arguments the conclusions of which are necessarily true, and arguments the premises of which are necessarily false. In classical logic, therefore, anything whatever follows from a contradiction. In R and some other relevance logics, however, the principle *ex contradictione quodlibet* no longer holds. A system which can tolerate inconsistency without trivialization is a 'paraconsistent logic.' Paraconsistent systems, anticipated by Vasiliev and by Jaśkowski, have been developed both within (e.g., by Routley) and without (e.g., by da Costa) the concern for relevance as a necessary condition for validity.

'Dialethic' logics are paraconsistent in a stronger sense; they not only deny that everything whatever follows from a contradiction, but also allow that contradictions are sometimes true. It is argued by Priest, for example, that dialethism is the appropriate response to the semantic paradoxes: the liar sentence is both true and false.

2.8 *Free Logic*

'Free logic,' so-called because its motivation is the idea that logic should be free of ontological commitments, usually deviates from classical logic only at the level of predicate calculus. Classical predicate calculus is not valid for the empty domain, since the theorem '(∃x) (Fx v -Fx)'—'there is something which either is or is not F'—implies that something exists; nor, in virtue of the rule of existential generalization (from 'Fa' to infer '(∃x) Fx') is it valid for non-referring terms. The first system of predicate logic valid in the empty domain was developed by Jaśkowski; the first system also to restrict the rule of existential generalization (to: from 'Fa, a exists' to infer '(∃x) Fx') by Leonard. Van Fraassen's 'presuppositional languages' are intended to supply a propositional basis for a free predicate calculus which is as it were quasi-classical; the 'supervaluational' semantics allow truth-value gaps, but, since they assign 'true' to any compound sentence to which all classical valuations would assign 'true,' exactly the classical theorems and inferences are sustained.

2.9 *Meinongian Logic*

Free logics restrict classical predicate calculus in the interests of ontological neutrality; a development of the 1980s is 'Meinongian logic,' which extends classical predicate calculus in the interests of ontological tolerance. The idea is that (as in the 'theory of Objects' proposed by Alexius Meinong) the domain is to include not only actual, existent objects, but also nonexistent and even impossible objects (the golden mountain, the round square). Meinongianism may (Routley) but need not (Parsons) be combined with paraconsistency.

3. Challenges to Classical Logic from Considerations of Language

Deviant logics have been developed sometimes out of purely formal interest; sometimes in anticipation of practical application in, especially, computing; sometimes prompted by considerations from metaphysics, philosophy of science or philosophy of mathematics; sometimes by considerations internal to the philosophy of logic; but frequently classical logic has been thought to stand in need of revision in order to accommodate such specifically linguistic phenomena as vagueness, reference failure, or semantic paradox.

3.1 *Regimentalism versus Naturalism in Logic*

Classical logic has the elegance of simplicity: a simplicity achieved in part by a high degree of abstraction and schematization relative to the complexities of natural languages. Regimentalists, as one might call them, such as Frege, Tarski, or Quine, hold that, from the point of view of the rigorous representation of what is valid in the way of argument, natural languages are not only unnecessarily complex but also in various ways defective, prone to ambiguity, vagueness, etc. Formal languages should be austere and simple, and must avoid such defects. Regimentalists tend to be hostile to proposals to revise logic so as to accommodate it better to natural language, preferring, when they cannot rule the unwelcome aspects of natural language outside the scope of logic, to impose a sometimes Procrustean regimentation to bring them within the classical apparatus. By contrast, Naturalists, as it seems appropriate to call the other party, think that formal logic should aspire to mirror the subtleties of natural languages, and tend to be more sympathetic to such proposals.

3.2 *Vagueness*

Frege and Russell deplored the vagueness of natural languages. When Peirce protested that '[l]ogicians

259

have been at fault in giving vagueness the go-by' he had in mind primarily indefiniteness in the sense in which an existential quantification ('a man', 'some animal') is indefinite, construing predicate vagueness as implicit quantification ('is bald in some sense of the term').

Those contemporary logicians who urge the merits of a nonstandard logic of vagueness are apt to have specifically in mind that in the presence of vagueness there will be borderline cases, cases where it is indeterminate whether or not a vague predicate such as 'short,' 'red,' 'bald,' 'pretty,' applies. When vague predicates are applied to borderline cases, the thought is, the result is a sentence which is neither true nor false, and this constitutes a challenge to classical, bivalent, logic.

The simple proposal that vague sentences be accommodated by a 3-valued system in which they take the third value, however, faces the difficulty that, though it no longer requires a sharp line to be drawn between cases in which a vague sentence is straightforwardly true and cases in which it is straightforwardly false, it still requires a sharp line to be drawn between cases in which the application of a vague predicate is borderline, and cases in which it is not. And this seems not so much to solve as to shift the problem.

With fuzzy logic the situation is much more complex, but not much more encouraging. The assumption here is that the meta-linguistic predicates 'true' and 'false' are themselves vague. Zadeh's linguistic evidence for this claim is questionable at best: 'very true,' surely, means 'true and important,' rather than 'true to a high degree'; and 'not very true' and 'rather true' are arguably not proper locutions at all. And in any case, despite Zadeh's suggestion that fuzzy logic is itself vague, in fact his approach requires an artificial imposition of precision more striking even than a 3-valued approach. Consider, for example, Zadeh's definition of '*true*':

$$true = \mathrm{df.}\; 0.3/0.6 + 0.5/0.7 + 0.7/0.8 + 0.9/0.9 + 1/1$$

i.e., as the fuzzy set to which degree of truth 0.6 belongs to degree 0.3, 0.7 to degree 0.5,..., 0.9 to degree 0.9, and 1 to degree 1; or his definition of '*very true*' as '*true²*.'

Since ruling vague sentences beyond the scope of logic may seem a little high-handed, and proposing that all vague discourse be 'precisified' before formalization may seem a little optimistic, there is something to recommend the 'supertruth' approach (Meehlberg, Przełecki, D. K. Lewis, Fine), which accommodates the phenomenon of vagueness within a classical framework, and arguably with less artificial precision than deviant logics of vagueness. This approach is motivated partly by the phenomenon of 'penumbral connection,' i.e., the fact that, despite their indefiniteness, there are logical relations among vague predicates: such as, that nothing can be both

red and orange at once. The suggestion is, roughly, that a vague sentence is to count as true if it would be true for all ways of making it precise. The 'supertruth' approach (which has an obvious affinity with the method of supervaluations) conceives of the truth-conditions of vague predicates as quasi-classical; and though it proposes a non-classical semantics it calls for no revision of the theorems or inferences of classical logic, since the principle that a vague sentence count as true if it would be true no matter how it was made precise preserves the classical tautologies even in instances involving vague predicates, such as 'Either Harry is bald or he isn't,' or 'If this patch is red, it is red.'

See: Vagueness.

3.3 Reference Failure, Fictional Discourse, etc.

Another challenge to classical logic derives from the phenomenon of reference failure, i.e., of sentences containing proper names (such as 'Mr Pickwick' or 'Odysseus') or definite descriptions (such as 'the present king of France' or 'the greatest prime number') which have no referent. Indeed, an argument to the effect that sentences containing proper names or definite descriptions presupposes that those names or descriptions refer, and thus, if there is failure of reference, are neither true nor false, is to be found in Frege.

Frege himself, however, regarded the phenomenon of reference failure much as he regarded ambiguity or vagueness, as a defect of natural languages to be extirpated from any acceptable formal language. His proposal was that a referent simply be arbitrarily supplied for any well-formed expression that would otherwise lack reference, and thus to preserve a bivalent logic.

It is now more usual for reference failure to be accommodated classically by means of Russell's Theory of Descriptions. 'The F exists' (e.g., 'the greatest prime number exists') is contextually defined as 'there is exactly one thing which is F' (e.g., 'there is exactly one thing which is prime and greater than any other prime'); 'the F is G' (e.g., 'the greatest prime number is odd') is defined as 'there is exactly one thing which is F, and whatever is F is G' (e.g., 'there is exactly one thing which is prime and greater than any other prime, and whatever is prime and greater than any other prime is odd'). 'The F is G,' on this account, does not presuppose, but entails, that the F exists, and is not truth-valueless, but false, if there is no, or no unique, F. Since Russell, like Frege, takes an ordinary proper name to be equivalent to a co-referential definite description, this also accommodates all cases of reference failure within a bivalent framework.

Skeptical, in any case, of the distinction between sense and reference ('*Sinn*' versus '*Bedeutung*') in the context of which Frege's account was set, Russell regarded Frege's approach as unacceptably artificial. The other foil to his theory of descriptions was Meinong's 'theory of Objects'—which Russell regarded as lacking that 'robust sense of reality' no less essential to a logician than to a zoologist. The capital letter in 'theory of Objects' signals that the word is used in a technical sense; the theory is about the *objects of thought*. According to Meinong some but not all Objects have Being—they either exist or, in the case of abstract Objects, subsist. But Objects *as such* are 'beyond being and notbeing'; that is, it is possible to think about something, and say true things about it, even if there is no such thing. 'The golden mountain is golden' and even 'the round square is round,' according to Meinong, are not false (as Russell would have it), or truth-valueless (as Frege's discussion might suggest), but true.

Some deviant logicians have been attracted by Frege's presupposition theory, others by Meinong's theory of Objects. The first party urges the merits of a nonbivalent logic in which the relation of presupposition may be formally represented. Smiley uses Bochvar's 3-valued logic for this purpose; Woodruff prefers Kleene's strong matrices. (Van Fraassen suggests remaining classical syntactically while adopting his nonbivalent presuppositional semantics.) The other party sympathizes with Meinong's objection that the Russellian approach betrays a 'prejudice in favor of the actual.' What the classical logician, and even the 3-valued presupposition theorist, sees as reference *failure*, the Meinongian logician construes as reference to an object which happens not to be real.

Even those who, reasonably enough, are alarmed by talk of unreal objects and the impossible inhabitants of impossible possible worlds, however, may have some sympathy with the thought that it may be inappropriate to treat fictional discourse, or discourse about propositional attitudes, on a par with those cases of reference failure which result from mistake or inadvertence, as alike defective.

This intuition might however be accommodated by other routes, requiring recourse neither to Meinongianism nor to any other nonstandard 'logic of fiction' (Woods', for example, analogous to a modal system, in which the operator 'O' is read 'Once upon a time ...'). The first step is to distinguish discourse *in* fiction from discourse *about* fiction. The latter can be acknowledged as straightforwardly true or false if construed as implicitly preceded by 'It says in the story that ....' The former may be best regarded not as unsuccessful fact-stating discourse, but simply as not making assertions at all. This would put fictional discourse, in the sense of 'discourse *in* fiction,' no longer in need of non-standard logical treatment, because ruled, with good reason, outside the scope of logic altogether.

Discourse about propositional attitudes, which may also involve nondenoting terms (as: 'The Vikings believed that Thor made thunder when he was angry,' 'Meinong believed that the round square was round

as well as square') obviously cannot be plausibly claimed not to be *bona fide* assertion-making discourse; and it must be conceded that a Russellian treatment leaves something to be desired. Such discourse may however be accommodated without the alarming ontological commitments of Meinongianism by adopting Burdick's construal of belief, etc., not as of some peculiar nonextensional object, but as of the ordered pair of an ordinary object and a predicate representing a 'mode of presentation.' In this treatment, beliefs, as we say, about nonexistent objects are construed as beliefs of the null set under a certain description ('The Vikings believed of ⟨Λ, "God of war"⟩ that he made thunder when angry'). Though it requires ascent to the formal mode in the introduction of modes of presentation, this maneuver maintains extensionality and avoids Meinongian ontological extravagance.

3.4 Semantic Paradox

If the liar sentence, 'This sentence is false' is true, what it says is the case, so it is false; while if it is false, since that is what it says, it is true. The classical, regimentalist line, paradigmatically represented by Tarski, is, maintaining the assumption that every legitimate declarative sentence is either true or else false, to draw the conclusion that the liar sentence is illegitimate. Semantically closed languages, therefore, which contain the means to refer to their own sentences and to predicate truth or falsity of them, are eschewed; in a well-behaved formal semantics the truth-predicate is deemed systematically ambiguous, with 'true-in-the-object-language' construed as a predicate in the °meta-language, 'true-in-the-meta-language' as a predicate of the meta-meta-language, etc. 'This sentence is false,' *simpliciter*, is not legitimate; 'this sentence is false-in-O' is a sentence of M, and not paradoxical. And Tarski's 'T-schema':

S is true if and only if p

where the expression on the left names a sentence, and the expression on the right is that sentence itself, can be sustained, relativized to a language ('S is true-in-O iff p').

Others, however, draw the conclusion that it is not the semantic closure of natural languages but bivalence that is at fault. This motivated Bochvar's 3-valued logic. It also motivates Kripke's diagnosis, and his resort to Kleene's 3-valued logic. According to Kripke, the truth-predicate is univocal, but only partially defined, undefined, in particular, for 'ungrounded' sentences like 'this sentence is true' and 'this sentence is false.' But repudiation of bivalence avoids the liar but not the strengthened liar: if the sentence 'this sentence is either false or truth-valueless' (or, 'this sentence is not true') is true, it is either false or truth-valueless; if it is false or truth-valueless, it is true. Kripke can, indeed, avoid the strengthened liar by ruling, consonant with his account of groundedness, that the predicate 'truth-valueless' belongs not to the object- but to the meta-language; but this is undeniably disappointing, given that the idea was to avoid the artificiality of the Tarskian hierarchy of languages.

The solution proposed by 'dialethic' logicians, that the Liar should be acknowledged to be *both true and false*, since no disastrous consequences need follow in a paraconsistent logic, may provoke outrage rather than disappointment. Dialethists see the semantic paradoxes, as Tarski did, as indicating the inconsistency of natural languages; but here intuition favors the Tarskian, Regimentalist response—'so much the worse for natural languages!'—over the dialethist's hospitality to contradictions.

4. A Challenge to Deviant Logic from Considerations of Language: The 'Meaning-Variance' Argument

The argument, due to Quine, is this: the deviant logician proposes a system in which some classical principles ostensibly fail; trying to 'deny the doctrine,' however, he succeeds only in 'changing the subject.' What he denies when he denies, say, that 'p or not p' is always true, is not what the classical logician asserts when he asserts that classical logic *is* always true; the fact that 'p v -p' is not a theorem shows that it is not the LEM that the 'deviant' logician denies, rather he is giving 'v' or '-' or both a new meaning.

Quine offers the example of a fictional, ostensibly deviant logic where the wff 'p & -p' is a theorem, but '&' turns out to be merely a 'perverse notation' for 'v,' and the appearance of disagreement *mere* appearance. The argument, however, shows less than Quine supposes. Granted—at least if one takes the meaning of logical connectives to be determined primarily by the syntax and/or semantics of the system in which they occur, rather than by the natural-language readings they are given—there may be room for doubt whether, say, the intuitionist logician means by his negation, for example, exactly what the classical logician means by his. (The more so because it is possible to represent Heyting's logic as a notational variant of the modal system S4, which might suggest that the Intuitionist's 'it is not the case that' could be construed as 'it is impossible that.') But it wouldn't follow that ostensibly deviant logics are really no more than a representation of classical logic in a nonclassical notation; only, at most, that the distinction between the correctness of classical logic and a challenge to the adequacy of its vocabulary, between deviant and extended logics, would begin to blur.

5. Conclusion

Before the development of modern formal logic, in his *Logik* of 1800, Kant wrote that '[t]here are ... few sciences that can come into a permanent state, which

admit of no further alteration.' But logic, he continued, was such a science: 'Aristotle has omitted no essential point ....' 'In our own times,' he went on, 'there has been no famous logician, and indeed we do not require any new discoveries in logic ....'

Less than a century later, with the work of Boole, Peirce and Frege, logic had been transformed by the new, powerful vocabulary and techniques of what is now called 'classical logic.' By 1923 C. I. Lewis was insisting that 'those who suppose that there is *a* logic which everyone would agree to if he understood it ... are more optimistic than those versed in the history of logic have a right to be.' Even if none of the deviant logics so far devised seem either so appealing mathematically or so well-motivated philosophically as seriously to threaten the position of classical logic, it is as well to recall Russell's observation, made in 1906, that 'since one never knows what will be the line of advance, it is always most rash to condemn what is not quite in the fashion of the moment.'

See also: Fiction, Logic of; Intuitionism; Paradoxes, Semantic; Relevant Logic.

Bibliography

Anderson A R, Belnap, N D Jr 1975 *Entailment*: volume 1. Princeton University Press, Princeton, NJ
Anderson A R, Belnap N D Jr, Dunn J M 1992 *Entailment*, volume 2. Princeton University Press, Princeton.
Burdick H 1982 A logical form for the propositional attitudes. *Synthese* 52: 185–230
Dunn J M, Epstein G 1977 *Modern Uses of Multiple-Valued Logic*. Reidel, Dordrecht
Fisch M, Turquette A 1961 Peirce's triadic logic. *Transactions of the C. S. Peirce Society* 2: 71–85
Fraassen B C Van 1969 Presuppositions, supervaluations and free logic. In: Lambert K (ed.) *The Logical Way of Doing Things*. Yale University Press, New Haven, CT
Gabbay D, Guenther F, eds 1986 *Handbook of Philosophical Logic, volume 3, Alternatives to Classical Logic*. Reidel, Dordrecht
Haack S 1978 *Philosophy of Logics*. Cambridge University Press, Cambridge
Haack S 1996 *Deviant Logic, Fuzzy Logic: Beyond the Formalism*. University of Chicago Press, Chicago
Heyting A 1966 *Intuitionism*. North Holland, Amsterdam
Kosko B 1993 *Fuzzy Thinking: The New Science of Fuzzy Logic*. Hyperion, New York
Lane R forthcoming Peirce's 'Entanglement' with the Principles of Excluded Middle and Contradiction. *Transactions of the C. S. Peirce Society*
Norman J, Sylvan R, eds 1989 *Directions in Relevant Logic*. Reidel, Dordrecht. [Sylvan R was formerly known as Routley R.]
Parsons T 1980 *Non-Existent Objects*. Yale University Press, New Haven, CT
Priest G, Routley R, Norman J (eds.) 1989 *Paraconsistent Logic*. Philosophia Verlag, Munich
Priest G 1987 *In Contradiction: A Study of the Transconsistent*. Martinus Nijhoff, Dordrecht
Quine W V O 1970 *Philosophy of Logic*. Prentice Hall, Englewood Cliffs, NJ

Rescher N 1969 *Many-Valued Logic.* McGraw Hill, New York

Routley R, Meyer R K, Plumwood V, Brady R T 1982 *Relevant Logics and Their Rivals.* Ridgeview, Atacasdero, CA

Schock R 1968 *Logics Without Existence Assumptions.* Almqvist and Wiksell, Stockholm

Synthese 1975 Vol. 30 (special issue devoted to logic and semantics of vagueness)

Woods J H 1974 *The Logic of Fiction.* Mouton, The Hague

Entailment

S. Read

The phrase '*p* entails *q*' was introduced in Moore 1922 to describe the internal relation between two propositions when the one, *q*, follows from the other, *p*. Different theories of this relation have been proposed.

1. The Classical View

The orthodox view, sometimes called the 'classical view,' is that *p* entails *q* when it is impossible for *p* to be true and *q* false. This view was codified by C. I. Lewis in his theory of 'strict implication.' It is thought to have some strange and unintuitive consequences, often called the 'paradoxes of strict implication,' that inconsistent propositions entail any proposition (for if they are inconsistent, they cannot be true, and so it is impossible they are true and any other proposition false) and that necessary propositions are entailed by any proposition (for a similar reason—being necessary they cannot be false). These paradoxes are either explained and justified, or lead to abandoning this theory for another (see Sects. 3 and 5). One attempt at justification was given by Lewis, in an argument originally developed in the twelfth-century school of Petit-Pont in Paris, to show that a contradiction entails any proposition. The argument proceeds by intuitively sound steps from *p* and not-*p*, to *p*, to *p* or *q*, and also to not-*p*, and so to *q*.

2. Material Implication

A view which was attributed by Lewis (1912) to Russell, the 'material implication' view, is that *p* entails *q* when either *p* is false or *q* is true. This view is thought to have similar paradoxical consequences, called the 'paradoxes of material implication,' that a false proposition entails any proposition and that a true one is entailed by any proposition.

3. The Logic and Relevance and Necessity

Following earlier work by E. Nelson, Wilhelm Ackermann presented in 1956 a codification of an account of entailment in which a 'logical connection' between *p* and *q* is demanded. His work was extended by Alan Anderson and Nuel Belnap Jr. and given the presumptive title, 'the logic of entailment,' drawing from Lewis a requirement of necessity and from Ackermann a requirement of relevance.

4. The Rejection of Transitivity of Entailment

One answer to Lewis's argument, from *p* and not-*p* to *q*, is to admit that every step in the argument is sound, but to deny the transitivity of entailment, that the succession of sound steps builds into a single sound step. One explication of this idea, due to von Wright and Geach, restricts sound entailments '*p* entails *q*' to substitution-instances of classically valid entailments $A \rightarrow B$ in which A is not logically false and B is not logically true.

5. Connexive Logics

Another account of entailment draws inspiration from some remarks of Aristotle's, when he appears to say that no proposition entails both some other proposition and its contradictory. McCall has developed logics containing such theses as $(p \rightarrow q) \rightarrow \sim (p \rightarrow \sim q)$, $\sim (p \rightarrow \sim p)$, and $\sim ((p \rightarrow q).(p \rightarrow \sim q))$. However, as Routley and Montgomery (1968) show, any consistent system of logic incorporating such theses as those above must lack very many principles which one would think highly desirable. Their main objection is that the failure of these principles makes it hard to conceive of a suitable semantic interpretation of the logic.

See also: Deviant Logics; Logic: Historical Survey; Relevant Logic.

Bibliography

Anderson A R, Belnap N D Jr 1975, 1992 *Entailment*, 2 vols. Princeton University Press, Princeton, NJ

Geach P T 1972 Entailment again. In: Geach P T *Logic Matters*. Blackwell, Oxford

Lewis C I 1912 Implication and the algebra of logic. *Mind* 21: 522–31

Moore G E 1922 External and internal relations. In: Moore G E *Philosophical Studies*. Routledge and Kegan Paul, London

Routley R, Montgomery H 1968 On systems containing Aristotle's thesis. *Journal of Symbolic Logic* 33: 82–96

Fiction, Logic of

D. E. B. Pollard

The term 'fiction' commonly connotes something made up or imagined. The items of most relevance to students of language are obviously those expressed in a linguistic medium, such as stories, novels, and plays. The term 'logic of fiction,' however, is susceptible of both wide and narrow definition. It can mean any account which explains in abstract and general terms the distinction between fiction and nonfiction, and by implication the distinction between fictional and nonfictional discourse. More narrowly, the term can connote any attempt to accommodate the salient features of fiction within the purview of a logical or technical semantic theory.

1. Problems and Distinctions

Some of the difficulties encountered in developing a logic of fiction can be traced to pretheoretical intuitions. On the one hand, there are texts which are both meaningful and in some sense 'about' characters and imagined events. On the other, there is the understanding that one is not being informed about real things. This immediately raises questions concerning reference and truth: how can one refer to what does not exist or make true statements about it? Talk about fictional characters is not readily equated with factual error. Moreover, the sense in which terms in fiction lack reference is not the same as that in which say, an obsolete term like *phlogiston* lacks reference. The latter case is one of failure of reference; but in the fictional case there is no intention to refer to any real entity. Yet people in general, and not just literary critics, are prepared both to make truth claims about fiction and also what seem to be acceptable inferences from the textual content of works of fiction. In this connection, one important distinction is to be made is that between 'discourse within fiction' and 'discourse about fiction,' where the former is the language in which the author creates the work, and the latter is the language in which readers and critics discuss or express their reasoning about it. It is moot whether this distinction requires correspondingly distinct logics.

2. Theoretical Perspectives

The most conspicuous contributions to this topic have a philosophical provenance. Two broad approaches can be distinguished: (a) theories which explain language in relation to the beliefs and intentions of its users and the types of linguistic act involved in communication; (b) theories which view language as an abstract system whose components are characterized independently of concrete contexts of use or speakers' intentions.

2.1 Pragmatic Theories

According to one very influential theory, the writer of fiction is performing a special kind of speech act in which the conventions of normal assertion are suspended. Typically, fiction is described as 'pretended assertion' and hence immune to assessment in terms of truth and falsity. It is not, therefore, an elaborate form of lying; the pretense is without intention to deceive. Since the usual conventions are in abeyance, notions like 'reference' are subject to different and nonsemantic conventions. So names of fictional characters or places, e.g., 'Sherlock Holmes' or 'Lilliput' might be said to 'refer' but in a sense which carries no implication of full-blooded existence. This approach has been open to the objection that it marginalizes fictional discourse as a 'nonserious' use of language.

Other theorists view fictional discourse as the communication of a special kind of intention on the part of the author. The author is seen as engaged, not in any kind of pretense, but rather in the attempt to secure a certain kind of conventional response in the reader. What is communicated to the reader is an invitation to engage in acts of imagination.

2.1 Logico-semantic Theories

Theories of this kind exhibit at least as much diversity as those already considered. Logicians have traditionally been concerned with the construction of formal systems equipped with a rigorous semantics.

Notions of reference and truth are subjected to idealization. Factual discourse is given priority as being most amenable to formalization. One very influential assumption has been that language in its 'proper' use should be directed at the real world. It follows immediately, therefore, that there is a problem about discourse which traffics in fictional entities. This renders names like 'Sherlock Holmes' or 'Pickwick' anomalous and creates a difficulty in assigning any clear truth status (truth-value) to the sentences in which those expressions appear. One tactic is to deny fictional statements any truth-value whatever; another is to go beyond the confines of traditional two-valued logic and assign them a third value distinct from truth and falsity.

Among the most common strategies has been the resort to some form of paraphrase. After analysis, an example like 'Hamlet killed Polonius' is construed as a disguised way of talking either about Shakespeare or the play he wrote. The whole purpose of this analysis is to accommodate fictional discourse within the standard framework of truth and falsity. Other logicians have appealed to the notion of 'possible worlds.' On this approach, it makes sense to say, for example, that Sherlock Holmes exists and plays the violin in some worlds other than the actual world. Thus the name 'Sherlock Holmes' has a reference in some worlds and not others, and the proposition that he plays the violin is true in some worlds, false or even lacking a truth-value in others. Apart from difficulties with the idea of 'possible worlds' itself, there are problems peculiar to fiction and its 'objects.' Unlike real things, the entities of fiction are incomplete. While the proposition that Napoleon disliked cats is in principle decidable, the proposition that Sherlock Holmes disliked cats is not. On this latter issue, Conan Doyle's texts are silent. Furthermore, according to so-called 'classical' logic, anything whatever follows what is false. If the statements of fiction are taken as false, then what might seem to be perfectly acceptable inferences made by readers are rendered arbitrary: it would be as reasonable to infer from Conan Doyle's novels that the moon is made of green cheese as it would to infer that Holmes was cleverer than Inspector Lestrade. Worse still, some instances of fiction (science fiction or fantasy tales) are paradoxical or logically inconsistent and therefore violate the constraints on what can count as a 'possible world.'

3. Further Developments

In addition to attempts to marry some of the approaches outlined, some logicians have developed new systems of logic which tolerate the inconsistencies and anomalies prohibited by more 'classical' conceptions. According to some proponents of these newer systems, the idea that there is any one logic of fiction may itself be questionable. It suffices to say here that these new proposals remain controversial.

Bibliography

Crittendon C 1991 *Unreality: The Metaphysics of Fictional Objects*. Cornell University Press, Ithaca, NY
Currie G 1990 *The Nature of Fiction*. Cambridge University Press, Cambridge
Donnellan K 1974 Speaking of nothing. *Philosophical Review* **83**: 3–31
Lamarque P V, Olsen S H 1994 *Truth, Fiction, and Literature: A Philosophical Perspective*. Clarendon Press, Oxford
Lewis D 1978 Truth in fiction. *American Philosophical Quarterly* **15**(1): 37–46
Rorty R 1982 Is there a problem about fictional discourse? In: Rorty R *Consequences of Pragmatism*. Harvester, Brighton
Searle J R 1974–75 The logical status of fictional discourse. *New Literary History* **6**: 319–32
Walton K 1990 *Mimesis as Make-believe*. Harvard University Press, Cambridge, MA
Woods J H 1974 *The Logic of Fiction*. Mouton, The Hague

Identity

A. A. Brennan

The topic of identity is fundamental in twentieth-century philosophy. It has been central to many of the most vexed problems and debates in philosophy of language, metaphysics, and the philosophy of science. Yet the logic of identity is extremely simple and gives little hint of the philosophical dividends which have flowed from its discovery and application. Identity is, technically, a congruence relation, that is, a relation that each thing has to itself and to nothing else. The identity relation can be added to predicate logic to yield the enriched language of predicate logic with identity. Thus enriched, the predicate calculus can express numerical sentences, ones that capture the exclusive sense of 'else' in English and can also provide contextual definitions of descriptive phrases in the fashion pioneered by Bertrand Russell in his theory of descriptions.

1. Defining Identity

There are several ways of defining the identity relation. Among the most common are those that call attention to its reflexiveness, on the one hand, and to its obedience to Leibniz's Law on the other. Reflexiveness is the property a relation has if, for everything, the relation holds between that thing and itself; in symbols, $\forall x$ $(x = x)$, with ' $=$ ' used as the sign for identity. Leibniz's Law is the principle of the indiscernibility of identicals, namely that if x and y are identical, then anything that can be truly predicated of x can also be predicated truly of y. In symbols, there is the scheme $(x = y$ & $Fx) \rightarrow Fy$. Reflexiveness and Leibniz's Law define numerical identity, that is sameness of object, and not qualitative identity (sameness of property or quality). In everyday situations, we often say items are identical when we mean they are exactly similar (identical in all their properties, but not numerically one and the same thing).

Given these principles, it is easy to define other standard properties of identity, for example, that it is transitive (if x is identical with y and y is identical with z, then x is identical with z). One principle, however, that can be derived has itself been the subject of controversy (Peirce for example, called it 'all nonsense'). This is the principle of the identity of indiscernibles, in symbols, where F is any predicate, $(Fx$ & $Fy) \rightarrow x = y$.

2. Applications in Predicate Logic

Extended with the identity relation, predicate logic can give symbolic versions for numerical claims. To say there are at least two dialects of English, for example, is to say that there is at least one thing, x, such that x is a dialect of English, and one thing, y, such that y is a dialect of English, and that x is not identical with y. To say there are exactly two truth values is to say

$$\exists x \exists y ((x \text{ is a truth value } \& \, y \text{ is a truth value}) \& \sim (x = y)) \& \\ \forall z (z \text{ is a truth value} \rightarrow z = x \text{ or } z = y))$$

in words, there are two nonidentical things, x and y which are truth values, and anything z which is a truth value is the same thing as x or the same thing as y.

The expressive power of the notation also includes capturing the exclusive force of 'else' in sentences like

Jane can run faster than anyone else on the team.

which is taken to mean

Jane can run faster than anyone on the team who is not identical with Jane.

3. Russell's Theory of Descriptions

The ability to capture numerical claims is connected to Russell's famous attempt to give contextual definitions of sentences containing definite descriptions. Russell took such sentences to have a truth value whether or not the descriptive phrase in them referred

to anything. Those with nonreferring descriptive phrases come out as uniformly false under his analysis. Russell was thus able to maintain the principle of bivalence (that each sentence is determinately either true or false).

One supposed advantage of Russell's theory of descriptions was getting round the problem of 'about' in the following form. 'The present King of France is wise,' like 'the golden mountain is made of gold,' seem to be sentences that are about something. Yet there is no present King of France, just as there is no golden mountain. If one accepts that well-formed subject-predicate sentences are about their subjects, then these sentences give rise to deep and challenging puzzles. Since there is no present King of France, is there some nonexistent 'thing' having wisdom predicated of it? Since there is no (actual) golden mountain, is it some possible (but unactualized) golden mountain which is made of gold?

Russell tackled this problem by providing a contextual paraphrase for whole sentences containing definite descriptions under which the problematic descriptive phrases are supplanted by predicates. The surface, subject-predicate form of sentences with definite descriptions is, according to him, a poor guide to their logical form. The latter is given by treating sentences containing descriptions as conjunctions. Corresponding to:

The golden mountain is made of gold

is the conjunction:

at least one thing is a golden mountain and

at most one thing is a golden mountain and

anything which is a golden mountain is made of gold.

Under this analysis, the expression 'golden mountain' occurs only as a fragment of a predicate; thus there is no commitment to the existence of some unique subject of which 'made of gold' is predicated.

In standard notation, the conjunction of three sentences giving the Russellian analysis can be expressed as follows (with 'Gx' for 'x is golden (or is made of gold),' 'Mx' for 'x is a mountain'):

$$\exists x (Gx \& Mx) \& \forall x \forall y (((Gx \& Mx) \& (Gy \& My) \rightarrow x = y)) \& \\ \forall x ((Gx \& Mx) \rightarrow Gx)$$

This formula is provably equivalent to the shorter form:

$$\exists x ((Gx \& Mx) \& \forall y ((Gy \& My) \rightarrow x = y) \& Gx)$$

Although it might seem as if the above sentence should be true, Russell's analysis yields the value false (since the existential claim that there is a golden mountain is false). Russell regarded it as a virtue of the theory that it yielded a uniform result for every sentence containing a vacuous definite description; namely, that the sentence turned out false.

In a development of Russell's ideas W V O Quine has argued that Russell's theory allows one to parse proper names as well as descriptions. Since both definite descriptions and proper names purport to denote exactly one entity, Quine suggests that both should be given a similar treatment from the point of view of logical form. Hence, 'Cerberus barks' is analyzed as:

At least and at most one thing is Cerberus and it barks.

Notice that Quine's proposal does not mean eliminating reference to a unique individual, but rather reconstrues such reference as best expressed through the apparatus of quantification rather than by a proper name. A logical regimentation of natural language would, for Quine, thus dispense with any expressions carrying the semantic role of proper names and definite descriptions.

4. Statements of Identity

Identity has had an important role in other parts of philosophical and semantic theory. It was a puzzle about the meaning of identity statements which led Gottlob Frege to the hypothesis that names, and other semantically relevant components of sentences, must have both a sense and a reference. In his early work, he took identity to be a relation between signs but later realized that in sentences such as:

The morning star is the evening star

the identity in question is of one and the same celestial body with itself. What makes the statement informative, according to Frege, is that the expressions on either side of the 'is' of identity differ in sense even though they both name the planet Venus. Some philosophers, like Strawson and Lockwood, have argued that one role of identity statements is to enable speakers to collapse separate files of information held of an object into one larger file. Someone who had separate files of information held under the labels 'morning star' and 'evening star' would, once they accepted the above identity, be able to reorganize their information store.

Not all uses of 'is' in English involve identity. Writers have attempted to distinguish the 'is' of identity, as in the above example, from the 'is' of predication (e.g., 'Jane is a pilot') and the 'is' of constitution (e.g., 'the bust is bronze'). It is easier to have an intuitive grasp of these distinctions than to give satisfactory definitions of them. Recognizing that 'is' can be used to mean 'is constituted from' saves us from being misled by stories like the following. Suppose a sweater made of wool is unraveled and then the same wool is knitted into a scarf. Since the sweater is wool and the scarf is wool, and the wool is the same in each case, there might be a temptation to think the sweater is the scarf. However, the 'is' of constitution does not have the same logic as the 'is' of identity.

David Wiggins has been a prominent defender of the view that any statement of the form '*a* is the same as *b*' is indefinite until an answer is given to the question 'The same what?' The issue of whether genuine identity statements do require such clarification, like the issue of whether identity is relative, has been debated in recent analytic philosophy. Such debates lead rapidly into metaphysical problems concerning the identity or unity of objects. Theorists generally distinguish two kinds of unity question: unity at a time (synchronic unity) and unity or identity through time (diachronic). One special focus of interest in this area is the topic of personal identity and the role of psychological and physical features in determining the unity of the self.

5. Identity and Possible Worlds

With the increasing interest in modal logic since the 1960s, has come also an interest in the issue of identity across possible worlds. Exploring this issue provides a convenient way into the debate between modal realists (such as David Lewis) who believe that objects are tied to particular worlds and have counterparts in other worlds, and others like Saul Kripke who believe that a genuine proper name (a 'rigid designator') denotes one and the same object in any world in which it designates at all. Kripke's account associates well with the causal theory of reference, and has helped establish a new philosophical orthodoxy about statements of identity. This is that any identity statement using proper names (or any other designators that are 'rigid' in the Kripke sense) is necessarily true, if it is true at all.

This can be shown by an argument depending only on Leibniz's Law as given at the start of this article, together with the fact that, in standard versions of modal logic, any logical truth is a necessary truth. Thus, provided that '$\forall x\,(x = x)$' is necessarily true, it follows that it is necessary that Cicero = Cicero. Now suppose 'Tully' is another name for Cicero. It follows by Leibniz's Law that, since 'Cicero = Tully' is true, anything true of Cicero is also true of Tully. But it is necessarily true of Cicero that he is identical with Cicero, so the same thing (that it is necessarily true he is identical with Cicero) is also true of Tully. So if it is true that Cicero is Tully then it is necessarily true that he is Tully.

This particular claim about identity has led to significant developments in the understanding of natural kind terms. Kripke, Hilary Putnam and others have argued that it is a contingent feature of English that terms like 'water', 'gold,' and 'hydrogen' refer to the stuff they do. However, it is a necessary feature of something's being water that it is largely H_2O, and likewise necessary for a gas's being hydrogen that it has atomic number 2. Since discovering the nature of water and hydrogen involved empirical study, the truth that water is H_2O is both necessary, but known a posteriori (through experience). Putnam coined the term 'deictic–nomological' for this theory of natural-kind words, to call attention to the context-dependence of their introduction, together with the lawful (nomological) necessity of identity statements like 'water is H_2O.'

See also: Necessity; Possible Worlds.

Bibliography

Brennan A 1988 *Conditions of Identity.* Clarendon Press, Oxford
Kripke S 1980 *Naming and Necessity,* rev. edn. Basil Blackwell, Oxford
Morris T V 1984 *Understanding Identity Statements.* Aberdeen University Press, Aberdeen
Putnam H 1973 Meaning and reference. *Journal of Philosophy* **70**: 699–711
Quine W V O 1960 *Word and Object.* MIT Press, Cambridge, MA
Russell B 1905 On denoting. *Mind* **14**: 479–93
Salmon N 1982 *Reference and Essence.* Basil Blackwell. Oxford
Wiggins D 1967 *Identity and Spatio-Temporal Continuity.* Basil Blackwell, Oxford
Wiggins D 1980 *Sameness and Substance.* Basil Blackwell, Oxford

Intuitionism

A. Weir

Intuitionism is a school in the philosophy of mathematics founded by the Dutch mathematician L. E. J. Brouwer. The name derives from Brouwer's agreement with Kant that arithmetic deals with mental constructions derived from a priori intuitions concerning the structure of temporal succession. Brouwer's constructivism led him to reject large parts of standard mathematics as illegitimate. In particular, the intuitionists reject the idea of completed infinite sequences or totalities. Since arithmetic deals with finite mental constructions, infinity must always be conceived of as potential. An infinite sequence is to be interpreted as a rule for indefinitely extending finite initial segments without ever reaching a completed infinite totality. This has radical consequences which become obvious in analysis, many of whose standard results are rejected by the intuitionist as false of the continuum, correctly conceived; hence some intuitionist theorems contradict (at least at face value) those of classical mathematics. These radical mathematical ideas led Brouwer to argue against standard classical logic, claiming that certain of its principles, while valid for finite surveyable domains, were not legitimately extendible to the infinite. Brouwer's impact on contemporary philosophy of language has perhaps arisen mainly from the formalization of his logical ideas by Kolmogorov and, more influentially, Heyting, though many who espouse intuitionism in logic do so from a perspective far removed from the Kantianism which motivated Brouwer.

1. Intuitionist Logic: Bivalence and Excluded Middle

Whereas the father of modern logic, Gottlob Frege, had sought to find a foundation for mathematics in logic, Brouwer's approach to logic is almost the reverse. For him, one first establishes the correct principles of reasoning in mathematics and then distills logic out of reflection on those. Hence Brouwer was led to reject the law of excluded middle: the law that for any proposition p, either p holds or p does not hold. If one ascends to a metalinguistic formulation of the excluded middle principle and equates 's is false' with 's is not true' it becomes the principle of bivalence: every sentence is either true or false.

Now one can reject the principle of bivalence and still retain classical logic and all its theorems. One might, for instance, propose intermediate grades of truth in order to cope with such phenomena as vagueness; there are ways of doing this (though not perhaps the most plausible), which retain classical logic. But the intuitionistic rejection of classical logic is motivated by entirely different considerations and holds even for propositions which are taken to have perfectly definite meanings, such as the propositions of mathematics.

In particular, intuitionists agree with classical mathematicians that there is no third possibility between truth and falsity (*tertium non datur*). Although they deny that every proposition is either true or false, it does not follow from this, in intuitionistic logic, that there is some proposition which is neither. In fact, the double negation of each instance of the principle of excluded middle, namely, $\neg\neg(p \lor \neg p)$ (here '$\neg$' is the negation symbol, 'v' the disjunction symbol) is a theorem of intuitionistic logic. For the intuitionist, as for the classicist, to reject (p $\lor$ $\neg$p) is absurd, equivalent to affirming the existence of true contradictions. But whilst accepting, for any p, that $\neg\neg(p \lor \neg p)$ holds, intuitionsts do not thereby infer that (p $\lor$ $\neg$p), for they reject the principle of double negation elimination, from $\neg\neg$p conclude p.

Now the rule of double negation elimination is a very simple rule which has seemed self-evident to many. The intuitionists explain their rejection of it along these lines: to have a proof of ¬p is to have a proof that p will never be proved. Thus a proof of ¬¬p is a proof that ¬p will never be proved, that is, a proof that one cannot prove that p is unprovable. But such a proof of ¬¬p is entirely distinct from a proof of p itself. Hence since a proof of ¬¬p cannot be transformed into one of p, the latter does not follow from the former.

2. Intuitionism in Contemporary Philosophy of Language

The intuitionist explanation of the meaning of the logical operators in general takes the same overall form as that for negation: it focuses on the ways in which proofs of complex sentences built up by means of the operators are constructed from proofs for their components. Thus the meaning of 'v' for the intuitionist is given by the rule that a proof of p v q is either a proof of p or else a proof of q.

This proof–theoretic account of the meaning of logical operators has been taken over by Michael Dummett and generalized to take in their application to empirical as well as mathematical sentences, verification and falsification playing the role which proof does in mathematical discourse. Dummett's motivation is very different from Brouwer's—based on the Wittgensteinian slogan that meaning is use and on an empiricist view of language acquisition. The result is a type of verificationist theory of meaning.

For according to Dummett, one can be credited with full understanding of undecidable sentences (sentences for which at present there is no effective method for determining whether they are true or false) only if one has the capacity to recognize verifications and falsifications of the sentences if presented with them. But if one does not have the further capacity to decide the sentence's truth value then one cannot be credited with a grasp of a content for the sentence which determines that it must be either true or false. Since, however, the sentence is undecidable, one cannot rule out coming to have a decision procedure in future, in

which case the sentence would then become determinately true or false. Hence intuitionism, with its rejection of excluded middle but also of *tertium non datur*, is the correct logic.

Against Dummett one might ask why the capacity to recognize verifications and falsifications, if forthcoming, is not sufficient grounds to credit someone with grasp of bivalent propositions. Moreover the Dummettian generalization of intuitionism to ordinary language runs into problems coping with the absence of anything like the conclusive verification one has in mathematics.

3. Conclusion

One final, and fundamental, question which arises with intuitionism is whether there really is a substantive debate between intuitionist and classicist. Brouwer, in rejecting bivalence, often presented it not as standardly understood—every proposition is either true or false—but as a modal principle to the effect that every proposition is either correct or impossible. Intuitionists went on to explain the connectives in terms of proof and provability. If one takes these explanations at face value one can translate (albeit with some loss of content) intuitionist language into classical language plus a modal operator □ read as 'it is provable that.' Gödel showed that the result is a classical modal logic known as S4 in which the intuitionist excluded middle p v ¬p gets translated as (□ p ∨ □−□p) ('∨' for classical disjunction '−' for classical negation) read as p is provable or else provably not provable. And the classicist can agree with the intuitionist that this sentence is not provable for all propositions p. So the ever-present danger, in debates about fundamental principles, that the dispute is really just terminological, seems a real one in this case.

Bibliography

Brouwer L 1967 On the significance of the principle of excluded middle. In: van Heijenoort (ed.) *From Frege to Gödel*. Harvard University Press, Cambridge, MA
Dummett M A E 1977 *Elements of Intuitionism*. Clarendon Press, Oxford
Heyting A 1956 *Intuitionism*. North-Holland, Amsterdam

Logic: Historical Survey

S. D. Guttenplan

The history of formal logic presents an interesting and initially mysterious phenomenon. Compared to almost any intellectual discipline outside of perhaps philosophy itself (of which it is often taken to be a

part) it has the longest history. But that history is by no means a continuous record of progress and achievement. It is only a slight exaggeration to say that, after a spectacular beginning which culminated in the work of Aristotle (d. 322 BC), logic went through a period of general stagnation relieved only by relatively isolated contributions until the late nineteenth and early twentieth centuries, when logic was transformed by discoveries which eclipsed even the brilliance of Aristotle's work. This article will give an outline of this history, particularly as it bears on topics relating to language and linguistics.

1. The Study of Logic and Related Subjects

Perhaps the fact that a subject should begin well and then remain in the shadows for a long time will not seem so surprising. After all, there are fashions in the intellectual world as in any other. However, what deepens the mystery of the history of logic is that its period of stagnation did not coincide with one of neglect. On the contrary, for all the centuries it remained largely unchanged, it continued to play a special and prominent role in the liberal education offered in every place of learning. If there is one species of textbook in the university tradition which has at once the longest and most curious history it is that of the logic text. The form may vary from period to period, but, if one surveyed what counted as logic texts from the period after Aristotle to the present day, one would see the point about the history of logic illustrated in a most graphic way. There are certainly thousands of different exemplars of the type 'logic textbook,' and they were used continuously in the educational tradition of the west. Yet there was a period of over a thousand years in this tradition when the formal logical content of these textbooks changed very little. The difference between the logic texts of the early medieval period and the middle nineteenth century would be real but of no real significance in comparison to the change which has taken place since then. It is a simple fact that the standard present text in formal logic contains very little of what would have figured centrally in the text of about a hundred years before.

Here something should be added to soften the stark picture just painted. As was noted, that part of logic which remained such an unchanged part of the syllabus for so long was formal logic. But there are other aspects of the subject which are woven around the formal core. Logic began as the study of inference and validity, and through the work of Aristotle the formal study of inference was born. This formal study (known best under the heading of the 'syllogism,' details of which follow in Sect. 3) was the relatively unchanging core of the subject from after Aristotle until the beginning of the present century. Around this core there revolved a great many topics which nowadays would be classified under the headings 'philosophy of logic' and 'philosophy of language.' Here are found questions about the nature of premises and conclusions of arguments, whether they are sentences, thoughts, propositions distinct from either of these, as well as

questions about concepts ranging from those about individuals and species to those about modality (notions such as possibility) and logical form (notions such as universality, particularity, conditionality and disjunction). In many and subtle ways there was a gradual growth in wisdom about this latter subject matter—the philosophies of logic and language—and this is especially evident when one goes back to medieval texts with the hindsight gained from modern discussions. However, it can seem surprising that the advances made in these areas had so little impact on the development of formal logic itself: time and again one sees suggestions here and there in the history of the subject where one feels that 'if only this suggestion were followed through and applied to formal methods, a large part of what now goes on in logic would have developed hundreds of years earlier.'

The reason for this curious situation is particularly important in the present context. For what has largely made the difference necessary for the revolutionary changes in logic in the twentieth century has been a change in the framework within which the subject is studied, and that change has brought about a situation in which formal logic is a crucial part, not merely of the study of inference, but in the study of language and linguistics. Essentially what seems to have happened is that the formal study of inference, and the related unsystematic studies of philosophy of language and logic, existed side-by-side, but without any coherent metatheory to unite them. Since the 1890s, and especially due to the work of Gottlob Frege, a fundamentally different notion of the role of formal logic in the context of philosophy of logic and language has arisen. Along with this change have come revolutionary changes in formal methods themselves. But what is most important in the present context is that the changed perspective on logic has made it a fundamental aspect of the study of natural language. Of course, the study of inference still remains the starting point for logic, and important branches of the subject have very little directly to do with natural language, but it is now seen that in studying inference one is also systematically studying the rich linguistic structure which is expressed in natural languages. For, in their myriad different ways, all natural languages are capable of expressing thoughts that it is the business of logic to capture in precise form. Indeed, it has even been thought that the formal languages of logic give the deep structure of the thoughts expressed in natural languages. However, whether or not logical languages have this exact role, there is no doubt that the study of logic now plays almost as central a part in linguistics as it does in philosophy itself.

2. Logic Before Aristotle

The study of inference could have begun almost anywhere, since the use of argument and reason is as widespread as humanity itself. Thus, one can only speculate as to why the origins of logic were in Greece. Perhaps the closest to an explanation comes with the recognition that the Greeks began the systematic study of philosophy—a discipline within which argument plays perhaps a larger part than it does elsewhere, at least as practiced by the Greeks. It has been observed that the Greeks of the fifth and fourth centuries BC were 'intoxicated' with argument, so it should not be all that surprising that they were also the first to investigate systematically the inferences on which their argumentation was based.

The formalization of logic and the attempt to codify the principles of valid inference were Aristotle's great contributions to the subject. However, it is worth remarking on his predecessors, since their less formal work is what stimulated Aristotle, and provided him with the necessary materials. There are three different strands to the logical tradition before Aristotle. The first was the mathematical: Greek geometers, most particularly Pythagoras and those of his school (sixth century BC) sought proofs of the truths which, in many cases, had merely been 'observed' to be true by the Egyptians. Since a proof is a special kind of argument—one used to demonstrate the truth of its conclusion from a set of truths (axioms) fully accepted as true—this area provided Aristotle with a great many of his examples. Moreover, it is clear that Aristotle thought of demonstrative reasoning as the most representative form of inference, and this came to be reflected in his choice of formal methods.

The second pre-Aristotelian strand centers on philosophy and, in particular, metaphysics and epistemology. Philosophy in the Greek world was bound up with debate and argument. The Greeks found such argument fascinating, even more so when there was something paradoxical or puzzling in the result. Zeno of Elea, Euclides, and his pupil Eubulides, and, above all, Plato made argument the primary tool in the endeavor to understand the structure of the world and our place in it. The dialogues of Plato are a vast repository of such metaphysical argument (generally known as 'dialectic'), and Aristotle, student as he was of Plato, was deeply influenced by them in at least two important ways. First, he shared with Plato the conviction that dialectical argument was a necessary feature of acquiring philosophical wisdom; and, second, he had to hand, in the Platonic teaching, a great many specific examples of such argument together with a conception of the nature and purpose of inference. For, though Plato did not himself introduce the formal methods into logic, he certainly did contribute a great deal to the philosophies of logic and language mentioned above. Indeed, it would be difficult to imagine how Aristotle could have taken the further steps he did except against this background. That he differed greatly from his teacher is certain, but Aristotle did take from Plato a set of questions about inference and validity which made his own contribution possible.

Moreover, even in his rejection of things Platonic, Aristotle shows a certain indebtedness. One may speculate that Aristotle's conviction that demonstrative reasoning, rather than dialectic, is the paradigm of codifiable inference is of a piece with his rejection of so many of the specific doctrines of his teacher.

The third strand of the pre-Aristotelian origins of logic is located in the social and cultural milieu rather than in the work of specific thinkers. In Athens and other Greek city states, the ability to win arguments in public debate was considered an important accomplishment for the ambitious citizen. This meant that instruction in the formal methods of debate was sought after, and there was a group of specialists in this type of instruction who were known as 'sophists.' Aristotle himself wrote a work giving hints as to how most effectively to present winning arguments, whether for their own sake or in, for example, courts of law. Clearly, this focus on the nature of debate and argument contributed hugely to the development of logic, though it also encouraged that rather negative view of logic which persists in the pejorative word 'sophistry.'

See: Plato and his Predecessors.

3. Aristotle's Contribution to Logic

Aristotle died in 322 BC and his work was collected by his pupils. The result of this was a corpus of work on logic and reasoning that some time after his death came to be called the 'Organon' or 'instrument of science.' Whether this classification is fully justified is not at all agreed. Certainly, there is work in the *Organon* which would be better classified as metaphysics or philosophy of language, but there can be no question of the importance of this classification for the history of logic. It came to be thought that the very boundaries of logic were to be identified with the various subject matters of the *Organon*.

The works in the *Organon* are as follows: (a) the *Categories* in which Aristotle examines among other things the kinds of predication (substance, quantity, quality, relation, place, time, situation, state, action and passion) which can be made in respect of a subject; (b) the *Topics* and its appendix, *De Sophisticis Elenchis* which together contain Aristotle's contribution to the art of dialectical debate as described earlier; (c) *De Interpretatione* in which are discussed the various ways in which pairs of statements can be opposed (as, for example, by being contradictory of one another); (d) the *Prior Analytics* in which Aristotle offers his system for the analysis of the logical form of arguments; and, finally, (e) the *Posterior Analytics* which is largely a philosophical treatise about demonstrative and other sorts of reasoning. The particular formal logic (the 'syllogistic') which has always been associated with Aristotle, and which so shaped the history of the subject for more than two thousand years, comes in

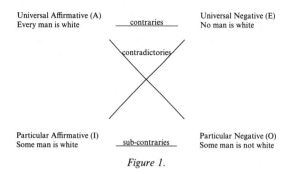

Figure 1.

chs. 5–8, 10, 11, 14 of *De Interpretatione* and *Prior Analytics, i, 1–7.*

In *De Interpretatione*, after an initial discussion of certain issues in the philosophy of logic, Aristotle investigates the question of which statements can be said to be some sort of denial of some given statement. Almost exclusively, these statements are all general subject-predicate claims. Aristotle's own examples are as follows (1):

> Every man is white, (1)
> No man is white,
> Some man is white,
> Some man is not white.

Additionally, Aristotle introduces and discusses various further relations between statements of the above forms, relations we would now consider to be inferential. Thus, he discusses the issue of whether 'Every man is white' implies 'Some man is white' (a relationship which has been called 'subalternation') and whether 'No man is white' is equivalent to 'Every man is nonwhite.' This latter relation is called 'obversion' and Aristotle decides that it is valid in one direction, but is not an equivalence relation.

When the four forms of general statement are arranged spatially as in Fig. 1, the result is the famous square of opposition. This was the starting point for all teaching of Aristotelian logic in the middle ages and beyond, though in this precise form it is not in Aristotle's text. The details of the square of opposition are not important here, but what is crucial to recognize is that Aristotle's whole further development of logic is based upon sentences of the above forms—sentences which are known as categorical. The syllogistic, which will be surveyed shortly, is a restricted system of inferences all of whose premises and conclusions are drawn from the set of four types of statement that figure in the square of opposition.

Why did Aristotle find these sorts of categorical general statement so central to the study of inference? There is no fixed view about this, but it does seem likely that his interest in what was described above as 'demonstrative' inference was crucial here. From a modern day perspective this can seem odd, since one thinks of all sorts of deductive inference as demonstrative, but a little imagination should show the way. If one thinks about what goes on in school geometry, then one can get the appropriate flavor. A great deal of what the geometer does is to assert categorically of various classes of things (circles, triangles, lines joining midpoints, parallels, etc.) that they are or are not members of some further class. If one took the reasoning of the geometer as the central case of reasoning in general, then it would seem reasonably natural to regard the categorical sentences of the square of opposition as central and typical of a type of reasoning (demonstrative) that it was worth capturing.

The doctrine of the syllogism is described in the *Prior Analytics*. In barest outline it consists in the study of those forms of inference which contain two categorical premises and which validly imply some further categorical conclusion. A typical example of such an inference is (2):

> Every dog is a mammal. (2)
> Every mammal is warm-blooded.
> Therefore, every dog is warm-blooded.

The sentences in this example do not have the precise syntactical form of any example of Aristotle's, and this is itself important. For it is no easy matter to translate directly from Greek into fluent English whilst preserving the precise syntactical structure of the Greek. In the Greek of Aristotle and Plato there is often a complicated and clumsy use of pronouns in connection with general statements. Perhaps because of the awkwardness of categorical statements in Greek (especially when studying inferences between them) Aristotle introduced (but without explanation) the use of letters as variables standing for the terms in categorical sentences. Thus, the above syllogism is said to have the following structure of terms (3):

> A—B (3)
> B—C
> A—C

This use of symbols is the first of its kind in logic, and it represents the beginnings of the formalization of inference. As used of categorical sentences and syllogisms, this formalization may not seem revolutionary, but this is perhaps because we have come to take such a use of symbols for granted. What Aristotle achieved here was truly remarkable: he presented a pattern of inference in a precise enough way for it to become an object of purely formal or syntactical study. Thus, by thinking of the A's, B's, and C's as forming patterns, it is possible to study the validity of syllogistic inferences by reference to these patterns and, of course, by reference to the quantifier words (every, some, none) which modify each line of the pattern.

The logicians of the Middle Ages carried this study much further—some might even say to extremes. And this is especially unfortunate given the very restricted range of inferences that are possible within the syllogistic. But the idea of the symbolism was epochal in the history of logic.

See: Aristotle and the Stoics; Aristotle and Logic.

4. Stoic Logic

Developed by Chrysippus and the Megarians, Stoic logic constitutes a second major tradition in the subject to be put alongside that engendered by Aristotle. From our perspective, it is difficult to understand fully why the Aristotelian and Stoic traditions should have been thought of as having such separate identities—identities which remained distinct until much nearer the twentieth century. This is because the sorts of subject matter that figured in Stoic logic are now fully integrated with those that concerned Aristotle, and it is not easy to imagine them as distinct. As was mentioned earlier, perhaps the only way to understand this aspect of the history of logic is by allowing due weight to the fact that the ancient world thought of demonstrative reasoning as a different kind of subject matter from that of philosophical or metaphysical reasoning. It is as if inference was classed in terms of its field of action, rather than, as now, thought of as a unified subject which applied indifferently to different areas of human knowledge. Moreover, it seems clear that there were clashes of personality involved. The Megarian logicians' attacks on Aristotle contributed to the view of their logic as somehow an alternative, when to us it is so clearly a contribution to the same study.

By and large it is fair to describe the main contribution of Stoic logic as coming under the headings of philosophy of logic and philosophy of language. There was in their work nothing that compares to the Aristotle's formalization of logical inference. The three main subheadings under which one can classify the Stoic contribution to logic are: the study of logical paradoxes, the study of conditional or hypothetical assertions, and the study of modal notions.

4.1 Paradoxes

The four most famous logical paradoxes discussed in the Megarian and Stoic corpus were:

  (a) *The Liar*: John says that he is speaking falsely. Is he speaking truly? Clearly, if yes, then no and if no, then yes.
  (b) *The Unnoticed Man*: if John knows Jim, but doesn't recognize him on some occasion then he does not know him.
  (c) *The Heap*: one grain of sand does not make a heap, and if you add another single grain you do not get a heap. So, there is no number of grains you can add to get a heap.
  (d) *The Horned Man*: what John has not lost he

still has. He has not lost horns, so he still has them.

Unfortunately, it is not known what the originator (probably Eubulides) or his later followers thought of these paradoxes—what they used them to illustrate or how they saw them as fitting in with logic. However, in their different ways each of them has been influential in the study of logic and language. For, aside from their curiosity value, each of them has important consequences in the study of the semantics of both natural and formal languages. The Liar has been the basis for a great deal of philosophical work on truth and meaning as well as having a crucial role in our construction of modern theories of formal semantics. The Unnoticed Man focuses on the logic of epistemic notions such as knowledge and belief, and treatments of this and cognate puzzles figure centrally in contemporary philosophy of language. The Heap arises because of the vagueness inherent in predicates of natural language, and it forces us to recognize a certain recalcitrance in such predicates. And the Horned Man can be seen as an early worry about the notion of presupposition.

4.2 Conditionals

The Stoic interest in conditionals (assertions of the form, if . . . then) probably have their origin in the use of conditional arguments of the form (4):

> If P then Q. (4)
> If P then not Q.
> Therefore, it is impossible that P.

This form of argument was used before Aristotle's time in metaphysical contexts by Zeno of Elea, and is of course one form of the *reductio ad absurdum* argument which entitles us to conclude the negation of a given statement if it can be shown to lead to a contradiction. In any case, it is clear from what we do know about the Stoics, and, in particular, Chrysippus (d. 207 BC) and his follower Philo, that they studied both the conditional form of statement and conditional arguments in a strikingly modern way. They seem to have isolated and wrestled with some of the philosophical and linguistic problems that we now think of as problems about the relation between formal renderings of the conditional, and natural language conditionals. Indeed, Philo may well be the first philosopher to have formulated and worried about the truth conditions of the material conditional.

4.3 Modality

What Stoic and Megarian logic is perhaps most closely associated with is its contribution to ideas about modal notions such as possibility and necessity. Most prominent here is Diodorus Cronus whose work dates from some 25 years after the death of Aristotle. Diodorus's name is with the so-called 'Master' argument whose conclusion is that the future is necessary, i.e., that it is in some way predestined. Accounts of this argument are very sketchy, deriving from a not wholly convincing outline given some hundreds of years later by Epictetus, but it is fairly clear that Diodorus thought of necessity and possibility as applying to some such item as a sentence (or proposition or statement). He defines these notions in a temporal way, as would be expected if they are to serve in an argument for fatalism, so that, for example, necessity is that which is true and will never be false, whilst possibility is that which is either true or will be.

Later philosophers in this tradition came to think of the modal notions in a nontemporal way. Thus, necessity is defined as that which is true and does not admit of falsehood. Of course, unlike the Diodorus definition, this latter definition does not eliminate modality. For, one cannot so much as understand the definition without already possessing the idea of 'not admitting of falsehood,' and this latter notion is clearly itself modal, i.e., it means roughly 'cannot possibly be false.'

See: Aristotle and the Stoics.

5. Roman, Medieval, and Renaissance Logic

Clearly it is impossible to include in this survey any detailed discussion of individual works. However, it is necessary to have some general idea about these periods in order to grasp the changes that came to take place later.

5.1 The Roman Contribution

The period from the second century BC to the sixth century AD was one of consolidation and transmission of ideas rather than innovation. Early in this period, Cicero provided some Latin translations of Greek work in logic, both Aristotelian and Stoic. In the second century AD, the physician, Galen, produced a number of treatises on logic, only a small portion of which survive, though they were influential in his time. And in the third and fourth centuries, writers such as Alexander of Aphrodisias, Sextus Empiricus, and Porphyry produced works which remain important sources for today's knowledge of Greek logic. It was in this period that the bitter rivalry between Aristotelian and Stoic logic was at its height. As was mentioned earlier, it is difficult to understand why there should have been such rivalry, since from today's perspective there is only one overall framework in which formal and informal logic is conducted. However, in the absence of some such framework, the clear differences in schools and personalities tended to exaggerate the smallest differences in content and presentation.

The culmination of this period comes with the work of Boethius (470–524 AD). It was his work which was to influence the whole of medieval logic, though this was more because of his scholarly abilities than

because they contained any advances. However, it is important to note that in several ways, his commentaries and glosses on Greek logic were responsible for the different emphases one finds in medieval logic. In particular, he did seem to think of logic as embedded somehow in the study of language, and he did preserve the discussion of conditional statements which eventually led to the study of so-called 'consequentiae' in the Middle Ages. Exactly in what way Boethius thought of the relationship between logic and language is not clear, since it is not clear whether he separated the idea of language from that of thought itself. But there is certainly a difference in emphasis between Boethius and his master Aristotle in this respect, and that was perhaps enough to encourage the kind of philosophy of logic and language that developed in the Middle Ages.

5.2 Medieval Logic

The logic of the Middle Ages is at once frustratingly stationary and full of fascinating detail of argument and discussion. Certainly, it is the one period in the subject which one cannot even begin to treat in a survey of this breadth. Indeed, a simple list of names of those who either wrote textbooks in the subjects or ventured speculations about this or that specific topic would be longer than there is place for here. For the obsession with detail and close argument that have come to be associated with the Middle Ages, especially in the later period after the firm establishment of the universities, is nowhere shown more clearly than in logic. Nonetheless, and leaving names aside, there are two main areas which were of special concern to logicians in the Middle Ages, though the work done in these areas did little to change the fundamental role played in formal logic by the syllogistic.

The first of these was a study of the signification of words—a study now located firmly in the philosophy of language. The tortuous path of this work, and the myriad distinctions to which it gave rise, cannot even be summarized here. However, it is clear that whilst little was done to extend the range of formal logic beyond categorical and some conditional forms, this study (known as 'proprietates terminorum') had a depth and generality which went beyond anything in Aristotle. Worries about what kind of signification belonged to logical words, names, adjectives, the copula, and even worries about the levels at which linguistic items were discussed (as elements of sound, thought, or in terms of connection to universals or some such), all figured in these debates.

The second main area of inquiry was into the form and logic of conditional statements. The impetus for this study comes from Abelard who lived in the early part of the twelfth century. In his *Dialectica* he sharply distinguishes between the use of devices such as 'if ... then' to indicate passages of argument and as devices for making complex statements out of simpler ones.

In short, he distinguished between conditional propositions and argument structures. Indeed, in later developments in this subject area of *consequentiae*, it came to be recognized that there was a close relationship between the validity of an argument and the necessary truth of the conditional connecting the conjoint premises and conclusion. Also, in the intricate debate surrounding this subject there was a no less lively appreciation of the material conditional than one finds in debates about this subject today.

See: Medieval Philosophy of Language.

5.3 *The Renaissance up to the Eighteenth Century*

The rise of what is known as 'humanism' in the Renaissance coincided with the new availability of ancient texts of Plato and Aristotle which had not been known in the west during the Middle Ages. This gave rise to new studies across a broader range of subjects than had been possible before, and included a new interest in the scientific study of the world, including mathematical study. The effect of these changes on logical studies was significant. On the one hand, there was a tendency to downgrade the importance of logic. The complexities of medieval discussions of logic were not seen as having produced any significant addition to knowledge, whereas the study of mathematics and science was seen as offering some hope in this direction. (Interestingly, it was not until the twentieth century that medieval studies came to be seen as having made a contribution to the philosophy of logic and language.) On the other hand, though there was criticism of logic, there was no real attempt to reform or change the subject in any important way. By and large, the logic syllabus in the universities remained the same, whilst interest in the subject withered. At the end of the seventeenth century, it had almost become fashionable to show a sort of contempt for the study of logic as done in the universities. John Locke himself wrote (in his *Essay Concerning Human Understanding*): 'God has not been so sparing to men to make them barely two-legged creatures, and left it to Aristotle to make them rational.'

The attitude of the philosophers of these centuries to logical studies illustrates what has been a background theme of this survey. They bitterly criticized the logic they had been forced to study at university, but did not see their own work as in any way contributing to change that study itself. Though there were no doubt complex social and institutional causes of these attitudes, the absence of a coherent view about the place of logic in the study of mind and language was certainly a contributing factor. By the seventeenth and eighteenth century, the detailed study of a very restricted form of inference (the syllogism) based on a narrow selection of sentence types (categoricals) simply could not serve as the basis for incorporating formal methods into the study of language and reasoning in a wider context.

In this connection something should be said about the famous *Port Royal Logic* of Pierre Nicole and Antoine Arnauld. This work, whose title was *La Logique ou l'Art de Penser*, was a new style of textbook in logic published in the seventeenth century, and it had a considerable influence on logic for more than a century. Essentially what it did was to combine the formal logic of the syllogism with the then modern conception of reasoning which had its origins in the epistemological concerns of Descartes and his followers. Logic was understood as the art of directing thought so as to yield knowledge of the world, and the most novel part of the book contains interesting discussions of method and clear thinking. What should be stressed in the present context is how strange it now appears that the limited syllogistic should continue to be the core of formal logical methods in a work whose subject matter is inquiry in general. The partnership between formal methods of logic, a general conception of reasoning, and a philosophy of language appropriate to these had yet to be made. Certain of the basic ingredients of philosophy of logic and language were around, but at this point, the formal methods available were both inadequate, and yet not fully seen to be so.

6. Logic and Mathematics

The period beginning with Leibniz (1646–1716) and leading to Frege's work at the end of the nineteenth century sees the development of formalisms of considerably more sophistication than the syllogistic. Moreover, since these formalisms by and large developed through various attempts to bring logic and mathematics together in certain ways, it is not unreasonable to think of the theme of the period as the 'mathematization' of logic.

6.1 *Leibniz*

G. W. Leibniz is an exceptional figure in the history of logic, philosophy, and mathematics. In each of these areas he produced work, often sketchy or incomplete, which was both original and fundamental. Indeed, in some ways, his ideas suffered from the fact that there was little or no context into which they could be fitted. Aside from being one of the 'standard' philosophers in the present syllabus, he was (with Newton) an originator of the differential calculus, and a pioneer in work on probability theory. From the point of view of this survey, his most interesting work is that on the idea of a so-called 'universal character.'

Along with many writers at that time, Leibniz thought that language somehow obscured or hampered clear thinking about the world. The general opinion, which Leibniz shared, was that it should be possible to reform language so as to make it an instrument of instruction and knowledge rather than an obstacle. For example, it was noted (the example is not Leibniz's own) that English speakers have to learn the word 'cow' in order to be able to refer to these creatures, but that the effort put into this gives the learner little more return than the piece of knowledge that 'cow' (this particular sound pattern) refers to cows. How much better it would be if, in learning the word, one also learned some information about cows. That is, why not redesign language so that it forms reflected scientific knowledge of the world? In this way, when someone went to the trouble of learning the language, he would as well learn, from the symbolism itself, a lot about cows.

The 'universal character' of Leibniz had the above as one of its goals. This goal required, improbably, that knowledge be complete or nearly so, but that did not seem an obstacle to Leibniz and others. But Leibniz's project had a feature that distinguished it from other such projects—a feature that is important for the development of logic. For Leibniz thought that the construction of the universal character could go hand in hand with a mechanization of reasoning. That is, he thought that one could develop a set of rules which could be mechanically applied to the premises of any argument (formulated in the universal character) so that the conclusion would then arise by a calculation not unlike that in algebra. Most famously, he thought that disputes could be settled not by the usual wrangling, but by participants sitting down to calculate. In aid of this project, Leibniz investigated syntax or purely formal structure, hoping to develop a general theory of reasoning by this means. In conception if not in execution, his efforts in this direction bear a striking resemblance to projects that came later, and which culminated in the formal systems of logic we have today.

In spite of his innovative thinking about logic and language, Leibniz did not advance the subject in a detailed way, nor did he have much direct influence on his contemporaries. Part of the problem here is that Leibniz stubbornly resisted any move away from the categorical form of sentence at the heart of the syllogistic. He saw that there were special problems about the logic of relations, but he did not carry through his mechanization of reason so as to deal with them.

There is no space to discuss their work in detail, but in their different ways, Bernard Bolzano (1781–1848) in Prague and John Stuart Mill (1806–73) in Britain made important contributions to the philosophy of logic and language. It is not easy to place Bolzano in the history of the subject, inasmuch as he drew inspiration from a wide variety of sources and was distinctly original. However, it is not unreasonable to see him as continuing in the broad tradition of Leibniz. On the other hand, Mill's *System of Logic* (1843)

was clearly within the empiricist tradition, and can be seen as an attempt to provide a clear home for logic, including formal logic, within that tradition. This latter task was necessary, for, as already shown, empiricists from Hobbes and Locke onwards tended to view logic as of no particular philosophical or scientific importance. However, it should be pointed out that neither Bolzano nor Mill made any significant contribution to the formal methods of logic.

See: Leibniz, G W.

6.2 The Algebra of Logic

The period after Leibniz saw great advances in various branches of mathematics, from analysis to number theory, algebra and geometry. One particularly important feature of these advances came ultimately to have crucial importance for the development of logic. That feature is usually called 'generality.' With the increasing sophistication of mathematics, it came to be appreciated that results in one branch of the quickly ramifying subject could have important consequences for other branches. Moreover, the way in which these consequences were often realized was not so much by direct methods, as by a process mathematicians call 'generalization.' In this method, one takes certain features of one subject matter and thinks of them in a sufficiently abstract way to allow them to be used of a completely different subject matter. This sort of thinking might be illustrated with the very simple example in the development of the number series. If one persists in thinking of the numbers as related directly to objects that one needs to count, then negative, rational, real, and complex numbers will remain forever beyond one's ken. But if one comes to have a conception of a number series as a kind of purely formal order generated by certain operations on its elements, it will be reasonable to think of there being different sorts of numbers related to different sorts of operation.

In 1847, George Boole published *Mathematical Analysis of Logic*. The basic idea behind this work was that it was possible to apply algebraic laws to elements which were not themselves numbers. What was important to Boole were the relationships between the elements rather than their nature. Moreover, in using algebraic relationships between these undefined elements, Boole saw no reason to keep the relationships fixed to those obtaining between numbers. For example, Boole came to think of the equation '$x = 1$' as capable of expressing the claim that the proposition x is true, and '$x = 0$' as expressing the falsity of x. This allows a nice analogy between multiplication of 1's and 0's and conjunction: 'proposition x and proposition y' functions in this way just like '$x . y$.' However, since the complex proposition 'x or y' will have the value false when x and y are both false, and true otherwise, it seems at first impossible to extend the analogy in the natural way to disjunction, i.e., by treating disjunction as '+.' For, the sum of two 1's is 2. However, Boole proposed that one think of the 'or' relationship as following slightly different rules from those obtaining in the number series. What results is an algebra in which $1 + 1 = 1$.

By thinking in this way, Boole not only invented a special class of algebras, but he encouraged the idea that there could be a connection between mathematics and logic at a level above that of specific content (numbers or propositions). This way of thinking was to have profound consequences for the development of logic as well as mathematics.

7. Frege

Gottlob Frege (1848–1925), was a German mathematician who, during his lifetime, remained an obscure professor in Jena. Nonetheless, it could be argued that he achieved more important breakthroughs in logic than any other single individual with the possible exception of Aristotle. He created modern logic through the use of an artificial language, named 'conceptual writing' (or ideography), which he used to make extensive investigations into the logical structure of natural as well as mathematical languages; he was the first to construct a formal deductive logical system, and also to investigate the logical foundations of arithmetic.

His first published work, entitled *Conceptual Notation, a formula language, modeled upon that of Arithmetic, for pure thought* (1879) (commonly known as *Begriffsschrift*), was meant to provide mathematics with an expressive tool capable of displaying the full rigor needed for a precise notion of mathematical proof. The specific goal Frege had in mind in developing such a tool was to show that ultimately mathematical notions—such as 'number' or 'hereditary property in a sequence'—could be defined using only logical notions and, furthermore, that mathematical truths could be derived as theorems from a system whose axioms included only 'logical laws.' In essence, what Frege wanted to show was that mathematical notions were in effect extensions of logical concepts, and that these latter concepts could be given a precise axiomatic basis. This project, attempted in more detail in 1884 in *The Foundations of Arithmetic*, and in the 1893–1903 *Basic Laws of Arithmetic*, has since been named 'the logicist stance' in the philosophy of mathematics. However, it became quite apparent to those who did read Frege (and here the English philosopher and logician Bertrand Russell figures importantly), that the conceptual notation provided the basis for a more general account of reasoning and proof than that connected solely with mathematics.

See: Frege, Gottlob.

7.1 Conceptual Notation

According to Frege, using a purely logical notation allows one to represent inferential transitions in a precise way and without undetected appeals to intuition. It also allows the concepts used to be displayed in a more determinate and rigorous way than is permitted by ordinary language. As is indicated in the subtitle of the work, Frege's ideography is inspired by arithmetical formulas, and this puts one in mind of the work of Leibniz as well as Boole. But the analogy between both symbol systems (arithmetic and logic) is not grounded, as was the case for Leibniz and Boole, on arithmetical operations themselves being chosen as basic relations. Instead of using arithmetical ideas as the basis for logic, Frege's conceptual notation uses certain notions implicit in logical structures as would be found in certain natural language constructions. Thus, the conceptual notation is not a mathematization of logic so much as a genuine formalization of logical notions.

The logical ideography is essentially a notation for representing the detailed logical form of sentences such as might be found in natural language, though it is not conceived of as a notation tied to natural language. Frege thought, and he was not alone in thinking, that natural language was too vague and confused to serve as the basis of logical inference. In the notation, constant terms are distinguished from variable signs, and these latter are seen as possible fillings for 'function' terms. Frege conceived of a judgment as a structure resembling a mathematical function (such as the function 'square root') filled out with argument places (as in 'square root of 2,' in which '2' is the argument). A full-blown judgment such as might be expressed in a complete sentence obtains when the empty space in a function term is filled by an argument term of the correct kind, for example, a proper name. Thus, 'is a horse' can be considered a one-place function and 'Desert Song' as an argument to get the judgment 'Desert Song is a horse,' though this would be written in something more like this form: 'Is a horse (Desert Song),' following the practice used by mathematicians in writing functions. This type of symbolism proves much more flexible than the classical subject-predicate analysis of the proposition for two reasons. First, since it is possible for functions to have more than one place, one can deal with relational sentences. For the first time, logical notation had moved beyond the restrictive subject-predicate structure bequeathed to us by Aristotle. Second, one could use variables in argument places and achieve judgments by attaching quantifiers to these variables. This was an enormous advance which, together with the possibility of multiple-place functions, gives the logic a great deal of expressive power.

The goal of the notation is not only to solve problems: it is not only meant as a *calculus ratiocinator*, it also aims at elucidating the conceptual contents of functional expressions. That is, it aims to be a notation for expressing precisely complex concepts as constructed from basic elements. Moreover, these analyses use the very same formal resources as the ones used in proof itself—resources such as quantification, implication and negation. Frege's formal notation thereby achieves a unification of two domains which traditional logics always treated separately, the *construction* of concepts and the *derivation* of propositions.

The *Begriffsschrift* contains the first full exposition of propositional calculus, presented in an axiomatic and fully formal way. But few among Frege's contemporaries were able to appreciate the importance of his contribution, not least because of his choice of a cumbersome and daunting notation system. (The notation relied heavily on spatial arrangements and did not resemble the linear notations used in mathematics and, for that matter, natural languages.) This notation did not survive Frege, and the current logical symbolism is largely derived from Peano's *Formulaire Mathematique*, which was taken up by Russell's *Principia Mathematica*.

7.2 Formal Notation and Natural Language

In a series of papers many of which remained unpublished in his lifetime, Frege used the resources of the conceptual notation to explore the logical structures of language and judgments that can be made within it. He considered his ideography as related to ordinary language in the way that a microscope is related to the naked eye: it enables one to perceive distinctions which remain blurred or even totally blacked out in the ordinary language. For example, in ordinary language the word 'is' expresses the following possible relations:

(a) the relationship between an object and the concept under which it can be subsumed. That is, 'Julius is a man' has the logical form: Fa.

(b) The relationship of subordination between concepts, as in 'man is a rational animal,' whose logical form contains the complex predicate: $Fx \supset Gx$.

(c) The relation between a first order and a second order concept, named 'inherence,' as in 'there is a mortal human' which is written as: $(\exists x)(Fx \& Gx)$. Here the quantifier serves as a second order concept linking the two first order concepts.

(d) The relationship of identity between two objects, as in 'Hesperus is Phosphorus,' whose logical form is expressed by the mathematical symbol for equality, used here as an identity between two proper names: $a = b$.

Failure to distinguish such differences in the logical structures of sentences containing 'is' not infrequently led to the drawing of false inferences. Famous proofs of the existence of God, based upon a confusion of

(c) with (a) above, treated existence as a first order property of an individual. Not only did the analysis 'subject-copula-predicate' of the standard Aristotelian logic encourage, in Frege's view, this type of confusion; it was also responsible for a failure to reveal the ways in which sentences having a different subject and a different predicate may nevertheless have the same meaning, as in 'Titus killed Caius' and 'Caius was killed by Titus.'

In a paper published in 1892, 'On Sense and Reference,' Frege examined what is required of the relation of identity. Contrary to what he himself had claimed in his 1879 *Begriffsschrift*, he revised his account of identity, and no longer thought it could be treated simply as a relationship between signs. In doing this, he realized that the very conception of a sign had to be revised. The new view was that every sign expresses both a sense and a reference. In the case of proper names, the sense of the name-sign is a way in which the reference is given, and the reference is the object named. However, in the case of predicates, the predicate sign refers to a concept, and the extension of the predicate (the items in the world to which it applies) plays a different role. Using a famous example in the arena of proper names, this distinction allowed Frege to claim that sentences such as (5 and 6):

Hesperus is Hesperus   (5)

Hesperus is Phosphorus   (6)

are identical in terms of reference though they differ in 'cognitive value,' that is, in the way that they enter into our understanding of beliefs and inferential processes. Thus, though the ancient astronomers would have assented to (5) on straightforward logical grounds, they would have dissented from (6) because they believed that the evening star (Hesperus) was a different heavenly body from the morning star (Phosphorus). However, as it happens both 'stars' are in fact the planet Venus, so Frege's distinction between sense and reference allowed him to treat both (5) and (6) as trivially claiming the self-identity of Venus, whilst at the same time maintaining that (5) and (6) could be understood differently by the ancient astronomers. This was because it was sense that mattered at the level of understanding, and the two proper names differ in sense, though not in reference. Frege extended this sense-reference distinction to what could be called propositions or sentences asserted. He claimed that the sense of a sentence was the thought it expressed, and its reference was either the value True or False.

Aside from providing a detailed and more convincing analysis of natural language structures than was possible in the traditional logic, Frege also made suggestive remarks about what might be called the 'nonstructural' aspects of ordinary language. In his view, a logical analysis of natural language should carefully distinguish the two levels or functions of an utterance, its expressing a sense and referring to a truth value, from a third function, which is to raise 'associated representations,' or provide a specific coloring for the thought. This function does not properly concern logic, but helps expressing emotions or highlights pragmatic factors relevant only for specific communicative purposes.

7.3 Logic, Mathematics, and Paradox

The major logical work of Frege is his *Basic Laws of Arithmetic*, in which he develops a 'system of logical laws' from which the theorems of arithmetic can be derived with the help of suitable definitions. Such a system includes seven axioms which give the conditions of use for basic signs such as implication, negation, identity, and quantification over first and second order functions. Law V allows transformations between one function and another when their ranges (i.e., the mappings associating a value to each argument) are identical. That law is considered by Frege as 'essential in logic when concept extensions are being dealt with.' Unfortunately, it was that very principle which was responsible for the paradox which Russell noted.

Notational innovations include replacing the equivalence sign with an identity sign (as has been noted in the case of proper names), and introducing a set of new signs to express the range of a function. It is characteristic of Frege's idea of a formal system that syntactical rules should not be divorced from semantic interpretation. What he calls 'the highest principle for definitions' requires that 'well-formed names always have a reference.' Frege uses a set of rules to make sure that the principle will be correctly applied while introducing any new expression in the system. Taking his starting point in the fact that the names for truth values do refer, he shows that the various basic terms of his logical symbolism also have a determinate reference.

In a letter dated June 16, 1902, Russell indicated to Frege that a contradiction could be derived in the system of his *Basic Laws*. Frege's ideography makes it possible to express the fact that a class does not belong to itself; it is true in the system for example, that the class of men is not a man. But one may then define a concept K as 'concept such that its extension does not belong to itself,' and show that the extension of K both belongs and does not belong to itself. Given the importance of Law V for Frege, and his insistence on every expression having determinate reference, this was disastrous.

Various solutions were explored by Frege, Russell, and later logicians to remedy Russell's paradox. Frege himself finally rejected all the available solutions, such as Russell's type theory, insofar as it led to what appeared to him to be unnatural ways of representing logical laws. In spite of Frege's own sense of having failed to achieve a logical reduction of arithmetic truths, the very contradiction shown to be infecting his system helped later logicians to come to understand some of the properties of formal systems revealed through various puzzles and antinomies. Research done later by Tarski, Gödel, and Carnap led to the idea of clearly distinguishing between claims made inside a language and the rules being expressed about the language. This is the distinction so fundamental now to logic between object and metalanguages. A powerful method, first devised by Hilbert, named arithmetization, allowed Gödel to show that there were severe, principled limitations to what could be proven inside a formal system including a representation of arithmetic such as Frege's.

See: Paradoxes, Semantic; Russell, Bertrand; Tarski, Alfred.

8. After Frege

Frege's work initiated a complete renaissance in logical studies, and deepened the understanding of the structure of natural language. Although logicism understood as the project of reducing mathematics to logic would only survive in a weakened form, Frege's effort to develop a formal symbolism adequate for expressing the relations of propositions in a system broke new theoretical ground, for logicians, mathematicians, linguists, and philosophers. Two influential schools in philosophy derived their basic claims from Frege's lessons, and it cannot be chance that they were headed by two former students or admirers of Frege: Carnap and Wittgenstein. The logical positivists, including Carnap, continued the exploration of the properties of formal systems and their foundational relevance for science in general. And the continuing tradition of analytic philosophy extended Frege's effort at elucidating the logical structure of ordinary language and dissolving, through logical scrutiny, some of the traditional dialectical illusions, now seen as originating in natural language. With Frege, not only logic itself, but the theoretical background to logic—its connection to philosophy and language studies generally—changed out of all recognition.

There are three directions in which logic has developed since Frege. On the one hand, the formalization of logic and the study of such formal systems has led to a major branch of mathematics. This work began with Frege, but continued with the publication in 1910–13 of Russell's and Whitehead's *Principia Mathematica*. Perhaps the two most important names in this field are Kurt Gödel and Alfred Tarski, but the technical details of their work lies beyond this survey.

The second area of research is that of computer science. In a slightly different idiom, some of the results of Gödel and Tarski have proven important to the development of the theory of computation. The name of Alan Turing, the English mathematician, is most well-known here.

Finally, the development of complex formal systems capable of expressing many of the nuances of natural language has made logic into one of the most important philosophical and linguistic tools in the current literature. One only has to look at journals in these areas to see this. So, after a very checkered history, the various strands of logic have now come together: it is now a fundamental part of our understanding of language and the mind in the way that it always promised to be in its earliest stages.

See also: Natural Deduction; Reasoning; Entailment; Deviant Logics.

Bibliography

Bochenski J I M 1970 *A History of Formal Logic*. Chelsea Publishing, New York

Kneale W, Kneale M 1962 *The Development of Logic*. Oxford University Press, Oxford

Moody E A 1953 *Truth and Consequence in Medieval Logic*. Amsterdam

Nagel E, Newman J R 1958 *Gödel's Proof*. New York University Press, New York

Van Heijenoort J (ed.) 1967 *From Frege to Gödel: A Source Book in Mathematical Logic*. Harvard University Press, Cambridge, MA

Logical Form

A. A. Brennan

Logic is the study of form rather than content. This simple observation gives little clue to the difficulties inherent in giving a satisfactory account of logical form. Although the formulae of truth-functional, or sentential, logic seem to provide a skeletal form for the corresponding sentences of natural language, the structures of the logic of quantifiers are somewhat remote from their natural language counterparts. It can be helpful to think of logic as providing a translation of sentences of natural language into those of a formal (that is, symbolic) language, rather than as revealing anything about the form (logical, grammatical, or semantic) of sentences in natural languages (see Guttenplan 1986).

1. Logical Form and Natural Language

The exploration of logical form, however, has been an important stimulus in both philosophy and linguistics. Gottlob Frege tried to give an account of the semantics of natural languages based on the assimilation of their features to those of formal languages. Ludwig Wittgenstein regarded logic, in his early period, as 'the great mirror,' its forms revealing not only something about the forms of natural language sentences, but also something about the forms of objects themselves and the possibilities of their relations with other objects. Logical form, then, for Wittgenstein, was critical both to semantics and to ontology, and a major concern of his *Tractatus Logico–Philosophicus* is the search for the general form of the sentence. The search was flawed, however, since Wittgenstein assumed wrongly that the form of all natural language sentences could be given using only the apparatus of truth-functions.

1.1 Sentential Connectives

To grasp the central idea of logical form, it is helpful to distinguish between certain 'logical' words, such as *if*, *and*, *or*, *not*, *all*, and *some*, and other, 'nonlogical' words. Thus, the sentence *it is raining and it is wet* is analyzed as consisting of two simpler sentences connected using the logical word *and*. Using letters to replace the sentences, and the sign ' $\wedge$ ' for *and*, the logical counterpart of the sentence reads $p \wedge q$. This is held to reveal the logical form of the original sentence in that the substitution of any other sentences for p and q will change only the content, not the form, of the original. For the truth-functions, the interpretation of each sentence consists simply in assigning to it one of the two truth-values, 'true' or 'false.' Where a sentence is a compound of simple sentences, the method of truth tables gives a vivid representation of how the interpretation (truth-value) of the whole sentence depends systematically on the truth-values of its parts.

1.2 Predicate Logic

The introduction of the quantifiers *all* and *some* involves considerable rephrasing of the natural language counterparts before reaching the logical forms. Classical logic, as expounded in the nineteenth century, notably by Frege, treats universal sentences as conditionals and existential sentences as conjunctions. Hence, the logical form of (1):

All fish swim (1)

is (2):

All things, x, are such that if x is a fish, (2)
then x swims

or (3):

> For any thing, x, if x is a fish, then x swims. (3)

The logical form of (4):

> Some fish swim (4)

is (5):

> There is (that is, exists) at least one thing, x; (5)
> such that x is a fish and x swims.

Using standard signs for the quantifiers, and using '⊃' for *if..., then...*, these sentences receive the final symbolism in (6) and (7):

> All fish swim $\forall x(Fx \supset Gx)$ (6)

> Some fish swim $\exists x(Fx \wedge Gx)$. (7)

The x in these formulae is known as the *variable of quantification*, and—as Frege first observed—has a role akin to an anaphoric pronoun.

These logical forms suggest that sentences that seem simply to predicate *swim* of the subject *all fish* or *some fish* in fact involve something much more complex. Each involves two contained sentences, within which something is predicated of the variable of quantification taken as subject. The discovery of these forms was of supreme importance in dislodging various traditional doctrines. For example, the symbolic versions above make clear that *all fish swim* does not imply that some fish swim (contrary to the medieval understanding of Aristotle's logic). For, in a world containing no fish at all, it would be true that all fish swim, but false that there exists at least one thing which is both a fish and also swims. Frege made much of the fact that (in his version of the above symbolic forms) it is clear that the semantics of names is quite distinct from the semantics of quantifiers.

In the theory of quantification, the open sentence *Fx* is interpreted by giving some predicate of natural language to put in place of the predicate-letter, *F* (hence, *x is red*, *x is a fish*, and so on). Likewise, polyadic predicates provide interpretations for open sentences like *Fxy*, *Gxyz*, and so on (for example, *x is east of y*, *x is between y and z*). Natural language often

deals with polyadic matters using sentences containing names, and these have their symbolic counterparts in constants (sometimes also called 'parameters'). Hence, *Adelaide is between Perth and Sydney* might be represented as *Gabc*, where *a*, *b*, and *c* are constants, rather than variables.

2. Logical Truth and Logical Consequence

Once the forms are understood, it becomes easy to settle the key issues of logical truth and logical consequence. A logical truth is a sentence whose symbolic paraphrase is true under all interpretations (in every nonempty universe). One sentence is a logical consequence of another (or of a set of sentences) if every interpretation (in every nonempty universe) which makes the latter true also makes the former true. Alternatively, if there is an interpretation of the set of sentences {*A, B, C, D*}, which makes them all true, while—under the same interpretation—a further sentence, *E*, is false, then *E* is not a logical consequence of the set {*A, B, C, D*}.

Thanks to the completeness and consistency of both truth-functional logic and the general logic of quantifiers, various methods of proof (axiomatic, natural deduction, and tableau procedures) are able to give straightforward verdicts on logical truth and logical consequence. This fact is sometimes described by saying that semantic validity (logical truth) matches syntactic validity (logical provability). However, although truth tables provide a mechanical procedure for determining logical truth and consequence for truth-functions, there is no similar method available for predicate logic in general.

See also: Logic: Historical Survey; Natural Deduction.

Bibliography

Frege G 1964 *The Basic Laws of Arithmetic*. University of California Press, Berkeley, CA
Guttenplan S 1986 *The Languages of Logic: An Introduction*. Basil Blackwell, Oxford
Jeffrey R 1990 *Formal Logic: Its Scope and Its Limits*, 3rd edn. McGraw Hill, Maidenhead
Wittgenstein L 1961 *Tractatus Logico–Philosophicus*. Routledge and Kegan Paul, London

Natural Deduction

A. Fisher

There is nothing very 'natural' about 'natural deduction' systems. They are systems of rules for checking whether one 'logical formula' is provable from other logical formulas in given systems of logic. As such they belong to the proof–theoretic approach, to logic, rather than to the model–theoretic approach: they are based on ideas about what is provable rather than on semantic ideas like 'truth' and 'counter-example.'

1. Propositional Logic and Truth Tables

Consider the case of classical, two–valued, propositional logic. This is the system of logic which assumes that every proposition is either true or false (and not both) and whose logical connectives ('not,' 'and,' 'or' and 'if . . . then') are defined by the following truth-tables (where T = true and F = false):

(notP)	(P and Q)	(P or Q)	(if P then Q) (1)
−P	P & Q	P v Q	P ⊃ Q
FT	T T T	T T T	T T T
TF	T F F	T T F	T F F
	F F T	F T T	F T T
	F F F	F F F	F T F

A formula of this system of logic is said to be a 'tautology' or 'valid,' provided it is true whatever the value of its constituent propositions (provided it always has the value T under the main connective of its truth-table). If this is *not* the case, there is a 'counter-example' to the formula, and it is said to be 'invalid.'

With these basic ideas one can test (some) natural language arguments for validity by translating them into the notation of propositional logic and using truth-tables; either one finds a counter-example or the argument is valid. For example, many 'logical principles' which people intuitively accept can be shown to be valid:

P or not P   (2)

if P implies Q and Q is false then P must be false.   (3)

if P implies Q and Q implies R then P implies R.   (4)

if P or Q are true and Q is false then P must be true.   (5)

2. Natural Deduction and Proof

Natural deduction methods proceed quite differently. Keeping to the example of classical propositional logic, the same underlying semantic ideas can be found, but everything is articulated in terms of what is *provable* from what—in terms of 'proof-rules' or 'inference-rules.' For example, one of the rules will say that from the conjunction 'P & Q' one can derive 'P'; another will say that from '−−P' one can derive 'P'; another will say that from the formula 'P' one can derive 'P v Q'; another will say that if you can derive both 'Q' and '−Q' from 'P,' then '−P' is provable, etc. The rules consist of 'introduction rules' and 'elimination rules': the elimination rules permit the 'elimination' of a logical connective from a formula, that is, they show which logically simpler formulas can be derived from a formula containing a given logical connective (like the examples concerning '&' and '−−' above); the introduction rules permit the 'introduction' of logical connectives, that is, they show which logically more complex formulas can be derived

from other formulas (like the examples concerning 'v' and '−' above). Each logical connective must have both introduction and elimination rules.

These rules are then used to check which logical formulas can be derived from which. For example, suppose one wished to show that example (4) above was provable in a natural deduction system for classical propositional logic, then a finite sequence of formulas would be constructed as follows:

(1)		P	Assumption	(6)
(2)		P⊃Q	Assumption	
(3)		Q⊃R	Assumption	
(4)	1, 2	Q	From 1 and 2 by ⊃-elimination (modus ponens)	
(5)	1, 2, 3	R	From 3 and 4 by ⊃-elimination	
(6)	2, 3	P⊃R	From 1 and 3 by ⊃-introduction	

where the numbers without brackets list the formulas on which the formula to their right 'depends.' This finite sequence of formulas shows that the formal equivalent of example (4) above is provable in standard natural deduction systems for classical propositional logic (with the rules indicated; for a detailed exposition of such a system see Lemmon 1965).

A natural deduction system for classical propositional logic then consists of a set of inference rules, like those mentioned above, and one uses these rules to test whether a given formula can be derived from other formulas. This is different from testing for validity by constructing truth- tables. On the natural deduction approach one constructs finite sequences of formulas, each of which is either an assumption made for the purpose of the test, or is derived from other formulas in the sequence by one of the rules of the natural deduction system. The object is to see if one can derive the conclusion of an argument from its premises using valid rules of inference.

The rules of 'natural deduction' systems are frequently rather 'unnatural' (especially for systems richer than propositional logic), and the process of constructing a proof sequence within such a system is often counterintuitive. However, it is fair to say that natural deduction systems are more 'natural' than 'axiomatic' approaches to logic. Gottlob Frege was the first person to articulate the principles of modern logic, in his *Begriffsschrift* (1879), and his presentation of logic was axiomatic (i.e., resembling Euclid's axiomatic presentation of geometry). Russell and Whitehead's *Principia Mathematica* (1910–13) was similar in its axiomatic approach to logic. S. Jaskowski and G. Gentzen independently devised natural deduction approaches to logic in the early 1930s. However, the method of 'semantic tableaux' (due to E. Beth in the mid-1950s) is probably the most 'natural' way of testing the validity of arguments (for a good exposition, see Jeffery 1967; for more on the history and development of natural deduction systems see Kneale and Kneale 1962: 538).

Bibliography
Jeffery R C 1967 *Formal Logic: Its Scope And Limits.* McGraw-Hill, New York
Kneale W, Kneale M 1962 *The Development of Logic.* Oxford University Press, Oxford
Lemmon E J 1965 *Beginning Logic.* Nelson, London
Quine W V 1952 *Methods of Logic.* Routledge and Kegan Paul, London
Tennant N 1978 *Natural Logic.* Edinburgh University Press, Edinburgh

Necessary and Sufficient Conditions

A. A. Brennan

A standard form of explicit definition consists in specifying necessary and sufficient conditions for the truth of a sentence. The notions of necessity and sufficiency are sometimes defined simply by reference to the 'truth-functional' account of the conditional. A conditional sentence of the form 'if p, then q' is false, according to classical logic, only when the antecedent (the *if*-clause) is true and the consequent (the *then*-clause) is false. In all other cases, the conditional is true. It appears to follow that if a conditional is true and has a true antecedent, then its consequent will be true. The truth of the antecedent, then, might be said to be sufficient for the truth of the consequent, and the truth of the consequent said to be, in its turn, necessary for the truth of the antecedent. The latter usage reflects the fact that equivalent to 'if p, then q' is the form 'if not q, then not p.' A necessary condition, in other words, is one whose truth is a sine qua non of the truth of the other condition (for a discussion, and criticism, of definitions in terms of necessary and sufficient conditions see *Family Resemblance*).

1. Problems with a Truth-functional Account

Standardly, the vocabulary of necessary and sufficient conditions is made to apply to sentences which are related either logically or nonlogically. Thus, to take a case of physically necessary and sufficient conditions, consider the conditional:

If the car starts there is charge in the battery.   (1)

Here the truth of the condition 'the car starts' is usually said to be sufficient for the truth of the claim 'there is charge in the battery.' Likewise, the truth of 'there is charge in the battery' is a (physically) necessary condition for the truth of 'the car starts.' The vocabulary is often used of the physical situations themselves. Thus one could say that the car's starting is a sufficient condition of there being charge in the battery. Likewise, there being charge in the battery is a necessary condition of the car's starting (for if there were not charge in the battery, the car would not start).

This way of explaining the distinction runs up against counterintuitive results if the conditional in the above example is taken to be truth-functional. A sufficient condition is meant to guarantee the truth of a certain further sentence. Now, provided it is true that the sun is shining and true that Jane is eating a cheese cracker, the truth-functional conditional 'If Jane is eating a cheese cracker then the sun is shining' is also true. Yet it would be implausible to claim that the truth of the sentence 'Jane is eating a cheese cracker' guarantees the truth of the sentence 'the sun is shining.'

A similar problem arises if the notions of necessary and sufficient conditions are defined by reference to inferential relations understood in the fashion of classical logic. Although in a deductive argument the truth of the premises is meant to guarantee the truth of the conclusion, there is no requirement that the premises be relevant to the conclusion. Likewise, in the same sort of argument, if the conclusion is false, then at least one of the premises is false: but there may well be no connection of the sort that makes it seem reasonable to describe the truth of the conclusion as necessary for the truth of the premises.

2. An Alternative to the Truth-functional Account

Rather than defining necessary and sufficient conditions by reference to the truth-functional conditional, then, it may be more straightforward to do this in terms of the natural-language use of 'if' where the truth of the antecedent is held to provide at least some relevant reason for thinking that the consequent is true, if not an explanation of why the consequent is true. For such conditionals, the truth of the antecedent is sufficient for the truth of the consequent, while the truth of the consequent, in turn, is necessary for the truth of the antecedent. That the car starts gives reason for thinking that there is charge in the battery, and so constitutes a plausible sufficient condition of there being charge in the battery. Moreover, the battery's having charge is a necessary condition for starting the car, in that its being dis-

283

charged would (at least in part) explain the car's not starting.

By extension from the physical—or causal—cases, it is possible to define various other kinds of necessary and sufficient condition—including nomic and conceptual ones. For example, it appears to be a necessary, but not sufficient, condition of speaking a sentence that the subject utter words. In this example, there is a claimed conceptual connection between speaking and uttering. Likewise, in the conceptual analysis of memory, that it is of the past seems to be a necessary condition for something's being a memory.

That a ball is red is a logically necessary condition of its being red and made of vinyl (and the latter is a logically sufficient condition of its being red). This is so because of the deductive relation between:

> The ball is red and made of vinyl   (2)

and:

> The ball is red.   (3)

Perhaps in this case, the truth-functional account of necessary and sufficient conditions comes as close to being acceptable as it is ever likely to. Even so, counterintuitive consequences obtrude. For instance, any logically true sentence would now be a necessary condition of every sentence (for example, anything of the form 'p ∨ ~p' is a logical truth, and so the conditional 'q → (p ∨ ~p)' is therefore true no matter what sentence 'q' represents). Classical logicians may be prepared to accept this kind of result as a corollary of the so-called 'paradoxes of material implication.'

See also: Deviant Logics; Entailment; Relevant Logic.

Bibliography

Anderson A R, Belnap N 1975 *Entailment the Logic of Relevance and Necessity*. Princeton University Press, Princeton, NJ
Wilson I R 1979 Explanatory and inferential conditionals. *Philosophical Studies* **35**: 269–78

Necessity

G. Forbes

Philosophers have long supposed that certain propositions are not merely true but necessarily true: they could not possibly be false. The search for such propositions and attempts to explain the source of their necessity have occupied a central place in the history of philosophy. Many of the great problems of philosophy may be formulated in terms of the modal concepts of necessity, contingency, and possibility. Aristotle's problem of the open future is the problem whether, if it is true that something is going to happen, them it *must* happen. Hume's problem of causation is the problem of whether an event E can have an effect which in some sense *must* occur, given the occurrence of E. Kant's problem of free will is the problem of whether in a world governed by laws of nature there is any sense in which agents *can* act otherwise than they do. Examples may be multiplied. In contemporary philosophy, the analysis of modal concepts themselves has also flourished, hand in hand with a revived interest in such central issues in modal metaphysics (Kripke 1980; Lewis 1986a; Van Inwagen 1983). Both the analytical and the metaphysical aspects of the debate are discussed.

1. Varieties of Necessity

As the problems of Aristotle, Hume, and Kant make plain, there is more than one notion of necessity. Some

notions are epistemic, such as the notion of what is implied by what we know, but the concern here is not with epistemic concepts. The most important non-epistemic notions are these, from least to most constrained: (a) (narrow) logical necessity; (b) mathematical necessity; (c) metaphysical necessity (sometimes called 'broadly logical necessity'); and (d) physical necessity. Logical necessity belongs to the validities of logic, mathematical necessity belongs to the truths of mathematics, metaphysical necessity to the truths of metaphysics, and physical necessity to laws of nature.

Three questions may be raised about each type of necessity: (i) how does that type of necessity relate to the others, and in particular, is it 'reducible' to any of the others?, (ii) what are specific examples of propositions which are necessities of that type?, and (iii) wherein lies the source of the type of necessity in question? For example, with regard to (i), the logicist movement in philosophy of mathematics was concerned to show that mathematical truth reduces to logical truth, a thesis which has as a corollary that mathematical necessity reduces to logical necessity. With regard to (ii), there has been considerable recent discussion of certain putative metaphysical necessities (Kripke 1980; Putnam 1975). And with regard to (iii), the problem of the source of necessity has prompted a range of proposals from conventionalism at one extreme (Wright 1980; Sidelle 1989) to unqualified realism at the other (Lewis 1986b).

2. Mathematical and Logical Necessity

According to the mathematical Platonist, mathematics is the study of certain abstract objects such as numbers and functions. These objects exist necessarily and their intrinsic properties, as well as their relations amongst themselves, are also necessary: it is necessary that the number 3 exists, necessary that it is prime, and necessary that it is greater than the number 2. For a mathematical Platonist, mathematical necessity is *sui generis*, deriving from the peculiar nature of the subject matter of mathematics.

The most important movement in modern philosophy of mathematics has been the logicist movement, founded by Frege and Russell (Frege 1986; Russell 1919). The logicists proposed to reduce mathematics to logic (so they were not 'mathematical' Platonists), but the actual reductions which Frege and Russell produced were to set theories and type theories which it would require exceptional generosity to classify as logic. For these theories have substantial existential import (a set theory to which number theory reduces has only infinite models), and it is hard to see how logic alone, or logic and definitions, could give rise to any existential consequences whatsoever; even classical logic's theorem 'something exists' is somewhat objectionable, and a free logic where it fails is preferable. So the logicism of Frege and Russell does not provide a good reason for thinking that mathematical necessity is a species of logical necessity.

However, there is an interesting contemporary variant of logicism to which the objection from unwanted existential import does not arise. Hartry Field has argued that mathematical necessity is a species of logical necessity, but not because mathematical truth reduces to logical truth. Field is an instrumentalist about mathematics, and holds that the statements of mathematics are not bearers of truth and falsity at all. However, there is such a thing as mathematical knowledge. Mathematical knowledge is knowledge of the form *it is logically consistent (possible) that A* where *A* is the conjunction of the axioms of a mathematical theory, or of the form *it is logically necessary that if A then B*, where *B* is some sentence which follows from the axioms *A*. Field elaborates these basic ideas to accommodate nonfinitely axiomatized theories and develops a modal logic for the logical possibility and necessity operators (Field 1989). On this approach, then, one can trace the appearance of necessity in a theorem *B* to the necessity of the conditional *if A then B*. But clearly, there is a controversial question whether this approach is successful in the special case where *B* is one of the conjuncts of *A* (i.e., an axiom). That is, can the apparent necessity of *if x and y have identical successors then x and y are identical* be explained merely by its being a consequence by &-Elimination of the collection of logically consistent statements that make up Peano's axioms for arithmetic?

3. Some Metaphysical Necessities

Logical necessity narrowly construed allows as possibilities some things which seem in a substantial sense to be impossible; one says they are metaphysically impossible. For example, it is impossible that an object which is red all over at a time *t* is also green all over at *t*, but logic alone cannot discover a contradiction in the hypothesis that it is both. More interestingly, it also seems impossible that I, the present writer, could have been a musical score, or a tree, or an insect, rather than a human being: the kind of thing I am seems to be 'essential' to me (Wiggins 1980). An essential property of an object *x* is a property *x* could not have lacked except by failing to exist; so it is necessary that if *x* exists, it has the property. The interesting examples of impossibilities not precluded by logic (or mathematics) are examples of this sort, where we have the intuition that there is no genuinely possible way things could have gone (no genuinely possible world) in which the relevant object *x* lacks the property. These examples involve specific objects or kinds of objects, and for that reason the necessities have been traditionally known as 'de re' necessities, necessities concerning objects.

Following on work of Kripke (1980), two of the most widely discussed de re necessities are the 'necessity of identity' and the 'necessity of origin.' Suppose the Superman story is fact. Then Clark Kent = Superman. Is this a necessary or contingent fact? There is some impulse to say it is contingent, but Kripke argues that this is a confusion. It is true that, in advance of detailed investigation, what someone knows may be 'consistent' with Superman being someone other than Clark Kent, but this is merely an epistemic possibility and is therefore irrelevant to the question whether, granted that Superman in fact *is* Clark Kent, there is a genuinely possible world in which Superman is not Clark Kent. There is certainly a world in which Superman is not the person *called* 'Clark Kent,' but that is quite different from not *being* Clark Kent; after all, there is a world in which Clark Kent is not the person called 'Clark Kent.' The strongest argument that there is no possible situation in which Clark Kent is not Superman is that such a situation would be one in which, *per impossibile*, Superman is not Superman. For if Superman and Clark Kent are the same person, anything possible for one is possible for the other, so if not being Clark Kent is possible for Superman, not being Clark Kent is possible for Clark Kent. And such a possibility is hard to understand.

There is no comparably simple argument for the necessity of origin, according to which a particular organism *O* which actually originates from a cell *C* could not have originated from any distinct cell *D*. Or as Kripke puts it rhetorically, 'How could a person originating from different parents, from a totally different sperm and egg, be *this very woman*?' (Kripke 1980: 113). Subsequent work on this topic has shown that Kripke's intuition can be traced to principles about the acceptability of criteria for determining the identity of an object in a possible world, but whether these principles are correct is itself a matter of controversy (Forbes 1985).

4. The Source of Necessity

Quine has argued that the various kinds of necessity discussed here are creatures of darkness to the extent that they go beyond some explicit notion of formal validity which can be expressed in a predicate (Quine 1976: paper 15). But few have been persuaded by his skepticism, and thus the majority of philosophers incur the problem of the source of necessity.

On the conventionalist account, logical, mathematical, and metaphysical necessity can be traced to conventions governing the use of language. But conventionalism has hardly been a success even in the easiest case of logical necessity (Quine 1976: paper 11), and it is hard to see how it could explain de re metaphysical necessities. That there is a convention, for each organism *x* and propagule *y* from which *x* originates, to treat any assertion to the effect that *x* originates from *y* as a necessary truth, seems an unpromising account of how such necessity arises (but see Sidelle 1989: Chap. 3).

Conventionalism is one flavor of the position that necessity must ultimately reduce to facts about meaning or concepts: the necessity of 'all bachelors are unmarried' is the paradigm, and all other necessities are to be somehow reduced to the case of straightforwardly analytic truths. But the de re necessities mentioned above appear to constitute very great stumbling blocks to such linguistic approaches to necessity.

At the opposite end of the spectrum of views about the source of necessity there is David Lewis's position (Lewis 1986b), which removes the source of necessity from language and thought as far as can be. According to Lewis, a necessary truth is one which holds in every possible world, and a possible world is a complete way things could have been which exists in exactly the way the actual world exists: *this* world is to other worlds as *this* place is to other places. It seems that no further account of the source necessity could be given: the necessities are just those things which 'happen' to hold in all worlds.

An intermediate but still realist position is one which discerns the source of necessity in the structure of properties. Such a view appears to have a good chance of dovetailing with a plausible epistemology of modality, whose task is to explain how we know what is necessary and what is not. Both the source problem and the epistemological problem are important areas of future research (see Fine 1994).

See also: Essentialism; Modal Logic.

Bibliography

Field H 1989 *Realism, Mathematics and Modality*. Basil Blackwell, New York
Fine K 1994 Essence and modality. In: Tomberlin J (ed.) *Philosophical Perspectives*, vol. 8. Ridgeview, Atascadero, CA
Forbes G 1985 *The Metaphysics of Modality*. Clarendon Press, Oxford
Frege G 1986 *The Foundations of Arithmetic*. Basil Blackwell, Oxford
Kripke S A 1980 *Naming and Necessity*. Blackwell, Oxford
Lewis D K 1986a *Philosophical Papers*, vol. II. Oxford University Press, New York
Lewis D K 1986b *On The Plurality of Worlds*. Basil Blackwell, Oxford
Putnam H 1975 *Mind, Language and Reality: Philosophical Papers*, vol. 2. Cambridge University Press, Cambridge
Quine W V O 1976 *The Ways of Paradox*. Harvard University Press, Cambridge, MA
Russell B 1919 *Introduction to Mathematical Philosophy*. Allen and Unwin, London
Sidelle A 1989 *Necessity, Essence and Individuation*. Cornell University Press, Ithaca, NY
Van Inwagen P 1983 *An Essay on Free Will*. Clarendon Press, Oxford
Wiggins D 1980 *Sameness and Substance*. Blackwell, Oxford
Wright C 1980 *Wittgenstein on the Foundations of Mathematics*. Duckworth, London
Yablo S 1992 Cause and essence. *Synthese* **93**: 403–49

Occasion Sentences and Eternal Sentences

C. J. Hookway

The distinction between occasion sentences and eternal sentences is important in the philosophy of Quine. The truth value of a sentence such as 'That bird is a seagull' will vary with the context of utterance. 'I was angry with you yesterday' is similarly true on some occasions, false on others, depending upon the speaker, the addressee, and the time of utterance. Quine calls such sentences occasion sentences, contrasting them with standing sentences whose truth value is less context-dependent. Once I have decided to assent to 'Apples grow on trees,' I shall do so in any context.

1. A Matter of Degree

The distinction is a matter of degree. 'Rome is the capital of Italy' is hardly an occasion sentence but political change could make it false. An eternal sentence is a standing sentence 'of an extreme kind': 'its truth value stays fixed through time and from speaker to speaker' (Quine 1960: 193). Examples include truths of scientific theory and mathematics, and descriptions of particular events can also be provided by eternal sentences: tense, personal pronouns, and demonstratives can be replaced by descriptions of the time, place, and people and things involved. Thus 'The bird that was observed by so-and-so at 3 pm on June 3, 1990 at such-and-such place was a seagull' is an eternal sentence describing the event mentioned in our first example. Not all standing sentences are eternal: for example, 'Germany has been unified.'

2. Eternal Sentences and Propositions

If I say 'You are angry' and you subsequently say 'I was then angry,' then, in one sense, we say the same thing: i.e., express the same proposition; the utterances are either both true or both false. Many philosophers have argued that propositions, abstract objects which are expressed by utterances, do not exist: they hold that no clear account of them has been provided. Eternal sentences can serve as surrogates for propositions: the same eternal sentence could have been uttered on both occasions. Truth and falsehood can be seen as straightforward properties of eternal sentences, and no relativity to context is required. Logical laws are also normally formulated for propositions rather than sentences: this illuminates the systematic relations between the truth values of different occasion sentences in related contexts and simplifies the formulation of the laws. The same benefits are obtained if the laws are formulated for eternal sentences.

One cannot always find an eternal sentence which gives the content of a thought. The belief that a meeting is beginning now can move one to act although the thought that the meeting is at 3 pm would not, since one may not know that it is now 3 pm (Perry 1979). It is compatible with this that the facts of nature can all be expressed by eternal sentences.

See also: Indeterminacy of Translation; Proposition; Truth.

Bibliography

Perry J 1979 The problem of the essential indexical. *Nous* **13**: 3–21
Quine W V O 1960 *Word and Object*. Technology Press of the MIT, Cambridge, MA
Quine W V O 1970 *Philosophy of Logic*. Prentice-Hall, Englewood Cliffs, NJ

Proposition

M. Crimmins

The idea of a proposition has played a central role in the development of logic, philosophy of language, philosophical psychology, and theoretical linguistics. A simple example illustrates the features of propositions that help explain their usefulness. I say that King is a scary dog; you believe it, remember it, and say it yourself at times—usually in English, but sometimes in French or German; whether or not it is true depends only on a fact about King; if it is true, it never was nor will be false (though it might have been false); it implies that King is a dog, and it is compatible with King's being a German Shepherd dog. Propositions, then, as standardly understood, are contents of utterances and of propositional attitudes, they are not individuated in terms of any particular language, they are tightly bound up with, or identical to, their truth conditions, they are unchanging bearers of truth, falsity, contingency, or necessity, and they stand in relations of entailment, exclusion, and compatibility.

1. The Theoretical Status of Propositions

The usefulness of propositions does not arise simply from the number and importance of these individual uses; the real work is done by the systematic connections propositions allow us to make among language, thought, truth, and the world. Communication involves (often) saying something one believes—and thereby causing others to believe the same thing. Truthfulness and knowledge involve uttering and believing things that are true. Representation and communication are just the storage and exchange of information (including misinformation), and propositions are taken to be the principal values of all the various currencies of information.

The theoretical status of propositions can be seen in at least two ways. First, propositions might be considered theoretical posits: entities which one believes in precisely because they explain talk of what people say, believe, hope, and so on, and because they explain central features of the processes of communication and psychological inference. If this is right, then empirical facts about the use of propositional attitude sentences (see Sect. 6 below) and about communication and inference, will count as data to which a theory of propositions must be adequate—it is an empirical task to discover what propositions are. Second, propositions might be thought of as theoretical constructs which allow the organization and unification of theoretical explanations of the various semantic, mental, and other phenomena. Seen in this way, one is oneself in control of what propositions are; what is open to empirical question is rather their theoretical utility.

2. Propositions, Sentences, Meanings, Facts

Since it is possible to say the same things with different words, and even in different languages, the things people say, propositions, are not simply the sentences they utter; nor, clearly, are they the utterances themselves (statements, in the case of assertion). Neither are propositions the meanings of sentences: the sentence 'I am hungry' has just one meaning when you and I utter it, but you express a proposition about yourself, and I do not. The relationship seems to be this: a statement consists of a speaker assertively uttering a sentence with a certain meaning, thereby expressing a certain proposition, and taking on a commitment to its truth. Other forms of utterance, including questions and commands, involve propositions in parallel ways.

Propositions often are distinguished not only from sentences and statements, but also from facts and states of affairs. A proposition might be true or false, whereas facts can only exist, and states of affairs can either be the case (alternatively: hold, be factual) or not. These distinctions are important only in certain theories, like situation semantics, which make use of more than one of these kinds of entity.

Propositions and truth conditions are at the very least intimately related. A proposition is an abstract claim that things are a certain way. Truth conditions (of a statement, sentence, proposition, or whatever) are simply the conditions that must hold if the thing under consideration is to be true. The conditions that must hold and the abstract claim that they do in fact hold are difficult to tell apart, so many theorists stipulate that propositions simply are their truth conditions, and are as well the truth conditions of statements, beliefs, and so on. Others have preferred to hold that propositions have their truth conditions essentially, but are not identical to them.

Even among the philosophers and linguists who agree that propositions ought to play a crucial theoretical role, there is little agreement about precisely what they are. Among the many different conceptions of proposition relevant to the study of language, the most prominent include Frege's 'thoughts' (based on Platonic universal entities he calls 'senses'), Russell's 'structured propositions' (which contain concrete objects as well as universals; this conception is explained well in Soames 1987), and Carnap's 'intensions' (based on the notion of a complete description of the world in an ideal language). Refined versions of Carnap's conception survive in theories of possible worlds (Lewis 1986; Stalnaker 1984) and in early situation theory (Barwise and Perry 1983). One's choice of a particular conception of proposition should be motivated by considerations about what kinds of entities are suited to the roles propositions play, and how they must be individuated (distinguished from one another).

3. Individuating Propositions

It is usually agreed that if propositions are to be bearers of truth and objects of attitudes like belief, then simply by the indiscernibility of identicals, it follows that they must be individuable by a *truth test* and by a *belief test*: if p is true (or might have been true) and q is false (or might then have been false), then p and q cannot be the same proposition; if p is an object of belief for an agent and q is not, then p and q cannot be the same proposition. These tests, it may seem, can provide data to be explained by a theory of what propositions are.

3.1 Talking about Propositions

As important and as legitimate as these tests are, however, their application in any particular case is by no means straightforward, largely because of difficulties concerning the logical form of devices for talking about propositions, and accompanying difficulties in securely hanging on to p and q from the premises to the conclusions of the tests. For instance, one might have thought it clear that, since Tom can believe the proposition that Cicero was an orator while not believing the proposition that Tully was an orator, then the proposition that Cicero was an orator must be different from the proposition that Tully was an orator, in spite of the fact that Cicero is the same person as Tully. But even given the truth of the premises about Tom's beliefs (for some philosophers doubt that these premises can possibly be true), the conclusion follows only if one assumes (a) that the belief reports used in the premises have a very straightforward logical form (say, reporting simply that the belief-relation holds between Tom and a specified proposition), and (b) that there are no shifting contextual features that cause the propositions specified in the premises to differ from those specified in the conclusion (i.e., that what proposition is specified by a description of the form 'the proposition that *s*' does not subtly vary with the evolving context of discourse). Since these assumptions are hard to defend without the help of well-developed theories about propositions, semantics, and belief, it is problematic to use such a 'test' to provide data for such theories. Of course, any plausible accounts of these matters must give explanations for divergences from the natural, naive views that reports of propositional attitudes straightforwardly report relations to propositions, and that specifying a proposition is a straightforward matter without a great deal of subtle contextuality. But there are independent reasons to think that subtle features of context can be crucial to the truth of propositional attitude reports (see Kripke 1979; Crimmins and Perry 1989).

3.2 Propositional Content

Another stumbling block in individuating propositions is that intuitions about the identity and difference of 'what is expressed' in statements (or of 'what is believed' in cases of belief) can at times be uncertain, and so theories of semantics and propositions that do not reflect these uncertainties have some explaining to do. There are at least two kinds of uncertainty worth mentioning.

First, between clear cases of identity and difference of proposition expressed, there may be grades and shades. Consider these pairs of statements: 'John and Bill have kissed Mary' and 'John has kissed Mary, Bill has kissed Mary'; 'John kissed Mary' and 'Mary was kissed by John'; 'John bought a car' and 'John was sold a car'; 'This triangle is equilateral' and 'This triangle is equiangular'; 'Line *a* is parallel to line *b*' and 'The direction of line *a* is the same as the direction of line *b*'; 'John shaved John' and 'John shaved himself.' Are these different ways of saying the same things, or are different but closely related things expressed?

Second, there are conflicts of reference and perspective: for you to believe or say the same thing as I do when I believe or say that I am hungry, must you believe that *I* am hungry, or that *you* are hungry? In this particular case, there seem to be two dimensions of what we say that we can compare; perhaps if you are to say something with the same meaning you must say that you are hungry, and if you are to say something with the same truth conditions, you must say that I am hungry. Things are more complicated, however, with my statement of 'my fork is to the left of your spoon.' Here, there are several different candidates for sentences you might use to say the same thing I have said, obtained by varying the different elements of the sentence to maintain either reference

or perspectival similarity. The general problem is that intuitions about saying or believing the same thing are sensitive both to reference and to perspective, and so in general these intuitions cannot be explained by citing just one 'thing said' in a statement or 'thing believed' in a belief.

4. Structured Propositions

Theories of structured propositions take propositions to be abstract, structured entities, typically containing individuals and properties as constituents (see Cresswell 1985; Katz 1977; Salmon 1986). One such theory would take a proposition to be a sequence containing a property or relation as its first constituent, and other entities as its other constituents. For instance, if *FatherOf* is a binary relation and John and Tom are individuals, then the sequence ⟨*FatherOf*, John, Tom⟩ is the proposition that John is the father of Tom. Logical connectives and quantifiers can be accommodated in any of several ways, including by treating 'logical constants' as relations between propositions, as in (1):

$$\langle Or, \langle White, \text{Snow} \rangle, \langle Green, \text{Grass} \rangle \rangle \tag{1}$$

The great usefulness of structured propositions in semantics comes from facts about the compositional way in which the proposition expressed by a statement depends on the objects, properties, relations, and so on expressed by its component expressions. The sentence 'John is the father of Tom' expresses the proposition just described because the use of 'John' refers to John, the use of 'Tom' refers to Tom and the use of 'is the father of' expresses the relation *FatherOf*. By mirroring the syntactic structure of the sentences used to express them, structured propositions are naturally suited for playing the role of the semantic values of statements.

A problem somewhat special to this account of propositions is that it can seem to mistakenly distinguish identical propositions. For instance, the proposition that two is less than three will count as different from the proposition that three is greater than two; and one might have thought these were the same, that the claims are identical. This might be remedied by a modification in which the argument roles of relations are not ordered (so that 'is less than' and 'is greater than' express the same relation), but other cases of this kind may persist in which propositions are incorrectly distinguished.

5. Propositions as Sets of Possible Worlds

In possible-worlds theory (see Lewis 1986; Stalnaker 1984), a proposition is a set of possible worlds. The proposition expressed by 'John is the father of Tom' is the set containing exactly those possible worlds in which John is Tom's father. The actual world is a possible world (at least on many theories; otherwise it is not a world, but corresponds to a unique world), and is a member of every true proposition. If John really is Tom's father, then the actual world is one in which John is Tom's father, so it is a member of the proposition that John is Tom's father. Sets of worlds bear relations to each other of inclusion, exclusion, and so on, and in possible-worlds' theory these become logical relations. For instance, if proposition P is a subset of proposition Q, then P entails Q. The set of worlds in which grass is green and snow is white is a subset of the set of worlds in which snow is white. Possible-worlds propositions are in this way neatly suited to tasks of set-theoretically modeling logical relations.

Construed in this way, propositions have constituents, but these are worlds, as opposed to individuals and properties or concepts. So their structure is nothing like the structure of statements that express them. For instance, conjunctions usually have fewer constituents than their conjuncts, and all necessarily true propositions have exactly the same constituents (and are identical). So while possible-worlds propositions may do semantic duty as truth conditions of statements, they are not useful as semantic 'structures' reflecting the way in which the truth conditions of a statement depend on its parts.

While possible-world semantics seems not to make the mistake of distinguishing between identical propositions, it does seem to make the opposite mistake, of conflating distinct propositions. According to possible-worlds' theory, all necessarily equivalent propositions are identical, since they are true in all the same worlds. Thus, the conjunctive proposition that snow is white and two equals two, is on this view identical to the proposition that snow is white. In addition, all true mathematical claims express the same proposition (the necessary one containing all possible worlds).

6. Propositional Attitudes

Part of the intuitive motivation for using propositions as central theoretical tools comes from their serving not only as the things one claims, but also as the things one believes, hopes, doubts, and so on. The difficulty in explaining semantically linguistic practices of talking about these propositional attitudes has led to an embarrassment for theorists who have long since adopted propositions for theoretical use.

The naive semantic view of belief reports, for example, is just this: a use of '*A* believes that *p*,' expresses the proposition that *A* bears the relation of belief to the proposition expressed by *p*. This view has been held in very different forms by Frege, Russell, Carnap, Barwise and Perry, Salmon, and Soames. Yet, the view in all its forms has never been able satisfactorily to handle the simple, though stubborn, puzzles about

substitution, including Frege's example of the agent who believes that Hesperus is seen in the morning, yet does not believe that Phosphorus is seen in the morning (where Hesperus and Phosphorus are really both the planet Venus). The problem seems to result from a tension between on the one hand the theoretically useful *public* nature of propositions, and on the other the fact that belief reports seem to make very fine, idiosyncratic distinctions among beliefs.

Frege and his followers opt to solve the problem by holding that just which proposition is expressed by a sentence is a very idiosyncratic, speaker-relative matter, which cannot be determined simply by the individuals and properties referred to by the words and phrases in the sentence uttered. Thus it is no surprise that someone can believe that Hesperus is seen in the morning, but not that Phosphorus is seen in the morning (because the sentences 'Hesperus is seen in the morning' and 'Phosphorus is seen in the morning' can express very different propositions). One trouble with this approach is in connecting the proposition that the speaker of such a belief report expresses by uttering, say, 'Hesperus is seen in the morning,' with a proposition that the agent might really believe. If propositions are idiosyncratic for given speakers and believers, then it is difficult to ensure that what an agent believes is ever what we say she believes.

Another way out is to explain away the intuition that an agent really can believe something about Hesperus without believing the same thing about Phosphorus. The prevalent view of this sort (see Barwise and Perry 1983; Salmon 1986; Soames 1987) involves holding that it is strictly speaking true, but very misleading, to say that the agent believes that Phosphorus is seen in the morning. It is wrong, though not necessarily false, to say things that are misleading, so one would not be comfortable in saying that the agent believes that Phosphorus is seen in the morning— though in fact one is wrong in one's naive intuitions about the truth of that claim, according to these theorists.

Responses to these problems have emphasized the context sensitivity of propositional attitude statements, and have abandoned the naive view that such a statement simply claims that an agent is related to a proposition (see Asher 1986; Crimmins and Perry 1989; Richard 1990). This allows these semanticists to retain the picture of propositions as public entities that people state, believe, hope, and so on, while still allowing for the idiosyncrasy and speaker relativity of attitude *reports*. The idiosyncrasy is traced not to idiosyncratic propositional contents of beliefs, hopes, and statements, but rather to idiosyncratic contextually determined conditions that reporters claim to hold of agents' beliefs, hopes, and statements, beyond merely having a certain content. Thus, to claim that the agent believes that Hesperus is seen in the morning and that the agent does not believe that Phosphorus is seen in the morning may be to ascribe a belief *meeting a certain condition* in a proposition and lack of any belief *meeting a different condition* in the same proposition (where the conditions are specified contextually).

See also: Intensionality; Propositional Attitude; Sense; Truth.

Bibliography

Asher N 1986 Belief in discourse representation theory. *Journal of Philosophical Logic* **15**: 127–89
Barwise J, Perry J 1983 *Situations and Attitudes*. MIT Press, Cambridge, MA
Cartwright R 1987 Propositions. In: *Collected Papers*. MIT Press, Cambridge, MA
Cresswell M J 1985 *Structured Meanings*. MIT Press, Cambridge, MA
Crimmins M, Perry J 1989 The prince and the phone booth: Reporting puzzling beliefs. *Journal of Philosophy* **86**: 685–711
Crimmins M 1992 *Talk About Beliefs*. MIT Press, Cambridge, MA
Crimmins M 1995 Quasi-Singular Propositions: The Semantics of Belief Reports. *Proceedings of the Aristotelian Society*. Suppl. vol 69: 195–209
Katz J J 1977 *Propositional Structure and Illocutionary Force*. Harvester, Hassocks
Kripke S A 1979 A puzzle about belief. In: Margalit A (ed.) *Meaning and Use*. Reidel, Dordrecht
Lewis D 1986 *On the Plurality of Worlds*. Blackwell, Oxford
Récanati F 1995 Quasi-Singular Propositions: The Semantics of Belief Reports. *Proceedings of the Aristotelian Society*. Suppl. vol 69: 175–193
Richard M 1990 *Propositional Attitudes*. Cambridge University Press, Cambridge
Salmon N 1986 *Frege's Puzzle*. MIT Press, Cambridge, MA
Soames S 1987 Direct reference, propositional attitudes and semantic content. *Philosophical Topics* **15**: 47–87
Stalnaker R C 1984 *Inquiry*. MIT Press, Cambridge, MA

Propositional Attitudes

R. A. Muskens

Verbs such as *know, believe, hope, fear, regret,* and *desire* are commonly taken to express an attitude that one may bear towards a proposition and are therefore called verbs of propositional attitude. Thus in (1) below the agent Cathy is reported to have a certain attitude—namely that of regret—towards the proposition that is the meaning of the embedded sentence:

Cathy regrets that Jim didn't call her. (1)

This immediately raises the question what it is exactly that can be the object of an attitude. Attitude reports produce a context in which to study this issue and thus have a central importance for the semantics of natural language. However, the study of propositional attitudes mainly helps to reveal what meanings are *not*. Unfortunately it does not give much clue about what meanings are.

1. The Object of an Attitude as a Truth Value

A widely accepted principle in semantics is that if two sentences have different truth values, they cannot have the same meaning (see Cresswell 1982 for a particularly clear statement of the role of this principle). On a naïve account of semantics it might even be thought that meanings just *are* truth values. Of course a theory to this effect would be rather hard to accept, since intuitively there are myriads of meanings while there are only two truth values, truth and falsity.

Attitude reports provide a way to refute such a theory. Contrast sentence (1) with sentence (2):

Cathy regrets that Joe didn't call her. (2)

Now suppose that in fact neither Jim nor Joe called Cathy. If the meanings of the embedded sentences would simply be their truth values then, since they are both true, they would have the same meaning and Cathy would bear the relation of regret to one precisely if she would bear that relation to the other. Thus the theory predicts that (2) follows from (1). This is absurd of course, and it may be concluded that meanings are not simply truth values.

Note the structure of the argument. The starting point was the supposition that meanings were to be equated with certain entities. From this it was derived that two given sentences had the same meaning and that therefore bearing some attitude towards one implied bearing the same attitude towards the other. This turned out to be absurd and it was concluded that meanings were not the things they had been supposed to be. This sort of argument can be brought up against many proposals about the nature of meaning and it can be used to show that there is no real sameness of meaning in natural language, except of course the trivial synonymy that obtains between an expression and itself.

2. The Possible Worlds Account of the Attitudes

Perhaps the standard view about meaning is the view that the meaning of a sentence is the set of all circumstances in which it is true and the most elegant formalization of this theory is given in the possible worlds semantics that also underlies modal logic. On this account a verb of propositional attitude denotes a relation between an agent and a set of possible worlds, the set of worlds in which the sentential complement of the attitude verb is true. According to this theory, the meaning of (3) can be formalized as formula (4), an expression that denotes the set of all worlds j such that something is a man in j and likes Cathy in j. The theory also provides a way to formalize propositional attitude reports. Sentence (5), for instance, can be rendered as (6), an expression that has for its extension the set of all worlds where the belief relation obtains between Cathy and (4):

Some man likes Cathy. (3)

$\lambda j. \exists x (M(x, j) \wedge L(x, c, j))$ (4)

Cathy believes that some man likes her. (5)

$\lambda i. Bel(c, \lambda j. \exists x (M(x, j) \wedge L(x, c, j)), i)$ (6)

Formula (6) gives the nonspecific reading of (5), the reading where Cathy believes that at least one man likes her. One virtue of the possible world analysis of the attitudes is that it allows for a second reading of the sentence in question, the reading where (5) states that there is some particular man of whom Cathy believes that he likes her. This reading can be formalized as (7) below. It is called the *de re* reading of (5), while (6) is its *de dicto* reading.

$\lambda i. \exists x (M(x, i) \wedge Bel(c, \lambda j. L(x, c, j), i))$ (7)

There is another phenomenon that is nicely explained by the possible worlds analysis of the propositional attitudes. Consider the invalid argument (8):

Sue knows that the tallest spy is a spy. (8)
Tim is the tallest spy.

Sue knows that Tim is a spy.

Sue may know that the tallest spy is a spy without knowing that Tim, who actually is the tallest spy, is a spy. But how can it be that, Tim and the tallest spy being one and the same person, the open sentence 'Sue knows that____is a spy' is true of one but not of the other? A possible worlds analysis solves the riddle, for even if Tim and the tallest spy are the same in this world, there may be other worlds where this is not so. Therefore Sue may bear an attitude towards the set of all worlds in which the tallest spy has a certain property without having that same attitude towards the set of all worlds in which Tim has that property.

However, it is disputed whether the possible worlds theory can handle all such replacements of coreferential noun phrases in contexts of propositional attitude. In particular this may not be so if the two coreferential noun phrases are names. A standard example here (derived from Frege (1892)) chooses Hesperus and Phosphorus, two names for the planet Venus, as the pair of coreferential names that are not interchangeable. Hesperus is the Evening Star, Phosphorus the Morning Star and in ancient times it still was unknown that these two heavenly objects were one and the same planet. This means that the argument given as (9) below is not valid:

The Ancients knew that Hesperus was Hesperus. (9)
Hesperus is Phosphorus.

The Ancients knew that Hesperus was Phosphorus.

The possible worlds account of the fact that (8) is not valid made crucial use of the possibility that although 'Tim' and 'the tallest spy' may refer to the same person in the actual circumstances they may refer to different persons in other possible worlds. In order to analyze the Hesperus–Phosphorus paradox along the same lines one must allow for the possibility that although Hesperus and Phosphorus are in fact the same planet, they are only contingently so. This means that one must allow that there might have been situations in which Hesperus and Phosphorus were not the same planet. But some philosophers, especially Kripke (1972, 1979), have argued forcefully against this possibility and hold that denotations of proper names cannot vary across possible worlds. If this 'rigid designator' view of proper names is indeed correct then the sentence 'Hesperus is Phosphorus' is true in all possible worlds and thus has the set of all worlds as its semantic value. Since 'Hesperus is Hesperus' has the same value, the first premise and the conclusion of (9) cannot but have the same truth value and the argument is predicted to be valid, contrary to standard intuition.

Hintikka (1962) gives an attractive specialization of the possible worlds approach that should be mentioned here. In general the possible worlds approach to the propositional attitudes is committed to the view that the intension of a verb of propositional attitude is a relation between an agent, a set of possible worlds and a world of evaluation; it is not committed to any particular analysis of this relation. But such a further analysis can have its own merits and Hintikka proposes to define the relation in terms of a simpler one. The attitude of belief, for example, is analyzed in terms of the 'doxastic alternative' relation, which holds between an agent x, a world j, and a world i intuitively if j is compatible with everything that x believes in world i. The report that x believes p is analyzed now as the statement that p holds in all of x's doxastic alternatives. Writing $B(c, j, i)$ for 'j is one of Cathy's doxastic alternatives in i' sentence (5) can be reformulated as formula (10):

$$\lambda i. \forall j(B(c, j, i) \rightarrow \exists x(M(x, j) \wedge L(x, c, j))) \qquad (10)$$

It should be stressed that there is no incompatibility between this new formalization and the one given in (6). The relation between (6) and (10) is one of specialization. The belief relation is merely redefined in terms of the relation of doxastic alternatives: $\text{Bel}(x, p, i)$ now holds if and only if $\forall j(B(x, j, i) \rightarrow p(j))$ does.

3. The Problem of Logical Omniscience

If one compares the possible worlds analysis of meaning with the theory that meanings are simply truth values one finds that, where the latter account is extremely coarse-grained in the sense that it distinguishes only two meanings, the former approach individuates infinitely more meanings and in general is much more subtle. But even in the case of the possible worlds theory contexts of propositional attitude can help us to see that the individuation of meanings is still not fine-grained enough. The Hesperus–Phosphorus paradox that was mentioned (Sect. 2) is one argument that points in this direction, but it is dependent upon the view that names are rigid designators. This view is not universally accepted, but there are other problems with the possible worlds analysis that also suggest that meanings should be discriminated more fine-grainedly. One hard nut is the problem of so-called 'logical omniscience,' the false prediction that if somebody knows that φ he also knows that Ψ, where Ψ is any sentence that is logically equivalent with φ. In order to see that this prediction is indeed false, the following example, adapted from Moore (1989), may be considered.

Suppose some person called Jones wants to enter a building that has three doors, A, B, and C. The distances between any two of these doors are equal. Jones wants to get in as quickly as possible, without making detours and he knows that if A is locked B is not. Now, if our agent tries to open door B first and finds it locked, there might be a moment of hesitation. The reasonable thing for Jones is to walk to A, since if B is locked A is not, but he may need some time to infer this. This contrasts with the case in which he tries A first, since if he cannot open this door he will walk to B without further ado. The point is that one may well fail to realize (momentarily) that a sentence is true, even when one knows the contrapositive to hold. For a moment (11) might be true while (12) is false:

Jones knows that if A is locked B is not locked. (11)

Jones knows that if B is locked A is not locked. (12)

It follows that the two embedded sentences cannot have the same semantic value, even though they are logically equivalent on the usual account. The possible worlds analysis, on the other hand, predicts that logically equivalent sentences are true in the same possible worlds and thus have the same semantic value. In particular it predicts that the embedded sentences of (11) and (12) have the same meaning and thus that (11) and (12) themselves have the same truth values.

All reasoning takes time. This means that (13):

Jones knows that φ. (13)

need not imply (14):

Jones knows that Ψ. (14)

even if φ and Ψ are logically equivalent. If the embedded sentences are syntactically distinct then, since Jones needs time to make the relevant inference, there will always be a moment at which (13) is true but (14) is still false.

This is a problem for the analysis of the attitudes in terms of possible worlds, but worse even, it seems to be a problem for any analysis that is based on some form of standard logic. All ordinary logics allow logical equivalents to be interchanged, but we see here that contexts of propositional attitude do not admit of such replacements. Many researchers therefore have proposed logics that do not support the full interchangeability of logical equivalents. The bibliography contains a selection of such proposals.

See also: Proposition.

Bibliography

Barwise J, Perry J 1983 *Situations and Attitudes*. MIT Press, Cambridge, MA

Church A 1950 On Carnap's analysis of statements of assertion and belief. In: Linsky L (ed.) 1971 *Reference and Modality*. Oxford University Press, London

Cresswell M J 1972 Intensional logics and logical truth. *Journal of Philosophical Logic* **1**: 2–15

Cresswell M J 1982 The autonomy of semantics In: Peters S, Saarinen E (eds.) *Processes, Beliefs and Questions*. Reidel, Dordrecht

Fagin R, Halpern J Y 1988 Belief, awareness and limited reasoning. *Artificial Intelligence* **34**: 39–76

Frege G 1892 Über Sinn und Bedeutung. In: Frege G 1962 *Funktion, Begriff, Bedeutung. Fünf Logische Studien*. Vandenhoeck, Göttingen

Hintikka J 1962 *Knowledge and Belief: An Introduction to the Logic of the two Notions*. Cornell University Press, Ithaca, NY

Hintikka J 1975 Impossible possible worlds vindicated. *Journal of Philosophical Logic* **4**: 475–84

Konolige K 1985 Belief and incompleteness In: Hobbs J R, Moore R C (eds.) *Formal Theories of the Commonsense World*

Kripke S 1972 Naming and necessity. In: Davidson D, Harman G (eds.) *Semantics of Natural Language*. Reidel, Dordrecht

Kripke S 1979 A puzzle about belief. In: Margalit A (ed.) *Meaning and Use*. Reidel, Dordrecht

Levesque H J 1984 A logic of implicit and explicit belief. In: *Proceedings AAAI-84*. Austin, TX

Mates B 1950 Synonymity. In: Linsky (ed.) 1952 *Semantics and the Philosophy of Language*. The University of Illinois Press, Urbana, IL

Moore R C 1989 Propositional attitudes and Russellian propositions. In: Bartsch R, van Benthem J F A K, van Emde Boas P (eds.) *Semantics and Contextual Expression: Proceedings of the Sixth Amsterdam Colloquium*. Foris, Dordrecht

Moore R C, Hendrix G C 1982 Computational models of belief and the semantics of belief sentences. In: Peters S, Saarinen E (eds.) *Processes, Beliefs and Questions*. Reidel, Dordrecht

Muskens R A 1991 Hyperfine-grained Meanings in Classical Logic. *Logique et Analyse* **133–134**: 159–76

Muskens R A 1995 *Meaning and Partiality*. CSLI, Stanford, CA

Quine W V O 1966 Quantifiers and propositional attitudes. In: *The Ways of Paradox*. Random House, New York

Rantala V 1982 Impossible worlds semantics and logical omniscience. In: Niiniluoto J, Saarinen E (eds.) *Intensional Logic: Theory and Applications*. Helsinki

Stalnaker R 1984 *Inquiry*. The MIT Press/Bradford Books, Cambridge, MA

Thomason R H 1980 A model theory for propositional attitudes. *LaPh* **4**: 47–70

Wansing H 1990 A general possible worlds framework for reasoning about knowledge and belief. *Studia Logica* **49**: 523–39

Reasoning

A. Fisher

The study of reasoning has entered into a new phase since the 1970s. For two thousand years the 'science of reasoning' was, essentially, the Aristotelian tradition; then in the nineteenth and twentieth centuries it took a distinctly mathematical turn: but since the 1970s it has returned to studying 'real reasoning'—reasoning which people actually use in order to convince one another—and this is leading to new ideas about the nature, structure, and evaluation of reasoning, particularly from the perspectives of informal logic, linguistics, and cognitive psychology.

1. Historical Background

Though the Stoics invented propositional logic, Aristotle was undoubtedly the key figure in the 'science of reasoning' until the nineteenth century. Aristotle distinguished three different kinds or aspects of reasoning. These were: (a) 'analytic'—the science of demonstrative reasoning, the kind of reasoning which is characteristic of mathematics; (b) 'dialectic'—the science of argumentative dialogue; and (c) 'rhetoric'—the science of persuasion. Aristotle's analytic is the beginning of what is called 'logic' and is to be found mainly in his *Prior Analytics* and *Posterior Analytics*. His theory of argumentative debate is to be found in his *Topics* and *De Sophisticis Elenchis*, and his theory of good and convincing oratory is to be found in his *Rhetoric*. The theory of the syllogism is probably Aristotle's most famous contribution to the theory of reasoning and is still widely studied. A syllogism is an argument with two premises and a conclusion, where all three sentences are of one of the following forms,

(A) 'All As are Bs,' (E) 'No As are Bs,' (I) 'Some As are Bs,' (O) 'Some As are not Bs,' and the premises have one term in common, as in:

All crocodiles are amphibious creatures	(A)
No amphibious creatures are lovable	(E)

Therefore

No crocodiles are lovable.	(E)

where 'amphibious creature' is the term common to both premises. Prior (1962) contains an excellent account of Aristotle's theory of the syllogism.

In the medieval world Aristotle's theory of the syllogism was studied; 'disputations' were conducted according to strict rules deriving from the theory of dialectic; and rhetoric also remained of central importance. However, with the rise of science, dialectic and rhetoric declined in importance and the study of reasoning became increasingly the study of analytic. Furthermore, the methods by which reasoning was studied became increasingly mathematical. Some of the most important figures in this development were Leibniz, Bolzano, Boole, and De Morgan, but by far the most important was Gottlob Frege (1848–1925), and modern logic is universally recognized to date from the publication of his *Begriffsschrift*; (1879).

2. The Influence of Frege

Frege was a mathematician who was mainly interested in studying mathematical reasoning by mathematical methods. He generalized certain mathematical ideas, notably those of 'variable' and 'function,' to produce the notational ideas which are now universally used to articulate the logical form of sentences and the logical structure of reasoning. The essentials of this notation are variables, predicates, and quantifiers. Variables, like x, y, z, function in logical notation very much as variables function in mathematical expressions, i.e., they mark a 'gap' in an expression which can be filled by a name or which can be quantified over to yield a true or false sentence. 'Predicate letters,' like F, G, and H, stand for something different from ordinary grammatical predicates and something more like mathematical functions. For example, in *All crocodiles are amphibious creatures* the grammatical subject is 'all crocodiles' and the grammatical predicate is 'are amphibious creatures.' In logic, 'all' is a 'quantifier,' a word of quantity, and the *logical* predicates are ' . . . is a crocodile' and ' . . . is an amphibious creature.' Logical predicates are commonly thought of as 'what is left' when names are removed from simple sentences; for example, *John is a crocodile, John is scalier than Mary,* and *John is between Mary and Peter* yield the logical predicates 'x is a crocodile,' 'x is scalier than y,' and 'x is between y and z,' written Fx, Gxy, and Hxyz respectively, where the variables mark gaps as explained above. The *quantifiers* are the words 'all' and 'some' (and their synonyms), and are commonly written ∀x and Ex respectively. To return to the simple example, *All crocodiles are amphibious* is construed as saying, 'For all x, if x is a crocodile then x is an amphibious creature' which is written in logical notation as ∀x (Fx ⊃ Gx).

Frege's system provided a considerably more powerful and flexible instrument for representing patterns of reasoning involving quantifiers than did Aristotle's syllogistic, and the Fregean tradition, with important contributions from Bertrand Russell and others, dominated thinking about reasoning until the 1970s. It produced many remarkable results, especially about mathematical reasoning: some of the most notable of these were Church's theorem that elementary predicate logic is undecidable, Tarski's theorem that 'truth' cannot be defined within elementary arithmetic, and Gödel's theorems that one cannot prove the consistency of elementary number theory without assuming it and that one cannot completely axiomatize elementary number theory. This remarkable tradition is the theoretical basis of the whole of the modern computing and information technology industry and much research is continuing along these lines.

3. Recent Developments

However, since the 1970s there has been an upsurge of interest in the study of reasoning which derives from several quite different perspectives, including those of informal logic, argumentation theory, and cognitive psychology.

3.1 Informal Logic

The informal logic tradition has emerged mainly in North America, among logicians and philosophers who used to teach modern formal logic partly in the hope of improving students' reasoning skills. Partly because this hope was not realized, and partly because of the difficulty of *applying* modern logic to much 'real reasoning'—reasoning of the kind people actually use in order to try to convince others—modern informal logic focuses on the study of such real reasoning. It pays particular attention to the language and structure of reasoning, and to fallacies. Though there were earlier works in this tradition, the publication of Michael Scriven's book, *Reasoning* (1976), is widely regarded as the moment when the subject came of age. Good examples of works in this tradition are Govier (1985); Johnson and Blair (1977); and Freeman (1988) For a scholarly account of the theoretical problems in this tradition, and some possible solutions see Freeman (1991).

3.2 Argumentation

The 'argumentation' tradition has arisen mainly in Holland, and derives its inspiration particularly from the speech–act theory of J. L. Austin as developed by J. R. Searle. However, it also owes a great deal to modern logic, to the theory of dialectic, and to Perelman's work on rhetoric. Argumentation theory also focuses on 'real argumentation'; it describes its program as belonging to 'normative pragmatics,' and it assesses argumentation by reconstructing it in terms of an ideal dialectical model (for this approach to the study of argument see especially Eemeren, et al. 1984; 1987).

3.3 Cognitive Psychology

In recent years cognitive psychologists have given increasing attention to the study of reasoning. Interesting developments here, with far–reaching implications for the whole field, are particularly associated with the work of Philip Johnson-Laird, especially with his contention that people reason, not by any kind of reference to 'logical rules' (as Piaget and many others have thought), but by means of 'mental models' (for a good exposition of these ideas see Johnson-Laird 1983, 1991).

4. Summary

In summary, the study of reasoning began with the ancient Greeks, remained in the Aristotelian tradition for nearly two thousand years, then took a mathematical turn, and has in the latter part of the twentieth century returned to a broad approach to the subject, and is focusing, in the 1990s, on real reasoning—reasoning of the kind people actually use with a view to convincing others, and which is only rarely about crocodiles!

See also: Logic: Historical Survey.

Bibliography

Blair J A, Johnson R H 1980 *Informal Logic; The First International Symposium*. Edgepress, Pt Reyes, CA

Eemeren F H van, Grootendorst R, Kruiger T 1987 *Handbook of Argumentation Theory*. Foris, Dordrecht

Eemeren F H van, Grootendorst R 1984 *Speech Acts in Argumentative Discussion*. Foris, Dordrecht

Freeman J B 1988 *Thinking Logically*. Prentice Hall, Englewood Cliffs, NJ

Freeman J B 1991 *Dialectics and the Macrostructure of Argument: A Theory of Argument Structure*. Foris Publications, Berlin/New York

Frege G 1879 *Begriffsschrift*. Louis Nebert, Halle

Govier T 1985 *A Practical Study of Argument*. Wadsworth, Belmont, CA

Johnson R H, Blair J A 1977 *Logical Self-Defense*. McGraw-Hill, New York

Johnson-Laird P N 1983 *Mental Models*. Cambridge University Press, Cambridge

Johnson-Laird P N 1991 *Deduction*. Lawrence Erlbaum, Hove

Kneale W, Kneale M 1962 *The Development of Logic*. Oxford University Press, Oxford

Perelman C, Olbrechts-Tyteca 1969 *The New Rhetoric: A Treatise on Argumentation*. University of Notre Dame Press, Notre Dame, IN

Prior A N 1962 *Formal Logic*. Oxford University Press, Oxford

Scriven M 1976 *Reasoning*. McGraw-Hill, New York

Relevant Logic

S. Read

An orthodox account of logical consequence requires that one proposition is a consequence of others if the latter cannot be true and at the same time the former false. This view would seem, however, to ignore any connection of relevance between the propositions involved. An alternative account, designed to explicate this notion of logical relevance of one proposition to another, was developed by Anderson and Belnap out of earlier work by Ackermann. It is called 'relevant,' or 'relevance,' logic.

1. Relevance

Anderson and Belnap focused on two aspects of relevance:

1.1 Meaning-connection

If one proposition entails another, there must, they said, be some connection of meaning between them. How can this be explicated in the context of modern formal logic? Anderson and Belnap concentrated initially on propositional logic, and within that on so-called first-degree entailments, entailments of the form A→B, where A and B contain no occurrences of the entailment connective '→,' but only truth-functional connectives '&' (and), '∨' (or), and '∼' (not). Belnap proposed a test of meaning-connection relevance in this context, that of variable-sharing. A necessary condition for A to entail B is that A and B (combinations of propositional variables) should share a variable.

1.2 Derivational Utility

Variable-sharing can be criticized as over-technical and parochial, and difficult to generalize beyond prop-

ositional logic. An alternative criterion which Anderson and Belnap developed is based on the idea of the use of an assumption in a chain of derivations. Only what has actually been used in some essential way is relevant. However, what is essential is difficult to pin down. It cannot mean 'necessary,' given that they accept the validity of $(p{\rightarrow}q){\rightarrow}((q{\rightarrow}p){\rightarrow}(p{\rightarrow}q))$; and it must be restricted to occurrences or tokens, since they reject $p{\rightarrow}(p{\rightarrow}p)$.

2. Entailment and Relevant Implication

Anderson and Belnap's first interest was in the logic of entailment, E, which respects considerations of both relevance and necessity. Before long, however, a theory of a non-modal conditional connective was developed, called the calculus of relevant implication, R. In the early 1970s, it was discovered (by Maximova) that extending relevant implication by an S4-type modal connective, yielding the system $R^{\square}$, did not give a theory identical to that of entailment, and since then interest in the calculus E of entailment has waned in favor of R and $R^{\square}$.

3. Semantics

3.1 Relational Semantics

At the end of the 1960s, relevant logic was well-worked out as a formal syntactic theory, but it had no real semantics. Following Kripke's lead in providing a set-theoretic semantical analysis of modal logic, several authors independently hit upon the way to provide a similar semantics for relevant logic. The preferred version has settled on a relational semantics, in which the conditional '→' receives its truth-condition relative to a ternary relation of accessibility between worlds or indices: 'A→B' is true at x if B is true at z whenever A is true at y and $Rxyz$—where $Rxyz$ can be read as 'x and y are compossible at z'.

3.2 Other Semantic Analyses

The ternary relation $Rxyz$ obeys the same principles as a basic relation of spherical geometry: 'z lies within the minor arc of the great circle through x and y.' The worlds semantics also has an algebraic counterpart— the Lindenbaum algebra is a distributive lattice with a semigroup operation, called a De Morgan monoid, whose prime filters correspond to the worlds. By focusing on the semigroup operation ∘ and all the filters one can also develop an elegant operational semantics, whose truth clause for '→' reads: 'A→B' is true at x if and only if whenever A is true at y, B is true at $x \circ y$.

4. Decidability

It was thought for some time that R (and E) were decidable, that is, that there was an effective method for testing for validity in them. No proof could be found, however, and eventually in the early 1980s Urquhart established their undecidability.

Perhaps the most famous thesis valid in classical logic but invalid in R and E is the inference from A ∨ B and ∼A to B, Disjunctive Syllogism. The corresponding rule form, that if A ∨ B and ∼A are in some theory T then so is B, is known as the Gamma conjecture for T. (γ was Ackermann's name for this rule in his forerunner of E.) E and R are Gamma-theories. Much work in the 1970s and 1980s focused on $R^{\#}$, effectively Peano arithmetic based on R. To much surprise, this was found in 1987 not to be a Gamma-theory.

5. Quantified Relevant Logic

With the exception of the study of $R^{\#}$, much of the work on relevant logic has concentrated on the propositional fragment (indeed, in its first phase, the first-degree part—theses A→B where A and B contain no arrows—dominated discussion), perhaps in the belief that the extension to first order and quantifiers was relatively straightforward. In point of fact, there are two tricky problems here. The first concerns the correct analysis of *All As are B*. If it is represented as $(\forall x)(Ax \rightarrow Bx)$, with the '→' of relevant logic, while *Some As are B* remains as $(\exists x)(Ax \ \& \ Bx)$, then *Not all As are B* and *Some As are not B* are no longer equivalent. This is counter-intuitive. Second, straightforward extensions of the proof theory and semantics in fact result in incompleteness, as shown in Fine 1988. This was rectified in Fine 1989 by revising the semantics. Quantified relevant logic is still a fairly unstable theory.

6. Substructural Logics

Research into relevant logics since 1990 has been subsumed within the broader genus of sub-structural logics, a neologism coined to denote logics with restricted structural rules—rules such as Contraction, Weakening, Permutation etc.; and the rise of linear logic in theoretical computer science, in which the tracking of resources is a central concern, has both drawn on earlier results in relevant logic and has extended them, as a closely related substructural logic.

See also: Deviant Logics; Formal Semantics; Modal Logic.

Bibliography

Anderson A R, Belnap N D 1975, 1992 *Entailment,* 2 vols. Princeton University Press, Princeton, NJ
Avron A 1992 Whither relevance logic? *Journal of Philosophical Logic* 21: 243–81
Dunn J M 1986 Relevance logic and entailment. In: Gabbay D M, Guenthner F (eds.) *Handbook of Philosophical Logic,* vol. III. Reidel, Dordrecht
Fine K 1988 Semantics for quantified relevance logic. *Journal of Philosophical Logic* 17: 27–59
Fine K 1989 Incompleteness for quantified relevance logics. In: Norman J, Sylvan R (eds.) *Directions in Relevant Logic.* Kluwer, Dordrecht
Read S 1988 *Relevant Logic.* Blackwell, Oxford
Routley R, Plumwood V, Meyer M K, Brady R T 1982 *Relevant Logics and Their Rivals.* Ridgeview, Atascadero, CA
Schroeder-Heister P, Dosen K (eds.) 1993 *Substructural Logics.* Clarendon Press, Oxford

Singular/General Proposition

M. Crimmins

Many propositions depend for their truth values on facts about particular individuals, but only singular propositions are directly *about* individuals. The proposition that the President of the USA is not tall, depends for its truth value on the height of a particular person, for example Bill Clinton, but it is not directly about him (though it is directly about the USA). If Clinton were never to have existed, the proposition that the President of the USA is not tall would still exist and could be stated in the same way; it is not *internally* related to Clinton; it is not identified by reference to Clinton, but only to the property of being the President of the USA; it might have been true even if Clinton were tall (so long as the President of the USA was not). The proposition that Bill Clinton is not tall, on the other hand, is internally related to Clinton. It is directly *about him*; it could not be stated (in the same way) if he never had existed; it is identified by reference to him; it could not be true unless Clinton himself was not tall. Singular propositions are those of this latter kind, which are directly about particular individuals. General propositions are about no particular individuals, but only about properties. Some paradigm general propositions are that all snow is white, and that the shortest spy is human. Paradigm singular propositions include that the earth is round, and that Nixon was President of the USA. In theories of structured propositions, singular propositions are held to contain the individuals they are about as constituents, whereas general propositions contain only properties.

See also: Proposition; Reference: Philosophical Issues.

Bibliography

Evans G, McDowell J (eds.) 1982 *The Varieties of Reference.* Clarendon Press, Oxford

Type/Token Distinction

M. Crimmins

The type/token distinction, attributed to philosopher C. S. Peirce, is usually explained by example. Thus, there are two possible correct answers to these questions: how many words are uttered in saying 'Home, sweet home'? how many numerals are written in writing '422'? In each case the answer is *two* if 'types' of symbol are counted, and *three* if 'tokens' are counted. The general terms 'word,' and 'numeral,' then, are ambiguous; they might stand for categories either of types or of tokens.

1. Putative Definitions

There are no generally received definitions of type and token; the closest candidate would be: tokens are simply particulars, types are universals (properties), and a given token is *of* a given type if it falls under that universal (has that property). In practice, not all properties are such that it is natural to call them types and to call the things that have them tokens (are you a token of the property of being far from the North Pole?); it seems natural only where the property itself (the type) can be classified with a common noun ('home' is a word, '2' a numeral, toothache a sensation), and only where having that property (being of the type) is crucial for the relevance to some inquiry of the things (tokens) having the property.

2. The Distinction Applied to Language

In linguistics, the most frequently discussed types are expressions such as words, phrases, and sentences, and theoretical entities like parse trees. The tokens of these types are (said to be) utterances and inscriptions.

Every utterance or inscription of the word (type) 'now' is a token of that word-type. An utterance is relevant to the study of a language—it is *in* the language—because it is a token of an expression-type of that language, and perhaps also because it is intended so to be.

It is usual to say that the question of *truth* arises not for sentence types but for token utterances and inscriptions, since tokens, not types, are associated with specific truth-evaluable claims, thoughts, or propositions. The sentence type 'I am hungry,' is not itself true or false, but various tokens of it are true or false. Types, on the other hand, are associated with lexical *meanings* and other meaning rules and conventions of language. The sentence type 'I am hungry' has a specific meaning in English independent of any particular occasion of its use (there are no actual tokens of many or even most meaningful sentence types). Lexical ambiguity involves an expression type (like 'bank') having multiple meanings.

3. Complications for the Distinction

It should be recognized that the type/token distinction is not as clear as it may sometimes seem. Complications arise in the case of reused tokens, such as a recording on an answering machine or an 'out to lunch' sign on the door of a business. Here it may be useful to distinguish between an occasion of use of an expression and the physical 'vehicle' carrying the expression on that occasion (the inscription, or the recording); which of these should count as the token is not clear. A token is to be distinguished also from an 'occurrence' of a type: in the 'sentence type' 'Home, sweet home,' there are two occurrences of the 'word type' 'home,' and so there are two tokens of that word type in every token of the sentence type.

4. On the Primacy of One Over the Other

The history of semantics has seen significant swings in the importance attached to features of tokens beyond simply those of the expression types of which they are tokens. First there was nearly exclusive concern with formalized languages, in which all semantic features like reference, meaning, and truth attach to (or are determined by) expression types, and actual use of these expressions is irrelevant to semantic questions. The later Wittgenstein and 'ordinary language' phil-osophers, who saw meaning of expression types as arising out of actual token uses of expressions in communication and other activities, took as the unit of investigation the token utterance, embedded in a rich conversational context (this tradition continues in the late twentieth century in the theory of speech acts). Successes in possible-world semantics for modal logics led in the 1960s and 1970s to renewed interest in type-driven semantics in which tokens often were ignored except for such obviously context-sensitive expressions as demonstratives. Much late twentieth-century work in semantics and pragmatics again emphasizes the primacy of the token, and the semantic importance of such complex features of context as salience, relevance, and mutual belief.

See also: Categories and Types.

SECTION VII

Formal Semantics

Categorial Grammar

M. Steedman

Categorial Grammar (CG) is a term which covers a number of related formalisms that have been proposed for the syntax and semantics of natural languages and logical and mathematical languages. All are generalizations of a core context-free grammar formalism first explicitly defined by Ajdukiewicz in 1935, but with earlier antecedents in the work of Husserl, Leśnewski, Frege, Carnap, and Tarski on semantic and syntactic categories, ultimately stemming from work in the theory of types (a tradition to which some work in CG shows signs of returning). The distinguishing characteristics of these theories are: an extreme form of 'lexicalism' where the main and even entire burden of syntax is borne by the lexicon; the characterization of constituents, both syntactically and semantically, as 'functions' and/or 'arguments'; the characterization of the relation between syntax and semantics as 'compositional,' with syntactic and semantic types standing in the closest possible relation, the former in many cases merely encoding the latter; a tendency to 'freer surface constituency' than traditional grammar, the previously mentioned characteristic guaranteeing that all the nonstandard constituents that CG sanctions are fully interpreted semantically.

Such grammars have been implicated in much work at the foundation of modern theories of natural language semantics. Like their theoretical cousins Tree Adjoining Grammars (TAG), Lexical Functional Grammar (LFG), Generalized Phrase Structure Grammar (GPSG), and Head-driven Phrase Structure Grammar (HPSG), they have also, in the early 1990s, provided an important source of constrained alternatives to transformational rules and their modern derivatives for formal theories of natural language syntax. In the syntactic arena, categorial grammars have been claimed to have significant advantages as explanatory and unifying theories of unbounded constructions including coordination and relative clause formation, of constructions that have been held to involve 'reanalysis,' of phonological phrasing associated with intonation, of numerous clause-bounded phenomena including reflexive binding, raising, and

control; and also of analogous discontinuous phenomena in morphology.

1. Pure Categorial Grammar

In a categorial grammar, all grammatical constituents, and in particular all lexical items, are associated with a 'type' or 'category' which defines their potential for combination with other constituents to yield compound constituents. The category is either one of a small number of 'basic' categories, such as *NP,* or a 'functor' category. The latter have a type which identifies them as functions mapping arguments of some type onto results of some (possibly different) type. For example, English intransitive verbs like *walks* are most naturally defined as functions from nounphrases *NP* on their left to sentences *S*. English transitive verbs like *sees* are similarly defined as functions from nounphrases *NP* on their right to the aforementioned intransitive verb category. Apart from a language-particular specification of directionality, such categories merely reflect the types of the semantic interpretations of these words.

There are several different notations for directional categories. The most widely used are the 'slash' notations variously pioneered by Bar-Hillel/Lambek (1958), and subsequently modified within the group of theories that are distinguished below as 'combinatory' categorial grammars. These two systems differ slightly in the way they denote directionality, as illustrated in the following categories for the transitive verb *sees* (1):

Lambek CG:	$sees := (np \backslash s)/np$	(1a)
Combinatory CG:	$sees := (S \backslash NP)/NP$	(1b)

(Both notations reflect the assumption that multi-argument functions like transitive verbs are 'curried.' Other notations allow 'flat' multi-argument functions. Under an equivalence noted by Schönfinkel in 1924, the assumption is merely one of notational convenience. The categories as shown are simplified by the omission of number and person agreement specifications. In common with most theories, it is assumed that the categories here represented as atomic NPs are in fact feature bundles including agreement features which must unify with corresponding features of their arguments. *np* has been used as the type of NPs in Lambek's notation, rather than *n*, as in the original.)

Lambek's notation encodes directionality in the slash itself, forward slash / indicating a rightward argument and backward slash \ indicating a leftward argument. However, for reasons which will become apparent when the Lambek calculus is examined in detail, Lambek chose to make leftward arguments appear to the left of their (backward) slash, while rightward arguments appeared to the right of their (forward) slash. This notation has many attractive features, but lacks a consistent left to right order of domain and range. It is therefore rather harder than it might be to comprehend categories in this notation. Readers may judge this difficulty for themselves by noting how long it takes them to decide whether the two functions written $(a/b)\backslash(c/d)$ and $(d\backslash c)/(b\backslash a)$ do or do not have the same semantic type. This property tends to make life difficult, for example, for linguists whose concern is to compare the syntactic behavior of semantically related verbs across languages with different base constituent orders.

It was for this last reason that Dowty and Steedman proposed an alternative notation with a consistent left-to-right order of range and domain of the function. In this notation, arguments always appear to the right of the slash, and results to the left. A rightward-leaning slash means that the argument in question is to the right, a leftward-leaning slash, that it is to the left. The first argument of a complex function category is always the rightmost category, the second argument the next rightmost, and so on, and the leftmost basic category is always the result. It is therefore obvious in this notation that the two categories instanced in the last paragraph, which are now written $(C/D)\backslash(A/B)$ and $(C\backslash D)/(A\backslash B)$, have the same semantic type, since the categories are identical apart from the slashes.

All the notations illustrated in (1) capture the same basic syntactic facts concerning English transitive sentences as the familiar production rules in (2):

$$S \rightarrow NP\ VP \qquad (2)$$

$$VP \rightarrow TV\ NP$$

$$TV \rightarrow sees$$

That is to say that in order to permit parallel context-free derivations it is only necessary to include the following pair of rules of functional application (3); allowing functor categories to combine with arguments (the rules are given in both notations):

Functional Application:	Functional Application:	(3)
(i) $x/y\ y \Rightarrow x$	(i) $X/Y\ Y \Rightarrow X$	
(ii) $y\ y\backslash x \Rightarrow x$	(ii) $Y\ X\backslash Y \Rightarrow X$	
(a) Lambek	(b) Combinatory	

These rules have the form of very general binary PS rule schemata. Clearly CG is context free grammar which happens to be written in the accepting, rather than the producing, direction, and in which there has been a transfer of the major burden of specifying particular grammars from the PS rules to the lexicon. (CG and CFPSG were shown to be weakly equivalent by Bar-Hillel et al. in 1960.) While it is now convenient to write derivations in both notations as follows (4), they are clearly just familiar phrase-structure 'trees' (except that they have the leaves at the top, as is fitting):

Gilbert	sees	George		Gilbert	sees	George	(4)
np	(np\s)/np	np		NP	(S\NP)/NP	NP	
	np\s				S\NP		
	s				S		
	(a) Lambek				(b) Combinatory		

(The operation of combination by the application rules is indicated by an underline annotated with a rightward or leftward arrow.) It will be clear at this point that Lambek's notation has the very attractive property of allowing all 'cancelations' under the rules of functional application to be with adjacent symbols. This elegant property is preserved under the generalization to other combinatory operations permitted by the generalization to the Lambek calculus. (However, it will be shown that it cannot be preserved under the full range of combinatory operations that have been claimed by other categorial grammarians to be required for natural languages.)

Grammars of this kind have a number of features that make them attractive as an alternative to the more familiar phrase structure grammars. The first is that they avoid the duplication in syntax of the subcategorization information that must be explicit in the lexicon anyway. The second is that the lexical syntactic categories are clearly very directly related to their semantics. This last property has always made categorial grammars particularly attractive to formal semanticists, who have naturally been reluctant to give up the belief that natural language syntax must be as directly related to its semantics as that of arithmetic, algebra, or the predicate calculus, despite frequent warnings against such optimism from linguistic syntacticians.

At the very time Bar-Hillel and Lambek were developing the earliest categorial grammars, Chomsky was developing an argument that many phenomena in natural languages could not be naturally expressed using context free grammars of any kind, if indeed they could be captured at all. It is therefore important to ask how this pure context-free core can be generalized to cope with the full range of constructions found in natural language.

2. Early Generalizations of Categorial Grammar

Three types of proposal that came from categorial grammarians in response to this challenge should be distinguished. The first was simply to take over the Chomskyan apparatus of transformations, replacing his CFPS base grammar with a pure CF categorial grammar. This proposal was influentially advanced by Lyons (1968: 227ff., 327ff.), and endorsed by Lewis in 1970. Lyons's arguments were based on the advantages of a categorial base for capturing the word-order generalizations associated with the then nascent $\bar{X}$-theory (which were explored in categorial terms by Flynn), and were prescient of the subsequent tendency of Chomsky's theory towards lexicalism and a diminished role for PS rules. However, there was increasing awareness at this time that transformational rules themselves needed replacing by some more constrained formal mechanism, and this awareness gave rise to several more radical categorially based alternative proposals.

The paper in which Lewis endorses Lyons's proposal for a categorially based transformational grammar is in fact only peripherally concerned with syntax. Its more central concern is quantifier scope, which motivates Lewis to introduce a transformational rule which would nowadays be recognized as 'quantifier raising,' complete with the suggestion that this rule should operate '*beneath . . .* the most ordinary level of deep structure'—that is at what would be called the level of logical form. However, Lewis's account also involves an abstraction operator equivalent to Church's λ, in the form of Ajdukiewicz's operator κ. Implicit in Montague's general approach (though not in his practice), and explicit in the approach of Keenan, Venneman, and the 'λ-categorial' grammars of Cresswell (1973: 7) and von Stechow (1974), is the proposal that with the abstraction operator there is no need for independent movement transformations at all. Compositional interpretations can be assembled on the basis of surface grammar augmented by the completely general variable-binding operation of λ-abstraction, a proposal that was implicit in Ajdukiewicz.

This bold approach was also prescient of coming moves within the transformational mainstream, anticipating (and possibly, via work in Montague Grammar helping to precipitate) the move in Chomsky's theory to small numbers of general purpose movement transformations, perhaps confined to a single most general rule '*move α,*' and the realization that all such 'movements,' even those involving *Wh*-elements and their traces, could be regarded as base-generated. (O'Grady, who combines a categorial base with rules for combining nonadjacent elements, can be seen as continuing this tradition within CG.) However, by the same token, the essential equivalence between λ-abstraction ('bind a variable anywhere in the domain') and *move-α* ('co-index any items in the domain') means that the abstraction device is potentially very unconstrained, as Cresswell recognized (1973: 224–27). The approach remains immensely pro-

ductive in the semantic domain. It remains less clear whether there is any distinct advantage inherent in the syntactic aspects of λ-categorial grammar. Nevertheless, it has made the important contributions of providing a clear and simple interpretation for the notion of movement itself, which might otherwise have appeared semantically unmotivated, and of having directly led, via the work of Emmon Bach, to the third, most recent, and most radical group of proposals for generalizing pure categorial grammar.

As a part of a wider tendency at the time to seek low-power alternatives to transformations, there were during the 1970s a number of proposals for augmenting categorial grammar with additional operations for combining categories, over and above the original rules of functional application. In contrast to the λ-categorial approach, these operations were less general than the abstraction operator of λ-categorial grammar, the chief restriction being that, like the application rules themselves, these operations were confined to the combination of nonempty string-adjacent entities, and were dependent on the directionality of those entities. These proposals had an important historical precedent in the work by Lambek (1958) referred to earlier.

Lambek's short paper can be seen as making two quite separate points. The first was that a number of simple functional operations, importantly including functional composition and type-raising, looked as though they were directly reflected in natural syntax. His second point was that these very operations, together with an infinite set of related ones, could be generated as theorems of a quite small set of axioms and inference rules. In this he drew on even earlier traditions of natural deduction in the work of Gentzen, and the analogy drawn between logical implication and functional types by Curry (e.g., Curry and Feys 1958), which he deployed in an important proof of decidability for his syntactic calculus. The effect was to define this version of categorial grammar as a restricted logic.

These two proposals can be seen as reflected in two distinct styles of modern categorial grammar. On the one hand, there is a group of linguists who argue that the addition of a few semantically simple primitive combinatory operations like functional composition yields grammars that capture linguistic generalizations. Sometimes these operations are individual theorems of the Lambek calculus, and sometimes they are not. These theorists are typically not concerned with the question of whether their operations can be further reduced to an axiomatic calculus or not (although they are of course deeply concerned, as any linguist must be, with the degrees of freedom that their rules exhibit, and the automata-theoretic power implicit in their theory).

The other modern school of categorial grammarians is more concerned to identify additional sets of axiom-schemata and inference rules that define other syntactic calculi, primarily as a way of looking at relations among logics, particularly intuitionistic or constructive ones, including modal logics, linear logic, and type-theory. The relation of such logics to natural grammars is often not the central issue.

It will be easiest to discuss Lambek's original proposal in the light of these more recent developments. In adopting this narrative tactic, the history of the subject is recapitulated, for the significance of Lambek's proposals was not appreciated at the time, and his paper was largely forgotten until the rediscovery of many of its principles in the 1970s and early 1980s by Geach, Bach, Buszkowski, and others.

3. Modern Categorial Theories of Grammar

This section begins by examining the 'combinatory' style of categorial grammar, before returning to the 'Lambek' style including Lambek's original proposal. Each of these subsections ends with a brief discussion of the automata-theoretic power inherent in each system. It is convenient to further distinguish certain theories within both frameworks that are mainly concerned with the semantics of quantifier scope, rather than with purely syntactic phenomena. This work is discussed in a separate section.

3.1 'Combinatory' Categorial Grammars

A major impulse behind the development of generalized categorial grammars in this period was an attempt to account for the apparent vagaries of coordinate constructions, and to bring them under the same principles as other unbounded phenomena, such as relativization.

To begin to extend categorial grammar to cope with coordination a rule is needed, or rather a family of rules, of something like the following form (5):

Coordination Rule ($\langle\&\rangle$):   (5)
X' *conj* $X'' \Rightarrow X'''$

This rule captures the ancient intuition that *coordination is an operation which maps two constituents of like type onto a constituent of the same type*. That is, X', X'', and X''' are categories of the same type X but different interpretations, and the rule is a schema over a finite set of rules whose semantics will be ignored here.

Given such a rule or rule schema, derivations like the following are permitted (6):

Harry	cooked	and	ate	apples	(6)
NP	$(S\backslash NP)/NP$	*conj*	$(S\backslash NP)/NP$	NP	

$$\frac{\qquad\qquad}{(S\backslash NP)/NP}\langle\&\rangle$$

$$\frac{\qquad\qquad\qquad}{S\backslash NP}$$

$$\frac{\qquad\qquad\qquad\qquad}{S}\langle$$

The driving force behind much of the early development of the theory was the assumption that *all* coordination should be this simple—that is, combinations of 'constituents' without the intervention of deletion, movement, or equivalent unbounded coindexing rules. Sentences like the following are among the very simplest to challenge this assumption, since they involve the coordination of substrings that are *not* normally regarded as constituents (7):

(a) Harry cooked, and *might eat, * some apples   (7)
(b) Harry cooked, and *Mary ate,* some apples
(c) Harry will copy, and *file without reading,* some articles concerning Swahili.

The problem can be solved by adding a small number of operations that combine functions in advance of their arguments. Curry and Feys (1958) offer a mathematics for capturing applicative systems equivalent to the λ-calculi entirely in terms of such operators, for which they coined the term 'combinator'—hence the term 'combinatory' categorial grammars.

3.1.1 A Note on Combinators

A combinator is an operation upon sequences of functions and/or arguments. Thus, any (prefixed) term of the λ-calculus is a combinator. This article will be interested in combinators that correspond to some particularly simple λ-terms. For example, (8):

(a) $\mathbf{I} \equiv \lambda x[x]$ (8)
(b) $\mathbf{K}y \equiv \lambda x[y]$
(c) $\mathbf{T}x \equiv \lambda F[Fx]$
(d) $\mathbf{B}FG \equiv \lambda x[F(Gx)]$
(e) $\mathbf{C}Fy \equiv \lambda x[Fxy]$
(f) $\mathbf{W}F \equiv \lambda x[Fxx]$
(g) $\mathbf{S}FG \equiv \lambda x[Fx(Gx)]$
(h) $HFG \equiv \lambda x[H(Fx)(Gx)]$
where x is not free in F, G, H, y.

(A convention of 'left-associativity' is assumed here, according to which expressions like $\mathbf{B}FG$ are implicitly bracketed as $(\mathbf{B}F)G$. Concatenation as in $\mathbf{T}x$ denotes functional application of $\mathbf{T}$ to x.)

The above are equivalences, not definitions of the combinators. The combinators themselves can be taken as primitives, and used to define a range of 'applicative systems,' that is systems which express the two notions of 'application' of functions to arguments, and 'abstraction' or definitions of functions in terms of other functions. In particular, surprisingly small collections of combinators can be used as primitives to define systems equivalent to various forms of the λ-calculus, entirely without the use of bound variables and the binding operator λ.

3.1.2 BTS *Combinatory Categorial Grammar* (CCG)

One combinatory generalization of categorial grammar adds exactly three classes of combinatory rule to the context-free core. Since two of these types of rule—namely composition and type-raising—have been at least implicit in the majority of combinatory generalizations of categorial grammars, and since a third operation is provably necessary, this system will be taken as the canonical exemplar, comparing it later to a number of variants and alternatives. (This variety, with whose development the present author has been associated is sometimes referred to as CCG (for Combinatory Categorial Grammar), although it is only one of the possible combinatory versions of CG.) The combinatory rules have the effect of making such substrings into grammatical constituents in the fullest sense of the term, complete with an appropriate and fully compositional semantics. All of them adhere to the following restrictive assumption (9):

> The Principle of Adjacency: Combinatory rules (9) may only apply to entities which are linguistically realized and adjacent.

The first such rule-type is motivated by examples like (7a), above. Rules of functional composition allow functional categories like *might* to combine with functions into their argument categories, such as *eat* to produce nonstandard constituents corresponding to such strings as *might eat*. The rule required here (and the most commonly used functional composition rule in English) is written as follows:

> Forward Composition ($>$B): (10)
> $X/Y \quad Y/Z \Rightarrow_B X/Z$

The rule permits the following derivation for example (7a):

Harry	cooked	and	might	eat	some apples	*(11)*
NP	$(S\backslash NP)/NP$	conj	$(S\backslash NP)/VP$	VP/NP	NP	

$$\frac{}{(S\backslash NP)/NP} \text{B}$$

$$\frac{}{(S\backslash NP)/NP} \langle \& \rangle$$

$$\frac{}{S\backslash NP}$$

$$\frac{}{S} <$$

It is important to observe that, because of the isomorphism that CG embodies between categories and semantic types, this rule is also *semantic* functional composition. That is, if the interpretations of the two categories on the left of the arrow in 10 are respectively *F* and *G,* then the interpretation of the category on the right must be the composition of *F* and *G.* Composition corresponds to Curry's composition combinator, which he called **B**, defined earlier as (8d). Hence, the combinatory rule and its application in the derivation are indexed as $>$B because it is a rule in which the main functor is rightward-looking, and has composition as its semantics. Hence also, the formalism guarantees without further stipulation that this operation will compose the interpretations, as well as the syntactic functional types. Formal discussion

of this point is deferred, but it should be obvious that if the mapping from VP interpretations to predicate interpretations is known that constitutes the interpretation of *might,* and the mapping from NP interpretations to VP interpretations corresponding to the interpretation of *eat* is known, then everything necessary to define their composition is known, the interpretation of the nonstandard constituent *might eat.*

The result of the composition has the same syntactic and semantic type as a transitive verb, so when it is applied to an object and a subject, it is guaranteed to yield exactly the same interpretation for the sentence *Harry might eat some apples* as would have been obtained without the introduction of this rule. This nonstandard verb *might eat* is now a constituent in every sense of the word. It can therefore coordinate with other transitive verbs like *cooked* and take part in derivations like (11). Since this derivation is in every other respect just like the derivation in (6), it too is guaranteed to give a semantically correct result.

Examples like the following (12), in which a similar substring is coordinated with a *di*-transitive verb, require a generalization of composition proposed by Ades and Steedman in 1982:

> I *will offer, and* $[may]_{(S\backslash NP)/VP} [sell]_{(VP/PP)/NP}$, (12)
> my 1959 pink cadillac to my favourite brother-in-law.

To compose the modals with the multiple-argument verbs, the following relative of rule 10 is needed (13):

> Forward Composition ($>$B2): (13)
> $X/Y \quad (Y/Z)/W \Rightarrow_{B^2} (X/Z)/W$

This corresponds in combinatory terms to an instance B^2 of the generalization from **B** to B^n (cf., Curry and Feys 1958: 165, 185). It can be assumed, at least for English, that *n* is bounded by the highest valency in the lexicon, which is about 4.

The second novel kind of rule that is imported under the combinatory generalization is motivated by examples like (7b) above, repeated here (14):

> Harry cooked, and Mary ate, some apples. (14)

If the assumption is to be maintained that everything that can coordinate is a constituent formed without deletion or movement, then *Harry* and *cooked* must also be able to combine to yield a constituent of type S/NP, which can combine with objects to its right. The way this is brought about is by adding rules of type-raising like the following (15) to the system:

> Forward Type-raising ($>$T): (15)
> $Y \Rightarrow_T X/(X\backslash Y)$

This rule makes the subject NP into a function over predicates. Subjects can therefore compose with functions *into* predicates—that is, with transitive verbs, as in the following derivation (16) for (14):

Harry	cooked	and	Mary	ate	some apples	(16)
NP	$(S\backslash NP)/NP$	*conj*	NP	$(S\backslash NP)/NP$	NP	

$$\xrightarrow{\quad} T$$
$$S/(S\backslash NP) \qquad\qquad\qquad\qquad S/(S\backslash NP)$$
$$\xrightarrow{\qquad\qquad\qquad\qquad} B \qquad\qquad\qquad\qquad\qquad\qquad\qquad \xrightarrow{\qquad\qquad\qquad\qquad} B$$
$$S/NP \qquad\qquad\qquad\qquad\qquad\qquad\qquad S/NP$$
$$\langle\&\rangle$$
$$S/NP$$
$$S$$

Type-raising corresponds semantically to the combinator **T**, defined at (8c). It will be shown later that type-raising is quite general in its application to NPs, and that it should be regarded as an operation of the lexicon, rather than syntax, under which all types corresponding to functions into *NP* (etc.) are replaced by functions into the raised categor(ies). However, for expository simplicity it will continue to be shown in derivations, indexing the rule as $>$T. When the raised category composes with the transitive verb, the result is guaranteed to be a function which, when it reduces with an object *some apples*, will yield the same interpretation that would have obtained from the tra-

Harry will copy, and file without reading,   (18)
   some articles concerning Swahili.

Under the simple assumption with which this article began, that only like 'constituents' can conjoin, the substring *file without reading* must be a constituent formed without movement or deletion. What is more, it must be a constituent of the same type as a transitive verb, *VP/NP*, since that is what it coordinates with. It follows that the grammar of English must include the following operation (19), first proposed by Szabolsci:

Backward Crossed Substitution ($<$Sx)   (19)
$Y/Z \quad (X\backslash Y)/Z \Rightarrow_s X/Z$

Harry will	copy	and	file	without	reading,	some articles	(20)
S/VP	VP/NP	*conj*	VP/NP	$(VP\backslash VP)/VPing$	$VPing/NP$	NP	

$$\xrightarrow{\qquad\qquad} B$$
$$(VP\backslash VP)/NP$$
$$\xleftarrow{\qquad\qquad\qquad\qquad} Sx$$
$$VP/NP$$
$$\langle\&\rangle$$
$$VP/NP$$
$$\xrightarrow{\qquad\qquad} B$$
$$S/NP$$
$$S$$

ditional derivation. This interpretation might be written as follows (17):

   cook' apples' harry'.   (17)

(Here again a convention of 'left associativity' is used, so that the above applicative expression is equivalent to (*cook'* apples') harry'.) It is important to notice that it is at the level of the interpretation that traditional constituents like the VP, and relations such as *c*-command, continue to be embodied. This is an important observation since as far as surface structure goes, both have now been compromised.

Of course, the same facts guarantee that the coordinate example above will deliver an appropriate interpretation.

The third and final variety of combinatory rule is motivated by examples like (7c), repeated here (18):

This rule permits the derivation shown in (20) for sentence (18). (Infinitival and gerundival predicate categories are abbreviated as *VP* and *VPing*, and NPs are shown as ground types.)

It is important to notice that the crucial rule resembles a generalized form of functional composition, but that it *mixes* the directionality of the functors, combining a leftward functor over *VP* with a rightward function into *VP*. Therefore it must be predicted that other combinatory rules, such as composition, must also have such 'crossed' instances. Such rules are not valid in the Lambek calculus.

Like the other combinatory rules, the substitution rule combines the interpretations of categories as well as their syntactic categories. Its semantics is given by the combinator **S**, defined at (8g). It follows that if the constituent *file without reading* is combined with an object *some articles* on the right, and then combined with *Harry will*$_{S/VP}$, it will yield a correct interpretation. It also follows that a similarly correct interpretation will be produced for the coordinate sentence (18).

These three classes of rule—composition, type-raising, and substitution—constitute the entire inventory of combinatory rule-types that this version of combinatory CG adds to pure categorial grammar. They are limited by two general principles, in addition to the principle of adjacency (9). They are the following (21 and 22):

> The Principle of Directional Consistency: All (21) syntactic combinatory rules must be consistent with the directionality of the principal function.

> The Principle of Directional Inheritance: If the (22) category that results from the application of a combinatory rule is a function category, then the slash defining directionality for a given argument in that category will be the same as the one defining directionality for the corresponding argument(s) in the input function(s).

Together they amount to a simple statement that *combinatory rules may not contradict the directionality specified in the lexicon.* They drastically limit the possible composition and substitution rules to exactly four instances each. It seems likely that these principles follow from the fact that directionality is as much a property of 'arguments' as is their syntactic type. This position is closely related to Kayne's notion of 'directionality of government.'

The inclusion of this particular set of operations makes a large number of correct predictions. For example, once it is seen fit to introduce the forward rule of composition and the forward rule of type-raising into the grammar of English, the degrees of freedom in the theory are not increased any further by introducing the corresponding 'backward' rules. Thus the existence of the coordinate construction in (23) is predicted without further stipulation, as noted

Dowty and others, and constitute strong evidence in support of the decision to take type-raising and composition as primitives of grammar, and moreover for the relegation of raised categories to the lexicon.

The analysis also immediately entails that the dependencies engendered by coordination will be unbounded, and free in general to apply across clause boundaries. For example, all of the following examples parallel to those in (7) with which the section began are immediately accepted, without any further addition to the grammar whatsoever (24).

(a) Harry cooked, and *expects that Mary will* (24) *eat,* some apples

(b) Harry cooked, and *Fred expects that Mary will eat,* some apples

(c) Harry cooked, and *Fred expects that Mary will eat without enjoying,* some apples that they found lying around in the kitchen.

Moreover, if it is assumed that nominative and accusative relative pronouns have the following categories (which simply follow from the fact that they are functions from properties to noun modifiers), then the relative clauses in (26) below are also accepted:

(a) *who/that/which*$:=(N\backslash N)/(S\backslash NP)$ (25)
(b) *who(m)/that/which*$:=(N\backslash N)/(S/NP)$

(a) a man who *(expects that Mary) will eat some* (26) *apples*

(b) some apples that *(Fred expects that) Mary will eat*

(c) some apples that *(Fred expects that) Mary will eat without enjoying*

The generalization that 'Wh-movement' and 'right node raising' are essentially the same and in general unbounded is thereby immediately captured without further stipulation.

Rules like the 'direction mixing' substitution rule (19) are permitted by these principles, and so are composition rules like the following (27):

$$Y/Z \quad X\backslash Y \Rightarrow X/Z \qquad (27)$$

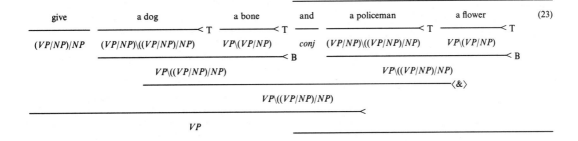

by Dowty. This and other related examples, which notoriously present considerable problems for other grammatical frameworks, are extensively discussed by

Such a rule has been argued to be necessary for, among other things, extractions of 'non-peripheral' arguments, as in the derivation (28).

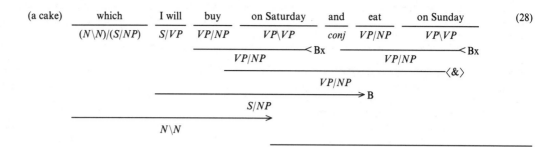

Such rules allow constituent orders that are not otherwise permitted, as the example shows, and are usually termed 'non-order-preserving.' It will be shown later that such rules are not theorems of the Lambek calculus. Friedman et al. showed that it is the inclusion of these rules, together with the generalization to instances of rules corresponding to $\mathbf{B}^2$ (cf. 13) that engenders greater than context free power in this generalization of CG. A language which allowed non-order-preserving rules to apply freely would have very free word order, including the possibility of 'scrambling' arguments across clause boundaries. It is therefore assumed in this version of combinatory categorial grammar that languages are free to restrict such rules to certain categories, or even to exclude some of them entirely.

One of the most interesting observations to arise from the movement analysis of relatives is the observation that there are a number of striking limitations on relativization. The exceptions fall into two broad classes. The first is a class of constraints relating to asymmetries with respect to extraction between subjects and objects. This class of exceptions has been related to the 'empty category principle' (ECP) of GB. In the terms of the combinatory theory, this constraint arises as a special case of a more general corollary of the theory, namely that arguments of different directionality require different combinatory rules to apply if they are to extract, as inspection of the following examples will reveal. The possibility for such asymmetries to exist in SVO languages because of the exclusion of the latter nondirection preserving rule is therefore open, for example, (29):

(a) (a man whom) [I think that]$_{S/S}$ [Mary likes]$_{S/NP}$ (29)
(b) *(a man whom) [I think that]$_{S/S}$ [likes Mary]$_{S\backslash NP}$

Indeed, a language like English *must* limit or exclude this rule if it is to remain configurational.

The second class is that of so-called 'island constraints,' which have been related to the principle of 'subjacency.' The fact that adjuncts and NPs are in general islands follows from the assumption that the former are backward modifiers, and that type-raising

is lexical and restricted to categories which are arguments of verbs, such as NPs. This can be seen from the categories in the following unacceptable examples (30):

(a) * a book [which]$_{(N\backslash N)/(S/NP)}$ [I will]$_{S/VP}$ [walk]$_{VP}$ (30) [without reading]$_{(VP\backslash VP)/NP}$
(b) * a book [which]$_{(N\backslash N)/(S/NP)}$ [I met]$_{S/NP}$ [a man who wrote]$_{(S\backslash(S/NP))/NP}$

The possibility of exceptions to the island status of NPs and adjuncts, and their equally notorious dependence on lexical content and such semantically related properties as definiteness and quantification, can be explained on the assumption that verbs can be selectively type-raised over such adjuncts, and lexicalized. Thus the possibility of exceptions like the following (and the generally uncertain judgments that are associated with sentences involving subjacency violations) are also explained (31):

(a) ?a man who I painted a picture of   (31)
(b) ?an article which I wrote my thesis without being aware of.

(The subjacency constraints are treated at length by Szabolcsi and Zwarts, and Hepple.)

Other theories on this branch of the categorial family have proposed the inclusion of further combinators, and/or the exclusion of one or more of the above. Perhaps the first of the modern combinatory theories, that of Bach, proposed an account of certain bounded constructions, including passive and control, by a 'wrapping' operation which combined functions with their second argument in advance of their first, an analysis which has been extended subsequently. Such operations are related to (but not identical to) the 'associativity' family of theorems of the Lambek calculus. They are also closely related to the $\mathbf{C}$ or 'commuting' family of combinators. They can also be simulated by, or defined in terms of, the composition and type lifting combinators, as seen in example (31). Curry's combinator $\mathbf{W}$ has also been implicated in some analyses of reflexives. The theory of related constructions exploits functional composition in accounting for raising, equi, and the like, with important implications for the treatment of VP anaphora.

Since all of the above constructions are bounded, the theories in question can be viewed as combinatory theories of the lexicon and of lexical morphology (however, there are arguments against too simplistic an interpretation of this view). To that extent, the above theories are close relatives of the theories of Keenan and Faltz and of Shaumyan. All of these theories embody related sets of operations in lexical semantics. Shaumyan in particular explicitly identifies these operations with a very full range of Curry's combinators.

3.1.3 Power of Combinatory Grammars

One may ask at this point what the power of such grammars is. Curry and Feys show that collections of combinators as small as the pair **SK** may have the full expressive power of the lambda calculus. **BCWI** and **BCSI** are also implicitly shown by Curry and Feys to be equivalent to the λI-calculus—that is, the lambda calculus without vacuous abstraction. The system of (typed) **BST** is also essentially equivalent to the (simply typed) λI-calculus, although technically it may be necessary to include the ground case of I where its argument is a single variable as a special case. This equivalence means that any restrictiveness that inheres to the theory in automata-theoretic terms stems from the directional sensitivity inherent in the lexicon and in the Principles of Consistency (21) and Inheritance (22) alone.

Joshi et al. have shown that a number of 'mildly non-context-free' grammar formalisms including Joshi's Tree-Adjunction Grammars (TAG), Pollard's Head Grammars (HG), and the version of combinatory categorial grammar sketched here can be mapped onto Linear Indexed Grammars.

The consequences of equivalence to linear indexed grammars are significant, as Joshi et al. show. In particular, linear indexed grammars, by passing the stack to only one branch, allow divide-and-conquer parsing algorithms. As a result, these authors have been able to demonstrate polynomial worst-case limits on the complexity of parsing the version of combinatory CG described above.

3.2 Lambek-style Categorial Grammars

Lambek's original proposal began by offering intuitive motivations for including operations of composition, type-raising, and certain kinds of rebracketing in grammars. All of the operations concerned are, in terms of an earlier definition, *order preserving*. The first two operations are familiar but the last needs some explanation. Lambek notes that a possible 'grouping' of the sentence (*John likes*)(*Jane*) is as shown by the brackets. (He might have used a coordinate sentence as proof, although he did not in fact do so.) He then notes that the following operation would transform a standard transitive verb into a category that could combine with the subject first to

yield the desired constituency (the rule is given in Lambek's own notation, as defined earlier (32)):

$$(np\backslash s)/np \rightarrow np\backslash(s/np) \tag{32}$$

There are two things to note about this operation. One is that it is redundant: that is, its effect of permitting a subject to combine before an object can be achieved by a combination of type-raising and composition, as in example (16). The second is that, while this particular operation is order preserving and stringset-preserving, many superficially similar operations are not. For example, the following rule (33) would not have this property:

$$* (s/np)/np \rightarrow s/(np/np) \tag{33}$$

That is, rebracketing of this kind can only apply across opposite slashes, not across same slashes.

However, Lambek was not proposing to introduce these operations as independent rules. He went on to show in his paper that an infinite set of such-order preserving operations emerged as theorems from a logic defined in terms of a small number of axiom schemata and inference rules. These rules included an identity axiom, associativity axiom schemata, and inference rules of application, abstraction, and transitivity. The theorems included functional application, the infinite set of order-preserving instances of operations corresponding to the combinators $\mathbf{B}, \mathbf{B}^2, \ldots, \mathbf{B}^n$, and the order-preserving instances of type-raising, $\mathbf{T}$. They also included the rule shown in (32) and a number of operations of mathematical interest, including the Schönfinkel equivalence between 'flat' and 'curried' function-types, and a family of 'division rules' including the following (34):

$$z/y \rightarrow (z/x)/(y/z) \tag{34}$$

The latter is of interest because it was the most important rule in Geach's proposal, for which reason it is often referred to as the 'Geach Rule.'

This last result is also of interest because an elegant alternative axiomatization of the Lambek calculus in terms of the Geach rule was provided by Zielonka, who dropped Lambek's associativity axioms, substituting two Geach Rules and two Lifting Rules, and dropping the abstraction and transitivity inference rules in favor of two derived inference rules inducing recursion on the domain and range categories of functors. Zielonka's paper also proved the important result that no finite axiomatization of the Lambek calculus is possible without the inclusion of some such recursive reduction law. Zielonka's calculus differs from the original in that the product rule is no longer valid, for which reason it is sometimes identified as the 'product-free' Lambek calculus.

The Lambek calculus has the following properties. If a string is accepted on some given lexical assignment, the calculus will allow further derivations corresponding to all possible bracketings of the string.

That is, the calculus is 'structurally complete.' Curiously, while Buszkowski showed that a version of the calculus restricted to one of the two slash-directions was weakly equivalent to context-free grammar, the nonfinite-axiomatization property of the calculus meant that for many years no proof of the same weak equivalence for the full bidirectional calculus was available. Nevertheless, everyone had been convinced since the early 1960s that the equivalence held, and Buszkowski et al. (1988) had presented a number of partial results. A proof was finally published in 1993 by Pentus.

If the Lambek calculus is compared with the combinatory alternative discussed earlier, then the following similarities are seen. Both composition and type-raising are permitted rules in both systems, and both are generalized in ways which can be seen as involving recursive schemata and polymorphism. However, there are important divergences between these two branches of the categorial family. The most important is that many of the particular combinatory rules that have been proposed by linguists, while they are *semantically* identical to theorems of the Lambek calculus, are not actually theorems thereof. For example, Bach's rule of 'right-wrap,' which shares with Lambek's rebracketing rule (32) a semantics corresponding to the commuting combinator **C**, is not Lambek-provable. Similarly, examples like (28) have been used to argue for 'nonorder-preserving' composition rules, which correspond to instances of the combinator **B** that are also unlicensed by the Lambek calculus. It is hard to do without such rules, because their absence prevents all nonperipheral extraction and all non-context-free constructions (see below). Finally, none of the rules that combine arguments of more than one functor, including Geach's semantic coordination rule, the coordination schema (5), and Szabolsci's substitution rule (19) are Lambek theorems.

The response of categorial grammarians has been of two kinds. Many linguists have simply continued to take non-Lambek combinatory rules as primitive, the approach discussed in the previous sections. Such authors have placed more importance on the compositional semantics of the combinatory rules themselves than on further reducibility to axiom systems. Others have attempted to identify alternative calculi that have more attractive linguistic properties.

Lambek himself was the first to express scepticism concerning the linguistic potential of his calculus, a position that he has maintained to the present day. He noted that, because of the use of a category $(s\backslash s)/s$ for conjunctions, the calculus not only permitted strings like (35a), below, but also ones like (35b):

(a) Who walks and talks?   (35)
(b) *Who walks and he talks?

The overgeneralization arises because the conjunction

category, having applied to the sentence *He talks* to yield $s\backslash s$, can *compose* with *walks* to yield the predicate category $np\backslash s$. It is exactly this possibility that forces the use of a syncategorematic coordination schema such as (5) in the combinatory approach. However, it has been shown that such rules are not Lambek calculus theorems. Lambek's initial reaction was to restrict his original calculus by omitting the associativity axiom, yielding the 'nonassociative' Lambek calculus. This version, which has not been much used, is unique among extensions of categorial grammar in disallowing composition, which is no longer a theorem.

Other work along these lines, notably by van Benthem (1991), Moortgat (whose 1989 book is the most accessible introduction to the area), and Morrill (1994), has attempted to generalize, rather than to restrict, the original calculus. Much of this work has been directed at the possibility of restoring to the calculus one or more of Gentzen's 'structural rules,' which Lambek's original calculus entirely eschews, and whose omission renders it less powerful than full intuitionistic logic. In CG terms, these three rules correspond to *permutation of adjacent categories,* or 'interchange,' *reduction of two instances of a category to one,* or 'contraction,' and *vacuous abstraction,* or 'thinning' (sometimes termed 'weakening'). In combinatory terms, they correspond to the combinator-families **C**, **W**, and **K**. As Lambek points out, a system which allows only the first of these rules corresponds to the linear logic of Girard, while a system which allows only the first two corresponds to the relevance logic **R**₋, and the 'weak positive implicational calculus' of Church, otherwise known as the λ_I-calculus.

3.2.1 Power of Lambek-style Grammars

Van Benthem (1991) examined the consequences of adding the interchange rule, and showed that such a calculus is not only structurally complete but 'permutation-complete.' That is, if a string is recognized, so are all possible permutations of the string. He shows (1991: 97) that this calculus is (in contrast to the original calculus) of greater than context-free power. For example, a lexicon can readily be chosen which accepts the language whose strings contain equal numbers of a's, b's, and c's, which is non-context free. However, Moortgat (1989: 118) shows that the theorems of this calculus do not obey the principles of directional consistency (21) and directional inheritance (22)—for example, they include all sixteen possible forms of first-order composition, rather than just four. Moortgat also shows (1989: 92–3) that the mere inclusion in a Lambek-style axiomatization of slash-crossing composition rules like (27) (which of course are permitted by these principles) is enough to ensure collapse into van Benthem's permuting calculus. There does not seem to be a natural Lambek-style system in between.

However, Moortgat does offer a way to generalize the Lambek calculus without engendering collapse into permutation-completeness. He proposes the introduction of new equivalents of slash, including 'infixing' slashes, together with axioms and inference rules that discriminate between the slash-types (cf. 1989: 111, 120), giving the system the character of a 'partial' logic. While he shows that one such axiomatization can be made to entail the generalizations inherent in the principles of consistency and inheritance, it seems likely that many equally simple formulations within the same degrees of freedom would produce much less desirable consequences. Moreover, unless the recursive aspects of this axiom-schematization can be further constrained to limit such theorems as the composition family $\mathbf{B}^n$ in a similar way to the combinatory alternative, it appears to follow that this calculus is still of greater power than linear indexed grammar.

In the work of Moortgat, the combinatory and Lambek-style traditions of CG come close to convergence. Without the restrictions inherent in the principles of consistency and inheritance, both frameworks would collapse. The main difference between the theories is that on the combinatory view the restrictions are built into the axioms and are claimed to follow from first principles, whereas on the Lambek view, the restrictions are imposed as filters.

4. Categorial Grammars and Linguistic Semantics

There are two commonly used notations that make explicit the close relation between syntax and semantics that both combinatory and Lambek-style categorial grammars embody. The first associates with each category a term of the lambda calculus naming its interpretation. The second associates an interpretation with each basic category in a functor, a representation which has the advantage of being directly interpretable via standard term-unification procedures of the kind used in logic programming languages such as PROLOG. The same verb *sees* might appear as follows in these notations, which are here shown for the combinatory categories, but which can equally be applied to Lambek categories. In either version it is standard to use a colon to associate syntactic and semantic entities, to use a convention that semantic constants have mnemonic identifiers like *see'* distinguished from variables by primes. For purposes of exposition it will be assumed that translations exactly mirror the syntactic category in terms of dominance relations. Thus a convention of 'left associativity' in translations is adopted, so that expressions like *see' y x* are equivalent to *(see' y) x* (36):

(a) λ-term-based: $\quad sees := (S \backslash NP)/NP : \lambda y \lambda x[see' \, y \, x]$ (36)
(b) Unification-based: $sees := (S : see' \, y \, x \backslash NP : x)/NP : y$

The advantage of the former notation is that the λ-calculus is a highly readable notation for functional

entities. Its disadvantage is that the notation of the combinatory rules is complicated to allow the combination of both parts of the category, as in (37a), below. This has the effect of weakening the direct relation between syntactic and semantic types, since it suggests rules might be allowed in which the syntactic and semantic combinatory operations were *not* identical. In the unification notation (37b), by contrast, the combinatory rules apply unchanged, and necessarily preserve identity between syntactic and semantic operations, a property which was one of the original attractions of CG.

Forward Composition: (37)
$X/Y : f \quad Y/Z : g \Rightarrow X/Z : \lambda x[f(g \, x)]$

(a) λ-term-based

Forward Composition:
$X/Y \quad Y/Z \Rightarrow X/Z$

(b) Unification-based

Because of their direct expressibility in unification-based programming languages like PROLOG, and related special-purpose linguistic programming languages like PATR-II, the latter formalism or notational variants thereof are widespread in the computational linguistics literature. Derivations appear as follows (for simplicity, type-raising is ignored here):

Gilbert	sees	George	(38)
$NP : gilbert'$	$(S : see' \, y \, x \backslash NP : x)/NP : y$	$NP : george'$	

$S : see' \, george' \, x \backslash NP : x$

$S : see' \, george' \, gilbert'$

All the alternative derivations that the combinatory grammar permits yield equivalent semantic interpretations, representing the canonical function-argument relations that result from a purely applicative derivation. In contrast to combinatory derivations, such semantic representations therefore preserve the relations of dominance and command defined in the lexicon, a point that has obviously desirable consequences for capturing the generalizations concerning dependency that have been described in the GB framework in terms of relations of c-command and the notion of 'thematic hierarchy.' This point is important for example, to the analysis of parasitic gaps sketched earlier, since parasitic gaps are known to obey an 'anti-c-command' restriction.

By the very token that combinatory derivations *preserve* canonical relations of dominance and command, one must distinguish this level of semantic interpretation from the one implicated in the proposals of Geach and others. These authors use a very similar range of combinatory operations, notably including or entailing as theorems (generalized) functional composition (lexical, polymorphic), type-lifting, and (in the case of Geach) a coordination schema of the kind introduced in Sect. 2, in order to free the scope of quantifiers from traditional surface syntax, in order to capture the well-known ambiguity of sentences like the following (39):

Every woman loves some man. (39)

On the simplest assumption that the verb is of type $e \rightarrow (e \rightarrow t)$, and the subject and object are corresponding (polymorphic) type-raised categories, the reading where the subject has wide scope is obtained by a purely applicative reading. The reading where the object has wide scope is obtained by composing subject and verb before applying the object to the result of the composition. In this their motivation for introducing composition is the combinatory relative of the λ-categorial grammars of Lewis, Montague, and Cresswell (see above). Indeed, one must sharply distinguish the *level* of semantic representation that is assumed in these two kinds of theory, as Lewis in fact suggested (1972:48), ascribing all these authors' operations to the level of logical form. Otherwise one must predict that those sentences which under the assumptions of the combinatory approach *require* function composition to yield an analysis (as opposed to merely allowing that alternative), such as right node raising, must yield only one of the two readings. (Which reading is obtained will depend upon the original assignment of categories.) However, this prediction would be incorrect: both scopings are allowed for sentences like the following (40), adapted from Geach:

Every girl likes, and every boy detests, some (40)
saxophonist.

That is not to say that the categorial analysis is without advantages. As Geach points out, one does *not* appear to obtain a third reading in which two instances of the existential each have wide scope over one of the universals, so that all the girls like one particular saxophonist, and all the boys detest one particular saxophonist, but the two saxophonists are not the same. This result is to be expected if the entire substring *Every girl likes and every boy detests* is the syntactic and semantic constituent with respect to which the scope of the existential is defined. However, it remains the case that there is a many-to-one relation between semantic categories at this level and categories and/or rules at the level which has been considered up to now. The semantics itself and the nature of this relationship are a subject in their own right which it is not possible to do justice to here, but the reader is referred to important work by Partee and Rooth, and Hendriks on the question. Much of this work has recently harked back to axiomatic frameworks related to the Lambek calculus.

5. Further Reading

Two indispensible collections of readings in categorial grammar between them contain many important pap-

ers in the area, including many of those cited above. Buszkowski et al. (1988) includes a number of historically significant older papers, including those by Lambek (1958) and Geach (1970). The most important omissions in the otherwise excellent historical coverage afforded by the Buszkowski volume are the original paper by Ajdukiewicz (1935), which is translated together with other historically relevant material in McCall (1967), and the work of Bar-Hillel (1964). Certain papers crucial to the prehistory of CG, including Schönfinkel (1924), are collected in translation in van Heijenoort (1967). The review articles by the editors contain valuable survey material in many of the areas touched on here, and the collection is particularly valuable as a source of mathematical results concerning the Lambek calculus and its extensions. The collection edited by Oehrle et al. (1988) also contains important survey articles, largely non-overlapping with those in the previous collection. The overall slant is more linguistic, and the collection includes a large number of important papers which continue to influence current work in natural language syntax and semantics. To some extent, these largely complementary collections epitomize the two approaches distinguished at the start of Sect. 3.

Besides the valuable introductory essays to these two collections, the relevant section of Lyons (1968), which heralded the revival of categorial grammar as a linguistic theory, remains one of the most accessible and inspiring brief introductions to categorial grammar for the general linguist. The 1993 book by Wood (which has appeared since the first version of this article was written) is the most complete review of the whole area.

As far as the mathematical foundations of CG go, the most intuitive introduction to the relation between combinators and the λ-calculus remains Curry and Feys (1958: ch. 5 and ch. 6). Hindley and Seldin (1986) provide an excellent modern introduction. Smullyan (1985), in which the combinators take the form of birds, is undoubtedly the most entertaining among recent presentations of the subject, and is a goldmine of useful results. The papers of Richard Montague were collected in Thomason (1974). The related λ-categorial approach of Cresswell is presented in a series of books of which the first appeared in 1973. Important work in Lambek-style categorial grammars is to be found in Moortgat (1989) and van Benthem (1991), the former being aimed at the linguist, the latter at the mathematical logician. Morill (1994) extends this work.

A number of collections bringing together papers on recent linguistic theories include papers on CG, and relate it to other contemporary approaches. The collections by Jacobson and Pullum (1982), Huck and Ojeda (1987), Baltin and Kroch (1989) and Sag and Szabolsci (1992) are useful in this respect. These and the two collections mentioned earlier provide references to a large and diverse literature constituting the foundations of the categorial approach. However, for current linguistic work in this rapidly evolving area one must turn to the journals and conference proceedings. Among the former, *Linguistics and Philosophy* has been a pioneer in presenting recent categorial work. Among the latter, the annual proceedings of the West Coast Conference on Formal Linguistics is one important source. Much computational linguistic work in CG also remains uncollected, and here again one must turn to journals and conference proceedings, among which *Computational Linguistics* and the annual proceedings of the meetings of the Association for Computational Linguistics (and of its European Chapter) are important. A more complete bibliography can be found in Steedman (1993).

Bibliography

Baltin M, Kroch A S (eds.) 1989 *Alternative Conceptions of Phrase Structure*. Chicago University Press, Chicago, IL

Bar-Hillel Y 1964 *Language and Information*. Addison-Wesley, Reading, MA

Buszkowski W, Marciszewski W, van Benthem J (eds.) 1988 *Categorial Grammar*. Benjamins. Amsterdam

Cresswell M 1973 *Logics and Languages*. Methuen, London

Curry H, Feys R 1958 *Combinatory Logic*, vol. I. North-Holland, Amsterdam

Hindley R, Seldin J 1986 *Introduction to Combinators and λ-calculus*. Cambridge University Press, Cambridge

Huck G, Ojeda A (eds.) 1987 *Syntax and Semantics 20: Discontinuous Constituency*. Academic Press, New York

Jacobson P, Pullum G K (eds.) 1982 *The Nature of Syntactic Representation*. Reidel, Dordrecht

Lambek J 1958 The Mathematics of Sentence Structure. In: Buszkowski, et al. (eds.) 1988

Lewis D 1970 General Semantics. *Synthese* **22**: 18–67

Lyons J 1968 *Theoretical Linguistics*. Cambridge University Press, Cambridge

McCall S (ed.) 1967 *Polish Logic 1920–1939*. Clarendon Press, Oxford

Moortgat M 1989 *Categorial Investigations*. Foris, Dordrecht

Morrill G 1994 *Type-logical Grammar*. Kluwer, Dordrecht

Oehrle R T, Bach E, Wheeler D (eds.) 1988 *Categorial Grammars and Natural Language Structures*. Reidel, Dordrecht

Sag I, Szabolsci A (eds.) 1992 *Lexical Matters*. CLSI/Chicago University Press, Chicago, IL

Smullyan R 1985 *To Mock a Mockingbird*. Knopf, New York

Steedman M 1993 Categorial Grammar. *Lingua*

Thomason R (ed.) 1974 *Formal Philosophy: The Papers of Richard Montague*. Yale, New Haven, CT

van Benthem J 1991 *Language in Action*. North-Holland, Amsterdam

van Heijenoort J (ed.) 1967 *From Frege to Gödel*. Harvard University Press, Cambridge, MA

Wood M 1993 *Categorial Grammars*. Routledge, London

Categories and Types

H. L. W. Hendricks

Within theories of formal grammar, it has become customary to assume that linguistic expressions belong to syntactic 'categories,' whereas their interpretations inhabit semantic 'types.' This article aims to set out the basic ideas of logical syntax and semantics as they are found in categorial grammar and lambda calculus, respectively, and to focus on their convergence in theories of linguistic syntax and semantics.

The philosophical idea that the objects of thought form a hierarchy of categories is almost as old as philosophy itself. That this hierarchy may be based on function–argument relationships was realized by two eminent mathematicians/philosophers in the nineteenth century, namely Frege and Husserl. Their influence may be traced in two subsequent streams of logical investigation. One is that of mathematical ontology, where Russell developed his theory of types which describes mathematical universes of individual objects, functions over these, functionals over functions, etc. Although Zermelo-style axiomatic set theory, rather than type theory, became the received

mathematical view, the type-theoretic tradition in the foundations of mathematics has persisted, inspiring important specific research programs such as lambda calculus in its wake. A second stream developed in philosophy, where Leśniewski and Ajdukiewicz developed a technical theory of categories which eventually became a paradigm of linguistics known as 'categorial grammar.'

A first convergence of both streams may already be observed in the work of Montague (1974), where mathematically inspired type theories supply the semantics for a categorially inspired syntax of natural languages. Since 1980, a more principled connection between categories and types has emerged from work building on Lambek's extension of classical categorial grammar.

1. Types

In 1902, Russell showed (in a famous letter to Frege) that a naive principle of set comprehension leads to a paradox for the set $A = \{x \mid x \notin x\}$: $A \in A$ if and only if $A \notin A$. Russell solved the problem by simply excluding

$x \in x$ from the set of well-formed formulas. Roughly, every variable $x, y, z, \ldots$ is annotated (typed) with an index $n \in N$, and $x_n \in x_m$ is acceptable only if $m = n + 1$. Within set theory, this theory of types was superseded by Zermelo's axiomatization, where the axiom of foundation requires that each set be well-founded.

The idea of typing recurred in the context of lambda calculus, which was originally conceived by Church (1932–33) as part of a general theory about functions and logic, and intended as a foundation for mathematics. Although the full system turned out to be inconsistent, the subsystem dealing with functions only turned out to be a successful model for computable functions. This system, the pure lambda calculus, is a type-free theory about functions as 'rules' (prescriptions). Typed lambda calculus can be seen as a theory about functions as 'graphs' (sets of ordered pairs). In the (Church-style) typed lambda calculus under consideration here, every term has a unique type: it is an annotated version of a type-free lambda term. Within this theory, all usual logical operators (Boolean connectives and quantifiers) are definable in terms of application, abstraction, and identity.

The set of 'types' consists of primitive types and types formed out of them by means of certain operations. Common primitive types in logical semantics include e (entities) and t (truth values). Only the type-forming operator that forms function types (a, b) out of types a and b will be used. A 'frame' $\mathbf{D}$ is a family of domains $\mathbf{D}_a$, one for each type a, such that $\mathbf{D}_e$ is an arbitrary nonempty set (the set of individuals), $\mathbf{D}_t = \{0, 1\}$, the set of truth values, and $\mathbf{D}_{(a,b)} = \mathbf{D}_b^{\mathbf{D}_a}$ the set of functions from objects in $\mathbf{D}_a$ to objects in $\mathbf{D}_b$. (Using 'Schönfinkel's trick' (1924), the functions of several arguments can be obtained by iteration of application.)

The formal 'language' to refer to objects in such structures consists of the following 'terms': infinitely many variables x_a of each type a; some typed constants c_a; and the following compound terms: if $\sigma_{(a,b)}$ and τ_a are terms, then $\sigma(\tau)$ is a term of type b ('application'); if σ_b is a term and x_a is a variable, then $\lambda x \cdot \sigma$ is a term of type (a, b) ('abstraction'); and if σ_a and τ_a are terms, then $\sigma = \tau$ is a term of type t ('identity').

A 'model' $\mathbf{M}$ is an ordered pair $\langle \mathbf{D}, \mathbf{I} \rangle$, where $\mathbf{D}$ is a frame, and $\mathbf{I}$ is an 'interpretation function': a function such that $\mathbf{I}(c_a) \in \mathbf{D}_a$ for each constant c_a. The 'extension' or 'interpretation' $|\sigma|^{\mathbf{M},g}$ of a term σ in a model $\mathbf{M}$ under a 'variable assignment' g (i.e., a function such that $g(x_a) \in \mathbf{D}_a$ for each variable x_a; $g[d/x]$ is the assignment g' such that $g'(x) = d$ and $g'(y) = g(y)$ if $x \neq y$) is defined as follows: $|c|^{\mathbf{M},g} = \mathbf{I}(c)$; $|x|^{\mathbf{M},g} = g(x)$; $|\sigma(\tau)|^{\mathbf{M},g} = |\sigma|^{\mathbf{M},g}(|\tau|^{\mathbf{M},g})$; $|\lambda x \cdot \sigma|^{\mathbf{M},g} = f \in \mathbf{D}_b^{\mathbf{D}_a}$ such that for all d: $f(d) = |\sigma|^{\mathbf{M},g[d/x]}$; and $|\sigma = \tau|^{\mathbf{M},g} = 1$ iff $|\sigma|^{\mathbf{M},g} = |\tau|^{\mathbf{M},g}$.

An example: let $P_{(e,t)}$ and x_e be variables which (due to their type) range over (characteristic functions of) sets of individuals and individuals, respectively. Let $\text{MAN}_{(e,t)}$ and $\text{WALK}_{(e,t)}$ be constants interpreted as (the

characteristic function of) the set of men and the set of walkers. Then $\lambda P \cdot \exists x[\text{MAN}(x) \& P(x)]$ is a complex term of type $((e,t), t)$ which denotes the function from sets of individuals to truth values such that a set is assigned the value 1 iff there is a man in that set: a plausible interpretation for the noun phrase *a man*. Now, consider the term $\lambda P \cdot \exists x[\text{MAN}(x) \& P(x)](\text{WALK})$ of type t. The value of this term is the above function applied to the set of walkers. It will be 1 iff there is a man who walks. In fact, the latter term is equivalent to $\exists x[\text{MAN}(x) \& \text{WALK}(x)]$.

There are various alternatives in setting up typed lambda calculus. For example, Montague's IL (intensional logic (1974)) is a version of type theory which enables one to form 'intensional' types (s, a) out of a type a. His frames include an additional nonempty set $\mathbf{W}$ (of possible worlds), and the definition of domains is extended with the clause that $\mathbf{D}_{(s,a)} = \mathbf{D}_a^{\mathbf{W}}$, that is, the set of functions from possible worlds to objects in $\mathbf{D}_a$. Together with appropriate adaptions of the formal language and its interpretation, this version allows a formal reconstruction of semantic notions such as properties, propositions, and individual concepts. Gallin (1975) has shown that IL can be embedded into the extensional theory outlined above if it is enriched with a basic type s, such that $\mathbf{D}_s = \mathbf{W}$. The resulting system is called 'two-sorted type theory.'

Moreover, the whole format of presentation can be shifted. Thus, Orey (1959) proposed to interpret the calculus in hierarchies of 'relations,' rather than functions. Muskens (1989) has argued that this relational interpretation is more convenient if the objective is to 'partialize' semantics, a move motivated by various linguistic considerations involving the semantics of so-called 'attitude reports' in natural language.

2. Categories

According to Ajdukiewicz (1935), natural language expressions exhibit a function/argument structure, symbolized in the category (A, B) for expressions needing an expression of category A to yield an expression of category B, plus the axioms $(A, B), A \Rightarrow B$ and $A, (A, B) \Rightarrow B$. However, in natural languages these functors usually have a direction in which they look for their arguments. Therefore, Bar-Hillel (1953) proposed a 'directed' variant, the so-called 'Ajdukiewicz/Bar-Hillel calculus' (AB), where left-looking and right-looking functors each have their own axiom: $B/A, A \Rightarrow B$ and $A, A \backslash B \Rightarrow B$. When a Cut rule is added: if $T \Rightarrow A$ and $X, A, Y \Rightarrow B$, then $X, T, Y \Rightarrow B$ (where A, B are categories, T, X, Y finite sequences of categories, and T is nonempty), AB can be used for language recognition.

Notice that AB grammars are extremely lexicalist. They only have universal axioms, a universal cut rule, and a lexicon. There are no fragment-specific rules for combining expressions. Assume, for example, the lexical category-assignments *George* → *NP*, *saw* →

$NP\backslash(S/NP)$, $a \rightarrow NP/N$, and $man \rightarrow N$. Then it can be shown that *George saw a man* is a sentence (S) by proving the theorem $NP, NP\backslash(S/NP), NP/N, N \Rightarrow S$.

$$\frac{\dfrac{NP, NP\backslash(S/NP) \Rightarrow S/NP \qquad S/NP, NP \Rightarrow S}{NP, NP\backslash(S/NP), NP \Rightarrow S} \qquad NP/N, N \Rightarrow S}{NP, NP\backslash(S/NP), NP/N, N \Rightarrow S}$$

Bar-Hillel, et al. (1960) proved that AB grammars and context-free grammars recognize exactly the same set of languages.

Lambek (1958) proposed an important extension of AB. The (product-free part of this) calculus (L) consists of one axiom and five inference rules.

[Ax] $A \Rightarrow A$

[/L] $\dfrac{T \Rightarrow A \quad U, B, V \Rightarrow C}{U, B/A, T, V \Rightarrow C}$ [/L] $\dfrac{T \Rightarrow A \quad U, B, V \Rightarrow C}{U, T, A\backslash B, V \Rightarrow C}$

[/R] $\dfrac{T, A \Rightarrow B}{T \Rightarrow B/A}$ [\R] $\dfrac{A, T \Rightarrow B}{T \Rightarrow A\backslash B}$

[Cut] $\dfrac{T \Rightarrow A \quad X, A, Y \Rightarrow B}{X, T, Y \Rightarrow B}$

It is easily seen that $L - \{[/R], [\backslash R]\}$ is equivalent to $AB \cup \{[Ax]\}$. Notice, however, that the introduction of [/R] and [\R] essentially enlarges the set of theorems. For example, L allows the derivation of theorems like $A \Rightarrow B/(A\backslash B)$ ('raising'), $A/B, B/C \Rightarrow A/C$ ('composition'), $A\backslash(C/B) \Leftrightarrow (A\backslash C)/B$ ('associativity'), and $A/B \Rightarrow (A/C)/(B/C)$ ('division').

By showing that the set of theorems is not affected by leaving out [Cut], Lambek established the decidability of L. Moreover, Buszkowski, in Buszkowski, et al. (1988) has proved that L is complete (and AB, therefore, incomplete) with respect to the intuitive interpretation of categories as sets of expressions (S is the set of finite sequences of lexical items): that is, for $A\backslash B = \{x \in S \mid \forall y \in A : xy \in B\}$ and $B/A = \{x \in S \mid \forall y \in A : yx \in B\}$ it holds that $T \Rightarrow C$ iff $T \subseteq C$. Finally, Pentus (1993) has proved that the generative capacity of L is the same as that of context-free grammars.

3. Types and Categories

As noted in the introduction, the first gathering of syntactic categories and semantic types can be discerned in the linguistic papers of Montague. The most influential one (1974: ch. 8) presents a grammar for a fragment of English with a semantic component, where the expressions defined by the syntactic component are translated into expressions of the logical language IL. These IL expressions receive their model-theoretic interpretation in the usual way. Thus, the English expressions are indirectly assigned a semantic interpretation, viz., via the interpretation of the logical expressions into which they are translated.

In syntax, all expressions belong to categories. For these categories, Montague uses a notation familiar from categorial grammar: besides basic categories, there are compound categories A/B and $A//B$. The syntactic category of an expression determines the semantic type of its interpretation (or rather: its IL translation), in that basic categories C are assigned some type TYPE(C), and A/B and $A//B$ both get the type $((s, \text{TYPE}(B)), \text{TYPE}(A))$. However, the categorial influence does not go further: there are fragment-specific rules which give a recursive definition of the set of English expressions, and these rules do much more than merely concatenating expressions. They involve morphological retrieval, insertion of syncategorematic expressions, substitution, etc. Thus one cannot simply say that expressions of category A/B are the ones which combine with an expression of category B on their right-hand side to yield an expression of category A (or, more formally, that $B/A = \{x \in S \mid \forall y \in A : yx \in B\}$).

In Montague's work, the category-to-type assignment, TYPE, is a *function*. If an expression belongs to a category C, then its translation is rigidly and invariably of the unique type assigned to C, TYPE(C). This entails that one has to employ a strategy of generalizing to the worst case: uniformly assign *all* expressions of a certain syntactic category the 'worst' (most complicated) type needed for *some* expression in that category. *John*, for instance, belongs to the same category as *a man*. But as the latter noun phrase needs an (extensional) interpretation of type $((e, t), t)$ (cf. above), the former will have to have such an interpretation as well. (Luckily, $\lambda P \cdot P(j)$ will do.) This aspect has been criticized by Partee and Rooth (1983), among others. They argue that scope ambiguities in natural languages show that there is not always a worst case to generalize to, and propose a reverse, flexible strategy instead: an expression gets a lexical translation of the minimal type available for that expression, and general rules derive the necessary translations of more complicated types.

In the 1960s and 1970s, various proposals were made for strengthening the basic (AB) framework of categorial grammar. As a matter of historical irony, most of these proposals were already present in Lambek (1958). Around 1980, the rediscovery of this seminal paper led to a renaissance of categorial research, partly also inspired by Montague's work on the semantics of natural language. In view of its origins, categorial grammar is a formalism which can accommodate both syntactic categories of expressions and semantic types of objects. In fact, van Benthem (1986) showed that both perspectives can be systematically related. Product-free L, for instance, can be assigned a straightforward semantic interpretation in which all categories C are provided with a typed lambda term τ (rendered as $C : \tau$ below). The type of τ is determined by C: basic categories C are associated with some type TYPE(C), and compound categories

$A\backslash B$ and B/A with the type $(\text{TYPE}(A),\text{TYPE}(B))$. [/L] and [\L] correspond to 'application,' [/R] and [\R] to 'abstraction,' and [Ax] and [Cut] to 'identity':

$$[/L] \quad \frac{T\Rightarrow A:\alpha \qquad U, B:\beta(\alpha), V\Rightarrow C}{U, B/A:\beta, T, V\Rightarrow C}$$

$$[\backslash L] \quad \frac{T\Rightarrow A:\alpha \qquad U, B:\beta(\alpha), V\Rightarrow C}{U, T, A\backslash B:\beta, V\Rightarrow C}$$

$$[/R] \quad \frac{T, A:x\Rightarrow B:\tau}{T\Rightarrow B/A:\lambda x\cdot\tau}$$

$$[\backslash R] \quad \frac{A:x, T\Rightarrow B:\tau}{T\Rightarrow A\backslash B:\lambda x\cdot\tau}$$

$$[Cut] \quad \frac{T\Rightarrow A:\tau \qquad X, A:\tau, Y\Rightarrow B}{X, T, Y\Rightarrow B}$$

$$[Ax] \quad A:\tau\Rightarrow A:\tau$$

As for the relationship between categories and types, Montague's semantics and categorial grammar underwent a parallel development. In AB grammars, each expression is assigned exactly one category. L is far more flexible; the presence of theorems like raising (cf. above) entails that an expression belongs to an infinite number of syntactic categories, and its interpretations in those categories to an infinite number of semantic types. This increased syntactic/semantic flexibility mirrors (but can be distinguished from) the purely semantic flexibility argued for within Montague grammar. In conjunction with additional lexical polymorphism, categorial flexibility has been successfully exploited in categorial accounts of nonconstituent coordination, scope ambiguities, negative polarity, and other linguistic phenomena.

Research within categorial grammar has headed towards the incorporation of new type-forming operators, to be used for the description of extraction, gapping, locality facts, etc. In this area, work on linear logic (cf. Girard 1987), of which L turned out to be a weak, noncommutative implicational fragment, has proved to be a valuable heuristic tool.

See also: Categorial Grammar; Montague Grammar.

Bibliography

Ajdukiewicz K 1935 Die syntaktische Konnexität. *Studia Philosophica* 1: 1–27

Bar-Hillel Y 1953 A quasi-arithmetical notation for syntactic description. *Lg* 29: 47–58

Bar-Hillel Y (ed.) 1964 *Language and Information*. Addison-Wesley, Reading, MA

Bar-Hillel Y, Gaifman C, Shamir E 1960 On categorial and phrase structure grammars. *The Bulletin of the Research Council of Israel* 9: 1–16

Barendregt H 1981 *The Lambda Calculus: Its Syntax and Semantics*. North-Holland, Amsterdam

Benthem J van 1986 *Essays in Logical Semantics*. Reidel, Dordrecht

Buszkowski W 1997 Mathematical linguistics and proof theory. In: Benthem J van, Meulen A ter (eds.) *Handbook of Logic and Language*. Elsevier Science, Amsterdam

Buszkowski W, Marciszewski W, Benthem J van (eds.) 1988 *Categorial Grammar*. Benjamins, Amsterdam

Church A 1932–33 A set of postulates for the foundation of logic. *Annals of Mathematics* 33: 346–66; 34: 839–64

Gallin D 1975 *Intensional and Higher-order Modal Logic*. North-Holland, Amsterdam

Gamut L T F 1990 *Logic, Language and Meaning*, vol. II. University of Chicago Press, Chicago, IL

Girard J Y 1987 Linear logic. *Theoretical Computer Science* 50: 1–102

Lambek J 1958 The mathematics of sentence structure. *American Mathematical Monthly* 65: 154–70

Montague R 1974 *Formal Philosophy*. Yale University Press, New Haven, CT

Moortgat M 1997 Categorial type logics. In: Benthem J van, Meulen A ter (eds.) *Handbook of Logic and Language*. Elsevier Science, Amsterdam

Muskens R 1989 Meaning and partiality. (Doctoral dissertation, University of Amsterdam)

Oehrle R, Bach E, Wheeler D (eds.) 1988 *Categorial Grammars and Natural Language Structures*. Reidel, Dordrecht

Orey S 1959 Model theory for the higher-order predicate calculus. *Transactions of the American Mathematical Society* 92: 72–84

Partee B, Rooth M 1983 Generalized conjunction and type ambiguity. In: Bäuerle R, Schwarze C, Stechow A von (eds.) *Meaning, Use and Interpretation of Language*. De Gruyter, Berlin

Pentus M 1993 Lambek Grammars are context free. In: *Proceedings of the Eighth Annual IEEE Symposium on Logic in Computer Science*. Montreal

Schönfinkel M 1924 Über die Bausteine der mathematischen Logik. *Mathematische Annalen* 92: 305–16

Turner R 1997 Types. In: Benthem J van, Meulen A ter (eds.) *Handbook of Logic and Language*. Elsevier Science, Amsterdam

De Dicto/De Re

G. Forbes

The *de dicto/de re* distinction is a classification usually effected on sentences which contain 'modal' contexts (e.g., *it is possible that* or a subjunctive verb) or 'epi-stemic' contexts (*Ralph believes that* or *it is a priori that*). For some it is primarily a syntactic classification and for others primarily a semantic one, and one important question is to what extent the syntactic and semantic viewpoints can be harmonized.

1. Syntactic and Semantic Contrasts

Here are two pairs of examples (1–2), one modal and the other epistemic, which illustrate the distinction (Quine 1976):

$$\Box(\exists x)(x \text{ is greater than } 7) \tag{1a}$$

$$(\exists x)\Box(x \text{ is greater than } 7) \tag{1b}$$

$$\text{Ralph believes that } (\exists x)(x \text{ is a spy}) \tag{2a}$$

$$(\exists x) \text{ Ralph believes that } x \text{ is a spy.} \tag{2b}$$

(1a) and (2a) are *de dicto*, for each has a complete proposition in the scope of its governing context. But (1b) and (2b) are *de re*, for each has a variable which is free within the modal or epistemic context. This syntactic difference corresponds to an obvious semantic one: (1b) and (2b) say that there is an object such that *it* is necessarily greater than 7 or that *it* is believed by Ralph to be a spy, which explains the label '*de re*.' Contrast (2a): it does not say that there is any particular object which Ralph believes to be a spy.

However, there is a problem about classifying sentences with expressions which pick out specific individuals, for example, in (3–5):

$$\Box(\text{Aristotle is a member of the species } homo\ sapiens) \tag{3}$$

$$\text{Ralph believes that you are a spy} \tag{4}$$

$$\text{Ralph believes that the shortest spy is a spy.} \tag{5}$$

The problem is whether each should be classified as *de dicto*, since each contains a complete proposition within the scope of the governing context, or as *de re*, since each seems to concern a specific object.

2. The Modal Case

The syntactic and semantic classifications for modal contexts can be harmonized by making use of the notion of a 'rigid designator' (Kripke 1980). A rigid designator is an expression such that, whenever it picks out x at one world and y at another, then $x = y$. So 'Aristotle' and 'you' (relative to a fixed context of utterance) are rigid while 'the shortest spy' is nonrigid. One can then define a '*de dicto* sentence' of a modal language to be one which contains no occurrence of a rigid designator within the scope of a modal operator, and no occurrence of a variable within the scope of an operator whose binding quantifier is not within the scope of that operator. Example (3) is therefore *de re* (for (4) and (5), see below).

One can now explain exactly what the *de dicto/de re* distinction amounts to in the modal case. A possible worlds' model $\mathcal{M}$ for a language $\mathcal{L}$ consists in a collection of worlds W (with one singled out as the actual world) and a collection of possible objects X together with, for each $w \in W$, a description which says, for

each n-place atomic relation-symbol R of $\mathcal{L}$, which n-tuples of members of X satisfy R at w and which do not, and for each rigid designator of $\mathcal{L}$, which object it designates at w. If $w \in W$, then a 'qualitative duplicate' w' of w can be constructed by choosing a set Y of the same size as X such that Y contains every $x \in X$ denoted in $\mathcal{M}$ by a rigid designator of $\mathcal{L}$, and a particular 1–1 correspondence f between X and Y, and then by replacing $x \in X$ with $f(x) \in Y$ throughout the description of w (the denotations of the rigid designators stay the same). Then if $\mathcal{M}$ is a possible worlds model, one defines a *Fine-weakening* of $\mathcal{M}$ to be a model $\mathcal{M}'$ with the same actual world as $\mathcal{M}$ but in which each other world has been replaced by a qualitative duplicate (allowing different choices of Y or f for different $w \in W$). Next, one can say that a sentence is *essentially de re* if it is not equivalent to a *de dicto* sentence: '$(\forall x)\Box(Fx \supset Fx)$' is *de re* but not essentially so, since it is equivalent to '$\Box(\forall x)(Fx \supset Fx)$.' The main result, due to Fine, is that a sentence σ is essentially *de re* if there are models $\mathcal{M}$ and $\mathcal{M}'$, $\mathcal{M}'$ a Fine-weakening of $\mathcal{M}$, such that σ holds in one model but not the other (Fine 1978). Reflection on these definitions indicates that what is disrupted in the move from $\mathcal{M}$ to $\mathcal{M}'$ is the pattern of recurrence of specific objects from world to world. This precisely pins down the semantic feature of *de re* sentences underlying the syntactic criterion.

3. The Epistemic Case

There is little prospect of anything comparably rigorous and comparably significant for epistemic contexts. On one view, the very legitimacy of such forms as (2b) and (4) can be disputed, on the grounds that the position of the term in (4) is not open to substitution by a coreferential term (even if you are John Smith, Ralph might deny that John Smith is a spy) and hence not open to quantificational binding (Quine 1976). In reply, one could challenge either the failure of substitution claim, for there is no failure of substitution of rigid designators in the modal case, or else the idea that quantification is acceptable only if substitution does not fail (Salmon 1986; Kaplan 1986). To make further progress, one would then have to work out the semantic intuition underlying the *de re* label in the epistemic examples, the intuition that in (2b) and in (4) Ralph's belief is in some sense about an object, while in (5), assuming he deduced 'the shortest spy is a spy' from 'there are finitely many spies and no two have the same height,' his belief in that same sense is *not* about an object. The nature of this contrast is still controversial (Burge 1977; Forbes 1987).

See also: Modal Logic; Necessity; Reference: Philosophical Issues.

Bibliography

Burge T 1977 Belief De Re. *The Journal of Philosophy* **74**: 338–62

Fine K 1978 Model theory for modal logic part one: The *de re/de dicto* distinction. *The Journal of Philosophical Logic* **7**: 125–56

Forbes G 1987 Indexicals and intensionality: A Fregean perspective. *The Philosophical Review* **96**: 3–31

Kaplan D 1986 Opacity. In: Hahn L E, Schilpp P A (eds.) *The Philosophy of W. V. Quine*. Open Court, La Salle, IL

Kripke S A 1980 *Naming and Necessity*. Harvard University Press, Cambridge, MA

Quine W V 1976 *The Ways of Paradox*, rev. enl. edn. Harvard University Press, Cambridge, MA

Salmon N 1986 *Frege's Puzzle*. MIT Press, Cambridge, MA

Formal Semantics

J. van Eijck

Formal semantics of natural language is the study of the meaning of natural language expressions using the tools of formal or symbolic logic. The ultimate aim of the discipline is commonly taken to include the following: to give an explication of the concept of meaning and to use this explication to provide an account of the role of language in the activity of drawing inferences (the individual processing of information), and of the role of language in the activity of sharing or communicating information (the collective processing of information).

This article provides an introduction to formal theories of meaning and to the logical analysis of language in the footsteps of Gottlob Frege, the founding father of the enterprise. The process of composition of meaning and the relations between the concepts of meaning, inference, and truth are presented, and contextual aspects of meaning are discussed. The article ends with a sketch of the emerging perspective of a dynamic theory of meaning.

1. The Composition of Meaning

Introductory logic textbooks usually include a selection of exercises for translating natural language sentences into first-order logic. Invariably, these exercises assume that the student already has a firm grasp of what the sentences mean. The aim of such exercises is to expand the student's awareness of the expressive power of predicate logic by inviting him/her to express an (intuitively) well-understood message in the new medium. Because of this presupposed understanding of the original message, such translations cannot count as explications of the concept of meaning for natural language.

It is necessary to ask under what conditions a translation procedure from natural language into some kind of logical representation language can count as an explication of the concept of meaning. Obviously,

the procedure should not presuppose knowledge of the meaning of complete natural language sentences, but rather should specify how sentence meanings are derived from the meanings of smaller building blocks. Thus, the meanings of complex expressions are derivable in a systematic fashion from the meanings of the smallest building blocks occurring in those expressions. The meaning of these smallest building blocks is taken as given. It has been argued that the real mystery of semantics lies in the way human beings grasp the meaning of single words; see, for example, Percy (1954), or Plato's dialogue *Cratylus*.

Formal semantics has little or nothing to say about the interpretation of semantic atoms. It has rather a lot to say, however, about the process of composing complex meanings out of smaller building blocks. The intuition that this is always possible can be stated somewhat more precisely; it is called the Principle of Compositionality and defined as follows:

> The meaning of an expression is a function of the meanings of its immediate syntactic components plus their syntactic mode of composition.

The principle of compositionality is implicit in Gottlob Frege's writings on philosophy of language; it is made fully explicit in Richard Montague's approach to natural language semantics. Rather than indulge in philosophical reflections on the meaning of compositionality, the principle will be illustrated here by showing how Alfred Tarski's definition of the semantics of 'first-order predicate logic' complies with it.

From the end of the nineteenth century until the 1960s the main tool of semantics was the language of first-order predicate logic, so-called because it is a tool for describing properties of objects of the first order in Bertrand Russell's hierarchy of 'things,' 'properties of things,' 'properties of properties of things,' etc. Essentially, predicate logic was first presented in 1879 by Frege.

Modern semantic theories of natural language are generally not based on first-order logic but on typed intensional logic, because of its still larger scope and because of the fact that this tool is more suited for a compositional treatment of the semantics of natural language. 'Typed logics' and 'intensionality' will be discussed further on in this article.

2. Meaning in Predicate Logic

According to Frege, the key concept of semantics is reference in the real world. For sentences, this boils down to truth *simpliciter*. Proper names are assumed to refer to individuals in the real world bearing those names, common nouns to sets of things in the real world having the appropriate properties, and so on. Because in this view any name names only one object, a sharp distinction between name and object is not crucial. At the start of the development of predicate logic, no sharp distinction was made between syntax and semantics.

Later on, there gradually emerged a clearer distinction between the *syntax* and the *semantics* of formal representation languages. The semantics of sentences of first-order logic is then given in terms of classes of models in which the sentences are true. The validity of inferences in first-order logic, from a set of premises to a conclusion, is in turn described in terms of truth: the valid inferences are precisely those with the property that any model in which all the premises are true makes the conclusion true as well.

This habit of generalizing over models is a typical feature of formal semantics. The generalization reflects the fact that validity of inferences concerns the form of the inferences, not their content. It should be borne in mind, though, that this concept of form is arrived at by generalizing over content. As far as semantics is concerned with interpretation of language in appropriate models, the discipline is concerned with (semantic) content as opposed to (syntactic) form.

The first clear discussion of the discipline of semantics conceived as the study of the relations between the expressions of a logical language and the objects that are denoted by these expressions is due to Tarski (1933) (see Tarski 1956 for an English translation). The nonlogical vocabulary of a predicate logical language L consists of (1–3):

a set $C = \{c_0, c_1, c_2, \ldots\}$
of names or individual constants, (1)

for each $n > 0$ a set $P^n = \{P^n_0, P^n_1, P^n_2, \ldots\}$
of n-place predicate constants, (2)

and for each $n > 0$ a set $f^n = \{f^n_0, f^n_1, f^n_2, \ldots\}$
of n-place function constants. (3)

Note that not all of these ingredients have to be present: in most cases, most of the P^n and f^n will be empty. A typical value for the highest n with either P^n or f^n nonempty is 3, which is to say that predicate or func-

tion constants with higher arity than 3 are quite rare. The 'arity' of a predicate or function constant is its number of argument places.

The logical vocabulary of a predicate logical language L consists of parentheses, the connectives —, &, $\vee$, $\rightarrow$, and $\equiv$, the quantifiers $\forall$ and $\exists$, the identity relation symbol $=$, and an infinitely enumerable set V of 'individual variables.'

If the nonlogical vocabulary is given, the language is defined in two stages. The set of 'terms' of L is the smallest set for which the following hold:

(a) If $t \in V$ or $t \in C$, then t is a term of L.
(b) If $f \in f^n$ and $t_1, \ldots, t_n$ are terms of L, then $f(t_1 \cdots t_n)$ is a term of L.

This definition says that terms are either individual variables or constants, or results of writing n terms in parentheses after an n-place function constant. Terms are the ingredients of formulae. The set of 'formulae' of L is the smallest set such that the following hold:

(a) If t_1, t_2 are terms of L, then $t_1 = t_2$ is a formula of L.
(b) If $P \in P^n$ and $t_1, \ldots, t_n$ are terms of L, then $Pt_1 \cdots t_n$ is a formula of L.
(c) If φ is a formula of L, then $-\varphi$ is a formula of L.
(d) If φ, ψ are formulae of L, then $(\varphi \& \psi)$, $(\varphi \vee \psi)$, $(\varphi \rightarrow \psi)$ and $(\varphi \equiv \psi)$ are formulae of L.
(e) If φ is a formula of L and $v \in V$, then $\forall v \varphi$ and $\exists v \varphi$ are formulae of L.

This completes the definition of the syntax. The semantic account starts with the definition of models. A 'model' M for L is a pair $\langle D, I \rangle$ where D is a nonempty set and I is a function that does the following:

(a) I maps every $c \in C$ to a member of D.
(b) For every $n > 0$, I maps each member of P^n to an n-place relation R on D.
(c) For every $n > 0$, I maps each member of f^n to an n-place operation g on D.

D is called the 'domain' of the model M, I is called its 'interpretation function.'

Sentences involving quantification generally do not have sentences as parts but open formulae, that is, formulae in which at least one variable has a free occurrence. As it is impossible to define truth for open formulae without making a decision about the interpretation of the free variables occurring in them, infinite 'assignments' of values are employed to the variables of L, that is to say functions with domain V and range $\subseteq D$. However, it is easy to see that only the finite parts of the assignments that provide values for the free variables in a given formula are relevant.

The assignment function s enables definition of a 'value' function for the terms of L. Let the model $M = \langle D, I \rangle$ be fixed and let s be an assignment for L in D. The function vs mapping the terms of L to elements of D is given by the following clauses:

(a) If $t \in C$, then $v_s(t) = I(t)$.
(b) If $t \in V$, then $v_s(t) = s(t)$.

(c) If t has the form $f(t_1 \cdots t_n)$, for some $f \in f^n$, then
$$v_s(t) = I(f)(v_s(t_1), \ldots, v_s(t_n)).$$
Note that the clause for function terms is recursive, and moreover, it precisely follows the recursion in the syntactic definition of such terms.

The second stage of the semantic definition process consists of explaining what it means for an arbitrary formula φ of L to be true in the model relative to an assignment s. One may recursively define a function $[\![\cdot]\!]_s$ mapping the formulae of L to the set of truth values $\{0, 1\}$ (0 for falsity, 1 for truth). The recursive definition follows the syntactic definition of the formulae of the language. First, the basic case is handled where φ is an atomic formula.

(a) If φ has the form $t_1 = t_2$, then $[\![\varphi]\!]_s = 1$ if and only if $v_s(t_1) = v_s(t_2)$.

(b) If φ has the form $Pt_1 \cdots t_n$, then $[\![\varphi]\!]_s = 1$ if and only if $\langle v_s(t_1), \ldots, v_s(t_n) \rangle \in I(P)$.

The logical connectives are treated as follows:

(c) If φ has the form $\neg\psi$, then $[\![\varphi]\!]_s = 1$ if and only if $[\![\psi]\!]_s = 0$.

(d) If φ has the form $(\psi \& \chi)$, then $[\![\varphi]\!]_s = 1$ if and only if $[\![\psi]\!]_s = [\![\chi]\!]_s = 1$.
If φ has the form $(\psi \vee \chi)$, then $[\![\varphi]\!]_s = 1$ if and only if $[\![\psi]\!]_s = 1$ or $[\![\chi]\!]_s = 1$.
If φ has the form $(\psi \rightarrow \chi)$, then $[\![\varphi]\!]_s = 0$ if and only if $[\![\psi]\!]_s = 1$ and $[\![\chi]\!]_s = 0$.
If φ has the form $(\psi \equiv \chi)$, then $[\![\varphi]\!]_s = 1$ if and only if $[\![\psi]\!]_s = [\![\chi]\!]_s$.

Finally, the quantifiers $\forall$ and $\exists$ are considered. To start with a simple example, suppose the object is to describe the circumstances under which $\forall x Px$ is true. In the description we want to refer to information about the truth or falsity of Px, for we want the account to be compositional. Saying that Px must be true in the model, given s, is not enough, because $[\![Px]\!]_s$ depends on the value that s assigns to x: $[\![Px]\!]_s = 1$ if and only if $s(x) \in I(P)$. What we want to say is something different: Px is true no matter which individual is assigned to x. This means that we are interested in assignments that are like s except for the fact that they may assign a different value to some variable v. Here is a precise definition (4):

$$s(v \mid d)(w) = \begin{cases} s(w) & \text{if } w \neq v \\ d & \text{if } w = v. \end{cases} \tag{4}$$

Armed with this new piece of notation the quantifier case can be disposed of:

(e) If φ has the form $\forall v\psi$, then $[\![\varphi]\!]_s = 1$ if and only if $[\![\psi]\!]_{s(v \mid d)} = 1$ for every $d \in D$.
If φ has the form $\exists v\psi$, then $[\![\varphi]\!]_s = 1$ if and only if $[\![\psi]\!]_{s(v \mid d)} = 1$ for at least one $d \in D$.

This completes the definition of the function $[\![\cdot]\!]_s$. If $[\![\varphi]\!]_s = 1$ we say that assignment s satisfies φ in the model, or that φ is true in the model under assignment s.

As was remarked above, truth or falsity of a formula in a model under an assignment s only depends on the finite part of s that assigns values to the free variables of the formula. Sentences do not contain free variables, so the truth or falsity of a sentence in a model does not depend on the assignment at all. We say that a sentence φ of L is true in a model if φ is true in the model under every assignment s. Equivalently, we could have said that φ is true in the model if φ is true under some assignment. The notion of an assignment was a tool that can now be discarded.

The main feature of the Tarski semantics for predicate logic is its recursive nature: the meaning of a complex formula is recursively defined in terms of the meanings of its components. This is what compositionality is all about.

3. Abstraction and Quantification

In the above presentation of the semantics of first-order predicate logic, quantifiers were introduced syncategorematically, which is to say that they are not regarded as building blocks of the language in their own right. It follows that the quantifiers do not have meanings of their own. The compositional semantics of first-order predicate logic would look more elegant if the quantifiers were to be considered building blocks. This can be done by means of the concept of *abstraction*.

Abstraction as a conceptual tool is already used by Frege, but his notation is rather awkward. Rather than stick with Frege's presentation a version using lambda operators or λ-operators is presented. Lambda operators were introduced by Alonzo Church (1940). This device can be used to construct meanings for separate building blocks of languages. In doing so a version of typed logic is sketched. Typed logics are currently the most widely used tools for representing the semantics of natural language expressions.

The fact that in example (5) *John* can be replaced by *Fred* to form a new sentence shows abstraction focused on *John*.

John respects Bill. $\qquad\qquad$ (5)

This process of abstraction starts with a sentence, removes a proper name, and yields a function from proper names to sentences, or semantically, a function from individuals to truth values, that is, a characteristic function. Lambda operators allow this function to be referred to explicitly (6):

$\lambda x.x$ *respects Bill.* $\qquad\qquad$ (6)

The function denoted by (6) corresponds to the property of respecting Bill. For convenience functions of this type are called 'properties.' Next, an abstraction can be made from the second proper name, and a functional expression denoting the relation of respecting is produced (7):

$\lambda y \lambda x . x \, respects \, y.$ (7)

Expression (7) denotes the relation of respecting by presenting it as a function that combines with an individual to form a property (a function from individuals to truth values). Actual variable names are unimportant but binding patterns matter: (7) and (8) are (logically equivalent) alphabetic variants.

$\lambda x \lambda y . y \, respects \, x.$ (8)

The relation of being respected is denoted by a slightly different lambda expression (9).

$\lambda x \lambda y . x \, respects \, y.$ (9)

The distinction between the active and passive voice is reflected in the different binding patterns of (8) and (9).

In the context of lambda operators, quantifiers can be viewed as higher order functions. The quantifier $\forall$ combines with the expression $\lambda x . \varphi$, where φ is a sentence, to form a sentence $\forall \lambda x . \varphi$ (written here as $\forall x \varphi$). Observe that the quantifier itself does not have to act as a binder any more. The binding mechanism is taken over by the lambda operator. The sentence $\forall x \varphi$ is true if and only if $\lambda x . \varphi$ denotes a function which gives true for every argument. Thus, $\forall$ denotes a function from characteristic functions to truth values. It maps every characteristic function that always gives true to true, and every other characteristic function to false. Similarly, $\exists$ denotes the function from characteristic functions to truth values which maps every function that for some value assumes the value true, to true, and the function that assigns false to every argument, to false.

Lambda abstraction and quantifiers make it possible to express what it means to admire an attractive girl (10).

$\lambda x . \exists y (girl \, y \, \& \, attractive \, y \, \& \, x \, admires \, y).$ (10)

To be courted by every unmarried man, on the other hand, is something quite different, as expression (11) makes clear.

$\lambda x . \forall y ((man \, y \, \& -married \, y) \rightarrow y \, courts \, x).$ (11)

It is also possible to abstract over objects of more complex types. Again starting from (5), an abstraction can be made over the transitive verb or over the predicate. Abstracting over the predicate yields (12), an expression which combines with a property denoting expression (i.e., a predicate) to form a sentence.

$\lambda P . P(John).$ (12)

Interestingly, (12) is an expression of the same type as that of quantified noun phrases. The quantified noun phrase *every man* combines with a property denoting expression to form a sentence, so (13) is an appropriate translation.

$\lambda P . \forall x (man \, x \rightarrow P(x)).$ (13)

Combining (13) with (6) gives the expression in (14). In fact, for convenience (6) has been replaced with an alphabetic variant (an expression using different variables to effect the same binding pattern). This kind of conversion is called α conversion.

$\lambda P . \forall x (man \, x \rightarrow P(x))(\lambda y . y \, respects \, Bill).$ (14)

Expression (14) is the result of combining the translation of *every man* with that of *respects Bill*. The result should be a sentential expression, that is, an expression denoting a truth value. To see that this is indeed the case, a reduction of the expression is necessary. All expressions of the form $\lambda v . E(A)$ are reducible to a simpler form; they are called 'redexes' (*red*ucible e*x*pressions).

4. Reducing Lambda Expressions

To reduce expression (14), Sect. 3 above to its simplest form, two steps of so-called β conversion are needed. During β conversion of an expression consisting of a functor expression $\lambda v . E$ followed by an argument expression A, basically the following happens. The prefix $\lambda v .$ is removed, the argument expression A is removed, and finally the argument expression A is substituted in E for all free occurrences of v. The free occurrences of v in E are precisely the occurrences which were bound by λv in $\lambda v . E$.

There is a proviso. In some cases, the substitution process described above cannot be applied, because it will result in unintended capturing of variables within the argument expression A. Consider expression (15):

$(\lambda x \lambda y . R(y)(x))(y).$ (15)

In this expression, y is bound in the functional part $\lambda x \lambda y . R(y)(x)$ but free in the argument part y. Reducing (15) by β conversion would result in $\lambda y . R(y)(y)$, with capture of the argument y at the place where it is substituted for x. The problem is sidestepped if β conversion is performed on an alphabetic variant of the original expression, say on $(\lambda x \lambda z . R(z)(x))(y)$.

Another example where α conversion (i.e., switching to an alphabetic variant) is necessary before β conversion to prevent unintended capture of free variables is the expression (16):

$\lambda p . \forall x (A(x) \equiv p)(B(x)).$ (16)

In (16), p is a variable of type truth value, and x one of type individual entity. Then x is bound in the functional part $\lambda p . \forall x (A(x) \equiv p)$ but free in the argument part $B(x)$. Substituting $B(x)$ for p in the function expression would cause x to be captured, with failure to preserve the original meaning. Again, the problem is sidestepped if β conversion is performed on an alphabetic variant of the original expression, say on $\lambda p . \forall z . (A(z) \equiv p)(B(x))$. The result of β conversion then is $\forall z . (A(z) \equiv B(x))$, with the argument of B still free, as it should be.

Using $[A/v]$ for the substitution operation, the β-

321

reduction step can be expressed formally as follows. Suppose $\lambda v.E(A)$ is an expression where all bound variables are different from the free variables. This condition constitutes a straightforward way of making sure that the problem mentioned above will not occur. Then $\lambda v.E(A)$ β-reduces to $[A/v]E$.

Applying the procedure of β reduction to (14), a first β conversion step reduces (14) to (17), and a second, internal, β conversion step then yields (18).

$$\forall x(man \; x \rightarrow \lambda y.y \; respects \; Bill(x)). \tag{17}$$

$$\forall x(man(x) \rightarrow x \; respects \; Bill). \tag{18}$$

The process of reducing lambda expressions has drastic consequences for their syntactic appearance. Historically, the syntactic form of logical expressions translating natural language sentences was taken to reflect the *logical form* of these sentences. In Sect. 5 it is pointed out that the metamorphosis of β conversion bears on certain historical problems of logical form.

5. Misleading Form and Logical Form

From *John walked* it follows that someone walked, but from *No one walked* it does not follow that someone walked. Therefore, logicians such as Frege, Russell, Tarski, and Quine have maintained that the structure of these two sentences must differ, and that it is not enough to say that they are both compositions of a subject and a predicate.

The logicians who used first-order predicate logic to analyze the logical structure of natural language were struck by the fact that the logical translations of natural language sentences with quantified expressions did not seem to follow the linguistic structure. In the logical translations, the quantified expressions seemed to have disappeared. The logical translation of (19) does not reveal a constituent corresponding to the quantified subject noun phrase.

Every unmarried man courted Mary. (19)

$$\forall x((man \; x \; \& - married \; x) \rightarrow x \; courted \; Mary). \tag{20}$$

In the translation (20) the constituent *every unmarried man* has disappeared: it is contextually eliminated. Frege remarks that a quantified expression like *every unmarried man* does not give rise to a concept by itself (*eine selbstandige Vorstellung*), but can only be interpreted in the context of the translation of the whole sentence. Applied to this particular example: the literal paraphrase of (20) is:

All objects in the domain of discourse have the property of either not being unmarried men or being objects who courted Mary. (21)

In restatement (21) of sentence (19) the phrase *every unmarried man* does not occur any more.

The logical properties of sentences involving quantified expressions (and descriptions, analyzed in terms of quantifiers) suggested indeed that the way a simple noun phrase such as a proper name combines with a predicate is logically different from the way in which a quantified noun phrase or a definite description combines with a predicate. This led to the belief that the linguistic form of natural language expressions was misleading.

The application of the logical tools of abstraction and reduction allow one to see that this conclusion was unwarranted. Using translation of natural language in expressions of typed logic it is seen that natural language constituents correspond to typed expressions that combine with one another as functions and arguments. After full reduction of the results, quantified expressions and other constituents may have been contextually eliminated, but this elimination is a result of the reduction process, not of the supposed misleading form of the original natural language sentence. Thus, while fully reduced logical translations of natural language sentences may be misleading in some sense, the fully unreduced original expressions are not.

As an example of the way in which the λ tools smooth logical appearances, consider the logic of the combination of subjects and predicates. In the simplest cases (*John walked*) one could say that the predicate takes the subject as an argument, but this does not work for quantified subjects (*no one walked*). All is well, however, when we say that the subject always takes the predicate as its argument, and make this work for simple subjects by logically raising their status from argument to function. Using λ, this is easy enough: *John* is translated not as the constant j, but as the expression $\lambda P.P(j)$. This expression denotes a function from properties to truth values, so it can take a predicate translation as its argument. The translation of *no one* is of the same type: $\lambda P. - \exists x.(person \; x \; \& \; P(x))$. Before reduction, the translations of *John walks* and *no one walks* look very similar. These similarities disappear only after both translations have been reduced to their simplest forms.

6. Meaning in Natural Language

In a Montague-style approach to natural language, one takes for the natural language syntax some version of categorial grammar enriched with quantifying in rules (to be discussed at the end of this section), and for the semantics some form of typed logic. The combination of categorial grammar and typed logic allows the link between syntax and semantics to be of the utmost simplicity. Lexical items are assigned categories such as CN for common nouns, IV for intransitive verbs, S/IV for noun phrases (these take intransitive verb phrases on their right to form sentences), (S/IV)/CN for determiners (these take common nouns on their right to form noun phrases), IV\IV for adverbial modifiers (these take intransitive verb phrases on their left to make new intransitive verb phrases).

Next, the lexical items get assigned translations with types matching the syntactic categories. In the simplest possible approach, the translation types are defined in terms of simplest types e (for entities), and t (for truth values). Formulae have type t, individual terms have type e. Expressions denoting functions from type A to type B have type (A, B). It follows from this rule that property denoting expressions have type (e, t). In general, if variable v has type A and expression E has type B, then $\lambda v.E$ has type (A, B). If E has type (A, B) and a has type A, then the expression $E(a)$ is well-formed and has type B.

It is not difficult to see which types are suitable for which syntactic categories. Sentences, category S, should translate into formulae, with type t. Intransitive verbs, category IV, translate into properties, type (e, t). Common nouns, category CN, also translate into properties. The rest of the category-to-type match is taken care of by a general rule. If category X translates into type A, and category Y translates into type B, then categories X/Y (takes a Y to the right to form an X) and Y\X (takes a Y to the left to form an X) translate into type (A, B).

The rules for syntactic function application are then matched by rules for semantic function application. The meaning of *John loves Mary* is derived in two steps. First *loves* and *Mary*, with categories IV/(S/IV) and S/IV respectively, combine to form *loves Mary*, with category IV. The meaning of this expression is derived from the meanings of the components by function–argument application. Next *John* and *loves Mary*, with categories S/IV and IV respectively, are combined to form *John loves Mary*, with category S. Again, the meaning is derived from the meanings of the components by function–argument application.

One should now briefly examine the notion of 'ambiguity' for fragments of natural language with a compositional semantics. If a natural language expression E is ambiguous, that is, if E has several distinct meanings, then, under the assumption that these meanings are arrived at in a compositional way, there are three possible sources for the ambiguity (combinations are possible, of course):

(a) The ambiguity is lexical: E contains a word with several distinct meanings. Example: *a splendid ball*.

(b) The ambiguity is structural: E can be assigned several distinct syntactic structures. Example: *old [men and women]* versus *[old men] and women*.

(c) The ambiguity is derivational: the syntactic structure that E exhibits can be derived in more than one way. Example: *Every prince sang some ballad* is not structurally ambiguous, but in order to account for the ∃∀ reading one might want to assume that one of the ways in which the structure can be derived is by combining *some ballad* with the incomplete expression *every prince sang —*.

Derivational ambiguities are very much a logician's ploy. In an essay on philosophical logic by P. T. Geach they are introduced as follows:

> [...] when we pass from 'Kate/is loved by/Tom' to 'Some girl/is loved by/every boy,' it does make a big difference whether we first replace 'Kate' by 'some girl' (so as to get the predicable 'Some girl is loved by —' into the proposition) and then replace 'Tom' by 'every boy,' or rather first replace 'Tom' by 'every boy' (so as to get the predicable '— is loved by every boy' into the proposition) and then replace 'Kate' by 'some girl.' Two propositions that are reached from the same starting point by the same set of logical procedures (e.g., substitutions) may nevertheless differ in import because these procedures are taken to occur in a different order.
>
> (Geach 1968, Sect. 64)

This is exactly the mechanism that has been proposed by Richard Montague to account for operator scope ambiguities in natural language. Montague introduces a rule for the 'quantifying in' of noun phrases in incomplete syntactic structures. The wide scope ∃ reading for the example *Every prince sang some ballad* is derived by using a rule Q_i to quantify in *some ballad* for syntactic index i in the structure *Every prince sang PRO_i*. In more complex cases, where more than one occurrence of PRO_i is present, the appropriate occurrence is replaced by the noun phrase, and the other occurrences are replaced by pronouns or reflexives with the right syntactic agreement features (see Montague (1973) for details).

The Montagovian approach to scope ambiguities does not account for restrictions on possible scope readings. It is not denied that such restrictions should be imposed, but they are relegated to constraints imposed by lexical features of determiner words. A problem here is that scope behavior of certain natural language expressions seems to be influenced by the wider syntactic context.

7. Meaning, Truth, and Inference

Typed logics are the proper logical tool for describing the semantics of natural language. One way to go about generalizing the model concept of predicate logic for languages of typed logic is as follows. A model for a typed logic based on individual objects and truth values starts out with a universe U for the domain of individual objects, and the set $\{1, 0\}$ for the domain of truth values. Next, more complex domains are construed in terms of those basic domains. The domain of properties is the set of functions $U \to \{1, 0\}$, that is, the set of all functions with U as domain and the truth values as co-domain. The domain of characteristic functions on properties (the type of things to which the quantifiers $\forall$, $\exists$ belong) is the set $(U \to \{1, 0\}) \to \{1, 0\}$, and so on. Another generalization is also possible, by defining so-called *general models*.

Models for typed logical languages can be used to

define functions $\llbracket \cdot \rrbracket$ which map all expressions of the language to objects of the right types in the model: sentence type expressions to truth values, property type expressions to properties, object-to-property type expressions to functions from objects to properties, and so on. If one assumes for a moment that the basic domain U is the set of natural numbers, and that the predicate letter O stands for being an odd number, then the interpretation of a property expression $\lambda x.O(x)$, notation $\llbracket \lambda x.O(x) \rrbracket$, is a function f which yields 1 for every $u \in U$ which is an odd number, and 0 for all even numbers. The property expression $\lambda x.{-}O(x)$ has the characteristic function of all even numbers as its interpretation. The interpretation of $\lambda P.\forall P$ (universal quantification over individuals), notation $\llbracket \lambda P.\forall P \rrbracket$, is the function $F \in (U \to \{1,0\}) \to \{1,0\}$ with $F(f)=1$ for the function f in $U \to \{1,0\}$ with $f(u)=1$ for all $u \in U$, and $F(g)=0$ for all $g \neq f$. As a final example, $\lambda P.\forall x.({-}O(x) \to P(x))$ has as its interpretation the characteristic function F which maps every function $f \in U \to \{1,0\}$ mapping every even number to 1, to 1, and all other functions in $U \to \{1,0\}$ to 0. Note that $\lambda P.\forall x.({-}O(x) \to P(x))$ would be an appropriate translation for the natural language phrase *every non-odd thing*.

The model theoretic approach to meaning now equates the intuitive concept of 'meaning' with the precise model theoretic concept of 'interpretation,' that is, with values of a function $\llbracket \cdot \rrbracket$ generated by an appropriate model. Note that $\llbracket \cdot \rrbracket$ is ultimately defined in terms of the interpretations of certain basic expressions in the model (for instance, predicates like O, universal quantification over individuals). The interpretation of these basic expressions can be described in terms of truth in the model, modulo appropriate assignments to free variables. The meaning of O reduces to the truth or falsity of $O(x)$ in the model, relative to assignments of individuals to x, the meaning of universal quantification over individuals reduces to truth or falsity of $\forall x.\varphi$ in the model, relative to assignments of properties to $\lambda x.\varphi$, and so on. Thus it can be said that meaning is ultimately defined in terms of truth in a model.

Next, logical validity of inferences is defined in terms of truth, by saying that an inference from premises φ_1 through φ_n to conclusion ψ is valid if and only if every model in which all of φ_1 through φ_n evaluate to true will make ψ true as well. In fact, for typed languages, the concept of logical validity can be extended to arbitrary expressions denoting characteristic functions. Let E_1 and E_2 be expressions for characteristic functions of the same type. If one characteristic function F_1 involves another one, F_2, if F_1 and F_2 have the same types and F_2 yields 1 for every argument for which F_1 yields 1, then E_1 logically involves E_2 if and only if in every model, $\llbracket E_1 \rrbracket$ involves $\llbracket E_2 \rrbracket$. To give a rather trivial example, $\lambda x.{-}O(x)$ logically involves $\lambda x.(O(x) \vee {-}O(x))$. Typed languages

are powerful enough to express involvement in a formula. E_1 logically involves E_2 if and only if the formula $\forall P.(E_1(P) \to E_2(P))$ is true in every model. Here P is a variable of the right type for arguments of E_1 and E_2.

Conversely, one may want to impose certain restrictions on the possible interpretations of the basic vocabulary by stipulating that certain concepts should involve others. For instance, one may want to ensure that the concept of walking involves the concept of moving relative to something. Assuming that these are expressions $\lambda x.W(x)$ for walking and $\lambda y\lambda x.M(x,y)$ for moving with respect to, one can express the requirement as: $\lambda x.W(x)$ should involve $\lambda x.\exists y.(object(y) \,\&\, M(x,y))$. The semantic requirement is then imposed by restricting attention to models in which the first concept does indeed involve the second one. The desired involvements can be expressed as formulae. Such formulae, intended to constrain the class of possible models with the purpose of enforcing certain relations between elements in the vocabulary of the language, are called 'meaning postulates.' Given a natural language fragment and a set of meaning postulates for that fragment, a sentence of the fragment is 'analytic' if it is true in any model satisfying all the meaning postulates. A sentence of the fragments is 'synthetic' if it does have counterexamples among the models satisfying all the meaning postulates. Given that the meaning postulates constrain the meanings of the vocabulary in the right way, one may assume that the real world (or some suitable aspect of it) will make all the meaning postulates true, so the synthetic sentences are precisely those that the world could be in disagreement with. The logically valid sentences are those that are true in any model of the language, irrespective of any meaning postulates.

This overview of models, interpretations, logical inference, logical involvement, and the analytic/synthetic distinction makes clear that truth is the tortoise which carries the whole edifice of semantics on its back.

8. Meaning in Context

The very simple account of meaning given in the previous sections breaks down if one wants to extend the treatment to intensional phenomena. Consider example (22).

John seeks a girlfriend. (22)

Example (22) might mean that John is looking for Sue, who happens to be his girlfriend, but it might also mean that John is answering small ads in the lonely hearts column because he wants to create a situation in which he has a girlfriend.

The setup of the previous sections would only give the first sense of the sentence. A standard way to get the second sense is by making a distinction between 'extensional' and 'intensional' interpretations of phrases. The extensional interpretation of a phrase is its interpretation in a given context. The intensional interpretation is somewhat more involved: it is a function from contexts to (extensional) interpretations in those contexts. Under the second reading of (22), John is related, not to an individual, but to the set of possible contexts which contain a girlfriend for him. Such possible contexts are often called 'possible worlds.' Following Lewis (1970), the set of all properties of a thing is called the 'character' of the thing. For example, some reflection will show that expression (23) denotes the characteristic function of the character of a girlfriend:

$$\lambda P.\exists y(girlfriend(y)\, \&\, P(y)). \tag{23}$$

Expression (23) gives the character of a girlfriend in the actual context, but that is not quite what is wanted. To achieve this one must interpret basic expressions such as common nouns relative to contexts, with *girlfriend*(y, c) meaning that y is a girlfriend in context c. Expression (24) gives a mapping from contexts to characters of girlfriends in these contexts.

$$\lambda c\lambda P.\exists y(girlfriend(y, c)\, \&\, P(y, c)). \tag{24}$$

When John is seeking a girlfriend in the intensional sense he is related to the item specified by (24).

Intensional interpretations are also useful for interpreting propositional attitude sentences, such as the example in (25).

John believes that a ghost is haunting his house. (25)

The embedded that–clause in this example cannot have its extensional interpretation, for if, in fact, no ghost is haunting John's house then the extensional interpretation is just the truth value 'false,' and John's beliefs are not as closely tied to the actual world as that. Rather, (25) is true just in case any situation or context compatible with John's belief is such that in that context a ghost is haunting his house. The translation for the embedded clause that is needed to get this is given in (26).

$$\lambda c.\exists y(ghost(y, c)\, \&\, haunt(y, house\text{-}of(John, c), c)). \tag{26}$$

Note that the common noun translations and the translation of the transitive verb *haunt* all have an extra argument for the context. The translation of the proper name does not, for we take it that proper names denote the same individual in any context. One way to tackle Frege's famous Morning Star/Evening Star paradox in terms of intensions would be to make names context-sensitive too. Details will not be spelled out, as such a solution is not without its philosophical difficulties. The source of the paradox is not so much change of reference of proper names in other contexts, but incomplete information about the identity relation in those contexts.

It should be noted that the shift from extensional to intensional interpretations by no means solves all problems of sense and reference. Intensions are still not fine-grained enough to distinguish between equivalent statements of logic. Because logical truths are true independent of context, *2+2=4* is true in all contexts, and so is *Zorn's lemma is equivalent to the Axiom of Choice*. Still, *John knows that 2+2 equals 4* hardly warrants the conclusion *John knows that Zorn's lemma is equivalent to the Axiom of Choice*. John may never have heard about set theory in the first place. One possible way out is to make meanings still more fine-grained, by taking them to be structured trees with intensions at their leaves (see Lewis (1970) for details). Indeed, Lewis reserves the term 'meaning' for such structured objects.

As contexts have been mentioned, the fact should be acknowledged that the context in which a natural language statement is made—let us call it the current context—plays a very special role in the interpretation of the sentence. Tense operators are interpreted with respect to the time of utterance, personal pronouns *I, you,* are interpreted as speaker and addressee in the current context, demonstratives can be used to 'anchor' the discourse to items in the current context. The anchoring mechanism has to be defined with some care, for it should be able to account for the anchoring of sentences like *This is cheaper than this, but this is nicer than this* (with four acts of pointing to different objects while the sentence is being uttered) (again, see Lewis (1970) for some suggestions).

In the above contexts have been more or less equated with possible worlds, that is, alternative complete pictures of what the world might have been like. It is argued in Barwise (1981) that some contexts of linguistic utterance are essentially incomplete. This observation has led to the development of strategies for interpreting natural language with respect to 'partial models' or 'situations.' (See *Situation Semantics* for a full-fledged theory along these lines, and Muskens (1989) for an attempt to incorporate partiality in a more traditional account.)

9. The Meanings of Nonindicative Expressions

It has been seen that the extensional interpretation of a declarative sentence is a truth value, and its intensional interpretation a set of contexts. The extensional interpretation of *John loves Mary* in a model is either the value true or the value false. The intensional interpretation of this sentence is the set of contexts where the sentence has the value true. The intensional interpretation is needed in cases where the sentence occurs in embedded contexts, such as *Bill believes that John loves Mary,* which is standardly interpreted as true just in case *John loves Mary* is true in any context which is compatible with everything that Bill believes. So much for the semantics of the indicative mood. How about such nonindicative moods as questions and commands? Can their semantics be related to the semantics of the indicative mood?

Broadly speaking, the indicative mood is for *descri-*

bing situations, the interrogative mood for *checking* situations, and the imperative mood for (giving directions for) *changing* situations. A declarative sentence picks out a set of contexts where the sentence is true; its (intensional) meaning has the form $\lambda i.Pi$, where P is a predicate of contexts. Now take simple yes/no questions, for example. A yes/no question such as *Does John love Mary?* is an invitation to check whether the indicative root of the question, namely the statement *John loves Mary*, is true in the given situation. A check is an action, and actions are transformations from situations to other situations. Thus, a yes/no question $P?$ denotes a relation $\lambda i\lambda j.(i=j \ \& \ Pj)$. In other words, a yes/no question relates the set of states of the world to the set of states where the answer to the question is *yes*. This dynamic view of questions can be related to a more static picture. (See Hintikka (1976) or Groenendijk and Stokhof (1984, 1988) for the static semantics of questions, Van Benthem (1991) for relations between a static and a dynamic view.)

Utterances in imperative mood can be interpreted as commands to change the context, that is, as mappings from contexts to intended contexts which are the result if the command is obeyed. Again, a dynamic perspective naturally presents itself. The command *Close the door!* relates situations to new situations where the door is closed. A command $P!$ denotes a relation $\lambda i\lambda j.Pj$. In other words, a command relates the set of states of the world to the set of states of the world where the command is fulfilled. Of course, there is much to be said about felicity conditions of imperatives (*Close the door!* only makes sense when the door is open), but likewise there is much to be said about felicity conditions of questions and declaratives.

What matters here is that a command like *Close the door!* can be interpreted as a relation between the current context c_0 and the set of all contexts which are the result of performing the action of closing the door in c_0 in some way or other. The result of uttering the command need not be that one ends up in a context like c_0 but with a closed door (not all commands are obeyed, fortunately), but that does not matter to the principle of the account. Note that, just as in the dynamic account of questions, the concept of truth continues to play an important role. The contexts that are like the current context but where the command has been obeyed are contexts where the sentence which is the declarative root of the imperative is true.

10. The Dynamics of Meaning

In Sect. 9 one has started to look at meaning in a dynamic way. Instead of focusing on the question 'How are linguistic expressions semantically linked to a (static) world or model?' one has switched to a new question: 'How do linguistic messages viewed as actions change the current situation?' Not only a question or a command, but every linguistic utterance can be viewed as an action: it has an effect on the state

of mind of an addressee, so one could say that the dynamic meaning of a natural language utterance is a map from states of mind to states of mind. Such talk about influencing states of mind is no more than a metaphor, of course; to make this precise one needs to replace 'state of mind' by a more precise concept of 'state.' An obvious place to look for inspiration is the semantics of programming languages, where the meaning of a program is taken to be the effect that it has on the memory state of a machine: the dynamic meaning of a computer program is a mapping from memory states to memory states. Van Benthem (1991) looks at the link between programing language semantics and natural language semantics in some detail and presents a uniform picture of how static and dynamic views of language are related.

In imperative programing, for example, in a language like PASCAL, on program startup part of the storage space of the computer is divided up in segments with appropriate names. These are the names of the so-called 'global variables' of a program, but in order to avoid confusion with logical variables these will be called 'store names.' The effect of a program can be specified as a relation between the states of the stores before the execution of the program and the states of the stores afterward. A memory state is a specification of the contents of all stores, in other words, it is a function from the set of stores to appropriate values for the contents of these stores. Equivalently, one can look at each individual store as a function from states to appropriate values for that store. In this perspective on stores as functions from states to values, one can say things like $v_1(i)=3$, meaning that the content of store v_1 in state i is 3.

Suppose a program consists of one command, $v_1:=3$, the command to put the value 3 in the store with name v_1. Then the effect of this program on a given state i is a new state j which is just like i except for the fact that $v_1(j)=3$ (where the value for v_1 in i might have been different). The abbreviation $i[v]j$ for 'state i and state j differ at most in the value store v assigns to them' will be used. It will be assumed that if i is a state and v a store, then there will always exist a state j with $i[v]j$.

In a language like PASCAL every store has a specific type: some stores are reserved for storing strings, others for integer numbers, others for real numbers, and so on. For a rough sketch of how to use the dynamics metaphor for an account of anaphoric linking in natural language, these storage types do not matter. One will assume all stores to be of the same type, taking it that they are all used to store (names of) entities. One can again use typed logic as a medium of translation, but now an extra basic type s is needed. For ease of exposition, one forgets about contexts and intensionality again, and goes back to an extensional treatment. Using s for the type of states and e for the type of entities, one can express the assumption that all stores store entities as follows: every store is of type (s, e).

Suppose there is a list of store names $V = v_1, v_2, \ldots$. One wants to account for anaphoric links as in example (27). The intended anaphoric links are indicated by subscripts.

A_1 man loves a_2 woman. He$_1$ kisses her$_2$.   (27)

The difficulty with the traditional account of the semantics of (27), where the anaphoric links are established by a variable binding mechanism, is that the pronouns in the second sentence can only be translated as variables bound by the existential quantifiers in the first sentence if the quantifiers extend their scopes beyond the sentence limit. The scope of an existential quantifier has to be closed off somewhere, but there appears to be no natural place for a boundary. Wherever one puts the closing-off point, beyond it pronouns might still turn up that have to be linked to the same antecedent. Some theories have tried to solve this problem by translating indefinite and definite noun phrases as some sort of free variables. The following illustrates how a dynamic approach to pronoun–antecedent linking can be integrated in a traditional Montague-style grammar.

In the dynamic approach, sentences are translated as relations between states, in other words, sentences are of type $(s, (s, t))$: a sentence interpretation takes two states and then gives a truth value. Sentences that do not have a dynamic effect will not change the state, for instance the 'dynamic' translation of *John loves Mary*, in typed logic, will be something like (28).

$$\lambda i \lambda j.(i = j \,\&\, love(John, Mary)).$$ (28)

The translation of *A_1 man loves a_2 woman*, on the other hand, does involve state changes, because the dynamic interpretation of the indefinite noun phrases involves assigning values to stores. The interpretation of *a_1 man* is a relation between states i and j which holds just in case $i[v_1]j$ and the value of v_1 in state j is indeed a man.

$$\lambda P \lambda i \lambda j.(i[v_1]j \,\&\, man(v_1 j) \,\&\, P(v_1 j)).$$ (29)

Note that $i[v_1]j$ is used here as abbreviation for the appropriate expression of typed logic. The translation of the common noun *man* in (29) does not involve states, and neither does the variable P that is proxy for the translation of the verb phrase. This is not quite right, for common nouns can contain relative clauses with dynamic effects, and verb phrases can have dynamic effects as well, so translations of common nouns and verb phrases must contain the means to accommodate these. In other words, the states must be 'threaded' through all these constituents. In case of a lexical noun such as *man* the net effect of the threading is nil, but the variable P must be of type $(s, (s, (e, t)))$ to cater for state switches in the verb phrase. The translation for *a_1 man* now looks like (30).

$$\lambda P \lambda i \lambda k. \exists j (i[v_1]j \,\&\, man(v_1 j) \,\&\, P(v_1 j, j, k)).$$ (30)

Here is the dynamic translation for *A_1 man loves a_2 woman*.

$$\lambda i \lambda k. \exists j (i[v_1]j \,\&\, man(v_1 j) \,\&\, j[v_2]k$$
$$\&\, love(v_1 k, v_2 k) \,\&\, woman(v_2 k)).$$ (31)

The interpretation for the pronoun *he$_1$* makes use of the contents of store v_1. Thus, the anaphoric links are provided by the retrieval of stored values. Expression (32) gives the translation for the pronoun *he$_1$* that has the desired effect; P is again a variable of type $(s, (s, (e, t)))$.

$$\lambda P \lambda i \lambda j.P(v_1 i, i, j).$$ (32)

The translation of the whole discourse (27) is left to the reader. A pioneer paper on dynamic interpretation of natural language is Barwise (1987). Groenendijk and Stokhof (1990) and Muskens (1991) contain worked-out proposals.

See also: Game-theoretical Semantics; Montague Grammar; Paradoxes, Semantic; Situation Semantics.

Bibliography

Barwise J 1981 Scenes and other situations. *The Journal of Philosophy* **78**: 369–97

Barwise J 1987 Noun phrases, generalized quantifiers and anaphora. In: Gärdenfors P (ed.) *Generalized Quantifiers/Linguistic and Logical Approaches*. Reidel, Dordrecht

Barwise J, Cooper R 1981 Generalized quantifiers and natural language. *LaPh* **4**: 159–219

Church A 1940 A formulation of the simple theory of types. *Journal of Symbolic Logic* **5**: 56–68

Dowty D R 1976 *Word Meaning and Montague Grammar*. Reidel, Dordrecht

Dowty D R, Wall R E, Peters S 1981 *Introduction to Montague Grammar*. Reidel, Dordrecht

Frege G 1879 *Begriffsschrift*. In: Heyenoort J van (ed.) 1970 *Frege and Gödel: Two Fundamental Texts in Mathematical Logic*. Harvard University Press, Cambridge, MA

Geach P T 1968 *Reference and Generality: An Examination of some Medieval and Modern Theories*. Cornell University Press, Ithaca, NY

Groenendijk J, Stokhof M 1984 Studies on the semantics of questions and the pragmatics of answers. (PhD thesis, University of Amsterdam)

Groenendijk J, Stokhof M 1988 Type shifting rules and the semantics of interrogatives. In: Chierchia G, Partee B H, Turner R (eds.) *Properties, Types and Meaning*, vol. II. Kluwer, Dordrecht

Groenendijk J, Stokhof M 1990 Dynamic Montague Grammar. In: Kálmán L, Pólos L (eds.) *Papers from the Second Symposium on Logic and Language*. Akadémiai Kiadó, Budapest

Hintikka K J 1976 The semantics of questions and the question of semantics. *Acta Philosophica Fennica* **28**

Kamp H 1981 A theory of truth and semantic representation. In: Groenendijk J, Stokhof M (eds.) *Formal Methods in the Study of Language*. Mathematisch Centrum, Amsterdam

Lewis D 1970 General semantics. *Synthese* **22**: 18–67

Montague R 1973 The proper treatment of quantification in ordinary English. In: Hintikka K J J, Moravscik J M E, Suppes P (eds.) *Approaches to Natural Language*. Reidel, Dordrecht

Muskens R 1989 Meaning and partiality. (PhD thesis. University of Amsterdam)

Muskens R 1991 Anaphora meaning, context and the logic of change. In: Eijck J van (ed.), *Logics in AI*. Springer, Berlin

Partee B H 1975 Montague Grammar and Transformational Grammar. *LIn* **6**: 203–300

Partee B H (ed.) 1975 *Montague Grammar*. Academic Press, New York

Percy W 1954 *The Message in the Bottle*. Farrar, Straus and Giroux, New York

Pereira F, Shieber S 1985 *Prolog and Natural Language Analysis*. CSLI Lecture Notes 10, Stanford, CA (Distributed by University of Chicago Press, Chicago, IL)

Tarski A 1956 The concept of truth in formalized languages. In: Tarski A (trans. Woodger J H) *Logic, Semantics, Metamathematics: Papers from 1923 to 1938*. Clarendon Press, Oxford

Van Benthem J F A K 1986 *Essays in Logical Semantics*. Reidel, Dordrecht

Van Benthem J 1991 General dynamics. *Theoretical Linguistics:* 159–201

Game-theoretical Semantics

Ö. Dahl

The term 'game-theoretical semantics' is used to refer to systems of formal semantics in which the semantic rules are formulated as rules in a game of some kind. The term 'game-theoretical' suggests a rather direct connection to mathematical game theory as developed by von Neumann and others, the main source of inspiration for extant proposals for game-theoretical semantics has rather been Wittgenstein's concept of 'language game' than game theory.

Although the notion of a language game has been employed in semantics by various people over the years, the term 'game-theoretical semantics' is mainly associated with the work of Jaakko Hintikka and his followers. Hintikka first developed his system of game-theoretical semantics for formal languages but later applied it also to natural language. The rules given below are Hintikka's (1983) for first-order predicate calculus, but the rules for ordinary English would be analogous.

The semantical game in terms of which a sentence S is interpreted in Hintikka's system involves two players, called 'Myself' or 'I' and 'Nature,' whose aims in the game are to show that S is true and false, respectively. Complex sentences are interpreted stepwise, by applying the game rules in a *top-down* fashion, until an atomic sentence is reached. If it is true, I/Myself have won; if it is false, Nature has won. Another way of expressing this is to say that a sentence is true if there is a winning strategy for 'Myself' in the game; if it is false, there is a winning strategy for 'Nature.'

The rules applied are the following:

(a) (G. A) If A is atomic, I have won if A is true and Nature has won if A is false.

(b) (G. &) G (S$_1$ & S$_2$) begins by Nature's choice of S$_1$ of S$_2$. The rest of the game is G(S$_1$) or G(S$_2$) respectively.

(c) (G. ∨) G(S1 ∨ S2) begins by Myself's choice of S1 or S2. The rest of the game is G(S1) or G(S2) respectively.

(d) (G. ∀) G(∀x(S(x)) begins by Nature's choice of a member of the domain. Let the name of the member chosen be arbitrarily determined as 'b.' The rest of the game is then G(S(b)).

(e) (G. ∃) G(∃x(S(x)) is defined likewise except that the member of the domain is chosen by Myself.

(f) (G.—) G(—S) is played like G(S) except that the roles of the two players (as defined by these rules) are interchanged.

Hintikka attributes particular significance to the treatment of quantifiers in his semantics. It is meant to make explicit the intuition that an existential sentence is true if a value can be found for the existentially bound variable that makes the sentence in the scope of the quantifier true. In the rule above, this is formulated in terms of 'Myself' choosing a value for the variable. In the case of the universal quantifier, it is 'Nature' that makes the choice.

Hintikka's theory of game-theoretical semantics has been applied to various problems in semantics, notably branching quantifiers, the choice between *some* and *any* in English, 'donkey sentences,' intentional identity, tense, and others.

Bibliography

Hintikka J 1973 *Logic, Language-Games, and Information: Kantian Themes in the Philosophy of Logic*. Clarendon Press, Oxford

Hintikka J (in collaboration with Kulas J) 1983 *The Game of Language*. D Reidel, Dordrecht

Saarinen E (ed.) 1979 *Game-theoretical Semantics*. D Reidel, Dordrecht

Intension

J. van der Does

In the *Republic*, Plato distinguishes between the objects a class-name applies to and the idea or concept associated with that name. This distinction has figured in philosophy ever since, be it under different names. In the logic treatises of Port-Royal, one respectively spoke of the *extension* and *compréhension* of a class-name, while Leibniz preferred the terms 'extension' and 'intension.' Other pairs of terms which are used for this purpose are Mill's 'denotation–connotation' and Frege's 'reference-sense,' but Leibniz's terminology is adopted here.

Frege (1892) argues that the distinction should also be made to apply to sentences, proper names, and definite descriptions and due to the work of Montague, among others, all linguistic categories are attributed with intensions and extensions. In general terms the extension of an expression is what it refers to, while its intension is the way in which this extension is presented (see the tables in *Intensionality*).

1. Extensionality versus Intensionality

Whatever its intension may be, the extension of a sentence is often taken to be a truth value; i.e., either true or false (other possibilities are sometimes considered as well). Extensionally, the meaning of a sentence consists of its truth conditions: the conditions which a situation has to satisfy in order to make the sentence true.

That extensions do not in general suffice to give a satisfactory compositional semantics, has been argued most forcefully by Frege (1892). In an extensional semantics, expressions with identical extensions can be substituted for each other within a sentence preserving its truth value. But plainly this is not always so, as is shown by the invalidity of the following argument:

> Isolde thinks that Tristan is admirable.
> Tristan is the murderer of Isolde's fiancé.
> not ∴ Isolde thinks that the murderer of her fiancé is admirable.

Even if the extension of the proper name Tristan, i.e., Tristan himself, is identical to the extension of the definite description, 'the murderer of Isolde's fiancé,' the first premiss may be true and the conclusion false.

2. Matters of Priority

When formalizing these notions, one has to ask what comes first: the intension or the extension of an expression? In the literature one finds three answers to this question. The work in the tradition of Frege, Carnap, and Montague reduces intensions to extension, while property theories take the inverse route. In turn, nominalists like Quine 'unask' the question. According to them intensions should be disallowed to begin with, since such obscure abstract objects lack explanatory power.

Above, the extension and intension of an expression are distinguished as follows: the extension is what the expression refers to and its intension is the manner in which its extension is presented. Of course, these descriptions are vague, but there are different proposals to make these notions more precise.

The most influential theory is that of Richard Montague. In his intensional type logic, Montague defines intensions in terms of extensions using the tools of possible worlds semantics. On this view, the intension of an expression is a rule that allows one to determine its extension in each context. For convenience, contexts are taken to be possible worlds, which are perhaps best thought of as conceivable alternatives to the actual world, but richer contexts are used as well. The intensions are identified as functions from contexts to extensions in a context. For example, the intension of a common noun is a function from possible worlds to sets of individuals, whereas the proposition expressed by a sentence is a function from possible worlds to truth values, or, equivalently, a set of possible worlds. Since sets themselves are highly extensional objects—they are fully determined by their elements—this manner of modeling propositions immediately leads to the problem of omniscience when combined with a principle of compositionality. Within such a framework, attitude verbs like 'to doubt' denote relations among an individual and a proposition. It follows that if *a* doubts *p*, he cannot escape doubting all sentences that also denote *p*. For example, the sentence, 'Fermat's last theorem is true' is either equivalent with 'two plus two is four,' if the theorem holds, or with 'two plus two is three,' if it does not. Let us suppose the theorem is true, then it still does not follow from, 'Fanny doubts that Fermat's last theorem is true' that 'Fanny doubts that two plus two is four.' Similar problems arise with regard to other intensional contexts.

In Property theories one works on the assumption that intensions are primitive notions, not to be defined in terms of more basic ones. Extensions in contrast should be derived from intensions by means of the two-place relation, 'applies to,' which is also primitive.

For instance, the common noun 'red' is associated with the given property red, and its extension is defined to be the class of all individuals to which this property applies. Property theories circumvent the problem of omniscience. To continue the above example, the sentence, 'Fermat's last theorem is true' refers to a proposition and so does the sentence, 'Two plus two is four.' But since propositions are primitive, these will be different objects, and hence the faulty inference is blocked. (There are, in fact, property theories which obtain propositions from other intensional objects. They block the inference, since the structure of the propositions involved will differ.) However, property theories face another problem, in that the intensional objects they use are often too fine-grained. For instance, it seems that the proposition expressed by 'John walks and talks' is exactly that of 'John walks and John talks,' but this is not always guaranteed in such theories. Consequently, the quest is for objects which have a granularity intermediate between the fine non-compound abstract objects and the coarse sets of possible worlds.

Much in the above '... offends the aesthetic sense of those who have a taste for desert landscapes' (Quine 1961: 4). On the nominalistic view, of which Quine and Goodman are ardent defenders, explaining meaningful language in terms of abstract entities is explaining the obscure by the still more obscure. They strive to give an explanation in terms of particulars. The sole intensionality they would allow is that of the linguistic sign, which is identified with the heterogeneous space–time region comprising all of its uses. This, too, is an extremely fine-grained notion of intensionality, for changing but one word in a sign results in a completely different particular.

3. Sentence Meanings

In translating a text, preservation of meaning or intension is often stated to be the main aim. But what are the philosophical positions concerning the nature of meaning? These questions, evoked by the phenomenon of sameness of meaning, are closely related to the problem of universals, evoked by the phenomenon of sameness of attributes, which has haunted philosophy. It is therefore no surprise that none of the theories of meaning proposed thus far is accepted by all workers in the field. Here, some of the main positions are sketched using the familiar tripartition from the literature on universals; namely the realistic, the mentalistic, and the nominalistic position.

Frege (1892, 1918) held the realistic view that the intension of a sentence was the thought it expresses. These thoughts were taken to be free from the subjective, poetic qualities which are attached to our everyday thoughts. Instead, Frege took them to be abstract entities existing independently of our human minds in a Platonistic realm different from either physical or

cognitive states and processes. In the *Tractatus* (1922), Wittgenstein, too, holds that the meaning of a simple sentence is an objective structure, but rather than Fregean thoughts these entities are identified as possible states of affairs in logical space. The world consists of the states of affairs which are realized, and hence a sentence would be true if its sense were to correspond to such actual states of affairs.

The semantics of Frege and the early Wittgenstein make use of notions which are far removed from actual linguistic practice. So these semantics leave open the important question of how to explain, in terms of these concepts, the ability to use language in order to make statements, queries, and the like.

According to a 'mentalistic' view on meaning, intensions only exist within a mind. Meaningful language is now seen as a speaker's main tool to communicate the thoughts and pictures he senses. In order to do so, he somehow codes these subjective experiences in the form of perceptible signs, often written or spoken sentences. A hearer, in turn, decodes these signs resulting in subjective experiences akin to those the speaker wished to express.

In this strongly simplified picture, there is an apparent danger of misunderstanding: how to find out whether the decoded message is the one intended? In order to bar the conclusion that misconstrual of intension is almost inevitable, one often appeals to universal principles governing the human mind, which would secure at least the possibility of successful transfer of information. What these principles are is a matter for science to decide. Such 'innate knowledge' is also used to answer the question of how the signs come to have the meaning they in fact have. Some hold that there is stock of basic concepts, present at birth, perhaps in a mental language linked by convention to a spoken language, which gives the foundation for becoming a native speaker when exposed to a sufficiently rich linguistic environment. As will be seen shortly, the idea that meaningful language can be explained in this subjective mentalistic manner, is criticized by Wittgenstein (1953).

On the 'nominalistic' view, one strives to explain meaningful language in terms of particulars, rather than in terms of objective or subjective abstract entities. As was said in the previous section, these particulars induce a fine-grained notion of intensionality. In contrast, the abstract entities posited as meanings are often much coarser, in that they are said to remain constant across different languages. The feeling that such constancy occurs, prompted their use to begin with. This constancy is hard to explain on the nominalistic view, but Quine's argument of the indeterminacy of translation purports to show that the assumed preservation of meaning is an illusion.

4. Analytic versus Holistic Theories of Meaning

Until the 1990s sentences were taken to have meaning

in isolation, but on this score philosophers have different opinions, too.

According to the influential dictum of Frege (1884: Introduction), which states that the meaning of words should be studied within the context of a sentence, sentences are the primary bearers of meaning, so that the meaning of smaller units (words and morphemes) and of larger units (discourses and theories) should be derived from sentence meaning. This view can be called *analytical*: the meaning of a sentence is analyzed in terms of the contribution of its smaller units and the way in which they are combined.

In contrast, Quine (1961: ch. 2) defends the *holistic* view that '...in taking the statement as unit we have drawn our grid too finely. The unit of empirical significance is the whole of science.' According to Quine, only an entire language, varying from chatter to science and logic, can be said to be meaningful. In particular, the empirical content of a language is spread over the maze of interconnections that happen to exist among its sentences. Consequently, all talk of the meaning of a sentence should be construed as a manner of speech. One such construction is based on the observation that each language L comes with an equivalence relation among its sentences: sentence 1 is synonymous in L to sentence 2. Since this equivalence relation induces a partition of L's expressions, the meaning of a sentence S can be identified with a member of this partition, namely the class of expressions synonymous to S. Quine strives to explain the synonymy-relation in a behavioristic fashion, in terms of language use and of dispositions to such use. The dispositions, in turn, are hoped to get a neurophysiological explanation.

It should be noted that a sentence meaning induced by synonymy is highly language dependent since synonymy itself is. They are not the kind of objects to explain preservation of meaning under translation. But if Quine's controversial argument concerning the indeterminacy of translation is cogent, this is exactly what one should expect. Note also that this extreme version of a holistic view on language makes it unlikely that anyone could master a language in all its details. It must even be conceded that extensive parts, in particular the more stable ones such as science and mathematics, are unknown to most of us. One may thus wonder how the tiny fragments with which one is normally acquainted, suffice to form native speakers.

Another view on language which is not obviously molecular, is to be found in Wittgenstein's later writings. In his 'Philosophical Investigations,' Wittgenstein aims to show that the meaning of a linguistic sign is its use. It is not entirely clear, though, whether meaning and use are identical. The meaning of an expression should give sufficient ground for its correct use, but perhaps such use is only partly determined by its meaning. However, some of Wittgenstein's arguments make it hard to conceive of meaning as something separate from the sign.

Wittgenstein is strongly opposed to the view that the meaning of an expression consists of a mental picture which is somehow correlated to the linguistic sign. This correlation should be given in terms of rules and, in order to bar an infinite regress, one must assume that the relation between a picture and its accompanying rules is at most partly dependent on other rules. But a picture in isolation does not show how it should be applied; its significance depends crucially on factors external to the picture (a picture which seems to contain its rules of application remains a picture). The famous private language argument sets out to show that in general these external factors are different from mental acts. Instead, a sign gets its meaning from conventions—we decide whether to use a particular sign for a particular purpose—and from customs which are entrenched in a wider context, a 'form of life' that makes them useful.

These arguments against meaning as mental pictures hold as well if such pictures are 'objectivized' one way or another. Wittgenstein often states that replacing the elusive mental pictures by more concrete objects does not make a crucial difference. If so, his arguments would hold against all theories that propose meanings as things which are rather remote from the signs to which they are said to be linked. As soon as one separates meaning from a sign, there is no way to get them back together again.

See also: Intensionality.

Bibliography

Frege G 1892 Sinn und Bedeutung. In: Pätzig G (ed.) 1962 *Funktion, Begriff, Bedeutung.* Vandenhoeck and Ruprecht, Göttingen

Frege G 1918 Der Gedanke—Eine Logische Untersuchung. In: Pätzig G (ed.) 1966 *Logische Untersuchungen.* Vandenhoeck und Ruprecht, Göttingen

Quine W V O 1960 *Word and Object.* MIT Press, Cambridge, MA

Quine, W V O 1961 *From a Logical Point of View.* Harvard University Press, Cambridge, MA

Wittgenstein L 1922 *Tractatus Logico-philosophicus.* Routledge and Kegan Paul, London

Wittgenstein L 1953 *Philosophische Untersuchungen.* Basil Blackwell, Oxford

Intensionality

J. van der Does

A Fregean theory of meaning has a tripartite character: it combines a theory of the extensions of expressions with one of their intension and their force. Sentence (1), for instance, has a truth value as its extension—it is either true or false—while its intension is the thought it expresses.

> William will buy this Breitner. (1)

The force of a sentence determines its function. In particular, (1) can be used to assert that the thought it expresses is true, but one could also use the corresponding interrogative to query whether that thought is true; similarly for promises, commands, and the like.

In logical semantics it is often assumed that the intension of an expression is the core of its meaning, so that most proposals in this area are intensional. In particular, work in the tradition of Richard Montague is based on this presumption. The force of an expression, in contrast, is the locus of much research in speech act theory.

Prior to discussing intensional phenomena in more detail, Table 1 gives the intension of some important classes of expressions:

Table 1.

Expression	Intension
proper names, definite descriptions	individuals
sentences	propositions
common nouns, intransitive verbs	first-order properties
transitive verbs	two-place relation between individuals and properties of sets of individuals
determiners	two-place relations between properties
conjunctions	two-place functions from propositions to propositions

A more formal account of the references associated with these categories is given below.

1. Opaque Contexts

Intensional constructions are constructions which violate a principle of extensionality:

> If $t = t'$, then $[t/x]t''(x) = [t'/x]t''(x)$

(Here, the notion of substituting a term t for a free variable x in a term t' is employed; notation: $[t/x]t'$). Following Quine, these intensional constructions are said to create 'opaque' or 'intensional contexts.' So

the context $t''(x)$ is opaque if the corresponding substitution principle fails. This is in contradistinction to the so-called 'transparent' or 'extensional contexts' for which these substitution principles do hold. For example, the context 'x compiled a thesaurus' is transparent, as the following valid reasoning indicates:

> Roget compiled a thesaurus.
> Roget is Romilly's grandfather.
> ∴ Romilly's grandfather compiled a thesaurus.

It is far from true that all expressions are extensional. Here are some constructions which give rise to opaque contexts, together with examples which show that they violate the principle of extensionality:

Quotation. Sentence (4) does not follow from (2) and (3):

> The gladiator spoke the words 'Ave Caesar.' (2)

> Caesar is Gaius Julius. (3)

> The gladiator spoke the words 'Ave Gaius Julius.' (4)

Indirect speech. Sentence (7) does not follow from (5) and (6):

> Harry said that John kissed Mary. (5)

> John is the smartest boy in the class. (6)

> Harry said that the smartest boy in the class kissed Mary. (7)

Propositional attitudes, i.e., relations denoted by verbs like 'to discover,' 'to believe,' 'to suspect,' and 'to know.' Sentence (10) does not follow from (8) and (9):

> The detective knows that the thief entered through the skylight. (8)

> Biggles is the thief. (9)

> The detective knows that Biggles entered through the skylight. (10)

Intensions, i.e., relations denoted by verbs such as 'to look for,' 'to wish for,' and the like. Sentence (13) does not follow from (11) and (12):

> John is looking for the supreme commander of the Armed Forces of the United States of America. (11)

> The President of the United States of America is the supreme commander of the United States Armed Forces. (12)

> John is looking for the President of the United States of America. (13)

Temporal designation. Sentence (16) does not follow from (14) and (15):

George Bush is President of the United States. (14)

In 1963, the President of the United States was
assassinated in Dallas, Texas. (15)

In 1963, George Bush was assassinated in
Dallas, Texas. (16)

Modality. It is a necessary truth that nine exceeds
seven, and it is a fact that the number of planets is
nine. Yet (17) is not necessarily true:

The number of the planets exceeds seven. (17)

The truth or otherwise of (17) is not to be determined
solely on the basis of the expressions it contains. In
fact (17) expresses a contingent astronomical fact.
That there are more than seven planets is something
which has been discovered through intensive observations and inference. So (20) does not follow from
(18) and (19):

Nine necessarily exceeds seven. (18)

Nine is the number of the planets. (19)

The number of the planets necessarily exceeds
seven. (20)

Besides these, there are many more constructions
giving rise to opaque contexts. Just about every category of expressions contains elements which can create opaque contexts, for example, adjectives such as
'suspected' and 'alleged,' adverbs such as 'apparently,'
and so on.

2. Modalities de dicto and de re

Philosophers react differently to the principle of extensionality in the case of opaque contexts. It might be
argued that there is a reading for (20) in which this
sentence does indeed follow from (18) and (19). This
reading can be paraphrased as follows: that number
which is in fact the number of the planets is necessarily
greater than seven. Formally, this can be expressed in
a predicate–logical language with a necessity operator
$\square$ and a possibility operator $\diamond$ added (see Gamut
1991: ch. 3). These operators make formulas out of
formulas. The resulting $\square\varphi$ should be read as: necessarily φ, and $\diamond\varphi$ as: possibly φ. In this language, the
reading of (20) in which it does follow from (18) and
(19) translates as (21), whereas the reading in which it
does not may be rendered as (22):

$\exists x(x = \text{the number of planets} \wedge \square x > 7)$ (21)

$\square\exists x(x = \text{the number of planets} \wedge x > 7)$ (22)

Reading (22) says that in every possible situation the
number of the planets, whatever it happens to be, will
exceed seven. These two readings (21) and (22) of
(20) comply with a distinction traditionally drawn in
modal logic between modalities de dicto and de re, a
distinction which can be made precise in terms of the
scope of $\square$.

Consider the somewhat simpler examples (23) and
(24), and their translations (25) and (26):

Necessarily there is something which is greater
than seven. (23)

There is something which is necessarily greater
than seven. (24)

$\square\exists x(x > 7)$ (25)

$\exists x\square(x > 7)$ (26)

In (25) the scope of $\square$ contains $\exists x(x > 7)$, and in (26)
it contains $x > 7$. The scope of an occurrence of $\square$
may be considered to be the opaque context created
by this operator. If the formula within the scope of $\square$
is a sentence, i.e., a formula with no free variables,
then $\square$ is said to be a modality de dicto. As examples,
then, one has (22) and (25). If on the other hand there
is a free variable within the scope of $\square$, that is to say
a variable which may be bound by a quantifier outside
the scope of $\square$, then $\square$ is said to be a modality de re.
Sentences (21) and (26) are examples of this modality.
Traditionally, a modality de dicto was seen as an
attribution of necessary (or possible) truth to a proposition (dictum) and a modality de re was seen as an
attribution of a necessary (or possible) property to an
entity (res). The traditional distinction does correspond to the formal one. In asserting the truth of
(25) one does indeed assert that the proposition
$\exists x(x > 7)$ is necessarily true; while in asserting the truth
of (26) one asserts the existence of an entity which
necessarily has the property of being greater than
seven.

Some philosophers have objected to de re modalities. For them, recognition of such modalities amounts
to a revival of 'essentialism,' a philosophical position
which distinguishes between accidental and essential
properties of things. They have their objections to any
such position and therefore reject modalities de re as
meaningless and thus useless, at best suggesting to
reduce modalities de re to modalities de dicto. One
such vigorous opponent of modalities de re has been
the philosopher and logician Quine.

Even leaving aside the question of whether recognizing modalities de re does indeed lead to essentialism, it would seem that a position like this is
particularly unsuited to the present purposes. It can
be argued that philosophical objections may never be
allowed to weigh heavily if the aim is the description
of natural language. For the aim is to give descriptions
of how in fact we speak, not of how we would have to
speak in order to carry the approval of philosophers. It
is quite possible that speakers of natural languages
do indeed make philosophically dubious assumptions,
but that is a fact of life which should not be swept
under the carpet of some philosophically more sophisticated reformulation. Now, that modalities de re
occur in natural language seems indisputable. One
example is (27):

333

Each of those present may have committed the
murder. (27)

It is clear what this means. Sentence (27) may be
formalized as $\forall x \Diamond Mx$. It certainly does not mean the
same thing as $\Diamond \forall x Mx$, which is the translation of
(28):

It is possible that each of those present has
committed the murder. (28)

It is not at all clear how a de re modality like (27)
could be reduced to a de dicto modality. And besides,
possible worlds semantics does provide a clear
interpretation for modalities de re.

3. Intensional Type Theory

A type theory has expressions which are interpreted
according to the type associated with them. In the
particular case of Montague's intensional type theory,
the set of types is the smallest set which contains:
  (a) Two basic types: e (for: entity or thing) and t
      (for: truth value);
  (b) All types (α, β), where α and β are types;
  (c) All types (s, α), where α is a type.
The first two clauses are identical to those for extensional types. The third clause is new, and allows one
to form intensional types. Note that s itself is not a
type; its only purpose is to enable to form composite
intensional types. Informally, expressions of type
(α, β) denote functions that map objects of type α to
objects of type β. The expressions of type (s, α) denote
intensional entities: functions from possible worlds to
objects of type α.

Among the expressions, there are infinitely many
variables x_α for each type α, but there may also be
constants c_α. The variables and constants of type α
constitute the basic or noncompound expressions of
that type. The compound expressions are defined by:
  (a) If t_β is an expression of type β and x_a is a
      variable of type α, then $\lambda x_\alpha.t_\beta$ is an expression
      of type (α, β).
  (b) If $t_{(\alpha,\beta)}$ is an expression of type (α,β) and t_α
      is an expression of type α, then $t_{(\alpha,\beta)}(t_\alpha)$ is an
      expression of type β.
  (c) If t_α is an expression of type α, then $^\wedge t_\alpha$ is an
      expression of type (s, α).
  (d) If $t_{(s,\alpha)}$ is an expression of type (s, α), then $^\vee t_{(s,\alpha)}$
      is an expression of type α.
  (e) If t_t is an expression of type t, then $\Box t_t$ is an
      expression of type t.
  (f) If t and t' are typed expressions, then $t = t'$ is
      an expression of type t.
In a term of the form $\lambda x_\alpha.t_\beta$, the variable x_α is said to
be bound by λx_α. Variables which are not bound, are
free.

In order to interpret the expressions, one first has
to introduce the domains in which the expressions take
their semantical value and then to map the expressions
onto objects of the appropriate kind by means of an

interpretation function. To this end, with each type a
a domain D_a of objects of type a is associated. For the
basic type e and t the domains are respectively a given
nonempty set of individuals D and the set of truth
values:

$$D_e = D$$

$$D_t = \{0, 1\}$$

The domains for the complex types are so-called function spaces. In case of type (s, α), a given nonempty
set W of possible worlds is used:

$$D_{(\alpha,\beta)} = \{f: f \text{ is a function from } D_\alpha \text{ to } D_\beta\}$$

$$D_{(s,\alpha)} = \{f: f \text{ is a function from } W \text{ to } D_\alpha\}$$

A model $M = \langle F, [\![-]\!] \rangle$ for intensional type theory
consists of a frame: $F = \{D_\alpha: \alpha \text{ is a type}\}$ and an
interpretation function $[\![-]\!]$. In extensional type theory the interpretation function assigned an element of
D_α to each constant of type α. However, in case of
intensional type theory the extension of a constant
should be able to vary from context to context. That
is why constants of type α are interpreted as functions
of possible worlds onto elements of type α. So
$[\![c_\alpha]\!](w) \in D_\alpha$, for each $w \in W$. Individual constants c_e,
however, are often required to be 'rigid designators,'
so that $[\![c_e]\!]$ takes the same value at all worlds.

Given an assignment a for a model M, i.e., a function from variables of type a to objects in M of type
α, the interpretation function $[\![-]\!]$ is extended to
associate each expression t with its extension in possible world w under a; notation: $[\![t]\!]_{a,w}$, using the following recipe:

(i) $[\![x_\alpha]\!]_{a,w}$ $= a(x_\alpha)$
(ii) $[\![c_\alpha]\!]_{a,w}$ $= [\![c_\alpha]\!](w)$
(iii) $[\![\lambda x_\alpha.t_\beta]\!]_{a,w}$ $=$ the function f from D_α to D_β
                defined by, for all $d \in D_\alpha$:
                $f(d) := [\![t_\beta]\!]_{a[x_\alpha:=d],w}$,
(iv) $[\![t_{(\alpha,\beta)}(t_\alpha)]\!]_{a,w}$ $= [\![t_{(\alpha,\beta)}]\!]_{a,w}([\![t_\alpha]\!]_{a,w})$
(v) $[\![^\wedge t_\alpha]\!]_{a,w}$ $=$ the function g from W to D_α
                defined by, for all $w' \in W$:
                $g(w') := [\![t_\alpha]\!]_{a,w'}$.
(vi) $[\![^\vee t_{(s,\alpha)}]\!]_{a,w}$ $= [\![t_{(s,\alpha)}]\!]_{a,w}(w)$
(vii) $[\![\Box\varphi]\!]_{a,w} = 1$ iff $[\![\varphi]\!]_{a,w'} = 1$ for all $w' \in W$
(viii) $[\![t = t']\!]_{a,w} = 1$ iff $[\![t]\!]_{a,w} = [\![t']\!]_{a,w}$

Some comments may be in order. Clause (ii) stipulates
that the extension of a constant of type α in a world
w is an object of type α. Given the definition of assignments, clause (i) stipulates the same for variables.
Clause (iii), the most complicated one, makes use of
the assignment $a[x_\alpha := d]$. By definition, this is the
assignment which is identical to a, except perhaps for
the value at x_α, which is given by: $a[x_\alpha := d](x_\alpha) = d$. (If
$a(x_\alpha) = d$, the assignments are identical.) Since
$[\![t_\beta]\!]a[x:=d],w$ is an object of type β, $[\![\lambda x_\alpha.t_\beta]\!]a,w$ is a
function from D_α to D_β. Clause (iv) makes $t_{(\alpha,\beta)}(t_\alpha)$
denote an object of type β in w, for in that world t_α is

an object of type α and $t_{(\alpha,\beta)}$ a function from objects of type α to objects of type β. Note that clause (v) is rather similar to clause (iii), and clause (iv) to (vi). The reason is that the cap-operator '$^\wedge$' functions much like the lambda-abstractor 'λ'; it abstracts, so to speak, only over objects of type s. Since s is not really a type in this system so that variables of that type are disallowed, one has to introduce a separate operator to be able to denote the intension of an expression into the formal language. Similarly, the cup-operator is a form of function application; it yields the value of an intension at the present world. According to clause (vii), finally, the necessity operator captures universal necessity.

Table 2 gives the intension of the expressions in Table 1 in terms of types:

Table 2.

Expression	Type
proper names, definite descriptions	e
sentences	(s, t)
common nouns, intransitive verbs	$(s, (e, t))$
transitive verbs	$(s, ((s, ((e, t), t)), (e, t)))$
determiners	$(s, ((s, (e, t)), (s, ((e, t), t))))$
conjunctions	$(s, ((s, t), (s, t), t)))$

In the case of proper names, definite descriptions, and sentences, it is plain that the types of objects are identical to the objects given in Table 1. But this also holds good for the other kinds of expression. For instance, objects of type $(s, (e, t))$ are functions from possible worlds to sets of individuals. Similarly, objects of type $(s, (((s, (e, t)), t), (e, t)))$, the transitive verbs, are functions from possible worlds to objects of type $(((s, (e, t)), t), (e, t))$. The latter objects, in turn, are best seen as two-place relations among objects of

type $(s, ((e, t), t))$, i.e., properties of sets of individuals, and objects of type e individuals.

Unlike predicate logic and extensional type theory, intensional type theory does not satisfy a so-called replacement theorem:

Replacement theorem

If $[\![\,t = t'\,]\!]_{a,w} = 1$, then $[\![\,[t/x]t' = [t'/x]t''\,]\!]_{a,w} = 1$.

This principle still does hold, though, if the type of t'' is extensional; that is to say: intensional type theory generalizes extensional type theory.

A counterexample to the replacement theorem is the context $\square(x_e = {}^\vee (the\ tallest\ man))$. Here, 'the tallest man' is interpreted as an object of type (s, e); namely, the function that assigns to each possible world the tallest man in that world. Then, even if:

$$[\![\,john\,]\!]_{a,w} = [\![\,{}^\vee (the\ tallest\ man)\,]\!]_{a,w}$$

it may still be so that:

$$[\![\,[john/x]\square(x_e = {}^\vee (the\ tallest\ man))\,]\!]_{a,w}$$
$$\neq [\![\,[{}^\vee (the\ tallest\ man)/x]\square(x_e = {}^\vee (the\ tallest\ man))\,]\!]_{a,w}$$

John may be the tallest man in world w, but of course it is not necessary that he is the tallest man in any world. So $[\![\,[john/x]\square(x_e = {}^\vee (the\ tallest\ man))\,]\!]_{a,w}$ may be false. On the other hand, in each world the tallest man is necessarily the tallest man: $[\![\,[{}^\vee (the\ tallest\ man)/x]\square(x_e = {}^\vee (the\ tallest\ man))\,]\!]_{a,w}$ is always true. In short, one has a counterexample to the invalid reasoning:

> John is the tallest man.
> Necessarily, the tallest man is the tallest man.
> ∴ Necessarily, John is the tallest man.

See also: De Dicto/De Re; Intension; Modal Logic.

Bibliography

Gamut L T F 1991 *Logic Language and Meaning. Vol. 2: Intensional Logic and Logical Grammar*. University of Chicago Press, Chicago, IL

Metalanguage versus Object Language

J. van Eijck

Mathematical logic studies formal languages. The language which is the object of logical study is called the 'object language,' the vehicle of thought in studying it is the 'metalanguage.' Generally, the syntax of the object language is rigorously defined, that of the metalanguage is not. The object language might be the first-order language of arithmetic, with a fixed

logical and nonlogical vocabulary and unambiguous formation rules. The metalanguage is the informal language of mathematics with some additional formal elements such as elements of set theoretic notation and abbreviations like *iff* (for: 'if and only if') and ⇒ (for: 'only if'). Because the object language was devised to formalize mathematical reasoning, the logical vocabulary of the object language will have counterparts in the metalanguage, for instance, the material implication symbol → at object-language level reflects the *only if* or ⇒ at metalevel, the material implication symbol ≡ at object level the *iff* or ⇔ at metalevel, and so on.

The question of which concepts belong to the object language and which to the metalanguage is a key problem of logic. Alfred Tarski has argued that truth is essentially a metalanguage concept. His argument is based on a well-known semantic paradox dating from Antiquity, the Paradox of the Liar. Consider sentence (1):

> This sentence is false. (1)

Sentence (1) is paradoxical. This can be seen as follows. First assume that (1) is true. Then because of what (1) says, it must be false. Contradiction. Now assume that (1) is false. Then what the sentence says is not true, that is, it is not true that (1) is false. In other words, (1) is true. Contradiction again.

Given the presence of a truth predicate T in the object language, the Liar Paradox can be formalized in first-order logic. Let $\lceil \ \rceil$ be a function mapping the formula φ to a term $\lceil \varphi \rceil$. Then the fact that T is the truth predicate makes the following principle (2) true, for arbitrary sentences φ.

$$\varphi \equiv T \lceil \varphi \rceil . \tag{2}$$

Modulo some assumptions about the possibility of encoding syntactic operations as functions on codes of syntactic objects, it can be shown that there exists a sentence ψ for which the equivalence (3) is true (in some suitable model).

$$\psi \equiv - T \lceil \psi \rceil . \tag{3}$$

Equivalence (3) is a formalized version of Liar sentence (1), and the combination of (2) and (3) gives rise to a paradox in first-order logic. (Further details can be found in *Formal Semantics*.)

In Tarski's view, the Formalized Liar Paradox arises because the concept of truth is used at the wrong level. It cannot be denied that natural languages do contain a truth predicate, so Tarski's argument is relevant for natural language semantics. Tarski simply dismissed natural languages as unable to withstand logical scrutiny, but there are several ways to get around his conclusion. First, one can take care always to restrict semantic accounts for natural language to 'fragments,' in such a way that no fragment contains a truth predicate for the sentences of the fragment itself, although a fragment might contain a truth predicate for embedded natural-language fragments. This approach might lead to a hierarchy of an object fragment, a metafragment, a meta-metafragment, and so on. A second solution is the observation that one half of (2) is harmless: weakening (2) to $\varphi \rightarrow T \lceil \varphi \rceil$ blocks the paradox. Saul Kripke has shown that it is indeed possible to define a partial truth predicate in the object language satisfying $\varphi \rightarrow T \lceil \varphi \rceil$. His definition is outside the scope of the present article.

See also: Formal Semantics; Paradoxes, Semantic; Truth.

Bibliography

Kripke S A 1975 Outline of a theory of truth. *The Journal of Philosophy* **72**: 690–716
Tarski A 1956 The concept of truth in formalized languages. In: Tarski A (ed.) *Logic, Semantics, Metamathematics*. Clarendon Press, Oxford

Modal Logic

M. Davies

Modal logic is the logic of necessity and possibility—intuitively, of the ways things must be, and the ways things might have been. For example, it is not a mere contingency about the world that all grandmothers are mothers of parents: that is something that must be the case. On the other hand, if Jane is not in fact a grandmother, that is merely contingent: Jane might have been a grandmother if things had gone differently. Modal logic is a means of formalizing the claim that *it is necessary that* all grandmothers are mothers of parents, and the claim that *it is possible that* Jane should have been a grandmother.

1. The Origins of Modal Logic

In ancient philosophy, modal notions loom large in discussions of fatalism, determinism, and divine foreknowledge, although it is arguable that before the work of Duns Scotus in the late thirteenth century these discussions did not clearly distinguish between genuinely modal ideas (e.g., what is not actually so, but might have been so) and temporal ideas (e.g., what is not now so, but sometime will be so). In any case, the modern origins of modal logic lie in the work of Lewis on the notion of strict implication (see Lewis 1912; Lewis and Langford 1932).

For the material implication '⊃' of classical logic, the schemas in (1–3) are all valid.

$$A \supset (B \supset A) \tag{1}$$

$$\sim A \supset (A \supset B) \tag{2}$$

$$(A \supset B) \vee (B \supset A) \tag{3}$$

However, for the intuitive notion of entailment, or strict implication, one may first consistently accept that Jane is a grandmother (A), while denying that the proposition that penguins waddle (B) entails that Jane is a grandmother (A). Second, one may consistently accept that Jane is not a politician ($\sim$A) while denying that the proposition that Jane is a politician (A) entails that penguins fly (B). And third, one may consistently deny that the proposition that Jane is a politician (A) entails that penguins waddle (B) while also denying that the proposition that penguins waddle (B) entails that Jane is a politician (A). In short, the three schemas that are valid for material implication are intuitively not valid for entailment, or strict implication. (Schemas (1) and (2) are sometimes called the 'paradoxes of material implication.') Modal logic was designed to permit the formalization of statements about strict implication, such as the statement that the proposition that Jane is a grandmother *strictly implies* that Jane is the mother of a parent.

The notation of modal logic results from adding to the notation of ordinary propositional or predicate logic the one-place sentence operators '□' (box) and '◇' (diamond), and the two-place sentence operator '-з' (fish-hook), expressing necessity, possibility, and strict implication, respectively. Recall that in the case of propositional logic one can define '∨' in terms of '&' and '$\sim$,' for example. Similarly, in the case of the modal operators, one does not have to take all three as new primitive operators. If '□' is taken as primitive, then one can define '◇A' as '$\sim$□$\sim$A' and 'A-з B' as '□(A⊃B).' Similarly, if '◇' is taken as primitive, then one can define '□A' as '$\sim$◇$\sim$A' and 'A-з B' as '$\sim$◇(A&$\sim$B).' Finally, if '-з' is taken as primitive, then one can define '□A' as '((A∨$\sim$A)-з A)' and '◇A' as '$\sim$(A-з(A&$\sim$A)).'

2. Propositional Modal Logic

The language of propositional modal logic is the result of adding some of the modal operators to the language of propositional logic. In fact, '□' will here be added as the only new primitive operator; and the definition of 'well-formed formula' (WFF) will be extended by allowing '□' the same privileges of occurrence as '$\sim$.'

2.1 The Systems K and T

There are many different systems of propositional modal logic, differing in their proof-theoretic resources. But all so-called 'normal' modal propositional systems are based upon a common core. This core is made up of three components. First, there is

some complete proof system for classical propositional logic, including the rule of *modus ponens*:

From: A and A ⊃ B
Infer: B.

Second, there is an axiom schema:

K. □(A ⊃ B) ⊃ (□A ⊃ □B).

Third, there is a rule of proof, called 'Necessitation':

If ⊢ A, then ⊢ □A.

Here, the turnstile 'X ⊢ Y' is to be read as 'there is a proof of Y from assumptions X.' The rule of Necessitation thus says that if there is a proof of A from no assumptions, then there is also a proof of □A from no assumptions.

It has already been seen that one can prove all instances of the schemas (1) and (2)—the paradoxes of material implication—from no assumptions, given propositional calculus resources alone. Consequently, one can prove all instances of □(A ⊃ (B ⊃ A)) and □($\sim$A ⊃ (A ⊃ B)) by the rule of Necessitation. Thence, by the schema K and the definition of '-з,' one obtains (4) and (5):

$$\Box A \supset (B \text{-з} A) \tag{4}$$

$$\Box \sim A \supset (A \text{-з} B). \tag{5}$$

These schemas are known as the 'paradoxes of strict implication.'

The rule of Necessitation certainly does not say that from A as an assumption one can prove □A. If it did, then it would trivialize modal logic. However, given the rule of Necessitation and the axiom schema K, one can derive a rule about proofs from assumptions, namely:

N. If $A_1, \ldots, A_n \vdash B$, then $\Box A_1, \ldots, \Box A_n \vdash \Box B$.

For suppose that $A_1, \ldots, A_n \vdash B$. Then, just as in non-modal propositional logic, one obtains

$$\vdash (A_1 \supset (\ldots (A_n \supset B) \ldots)).$$

Thence, by the rule of Necessitation,

$$\vdash \Box (A_1 \supset (\ldots (A_n \supset B) \ldots)).$$

By n − 1 applications of K, one obtains

$$\vdash \Box A_1 \supset (\ldots (\Box A_n \supset \Box B) \ldots);$$

and so, by n − 1 applications of *modus ponens*, $\Box A_1, \ldots, \Box A_n \vdash \Box B$, as required. Rule N says that the class of necessary truths is closed under deductive consequence.

The propositional modal system which contains just the core comprising propositional logic, Necessitation, and the schema K, is itself called 'K.'

The first extension of K to consider is the system T, which results by adding to the system K the further axiom schema:

T. □A ⊃ A.

Given the definition of '◇' in terms of '□,' all instances of the schema

$$A \supset \Diamond A \qquad (6)$$

are also theorems of the system T.

These schemas T and (6) are clearly faithful to the intuitive notions of necessity and possibility from which this discussion began. What is necessarily the case—for example, that all grandmothers are mothers of parents—is surely true; and what is true—for example, that Jane is not in fact a grandmother—is by that very fact shown to be possible. Consequently, the system K—which does not contain these plausible schemas—may seem a counterintuitive candidate for a logic of necessity and possibility. However, there are other notions of necessity and possibility to which the resources of modal logic have been applied.

2.2 Deontic, Doxastic, and Epistemic Logics

One notion that is sometimes treated in the style of modal logic is deontic necessity: what ought to be the case, or what is obligatory. The corresponding notion of possibility is: what is allowed to be the case, or what is permissible. It is certainly not true that everything that ought to be the case is the case. So, in 'deontic logic,' one will require to consider modal systems that do not contain schema T (see, for example, Smiley 1963; Åqvist 1984). However, to the extent that what is obligatory is ipso facto permissible, one may want to include the weaker schema $\Box A \supset \Diamond A$ in deontic logics.

A good deal of discussion of deontic logic centers around the schema

$$\sim(\Box A \& \Box \sim A). \qquad (7)$$

For in any normal deontic logic (that is, a logic that contains K, and hence rule N), schema (7) is a consequence of the schema

$$\sim \Box (A \& \sim A). \qquad (8)$$

But while schema (8) looks innocuous, schema (7) is much more controversial, since it seems to rule out the possibility of certain kinds of moral dilemmas (see Chellas 1980: ch. 6).

The resources of modal logic have also been applied to the notions of belief and knowledge. The operator '□' is read, for example, as 'Jane believes that,' or as 'Jane knows that.' In the latter case—epistemic logic—the schema T is, of course, correct; but it is not correct in the former case—doxastic logic.

Normal epistemic and doxastic logics both face the problem that, according to rule N, what a person knows or believes is closed under deductive consequence. That is, a person knows all the deductive consequences of what he or she knows, and believes all the deductive consequences of his or her beliefs. This closure property clearly does not hold for the ordinary notions of knowledge and belief; and the

difficulty thus posed is known as the 'problem of logical omniscience.' (For a discussion of differences between the logical properties of metaphysical necessity and of belief or knowledge, see Forbes 1988.)

2.3 Modal Logic and Provability

There is another important example of a propositional modal system without the schema T; this is the system G, which goes beyond K in containing the axiom schema:

$$\Box(\Box A \supset A) \supset \Box A.$$

The system G is used in the study of provability in first-order arithmetic (Peano arithmetic) (see Smiley 1963; Boolos 1979; Boolos and Jeffrey 1989).

It is possible to express, within the language of arithmetic, the claim that a given sentence of that language is provable. Gödel's Second Incompleteness Theorem states that a sentence of arithmetic that expresses the claim that arithmetic is consistent is not itself provable in arithmetic. (A sentence could express the consistency claim by saying that $0 = 1$, for example, is not provable in arithmetic.) Furthermore, it is possible to set up a scheme of translation between the modal language and the language of arithmetic, with the property that:

> Every translation of a theorem of the modal system G is provable in arithmetic.

Finally, the translation of $\Box A$ is always the sentence of arithmetic that expresses the claim that the translation of A is provable in arithmetic.

Now, suppose that this modal system, G, were to contain the schema T: $\Box A \supset A$. Then, a sentence of the language of arithmetic expressing the claim:

> If '$0 = 1$' is provable in arithmetic, then $0 = 1$

would be provable in arithmetic. It can certainly be proved in arithmetic that $0 \neq 1$. Consequently, by *modus tollens*, a sentence expressing the claim that '$0 = 1$' is not provable in arithmetic would be provable in arithmetic. But that would contradict Gödel's Second Incompleteness Theorem.

The interpretation of the modal operator '□' as expressing provability—a property of sentences—escapes some objections to modal logic that are due to Quine (1976; 1960: 195–200). Quine urges that the historical foundations of modal logic involve a confusion between use and mention, since 'implies' properly expresses a relation between sentences. The sentences that flank the '-3' of modal logic are apparently used, rather than mentioned; but the correct form for a statement about (strict) implication would be, for example:

> 'Jane is a grandmother' implies 'Jane is the mother of a parent,'

where the two sentences about Jane are mentioned,

rather than used. Similarly, Quine urges that the notion of necessity itself is innocent of confusion only if it is construed as a property of sentences.

Montague (1963) proves that, even in a very weak theory of arithmetic, no predicate of sentences can be awarded the basic properties of the modal operator '□' without resulting in inconsistency. Montague's result certainly shows that no predicate of sentences of arithmetic can consistently have the properties enjoyed by '□' in the system T; and he concludes that the interpretation of the modal operator as a predicate of sentences would involve sacrificing the greater part of modal logic. Work on the system G demonstrates, however, that a substantial and interesting system of modal logic—though not including T—can be based upon an interpretation of '□' as a predicate of sentences. Whether Quine's objections should be regarded as casting suspicion on other systems of modal logic is, of course, a further question.

2.4 Modal Systems that Extend T

The language of propositional modal logic permits a modal operator to occur embedded within the scope of another modal operator. Thus, for example, instances of the schema $\Box(A \lor \Diamond B)$ are WFFs of modal logic. In particular, modal operators can occur alongside one another to form 'iterated modalities': $\Box\Box A$, $\Box\Diamond A$, $\Diamond\Box A$, $\Diamond\Diamond A$, and so on.

All instances of the schemas $\Box\Box A \supset \Box A$ and $\Box\Diamond A \supset \Diamond A$ are already instances of the schema T. The two best-known propositional modal systems extending T are obtained by adding to T the converses of these schemas. Thus, S4 is the system that results by adding to T the schema

S4. $\Box A \supset \Box\Box A$,

and S5 is the system that results by adding to T the schema

S5. $\Diamond A \supset \Box\Diamond A$.

The S4 schema is in fact a theorem schema in S5, so that the system S5 contains the system S4. In fact, S5 can be characterized as the system that results by adding to S4 the schema

B. $A \supset \Box\Diamond A$.

The schema B is called the 'Brouwersche' axiom because of connections with Brouwer's work on the foundations of intuitionist mathematics. If the schema B is added directly to T, then the resulting system is B. Thus, S4 and B are systems that each extend T, and S5 is the smallest system that includes them both.

In S5, iterated modalities collapse into the final member of the string. Thus, for example, $\Diamond\Box\Box\Diamond\Diamond\Box\Diamond A \equiv \Diamond A$. This is because S5 contains the equivalences:

$$\Box\Box A \equiv \Box A \qquad (9)$$

$$\Box\Diamond A \equiv \Diamond A \qquad (10)$$

$$\Diamond\Box A \equiv \Box A \qquad (11)$$

$$\Diamond\Diamond A \equiv \Diamond A. \qquad (12)$$

Schemas (9) and (10) are immediate from T and S4, and T and S5, respectively. To establish schema (11), consider that by T one obtains $\Box A \supset \Diamond\Box A$; so one only needs to prove $\Diamond\Box A \supset \Box A$. It suffices to prove the contrapositive, $\sim\Box A \supset \sim\Diamond\Box A$. Because of the way that '$\Diamond$' and '$\Box$' are related, $\sim\Box A$ is equivalent to $\Diamond\sim A$; likewise, $\sim\Diamond\Box A$ is equivalent to $\Box\Diamond\sim A$. Consequently, it suffices to prove

$$\Diamond\sim A \supset \Box\Diamond\sim A.$$

But all instances of this schema are already instances of the schema S5; so we are done. Schema (12) is established similarly, but using S4 instead of S5.

In fact, S5 has an even stronger property. Any WFF of S5 is equivalent to a WFF in which no modal operator occurs within the scope of another modal operator. For example, $\Box(A \lor \Diamond B)$, in which '$\Diamond$' occurs within the scope of '$\Box$,' is equivalent to $\Box A \lor \Diamond B$, in which neither modal operator is within the scope of the other (for all cases of this reduction, see Hughes and Cresswell 1968: 50–54).

The systems K, G, T, B, S4, and S5 are just a few from the host of propositional modal systems that have been studied (Hughes and Cresswell 1968; Bull and Segerberg 1984). There have been, for example, detailed investigations of many systems that are intermediate between S4 and S5. As it happens, the schema S4 is also a theorem schema of the system G (Boolos 1979: 30), although G—as already noted—does not contain T. The system intermediate between K and G is K4, resulting by the addition of the schema S4 directly to K. Further systems could be obtained by adding the schema B or S5 directly to K.

Despite this great variety of modal systems weaker than S5, it is very plausible that the axioms of S5 are all intuitively valid for the notion of necessity that has loomed large in philosophical work: metaphysical necessity (Kripke 1980), or 'broadly logical' necessity (Plantinga 1974). Consequently, S5 is widely used as the formal basis for philosophical discussions of necessity.

3. Model-theoretic Semantics for Propositional Modal Logic

The semantics for nonmodal propositional logic is very simple. A model or valuation is determined by an *assignment* of truth-values to sentence letters. By way of the familiar truth-tables for the connectives, the assignment is extended to evaluate each WFF as true or false. A WFF is then said to be 'valid'—or a tautology—if it is evaluated as true on every assignment: if it is true in every model. An argument from $A_1, \ldots, A_n$ to B is then said to be valid if the conclusion

B is evaluated as true on every assignment on which all the premises $A_1, \ldots, A_n$ come out true. Finally, the notion of provability is linked with that of validity by demonstrating that every WFF that is provable is valid ('soundness') and that every WFF that is valid is provable ('completeness').

These resources are not adequate for propositional modal logic, since the modal operators are not truth-functional. In the case of modal logic, the intuitive semantic idea—which goes back to Leibniz—is that necessary truth is truth in all possible worlds. The intuitive idea was turned into model-theoretic semantics for several modal systems by Kripke (1963). A modal model involves not just one assignment of truth-values to sentence letters, but a whole set of assignments: each assignment can be thought of as describing a possible world. The simplest way to develop the Leibnizian idea of necessity would then be to say that the truth of $\Box A$ on any one assignment requires the truth of A on every assignment in the set. However, Kripke's model theory introduces a further element: a relation of accessibility between assignments. The truth of $\Box A$ on any one assignment requires the truth of A on every asignment that is accessible from that one.

In the formal development of the semantics, a modal model is a triple $\langle W, R, V \rangle$, where W is a set (the set of possible worlds), R is a binary relation on W (the accessibility relation), and V is a function from ordered pairs of sentence letters and worlds to truth-values (the valuation). The valuation V thus determines an assignment of truth-values to sentence letters corresponding to each world w in the set W.

The valuation V is then extended—by induction on the complexity of WFFs—to an evaluation of each WFF as true or false at each world. For example, a negation $\sim A$ is true at a world w if and only if A is not true at w; a conjunction A&B is true at a world w if and only if each conjunct A and B is true at w; and so on for the other truth-functional connectives. Finally, $\Box A$ is true at a world w if and only if A is true at every world that is R-related to w, that is, every world w' such that $R(w, w')$.

A WFF of propositional modal logic is then 'valid' if it is true at every world in every model. Similarly, an argument in propositional modal logic is valid if, whenever all the premises are true at a world in a model, the conclusion is also true at that world in that model. In addition, a WFF is said to be 'valid in a model' if it is true at every world in that model; and a WFF is said to be 'valid in a class of models' if it is valid in every model in the class.

If every theorem of a given modal system is valid in a class of models, then the system is said to be 'sound' with respect to that class. If every WFF that is valid in a class of models is a theorem of a given modal system, then the system is said to be 'complete' with respect to that class.

340

3.1 Soundness Results

The system K is sound with respect to the class of *all* modal models. This is to say that every theorem of the system K is valid; that is, valid in every model. In order to see that this is so, one needs to consider the three components of the system K. First, it is clear that any WFF that is a substitution instance of a tautology of nonmodal propositional logic will be evaluated as true at every world in every model. Furthermore, the rule of *modus ponens* preserves validity. Second, one has to establish the validity of every instance of the schema

K. $\Box(A \supset B) \supset (\Box A \supset \Box B)$.

If $\Box(A \supset B)$ and $\Box A$ are both true at a world w, then $A \supset B$ and A are both true at every world w' accessible from w. But then, by the truth-table for '$\supset$,' B is also true at every such w', and so $\Box B$ is true at w, as required. Third, it is necessary to check that the rule of Necessitation preserves validity: if A is valid, then $\Box A$ is also valid. Assume that A is true at every world in every model, and suppose that for some world w, in some model, $\Box A$ is not true at w. Then there is some world w' accessible from w in the model, such that A is not true at w'. But this contradicts the assumption that A is true at every world in every model. So, $\Box A$ is after all true at every world in every model.

The system T is not sound with respect to the class of all modal models. It is a straightforward matter to construct a model in which some instance of the schema T is false at some world. For example, suppose that $W = \{w_1, w_2\}$, that w_1 is R-related to w_2 and to no other world, and that for some sentence letter p, $V(p, w_1) = $ False while $V(p, w_2) = $ True. Then $\Box p$ is true at w_1 while p is false at w_1. So, $\Box p \supset p$ is false at w_1 in this model.

The system T is, however, sound with respect to the class of all models in which the R-relation is 'reflexive'; that is, in which, for every world w, $R(w, w)$. (It is a routine matter to check this.) For short, T is said to be sound with respect to the class of all reflexive models.

There are similar soundness results for the systems S4, B, and S5. The system S4 is sound with respect to the class of all models in which R is both *reflexive and transitive*. (R is transitive if, whenever $R(u, v)$ and $R(v, w)$, one also has $R(u, w)$.) The system B is sound with respect to the class of all models in which R is both *reflexive and symmetric*. (R is symmetric if, whenever (u, v), one also has $R(v, u)$.) The system S5 is sound with respect to the class of models in which R is *reflexive, transitive, and symmetric*; that is, in which R is an 'equivalence' relation.

Furthermore, the system K4 is sound with respect to the class of models in which R is transitive. There is also a soundness result for the system G; but the crucial property of the R-relation is more complex. G is sound with respect to the class of models in which R is transitive and there is no infinite sequence of worlds w_1, w_2, w_3,... such that $R(w_1, w_2)$, and $R(w_2, w_3)$ and ....

It is important to note that if a system is sound with respect to a class of models, it by no means follows that these are the only models in which the theorems of the system are all valid. In the case of T, for example, there are certainly models which are not reflexive, yet in which all the theorems of T are valid.

3.2 Completeness and Canonical Models

The system K is complete with respect to the class of *all* modal models. This is to say that every WFF that is valid—that is, valid in every model—is a theorem of the system K.

The fundamental idea behind a proof of completeness is familiar from nonmodal propositional and predicate logic. The aim is to show that every WFF that is not a theorem is not valid. Then, one notes that A is not a theorem if and only if $\sim$A is consistent (that is, no contradiction can be proved from $\sim$A), and that A is not valid if and only if $\sim$A is satisfiable. So, to demonstrate completeness, it is sufficient to show that if a WFF is consistent, then it is satisfiable—which, in the case of modal systems, means that it is true at some world in some model. Usually, the aim is to prove a stronger result; namely, that if a *set* of WFFs Σ is consistent, then there is a world in some model such that all the WFFs in Σ are true at that world. Such a world is said to satisfy Σ. In this statement of 'strong completeness,' the set Σ may be infinite.

In the case of normal modal systems, it is possible to establish an even stronger completeness result. In the case of the system K, for example, it can be shown that there is a single modal model—the 'canonical model' for K—with the property that each set of WFFs Σ that is consistent in K is satisfied by some world in that model. (The method of canonical models was introduced by Lemmon and Scott (1977); for a later exposition, see Hughes and Cresswell (1984).)

Clearly, the existence of this canonical model for K shows that K is complete with respect to the class of all modal models. The method of canonical models can also be applied to T, to yield a model in which each set of WFFs that is consistent in T is satisfied by some world. Furthermore, this canonical model for T is a reflexive model; and that suffices to show that T is complete with respect to the class of reflexive models. In a similar way, the method of canonical models can be used to show that the systems K4, S4, B, and S5 are complete with respect to the classes of models in which the R-relation is transitive (K4), reflexive and transitive (S4), reflexive and symmetric (B), and an equivalence relation (S5) respectively.

The application of the method of canonical models to the system G is more indirect (Boolos 1979). But for each of the other systems, this establishes a class

of modal models with respect to which the system is both sound and complete.

3.3 Characterization and Frames

For each of the six modal systems K, K4, T, S4, B, and S5, there is a class of models that exactly characterizes the system, in the sense that the theorems of the system are exactly the WFFs that are valid in all models in that class. Furthermore, in each case, the class of models is defined in terms of a condition upon the R-relation (or no condition in the case of K).

However, quite generally, there will be many different classes of models that characterize the same system. The system K, for example, is characterized by the class of all modal models. But it is also characterized by the class of all models in which the R-relation is irreflexive; that is, in which, for each world w, w is not R-related to itself.

The system T is characterized by the class of reflexive models, but—as already noted—there are models for T in which the R-relation is not reflexive. So, the class of models in which all the theorems of T are valid is more inclusive than the class of reflexive models. The canonical model for T is, of course, a model for T, and so belongs to this more inclusive class; so, for each WFF that is not a theorem of T, there is a model in the class in which that WFF is not valid. Consequently, the class of all models for T characterizes the system T. Similarly, it can be seen that the class of models comprising just the canonical model for T characterizes the system T. In fact, for any normal modal system, the class of all models for the system, and the class comprising just the canonical model for the system, will each characterize the system.

The class of reflexive models is far from being the unique class of models that characterizes the system T. In particular, it has been seen that a class including nonreflexive models characterizes T. The discussion now introduces the notion of a frame: a pair $\langle W, R \rangle$, where W is a set (the set of possible worlds) and R is a binary relation on W (the accessibility relation). A WFF of propositional modal logic is 'valid on a frame' $\langle W, R \rangle$ if it is valid in every model $\langle W, R, V \rangle$ based upon that frame. A frame $\langle W, R \rangle$ is said to be a 'frame for a modal system' if every theorem of that system is valid on $\langle W, R \rangle$.

It is possible to show that if $\langle W, R, V \rangle$ is a non-reflexive model for T, then there is another model $\langle W, R, V' \rangle$ on the same frame $\langle W, R \rangle$ in which some theorem of T is not valid. Thus, if $\langle W, R \rangle$ is a frame for T, then R is reflexive (in which case the frame is also said to be reflexive). As a consequence, one can say not only that the class of reflexive frames characterizes T, but also that the class of reflexive frames is the most inclusive class of frames that characterizes T.

Similarly, it is also possible to show that any frame

for K4 is transitive, any frame for S4 is reflexive and transitive, any frame for B is reflexive and symmetric, and any frame for S5 is reflexive, symmetric, and transitive. A great deal of work in modal logic is concerned with the characterization of modal systems by classes of frames (Hughes and Cresswell 1984).

3.4 Simpler Semantics for S5

The system S5 is characterized by the class of models $\langle W, R, V \rangle$ (and by the class of all frames $\langle W, R \rangle$) in which R is an equivalence relation. An equivalence relation divides its domain—the set of worlds W in this case—into equivalence classes: the worlds in one equivalence class are R-related to each other and to no worlds outside that equivalence class. It is straightforward to show that S5 is characterized by the class of models in which R is an equivalence relation with only one equivalence class.

The system S5 is clearly sound with respect to this class of models. It is also complete with respect to this class; but this cannot be established directly by the method of canonical models. The canonical model for S5 contains more than one equivalence class, since for a sentence letter p both the set $\{\Box p\}$ and the set $\{\sim p\}$ are consistent. Therefore, in the canonical model, there will be a world w_1 at which $\Box p$ is true, and a world w_2 at which $\sim p$ is true. But then w_1 and w_2 must be in different equivalence classes, since the truth of $\Box p$ at w_1 requires the truth of p at every world that is R-related to w_1.

However, suppose that Σ is a set of WFFs that is consistent in S5. Then there is a world w in the canonical model for S5 at which all the WFFs in Σ are evaluated as true. The evaluation of WFFs at w depends only upon the evaluation of WFFs at other worlds that are accessible from w. Consequently, it would make no difference to the evaluation of WFFs at w if one were to remove from the canonical model all those worlds that lie outside the equivalence class to which w belongs. If one removed all those worlds, then one would be left with a model with only one equivalence class, containing a world w at which all the WFFs in Σ are evaluated as true. Consequently, for every consistent set of WFFs Σ, there is a model with only one equivalence class, containing a world w that satisfies Σ.

If a model contains only one equivalence class, then every world is accessible from every other world, and so there is no need to specify the accessibility relation separately. Consequently, a 'simple S5 model' is a pair $\langle W, V \rangle$, where W is a set of worlds, and V is a function from ordered pairs of sentence letters and worlds to truth-values. The valuation V is extended to an evaluation of each WFF as true or false at each world just as before, save that $\Box A$ is true at a world w if and only if A is true at *every world in W*. Thus, in the case of S5, one returns to the original Leibnizian idea that necessary truth is truth in all possible worlds.

It has already been noted that the axioms of S5 are plausibly valid for the notion of metaphysical, or broadly logical, necessity. Simple S5 models are typically used as the semantic basis for philosophical discussions of necessity (Plantinga 1974; Forbes 1985). However, these discussions cannot proceed very far without the resources of quantified modal logic.

4. Quantified Modal Logic

Suppose that modal operators are added to the language of predicate logic, while still allowing '$\Box$' the same privileges of occurrence as '$\sim$.' Then, not only sentences of the form $\Box(\exists x)F(x)$ are permitted, where the '$\Box$' has a complete sentence within its scope, but also sentences of the form $(\exists x)\Box F(x)$, where the '$\Box$' has only an open sentence within its scope.

Quine (1960; 1976) points out that this—the third 'grade of modal involvement'—is only very dubiously intelligible if the modal operator is properly conceived as expressing a property of sentences. If the property of sentences is expressed by a predicate 'Nec,' then the problem can be seen very clearly by considering an expression of the form $(\exists x)Nec('F(x)')$. For here, the used quantifier does not bind the mentioned variable, and so is vacuous.

The only circumstances in which this problem can clearly be overcome are those in which each object in the domain of quantification has a uniquely canonical name. In those circumstances, a sentence of the form $(\exists x)\Box F(x)$ can be interpreted as saying that there is an object z such that the property expressed by 'Nec' applies to the sentence of the form F(n) that results by replacing the variable with the canonical name of z. One case in which these requirements are met is provided by the language of arithmetic, where each natural number has a numeral as its canonical name. Consequently, the use of modal logic in the study of provability can proceed from the propositional modal system G to the corresponding quantified modal system, without any risk from Quinean objections.

Where there are not uniquely canonical names, quantification into the scope of a modal operator cannot be rendered intelligible in this way, and so the conception of the modal operator as expressing a property of sentences must be given up. Quine's objection to this is that it leads to 'Aristotelian essentialism': the doctrine that an object has some of its properties essentially, and others only contingently. For a sentence of the form $(\exists x)\Box F(x)$ says that there is an object that necessarily has such-and-such a property. Quine (1976: 175) also notes that in quantified modal logic one will almost inevitably obtain the theorem

$$(\forall x)(\forall y)(x = y \supset \Box(x = y))$$

which says that 'identity holds necessarily if it holds at all.'

These two features of quantified modal logic—that it is committed to the intelligibility of essentialist claims and to the necessity of identity—are regarded by Quine as unattractive. However, in philosophical use of quantified modal logic (particularly following Kripke 1980), they are accepted as foundational.

4.1 Model-theoretic Semantics for Quantified Modal Logic

The key idea in the semantics for quantified modal logic is once again that of a possible world. In the case of propositional modal logic, each world was associated with an assignment of truth-values to sentence letters and then—by an induction on the complexity of WFFs—with an evaluation of every WFF as true or false. In the case of quantified modal logic, each world must be associated with a domain of objects and an interpretation of each constant and atomic predicate in that domain. In effect, each world determines a structure that is a model for the corresponding nonmodal predicate calculus language. Given that structure, a complex WFF can be evaluated as true or false (relative to a sequence of objects assigned to free variables). If the modal system is a quantified version of S5, then $\Box$A will be true at a world if A is true at every world. (For a brief discussion of the axiomatization and model theory for quantified versions of S5 and other modal systems, see Hughes and Cresswell 1984: ch. 9).

A version of the semantics for quantified S5 can be sketched by first making two simplifying assumptions. First, one assumes that every object in the domain has at least one name in the predicate calculus language to which the modal operator '$\Box$' is added. Second, one ignores the fact that which objects exist is itself a contingent matter. That is, one ignores the fact that different worlds should have different domains of objects associated with them, and assumes that the domain is the same for all worlds in the set W.

With these assumptions in place, a quantified S5 model (with fixed domain) is said to be a triple $\langle W, D, I \rangle$, where W is a set of worlds, D is a domain of objects, and I is an interpretation function. The function I maps constants (names) to objects in D, and maps each ordered pair of a closed atomic WFF and a world to a truth-value. Thus, I determines an extension for each atomic predicate at each world. The extension of I to an evaluation of each closed WFF as true or false at each world is then straightforward. The truth-functional connectives and the modal operator are treated just as in the case of the simple semantics for propositional S5. The quantifiers are treated just as in the case of nonmodal predicate calculus when every object in the domain has a name. Thus, for example, $(\exists x)C(x)$ is true at a world w if and only if some substitution instance C(m) is true at w. Because of the second assumption, all instances of the schema

$$(\forall x)\Box F(x) \supset \Box(\forall x)F(x) \qquad (13)$$

(the Barcan formula; Marcus 1962) and the schema

$$\Box(\forall x)F(x) \supset (\forall x)\Box F(x) \qquad (14)$$

(the converse Barcan formula) are valid.

Once the first assumption is removed, the notion of truth needs to be replaced with that of satisfaction by sequences, or truth relative to an assignment of objects to free variables, just as in the case of nonmodal predicate calculus.

More importantly, once the second assumption is removed, one is faced with several choices. Suppose that a quantified S5 model (with varying domain) is said to be a triple $\langle W, d, I \rangle$ where d is now a function from worlds in w to sets of objects. Thus, d(w) is the domain of the world w; intuitively, the set of objects that exist at w. One lets $D = \bigcup \{d(w): w \in W\}$ (and simplifies the description of the choices by retaining the first assumption: every object in D has a name in the language).

The first choice to be faced concerns atomic predicates. The question is whether the interpretation function I should assign to each atomic predicate, at world w, an extension in the set D, or an extension that lies wholly within the domain of w, d(w). The standard presentations of model-theoretic semantics for quantified modal logic (Kripke 1963; Fine 1978) do not impose the restriction that the extension of an atomic predicate at world w should lie within the domain of w. Thus they allow that, so far as the model theory is concerned, an atomic sentence of the form Fm may be true at a world even though the object named by m does not exist at that world. The opposite choice would correspond to the requirement that an atomic sentence should be false at a world if any of the objects named in it fails to exist at that world. This requirement is called the 'falsehood principle.'

The second choice to be faced concerns the quantifiers. In the evaluation of WFFS as true or false at a world w, the question is whether the quantifiers should be interpreted as ranging over the domain of that world, d(w), or as ranging over the larger set D. The standard presentations have the quantifiers ranging only over d(w). This is sometimes called the 'actualist' interpretation of the quantifiers. The opposite choice is the 'possibilist' interpretation (see Forbes (1988) for detailed discussion).

Given the actualist interpretation of the quantifiers, the Barcan formula at (13) above is not generally valid. Intuitively, the reason is as follows. It may be that all the objects that exist at world w have a certain property P at every world, but that at some world w' there are other objects that lack the property P.

The third choice to be faced concerns the modal operators. In the evaluation of modal WFFS as true or false at a world, the question is whether the truth of $\Box$A should require the truth of A at every world or only the truth of A at every world in which the objects named in A exist. In standard presentations, the former option is taken, so that '$\Box$' expresses *strong necessity*. On the latter option, '$\Box$' expresses *weak necessity* (see Davies 1978). One apparent advantage of the 'weak necessity' option is that it permits a very direct formulation of typical essentialist claims. The claim that Socrates is necessarily human, for example, is the claim that it is not possible that Socrates should exist without being human. One disadvantage is that the 'weak necessity' option provides no way of expressing claims of necessary existence.

Given the actualist interpretation of the quantifiers, and the interpretation of '□' as expressing strong necessity, the converse Barcan formula at (14) above also fails. Intuitively, the reason is as follows. It may be that, for every world w, all the objects that exist at w have a certain property P at w, but that some object that exists at a world w' fails to exist at another world w'' and furthermore lacks property P at w''.

See also: Formal Semantics; Necessity; Possible Worlds.

Bibliography

Åqvist L 1984 Deontic logic. In: Gabbay D, Guenthner F 1984

Boolos G 1979 *The Unprovability of Consistency*. Cambridge University Press, Cambridge

Boolos G, Jeffrey R 1989 *Computability and Logic*, 3rd edn. Cambridge University Press, Cambridge

Bull R, Segerberg K 1984 Basic modal logic. In: Gabbay D, Guenthner F 1984

Chellas B F 1980 *Modal Logic: An Introduction*. Cambridge University Press, Cambridge

Davies M K 1978 Weak necessity and truth theories. *Journal of Philosophical Logic* 7: 415–39

Fine K 1978 Model theory for modal logic. Part I: The *de re/de dicto* distinction. *Journal of Philosophical Logic* 7: 125–56

Forbes G 1985 *The Metaphysics of Modality*. Oxford University Press, Oxford

Forbes G 1988 *Languages of Possibility: An Essay in Philosophical Logic*. Basil Blackwell, Oxford

Gabbay D, Guenthner F 1984 *Handbook of Philosophical Logic*, vol. 2. *Extensions of Classical Logic*. Reidel, Dordrecht

Hughes G E, Cresswell M J 1968 *An Introduction to Modal Logic*. Methuen, London

Hughes G E, Cresswell M J 1984 *A Companion to Modal Logic*. Methuen, London

Kripke S A 1963 Semantic considerations on modal logic. *Acta Philosphica Fennica* 16: 83–94

Kripke S A 1980 *Naming and Necessity*. Basil Blackwell, Oxford

Lemmon E J, Scott D S 1977 *The 'Lemmon Notes': An Introduction to Modal Logic*. Basil Blackwell, Oxford

Lewis C I 1912 Implication and the algebra of logic. *Mind* 21: 522–31

Lewis C I, Langford C H 1932 *Symbolic Logic*. Century, New York. 2nd edn., 1959, Dover, New York

Marcus R B 1962 Interpreting quantification. *Inquiry* 5: 252–59

Montague R 1963 Syntactical treatments of modality. *Acta Philosophica Fennica* 16: 153–67

Plantinga A 1974 *The Nature of Necessity*. Oxford University Press, Oxford

Quine W V O 1960 *Word and Object*. MIT Press, Cambridge, MA

Quine W V O 1976 Three grades of modal involvement. In: *The Ways of Paradox and Other Essays*. Harvard University Press, Cambridge, MA

Smiley T J 1963 The logical basis of ethics. *Acta Philosophica Fennica* 16: 237–46

Montague Grammar

T. M. V. Janssen

Montague grammar is a model for grammar that deals with the syntax and semantics of natural language. The emphasis lies on phenomena that are interesting from a semantic point of view (see Sect. 2). A salient aspect of Montague grammar is its methodology, which is characterized by the principle of compositionality of meaning (Sect. 3). This methodology has as a consequence that there is a systematic relation between syntax and semantics: though distinct, they are forced to remain in step with each other. Montague grammar constituted a fundamentally new approach to the semantics of natural language because of this systematic relation and the application of methods from mathematical logic (Sect. 1). Semantics is, in Montague grammar, model-theoretic semantics (Sect. 4). Meanings are formalized as intensions (Sect. 5), and represented using intensional logic (Sect. 6). An impression of Montague's most influential article (Montague 1973) is given in Sects. 6 and 7. An overview of the subsequent developments is given in Sect. 8.

1. Historical Background

Montague grammar emerged around 1970, and constituted a fundamentally new approach to the semantics of natural language. In order to understand the importance of this approach, it is useful to consider the situation in that period of some neighboring disciplines of semantics: philosophy of language, philosophical logic, and linguistics. These subjects are considered below, a more extended picture of the historical background is given by Partee and Hendricks (1977).

One of the subjects studied in philosophy of language was meanings of natural language, and these were (before 1970) sometimes represented in some or other logic. The mapping between a sentence and its logical representation was made in an ad hoc way: it was more or less stipulated which formula was the correct meaning representation of a given sentence. The situation could be characterized as follows: a 'bilingual logician,' who knew logic and who knew a natural language, provided the formula. It was noticed that there could be a large difference between the sentence and the formula, and a dominant view of these matters at that time was the so-called 'misleading form thesis,' saying that there is a sharp distinction between the grammatical and the logical form of sentences, and that the grammatical form disguises the logical form to such an extent that they cannot be related in a systematic way. It was sometimes even proposed to design for certain purposes an improved version of natural language in which the form does not obscure the meaning.

In philosophical logic, there has always been an interest in philosophically interesting notions that occur in natural language, such as 'necessarily' and 'possibly.' Axiom systems for these notions were designed which expressed their properties. A jungle of systems of modal logics arose, motivated by different properties of embeddings of these notions. Kripke brought about, in the mid-1960s, an enormous change in this field. He introduced semantic models for modal logics, thereby making it possible to conceive modal logic in the same way as mathematical logic: as a formal language with a model-theoretic semantics. The variety of systems could be structured by conceiving them as expressing relations between possible worlds in a model.

Around 1960, Chomsky brought about great changes in linguistics by introducing mathematical standards of explicitness. He developed the tools for this (context-free grammars and transformations), and syntax became a flourishing branch of linguistics. There was some attention to semantic issues, such as whether transformations were meaning-preserving, or what would be the input for a semantic component, but the theory was a theory about syntax that did not deal explicitly with semantics.

These three lines were brought together by Richard Montague. He was a mathematical logician who had made important contributions to the foundations of set theory. He was attracted by Chomsky's formal treatment of natural language, but unsatisfied by its (lack of) treatment of semantics. Therefore he developed an alternative to the Chomskyan approach

that satisfied his (logical) standards. He presented a fragment of English and provided it with a rigorous model-theoretic interpretation. Most important is the fact that the relation between a sentence and its meaning is defined in a systematic way. It became possible, for the first time in history, to calculate which meaning is associated with any given sentence, hence to make predictions concerning semantics.

By developing his grammar model, Montague provided evidence for his opinion that there is no important theoretical difference between natural languages and the languages studied by logicians: both can be dealt with using the same methods and with the same mathematical rigor (Montague 1970a: 189; Montague 1970b: 313; Thomason 1974: 188, 222). The title of one of Montague's first publications on this subject provides clear evidence of his position: 'English as a formal language' (Montague 1970a).

2. Aims

The aim of Montague grammar is to describe, predict, and explain semantic relations between natural language utterances, an aim it shares with other theories of grammar that deal with semantics. In the present section, some important semantic relations between natural language utterances will be introduced by means of examples, viz. entailment, valid reasoning, synonymy, and ambiguity. The examples given here are realistic in the sense that they are treated within the field of Montague grammar, thus giving an impression of the variety of phenomena that are studied. The examples that occur without reference are within the fragment of Montague (1973), or are variants of his examples.

An important semantic relation is the 'entailment' relation between sentences, say A and B. This means that whenever A is accepted as being true, B must also be accepted as being true, on grounds of meaning properties. Sentence (1) entails sentence (2):

Mary is singing and dancing. (1)

Mary is singing. (2)

This entailment, however, does not hold for all grammatical subjects: witness (3) and (4), where in fact the inverse relationship holds.

No-one is singing and dancing. (3)

No-one is singing. (4)

This means that the noun phrases have to be divided into two classes, one for which the entailment holds, and one for which it does not. Then one would like to have an explanation of why precisely *two girls* and *both girls* are in different classes (*Both/precisely two girls were singing and dancing*), and a prediction concerning compound terms like *few girls and many boys*. For an overview of properties of quantified noun phrases, see Keenan and Westerstahl 1997.

An example of a different nature is the following: (5) entails (6) (see Dowty 1979):

> John cools the soup. (5)

> The soup cools. (6)

Here, one would like to have a description of the relation between the meaning of *cool* as a transitive causative verb and *cool* as an intransitive verb. And one would like to know why the implication holds for *boil* but not for *stir*.

A 'valid reasoning' is a generalization of entailment that involves more sentences than two. If someone accepts (7) and (8), they may conclude correctly (9):

> John sings. (7)

> John is a man. (8)

> A man sings. (9)

A more intricate example is (Groenendijk and Stokhof 1982):

> John knows whether Mary comes. (10)

> Mary comes. (11)

> John knows that Mary comes. (12)

Here, one sees that there is a relation between the meaning of the *whether* clause and the *that* clause. It seems that the latter is weaker. However, the relation is more complicated: if one has the negated version (11a), then (12a) follows from (10) and (11a).

> John knows whether Mary comes. (10)

> Mary does not come. (11a)

> John knows that Mary does not come. (12a)

Hence the relation between the *whether* clause and the *that* clause depends on the factual situation.

A special case of entailment is 'synonymy.' Sentences are called synonymous just in case they entail each other. For example, sentences (13) and (14) are synonymous:

> John or Mary comes. (13)

> John comes or Mary comes. (14)

Another example of synonymy is (Partee and Bach 1981):

> Mary admires herself, and Sue does too. (15)

> Mary admires herself, and Sue admires herself. (16)

It may seem that the meaning of the *does too* clause can be found by the substitution of a phrase that occurs elsewhere in the sentence. This is, however, not always the case. It is, for instance, possible to conclude from (17) to (18).

> Mary believes that she is ill, and Sue does too. (17)

> Mary believes that she is ill, and Sue believes that Mary is ill. (18)

This illustrates the important phenomenon of 'ambiguity.' Sometimes a sentence can be understood in two or more ways corresponding with distinct consequences. From (17), one may either conclude that

> Sue believes that Mary is ill (19)

or that

> Sue believes that she (= Sue) is ill. (203)

Another example of ambiguity is (e.g., Janssen 1983, 1986b):

> Ten years ago, John met the president of the USA. (21)

> The president of the USA is Bush. (22)

On the one reading of (21), one may conclude that ten years ago John met Mr Bush. On the other reading, this does not follow since John met the person who was president ten years ago. This ambiguity clearly concerns the functioning of tense operators.

The decision whether a sentence is ambiguous or vague is not always clear. Consider (23):

> Two girls ate five sandwiches. (23)

One may ask what counts as a source of semantic ambiguity; if it makes a difference whether they shared all five sandwiches; whether the sandwiches were distributed between the girls; or if it makes a difference whether they ate together or whether each girl ate on her own. Maybe the issue would be more exciting if the sentence was *Two girls shot five men* and one had to judge the girls. Verkuyl and Van der Does (1996) argue that (23) has one meaning, whereas they refer to other authors who argue for a fourfold or even ninefold ambiguity.

So far, only examples of relations between declarative sentences have been cited. Other types of sentences take part in 'other semantic relations,' as between the questions (24) and (25):

> Which girls came to the party? (24)

> Did Mary come to the party? (25)

In this example, there is nothing like the acceptance of a premise or of a conclusion. Nevertheless, there is a relation: every answer to the first implies an answer to the second question. The meanings assigned to these questions should account for this (Groenendijk and Stokhof 1989).

Sequences of sentences likewise have logical properties. Consider (26) and (27).

> A man walks in the park. He whistles. (26)

> A man in the park whistles. (27)

This example puts a requirement on the treatment of texts. The meaning of the two sentences together should be equivalent to the meaning of the single sentence.

All examples discussed in this section have the common feature that they do not depend on specific details of the meanings of the words involved (except for logically crucial words such as *not* or *and*). It is, for example, possible to account for the inference from (1) *Mary is singing and dancing* to (2) *Mary is dancing* without describing the differences between *dancing, jogging,* and *walking.* Each of the examples can be replaced by another which exhibits the same pattern but uses other words. The examples illustrate that in Montague grammar one is mainly interested in structural aspects of the semantic relations between sentences, that is, in the systematic aspects of meaning. The formalization of what meanings are does not need to go further than is required for an adequate account of these structural aspects.

3. The Compositional Approach

The most salient aspect of Montague grammar is the systematic way in which natural language expressions are connected with their respective meanings. This relation is characterized by the principle of compositionality of meaning. Such a principle can, in several formulations, be found in many disciplines that deal with semantics, such as linguistics, philosophy, and computer science. In philosophy of language, it has a long tradition and is often called 'Frege's principle.' The version of this principle that describes the method of Montague grammar most explicitly is (Partee, et al. 1990: 318):

> The meaning of a compound expression is a function of the meanings of its parts and of the syntactic rules by which they are combined.

The formulation of the principle contains several vague terms, and a proper application of the principle requires a more formal interpretation (for a discussion of the principle, its formalization, consequences, and its status, see *Compositionality of Meaning*). The main points of its formalization are summarized here.

The syntax of the grammar consists of rules which express how new expressions can be formed from already available ones. The rules are, therefore, operations which act on inputs and yield an output. If an expression E is the output of the application of a rule R, then the inputs that form E are defined as being the parts of E in that derivation. The semantic component is organized in a parallel way: there are semantic rules that operate on input meanings and yield an output meaning. The crucial factor for obeying compositionality is that there is a strict correspondence between syntax and semantics. For each syntactic rule, there should be a corresponding semantic rule expressing the semantic effect of that syntactic rule. Compositionality is taken to be not an empirically verifiable property of natural language but a methodological principle: it constrains the organization of the grammar.

Consider example (28):

Penguins do not fly. (28)

A very simple grammar will be considered, naively as regards its meaning. For example, it will be assumed that the sentence says something about all penguins, whereas plurals without article usually have a more subtle meaning. The intention of this example is, however, only to illustrate the *method* of compositionality.

Suppose the grammar has as basic expressions the plural noun phrase *penguins* and the verb *fly.* A rule (say R1) forms the verb phrase *do not fly* from this verb. Furthermore, there is a rule (R2) combining a noun phrase with a verb phrase to form a sentence, by concatenating them and performing the required changes in the verb phrase for agreement and similar trimmings. Then sentence (28) has, according to this grammar, two parts: *penguins* and *do not fly,* and the latter phrase has in turn one part: *fly.*

This derivation might be represented in the form of a tree, as in Fig. 1. Note that this tree does not depict the constituent structure of the sentence; for example, there are no separate nodes for *do* and *not.* The tree shows how the sentence is formed; it is a construction tree or derivation tree. There is no a priori reason why the derivation would be identical to the constituent structure of the result (one might impose this as an additional requirement).

Of course, there might be good arguments for preferring a different grammar. Thus, one might construct (28) out of the positive sentence *Penguins fly* or, alternatively, from *penguins, fly,* and *not.* In the former case the rule has one part, and in the latter case three parts. Compositionality as such provides no criterion for such issues. The best choice is probably to be discovered by considering more examples and larger fragments.

The principle of compositionality states that the meaning of the sentence is a function of the meanings of its parts, hence (according to the given grammar) of *penguins* and *do not fly.* Of course, the meaning of the latter is, in turn, a function of the meaning of its part *fly.* So, in the end, the meanings of the basic expressions are attained. Adopting for the moment a very simple conception of meaning that will be revised in the next section, one can take the meaning of *fly* to be the set of individuals who fly, and the meaning of *penguins* to be the set of individuals who are penguins.

According to the rules, the verb phrase *do not fly*

Figure 1.

has only *fly* as a part, and therefore the meaning of this verb phrase has to be formed out of the meaning of *fly*. So there has to be a semantic operation that expresses the meaning of negating a verb. For the moment, the meaning of *do not fly* is, in analogy of that of *fly,* the set of individuals who do not fly. The operation that forms this meaning from the meaning of *fly* is the formation of a set complement. In line with the above assumptions about meaning, one may say that the sentence means that the set of penguins is included in the set of nonflying individuals. This meaning is to be obtained from the meanings of its parts: from the set of penguins, and from the set of individuals who do not fly. This can indeed be done.

The situation is as follows. Two syntactic rules (R1 and R2) are each accompanied by a semantic interpretation (M1 and M2 respectively):

R1: negating a verb
M1: complement formation
R2: concatenating a noun phrase with a verb phrase, performing agreement changes
M2: set inclusion

In this section, the method of compositionality has been exemplified. The crucial aspect is the correspondence between syntax and semantics. One might change the concept of meaning used above (as will be done in Sect. 5), or change the syntax used (see Sect. 7); but as long as the correspondence remains intact, the grammar can be seen as an instance of Montague grammar. This characterization of Montague's method is given in a formal mathematical terminology in his paper 'Universal grammar' (Montague 1970b).

4. Interpretation in a Model

In Montague grammar, as well as in all other formal theories of semantics, the natural language expressions are interpreted in a class of abstract models. For example, a name like *John* is associated with an individual in such models, and an adjective like *brave* is a property. Each model is constructed out of a number of basic sets by means of standard constructions, and the result can be restricted by 'meaning postulates.' The most characteristic feature of the models in Montague grammar is the distinction made between the 'extension' of an expression and its 'intension,' a distinction that will be the topic of the next section. In the present section, the status of the model and its connection with natural language will be considered.

The model in which humans interpret natural languages has, of course, a certain resemblance to the real world, but it should not be conceived of as a model of the real world. There are two differences. First, in language, one speaks not only about the real world, past, present, and future, but also about situations that might be the case. Even though uni-

corns do not exist, one can speak about them, and the sentences used have semantic properties that should be dealt with. The model thus embraces much more than reality.

Second, as far as the model is connected with reality, it is a model of how natural language 'conceives' of it. This conception might be different from the real situation. Examples are mass nouns like *water* or *air*. In natural language, they are used in a different way from count nouns such as *chair* or *flower*. The mass noun *water* is used as if every part of a quantity of water is again water; as if it had no minimal parts. The same holds for *air*. Although in reality water has minimal molecules, and air is a mixture, the model will not reflect that fact (Bunt 1979).

Although the model does not reflect reality, one can be interested in the relation which it has with reality. Examples are the relation between *blue* and the frequencies of light, or the number of exceptions accepted when it is said that *all ravens are black*. This kind of research is rare in Montague grammar, however, because it amounts to the analysis of specific words, whereas in Montague grammar one is mainly interested in the more structural aspects of the semantics of natural language.

The model, not being a model of reality, might be regarded as a model of how the human mind conceives reality. Although psychological reality is not one of the claims of Montague grammar (it is so in some other theories), the issue has received some attention (Partee 1977; Dowty 1979: ch. 8).

The connection between natural language and the model can be made in two ways. One method, the direct one, was followed in Sect. 3: for a word, some element (set, function) in the model is given as the meaning of that word, and for a syntactic rule a corresponding meaning operation is given. This method is used in Montague's first publication (Montague 1970a), and in a few other publications as well (e.g., Keenan and Faltz 1985). The other method is the indirect one: natural language is translated into some logical language, which is interpreted in a model. If this translation is compositional, and the interpretation of the logical language is compositional, then the combination of the two processes is a compositional process of meaning assignment. Care has to be taken that the logic is used as an auxiliary language only, so that this intermediate language can in principle be eliminated. This implies that every operation that is performed in the logic should have an interpretation in the model. This indirect method is the standard method in Montague grammar; usually, (variants of) intensional logic are used as the intermediate language.

5. Extension and Intension

An important decision concerns the question of how to model meaning. In Sect. 3, the meaning of *penguins* was defined as the set of penguins, and of *fly* as the set of flying individuals. Applying the same approach to *the president of the USA* (example (22), Sect. 2) would yield as meaning the individual Clinton, and applied to *unicorn* (assuming there are none) the empty set. This approach would, however, give results that are intuitively incorrect. It would have the consequence that in case neither unicorns nor centaurs exist, the meaning of *unicorn* would be equal to the meaning of *centaur*. As for *the president of the USA*, it would have the undesirable consequence that its meaning changes after each election. Examples like these have led to the distinction between two kinds of interpretation: extension and intension.

At the time of writing, the president of the USA is Mr Clinton, but at other moments in time a different person will be president, and in another course of events Mr Clinton could have lost the election and Mr Dole would be president. The model in which natural language is interpreted has components dealing with this. It has a collection of time points for dealing with changes in the course of time, and it has a collection of so-called 'possible worlds.' These possible worlds represent the possibility that Dole has won. They also represent the possibility that unicorns exist. Intensions are functions with possible worlds and time points as domain. The intension of *the president of the USA* is a function from time points and possible worlds that yields an individual (the president at that moment in that possible world), and the intension of *unicorn* is the function that yields for each possible world and time point a set of individuals (the unicorns). The extension of an expression is the value of the intension function with respect to a given world and time point, for example, the moment now in the actual world. Then the extension of *the president* is the president now (Mr Clinton), and the extension of *unicorn* is the actual set of unicorns. The extension of a sentence is traditionally identified with its truth value. Thus, the extension of *John kisses Mary* is true just in case John kisses Mary. The intension is the function which says, for each possible world, in which moments John kisses Mary.

Since there are possible worlds in which there are unicorns but no centaurs, the words *unicorn* and *centaur* have different intensions. As a consequence, sentences (29) and (30) will have different intensions too.

John seeks a unicorn. (29)

John seeks a centaur. (30)

Thus, using intensions, the nonsynonymy of (29) and (30) can be accounted for. For this purpose, no further information concerning relations between different possible worlds is needed, nor any information concerning relations between time points. This holds for all examples mentioned in Sect. 2, and therefore the set of possible worlds and the set of time points are usually introduced as just one set, without further specification. This is, however, not always sufficient.

If one is interested in tense phenomena in natural language, then more has to be said about the moments of time, for example that they are linearly ordered, and whether they are indivisible points or intervals with a duration. If one is interested in causatives (*John broke the glass*) or counterfactuals (*If Mary did not come, John would fly*), then the set of possible worlds needs more structure. For dealing with these phenomena, it is crucial to know how the world was just before the breaking of the glass, or which world resembles the present one except for the coming of Mary.

The above discussion shows that the formalization of the intuitive notion of meaning as intension is much better than as extension. However, intensions only deal with those aspects of meaning that have to do with truth and denotation, and neglect aspects such as style, new information versus old information, etc. Therefore, they can only be regarded as a restricted approximation of meaning. Even accepting this limitation, however, intensions are still not completely satisfactory. An important shortcoming concerns tautologies. Consider (31):

Bill comes or does not come. (31)

The intension of this sentence is the function that always yields 'true.' Hence (32) and (33) have the same intension:

John comes. (32)

John comes and Bill comes or does not come. (33)

This causes problems with embedded clauses. Sentences (34) and (35) will have the same intension, whereas they should not be equivalent since Mary's beliefs in (34) do not concern Bill; she may not even know about his existence.

Mary believes that John comes. (34)

Mary believes that John comes and that Bill comes or does not come. (35)

The conclusion is that intensions are not fine-grained enough to distinguish the meanings of sentences like (34) and (35). Several improvements have been proposed, such as structured intensions (Lewis 1970), and an approach based on partial functions (Muskens 1989).

6. A Small Fragment

This section considers as examples three sentences and their treatment. The treatment given in Montague (1973) will be followed, except for one detail (see Sect. 7). In the course of the presentation, some important features of intensional logic will be explained.

The sentences are:

John walks. (36a)

A man walks. (37a)

Every man walks. (38a)

These sentences are very simple, and it is easy to present their interpretation in traditional predicate logic:

walk(john) (36b)

$\exists x[man(x) \land walk(x)]$ (37b)

$\forall x[man(x) \rightarrow walk(x)]$ (38b)

One immediately sees that these three sentences are syntactically much alike (a subject and a verb), but the formulas in predicate logic are rather different: two with a quantifier (different ones!), and in each case another main operator ($\rightarrow$, $\land$, and predicate application). What makes it interesting to present these examples here is not the meaning assigned to them, but the fact that these very different meanings can be derived compositionally from the corresponding sentences.

All three sentences are built from a singular noun phrase and the verb *walks,* and for this reason one can design a syntactic rule that combines a noun phrase and a verb. Since in Montague grammar there is a correspondence between syntactic rules and semantic rules, one also has to design a rule that combines the meaning of the verb with the meaning of the noun phrase. This in turn requires that there be meanings for verbs and for noun phrases. These meanings will be discussed first, then the semantic rule will be designed.

As explained in Sect. 5, predicates are given intensions as meanings: functions from possible worlds and moments of time to sets of individuals. Thus, the intension, or meaning, of the verb *walk* is a function from possible worlds and moments of time to sets: for each possible world and each moment of time, there is a set (possibly empty) of individuals who walk. Such an intension is called a 'property.' For the noun phrases, it is more difficult to select a format that allows these meanings to be rendered uniformly. In order to keep the calculus going in a maximally uniform way, all noun phrase meanings should preferably be of the same type. This requirement is easily seen to be nontrivial, as, for example, the expression *every man* extends over sets of possibly many individuals, where *John* seems to refer to one individual only.

Montague, proposed (1973) to model the meaning of a noun phrase as a set ('bundle') of properties. An individual is, in this approach, characterized by the set of all its properties. This is possible since no two individuals share all their properties at the same time, if only because the two cannot be at the same place at the same time. This approach permits generalization over all noun phrases referring to (sets of) individuals (see also Lewis 1970).

Meanings of linguistic expressions (functions from world–time pairs to specific world extensions) are denoted by formulas in the language of intensional logic. The meaning of *John* will be denoted by:

$\lambda P[{}^\vee P(john)]$ (39)

To explain this formula, the variable

P (40)

is a variable over properties of individuals: P may be replaced, for example, by the property 'walking.' The expression

${}^\vee P$ (41)

denotes the extension of the property expressed by any predicate P in any given world at a given moment of time. Thus, for the actual world now,

${}^\vee P(john)$ (42)

is true if the predicate ${}^\vee P$ holds for John now, in this world, and false otherwise. Any property denoted by P can be abstracted by means of the lambda operator: λP. Lambda abstraction of P gives:

$\lambda P[{}^\vee P(john)]$ (43)

which is the same as (39) above. This expression denotes a function which says, for any property α, given a world–time pair $\langle w, t \rangle$, whether John belongs to the extension of that property in $\langle w, t \rangle$. Let this function be called X_j. Some properties of this function will now be investigated.

According to the definition of X_j,

$X_j(\alpha)$ is true iff α now holds for the individual (I)
John, i.e., iff $\alpha(john)$ is true, and false otherwise.

X_j is, therefore, the characteristic function of the set of properties that can be predicated of John. As usual in logic, this characteristic function can be identified with the set of properties that John has. X_j can therefore be seen as a formalization of the idea that the meaning of *John* is a set of properties.

This function X_j can be evaluated with, as argument, the property of being a man, that is, the function that yields for each index (i.e., for each world and time) the extension of the predicate *man*. The notation for this argument is:

${}^\wedge man$ (44)

The symbol ${}^\wedge$ translates the predicate *man* into the language of intensional logic, where ${}^\wedge man$ denotes the intension associated with *man*. X_j is now applied to this argument to obtain, using result (I),

$X_j({}^\wedge man)$ is true iff ${}^\wedge man$ now holds for the (II)
individual John, i.e., iff ${}^\vee{}^\wedge man(john)$ is true,
and false otherwise.

In the expression $X^j({}^\wedge man)$, X_j can be replaced by its original definition (viz. (43)). Then, (45) is obtained:

$$\lambda P[\check{\ }P(john)](\hat{\ }man) \tag{45}$$

Result (II) now states that this is equivalent with

$$\check{\ }\check{\ }man(john). \tag{46}$$

Thus, it has been shown, using semantic considerations, that it is allowed to substitute the argument $\hat{\ }man$ for the variable P, an operation known as 'lambda conversion.' According to the definitions given with (41) and (44), $\check{\ }\hat{\ }man$ denotes the present value of the property of being a man. Hence (46) and (45) are equivalent with (47)

$$man(john). \tag{47}$$

Summarizing, the variable P in (45) has been replaced with the property κman which is in the range of P, and $\check{\ }\hat{\ }man$ has been reduced to just *man*. As the operations concerned are admissible independently of the particular choice of the predicate *man*, the procedure can be generalized to all predicates of the same class (type).

To revert to the treatment of the simple sentence *John walks*, the syntax has, as stipulated earlier, a rule that combines a noun phrase with a verb to form a sentence. What is still needed is a semantic operation that matches the syntactic rule with its semantic consequences. The operation that does this is so-called 'function application': one of the two syntactic constituents acts as a function, while the other acts as argument (input). In this case, the verb meaning is allowed to act as the argument, and the noun phrase meaning as the function. The result of function application, in this case, is a function from world–time pairs to truth-values, or the set of world–time pairs where John walks.

According to the rule just given, the meaning of *John walks* is found by application of the meaning of *John*, that is, (43), to the meaning of *walk*. This is denoted by:

$$\lambda P[\check{\ }P(john)](\hat{\ }walk) \tag{48}$$

This, as seen above, can be reduced, in two steps, to:

$$walk(john) \tag{49}$$

which now gives the meaning representation aimed at.

For the other sentences, one proceeds analogously. The noun phrase *a man* is likewise translated as a set of properties:

$$\lambda P[\exists x[man(x) \wedge \check{\ }P(x)]] \tag{50}$$

This denotes the characteristic function of the set of properties such that for each property in the set there is a man that has that property. The sentence *A man walks* is then represented as:

$$\lambda P[\exists x[man(x) \wedge \check{\ }P(x)]](\hat{\ }walk) \tag{51}$$

which reduces to:

$$\exists x[man(x) \wedge walk(x)] \tag{52}$$

Analogously, every man walks is represented as:

$$\lambda P[\forall x[man(x) \rightarrow \check{\ }P(x)]](\hat{\ }walk) \tag{53}$$

or equivalently

$$\forall x[man(x) \rightarrow walk(x)] \tag{54}$$

This treatment illustrates some of the power of lambda abstraction and lambda conversion. The meaning of the verb is 'plugged into' the meaning of the noun phrase in the right position. Lambda calculus is frequently used in Montague grammar. Without the lambda operator, it would be impossible to maintain compositionality. Impressed by the power of lambdas, Barbara Partee once said: 'Lambdas really changed my life.' What has been, in the end, obtained as meaning representations for the three sentences discussed is nothing more than the formulas usually associated with them in elementary logic courses. There, however, they are found on intuitive grounds, whereas in Montague grammar they are the result of a formal system which relates syntax and semantics in a systematic way.

7. Some PTQ Phenomena

Montague worked out his ideas in a number of papers, the most influential of which is 'The proper treatment of quantification in ordinary English,' henceforth PTQ (Montague 1973). This paper deals with some semantic phenomena, all connected with quantifiers. Three such phenomena will be discussed here: identity and scope ambiguities (both presented here because they have been the subject of a great deal of discussion since the publication of PTQ), and the 'de dicto–de re' ambiguity, central to Montague grammar, and the origin of its trade mark, the unicorn.

The first phenomenon concerns problems with identity. Consider:

The price of one barrel is \$1.00.	(55)
The price of one barrel is rising.	(56)
\$1.00 is rising.	(57)

It is obvious that (57) must not be allowed to follow logically from (55) and (56), as \$1.00 will remain \$1.00 and will neither rise nor fall. The same phenomenon occurs with temperatures, names, telephone numbers, percentages, and in general with all nouns which may denote values. The PTQ treatment of such cases is as follows. Prices, numbers, etc. are treated as basic entities, just as persons and objects. The expression *the price of one barrel* is semantically a function that assigns to each world–time index a particular price. Such a function is called an 'individual concept.' In (55) an assertion is made about the present value of this function, but in (56) an assertion is made about a property of the function. Thus, the expression *the price of one barrel* is considered ambiguous between a value reading and a function reading. The difference in readings blocks the false conclusion (57).

In spite of criticisms, mainly related to the treatment of such nouns as basic entities (e.g., Bennett 1976), the notion of individual concepts also seems useful to account for cases like the following (Janssen 1984):

> The treasurer of the charity organization is the   (58)
> chairman of the hospital board.

> The treasurer of the charity organization has resigned.
>   (59)

> The chairman of the hospital board has resigned.   (60)

Here, substitution *salva veritate* of terms under an identity statement seems to be running into difficulty. Again, one can say that (58) is a statement about the identity of the values of two different functions at a given world–time index, whereas (59) is a statement about the function (in Frege's terms, about the *Wertverlauf*). Hence the nonvalidity of (60) as a conclusion.

The second phenomenon is scope ambiguity. Consider

> Every man loves a woman.   (61)

In PTQ, this sentence is considered to be ambiguous (though many linguists would disagree; see below). In the one reading, one particular woman is loved by all men, and in the other every man has at least one woman whom he loves. The first reading is given in (62), and is called the specific reading, or the wide scope reading for *a woman*. The second reading is given in (63); it is called the 'narrow scope reading.'

$$\exists x[woman(x) \wedge [\forall y\, man(y) \rightarrow love(y, x)]]   \quad (62)$$

$$\forall y[man(y) \rightarrow [\exists x\, woman(x) \wedge love(y, x)]]   \quad (63)$$

Many linguists consider (61) to be unambiguous. Well-known is the principle (Seuren 1969; Jackendoff 1972) which states that the most plausible reading is given by the surface order of the quantified NPs and of the negation. Following this principle, (61) has only one reading, viz. (63). Note that the reading expressed by (62) is a special case of (63). The principle has not remained unchallenged. Witness (64), where the most plausible reading is not given by the surface order.

> At the finish, a medal is available for all participants
> in the race.

There are other linguistic theories which also assign one reading to (62). But whether (61), the PTQ example, really is ambiguous is less relevant as long as there are sentences that do show scope ambiguities, which seems beyond doubt. For instance, in Sect. 2 an example involving tense was given (*Ten years ago, John met the president*). The machinery of PTQ for dealing with scope ambiguities is presented below.

Since the scope ambiguity does not seem to have a lexical source, the principle of compositionality of meaning requires the construction of two different derivations for the two readings. In PTQ, this is done as follows. First, the basic sentence (65) is formed, in which neither of the two noun phrases occurs but which contains indexed variables (*he$_n$*) instead:

> he$_1$ loves he$_2$.   (65)

Next, noun phrases are substituted for the variables. This can be done in two different orders. The noun phrase that is substituted last gets the widest reading. Thus, the specific reading (wide scope for *a woman*) is obtained from (65) by first forming (66):

> Every man loves he$_2$ (66)

and then

> Every man loves a woman.   (67)

These rules are called 'quantification rules.' The corresponding semantic rule leads to an interpretation equivalent to that of (62). For the other reading, the reverse order of quantifier substitution is used.

These quantification rules have met with some resistance from linguistic quarters, where they are looked upon as unusual creatures. Other solutions have been attempted, where the disambiguation is not done in the syntax. Cooper (1979) deals with scope phenomena in a separate component, a 'storage' mechanism. Hendriks (1987) uses rules which change the meaning of a noun phrase from a narrow scope reading to a wider scope reading.

The third phenomenon is the ambiguity of 'de dicto' versus 'de re' readings. To see the difference, first consider (68) and (69):

> John finds a unicorn.   (68)

> There is a unicorn that John finds.   (69)

Sentence (69) follows from (68). Yet (71) does not follow from (70):

> John seeks a unicorn.   (70)

> There is a unicorn that John seeks.   (71)

In fact, (70) is ambiguous between a specific reading in which there is a specific unicorn that John seeks, and an intensional reading where John is said to engage in the activity of seeking a unicorn and nothing is implied about the real existence of such animals. The latter reading is usually called the 'de dicto' reading ('de dicto': Latin for 'about what is said'). The former reading is the 'de re' reading ('de re': Latin for 'about the thing'). The ambiguity is accounted for, in principle, in the following way. In the 'de re' reading, a relation is asserted to hold between two individuals. The 'de dicto' reading establishes a relation between John and the set of properties of a unicorn (i.e., the interpretation of the noun phrase *a unicorn*). Whether this way of analyzing and accounting for the 'de dicto' reading is satisfactory in all respects is a question still widely debated (see e.g., Gamut 1991).

The two readings of *John seeks a unicorn* are obtained in the following way. For the 'de re' reading, a quantification rule introduces the expression *a unicorn*. And if the expression *a unicorn* is introduced directly, that is, without the intervention of a quantification rule, the result is the 'de dicto' reading. In principle, this method is analogous to the method used to express scope differences. One may, in fact, regard the distinction between 'de dicto' and 'de re' readings as a distinction due to scope differences of the intensional operator *seek*.

8. Developments

PTQ (Montague 1973) signaled the start of a large amount of formal semantic research. This section reviews some of the developments that emanated from PTQ.

PTQ is restricted in at least two ways. First, it restricted itself to a 'fragment' of English, which in itself consituted a severe limitation as regards its coverage. In the majority of publications that were inspired by PTQ, attempts are made to extrapolate from Montague's fragment to larger areas of English and other languages. Second, the formal tools of PTQ are restricted. For instance, it uses a primitive kind of syntax, has semantic models of a certain type, and deals only with isolated declarative sentences. Several attempts have been made at improving the situation without losing any of the benefits already achieved. This section concentrates on this second class of publications because they give a perspective on the present-day possibilities in Montague grammar. Thereafter, the first class of publications will be considered briefly.

The relative lack of syntactic sophistication in PTQ appears, for example, from the absence of syntactic features, well-motivated constituent structures, and grammatical functions, and from the occurrence of several clearly ad hoc rules. As far back as the earliest years of Montague grammar, proposals were made to incorporate syntactic know-how as developed in linguistics into Montague grammar. The theory of transformational grammar was, of course, a prominent source of inspiration in this respect. It was this theory that led some reasearchers (Partee 1975; Dowty 1982) to devise systems where the rules of syntax operate on tree structures (constituent structures) rather than on strings, as is done in PTQ. Partee's ideas on how to combine Montague grammar with transformational grammar are worked out in the very large grammar used in the machine translation project ROSETTA (Rosetta 1994).

The syntactic rules used in PTQ are not subject to any formal restriction. They may carry out any formally well-defined operation on syntactic material. For logicians, this is a comfortable situation, as they can now focus on the semantic problems and are not hampered by syntactic qualms. In linguistics, on the other hand, this is felt as a severe loss in empirical force, as unrestricted rule systems may generate any formally defined language, and not just the restricted class of natural languages. Several proposals have been offered by linguists to restrict the format of syntactic rules in a Montague grammar context. Partee (1979) aims at allowing only a few basic operations in the syntax, and at restricting the relations between syntactic and semantic rules. Hausser (1984) claims what he calls 'surface compositionality' for syntactico–semantic analyses. Generalized phrase structure grammar, or GPSG (Gazdar, et al. 1985), is a special form of Montague grammar in which the rules are context-free. Categorial grammar can be seen as a further restriction on the syntax.

The smallest units in PTQ are the words of a sentence. Their meanings are regarded as basic and remain unanalyzed except for a few logically interesting words such as the quantifiers and the verb *be*. Often, however, it is linguistically interesting to carry the internal analysis of word meanings further. In Sect. 2, examples (5) and (6) featured the word *cool,* which can be an adjective, an intransitive verb, and a causative verb (Dowty 1979). Tense phenomena require an analysis of verb forms and temporal adverbials (Dowty 1979). Compound words allow sometimes for an analysis in terms of their parts (Moortgat 1987).

Certain meaning assignments in PTQ seem counterintuitive. The noun phrase *John,* for example, is not interpreted as denoting an individual, but as denoting a set of properties, only because other noun phrases in the same syntactic position require this semantic type (see Sect. 6). This strategy is frequently followed and is called 'generalization to the most difficult case.' Yet other strategies are easily imaginable. One could, for example, stick to the intuitive notion that the expression *John* denotes an individual and introduce rules that raise interpretations to a higher type whenever required. Type-shifting rules make for greater flexibility in the relation between a word and its semantic type, a property which has earned this approach the name of 'flexible Montague grammar' (see, for example, Partee and Rooth (1983), Keenan and Faltz (1985), Hendriks (1987), Groenendijk and Stokhof (1989)).

The largest linguistic units in PTQ are the sentences. The task of extending Montague's method to discourses looked unrewarding at first, in particular in view of cross-sentential anaphora phenomena. The first Montague-inspired attempt to widen the coverage of the theory to discourses (Kamp 1981) was not entirely compositional. Groenendijk and Stokhof (1991) later provided a fully compositional way of doing this. This makes it possible to incorporate on the text level results obtained earlier in Montague grammar on the sentence level (see Van Eijck and Kamp 1997).

PTQ deals with only one type of sentence, declarative sentences, whose meanings can be described in terms of truth-conditions with respect to world–time indexes. This may be due to the fact that Montague grammar has its roots in mathematical logic. Yet other authors have tried to overcome this limitation by working on the semantics of questions and wh-complements (Karttunen 1977; Groenendijk and Stokhof 1982, 1997).

The PTQ model is based on a hierarchy of typed sets. Yet certain phenomena seem to resist such a treatment. Mass nouns seem to require sets without elements (Bunt 1979). Nominalizations seem to require a domain in which functions can have themselves as arguments (e.g., *I love loving;* see Chierchia 1982). Perception verbs challenge the basic role of possible worlds, which are abandoned by Barwise and Perry (1983), who replace them with 'situations' (though a classical model with partial functions (Muskens 1989) can be used as well).

Much research in Montague grammar is, however, of a different nature, in that it aims less at improvement of the formal tools than at a widening of the range of phenomena treated. A characteristic example is Bennett (1976): 'A variation and extension of a Montague fragment of English.' Often, such publications contain interesting observations, discussions with other theories, and an ingenious solution exhibiting some hidden regularity and providing an explanation. Thus one finds treatments of relative clauses, passives, scope phenomena, control, numbers, plurals, generics, complement structures, and deictic pronouns. Such publications are important because they carry out Montague's program of giving a systematic account of the syntax and the semantics of natural languages (for specific references, the reader may consult the extensive bibliographies in Gamut (1991) and Dowty, et al. (1981)), and Partee and Hendriks (1997).

See also: Compositionality of Meaning; Intension; Intensionality; Meaning Postulate.

Bibliography

An introductory article on PTQ (Montague 1973) is van Eynde (1991), an introduction especially for linguists is Partee (1975), and a rather extended introduction is Gochet and Thayse (1989). A book that is frequently used as introduction to PTQ is Dowty, et al. (1981). An excellent introduction to Montague grammar, with much attention to motivations and justifications, is Gamut (1991). An introductory article on 'Universal grammar' (Montague 1970b) is Halvorsen and Ladusaw (1979); its mathematical background is investigated in Janssen (1986a).

Many publications on Montague grammar have appeared in the proceedings of the Amsterdam Colloquia (Groenendijk, et al. (eds.) 1981 1984); Landman and Veltman 1984; Groenendijk, et al. (eds.) 1986a and b; Bartsch, et al.

1989). Publications on Montague grammar often appear in *Linguistics and Philosophy*. For more references, see Dowty, et al. (1981), Gamut (1991) and Partee and Hendriks (1997).

Bartsch R, Benthem J van, Emde Boas P van 1989 *Semantics and Contextual Expression*. Grass-series 11. Foris, Dordrecht

Barwise J, Cooper R 1981 Generalized quantifiers and natural language. *Linguistics and Philosophy* 4: 159–219

Barwise J, Perry J 1983 *Situations and Attitudes*. Bradford Books, Cambridge, MA

Bennett M 1976 A variation and extension of a Montague fragment of English. In: Partee B H (ed.) 1976

Benthem J van, Meulen A ter 1996 *Handbook of Logic and Language*. Elsevier and MIT Press, Amsterdam and Cambridge, MA

Bunt H C 1979 Ensembles and the formal properties of mass terms. In: Pelletier F J (ed.) *Mass Terms*. Reidel, Dordrecht

Chierchia G 1982 Nominalization and Montague grammar: A semantics without types for natural languages. *Linguistics and Philosophy* 5: 303–54

Cooper R H 1979 The interpretation of pronouns. In: Heny F, Schnelle H S (eds.) 1979

Dowty D R 1979 *Word Meaning and Montague Grammar*. Synthese Language Library 7. Reidel, Dordrecht

Dowty D 1982 Grammatical relations and Montague grammar. In: Jacobson P, Pullum G K (eds.) 1982 *The Nature of Syntactic Representation*. Reidel, Dordrecht

Dowty D R, Wall R E, Peters S 1981 *Introduction to Montague Semantics*. Synthese Language Library 11. Reidel, Dordrecht

Eijck J van, Kamp H 1996 Representing discourse in context. In: Benthem J van and Meulen A ter, *Handbook of Logic and Language*. Elsevier and MIT Press, Amsterdam and Cambridge, MA

Gamut L T F 1991 *Logic, Language and Meaning, vol. II. Intensional Logic and Logical Grammar*. University of Chicago Press, Chicago, IL

Gazdar G, Klein E, Pullum G, Sag I 1985 *Generalized Phrase Structure Grammar*. Basil Blackwell, Oxford

Gochet P, Thayse A 1989 Intensional logic and natural language (ch. 2), Montague grammar (ch. 3). In: Thayse A (ed.) *From Modal Logic to Deductive Databases*. J. Wiley and Sons, Chichester

Groenendijk J A G, Janssen T M V, Stokhof M B J (eds.) 1981 *Formal Methods in the Study of Language. Proceedings of the Third Amsterdam Colloquium*. MC-Tracts 135 and 136. CWI, Amsterdam

Groenendijk J, Janssen T M V, Stokhof M (eds.) 1984 *Truth, Interpretation, and Information. Selected Papers from the Third Amsterdam Colloquium*. Grass-series 2. Foris, Dordrecht

Groenendijk J, Jongh D de, Stokhof M (eds.) 1986a *Foundations of Pragmatics and Lexical Semantics*. Grass-series 7. Foris, Dordrecht

Groenendijk J, Jongh D de, Stokhof M (eds.) 1986b *Studies in Discourse Representation Theory and the Theory of Generalized Quantifier*. Grass-series 8. Foris, Dordrecht

Groenendijk J, Stokhof M 1982 The syntax and semantics of wh-complements. *Linguistics and Philosophy* 5: 175–233

Groenendijk J, Stokhof M 1989 Type-shifting rules and the semantics of interrogatives. In: Chierchia G, Partee B H, Turner R (eds.) *Properties, Types and Meaning, vol. II. Semantics Issues*. Kluwer, Dordrecht

Groenendijk J, Stokhof M 1991 Dynamic predicate logic. *Linguistics and Philosophy* 14: 39–100

Groenendijk J, Stokhof M 1996 Questions. In: Benthem J van, Meulen A ter, *Handbook of Logic and Language*. Elsevier and MIT Press, Amsterdam and Cambridge, MA

Halvorsen P K, Ladusaw W A 1979 Montague's 'Universal Grammar.' An introduction for the linguist. *Linguistics and Philosophy* 3: 185–223

Hausser R R 1984 *Surface Compositional Grammar*. Studies in Theoretical Linguistics. Fink Verlag, Munich

Hendriks H 1987 Type change in semantics: The scope of quantification and coordination. In: Klein E, Benthem J van (eds.) *Categories, Polymorphism and Unification*. Institute for Language, Logic and Information, University of Amsterdam

Heny F, Schnelle H S (eds.) 1979 *Selections from the Third Groningen Round Table*. Syntax and Semantics 10. Academic Press, New York

Jackendoff R 1972 *Semantic Interpretation in Generative Grammar*. MIT Press, Cambridge, MA

Janssen T M V 1983 Scope ambiguities of tense, aspect and negation. In: Heny F, Richards B (eds.) *Syntactic Categories, Auxiliaries and Related Puzzles*. Synthese Language Library 20. Reidel, Dordrecht

Janssen T M V 1984 Individual concepts are useful. In: Landman F, Veltman F (eds.) 1984

Janssen T M V 1986a *Foundations and Applications of Montague Grammar, Part 1: Foundations, Logic, Computer Science*. CWI Tract 19. Center for Mathematics and Computer Science, Amsterdam

Janssen T M V 1986b *Foundations and Applications of Montague Grammar, Part 2: Applications to Natural Language*. CWI Tract 28. Center for Mathematics and Computer Science, Amsterdam

Janssen T M V 1996. Compositionality. In: Benthem J van, Meulen A ter, *Handbook of Logic and Language*. Elsevier and MIT Press, Amsterdam and Cambridge, MA

Kamp H 1981 A theory of truth and semantic representation. In: Groenendijk J, Janssen D de, Stokhof M (eds.) 1981

Karttunen L 1977 Syntax and semantics of questions. *Linguistics and Philosophy* 1: 3–44

Keenan E L, Faltz L M 1985 *Boolean Semantics for Natural Language*. Kluwer, Dordrecht

Keenan E L, Westerstahl D 1996 Generalized quantifiers in linguistics and logics. In: Benthem J van, Meulen A ter, *Handbook of Logic and Language*. Elsevier and MIT Press, Amsterdam and Cambridge, MA

Landman F, Veltman F (eds.) 1984 *Varieties of Formal Semantics*. Grass-series 3. Foris, Dordrecht

Lewis D 1970 General semantics. *Synthese* 22: 18–67. Reprinted in: Davidson D, Harman G (eds.) 1972 *Semantics of Natural Language*. Synthese Library 40, Reidel, Dordrecht

Montague R 1970a English as a formal language. In: Visentini, et al. 1970 *Linguaggi nella società et nella technica*. Edizioni di communità (distributed by the Olivetti Corporation, Milan). Reprinted in: Thomason R H (ed.) 1974

Montague R 1970b Universal grammar. *Theoria* 36: 373–98

Montague R 1973 The proper treatment of quantification in ordinary English. In: Hintikka K J J, Moravcsik J M E, Suppes P (eds.) *Approaches to Natural Language*. Synthese Library 49. Reidel, Dordrecht

Moortgat M 1987 Compositionality and the syntax of words. In: Groenendijk J, Jongh D de, Stokhof M (eds.) 1986a

Muskens R 1989 Going partial in Montague grammar. In: Bartsch R, Benthem J van, Emde Boas P van (eds.) 1989

Partee B 1975 Montague grammar and transformational grammar. *Linguistic Inquiry* 6: 203–300

Partee B H (ed.) 1976 *Montague Grammar*. Academic Press, New York

Partee B H 1977 Possible world semantics and linguistic theory. *The Monist* 60: 303–26

Partee B H 1979 Montague grammar and the well-formedness constraint. In: Heny F, Schnelle H S (eds.) 1979

Partee B, Bach E 1981 Quantification, pronouns and VP-anaphora. In: Groenendijk J, Janssen D de, Stokhof M (eds.) 1981

Partee B H, Meulen A ter, Wall R E 1990 *Mathematical Methods in Linguistics*. Kluwer, Dordrecht

Partee B, Rooth M 1983 Generalized conjunction and type ambiguity. In: Bäuerle R, Schwarze Ch, Stechow A von (eds.) *Meaning, Use and Interpretation of Language*. Walter de Gruyter, Berlin

Partee B H, Hendricks H 1996 Montague grammar. In: Benthem J van, Meulen A ter, *Handbook of Logic and Language*. Elsevier and MIT Press, Amsterdam and Cambridge, MA

Rosetta M T 1994 *Compositional Translation*. Kluwer, Dordrecht

Seuren P A M 1969 *Operators and Nucleus: A Contribution to the Theory of Grammar*. Cambridge University Press, Cambridge

Thomason R H (ed.) 1974 *Formal Philosophy: Selected Papers of Richard Montague*. Yale University Press, New Haven, CT

Verkuyl H, van der Does J 1996 The semantics of plural noun phrases. In: J van der Does, *Quantifiers, Logic and Language*, CSLI lecture notes 54, CSLI, Stanford, CA

Possible Worlds

J. van der Does

There seems to be at least one possible world; the actual world we are living in. But there may also be others. Here, the main problem is to clarify the precise status of possible worlds. A skeptic would have little patience with this issue and hold that these worlds are at most an unfortunate manner of speech which, if allowed at all, should be analyzed in terms of harmless modes of expression. Yet, possible worlds have been fruitfully used in mathematics, logical semantics, and even in science. For this reason philosophers such as Kripke, Lewis, and Stalnaker, among others, have concerned themselves with the issue of whether possible worlds are as real as the actual one, or whether they are abstract alternatives to the real world they might represent.

1. History

A famous use of possible worlds is by Leibniz (1646–1716) in his *Monadology* and *Theodicy*. Facts are contingent; they could have been otherwise. So, he poses the question, why are the present facts realized and no others? In particular, if God in his infinite wisdom chose this world to exist, why is it so much worse than we can imagine? Leibniz answered these questions in the *Monadology*, §53–55:

> (53) Now, as there is an infinity of possible universes in the ideas of God, and as only one of them can exist, there must be a sufficient reason for God's choice, which determines him to one rather than another.
>
> (54) And this reason can only be found in the *fitness* or in the degrees of perfection that these worlds contain, each possible world having the right to a claim to existence to the extent of the perfection it enfolds.
>
> (55) And this is the cause of the existence of the best: that his wisdom makes it known to God, his Goodness makes him choose it, and his power makes him produce it.

In the late twentieth century, most philosophers would find Leibniz's solution an amazingly clever tale, but no more than that: a tale. Also, some of his followers used it to justify a superficial 'optimism,' which brings along an ethical inertia in a world full of tragedies and disasters. This aspect of the doctrine is ridiculed by Voltaire (1694–1778) in his *Candide*. It tells the story of a young optimist who is raised in the most beautiful and delightful of all possible mansions, the country seat of Baron Thunder-ten-tronck. Candide remains indifferent to a terrible amount of anguish, mainly suffered by others, for the metaphysico-theologo-cosmolo-nigologist Pangloss taught him that all is for the best in the best of all possible worlds.

2. Philosophy

The interest in possible worlds does not survive for theological or ethical reasons. Most rational human activities—such as anticipation of future events, investigation and explanation, fiction—involve a consideration of alternatives to the ways things are. This is reflected in the distinctively modal flavor of parts of speech and some of the relations between them: counterfactual conditionals, modal adverbs, and auxiliaries, and implication, among other things. Until

the 1960s, the semantics of these expressions was opaque. But the development of possible world semantics, made famous by the young Kripke, clarified the semantics of modal expressions by means of 'the same set-theoretic techniques of model theory that proved so successful when applied to extensional logic' (Kripke 1980: 19).

In possible world semantics, one takes the notions of a 'possible world' and an 'accessibility' or a 'similarity' relation among them as primitives. Propositions are defined as sets of possible worlds. The truth of a sentence in a world may depend on what is the case in the worlds which are accessible from or similar to that world.

In taking possible worlds and the relations among them as primitives, the claim is not that no more could or need be said about them, but that it is fruitful to work at 'a certain level of abstraction, a level that brings out what is common in a certain range of otherwise uncommon activities' (Stalnaker 1984: 57). This is not unlike the use of individuals in extensional semantics. Despite its more familiar appearance, the general notion of an 'individual' seems as elusive as that of a 'possible world.' To elucidate, for example, the relation of consequence for a first-order logic—the only significant aspect of individuals is that they have properties or may be related to each other. The elucidation could even be so successful that many people are happy to adopt the instrumentalist view. On this view, the primitive notions are seen as convenient fictions which help to make a workable and perspicuous theory. However, with respect to possible world semantics, the instrumentalist view is rarely defended. Instead, one finds different forms of realism, which are discussed under the headings 'real worlds' and 'abstract worlds' below.

3. Real Worlds

'I believe there are possible worlds other than the one we happen to inhabit.' This statement gives a flavor of the modal realism defended by David Lewis (1973, 1986). According to him, possible worlds are the objects we existentially quantify over when holding, as many of us do, that there are many ways things could have been. Lewis's position can be summarized in four theses (cf. Lewis 1973: 84–86; Stalnaker 1984: 45):

> (i) Possible worlds exist. (ii) Other possible worlds are things of the same sort as the actual world. (iii) The indexical analysis of the adjective 'actual' is the correct analysis. (iv) Possible worlds cannot be reduced to anything more basic.

The third thesis should be understood as saying that the phrase 'the actual world' is always used by speakers to single out the world they are in. In absence of a further specification of what kind of entities 'possible worlds' are, the theses (i), (iii), and (iv) are rather harmless. It is only in combination with thesis (ii), which postulates a super universe where our world is found among other worlds, that they yield a strong form of realism. Note that on this view the actual world is not identified with the totality of all there is, as is commonly done. The actual world is one out of many worlds which differ in what goes on in them but are all of the same kind.

Robert Stalnaker (1984: 44–50) argues for what he calls a 'moderate realism.' He holds against Lewis, not that there may be modal facts which might never be known of, but rather that on Lewis's view all modal facts are in principle unknowable:

> Presumably, any part of reality that is spatially or causally connected with something in the actual world is itself part of the actual world.... But if other possible worlds are causally disconnected from us, how do we know anything about them?
>
> (Stalnaker 1984: 49)

Most people find it reasonable to hold that there are countless ways in which things might have been. However, the reasonableness of this view is hard to come by if it depends on the existence of worlds which are farther removed from us than the remotest corners of our universe. The problem is how talk about such alien entities could play a role in the semantics of ordinary everyday speech.

This argument against Lewis strongly depends on the assumption that the worlds in the super universe are spatially and causally disconnected, and hence inaccessible. But a modal realist does not seem to be committed to such a universe. Perhaps, it is more like the universe used in the many-worlds interpretation of quantum mechanics, developed by Everett and Wheeler in 1957, where the worlds are paths through a many-dimensional branching structure (a popular account is in Gribbin 1985). Branching occurs when there are different possibilities; a point which is nicely illustrated by means of Schrödinger's cat paradox. (Lewis 1986: 124–25, discusses an ethical variant of this example invented by Larry Niven.)

Imagine a nontransparent box with a live cat in it beside a fully random device which might break a bottle of poison. Due to the randomness of the device one is totally ignorant of whether or not the cat is still alive, unless one opens the box. Now, before observing the cat, is it alive or dead? On one interpretation the states of the cat are undetermined, for equally probable. The poison is definitely emitted and the cat definitely dead only the instant one looks in the box and finds the cat in that state. Before that moment the living cat and the dead cat are equally probable and therefore equally 'unreal.' On Everett's interpretation both cats are real but located in different worlds. There are no nonactual possibilities which become actual through observation. All possibilities exist, though in different mutually incompatible worlds.

In Everett's interpretation there is a universe in which the worlds may be spatially or causally related to each other. Yet from within a world all other worlds are inaccessible. What is important here is that this inaccessibility, so crucial for Stalnaker's argument, does not prevent one from reasoning about the non-actual possibilities. In particular, the reasonableness of holding that there are many ways in which things that might have been can be sustained even in the absence of immediate access to the alternatives themselves. What is required is, rather, some insight into how the alternatives come about.

It may also be concluded that one should resist taking the entire structure to be the actual world; a world that happens to have many world-like parts. It might appear that such a move is mainly terminological, but this is not so. For on the new interpretation, all world-like parts are actual in an absolute sense. As a consequence, the desired contingency is absent because there are no alternatives and hence nothing to vary. Contingency just occurs if the branches themselves are the worlds, each one actual for its inhabitants.

4. Abstract Worlds

Only a few philosophers feel comfortable with the modal realism defended by Lewis. They say that his position, which takes possible worlds as concrete particulars, is induced by an unfortunate terminology. The use of 'possible world' suggests the possibilities to be the wrong kind of entity. Nobody mistakes the euphoric state of John for John himself. Similarly, a state the actual world might be in should not be conflated with that world itself. The world is a particular, the largest one possible, but its states are abstract 'ways things might have been.' Therefore it would have been better, if they had been called 'possible states,' 'histories,' or 'counterfactual situations' (Kripke 1980: 20).

On this view, perhaps more needs to be said about the states and how they relate to the unique concrete world. There are some proposals that try to do so. Most of them are variants of Carnap's 'state-descriptions' (Carnap 1956: 9), where possible worlds are maximal consistent sets of basic sentences (a basic sentence is either an atomic sentence or the negation thereof). In this case a possible world is a structured object built from basic sentences by set-theoretical means. A possible world is related to the real world via the basic sentences. It is actual, yet abstract, if and only if all its basic sentences are true (they correspond to the atomic facts in the real world).

As Lewis (1986: §3.1) points out, there are some objections to this approach, only some of which can be countered. For one, it must be assumed that everything has a name. Otherwise some individuals cannot be represented within a possible world, so that not all alternatives are present. On the other hand, the names must be unique in order to preclude hidden inconsistencies (Mister X named as 'Peter' is blond but named as 'Paul' is not). A convenient way to realize the appropriate naming is to let the objects themselves figure as their own names. Similarly, the properties and relations among the objects can be taken as 'relation signs.' Note in passing that this strategy is quite like the one used by Barwise and Perry to obtain abstract situations. The strategy undermines two objections to state-descriptions, namely: (a) that worlds are unlike sets of sentences; and (b) that maximal consistent sets are not numerous enough. In the abstract, the worlds are made up of real objects and real relations. And using the objects and relations themselves removes cardinality and other restrictions which are sensible for languages (e.g., that the language is countable). Still, this liberal version of state-descriptions, far removed from Carnap's original proposal, has to face a serious problem: it takes modality as a primitive. It does so mainly via consistency. A set of sentences is maximal if and only if adding new sentences makes it inconsistent (i.e., not consistent). But it is consistent if and only if its sentences *could* all be true. In short, this way of explaining modal phenomena achieves at most a reduction of all modal phenomena to a modality of a particular kind (the one taken as primitive). Whether or not this reduction is substantial depends on a further analysis of the primitive notion.

An important virtue of the proposals that identify possible worlds with concrete particulars or with maximal consistent sets is that they are specific. Often one has to make do with less detail. For instance, Kripke (1980: 20) uses the image that 'possible worlds' are little more than the miniworlds of school probability blown large. And in the moderate realism of Stalnaker their existence is 'inferred or abstracted from the activities of rational agents,' so that claims about possible worlds should be located 'in a theory of rational activities' (Stalnaker 1984: 50–55). His realism 'need not take possible worlds among the ultimate furniture of the world.' They are useful primitives in theorizing about activities at a certain level of abstraction. What the abstract worlds are may depend on the context, and especially on the kind of activity considered (1984: 57–58). Now, these statements point to interesting ways of clarifying the use of possible worlds, but as they stand they are rather programmatic (and are intended as such). Among other things, they leave in the dark how a state, an unanalyzed 'way things might have been' is related to the

one real world, that is, what it is that makes a state not merely possible, but actual. Lewis on the 'Ersatzist Programme' (1986: §3) has an extensive discussion of the issues at hand. He also discusses other alternatives.

5. Occam's Razor

One option is to do without possible worlds and limit ourselves to less troublesome individuals. This most radical use of Occam's razor would deprive us of a useful tool in describing semantic phenomena. After all, the metaphysics necessary to explain natural language may involve the use of entities which are suspect for the critical philosopher. For want of an analysis which is as perspicuous and successful as possible world semantics one has to choose among the modal realism of Lewis and the 'moderate' versions of realism. The question is how to apply the razor in this case; whether it should cut the number of entities posited, or only the number of kinds of entity. In both cases, Lewis seems to be better off. Although his worlds appear grandiose, they are all of the same kind. In contrast, the moderate realist has to distinguish between the real world and abstract world representations. And since the moderate realist will want his distinctions to be as fine grained as those of Lewis, he needs to have as many representations as Lewis needs worlds (see Lewis 1973: 87). The main virtue of the moderate realist position appears to be that the use of abstractions leaves the possibility that these may be eliminated in favor of more 'respectable' entities. In the absence of such an analysis, the case is not so clear.

See also: Modal Logic.

Bibliography

Carnap R 1956 *Meaning and Necessity*, 2nd edn. University of Chicago Press, Chicago, IL
Gribbin J 1985 *In Search of Schrödinger's Cat*. Corgi Books, London
Hintikka J 1969 *Models for Modalities*. Synthese Library 23, Reidel, Dordrecht
Kripke S A 1980 *Naming and Necessity*. Harvard University Press, Cambridge, MA
Leibniz G W 1991 *Monadology*. Routledge, London
Lewis D 1973 *Counterfactuals*. Blackwell, Oxford
Lewis D 1986 *On the Plurality of Worlds*. Blackwell, Oxford
Stalnaker R C 1984 *Inquiry*. Bradford Books, MIT Press, Cambridge, MA
Voltaire 1947 (trans. Butt J) *Candide or Optimism*. Penguin Books, London

Presupposition

P. A. M. Seuren

A presupposition is a property of a sentence, making that sentence fit for use in certain contexts and unfit for use in other contexts. Most natural language sentences carry one or more presuppositions. If a sentence B carries a presupposition A (B ≫ A), then A must be true for B to be true, or more precisely, the proposition expressed by A must be true for the proposition expressed by B to be true. (From here on, when necessary, a reference to a sentence is to be taken as a reference to the proposition expressed by it in every context of use.) Thus, A is an entailment of B (B ⊨ A). Since entailments are the business of logic, this implies that presupposition is in any case relevant in the logical analysis of natural language. Presuppositional entailments distinguish themselves, however, from other, 'classical,' entailments in that in an orderly presentation, transfer, and storage of information, that is, in a coherent discourse, they are, in some sense, prior to their carrier sentences. They restrict the domain within which their carrier sentence is interpretable. This, in turn, implies that presupposition is relevant in the analysis of the cognitive processes involved in the linguistic transfer of information. Such properties are commonly called 'discourse-related properties' of language.

The following examples illustrate the difference between classical and presuppositional entailments. In (1a, b), the first sentence classically entails (⊨c) the second; in (2a–d) the first sentence presupposes (≫) the second:

The king has been assassinated ⊨c The king is dead.	(1a)
Nob works hard ⊨c Nob works.	(1b)
Nob lives in Manchester ≫ There exists someone called 'Nob.'	(2a)
Sue has forgotten that Nob was her student ≫ Nob was Sue's student.	(2b)
Nob has come back ≫ Nob went away.	(2c)
Nob still lives in Manchester ≫ Nob lived in Manchester before.	(2d)

In (2a) one finds an example of so-called 'existential presuppositions.' These were the main starting point for presupposition theory in philosophy. Number (2b) exemplifies 'factive presuppositions' (Kiparsky and Kiparsky 1971); the truth of the *that*-clause is presupposed. In (2c) we have a case of 'categorial presupposition'; these are directly derived from the lexical meaning of the main predicate (*come back*). And (2d) belongs to a 'remainder category'; the presupposition being due to the adverb *still*.

The distinction between classical and presuppositional entailments gives rise to the question of whether the distinction is purely logical, or partly logical and partly to do with the orderly transfer of information—i.e., discourse-related, or entirely discourse-related, and hence irrelevant to logic. Answers to this question will be heavily theory-dependent and bound up with the question of how the disciplines concerned—mainly logic, semantics, and pragmatics—are to divide the labor. A decision will involve a whole theoretical paradigm, and only a wide variety of data, analyses, and other kinds of considerations will be able to tip the balance.

For some, discourse-related properties are *pragmatic*. The tendency here is to equate the logic and the semantics of language, the logic being classical and thus bivalent. Anything falling outside classical logic is taken to be pragmatic, including all discourse-bound aspects. In this view, presupposition is nonlogical and purely pragmatic, and the entire burden of explanation is thus placed on a pragmatic theory still largely to be developed.

Others take presupposition to be a *semantic* property. They make a primary distinction between what is part of the linguistic system, that is, at 'type'-level, and what results from the interaction of the linguistic system with any contingent state of affairs in the actual or any imagined world, that is, at 'token'-level. In this view, all systematic linguistic aspects of the machinery, whereby speakers' cognitive contents (mental propositions) representing possible states of affairs are signified by uttered sentences and hence transferred to listeners, are considered to be semantic, whereas aspects to do with conditions of use are called pragmatic. Typically, in this view, semantics is taken to comprise a great deal more than what is provided by logic, and the logic to be adopted may well, if it incorporates the notion of presupposition, turn out to deviate from classical bivalent logic. In this semantic view, presupposition is at least partly, and for some entirely, a logical phenomenon. The terminological difference thus reflects different attitudes regarding the status of logic vis-à-vis semantics and the autonomy of the linguistic system, that is, the grammar and the semantics, of a natural language.

Finally, there is a diminishing school that looks upon presupposition as a purely *logical* phenomenon, requiring a nonclassical logic.

1. Operational Criteria

Whichever position one takes, it is clear that presuppositions are systematic properties of sentences, detectable ('observable') irrespective of actual conditions of use, though, apparently, their rationale is to restrict the usability of sentences to certain classes of context (discourse). This appears from the fact that, like classical entailments, presuppositions can be read off isolated sentences, such as those in (2), given without any special context. Yet these sentences *evoke* a certain context or class of contexts. Example (2a) evokes a context in which there is someone called 'Nob'; (2b) requires it to be given in the context, and thus evokes such a context, that Nob was Sue's student; (2c) requires it to be given that Nob was away; and (2d) that he lived in Manchester before. This, together with the logico-semantic property of entailment, provides a set of operational criteria to distinguish and recognize actual presuppositions of sentences.

First, if $B \gg A$ then in any case $B \vDash A$. This can be operationally tested (not defined) as follows. If the conjunction of sentences 'maybe not A, yet B' is recognized as per se incoherent then $B \vDash A$. Clearly, in all cases of (1) and (2) above, this test yields a positive result. For example, sentence (1a′) is clearly per se incoherent (signaled by '!'):

> !Maybe the king is not dead, yet he has been   (1a′)
> assassinated.

But it yields a negative result when applied to (3a, b), since (3c) is coherent. Therefore, (3a) does not entail (3b) (i.e., (3a) $\nvDash$ (3b)). The relation between these two sentences is of a different kind:

> Lady Fortune neighs.   (3a)

> Lady Fortune is a horse.   (3b)

> Lady Fortune may not be a horse, yet she   (3c)
> neighs.

The customary heuristic criterion for the entailment relation in $B \vDash A$ is the incoherence of 'not A, yet B.' This, however, is too strong, since it would incorrectly make (4a) entail (4b), given the incoherence of (4c). Example (4d), on the other hand, is still coherent:

> The king may have been assassinated.   (4a)

> The king is dead.   (4b)

> !The king is not dead, yet he may have been   (4c)
> assassinated.

> The king may not be dead, yet he may have   (4d)
> been assassinated (and thus be dead).

The difference is caused by the fact that natural language operators of epistemic possibility, such as English *may*, require compatibility of what is said in their scope with what is laid down as being the case in adjacent discourse (or in any knowledge store operational during the discourse). But they do not bring along the *entailment* of everything that is compatible with what is in their scope. Generally, if $B \vDash A$ (and A

is not logically necessary), then *Possibly*(B) $\nvDash$ A. Yet *not*-A *but Possibly*(B) is incoherent for reasons to do with discourse construction: B (the scope of *Possibly*) is incompatible with the negation of its entailment A. But since B is in the scope of the entailment-canceling operator *Possibly*, no conclusion can be drawn with respect to the entailment properties of B. In the configuration *Possibly*(*not*-A), *yet* B, there is again discourse incoherence if $B \vDash A$, and for the same reason. But now B does not stand under any entailment-canceling operator, and it is thus legitimate to draw a conclusion with respect to the entailment properties of B.

The 'entailment criterion,' that is, the incoherence of 'maybe not A, yet B,' yields identical results for all entailments, whether classical or presuppositional, and thus does not distinguish between the two categories. There is, however, a corollary which does make the distinction. If $B \gg A$ and B is the scope of an entailment-canceling operator, A will survive not as an entailment but as a more or less strongly invited inference. Generally, $O(B_A) > A$, where 'B_A' stands for 'B presupposing A,' 'O' stands for any entailment-canceling imbedding operator, and '$>$' stands for invited inference. In standard terminology it is said that the presupposition of B is 'projected' through the imbedding operator. The conditions under which presuppositions of imbedded clauses are projected through imbedding operator structures constitute the well-known 'projection problem' of presupposition.

Projection is typical of presuppositions, not of classical entailments, of imbedded clauses. Thus, (5a) > (5b), but (6a) $\ngtr$ 6b), precisely because (5b) is a presupposition of the imbedded clause *Nob lives in Manchester*, whereas (6b) is a classical entailment of *The king has been assassinated*.

> Sue believes that Nob lives in Manchester.   (5a)

> There exists someone called 'Nob.'   (5b)

> Sue believes that the king has been assassinated.   (6a)

> The king is dead.   (6b)

The projection criterion is most commonly used with the negation as the entailment-canceling operator. Strawson (1950; 1952) observed that presupposition is preserved as entailment under negation. In his view, a sentence like:

> The present king of France is not bald   (7)

still presupposes, and thus entails, that there exists a king of France, who therefore, if (7) is true, must have hair on his head. Strawson's observation was perhaps made without due consideration of the complications involved, since in many but not all cases presupposition is weakened to invited inference under negation. In any case, it was highly influential, and the so-called 'negation test' became the standard test for presupposition in much of the literature. Provided the notion of entailment is replaced by that of invited inference, this test is sound.

A further criterion to separate classical from presuppositional entailments is the 'discourse criterion.' Any bit of discourse 'A and/but B_A' (taking into account anaphoric processes) will be felt to be orderly and well-planned. We shall use the term 'sequential' to refer to the typical quality of presuppositionally well-ordered texts, without implying that texts that are not, or not fully, sequential are therefore unacceptable in some sense. The concept of sequentiality is used only to characterize stretches of acceptable texts that have their presuppositions spelled out. Fully sequential texts will tend to be dull, but well-ordered. This is demonstrated by the following bits of discourse ('$\sqrt{}$' signals sequentiality):

$\sqrt{}$ There exists someone called 'Nob,' and he (8a)
lives in Manchester.

$\sqrt{}$ Nob was Sue's student, but she has forgotten (8b)
that he was.

$\sqrt{}$ Nob was away, but he has come back. (8c)

$\sqrt{}$ Nob lived in Manchester before, and he still (8d)
lives there.

Classical entailments generally lack this property. When a classical entailment or an inductive inference precedes its carrier sentence the result may still be acceptable, yet there is a clear qualitative difference with sequential texts, as is shown in (9a, b), where a colon after the first conjunct is more natural ('#' signals nonsequential discourse):

\# The king is dead, and/but he has been (9a)
assassinated.

\# Nob earns money, and/but he has a job now. (9b)

The discourse criterion still applies when a presupposition is weakened to an invited inference. A discourse 'A and/but $O(B_A)$' will again be sequential:

$\sqrt{}$ Nob really exists, and Sue believes that he (10a)
lives in Manchester.

$\sqrt{}$ Nob was Sue's student, but she has probably (10b)
forgotten that he was.

$\sqrt{}$ Nob went away, and he has not come back. (10c)

$\sqrt{}$ Nob lived in Manchester before, and he may (10d)
still live there.

In practice, the combination of these tests will reliably set off presuppositions from classical entailments.

2. The Logical Problem

2.1 The Threat to Bivalence

The first to signal the fact that presuppositions are a threat to standard logic was Aristotle's contemporary, Eubulides of Miletus (Kneale and Kneale 1962: 113–17). He is known for his arguments against the Aristotelian logical axiom of 'strict bivalence,' also called the 'principle of the excluded third' (PET). This principle consists of two independent subprinciples: (a) all sentences always have precisely one truth-value (hence no truth-value gaps), and (b) there are precisely two truth-values, 'true' and 'false' (weak bivalence). Eubulides formulated a few so-called 'paradoxes' (the most famous of which is the liar paradox), including the 'Paradox of the horned man' (Kneale and Kneale 1962: 114): 'What you have not lost you still have. But you have not lost horns. So you still have horns.'

This paradox rests on presuppositional phenomena. Let B be *You have lost your horns*, and A *You had horns*. Now $B \gg A$, but $not(B) \not\gg A$, though $not(B) > A$. Eubulides, like Strawson, wanted presupposition to hold for the carrier sentence both with and without the negation. Then there would be both $B \vDash A$ and $not(B) \vDash A$, which, under PET, would mean that $not(A) \vDash not(B)$ and $not(A) \vDash B$. In other words, $not(A)$ would have contradictory entailments, and thus be a necessary falsehood. A would thereby be a necessary truth, which, of course, is absurd for such a typically contingent sentence as *You had horns*. To avoid this, PET would have to be dropped. Although Aristotle himself was unable to show Eubulides wrong, there is a flaw in the paradox of the horned man. It lies in the first premiss *What you have not lost you still have*. For it is possible not to have lost something precisely because one never had it.

In the early 1950s, Eubulides' point was taken up by Strawson, who also posited the preservation of presupposition under negation. In Strawson's view, nonfulfillment of a presupposition leads to the carrier sentence A, and its negation, lacking a truth-value altogether. In allowing for truth-value gaps he thus denied subprinciple (a) of PET.

From a different angle, Frege (1892) had come to the same conclusion, at least for existential presuppositions. A sentence like:

The present king of France is bald (11)

is analyzed by Frege in the traditional way as 'Bald(the present king of France),' i.e., as a predicate with its subject argument term. The predicate *bald* extends over all bald individuals in this or any world. Now, to decide whether (11) is true, or false an individual i referred to by the definite description *the present king of France* is needed. If i is a member of the set of bald individuals the sentence is true; if not it is false. In the absence of any present king of France there is thus no way, in Frege's analysis, of computing the truth-value of either that sentence or its negation (i.e., (7)). Both will, therefore, fall into a truth-value gap.

Frege's argument posed a profound problem for standard logic. If sentence (11) is analyzed in the Fregean way then, in any strictly bivalent logic, the sentence *There is a king of France* must be considered a necessary truth, which is absurd. Put differently, the applicability of standard logic to English would have to be made dependent on the contingent condition of there being a king of France—a restriction no true logician will accept. Subsequently, two traditions developed in the effort to solve this problem, the Russell tradition and the Frege–Strawson tradition. In their present form, the two have begun to converge, yet they remain stuck in certain stubborn inadequacies. A third solution is beginning to present itself.

2.2 The Russell Tradition

It was this problem of empty reference that stirred the young Bertrand Russell into action. Having devised his solution to the problem of universal quantification over empty sets (*All square circles are in London*: true or false?), which had beset traditional predicate calculus ever since its Aristotelian beginnings, he now proceeded to solving the problem of definite descriptions without a reference object. In 1905, Russell published his famous article *On referring*, where he proposed that a sentence like (11) should not be analyzed in the traditional (Fregean) way. Putting the new theory of quantification to use, he argued that (11) should be analyzed as follows:

$$\exists x[KoF(x) \wedge Bald(x) \wedge \forall y[KoF(y) \rightarrow x = y]] \qquad (12)$$

or: 'There is an individual x such that x is now king of France and x is bald, and for all individuals y, if y is now king of France, y is identical with x.' In other words: 'There is now precisely one king of France, and he is bald.' In order to save bivalence, Russell thus rejected the time-honored subject–predicate analysis used in logic as well as in grammar, replacing it by an analysis in terms of existential and universal quantification. The definite description *the present king of France* thus no longer forms a structural constituent of the logically analyzed sentence. It is dissolved into quantifiers and propositional functions.

The negation of (11), that is, (7), should be analyzed logically as (12) preceded by the negation operator, i.e., as (13a). However, for reasons best known to themselves, speakers often prefer to interpret (7) as (13b), with the negation restricted to the propositional function 'Bald(x)':

$$\neg[\exists x[KoF(x) \wedge Bald(x) \wedge \forall y[KoF(y) \rightarrow x = y]]] \qquad (13a)$$

$$\exists x[KoF(x) \wedge \neg[Bald(x)] \wedge \forall y[KoF(y) \rightarrow x = y]] \qquad (13b)$$

In practice, therefore, a sentence like (7) is ambiguous.

This proposal, known as Russell's *Theory of Descriptions*, quickly became standard among logicians and philosophers of language, precisely because it saved classical logic, with its cherished PET, from Frege's problem. At the same time, however, it brought about a deep rift between logic and grammar, since the Russellian way of analyzing sentences ran counter to any accepted notion of linguistic structure. From 1900 onward, grammarians (linguists) preached

the irrelevance of logic to the study of language, and not until the 1970s did a rapprochement come about.

Although Russell's *Theory of Descriptions* saves classical logic, it fails to save the facts of natural language. Those who recognized this, modified Russell's analysis in various ways, without, however, giving up the original idea. There thus came about a 'Russellian tradition' in the analysis of definite descriptions, and presuppositions in general.

The first, and most obvious, objection concerns the so-called 'uniqueness clause' in (12)—$\forall y[KoF(y) \rightarrow x = y]$—which is meant to ensure that only one king of France is said to exist and thus to account for the uniqueness expressed by the definite article. It is clear, however, that the use of the definite article involves no claim to uniqueness of existence, but only to discourse-bound uniqueness of reference. The uniqueness clause was thus quietly dropped early on in the piece.

Another objection is that this theory is limited to definite descriptions and thus in principle is unable to account for other than existential presuppositions. Factive and categorial presuppositions, as well as those derived from words like *all, still*, or *only*, fall in principle outside its scope. Yet analogous problems arise. For example, (14a)≫(14c), yet likewise (for reasons to be discussed below) (14b)≫(14c), and (14b) is, to the best of our analytical powers, the logical negation of (14a):

Only Nob laughed.	(14a)
Not only Nob laughed.	(14b)
Nob laughed.	(14c)

Likewise (15a)≫(15c), and (15b)≫(15c) even though (15b) is the negation of (15a):

That Nob laughed surprised Sue.	(15a)
That Nob laughed did not surprise Sue.	(15b)
Nob laughed.	(15c)

The presupposition structurally associated with cleft and pseudocleft sentences behaves in the same manner, as is seen from (16) and (17), exemplifying clefts and pseudoclefts, respectively:

It was Nob who laughed.	(16a)
It wasn't Nob who laughed.	(16b)
Someone laughed.	(16c)
Who laughed was Nob.	(17a)
Who laughed wasn't Nob.	(17b)
Someone laughed.	(17c)

Both (16a) and its negation (16b) presuppose (16c), and likewise for (17).

These are cases, overlooked by Eubulides, Strawson, and others, where presupposition is indeed fully preserved under negation. Consequently, in classical bivalent logic the presuppositions of sentences like (14a, b), (15a, b), (16a, b), or (17a, b) would be necessary truths.

Presupposition theorists see the same problem in (18), where both (18a) and its negation (18b) presuppose (18c):

All men are mortal. (18a)

Not all men are mortal. (18b)

There exist men. (18c)

In Russellian predicate calculus, however, (18a) does not entail (18c), and thus cannot presuppose it, whereas (18b) ⊨ (18c). Yet presupposition theorists will maintain that (18a) does entail (18c)—in fact, *There may not be any men, yet all men are mortal* is grossly incoherent—and that (18b) does not classically entail but presuppose (18c): *There exist men and/but not all men are mortal* is an acceptable discourse. Russellian predicate calculus thus seems to fit the presuppositional facts badly.

In order to generalize the *Theory of Descriptions* to other than existential presuppositions, some logicians have proposed to modify Russell's analysis as given in (12) to:

$$\exists x[KoF(x)] \wedge Bald(he) \qquad (19)$$

or 'There is now a king of France, and *he* is bald.' The bracketing structure is changed: The subject *he* of 'Bald' is no longer a bound variable, but an anaphoric expression. If a mechanism for this kind of anaphora can be provided, the analysis can be generalized to all kinds of presupposition. A sentence A_B is now analyzed as 'B and A_B,' and $\neg A_B$ can be said to be normally analyzable as 'B and $\neg A_B$,' with small scope for *not*, though discourse conditions may force the analysis '$\neg$[B and A_B],' with large scope for the negation. This analysis, which saves PET, is known as the 'conjunction analysis for presupposition.' Kamp (1981) and Groenendijk and Stokhof (1991), each with a specific anaphora mechanism, defend this analysis for existential presuppositions.

The introduction of an anaphora mechanism is necessary anyway, since the original Russellian analysis as given in (12) fails for cases like (20), where classical quantifier binding is impossible for the anaphoric expression *it (the dog)*, which is in the scope of *I hope* whereas *I hope* is not in the scope of *I know*:

I know that there was a dog and I hope that it (20)
(the dog) was white.

Geach argued (1972: 115–27) that a sentence like:

There was a dog and it was white. (21)

should be analyzed not with an anaphoric *it*, analogous to (19), but as $\exists x[Dog(x) \wedge White(x)]$, on the grounds that this is fully compatible with

$\exists x[Dog(x) \wedge \neg White(x)]$, just as (21) is fully compatible with:

There was a dog and it was not white. (22)

In the conjunction analysis, however, there is incompatibility between $\exists x[Dog(x)] \wedge White(it)$ on the one hand, and $\exists x[Dog(x)] \wedge \neg White(it)$ on the other, since $A \wedge B$ and $A \wedge \neg B$ are incompatible (contrary). Cases like (20), however, show that the bound variable analysis favored by Geach lacks generality (see Seuren 1977; 1985: 319–20).

Even so, the incompatibility problem remains for the conjunction analysis, which is unable to account for the fact that (23a) is coherent but (23b) is not:

There was a dog and it was white, and there (23a)
was a dog and it was not white.

! There was a dog and it was white and it was (23b)
not white.

Clearly, in (23a) there are two dogs, due to the repetition of *there was a dog*, but in (23b) there is only one. Yet the conjunction analysis cannot make that difference, since the repetition of *there was a dog* makes no semantic difference for it. Recently, attempts have been made to incorporate this difference into the logic (e.g., Kamp 1981; Heim 1982; Groenendijk and Stokhof 1991). The usual procedure is to attach a memory store to the model theory which keeps track of the elements that have so far been introduced existentially, i.e., some form of discourse-based semantics. Now, the second occurrence of *there was a dog* in (23a) represents a different proposition from the first, so that the propositional analysis is no longer $[a \wedge b] \wedge [a \wedge \neg b]$ but $[a \wedge b] \wedge [c \wedge \neg d]$, which shows no incompatibility.

The common motivation in this Russellian tradition of analyzing definite descriptions was always the wish to do justice to the facts of language without giving up PET as a logical axiom. In its latest forms, the conjunction analysis deviates in certain ways from Russell's predicate calculus, yet it leaves PET unaffected. Not all philosophers of language, however, were so attached to PET. Some felt that both the theory and the facts are better served without it.

Even in its most up-to-date versions, the conjunction analysis still has to cope with a number of problems. Thus, without ad hoc provisions it still seems necessary to postulate existence for term referents that are explicitly said not to exist:

The monster of Loch Ness does not exist. (24a)

The imaginary conspiracy was widely (24b)
publicized.

Clearly, analyses like 'there exists a monster of Loch Ness and/but it does not exist' or 'there existed an imaginary conspiracy and/but it was widely publicized' do injustice to both the logic and the semantics of such sentences. Moreover, the conjunction analysis forces one to say that the negation, in, for example, *John did not buy a car* is sentence negation, but in *John did not buy the car* it normally only negates the second conjunct and thus does not function as sentence negation. And if, in the latter case, the negation is indeed full sentence negation and thus cancels presuppositions, that is, as '¬[B and A$_B$],' then the conjunction analysis fails to account for the discourse-correcting 'echo' effect of such sentences. This use of negation is highly marked and pragmatically plausible only in contexts where a previously uttered or suggested A$_B$ is radically denied because of presupposition failure.

2.3 The Frege–Strawson Tradition

Strawson (1950; 1952) was the first to oppose the Russell tradition. Rejecting the *Theory of Descriptions*, he reverted to the traditional subject–predicate analysis for sentences with definite descriptions as their subject. He discussed existential presuppositions only, and only under extensional predicates, excluding cases like those in (24). He moreover neglected the Russellian wide-scope reading of negation, considering only the presupposition-preserving reading, interpreting that as the normal logical sentence negation. For Strawson, if B ≫ A then also *not*(B) ≫ A, and when A fails to be true (presupposition failure), both B and *not*(B) lack a truth-value. The definition of presupposition is strictly logical: B ≫ A =$_{Def}$ B ⊨ A and *not*(B) ⊨ A and non-truth of A necessarily goes with both B and *not*(B) lacking a truth-value.

The logic of this system is bivalent with gaps, i.e., sentences without a truth-value in models where B is not true. Since lack of truth-value is hardly a valid input for a truth-function, Strawson's 'gapped bivalent propositional calculus' (GBC) is best reconstructed as shown in Fig. 1 (where the symbol '∼' stands for presupposition-preserving negation, '1' for truth, '2' for falsity, and '*' for lack of truth-value).

Insofar as truth-values are assigned, this calculus preserves the classical tables. Moreover, * ('unvalued') is 'infectious': wherever it appears in the input to a truth-function, the output is unvalued. GBC has the remarkable property of limiting the applicability of (bivalent) logic to cases where the, mostly contingent, presuppositions of the sentences involved are fulfilled (true). If U is the set of all possible states of affairs,

then GBC operates in a different U for different sets of sentences. GBC is subject to a flexible, or 'dynamic' U$_S$, defined for any specific set of sentences S, and it can express propositions about states of affairs outside U$_S$ only by the addition of existentially quantified sentences without presuppositions.

This analysis of presupposition was, partly successfully, criticized by Wilson (1975) and Boër and Lycan (1976). These authors side with Russell and show that in a sentence like (7) the negation is not presupposition-preserving since entailment does not hold. A sentence like (25) is coherent, though it requires emphatic, discourse-correcting accent on *not*:

> The present king of France is NOT bald. There (25)
> is no king of France!

Wilson, in particular, gives many examples of presuppositions of negated carrier sentences where presuppositional entailments are canceled under emphatic negation. The projection of the presupposition through negation, as well as the satisfaction of the discourse criterion are to be explained by a separate pragmatic theory. Logically speaking, presuppositions are simply entailments, though they have their own pragmatic properties. Logic has no place for them. Hence, these authors say, there is nothing amiss with classical bivalent logic as an analytic tool for language. This analysis may be called the 'entailment analysis' of presupposition.

If presuppositional entailments were *always* canceled by negation, little could be said against the entailment analysis (but for the failure of any pragmatic theory to account in anything like a satisfactory way for the projection and discourse properties of presuppositions of negated carrier sentences). But this is not so. Under certain definable conditions, natural language *not* is clearly presupposition-preserving (Seuren 1985: 228–33). Thus, in English, when sentence-negating *not* occurs in any other than the canonical position of negation, that is, in construction with the finite verb, it is per se presupposition-preserving. Examples (14b) and (18b) above, with fronted *not*, preserve their presuppositions. And in (26), *not* is in construction with the infinitive *to realize*, and therefore also preserves the factive presupposition induced by this verb:

> Nob seems not to realize that he is in trouble. (26)

Furthermore, as illustrated in (15) above, factive *that*-clauses in fronted position cause the negation over the factive main predicate to preserve the factive presupposition. Then, cleft and pseudocleft presuppositions are always saved under negation, as is seen in (16) and (17). In fact, the kind of discourse-correcting highly marked 'echo' negation found in (25) and similar examples is impossible for all the cases in (27):

~A	A	∧ B 1	2	*	∨ B 1	2	*
2	1	1	2	*	1	1	*
1	2	2	2	*	1	2	*
*	*	*	*	*	*	*	*

Figure 1. Gapped bivalent propositional calculus (GBC)

!**Not** only Nob laughed. He dídn't laugh! (27a)

!**Not** all men are mortal. There dón't exist any men! (27b)

!Nob seems **not** to realize that he is in trouble. He ísn't in trouble! (27c)

!That Nob laughed did **not** surprise Sue. He dídn't laugh! (27d)

!It was **not** Nob who laughed. Nóbody laughed! (27e)

!Who laughed was **not** Nob. Nóbody laughed! (27f)

The same holds for the negation that is required with 'negative polarity items' (NPIs) in simple assertive main clauses (the NPIs are italicized):

!Nob did **not** laugh *at all*. He doesn't exist! (28a)

!Nob does **not** *mind* that he is in trouble. He ísn't in trouble! (28b)

!Nob does **not** live in Kentucky *any longer*. He never lived there! (28c)

!Nob has **not** come back *yet*. He never went away! (28d)

!Sue has **not** seen Nob *in weeks*. She doesn't exist! (28e)

This test to show the canceling of presuppositional entailment, applied in (25), (27), and (28) and used by Wilson as well as Boër and Lycan, is none other than the customary entailment criterion 'not A, yet B' mentioned earlier. It involves, moreover, the typical marked discourse-correcting emphatic *not* with 'echo'-effect. Application of the more refined test 'maybe not A, yet B' yields identical results for the cases at hand:

!Maybe Nob didn't laugh, yet not only Nob laughed. (29a)

!Maybe there exist no men, yet not all men are mortal. (29b)

!Maybe Nob is not in trouble, yet he seems not to realize that he is. (29c)

!Maybe Nob didn't laugh, yet that he laughed did not surprise Sue. (29d)

!Maybe no one laughed, yet it wasn't Nob who laughed. (29e)

!Maybe no one laughed, yet who laughed wasn't Nob. (29f)

!Maybe Nob isn't in trouble, yet he doesn't *mind* that he is. (29g)

!Maybe Nob never went away, yet he hasn't come back *yet*. (29h)

!Maybe Nob never lived in Kentucky, yet he doesn't live there *any longer*. (29i)

Curiously, however, application of the more refined

test yields positive results for *all* presuppositions, not only those under presupposition-preserving negation:

!There may not be a king of France, yet he is not bald. (30a)

!Maybe Nob wasn't Sue's student, yet she has not forgotten that he was. (30b)

!Maybe Nob didn't go away, yet he hasn't come back. (30c)

This would mean that negation does, after all, preserve presuppositions as full entailments. One notes, however, that when the more refined test is applied, as in (29) and (30), there is no way one can assign emphatic accent to *not*, because there is no discourse correction and hence no 'echo'-effect. The use of *not* in (29) and (30) is thus seen to be different from (25), and in general all similar cases presented in Wilson (1975) and elsewhere. And this use of *not* does preserve presuppositions.

This observation, together with the fact that under certain structurally definable conditions negation does preserve presuppositional entailments, renews the threat to classical bivalent logic. One proposal to solve this logical problem is to say that language conforms to a three-valued (trivalent) logic, which is identical to classical bivalent logic but for a distinction made between two kinds of falsity, each turned into truth (designated) by a separate negation operator. 'Minimal falsity' ('2') results when all presuppositions are true but not all classical entailments. 'Radical falsity' ('3') results when one or more presuppositions fail to be true. Correspondingly, 'minimal negation' ($\sim$) turns minimal falsity into truth, and truth into minimal falsity, leaving radical falsity unaffected, while 'radical negation' ($\simeq$) turns radical falsity into truth, and both truth and minimal falsity into minimal falsity. The radical negation enables one to utter a proposition about states of affairs falling outside the subuniverse for the discourse at hand, something which Strawson's GBC does not allow for.

From this point on there are two known ways to generalize 'classical bivalent propositional calculus' (CBC) to more values. The first is Kleene's (1938) 'trivalent generalized calculus' (TGC[1]). It aims at preserving all theorems of CBC with bivalent $\neg$ replacing trivalent $\sim$. This is what the truth-tables of Fig. 2 do. The generalization is that $\wedge$ yields '2' whenever either conjunct is valued '2,' '1' only if both conjuncts are valued '1,' and '3' otherwise. Analogously, $\vee$ yields '1' whenever either conjunct is valued '1,' '2' only if both conjuncts are valued '2,' and '3' otherwise.

This system is widely used by presuppositional logicians (e.g., Blau 1978; Blamey 1986). One notes that TGC[1] lacks the radical negation ($\simeq$), but the system will come to no harm if it is added, so that the two negations can formally distinguish between minimal and radical falsity.

		∧ B			∨ B		
~A	A	1	2	3	1	2	3
2	1	1	2	3	1	1	1
1	2	2	2	2	1	2	3
3	3	3	2	3	1	3	3

Figure 2. Trivalent generalized calculus 1 (TGC^1)

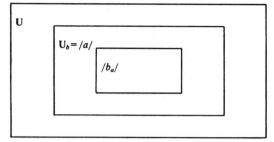

Figure 4. Valuation space construction of /b$_a$/ and U_b in U

The other generalization of CBC to more values is found in Seuren (1985; 1988). The operators ∧ and ∨ select, respectively, the highest and the lowest of the component values. This results in truth-tables as shown in Fig. 3. Note that classical negation (¬), which has been added for good measure, is the union of ~ and ≃, as is likewise the case in TGC^1. In Seuren's view (as expressed in Seuren 1985; 1988), ¬ does not occur in natural language, which has only ~ and ≃.

It has been shown (Weijters 1985) that TGC^2 is equivalent with classical bivalent logic if only the operators ¬, ∧, and ∨ are used. Thus, closed under {¬, ∧, ∨} classical bivalent logic is independent of the number of truth-values (tv) employed, though any tv > 2 will be vacuous.

Moreover, in both generalizations with n truth-values (n ≥ 2), there is, for any tv i ≥ 2, a 'specific negation' N_i turning only that tv into truth, lower values into '2,' and leaving higher values unaffected. Thus, in TGC^2, as in Fig. 3, N_2 is ~ and N_3 is ≃. Classical bivalent ¬ is the union of all specific negations. Consequently, in CBC, ¬ is both the one specific negation allowed for and the union of all specific negations admitted. CBC is thus the most economical variety possible of a generalized calculus of either type, with just one kind of falsity.

The distinction between the two kinds of falsity is best demonstrated by considering valuation spaces. Let U (the 'universe') be again the set of all possible states of affairs (valuations), and /A/ (the 'valuation space' of A) the set of all possible valuations in which A is true (A, B, ... being metavariables over sentences $a, b, c, d, ...$ and their compositions in the language L). We now define U_A (the 'subuniverse' of A) as *the set of all possible valuations in which the conjunction of all presuppositions of A is true*. Since A ⊨ A, /A/ is the valuation space of the conjunction of all entailments of A. And since A ⊯ A, /A/ ⊂ U_A. /~A/ is the comp-

lement of /A/ in U_A, whereas /≃A/ is the complement of U_A in U. Clearly, /≃A/∪/~A/ = /¬A/. If A has no presuppositions, then /~A/ = /≃A/ = /¬A/. Conjunction and disjunction denote, as standard, intersection and union, respectively, of valuation spaces. For any valuation v_n, if $v_n∈$/A/, v_n(A) = 1. If $v_n∈U_A$, v_n(A) = 2 and v_n(~A) = 1. If $v_n∈U - U_A$, v_n(A) = 3 and v_n(≃A) = 1 (for more details, see Seuren 1988).

The normal negation in language is the minimal negation (~), denoting the complement of a sentence's valuation space within its subuniverse. And the normal truth-values speakers reckon with in undisturbed discourse are '1' and '2.' The function of the subuniverse of a sentence A, that is, U_A, is, typically, to limit the set of states of affairs (valuations) in which A can be uttered while being true or minimally false. Since presuppositions are type-level properties of sentences and thus structurally derivable from them, competent speakers immediately reconstruct U_A on hearing A (this fact underlies the phenomenon of 'accommodation' or 'post hoc suppletion'; see below). And since they proceed on the default assumption of normal undisturbed discourse, the default use of negation will be that of ~, ≃ being strongly marked in that it provokes an 'echo' of the non-negated sentence (which, one feels, has been either uttered anyway 'in the air' in immediately preceding discourse), and calls for a correction of preceding discourse.

The question of whether TGC^2 or TGC^1 is preferable for the description and analysis of presuppositional phenomena is hard to decide if presupposition is defined as follows (varying on Strawson's definition mentioned above):

$$B ≫ A =_{Def} B ⊨ A \text{ and } {\sim}B ⊨ A \text{ and } {\sim}A ⊨ {\simeq}B \qquad (31)$$
$$\text{and } {\simeq}A ⊨ {\simeq}B$$

According to this purely logical definition in trivalent terms, if nontruth of A necessarily leads to radical falsity of B, then B ≫ A. Extensive testing shows that, on this definition, both TGC^2 and TGC^1 suffer from empirical inadequacies.

TGC^2 is at a disadvantage for conjunctions of the form A ∧ B$_A$, since it predicts that A ∧ B$_A$ ≫ A (non-

				∧ B			∨ B		
¬A	≃A	~A	A	1	2	3	1	2	3
2	2	2	1	1	2	3	1	1	1
1	2	1	2	2	2	3	1	2	2
1	1	3	3	3	3	3	1	2	3

Figure 3. Trivalent generalized calculus 2 (TGC^2)

truth of A gives radical falsity of B_A and thus of $A \wedge B_A$). A sentence like:

Nob's dog has died and he is sad about it. (32)

should thus presuppose that Nob's dog has died, which is not what the operational criteria tell us. TGC^1 fares better for this type of conjunction, since here, if $v_n(A) = 2$, $v_n(B_A) = 3$, and therefore, $v_n(A \wedge B_A) = 2$.

Both TGC^1 and TGC^2 make incorrect predictions for disjunctions (and hence conditionals). In both systems, the following theorem holds:

$$(\sim A \vee B_A) \wedge (\sim B_A \vee C_A) \gg A \quad (33)$$

Thus, a sentence like:

If Nob's dog has died Nob knows it, and if he (34)
knows it he is sad about it.

is said to presuppose that Nob's dog has died. And a sentence like:

If Nob's dog has died Nob knows it or he (35)
doesn't know it,
and if he knows it he is drunk,
and if he doesn't know it he is sober

presupposes that Nob's dog has died in TGC^1, while it is entailed in TGC^2. Both are thus seen to make incorrect predictions if *and* is made to translate $\wedge$, and 'if A then B' stands for $(\sim A \vee B)$.

3. The Discourse Approach

The problems raised by a purely logical definition of presupposition are compounded by the fact that a *logical* definition of presupposition, such as (31), inevitably entails that any arbitrary sentence will presuppose any necessary truth, which would take away all empirical content from the notion of presupposition. Attempts have therefore been made (for example, Gazdar 1979; Heim 1982; Seuren 1985) at viewing a presupposition A of a sentence B_A as restricting the interpretable use of B to contexts that admit of, or already contain, the information carried by A. If one sticks to trivalence, (31) may be weakened from a definition to a mere logical property:

If $B \gg A$ then $B \vDash A$ and $\sim B \vDash A$ and $\sim A \vDash \simeq B$ (36)
and $\simeq A \vDash \simeq B$

One advantage of this approach is that it leaves room for an account of the discourse-correcting 'echo' function of radical NOT. Horn (1985; 1989) says, no doubt correctly (though his generalization to other metalinguistic uses of negation is less certain), that NOT is 'metalinguistic,' in that it says something about the *sentence* in its scope. Neither TGC^2 nor TGC^1 accounts for this metalinguistic property. What NOT-('B_A') says about the sentence 'B_A' is that it suffers from presupposition failure, and thus cannot be coherently used in a discourse where A has been denied truth. NOT is interpreted as the complex predicate 'belongs to the non-language for the discourse at hand.' The notion of 'non-language' is defined in terms of 'sequential discourse incrementation.'

The 'sequential incrementation' of a (monologue) discourse D is a process restricting D to specified valuation spaces. Intuitively, it locates the situation to be described in a progressively narrower section of U. Incrementation involves the assignment of the value '1' or '2' to sentences of the language L. The result of the sequential incrementation of A, or i(A), is a (further) restriction of the D under construction to the intersection of $/D/$ and $/A/$. $D+A$ is thus equivalent to $D \wedge A$: D can be considered the conjunction of all its sentences. The initial valuation space is U.

The 'sequentiality criterion' requires that:
(a) if $B \gg A$ then i(A) must precede i(B),
(b) i(A $\wedge$ B) consists of i(A) followed by i(B),
(c) for any D, $/D/ \supset /D+A/$,
(d) no i(A) may result in the empty valuation space.

Condition (a) requires that if A has not already been incremented prior to i(B_A) it is quietly 'slipped in.' This process is called 'accommodation' or 'post hoc suppletion.' A text requiring accommodation is not fully sequential. Condition (b) splits up a conjunction into separate subsequent incrementations of its conjuncts. Condition (c) is the 'informativeness condition.' It requires that every subsequent incrementation restricts the valuable space of D, thus specifying further the situation to be described. Condition (d) prevents logical inconsistency in any D. Again, the sequentiality criterion does not imply that a discourse or text not satisfying it is unacceptable in some sense. It only sets out the prototypical conditions of a possibly unexciting but well-ordered discourse.

If A is valued '2,' then B_A is excluded from D since now both B_A and $\sim B_A$ are valued '3,' which is not allowed in D: neither B nor $\sim B$ can be processed in D. Thus, at each stage Q in the development of D there is a set of sentences of L that are excluded from the further development of D, and also a set of sentences that can still be processed. The former is the 'nonlanguage' of D at Q, or $NL(D)^Q$; the latter is the 'presuppositional language' of D at Q, or $PL(D)^Q$. $PL(D)^Q$ is thus defined by the constraint that D contains no negation of any of the presuppositions of the sentences of $PL(D)^Q$.

For example, let D consist of the sentences a, b_a, and $\sim c_b$, in that order (b_a has no presuppositions beyond a, and analogously for c_b). Now $d_c \in NL(D)^c$, since c is valued '2.' The sentence NOT('d') is now true, as it says precisely this. In this interpretation, NOT('d') is incremented the way sentences normally are: $/D/$ will contain states of affairs involving sentences, which are objects like other objects. But the logical relation of NOT('d') with respect to $\sim d$ and d cannot be expressed due to the metalevel shift. NOT('d') is now understood as 'the truth-commitments entered into so far are satisfied and d suffers from presupposition failure; it therefore belongs to $NL(D)^C$.' Both i(d) and i($\sim d$)

367

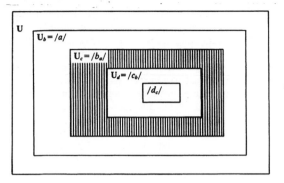

Figure 5. Valuation space construction of $/\sim c_{ba}/$ and $/d_c/$

result in the empty valuation space, as $(/d/ \cup /\sim d/) \cap /\sim c/ = \varnothing$. This is illustrated in Fig. 5, where the area covered by vertical lines is $/\sim c/$.

Under this construal of the notion of sequential discourse, we are practically back at Strawson's GBC (Fig. 1), but with the extra provision of sentences (and other linguistic objects) as possible reference objects. It follows from this analysis that natural language negation is ambiguous between $\sim$ and NOT, the latter being interpretable as 'belongs to $\mathbf{NL(D)}^{\text{now}}$,' and thus providing a functional instrument for correcting any discourse whose sequential reconstruction (that is, with full post hoc suppletion of all implicit presuppositions) is inconsistent.

This may provoke fears of a resurrection of the 'liar paradox.' Yet this fear is unfounded. Following the medieval solution to this paradox in terms of *vacatio*, that is, lack of reference (Bottin 1976; Seuren 1987), we say that the sentence *This proposition is false* fails to deliver a reference object for the subject term *this proposition*, so that the sentence fails to deliver a truth-value. This solution implies an infraction of PET, but so does the whole analysis.

A generalized trivalent logic is still useful in that it can express the logical properties of NOT. If NOT('d') (in the example of Fig. 5) is interpreted, after $\sim c_d$, as $\simeq d$, that is, as the intersection of $/\sim c/$ and $/\simeq d/$ ($= /\sim c/$ since $/\simeq d/ = U-/c/$), it is valued '1,' yet has no effect on the incrementation of D: it does not restrict further the valuation space of D and thus violates condition (c) of the sequentiality criterion. But now the metalinguistic character of NOT is ignored and i($\simeq d$) is true but not informative.

From this point of view, TGC^1 and TGC^2 differ as follows. In TGC^1, as can be seen from Fig. 2, $U^A \wedge {}^B = (U_A \cap U_B) \cup /\sim A/ \cup /\sim B/$. Thus, if A has no presuppositions, $U_{A \wedge B_A} = (U \cap /A/) \cup (U-/A/) \cup (/A/-/B/) = U$. Consequently, $/\sim B_A/ = /A/-/B/$, but $\sim(A \wedge B_A) \equiv \neg B_A$, even though $/B_A/ = /A \wedge B_A/$. A fully sequential discourse will thus never be radically false in TGC^1, even when A is minimally false and all

the remaining sentences are therefore radically false. But a discourse $[B_A + C_B + D_C + \ldots]$ (that is, with the initial presupposition kept implicit) will be radically false just in case A is not true. In TGC^2, on the other hand, the subuniverses for conjunction (and disjunction) run parallel: $U^A \wedge {}^B = (U_A \cap U_B)$ (and $U^A \vee {}^B = (U_A \cup U_B)$). Thus, $U_{[A+B_A+C_B+D_C]} = U_{[B_A+C_B+D_C]} = /C/$, as it makes no difference whether the presupposition is implicit or explicit. Since it makes a D radically false as soon as a radically false sentence is added, it allows for the rule that a minimally false D is made true simply by negating all its false sentences, without any sentence having to be rejected as belonging to $\mathbf{NL(D)}$, whereas a radically false D is made true by negating all its minimally false sentences and eliminating all sentences valued '3.' Such a trivalent logic requires that the notion of presupposition be limited to single increment units. In TGC^2, conjunctions (discourses) have subuniverses, but no presuppositions.

4. The Structural Source of Presuppositions

The structural source of three of the four types of presupposition that were distinguished at the outset of Sect. 1 can be identified uniformly: it lies in the lexical meaning conditions of the main predicate of the sentence (clause) in question. The lexical conditions of a predicate P^n over individual objects are the conditions that must be satisfied for any object, or n-tuple of objects, to be truthfully predicated by means of P^n. Thus, for the unary predicate *bald* the conditions must be specified under which any object can truthfully be called 'bald.' Or for the binary predicate *wash* it must be specified under what conditions it can truthfully be said of any pair of objects $\langle i, j \rangle$ that 'i washes j.' Analogously for predicates whose terms refer to things other than individual objects, such as sets of objects, or facts, or imbedded propositions.

In the light of presupposition theory, one can now, following Fillmore (1971), make a distinction between two kinds of lexical conditions, which we shall call the 'preconditions' and the 'satisfaction conditions.' The criterion distinguishing the two is that when any precondition is not fulfilled the sentence is radically false, whereas failure of a satisfaction condition results in minimal falsity. Fulfillment of all conditions results in truth.

The following notation makes the distinction formally clear. Let the extension of a predicate P^n be characterized by the function symbol σ. Then an n-ary predicate P^n over individuals will have the following schema for the specification of its lexical conditions:

$$\sigma(P^n) = \{\langle i^1, i^2, \ldots, i^n \rangle : \ldots (\text{preconditions}) \ldots | \ldots \quad (37)$$
$$(\text{satisfaction conditions}) \ldots \}$$

or: 'the extension of P^n is the set of all n-tuples of individuals $\langle i^1, i^2, \ldots, i^n \rangle$ such that $\ldots$ (preconditions) $\ldots$ and $\ldots$ (satisfaction conditions) $\ldots$' The preconditions and satisfaction conditions may affect any or all of the members of the n-tuple. The predicate *bald*, for example, can be considered to have a lexical specification of the following structure (without any pretension to lexicographical adequacy):

$$\sigma(\text{bald}) = \{i : i \text{ is normally covered, in} \quad (38)$$
$$\text{prototypical places, with hair, fur,}$$
$$\text{or pile; or } i \text{ is a tire and normally}$$
$$\text{covered with tread} \mid \text{the normal covering}$$
$$\text{is absent}\}$$

Categorial presuppositions are thus clearly derivable from lexical preconditions. The same holds for factive presuppositions, to be derived from a precondition associated with the factive predicate in question to the effect that the proposition expressed by the factive *that*-clause must be true. Discourse-semantically this means that the factive *that*-clause must be incremented in the truth-domain of D, or anyway in the same (sub)-D as the carrier sentence, and prior to it.

A similar treatment is now obvious for existential presuppositions. An existential presupposition is associated with a particular argument term of a given predicate P^n, and derivable from the precondition that the reference object of that argument term must exist in the real world. It is then said that P^n is 'extensional with respect to that argument term.' The predicate *talk about*, for example, is extensional with respect to its subject term, but not with respect to its object term, since one can very well talk about things that do not exist. Most predicates are extensional with respect to all of their terms, so that one may consider extensionality to be the default case. From a notational point of view it is therefore preferable to mark the nonextensional arguments of a predicate, for example, by means of an asterisk. The lexical description of *talk about* will then be structured as in (39), where the asterisk on 'j' (that is, the reference object of the object term) indicates that this predicate is nonextensional with respect to its object term:

$$\sigma(\text{talk about}) = \{\langle i, j^* \rangle : \ldots (\text{preconditions}) \ldots \quad (39)$$
$$\mid \ldots (\text{satisfaction conditions}) \ldots \}$$

The predicate *exist* is to be specified as nonextensional with respect to its subject term:

$$\sigma(\text{exist}) = \{i^* \mid i \text{ is in the real world}\} \quad (40)$$

Discourse-semantically, this means that a definite subject of the verb *exist* must be represented somewhere in D, but not necessarily in the truth-domain of D. It may very well be located in some intensional subdomain, for example, the subdomain of things that Nob keeps talking about, as in:

The machine that Nob keeps talking about (41)
really exists.

The incremental effect of (41) is that the representation

of the thing that is said to exist is moved up to the truth-domain of D.

The remainder category of presuppositions, induced by words like *only, no longer, still*, or by contrastive accent and (pseudo)cleft constructions, appears not to be derivable in this way. The choice here is either to derive them by adhoc rules, or to adopt a syntactic analysis in terms of which these words and constructions figure as (abstract) predicates at the level of representation that is taken as input to the incrementation procedure. On the whole, the literature is remarkably silent on this question. In general, the prefference is for adhoc derivations of presuppositions (e.g., Gazdar 1979).

See also: Presupposition, Pragmatic.

Bibliography

Blamey S 1986 Partial logic. In: Gabbay D, Guenthner F (eds.) *Handbook of Philosophical Logic*, vol. 3. Reidel, Dordrecht

Blau U 1978 *Die dreiwertige Logik der Sprache. Ihre Syntax, Semantik und Anwendung in der Sprachanalyse*. De Gruyter, Berlin

Boër S E, Lycan W G 1976 The myth of semantic presupposition. *Working Papers in Linguistics* 21: 2–90

Bottin F 1976 *Le antinomie semantiche nella logica medievale*. Antenore, Padua

Fillmore C J 1971 Types of lexical information. In: Steinberg D D, Jakobovits L A (eds.) 1971

Frege G 1892 Ueber Sinn und Bedeutung. *Zeitschrift für Philosophie und philosophische Kritik* 100: 25–50

Gazdar G 1979 *Pragmatics. Implicature, Presupposition, and Logical Form*. Academic Press, New York

Geach P T 1972 *Logic Matters*. Blackwell, Oxford

Groenendijk J, Stokhof M 1991 Dynamic predicate logic. *La Ph* 14: 39–100

Heim I 1982 The semantics of definite and indefinite noun phrases. (Doctoral dissertation, University of Massachusetts at Amherst)

Horn L R 1985 Metalinguistic negation and pragmatic ambiguity. *Lg* 61: 121–74

Horn L R 1989 *A Natural History of Negation*. University of Chicago Press, Chicago, IL

Kamp H 1981 A theory of truth and semantic representation. In: Groenendijk J, Janssen T, Stokhof M (eds.) *Formal Methods in the Study of Language I*. Mathematisch Centrum, Amsterdam

Kempson R M 1975 *Presupposition and the Delimitation of Semantics*. Cambridge University Press, Cambridge

Kiparsky P, Kiparsky C 1971 Fact. In: Steinberg D D, Jakobovits L A (eds.) 1971

Kleene S 1938 On notation for ordinal numbers. *Journal of Symbolic Logic* 3: 150–55

Kneale W C, Kneale M 1962 *The Development of Logic*. Clarendon Press, Oxford

Russell B 1905 On denoting. *Mind* 14: 479–93

Seuren P A M 1977 Forme logique et forme sémantique: Un argument contre M. Geach. *Logique et Analyse* 20: 338–47

Seuren P A M 1985 *Discourse Semantics*. Blackwell, Oxford

Seuren P A M 1987 Les paradoxes et le langage. *Logique et Analyse* 30: 365–83

Seuren P A M 1988 Presupposition and negation. *Journal of Semantics* **6**: 175–226

Steinberg D D, Jakobovits L A (eds.) 1971 *Semantics. An Interdisciplinary Reader in Philosophy, Linguistics, and Psychology*. Cambridge University Press, Cambridge

Strawson P F 1950 On referring. *Mind* **59**: 320–44

Strawson P F 1952 *Introduction to Logical Theory*. Methuen, London

Weijters A 1985 Presuppositional propositional calculi. Appendix to Seuren P A M 1985

Wilson D 1975 *Presuppositions and Non-Truth-Conditional Semantics*. Academic Press, London

Semantics versus Syntax: Perspectives on Natural Language Content
R. M. Kempson

The period between 1972 and the early 1990s was a period of an assumed dichotomy between syntactic and semantic forms of explanation. However, at the end of this period, the sharpness of the division is being questioned as problems of interpretation emerge that need structural solutions. As will be demonstrated, the resolution of this dichotomy involves an accompanying shift in assumptions about the language faculty itself.

In 1972, the battlelines between syntactic and semantic investigations into properties definitive of natural language were drawn up by Lewis (1972): semantics was announced to be the articulation of truth-theoretic content, and representational approaches to content were dismissed as 'markerese' with the comment that 'one might just as well translate into Latin.' These antimarkerese arguments were addressed against Katz's theory of semantic markers (cf. Katz 1972), but were taken as applying to any characterization of meaning which advocated meaning representations intermediate between syntactic explications of structure and the semantic objects which constitute the interpretation of that structure. Chomsky responded to this challenge with the retort (articulated in most detail in Chomsky 1986) that semantics was not part of any natural language grammar, hence *a fortiori* not definitive of the language faculty. These two positions became ideological stances, the Lewis approach to natural language understanding developed by those working in the Montague paradigm (Thomason 1974; Dowty 1979; Dowty, et al. 1981; Chierchia and McConnell-Ginet 1990), while the Chomskian concept of natural language developed into the 'government and binding paradigm' (Chomsky 1982; May 1985; Chomsky 1986).

A phenomenon which poses both sides of the divide with problems of equal severity (though recognized only within semantics, cf. Partee 1984b) is the phenomenon of context dependence. The information conveyed by natural language expressions varies from context to context, and the process whereby we as hearers establish such values involves processes of general reasoning. The simplest examples involve pronouns indexically used. Example (1) can be an assertion about Tom, Dick or Harry, depending on who is being talked about:

He is sick. (1)

By model-theoretic criteria, the sentence is ambiguous, having different interpretations as the referent varies. The phenomenon of multiple ambiguity is by no means restricted to such indexical uses. There is an array of different kinds of interpretation assigned to pronominal expressions, labeled variously as bound-variable pronouns, discourse coreference (Reinhart 1983, 1986), E-type pronouns (Evans 1980; Heim 1982), donkey-type pronouns (Kamp 1981; Heim 1982), and lazy pronouns (Karttunen 1968; Cooper 1979). All share the property that the interpretation of the pronoun is determined by some form of linkage with an antecedent, but the type of linkage varies, as does the type of model-theoretic content):

John came in. He was sick. (2)

Every student worries that she is going to fail. (3)

Joan worries that she's going to fail. (4)

Only a few students entered the exam, but they were confident they would pass. (5)

Every student who entered for an exam, passed it. (6)

Every student who puts her cheque in the building society is more sensible than the student who puts it in her current account. (7)

With model-theoretic assumptions underpinning the concept of linguistic content, the full set of pronominal uses is nonunitary. Such assumptions thus fail to provide a semantic basis for characterizing the information conveyed by a pronoun qua pronoun (there is a voluminous literature on the degree to which the heterogeneity of this phenomenon can be reduced, cf. Cooper 1979; Hausser 1979; Kamp 1981; Heim 1982; Kempson 1988; Heim 1990; Chierchia 1995; Kamp and Reyle 1993; van Eijk and Kamp 1997).

This proliferation of ambiguities is across the board. All anaphoric expressions depend for their interpretation on some concept of context of utterance giving rise to a range of truth-theoretically discrete types of meaning. Examples (8)–(17) display an array of VP, nominal, and demonstrative anaphoric dependencies, having in common only this property of dependency on their immediate surrounding context for assignment of some interpretation:

John likes Mary, but I don't. (8)

Everyone worries about their logic paper, (9)
except Marcelo, who never does.

John kissed everyone that Sue didn't. (10)

Don't. (11)

Most students like Maths, but I know at least (12)
one who does not

One will do. (13)

Jo telephoned a journalist every time Sue (14)
interviewed one.

That man is a nuisance. (15)

She made a cake for John and that bastard never (16)
thanked her.

Every time she had a coke, she knew that later, (17)
that week she'd have a headache.

The phenomenon is not even restricted to explicitly anaphoric processes. It can apply to tense construal (Partee 1984b), to the interpretation of adjectives (Klein 1980), adverbs (Stump 1985), and so on. Indeed natural-language expressions, both simple and complex, are invariably construed relative to some unfolding concept of context. We seem faced with a multiplicity of ambiguities far beyond what any lexical sources of ambiguity would lead us to expect.

This phenomenon is additionally problematic for the Montague program, because it conflicts with a central cornerstone of the program—the compositionality principle. According to this principle, the meaning of any compound expression is recursively defined as a function of the meaning of its elementary parts. Indeed the force of model-theoretic semantics lies in large measure in the substance it provides to the claim that the truth-theoretic content for sentence-sized expressions is a function of the way in which the content of lexical elements combines together to yield a truth-evaluable whole. But as Kamp pointed out in 1981, it is not obvious in what sense the sentence *He was sick* in (2) has a truth-evaluable content as a sentence—rather the truth-evaluable content that it has is dependent on the evaluation of the previous

sentence *John came in* and the relation between the two.

The solution Kamp proposed to these problems became the first model to blur the syntax–semantics dichotomy, and this analysis was the first dynamic model of semantic evaluation (Kamp 1981). He defined an intermediate level of characterization called 'discourse representation structure' (DRS), a structure defined by an algorithm whose role was to assign values to anaphoric expressions as part of the mapping from syntactic construct to DRS. The DRS so assigned to a sentence was then subject to model-theoretic evaluation. So rather than interpreting the sentence *John came in,* and only then, independently interpreting *He was sick,* the algorithm projects a DRS for the first sentence (I), and extends this by the information provided by the second sentence to create the new DRS II:

$$
\boxed{\begin{array}{l} u \, . \\ \text{John}(u) \\ \text{came in}(u) \end{array}} \qquad \text{DRS I}
$$

$$
\boxed{\begin{array}{l} u \, . \, v \, . \\ \text{John}(u) \\ \text{came in}(u) \\ v = u \\ \text{sick}(v) \end{array}} \qquad \text{DRS II}
$$

A DRS is a partial model containing some nonempty set of entities called discourse referents, and predicates on those entities. Truth is then defined for a DRS in terms of its embeddability in some total model, and not as a property of sentences directly. Despite the model-theoretic status of these mini-models, the internal structure of such DRS's has played an important role in the way the theory has developed. There is for example a stated locality condition on the identification of a discourse referent for pronouns that they be identified from some 'higher' DRS. This structural condition on pronominal identification led in its turn to a rule moving elements from some subordinate box to some higher DRS. For example the two readings of (18) according as the indefinite is or is not internal to the conditional are distinguished as the discourse referent for the indefinite is or is not moved to the 'top box':

If a friend of mine comes to see me, let her in. (18)

Such locality conditions and/or movement processes critically invoke properties of the DRS qua representation in ways not naturally reducible to some model-theoretic image. Thus we get the first blurring of semantic and syntactic constructs—constructs defined in semantic terms but manipulated in terms of their configurational properties. There is also unclarity in the status of such intermediate representations. Are they a set of representations internal to the natu-

371

ral-language grammar, or are they rather part of some general model structure onto which natural-language strings are mapped. A formal algorithm is defined from natural language expressions onto DR structures, suggesting that they are envisaged as being part of natural-language grammars. Yet they are defined for entities for which those grammars do not provide input—viz., sequences of sentences. This is the problem which lies at the heart of the context-dependency phenomenon: the articulation of truth-evaluable vehicles is not defined over sentence-strings as determined by principles internal to the grammar alone, but by such principles in combination with something else. If we are to isolate a concept of natural language content attributable to natural language expressions independent of context, then we have to model two related phenomena: (a) the underdeterminacy displayed by many natural language expressions, simple and complex, vis-à-vis the truth-theoretic content attributable to them; and (b) the process whereby the lexically-assigned natural-language content is enriched to yield some such complete specification. DRT was one of the first theories of semantic modeling to seriously grapple with this problem (cf. also Heim 1982; Barwise and Perry 1984).

The context-dependency of truth-theoretic content is no less problematic for standard syntactic assumptions, for the recognition that grammar-internal specification of anaphoric expressions very considerably underdetermines interpretation conflicts with familiar syntactic distinctions. There is claimed to be a distinction between discourse coreference and bound variable anaphora, the latter (but not the former) being subject to a c-command restriction between it and the operator on which it is dependent (Reinhart 1983, 1986). Hence the widely adopted grammar-internal characterization of bound-variable anaphora. This assumption that some anaphoric dependencies are determined exclusively by grammar-internal principles cannot be sustained. The reason is this: for every anaphoric linkage, howsoever established, there is a corresponding bound-variable analogue. In particular there are anaphoric linkages demonstrating two major central cognitive activities:

(a) logical deduction

Joan isn't so anti-private practice as not to have (19)
any private patients, but she's always
complaining that they treat her as a servant.

(b) retrieval from memory of contingently known information associated with specified objects

The fridge is broken. The door needs mending. (20)

Establishing the anaphoric linkage in (19) involves a step of 'double negation elimination': establishing the anaphoric linkage in (20) involves making a link in virtue of the knowledge that fridges have doors. Both processes are central to any account of human reason-

ing of the most general sort, and are not properties of the language faculty itself. But these examples have straightforward analogues in which the pronominal linkage involves central cognitive processes while yet licensing a bound-variable interpretation:

Every one of my friends who isn't so anti- (21)
private practice as not to have any private
patients is complaining that they treat her as a
servant.

Every fridge needs the door mending. (22)

These data pose us with a number of alternatives, only one of which is free of inconsistency. They display an interaction precluded by all standard theories of syntax, that between general cognitive processes and constraints said to be subject to grammar-internal explication. It appears that the output of such general cognitive processes has to be checked against a syntactic restriction on interpretation. We could take these data as evidence that the encapsulation of the language faculty should simply be abandoned and free interaction of processes internal to the language faculty and central cognitive processes should be allowed. Since this would involve jettisoning all possibility of characterizing properties specific to language, this alternative is not acceptable. Notice however that the alternative of invoking the ambiguity of bound-variable anaphora and discourse coreference as a means of dividing off grammar-internal processes from general cognitive processes is not a viable option. To postulate ambiguity here is no help—the grammar-internal phenomenon still involves interaction with the relevant central cognitive processes. And to stipulate double negation elimination or bridging cross-reference as a grammar-internal phenomenon is to incorporate central cognitive processes into the grammar, and this too involves reneging on the language-encapsulation view. Our only recourse is to grant the underdeterminacy of all anaphoric expressions, allow the phenomenon of anaphoric dependence to be characterized as part of the pragmatic process of assigning interpretation to utterances, and characterize the constraint on bound-variable interpretations in like manner to the disjointness requirement on pronominal anaphora (principle B) as a filter on licit choices of anaphoric dependence made as part of this pragmatic process.

Exploring this last route gives us a much more syntactic view of content. We need to define concepts of locality, c-command, etc., over configurations licensed both by grammar-internal processes and by general cognitive processes. There is evidence that this is the right direction in which to look for a solution. Elliptical processes display the underdeterminacy of natural-language expressions vis-à-vis the interpretation assigned to them even more dramatically than anaphora, but are yet subject to familiar grammar-internal constraints such as the so-called 'island' constraints precluding dependency into a relative clause for example (cf. Morgan 1973). Thus bare argument fragments can be interpreted in context as expressing whole propositions, reconstructing complex propositional structure from some antecedent source:

Joan wants Sue to visit Bill in hospital. And Mary too. (23)

The elliptical *And Mary too,* which can be uttered by some other speaker, can be reconstructed either as (a) 'Mary wants Sue to visit Bill in hospital,' or (b) 'Joan wants Mary to visit Bill in hospital,' or as (c) 'Joan wants Sue to visit Mary in hospital.' However, just as *wh*- questions cannot license binding of the *wh*-expression into a relative clause, so these fragments cannot be reconstructed as replacing some expression inside a relative clause:

Joan visited the woman who likes Bill, in hospital. (24)
And Mary too.

The fragment in (24) can be construed as 'Mary visited the woman who likes Bill in hospital,' and as 'Joan visited Mary in hospital.' But it cannot be interpreted as 'Joan visited the woman who likes Mary, in hospital.' This island-constraint phenomenon is generally taken as definitive of a grammatical phenomenon. But there is independent reason to consider that the interpretation of fragments is a pragmatic process, sensitive to general on-line constraints on utterance interpretation—just as is anaphora. If we are not to abandon all hope of retaining the concept of grammar as some encapsulated language-specific faculty, we have to state grammar-internal processes in such a way that they are able to be implemented over pragmatically induced configurations. We need to define utterance interpretation as a structure-building process from the under-determining input provided by grammar-internal principles, and construe all configurational constraints on interpretation as constraints on that structure-building process. We thus arrive at the conclusion that processes of interpretation need to be just as syntactic as the configurations familiar from syntactic theory. The boundaries between syntax and interpretation need to be blurred yet further.

The exploration of such processes of interpretation is taking several routes. There is Discourse Representation Theory, with its intermediate hybrid representations, part semantic, part syntactic (Kamp and Reyle 1993). There is so-called 'structured semantics,' in which structure is superimposed on the model itself (cf. Cresswell 1985). And there is a proof-theoretic route whereby utterance interpretation is characterized as an inferential process of syntactically building a proof structure. This was first proposed by Sperber and Wilson (1986) as one aspect of their overall theory of utterance interpretation. Here a formal model of this option is outlined (Gabbay and Kemp-

son 1992; Kempson and Gabbay in press), showing how it predicts directly the interaction between familiar syntactic constraints and processes of general reasoning without abandoning the encapsulation of the language faculty as an independent input to processes of general reasoning. (This model has been further developed by Kempson, Gabbay and Meyer-Viol; cf. Kempson, et al. in press.)

Suppose we assume that stored in the lexicon for each lexical item is a specification of its contribution to utterance interpretation. In the simple cases, this takes the form of a pair—a conceptual expression, and a specification of its logical type (expressed as in Montague semantics in terms of the two primitives: e, an individual denoting expression; and t, a truth-bearing entity; and combinatorial functions on these). A verb such as *swim* for example, expresses the two-place relation swim', an expression of logical type $\langle e, \langle e, t \rangle \rangle$. Expressing types as propositions and taking the corresponding logical expression as a matching label for its twinned type, we can view this lexically stored information as labeled premises in a logic—premises which will combine together to deduce the proposition expressed by an uttered sentence, as conclusion. Thus in a sentence such as *John loves Mary,* we have three words:

John, loves, Mary

yielding from the lexicon three premises:

John' : e
love' : $e \rightarrow (e \rightarrow t)$
Mary': e

Assuming here concepts of subject and tense, information from the lexicon will lead by two steps of modus ponens to the proposition:

love' (Mary') (John') : t

For every step of modus ponens taken, the information in the labels builds up, recording the assumptions used and their mode of combination, the resulting conclusion a well-formed formula of a predicate logic labeling the logical type t (the logic assumed is the labeled natural deduction system of Gabbay 1996).

Such a sentence as this displays no obvious under-determinacy, but the phenomenon of anaphora can be reconstructed, with its under-determining input, and dependency established in context, as a process of natural deduction. An initiating assumption of some metavariable over labels is entered as the premise lexically associated with the pronoun, an assumption which is discharged by identification with some information independently recoverable from the inference-structure already presented—in effect, the natural deduction moves of the Rule of Assumptions, reiteration of a premise from one inference-structure to another, and assumption discharge:

John loves Mary. She loves him.

> John' : *e*
> love' : *e* → (*e* → *t*)
> Mary' : *e*
> love' (Mary') : *e* → *t*   Modus Ponens
>   love' (Mary') (John') : *t*   Modus Ponens

---

u : *e*	condition: Θ*u* ∉ local proof-structure female(Θ*u*) [Θ an instantiation function]		
Mary' : *e*	Reiteration		
CHOOSE Θ*u* = Mary'			
love' : *e* → (*e* → *t*)			
v : *e*	condition: Θ*v* ∉ local proof-structure male(Θ*v*)		
John' : *e*	Reiteration		
CHOOSE Θ*v* = John'			
love' (John') : *e* → *t*	Modus Ponens		
love' (John') (Mary') : *t*	Modus Ponens		

Reconstructed this way, anaphoric linkage is a relation established across structure—proof-theoretic structure. Locality restrictions on this process, whether to some non-local domain as with pronominals, or to some local domain as with anaphors, are naturally expressible as side conditions on the process of instantiating the initiating assumed variable. We have principle A and principle B of the binding theory stated directly as a specification given in the lexicon as definitional of anaphors/pronominals but implemented on proof structures as part of the process of arriving at some labeled conclusion, here:

love' (John') (Mary') : *t*.

Utterance interpretation can now be defined as a process of natural deduction from some initiating set of premises to some conclusion *a* : *t*, *a* being the proposition expressed, with some of the words presented as premises to that conclusion, others determining how the conclusion is reached. With this mode of explanation the concept of interpretation is essentially structural: linguistic content is characterized in various ways according as the lexical item contributes to this process of proof-unfolding. Lexical items such as *love* contribute labeled premises:

love   love' : *e* → (*e* → *t*).

Items such as pronouns and anaphors contribute premises labeled by a metavariable with some associated side condition determining how that variable is to be identified:

he   *u* : *e* CONDITION   Θ*u* ∉ local proof structure male(Θ*u*)
            (Θ an instantiating function)

And some expressions contribute solely by providing some constraint on the proof process. Relative clause markers, for example, are a means of linking one local piece of reasoning with another—through some unifying variable. Suppose, for example, we wish to link together two pieces of information, that a man fainted and that that man smiled. We can do so through the relative clause structure:

A man who smiled fainted.   (25)

The relative marker provides a means of constructing such linked pieces of information, through common use of some unifying variable. Reflecting this, *wh-* can be characterized as initiating, from the lexicon, a database to be so linked. The logic defines a concept of linked databases, two databases being linked if and only if some free variable in each is replaced by some common unifier. And we assign to *wh-* the lexical specification that it impose the requirement that its containing proof structure lead to a conclusion of type *t* labeled by some open formula containing a variable, a structure which can then be linked through some associated determiner:

wh- {......} ⊢ α(u) : *t*

The lexical content of *wh-* does not itself constitute a premise to be manipulated in any proof structure—rather it provides a restriction on the form of conclusion that must be established.

We now have a new construal of the nature of interpretation—lexical items contain specifications which constrain the building of a proof-structure from which the more orthodox concept of truth-content will be derivable. The essence of linguistic content so defined is that it is meta to any such level and hence essentially syntactic. Furthermore, the building of this configurational structure is not characterized as a grammar-internal process but as a process of central cognitive reasoning. We have arrived at a conclusion which not only blurs syntactic and semantic distinctions but sets a different boundary between grammar-internal and central cognitive processes. Yet despite the apparent merging of syntax and logical deduction, the language faculty itself remains as a discrete construct. The input information, characterized as the lexicon, is the necessary input to the deduction process, its own internal statements encapsulated from and not affected by any subsequent processes of deduction. We abandon the concept of the language faculty as a body of knowledge entirely divorced from our faculty for reasoning, but we retain the concept of encapsulation vis-à-vis its a priori nature, the essential input to any cognitive processing of linguistic stimuli. The apparent interaction of syntactic and cognitive constraints is now unproblematic. The linguistic input severely underdetermines the output structure constituting its interpretation, and the entire process of actually building that structure is a process of reasoning. Many so-called syntactic phenomena emerge as consequences of the proof discipline itself. One such is the island constraint phenomenon displayed in the interpretation of elliptical fragments.

Recall first (23) (repeated here):

Joan wants Sue to visit Bill in hospital. And Mary too.
(23)

We have in the interpretation of the first sentence some complex database leading to the conclusion:

want' (visit' (Bill') (Sue')) (Joan')) : *t*.

With the fragment *and Mary too,* the hearer faces the goal-directed task of reaching some conclusion $\alpha : t$ but here he has only *Mary* provided as input. In order to arrive at some conclusion, he must create the necessary propositional structure. To do this, he reuses the entire previous clause, creates a one-place predicate out of it, and reapplies this result to the new argument *Mary.* This step of building a lambda-abstract is licensed because it is a move from some premise of the form $\alpha : t$ to a premise of the form $\lambda x(a) : e \rightarrow t$, a perfectly licit step of conditional-introduction. Depending upon which position is abstracted over, we can create for (23) any of the interpretations (a)–(c) above. Relative clauses being two such local reasoning structures linked together through a common variable, the relative-clause island phenomenon follows directly:

Joan visited the woman who likes Bill in (24)
hospital. And Mary too.

We build for an interpretation of the first sentence of (24) the linked database:

Joan' : *e*
visited' : $e \rightarrow (e \rightarrow t)$
u : *e*
in-hospital' : $(e \rightarrow t) \rightarrow (e \rightarrow t)$

$\uparrow$

u : *e*
woman' : $e \rightarrow t$

$\uparrow$

u : *e*
likes' : $e \rightarrow (e \rightarrow t)$
Bill' : *e*

To reconstruct the fragment we need to take one step of conditional introduction, but on which local structure should we carry out this step? In order to create the complex reading substituting Mary in place of Bill in the relative clause, we would need to carry out conditional introduction on the first of these local structures (corresponding to the matrix clause). But the premise which we wish to withdraw is not there—it is only in some separate, albeit linked, structure. But conditional introduction is a local step of reasoning—it cannot be vacuously carried out in one struc-

ture as a record of some such step in another structure. The logic itself precludes any such interpretation. Hence the island constraint phenomenona are a direct consequence of the logic discipline adopted. The apparent puzzle of interaction between grammar-internal constraints and the pragmatic process of utterance interpretation is resolved. Syntactic phenomena are explained not by properties definitional of a discrete encapsulated language faculty but by the logic discipline in which the language faculty is embedded. But to do so, we have had to abandon Lewis's stricture and set up a syntactic concept of interpretation, manipulating semantic constructs (such as the type vocabulary) as expressions in a calculus for which inference is syntactically defined.

Within this new perspective, we are able to retain both the concept of a universal human capacity for constructing and manipulating structural configurations through the medium of language; and the concept of parametric variation between languages. Each language is a logic, with its own internal constraints on how the building up of proof-theoretic structures is controled—with idiosyncratic locality restrictions (parametric variation in anaphor binding, for example), with idiosyncratic specification of how one structure is linked online to another (parametric variation in the value of *wh-* dependencies), and so on. But any one such logic falls within the general family of logics defined by the 'labeled deductive system': all such logics are natural deduction systems which model our ability to take elementary concepts, progressively build them up to form complex structured concepts, and then reason with those complex structures as wholes. Our innate language capacity is, that is to say, firmly embedded in our capacity for reasoning.

Bibliography

Barwise J, Perry J 1984 *Situations and Attitudes.* MIT Press, Cambridge, MA

Chierchia G 1995 *The Dynamics of Meaning.* University of Chicago Press, Chicago, IL

Chierchia G, McConnell-Ginet S 1990 *Meaning and Grammar: An Introduction to Semantics.* MIT Press, Cambridge, MA

Chomsky N 1982 *Lectures on Government and Binding.* Foris, Dordrecht

Chomsky N 1986 *Knowledge of Language.* Praeger, New York

Cooper R 1979 The interpretation of pronouns. In: Heny F, Schnelle H (eds.) *Syntax and Semantics,* vol. 10. Academic Press, London

Cresswell M J 1985 *Structured Meanings.* MIT Press, Cambridge, MA

Dowty D R 1979 *Word Meaning and Montague Grammar.* Reidel, Dordrecht

Dowty D R, Wall R E, Peters S 1981 *Introduction to Montague Semantics.* Reidel, Dordrecht

Evans G 1980 Pronouns. *Linguistic Inquiry* **11**: 337–62

Gabbay D 1996 *Labelled Deductive Systems.* Blackwell, Oxford

Gabbay D, Kempson R 1992 Natural-language content: A truth-theoretic perspective. In: *Proceedings of the 8th Amsterdam Formal Semantics Colloquium,* Amsterdam

Hausser R R 1979 How do pronouns denote? In: Heny F, Schnelle H (eds.) *Syntax and Semantics,* vol. 10. Academic Press, London

Heim I 1982 The semantics of definite and indefinite noun phrases (Doctoral thesis, University of Massachusetts)

Heim I 1990 E-type pronouns and donkey anaphora. *Linguistics and Philosophy* 13: 137–78

Kamp H 1981 A theory of truth and discourse representation. In: Groenendijk J A G, Janssen T M V, Stokhof M B J (eds.) *Formal Methods in the Study of Language.* Mathematisch Centrum, Amsterdam

Kamp H, Reyle U 1993 *From Discourse to Logic.* Reidel, North-Holland

Karttunen L 1968 *What do Referential Indices Refer to?* Santa Monica publication no. P-3554

Katz J J 1972 *Semantic Theory.* Harper and Row, New York

Kempson R 1988 Logical form: The grammar-cognition interface. *Journal of Linguistics* 24(2): 393–431

Kempson R, Gabbay D in press Crossover: a unified view. *Journal of Linguistics*

Kempson R, Meyer-Viol W, Gabbay D in press Syntactic computation as labelled deduction. In: Borsley R, Roberts I (eds.) *Syntactic Categories.* Academic Press, New York

Klein E 1980 A semantics for positive and comparative adjectives. *Linguistics and Philosophy* 4: 1–45

Lewis D 1972 General semantics. In: Davidson D, Harman G *Semantics of Natural Languages.* Reidel, Dordrecht

May R 1985 *Logical Form: Its Structure and Derivation.* MIT Press, Cambridge, MA

Morgan J 1973 Sentence fragments and the notion 'sentence.' In: Kachru B B, Lees R B, Malkiel Y, Pietrangeli A, Saporta S (eds.) *Issues in Linguistics: Papers in Honor of Henry and Renee Kahane.* University of Illinois Press, Urbana, IL

Partee B H 1984a Nominal and temporal anaphora. *Linguistics and Philosophy* 13: 243–86

Partee B 1984b Compositionality. In: Landman F, Veltman F (eds.) *Varieties of Formal Semantics.* Foris, Dordrecht

Reinhart T 1983 Coreference and bound anaphora: A restatement of the anaphora question. *Linguistics and Philosophy* 6: 47–88

Reinhart T 1986 Center and periphery in the grammar of anaphora. In: Lust B (ed.) *Studies in the Acquisition of Anaphora,* vol. 1. Reidel, Dordrecht

Sperber D, Wilson D 1986 *Relevance: Communication and Cognition.* Blackwell, Oxford

Stump G T 1985 *The Semantic Variability of Absolutive Constructions.* Reidel, Dordrecht

Thomason R H (ed.) 1974 *Formal Philosophy: Selected Papers of Richard Montague.* Yale University Press, New Haven, CT

van Eijk J, Kamp H 1997 Representing discourse in context. In: van Benthem J, ter Meulen A (eds.) *Handbook of Logic and Language.* MIT Press, Cambridge, MA

Situation Semantics

P. J. E. Dekker and H. L. W. Hendriks

The term 'situation semantics' covers a variety of theories and conceptions of meaning and the logic of information, and, particularly, the development of a partial semantics for natural language. Within this context, situations are the basic building blocks of reality. They constitute the cornerstones of a theoretic framework that allows for an integrated classification of the world, of meaning, and of the mental states that cognitive beings can be in.

At the heart of the enterprise lies the work of the founding fathers of situation semantics: Jon Barwise and John Perry. In the early 1980s they launched a campaign for a more 'realistic,' situation-based semantics, and against traditional formal semantic theories which were rejected as too coarse-grained. A series of publications culminated in the still canonical book on the subject: *Situations and Attitudes* (Barwise and Perry 1983; *S&A* henceforth). The book introduced the basic themes which, even 10 years after,

continued to engage the situation semantic entrepreneurs.

In this article some of those themes are addressed. In the first section, the key notions 'meaning,' 'realism,' 'partiality,' and 'relativity' are explained. The second section is a short introduction to situation theory, a theory of the classification of reality and meaning. Then there is a sketch of how a situation theoretic semantics of natural language can be built up, including a treatment of the notoriously problematic 'propositional' attitude reports. The last section surveys a number of extensions and developments.

1. Key Notions

1.1 Meaning and Information

Traditionally, formal semantics has focused on developing a theory of truth and truth-preserving inference. The descriptive content of an indicative sentence is explained in terms of its truth conditions, and an inference is called 'valid' if the truth conditions of the premises are at least as strong as the truth conditions of the conclusion.

Situation semantics is more ambitious. Following Dretske (1981), who takes information as the basic notion of the domain of knowledge and communication, it considers a semantics based on truth conditions much too abstract for the analysis of everyday reasoning and the exchange of information in natural language. Instead, it tries to supply a general theory of information extraction and processing which applies to linguistic information exchange as a special case. Within such a theory, truth and validity will only be derivative.

The guiding idea is that meaning is not some idealized or idealizable relation between language and the world, but a very real thing in the world itself. The world is full of information: events happening in one part of the world carry information about events in other parts of the world, and living organisms are able to pick up such information and react accordingly. For instance, the presence of smoke may carry the information that there is fire, and, likewise, the exclamation 'Fire!' may inform us about the same thing: that there is a fire. Individuals seeing the smoke, or hearing somebody shout 'Fire!' may well be disposed to run away. In both cases, the informational link can be expressed by the word 'means': smoke means fire and 'Fire!' means fire. Of course, smoke's (naturally) meaning fire and Fire!'s (conventionally) meaning fire are not the same thing, but they are 'very much the same' from the perspective of an information-processing agent. Situation theory classes the different species of informational links under a common genus. These links may be natural laws, but they are also linguistic conventions.

1.2 Realism and Attunement

Mere regularities do not give rise to meaning. One can speak of meaning when organisms become 'attuned' to the regularities in their environment, and start to anticipate events on the basis of obtaining events.

Basically then, meaning is taken to be a discriminated relation between real events or situations. However, the perceptual and cognitive capacities of living organisms enable a more fine-grained classification of their environment. Organisms may individuate objects, relations, and locations, and classify situations according to whether they support the state of affairs that certain objects stand in certain relations at certain locations. Yet, these objects and relations are considered 'real,' since they are 'uniformities' across situations. Hence, meanings can be derivatively, but realistically, seen as relations between compounds of aspects of real events, between situations of certain types.

1.3 Partiality and Situations

The most important feature of situation semantics is its partiality. In general, information is a partial description of situations, which are themselves parts of the world. This is consistent with the general idea that meaning is situated in reality. First, information for living organisms concerns their environment, the part of reality in which an organism finds itself. Second, the regularities that enable organisms to extract information obtain between (types of) situations, not between complete worlds. Besides, these regularities usually hold only in parts of the world, for instance in the natural environment of the individual. As was pointed out, the relevant regularities for organisms are generally not full-blown natural laws; they include conventional regularities connecting utterances with the things they mean.

1.4 Relativity and Efficiency

The notion of meaning as a relation between situations is another hallmark of the theory. In the situation semantic perspective it is not sentences that convey information or entail one another, but statements, i.e., sentences uttered on a specific occasion. Linguistic meaning is a relation between utterance situations and interpretations, and the meaning of an assertively used indicative sentence ϕ is a relation between situations in which ϕ is uttered on the one hand, and the collection of described situations that constitute ϕ's interpretation on the other. This relational account of meaning sheds new light on the so-called 'efficiency of language.' This phenomenon, more familiarly known as 'context dependence,' is the connection between described situations and the (partial) contexts in which language is used. For example, it is (part of) the meaning of the personal pronoun 'I' that it refers to the speaker—not some unique speaker in the whole wide world, but the unique speaker in an utterance situation. More generally, the notion of meaning as a relation between (types of) situations can exploit all kinds of facts in the utterance situation which are relevant for establishing the interpretation of that utterance.

2. Situation Theory

The major tenet of situation theory is that reality consists of situations. Situations can be perceived and stand in causal relations to one another. They exhibit uniformities to living organisms. The basic uniformities that human beings recognize are individuals $(a, b, \ldots)$, n-ary relations $(r^n, \ldots,$ where $n \geqslant 0)$, and locations $(l, l', \ldots)$. These uniformities we find reflected in human languages. Individuals are thought of as the real things known to us, which figure in different situations. Relations (including properties) are also seen as invariants across real situations. Locations are taken to be regions of space–time. They may temporally precede, and spatially or temporally overlap or include one another.

From these 'primitives' and $\{0, 1\}$, an additional set of 'polarity markers' ($\{no, yes\}$ in *S&A*), other situation theoretic objects can be built up. First, sequences of basic information units, 'infons,' are constructed: $\langle\!\langle R^n, l, a_1, \ldots, a_n; i\rangle\!\rangle$ consisting of an n-ary relation R^n, a location l, a sequence of n individuals $a_1, \ldots, a_n$, and a polarity marker i. Such sequences reflect the fact that the individuals $a_1, \ldots, a_n$, do (in case $i = 1$) or do not (in case $i = 0$) stand in relation R^n at location l in some situation. (In *S&A* the location argument of an infon is fronted: $\langle l, \langle R^n, a_1, \ldots, a_n; i\rangle\rangle$. In more recent work, it has become optional.) For instance, the infon $\langle\!\langle$ *LOVES, here&now, Jon, John;* $1\rangle\!\rangle$ reflects the fact Jon loves John here and now, and $\langle\!\langle$ *LOVES, here&now, Jon, John;* $0\rangle\!\rangle$ reflects the fact that Jon does not love John here and now. Notice that facts are talked about here without making reference to situations. The connection between facts and the reality of situations comes about by what is called the 'supports'-relation. If an infon i is a fact in a real situation s, then s is said to support i, which is written as: $s \vDash i$. So if $s \vDash \langle\!\langle$ *LOVES, here&now, Jon, John;* $0\rangle\!\rangle$, then in s Jon does not love John at the location here and now. Furthermore, $s \vDash \langle\!\langle$ *LOVES, here&now, Jon, John;* $0\rangle\!\rangle$ itself is called a proposition which is either true or false.

Infons are the basic information units of situation theory. More complex information is gathered in sets of infons, called 'abstract situations.' So real situations, parts of the world which are recognized as such by agentive organisms, are distinguished from abstract situations (or just 'situations'), mathematical compounds of primitives abstracted from real situations. Notice that real situations are even more primitive than the theoretical primitives from which abstract situations are built up. (In *S&A*, abstract situations are called 'courses of events.' Certain courses of events are called 'states of affairs,' situations whose infons all have the same location argument.) Abstract situations s may also be said to support an infon i, where, of course, $s \vDash i$ if and only if $i \in s$. Furthermore, real and abstract situations can be related in the following way. An abstract situation s corresponds to a real situation s iff for all infons $i: i \in s \Leftrightarrow s \vDash i$. If an abstract situation corresponds to some real situation then it is said to be 'actual.' A weaker notion is in use as well. An abstract situation s classifies a real situation s iff for all infons i: if $i \in s$ then $s \vDash i$. In case an abstract situation classifies some real situation, then it is called 'factual.' In a sense, then, an actual situation is some kind of complete factual situation: if some situation s is factual, then there is some actual situation s' such that $s \subseteq s'$.

A situation can leave the issue whether certain individuals stand in a particular relation undecided. Neither $\langle\!\langle$ *WALK, here&now, Jon;* $1\rangle\!\rangle$ nor $\langle\!\langle$ *WALK, here*

&*now, Jon;* $0\rangle\!\rangle$ needs to be a member of s, and this possibility captures the credited partiality of real situations. But it is also possible that both an infon and its negation are an element of a situation. This possibility does not seem to be grounded in reality. (However, in the context of attitude reports (cf. below) this possibility might be useful again.) An important notion, therefore, is that of a coherent situation: a situation s is coherent if, for no $R^n, l, a_1, \ldots, a_n$, both $\langle\!\langle R^n, l, a_1, \ldots, a_n; 1\rangle\!\rangle$ and $\langle\!\langle R^n, l, a_1, \ldots, a_n; 0\rangle\!\rangle$ are in s. It will be assumed that all actual situations are coherent.

It was said above that meaning in situation semantics is, basically, a relation between situations, a relation which itself is considered 'real.' However, in order to account for this relation, more complex uniformities need to be introduced—so-called 'situation types.' For that purpose 'basic indeterminates' (also called 'parameters') are introduced. These are abstract stand-ins for real primitives: $a, b, \ldots$ for individuals; $r, r', \ldots$ for relations; and $l, l', \ldots$ for locations. An indeterminate (or 'parametrized') infon is a sequence $\langle\!\langle R^n, l, a_1, \ldots, a_n; i\rangle\!\rangle$ where $R^n, l, a_1, \ldots, a_n$ are indeterminates or real primitives, and i is a polarity marker. A 'situation-type' (or 'parametrized situation') is a set of indeterminate infons, i.e., an abstract situation in which zero or more indeterminates are substituted for real primitives. An example: situation-type $S = \{\langle\!\langle LOVES, l, a, b; 1\rangle\!\rangle\}$ contains one indeterminate infon $\langle\!\langle LOVES, l, a, b; 1\rangle\!\rangle$, with three indeterminates: $l, a,$ and b. Note that, since every infon is also an indeterminate infon (one with zero indeterminates), every situation is a situation type.

Situation types are conceived of as uniformities in their own right. They may be used to classify situations and can be linked up with situations using anchors. 'Anchors' are partial functions from individual, relation, and location indeterminates to individuals, relations, and locations, respectively. An anchor f is a total anchor for situation-type S if f is defined on all indeterminates in S. Write $S[f]$ for the situation-type S' which results from simultaneously substituting $f(x)$ for x in S for all indeterminates x in the domain of f. Then can be defined: s *is of type* S (also written as $s: S$) if there is a total anchor f for S such that $S[f] \subseteq s$. For instance, $f = \{\langle l, here\&now\rangle, \langle a, Jon\rangle, \langle b, John\rangle\}$ is a total anchor for situation-type $S = \{\langle\!\langle LOVES, l, a, b; 1\rangle\!\rangle\}$, and $S[f] = \{\langle\!\langle LOVES, here\&now, Jon, John; 1\rangle\!\rangle\} = s$. Since $S[f] = s, s$ is of type S. However, observe that also $s' = \{\langle\!\langle LOVES, here\&now, Jon, John; 1\rangle\!\rangle, \langle\!\langle SMOKE, there\&then; 0\rangle\!\rangle\}$ is of type S.

The notion 'constraint' models the idea that meanings reside in the world, as regularities which allow attuned agents to derive information about situations from situations. It is a fact that situations of a certain kind entail the presence of situations of another kind. In situation theory this fact is captured by infons of the form $\langle\!\langle INVOLVES, S, S'; 1\rangle\!\rangle$. S and S' are situation-types and INVOLVES is a primitive binary relation between situation-types. Infons of this form are called (unconditional) constraints. However, constraints by themselves do not constrain reality. The factuality of an infon $\langle\!\langle$ INVOLVES, S, S'; $1\rangle\!\rangle$ as such is no guarantee that situations of type S' always come along with situations of type S. It is only in structures of situations that constraints correspond to regularities between situations. Structures of situations are models of reality. In keeping with the slogan 'Reality consists of situations—individuals having properties and standing in relations at various spatiotemporal locations' (S&A: 7), a 'structure of situations' M is a collection of abstract situations, i.e., a collection of sets of infons. M consists of a collection, M, of factual situations, with a nonempty subcollection, M_0, of actual situations. It observes four conditions:

(a) every s in M is coherent;
(b) if $s \in M_0$ and $s' \subseteq s$, then $s' \in M$;
(c) if X is a sub*set* (with stress on *set*) of M, then there is an $s \in M_0$ such that $\bigcup X \subseteq s$ ($\bigcup X$ is the set of infons i for which there is an $s \in X$ such that $i \in s$);
(d) if C is a constraint in M, then M respects C.

Condition (a) states that reality is consistent. Condition (b) models the fact that parts of real (actual) situations are also (factual) situations. Condition (c) requires that the infons involved in a 'set' of factual situations be also members of an actual situation. Recall that M_0 was defined as a 'collection' of abstract situations, so it need not be a set—it could be a proper class: too large to be countenanced as a set. But if M_0 actually were a set, then (c) would entail the existence of a situation $s \in M_0$ such that $\bigcup M_0 \subseteq s$, so $\forall s' \in M_0: s' \subseteq s$. Such a situation, if present, might be called a world in M.

Condition (d) relates constraints to the regularities in reality that underlie the possibility of extracting information about situations from other situations. Intuitively, if constraints are conceived of as laws, what this clause says is that reality behaves in conformity with the laws it contains. The relevant notion of a structure of situations M respecting such a constraint is therefore defined as follows: M respects $\langle\!\langle$ INVOLVES, S, S'; $1\rangle\!\rangle$ iff $\forall s \in M_0: \exists s' \in M: \forall f:$ if f is an anchor for exactly the indeterminates of S, and $S[f] \subseteq s$, then $\exists g: (S'[f])[g] \subseteq s'$. This says that for every situation of type S there is a situation s' of type S' such that all ways of anchoring S in s are ways of (partially) anchoring S' in s'.

Notice that S and S' are arbitrary situation-types, so S' can contain indeterminates absent from S. In Barwise and Perry (1983: 146), this is considered 'a mistake.' Accordingly, Barwise (1989: 114) simply stipulates that every parameter in S' will also be a parameter in S. This enables us to simplify the definition considerably: M respects $\langle\!\langle$ INVOLVES, S, S'; $1\rangle\!\rangle$ iff $\forall s \in M_0: \exists s' \in M: \forall f:$ if $S[f] \subseteq s$, then $S'[f] \subseteq s'$. For

example, the constraint $\langle\!\langle$ INVOLVES, $\{\langle\!\langle$ SMOKE, l; $1\rangle\!\rangle\}$, $\{\langle\!\langle$ FIRE, l; $1\rangle\!\rangle\}$; $1\rangle\!\rangle$ is respected by M iff $\forall s \in M_0: \exists s' \in M: \forall f:$ if $\{\langle\!\langle$ SMOKE, l; $1\rangle\!\rangle\}[f] \subseteq s$, then $\{\langle\!\langle$ FIRE, l; $1\rangle\!\rangle\}[f] \subseteq s'$. This amounts to $\forall s \in M_0: \exists s' \in M: \forall l:$ if $\{\langle\!\langle$ SMOKE, l; $1\rangle\!\rangle\} \subseteq s$, then $\{\langle\!\langle$ FIRE, l; $1\rangle\!\rangle\} \subseteq s'$. So, for every situation s in M_0 with smoke at a number of locations, there is a situation s' in M with fire at those locations.

Having defined the notion 'M respects C,' what the interpretation of situations is given a certain constraint can be defined. The 'interpretation' of a situation s of type S with respect to a constraint C, $[s]_C$, where $C = \langle\!\langle$ INVOLVES, S, S'; $1\rangle\!\rangle$, is the collection of situations s' such that $\forall f:$ if f anchors exactly the indeterminates of S and $S[f] \subseteq s$, then s' is of type $S'[f]$.

So, for $C = \{\langle\!\langle$ INVOLVES, $\{\langle\!\langle$ SMOKE, l; $1\rangle\!\rangle\}$, $\{\langle\!\langle$ FIRE, l; $1\rangle\!\rangle\}$; $1\rangle\!\rangle$, and $s = \{\langle\!\langle$ SMOKE, here&now; $1\rangle\!\rangle\}$, $[s]_C$ is the collection of all situations s' such that $\{\langle\!\langle$ FIRE, here&now; $1\rangle\!\rangle\} \in s'$. In other words, the interpretation with respect to C of a situation with smoke here and now consists of involved situations with fire here and now.

3. Situation Semantics

Assuming that linguistic meanings of expressions are conventional constraints on utterances and that the primary function of language is to convey information, situation semantics describes the meaning of an assertively used indicative sentence ϕ as a relation $u[\phi]s$ between situations u in which ϕ is uttered and situations s described by such utterances. This is called 'the relational theory of meaning.' In other semantic approaches, the constraints ϕ puts on u have been put away in so-called 'context sequences.' Within situation semantics, the context of a sentence is the same type of thing as the thing the sentence is about, which allows an account of the 'efficiency of language' alluded to above.

An utterance situation u comprises the utterance of an expression ϕ (an aspect of u which is made explicit in the notation '$u[\phi]s$' we use) by one speaker to one addressee at one location. Moreover, u determines a number of 'speaker connections,' which specify the referents the speaker intends to denote by uttering certain subexpressions of ϕ. For instance, they specify the intended referents of proper names and the (temporal) locations that serve as intended referents of tenses of verbs.

The 'meanings' of lexical and compound expressions exploit these features of u. For example, a sentence like 'I am stroking Jackie' is assigned the meaning $u[I\ am\ stroking\ Jackie]s$ iff $\langle\!\langle$ STROKE, l, a, b; $1\rangle\!\rangle \in s$, where $l = u(am)$, l temporally overlaps with the location of u, a is the speaker in u, and $b = u(Jackie)$. The interpretation of coordinated sentences is straightforward: $u[\phi\ and\ \psi]s$ iff $u[\phi]s$ and $u[\psi]s$; $u[\phi\ or\ \psi]s$ iff $u[\phi]s$ or $u[\psi]s$.

A 'statement' consists of the utterance of an indicative sentence ϕ in an utterance situation: $u: \phi$. Whereas sentences have meanings, a statement $u: \phi$ is assigned an 'interpretation' $[u: \phi] = \{s \mid u[\phi]s\}$. The interpretation of the statement u: *I am stroking Jackie* is the collection of situations s such that $\langle\!\langle STRO\text{-}KE, l, a, b; 1\rangle\!\rangle \in s$, where l, a, b are as above. This collection contains possible situations, but also impossible (incoherent) ones. Notice that for simple positive sentences ϕ like 'I am stroking Jackie,' $[u: \phi]$ is 'persistent': if $s \in [u: \phi]$ and $s \subseteq s'$, then $s' \in [u: \phi]$. Truth is a property of statements, not of sentences. A statement $u: \phi$ is 'true' in M iff there is an s such that $s \in M_0$ and $s \in [u: \phi]$.

In keeping with the underlying philosophy, there are two notions of logical consequence for statements. If Φ and Ψ are statements, then Ψ is a 'strong consequence' of Φ iff $[\Phi]$ is a subcollection of $[\Psi]$, and Ψ is a 'weak consequence' of Φ iff Ψ is true in every M where Φ is true. The notion of strong consequence is relevant for the logic of information containment: if someone knows that Φ, and Ψ is a strong consequence of Φ, then (s)he knows that Ψ. The notion of weak consequence is more traditional. If Φ is true, and Ψ is a weak consequence of Φ, then Ψ must be true as well. Note, however, that the weak consequences of a statement do not completely coincide with the consequences in classical logics.

The relational theory of meaning, in which u and s are the same type of thing, easily explains the phenomenon of 'inverse information.' An utterance can convey information about a described situation, but also about the utterance situation. Suppose someone next door says 'I am Jon.' This utterance describes situations in which the speaker of the utterance is called Jon. However, for someone who knows Jon, the utterance may convey information about the utterance situation: he is speaking there! Note that this information is not part of the linguistic interpretation of the utterance.

From the outset, situation semantics has been concerned with attitude reports, utterances of sentences containing verbs like 'see (that),' 'know that,' 'believe that,' which are used to report perception and cognition. The seminal paper 'Scenes and Other Situations' (1981, reprinted in Barwise 1989) studies the semantics of sentences reporting visual perceptions. Syntactically, one can distinguish at least two kinds of those reports. In (1), the verb 'see' has an untensed sentence (or 'naked infinitive') as its complement; in (2), it selects a *that*-complementizer followed by a tensed sentence:

> John saw Jackie bite Molly. (1)

> John saw that Jackie bit Molly. (2)

Semantically, 'epistemically neutral' 'see' can be contrasted with 'epistemically positive' 'see that': 'To prove the first (and weaker) claim, one has to show that [John] had his eyes open and functioning, and that an event of a certain sort was taking place before him. To prove the stronger claim, one needs to prove something about what he recognized and what thoughts were going through his mind' (S&A: 179). *See-* reports like (1) are considered paradigmatic for a semantics of the attitudes. One reason for this is that they report, in a sense, the most realistic attitude; what is seen is real. Another reason is that they have the least controversial semantic properties, like:

(a) *Veridicality*: if a sees ϕ, then ϕ^*, where ϕ^* is the tensed version of ϕ. *Jackie sees Molly scratch. So, Molly scratches.* (ϕ must be a sentence giving rise to a persistent interpretation. It does not follow that if Alice is seeing no one walk on the road, then no one is walking on the road.);

(b) *Conjunction Distribution*: if a sees ϕ and ψ, then a sees ϕ and a sees ψ;

(c) *Disjunction Distribution*: if a sees ϕ or ψ, then a sees ϕ or a sees ψ.

Properties like these should shed light on the proper treatment of *see*-reports. Standard possible world semantics assumes that the semantic value of embedded clauses is the set of possible worlds in which they are true. This leads to the problem that if a sees ϕ and ϕ is logically equivalent to ψ, then a sees ψ. Hence, *John saw Jackie bite Molly* entails *John saw Jackie bite Molly and Tully scratch or not scratch,* since *Jackie bite Molly* and *Jackie bite Molly and Tully scratch or not scratch* denote the same set of possible worlds.

In the special case of verbs like 'see,' this assumption has even worse implications. Using veridicality, conjunction distribution, and disjunction distribution, one can derive 'omnipercipience' ('you've seen one, you've seen them all'): if for some ϕ, a sees ϕ, then for all true ψ, it must hold that a sees ψ.

Situation semantics solves those problems by assigning clauses a more fine-grained semantic value: situations. *See* denotes a primitive relation, SEE, between a location, an individual (the agent), and a situation. The infon $\langle SEE, l, a, e; 1\rangle$ corresponds to the fact that a sees e at l, and *see*-reports are interpreted in the following way: $u[$ *John is seeing Jackie bite Molly*$]s$ iff $\langle SEE, l, a, s'; 1\rangle \in s$ and $\langle BITE, l, b, c; 1\rangle \in s'$, where $l = u(is)$, l temporally overlaps with the location of u, $a = u(John)$, $b = u(Jackie)$, and $c = u(Molly)$.

It is easy to see that this analysis validates conjunction and disjunction distribution. However, veridicality is not yet guaranteed. If $\langle SEE, l, a, s'; 1\rangle \in s$, and s is actual, nothing follows about s' being actual or factual; s' is just a possible (or even impossible) situation doing duty as a constituent of a fact. To get veridicality, a constraint is needed: $\langle INVOLVES, S, S'; 1\rangle$, with $S = \{\langle SEE, l, a, s; 1\rangle\}$ and $S' = s$ (where s is a situation indeterminate).

The effect of this constraint is that for every actual s', there is a factual $s\rangle$ such that for all locations l, individuals *a*, and situations *s* such that $\{\langle see, l, a, s; 1\rangle\} \subseteq s'$, it holds that $s \subseteq s'$. Every factual situation is a subset of an actual situation. So, if the interpretation of the embedded sentence is persistent, then the fact that it contains a factual situation entails that it also contains an actual situation. Hence, the sentence must be true.

'Less realistic' attitude reports like 'Jon believes that Jackie bites Molly' obey different semantic principles. Veridicality does not apply to *believe that*-reports, since one can believe things that are not true. Neither does disjunction distribution: it is possible that 'Jon believes that Jackie or Molly has fleas' is true, whereas both 'Jon believes that Jackie has fleas' and 'John believes that Molly has fleas' are false. On the other hand, conjunction distribution is valid for *believe that*.

Situation semantics not only wants to account for these logical facts, but also for the way in which attitude reports are used in explanations of what people think and do. There is, for example, a big difference between John believing that Jon is ill and Jon believing that Jon (i.e., he himself) is ill. Yet on an account which construes believing as a relation between individuals and situations, John and Jon stand in exactly the same relation to the same situations if they both believe that Jon is ill, though Jon is the one to get up and go see the doctor. There is some intuitive sense in which John and Jon have different beliefs (i.e., are in different mental states) if they both believe that Jon is ill. Accordingly, situation semantics analyses *believe that*-reports in terms of represented belief.

The basic idea is to use situation-types to classify both what is believed and how it is believed. This does justice to the commonsense intuition that there are different ways of believing the same thing. Individuals *a* at locations *l* are in 'cognitive states': frames of mind which are related to the world by a setting. A frame of mind is given by a situation-type *S*, and a setting consists of an anchor *f* (assume that *f* is a total anchor for *S*). A belief, therefore, is a pair $\langle S, f\rangle$, written as $\langle BR, l, a, S, f; 1\rangle$ (*br* abbreviates 'represented belief').

Now, John's believing at *l* in *s* that Jon is ill at *l'* can be rendered as: $\langle BR, l, \text{John}, S, f; 1\rangle \varepsilon s$, where $S = \{\langle ILL, l, a; 1\rangle\}$, $f(l) = l'$, and $f(l) = Jon$. The fact that Jon is in a different mental state from John when he believes that Jon is ill is expressed by using the *role i* in his frame of mind, an indeterminate associated with the agent of a situation. (Roles will be discussed below.)

The semantics of *believe that*-reports is phrased in terms of situation-types and anchors. It is simply required that the agent has some belief $\langle S, f\rangle$ such that the anchoring of *S* by *f* classifies the interpretation of the embedded sentence. On this analysis, if *a* believes that ϕ, and the statement that ψ is a strong consequence of the statement that ϕ, then *a* believes that ψ. So, conjunction distribution is valid (whereas disjunction distribution and veridicality fail).

4. Extensions and Developments

Barwise and Etchemendy's *The Liar* (1987) is a thorough study of the liar paradox and related cases of circularity or self-reference. Assertions like 'I am now lying, 'What I am now saying is false,' This proposition is not true' are paradoxical, since if they were true, then what they claim would have to be the case, and so they would be not true. Conversely, if they are not true, then what they claim to be the case is in fact the case, so they must be true. Whereas the liar paradox has been known since antiquity, no satisfactory analysis of it has yet been given. In formal semantic practice, one usually follows Tarski's (1956) approach of avoiding the paradox by denying languages their own truth predicate. Saul Kripke, however, has shown that circular reference of the sort involved in the liar is not only a much more common phenomenon than had been supposed, but also that whether a given utterance is paradoxical may well depend on nonlinguistic, empirical facts. Ergo: 'there can be no syntactic or semantic "sieve" that will winnow out the "bad" cases while preserving the "good" ones' (Kripke 1975). Barwise and Etchemendy's analysis of languages that admit circular reference and contain their own truth predicate supplements situation theory with the theory of non-wellfounded sets developed by Peter Aczel.

Aczel (1988: ii) introduces non-wellfounded ('extraordinary') sets with a quotation from Mirimanoff (1917): 'Let *E* be a set, *E'* one of its elements, *E*⟩ any element of *E'*, and so on. Call a *descent* the sequence of steps from *E* to *E'*, *E'* to *E*⟩, etc. ... I say that a set is *ordinary* when it only gives rise to finite descents; I say that it is *extraordinary* when among its descents there are some which are infinite.' The standard system of axiomatic set theory, ZFC, includes the foundation axiom FA. This axiom expresses that all sets are ordinary (i.e., wellfounded), thus giving rise to the familiar 'cumulative hierarchy of sets.' Instead, Aczel proposes an antifoundation axiom (AFA) which entails the existence of non-wellfounded sets such as Ω: the unique set such that $\Omega = \{\Omega\}$. Using a version of Aczel's set theory with atoms, Barwise and Etchemendy arrive at a notion of circular situations and circular propositions. On their view, truth is not a property of sentences, but of statements or propositions. Sentences may well fail to express a proposition, and so fail to have a truth value. This does not hold for propositions, the kind of thing asserted by a successful statement: if a proposition is not true, then it is false. *The Liar* discusses two accounts of the relation between sentences and the propositions they express, the Russellian and the Austinian view.

According to the Russellian view, sentences are used to express propositions, claims about the world, and these claims are true just in case the world is as it is claimed to be. Relevant is that the truth of the proposition is arbitrated by the world as a whole. On the Russellian analysis, the liar sentence 'This proposition is not true' expresses the unique (non-wellfounded) proposition f satisfying $f = [FALSE\,f]$.

According to the truth scheme introduced by Austin (1961), an assertively used declarative sentence S contributes two things: the descriptive conventions of language yield a certain type of situation S that is expressed by ϕ, whereas the demonstrative conventions refer to an actual, 'historic' situation s. So, an Austinian proposition can be written as a claim $s\!:\!S$ (cf. Sect. 2 above). The rule of truth is simply that $s\!:\!S$ is true if s is of type S. This holds in general, independently of the presence of indexical expressions in ϕ. On the Austinian analysis, there are many different propositions that can be expressed using the liar sentence.

Comparing the two accounts, Barwise and Etchemendy show that while the Russelian view is crucially flawed in limiting cases, the Austinian view can be seen as a refinement which avoids the paradox while providing a straightforward understanding of the semantic intuitions that give rise to it.

On the basis of various examples involving inherently circular situations (aspects of perceptual knowledge, self-awareness, Gricean intentions of speakers and hearers, shared information), Barwise (1989: ch. 8) argues that reality, unlike the cumulative hierarchy of sets, is not wellfounded. Consistent with the assumption that situations are parts of reality (families of facts) that can be comprehended as completed totalities, i.e., as sets, this article has been modeling situations as sets of infons, and infons as sequences $\langle\!\langle R^n, l, a_1, \ldots, a_n; i\rangle\!\rangle$ consisting of an n-ary relation R^n, a location l, a sequence of n arguments $a_1, \ldots, a_n$ (the constituents of the infon, which can be primitives, situations, or situation-types), and a polarity marker i. Now, if this sort of set theoretical model is to be used, then non-wellfounded sets are essential when circular situations are to be represented. Thus it should be possible that a situation s contains infon $\langle\!\langle R^n, a_1, \ldots, a_n; i\rangle\!\rangle$ as a member, while s itself also is (a constituent of a member of . . .) a member of a_1 or . . . or a_n.

In an interesting case study of non-wellfoundedness, Barwise (1989: ch. 9) addresses the phenomenon of common knowledge, which is crucial for an understanding of communication. Common knowledge arises for instance when a card player (Jon, say), receives a card (e.g., the queen of clubs) that everyone (viz., Jon and John) can see. The orthodox 'iterate' account analyzes this in terms of an infinite hierarchy of iterated attitudes: (0) Jon has the queen of clubs; (1) Jo(h)n knows Jon has the queen of clubs: (2) Jo(h)n knows that Jo(h)n knows that Jon has the queen of clubs; and so on. Barwise contrasts this account with non-wellfounded approaches, and shows that it is inadequate. Moreover, it turns out that common knowledge is better analyzed in terms of shared information.

In spite of its pervasively indexical, 'efficient,' character (witness the speaker connections), the situation semantics outlined in Sect. 3 is essentially Russelian. More recent contributions, however, have incorporated the inherently indexical Austinian approach sketched in the present section. Gawron and Peters (1990), a book on quantification and anaphora, is a case in point.

Situation semantic accounts of anaphora and quantification make frequent use of so-called 'restricted parameters' or 'roles' (see *S&A*: 80–90; Gawron and Peters 1990; Devlin, et al. and Westerståhl in Cooper, et al. 1990). A restricted parameter is an indeterminate subscripted by a situation-type that contains the indeterminate. The idea is that the situation-type restricts the domain of things onto which the indeterminate can be anchored. If r is a restricted indeterminate x_S, then an anchor f for r in situation s must be such that f anchors all parameters in S (among which may be restricted ones), $S[f] \subseteq s$, and $f(r) = f(x)$. Suppose $S = \langle\!\langle MAN, x, 1\rangle\!\rangle$; then x_S can only be anchored to individuals a in s if a is a man in s. It is clear that restricted parameters introduce a form of restricted existential quantification. For instance, the proposition $s \vDash \{\langle\!\langle WALKS, x_S; 1\rangle\!\rangle\}$, where S is as above, expresses that in s an individual a walks who is a man. Notice that s itself is not required to contain the information that a is a man, provided that some other situation s' does (Devlin, in Cooper, et al. 1990: 84). Instead of situation-types it is also possible to have propositions as restrictions on parameters (Gawron and Peters 1990). Such a proposition explicitly addresses a resource situation where the restriction is required to be satisfied. For example, if r is the parameter $x_{s \vDash S}$, where S is as above, then $s \vDash \langle\!\langle WALKS, r; 1\rangle\!\rangle$ expresses that someone who is a man in s walks in s. (Resource situations were already introduced in $S_{\&}A$. These situations are exploited by speakers and they figure as a kind of domains for reference and quantification.)

Gawron and Peters (1990; and in Cooper, et al. 1990) give a more or less uniform treatment of natural language noun phrases using restricted parameters. Proper names, pronouns, definite, and indefinite descriptions contribute restricted parameters to the interpretations of sentences. A use of the proper name 'John' introduces a parameter $x_{(r \vDash \langle\!\langle NAMED, x, 'John'\rangle\!\rangle)}$ that restricts x to be anchored to an individual named 'John' in the resource situation. Definite descriptions like 'the dog' introduce a parameter that is restricted to be anchored to the unique dog in a resource situation, if there is one. The content of the pronoun 'she' is captured with a parameter that is restricted to be anchored to females in a resource situation. Here the utterance situation (Gawron and Peters use the term 'circumstances') contains the information whether the pronoun is used deictically or anaphorically, and what the resource situation is. The first person pronoun I

yields a parameter restricted to be anchored to its utterer. Anaphoric pronouns are simply reused parameters, with additional restrictions due to their gender.

An interesting possibility is that an anaphoric pronoun may pick up a parameter associated with either the argument slot of a verb or the noun phrase that fills the argument slot. This enables Gawron and Peters to treat so-called 'sloppy' readings of sentences like 'Only John expected that he would lose.' On the sloppy reading John is the only one that expected 'himself' to lose. Here the pronoun is linked up with the subject–argument–role of the EXPECT-relation. On the strict reading, where the pronoun is coparametric with the subject 'John' itself, nobody expected that John would lose, except John.

Gawron and Peters (1990) also treat quantified noun phrases. A quantified phrase like 'Every N' is analyzed in terms of a determiner relation with a domain-type constructed from the common noun N. A determiner is a relation between properties and this relation is said to hold of the domain-type and the property expressed by the surrounding utterance. Circumstances determine which part of the utterance is in the scope of the quantifier, and hence resolve possible scope ambiguities. Essential in this treatment is the restriction that a determiner like EVERY holds of two properties P_1 and P_2 if all objects that have property P_1 also have property P_2. Again, the first property (the domain-type) is constructed relative to a resource situation for the utterance.

In their contribution to Cooper, et al. (1990), Gawron and Peters treat quantified noun phrases more on a par with nonquantified noun phrases. Quantified noun phrases initially contribute a parameter r to the interpretation of an utterance, with a restriction imposed by their common noun. The determiner is interpreted as a property of properties P which relates the appropriate anchors of r (the anchors that satisfy the restriction on x) to the objects having P. A generalization of this mechanism allows a treatment of the so-called 'donkey-anaphor' *it* in a sentence like 'Every farmer who owns a donkey beats it.'

For alternative treatments of quantification within situation semantics see Barwise and Perry in Cooper (1985: 144–147); Cooper (1987); Devlin in Cooper, et al. (1990). Fenstad, et al. (1987) account for donkey-anaphora as well. Dynamic approaches to semantics are also treated by Ruhrberg, who discusses the concept of simultaneous abstraction in Seligman and Westerstahl (1996). Ter Meulen (1995) studies the representation of temporal information in a related framework, as do Seligman and ter Meulen (1995). Conditionals are addressed in Barwise (1989) and Cavedon (1995, also in Seligman and Westerstahl 1996). Poesio addresses definite descriptions in Aczel, et al. (1993). Glasbey provides a situation theoretic account of the progressive, Cooper and Ginzburg deal with attitude reports, both in Seligman and Westerstahl (1996).

5. Suggestions for Further Reading

In addition to the books and papers that were referred to above, Seligman and Moss (1997) is recommended to the reader who would like to know more about situation theory (rather than situation semantics, which we have been mainly concerned with). Another introduction to that topic is Devlin (1991). Cooper (1991) could be read as an introduction to situation semantics. The majority of research papers in situation theory and situation semantics are contained in collections entitled 'Situation Theory and its Applications,' volumes 1, 2 and 3 (Cooper, et al. 1990; Barwise, et al. 1991; Aczel, et al. 1993), and 'Logic, Language and Computation' (Seligman and Westerstahl, 1996). These contain selections of papers presented at a biannual conference. The name of that conference was changed in 1994 to 'Information-Theoretic Approaches to Language, Logic and Computation.'

Bibliography

Aczel P 1988 *Non-Well-Founded Sets*. CSLI Publications, Stanford, CA

Aczel P, Israel D, Katagiri Y, Peters S (eds.) 1993 *Situation Theory and Its Applications*, vol. 3. CSLI Publications, Stanford, CA

Austin J L 1961 Truth. In: Urmson J O, Warnock G J (eds.) *Philosophical Papers*. Oxford University Press, Oxford

Barwise J 1989 *The Situation in Logic*. CSLI Publications, Stanford, CA

Barwise J, Etchemendy J 1987 *The Liar. An Essay on Truth and Circularity*. Oxford University Press, New York

Barwise J, Gawron J M, Plotkin G, Tutiya S (eds.) 1991 *Situation Theory and Its Applications*, vol. 2. CSLI Publications, Stanford, CA

Barwise J, Perry J 1983 *Situations and Attitudes*. Bradford Books, MIT Press, Cambridge, MA

Cavedon L 1995 A Channel-Theoretic Approach to Conditional Reasoning. (PhD Thesis, Centre for Cognitive Science, University of Edinburgh)

Cooper R (ed.) 1985 Situations and attitudes. aPh 8: 1

Cooper R 1987 Preliminaries to the treatment of generalized quantifiers in situation semantics. In: Gärdenfors P (ed.) *Generalized Quantifiers: Linguistic and Logical Approaches*. Reidel, Dordrecht

Cooper R 1991 Three lectures on situation theoretic grammar. In: Filgeiras M, et al. (eds.) *EAJA 90 Proceedings*. Lecture Notes in Artificial Intelligence, Volume 476. Springer, New York

Cooper R, Mukai K, Perry J (eds.) 1990 *Situation Theory and its Applications*, vol. 1. CSLI Publications, Stanford, CA

Devlin K 1991 *Logic and Information*. Cambridge University Press, Cambridge

Dretske F I 1981 *Knowledge and the Flow of Information*. Basil Blackwell, Oxford

Fenstad J E, Halvorsen P K, Langholm T, Van Benthem J (eds.) 1987 *Situations, Language and Logic*. Reidel, Dordrecht

Gawron J M Types, contents and semantic objects. *LaPh* 9: 427–76

Gawron J M, Peters S 1990 *Anaphora and Quantification in Situation Semantics*. CSLI Publications, Stanford, CA

Kripke S 1975 Outline of a theory of truth. *The Journal of Philosophy* 72: 690–716

Langholm T 1988 *Partiality, Truth and Persistence*. CSLI Publications, Stanford, CA

Pratt I 1987 Constraints, meaning and information. *LaPh* 10: 299–324

Seligman J, Moss L 1997 Situation theory. In: van Benthem J, ter Meulen A (eds.) *Handbook of Logic and Language*. Elsevier Science, Amsterdam

Seligman J, ter Meulen A 1995 Dynamic aspect trees. In: Polos L, Masuch M (eds.) *Applied Logics, How, What and Why*. Kluwer, Dordrecht

Seligman J, Westerstahl D 1996 *Logic, Language and Computation*. CSLI Publications, Stanford

Stalnaker R C 1986 Possible worlds and situations. *Journal of Philosophical Logic* 15: 109–23

Tarski A 1956 The concept of truth in formalized languages. In: *Logic, Semantics, Metamathematics*. Clarendon Press, Oxford.

ter Meulen A 1995 *Representing Time in Natural Language. The Dynamic Interpretation of Tense and Aspect*. Bradford Books, MIT Press, Cambridge, MA

Truth and Paradox

J. van Eijck

In natural languages, extensive use is made of a truth predicate. We continually say things like *What John has just said is false; Most statements made by the government spokeswoman are true*, etc. This article discusses the relevance of the paradox of the liar for the concept of truth in formal and natural languages. The first part of the article focuses on first order logic; it explains the problem posed by the liar for the incorporation of a truth predicate in first order languages, or in any language with at least the same expressive power. The second part shows how a dynamic perspective on arriving at truth through revision can yield a predicate which accurately reflects truth for all non-paradoxical sentences. This result applies to both formal and natural languages.

1. The Liar Paradox and the *T*-Principle

In its simplest guise, the liar paradox revolves around sentence (1):

This sentence is false.　　　　　　　　　　　(1)

Sentence (1) is paradoxical, for both the assumption that it is true and the assumption that it is false lead to a contradiction. For instance, assume that (1) is true. Then because of what (1) says, it must be false. Contradiction. Now assume that (1) is false. Then what the sentence says is not true, that is, it is not true that (1) is false. In other words, (1) is true, and contradiction again.

Suppose first order language L has a predicate T, to be interpreted as 'true in model M,' where M is some intended model of L. To make this work, one has to assume that there is a function $\ulcorner\ \urcorner$ mapping the (closed or open) formula φ to a term $\ulcorner \varphi \urcorner$ denot-

ing an individual in the domain of M. Given such a function, we can say that the term $\ulcorner \varphi \urcorner$ represents the formula φ. The representation trick can be pulled off by including the natural numbers in the domain of M and devising an encoding of formulas as numbers. The encoding can be made to work for all syntactic objects; for instance, $\ulcorner x \urcorner$ is the term representing the variable x. Note that $\ulcorner x \urcorner$ is a closed term: the variable x does not occur freely in it, because $\ulcorner x \urcorner$ is just a name for a number, namely the number representing x. More generally, $\ulcorner t \urcorner$ is the closed term representing the open or closed term t.

Give the encoding function, one would expect the following principle to hold in model M for all sentences φ of L:

$$\varphi \equiv T \ulcorner \varphi \urcorner \qquad (2)$$

We call this the *T*-principle; sometimes it is also referred to as the convention *T*. What the *T*-principle says, in fact, is that the truth predicate holds precisely of the representations of the sentences which are true (in M). We now proceed to show that there is something very wrong with the *T*-principle.

When φ is a formula with x among its free variables, and t is a term, then we use $[t/x]\varphi$ for the result of substituting t for x in φ. Next, we mirror this substitution operation at the level of encodings. If φ is a formula with x among its free variables and t is a term, then we use $sub_x(\ulcorner \varphi \urcorner, \ulcorner t \urcorner)$ for $\ulcorner[t/x]\varphi\urcorner$. Thus, sub_x is a function mapping pairs of code numbers to new code numbers. The proof that sub_x can be constructed from $\ulcorner\ \urcorner$ is outside our scope (see Enderton 1972). Note that x is not a free variable in sub_x.

Encodings, the T predicate and the sub_x function, are the ingredients of the recipe for the formal reconstruction of the liar. The key formula that we need now is $-Tsub_x(x, x)$. Call this formula φ. What φ means may be a bit hard to grasp at first reading. The diligent reader is asked to check that φ is true of all numbers which encode formulas that, when their own code number is substituted in them for the variable x, yield sentences with code numbers that do not satisfy T.

Let n be the code number of φ, that is, $n = \lceil \varphi \rceil$. Next, let ψ be the formula $[n/x]\varphi$. The formalized liar is sentence (3):

$$\psi \equiv -T\lceil \psi \rceil \qquad (3)$$

It will be shown that now sentence (3) is true in M. Truth of ψ is equivalent to truth of $[n/x]\varphi$, because $\psi = [n/x]\varphi$. Truth of $[n/x]\varphi$ is equivalent to truth of $-Tsub_x(n, n)$, since $\varphi = -Tsub_x(n, n)$ and n is substituted for x in φ. Truth of $-Tsub_x(n, n)$ is equivalent to truth of $-Tsub_x(\lceil \varphi \rceil, n)$, since $n = \lceil \varphi \rceil$. Truth of $-Tsub_x(\lceil \varphi \rceil, n)$ is equivalent to truth of $-T\lceil [n/x]\varphi \rceil$, from the definition of sub_x. Finally, truth of $-T\lceil [n/x]\varphi \rceil$ is equivalent to truth of $-T\lceil \psi \rceil$, since $\psi = [n/x]\varphi$. This shows the equivalence of ψ and $-T\lceil \psi \rceil$ in M, so (3) is true in M.

Next, (3) and the T-principle can be used to derive a contradiction. Assume ψ is true (in M). Then, because of (3), $-T\lceil \psi \rceil$ is true, so $T\lceil \psi \rceil$ is false, and, because of (2), ψ is false. Contradiction. Assume ψ is false. Consequently, because of (3), $-T\lceil \psi \rceil$ is false, so $T\lceil \psi \rceil$ is true and, because of (2), ψ is true. Contradiction again. This paradox is closely related, in fact, to the half-paradox used by Kurt Gödel to show the incompleteness of the first order theory of arithmetic and to derive the undecidability of first order predicate logic.

As the logical representation languages used for natural language semantics have at least the same expressive power as first order predicate logic, the above result applies to them as well. Tarski has drawn the conclusion that providing a precise semantic account of the concept of truth in natural languages is a more or less hopeless enterprise.

2. The Revision Theory of Truth

Fortunately, things are not quite as gloomy as they look. Consider an arbitrary language L with a truth predicate T, and a device for naming sentences of the language by means of encoding or by some other means; $\lceil \varphi \rceil$ will continue to be used as a name for the code of φ. It turns out that a truth predicate T for L can be constructed by switching to a dynamic perspective on how T gets its proper extension.

Initially there is a model where the one place predicate T has some arbitrary initial extension, and then iterates through an infinite series of T revision steps. In the course of these revisions the interpretation of

T in the startup state of the model will become less and less significant. Every revision step influences the interpretation of the terms which are codes of formulas, as follows:

If at a given stage, $[\![\varphi]\!] = 1(0)$, then at the next stage, $[\![T\lceil \varphi \rceil]\!] = 1(0)$.

For nonparadoxical sentences, it is seen that through the revisions, gradually the T predicate approaches closer and closer to the status of a real truth predicate. In the initial stage, only the interpretations of the sentences that do not involve truth are guaranteed to be right. At the starting point, sentences like *Snow is white* will be true, but *It is true that snow is white; It is true that it is true that snow is white*, and so on, will have arbitrary truth values, since the predicate T occurs in them. The interpretation of T has to be revised. In the first step all (codes of) sentences which are true at the starting point are put in the extension of T, and T will be false of all (codes of) sentences which are false at the starting point (and all objects which are not codes of sentences at all). The result is that at this stage sentences such as *It is true that snow is white* become true. This process is then iterated. To see that this has to go on for quite a long time, consider an infinite set of sentences *Snow is white; It is true that snow is white; It is true that it is true that snow is white*, and so on. Call this set S. It is desirable to be able to say that all sentences in S are true; this can certainly be asserted in natural language (and the assertion would of course be true). To take such cases into account the process of revising the interpretation of T must be carried through into the transfinite.

It can be shown that there is some transfinite stage α at which the process stabilizes: at this stage, all sentences that eventually stop flipflopping are stable already. At this level T is still unstable for paradoxical sentences. To see why this is so, consider the formalized liar (3), the formula $\psi \equiv -T\lceil \psi \rceil$. By the reasoning that was given above, (3) is true in the initial stage of our model, and in all further stages (the reasoning does not depend on the extension of T). The extension of T at the initial stage was arbitrary. Let us suppose $[\![T\lceil \psi \rceil]\!] = 1$ at this stage. Then at the initial stage, $[\![\psi]\!] = 0$, because of what (3) says. Then after one revision, $[\![T\lceil \psi \rceil]\!] = 0$, because of what the revision instruction says, and because of (3), $[\![\psi]\!] = 1$ at this stage. And so on. Thus, the values of $[\![\psi]\!]$ and $[\![T\lceil \psi \rceil]\!]$ will continue to flipflop through the revision stages.

All sentences whose truth or falsity depends ultimately on factors that do not involve the concept of truth will be stable at the stabilization stage α, and their truth value at this stage will be independent of the T interpretation we started out with. All paradoxical sentences will be unstable at α. A sentence such as *This sentence is true* will be stable as well, but which truth value it will have will depend on the original interpretation of T. If at the initial stage the code of this sentence is in the extension of T, then this value will not change. In the other case it will not change either. The reason is that both the assumption that *This sentence is true* is true and the assumption that it is false are coherent.

Under a suitably dynamic perspective on the action of 'calling a sentence true,' it is possible, contrary to what Tarski believed, to make semantic sense of the everyday usage of the truth and falsity predicates of natural language. The revision perspective on truth was developed by Gupta and Herzberger under the influence of Kripke (1975). (See Visser (1984) for an overview; important source papers are collected in Martin (1984). Barwise and Etchemendy (1987) and the article *Paradoxes, Semantic* also provide further details and discussion.)

See also: Paradoxes, Semantic; Truth.

Bibliography

Barwise J, Etchemendy J 1987 *The Liar. An Essay on Truth and Circularity*. Oxford University Press, New York and Oxford

Enderton H B 1972 *A Mathematical Introduction to Logic*. Academic Press, New York

Kripke S A 1975 Outline of a theory of truth. *The Journal of Philosophy* **72**: 690–716

Martin R L (ed.) 1984 *Recent Essays on Truth and the Liar Paradox*. Oxford University Press, Oxford

Tarski A 1956 The concept of truth in formalized languages. In: Tarski A *Logic, Semantics, Metamathematics*. Oxford University Press, Oxford

Visser A 1984 Semantics and the liar paradox. In: Gabbay D, Guenthner. *Handbook of Philosophical Logic*, vol. IV. Reidel, Dordrecht

Pragmatics and Speech Act Theory

Ambiguity

K. Wales

The concept of 'ambiguity,' much discussed in semantics, is of crucial concern in the study of literary language. This article first looks at the linguistic definition of ambiguity, and then considers some of its pragmatic and stylistic implications.

1. Linguistic Ambiguity

Ambiguity describes the linguistic phenomenon whereby expressions are potentially understood in two or more ways; an ambiguous expression has more than one interpretation in its context.

Multiple meaning seems to be universal in human language, because of the arbitrary relationship between sign and referent. The two main kinds of multiple meaning are 'polysemy' (when an expression has developed more than one meaning, e.g., 'plot'; 'branch'); and 'homonymy' (when an expression has the same form as another, but a different etymology and meaning: e.g., 'port'; 'flock'). The lexicon of English is particularly rich in multiple meaning because of its varied history: the first edition of the *Oxford English Dictionary* (*OED*), for instance, records 154 sense divisions under the word *set*. What is remarkable is that such a 'heavy' semantic load, which applies similarly for a large number of common core lexical items, can be tolerated in everyday usage without ambiguity inevitably occurring. Yet the main causes of lexical ambiguity are indeed polysemy and homonymy. The answer lies in the notion of context: for an expression to be ambiguous, the two or more acts of interpretation must take place simultaneously, and in the same context. Speakers of English are not normally likely to confuse or bring together the different senses of *plot* ('action of story' and 'piece of land'). But when this happens, ambiguity can be the result.

It is important to stress the 'can be.' Even granted that it is explained as a semantic phenomenon, from a pragmatic point of view ambiguity does not necessarily arise even when linguistic conditions seem ideal for it. For communication does not take place in a vacuum: one's interpretation of a sentence in a written text will take into account the whole co-text; the interpretation of a spoken utterance will take into account the natural redundancy of language, and also the whole situational context surrounding speech. But certainly the absence of such a context probably explains why ambiguity is commoner in writing, especially in registers where the co-text itself is unelaborated: e.g., notices, headlines, and slogans ('Dogs must be carried on escalators'; 'Free women'). It is in writing that 'grammatical ambiguity' is particularly noticeable, where more than one structural interpretation is possible: 'Free women' as an imperative, or a noun phrase, for instance. Grammatical ambiguity was one of the main arguments used for establishing 'deep' and 'surface' structures in transformational grammar of the 1960s. In speech, stress and intonation help usefully to distinguish syntactic structures, clues which are absent in writing, so giving rise to further causes of ambiguity: 'Flying planes can be dangerous,' for example. There is also the obvious point, but which has important implications for the written medium, that if a spoken utterance is ambiguous, the addressee can ask the speaker directly for clarification.

2. Ambiguity and Ambivalence

In ordinary parlance ambiguity often has pejorative overtones, regarded as a stylistic fault, like vagueness and obscurity. For as Grice (1975) has stressed, it is a fundamental principle of 'normal' communication that people work cooperatively together to achieve coherent and effective exchanges. And by what Grice calls the 'maxim of manner' one normally tries to be clear, and so avoid obscurity and ambiguity, etc. Hence readers might be irritated by an ambiguous newspaper headline like 'British teachers amongst poorest in Europe.'

The 'cooperative principle' puts the burden of responsibility for effective communication on the speaker or writer. The implication is that ambiguity could be avoided and that it is due to carelessness. But there is another kind of ambiguity that is in contrast intentional. In Orwellian terms, this has been dubbed 'doublespeak.' For various motives speakers or writers may be equivocal or ambivalent: to avoid committing themselves, to save face, etc. The domains of political oratory and advertising frequently present examples of this.

In pragmatics, the term 'ambivalence' is now used for utterances with more than one illocutionary force. In traditional rhetoric this was termed 'amphibology' or 'amphiboly' ('ambiguity'), and interestingly it seems mainly to have been used in contexts that were open to intentional abuse rather than unintentional misinterpretation. So Chaucer writes in *Troilus and Criseyde*:

'For goddes speken in amphibologies,
And for one soth ('truth') they tellen twenty lyes . . . '

In Shakespeare's *Richard II*, Bolingbroke's 'Have I no friend will rid me of this living fear?' (v. iv) is interpreted by Exton as a command to kill Richard; Bolingbroke himself, however, publicly claims after the event that it was merely a wish (v. vi).

3. Literary Ambiguity

There is another kind of doublespeak with intention, that is termed 'punning.' Puns exploit the same lexical and grammatical ambiguities referred to above, but for comic effect: common in jokes, riddles, and advertising ('Thames Water Board: running water for you').

Here the clarity maxim is overridden by the ludic. The thin line between ambiguity and punning is revealed by examples where the comic intent cannot be known for sure, even if the effect is comic: e.g., the newspaper headline 'Planting of evidence at flower show alleged.' The expectation of humor in headlines are as yet ambivalent.

In literary language, however, readers expect multiple meaning, and do not question it. One is accustomed to tropes like metaphor, allegory, and irony, which also give rise to two or more interpretations in a single context. One has come to expect 'indeterminacy,' as reader-response criticism confirms; and the endless play of signification from deconstruction theory. And since the work of Empson (1949), ambiguity in the widest sense has been seen as crucial to literary, especially poetic, language and its interpretation. For Empson, any verbal nuance which gives room for alternative reactions is a type of ambiguity.

Bibliography

Empson W 1949 *Seven Types of Ambiguity*, 2nd edn. Chatto and Windus, London
Grice H P 1975 Logic and conversation. In: Cole P, Morgan J L (eds.) *Syntax and Semantics 3: Speech Acts*. Academic Press, New York
Leech G N 1983 *Principles of Pragmatics*. Longman, London
Nowottny W 1962 *The Language Poets Use*. Athlone Press, London

Conversational Maxims

J. Thomas

H.P. Grice had worked with the philosopher J.L. Austin at Oxford in the 1940s and 1950s. Grice's work on the cooperative principle and its related conversational maxims arises from the same tradition of ordinary language philosophy. In his book *How to Do Things with Words* (1962; 2nd edn. 1976), Austin made the distinction between what speakers say and what they mean. Grice's theory tries to explain how a hearer might get from the level of expressed meaning to the level of implied meaning.

It is perhaps easiest to begin with a concrete example of the type of problem which Grice's theory was designed to handle. On a visit to London, two friends returned to their parked car to find that it had been wheel clamped by the police. The driver turned to his passenger and said: *Great, that's just what I wanted!* It would doubtless have been clear to the passenger,

as it would have been to any competent interactant, that what the driver intended to imply was very different (just the opposite, in fact) from what he actually said. Grice set out to explain the mechanisms by which such implicatures are generated and interpreted.

Grice first outlined his theory in the William James lectures, delivered at Harvard University in 1967 (a version of which was published in 1975 in his paper 'Logic and Conversation'), and expanded upon it in papers published in 1978 and 1981. Grice never fully developed his theory—there are many gaps and several inconsistencies in his writings. Yet it is this work—sketchy, in many ways problematic, and frequently misunderstood—which has proved to be one of the most influential theories in the development of pragmatics.

1. The Four Conversational Maxims

Grice (1975) proposed the four maxims of 'quantity,' 'quality,' 'relation,' and 'manner,' which were formulated as follows (1):

Quantity: Make your contribution as informative   (1)
as is required (for the current purpose of
the exchange).
Do not make your contribution more
informative than is required.
Quality: Do not say what you believe to be false.
Do not say that for which you lack
adequate evidence.
Relation: Be relevant.
Manner: Avoid obscurity of expression.
Avoid ambiguity.
Be brief (avoid unnecessary prolixity).
Be orderly.

A speaker might observe all the maxims, as in the following example (2):

Father: Where are the children?   (2)
Mother: They're either in the garden or in the
playroom, I'm not sure which.

The mother has answered clearly (manner), truthfully (quality), has given just the right amount of information (quantity), and has directly addressed her husband's goal in asking the question (relation). She has said precisely what she meant, no more and no less, and has generated no implicature (that is, there is no distinction to be made here between what she says and what she means).

Grice was well aware, however, that there are very many occasions when people fail to observe the maxims (this might be because, for example, they are incapable of speaking clearly, or because they deliberately choose to lie). In his writings, he discussed each of these possibilities, but the situations which chiefly interested him were those in which a speaker *blatantly* fails to observe a maxim, not with any intention of deceiving or misleading, but because the speaker wishes to prompt the hearer to look for a meaning which is different from, or in addition to, the expressed meaning. This additional meaning he called 'conversational implicature,' and he termed the process by which it is generated 'flouting a maxim.'

2. Flouting a Maxim

A 'flout' occurs when a speaker *blatantly* fails to observe a maxim at the level of what is said, with the deliberate intention of generating an implicature. There follow examples of flouts of each of the maxims in turn, and also a review of Grice's discussions of the reasons for flouting a maxim.

2.1 Flouts Necessitated by a 'Clash between Maxims'

A speaker flouts the maxim of quantity by blatantly giving either more or less information than the situation demands. For example, imagine someone asked a departmental colleague who was standing next to the clock if he would tell them the time. Imagine he replied: *Well, according to this clock it's a quarter to four,* when he could simply have said: *It's a quarter to four.* According to Grice, such a response would set in motion a process of informal reasoning which would lead one to derive an additional piece of information. This might work in the following way (3):

(a) Your colleague has clearly given you more   (3)
information than you required. He appears to
have breached the maxim of quantity.
(b) However, you have no reason to believe that
he is being deliberately uncooperative (i.e.,
that he is failing to
observe the cooperative principle (CP)).
(c) You must conclude that his failure to
observe the maxim of quantity is due to his
wish to observe the CP in some
other way. You must work out why the CP
should force
your colleague to give more information
than you requested.
(d) The failure to observe the maxim of quantity
can be explained if you assume that your
colleague also
wishes to observe the maxim of quality. You
conclude that for some reason he is
confronted with a clash between these
maxims (either he tells the truth
or he gives you just the right amount of
information).
(e) His reply is a compromise, which leads you
to deduce that he is not sure that he has
given you the exact time
because the clock in the department is often
inaccurate.

Thus, Grice's explanation for the nonobservance of the maxim of quality in this instance is that the speaker was faced with a clash of maxims. The speaker found himself unable simultaneously to observe the maxims of quality and quantity, signaled his dilemma by flagrantly failing to give the right amount of information, and prompted his interlocutor to draw an inference. A similar explanation might be offered for the following instance of nonobservance of the maxim of quantity. In this case, the second speaker gives less information than the situation demands (4):

A: Has Chris given up smoking?   (4)
B: Well, he's certainly stopped buying his own.

B might simply have replied: 'No.' It would be possible to argue that his failure to do so stems from a clash between the maxims of quantity and quality (B does not know for sure whether Chris has given up smoking, and speaks only on the basis of the evidence he has). But this explanation is rather implausible. It is better explained by what Grice terms 'exploiting' the maxims.

2.2 Flouts which 'Exploit' a Maxim

According to Grice's theory, interlocutors operate on the assumption that, as a rule, the maxims will be observed. When this expectation is confounded and the listener is confronted with the blatant non-observance of a maxim (that is, the listener has discounted the possibility that the speaker may be trying to deceive, or is incapable of speaking more clearly, succinctly, etc.), he or she is again prompted to look for an implicature. Most of Grice's own examples of flouts involve this sort of 'exploitation.'

Flouts which exploit the maxim of quality, for example, occur when the speaker says something which is blatantly untrue or for which she or he lacks adequate evidence. In the 'wheel clamping' example given in the opening section, an implicature is generated by the speaker's saying something which is patently false. Since the speaker does not appear to be trying to deceive the listener in any way, the listener is forced to look for another plausible interpretation. According to Grice, the deductive process might work like this (5):

(a) A has expressed pleasure at finding his car (5)
    clamped.
(b) No one, not even the most jaded masochist,
    is likely to be pleased at finding his car
    clamped.
(c) His passenger has no reason to believe that
    A is trying to deceive him in any way.
(d) Unless A's utterance is entirely pointless, he
    must be trying to put across to his
    passenger some
    other proposition.
(e) This must be some obviously related
    proposition.
(f) The most obviously related proposition is
    the exact opposite of the one he has expressed.
(g) A is extremely annoyed at finding his car
    clamped.

The following example (6) works in much the same way, but this time involves what Grice rather vaguely terms 'generating a conversational implicature by means of something like a figure of speech'. The speaker is the *Peanuts* character, Linus, who comments wearily: *Big sisters are the crab grass in the lawn of life*.

(a) It is patently false that big sisters are crab (6)
    grass.
(b) Linus does not appear to be trying to make
    readers believe that big sisters are crab
    grass.
(c) Unless Linus's utterance is entirely
    pointless, he must be trying to put across
    some other proposition.
(d) This must be some obviously related
    proposition.
(e) The most obviously related proposition is
    that, like crab grass in lawns, big sisters are a
    bane.

What Grice's theory (at least as originally formulated) fails to say is why in this example one is expected to seek a comparison between crab grass in lawns and big sisters in life, whereas in the previous example one looked for a proposition which was the exact opposite of the one expressed. Developments in relevance theory (Sperber and Wilson 1986) could help to rescue Grice's theory at this point.

Examples of floutings of the maxim of relation are legion. The one in (7) is typical (it has to be assumed that it is clear in the context that B has heard and understood A's question):

A: Who was that you were with last night? (7)
B: Did you know you were wearing odd socks?

It would be tedious once again to work through all the steps in the informal deductive process— suffice it to say that A is likely to come to the conclusion that B is irritated or embarrassed by the question and wishes to change the subject. Again, Grice's theory fails to address a very important issue, viz. why does B choose to indicate only indirectly that she is irritated or embarrassed? After all, if A were a particularly insensitive person, there is the risk that she might ignore B's hint and pose the question again. B could remove that possibility by saying: *Mind your own business*! In the 1970s and 1980s, much effort in the field of pragmatics was put into developing theories of politeness (see, for example, Brown and Levinson (1987) and Leech (1983)) which, proponents argue, 'rescue' Grice's theory by explaining the social constraints governing utterance production and interpretation.

The following example (8) illustrates a flout of the maxim of manner. It occurred during a radio interview with an unnamed official from the United States Embassy in Port-au-Prince, Haiti:

Interviewer: Did the United States Government (8)
              play any part in Duvalier's depar-
              ture? Did they, for example, actively
              encourage him to leave?
Official: I would not try to steer you away
              from that conclusion.

The official could simply have replied: 'Yes.' Her actual response is extremely long-winded and convoluted, and it is obviously no accident, nor through any inability to speak clearly, that she has failed to observe the maxim of manner. There is, however, no reason to believe that the official is being deliberately unhelpful (she could, after all, have simply refused to answer at all, or said: *No comment*).

The hearer must therefore look for another explanation, and, once again, there is nothing in Grice's theory to help explain the official's flouting of the maxim of manner. In this case, it is not a clash of maxims which has caused her to flout the maxim of manner in this way. Rather, it is occasioned by the desire to claim credit for what she sees as a desirable outcome, while at the same time avoiding putting on record the fact that her government has intervened in the affairs of another country. In fact, this exchange was widely reported and the implicature spelt out in news broadcasts later the same day: *Although they have not admitted it openly, the State Department is letting it be known that the United States was behind Jean-Paul Duvalier's decision to quit the island.* Nor can one sensibly ascribe the speaker's use of indirectness to any desire to be 'polite' (at least, in the normal sense of the term)—it appears to be motivated by the fact that she has two goals which are difficult to reconcile. This 'desire to say and not say' something at the same time is lucidly discussed by Dascal (1983), together with other social factors which lead speakers to employ indirectness.

The important thing to note in each of these cases is that it is the very blatancy of the nonobservance which triggers the search for an implicature. The same is true in each of the cases which follow.

3. Common Misrepresentations of Grice's Theory

There are many criticisms which can be made of Grice's work. However, there are four criticisms of his work which are made very frequently (particularly by nonspecialists) and which are totally unfounded. The first is that Grice had a ludicrously optimistic view of human nature: that he saw the world as a place full of people whose one aim in life was to cooperate with others. This is a complete misreading of Grice's work and is discussed in detail in the *Cooperative Principle* article.

The second unfounded criticism is that Grice was proposing a set of rules for good (conversational) behavior. This misunderstanding probably stems from the unfortunate fact that Grice formulated his maxims as imperatives. But it is clear from everything else he wrote on the subject that his chief objective was simply to describe linguistic behaviors which, by and large, people do observe in conversation unless they wish to generate an implicature, or are deliberately setting out to mislead, or are prevented for some reason from so doing (e.g., nervousness, an inadequate grasp of the language).

The third misconception represents Grice as believing that his maxims are always and invariably observed. This is simply false—such a claim would make complete nonsense of his theory. Discussing the maxims in his 1978 and 1981 papers, Grice refers to them as being:

> standardly (though not invariably) observed by participants in a talk exchange.

> desiderata that normally would be accepted by any rational discourser, though, of course, they could be infringed and violated.

The fourth misunderstanding is to confuse the different types of nonobservance of the maxim. This seems to come from an incomplete reading of Grice's articles, or a reliance on second-hand accounts (few general linguistics textbooks discuss any categories other than flouting). A typical criticism of this order (this one is from Sampson 1982: 203) runs as follows:

> people often flout his [Grice's] maxims. To anyone who knew, for instance, my old scout at Oxford, or a certain one of the shopkeepers in the village where I live, it would be ludicrous to suggest that as a general principle people's speech is governed by maxims such as 'be relevant'; 'do not say that for which you lack adequate evidence'(!); 'avoid obscurity of expression, ambiguity or unnecessary prolixity'(!). In the case of the particular speakers I am thinking of... the converse of Grice's maxims might actually have greater predictive power.

What Sampson is discussing is not the flouting of a maxim (that is, the blatant nonobservance for the purpose of generating an implicature). What he is describing is the unmotivated or unintentional nonobservance of a maxim, which Grice calls 'infringing' (see Sect. 4.2).

Grice was well aware that there are many occasions on which speakers fail to observe the maxims, even though they have no desire to generate an implicature, and even though his categories seem to cover all possible instances of nonobservance.

4. Categories of Nonobservance of the Conversational Maxims

In his first paper (1975: 49), Grice listed three ways in which a participant in a talk exchange may fail to fulfill a maxim: the speaker may flout a maxim, 'violate' a maxim, or 'opt out' of observing a maxim. He later added a fourth category of nonobservance: 'infringing' a maxim. Several writers since Grice have argued the need for a fifth category—'suspending' a maxim, and this category is considered along with the others. Having made all these distinctions, it is irritating to note that Grice himself does not always use the terms consistently, and that remarkably few commentators seem to make any attempt to use the terms correctly. The distinctions which Grice originally made are important for a full understanding of his theory. Flouting has already been examined in detail, and each of the others is now considered in turn.

4.1 Violating a Maxim

Many commentators incorrectly use the term 'violate' for all forms of nonobservance of the maxims. But in his first published paper on conversational cooperation (1975), Grice defines 'violation' very specifically as the *unostentatious* nonobservance of a maxim. If a speaker violates a maxim, he or she 'will be liable to mislead' (1975: 49).

Example (9) is an extract from an interaction between a headmaster and a pupil. It has already been established that the addressee, Hannah (a girl aged about 12), and her friend played truant from school. What is at issue now is where they went on the afternoon in question and, in particular, whether they had been to Simon Connolly's house:

Headmaster:	You know that I now know where	(9)
	you went, don't you?	
Hannah:	We were in the woods.	

It is later established that Hannah's assertion that they were in the woods is true, but not the whole truth (she does not volunteer the information that they had first been to Simon Connolly's house 'for a little while'). But there is nothing in the formulation of Hannah's response which would allow the headmaster to deduce that she was withholding information. This unostentatious violation of the maxim of quantity generates the (probably intentionally) misleading implicature that they went to the woods and nowhere else, that is, that they did not go to the boy's house.

Pragmatically misleading (or potentially pragmatically misleading) utterances of this sort are regularly encountered in certain activity types, such as trials, parliamentary speeches, and arguments. So regularly do they occur, in fact, that they could be seen as the norm for this type of interaction, and be interpreted in that light by participants. For more on this point, see Sect. 4.4.

Initially, it might appear that violating a maxim is the exact opposite of flouting a maxim. In the case of the violation by the schoolgirl, the speaker says something which is *true* (as far as it goes) in order to imply an untruth. In the case of a flout (as in the wheel-clamping example), a speaker may blatantly fail to observe the maxim of quality at the level of what is said, but nevertheless imply something which is true. All the examples of flouts which Grice himself gives are of this order. However, there is no principled reason to expect that an implicature will be *true*—a speaker can imply a lie almost as easily as he or she can say one.

4.2 Infringing a Maxim

As has been already noted, a speaker who, with no intention of generating an implicature, and with no intention of deceiving, fails to observe a maxim, is said to infringe the maxim. In other words, the nonobservance stems from imperfect linguistic performance, rather than from any desire on the part of the speakers to generate a conversational implicature (this is the phenomenon which ampson was describing above). This type of nonobservance could occur because the speaker has an imperfect command of the language, or because the speaker's performance is impaired in some way (nervousness, drunkenness, excitement), or because of some cognitive impairment, or simply because the speaker is constitutionally incapable of speaking clearly, to the point, etc.

4.3 Opting Out of a Maxim

A speaker opts out of observing a maxim by indicating unwillingness to cooperate in the way that the maxim requires. Examples of opting out occur frequently in public life, when the speaker cannot, perhaps for legal or ethical reasons, reply in the way normally expected. Alternatively, the speaker may wish to avoid generating a false implicature or appearing uncooperative. Here is an example from a British MP, who had been asked a question about talks he had had with the Libyan leader Colonel Gadaffi: *Well, honestly, I can't tell you a thing, because what was said to me was told me in confidence.*

When a speaker explicitly opts out of observing a maxim, she or he could be seen to provide privileged access into the way in which speakers normally attend to the maxims, which in turn offers prima facie evidence for Grice's contention that there exists on the part of interactants a strong expectation that, *ceteris paribus* and unless indication is given to the contrary, the CP and the maxims will be observed.

4.4 Suspending a Maxim

Several writers have suggested that there are occasions when there is no need to opt out of observing the maxims because there are certain events in which there is no expectation on the part of any participant that they will be fulfilled (hence the nonfulfillment does not generate any implicatures). This category is necessary to respond to criticisms of the type made by Keenan (1976), who proposed as a counterexample to Grice's theory of conversational implicature the fact that in the Malagasy Republic participants in talk exchanges 'regularly provide less information than is required by their conversational partner, even though they have access to the necessary information' (Keenan 1976: 70). Keenan's examples do not falsify Grice's theory if they are seen as instances where the maxim of quantity is suspended. There is no expectation at all on the part of interactants that speakers will provide precise information about their relatives and friends, in case they draw the attention of evil spirits to them. Although the Malagasy may appear to be underinformative at the level of what is said, the uninformativeness is nevertheless systematic, motivated, and generates implicatures which are readily interpretable by members of that community.

Suspensions of the maxims may be culture-specific (as in Keenan's examples) or specific to particular events. For example, in most cultures, the maxim of quantity appears to be selectively suspended in, for example, courts of law, committees of inquiry, or indeed in any confrontational situation where it is held to be the job of the investigator to elicit the truth from a witness. The witnesses are not required or expected to volunteer information which may incriminate them, and no inference is drawn on the basis of what they do not say (cf. the example of the schoolgirl in Sect. 4.1).

4.5 *Distinguishing between Different Types of Non-observance*

As has been seen, a flout is, by definition, so blatant that the interlocutor knows that an implicature has been generated. One very important point which Grice failed to address is how an interlocutor is supposed to distinguish between a violation, possibly intended to mislead, and an infringement, not intended to generate any implicature.

5. Conclusion

Grice first put forward his ideas concerning the conversational maxims in 1975, and his work continues in the early 1990s to serve as the basis for much (probably most) work in pragmatics. Yet, as this article demonstrates, the theory is full of holes. Some of those holes have been or are being plugged, particularly by people working in politeness theory and in relevance theory, but the fact of the matter is that, unsatisfactory as Grice's work is, it has yet to be replaced by anything better.

See also: Cooperative Principle; Relevance.

Bibliography

Austin J L 1976 *How to Do Things with Words*, 2nd edn. Oxford University Press, London
Brown P, Levinson S C 1987 *Politeness: Some Universals in Language Usage*. Cambridge University Press, Cambridge
Dascal M 1983 *Pragmatics and the Philosophy of Mind I: Thought in Language*. Benjamins, Amsterdam
Grice H P 1975 Logic and conversation. In: Cole P, Morgan J L (eds.) *Syntax and Semantics Vol. 3: Speech Acts*. Academic Press, New York
Grice H P 1978 Further notes on logic and conversation. In: Cole P (ed.) *Syntax and Semantics*, vol. 9. Academic Press, New York
Grice H P 1981 Presupposition and conversational implicature. In: Cole P (ed.) *Radical Pragmatics*. Academic Press, New York
Grice H P 1989 *Studies in the Way of Words*. Harvard University Press, Cambridge, MA
Keenan E O 1976 The universality of conversational postulates. *LiS* **5**: 67–80
Leech G N 1983 *Principles of Pragmatics*. Longman, London
Levinson S C 1983 *Pragmatics*. Cambridge University Press, Cambridge
Sampson G 1982 The economics of conversation: Comments on Joshi's paper. In: Smith N V (ed.) *Mutual Knowledge*. Academic Press, London
Sperber D, Wilson D 1986 *Relevance: Communication and Cognition*. Basil Blackwell, Oxford
Thomas J A 1995 *Meaning in Interaction: An Introduction to Pragmatics*. Longman, London

Cooperative Principle

J. Thomas

The cooperative principle (CP) was first proposed by H.P. Grice in a series of lectures given in 1967. It runs as follows: 'Make your contribution such as is required, at the stage at which it occurs, by the accepted purpose or direction of the talk exchange in which you are engaged.'

Already there is a problem. The way in which the CP is worded makes it seem as if Grice was telling speakers how they ought to behave. What he was actually doing was suggesting that in conversational interaction people work on the assumption that a certain set of rules is in operation, unless, that is, they receive indications to the contrary. In all spheres of life, assumptions are made all the time. For example, a car driver assumes that other drivers will observe the same set of regulations—the traffic system would grind to a halt if such assumptions were not made. Of course, there are times when a driver has indications that another driver may be liable to disobey the rules

(a learner, a drunk, a person whose car is out of control), or that he may be following a different set of rules (a car with foreign number plates), and on these occasions the usual assumptions have to be reexamined or suspended altogether. And, of course, there are times when a driver wrongly assumes that others are operating according to the rules, and then accidents occur. So it is with conversation. When talking, speakers operate according to a set of assumptions, and, on the whole, get by, although inevitably misunderstandings and mistakes occur and sometimes a speaker is deliberately misled.

Grice's work has been, and continues to be, extremely influential. It has also been widely criticized and widely misunderstood. This article discusses various interpretations of his work, and argues in favor of the weaker of the two most common interpretations of the notion of 'conversational cooperation.'

In setting out his cooperative principle, together

with its related maxims, Grice was interested in explaining one particular set of regularities—those governing the generation and interpretation of 'conversational implicature.' For example, my brother comes in carrying an ice cream and says: *I didn't bother buying one for you,* to which I reply: *That's uncommonly generous of you!* On the face of it, my reply is untrue. However, the CP would lead him to assume that, in spite of appearances, I was making an appropriate comment on his behavior. He would therefore conclude that I had sacrificed a conversational maxim at one level, in order to uphold it at another. In other words, I had said something false, but implied something that was true. Grice argues that without the assumption that the speaker is operating according to the CP, there is no mechanism to prompt someone to seek another level of interpretation.

1. Different Interpretations of the Notion of Conversational Cooperation

Many critics of Grice's work on conversational implicature (Grice 1975; 1978; 1981) have been arguing at cross-purposes, and one important reason for this is that the very term 'cooperation' is misleading, since what in everyday terms would be seen as 'highly uncooperative' behavior, such as arguing, lying, hurling abuse, may yet be perfectly cooperative according to some interpretations of Grice's (1975) term.

Grice's own definition of the cooperative principle is ambiguous and inconsistent, and this has enabled both those who have adversely criticized his work and those who have adopted his theories to interpret what he has written to suit themselves. The majority of interpretations, it should be said, can be justified in terms of what Grice actually *wrote,* although some appear to be rather perverse interpretations of what he *meant.* What is striking, however, is how few of those who have drawn so heavily on Grice's theories appear to have noticed the many ambiguities which exist in his work, or, if they have noticed, have taken the trouble to define the way in which they themselves have interpreted the concept of conversational cooperation or are using the term 'cooperative.'

Outlined below are the most strikingly divergent interpretations of Grice's theory, followed by discussion of the different shades within each view. Common to all interpretations is the assumption that the speaker (S) and hearer (H) have some shared interest in conforming to certain linguistic and pragmatic norms, and in a *typical* conversation they do so. However, the question is what it means to conform to linguistic and pragmatic norms.

The most extreme view, which is introduced here only in order to dismiss it totally as a complete misinterpretation of what Grice was concerned to do, says that the maxims of quality, quantity, relation, and manner must at all times be observed at the level of what is said. According to this view, the example given in the introductory section (*That's uncommonly generous of you!*) would be seen as an instance of uncooperative behavior. Now, Grice states unequivocally that the ostentatious nonobservance of a maxim at the level of what is said (that is, what he originally defined as a 'flout') in no way contravenes the CP. On the contrary, it is the mechanism which is required in order to generate an implicature.

The first view which is worthy of serious consideration (if only because it is so widely held) could be called 'real-world goal-sharing.' According to this interpretation, Grice is arguing that, in a 'normal' conversation, S and H actually have some shared interests which, by means of conversation, they 'jointly conspire to promote.' 'Real-world goal-sharing' refers to situations in which S shares with H some common aim or purpose beyond that of getting H to understand which proposition is being expressed or implied. According to this definition, compliance with the CP is possible only against a background of shared goals or interests, which might include (minimally) such local goals as 'keeping the conversation going,' but would generally involve a greater degree of 'real cooperation,' such as a shared interest in establishing the truth. Kiefer interprets Grice in this way:

> Now the Gricean maxims attempt to describe cooperative communication in which the participants strive after the same goal and are equally interested in achieving this goal, furthermore in which the participants have the same social status and finally in which the only goal of the communication is the transmission of information (in a maximally economical way).
>
> (1979a: 60)

According to a third school of thought, which could be called 'linguistic goal-sharing,' Grice intended the cooperative principle to have a much more limited scope. It applies only to the observance of linguistic conventions and presupposes no shared aim or purpose beyond that of establishing correctly S's illocutionary intent (that is, getting H to understand which proposition is being expressed or implied). In particular, it does not presuppose that the proposition which is expressed, entailed, or implied is necessarily polite, relevant to any of H's real-world (extralinguistic) social goals, or even presuppose (according to some interpretations) that it is truthful. This is the interpretation for which Holdcroft (1979) argues in his excellent discussion paper.

2. The Real-world Goal-sharing View of Cooperation

Apostel (1980), Bollobás (1981), Corliss (1981), Kasher (1976; 1977a), Kiefer (1979a), Pratt (1977; 1981), and Sampson (1982) are among the writers who understand Grice to be using the term 'cooperation' in what is called here the 'real-world goal-sharing' sense: that is, they believe that when Grice speaks of cooperation he means that S shares with H some common goal or purpose *beyond that of efficient message-communication.* (It should be pointed out that hardly any of these writers actually subscribe to the real-world goal-sharing view themselves—indeed, Apostel, Kasher, Kiefer, Pratt, and Sampson expressly dissociate themselves from it—but they do apparently believe Grice to have been propounding it.)

According to this view, Grice's CP 'rests on the assumption of cooperation and shared purposes' (Kasher 1976: 201–02; 1977a). That Kasher (1977a: 332) is using 'cooperation' in the 'real-world goal-sharing' sense becomes clear when he says that the principles which he himself proposes, unlike Grice's: 'do not presume the existence of mutual ends for talk-exchanges, but merely the existence of an advantage for limited cooperation.' Kasher's counter-examples only serve as such to the goal-sharing view of co-operation. Sampson (1982: 204) likewise interprets co-operation in the very strong real-world goal-sharing sense, and attacks Grice's putative view with some vehemence, criticizing the CP on the grounds that it 'embodies assumptions which . . . are very widely shared by students of language, but which imply a profoundly false conception of the nature of social life.'

Kasher, Kiefer, Pratt, and Sampson all believe that Grice's theory rests on a false view of the nature of participants in a conversation. Pratt (1981) caricatures the Gricean speaker as a 'cricketer-cum-boy-scout,' 'an honorable guy who always says the right thing and really means it!' All argue that Grice's explanation works only in the rather limited number of situations in which there is 'full cooperation.' They also consider that Grice's maxims apply only to 'co-operative communication in which participants strive after the same goal' (Kiefer 1979a: 60), situations which they do not see as representing any sort of conversational norm (Pratt 1981):

> only some speech situations are characterized by shared objectives among participants. Clearly it is at least as common for speakers to have divergent goals and interests in a situation . . . There is no good reason at all to think of shared goals as representing any kind of natural norm in verbal interaction.

Apostel, Kasher, Kiefer, Pratt, and Sampson are right to reject social goal-sharing as a realistic model of human interaction. Their mistake, however, is in assuming that Grice was proposing it as such, a confusion which presumably stems from Grice's over-reliance in his 1975 paper on the analogy between linguistic behavior and other forms of cooperative endeavor, such as repairing a car. It is perhaps significant that he does not pursue the analogy in either of his subsequent papers on the subject of conversational implicature (Grice 1978; 1981), but concentrates on linguistic behavior alone.

This article dismisses the notion of real-world goal-sharing, both as a realistic model of linguistic inter-action and as a reasonable interpretation of what Grice was concerned to do. It argues in favor of the linguistic goal-sharing view.

3. The Linguistic Goal-sharing View of Cooperation

The dispute between the social goal-sharers and the linguistic goal-sharers can be summarized as follows. For the linguistic goal-sharers, 'conversational co-operation' is concerned with the relationship between what is said and what is implied: 'Use language in such a way that your interlocutor can understand what you are saying and implying.' For the social goal-sharers, 'conversational cooperation' means: 'Tell your interlocutor everything s/he wants to know.'

Those linguists who consider that Grice's theory does have some explanatory power have assumed that the CP and its maxims relate to a theory of linguistic interaction alone, rather than to a more general theory of social interaction, and all their examples are concerned with relating utterances to (implied) propositions. This implies a rejection of the real-world goal-sharing interpretation of cooperation in favor of linguistic goal-sharing, though lamentably few state this explicitly. Honorable exceptions to this stricture are Holdcroft (1979) and Weiser. The latter states his position unambiguously:

> The observation that people follow Grice's cooperative principle in conversation doesn't mean that people are cooperating with each other, but that they are conscious of a system of [regularities] which allows others to make 'strong inferences' about them . . . If you ought to do something and you don't do it, others are entitled to make some inference about your omission. If you show that you're aware that you're not doing something you ought to, then other strong inferences will be made, depending on how you demonstrate your awareness . . .

For this group, the CP relates to a theory of linguistic interaction only, and is 'the general assumption on the part of H that S will not violate conversational procedures' (Grice 1981: 185). A further difficulty is introduced, however, when one considers precisely what constitutes for them 'a violation of conversational procedures.' It is clear that flouting, opting out, or unintentionally infringing a maxim do not constitute a 'violation of conversational procedures.'

What is not clear is whether Grice himself and/or the linguistic goal-sharers consider the unostentatious nonobservance of a maxim at the level of what is said to be a 'violation of conversational procedures.' Consider example (1):

A: Do you know where Paul is?   (1)
B: Are the pubs open yet?

On the face of it, B has flouted the maxim of relation

and has generated the implicature that he does not know for certain where Paul is, but it is very likely that he is at the pub. Now suppose that B actually knows full well where Paul is—he is at this moment breaking into A's toolshed. There is nothing whatever in the way in which B has responded which would indicate to A that B is implying something which is untrue.

The important question for the present discussion is: 'Was B being conversationally cooperative or not?' To answer 'no' would be to adopt the real-world goal-sharing fallacy—one knows that B was understood by A to have implied precisely what he intended to imply (viz. that he did not know exactly where Paul was, but was probably at the pub). The only reason for calling him 'conversationally uncooperative' in these circumstances would be on the grounds that he failed to tell his questioner exactly what his questioner wanted to know.

The linguistic goal-sharers would therefore have to reply 'yes,' arguing that the fact that what B implied was untrue has nothing to do with conversational cooperation or with a theory of implicature. The fact that B has deceived A is of no interest to the linguist (though it might be a suitable question for a social psychologist or a moral philosopher). However, to answer 'yes' in these circumstances makes it very difficult to say what, if anything, is not conversationally cooperative (that is, whether the concept of conversational cooperation is vacuous).

4. Conclusion

If one rejects the social goal-sharing interpretation of Grice's theory, then the concept of conversational cooperation does become trivially true. If, as some commentators maintain, even saying nothing or walking away is interpretable as 'opting out,' then it becomes difficult to find any instances of talk conducted in the presence of another person which do not *count* as cooperative.

Margolis (1979), in common with many others, has attacked Grice on the grounds that he provides only vague, sloppy, and circular notions of rules and discovery procedures. Margolis's criticisms (and similar ones proposed by Holdcroft 1979) that the CP is vacuous and unfalsifiable may be largely justified, but it would be a mistake to underestimate the insights which Grice has given into the process of utterance interpretation. To have pointed out what ordinary interactants take for granted is recognized within ethnomethodology, for example, as a major theoretical contribution. Altieri (1978: 92), commenting on Margolis's strictures, makes the following observation:

with Grice, charges like Joseph Margolis' claim that his

maxims are only principles of common sense may indicate his strength rather than his weakness. A *sensus communis* is not a bad ground on which to base our capacity to understand the pragmatics of meaning.

Grice can claim credit for asking a lot of exciting questions, which have led linguists to think about language in a completely new way. But in the end, what is left is a set of very informal procedures for calculating conversational implicature, which cannot really withstand close scrutiny. On the other hand, flawed as Grice's work is, no one else, in the view of this writer, has yet come up with anything better with which to replace it.

See also: Conversational Maxims.

Bibliography

Altieri C 1978 What Grice offers literary theory: A proposal for 'expressive implicature.' *Centrum* **6(2)**: 90–103
Apostel L 1979 Persuasive communication as metaphorical discourse under the guidance of conversational maxims. *Logique et Analyse* **22**: 265–320
Bollobás E 1981 Who's afraid of irony? An analysis of uncooperative behavior in Edward Albee's 'Who's afraid of Virginia Woolf?' *JPrag* **5(3)**: 323–34
Corliss R L 1972 A theory of contextual implication. *Philosophy and Rhetoric* **5**: 215–30
Grice H P 1975 Logic and conversation. In: Cole P, Morgan J L (eds.) *Syntax and Semantics Vol. 3: Speech Acts*. Academic Press, New York
Grice H P 1978 Further notes on logic and conversation. In: Cole P (ed.) *Syntax and Semantics,* vol. 9. Academic Press, New York
Grice H P 1981 Presupposition and conversational implicature. In: Cole P (ed.) *Radical Pragmatics*. Academic Press, New York
Grice H P 1989 *Studies in the Way of Words*. Harvard University Press, Cambridge, MA
Holdcroft D 1979 Speech acts and conversation I. *Philosophical Quarterly* **29**: 125–41
Kasher A 1976 Conversational maxims and rationality. In: Kasher A (ed.) *Language in Focus*. Reidel, Dordrecht
Kasher A 1977a Foundations of philosophical pragmatics. In: Butts R E, Hintikka J (eds.) *Basic Problems in Methodology and Linguistics*. Reidel, Dordrecht
Kasher A 1977b What is a theory of use? *JPrag* **1(2)**: 105–20
Kiefer F 1979a What do the conversational maxims explain? *Linguisticae Investigationes* **3(1)**: 57–74
Kiefer F 1979b A brief rejoinder. *Linguisticae Investigationes* **3(2)**: 379–81
Margolis J 1979 Literature and speech acts. *Philosophy of Literature* **3**: 39–52
Pratt M-L 1981 The ideology of speech act theory. *Centrum* [New Series]: 5–18
Sampson G 1982 The economics of conversation: Comments on Joshi's paper. In: Smith N V (ed.) *Mutual Knowledge*. Academic Press, London
Thomas J A 1995 *Meaning in Interaction: An Introduction to Pragmatics*. Longman, London

Felicity Conditions

K. Allan

A speech act is created when speaker/writer S makes an utterance U to hearer/reader H in context C. When S says 'I promise to take you to a movie tomorrow' s/he might mean it, in which case the illocutionary point of the utterance would be felicitous, or s/he might secretly intend not to carry out the promise, in which case the illocutionary point would be infelicitous. The question of S's sincerity is not the only felicity condition on an illocutionary act. In addition to (1) the sincerity condition, Austin argued for three additional kinds of felicity conditions: (2) a preparatory condition to establish whether or not the circumstances of the speech act and the participants in it are appropriate to its being performed successfully; (3) an executive condition to determine whether or not the speech act has been properly executed; and (4) a fulfillment condition determined by the perlocutionary effect of the speech act. If all the relevant felicity conditions were satisfied for a given illocutionary act, Austin described it as 'happy' or 'felicitous.'

Austin's felicity conditions were expressed as follows:

(A.1) There must exist an accepted conventional procedure having a certain conventional effect, that procedure to include the uttering of certain words by certain persons in certain circumstances, and further,

(A.2) the particular persons and circumstances in a given case must be appropriate for the invocation of the particular procedure invoked.

(B.1) The procedure must be executed by all participants both correctly and

(B.2) completely.

(Γ.1) Where, as often, the procedure is designed for use by persons having certain thoughts or feelings, or for the inauguration of certain consequential conduct on the part of any participant, then a person participating in and so invoking the procedure must in fact have those thoughts or feelings, and the participants must intend so to conduct themselves, and further

(Γ.2) must actually so conduct themselves subsequently. Now if we sin against one (or more) of these six rules, our performative utterance will be (in one way or another) unhappy.

(Austin 1975: 14f)

(A.1–2) describe preparatory conditions, (B.1–2) executive conditions, (Γ.1) a sincerity condition, and (Γ.2) a fulfillment condition. Each felicity condition will be examined in turn.

(A.1) 'There must exist an accepted conventional procedure having a certain conventional effect, that procedure to include the uttering of certain words by certain persons in certain circumstances.' These are preparatory conditions on the felicity of speech acts like:

I baptize you in the name of the Father and of the Son and of the Holy Spirit. (1)

I pronounce you man and wife. (2)

I dub thee 'Sir Caspar.' (3)

I declare the ball out. (4)

Out! [In the sense of (4)] (5)

Typically, there are only certain ceremonial conditions under which baptism, the effecting of a marriage rite, knighting someone, and umpiring, can legitimately take place; and the speech acts in (1–5) only come off under these conditions. Thus, although anyone at all can utter (1–5) under any circumstances whatever, the illocutionary act will be invalid unless certain conventional circumstances prevail. For instance, in most Anglophone communities the preparatory conditions on (2) are: (a) only certain legally defined members of the community can function as marriage celebrants; (b) only such marriage celebrants may felicitously effect a marriage rite uttering (2); (c) they can only do so under circumstances conventionally recognized as constituting a marriage ceremony; (d) the people to be married must be a man and a woman and both over the age of 16 or thereabouts; (e) only if neither is concurrently married. If we ignore a few local legal variations, the uttering of (2) under different circumstances will not effect a marriage, and the performative will be infelicitous. It is notable that in, say, a film or a play, a pretend marriage can be effected by the uttering of (2) under a proper model of the appropriate circumstances; but whereas the personae in the drama can subsequently be held to be married, the actors playing man and wife cannot. Comparable circumstances controlling the success of the illocutionary acts represented in the other sentences can readily be imagined. It is clear in all such cases that the speech act enacts the law (rules of society) or the rules of the game. (A.1) is very legalistic.

(A.2) 'The particular persons and circumstances in a given case must be appropriate for the invocation of the particular procedure invoked.' This condition seems to be largely included in (A.1), but concentrates on the participants rather than the circumstances in which the speech act takes place. For instance, a felicitous order can be performed by a colonel saying to a private soldier 'I order you to clean the latrines at

1100 hours' or 'Clean the latrines at 1100 hours.' But it would ordinarily be infelicitous for a private soldier to address such utterances to his/her colonel; the resulting performative would be, in Austin's words, 'null and void.' Similarly the participants in a marriage ceremony must be as they are described above, otherwise the marriage will be 'null and void.' No-one but a monarch (or their appointed agent) can legitimately utter (3) if Caspar is truly to be knighted. And only an umpire, referee, or their delegated minions have the power to declare a ball out of play; neither a television commentator, nor one of the players, has the power to make a declaration such as (5) stick without the umpire's say-so. (A.2) also covers such peculiarities as a driver saying to his car 'I bet you a dollar you run out of petrol before we get to a garage' because a car is not a suitable addressee for a bet.

In *Speech Acts* (1969: 63–67), John Searle identified preparatory conditions on a number of illocutionary acts, and we now turn our attention to his proposals. Searle identifies one of the preparatory conditions on promising as follows:

> H would prefer S to do A (i.e., carry out the promised act) to his not doing A, and S believes that H would prefer S's doing A to his not doing A.

S can only make the promise in the light of the second of these conjuncts. H's preferences lie outside of linguistic considerations, although it is likely that they are relevant to the perlocutionary effect of S's utterance. Linguists should ignore the first conjunct of Searle's preparatory condition on promising, and all comparable statements. The second preparatory condition on promising which Searle identifies is the following:

> It is not obvious to both S and H that S will do A in the normal course of events.

This condition, and all comparable statements within the preparatory conditions on other illocutionary acts, can be subsumed under the general conventions of the Gricean cooperative principle, in particular the maxim of quantity (cf. Allan 1986: ch. 1; Grice 1975; Levinson 1983: 241), and it would be redundant to include statements of such preparatory conditions within the definitions of every illocutionary act. Hence, Searle's preparatory conditions on promising can be pruned to:

> S believes that H would prefer S's doing A to S's not doing A.

If one examines promises in more detail, it turns out that this needs rewording (cf. Allan 1986); but it will suffice to exemplify the preparatory condition on promising. Among other (pruned) preparatory conditions identified by Searle are those on:

(a) requests—S believes H is able to do the act requested;

(b) assertions—S has evidence (reasons for believing etc.) the truth of *p*;

(c) thanks—S is grateful to H for having done deed D;

(d) advice—S believes there is reason for H to do A and that it will benefit H.

Preparatory conditions identify the particular circumstances and, perhaps, participants appropriate to performing a given illocutionary act. As Searle and Vanderveken (1985: 17) point out: 'In the performance of a speech act the speaker *presupposes* the satisfaction of all the preparatory conditions.' More precisely, they are what Seuren calls 'prejections' of U (see Seuren 1985: 272 ff). They are special clauses of the generally applicable cooperative conditions on utterances.

Austin's conditions (B.1–2) are executive conditions. (B.1) states that the procedure invoked by the illocutionary act 'must be executed by all participants correctly.' Austin (1975: 36) exemplifies (B.1) with 'I bet you the race won't be run today' said when more than one race was arranged for that day. If S knew there was more than one race, then s/he would be violating the cooperative maxim of manner by being ambiguous instead of saying precisely what s/he meant. The utterance would, in addition, violate the maxim of quantity if S knew there was more than one race, but didn't bother to make this clear. And if S didn't know, but did suspect that there would be more than one race on the day in question, then in making this utterance s/he would be violating the cooperative maxim of quality by failing to advert H of this suspicion. So these particular examples of mis-executions can all be dealt with under the generally applicable maxims of the cooperative principle. In any case, such misexecutions do not render the illocutionary act invalid, as Austin suggests they do. Under the circumstances described above, H can justifiably reply 'I'll take you on, provided you tell me what race you mean,' thereby demonstrating that the utterance addressed to H has successfully achieved the illocutionary point of offering a bet; the misexecutions ('misfires') Austin described don't affect this.

Some other misexecutions envisaged by Austin can also be dismissed, e.g., suppose the priest baptising a child, by a slip of the tongue, or an inconvenient hiccup, actually said (6) instead of (1):

$$I \left\{ \begin{matrix} \text{pronounce} \\ \text{marry} \\ \text{[hiccup]} \end{matrix} \right\} \begin{matrix} \text{you in the name of the Father and} \\ \text{of the Son and of the Holy Spirit.} \end{matrix} \quad (6)$$

Austin claims that in such circumstances the baptism would not be effected; but this is questionable. Such accidental quirks as slips of the tongue, or hiccups, should be dismissed as irrelevant performance variables (cf. Chomsky 1965: 4).

Declaratory speech acts bring about states of affairs such as baptism, marriage, knighting, job appointment/termination, consecrating, sentencing, etc., or express decisions on states of affairs. Because they rely for their success on S being sanctioned by the community, institution, committee, or even a single person within the group to perform the acts under stipulated conditions, a safeguard such as the following executive condition is needed:

> At the time of utterance, S, being of sound mind, consciously intends his/her utterance U to count as a declaration that A.

Suppose that S is a person sanctioned to terminate H's employment, and S says to H 'You're fired!'; H would most probably be held not to have been fired if S were found to be insane, talking in his/her sleep or in a drunken stupor, or kidding, etc. at the time of uttering those words. An alternative to having such an executive condition is to impose this constraint as a preparatory condition on the utterance; e.g., the preparatory conditions on a verdictive (S declares the verdict that *p*) should look something like the following:

> Members of group G are sanctioned to declare verdicts on a set of topics T in a set of situations K; and (i) S is a member of G; (ii) at the time of uttering U, S is of sound mind; (iii) the verdict that *p* is on a topic which is a member of T; (iv) the situation of utterance is a member of K.

These would be the preparatory conditions on, for example, a tennis umpire declaring a ball *Out!*, or a jury foreman announcing a guilty verdict; notice that G, T, and K are different for the two verdictives. Provided one recognizes the relevance of a condition such as (ii) within a specification for declaratory acts, it hardly matters whether one follows the Austinian tradition and calls it an executive condition or includes it within the preparatory conditions.

Austin's (B.2) states that the procedure invoked by the illocutionary act must be executed completely; and Austin saw this as a condition on the effectiveness of the illocution. Thus, an example of a (B.2) mis-execution would be where a clergyman says '*I*...' and chokes to death; and here it is true the baptism wouldn't have taken place. But this is a quintessential performance hitch, and no rule of language can or should be expected to cope with it. Another example, suggested by Austin, is that the act performed by S uttering, 'I bet you $10 that horse will win' is mis-executed if no-one takes up the bet. However, this is a failure to achieve the desired perlocutionary effect; the illocutionary point remains good, because if no-one takes up the bet S can legitimately continue 'Well, I offered a bet and I guess it's my loss if no-one takes me up on it, since I'm sure to win'; or when the horse has lost, H can respond with 'You bet me $10 that horse would win, and now I wish I'd taken you up on

it.' It can be concluded that Austin's condition (B.2) is not a condition on the performance of the illocutionary act, but rather on the perlocutionary effect of the utterance—and this lies outside the scope of a linguistic account of speech acts.

(Γ.1) is the sincerity condition, which can be identified with the cooperative maxim of quality: 'Where the procedure is designed for use by persons having certain thoughts or feelings, or for the inauguration of certain consequential conduct on the part of any participant, then a person participating in and so invoking the procedure must in fact have those thoughts or feelings, and the participants must intend so to conduct themselves.' For example, someone uttering, 'I promise to take you to a movie tomorrow' would not be making a sincere promise unless s/he intended taking H to a movie. This is called a 'false promise'; and a contravention of the sincerity condition usually leads to an illocutionary act being described as false. Thus a 'false apology' is an insincere one, e.g., saying '*I'm sorry*' when it is clear no sorrow is felt. False sympathy is sympathy not felt, although professed. False advice is advice given, but not what it purports to be. Austin (1975: 50) notes that the sincerity condition is applicable to statements, too: 'Suppose I did say "the cat is on the mat" when it is not the case that I believe the cat is on the mat; what should we say? Clearly it is a case of insincerity.' Following Searle (1968), one needs to take account of the fact that the word *statement* is ambiguous between 'act of stating' ('statement$_{act}$') and 'what is stated' ('statement$_{object}$'). The two senses are contrasted in (7).

> The 'statement$_{act}$' of the 'statement$_{object}$' that all men are mortal takes one second. (7)

The gerund *stating* is synonymous with 'statement$_{act}$' but not with 'statement$_{object}$,' and in (7) can replace the one but not the other. The sincerity condition Austin spoke of applies only to the 'statement$_{act}$,' cf. 'His falsely stating that the cat is on the mat when he knows it to be up a tree is despicable.' In observing the cooperative maxim of manner, we normally say 'falsely (or truly) stating' when referring to the sincerity of the act, but to assign a truth value to the 'statement$_{object}$' we usually speak of 'a true or false statement,' thus minimizing possible ambiguity. The distinction between 'statement$_{act}$' and 'statement$_{object}$' corresponds to a distinction between what S believes and asserts (or implies) to be the case as against what actually is the case; a similar distinction can be made for other speech acts. Consider just one other example: promising. Suppose S were to sincerely say 'I promise to give you my mother's ring when we get home.' On arriving home S finds his house burgled and the ring stolen, and so is prevented from fulfilling his promise because the facts are incompatible with what S sincerely believed to obtain. In such a case, it might be noted that in Austin's terminology the illocutionary act 'misfires,' but there is no 'abuse' of the preparatory condition. For a complementary case, suppose S had made this utterance insincerely, fully intending to kill H on the way home, but being prevented from doing so; on arrival home he actually carries out his stated promise, even though it was uttered insincerely. Here is an 'abuse' of the preparatory condition, but no 'misfire'; so S's insincerity can easily remain undiscovered. Another example would be a twelfth century jester who jokingly says 'The world is a sphere' and thus produces an insincerely meant true statement. What is interesting here is that at no time during the twelfth century could either S or H believe in the truth of this assertion—hence it could work as a jest then, but not now; in this case, S's insincerity is transparent to his audience, the preparatory condition is based on faulty knowledge/belief.

Thus sincerity conditions on speech acts involve S's responsibility for what s/he is saying (asking, etc.). If S is observing the cooperative maxim of quality, then s/he will be sincere: and, normally, H will assume that S is being sincere unless s/he has good reason to believe otherwise. Generally, scholars have assumed that different kinds of illocutionary acts involve different kinds of sincerity conditions: e.g., assertions and the like are sincere if S believes in the truth of the proposition asserted; requests are sincere if S believes H can do A and might be willing to do A; promises are sincere if S willingly intends to do A; declaratory acts are sincere if S believes s/he has the proper authority to make the declaration. It is obvious from these descriptions that sincerity underpins speaker-based aspects of preparatory (and, if they are retained, executive) conditions. Now, if preparatory conditions on a speech act are properly stated, only one sincerity condition should be necessary:

> In uttering U, S knows or believes (or believes s/he knows) that all clauses of the preparatory condition hold.

This puts a burden on precise statement of the preparatory conditions, but that seems exactly where the burden should lie because preparatory conditions identify the particular circumstances appropriate to performing a given illocutionary act. Thus when H perceives a violation of any clause within the preparatory condition on an illocutionary act, the typical response (here generalized) is, 'S has no right to make this particular illocutionary point under the prevailing circumstances; s/he must be either deluded, insane, or malicious.'

Austin's (Γ.2) is a fulfillment condition. It states that the participants in a speech act must conduct themselves in accordance with the thoughts and feelings invoked in the illocution. Thus, according to Austin, a promise is invalid unless it is carried out; a bet is invalid if the winner is not paid. But such fulfillment conditions hang on the perlocutions of the speech acts, and therefore stand outside an account of the specifically linguistic aspects of S's utterance U. The illocutions of, for example, promising and betting can be communicated, and the respective illocutionary acts effected, without the perlocution coming off (cf. 'You promised to dig my rose bed, but you haven't done it' or 'You bet me $1000, and if you don't pay up by midnight I'll break your legs.') Such sentences confirm that the illocutions of a promise and a bet were valid enough, it is merely the subsequent behavior that is at fault. Thus a fulfillment condition has no place within a linguistic theory of speech acts; though it is relevant to a theory of interpersonal behavior.

An illocutionary act is felicitous when all the felicity conditions stipulated in its definition are satisfied. Today it can be seen that felicity conditions are those applications of the cooperative principle that need to be specified in the definition of a particular illocutionary act. Though many scholars would disagree, the author suggests that only one sincerity condition need be stated for all illocutionary acts: S believes the relevant preparatory conditions on the act hold. Preparatory conditions identify the circumstances necessary for an illocutionary act to succeed. It is also suggested that executive conditions, which identify the attitude or behavior that must be observed by S when executing the illocutionary act for it to be felicitous, can be written into the preparatory conditions on the act. On this view, the whole burden of felicitous illocution will depend on proper observation of the preparatory conditions on each illocutionary act. These conditions provide the grounds for motivating S to make the utterance and grounds from which H will evaluate the illocutionary act expressed in the utterance.

See also: Speech Act Classification; Speech Act Hierarchy.

Bibliography

Allan K 1986 *Linguistic Meaning* (2 vols.). Routledge and Kegan Paul, London
Austin J L 1975 In: Urmson J O, Sbisà M (eds.) *How To Do Things With Words,* 2nd edn. Clarendon Press, Oxford
Chomsky N 1965 *Aspects of the Theory of Syntax.* MIT Press, Cambridge MA
Grice H P 1975 Logic and conversation. In: Cole P, Morgan J (eds.) *Syntax and Semantics 3: Speech Acts.* Academic Press, New York
Levinson S C 1983 *Pragmatics.* Cambridge University Press, Cambridge
Searle J R 1968 Austin on locutionary and illocutionary acts. *Philos. Review* 77: 405–24
Searle J R 1969 *Speech Acts.* Cambridge University Press, Cambridge
Searle J R, Vanderveken D 1985 *Foundations of Illocutionary Logic.* Cambridge University Press, Cambridge
Seuren P A M 1985 *Discourse Semantics.* Basil Blackwell, Oxford

Indirect Speech Acts

K. Allan

A speech act is created when speaker/writer S makes an utterance U to hearer/reader H in context C. This entry examines 'indirect' speech acts. Suppose S_1 utters (1) in C_1, where it answers the question *What's the time?* (1):

> It is 7.45.　　　　　　　　　　　　　　　(1)

Many scholars would call this a 'direct' speech act, because in uttering (1) S_1 means exactly and literally 'the time now is seven forty-five.' However, (2) is uttered in context C_2, in which S_2 and spouse H_2 share the car to work, and need to leave home by 7.45 in order to arrive on time.

> It's 7.45.　　　　　　　　　　　　　　　(2)

Although this is still a bald-on-record statement of the current time it is often called an indirect speech act because S_2 means at least 'it is time to leave for work'; and it is quite likely that S_2 further implies 'hurry up, you're making us late.'

> In indirect speech acts the speaker communicates to the hearer more than he actually says by way of relying on their mutually shared background information, both linguistic and nonlinguistic, together with general powers of rationality and inference on the part of the hearer.
> (Searle 1975: 61)

There is overwhelming evidence that speakers expect hearers to draw inferences from everything that is uttered—just as they do from visual and other data perceived and conceived of—no matter how direct. It follows that H will begin the inferential process immediately on being presented with the locution (the language expression used in the utterance). Recognition of the clause-type used within the locution identifies the primary (or initial) illocution in U, but not necessarily S's illocutionary point. The inferential process will be exemplified by discussion of (1) and (2).

　　There is a convention that S has some purpose for choosing to utter U_i in C_i instead of maintaining silence or making some other utterance U_x. H tries to guess this purpose in the course of figuring out the illocutionary point of U_i, and in doing so will consider U_i's relevance to the co-text and setting of the utterance in the light of beliefs about normal behavior in C_i, beliefs about S, and the presumed common ground. Details of the inferential processes with respect to (1) and (2) are as follows. Step one is for H to recognize S's utterance act. Step two is to use H's knowledge of the grammar, lexicon, semantics, and phonology of English to recognize that S's words *It's*

7.45 spoken with a certain pattern of pause, pitch level, stress, and tone of voice, mean 'S says it is seven forty-five.' The third step is to recognize what S's locution is being used to denote/refer to: by 'it' S denotes 'the time'; the tense of the main verb indicates that the time S refers to is the present. H therefore concludes: 'S says the present time is seven forty-five.' Step four is to recognize from H's linguistic knowledge that this meets the description for the primary illocution of a statement in which it is S's reflexive-intention that H believe that S believes that it is seven forty-five. Up to step four, the inferential process for (2) is identical with that for (1); but thereafter it diverges. In step five H seeks to establish S's illocutionary point by relating the primary illocution to C_i, in order to determine S's apparent purpose in uttering U_i. In C_1 utterance (1) was issued in answer to the question *What's the time?*, so it is reasonable for H_1 to assume that the primary illocution has identified the illocutionary point because, in saying *It's 7.45*, S_1 has satisfactorily answered the question, and there are no further inferences to be drawn. Turning to utterance (2): in C_2, H_2 knows that S_2 has not been asked to tell H_2 the time, therefore S_2 has some personal motivation for drawing the current time to H_2's attention; H_2 also knows that S_2 knows that S_2 and H_2 have been getting ready to leave at 7.45 for work. H_2 will therefore conclude that S_2's motivation must be that because it is 7.45, it is time to leave for work; in other words, S_2 reflexively-intends H_2 to recognize that 'S_2 is saying it is time to leave for work.' Step six is to decide either that this is the illocutionary point of (2) or that some further inference should be drawn. H_2 may reason that S_2 knows as well as H_2 does that if it is time to leave for work but S_2 and H_2 have not yet done so, then they must hurry. Let us stipulate that in C_2, H_2 has grounds for believing that S_2 believes that S_2 is ready to leave for work but S_2 may not believe that H_2 is also ready (this would be made more probable if S_2's tone of voice reveals that s/he is irritated). Given this belief, H_2 will conclude that S_2 reflexively-intends (2) to be taken as sufficient reason for H_2 to hurry up because H_2 is delaying their departure and so making them late. Because there is no further inference to draw, H_2 will conclude that this is the illocutionary point of (2).

　　It is often assumed that performative clauses express their illocutionary point directly (see Gazdar 1981); but the analysis of (1) makes this impossible: the primary illocution of a performative clause is that of a statement (see Cohen 1964; Lewis 1970; Bach and Harnish 1979; Allan 1986). Consider (3):

I promise to go there tomorow. (3)

Here the primary illocution, corresponding to step four in the previous analysis, is (slightly simplified): 'S_3 is saying that S_3 promises to go there tomorrow.' This is not the illocutionary point of (3), however. S_3 is using this primary illocution as a vehicle for a further illocution to be read off the performative verb; namely, S_3 reflexively-intends the (primary) statement to be a reason for H_3 to believe that S_3 undertakes and intends (i.e., promises) to go there tomorrow. There is no further inference to draw, so this is the illocutionary point of (3). By definition, then, the performative clause in (3) communicates an indirect illocution.

What additional evidence is there that performatives are statements? First, there is the obvious similarity between (3) and (4):

I promised to go there tomorow. (4)

Unlike (3), which is in the present (nonpast) tense and has the illocutionary point of a promise, (4) is past tense and has the illocutionary point of a statement about a promise made (in the past). The primary illocution of (4) is 'S_4 is saying that S_4 promised to go there tomorrow.' This is not the only parallel with (3), because H_4 will interpret this as follows: S_4 reflexively-intends the (primary) statement to be a reason for H_4 to believe that S_4 did undertake and intend (i.e., promised) to go there tomorrow. There is no further inference to draw, so this is the illocutionary point of (4). Note that the undertaking in both (3) and (4) remains to be fulfilled, and while S_4 is not actually making the promise in (4) as S_3 is in (3), nevertheless, provided all normal felicity conditions hold, S_4 is as much obliged to fulfill the promise reported in (4) as S_3 is in (3). The presumption that the primary illocution of explicit performatives is that of a statement permits a commonsensical account of the similarity and difference between (3) and (4).

Second, there is a distinction between *saying* Σ and *saying that* Σ: the former reports locutions, the latter reports statements. Imperatives and interrogatives do not make statements. Compare (5):

Go!	What's your name?	(5)
I said go.	I said what's your name?	
*I said that go.	*I said that what's your name?	
I said that you must go.	I said that I want to know your name.	

In order to be reported by *saying that*, the propositional content of imperatives and interrogatives needs to be recast as a statement; this is not the case with a performative because its primary illocution is that of a statement, for example, (6):

The beer's cold.	I promise to go there tomorrow.	(6)

I said the beer's cold.	I said I promise to go there tomorrow.
I said that the beer's cold.	I said that I promise to go there tomorrow.

Third, there is a set of adverbials which modify primary illocutionary acts, e.g., *honestly, for the last time, seriously, frankly, once and for all, in the first place, in conclusion* (see Allan 1986). Consider (7):

In the first place I admit to being wrong; (7)
and *secondly* I promise it will never happen again.

Example (7) can be glossed: 'The first thing I have to say is that I admit to being wrong; and the second thing I have to say is that I promise it will never happen again.' It is clear that *secondly* denotes a second act of stating, not a second act of promising; from which it may be deduced that *In the first place* identifies a first act of stating, not a first act of admitting. There is no space to consider more than these three arguments; but the evidence is strongly against the view that explicit performatives are direct (= primary) illocutions, because primary illocutions are read off the clause-type.

Now consider (8):

Can you open the window? (8)

Depending on tone of voice and the context of utterance, the locution in (8) could be a question about the openability of the window, about H's ability to open the window, or a request to have H open the window. The primary illocution of (8) is 'S is asking H whether or not H can open the contextually identified window, either right now or in the immediate future.' The next step is for H to relate the primary illocution to the context of utterance in order to determine S's apparent purpose in asking H whether or not H can open the window. S_a could be asking whether or not H_a is capable of opening the window. Perhaps if H_a had sustained some possibly incapacitating injury, S_a might be asking about H_a's strength; but (8) would be an unusually oblique way to ask about someone's physical condition. Imagine another context, C_b: the weather is so delightful and the room so stuffy that S_b presumes H_b would surely have opened the window if it were openable; or perhaps the window is perceptibly screwed shut; in either case the question focuses on the openability of the window rather than presupposing it. Again, suppose S_c is visiting H_c in H_c's apartment; it is a sunny spring day and the heating is on: S_c has just walked up three flights of stairs wearing outdoor clothing and has remarked wryly how warm it is in the apartment. In C_c it is most likely that S_c is presupposing (a) the openability of the window and (b) H's capability of opening it, so that the illocutionary point of (8) is to get H_c to open the window. S_c, who is a guest, has pointedly remarked on the closeness of the room thus implying s/he would prefer cooler, more airy, conditions. This will be S_c's reason for asking whether or not H_c can open the window, either right now or in the immediate future. H_c will conclude that S_c reflexively-intends (8) to be taken as a reason for H_c to open the window.

In (8) S uses a formula which questions the possibility for H to open the window—thus expressly giving H the option to refuse—rather than coercing H by using an imperative, which offers no such option. For H to do A it is necessary that H *can* do A—which is why polite refusals state or imply the inability to comply. Asking if H can do A is more tentative than asking if H *will* do A because a *will* request solicits the cooperative answer *I will,* in which H commits her/himself to complying. The mitigation of a face threat was the reason scholars once gave for the use of indirectness; there appears to have been some confusion between the notion of indirect speech acts, as they have been described here, and the notion of on-record versus off-record speech acts, such as are described by Brown and Levinson (1987). For someone who is not very close to you to respond to the invitation *Do you want to come to a movie tonight?* with the bald-on-record refusal *No* is outright offensive; to avoid giving offence interlocutors hedge, apologize, prevaricate, and speak off-record, giving reasons for not accepting the invitation or complying with the request. Thus to refuse the invitation politely one says things like (9):

> I have to wash my hair. (9)
> I'd love to, but my mother's coming to dinner tonight.

Like most speech acts, the illocutionary point of the utterances in (9) is indirect; but more significantly, these are off-record refusals.

Because all entailments and implicatures of a proposition within U are communicated, they give rise to indirect illocutions that are often, though not necessarily, intended to be communicated. For example, *Woody likes his new job* informs H that 'S believes Woody has a new job,' and S may have made the utterance partly to inform H of this fact. *Who phoned?* informs H that 'S believes that someone phoned.' *My sister's husband*—'S has a married sister.' *Max has one son and two daughters*—'S believes Max has no more than one son and two daughters.' Challenges such as (10) directly seek an explanation for or cessation of the offending act; and indirectly S informs H of S's belief that 'the music (hifi) is loud.'

$$\left\{ \begin{array}{c} \text{Why} \\ \text{Must you} \end{array} \right\} \text{play the hifi so loud?} \qquad (10)$$

If S likes loud music, and knows or assumes that H does too, s/he would know why the hifi was playing loud and would not have asked (10) but said something supportive (*Great sound! Let's turn up the hifi!*). Therefore, either S believes that H does not like loud music and is seeking an explanation for this uncharacteristic behavior, or—and much more likely—S does not like loud music and is making plain the opinion that 'the music is *too* loud.' A public condemnation like that of the woman at a party who cries out *Mrs Trumpington, will you please ask your husband to keep his hands off me?!* broadcasts (a) what Mr T is doing, (b) a request that he be stopped, (c) S's entailed belief that he will not stop of his own volition. Those are on-record indirect illocutions. Off-record, S indirectly intends not only that Mrs T condemn her husband for sexual harassment of S, but that everyone in earshot should do so too.

The illocutionary point of any utterance is discovered by an inferential process that attends to S's tone of voice and the context of utterance, knowledge of the language itself and of conversational conventions, and perhaps general knowledge. S knows this and speaks accordingly, aware that H—as a competent social being and language user—will recognize the implications of what s/he says. It is not enough to know a language, one must also know how to use it. Having recognized the existence of the utterance, the inferential process must start with the form; and the primary illocution is read off the clause-type used. The binary distinction 'direct' versus 'indirect' is not fine enough for a proper analysis of speech acts. Because the primary illocution is only occasionally the illocutionary point of the utterance, most illocutions are inferred as 'secondary,' or 'tertiary' illocutions. The last illocution that can be inferred is the (presumed) illocutionary point of the utterance.

See also: Speech Act Theory: Overview; Speech Acts and Grammar.

Bibliography

Allan K 1986 *Linguistic Meaning,* vol. 2. Routledge and Kegan Paul, London

Bach K, Harnish R M 1979 *Linguistic Communication and Speech Acts.* MIT Press, Cambridge, MA

Brown P, Levinson S 1987 *Politeness: Some Universals in Language Usage.* Cambridge University Press, Cambridge

Cohen L J 1964 Do illocutionary forces exist? *Philosophical Quarterly* **55**: 118–37

Gazdar G 1981 Speech act assignment. In: Joshi A et al. (eds.) *Elements of Discourse Understanding.* Cambridge University Press, Cambridge

Lewis D 1970 General semantics. *Synthese* **22**: 18–67

Searle J R 1975 Indirect speech acts. In: Cole P, Morgan J (eds.) *Syntax and Semantics 3: Speech Acts.* Academic Press, New York

Irony
M. Marino

A concept that ranges from the mere bagatelle of a devious sophist to the organizing principle of the universe is a truly seductive chimera. The word 'irony' is often intended and usually understood in a variety of ways in modern discussions; yet, as often as it has been left underdetermined no umbrella concept called irony has been developed. Its movement from Classical Greek lexeme to later Latin figure of speech to cosmic descriptor for the German romantics in the nineteenth century helped make the modern senses multifarious; American New Criticism privileged the word as a primary principle of structure in their textual manipulations, and Schlegel's moral and philosphical uses of it have recently returned to prominence. It does little good to make a neat formal definition that neither the language nor even individual scholars can observe. The chimera can be neither slain nor tamed.

1. A Nondefinition of Irony

The simpler earliest reflexes of Greek *eirein* 'to speak' seem to have coalesced in a narrowing and pejorative sense around the behavioral characteristics of dissemblance; Greek *rhetor*'s origin in the same etymon, Indo-European **wer-* 'to speak,' suggests the same progression from neutral discourse to suspect means of oratory manipulation. One of Socrates' targets in Plato's *Republic* is convinced that he has been conned by Socrates' *eironeia*; however, Cicero lauds the original Socratic irony, 'feigned ignorance in order to instruct.' In the political sphere, Demosthenes perceived the *eiron* as a civic evader of responsibility through feigned unfitness; yet again, Aristotle prefers the self-deprecating *eironeia* of Socrates to the bluster of *alazoneia* 'exaggerated misrepresentation.' If Freudian joke tendentiousness is part of the ironic process, perhaps the opposite views of the speakers and the victims help to explain the polarity that was evident even early in the use of the concept. Cicero's use marked the movement from a behavioral characteristic to a rhetorical figure that blames by praise or praises by blame. Latin *ironia* had at least these two meanings, and Quintilian seems to have expanded the circumscribed figure to the manner of whole arguments.

It is not simply the complex history of the word that makes it impossible to control; it is also that irony usually involves intentions and always involves contexts. Neither of these concepts has lent itself to analytic representation so that descriptions of irony are at best either weakly induced from the all too plentiful examples or artificially bounded for rhetorical purposes. Instances of irony might be best generalized as being set by a secondary representation that is in an opposition to a primary representation of the same territory; ironization occurs at the realization of a discrepancy between the two. 'To say the opposite of what one means' or the slightly less restrictive 'to say other than what one means' are the traditional formulations. Taking note of the opposition addresses how the ironic instance affects understanding. How one recognizes dual representation is intertwined with contextualization and the ironist's intentions, if indeed he or she happens to exist.

Reference to intent is at least plausible if one is dealing with the instrumentality of the ironist, but the accidental recognition of situational irony requires a shift so that the perceiver is the agentive ironist with a personal set of intentions; categorical collapses like self-irony require both the speaker and victim to be the same. Of course the description of irony as an instrument (trope, figure, mode, or structure) is much easier than the discovered situational ironies (accidental, cosmic, *zeitgeistentsprechenol*, or epistemological). If intentions which differentiate irony from metaphor, symbol, myth, allegory, jokes, riddles, and so on, were discoverable, then reductively defining irony as 'allegoria'—saying something and meaning something else—could be eliminated. All of the allegoria above suggest two scripts that are mediated by an opposition: metaphor has tenor and vehicle; allegory has extended narrative references and external references; the riddle confuses many possibilities and its inferrable solution. While lying has sometimes been included as a form of allegoria, a lie projects only one representation; like any utterance or situation it could be discovered to be ironic, or even intended as ironic, but only in ways that are incidental to its function as lying. A lie does not succeed at lying when it is penetrated as irony must be. The potential of anything to be situationally ironic confuses the discussion. While any of the other allegoria may seek to move the hearer toward the second script, only irony has the purpose of negating the first script as an inherent part of its structure.

There are three abstract participants in the ironic instance that are easily related to the grammatical categories of first, second, and third person. The postulated first-person speaker is the ironist; the second-person audience is the perceiver; the third person is the victim of the irony. The coincidence of any of these persons creates specialized situations like self-depreciation and instructive irony, but the concepts of speaker, victim, audience, and the act itself will need to be variously differentiated for any discussion. The ideas of literal message, intended message, and context further define a normative vocabulary for the approaches to irony.

2. Types of Irony

Four categories of irony have been pragmatically generated: verbal irony, dramatic irony, extant irony, and artifacted irony. Any claim to mutual exclusivity or comprehensiveness for these categories would be ironically naive.

2.1 Verbal Irony

Verbal irony is usually associated with a wide variety of Classical tropes. The heavy hand of sarcasm involves the knowledge by both the speaker and the victim of the irony while in irony proper only the speaker and audience need understand the multiple meanings. Both *hyperbole* and *meiosis* or *litotes* involve a discrepancy of degree between the literal message and the intended message, the first ironically overstated and the second pair understated. Innuendo suggests the subtle insinuation of an intended meaning by the speaker. The range of invective that exists from the personal lampoon to the more general burlesque (high, low, travesty, caricature, parody) can be captured in the manner called satire. Satire shares the derision and wit that are a part of irony; yet, one might say that like a modern sense of irony it also recognizes incongruities in human situations. O'Connor (1974) adds *antiphrasis* (contrast), *asteism* and *charientism* (jokes), *chleuasm* (mockery), *mycterism* (sneering), *mimesis* (ridiculing imitation) to the list of forms; he argues that pun, paradox, conscious naivete, parody, and more can be ironic secondary to their uses; the listing suggests any manipulation of language can be classified as ironic. The usual invocation of an opposite meaning seems far too strong since so many verbal ironies are only subtly different from their literal messages.

2.2 Dramatic Irony

Dramatic irony begins with the idea of a dramatist (speaker) putting words into the mouth of a character (victim) that have one meaning for him but another meaning for the audience; either the audience already knows more than the character or the other elements of the play demonstrate the discrepancy. The term has been applied beyond drama to other types of narratives and sometimes to actual situational discrepancies where someone else is aware of something that one of the participants is not. Although comedies can have dramatic ironies, it is in tragedies that the reversal of fortune is a natural context for dramatic ironies which are often called tragic ironies. Sophocles' Greek tragedies generate the homonymic term Sophoclean irony for tragic irony. Dramatic irony resides not so much in the contrast between what is said and what is meant as does verbal irony, but in the opposition between what is enacted and what exists either in the rest of the fiction or even the world.

2.3 Extant Irony

Extant irony suggests the existential condition and can be seen as an infinite form of the worldly situational irony that was an extended sense of dramatic irony. Cosmic irony suggests the universe's indifference to the efforts of man and can be expressed in a view that God, a god, or the universe manipulates outcomes in some way that is not known to human beings or considerate of their aspirations. The irony of events suggests a more modest view of man's lack of control over his situations, while the irony of fate looks back to events controlled by unmastered personalities or society or even the gods, particularly if one capitalizes Fate. The existentialism of the nineteenth and twentieth centuries in its recognition of the isolation of the individual in an indifferent universe has certainly encouraged the concept of cosmic irony, but it has always been a motif of the conscious human condition. Irony is extended to an organizing principle for the psychology of Lacan and the epistemology of Foucault and an important modality for many modern thinkers.

2.4 Artifacted Irony

Artifacted irony takes the making of irony beyond immediate ironic intentions. Romantic irony found the literary techniques of paradox suggested by the paradoxical nature of reality. While verbal ironies and dramatic ironies are certainly created and cosmic irony purports to be extant, some ironies are particularly artifacted for effects beyond their irony. Romantic irony created a particular illusion in order to destroy it later: a character might take over control of the writing of his own work, presenting a paradox. Such artifacting did not begin with the German romantics; however, they do seem to have made it their own, often paradoxically commenting on a work from within itself. As far back as Socrates, clearly artifacted special circumstances yielded the type of irony that bears his name; the naivete of the pose created allowed him subtly to expose the error of his victim and effectively to understate his own view of truth. And the relativism or perspectivism of the twentieth century has helped the New Critics to raise the ironic paradox to a central device in both art and its criticism: any stance would suggest its opposite, and the tension between these relative positions could become the organizing principle of thought. It can also be plausibly argued that irony is a prime operative in the efforts of deconstruction.

3. Studies of Irony

The existence of irony and appeals to it seem ubiquitous. However, linguistic and literary studies make up the vast majority of works devoted to the exploration of irony even though other disciplines do occasionally engage the concept. Most works have focused on the stimulus itself; cognitive–perceptual studies of the connection of the intended message to the literal message arise out of the almost universal attempts to explain irony by exemplifying it. Focusing on the relations of the speaker to the victim or the audience allows discussion of the social–behavioral effects. There are even a few studies that concern themselves with the personal responses of the participants and their psychopathology.

3.1 Irony and Psychology

Theories of psychotherapy usually pay very close attention to language, indeed closest attention to the discrepancy between what is said and what is meant. If, as Haley claims, the psychotherapeutic relationship has paradox inherent in it, attention to irony defines the patient, the Socratic stance of the therapist, and the realization of the irony that constitutes progress. It can be argued that psychotherapy is analogous to language, in which a message has meaning only as a context qualifies it; such qualification can be treated as a definition of irony. Indeed, Breuer states that modern literature's pervasive irony is a homeopathic cure for the schizophrenia that results from the modern abandonment of contact between the outer world and our inner selves.

3.2 Irony and Philosophy

The German romantics are usually credited with the first epistemological use of the concept of irony. Both a worldview and its creative representation are driven by this concept that allows for otherwise untenable contradictions. Kierkegaard also finds that irony allows him a privileged position above normal discourse to speak of philosophical and religious matters. His path to the final religious stage is founded in part on the dialectic of the bifurcate character of irony. Both Hegel and Kierkegaard find that the negative always implicit in irony drives their philosophies of process. A hypostatic concept of irony has been used to organize thought, destroy referentiality, disassociate the speaker from his audience or even the universe, or associate the speaker with his audience or even the universe in modern philosophy.

3.3 Irony and Literature or Rhetoric

The literary study of irony has produced by far the greatest number of works, and every year reveals multiple studies of irony in the works of particular authors or sets of works. The more general works on irony are modest but effective introductions. Muecke has created excellent starting places for the history of the concept, has presented fine arrays of illustrations of the nature and types of ironies, has represented a limited anatomy of irony, and has given generous indications of the practice of irony in literature. He supplies an effective heuristic for differentiating situational from verbal irony: one need only to finish the linguistic test frames of 'it is ironic that...' or 'he is being ironical about...' Booth attempts to show how irony is transferred from an author to his audience. The explanation is circumscribed by presuming that he is defining an art that expresses the author's intentions; he manages to sneak situational irony in by giving it rhetorical force when someone talks about it. While he offers no discovery procedures, he does supply four steps to reconstructing the irony intended by the author: (a) rejection of the literal meaning; (b) exercise of alternative interpretations or explanations; (c) a decision about the author's knowledge or beliefs; (d) the selection of a new meaning or cluster of meanings. His rhetoric naturally engages ironies that could be agreed on, stable ironies; unstable, infinitely undermined ironies are acknowledged at the end of the book, but he feels obliged to salvage even some of them by a leap of faith to the truth beyond the instabilities. Four coordinated essays in a special issue of *Linguistique et sémiologiques* titled *L'ironie* point toward the range of tentative analytic representations of structural, rhetorical, semiotic, and linguistic issues in the context of developing scholarship.

3.4 Irony and Linguistics

As the linguistic studies of irony have begun to exceed the centuries of taxonomic descriptions, they have begun to analyze the process of irony in interesting ways. Syntactic and lexical descriptions of negation, anaphora, deixis, intonational contours, word order, and the like continue to shed local light on particular examples of ironies. However, it is the pragmatics and suprasentential analyses of the early 1990s that are helping linguistics to add substantially to the theory of irony by taking formal analysis to higher levels. Austin's distinction between literal statements and their intended effects has allowed Grice's conversational postulates and Searle's rules for interpreting the illocutionary force of sentences to give the current generation of linguists the tools to begin to discuss the intentions and contexts necessary for a sufficient description of irony. Contextual semantics and script theory suggest how the larger situations of irony might be described. Logical form, discourse analysis, speech-act theory, and artificial intelligence are currently chipping away at the intractable character of the roles of values, world knowledge, intentions, and contexts.

Bibliography

Behler E 1981 *Klassische Ironie, Romantische Ironie, Tra-*

gische Ironie. Zum Ursprung dieser Begriffe. Wissenschaftliche Buchgesellschaft, Darmstadt

Booth W C 1974 *A Rhetoric of Irony*. University of Chicago Press, Chicago, IL

Culler J 1975 *Structuralist Poetics. Structuralism, Linguistics and the Study of Literature*. Cornell University Press, Ithaca, NY

Grice H P 1975 Logic and Conversation. In: Cole P, Morgan J L (eds.) *Syntax and Semantics. Vol. 3: Speech Acts*. Academic Press, New York

Haley J 1963 *Strategies of Psychotherapy*. Grune and Stratton, New York

Handwerk G J 1986 *Irony and Ethics in Narrative. From Schlegel to Lacan*. Yale University Press, New Haven, CT

L'ironie 1976 Special issue in: *Linguistique et sémiologie. Travaux du centre de recherches linguistiques et sémiologiques de l'université de Lyon* II. Presses Universitaires de Lyon, Lyon

Muecke D C 1969 *The Compass of Irony*. Methuen, London

Muecke D C 1982 *Irony and the Ironic*. Methuen, London

O'Connor W V 1974 Irony. In: Preminger A, Warnke F J, Harrison O B Jr (eds.) *Princeton Encyclopedia of Poetry and Poetics*. Princeton University Press, Princeton, NJ

Searle J R 1970 *Speech Acts*. Cambridge University Press, Cambridge

Sedgewick G G 1935 *Of Irony. Especially in Drama*. University of Toronto Press, Toronto

Thompson J A K 1926 *Irony. An Historical Introduction*. George Allen and Unwin, London

Negation

P. Ramat

Negation in natural languages is very different from, and much more complicated than, negation in logic or mathematics. In many languages, for instance, it is not true that two negations correspond to a positive value according to the well-known formula $\neg\neg P = P$. Even in Latin, where *non nullus* ('not nobody') means—according to Classical texts—'somebody,' it is possible to find two negative terms preserving a negative value: *iura te non nociturum esse homini . . . nemini* (Plautus) 'swear that you will not harm anybody'; cf. Cockney and Black English *I don't see nothin' nowhere* (for a not perfect correspondence between logical and linguistic negation see also Sect. 2 below).

Consider first the declarative negation which refers to a real state of affairs as in example (1). This declarative negation has to be distinguished from the prohibitive (e.g., 'Do not lean out') which does not refer to a real state of affairs and, on the contrary, is used in order to prevent the realization of a state of affairs (see Sect. 7).

The linguistic operation of negation (NEG) consists in denying the truth value of the negated sentence, or of a part of the sentence, by applying a NEG operator (π_{NEG}) to a sentence like:

John likes to work gives John does not like to work, (1a)
i.e., [it is not true that [John likes to work]];

John does not like beer at lunch (1b)
i.e., [John does like beer, π_{NEG} ADV SATELLITE at lunch]].

Negative sentences are most frequently used to correct states of affairs assumed by the speaker to be either shared knowledge or to represent the commonest ones to be expected in the context. 'The post hasn't been delivered this morning' is a felicitous message only under the assumption, shared by speaker and hearer, that the post has to be delivered every day. This is the reason why negative sentences are not normally used to introduce new propositions or new referents. The sentence 'A train didn't arrive yesterday,' extrapolated from a situational context which makes a sense possible, is deemed to be rather odd; not so its affirmative counterpart 'A train arrived yesterday.' Another example is *When didn't a/the train arrive?*—it does not make sense to ask when an event didn't happen.

The content resulting from a negated sentence can be either negative or positive: *I know → I do not know*; *I ignore → I do not ignore*.

There are no known languages which do not possess a means for negating the truth value of a positive sentence. NEG is a linguistic universal: for cognitive and pragmatic reasons every language *must* have the possibility of asserting that the state of affairs expressed by a sentence is not true.

1. The 'Scope' of NEG: Sentence versus Phrase Negation

By adducing examples (1a) and (1b), the notion of 'scope' has already been introduced implicitly. The widest 'scope' of NEG (i.e., its sphere or domain of operation) is the sentence (S), but NEG may apply also to sentence subunities, that is, to syntagms (noun phrases, prepositional phrases) or even lexemes:

$_s[_{NP}[Many\ arrows]\ hit\ the\ target]$ (2)
$\rightarrow {}_s[\pi_{NEG\ NP}[Not\ many\ arrows]\ hit\ the\ target]$;

$_s[Many\ stars\ are\ _{PRED}[visible]]$ (3)
$\rightarrow {}_s[Many\ stars\ are\ \pi_{NEG\ PRED}[invisible]]$;

$_s[_{ADV}[Consciously,]\ Mary\ smiled]$ (4)
$\rightarrow {}_s[\pi_{NEG\ ADV}[Unconsciously,]\ Mary\ smiled]$; etc.

Examples (2)–(4) are affirmative sentences (a negative counterpart of (2) would be 'Many arrows didn't hit the target').

It may be concluded that the phrase/lexeme negation operates by applying a π_{NEG} to the phrase/lexeme to be negated, i.e., by negating the truth condition or the existence of that phrase/lexeme.

But in the following:

Mary doesn't drive dangerously/like a stunt car driver (5)

NEG has in its scope just the modal and the sentence makes sense only if the presupposition is that Mary is capable of driving. Only when NEG applies to S and its predicative nexus does a negative sentence occur.

The English sentence:

You may not read the newspaper today (6)

has two different intonations (suprasegmental traits) which correspond to two different readings: 'You are not allowed to read the newspaper today' and 'You have the option of not reading the newspaper today.' Only the first interpretation gives a negative sentence; and, in fact, the scope of NEG includes in this case the entire predication. This is not the case with the second interpretation. This is precisely why negative quantifiers (the so-called 'negative pronouns') make a sentence negative (see Sect. 6):

Nobody knows my sorrow. (7a)

In other words, 'There is no x such that x knows my sorrow'—the entire predication lies in the scope of 'Nobody'. Note that this holds true also for negative quantifiers in object position:

John had nothing, he knew nobody. (7b)

Not every language possesses this kind of quantifier. For example, Danish:

Har du set noget?—Nej, jeg har ikke set noget. (8a)
Have you seen something?—No, I have not seen something.
'Have you seen anything?—No, nothing.'

versus

Har du ikke set noget?—Jo, jeg har set noget. (8b)
Have you not seen something?—Yes, I have seen something.
'Haven't you seen anything?—Yes, I have seen something.'

The opposition between 'nothing' and 'something/anything' is realized syntactically in the context and not lexically, and *noget* acquires a negative mean-

ing if it is in the scope of NEG (*ikke*), as in the answer of (8a) and in the question of (8b).

2. Negation and Presuppositions

Commenting on (5), reference has been made to the presuppositions which make a sentence felicitous or not (in Grice's sense). As may be argued from the 'tag question' at the end of:

They almost sold it, didn't they? (9)

the sentence is felt to be positive, even though the proposition it asserts entails the negative state of affairs that they did not sell it (see Taglicht 1983: 108).

Conversely, (5) does not imply that Mary does not drive, but, on the contrary, that she drives (cf., also (1b)). What determines the negative effect of π_{NEG} and its applications are the pragmatic presuppositions at the discourse and situation level.

3. Typology of Negation

The means for realizing π_{NEG}s show a large crosslinguistic variety, as may easily be seen by comparing the simple declarative negative English sentence (10a) with its translations in various languages:

John doesn't eat fish (10a)

French
Jean ne mange pas de poisson (10b)
J.   NEG eats   NEG PART fish
   (vs. *Jean mange du   poisson*
                PART+ART   )

German
Hans ißt keinen Fisch (10c)
J.   eats NO: ADJ fish
   (vs. *Hans ißt Fisch*
        J.   eats fish)

Finnish
Jukka ei   syö kalaa (10d)
J.   NEG-3SG eat fish
   (vs. *Jukka syö kalaa*
        J.   eats fish)

Turkish
John balık yemiyor (10e)
J.   fish eat-NEG-PRES(3SG)
   (vs. *John balık yiyor*
        J.   fish eats)

Japanese
John wa sakana wo tabenai (10f)
J.   TPC fish   OBJ eat-NEG
   (vs. *John wa sakana wo taberu*
        J.   fish   eats)

Welsh
Nid yw John yn bwyta pysgod (10g)
NEG is J. in eat   fish
   (vs. *Y   mae John yn bwyta pysgod*
        DECL is J.   in eat   fish   )

Russian
Ivan ne est rybu (10h)
J.   NEG eats fish

Guaraní (Tupí family)

> *Juán nd-o'u-i*   *pira* (vs. *Ivan est rybu*)
> J.   NEG-eats-NEG fish   (10i)

Notice that: (a) In English there exists a special auxiliary verb to form negative sentences, the semantically main verb remaining uninflected; (b) French and Guaraní have the so-called 'discontinuous NEG' around the verb (: *ne ... pas*).—French shows also a morphosyntactic alternation between *de* and *du* depending on whether the sentence is negative or positive; (c) in German the NEG may be expressed by an adjectival inflected form; (d) in Finnish there is an inflected NEG verb whereas the lexical verb remains uninflected; (e) Turkish agglutinates a NEG mark *-ma-/-me-* to the verbal accented stem, before other stem determinations (e.g., *-me + yor > -miyor*); (f) the Japanese NEG is a verbal negative form *-nai* suffixed to the indefinite verbal base; (g) and Welsh has a particle *(nid)* introducing NEG sentences parallel to the particles for declaratives *(y)* and interrogatives (*a*, as in: *a mae John yn bwyta pysgod?*) so that NEG is a modality of the sentence. Among the eight languages under scrutiny Finnish is from the typological viewpoint the nearest to English.

The phenomena here underlined by no means exhaust the phenomenology of NEG sentences. Kwaa (Niger–Congo family) expresses NEG via a modification of the word order. Dravidian languages have the possibility of a negative conjugation for every active, passive, 'neutral,' or even causative verb (and this may remind students of the Welsh examples). In Tamil the NEG mark is *-ā-;* but this *-ā-* agglutinating with the desinential vowel may disappear. The negative verb is therefore characterized by the absence of a specific mark (one of the not very common examples of unmarked forms for semantically and functionally marked meanings) : *kāṇ-p-ēṇ* 'I shall see'; *kaṇ-ṭ-ēṇ* 'I saw'; but simply *kāṇ-ēṇ* 'I do not / I shall not / I did not see.' However NEG forms usually contain one (or more) mark(s) more in comparison with the corresponding positive sentence, for instance (10c) and (10d). (In fact, from a philosophical point of view, it has been said by Bergson that, whereas the positive sentence has to be considered as a judgment, the negative is more complex, being a judgment on a judgment (see example (1) above: [[it is not true that] ...]).)

Basically the main strategies for sentence negation are (a) morphological: a NEG mark e.g., (10g), (10h) which can be integrated in the verb, e.g., (10e), (10f); (b) morphosyntactic: NEG is expressed by a particular verbal cluster with a negative auxiliary expressing tense, aspect, mood, and person, e.g., (10a), (10d); however, the verb categories may be distributed between the negative auxiliary and the main verb, as is the case for some Uralic languages. Purely syntactic strategies like specific word order rules as in Kwaa are rather exceptional; (c) lexical: as in (10c). Special lexemes, different from the corresponding affirmative

existential verb, can occur for the negative copula 'there is not, there does not exist,' as in Turkish *yok-* versus *var*, e.g.:

> Tu   *Ekmek yok*   vs. *Ekmek var*   (11)
>   bread   there is not   bread   there is
>   'There's no bread'   'There's bread'

Östen Dahl published in 1979 a large study on the expression of NEG in around 240 languages, which yielded the following results: NEG is most frequently expressed by either bound morphemes as part of the predicate (45 percent) or by separate particles (44.9 percent). NEG auxiliaries make out only 16 percent of Dahl's sample, while the use of dummy auxiliaries as in English is quite rare.

The expression of NEG (according to Dahl 1979)

		%
1.	morphologically as part of the predicate	45.0
2.	morphologically in an auxiliary verb	16.7
3.	by a separate negative particle	
	a. in preverbal position	12.5 ⎤
	b. in preauxiliary position	20.8 ⎥
	c. before verbal group	2.1 ⎥
	d. in postverbal position	1.2 ⎥ = 44.9%
	e. in postauxiliary position	3.7 ⎥
4.	by a separate negative particle	⎥
	a. in sentence-initial position	0.4 ⎥
	b. in sentence-final position	4.2 ⎦

(N.B. The total runs above 100% because a number of languages have more than one type of NEG)

4. Diachronic Evolution of NEG Markers

In several linguistic traditions a trend can be observed which moves toward the use of an invariant NEG particle (preferably in preverbal position: see below). This is actually the most natural NEG strategy and comes nearest to the transparency ('diagrammatic') principle of optimization, i.e., 'one meaning: one form.' Thus Estonian does not inflect the NEG verb *ei* (3SG) which in this way approaches the uninflected particle construction type, drifting away from the auxiliary construction of the Finno–Ugric languages, that is, shifting from a morphological to a syntactic strategy (see *John ei söö kala* 'J. does not eat fish' but also with a subject in plural *John ja Mary ei kohtunud koolis* 'J. and M. did not meet at school'; also the extension of *ain't* in Black English as generalized NEG form).

A very interesting case is represented by the French-based creoles:

Louisiana

> *mo kup pa*   and *mo pa kup*
> me cut NEG   me NEG cut: 'I don't cut.'   (12a)

Mauritius   (12b)

> *mo mõte pa pe travaj*
> my watch NEG PROGR work: 'my watch isn't working.'

Guyanese

mo pa ka dromi
me NEG FUT sleep: 'I shan't sleep.' (12c)

There is a clear tendency to place the NEG marker (< French *pas,* postponed to the inflected verbal form—see (10b)) before the verb and also before tense and aspect markers *(pe, ka).* Exactly the same trend has been observed for Maghreb Arabic dialects, where the discontinuous NEG *ma* + verb + *-š* tends to be replaced by a simple preverbal NEG. It may be inferred from this evolution that Jespersen was right in talking of (1917: 5) 'a natural tendency, also for the sake of clearness, to place the negative first, or at any rate as soon as possible, very often immediately before the particular word to be negatived (generally the verb),' in other words to construct negative sentences with the verb (i.e., the core of the predication) in the 'scope' of NEG (see Sect. 1). Danish, Norwegian, and Swedish are on the way to reintroducing preverbal NEG and English children may during their learning period produce sentences with preverbal NEG, for example, 'No wipe fingers' though their mother language has NEG after the inflected verbal form ('I do not wipe my fingers'). The same has been noticed also for Japanese adults learning English: though Japanese has NEG suffixed to the verb at the sentence end, as in (10f), students in the first stages of their learning process formed sentences like 'I no want many children,' 'I no like English,' and also 'He don't like it' where 'don't' is clearly perceived as a negation particle, simply a variant of 'no' (see *ain't,* above).

Also, from a diachronic point of view, postverbal NEG usually seems to imply preverbal NEG, via discontinuous NEG. French *pas* derives from Latin *passu(m)* 'step.' Together with other Romance NEG particles like French *goutte* 'drop,' Italian *mica* 'crumb,' Catalan *cap* (< Latin *capu(t))* 'head,' Sursilvan Romantsch *buc(a)* (< Latin *bucca)* 'cheek,' etc., *pas* represents a clear instance of a lexeme having developed into a NEG marker (first in postverbal position). The original meaning of *pas (goutte, cap,* etc.) wasn't at all negative—it was the 'measure' object of the verb occurring in postverbal position, as expected in an SVO language like Late (Vulgar) Latin, for example *non vado passum* 'I do not proceed a step' (> French [*je*] *ne vais pas); non video guttam* 'I do not see a tear,' meaning 'I'm so blind that I can't even see the tears in my eyes' (> French [*je*] *ne vois goutte).* The same evolution is found in the above-mentioned Arabic discontinuous NEG: *ma-katabuu-š* (Cairo Arabic) 'they did not write,' where the second NEG form derives from the indefinite accusative *šayʔ(an)* 'thing'—thus 'not + verb + a thing.'

By occurring mostly in sentences with negative meaning, terms like *pas, goutte, šayʔ(an),* etc., assumed negative value *per se* and became negative polarity items (NPIS), no longer bound to a semantically

congruent verb. Generalization of *pas* as a neg particle gives *je ne vois pas.* NPIS can thus occur only in negative contexts. But discontinuous constructs like *ne ... pas* are marked constructions and tend to be avoided: only 17 percent of languages (usually of the SVO type) have this kind of NEG. Actually, the preverbal, weakly articulated part of the French negative construct (i.e., [n]) is redundant: *je ne vais pas* > colloquial *je vais pas.* The NPI may also be emphatically reinforced— *pas* > *pas du tout,* literally 'not at all,' and become in its turn redundant—*pas du tout* > *du tout.* See, for instance:

Croyez-vous que je vous blâme? Du tout. (13)
'Do you believe that I blame you? No, I don't.'

Schematically the so-called 'NEG cycle' may be represented as follows (see Schwegler 1988):

$$ne + \text{verb} > ne + \text{verb} + pas > \text{verb} + pas$$
$$(> pas\ du\ tout > du\ tout).\quad (14)$$

The same holds true also for English and German where 'not' and *nicht* derive from *naught, nought* < OE *na-wiht* and OHG *niowiht* 'no-whit, no-thing':

English (15)
$ne + \text{verb} > ne + \text{verb} + not > \text{verb} + not;$
German
$ni/en/ne + \text{verb} > ni/en/ne + \text{verb} + niht > \text{verb} + nicht.$

As for the raising of NEG to preverbal position see example (12) from creole languages.

5. Pragmatics of Negation

As may be argued from the historical evolution sketched in the previous section, pragmatics plays an important role in NEG strategies, especially because of the wish to reinforce the negative value of the utterance. NPIS like *pas, goutte,* etc., are emphasizing expressions which originally served to underline the negative meaning of the sentence and then became grammaticalized as NEG markers. For example, in English 'I heard what you said'—'The deuce you did!' ('You didn't at all') (Jespersen 1917: 33).

As the 'natural' position of NEG is the preverbal one, so that the verb lies in the scope of NEG, it is odd that there are languages like German, Brazilian Portuguese, some Italian dialects, etc., which have postverbal NEG.

The origin of German *nicht* and its postverbal position have already been discussed. In Brazilian Portuguese or other Romance traditions:

(= 10 above) *O João (não) come peixe não.* (16a)

Compare also the very similar Afrikaans construction:

Jan eet nie vis nie (16b)
J. eats NEG fish NEG

where the first NEG comes after the verb, according to the Germanic pattern.

The first *não* may be omitted. Postverbal *não* is, with few exceptions, sentence-final. However, in subordinate clauses one does not find sentence-final NEG:

Eu imagino que você não tem dinheiro
I imagine that you not have money   (17a)

and not:

*Eu imagino que você tem dinheiro não.   (17b)

Note also
Eu não imagino que você tem dinheiro não   (17c)
'I do not imagine that you have money.'

The subordinate clause is not negated and the final *não* represents the second NEG marker of the main verb as in (16). This is exactly the case in Afrikaans too:

He het nie gesê, dat hy hierdie boek geskrywe het nie
he has NEG said that he this book written has NEG
'he has not said that he has written this book.'   (18)

All this hints at an 'afterthought' strategy as the origin of the sentence-final NEG, a kind of comment after an intonational break which later disappeared when the final position became grammaticalized as regular. Compare for this kind of pragmatic discourse strategy substandard English *I'm not gonna say it, nah;* or French *J'vais pas le dire, non.*

The afterthought strategy may account for sentence-final NEG occurring also in SVO languages like Portuguese. But this is not the only possible explanation. It is clear that diachronically there is a great difference between the *pas* or *not/nicht* cases (ancient postverbal 'measure objects') and that of Portuguese *não*. Synchronically, however, they belong to the same type of NEG. Many different sources may have contributed to the origin of postverbal(sentence-final) NEG (see also the end of this section).

A large-scale analysis of all the languages of the world which have sentence-final or postverbal NEG has however still to be done. In any case it seems that word order does not play a decisive role in assigning to NEG its position in the sentence—contrary to what was thought in the first attempts at typologizing according to the word order types (see Lehmann's 'structural principle' 1978: 18). It is, for instance, not true that the general rule for rigid and consistent SOV languages is to have NEG after the verb as is the case for Sinhalese (SOV) versus, for instance, Irish, a VSO language where NEG comes at the beginning of the sentence:

Sinh *Jōn ballavə däkke nā*
J. dog saw NEG   (19a)

versus

Ir *Ní fhaca Seán an madadh*
NEG saw John the dog   (19b)

both 'John didn't see the dog.'

In Dahl's language sample only Bengali and Tamil are in fact quoted as having the order SOV + NEG, where NEG is an uninflected particle which seems to have developed out of auxiliary verbs (see Dahl 1979: 94). This kind of historical development for syntactic negation has to be noticed as another possible diachronic explanation for sentence-final/postverbal NEG.

6. Syntax of Negation: NEG Quantifiers

There is an important topic to be dealt with partly related to what has been said so far about the NPIs, namely the so-called 'permeable' and 'impermeable' negation, which is relevant to the syntax of NEG. The term was suggested by Tesnière (1966: 235 f.). There are languages which repeat the negation on every element of the sentence which can be negated:

Ru *Nikto ni s kem ni o čëm ne*
govoril
Nobody NEG with anybody NEG about anything NEG spoke
'Nobody spoke with anybody about anything'   (20a)
Ru *Nikto nigde nikogda ètogo ne skazal*
Nobody nowhere never this NEG said   (20b)

On the other hand one finds:
Lat *nemo hoc unquam dixit*
nobody this ever said   (21a)
or:
numquam hoc ullus dixit
never this anybody said   (21b)

with just one negated element. NEG is not 'permeable.' The same holds for English (for counter-examples from substandard English see the first paragraph of this article):

Nobody ever said this, or *Never did anybody say this.*   (21c)

Between the two poles of highest permeability (as in the Russian examples) and highest impermeability (as in the Latin and English examples) there are intermediate stages along a 'continuum':

French *Pas une fois il n'a adressé la parole à*   (22a)
personne
'He has never spoken to anybody'

versus

Italian *Mai una volta ha rivolto la parola ad*
alcuno/nessuno   (22b)

and not:

*Mai una volta non ha rivolto...   (22c)

Italian uses a NEG (or two) less than French.

Returning to (21), (21b): *unquam* and *ullus* are quantifiers (an adverb and, respectively, a pronoun) which usually occur in the scope of NEG and therefore become NPIs. But NPIs which do not (yet) have full negative value must be preceded by a clear NEG mark. See, for instance:

French   *Jean n'a pas dormi de la nuit*   (23a)
         'John hasn't slept all night long'

where *de la nuit* is on the way to acquiring negative value. However it is not (yet) possible to say:

*Jean a dormi de la nuit   (23b)

without a clear NEG mark before the NPI (and the verb). On the contrary it is possible to say:

Je n'imagine pas que Jean ait dormi de la nuit   (24)
'I do not imagine that J. has slept at all during the night'

since the NPI appears in a sentence which is subordinated to a negative main sentence. The general rule for these quantifiers therefore is that in negative sentences an element clearly showing negative value must have in its scope (i.e., must precede) the NPIs and the verb. Compare:

Italian   *Nessuno venne* and *Non venne nessuno*   (25)
          both meaning 'Nobody/no people came.'

If an NPI comes first in a sentence then it means that its negative value has already fully developed, and no other NEG is strictly required before the verb.

It has already been stated that there may also be languages which do not have a lexeme for negative quantifiers (see examples (8a) and (8b)):

Hindi *koî*   *nahî âya   thâ*   (26)
      somebody NEG come was (same meaning as (25))

(Note that NEG precedes the verb and gives a negative meaning to the sentence.)

Four main types may be distinguished for quantifiers in negative sentences:

(a) existential quantifier + NEG as in Hindi (example (26));
(b) 'neutral' (not negative) quantifier + NEG as in English 'John did not see anybody';
(c) NEG + negative quantifier as in Italian *Giovanni non vide nessuno* (same meaning as the previous English sentence);
(d) negative quantifier without NEG as in German *Hans hat niemanden gesehen* (same meaning as above).

Otherwise languages may appeal to nonexistential constructions; e.g., Modern Standard Arabic:

fî bilâdi- nâ laysa   dayfan   (27)
in town 1PL NEG:EXIST visitor
'Nobody is a stranger in our town.'

Crosslinguistic comparison hints at the following hierarchy of negative quantifiers, when they exist (as in case (c) and (d) above):

	PERS. ANIM. PRON &	NTR. PRON >	TEMP >	LOC >	OTHER ADVs
Ru	*nikto*	*nicto, ničego*	*nikogda*	*nigde*	*nikak*
Eng	*nobody*	*nothing*	*never*	*nowhere*	(*no way*)
Mod Gk	*kaneís*	*típote*	*poté*	*pouθená*	
Sp	*ninguno*	*nada*	*nunca*		
Wel	*neb*	*dim* (*byd*)			

Moreover, inherently negative quantifiers may be restricted to some position. The Australian language Tiwi has *karəkuwani* 'noone' and *karəkamini* 'nothing' which are restricted to subject position (see Payne 1985: 238).

Another phenomenon of the syntax of negation which deserves to be dealt with and can be explained in terms of discourse pragmatics is the so-called 'NEG-raising':

John wants the secretaries not to leave early   (28a)

and:

John does not want the secretaries to leave early.   (28b)

These sentences are not completely synonymous. There is indeed a semantic–pragmatic difference. Example (28b) indicates a lesser degree of control on the part of John over the state of affairs, whereas (28a) states as a matter of fact what John's firm wish is. Moreover, the so-called 'raising' of NEG to be observed in (28b) is not possible with every verb. There are semantic constraints: only verbs which admit the possibility of being controlled by the 'subject' (first actant) like *think*, or *want*, may let NEG 'leak' into the main sentence. This is not possible with a verb like *fear*, although it belongs to the same class of opinion verbs as *think*:

I fear that he will not arrive tomorrow   (29a)

has a completely different meaning from:

I do not fear that he will arrive tomorrow.   (29b)

Now, a transformation rule (here 'move NEG') governed by semantic criteria is hard to accept in generative theory. Moreover, since there is no hint of any trace whatsoever left by the NEG in its original position before the movement, one cannot decide whether NEG has been 'raised' to the main sentence in (28b) or 'lowered' to the subordinate clause in (28a). There seems to be no use in adopting the generative point of view. The position of NEG is determined by the speaker's intentions of focusing this or that part of the message (see the different message organizations of (28a) versus (28b)).

7. Prohibitive NEG

The difference between declarative and prohibitive NEG was indicated above. Prohibitive is linked to imperative modality, which is often expressed by a different verbal form—namely a nonreality form (imperative, subjunctive, optative, etc.). There are languages that make use of the same NEG marker for both, and there are languages which distinguish between them:

You do not eat fish (declarative) (30)

as well as:

Do not eat fish, John! (imperative) (31)

The distinction rests in this case on the opposition between indicative form with obligatory pronoun and imperative form without pronoun.

On the other hand the following is found:

Mod Gk   *(Sú) dén tro−s psári* (32)
       you   NEG eat: 2SG fish (same meaning as (30))

versus:

Mền pernâs,   Giánnē
NEG cross: 2SG VOC (33)
'Do not cross, John!'

Notice that in Modern Greek indicative and subjunctive endings may not be distinguished: in this case the opposition is based solely upon the distinction *dé(n)/mế(n)*. Italian offers the reverse strategy—whereas NEG remains unchanged, the 2SG imperative has a special form:

Giovanni, non attraversare
J.   NEG cross: 2SG.IMPERAT (34)

versus:

Giovanni non attraversa (35)
J.   NEG cross: 3SG.INDIC
'John does not cross.'

Different verbal forms together with different NEG markers are found, albeit redundantly, in (36) versus (37), (38) versus (39):

Anc Gk   *mě m' eréθize* (36)
       NEG me make angry: 2SG.IMPERAT
       'don't make me angry'

versus:

ou m' ereθízeis
NEG me make me angry: 2SG.INDIC
'you do not make me angry'

Lat   *ne cantes* (38)
     NEG sing: 2SG.SUBJ
     'do not sing'

versus:

non cantas (39)
NEG sing: 2SG.INDIC
'you do not sing.'

In some cases there may be just an intonation difference:

French   *Jean ne traverse pas* (40)
       'John is not crossing'

versus

Jean, ne traverse pas! (41)
'John, do not cross!'

The cognitive–behavioral difference between declarative and prohibitive negation is basic and every language has a means to express the functional opposition. In order to show this large possible variety, the following scale for marking prohibitive negation could be tentatively drawn:

(a)   intonation only (example (41));
(b)   morphosyntax (examples (30/31));
(c)   different markings on NEG (examples (32/33));
(d)   different markings on verb (examples (34/35));
(e)   different markings on both NEG and verb (examples (36/37); (38/39));
(f)   different lexical choice: e.g.:

Lat   *noli*   *me tangere*
     don't want: 2SG.IMPER me touch (42)
     'don't touch me'

Wel   *Peidiwch â   siarad!*
     stop: 2PL with talk(ing) (43)
     'do not talk'

(see Bernini and Ramat 1996).

Bibliography

Bernini G, Ramat P 1996 *Negative Sentences in the Languages of Europe*. Mouton de Gruyter, Berlin/New York

Dahl Ö 1979 Typology of sentence negation. *Linguistics* **17**: 79–106

Forest R 1993 *Négations. Essai de Syntaxe et de Typologie Linguistique*. Klincksieck, Paris

Horn L 1989 *A Natural History of Negation*. Chicago University Press, Chicago, IL

Jespersen O 1917 Negation in English and other languages. In: *Selected Writings of Otto Jespersen*. Allen and Unwin, London

Lehmann W P (ed.) 1978 *Syntactic Typology. Studies in the Phenomenology of Language*. University of Texas Press, Austin, TX

Payne J R 1985 Negation. In: Shopen T (ed.) *Language Typology and Syntactic Description*, vol. 1. Cambridge University Press, Cambridge

Schwegler A 1988 Word-order changes in predicate negation strategies in Romance languages. *Diachronica* **5**: 21–58

Taglicht J 1983 *Message and Emphasis. On Focus and Scope in English*. Longman, London

Tesnière L 1966 *Eléments de syntaxe structurale*, 2nd edn. Klincksieck, Paris

Performative Clauses

K. Allan

This entry examines the characteristics of explicit performative clauses within the theory of speech acts. The discussion which follows is restricted to English performative clauses; but most of the characteristics identified are to be found in other languages, too.

A speech act is created when speaker/writer S makes an utterance U to hearer/reader H in context C. The S who utters (1) is using an explicit performative clause (underlined) to make a promise:

I promise to call Jo tomorrow. (1)

(For the sake of discussion assume all felicity conditions are satisfied.) S could have made the same illocutionary point by uttering (2) in which the promise is not explicitly spelled out in the semantics of the verb:

I'll call Jo tomorrow. (2)

(1) uses an explicit performative clause whereas (2) does not.

Austin (1975: 57) notes that the legalistic-sounding adverb 'hereby' can be inserted into a performative clause, and will mark the verb as performative provided that 'hereby' is used with the meaning 'in uttering this performative.' Thus, (3) can be glossed as (4):

I hereby charge you with attempting to bribe a policeman. (3)

In uttering the words 'I charge you,' I charge you with attempting to bribe a policeman. (4)

Contrast the explicitly performative (3) with the nonperformative (5) in which 'hereby' means 'using this' and refers to something in the context, namely the bribe:

I could hereby charge you with attempting to bribe a policeman. (5)

In (3), where the illocutionary point is described explicitly in the performative clause, S actually charges H with attempting to bribe a policeman—such that H will subsequently have to appear before a court. But in (5), S only threatens to charge H with this offence; so the illocutionary point of (5) is a threat.

The presence of 'hereby' meaning 'in uttering this performative' is a sufficient, but not necessary, condition on an explicit performative clause. The following conditions C1–C6 are necessary characteristics of explicit performative clauses.

C1. The clause complies with the normal rules of English grammar.

C2. The main verb in the performative clause must be a performative verb which spells out the illocutionary point of U, cf. 'I charge you' in (3–4). Here is a short list of such verbs:

> abjure, abolish, accept, acknowledge, acquit, admit, admonish, advise, affirm, agree to, announce, answer, apologize, ascribe, ask, assent, assert, assess, assume, authorize, baptize, beg, bet, bid, call upon, caution, charge, christen, claim, classify, command, commiserate, compliment, concur, congratulate, conjecture, convict, counsel, declare, declare out, delegate, demand, demur, deny, describe, diagnose, disagree, dispute, donate, dub, excuse, exempt, fire, forbid, give notice, grant, guarantee, guess, hire, hypothesize, identify, implore, inform, instruct, license, name, notify, offer, order, pardon, permit, plead, pray, predict, prohibit, promise, proscribe, query, question, rank, recommend, refuse, reject, renounce, report, request, require, rescind, resign, sanction, say, sentence, state, submit, suggest, summon, suppose, swear, tell, testify, thank, urge, volunteer, vouch for, warn, withdraw.

These verbs can be used as explicit performatives only when formal conditions C1–C6 are satisfied, otherwise the illocutionary point of U is not described by the meaning of the 'performative' verb and the so-called performative verb is used nonperformatively.

C3. The performative verb must be in the present (nonpast, nonfuture, nonperfect) tense, because the illocutionary act is defined on the moment of utterance.

Contrast performative (6) with nonperformative (7):

I promise to take Max to a movie tomorrow. (6)

I promised to take Max to a movie tomorrow. (7a)

I have promised to take Max to a movie tomorrow. (7b)

Saying 'I promise' in (6), S makes a promise; but the words 'I promised' and 'I have promised' in (7) do not constitute the making of a promise; instead, they report that a promise was made. Thus the illocutionary point of (6) is a promise, whereas the illocutionary point of either utterance in (7) is to make an assertion or to inform H of a fact.

C4. A performative clause must be 'realis,' i.e., denote an actualization of the illocutionary act. Therefore (a) a performative verb can only co-occur with 'realis,' and not with 'irrealis' modal auxiliaries; and (b) a performative clause must be in the indicative mood. If Max says to his aged aunt:

I will hereby promise to visit you next time I'm in town. (8)

but then doesn't pay that visit next time he is in town, his aunt can justifiably chide him 'But you promised to visit!' thus accusing him of breaking his promise. This is because (8) denotes an ongoing act that can be glossed 'I will with these words make the promise to visit you next time I am in town.' In (8) the modal *will* is used in its root meaning 'willfully insist' and is realis, i.e., denotes an actual event, namely the illocutionary act described by the performative verb 'promise.' Contrast the performative promise of (8) with the predicted (even promised!) promise in:

> Tomorrow when I see her, I will promise to visit
> next time I'm in town.   (9)

'Hereby' cannot legitimately be inserted between 'will' and 'promise' in (9); which confirms that 'promise' is not a performative verb. In (9) the modal 'will' is used in its epistemic intentional sense and is irrealis because it denotes an unactualized event, namely the future act of promising (to take place 'tomorrow').

The pattern established by 'will' holds generally for modal auxiliaries with performative verbs. Because by definition the performative actualizes an illocutionary act, the modal must be used in a sense which is realis, cf. the leave-taking in 'I must hereby take my leave of you'; the warning in 'Trespassers should hereby be warned that they will be prosecuted.' Example (10) is ambiguous:

> I can hereby authorize you to act as our agent
> from this moment.   (10)

If 'can' means 'have the power to' and 'hereby' means 'in uttering this performative,' then (10) effects an authorization (I have the power by the utterance of these words to authorize you . . .). However, if 'I can hereby' means, e.g., 'using this telex from head-office enables me to,' then (10) is not performative and has the illocutionary point of a statement about S's ability to convey the authorization to H. Some additional examples of nonperformative verbs with modals are:

> I might promise to visit you next time I'm in town. (11)

> I might hereby authorize your release.   (12)

> I could hereby sentence you to ten years imprisonment.
>   (13)

'Might' is never realis and it is obvious that (11) states the possibility that S will promise without actualizing a promise. The 'hereby' that occurs in (12) necessarily has the sense 'using this,' and refers to something in context other than the performative utterance, e.g., a confession from another party; thus (12) is nonperformative. Similarly (13) does not pass sentence; compare it with 'I hereby sentence you to ten years imprisonment.' In (13) 'could' is epistemic and irrealis, and 'hereby' once again means 'using this.'

Explicit performatives occur only in the indicative mood; though they can take either emphatic stress or

emphatic 'do.' For example, 'I do promise to come more often' makes an emphatic promise. Since commands and requests are themselves illocutions distinct from promises, there is no such thing as making an 'imperative promise,' or a 'requesting promise'; both are anomalous. An utterance of 'Promise to come and see me more often' would be an exhortation or plea that H make a promise; it cannot be used to (as it were) force S's promise onto H. 'Do I promise to leave soon?' is a rhetorical question about a promise; no promise is made in uttering this. And because no performative can be irrealis, none can occur in the subjunctive mood. 'If I should promise to leave early, will you come to the party with me?' does not make a promise.

C5. The subject of the performative clause is conditioned by the fact that the speaker S is agent for either him/herself or another, whichever takes responsibility for enforcing the illocution described by the performative verb.

More often than not this controls the form of the subject noun phrase. All the explicitly performative clauses instantiated so far have had a first person singular subject 'I'; but 'we' makes just as good a subject for a performative, e.g., it is 'we' who make the promise in 'We, the undersigned, promise to pay the balance of the amount within ten days'; and it is 'we' who make the authorization in 'We hereby authorize you to pay on our behalf a sum not exceeding $500.' 'We' can be regarded as referring to joint speakers; but this is not strictly necessary, because a performative can be uttered on behalf of someone else by an authorized agent, as when an officer of the court says, 'The court permits you to stand down.' '[P]ermits' is performative because it is the issuing of this utterance which actually grants the permission. Austin (1975: 57) offers the following example with a second person subject: 'You are hereby authorized to pay . . .' This is passive, and the authorization is made either by S him/herself, or by him/her on behalf of someone else; similarly: 'Notice is hereby given that trespassers will be prosecuted.' It is notable that when the subject of an explicit performative is not first person, the utterance is made by or on behalf of the person or persons or institution responsible for enforcing the illocution (promise, authorization, granting of permission, giving notice, warning, etc.) described in the performative verb. Just the same responsibility, in fact, is attendant on the first person subject of an explicit performative clause. The person(s) responsible for the illocution is/are represented by the agent of the performative clause.

C6. It is often said that a performative verb necessarily occurs in the *simple aspect;* and it does normally do so, perhaps for the same reason that the simple aspect is normal in on-the-spot reporting of football matches, baseball games, etc. However, there are occasions where a performative may occur in the *pro-*

gressive aspect, cf. 'I am requesting you (for the umpteenth time) to tell me your decision.' This has the illocutionary point of a request: the grounds for claiming it to be a statement about a request are no stronger than the grounds for claiming the same about 'I request you (for the umpteenth time) to tell me your decision.' A felicitously uttered 'That horse has won its third race in a row, and I'm betting you $10 it'll win on Saturday' has the illocutionary point of a bet, so H can justifiably reply, 'You're on!' thereby taking up the bet, and expecting S to pay up when s/he loses (or vice versa).

Explicit performatives can be negative, e.g., the illocutionary force of a refusal can be borne by either 'I refuse your request' or, less likely, by the negative performative:

$$\text{I dōnt grànt} \qquad (14)$$
$$/ \qquad \text{your requèst.}/$$

In 'I don't promise to come to your party, but I'll try to make it' S performs an act of not-promising (note the scope of the negative: an act of not-promising is entirely different from an act of promising not to do something, cf. 'I promise not to come to your party'). The illocution of a negative performative is sometimes contrasted with another illocution, e.g., in 'I don't order you to get home early, but I hope you won't be too late.' Here, the illocution of not-ordering is contrasted with the exhortation expressed in the second clause.

The negative with a performative cannot be used to deny that an (any) illocutionary act has taken place; but it can be used to deny a particular illocution. For instance, the words in (14) uttered with appropriate prosody (a disjuncture after 'don't,' and a lower pitch level for 'grant your request') will render it a paraphrase of (15):

$$\text{I don't [as you claim] 'grant your request.'} \qquad (15)$$

$$\text{I dòn't} \qquad (16)$$
$$/ \qquad / \text{grànt your requèst.}/$$

Examples (15–16) are not refusals, but statements about a refusal.

Because the negative performative describes an act of not-doing, the adverb 'hereby' meaning 'in uttering this performative' must be placed before the negative, and not between it and the verb, cf. 'I do hereby not grant your request for more funds' and 'I hereby don't grant your request for more funds.' However, 'I don't hereby grant your request for more funds' does not make a refusal as such, but is instead a statement about a refusal, and is interpreted, 'I am not using this to grant your request for more funds' or 'I deny that I said or meant that "I hereby grant your request for more funds."'

To sum up the characteristics of explicit performative clauses: they must contain a verb that names the illocutionary point of the utterance; they must be in the present tense; in English they are typically in the simple aspect, but may be progressive; a performative clause must be 'realis' and denote the actualization of the illocutionary act; S must be agent for whoever takes responsibility for enforcing the illocutionary point of the utterance. An explicit performative clause may be negative; it may be emphatic; and it may contain the adverb 'hereby' meaning 'in/by uttering this performative.'

See also: Indirect Speech Acts; Speech Act Hierarchy; Speech Act Theory: Overview; Speech Acts and Grammar.

Bibliography

Austin J L 1975 In: Urmson J O, Sbisà M (eds.) *How to do Things with Words,* 2nd edn. Clarendon Press, Oxford

Pragmatics
J. L. Mey

1. Introduction
1.1 The Origins of Pragmatics

Among pragmaticians, there seems to be no agreement as to how to do pragmatics, nor as to what pragmatics is, nor how to define it, nor even as to what pragmatics is *not* (see Mey 1989). There seems to be agreement on one thing, however: pragmatics is a 'young' science, or (if one persists), pragmatics is the youngest subdiscipline of the venerable science

called *linguistics* (more on this difficult and sometimes stormy relationship below, Sect. 1.2).

Geoffrey Leech (1983) remarks that 'Fifteen years ago, it [viz., pragmatics] was mentioned by linguists rarely, if at all' (1983: 1). And if indeed pragmatics was mentioned 'at all,' it was more in the guise of a 'ragbag' or, as the Israeli mathematician and formal linguistic philosopher Yehoshua Bar-Hillel (1971) once expressed it, a 'waste-paper basket' designed to absorb the overflow from semantics, in the same way that semantics itself, a decade earlier, had been assigned the task of explaining whatever transformational generative syntax had been proved unable to cope with (see further Haberland and Mey 1977).

Thus, it does not come as a surprise that the eminent British linguist, Sir John Lyons, could have written the following, only 15 years before the publication of Leech's book: '[there is] no conflict between the peculiarly abstract approach to the study of language which is characteristic of modern "structural" linguistics and more "practical approaches"' (1968: 50–51), without so much as mentioning pragmatics. Instead, Lyons indicates the existence of certain 'practical' and 'realistic' tendencies which, however, are not opposed (in his opinion) to 'real' linguistics, except in the minds of people who (for whatever reason) insist on creating such an opposition.

1.2 Pragmatics and Linguistics: Two Powers in Conflict?

In the above quote from Lyons's book, mention is made of a 'conflict' between certain 'structural' (read: 'theoretical,' since the linguistic theory of the day was mainly interested in the *structure*, the system of a language, not in its *use*) and what Lyons calls 'more practical approaches' (such as having to do with the way in which people use their language—an approach which, in the 1990s, would be called 'pragmatic').

Another, somewhat related way of expressing this supposed conflict between the theoretically oriented and the more 'practical' (read: 'pragmatic') approach is to distinguish between an abstract, 'formal' way of describing language and a description of its 'actual' use. However, as Lyons admonishes, '[h]owever abstract, or formal, modern linguistic theory might be, it has been developed to account for the way people actually use language' (ibid.); hence there should *not* be any conflict. The problem is, rather, that (despite the good intentions on the part of the linguists) certain people have seen fit to exploit an apparent 'conflict' to further their own aims. Linguistics, including pragmatics, is a *science*, and, as such, it is universal and nonpartisan, says Lyons:

> In this respect, linguistics is no different from any other science; and the point would not be worth stressing, if it were not the case that some linguists, out of sympathy with current developments, have seen a necessary opposition between what have been called 'formalism' and 'realism' in the study of language.
>
> (ibid.)

This last remark is indicative of the existence of what may perhaps be called a 'deeper' conflict: the people to whom Lyons refers are those who were also involved in the general move of the 1960s and 1970s to make science 'relevant' to the overall aims of society, rather than to the interests of the privileged few. One

has to recall that Lyons wrote his text at a time when the whole of the academic world was shaken by the violent upheavals that resulted from precisely such a deeper conflict: the year was 1968, and the conflict manifested itself most notably in the student movements of the 1960s and 1970s that started that same year in Paris.

Even though the 'current developments' have passed, their lasting effect is still felt throughout the world of science. In the early 1990s, the clamor for a 'socially relevant' science has largely been translated as a plea for an ecologically sound development of the sciences; still, it seems fair to say that the 'developments' that Lyons was thinking of have resulted in a wholly different look at those sciences which directly deal with humans and their lives. The conflict of the 1960s has resulted in a heightened awareness of the importance of the 'human factors' in science, and in a critical stance toward 'science for its own sake.' It is precisely in this sense that pragmatics can be said to have inherited the push for a human-centered practice of the language sciences from those 'current developments' of the 1960s. The conflict was never just in the minds of 'some linguists,' and its resolution has been one of the main motivations behind the development of modern pragmatics.

1.3 The Development of Pragmatics

Pragmatics, in the above context, thus appears to be the first, historically motivated approach towards a societally relevant practice of linguistics. Naturally, such an approach does not originate *ex nihilo*: at least three (and perhaps four) developments, or developmental tendencies, can be distinguished, which together (in unison or in counterpoint) have made pragmatics into what it is in the early 1990s.

1.3.1 The 'Antisyntactic' Tendency

This tendency can be seen as a reaction to the 'syntacticism' of the Chomskyan school of linguistics, whereby all of linguistic science (including phonology and semantics) was supposed to fit into the syntactic framework. Linguists such as George Lakoff and John Robert ('Haj') Ross were the first to protest against this syntactic straitjacket; of the numerous alternative 'frameworks' proposed in the late 1960s (such as 'Generative Semantics' by Lakoff: more on this below, Sect. 1.4), none was truly pragmatic in orientation. Furthermore, these alternatives were (naturally as well as geographically) limited to North America; they never caught on in Europe.

1.3.2 The 'Social–Critical' Tendency

This tendency had its origin and heyday in Europe (starting independently in the UK, in Germany, and in Scandinavia, and spreading over most of the continent and later also outside, especially to Australia). Characteristic of this tendency is the need for a socially

417

useful science of language, together with a wish to leave the narrow perspectives of the 'single discipline' behind. Not surprisingly, the effects of language on people's lives, especially in situations of unequal societal power, attracted the interest of these early pragmaticians (such as Basil Bernstein in England, or Dieter Wunderlich in (the then West) Germany); the impact of their work was felt throughout the 1970s and far into the 1980s (for more on this topic, especially Bernstein's work, see below, Sect. 4.6; also see Wunderlich 1970).

1.3.3 The Philosophical Tradition

Originating in the British critical tradition of language investigation (illustrated by names such as Bertrand Russell, Ludwig Wittgenstein, John L. Austin, Gilbert Ryle, and others of the school of 'ordinary language philosophy,' and many more), this tendency was virtually unknown outside the UK until the late 1960s. It was only after the publication of Austin's student John Searle's landmark work *Speech Acts* (1969) that the first inroads into what later became known as pragmatic territory were made by Chomsky's rebellious students; to their great surprise, they found the region populated and partly cultivated by people such as those mentioned above (to use Geoffrey Leech's colorful image):

> When linguistic pioneers such as Ross and Lakoff staked claim in pragmatics in the late 1960s, they encountered there an indigenous breed of philosophers of language who had been quietly cultivating the territory for some time. In fact, the more lasting influences on modern pragmatics have been those of philosophers; notably, in recent years, Austin (1962), Searle (1969), and Grice (1975).
>
> (1983: 2)

1.3.4 The Ethnomethodological Tradition

Finally, mention must be made of a 'Johnny-come-lately' (but a rather influential one): the so-called ethnomethodological tradition. In this tradition, the emphasis had always been on communication rather than on grammar; how people got their messages across was considered more important than the ways in which they constructed their sentences, or whether or not their utterances were syntactically correct or logically consistent.

The ethnomethodologists were clearly, in this respect as in many others, a different breed from the linguists and the philosophers (including those whose main interests had avowedly had been 'ordinary' or 'everyday' language). The notion of language as the object of a scientific investigation that will make possible the description, classification, and definition of language phenomena in an abstract way, with the aid of objective correctness criteria (interpreted as providing univocal answers to questions such as whether an utterance is 'in the language' or not, à la Chomsky), is never taken seriously in ethnomethodology. Conversely, most of the linguists of this early period never took the ethnomethodologists and their results, especially in the domain of conversation analysis, seriously either.

Saying that this research tradition came late in the day, relative to the other tendencies, is of course itself a relative assertion—relative, to be exact, to the point of time at which the linguists first started to recognize the ethnomethodologists, their methods, and their results. While the precise 'moment of truth' cannot be established, it seems safe to say that from the mid-1970s, references to ethnomethodological research start turning up in the linguistic literature. By the early 1980s, the ethnomethodologists are firmly ensconced in pragmatics; thus, Levinson devotes roughly a quarter of the entire text of his book *Pragmatics* (1983) to their ideas and techniques (ch. 6: 'Conversational Structure'). Names such as Harvey Sacks, Emanuel Schegloff, and Gail Jefferson became household words in linguistic circles after the publication of their ground-breaking article in the prestigious linguistics journal *Language* in 1974; their style of investigation (often referred to by the nickname of the 'Santa Barbara School') has been widely adopted also in other research environments.

Still, even in the 1990s, many (mostly pure-theory oriented) linguists deplore this intrusion into their discipline by methods that are not strictly linguistically accountable, inasmuch as they derive their proper object from sciences such as ethnology and anthropology.

1.4 The Case of Semantics: An Example

Above, the roles and relative positions of both philosophy and 'ethnomethodology' in the development of pragmatics were discussed. Since both tendencies (which, in many pragmaticists' opinions, belong to the most influential, albeit controversial, directions in pragmatics) are dealt with in detail elsewhere, it makes sense to follow up some details in another important tendency in the heretical movement that led to the establishment of modern pragmatics: early 'generative semantics' and the problem of presuppositions.

As Leech remarks, 'its [pragmatics'] colonization was only the last stage of a wave-by-wave expansion of linguistics from a narrow discipline dealing with the physical data of speech, to a broad discipline taking in form, meaning and context (1983: 2).

In this connection, Leech refers to a 1968 article by Lakoff, 'On generative semantics,' that supposedly documents the early anti-Chomsky rebellion which was mentioned in Sect. 1.2 (Lakoff 1971a). However, it seems more appropriate to consider another article by Lakoff as evidence here: viz., the one entitled 'Presupposition and relative well-formedness' (Lakoff 1971b, reprinted in the same volume), rather than the somewhat programmatic article mentioned by Leech. It is in this second article that Lakoff for the first time, publicly and in writing, opposes the well-known Chomskyan criterion of 'well-formedness' as the ultimate standard by which to judge a linguistic production.

In the Chomskyan linguistic tradition, well-formedness plays the role of the decision-maker in questions of linguistic 'belonging.' A language consists of a set of well-formed sentences: it is these that 'belong' in the language; no others do. This is the definition that—assumed implicitly or explicitly invoked—has been the bulwark of the Chomskyan system since the late 1950s; it is also the definition that, from the earliest times, has most often come under attack from the quarters of so-called 'Ordinary Working Linguists' (often called 'OWLs'), and the one that makes least sense if, for a moment, consideration is given to what it is that people *really* say, and how they judge their own language's 'well-formedness' or 'correctness.'

As Lakoff points out, this latter notion is a highly relativistic one; it has to do (and a lot to do) with what speakers know about themselves, about their conversational partners (often called 'interlocutors'), about the topic of their conversation, and about its 'progress' (or what is felt as such, versus 'not getting anywhere'; the notion of 'progress' in conversation is discussed extensively in Stalpers 1993). In the following, this problem is discussed on the basis of a concrete example.

In grammar, correctness, as prescribed by the grammarians, often collides with what the language user perceives as correct. Classical examples include the *constructio ad sensum*, by which a noun in the singular denoting a collective body takes a plural verb form, since the plurality of the 'sense' is perceived as more important than the command of the grammar to use the singular (e.g., 'The Board of Directors have decided not to pay dividends this year,' and similar constructions). The following example is another case in point.

There is a rule of English grammar that says the relative pronoun *who* should be used when dealing with a noun which is human (and animate, of course), whereas *which* should be used for a nonanimate (and usually also for a nonhuman) referent. Here are some examples:

The man who kissed my daughter ran away (*who* for a human subject).

versus

The car which hit John's bicycle disappeared around the corner (*which* for a nonanimate (and nonhuman) subject).

and

The bird which shat on my nose flew away (*which* for a nonhuman, although animate, subject).

Such are the rules. However, questions then arise as to how they are maintained, and whether they are always obeyed, or whether there are cases where rule observation is less 'correct' than breaking the rule. Consider some additional examples.

My cat, *who* believes that I'm a fool, enjoys tormenting me.

This sentence, due to George Lakoff (1971b), is not all bad, or always bad. It all depends on the cat, on the speaker, and on their relationship. Given a special, intimate connection between human and pet, it may even be the case that *which*, for a cat of a certain quality and lineage, is totally inappropriate, and even unthinkable; thus Lakoff: 'if I happen to have such a cunning feline' (1971b: 330).

The same is the case in the following extract, describing a program (called 'CREANIMATE') that will allow children to create animals of their choice, using the computer.

In a typical interaction, a student may indicate that he wants to create a bird that swims. The system may respond by discussing some existing aquatic birds such as ducks and penguins. It could display video sequences demonstrating how these birds use the ability to swim to help them survive in the wild. The tutor would try to get the student to refine his design by asking whether the bird will use *his* wings to swim, the way a penguin does, or *its* feet, the way a duck does.
(Schank and Edelson (1990: 9); emphasis added)

Strictly speaking, the above is not only ungrammatical: reference ('anaphora,' as it is called technically) is made to a nonhuman being (a penguin) by the human pronoun *who*, but, moreover, inconsistently: ducks are also nonhuman, but still they are referred to as *it*. However, this then raises the question of *why* a duck is 'it' and a penguin 'he.'

This is not a matter of mere humanlikeness in general (such as: penguins are 'dressed up' in black ties, like noble corporate gentlemen at a social occasion). The real clue to the different conceptualizations is in the total (not just linguistic) *context* and its attendant conceptualization. According to this, 'hand-swimming' is considered to be typically human, as opposed to 'doggie-style swimming' (with all four feet). Penguins, who swim with their 'hands,' are therefore practicing 'human-swim'; ducks, that swim with their feet, are like doggies, therefore they 'animal-swim.'

Notice furthermore that this is not a reference to the 'real world,' since humans do not swim only with their hands or arms, as everybody knows who practices the breast stroke. It is the legs that really provide the motive power, but they are not seen as such: visually and conceptually, the arms are what is somehow characteristic of human swimming. The language reflects this conceptual dichotomy by its different referential pronominalization; and the moral is that attention to this should be paid in categorizing or indexing 'cases,' as when an attempt is made to treat language with the help of a computer. Not all swimming is alike, and not all swimming in one language is called 'swimming' in some other (for example, inanimate objects such as logs can 'swim' in German, but not, it would seem, in any other Germanic language).

Note also that some languages do indeed have different words for motion verbs, where animals are concerned, as opposed to humans. In the Inuit language of (west) Greenland, a human *arpappuq*, an animal *pangalippuq*. Both mean 'he/she/it runs.'

What occurs here is an instance of a more general case, in which 'extralinguistic factors very often enter in judgments of well-formedness,' as Lakoff remarks (1971b). And it is precisely these 'extralinguistic factors' (often called 'presuppositions') which open the door to apparently ungrammatical behavior on the part of the language users.

Another matter is, of course, what is and what is not 'grammatical.' A favorite party game among linguists is to discuss whether or not a particular expression is 'correct.' Such discussions invariably end with one or more of the participants invoking the authority invested in themselves as native speakers of some dialect of English (or whatever), in which precisely such and such a construction is 'grammatical' or 'ungrammatical,' whichever the case might be. Robin Lakoff comments on this curious phenomenon as follows:

> So one linguist's intuitive judgment was equal to another's, and there was no way to discriminate. 'That's not in my dialect,' you could say to a colleague, but that didn't obligate him to change his mind. Hence Ross's version of the Linguist's National Anthem: 'Oh, see if you can say . . .'
>
> (1989: 60)

Levinson, in his discussion of the elementary pragmatic issues, remarks likewise that 'it is often in fact possible to imagine contexts in which alleged anomalies were after all quite usable—the reader can try . . .' (1983: 7).

1.5 Why Pragmatics?

It is a historical fact that, since the early 1970s or so, a great and growing interest in pragmatics and pragmatic problems has been witnessed worldwide. There have been four international conferences (Viareggio 1985, Antwerp 1987, Barcelona 1990, Kobe 1993); an International Pragmatics Association (IPrA) has been in existence since 1985; the international *Journal of Pragmatics* has increased its yearly volume from the original 400 published pages to 1,200 in 1993, and its frequency from 4 quarterly to 12 monthly issues; and many other (official and unofficial) publications have appeared (some of which have survived, some not). Add to this an unestablished number of working papers, theses, dissertations, etc., on pragmatic topics, and the picture is complete. Pragmatics has come into its own, and it is here to stay.

However, in order to establish where this interest comes from, how it can be justified, and what it means, it certainly will not do just to register the fact that 'pragmatic' has come to be a fully accepted term in linguistic circles (compared to earlier usage; see above); the query must go deeper.

Levinson (1983: 35f.) notes several 'convergent reasons' for this phenomenon. First of all, there are the historical reasons (mentioned in Sect. 1.3): the dissatisfaction with Chomsky's aseptic model of a grammar. But along with (and perhaps above) this, there are other, internal-linguistic reasons, such as the many unexplained (and indeed unexplainable) phenomena having to do with the existence of language in the real world, a world of real *users*.

This 'world of users' has come to play the same role in pragmatics as the concept of 'context' has done in more traditional linguistics (even though it was perhaps seldom recognized as such), viz., that of an *existential* condition. That is, the world of users is, for pragmatics, the very condition of its existence.

As for traditional linguistics itself, the role of the context as explanatory device has been made explicit (one might say 'contextualized') by pragmatics as a *user context*, a context in which the users are the paramount features of interest, inasmuch as they are the *primi motores* of the entire linguistic operation, both in its theoretical (grammar-oriented) and its practical (usage-bound) aspects.

If this world of users and usage is confronted with the world of *rules*, so characteristic of traditional linguistics, it is impossible not to marvel at the gap between the two, as well as at the bizarre fact that the practitioners of traditional linguistics seemingly did not care too much about this situation. This holds both for the purely syntactic rules (see the case of *who* versus *which*, discussed in Section 1.4) and for phenomena of a more content-oriented nature: semantic rules, as discussed in connection with so-called 'presuppositions,' 'speech acts,' and other phenomena too numerous to discuss here.

Perhaps one of the most effective incitements for the development of pragmatics has been the growing irritation, felt especially by many of the younger, 'nonaligned' linguistic practitioners, with the lack of interest among established linguists for what really goes on in language, for what people actually 'do with words,' to borrow from the title of one of the classic works in the speech act tradition, John L. Austin's *How To Do Things with Words* (1962). The title of Austin's book contains an implicit question, the answer to which is not, of course, that people should form correct sentences or compose logical utterances, but that they communicate with each other (and themselves) by means of language.

Such an attitude is rather far apart from what one famous representative of the linguistic profession once permitted himself to state in public, viz., that he was not so much interested in what people actually said as in the rules of the grammar, insofar as they appear in what people say; another famous linguist was wont to describe a 'good linguist' as one who did not know any languages (thereby defining the term in contrast to one of its common meanings in nontechnical or somewhat older English, where a 'linguist' precisely is a person with a good command of (preferably) many languages).

Faced with these testimonials, one can only wonder and ask (adopting a distinction that was originally established by Chomsky (1957, 1965) for a slightly different purpose, namely to exclude actual linguistic usage from the business of describing the language from a theoretical point of view) what caused this split between the competence of linguists, on the one hand, and the performance of language users, on the other?

1.6 The Logical Way

A final argument for the introduction of the pragmatic point of view also in the way people think, or could be brought to think, about their language and the way to use it, has to do with *logic*.

One of the most tenacious ideas promulgated in discussions of language is the notion that language is a matter of logic. This is taken to mean that a correct use of language presupposes the use of logic, and that any use of language which is not in accordance with the laws of logic is simply bad. Logic thus is prior to language; it is maintained that everyday language is a bastardized and illegitimate variant of the pure language of logic, as manifested in mathematics, formal logic, and maybe even abstract music. To express oneself in illogical terms is the same as to speak badly; logic may be the handmaiden of philosophy, but language is certainly the handmaiden of logic. To top it all off, even the Bible admonishes people (as some philosophers believe) to express themselves in simple, logical terms of affirmation and negation: 'Let your communication be Yea, Yea; Nay, Nay: for whatsoever is more than these cometh of evil' (Matthew 5:37).

In pragmatics, many of the early discussions on the foundation of this science have turned around the possibility and desirability of letting pragmatic conditions govern the correct use of logical propositions, when disguised as 'ordinary language' utterances. As the facts would have it, however, logic and language are strange fellow-travelers: the amount of ground that they cover between them is not very encouraging, at any rate for the logician. Consider a simple case.

According to a well-known rule from logic, when conjoining two propositions (call them p and q, and symbolize their conjunction by the formula $p \& q$), it is not important in which order the two constituents of the formula appear: $p \& q$ is equivalent to $q \& p$.

Next consider the following (Levinson 1983:35). Somebody utters the sentence *Getting married and*

having a child is better than having a child and getting married. Supposing the everyday language conjunction *and* can be identified with the logical conjunction '&,' this gives a logical proposition of the form p ('getting married') $\& q$ ('having a child'), expressed in everyday language by means of a sentence like the above. Such an utterance should then, by the laws of logic, be equivalent to the proposition q ('having a child') $\& p$ ('getting married'). Hence, the above utterance would be equivalent to *Having a child and getting married is better than getting married and having a child.*

But clearly, in everyday life as in everyday language use, the two sentences do *not* mean the same; far from it. Which of the two is 'true' depends, of course, on the actual circumstances in which the utterers of the sentence live, in particular with regard to the conditions of their (married) lives and to matters of childbearing and -rearing. These circumstances are not to be predicted from the language as such, but can only be discovered by looking at the total human *context of use*, as seen above. Either sentence can be the expression of complete stupidity or of age-old wisdom; it all depends on the context of culture and life. But one thing is certain: they are in no way equivalent in everyday life, whatever they may be in the world of logic. A logical conjunction, by itself, says nothing about the temporal sequence of the conjuncts: actually, such considerations of time are completely alien to (classical) logic.

A further, and perhaps even more profound, difficulty lies in the fact that there is no a priori guarantee that any logical symbols (such as *and*, or its logical 'sister' *or*) can be faithfully represented by the words of a natural language (such as *and, or* in English). Vice versa, the words of the language do not univocally belong to one particular logical entity: for instance, the conjunction *but* is very different from *and* in daily use, yet it normally does not have a separate logical symbol. Thus, a conjunction of two sentences in the language by the conjunction *and* cannot be said simply to represent a logical conjunction of the type *and*. Logic is in essence an abstraction from language, and should never be made into its dominant perspective.

2. On Defining Pragmatics

2.1 A New Paradigm

If pragmatics did not just 'happen'; if it did not come in from nowhere, one is led to ask how it could become such a popular trend in such a relatively short time.

The answer to this question will at the same time provide a first approximation to an understanding of what pragmatics is all about. A more elaborate, but still tentative, definition is given in Sect. 2.3.5; such a definition will necessarily have an 'intensional' touch to it (it will say something about *what* pragmatics is supposed to be). It will not be easy to supplement this with an 'extensional' definition, since it is notoriously difficult to limit the field in such a way that it can be said *where* pragmatics stops and the 'beyond' begins (more on this in Sect. 2.4, where a comprehensive definition will be offered. The allusion is to several well-known series of monographs and books published under the common name of *Pragmatics and Beyond* by John Benjamins since 1978.)

As outlined in Sect. 1.2, the first, tentative efforts at establishing something like a pragmatic approach date back to the early 1970s. What is being witnessed there is the collapse of earlier theories and hypotheses (in particular, of the 'pan-syntacticism' of the early Chomsky and his followers). Slowly and with intermittent success, a new model emerges: pragmatics is in the making, even though initially its practitioners are not even aware of this themselves. Briefly, what is happening is a 'paradigm shift' in the classical sense, as defined by Kuhn (1962).

2.2 Context and User

Levinson has described this process (and, in particular, the growing importance of the 'context') from a more technical–linguistic point of view as follows:

> as knowledge of the syntax, phonology and semantics of various languages has increased, it has become clear that there are specific phenomena that can only naturally be described by recourse to contextual concepts. On the one hand, various syntactic rules seem to be properly constrained only if one refers to pragmatic conditions; and similarly for matters of stress and intonation. It is possible, in response to these apparent counter-examples to a context-independent notion of linguistic competence, simply to retreat: the rules can be left unconstrained and allowed to generate unacceptable sentences, and a performance theory of pragmatics assigned the job of filtering out the acceptable sentences. Such a move is less than entirely satisfactory because the relationship between the theory of competence and the data on which it is based (ultimately intuitions about acceptability) becomes abstract to a point where counter-examples to the theory may be explained away on an ad hoc basis, *unless* a systematic pragmatics has already been developed.
>
> (1983: 36; emphasis in original)

It should be clear (in accordance with what was said above) that such a development of a 'systematic pragmatics' can of course only be seen as a contemporary need with the help of hindsight: from the vantage point of 15 or 20 years later, it may be possible to observe how the old paradigm came under attack, and how the contours of a new one gradually took shape. But at the time when all this happened, all that could be seen was a growing number of unexplained (and, in fact, unexplainable) phenomena, observed first of all on the boundaries of syntax and semantics.

To name a few: there was the emergent interest in the problems of speech acts; the growing awareness of context as a decisive factor (not only in the syntactic domain, where context-free and context-sensitive

rules had been among the staples of mainstream theory from the very beginning); and especially, in connection with the question of how to define the context, a heightened interest in the issue of what one might broadly call a 'user point of view.'

Here, one encounters notions such as the 'register' (determining whether an utterance is to be considered formal or relaxed, whether or not it connotes social prestige, and so on); the modal aspects of the utterance (having to do with speakers' and hearers' attitudes toward what is said); questions of rhetoric (e.g., 'how to get one's point across'), and similar issues that were almost totally neglected by linguistics (as they had been by mainstream philosophy ever since the demise of the Sophists); and so on.

If one chooses to apply the notion of 'shifting paradigm' to the 'pragmatic turn' in linguistics, a number of observations can be brought to the same practical denominator, viz., a shift from the paradigm of theoretical grammar (in particular, syntax) to that of the *language user*. As will be seen, the latter is what pragmatics is all about.

2.3 Toward a Definition

2.3.1 The User's Role

A new paradigm of research carries with it, at least implicitly, a new definition of the object of that research. With regard to pragmatics, it is not always easy to see what such a new definition should imply when it comes to establish the boundaries between the 'old' and the 'new' interpretations of the research object. A few of the major questions are: how pragmatics can be defined vis-à-vis syntax and semantics (not to mention phonology); the role of pragmatics in the classical 'hyphenated areas' of research (psycho-, socio-, ethnolinguistics etc.); and newer representatives such as text linguistics, mathematical and computational linguistics, and the vast field covered by the term 'applied' linguistics.

It seems safe to say that most definitions of pragmatics have been inspired by Charles Morris's famous definition of pragmatics as 'the study of the relation of signs to interpreters' (1938: 6), except that in the 1990s, in a less technical, more applied linguistic terminology, one would probably use words such as 'message' and 'language user,' rather than 'sign' and 'interpreter.' Pragmatics is the science of linguistics inasmuch as that science focuses on the language-using human; this distinguishes pragmatics from the classical linguistic disciplines, which first and foremost concentrated on the systematic result of the users' activity: language as system and as structure.

Consequently, one could imagine that the proper domain of pragmatics would be what Chomsky had called *performance*, that is, the way in which the individual user went about his or her language in everyday life. Such a practice would be in contrast to the user's abstract *competence*, understood as his or her knowledge of the language and its rules (as, for example, described in a generative transformational grammar).

If this opposition is kept as a valid one, the study of language can simply be divided into two largely independent parts: one a description of its *structure* (as dealt with in the classical descriptions or grammars), the other a description of its *use* (to be taken care of by pragmatics).

In Jerry Katz's words: 'Grammars are theories about the structure of sentence types... Pragmatic theories, in contrast, ... explicate the reasoning of speakers and hearers...' (1977: 19), when the latter try to establish a relation between what is said and the semantic 'proposition' that is behind it.

A preliminary result of the quest for a definition is that in pragmatics, the language user is at the center of attention. Thus, it is possible to say there is a 'user's point of view' as a common orienting feature for both linguists and philosophers.

However, this is not sufficient to define pragmatics as a science, as witness the varying conceptions in pragmatics of that user's role, as well as of what is implied by the term 'use of language.' For instance, one can either consider 'language use' to be whatever happens when users are 'doing things with words'; or, in a more restrictive procedure, one can demand that pragmatics refer *explicitly* to a user, whenever language is discussed.

Furthermore, from a social–scientific point of view, a theory of language as a user's interest should rest on a theory of the user. However, the user being a member of a particular human society, such a theory should encompass everything that characterizes the user as a societal being. This seems to be a logical extension of the notion of pragmatics as a theory of use, even though it entails a 'very broad usage of the term [pragmatics]' (Levinson 1983: 2); Levinson also comments, somewhat wistfully, it might seem, that this usage is 'still [!] the one generally used on the Continent' (ibid.).

2.3.2 Communication and Behavior

From yet another point of view, pragmatics can be defined as *behavior*. This is the approach advocated by some very early proponents of the pragmatic view, Watzlawick, et al., who back in 1968, expressed their discomfort with information science and linguistics, placing the emphasis on one-way transmission of signs without attention to either communication or interaction. As they say, 'from the perspective of pragmatics, all behavior, not only speech, is communication, and all communication—even the communicational clues in an impersonal context—affects behavior' (Watzlawick, et al. 1968: 22). These authors' approach to pragmatics is not linguistic, but communicational and behaviorist; in fact, for them, communication (including nonverbal communication) and behavior are more or less syn-onymous: pragmatics *is* behavior, *is* communication. Pragmatically speaking, one's communicative behavior is such that one cannot *not* communicate (1968: 72).

No wonder that one looks in vain for traces of influence from these quarters on the linguistic movements of the time, most of which were somehow indebted to the 'Chomskyan revolution' with its emphasis on the formal characterization of a language's syntactic properties. By contrast, the 'hope of abstracting the formal relations between communication and behavior' must be said to have been rather remote (1968: 13); as a result, the area of communication 'has received remarkably little attention,' as Watzlawick, et al. remark (1968: 18).

In the tradition of Watzlawick and his colleagues (which to a great extent had its roots in the study of abnormal, psychiatrically treated behavior), the question is not what a person *should* say, according to the grammar of a language, but what a person *does* actually try to communicate, using whatever language he or she has. In this framework, the key words are not 'rules,' but 'information,' 'redundancy,' and 'feedback' (terms taken from information theory, but not used in the formal abstract sense in which they are defined there); 'imperviousness,' 'paradox in interaction,' and 'double bind' (actually terms that have their origin in interaction theory and the treatment of the mentally ill). Thus, even the 'craziest' language of the schizophrenic ('schizophrenese': see Sect. 4.4) is said to have its communicative value and import.

Watzlawick, et al. were in many ways pioneers; in other respects, they were the 'voice[s] crying in the wilderness' (Matthew 3: 3). Not until the linguists themselves had turned to pragmatics (forced by the paradoxes of their own science) could they begin to understand the double binds that they had been caught in by positing, as the touchstone of their research, a model of a nonexistent, 'ideal speaker/hearer' (Chomsky 1965).

2.3.3 Grammar and Context

In contrast to these broader uses of the term 'pragmatics,' one finds others demanding a minimum of strictly *linguistic* involvement before one can begin to talk about pragmatics in the linguistic sense of the term. In Levinson's words: 'Pragmatics is the study of those relations between language and context that are *grammaticalized*, or encoded in the structure of a language' (1983: 9; emphasis in original).

Even though he does not say so explicitly, Levinson seems to detect a conflict between those language-context relations that are, and those that are not, 'grammaticalized' (the process of grammaticalization being understood as the expression of pragmatic relations with the help of strictly linguistic means, such as the rules of a grammar operating on phonological, morphological, and syntactic elements). This, in its turn, implies making a distinction between the 'grammatical' and the 'user' point of view on the basis of how language and context relate, whether they do this with, or without, grammar's helping hand. The important notion of *context*, however, and the role that it plays in the expression of grammatical and pragmatic relations, is not addressed.

Still, the difference between a 'grammatical' and a 'user-oriented' point of view is precisely *in* the context: on the first view, one considers linguistic elements in isolation, as syntactic structures or parts of a grammatical paradigm, such as case, tense, etc.; whereas on the second, the all-important question is how these linguistic elements are used in a concrete *setting*, that is, in a context.

A definition of pragmatics that limits 'context,' and references to context, to what is (or can be) grammatically expressed has, of course, a big advantage: it excludes a number of irrelevant factors from the scope of investigation. One could formally define pragmatics as 'the study of grammatically encoded aspects of contexts,' establishing a function 'that assigns to utterances the propositions that express their full meaning in context' (where *proposition* is to be understood as the logical equivalent of a sentence), or, alternatively, 'a function from utterances to contexts, namely the contexts brought about by each utterance' (Levinson 1983: 31). Among the irrelevant, excluded factors, one could mention (to take a classic example) the presence of food in the mouth while speaking; this may be part of some context, yet it is not a linguistic factor, and maybe not even a pragmatic one.

As Levinson has it, 'the main strength of this definition of pragmatics is that it restricts the field to purely linguistic matters' (1983: 11). So far, so good: but restricting the field of pragmatics to 'purely linguistic matters' does not seem to be too interesting a definition from a *pragmatic* point of view. Certainly, not all 'extralinguistic' factors can always and everywhere be safely excluded from a pragmatic evaluation. A truly pragmatic consideration has to deal with the context as a *user's context*, and cannot limit itself to the study of grammatically encoded aspects of contexts, as the 'grammaticalization requirement' seems to imply.

The next section examines the grammaticalization problem in more detail.

2.3.4 Why Grammar Fails: Implicatures and Presuppositions

In order to establish why a 'strictly grammatical' definition of pragmatics must fail, two cases will be looked into that are often used to illustrate the problems of the 'grammaticalization' of supposedly pragmatic relationships. The cases in question are *conversational implicature* and *presupposition*; together they constitute two of the most important disputed

areas in the borderland of logic, semantics, and pragmatics.

By *conversational implicature* is meant the principle according to which an utterance, in a concrete conversational setting, is always understood in accordance with what one can expect in such a setting. Thus, in a particular situation involving a question, an utterance that on the face of it does not make 'sense' can very well be an adequate answer. If speaker A asks speaker B

What time is it?

it makes perfectly good sense to answer

The bus just went by,

given a particular constellation of contextual factors, including the fact that there is only one bus a day, and that it passes B's house at 7:45 each morning; furthermore, that A is aware of this, and that A takes B's answer in the 'cooperative spirit' in which it was given, viz., as a relevant answer to a previous question. Notice, however, that there are no strictly 'grammaticalized' items in this interchange that could be identified as carriers of such information about the context. Hence, under the interpretation of pragmatics-as-strictly-grammatical, such relevant information about the users and their contexts is not taken into consideration (cf. Levinson 1983: 98).

The other example deals with *presuppositions*. It is by no means always the case that pragmatic meaning is linguistically (that is, grammatically) encoded; usually, it is said to be 'presupposed' (Lakoff's cat and assorted other animals, referred to in Sect. 1.4, are cases in point).

Compare also the following pair of utterances:

Gorbachev called Yeltsin a real Marxist, and then Yeltsin insulted *him*

and

Yeltsin called Gorbachev a real Marxist, and then Gorbachev insulted *him*.

The first sentence seems normal, given what is known from the early 1990s about the two statesmen and feelings about eastern European leaders. In the second sentence, however, Yeltsin is trying (rather unsubtly, perhaps) to shower praise on his former president—so Gorbachev could retort with an insult. But even though the second sentence is odd, there are no *grammatical* means of establishing or recognizing that oddity: the presuppositions are all hidden.

Things get even worse in the following pair of sentences:

Bush called Gorbachev a real Marxist, and then Gorbachev insulted *him*

and

Castro called Gorbachev a bad Marxist, and then Gorbachev insulted *him*.

Here, one has to know such things as that President Bush would never have used the expression 'real Marxist' as other than a compliment to a statesman whose political and personal views are known to be inspired by Marx; hence Gorbachev's would-be insulting retort makes no sense at all. On the other hand, among Marxists, one can imagine that being called a 'bad Marxist' is indeed an insult, so the second sentence makes perfect sense. Again, the problem is how to put such things in a grammatically identifiable shape.

For the time being, the findings may be recapitulated as follows. In the study of language, there seem to be certain features and elements that cannot be captured in a strictly linguistic (or grammatical) view on language. When one looks closer at these features and elements, they seem to be related in some way to the 'outer' world (what used to be called, somewhat denigratorily, the 'extralinguistic'), that is, to the world of the users and their societal conditions.

2.3.5 A Preliminary Definition

From what has been said so far, the following preliminary *definition* of pragmatics can be offered.

Pragmatics is the study of language in a human context of use. Language use is the process by which people communicate, for various purposes, using linguistic means. This process is governed by the conditions of society, inasmuch as these conditions determine the users' access to, and control of, those means. Hence, pragmatics can also be described as a societally oriented and societally bound linguistics.

A further elaboration of these societal aspects will be given in Sect. 4. The relationship of pragmatics to the 'linguistic means' mentioned above will be discussed in the following section.

2.4 Pragmatics and Linguistics: Delimiting and Defining

A definition of pragmatics would not be complete unless it took into account where pragmatics begins and, possibly, where it ends. 'To define' means 'to impose a boundary' (cf. the Latin word *finis* 'end'; plural *fines* 'frontier'). 'Defining pragmatics' thus implies determining its frontiers with other, adjoining fields of research within (and possibly also outside) linguistics.

Nobody has been able to postulate, in a convincing way, any such defining boundaries; nor have the definitions that have been offered provided any possibility of delimiting pragmatics clearly and neatly to everybody's satisfaction. A real 'definition' in this sense is thus just as impossible to provide as a 'grammatical' definition in the sense of the previous section. Most authors either confine themselves to a strictly linguis-

tically oriented definition (like the one criticized in Sect. 2.3.3) or resort to a definition that, while incorporating as much societal context as possible, necessarily remains somewhat diffuse as regards the relation between pragmatics and the other areas of linguistics, including their relative autonomy.

It seems natural at this point to raise the question of why such clear, sharply demarcated boundaries are needed at all, when pragmatics is apparently in a steady evolutionary flux, and boundary markers, once placed, will have to be removed constantly anyway. A 'pragmatic' definition of pragmatics is required that avoids the Scylla and Charybdis of the above alternatives.

In the literature, such an idea seems to have been received with some enthusiasm. The most prominent representative of this 'pragmatic eclecticism' is Geoffrey Leech, who advocates *complementarity* as his solution to the dilemma. This is what he says about the relation between pragmatics and its nearest linguistic neighbor, semantics:

> The view that semantics and pragmatics are distinct, though complementary and interrelated fields of study, is easy to appreciate subjectively, but is more difficult to justify in an objective way. It is best supported negatively, by pointing out the failures or weaknesses of alternative views.
>
> (1983: 6)

Leech distinguishes three possible ways of structuring this relationship: *semanticism* (pragmatics inside semantics), *pragmaticism* (semantics inside pragmatics), and *complementarism* (they both complement each other, but are otherwise independent areas of research).

As an instance of *semanticism*, one can mention the early suggestions for dealing with the 'presupposition problem' (see above); what the transformationalists called 'deep syntax' was in reality semantics-inspired, and the presuppositions (which, after all, had a pragmatic background) were forced inside the semantico-syntactic chimera called 'semantax' in order not to disturb the unity and indivisibility of linguistics under the watching eye of Divine Syntax.

In contrast to this, consider the way in which Austin dealt with the problem. For him, the only real issue at stake was the effect that 'words' have when uttered, and the 'things' that can be 'done' with them. In Leech's terminology, this means that the pragmatic aspect of language is the only really interesting one: clearly a case of *pragmaticism*.

Finally, it seems plausible to assume that the main reason why Austin's work remained unknown to so many linguists for such a long time was precisely the same anxiety that radical views traditionally inspire in those who are concerned about territorial rights and privileges, and who hence worry about boundaries. Obviously, being a syntactician or a semanticist, one wants to do linguistics in one's own, professionally established way; the moment other people start telling one what to do, one's territorial integrity is in danger. So, in order not to rock the boat, most traditionally oriented linguists prefer to assign pragmatics (especially of the more radical variety, as discussed above) to a quiet corner, preferably a little bit outside linguistics 'proper'; here, pragmaticists can do their own thing, in 'complementarity and interrelation' with the rest, but still clearly distinguished from it. In this way, the delimitation problem can be solved in a *complementarist* fashion.

This latter alternative seems, in the early 1990s, to be the preferred solution to the boundary problem. Levinson, discussing the relationship between semantics and pragmatics, remarks:

> From what we now know about the nature of meaning, a hybrid or modular account seems inescapable; there remains the hope that with two components, a semantics and a pragmatics working in tandem, each can be built on relatively homogeneous and systematic lines.
>
> (1983: 15)

Taking this notion of complementarity as the basic methodological tool, and, under the guidance of what has come to be recognized as the all-important aspect of pragmatics—the user context—the following *definition* may be formulated.

Pragmatics is the study of language from a user point of view, where the individual components of such a study are joined in a common, societal perspective. The problems of pragmatics are not confined to the semantic, the syntactic, or the phonological fields, exclusively. Pragmatics thus defines a cluster of related problems, rather than a strictly delimited area of research. (For the 'perspective' approach, see Sect. 3.2.)

3. Tasks and Functions of Pragmatics

3.1 Introduction: Theory and Practice

From a theoretical point of view, the tasks and functions of pragmatics can be characterized in different ways, depending on one's view of linguistics as such, and of the place of pragmatics in linguistics. Such a (more abstract) characterization will place emphasis on the function of pragmatics within linguistics, either as a 'component' (just as phonology, syntax, and semantics are components of the linguistic system), or as a 'perspective.' By this is suggested something which is not an independent agency in its own right but which pervades the other components and gives them a particular, pragmatic 'accent.'

A practical characterization of the tasks and functions of pragmatics takes as its point of departure the traditional problems that linguistic research has grappled with over the years, and for whose solution one looks to pragmatics (such as the problems discussed in Sect. 2.3).

Furthermore, pragmatics is often given the task of trying to solve the numerous practical difficulties that are inherent in the exercise of linguistic functions. Many of these problems and problem areas have been opened up to pragmatics by 'outside agents': problems of conversation and turn-control; problems of argumentation; problems of language use in educational settings (applied linguistics); problems of interaction between humans and computers; and, in general, all sorts of communicational problems in anthropology, ethnography, psychiatry, and psychology, the 'public' language, both inside and outside the social institutions and the media, educational settings, and so on.

3.2 Component or Perspective

The 'component' view of linguistics, popular ever since Chomsky's early works (1957, 1965) and maintained faithfully in generative transformational grammar despite all its internal differences, is essentially based on a 'modular' conception of the human mind (the different faculties are thought of as independent but cooperating unit, a conception which is also popular among cognitive scientists and computer-oriented psychologists). In contrast, a 'perspective' on a human activity such as the use of language and the system underlying it tries to emphasize certain aspects of that activity. For instance, the pragmatic perspective on phonology will emphasize the social values that are inherent in a certain phonetic system, as compared to other, perhaps theoretically equivalent, but pragmatically radically different systems. As an example, think of the theoretical statements about Black English dialects of the 'inner city' being as 'good' as any other dialect of English (Labov 1966), which make little sense from a pragmatic perspective: one simply cannot 'do the same things' with Black as with Standard English in any other surroundings than precisely the inner city.

The Belgian pragmatician Jef Verschueren has expressed this line of thinking in the following words:

> [We are dealing with] a radical departure from the established component view which tries to assign to pragmatics its own set of linguistic features in contradistinction with phonology, morphology, syntax and semantics. If pragmatics does not belong to the contrast set of these... components of the study of language, neither does it belong to the contrast set of... components such as psycholinguistics, sociolinguistics, etc. (each of which studies processes or phenomena which can be situated at various levels of linguistic structuring... and each of which typically relates such processes or phenomena to a segment of extra-linguistic reality).
>
> (1987: 6)

In the component view of linguistics, each 'module' works within a properly delimited domain, with proper, well-defined objects, and with an established method. Thus, phonology busies itself with the speech sounds or phonemes, and leaves syntactic objects such as sentences to the syntacticians; similarly, the syntactic component does not interfere in the workings of syntax except in a sideways fashion (the components are not separated by watertight dividers, of course, as even the staunchest 'componentialists' will admit).

By contrast, in a perspective view, pragmatics could be said to serve as an 'umbrella' for the modules of linguistics, its components. In the words of the Finn Jan-Ola Östman, pragmatics should probably not be seen as 'belonging to the contrast set of psycholinguistics, sociolinguistics, etc., but rather as being the *umbrella* term for these and other (semi-)hyphenated areas in linguistics' (1988: 28; italics added).

A natural extension of this view would be to let the 'component' and the 'perspective' conceptions exist side by side: after all, they both are metaphors designed to expand, not to narrow, the epistemological horizon. There could be a *structural component* (such as phonology, a part of the system of language) along with a *structural perspective*, that is, a way of looking at language (in this case, phonology) as a structured system. In the same vein, one could have a *pragmatic component*, understood as the set of whatever pragmatic functions can be assigned to language, along with a *pragmatic perspective*, that is, the way in which these functions operate within the single units of the language system, respectively of language use.

Summarizing this view, Östman uses an analogy: if 'the unit of analysis in semantics [is] simply *meaning*: the meanings of words, phrases, larger constructions, prosody, and so on, ... then by the same token, the "unit" of analysis for pragmatics could be said to be *the functioning of language* ...' (1988; emphasis in original).

Note also what Östman says in the next paragraph: 'Admittedly, that latter [unit] is to be seen as a process rather than as an "object," but it is doubtful in what sense any units of analysis for semantics are that much more object-like.'

3.3 The Functional Approach

The notion of language as a functional whole is (like other good ideas) by no means new. As early as 1934, the German psychologist Karl Bühler elaborated his famous functional triangle of *Ausdruck*, *Darstellung*, and *Appell* as characteristic of language; and in the 1960s, Roman Jakobson elaborated on this Bühlerian model by adding three more functions: code, channel, and poetic quality.

What these models of human language intend to impart is a feeling of the importance of the human user in the communicative process. Messages are not just 'signals,' relayed through abstract channels: the human expression functions as a means of social togetherness and of solidarity with, and appeal to, other users.

The result of adopting this way of looking at linguistic phenomena is vividly demonstrated by the fact that the different agendas which had been drawn up by the componentialists and the perspectivists respectively can be consolidated. Whereas representatives of the former line of thought are mainly interested in phenomena such as presuppositions, implicatures, deixis, and so on, a typical 'perspectivist' will deal with concepts such as 'negotiability, adaptability, and variability, motivations, effects, etc.' (Östman 1988: 29). In a functional synthesis, all this can be brought together: the most important criterion for language as it is used is whether it fulfills its functions of communication and interaction, not what it sounds like, or what kind of techniques it uses for getting its message across.

Neither can this be said to be a new idea. Austin and the early speech act theoreticians (such as Searle) realized that in speech acting, as in so many other ways of word(l)y behavior, 'what you get is what you expect.' Asking a passer-by what time it is, a person may use a question of the type *Can you tell me ...?* or even *Do you have ...?* (viz., *the time*). The questioner would certainly be greatly taken aback by an answer in the affirmative (*Yes*), without any further information being offered. The reason for this astonishment is that such a 'question' is really more of a 'request' than a question (cf. the 'polite imperative' of the type *please tell ...* or *please give ...*—expressions which, incidentally, are rarely found in situations like the above). Other examples, quoted endlessly in the linguistic literature, include such cases as: requesting that a window be closed by remarking on the temperature in the room (type: *It's cold in here, isn't it?*); requesting a passing of the salt by inquiring about one's neighbor's ability to do so (type: *Can you pass me the salt?*); and so on.

Linguistic functions of use are best studied in situations where people interact normally, using language face to face. Consequently, such situations are considered as the prime sources of information when it comes to studying this functional aspect of language: among these, everyday conversation among people takes a first seat.

There are basically two ways of going about studying conversation and other basic linguistic interaction. One way is simply to study what is going on, trying to describe it as exactly as possible, and figuring out what the options are for participants to join in at any given point, and what their choices are of expressing themselves to their own and others' satisfaction. This line of approach is followed by the so-called conversational analysts.

Another, more theoretical approach tries to go 'behind conversation,' as it were, establishing the minimal conditions for successful interaction both on

427

the linguistic and also (and maybe even more importantly) on the hidden levels of societal equality or inequality among people, prejudice and class feeling, education and culture—in short, the whole gamut of societal background information that is necessary to carry on a successful conversation, understood as 'the sustained production of chains of mutually dependent acts, constructed by two or more agents each monitoring and building on the actions of the other' (Levinson 1983: 44).

The latter approach, needless to say, comes closer to pragmatics as described here (Sect. 2.3 above); in the present context of writing, it is the linguistic dimension of social interaction (see Mey 1985 for an elaboration of this point of view).

3.4 A Division of Pragmatics

In view of the above, the following rough division of the pragmatic field can be offered (it should be emphasized that such a division has more to do with a division of labor than with a strict, conceptual delimitation of fields of research).

3.4.1 Micropragmatics

Micropragmatics is the study of language use in smaller contexts. Traditionally, this context is understood as comprising the sentence (and its immediate surroundings); thus, the theory of speech acts is essentially a study of what people do, or can do, in a limited illocutionary environment. Phenomena such as reference, deixis, anaphora, etc., which by their very nature may point to contexts that are larger than the single utterance, are still seen as 'anchored' in the sentence as the origin of their syntactic and semantic coordinates. Pragmatics is still circumscribed by the conventions of linguistic analysis.

With the discovery of the presupposition not only as a necessary condition for explaining certain linguistic phenomena (see Sect. 2.3.4), but also as the essential link with the larger context of human language use (the 'world'), one begins to see the contours of a larger structure. The users of language are no longer seen as individual agents, demonstrating linguistic behavior mainly for the benefit of the analyst; the question is raised of what these users are trying to *do with their words*: they are trying to get a point across, just making conversation, or begging for their lives (with or without success). These viewpoints had already been adumbrated in the study of speech acting under the general heading of 'perlocutionary' effects, but most linguists had been rather reluctant to engage themselves in what may be termed the field of macropragmatics.

3.4.2 Macropragmatics

Here, the emphasis is on what actually goes on in language use; the context of use is not limited in advance, and basically comprises the entire environment, both linguistic and 'extralinguistic' (to use a term which used to be a highly negative denominator for many linguists). In macropragmatics, the interest is focused on user interaction, in various ways, and in a number of settings. Conversational analysis is one big area of research here, bringing together workers from various 'extralinguistic' fields such as anthropology, sociology, and ethnology, as well as from linguistics proper. The various uses of institutional and institutionalized language have also caught the interest of pragmatic workers: one can mention the language use that is found to be typical for the medical environment, educational institutions, the workplace, the marketplace, the rock scene, politics, the media, the computer environment, and so on.

Important thematic areas that are covered in macropragmatics are, in general, those that deal with the 'transcendental' conditions for human language use. Thus, the problems of sex-related differences in language and language use have become a prominent field of study in the last decades of the twentieth century, as has the general question of the unequal distribution of societal power, in particular as this power relates to national and international politics, or differences due to differences in social privilege.

A special interest of macropragmatics has arisen due to the massive displacement of foreign workers since the Second World War, both in the USA and in Europe, as an auxiliary force in the low-paid industrial, agricultural, and service sectors; the need for a language policy in this domain has found expression in worries about the survival and continued dominant position of the mother tongue (compare the 'English as a First Language' movement in the USA), as well as in a concern for the growing numbers of adult speakers of no language at all. These people, having a mother tongue that is in dire need of development and/or repair, since they never received any formal instruction in it, and a second language that is only insufficiently mastered, constitute a prime example of linguistic underprivilege. The same concern for the inequality of linguistic resources, and for the consequences of such a state of affairs, has led many pragmaticists to speculate on the question of how language can be used for societal–remedial (so-called 'emancipatory'), rather than for repressive, purposes; on 'repressive' versus 'oppressive' use of language, see Sect. 4.2).

As a general cover term, the word 'discourse' (originally introduced in this sense by Michel Foucault; see Foucault 1969: 153–54) is used to indicate the ensemble of the conditions that determine use of language, yet are invisible to the (linguistically or otherwise) untrained eye. Another, more traditional use of the term 'discourse' is found in the expression 'discourse analysis,' as used by many to indicate a closer concern for traditional linguistic methods in dealing with everyday language use than is shown, for example, in conversation analysis. In this latter sense, discourse analysis is close to what is often called 'text linguistics'; a more pragmatically oriented approach to text production and consumption is often defined as a topic in its own right, called 'text pragmatics.'

A concern for the factors underlying the above-mentioned phenomena of societal underprivilege is often linked to the term 'critical' in the sense defined by the so-called 'Frankfurt School' of sociology (for example, by Jürgen Habermas). This use of the term is closely related to the field of study called 'societal pragmatics' (see Mey 1985 and Sect. 4 below).

The various avenues of pragmatic research and practice that have been indicated above naturally lead to an evaluation and a critical examination of what pragmatics is all about. Reflections of this sort have led to the rise of a subfield called 'metapragmatics,' in which such matters find their natural locus.

3.4.3 Metapragmatics

In accordance with established language use in the sciences, the prefix 'meta-' is used to indicate a shift of 'level': the following discussion is on a different ('meta-') level from its object. Thus, a 'metalanguage' indicates a language that is 'about' (a) language, one level 'up' from that language (also called (an) 'object language'; the terms were originally invented by the Polish logician Alfred Tarski in the 1930s.

A 'metalanguage' is thus a language that comments on, examines, criticizes, etc., what happens on the level of language itself, the 'object language.' In everyday life, metalanguage is used when things are put in (verbal or literal) parentheses or in quotes, for example, by saying

> This is strictly off the record, but … (verbal parenthesis)

or

> And he goes: 'Don't give me that nonsense' … (direct quote).

Metalanguage is also used to discuss the problems that occur in the daily, object language: thus, every grammatical statement of the form:

> The word for 'red' is an adjective in English, but a participle in Inuit (Eskimo)

is technically a part of the metalanguages of the respective grammars of English and Inuit.

In the same vein, metapragmatics is a (pragmatic) discussion on pragmatics. There are two basic considerations that come into play whenever pragmatics is mentioned. One is the fact that pragmatics, by itself, cannot explain or motivate its principles and maxims. The reasons that pragmaticians operate with, for example, a Cooperative Principle (with its attend four Maxims) cannot be found inside pragmatics; neither can such principles be deduced from the observation of pragmatic phenomena.

The other consideration is more complex. It has to do with the fact that the explanatory framework for the observed pragmatic facts cannot by definition be restricted to a single context. The world in which people live is one in which everything hangs together. None of the phenomena of daily or scientific life can be explained in isolation from the rest; neither can use of language. To take but one example: in pragmatics, not only are principles and rules specified, but those rules and principles are also commented on and interpreted from personal points of view. People make and break the rules—if they want, they can choose not to be polite, for example (this is called 'flouting the principle of politeness' by Grice), if circumstances are such that they think their aims and goals are better realized by not being polite. When someone says, for instance, *You did a great job, and I'm not being polite,* the latter half of the sentence is a metapragmatic statement.

More specifically, and on an even deeper level, metapragmatics should worry about the circumstances and conditions that allow people to use their language, or prevent them from using it (or using it adequately, as the case may be). An investigation into these conditions is necessary and timely, yet it cannot be dealt with on the level of the observed phenomena alone; which is technically why metapragmatics must be referred to for a discussion of such problems.

Some of the first approaches to metapragmatics were due not to linguists, but to philosophers of language such as Grice and Searle. They started reflecting on rules for linguistic usage that transcend the mere practical concerns of correctness that are used to characterize language in traditional linguistic thinking. When Searle, in his ground-breaking work on speech acts, followed Austin in positing certain conditions for the felicitous performance of a linguistic act, he was already deep into metapragmatics, even though it was not called that at the time. Similarly, the conditions postulated by Grice on successful communication (referred to above by the name of the 'Cooperative Principle') are of a metapragmatic nature, since they deal with the principles that control the pragmatic phenomena. Thus, an important part of metapragmatics deals with the pragmatic rules, principles, and maxims that have been formulated within pragmatics.

The question naturally arises whether those rules and principles are specific for any particular language, or if they can be formulated on a wider scale, so that it might be possible to speak of certain 'universal' principles; as examples, consider the Gricean maxims, or the principle of politeness, as formulated by Geoffrey Leech (1983). It seems unclear in what way such putative 'universals' should be formulated, if indeed they can be found, and how many such universal principles one should allow for. Also, with regard to speech acts, the question has been raised whether a speech act always, and necessarily, triggers (or is triggered by) a special lexical unit, mostly a verb, in order to be properly performed. The answer to this question seems to be in the negative, as witness the great variety among languages as far as speech act realization (usually in the form of verbs) is concerned.

Other metapragmatic questions concern the way in which pragmatics should be done, and what should properly be included in the field. These questions have barely begun to be raised, and in the early 1990s there no well-established pragmatic methodology (except for, perhaps, a certain consensus about what it should *not* be, viz., a return to the methods of classical linguistics). In any event, the problem is not one of linguistic theorizing alone: in many of the neighboring disciplines, such as anthropology, literary theory, philosophy of language, and so on, questions of the interpenetration of the various domains of human cultural endeavor have been fruitfully discussed.

The concern with the world as the final, and eventually decisive, context of all linguistic activity has given rise to the study of the societal conditions that govern this 'macrocontext.' In this connection, the all-important question is who the proper 'owners' of the language and whether there is such a thing as a right to speak, on analogy with, for instance, the right to vote, or the right to work? In other words, one may ask whether it makes sense to talk about a 'linguistic democracy,' as many have implicitly assumed, or whether human rights include conversation, as the Chilean author Jenaro Prieto once queried (see Ruíz Mayo 1989: 1009).

For a number of (especially Marx-inspired) linguists, the problem of the societal reasons behind linguistic inequality is one of the most important ones in pragmatics. In fact, it is the problem, according to these researchers (compare, for instance, Mey 1985, Mininni 1990), that metapragmatics should occupy itself with first and foremost; more is said on this in Sect. 4.

4. Societal Pragmatics

4.1 Linguistics and Society

The question of societal pragmatics is intimately connected with the relationship between linguistics as a 'pure' science and the practice of linguistics as applied to what people use their language for, to 'what they do with their words.' Traditionally, in linguistics this split reflects itself in the cleavage of the discipline into two major branches that do not seem to speak to each other: *theoretical* linguistics and *applied* linguistics.

Traditionally, too, the former kind of linguistics has carried all the prestige of a 'real' (some would say 'hard') science, whereas the latter was considered the soft underbelly of linguistics, prone to all sorts of outside and irrelevant, because 'extralinguistic,' kinds of influences.

It has been one of the hallmarks of pragmatics, ever since its inception as an independent field of study within linguistics, to want to do away with this split. Pragmatics admonishes the linguistic 'scientists' that they should take the users of language more seriously, as they, after all, provide the bread and butter of linguistic theorizing, and it tells the practical workers in the 'applied' fields of sociolinguistics, such as language teaching, remedial linguistics, and the like, that they need to integrate their practical endeavors toward a better use of language with a theory of language use. However, despite much goodwill, many efforts, and a generally propitious climate for such endeavors, the 'unification' of linguistics is not something that is easily achieved. Pragmatics will probably, for a long time to come, be considered by many linguists not so much a 'science' in its own right as an aspect (albeit a valuable one) of, and a complement (albeit a necessary one) to, traditional linguistics.

The *user* aspect has from the very beginning been the mainstay of pragmatics. Already in the very first mentions of the term (such as by Charles Morris (1938), following earlier work by Charles S. Peirce), the term 'pragmatics' is closely tied to the user of language; pragmatics is thus clearly distinguished from, even opposed to, both syntax and semantics, as isolated disciplines.

The users had not only to be discovered, however; they had to be positioned where they belonged, in their *societal context*, 'context' to be taken here not only as the developmental basis for their activity as language users, but as the main conditioning factor that made that activity possible. The question of how people acquire their language turned out to be more of a social than a developmental problem that could only be discussed in a strictly psychological environment (as had been hypothesized earlier). A societal window on language acquisition and language use was opened, and pragmaticists soon found themselves joining hands with sociologists and educationalists who had been working in these areas for many years.

The question naturally arises as to what distinguishes pragmatics from those neighboring disciplines (among which several others could have been mentioned). The answer is that pragmatics focuses on the user and his or her *conditions* of language use. By this is meant not only that the user is considered as being in the possession of certain language facilities (either innate, as some have postulated, or acquired, or a combination of both) which have to be developed through a process of individual growth and evolution, but, more specifically, that there are certain societal factors that influence the development and use of language, both in the acquisition stage and in usage itself.

Whereas earlier (according to mainstream, especially faculty psychology) the use of speech was said to develop only if it was stimulated during the so-called psychologically 'sensitive' period, it has become somewhat of a pragmatic tenet that such stimulation is social more than anything else. This entails that the social conditions for language use are 'built in,' so to say, to the very foundation of language acquisition and use; but also, that such conditions are difficult to detect and determine as to their exact effect: the results of linguistic development in very early life become only evident much later, when young people enter the first stages of their formal education by joining the school system.

It is therefore not surprising that some of the earliest research interests of a truly pragmatic nature concentrated precisely on the problems of school environment versus home environment. A positive correlation could be established between children's school performance and their social status; school achievement is in important respects dependent on the learner's earlier development in the home. White middle-class children, as a whole, could be shown to be significantly better school performers than their peers from lower strata of society, that is, from nonwhite and, in general, nonmainstream environments. (The name of Basil Bernstein is inextricably bound up with this important research, even though later workers came to have a more critical view of his conclusions; see below, Sect. 4.6.)

The case of the young person's school achievement is a good illustration of what pragmatics is really about, because it very clearly demonstrates why the pragmatic pattern of thinking originally met with such resistance, and why the earliest impulses to pragmatic research had to come from the outside, so to speak; from the ranks not of linguists, but of educationalists and sociologists. The core of the matter here is that the pragmatic determiners are nearly always totally hidden: one has to postulate them almost without any regard to initial plausibility. Social theory, at least as it was practiced until the mid-1960s, had no explanation to offer for its own statistical results. It was not until the hidden conditions of societal structure and domination were brought out into the open that certain pragmatic features could be identified as important for language use. One of the most crucial of these turned out to be the question of the 'ownership' of cultural goods, and how this ownership was administered through various patterns of 'hegemony' (a term originally due to the Italian Marxist theoretician and linguist Antonio Gramsci), in cultural as in other respects.

The following subsections deal with some of these hidden assumptions by playing some of the characteristic themes, all orchestrated as variations on the main theme: 'Whose language are we speaking, when we use "*our*" language?' (see Mey 1985).

4.2 Language in Education: A Privileged Matter

'Morals are for the rich,' Bertolt Brecht used to say, echoing an earlier saying by Georg Büchner (*Woyzeck*, 1838). With a slight variation on this dictum, it could be said that education is only for those who can afford it. Here, one must consider not only the prohibitively high costs of education in the so-called free enterprise system (at the beginning of the 1990s, tuition costs for US private universities ranged from $14,000 to over $20,000 a year; source: *Daily Northwesterner*, January 10, 1991), but also the affordances having to do with coming from the right social background. The same classes that have established the institutions of higher education have also been material in structuring that education and organizing their curricula; and here one is faced with a self-perpetuating, coopting system that favors those who are most similar to itself—*par nobis*, as the expression used to be.

One of the requirements for those who aspire to participate in any college or university program is to pass the appropriate tests. Characteristically, these tests are geared to the values of the white, middle-class, male-dominated segments of society; minority students typically do less well on these tests, as is the case with foreigners too. It is not uncommon to observe a foreign student who performs relatively well on the mathematical parts of the GRE (the 'Graduate Record Examination,' a prerequisite to entering graduate school), but who almost fails the verbal part; this alone should induce a healthy skepticism toward the value of such testing as a whole, and draw attention to the part that language plays in devising and administering the test.

At stake here is, among other things, what many educational researchers have dubbed the 'hidden curriculum.' Schools are not only supposed to mediate a professional subject matter through their teaching; equally important are the attitudes and beliefs that are fostered and reinforced through the educational institutions. If one asks what these attitudes are about, one has to go back once more to the question of societal *power*, raised earlier: the prevalent attitudes reflect the attitudes of the powerful segments of society, and are (implicitly or explicitly) geared toward perpetuating the possession of that power among the ruling classes.

This means, with respect to language, that those people who are able to decide what language can be deemed acceptable, which uses of language should be furthered and encouraged, and which demoted and discouraged, are in a position of power and hence can control the future of whole segments of the population by controlling their actual language behavior.

The classic case of this linguistic *oppression* (as it is called) is that of 'low' versus 'high' prestige dialects of one and the same language, or that of 'pidgin' versus 'standard' languages, where pidgins are considered to be mere deteriorated variants of some higher entity called 'the' language. Gross cases of oppressive linguistic behavior control include the total or partial criminalization of local or vernacular idioms, as in the case of the 'Basque stick' (a punitive device used in the schools of the Basque lands, by which pupils were forced to carry a stick on their outstretched arms as punishment for having used a Basque word or expression, to be relieved only by the next sinner in line; cf. Mey 1985: 27).

In a more profound sense, the question can be asked 'whose language' is the controlling norm and guideline for people's linguistic behavior. This question boils down to asking whose behavior is to be the standard of language use, and what aims such a use should set for itself. Such questions can be answered by referring back to Brecht, as quoted at the beginning of this section. If morals are indeed for the rich, moral behavior is something that one should be able to afford (but as a rule cannot). However, by appealing to some universally valid laws of justice and equity (which are strictly valid only under idealized circumstances, in a so-called perfect but nowhere existing society of the Utopian kind), the rich are allowed to get away with corruption and embezzlement, while the sheep thief and the poacher are strung up: 'One man can steal a horse and another cannot look over the fence' (cf. Brecht and Dudov 1932).

What is happening here is not only oppression, as defined above; it might also be called linguistic *repression*: a term covering the subtle but ever so pernicious form of social control through language, as characterized above (see further Mey 1985: 26; the distinction between 'oppression' and 'suppression' is originally due to Pateman 1980). The concept of repression plays an important role in defining and describing some pragmatic paradoxes that arise in late twentieth-century pedagogical thinking: either the student is considered to be a completely passive receptacle for the ideas and knowledge to be imparted by the teacher—the 'banking' concept, as Freire has aptly called it (e.g., Freire 1973; Freire and Macedo 1987: xvi)—or the students are supposed to be in the possession of exactly those qualifications, as prerequisites to learning, that the teaching is supposed to imbue them with. In either case, the under privileged student is doomed to come out a loser: either he/she enters the 'rat race' on the ruling classes' premises (and obtains the privilege of membership in the rat club), or he/she never makes it in society, owing to an underprivileged start in life.

4.3 Other Social Contexts

Even though the educational system is perhaps the most obvious instance of the unequal distribution of social privilege, as it reflects itself in and is perpetuated through language, it is by no means the only one. Among the cases of linguistic repression that have attracted most attention are the language of the media and the medical interview. In both these cases, hidden presuppositions of the same kind as the ones characterized above are to be found.

The French sociolinguist Michèle Lacoste has, in a thoughtful study (Lacoste 1981), drawn attention to the fact that the doctor–patient interview, despite its obvious usefulness and even necessity, sins gravely by way of linguistic repression. What the physician allows the patient to tell him or her, is not what the patient wants to tell, or is able to tell, but rather, what in the institutionalized 'discourse' of the doctor–patient relationship is *pragmatically* possible. That is to say, the pragmatic presuppositions that govern the use of language in this particular case are those that are defined by the social institution of the interview in which the interaction between doctor and patient takes place.

For the patient, talking in this way has nothing to do with expressing oneself or manifesting one's problems; it is more akin to filling out a form with preset categories of questions and answers, or to submitting oneself to a 'multiple choice' type of examination.

In Lacoste's case, an elderly lady is complaining to her doctor about pains in her spleen. However, the doctor denies this, and instead locates the pains in the lady's stomach. When the patient repeatedly and rather indignantly rejects this suggestion on the grounds that it is *her* body, and that she, if anyone, must be familiar with her own pains, the doctor cuts her off abruptly by saying that she does not even know what a spleen is, even less where it is located in the body.

This example shows two things: for one, the mere knowledge of a linguistic expression in medical terminology (such as 'spleen') and the ability to use it correctly are worth nothing, if the pragmatic preconditions for such a use are not met. The old lady's voice is not heard because she does not possess the necessary societal standing and clout to make herself understood. This observation is valid also in other connections, such as the tests mentioned in Sect. 4.2, where verbal abilities are gauged in situations of unequal social power; all such cases bear clear testimony to the importance of the *hidden conditions* that determine the use of language and that steer its users.

The other point to be made in this connection is that the linguistic repression which is taking place has some very dangerous side-effects. The powerlessness of the repressed can easily turn into self-incrimination (by which the powerless attribute their lack of societal value to factors such as fate, God's will, their predestined stance in society ('Know your place'), their own lack of capability and potential, and so on), or else result in resignation, as happens in the case of the old lady, who ends up saying: 'Whatever you say, doctor'—thereby possibly exposing herself to the risk of a faulty diagnosis, with all its concomitant dangers both to herself (as a patient) and to the physician (as the potential target of a malpractice suit). Clearly, what is needed here is some form of technique or strategy aimed at providing appropriate aid to the societally and linguistically repressed; more on this in Sect. 4.6.

Summing up, then, the case of the medical interview is a clear example of institutionalized discourse in which the value of the individual's linguistic expression is measured strictly by the place that he or she has in the system. Only utterances which meet the criteria of the official discourse are allowed, and indeed registered; others are either rejected or construed as symptoms of (physical or mental) illness, lack of knowledge or even intelligence, and in general of dependent or inferior status. Erving Goffman remarks, much to the point (his observation has primarily to do with mental institutions, but applies to all sorts of institutional discourses):

> Mental patients can find themselves in a special bind. To get out of the hospital, or to ease their life within it, they must show acceptance of the place accorded them, and the place accorded them is to support the occupational role of those who appear to force this bargain.
>
> (Goffman 1961: 386)

4.4 Language and Manipulation

Goffman's 'special bind' is a particularly clear case of what can be called *manipulation*, understood as making people behave in a certain way without their knowing why, and perhaps even against their best interests and wishes. Most often, the instrument of manipulation is language— hence the notions of linguistic manipulation and *manipulatory language*. The latter can be defined as the successful hiding (also called 'veiling'; see Mey 1985) of societal oppression by means of language.

A case in point is the professional manipulation in psychiatric environments of schizophrenic patients' speech ('schizophrenese'; see Sect. 2.3.2) and its classification as a 'nonlanguage,' that is, a symptom (so-called 'schizophasia') rather than a means of communication. To see this, consider the following two analogical cases.

Suppose that a political prisoner complains to his legal counsel about his letters being opened. Such a complaint makes sense in the context; the prisoner may not be successful in stopping the guards' practice of letter-opening, but his utterance *They are opening my mail* is at least taken seriously.

Not so with the psychiatric patient. The same utterance, in a psychiatric institutional context, is registered as a schizophrenic symptom, proving that the person who utters the sentence is duly and properly a resident of the State Hospital. The patient, by complaining about his or her letters being opened, has furnished conclusive proof of the fact that he or she is not normal, hence has no right to complain. So, ironically, and in accordance with Goffman's observation quoted above, the only correct way of complaining is not to complain; which of course is sheer

madness, and proves the point of the patient's being committed.

But it is not necessary to go as far as the psychiatric institutions to find examples of linguistic manipulation. Consider the following. Suppose I am looking for a job. I tell myself that I must make a good impression on my potential future employer; I put on my best suit and tie, and go to the interview in the hope that he will 'give me the job.' Now, I may not be so lucky: the employer may tell me that the job has been 'taken'; somebody else 'got it.' That means they 'have no work' for me, and so on and so forth. In this linguistic universe, employers give, and employees take: viz., jobs. Such is our language.

In real life, however, totally different picture emerges: it is the employer who takes the employee's labor and converts it to his own profit. The employee gives his or her labor power to the employer, in exchange for a salary offered; but there is one big catch: the wages, although they are called 'fair' and are arrived at in 'free' negotiation, represent a form of societal oppression: the employer knows that he must make the employee accept less than the value of his or her labor, or else there would not be any profits. The wages are not the equivalent of a certain amount of work: rather, they represent a period of time during which the employer is entitled to press all the labor out of the employee that he possibly can. Wages express the market relation between labor power as a commodity, and whatever else is bought and sold in the marketplace; hence the wages can be called 'fair' only in the sense that they reproduce the market laws, and not by their equitable representation of a certain amount of work.

In this case, too, the language that people use hides the real state of affairs: and thus people can be manipulated into doing whatever the powerful in society (such as employers and doctors) tell them to do. This is what the case of the medical/psychiatric consultation and the job interview have in common.

Somebody might object and say that the worker is not *obliged* to take the employment: an employee is a free agent, and can refuse the employer's offer, and also give notice at any time. However, the very expression of this idea is again a case of manipulatory language use: since a linguistic relation exists between the two nouns, *employer* and *employee*, being respectively active and passive, one is led to believe that the relation between the two 'bearers' of those names is equally symmetrical: the employer is at one end of the employment relation, the employee at the other; but basically it is the same relationship, only in inverse directions. The employer employs the employee, the employee is employed by the employer. Even the language shows us that this is a fair, symmetrical deal.

However, what the language does *not* tell, and this is the catch, is which of the two is the powerful one in the relationship. The employer is the one who has the sole right to employ or not to employ. Conversely, for the employee there is no right to *be* employed; which shows where the true power in this situation lies, despite the superficial linguistic symmetry of the employment relation and its manipulatory potential.

4.5 Wording the World

Much attention has been paid by researchers to language as a means of 'seeing' the world. In well-known studies, Lakoff and Johnson (1980) and Lakoff (1987) have investigated the importance of metaphor as one way of realizing this 'wording.'

Metaphorical wording is different from the classical, referential view of language according to which words are thought of as 'labeling' things in the 'real' world. Metaphors express a way of conceptualizing, of seeing and understanding one's surroundings; in other words, metaphors contribute to one's *mental* model of the world. Because the metaphors of a language community remain more or less stable across historical stages and dialectal differences, they are of prime importance in securing the continuity, and continued understanding, of language and culture among people.

While one may disagree with some aspects of this view of metaphor, it is certain that understanding the common, metaphorical use of language is essential for an understanding of how people communicate, despite differences in class, culture, and religion, across geographical distances and even across languages. The study of metaphors may thus be one of the keys to solving problems in foreign language understanding and acquisition.

However, the view of metaphor as the only way to understand human cognitive capability is too restrictive. True, metaphors are ways of wording the world. But this wording, in order to obtain the true pragmatic significance that it is usually assigned, should include and respect its own context, because after all, the contexts of people's lives determine what metaphors are available and what their wordings are going to be. An uncritical understanding of metaphor, especially as manifested in a purely descriptive way of dealing with the issue ('Look and describe, but ask no questions') is not only wrong, but downright dangerous from a pragmatic point of view (Mey 1985: 223). And even if our metaphors cannot provide all the answers, pragmatic questions still have to be asked. As an illustration, consider the following.

Lakoff and Johnson routinely assign the female human person to the metaphorical 'low' position, whereas the corresponding 'high' is taken up by the male; this happens about 10 times in the course of one and a half pages (1980: 15–16). Clearly, some explanation has to be found for this curious phenomenon, and it seems reasonable to assume that the authors' particular wording (that is, their choice of metaphors) has a lot to do with the way in which society is structured: men on top, women at the bottom of the 'power pyramid.'

The point here is not to move directly from one 'universe' to another (viz., from the universe of power to the universe of language), but to understand that the way we in which people *see* the world is dependent on the way in which they metaphorically *structure* the world, and that, vice versa, the way in which people see the world as a coherent, metaphorical structure helps them to deal with the world. Put in another way, metaphors are not only ways of solving problems: they may be, and in a deeper sense, ways of *setting* the problems. As Schön remarks, in an important earlier study,

> When we examine the problem-setting stories told by the analysts and practitioners of social policy, it becomes apparent that the framing of problems often depends upon metaphors underlying the stories which generate problem setting and set the directions of problem solving.
> (1979: 255)

There is, in other words, a dialectic movement that goes from word to world and from world to word. Neither movement is prior to the other, logically; ontologically, both movements arise at the same time in the history of human development. In particular, as regards the individual human's development, the child, in acquiring language, is exposed to 'worlding' at the same time as it begins its wording process; one cannot postulate any general, ontological priority of the world as entailing an epistemological or linguistic priority. As Franck and Treichler remark,

> [it can be] argue[d] that language constructs as well as reflects culture. Language thus no longer serves as the transparent vehicle of content or as the simple reflection of reality but itself participates in how that content and reality are formed, apprehended, expressed, and transformed.
> (1989: 3)

In order to determine what a particular wording is worth, therefore, one has to investigate the conditions of use that are prevalent in the context of the wording. As to metaphors, the question needs to be asked what kind of 'seeing' a metaphor represents, and in what way this 'seeing' affects one's thinking or determines a particular mind-set (for which it was developed in the first place, in all likelihood).

The consequences of this view of wording are that one cannot understand one's interlocutors unless one has a good grasp of their word-and-world context (which includes, but is not limited to, metaphoring). That is, in order to understand another person's wording, the language user has to participate in his or her contexts, to word the world with him or her. Thus, the pragmatic view of language (and, in general, of all societal activity; cf. the quote from Schön (1979) above) demands a 'sympathetic' understanding, as a practice of 'co-wording,' in solidarity with the context.

To understand an utterance, the language user would ideally have to be able to say it her/himself, in the context of her/his conversational partners—which, after all, is not more than is generally expected of interlocutors in any good conversation. Language-in-use (and in particular, the use of metaphor) is therefore at the same time a necessary instrument of cognition and the expression of that cognition itself: it is a user's language, a user's pragmatic precondition to understanding their context, and to being understood in and through that context (which includes other language users).

4.6 Pragmatics and the Social Struggle

The growing interest in pragmatics as a user-oriented science of language naturally leads to the question of the sense in which pragmatics is *useful* to the users. In particular, given the fact that a sizable portion of the users of any language are 'underprivileged' in their relation to language, and are so, on a deeper level, because of their underprivileged position in society, it seems only reasonable to assume that an insight into the causes of societal underprivilege could trigger a renewed insight into the role of language in social processes, and that, vice versa, a renewed consciousness of language use as the expression of social inequalities could result in what is often called an 'emancipatory' language use.

The first efforts at establishing 'remedial' programs of language training date back to the 1960s, when the so-called 'Head Start' programs endeavored to give underprivileged children from US urban ghettos a chance to keep up with their white, suburban peers by teaching them the extra skills (in particular, language capabilities) that they needed to follow the regular curriculum. The results of these programs, if there were any, usually did not last, because they concentrated on the pure transfer of skills, without any connection to the contexts in which these skills were going to be used, or to the real reasons for the lack of culture and educational privilege: the societal context of the children in question.

The insights that resulted from Basil Bernstein's (1971–90) work with underprivileged children came to serve as guidelines for much of western (European) sociolinguistic and pragmatically inspired research in the 1970s. The terminology that Bernstein developed (in particular, his distinction between an 'elaborated' and a 'restricted' code) was, for a decade or so, dominant in the discourse of emancipatory linguistics.

Briefly, according to Bernstein, lower-class children, by virtue of their social origin, do not have access to the 'elaborated' linguistic code that is used in schoolteaching. These children, being native speakers of a 'restricted' code, cannot identify with the school language (which simply is not theirs); therefore, their school achievements stay significantly below those of the other children, who are dealing with the school's 'elaborated' code as a matter of course, since they have been exposed to that code all their lives.

For all its good intentions, Bernstein's solutions to the problem of selective, deficient school instruction did not yield the desired results. For one thing, he focused exclusively on the formal (morphological, syntactic, etc.) aspects of the 'codes,' rather than on matters of content and how that content was transmitted. Also, he did not pay explicit attention to the societal background of his codes, except as descriptive scaffolding and motivational support. But on the whole, and from a general sociolinguistic standpoint, one can safely say that Bernstein's notion of the societal context, especially as this concept is manifested in his theory of social stratification, despite all its weaknesses, was significantly more relevant than the class analyses practiced by the majority of his contemporary American and earlier European colleagues (such 'analyses' mainly consisted in setting up levels of social standing depending on how much money people made, or how often they went to the theater or concert hall, and so on).

The question now is whether, in the face of these failed efforts to apply the findings of linguistics to the problems of society, there can be any hopes of practicing pragmatics in the sense of what is so hopefully called 'emancipatory' linguistics.

The answer to that question, of course, depends to a great extent on what is understood by 'emancipation.' If that concept is understood as the elimination of social injustice, as getting rid of the 'bonds' that are inherent in the very word 'emancipation,' then language is not the tool to use. However, if the focus is placed on the *consciousness* of the bondage that is instrumental in creating and maintaining the divisions in society, between haves and have-nots, between rich and poor, between male and female, young and old, and so on, then there are rich opportunities for pragmatic linguists to step into the fray and contribute positively to the outcome of the social struggles. The way to do this is for linguists to stay linguists, while orienting themselves toward the pragmatic aspects of their science, that is, focusing on the users. The question is thus simply how a 'raised-consciousness' linguistics can contribute to making the users more aware of the language they are using, and in particular, how it can make the underprivileged users 'transcend' the boundaries of their underprivileged ('restricted') use without having them buy into the myths and fantasies of the privileged classes; and vice versa, how the privileged users' consciousness can be raised, so that they no longer consider the privileges of their position as natural and uncontroversial, societally speaking.

Some of the best illustrations of the potential of this (admittedly modest) approach are the results that have been obtained in the 'linguistic war against sexism' that has been going on since at least the 1960s. Of course, the mere substitution of a combined pronoun such as *he/she* for the supposedly 'generic' *he* (understood as the assertion of '[t]raditional grammars ... that the word *man* functions ... to encompass human beings of both sexes'; Frank and Treichler 1989: 3) does not, in and by itself, change anything in the conditions of society that underprivilege its female members. But if it is true, as McConnell-Ginet says (1989), that 'earlier feminist research has established that *he*, no matter what its user intends, is not unproblematically interpreted as generic, and the consequent shift in the community's beliefs about how *he* is interpreted has influenced what one can intend the pronoun to convey,' then it is also permissible to use this example as one of the areas in which emancipatory linguistics has actually been successful, albeit to a modest degree, that is, by establishing a whole new code for the use of pronouns in English—pronouns that reflect the growing consciousness of women's presence in society, but that at the same time, and with apparent success, change the ways in which society's members (both female and male) speak, write, and think about women, treat women, and interact with women. As examples, compare the growing number of journals that subscribe to guidelines for 'nonsexist' use of language promulgated and adopted by various scientific societies and journals (such as the American Psychological Association, the Modern Language Association of America, the Linguistic Society of America, and their respective journals, the *Journal of Pragmatics*, and so on).

Language, in McConnell-Ginet's words, 'matters so much precisely because so little matter is attached to it; meanings are not given but must be produced and reproduced, negotiated in situated contexts of communication (1989: 49),' that is, between the users of language themselves in their social and communicative relations, in people's *pragmatic* interaction in and through *linguistic* structures.

Bibliography

Austin J L 1962 *How to Do Things with Words*. Clarendon, Oxford

Bar-Hillel Y 1971 Out of the pragmatic waste-basket. *Lln* **2(3)**: 401–07

Bernstein B 1971–90 *Class, Codes and Control*, 4 vols. Routledge and Kegan Paul, London

Brecht B, Dudov Z 1932 *Kühle Wampe, oder: Wem gehört die Welt?* Präsensfilm, Berlin

Bühler K 1934 *Sprachtheorie*. Fischer, Jena

Chomsky N 1957 *Syntactic Structures*. Mouton, The Hague

Chomsky N 1965 *Aspects of the Theory of Syntax*. MIT Press, Cambridge, MA

Foucault M 1969 *L'archéologie du savoir*. Gallimard, Paris

Frank F W, Treichler P A (eds.) 1989 *Language, Gender, and Professional Writing: Theoretical Approaches and Guidelines for Nonsexist Usage*. The Modern Language Association of America, Commission on the Status of Women in the Profession, New York

Freire P 1973 *Pedagogy of the Oppressed*. Seabury Press, New York

Freire P, Macedo D 1987 *Literacy: Reading the Word and the World*. Routledge and Kegan Paul, London

Goffman E 1961 *Asylums*. Doubleday, Garden City, NY

Gramsci A 1971 *Prison Notebooks*. Lawrence and Wishart, London

Grice H P 1975 Logic and conversation. In: Cole P, Morgan J L (eds.) *Syntax and Semantics. Vol. 3: Speech Acts*. Academic Press, New York

Haberland H, Mey J L 1977 Editorial: Linguistics and pragmatics. *J Prag* **1(1)**: 1–16

Jakobson R 1960 Closing statement: Linguistics and poetics. In: Sebeok T A (ed.) *Style in Language*. MIT Press, Cambridge, MA

Katz J J 1977 *Propositional Structure and Illocutionary Force*. Harvester Press, Hassocks

Kuhn T S 1962 *The Structure of Scientific Revolutions*. University of Chicago Press, Chicago, IL

Labov W 1966 *The Social Stratification of English in New York City*. Center for Applied Linguistics, Washington, DC

Lacoste M 1981 The old lady and the doctor. *J Prag* **5(2)**: 169–80

Lakoff G 1971a On generative semantics. In: Steinberg D D, Jakobovits L A (eds.) *Semantics: An Interdisciplinary Reader in Philosophy, Linguistics, and Psychology*. Cambridge University Press, Cambridge

Lakoff G 1971b Presupposition and relative well-formedness. In: Steinberg D D, Jakobovits L A (eds.) *Semantics: An Interdisciplinary Reader in Philosophy, Linguistics, and Psychology*. Cambridge University Press, Cambridge

Lakoff G 1987 *Women, Fire, and Dangerous Things: What Categories Reveal about the Mind*. University of Chicago Press, Chicago, IL

Lakoff G, Johnson M 1980 *Metaphors We Live By*. University of Chicago Press, Chicago, IL

Lakoff R 1989 The way we were; or, The real truth about generative semantics: A memoir. *J Prag* **13(6)**: 939–88

Leech G N 1983 *Principles of Pragmatics*. Longman, London

Levinson S C 1983 *Pragmatics*. Cambridge University Press, Cambridge

Lyons J 1968 *Introduction to Theoretical Linguistics*. Cambridge University Press, Cambridge

McConnell-Ginet S 1989 The sexual (re)production of meaning: A discourse-based theory. In: Frank and Treichler (eds.) 1989

Mey J L 1985 *Whose Language? A Study in Linguistic Pragmatics*. John Benjamins, Amsterdam

Mey J L 1989 The end of the Copper Age, or: Pragmatics 12 $\frac{1}{2}$ years after. *J Prag* **13(6)**: 825–32

Mey J L 1992 Metaphors and solutions: Towards an ecology of metaphor

Mey J L, Talbot M 1988 Computation and the soul. *Semiotica* **72**: 291–339

Mininni G 1990 'Common Speech' as a pragmatic form of socia reproduction. *J Prag* **14(1)**: 125–35

Morris C H 1938 *Foundations of the Theory of Signs* (original monograph). Reprinted 1969 in: Neurath O, Carnap R, Morris C (eds.) *Foundations of the Unity of Science Towards an International Encyclopedia of Unified Science*, vol. 1. University of Chicago Press, Chicago, IL

Östman J O 1988 Adaptation, variability and effect: Comments on IPrA Working Documents 1 and 2. In: *Working Document* no. 3. International Pragmatics Association, Antwerp

Pateman T 1980 *Language, Truth and Politics*. Stroud, Lewes

Ruíz Mayo J 1989 Rumor's Delict (Delight?), or: The pragmatics of a civil liberty. *J Prag* **13(6)**: 1009–12, 1034

Sacks H, Schegloff E A, Jefferson G 1974 A simplest systematics for the organization of turn-taking in conversation. *Lg* **50(4)**: 696–735

Schank R C, Edelson D 1990 A role for AI in education: Using technology to reshape education. *The Journal of Artificial Intelligence in Education* **1(2)**: 3–20

Schön D A 1979 Generative metaphor: A perspective on problem-setting in social policy. In: Ortony A (ed.) *Metaphor and Thought*. Cambridge University Press, Cambridge

Searle J R 1969 *Speech Acts: An Essay in the Philosophy of Language*. Cambridge University Press, London

Stalpers J 1993 *Progress in Discourse: The Impact of Foreign Language Use on Business Talk*. (PhD thesis, Tilburg University)

Verschueren J 1987 Pragmatics as a theory of linguistic adaptation. In: *Working Document* no. 1. International Pragmatics Association, Antwerp

Watzlawick P, Beavin J H, Jackson D D 1968 *Pragmatics of Human Communication*. Faber, London

Wunderlich D 1970 Die Rolle der Pragmatik in der Linguistik. *Der Deutschunterricht* **22(4)**: 5–41

Presupposition, Pragmatic
C. Caffi

Both concepts, 'pragmatic' and 'presupposition,' can be interpreted in different ways. Not being very remote from the intuitive, pretheoretical concept of presupposition as 'background assumption,' presupposition covers a wide range of heterogeneous phenomena. Because of the principle of communicative economy, balanced by the principle of clarity (Horn 1984), in discourse much is left unsaid or taken for granted.

In order to clarify the concept of presupposition, some authors have compared speech with a *Gestalt* picture, in which it is possible to distinguish a ground and a figure. Presuppositions are the ground; what is actually said is the figure. As in a *Gestalt* picture, ground and figure are simultaneous in speech; unlike the two possible representations in the *Gestalt* picture, speech ground and figure have a different status, for instance with respect to the possibilities of refutation. What is said, i.e., the figure, is open to objection; what is assumed, i.e., the ground, is 'shielded from challenge' (Givón 1982: 101). What restricts the analogy is the fact that discourse is a dynamic process; the picture is not. So, there is a level of implicit communication. When communicating, one is constantly asked to choose what to put in the foreground and what in the background. Discourses and texts are therefore multilevel constructions. Presuppositions represent at least a part of the unsaid.

The label 'pragmatic' can be used in different ways: it may refer to a number of objects of study or to a number of methods of analysis, linked by the fact that they take elements of the actual context into account.

The origin of the concept of pragmatic presupposition lies in the recognition by philosophers of language and logicians that there are *implicata* of utterances which do not belong to the set of truth conditions. The starting point is their awareness that there are other relations between utterances besides that of entailment.

Definitions of pragmatic presupposition proposed in the 1970s have brought about a pragmatic re-reading of a problem which was above all logical and which had not found adequate explanation in the available semantic theories. This re-reading was basically methodological.

Since Stalnaker's definition (1970), a pragmatic presupposition has no longer been considered a relation between utterances, but rather between a speaker and a proposition. This is a good starting point, but it is far from satisfactory if the label 'pragmatic' is meant to cover more than 'semantic and idealized contextual features,' i.e., if one adopts a radical pragmatic standpoint.

A pragmatic presupposition might be provisionally defined as a 'ménage à trois' between a speaker, the framework of his/her utterance, and an addressee. From a radical pragmatic standpoint, a substantivist view of presuppositions—what the presupposition of an utterance is—seems to be less promising than a functional, dynamic, interactional, contractual–negotiating view of how the presuppositional phenomena work in the communicative exchange. The pragmatic presupposition can be considered as an agreement between speakers. In this vein, Ducrot proposed a juridical definition, whereby the basic function of presuppositions is to 'establish a frame for further discourse' (1972: 94; trans. Caffi). Presuppositions are based on a mutual, tacit agreement which has not been given before, but which is constantly renewed or revoked during interaction. Presuppositions are grounded on complicity.

After having been the focus of lively discussions on the part of linguists and philosophers of language during the 1970s, presuppositions seemed to have gone out of fashion by the 1990s, and to have maintained their vitality only in the thin air of certain circles, such as generative grammar, far removed from pragmatic concerns. This decline is justified only insofar as more subtle distinctions between different phenomena are suggested, and a descriptively adequate typology of *implicata* is built. It is less justified if the substitution is only terminological, that is, if the concept of presupposition is replaced by a general concept such as implicature or inference without any increase in explanatory power. In the latter case, it is not clear what advantages might result from the replacement of the cover term 'presupposition.' The question is whether the term 'presupposition' refers to a range of heterogeneous phenomena or to a particular type of *implicatum* to which other types can be added.

But even before that, it should be asked whether, between the more credited semantic presupposition and the more recent notion of implicature, there is room for pragmatic presupposition. Before answering this question, the problem of the distinction of the latter from the two mentioned types of adjacent *implicata*, semantic presupposition and implicature, must be addressed briefly.

1. Relation with Semantic Presupposition

The concept of semantic presupposition is relatively clear. Its parentage is accredited: Frege, Russell, Strawson. Its lineage seems to be traceable back to Xenophanes, quoted in Aristotle's *Rhetoric*, via Port-Royal and John Stuart Mill. There is a substantial agreement about its definition: the presupposition of a sentence is what remains valid even if the sentence is negated; its truth is a necessary condition for a declarative sentence to have a truth value or to be used in order to make a statement. A respectable test has been devised to identify it—the negation test. There is a list of the linguistic facts (Levinson 1983: 181–85) which trigger the phenomenon of presupposition: 31 have been listed, from factive verbs (e.g., *know*, *regret*) to change-of-state verbs (e.g., *stop*, *arrive*), to cleft sentences, etc. Semantic presuppositions and conventional implicatures identified by Grice (1975), who exemplifies them with *therefore*, have much in common; both depend on a surface linguistic element which releases the presupposition.

The difference between semantic presuppositions and conventional implicatures is that the latter, unlike the former, are irrelevant to truth conditions.

Unlike semantic presuppositions and some conventional implicatures, pragmatic presuppositions are not directly linked to the lexicon, to the syntax, or to prosodic facts (cf. the contrastive accent in 'MARY has come'), but to the utterance act.

Types of *implicata* recorded by dictionaries and which are part of the semantic representation of a lexeme or are conveyed by given syntactic or prosodic structures, should be distinguished from *implicata* that are independent of both dictionary and grammar. Pragmatic presuppositions are triggered by the utterance and speech act; they are neither the presuppositions of a lexeme, of a proposition, nor of a sentence. They are presuppositions that a speaker activates through the utterance, the speech act, and the conversational or textual move which that speech act performs. Thus, pragmatic presuppositions do not concern imperative sentences but orders, not declarative sentences but assertions, and so on. In other words, one ought to stress the distinction between syntactic moods and pragmatic functions, where there is no one-to-one correspondence: the same linguistic structure, the same utterance can perform different functions, convey different speech acts and different sets of presuppositions. The acknowledgment of a further theoretical level is the sine qua non for the analysis of pragmatic presuppositions. Pragmatic presuppositions are related to knowledge which is not grammatical but encyclopedic, i.e., concerns our being in the world. Rather, they do not consist in knowledge, in something which is already known, but in something that is *given as such* by the speaker, in something that is *assumed as such* and is therefore *considered irrefutable* (Van der Auwera 1979).

Once the semantic nature of lexical and grammatical (syntactic and prosodic) presuppositions has been recognized, the connection between semantic and pragmatic presuppositions should be stressed. First, the connection is of a general nature and concerns the obvious (but not to be neglected) fact that, when not dealing with an abstraction but with a real utterance, the phenomenon of semantic presuppositions becomes one of the available means by which the speaker can change the communicative situation. If the link between, for instance, a certain lexeme and the presupposition which is triggered by it is semantic, the latter's analysis within an utterance and a context must face the pragmatic problem of their use and effects.

Second, at a closer distance, the connection regards the specific pragmatic functions performed by phenomena which can be labeled as semantic presuppositions. For instance, it is important to recognize the effectiveness of semantic *implicata* (lexical presuppositions, conventional implicatures, presuppositions linked to syntactic constructions such as cleft sentences, etc.) both in the construction of texts and in the pragmatic strategies of manipulation of beliefs, or, to use Halliday's categories, both in the textual function and in the interpersonal one. On the one hand, the analysis of the different types and functioning of anaphora whose antecedent is not what the preceding text has stated, but what it has presupposed, has both textual and pragmatic relevance. On the other hand, precisely because it is shielded from challenge, communication via presuppositions lends itself to manipulation: suffice it to compare the different persuasive effectiveness of the choice of an assertion embedded in a factive verb versus a simple assertion (e.g., 'People know that solar energy is wishful thinking' versus 'Solar energy is wishful thinking').

Having defined the semantic nature of different types of presuppositional triggers, one should then recognize the role of pragmatics in the study of the production and interpretation of these potentially highly manipulatory *implicata*. Obviously, it is more difficult to question something that is communicated only implicitly rather than something which is communicated openly, if only because what is implicit must be recognized before being attacked. This is proved by the highly polemical and aggressive value underlying any attack to presuppositions; such an attack is seriously face-threatening.

2. Relation with Conversational Implicature

The criteria put forward by Grice for distinguishing conversational implicature from other *implicata* (i.e., calculability, nondetachability, nonconventionality, indeterminacy, cancelability) have not proved entirely satisfactory, even when integrated with the further criterion of 'reinforceability' (Horn 1991). The criterion of cancelability, viewed as crucial by many authors, seems to be problematic (for a discussion, see Levinson 1983). And in any case, cancelability is linked to the degree of formality of the interaction; in unplanned speech it is easily tolerated.

If satisfied with an intuitive differentiation that nevertheless uses these criteria, it can be reasonably maintained that pragmatic presuppositions are oriented, retroactively, toward a background of beliefs, given as shared. Implicatures, on the other hand, are oriented, proactively, toward knowledge yet to be built. Besides (at least if as a prototypical case one thinks of the particularized conversational implicature, i.e., according to Grice, the kind of implicature strictly dependent on the actual context), such knowledge has not necessarily to be valid beyond the real communicative situation. Thus, in order to distinguish the two types of *implicata*, the criteria of the different conventionality (presuppositions being more conventional than implicatures) and of the different validity (more general in the case of pre-

suppositions, more contingent in the case of implicatures) are called into play. Presuppositions concern beliefs constituting the background of communication. They become the object of communication, thus losing the status of presupposition, only if something goes wrong; that is, if the addressee does not accept them or questions them, forcing the speaker to put his/her cards on the table. Implicatures, on the contrary, concern a 'knowledge' which is not yet shared and which will become shared only if the addressee goes through the correct inferences, while interpreting the speaker's communicative intention. It is thus more a matter of degree than a dichotomy: the latter, more than the former, requiring the addressee to abandon his/her laziness—the 'principle of inertia' as Van der Auwera (1979) has called it, or the speaker's reliance on shared beliefs—and to cooperate creatively with the discourse. With implicatures, a higher degree of cooperation and involvement is asked of the addressee (the more I am emotionally involved, the more I am willing to carry out inferential work; see Arndt and Janney 1987).

Presuppositions can remain in the background of communication and even remain unconsidered by the addressee without the communication suffering. Implicatures must be calculated for communication to proceed in the direction desired by the speaker. The role of presuppositions and implicatures as against the speaker's expectations and the discourse design is therefore different; the former are oriented toward the already constructed (or given as such); the latter toward the yet to be constructed, or rather toward the 'construction in progress'; the former concern a set of assumptions; the latter their updating.

Presuppositions are more closely linked to what is actually said, to the surface structure of the utterance; implicatures are more closely linked to what is actually meant. Their degree of cancelability also seems to be different: presuppositions are less cancelable than implicatures. The difference between presuppositions and implicatures with respect to the criterion of cancelability could be reformulated in terms of utterance responsibilities and commitment. With presuppositions and implicatures, the speaker is committed to different degrees—more with the former, less with the latter—with respect to his/her own *implicata*. Thus, a possible definition of pragmatic presuppositions is: that which the hearer is entitled to believe on the basis of our words. In the case of presuppositions, the commitment implicitly undertaken is stronger, and stronger too is the sanction where the presupposition should prove to be groundless. And the reason is that, in the case of presuppositions, an attempt to perform a given speech act, however implicit, has been made; the linguistic devices, however indirect, have traced out a detectable direction. The addressee is authorized to believe that the speaker's speech act was founded, i.e., that his/her own presuppositions were satisfied. A character in Schnitzler's *Spiel im Morgengrauen* implacably says to the second lieutenant, who has lost a huge amount of money playing cards with him and does not know how to pay him back, 'Since you sat down at the card-table, you must obviously have been ready to lose.' Communicating is somehow like sitting at the card-table: presuppositions can be a bluff.

The Gricean concept of implicature can be compared to Austin's concept of perlocution with which it shares the feature of nonconventionality: implicature is an actualized perlocution. From the utterance, 'My car broke down,' one can draw a limited number of presuppositions: 'there's a car,' 'the car is the speaker's,' 'the car was working before.' One can also draw an indefinite number of implicatures. 'Where's the nearest garage?/I can't drive you to the gym/Can you lend me some money to have it repaired?/Bad luck haunts me,' etc.

Finally, an interesting relationship is the symbiotic one between pragmatic presuppositions and implicatures in indirect speech acts: the presuppositions of the act (preparatory conditions in particular) are stated or questioned so as to release a (generalized conversational) implicature.

3. Definitions

Officially at least, pragmatic presuppositions have had a short life. The available registry data on pragmatic presuppositions reveal they were born 1970 (Stalnaker) died (and celebrated with a requiem) 1977 (Karttunen and Peters). The two latter authors proposed to articulate the concept of presupposition into: (a) particularized conversational implicature (e.g., subjunctive conditionals); (b) generalized conversational implicature (e.g., verbs of judgment); (c) preparatory condition on the felicity of the utterance; (d) conventional implicature (e.g., factives, *even, only, but*). The reader edited by Oh and Dinneen (1979) can also be seen as a post mortem commemoration.

Against the backdrop of the inadequacies of the concept of semantic presupposition, Stalnaker (1970: 281) introduces the concept of pragmatic presupposition as one of the major factors of a context. Pragmatic presupposition, which enables him to distinguish contexts from possible worlds, is defined as 'propositional attitude.' In the same paper, Stalnaker (1970: 279) adds that the best way to look at pragmatic presuppositions is as 'complex dispositions which are manifested in linguistic behavior.' Confirming the equivalence between pragmatic presupposition and propositional attitude, Stalnaker (1973: 448) defines pragmatic presupposition in the following way: 'A speaker pragmatically presupposes that B at a given moment in a conversation just in case he is disposed to act, in his linguistic behavior, as if he takes the truth of B for granted, and as if he assumes that his

audience recognizes that he is doing so.' Stalnaker's definition shows a tension between the definition of pragmatic presupposition, on the one hand as a disposition to act, and on the other as a propositional attitude: pragmatic terms and concepts ('disposition to act,' 'linguistic behavior') are used along with semantic terms and concepts ('the truth of B' in particular). In Stalnaker's treatment (1970: 277–81), a narrow meaning of the concept of 'pragmatic' is associated with an extended meaning of the concept of 'proposition,' which is the object both of illocutionary and of propositional acts.

Keenan (1971), distinguishing a logical from a pragmatic notion, defines pragmatic presupposition as a relation between 'utterances and their contexts' (p. 51). 'An utterance of a sentence pragmatically presupposes that its context is appropriate' (p. 49). In an almost specular opposition to Stalnaker, Keenan seems to have an extended view of pragmatics, which ends up coinciding with 'conventions of usage' as Ebert (1973: 435) remarks. He also seems, at the same time, to hold a restricted view of the phenomenon 'presupposition,' as exemplified by expressions that presuppose that the speaker/hearer is a man/woman (sex and relative age of the speaker/hearer), with deictic particles referring to the physical setting of the utterance and with expressions indicating personal and status relations among participants (e.g., French '*Tu es dégoûtant,*' lit: 'You (informal) are awful (male)').

Among other interesting definitions, is Levinson's (1983: 205): 'an utterance A *pragmatically presupposes* a proposition B if A is *appropriate* only if B is *mutually known* by participants.'

Givón (1982: 100) makes the requisite of mutual knowledge more articulate: 'The speaker assumes that a proposition **p** is *familiar* to the hearer, likely to be *believed* by the hearer, *accessible* to the hearer, within the reach of the hearer etc. *on whatever grounds.*'

Some conclusions are already possible.

(a) The two definitions of presupposition as semantic and pragmatic (Stalnaker) or as logical and discursive (Givón) are compatible (cf. Stalnaker 1970: 279).

(b) Logical presupposition is a sub-case of discursive presupposition: 'logical presupposition is [...] the *marked* sub-case of discourse backgroundedness' (Givón 1984: 328).

One definition occurs with particular frequency— that of presupposition as 'common ground.' The move from presupposition as propositional attitude to presupposition as shared knowledge, from the world of utterances to the world 'en plein air,' is Stalnaker's (1973).

Now, both in the narrow definition (presupposition as propositional attitude) and in the extended one (presupposition as shared belief), there is a high degree of idealization. What is common ground?

What is shared knowledge? Is there a different 'common ground' for different communities of speakers? And to what extent, and on the basis of what kind of conjecture, can one speak, even within the same community, of 'common ground'? Stalnaker (1974: 201) realizes the Platonic flavor of this notion when he gives examples of asymmetry in 'shared knowledge' (a conversation with the barber). The definition of presupposition in terms of common knowledge works '[i]n normal, straightforward serious conversational contexts where the overriding purpose of the conversation is to exchange information [...] The difficulties [...] come with contexts in which other interests besides communication are being served by the conversation.' But what are the criteria that define a conversation as 'normal,' 'straightforward,' and 'serious'? Further, are there no other interests beyond that of exchanging information that come into play in *every* conversation?

Finally, it is worth stressing that the concept of 'common ground' is effective only as a *de jure* concept, not as a *de re* concept, i.e., not as something ontologically stated, but as something deontically given by the speaker (Ducrot 1972), a frame of reference with which the hearer is expected to comply. On the one hand, a field of anthropological, sociological, and rhetorical investigation opens up. On the other, the characterization of presupposition as shared knowledge risks being static and idealizing, and contains a high amount of ideological birdlime.

4. Pragmatic Presuppositions as Felicity Conditions

At this point, a few other remarks are in order. First of all, the classic presuppositional model is semantic; even when a notion of pragmatic presupposition is invoked, an analysis of a semantic phenomenon is in fact presented. Pragmatic notions such as that of 'utterance' or 'context' are invoked with the main aim of avoiding the contradictions of semantic models. The most refined treatment of pragmatic presupposition, Gazdar (1979), does not escape this restriction.

Second, an assertive model is involved in the different definitions of pragmatic presupposition. A point of view centered on truth value is lurking behind alleged pragmatic presuppositions: the concept of proposition (content of an assertion, be it true or false), is the relevant theoretical unit. But can this theoretical construct work as the pragmatic unit of measure? Is it adequate to describe communicative behavior? Nothing seems to escape the tyranny of propositions, from the content of the actual utterance to a mental content (which, if not in propositional form, becomes so after being embedded in a predicate like 'know' or 'believe'), to a common or shared knowledge, to the representation that a logician or a philosopher gives of that content. To what extent is the concept of proposition adequate? Pragmatic presuppositions not only concern knowledge, whether true or false: they concern expectations, desires, interests, claims, attitudes toward the world, fears, etc. The exclusive use of the concept of proposition is idealizing and in the long run misleading, especially when it gives rise to the restoration of the dimension truth/falsehood as the only dimension of assessment of an utterance, whereas it is only one among the many possible ones.

The pragmatic level is not homogeneous with respect to the other levels of linguistic description, i.e., to the syntactic or the semantic one; it triggers other questions and anxieties. Pragmatic presuppositions are not a necessary condition on the truth or the falsehood of an utterance; rather, they are necessary to the felicity of an act.

Once the logical semantic level of analysis has been abandoned, once it has been decided to consider the data of the real communication as relevant, the fact that Oedipus has killed his father is—prior to being an entailment or a presupposition of '*Oedipus regrets having killed his father*'—knowledge common to a culture. 'Perched over the pragmatic abyss' (Givón 1982: 111), one feels giddy. Pragmatic presupposition can actually be God, or the autonomy of cats (if one excepts the logicians' cats, which, as is well known, invariably remain on their mats). The notion of presupposition is then drawn out so much as to run the risk of being useless. There is, though, a narrower and more technical meaning of pragmatic presupposition which is helpful in building up a protective wall at the edge of the abyss: it is that of pragmatic presuppositions as the felicity conditions of an illocutionary act.

Assume that the relevant unit to the concept of pragmatic presupposition is not the utterance, but the speech act. Pragmatic presuppositions can be regarded as felicity conditions or, according to Searle's model, as constitutive rules of conventional acts (e.g., promises, requests, assertions, etc.). If a presupposition functioning as a felicity condition of the act does not hold, the act fails. Note, incidentally, that a presupposition failure has different consequences, compared to the failure of an implicature: in fact, the failure of the latter has no bearing on the success of the illocutionary act.

The identification of presuppositions with felicity conditions is not a new idea: 'By the presuppositional aspect of a speech communication,' argues Fillmore (1971: 276), 'I mean those conditions which must be satisfied in order for a particular illocutionary act to be effectively performed in saying particular sentences. Of course, we need not be concerned with the totality of such conditions, but only with those that can be related to facts about the linguistic structure of sentences.' This definition can be shared to the extent that it draws attention to researching systematic relations between utterance function and form. It cannot be accepted to the extent that the felicity conditions can only be heterogeneous and involve also the extralinguistic world, since they concern the place in which language and world meet—the communicative situation.

In a first, extremely sketchy approach, it is possible to distinguish between constitutive and regulative rules (Searle 1969; for a discussion of the notion of 'rule,' see Black 1962). There are presuppositions acting as constitutive rules concerning *the what*: the performance of a given act. There are presuppositions acting as regulative rules concerning *the how*: style, degree of indirectness, politeness; Keenan (1971) was especially thinking of these.

Further, there are pragmatic presuppositions concerning: (a) communication in general, linked to the utterance act (e.g., preparatory conditions in the sense of Fillmore, absence of obstacles to communication, sharing a code); and (b) pragmatic presuppositions specific to the type of speech act. In any case 'we cannot hope to understand the way someone is using the word *presupposition* unless we are able to discover what is thought to result when a presupposition fails' (Garner 1971: 27).

In order to achieve this purpose, it would be useful to devise a typology of different kinds of presuppositional failures which is based on Austin's (1962) theory of infelicities (for semantic treatments see Vanderveken 1991). In order to overcome the distinction between constative utterances (true or false) and performative utterances (happy or unhappy), Austin identifies different ways in which both can fail, to conclude that assertions too, as acts, are subject to the infelicity of performatives. Conditions can be divided into two groups, according to the different kind of consequence brought about when something goes wrong with one of them. The first group is formed by those conditions which, if disregarded, make the act void (which is the case with misfires: the act is purported but void). The second group is made up of those conditions whose breach makes the act an abuse (the act is professed but hollow). This criterion distinguishes **A** and **B** conditions on the one hand and Γ conditions on the other (the Greek letter is used by Austin to stress the difference in nature of the latter conditions). **A** conditions concern the existence of a procedure (**A1**) and the right to invoke it (**A2**), whereas **B** conditions regard execution, which must be correct (**B1**) and complete (**B2**).

If **A** conditions (misinvocations) are not satisfied, the act is void. A failure in the act of reference belongs to this type. According to Austin, in the case of failure of an existential presupposition (e.g., 'G's children are bald, but G has no children,'), the utterance is void: the referential failure leads to an infelicity analogous to a failure of **A** conditions for performatives. Specifying Austin's characterization, one can establish with

Donnellan (1966) a difference between referential and attributive uses of definite descriptions. One can say 'The man in the purple turtleneck shirt is bald' (the example is Stalnaker's 1970) to qualify a specific person, Daniels, as bald. This is an example of referential use of the definite description which in such cases is just a means to identify the person about which one wants to speak, e.g., picking him out from a group. The same utterance can also be used when one, through ignoring who actually wears the purple turtleneck shirt, wants to qualify him as bald. This is an example of attributive use of the definite description. As Stalnaker (1970: 285) underlines, the consequences of a failure of referential presuppositions on the success of the speech act are marginal in the sense that the speaker 'may still have successfully referred to someone,' even if there is no entity that satisfies the description (if there is no man wearing the purple turtleneck shirt). The consequences of a failure of attributive presuppositions are, on the contrary, dramatic because 'nothing true or false has been said at all.' Or, one can suggest, with Lyons (1977: 602), a link between existential presupposition and theme: 'It is only when a refering expression is thematic that failure of the existential presupposition results in what Strawson [. . .] would call a truth–value gap.'

Also, a nonfulfillment of Austin's **B** conditions (misexecutions) makes the act void: Austin has in mind the ambiguity of reference in particular, the use of vague formulas and uncertain references (p. 36) (**B1**, flaws) or the lack of uptake on the part of the hearer (**B2**, hitches), especially as regards acts that require a specific uptake. Extending Austin's idea, one could consider also some conversational phenomena, such as turn taking and topic change or, in textual linguistics, the different conditions of coherence and cohesion as examples affecting the correctness and completeness of the execution of a procedure.

A nonfulfillment of Γ conditions, on the contrary, leads to an abuse: the act is performed, but is unhappy. This is the case with different kinds of insincerity, for example when not believing what one is saying (Γ**1**, insincerities), in the possible world opened up by the utterance, or in breaching a commitment later on (Γ**2**, 'breaches of commitment'), by not keeping a promise or, as far as assertions are concerned, by being incoherent in the world following the issue of the utterance.

5. Toward a Pragmatic Definition of Pragmatic Presupposition

The typology of Austin's infelicities is a philosophical approach to the problem of linguistic action, seen as a kind of social action. The types of infelicity are a step forward with respect to the recurring, undifferentiated notions, such as that of 'appropriateness,' in the definition of pragmatic presupposition. They help distinguish between presuppositions without which the act is not performed (e.g., promising somebody something which one does not have), and presuppositions which, if unsatisfied, make the act unhappy (e.g., promising something insincerely). There are presuppositions whose satisfaction can be seen in binary terms. For other presuppositions, satisfaction can be seen in scalar terms, in the sense that they can be more or less satisfied: these are the ones concerning the appropriateness of an act, on which it is possible to negotiate (an order, although impertinent, has been given; advice, although from an unauthoritative source, has been put forward, etc.). The role of nonverbal communication in the successful performance of acts has to a large extent still to be investigated (Arndt and Janney 1987). For example, if someone offers me congratulations on my promotion with a long face, can I still say s/he is congratulating me?

In any case, the different types of infelicity help recall the substantial homogeneity of linguistic action to action *simpliciter*: pragmatics must be connected to praxeology, to the study of actions which, before being true or false, appropriate or inappropriate, are effective or ineffective.

A decisive move for the analysis of pragmatic presuppositions is that of connecting the typology of infelicities to research which is empirically founded on the functioning of linguistic and nonlinguistic interaction. For example, in conversation, the typology can be related to the various mechanisms of repairs or, more generally, to research on misunderstandings in dialogue (e.g., Shimanoff 1980; Dascal 1985) and on pathological communication (Abbeduto and Rosenberg 1987). In the case of the 'disconfirmation' studied by the Palo Alto school, this may bring about the suspension of a background presupposition about the other's legitimacy as a speaker (and therefore on his/her legitimacy *tout court*).

To achieve a dynamic view of pragmatic presuppositions, it is crucial to consider presuppositions not only as preconditions of the act (e.g., Karttunen and Peters 1977), but also as effects: if the presupposition is not challenged, it takes effect retroactively. 'If you do not react against my order, you acknowledge my power'; 'if you follow my advice, you accept me as an expert who knows what is best for you'; 'if you do not question my assessment, you ascribe a competence to me' (see Ducrot 1972: 96–97; Sbisà and Fabbri 1980: 314–15; Streeck 1980: 145).

The analysis of *implicata* still requires much theoretical and applied work. It is possible to sum up some of the steps. One can imagine the *implicata* of which pragmatic presuppositions are a part, as types of commitments assumed by the speaker in different degrees and ways. The different degrees of cancelability according to which the types of *implicata* have been traditionally classified, are related to a stronger or weaker communicative commitment: the speaker is responsible for the *implicata* conveyed by his/her linguistic act; if the addressee does not raise any objection, he/she becomes coresponsible for it. A decisive step is that of leaving behind the truth–functional heritage: rather than recognizing a presupposition as true, the matter is to accept it as valid.

For a pragmatic analysis of pragmatic presuppositions, it is furthermore necessary to consider the following:

(a) *A sequential–textual dimension* (Eco 1990: 225). Presuppositional phenomena can be explained only by taking a cotextual, sequential dimension into account (which, however, is implicit, albeit in an idealized way, in Grice's criterion of cancelability), as well as a rhetorical dimension (which is implicit in the Sadock and Horn criterion of reinforceability). For a study of pragmatic presuppositions, it is necessary to move from an analysis of predicates within single sentences to the analysis of textual structures in which the presupposition is one of the effects. Presuppositions change the legal situation of speakers (Ducrot 1972: 90 ff.; Sbisà 1989), i.e., their rights and duties within a context which is being built up along the way. The projection problem (for a discussion, see Levinson 1983), namely the problem of how the presuppositions of a simple sentence are or are not inherited from a complex sentence, may be reformulated in a pragmatic and textual perspective as a problem of the constraints, not only thematic, on coherence and acceptability that arise in the construction of a discourse.

(b) *An anthropological–cultural–social dimension.* Much has still to be done in the research on shared knowledge, on the kinds of beliefs which can be taken for granted within a given cultural and social group. Presuppositions are a way of building up such knowledge and of reinforcing it. The social relevance of this research, which might be profitably connected to work in the theory of argumentation (e.g., Perelman and Olbrechts-Tyteca's 1958 analysis) is obvious. As Goffman (1983: 27) writes: 'the felicity condition behind all other felicity conditions, [is] ... *Felicity's Condition*: to wit, any arrangement which leads us to judge an individual's verbal acts to be not a manifestation of strangeness. Behind Felicity's Condition is our sense of what it is to be sane.'

(c) *A psychological dimension.* The analysis of implicit communication, though avoiding psychologism, does require a psychological adequacy. Thus, we tend to choose those topics which are at least partially shared, which enable one to be allusive and elliptical, we produce 'exclusive' utterances that only the addressee can understand at once. In other words, we enact the maximum of knowledge between us and (*only*) the addressee.

The pragmatic analysis of presuppositions is a task which, for the most part, still has to be performed: a truly vertiginous enterprise, yet one which cannot be abandoned if, beyond the logical relations between utterances, human communication is considered a relevant object of study.

See also: Pragmatics; Presupposition.

Bibliography

Abbeduto L, Rosenberg S 1987 Linguistic communication and mental retardation. In: Rosenberg S (ed.) *Advances in Applied Psycholinguistics. Vol. I: Disorders of First-Language Development.* Cambridge University Press, Cambridge

Arndt H, Janney R W 1987 *InterGrammar.* Mouton, Berlin

Austin J L 1976 *How to Do Things with Words,* 2nd edn. Clarendon Press, Oxford

Black M 1962 The analysis of rules. In: *Models and Metaphors.* Cornell University Press, Ithaca, NY

Conte A G 1977 Aspetti della semantica del linguaggio deontico. In: di Bernardo G (ed.) *Logica deontica e semantica.* Il Mulino, Bologna

Dascal M 1985 The relevance of misunderstanding. In: Dascal M (ed.) 1985 *Dialogue: An Interdisciplinary Approach.* Benjamins, Amsterdam

Donnellan K 1966 Reference and definite descriptions. *Philosophical Review* **75**: 281–304

Ducrot O 1972 *Dire et ne pas dire.* Hermann, Paris

Dummett M 1981 *Frege: Philosophy of Language,* 2nd edn. Duckworth, London

Ebert K 1973 Präsuppositionen im Sprechakt. In: Petöfi J S, Franck D (eds.) *Präsuppositionen in Philosophie und Linguistik.* Athenäum, Frankfurt

Eco U 1990 Presuppositions. In: *The Limits of Interpretation.* Indiana University Press, Bloomington, IN

Fillmore C 1971 Verbs of judging: An exercise in semantic description. In: Fillmore C J, Langendoen D T (eds.) *Studies in Linguistic Semantics.* Holt, Rinehart & Winston, New York

Garner R 1971 'Presupposition' in philosophy and linguistics. In: Fillmore C J, Langendoen D T (eds.) *Studies in Linguistic Semantics.* Holt, Rinehart & Winston, New York

Gazdar G 1979 *Pragmatics. Implicature, Presupposition, and Logical Form.* Academic Press, New York

Givón T 1982 Logic versus pragmatics, with human language as the referee: Toward an empirically viable epistemology. *JPrag* **6**: 81–133

Givón T 1984 *Syntax,* vol. I. Benjamins, Amsterdam

Goffman E 1983 Felicity's condition. *American Journal of Sociology* **1**: 1–53

Grice H P 1975 Logic and conversation. In: Cole P, Morgan J L (eds.) *Syntax and Semantics 3: Speech Acts.* Academic Press, New York

Horn L R 1984 Toward a new taxonomy for pragmatic inference. In: Schiffrin D (ed.) *Meaning, Form, and Use in Context.* Georgetown University Press, Washington, DC

Horn L 1991 Given as new: When redundant affirmation isn't. *JPrag* **15**: 313–36

Karttunen L, Peters S 1977 Requiem for presupposition. *Proceedings of the Third Annual Meeting of the Berkeley Linguistic Society*

Karttunen L, Peters S 1979 Conventional implicature. In: Oh C K, Dinneen D A (eds.)

Keenan E L 1971 Two kinds of presuppositions in natural language. In: Fillmore C J, Langendoen D T (eds.) *Studies in Linguistic Semantics.* Holt, Rinehart & Winston, New York

Levinson S C 1983 *Pragmatics.* Cambridge University Press, Cambridge

Lyons J 1977 *Semantics.* Cambridge University Press, Cambridge

Oh C K, Dinneen D A (eds.) 1979 *Syntax and Semantics: Presupposition.* Academic Press, New York

Perelman C, Olbrechts-Tyteca L 1958 *Traité de l'argumentation. La nouvelle rhétorique.* Presses Universitaires de France, Paris

Petöfi J S, Franck D (eds.) 1973 *Präsuppositionen in Philosophie und Linguistik.* Athenäum, Frankfurt

Sbisà M 1989 *Linguaggio, ragione, interazione.* Il Mulino, Bologna

Sbisà M, Fabbri P 1980 Models for a pragmatic analysis. *JPrag* **4**: 301–19

Searle J R 1969 *Speech Acts.* Cambridge University Press, Cambridge

Shimanoff S B 1980 *Communication Rules: Theory and Research.* Sage, Los Angeles, CA

Stalnaker R C 1970 Pragmatics. *Synthese* **22**: 272–89

Stalnaker R C 1973 Presuppositions. *Journal of Philosophical Logic* **2**: 447–57

Stalnaker R C 1974 Pragmatic presuppositions. In: Munitz M, Unger P K (eds.) *Semantics and Philosophy.* New York University Press, New York

Strawson P F 1950 On referring. *Mind* **59**: 320–44

Streeck J 1980 Speech acts in interaction: A critique of Searle. *Discourse Processes* **3**: 133–54

Van der Auwera J 1979 Pragmatic presupposition: Shared beliefs in a theory of irrefutable meaning. In: Oh C K, Dinneen D A (eds.)

Vanderveken D 1985 What is an illocutionary force? In: Dascal M (ed.) *Dialogue: An Interdisciplinary Approach.* Benjamins, Amsterdam

Vanderveken D 1991 *Meaning and Speech Acts. Vol. 2: Formal Semantics of Success and Satisfaction.* Cambridge University Press, Cambridge

Relevance

M. M. Talbot

Grice's 'maxim of relation' (viz: 'be relevant') has been elevated to the status of an overriding principle governing communication and cognition by Sperber and Wilson (1986, 1995). The principle of relevance is at the center of their claim of a new approach to the study of human communication. 'Relevance theory' (RT) purports to be a unified theory of cognition to serve as a foundation for studies in cognitive science. Relevance theory offers insights into, among other things, inferencing, implicature, irony, and metaphor. Its refinements in the study of implicature are presented briefly in Sect. 5 below. The aims of RT are ambitious, but it does have some defects which limit its usefulness. The theory relies heavily on the explication of the workings of a formal deductive system for its substance, rests on restricted, asocial conceptions of communication, language-users, and their cognitive environments, and ignores developments in both discourse analysis and artificial intelligence.

1. The Principle of Relevance

Sperber and Wilson formulate the 'principle of relevance' as follows:

> Every act of ostensive communication communicates the presumption of its own optimal relevance.
>
> (1986: 158)

(See Sect. 2 below for an explanation of the term 'ostensive.') The term 'relevance' is used in a technical sense to refer to the bringing about of contextual effect. An utterance is only relevant if it has some contextual effect. In Sperber and Wilson's words:

> The notion of a contextual effect is essential to a characterization of relevance. We want to argue that having contextual effects is a necessary condition for relevance, and that other things being equal, the greater the contextual effects, the greater the relevance.
>
> (1986: 119)

There are varying degrees of relevance. Sperber and Wilson claim that there is an inverse correlation of effort and relevance. In other words, the more processing it takes to work out what a speaker intends by an utterance, the less relevant that utterance is. As various critics have pointed out, this begs the questions: 'relevant to what?' (e.g., Clark 1987) and 'relevant to whom?' (Wilks 1987).

2. Ostensive-inferential Communication

Ostensive and inferential communication are two sides of the same process; a process which, Sperber and Wilson argue, is achieved because of the principle of relevance. A communicator is involved in ostension; a communicator's audience is involved in inferencing. A communicator's ostensive action comes with a 'guarantee of relevance' (1986: 50), such that what makes the intention behind the ostensive act manifest to an audience is the principle of relevance.

3. Informative and Communicative Intentions

A distinction in RT, upon which Sperber and Wilson place considerable importance, is between 'informative' and 'communicative' intentions, which underlie all communication. In the informative intention, a speaker (S) intends a hearer (H) to recognize S's intention to inform H of something: S intends to make manifest to an audience a set of assumptions (on 'manifestness' and 'assumptions,' see Sect. 4 below).

In the communicative intention, S intends H to recognize the informative intention; it is therefore a second-order informative intention.

4. Cognitive Environments, Assumptions, and Manifestness

Sperber and Wilson initially define assumptions as 'thoughts treated by the individual as representations of the actual world' (1986: 2). They give precedence to the cognitive function of language in RT. But a strength of it is its ability to include nonpropositional and expressive elements, to account for vague, ambivalent meanings or 'impressions,' which may not be verbally communicated. The authors account for explicitness of an informative intention in terms of the degree to which an assumption is made manifest. Before going into detail about degrees of manifestness, however, a fuller description of assumptions is needed.

Assumptions are composed of a structured set of concepts. A concept is located in the memory store and contains an address (its point of access in memory) and one or all of the following entries: encyclopedic, logical, and lexical (Sperber and Wilson 1986: 83). The human information-processor (see Sect. 5.3 below) manipulates the conceptual content of assumptions. The processing device has access to assumptions from four sources: (1) direct perception; (2) decoding of the encoded utterances of others; (3) its own memory store, and (4) deduction from assumptions accessible from sources 1 to 3. Together these assumptions from four sources make up an individual's cognitive environment.

In Sperber and Wilson's model, H can infer S's assumptions on the basis of knowledge of S's cognitive environment. They define a cognitive environment as follows:

> A cognitive environment is merely a set of assumptions which the individual is capable of mentally representing.
> (1986: 46)

Differences in the cognitive environments of two people are simply differences in individual possession of facts, experience, and ability; people's stocks of assumptions vary according to their physical environments and cognitive abilities. On the basis of a complex of assumptions, H can infer the relevance of S's ostension. Sperber and Wilson argue that this capacity to infer relevance is the fundamental human information-processing activity. (They compare this human capacity to various nonhuman information-processing abilities, one of which is the instinctive ability of a frog to track insects.)

The authors account for variations in the strength of assumptions in terms of the degree to which they are made 'manifest' to an individual. An assumption actually 'entertained' by an individual is knowledge of which s/he has a mental representation. Other assumptions are only potential; these are possible assumptions, which an individual may (but need not) have mental representations of, which are hence potentially part of his/her manifest knowledge. An individual's cognitive environment is all his/her manifest knowledge: 'An individual's total cognitive environment is the set of all the facts that he can perceive or infer: all the facts that are manifest to him' (1986: 39). The most strongly manifest (i.e., 'most readily assumable') assumptions are those derived directly from perceptual sources, and those with long processing histories. The weakest are assumptions that can only be derived with effort: potentially computable implications from entries in memory store, or deductions that can be made from other assumptions.

5. The Identification of Implicatures

In RT, the principle of relevance governs the recovery of implicatures; a speaker's expectations about how to be maximally relevant are the means by which implicatures can be worked out. The authors' exploration of implicature offers two useful innovations: a distinction between implicated premises and implicated conclusions, and an alternative to an untenably clearcut divide between determinate and indeterminate implicatures. Only the second of these innovations results from the elevation of the maxim of relevance to the status of an overriding principle.

6. An Asocial Model

In *Relevance*, human beings are viewed as information processors with an inbuilt capacity to infer relevance.

This single capacity is assumed to be the key to human communication and cognition. Around this assumption, the authors build a model which they claim offers a unified theory of cognition, to serve as the foundation for an approach to the study of human communication. A drawback of the model, however, is its lack of any social element.

6.1 Individuals and Cognitive Environments

Relevance theory hinges on S's intention to inform and H's corresponding recognition of this intention. This recognition requires H to infer a connection between some action performed by S and S's intention in carrying it out; in other words, H constructs a teleological explanation for S's action. Teleology alone, however, is not enough for a theory of social action. *Relevance* presents an intentionalist view of action. In it, people are depicted as individuals who confront unique problems in communication. In the real world, however, people are social beings who are working within preexisting conventions. This latter view of the language-user and the nature of communication is practiced in studies of discourse analysis, especially in certain later developments (e.g., Fairclough 1989).

In Sperber and Wilson's model, differences between people are depicted solely as differences between individuals' cognitive environments. These differences are assumed to stem from variations in physical environment and cognitive ability between people. Considerations of culture and society are notably absent in the characterization of individuals' cognitive environments. In *Relevance*, the authors work with a 'commonsensical' view of all individuals sharing essentially the same epistemological organization of the real world. This is not to say that Sperber and Wilson are claiming that the assumptions making up people's cognitive environments are necessarily facts; they insist that they are presenting a cognitive approach rather than an epistemological one. In this insistence, they are stressing that they are not concerned with the truth or falsity of assumptions. But even a cognitive approach must rest on some conception of epistemology; if this conception is not explicitly focused on, it will nevertheless be present but in an unreflective form.

The consequences of such disregard are serious. For if language analysts are to construct a teleological explanation for someone's action, they need to make assumptions about that person's knowledge structures. The analysts assume the actor's assumptions. Similarly, the hearer in Sperber and Wilson's model needs to make assumptions about the speaker's knowledge structures. The authors claim that H can infer (and therefore assume) S's assumptions on the basis of knowledge of S's cognitive environment. But they do not attend to how H might know (or make guesses at) S's cognitive environment. (For further discussion, see Mey and Talbot 1988.)

6.2 *Assumptions and Manifestness*

A cognitive environment is the total of an individual's manifest knowledge, a whole set of assumptions derivable from the four sources mentioned in Sect. 4 above. Within the framework given, there is no way of discussing any divergence of assumptions according to class, gender, or ethnicity. In the absence of any cultural perspective, the knowledge manifest to different individuals is largely the same (typical examples include knowledge of the weather, the pleasantness of sea air, and the price of cars). The effect is highly ethnocentric; one is left with the impression that everyone lives in the same kind of white, middle-class, educated world. While this may be true, to some extent, of the linguists and cognitive scientists comprising the authors' audience, it is a seriously inadequate provision of social context for a study of either communication or cognition. This ethnocentric bias is displayed particularly clearly by the authors' examples of derivable assumptions that are weakly manifest (e.g., 'Chomsky never had breakfast with Julius Caesar') (1986: 40). Their ad hoc choice of unrelated facts known both to themselves and their readers for the potentially endless production of negative assumptions betrays an unsystematic approach.

As an alternative to the concept of mutual knowledge which they consider to be problematic (and which indeed has its own problems), Sperber and Wilson put forward the concept of 'mutual manifestness' of assumptions. They dislike mutual knowledge because, as they see it, such a concept relies on positing consciously held knowledge which S and H both, by definition, know for certain that they share. As they say, this degree of certainty is an impossibility, rendering the concept useless:

> Mutual knowledge must be certain, or else it does not exist; and since it can never be certain it can never exist.
> (1986: 19–20)

In order to provide a viable alternative to this excessively rigid and unsatisfactory concept of mutual knowledge, Sperber and Wilson suggest instead the 'mutual manifestness' of knowledge. Similarities in individuals' cognitive environments make mutually manifest assumptions possible. However, mutually manifest knowledge is itself a problem; it has little more to offer than the concept of mutual knowledge that it is intended to replace. As knowledge-which-is-there-to-be-mutually-assumed it is in principle no different from mutual knowledge (see Gibbs 1987a, 1987b for discussion). In the absence of any social element, with which to locate and specify kinds of knowledge that might be mutually accessible to different individuals, this is inevitable.

6.3 *The Mind as Information Processor*

In RT, thought processes are assumed to be exclusively matters of information processing by a 'device.' The human mind is conceived to be a 'deductive mechanism' which has the capacity to manipulate the conceptual content of assumptions from a range of sources (see Sect. 4 above) and no more than this. Sperber and Wilson operate with the same kind of reductionist conception of human mental processes as is found in transformational generative grammar, namely the 'black box.' This view of the mind severely limits the scope of human mental activity and precludes any sociocultural perspective on the individual's construction of knowledge. Sperber and Wilson's favorite metaphor for the human mind is the computer. They limit their object of enquiry accordingly to how the human mind functions as a computer, i.e., to human information processing.

7. Conclusion

Sperber and Wilson's basic premise is that 'Human cognition is relevance oriented' (1987: 700). Their aim in creating RT was to provide a unified theory of cognition for studies in cognitive science. Such a unified approach was eagerly awaited and anticipated as a major breakthrough. When *Relevance* appeared in print in 1986 it was favorably received in many places and has made some contribution to developments in pragmatics (in particular, in the identification of implicatures; see Sect. 5 above). It generated a good deal of debate in the late 1980s. A new version with some revision and extension appeared in 1995. However, RT does not appear to have had much lasting influence or effect; nor has it proved to supply the unified theory that was anticipated.

See also: Conversational Maxims; Shared Knowledge.

Bibliography

Clark H H 1987 Relevance to what? *Behavioral and Brain Sciences* **10(4)**: 714–15
Fairclough N 1989 *Language and Power*. Longman, London
Gibbs R W 1987a Mutual knowledge and the psychology of conversational inference. *Journal of Pragmatics* **11(5)**: 561–88
Gibbs R W 1987b The relevance of Relevance for psychological theory. *Behavioral and Brain Sciences* **10(4)**: 718–19
Mey J L, Talbot M M 1988 Computation and the soul (Review article of Sperber and Wilson's *Relevance*). *Semiotica* **72(3/4)**: 291–339
Sperber D, Wilson D 1986 *Relevance: Communication and Cognition*. Basil Blackwell, Oxford
Sperber D, Wilson D 1987 Precis of *Relevance*: Communication and Cognition. *Behavioral and Brain Sciences* **10(4)**: 695–754
Sperber D, Wilson D 1995 *Relevance: Communication and Cognition*, 2nd edn. Basil Blackwell, Oxford
Wilks Y 1987 Relevance must be to someone. *Behavioral and Brain Sciences* **10(4)**: 735–36

Speech Act Classification

K. Allan

A speech act is created when speaker/writer S makes an utterance U to hearer/reader H in context C. The illocutionary force of U is what S *does* in U, for example, states or requests something, thanks someone, makes a promise, declares an umpiring decision, etc. Every speech act conveys at least one illocutionary force; most convey more than one. This article examines criteria for classifying illocutionary forces (loosely called speech acts) and for defining illocutions.

1. Two Approaches to Classification

There have been two approaches to classifying speech acts: one, following Austin (1962), is principally a lexical classification of so-called illocutionary verbs; the other, following Searle (1975), is principally a classification of acts.

1.1 Lexical Classification

Austin (1962), the founding father of speech act theory, identified five classes of illocutionary verbs, which were refined and extended to seven by Vendler (1972) as follows (glosses from Austin 1962: 151–61; N = noun phrase, V = verb, p = proposition (sentence), nom = gerund or other nominalization): (a) expositives 'expounding of views, the conducting of arguments and the clarifying of usages and of references' (N_i V *that* p), for example, *state, contend, insist, deny, remind, guess*; (b) verdictives 'the giving of a verdict' (N_i V N_j (as) N or Adj), for example, *rank, grade, call, define, analyze*; (c) commissives 'commit the speaker' (N_i V *to* V), for example, *promise, guarantee, refuse, decline;* (d) exercitives 'exercising of powers, rights, or influences' (N_i V N_j *to* V), for example, *order, request, beg, dare*; (e) behabitives 'reaction to other people's behavior and fortunes' (N_i V N_j P nom (past (V))), for example, *thank, congratulate, criticize*; and Vendler's two extra classes (f) operatives (N_i V N_j *to be/become* N_k), for example, *appoint, ordain, condemn*; (g) interrogatives (N_i V *wh*-nom (p)), for example, *ask, question*.

Katz (1977: 50–57) critically examines Vendler's analysis. A more extensive lexical classification is Ballmer and Brennenstuhl (1981): they present a thesauruslike lexicon where verbs are grouped according to an illocutionary property such as 'make a hidden appeal,' which includes *bitch at, carp about, grumble, murmur, mutiny, nag, pout, rumble, sulk, whine*, and *wrangle* (p. 73); and there is 'put someone to flight,' which includes *chase away, chase off, discharge, dismiss, drive away, drive back, force out, frighten away, kick out, oust, put to flight, scare off, see off, send packing, squeeze out,* and *throw out* (p. 100).

Ballmer and Brennenstuhl identified speech act verbs using the formula N V ((addressee) *by saying*)p as in *Jo whined 'Why me?'*; *Jay chased him off with 'Don't let me see you here again!'* Their classification of 4,800 verbs into 600 categories comprising 24 types in 8 groups was made (as it is by other scholars) on an intuitive basis in terms of semantic similarity. Wierzbicka (1987) makes a much more explicit semantic analysis of 270 speech act verbs, grouping them into 37 classes. Her 'promise' class contains *promise, pledge, vow, swear, vouch for,* and *guarantee*.

1.2 Classification of Acts

Searle (1975) lists 12 differences between speech acts that can serve as bases for classification:

(a) The point of the illocution: for example, a request attempts to get H to do something, a descriptive is a representation of how something is, a promise is the undertaking of an obligation that S do something.

(b) Direction of fit between the words uttered and the world they relate to: for example, statements have a words-to-world fit because truth value is assigned on the basis of whether or not the words describe things as they are in the world spoken of; requests have a world-to-words fit because the world must be changed to fulfill S's request.

(c) Expressed psychological states: for example, a statement that *p* expresses S's belief that *p*, a promise expresses S's intention to do something, a request expresses S's desire that H should do something.

(d) The strength with which the illocutionary point is presented: for example, *I insist that . . .* is stronger than *I suggest that . . . .*

(e) Relevance of the relative status of S and H: some illocutions, like commanding, are sensitive to participant status; others, like stating, are not.

(f) Orientation: for example, boasts and laments are S-oriented, congratulations and condolences are H-oriented.

(g) Questions and answers are adjacency pair parts; commands are not.

(h) Propositional content: for example, H to do A (i.e., perform some act) for a request, S to do A for a promise.

(i) Promising can only be performed as a speech act; classifying can be performed in other ways.

(j) Baptizing and excommunicating require institutional conditions to be satisfied; but stating does not.

(k) Not all illocutionary verbs are performative verbs, for example, *boast* and *threaten* are not.

(l) Style of performing the illocutionary act: for example, the difference between announcing and confiding.

To these can be added another:

(m) differences in the criteria that H will bring in evaluating a speech act, for example, judging whether or not a statement is credible; judging invitationals in terms of whether S really wants A to be done and, if so, whether H is both able and willing to do A.

Searle uses only four criteria to establish five classes of speech acts: representatives (called 'assertives' in Searle 1979), directives, commissives, expressives, and declarations. The first criterion is illocutionary point ((a) above):

If we adopt illocutionary point as the basic notion on which to classify uses of language, then there are a rather limited number of basic things we do with language; we tell people how things are, we try to get them to do things, we commit ourselves to doing things, we express our feelings and attitudes, and we bring about changes through our utterances. Often we do more than one of these at once in the same utterance.

(Searle 1975: 369)

In addition, he uses: (b) direction of fit; (c) S's psychological state; and (h) propositional content.

Representatives/assertives have a truth value, show words-to-world fit, and express S's belief that *p*. Directives are attempts to get H to do something, therefore they show world-to-words fit, and express S's wish or desire that H do A. Commissives commit S to some future course of action, so they show world-to-words fit, and S expresses the intention that S do A. Expressives express S's attitude to a certain state of affairs specified (if at all) in the propositional content (e.g., the underlined portion of *I apologize for stepping on your toe*). There is no direction of fit; a variety of different psychological states; and propositional content 'must ... be related to S or H' (1975: 357f.). Declarations bring about correspondence between the propositional content and the world, thus direction of fit is both words-to-world and world-to-words. Searle recognizes no psychological state for declarations.

Bach and Harnish (1979: 42–51, 110f.) employ all of Searle's criteria except direction of fit, giving predominant emphasis to S's psychological state—which they refer to as S's 'attitude.' They identify six classes: constatives express a belief, together with the intention that H form (or continue to hold) a like belief; directives express S's attitude toward some act that H should carry out; commissives express S's undertaking to do A; acknowledgments (= Searle's 'expressives') express, perfunctorily if not genuinely, certain feelings toward the hearer. Searle's 'declarations' are all 'conventional illocutionary acts' in Bach and Harnish, but split into effectives, which effect changes in insti-

tutional states of affairs, and verdictives, which have official binding import in the context of the institution for which they are made.

Searle's 'declarations' and Bach and Harnish's 'conventional illocutionary acts' are different from the other classes of acts—assertives, directives, commissives, expressives—which are interpersonal. Interpersonal acts are typically directed at individuals. To take effect, they require H to react to S's illocution—mere understanding of the illocutionary point is insufficient: it is pointless for S to tell H it is raining, warn H of danger, or offer H condolences, if H fails to react appropriately to what S says. Declarations, on the other hand, are typically broadcast within a social group, and rely for their success on S being sanctioned by the community, institution, committee, or even a single person within the group to perform such acts under stipulated conditions; H's reaction as an individual is irrelevant to the effectiveness of being baptized, disqualified from driving, fired, or any other declaration, provided that the stipulated conditions are met. It is the reaction of the group which sanctions S that is significant for declarations. Compare the interpersonal 'opine that *p*' (e.g., *I think history is bunk*) with the declaration 'declare the verdict *p*' (e.g., S, umpiring a game at the US Open Tennis Tournament, declares the ball *Out!*).

opine, assertive = interpersonal (cf. Allan 1986: 194; Edmondson 1981: 145f.)

⟨description⟩ S opines that *p*.

⟨preparatory condition⟩ S believes there is sufficient evidence to express a (perhaps hedged) belief that *p*.

⟨illocutionary intention⟩ S reflexively intends that U be a reason for H to believe that S holds (and can justify) the opinion that *p* (and perhaps that H come to hold the opinion that *p*).

declare a verdict, declaration (cf. Allan 1986: 203; Wierzbicka 1987: 349)

⟨description⟩ S declares the verdict *p*.

⟨preparatory condition⟩ Members of group G are sanctioned to declare verdicts on a set of topics T in a set of situations K; and (a) S believes there is sufficient evidence to support the opinion that *p;* (b) S is a member of G; (c) at the time of uttering U, S is of sound mind; (d) the verdict that *p* is on a topic which is a member of T; (e) the situation of utterance is a member of K.

⟨illocutionary intention⟩ S reflexively intends H to recognize that U declares the verdict *p*. (H is a member of the wider community of which G forms a proper part.)

Because declarations rely for their success on S being sanctioned by the community, etc., it may be necessary to safeguard society's interest with an executive condition which requires some watchdog other than S to ensure that clauses (b–e) of the preparatory condition hold.

Speech acts can be grouped into four classes if H's evaluations are used as criteria. Statements (including denials, reports, predictions, promises, and offers) can all be judged in terms of the question 'Is *p* credible?' These are principally expressions of S's belief about the way the world was, is, or will be, and are most typically formulated with a declarative clause. Invitationals are a proper subset of Searle's directives, and include requests, exhortations, suggestions, warnings, etc. They have acceptability values: 'Does S really want A to be done and, if so, is H both able and willing to do it?' These principally invite H's participation, and many are formulated in an interrogative clause. Authoritatives include the rest of Searle's 'directives' and his 'declarations' (i.e., commands, permissions, legal judgments, baptisms, etc.), for which H must consider the question 'Does S have the authority to utter U in the given context?' These principally have S 'laying down the law'; many of them are formulated in an imperative clause, the rest in a declarative. Expressives (greetings, thanks, apologies, congratulations, etc.) have social-interactive appropriateness values: 'Has something occurred which warrants S expressing such a reaction to it?' These principally express social interaction with H; many are idiomatic, the rest are in the default declarative clause format.

It is notable that all classes of speech acts can be conveyed using a declarative clause; but interrogatives typically indicate invitationals, imperatives authoritatives, and idioms expressives.

2. Comparing Definitions of Illocutionary Forces

There is great similarity in the speech act definitions of Searle (1969), Bach and Harnish (1979), Edmondson (1981), Levinson (1983), Allan (1986), and Wierzbicka (1987), despite the different perspectives of these scholars. To identify the critical components of a definition, six definitions of assertives are reviewed here. For easy comparison, clauses in the definitions of the different scholars which serve similar functions are identified by a common label.

assert, state (that), affirm (Searle 1969: 67). Given the conditions described, Searle says that the utterance of *p* constitutes an assertion, statement, or affirmation (on the distinctive characteristics of each, see Wierzbicka 1987: 321, 329, 323).

⟨propositional content⟩	*p*. [Searle's 'propositional content' is the complement of the speech act verb and excludes its meaning—unlike the ⟨description⟩ ascribed to other scholars.]
⟨preparatory condition⟩	(a) S has evidence (reasons, etc.) for the truth of *p*.
	(b) It is not obvious to both S and H that H knows (does not need to be reminded of, etc.) *p*.
⟨sincerity condition⟩	S believes *p*.
⟨illocutionary intention⟩	Counts as an undertaking to the effect that *p* represents an actual state of affairs. [Searle's term for this is 'essential condition.']

assertives (Bach and Harnish 1979: 42)

⟨description⟩	In uttering U, S asserts that *p* if S expresses
⟨preparatory condition⟩	(a) the belief that *p*, and
⟨illocutionary intention⟩	(b) the intention that H believe that *p*.

By 'intention,' they mean a 'reflexive-intention'.

claim (Edmondson 1981: 145)

⟨preparatory condition⟩	(a) S wishes H to believe that S believes [that *p*; that is] the information contained in the location by means of which the claim is made is true.
⟨illocutionary intention⟩	(b) In making a claim, S may be held to believe that S's doing so is in the

Table 1. A comparison of five classifications of illocutionary types.

Austin	Vendler	Searle	Bach & Harnish	Allan
Expositives	Expositives	Assertives	Assertives	Statements
Commissives	Commissives	Commissives	Commissives	
Behabitives	Behabitives	Expressives	Acknowledgments	Expressives
	Interrogatives			Invitationals
Exercitives	Exercitives	Directives	Directives	
	Verdictives		Verdictives	
Verdictives	Operatives	Declarations	Effectives	Authoritatives

interests of H. In making a claim, S commits S to believing what is entailed by the content of that claim.

Edmondson leaves the ⟨description⟩ to be inferred; his (c), which is a comment, is omitted here.

assertion (Levinson 1983: 277, following Gazdar 1981)
⟨description⟩ An assertion that *p* ⟨illocutionary intention⟩ is a function from a context where S is not committed to *p* (and perhaps, on a strong theory for assertion, where H does not know that *p*), into a context in which S is committed to ⟨preparatory condition⟩ the justified true belief ⟨illocutionary intention continued⟩ that *p* (and, on the strong version, into one in which H does know that *p*).

assertives (update on Allan 1986: 193)
⟨description⟩	S asserts that *p*.
⟨preparatory condition⟩	There is reason for S to believe that *p*.
⟨illocutionary intention⟩	S reflexively-intends that U be recognized as a reason for H to believe that (S believes that) *p*.

assert (Wierzbicka 1987: 321)
⟨description⟩	I say: *p*.
⟨preparatory condition⟩	I imagine some people would say this is not true. I can say that this is true.
⟨illocutionary intention⟩	I assume that people will have to think that it is true.
⟨sincerity condition⟩	I say this because I want to say what I know is true.

These definitions are an extension of the semantics of the key verb (e.g., *assert*) naming the illocution. However, most utterances do not contain such a verb, and H must recognize the illocution without its help. Nearly all scholars refer to utterance content (the components identified here as ⟨description⟩ and ⟨propositional content⟩), though Edmondson leaves it to be inferred. Searle's definition refers to the content of the proposition that is asserted (*p*) and, unlike most other scholars, does not include a description of utterance content as a whole. He (correctly) believes that the same proposition (phrastic) may be used to express different illocutionary forces which are indicated outside *p* by what he calls 'illocutionary force indicating devices' captured in his 'essential condition.' This causes a problem, for instance, in his definition of 'thank (for)': ⟨propositional content⟩ 'past act A done by H' (Searle 1969: 67). Compare this with other scholars' ⟨description⟩ of 'thank': 'In uttering U, S thanks H for D if S expresses . . .' (Bach and Harnish 1979: 52); 'S expresses thanks to H for D' (Allan 1986); 'I say: I feel something good towards you because of that' (Wierzbicka 1987: 214). Searle's ⟨propositional content⟩ is seen to have nothing in particular to do with thanking. Moreover, it is inaccurate for utterances such as *Thank you for joining me* or *Thanks*. The reader is left to decide whether it is preferable simply to rectify Searle's definition, or to abandon his ⟨prop-

ositional content⟩ component in favor of a ⟨description⟩ which will include it.

Both Searle's second preparatory condition, 'It is not obvious to both S and H that H knows (does not need to be reminded of, etc.) *p*' and Wierzbicka's 'I imagine some people would say this is not true' offer reasons for S making the assertion rather than keeping quiet. These scholars believe that such felicity conditions are part of the fine detail of a semantic definition, but others would include them within a general set of cooperative presumptions applicable to many, perhaps all, speech acts. In this instance, Wierzbicka identifies a class of people who disagree with S's belief and whom S hopes to persuade that *p* is true; this point is applicable to the semantics of *assert* but not of *state*.

Searle and Wierzbicka identify a sincerity condition; this is not a necessary component of the definition, because sincerity can be subsumed to the cooperative maxim of quality applicable to every speech act in a form such as 'S knows or believes (or believes that s/he knows) that all clauses of the preparatory condition hold.'

The illocutionary intentions for assertions fall into two parts: the first identifies S's commitment to belief that *p;* the second, S's presumed intention towards H. Arguably, the latter can be inferred from general cooperative presumptions about S's purpose in uttering the assertion to H, and so does not need to be stated in the definition.

It has been seen from the review of six definitions of assertives that the obligatory components of the definitions of speech acts are the *preparatory condition* and *S's illocutionary intention*. The same holds true for all other classes of speech act; for definitions of these, the reader should turn to the works cited.

See also: Felicity Conditions; Indirect Speech Acts; Speech Act Theory: Overview; Speech Acts and Grammar.

Bibliography

Allan K 1986 *Linguistic Meaning*, vol. 2. Routledge and Kegan Paul, London

Austin J L 1962 *How to Do Things with Words*. Clarendon Press, Oxford

Bach K, Harnish R M 1979 *Linguistic Communication and Speech Acts*. MIT Press, Cambridge, MA

Ballmer T, Brennenstuhl W 1981 *Speech Act Classification*. Springer-Verlag, Berlin

Edmondson W 1981 *Spoken Discourse*. Longman, London

Gazdar G 1981 Speech act assignment. In: Joshi A, Webber B, Sag I (eds.) *Elements of Discourse Understanding*. Cambridge University Press, Cambridge

Katz J J 1977 *Propositional Structure and Illocutionary Force*. Thomas Crowell, New York

Levinson S C 1983 *Pragmatics*. Cambridge University Press, Cambridge

Searle J R 1969 *Speech Acts*. Cambridge University Press, Cambridge

Searle J R 1975 A taxonomy of illocutionary acts. In: Gunderson K (ed.) *Language, Mind, and Knowledge.* University of Minnesota Press, Minneapolis, MN

Searle J R 1979 *Expression and Meaning: Studies in the Theory of Speech Acts.* Cambridge University Press, Cambridge

Vendler Z 1972 *Res Cogitans.* Cornell University Press, Ithaca, New York

Wierzbicka A 1987 *English Speech Act Verbs.* Academic Press, Sydney

Speech Act Hierarchy

K. Allan

Most people, including all speech act theorists, believe language to be a practical means of communication between human beings (contrast Chomsky, who writes 'Language ... is "essentially" a system for the expression of thought' 1975: 57). With very few exceptions, the purpose of speaking or writing is to cause an effect on the audience: we want our opinions to be recognized—if not adopted, our assertions to be agreed with, our requests to be enacted, questions answered, advice taken, warnings heeded, commands complied with, thanks appreciated, apologies accepted, and so forth. The implication is that speaking (and writing—which will from now on be properly included under 'speaking' for simplicity of exposition) is an *act*; to be more exact, it is a hierarchy of acts.

To begin with, language only comes into existence if someone performs an 'act of utterance,' i.e., when speaker S makes an utterance U to hearer H in context C. C is significant because an utterance is made at a certain time (establishing tense deixis), in a certain place (establishing locational deixis), by S to H (which establishes person deixis), and oftentimes in a discourse which establishes textual deixis, cotext, and the world being spoken of. We can readily recognize an utterance act in a language that is completely unknown to us, in which we cannot distinguish the sentences used, and therefore cannot tell what S is saying to H, or asking of H, or proposing to H that H do, etc., although we guess that S is doing one of these things. The utterance act is therefore distinguishable from the act of saying or asking or telling H something. In a language that we do know, two people necessarily perform separate utterance acts in order to say the same thing. A single speaker asking (or telling) someone the same thing on two different occasions, necessarily performs two different utterance acts. We recognize utterance acts on the basis of brute perception: by hearing them spoken, seeing them signed or written, feeling them impressed in braille.

One can make an utterance without using language; a dog can *utter* a bark: but such utterances lie outside of speech act theory. Speech act theory is concerned with utterances where S uses a language expression and thereby performs a 'locutionary act.' Different scholars offer slightly different definitions of the locutionary act (e.g., Austin 1962; Searle 1969; Bach and Harnish 1977; Recanati 1987); but let us say that in performing a locutionary act S uses an identifiable expression *e* from language L (where *e* is a sentence or sentence fragment) spoken with identifiable prosody π. (π is composed of the pattern of pause, pitch level, stress, tone of voice, and the like; its counterpart in the written medium is punctuation and typography.) Furthermore, the constituents and constituent structure of *e* and of π, together with their proper senses (intensions, meanings) are also identifiable to a typical fluent speaker of L. Recognizing the locution means recognizing that *e* spoken with prosody π, which we will symbolize $\langle \pi, e \rangle$, means 'μ'; consequently, a locution is produced and then recognized by someone who has knowledge of the grammar, lexicon, semantics, and phonology of L.

S uses a locution and applies it to a particular world w_i at time t_i; and this constitutes the 'act of referring' (or a 'denotational act'). Austin, whose *How To Do Things With Words* (1962) first awakened wide interest in speech acts, included the act of referring as part of the locutionary act (p. 109), and they were first separated by John Searle in *Speech Acts* (1969: 81ff). S's act of referring occurs at a certain time in a certain place in a certain context, and the reference is influenced by all those factors, whereas the sense and intension of the expression is not. What Speaker does is to use the intensions of language-expressions (*e* and its constituents) to identify things in the world s/he is speaking of. The locution *I totaled my car yesterday* has the (virtually) unchanging sense: 'Speaker did irreparable damage to his or her car the day before this sentence was uttered.' However, the denotation will depend on **who** makes the utterance—which determines between 'his' or 'her' car, and **when** it was uttered—which dates 'yesterday.' The locution *The prime minister is an old woman* has at least two senses: 'the chief minister within the national parliament is a woman of advanced years' and 'the chief minister within the national parliament is a man who complains too much and is over-concerned with trivia.' To decide which of these two senses S is using, H must determine S's act of referring, that is, determine what world and time S is talking about and, as part of that task, determine which entities in that world S is identifying, and what S is saying about (predicating of) those entities (cf. Allan 1986, 1988; Gernsbacher 1990). The same thing can be referred to by different locutionary acts; so, it was once possible for the following three locutions to have identical reference: (1) *The prime minister is an old woman*; (2) *Golda Meir is an old woman*; (3) *Golda Meir, the prime minister, is a woman of advanced years*. It is not quite accurate to report that speakers of (1), (2), and (3) have said the same thing; but we might agree that they have said almost the same thing, thereby implicitly recognizing the difference between the locutionary and referential acts. Similarly, the following three locutions could appear in three different utterances in three different languages yet refer to the same dog: (a) *The dog's barking!* (b) *Mbwa anabweka!* (Kiswahili); (c) *Hi:nk o g gogs!* (Tohono O'odham). Whereas locutions are defined on a particular language, denotation and reference are defined on particular worlds. However, because different speakers are involved in performing the acts, it seems necessary to conclude that the same reference can be made by different Speakers using different locutionary and utterance acts. Obviously, under normal conditions of use, Speaker makes an utterance, uses a locution, and refers with it, all at one and the same moment.

The most significant act in the hierarchy of speaking is the 'illocutionary act.' Austin (1962) awoke people to the fact that S *does* something in uttering U to H in context C, e.g., states a fact or an opinion, confirms or denies something, makes a prediction, a promise, a request, offers thanks or an invitation, issues an order or an umpire's decision, gives advice or permission, names a child, swears an oath. Thus U is said to have the 'illocutionary force' or 'illocutionary point' of a statement, a confirmation, a denial, a prediction, a promise, a request, and so forth. Many utterances are so-called indirect speech acts, in which case there is more than one illocutionary force present; usually, though, S has only one message to convey in U, and this is its illocutionary point. Etymologically 'illocution' is IN + LOCUTION because the illocution arises from what S does in using the locution. It was said earlier that the purpose of speaking is to cause an effect on the audience: this is called a 'perlocution' or 'perlocutionary effect,' an effect that arises through (= PER) the locution.

The perlocutionary effect of U is the consequence of H recognizing (what s/he takes to be) the locution and illocutionary point of U. When S says (1), S is performing the illocutionary act of making a statement about the location of a spider:

There's a spider on your hair. (1)

Given the widespread fear of spiders, it is likely that by uttering these words S will frighten H; in that case, S has performed the perlocutionary act of frightening H; put another way, the perlocution (perlocutionary effect) of U is that H is frightened. Take another example. The illocutionary point of *I bet you a dollar you can jump that puddle* would typically be to have H recognize that S is offering a bet; the acceptance or refusal of the challenge is the perlocutionary effect of the utterance. So, a perlocution is a behavioral response to the meaning of U—not necessarily a physical or verbal response, perhaps merely a mental response of some kind. Other perlocutions are such things as: alerting H by warning H of danger; persuading H to an opinion by stating supporting facts; intimidating H by threatening; and getting H to do something by means of a suggestion, a hint, a request, or a command.

An effect of U which does not result from H recognizing the locution and illocutionary point of U is NOT a perlocutionary effect. For instance, in uttering (1) it could be that S frightened H despite the fact that H either did not hear, or did not understand a word of what S said: perhaps H is profoundly deaf and was frightened by S's breath on his face; perhaps H was frightened by an unexpected voice; or perhaps H does not understand English and S frightened him by his facial expression or tone of voice. In these cases, it is not the particular utterance consisting of a particular locution and particular illocution that frightens H, but merely the utterance act.

Because the normal reason for speaking is to cause an effect on the hearer, most of what human beings say is aimed towards the success of perlocutionary acts; consequently, they are extremely significant within a theory of communication. But, strictly speaking, perlocutionary acts and perlocutionary effects fall outside of linguistics because they are not part of language per se, but instead responses to the illocutions in utterances. What linguists can properly look at, however, are the intentions of speakers to bring about certain perlocutionary effects; these so-called perlocutionary or illocutionary intentions appear in definitions of speech acts in, for example, Bach and Harnish (1977), and Allan (1986).

Bibliography

Allan K 1986 *Linguistic Meaning,* vol. 2. Routledge and Kegan Paul, London

Allan K 1998 *Natural Language Semantics.* Blackwell, Oxford

Austin J L 1962 *How To Do Things With Words*. Clarendon Press, Oxford.

Bach K, Harnish R M 1977 *Linguistic Communication and Speech Acts*. MIT Press, Cambridge, MA

Chomsky N 1975 *Reflections on Language*. Pantheon, New York

Gernsbacher M A 1991 *Language Comprehension as Structure Building*. Lawrence Erlbaum, Hillsdale, NJ

Recanati F 1988 *Meaning and Force*. Cambridge University Press, Cambridge

Searle J R 1969 *Speech Acts*. Cambridge University Press, Cambridge

Speech Act Theory: Overview

K. Allan

1. The Speech Act as an Aspect of Social Interactive Behavior

A speech act is created when speaker/writer S makes an utterance U to hearer/reader H in context C. Speech acts are a part of social interactive behavior and must be interpreted as an aspect of social interaction (cf. Labov and Fanshel 1977: 30). In the words of Habermas (1979: 2), S utters something understandably; gives H something to understand; makes him/herself thereby understandable; and comes to an understanding with another person. Habermas indicates further requirements on S: that S should believe the truth of what is said, so that H can share S's knowledge (cf. Grice's (1975) maxim of quality; see *Cooperative Principle*); S should 'express his/her intentions in such a way that the linguistic expression represents what is intended (so that [H] can trust [S])'— compare Grice's maxims of quantity and manner; S should 'perform the speech act in such a way that it conforms to recognized norms or to accepted self-images (so that [H] can be in accord with [S] in shared value orientations)' (1979: 29). Additionally, S and H 'can reciprocally motivate one another to recognize validity claims because the content of [S's] engagement is determined by a specific reference to a thematically stressed validity claim, whereby [S], in a cognitively testable way, assumes with a truth claim, obligations to provide grounds [,] with a rightness claim, obligations to provide justification, and with a truthfulness claim, obligations to prove trustworthy' (Habermas 1979: 65).

2. J. L. Austin

Interest in speech acts stems directly from the work of J. L. Austin, and in particular from the William James Lectures which he delivered at Harvard in 1955, published posthumously as *How to Do Things with Words* in 1962 (revised 1975). Austin came from the Oxford school of 'ordinary language philosophers,' which also spawned Geach, Ryle, Strawson, Grice, and Searle. It was intellectually engendered by Wittgenstein, who observed (e.g., 1963: Sect. 23) that logicians have had very little or nothing to say about many of the multiplicity of structures and usages in natural language. Austin's concern with speech acts exhibits an informal, often entertaining, philosopher's approach to some uses of ordinary language.

Austin insisted on a distinction between what he called constatives, which have truth values, and performatives which (according to him) do not (cf. Austin 1962, 1963). The distinction between truth-bearing and non-truth-bearing sentences has a long history. Aristotle noted that 'Not all sentences are statements [*apophantikos*]; only such as have in them either truth or falsity. Thus a prayer is a sentence, but neither true nor false [therefore a prayer is not a statement]' (*On Interpretation* 17a, 1). Later, the Stoics distinguished a judgment or proposition (*axíōma*) as either true or false whereas none of an interrogation, inquiry, imperative, adjurative, optative, hypothetical, nor vocative has a truth value (cf. Diogenes Laertius 1925: 65–68). For more than two millennia, logicians and language philosophers concentrated their energies on statements and the valid inferences to be drawn from them to the virtual exclusion of other propositional types (questions, commands, etc.). Austin was reacting to this tradition (cf. Hare 1971: ch. 6):

> The constative utterance, under the name so dear to philosophers, of *statement*, has the property of being true or false. The performative utterance, by contrast, can never be either: it has its own special job, it is used to perform an action. To issue such an utterance *is* to perform the action—an action, perhaps, which one scarcely could perform, at least with so much precision, in any other way. Here are some examples:
> I name this ship 'Liberté.'
> I apologise.
> I welcome you.
> I advise you to do it.
>
> (Austin 1963: 22)

Austin's point is that in making such utterances under

the right conditions, S performs, respectively, an act of naming, an act of apologizing, an act of welcoming, and an act of advising (it has become usual to speak of 'acts' rather than 'actions'). Performatives have 'felicity conditions' (see Sect. 5 below) in place of truth values. Thus according to Austin, (1) has no truth value but is felicitous if there is a cat such that S has the ability and intention to put it out, and infelicitous—but not false—otherwise:

I promise to put the cat out. (1)

This contrasts with (2), which is either true if S has put the cat out, or false if not:

I've put the cat out. (2)

Austin's claim that performatives do not have truth values has been challenged from the start, and he seems to be wrong. Roughly speaking, their truth value is less communicatively significant than what Austin called the 'illocutionary force' of U. He observed that utterances without performative verbs also perform speech acts, for example, (3) can be used to make a promise:

I'll put the cat out. (3)

Austin would say that (1) and (3) have the same illocutionary force of promising; the function of the performative verb in (1) is to name the 'illocutionary act' being performed. In the later lectures of Austin (1962), he identified two other components of a speech act: locution and perlocution. Linguists recognize three acts which Austin conflates into his locutionary act.

3. The Hierarchy within Speech Acts

Speaking (and writing—which will from now on be properly included under 'speaking' for simplicity of exposition) comprises a hierarchy of acts. To begin with, language only comes into existence if someone performs an 'act of utterance.' People recognize utterance acts on the basis of brute perception: by hearing them spoken, seeing them signed or written, feeling them impressed in braille. Individuals can readily recognize an utterance act in a language that is completely unknown to them, in which they cannot distinguish the words or sentences used. One can utter sounds which have nothing to do with language.

Speech act theory is concerned with utterances where S utters a language expression and thereby performs a 'locutionary act.' Performing a locutionary act, S uses an identifiable expression e from language L (where e is a sentence or sentence fragment) spoken with identifiable prosody π (the pattern of pause, pitch level, stress, and tone of voice; its counterpart in the written medium is punctuation and typography). The constituent structure of e and of π, together with their proper senses (meanings), are also identifiable to a typical fluent speaker of L. Recognizing the location means recognizing that e spoken with prosody π

means 'μ'; consequently, a locution is produced and then recognized by someone who has knowledge of the grammar, lexicon, semantics, and phonology of L.

S uses the senses of language-expressions in the locution (e and its constituents) to identify things in the particular world that s/he is speaking of. This constitutes the 'propositional act of referring' or 'denotational act.'

The final act in the hierarchy of speaking is the 'illocutionary act.' S *does* something in uttering U to H in context C, for example, states a fact or an opinion, confirms or denies something, makes a prediction, a promise, a request, offers thanks or an invitation, issues an order or an umpire's decision, gives advice or permission, names a child, swears an oath. Thus U is said to have the 'illocutionary force' or 'illocutionary point' of a statement, a confirmation, a denial, a prediction, a promise, a request, and so forth. Obviously, under normal conditions of use, S makes an utterance, uses a locution, denotes with it, and expresses at least one illocution, all at one and the same moment.

With very few exceptions, the purpose of speaking is to cause an effect on H (Austin described this as 'securing uptake'): speakers want their opinions to be recognized if not adopted, their assertions to be agreed with, their requests to be enacted, questions answered, advice taken, warnings heeded, commands complied with, thanks appreciated, apologies accepted, and so forth. These are called 'perlocutions' or 'perlocutionary effects.' The perlocutionary effect of U is the consequence of H recognizing (what s/he takes to be) the locution and illocutionary point of U— otherwise the effect is *not* perlocutionary. Although extremely significant within a theory of communication, perlocutionary acts/effects fall outside of linguistics because they are not part of language per se but instead responses to the illocutions in utterances. What linguists can properly look at, however, are the intentions of speakers to bring about certain perlocutionary effects; these intentions appear in definitions of speech acts as 'illocutionary intentions'.

See: Speech Act Hierarchy.

4. The Speaker's Reflexive-intention; Hearers, and Overhearers

In the spoken medium, there is never more than one S per utterance; however, two S's may utter identical U's in unison or S may speak on someone else's behalf. Coauthors generally take joint responsibility for what is written; but, normally, each writes only a part of the text. This all starkly contrasts with the number of H's which any given S may have for an audience.

H is anyone whom, at the time of utterance, S reflexively intends should recognize the illocutionary point of U. There are a couple of explanations to interject here. The simpler one is that the illocutionary point of U is S's message. The second point is that S tailors U to suit H, taking into account what s/he knows or guesses about H's ability to understand the message which S wants to convey. The notion of a reflexive-intention is S's intention to have a person in earshot recognize that S wants him/her to accept the role of H and therefore be the/an intended recipient of S's message and consequently react to it. This, of course, renders the definition of H circular, and so something closer to Grice's (1957, 1968, 1969) original proposal should be considered, adapted to our customary terminology and with some updating from Recanati (1987: ch. 7): S's reflexive-intention toward H is the intention to have H recognize that when uttering U in context C, S intends U to have a certain perlocutionary effect on H partly caused by H recognizing that S has the intention to communicate with him/her by means of U. This last intention is the illocutionary intention. (So, when Joe hears Sue talking in her sleep, he will not assume she has a reflexive-intention toward him, and therefore not expect that she intends her utterance to have any perlocutionary effect on him—though she might unintentionally keep him awake.)

Clark and Carlson (1982) distinguish between H as 'direct addressee' and H as 'ratified participant,' the latter being a member of the audience participating in the speech act (cf. Goffman 1981: 131). The notion of face (Brown and Levinson 1987) is useful in distinguishing between two kinds each of H's and overhearers. An 'addressee' is someone who cannot reject the role of H without serious affront to S's face. Direct address is determined contextually—by direction of gaze, pointing a finger, touching an arm, using a name, or on the basis of who spoke last; less commonly, the nature of the message will determine who is the intended addressee. Note the change of addressee in *Joan, Max bought me this beautiful ring for our anniversary, didn't you Max, you sweetie!* and the nonspecific addressee in *Congratulations, whoever came first!* A 'ratified participant' can reject the H role more freely than an addressee and with less of an affront to S's face. When S is speaking, all those who can reasonably consider themselves ratified participants are expected, as part of the cooperative endeavor, to keep tabs on what is said, so that if called upon to participate they may do so appropriately.

Any other person hearing U is an overhearer: either a bystander or an eavesdropper. People in earshot are expected to overhear, though not necessarily to listen; only H's are properly expected to listen. As everyone knows, it can happen that U is overheard by someone when there was no original specific intention on S's part that this should happen; to put it more precisely, S has a reflexive-intention towards H but not towards an overhearer. An overhearer may perchance understand the message the same way that H does; but,

because s/he is not necessarily party to the appropriate contextual information relevant to the correct interpretation of the utterance, it is possible that s/he may seriously misinterpret it. So, a bystander within earshot was not originally intended as a H and may, depending on circumstances, accept or reject the role of H without loss of face; consider an occasion where X is arguing with Y in earshot of Z:

[X to Y as addressee]	Shut up or I'll lay one on you.
[Y to Z as ratified participant]	You heard him threaten to hit me, didn't you?
[X to Z as bystander]	You mind your own business.
[Z to both X and Y, rejecting the role of H]	I wasn't listening.

An eavesdropper can only admit to listening in at the expense of their own positive face, because it makes her/him look bad, and sometimes also at the expense of S's negative (impositive) face, because S feels affronted by the intrusion.

5. Felicity Conditions

Austin argued for four kinds of felicity conditions: (a) a preparatory condition to establish whether or not the circumstances of the speech act and the participants in it are appropriate to its being performed successfully; (b) an executive condition to determine whether or not the speech act has been properly executed; (c) a sincerity condition—which has a similar function to Grice's (1975) maxim of quality; and (d) a fulfillment condition determined by the perlocutionary effect of the speech act. If all the relevant felicity conditions were satisfied for a given illocutionary act, Austin described it as 'happy' or 'felicitous.' One can immediately dismiss (d) as irrelevant to a linguistic theory of speech acts because it has only a contingent link with the meaning of U. The other three felicity conditions merit brief discussion here.

The statement of preparatory conditions is obligatory in definitions of illocutions. The preparatory conditions identify what ought to be presupposed in a felicitous use of the illocution. For example, the preparatory condition on an assertion such as *France is a republic* ($=p$) is 'S has reason to believe that p.' If S had said *France is not a republic,* S would be condemned for being ignorant, deluded, insane, or maliciously attempting to mislead H. It is notable that presupposition failure (in, say, *In 1990, the King of France died*) gives rise to exactly the same response. In both cases, Austin would say 'the utterance is void.' Condemnation as a response to preparatory condition failure is common to all illocutions. Take the preparatory condition on thanking: 'H, or someone or something in H's charge, has done some deed D with the apparent intention of benefiting S (directly or indirectly)'; if S thanks H for D when H never did D, H will conclude that S is either deluded or is being sarcastic. Finally, take the case of the tennis player in the US Open who claims that his opponent's ball is 'out' when the umpire disagrees: the claim has no standing because the player is not a person sanctioned by the preparatory conditions on this illocutionary act to declare the ball out of play. Again, by violating the preparatory condition, S risks condemnation. The question arises whether the preparatory conditions on an illocutionary act really are its presuppositions, as Karttunen and Peters (1979: 10) apparently believe. The problem, which cannot be solved here (cf. Allan 1998), is that only some illocutionary acts have truth conditions, yet the standard definition of presupposition is based on truth conditions (X is a presupposition of Y if it is true that Y entails X and also true that $\neg$Y entails X). As Seuren (1985: ch. 3) recognizes, some alternative definition of presupposition seems called for.

Austin requires that the procedure invoked by the illocutionary act 'must be executed by all participants correctly and completely.' He exemplifies this 'executive condition' with *I bet you the race won't be run today* said when more than one race was arranged for that day. But such misexecutions should be dealt with under generally applicable maxims of the cooperative principle. The only executive condition which still seems warranted to linguists is one on declarations which either bring about or express decisions on states of affairs such as marriage, job appointment/termination, or umpiring. Because they rely for their success on S being sanctioned by the community to perform the acts under stipulated conditions, it may be necessary to safeguard society's interest with an executive condition requiring some watchdog other than S to ensure that the sanctions are respected. These sanctions need to be written into the preparatory conditions on the act; they identify the attitude or behavior that must be observed by S when executing the illocutionary act in order for it to be felicitous.

The sincerity condition on a speech act involves S's responsibility for what s/he is saying (asking, etc.). If S is observing the cooperative maxim of quality, then s/he will be sincere; and, normally, H will assume that S is being sincere unless s/he has good reason to believe otherwise. Generally, scholars have assumed that different kinds of illocutionary acts involve different kinds of sincerity conditions: for example, assertions and the like are sincere if S believes in the truth of the proposition asserted; requests are sincere if S believes that H can do A and might be willing to do A; declarations are sincere if S believes that s/he has the proper authority to make the declaration. Obviously, sincerity reflects on whether or not S upholds the preparatory conditions, so only one sincerity condition should be necessary: in uttering U, S knows or believes (or believes s/he knows) that all clauses of the preparatory condition hold. This puts a burden on

precise statement of the preparatory conditions; but that seems exactly where it should lie, because preparatory conditions identify the particular circumstances appropriate to performing a given illocutionary act.

To sum up: the only one of Austin's original felicity conditions that remains obligatory in the definitions of all illocutions is the preparatory condition. An executive condition may be valid for declarations. Some scholars still include sincerity conditions within definitions for illocutionary acts, but sincerity can be captured by generally applicable conditions on language use. Finally, linguists rarely attend to fulfillment conditions, nor should they—though these will remain important to scholars in other disciplines concerned with perlocutionary effects of utterances. The burden of felicitous illocution will depend on proper observation of the preparatory conditions on each illocutionary act. These conditions provide the grounds for motivating S to make the utterance and grounds from which H will evaluate the illocutionary act expressed in the utterance.

See: Felicity Conditions.

6. Explicit Performative Clauses

The characteristics of explicit performative clauses are as follows. The clause must contain a verb that names the illocutionary point of the utterance, for example, *admit, advise, apologize, ask, assert, authorize, baptize, bet, charge, claim, command, congratulate, declare, order, pardon, permit, prohibit, promise, refuse, say, suggest, swear, tell, thank, urge.* It must be in the present tense; in English, it is typically in the simple aspect, but may be progressive: thus *I promise/am promising to accompany you* are performative; *I promised/have promised to accompany you* are not. An explicit performative clause may be negative; it may be emphatic; and it may contain the adverb *hereby*, meaning 'in/by uttering this performative' (but not meaning 'using this,' referring to something in the context). It must be 'realis' and denote the actualization of the illocutionary act; therefore *I must hereby take my leave of you* is a performative, *I might hereby authorize your release* is not. Finally, S must be agent for whoever takes responsibility for enforcing the illocutionary point of U.

See: Performative Clauses.

7. Classes of Speech Act

There have been two approaches to classifying speech acts: one, following Austin (1962), is principally a lexical classification of so-called illocutionary verbs; the other, following Searle (1975a), is principally a classification of acts. Lexical groupings of semantically similar illocutionary verbs are made on an intuitive basis, perhaps with some reference to the syntactic environment of the verb (as in Vendler's

1972 classes), for example, expositives N_i V *that* p, such as *state, contend, insist, deny, remind, guess* versus, say, commissives N_i V *to* V, such as *promise, guarantee, refuse, decline;* exercitives 'exercising of powers, rights, or influences' (N_i V N_j *to* V), for example, *order, request, beg, dare;* or behabitives (N_i V N_j P nom (past (V))), for example, *thank, congratulate, criticize),* or Ballmer and Brennenstuhl's (1981) formula N V ((addressee) *by saying*)p.

Searle (1975a) used four criteria—illocutionary point, direction of fit, S's psychological state, and propositional content—to establish five classes of speech acts. 'Representatives' have a truth value, show words-to-world fit, and express S's belief that *p.* 'Directives' are attempts to get H to do something, therefore they show world-to-words fit, and express S's wish or desire that H do A. 'Commissives' commit S to some future course of action, so they show world-to-words fit, and S expresses the intention that S do A. 'Expressives' express S's attitude to a certain state of affairs specified (if at all) in the propositional content (e.g., the underlined portion of *I apologize for stepping on your toe*). There is no direction of fit; a variety of different psychological states; and propositional content 'must... be related to S or H' (1975a: 357f.). 'Declarations' bring about correspondence between the propositional content and the world, thus direction of fit is both words-to-world and world-to-words. Searle recognizes no psychological state for declarations. Searle's classification has been widely adopted.

Using H's evaluations as criteria, it is possible to establish links between classes of illocution and major clause types. 'Statements' (including denials, reports, predictions, promises, and offers) are principally expressions of S's belief about the way the world was, is, or will be, and are most typically formulated with a declarative clause. They can be judged in terms of the question 'Is *p* credible?' 'Invitationals' are a proper subset of Searle's directives, and include requests, exhortations, suggestions, warnings, etc. which principally invite H's participation. Many are formulated in an interrogative clause and prompt the question 'Does S really want A to be done, and if so is H both able and willing to do it?' 'Authoritatives' include the rest of Searle's 'directives' and his 'declarations' (commands, permissions, legal judgments, baptisms, etc.) which have S 'laying down the law.' Many of them are formulated in an imperative clause, the rest in a declarative. For these, H must consider the question 'Does S have the authority to utter U in the given context?' 'Expressives' (greetings, thanks, apologies, congratulations, etc.) have social-interactive-appropriateness values: 'Has something occurred which warrants S expressing such a reaction to it?' These principally express social interaction with H; many are idiomatic, the rest are in the default declarative clause format. All four classes of speech acts can be conveyed using a declarative clause; but interrogatives typically indicate invitationals, imperatives authoritatives, and idioms expressives.

See: Speech Act Classification.

8. Definitions of Illocutions

Definitions of illocutions are an extension of the semantics of the key verb naming the illocution, for example, *assert, deny, boast, suggest, promise, threaten, offer, command, baptize,* etc. Such a verb is just one kind of illocutionary force-indicating device or IFID. Another kind of lexical IFID is *please:* compare the information-seeking question *Are you leaving?* with the request that H leave in *Are you leaving, please?* The hyperbole in *Your bedroom's a pigsty!* implies not only condemnation but also often the command to clear it up. Idioms like *Would you mind...* minimize an impending imposition. There are morphological IFIDS marking clause-type and politeness levels in Japanese and other oriental languages. There are syntactic IFIDS like word order and clause-type (mood), cf. *You can do A* versus *Can you do A?* versus *Would that you could do A.* Last, there is prosody or punctuation; contrast *Out?* with *Out!* In most utterances, the recognition of an illocution requires reference to cooperative conditions and/or the context of utterance (see Sects. 9, 10, 11 below).

Austin cleared the ground and laid the foundations for speech act theory, and to him goes the credit for distinguishing locution, illocution, and perlocution. But it was Searle (1969: ch. 3) who first established criteria for the definitions of illocutions, using promising as his example. (a) 'Normal input and output conditions obtain.' That is, the situation of utterance (including participants) is favorable to successful communication. (b) 'S expresses the proposition that *p* in [U].' (c) 'In expressing that *p*, S predicates a future act A of S.' Conditions (b) and (c) constitute the 'propositional content' referred to in specific definitions of illocutionary acts (in this instance, promising); scholars since Searle have usually extended this component of a definition to a description of utterance content that names the illocution, thereby including the IFID that Searle expressly omits (Vanderveken 1990–91 is an exception). Rules (d) and (e) identify 'preparatory conditions' on the illocution; (d) being specific to promising, and (e) being 'to the effect that the act must have a point.' Rule (e) should be enshrined within general statements of cooperative conditions on language use because it is normally relevant to all illocutionary acts and does not need to be stated within any particular definition. (f) is a sincerity condition (see Sect. 5 above). (g) 'S intends [U] will place him under an obligation to do A' is to be taken together with (h), which identifies S's reflexive-intention, 'S intends (i-i) to produce in H the knowledge (K) that [U] is to count as placing S under an obligation to do A. S intends to produce K by means of the recognition of i-ɪ, and he intends i-ɪ to be recognized in virtue of (by means of) H's knowledge of the meaning of [U].' Searle calls this 'counts as' condition 'the essential rule.' Others have adopted or adapted it into an 'illocutionary intention.'

A survey of speech act definitions in Searle (1969), Bach and Harnish (1979), Edmondson (1981), Levinson (1983), Allan (1986), and Wierzbicka (1987) reveals great similarity despite the different perspectives of these scholars. The obligatory components of the definitions of illocutions are the preparatory condition and S's illocutionary intention. The propositional or utterance content will be either given or inferable from one or both of these. Finally, as was suggested in Sect. 5, a single sincerity condition holds for all acts.

9. Being Literal or Nonliteral, Direct or Indirect, On-record or Off-record

An indirect speech act is one in which S performs one illocutionary act (e.g., stating *It's cold in here*), but intends H to infer by way of relying on their mutually shared background information, both linguistic and nonlinguistic, another illocution (e.g., requesting the heating to be turned up); cf. Searle (1975b: 61), Bach and Harnish (1979: 70). Sadock (1974) identified some exotic species of indirect acts: 'whimperatives' indirectly request (the function of the imperative in Sadock's view) by means of S directly asking a question, for example, *Can't you (please) do A?* and *Do A, will you?* (this analysis is criticized in Allan 1986: 216); using a 'queclarative,' S directly questions and indirectly makes an assertion—*Does anyone do A any more?* means 'Nobody does A any more'; 'requestions' are quiz questions to which S knows the answer, for example, *Columbus discovered America in?* Because the clause-type determines the direct or primary illocution, most speech acts are indirect; so, rather than postulating a binary distinction (direct versus indirect), it is preferable to allow for an open-ended series of illocutions ranged from the primary illocution (determined by clause-type) to the last illocution that can be inferred from a given utterance (which is the illocutionary point).

The study of indirect speech acts has overwhelmingly dealt with requests. Blum-Kulka, et al. (1989: 18) identify nine points on an indirectness scale for requests. Their 'direct strategies' are used when S is dominant: (a) imperative *Clean up that mess;* (b) performative *I'm asking you to clean up that mess;* (c) hedged performatives *I would like to ask you to come for a check-up;* (d) obligation statements *You'll have to move that car;* (e) want statements *I want you to stop calling me.* What they call 'conventionally indirect strategies' are H-oriented: (f) suggestory formulas *How about cleaning up?;* (g) query preparatory (Sadock's 'whimperatives') *Could/Will you clear up*

the kitchen, please? Finally, their 'nonconventionally indirect strategies' are off-record: (h) strong hints *You've left the kitchen in a dreadful mess;* (i) mild hints *I say, it's a bit chilly in here, isn't it?* (said when the heating is off and the window open).

The contrast between direct and indirect illocution is muddied by the related contrasts between being on-record versus off-record, and being literal or nonliteral. Blum-Kulka, et al.'s 'nonconventional indirect' requests could be classified 'off-record'; the 'direct' and 'conventionally indirect' ones 'on-record' because an on-record U spells out the message explicitly. Note that S can be on-record and either direct or indirect; but if S is off-record, s/he is necessarily indirect. For someone who is not very close to S to respond to the invitation *Do you want to come to a movie tonight?* with the bald-on-record refusal *No* is downright offensive. To avoid giving offence, people hedge, apologize, prevaricate, and speak off-record, giving reasons for not accepting the invitation or complying with the request. Thus, to politely refuse the invitation, one says things like *I have to wash my hair* or *I'd love to, but my mother's coming to dinner tonight.* Note that these might be literally meant on-record statements of S's plans, but their illocutionary point is indirect and off-record refusal.

A nonliteral U such as the sarcastic *I'm sure the cat likes you pulling its tail* is an indirect, off-record request for H to desist. What makes it nonliteral is that S does not really mean it as a direct assertion about what the cat likes; in other words, it is the illocution which is nonliteral. However, there is no reason to believe that the literal meaning of *Max is a bastard* is any more direct than an utterance intending the nonliteral meaning of 'bastard'; furthermore, both interpretations are on-record. The psycholinguistic evidence (cf. Gernsbacher 1990: 89) is that all possible senses of a language expression are activated, and context then suppresses the activation of inappropriate meanings; consequently, there is no reason to believe that the nonliteral meaning of a lexically ambiguous term takes longer to process than its literal meaning; and there are therefore no grounds at all for suggesting that it is less 'direct.' What is nonliteral in the last example is the locution, not the illocution. Take another, problematic example: *If it's not Schlitz, it's not beer.* This is a direct, on-record assertion, but it is nonliteral because S does not really mean that a can of Budweiser or Foster's is not beer, though S might literally mean that in S's opinion (but not everybody's) Budweiser and Foster's lack the properties necessary for it to be properly classified as beer. Thus, one concludes that S is indirectly asserting the opinion that Schlitz is the best beer—and literally means this; there will be different views on whether or not this opinion is on the record.

It is not enough to retain the term 'indirect illocution' only for an illocution that is either off-record or nonliteral or both. Suppose S asserts *Ted's BMW is crook*. This entails the on-record proposition that 'Ted has a BMW' and it is indirect because S does not directly assert it (pace Russell). Presumably S literally means 'Ted has a BMW' because s/he presupposes its truth (i.e., purports to do so). One concludes that illocutions which are on-record and apparently literally meant are 'indirect' if they are entailed or implicated in U; also if they are off-record, or nonliteral, or both. The so-called 'conventionally indirect' illocutions are on-record, not S-dominant but H-oriented: this solves the problem that they do not necessarily translate into other languages (see Sect. 14).

See: Indirect Speech Acts; Speech Acts: Literal and Nonliteral.

10. More Than One Illocution in U

Coordinate, conjoined, and appositive clauses contribute more than one illocutionary point to U. With *I resign from the board and promise not to speak to the press*, S resigns and makes a promise. With *Welcome to the show; now, what do you do for a living?*, S welcomes H and asks a question. With *I met Celia—Did you know she was married, by the way?—at a party last night, and she told me the latest scandal at number 25*, S performs an informative interrupted by a question and conjoins to the informative a report.

One serious weakness with speech act theory has been to pretend that each U has only one illocutionary point. As Labov and Fanshel (1977: 29f.) pointed out, 'most utterances can be seen as performing several speech acts simultaneously.... Conversation is not a chain of utterances, but rather a matrix of utterances and actions bound together by a web of understandings and reactions.... In conversation, participants use language to interpret to each other the significance of the actual and potential events that surround them and to draw the consequences for their past and future actions.' Speech acts must be interpreted with attention to their context and to their function as an integral part of social interactive behavior. Here is a common enough example:

S₁: Would you like another drink?
S₂: Yes, I would, thank you.

S₁ asks a question and concomitantly makes the offer to bring S₂ a drink, if that is what S₂ wants. S₂ responds positively both to the question and to the offer, and coordinates with these illocutions a statement of thanks. Some situations allow for quite a large number of illocutionary points to be scored. Consider a public condemnation like that of the woman at a party who cries out *Mrs Trumpington, will you please ask your husband to keep his hands off me?!* S does several things simultaneously: (a) she makes a literal on-record request to Mrs T that she ask Mr T to stop harassing S; (b) she broadcasts on-record, literally, but indirectly,

what Mr T is doing; (c) she makes a literal on-record indirect request that he stop—despite the on-record indirect expression of her belief that he will not stop unless coerced; (d) off-record, S indirectly intends not only that Mrs T condemn her husband for sexual harassment of S, but (e) that everyone in earshot should do so too.

Another weakness of speech act theory is to pretend that S's illocutionary intentions can be precisely pinned down. Suppose that one morning as H is getting ready for work, S volunteers *It's 7.45*. This informs H of the time. One may or may not be overestimating S's intention if one assumes that s/he thereby implies that it is past the time when H should have already left for work, hence warning H that s/he is running late and furthermore counseling H to hurry. U may merely have been intended to draw H's attention to the time, leaving H to draw whatever conclusion s/he wished. H might be grateful for having the matter brought to his/her attention; get angry with S for interfering; respond by hurrying; respond by suing for divorce; there are innumerable possible responses. S discovers only through H's response the perlocutionary effect of U, and thence whether his/her intentions have been realized—always assuming S has any clear idea what these are!

11. The Inferential Analysis of Speech Acts

The inferential theory of speech acts developed out of proposals originally made by Searle (1975b), subsequently refined in the 'speech acts schema' described by Bach and Harnish (1979), and in Allan (1986: ch. 8). When S wishes to communicate with H, s/he will express him/herself in a way that s/he presumes will enable H to comprehend the intended message. The inferential theory of speech acts presents an abstract model of each step necessary in H's reasoning out of S's illocutionary point(s) in uttering U. There is an assumption that both S and H are normal human beings—that is, neither is a genius, a clairvoyant, nor a fool; both know the language L and how to use it; and they have the general knowledge that one can reasonably attribute to such persons in the particular context of utterance.

The stages in H's reasoning are taken to be as follows:

(a) Perception and recognition of U as linguistic.
(b) Recognition of U as an expression *e* of language L spoken with prosody π, and of the sense or senses (intensions) of the locution. This is done on the bases of the cooperative principle (the term is used here to include the reasonableness condition, the communicative presumption, face concerns, and the like), and H's knowledge of lexiconic, syntactic, and prosodic contributions to meaning—all of which must be specified within a general theory of meaning, though not within a theory of speech acts.

(c) Recognition of what S is referring to in the world spoken of (which forms part of the context C).

(d) Recognition of the primary illocution of U on the basis of the mood of the clause in the locution, and the definitions of the five or so primary illocutionary acts which form part of the theory of speech acts.

(e) S's presumed reason for performing this primary illocution is sought in the light of various assumptions and presumptions of the cooperative principle, knowledge of L, and the use of L (including knowledge of the definitions of illocutionary acts), context, and background information of many kinds. This process may lead to a number of illocutions being inferred, ranged in a sequence from primary illocution to illocutionary point.

(f) The illocutionary point (or points) of U, that is, S's message in U, is recognized when at last no further illocutions can be inferred, and the inference schema shuts down.

An utterance such as (4) trades on the cooperative requirement that H should have a good reason not to comply with such a request:

Why don't you be quiet? (4)

Consider the following inference schema:

In uttering (4) S intends H to reason that:	*Basis:*
1. S utters U in C. [Recognition of the utterance act]	Hearing S utter U in C.
2. U consists of $\langle \pi, e \rangle$ in English, and $\langle \pi, e \rangle$ means 'S asks why don't you be quiet?' ($= '\mu'$) [Recognition of the locution]	1, cooperative principle, knowledge of English.
3. By 'you,' S means 'H.' S is using $\langle \pi, e \rangle$ to mean 'S asks H to give a reason not to be quiet'. [Recognition of reference]	2, semantic theory, context.
4. S reflexively-intends U to be taken as asking a reason to be given for H not to be quiet. [Recognition of the primary illocutionary intention]	3, definitions of illocutionary acts.
5. S is asking for a reason to be given for H not to be quiet. [Recognition of the primary illocution]	4, definition of interrogatives.
6. S's reason for asking this is to be informed of the reason for H not to be quiet; i.e. S reflexively-intends U to be taken as a reason for H to tell S H's reason not to be quiet. [Recognition of the secondary illocutionary intention]	5, cooperative principle, definitions of illocutionary acts.
7. S is questioning H as to H's reason not to be quiet. [Recognition of the secondary illocution]	6, definition of questions.
8. S's question presupposes that H has been noisy. Noise imposes on others; it seems it has imposed on S. It is impolite to impose on others, therefore the person doing it should desist or else give a reason for not being able to desist. Any other action is uncooperative, and S must know this.	7, semantic theory. encyclopedic knowledge, cooperative principle, and perhaps context.
9. Therefore S reflexively-intends that U be taken as a reason either for H to be quiet or to inform S of the reason for being unable to be quiet. [Recognition of the tertiary illocutionary intention].	7,8, definition of illocutionary acts.
10. S is requesting H either to be quiet, or to tell S the reason for being unable to be quiet. [Recognition of the tertiary illocution]	9, definition of requestives.
11. There is no reason to believe any further illocutionary intention can be inferred, therefore S is either requesting H to be quiet or questioning his reason for being unable to be quiet. [Conclusion as to the illocutionary point of U]	3, 10, definitions of illocutionary acts, encyclopedic knowledge.

People are not expected to expressly offer reasons for being cooperative, but they are expected to offer reasons for not being cooperative: which is why there is the disjunctive illocutionary point to (4). Notice how the question illocution is carried down through the schema to become one of the disjuncts of the illocutionary point of the speech act.

Having recognized the utterance act, H must recognize S's locution. To accomplish this, H must recognize that U consists of expression *e* from language L spoken with prosody π. The first step in the process is for H to make the communicative presumption that S intends to communicate with him/her using language as a medium. This presumption is based in part on a categorizing ability to which H must have recourse at various levels in the analysis of utterance meaning. H takes the sense data from constituents of U and categorizes them using his/her linguistic knowledge, so as to perceive them in terms of a linguistic category. Perhaps the initial categorization is to recognize U as made in language L; this might be crudely described as matching H's perception of U and its parts with the languages that s/he knows. In practice, H usually has a clear expectation about which language S is using because of former experience with S or the situation of utterance; where this is not the case, there will be a heuristic interactional process along the following lines: (a) U sounds as though it is made in L_b; (b) constituent e_i of U seems to be a constituent of L_b; (c) if constituent e_j also seems to be

461

a constituent of L_b, then e_k will be another; (d) if there is no counterevidence, then S is speaking L_b (this procedure is not experimentally tested). Having established that U is made in L, H must use his/her knowledge of L when categorizing what s/he perceives in U as particular lexiconic, syntactic, and prosodic constituents of L. For instance, H needs a knowledge of L's lexicon and how to use it, in order to match the appropriate set of lexicon entries with the lexicon items which s/he perceives S to use in U. H must use knowledge of the syntactic properties of lexicon items in establishing their scope relations and the syntactic structures which combine them in U. Once these are recognized, H can determine the meanings of e's constituents, and the meaning of e itself; H will then take into account the effect of the prosody π on the meaning of e in order to determine the sense or senses of the locution $\langle \pi, e \rangle$.

The next step for H is to recognize what S is referring to in the world spoken of. To do this, H will match the sense(s) of e's constituents with entities in the world spoken of, using knowledge of the correlation between sense and denotation/reference. Having determined the reference of U, H uses knowledge of the definitions of illocutionary acts to determine S's illocutionary intention in U. Once again, it is a matter for H's categorizing ability: this time, H perceives what S is denoting by means of the locution $\langle \pi, e \rangle$, and s/he must determine what kind of message S intends to communicate using this proposition. The set of illocutionary intentions is located among the definitions of illocutionary acts which constitute a part of H's linguistic knowledge (and are presumably located along with other information about meaningful properties and meaning relations). Recognition of the illocutionary intention will lead to the identification of the illocutionary act which it helps to define. There are only five or six primary illocutionary acts, each being determined by the form of the locution. To determine the illocutionary point of U, H invokes the reasonableness condition and seeks some reason for S's primary illocution in the context, C; the conversational maxim of relation (or relevance) will often be invoked too, and so may the other maxims of the cooperative principle—though these are more likely to be called upon at later stages. H will need to keep tabs on the meaningful properties of U and its constituents at this as in all subsequent steps leading to the decision on the illocutionary point of U; s/he must also constantly monitor the semantic relationships of U and its constituents to their textual environment; the semantic properties and relations of U may well be significant to its proper interpretation. In seeking a reason for the primary illocution, H looks to the context C, and will also check background knowledge of many kinds, including knowledge of the kinds of things that people might say in C, and the kinds of reasons that other speakers might have had when

employing a similar primary illocution; in other words, H uses knowledge of L and the use of L to infer from the primary locution and the circumstances of utterance what the illocutionary point might be. This may lead through a number of indirect illocutions. The illocutionary point is only recognized when H can infer no further illocutions in U. When H recognizes the illocutionary point, s/he has finally determined the meaning of U.

Although this description offers a rational model for H's understanding of U, it is misleading because it pretends that each step is completed before the next is begun. This cannot be true because, in reality, people interpret parts of utterances as they are presented. The inferential theory of speech acts needs to be reworked to allow for this.

12. Performative Analysis

Katz and Postal (1964) recognized the contribution that clause-type makes to meaning, and postulated dummy morphemes 'Q' for interrogatives, interpreted 'I request that you answer'; 'I' for imperatives, interpreted 'I request'; and no dummy for declaratives. Searle (1969: 64) commented '[if] we can reduce all illocutionary acts to some very small number of illocutionary types it would then seem likely that the deep structure of a sentence would have a simple representation of its illocutionary type.' R. Lakoff (1968) proposed that one of the pair of abstract performative verbs which she dubbed **imper* 'command' and **hort* 'exhort' underlie all imperative sentences in Latin. Lakoff was motivated by the principle of economy: constraints stated on these two abstract verbs apply to all the surface verbs of commanding and exhorting, and do not need to be repeated for each verb separately. Her proposal legitimized abstract verbs as theoretical constructs. Here were the seeds of the performative analysis theory of speech acts.

In its original form, the so-called performative analysis in transformational grammar postulates that 'every deep structure contains one and only one performative as its highest clause' (Ross 1970: 261). Illocutionary force was thought to be a property of sentences rather than utterances, and to capture the illocutionary point of a sentence Ross proposed that the highest clause of the deepest phrase marker underlying every sentence is performative, whether or not the surface sentence contains a lexical performative.

$$[_S[_{NP}I] [_{VP}\text{PERFORMATIVE VERB } (you)$$
$$[_S\text{NONPERFORMATIVE SENTENCES}_S]_{VP}]_S]$$

This was wrong, and so was the claim that a sentential phrase marker can contain one, and only one, performative: *I say ₍that₎ I promise to be home by eight* confutes both claims. Performative 'I say' is the highest clause, but the embedded performative 'I promise' indicates the illocutionary point. Furthermore, most surface sentences do not contain a performative verb, so the one postulated is abstract. Now, abstract verbs are figments of the linguist's imagination: by definition, they have no surface manifestation and must be argued for on circumstantial evidence. Having complicated the grammar by introducing an abstract verb into deep structure, the linguist is then forced to complicate the grammar yet further, by postulating a deletion rule to remove the abstract verb from the phrase marker at some point in the progression from deep to surface structure. For the case in hand, Fraser (1974) showed that a performative deletion transformation would be difficult to define—and, in fact, it never was defined.

Ross (1970) presented 14 arguments based on almost unrelated bits of data in support of the hypothesis that the highest clause of every declarative sentence is a performative verb of stating. Every one of Ross's arguments has been assuredly refuted (along with additional ones in G. Lakoff 1972 and Sadock 1974) by Anderson (1971), Fraser (1974), Harnish (1975), and Allan (1986: 258ff.). Despite the wealth of evidence to contradict Ross's hypothesis, it had tremendous impact when it appeared and was widely accepted. Although some of the more pernicious errors in Ross's formulation were later rectified, and his conception of deep structure was updated by, for example, G. Lakoff and Sadock, the idea that illocutionary force can be accounted for as one of the higher clauses in the deepest phrase-marker underlying a sentence persisted throughout the 1970s. The question arises whether the fault lies with particular versions of the theory, or with the theory itself. Whereas the inferential theory of speech acts is a theory of H's interpretation of S's utterance U to H in context C, the performative analysis theory is a theory of the illocutionary potential of a given sentence. The inferential theory is a pragmatic theory that invokes H's knowledge of language L, of the use of L, of the context C, and also S's general background knowledge. For the performative analysis theory, all the information contained within the inference schemas of the inferential theory must somehow be located within the deepest phrase marker of a transformational grammar, and rules have to be specified for converting such deep structures into a surface structure equivalent to the locution. For two main reasons, this is an aim that cannot be achieved. Very briefly, such a quantity of information cannot properly be accommodated within recursive structures of the kind generated by rewrite rules such as 'Sentence → NP VP,' 'VP → V (NP) Sentence' (nor the more recent versions of Chomsky-inspired grammar). Even if it could, it is very doubtful whether such deep structures could be converted into proper surface structures matching the locution, because of difficulties with lexical insertion and the assignment of prosody. One is forced to conclude that as a theory of speech acts, performative analysis was always a lame duck.

13. Toward a Formal Theory of Speech Acts

Linguistics has adopted two trends from language philosophy: the Fregean school of formal languages, which has developed the model-theoretic truth-conditional systems associated with the names of Montague and Cresswell; and the notably informal school of ordinary language philosophy (see Sect. 2 above), which developed speech act theory. The formalization of speech act theory bridges the gap between the two schools. The program is, in effect, to extend the Fregean tradition's formal semantics of sentences by adding a formal theory of illocutionary types together with a characterization of illocutionary success (identifying particular illocutions) and satisfactory correspondence between U and states of affairs in the world spoken of.

Katz (1977) embarked on such a program using the 'semantic markerese' of his semantic theory (Katz 1972). His theory of propositional types sets out to describe the illocutionary potential of sentences as part of their sense. He uses the terminology of his semantic theory (Katz 1972), which purportedly models the ideal speaker-hearer's competence (cf. Chomsky 1965: 4). According to Katz (1977: 24):

> The propositional type of a sentence (on a sense) is the information that determines the type of speech act that a token performs in a null context.
>
> The propositional content of a sentence (on a sense) is the information that determines the particular speech act (within the categories specified by its propositional type, and subtypes) a token performs in a null context.
>
> ... [A]lthough for convenience we speak about a token of a sentence type performing a speech act, this is to be understood to mean that the speaker performs the act in the use of the token.

Strictly speaking, Katz does not, therefore, offer a theory of speech acts: speech acts are quintessentially pragmatic events, and Katz eschews pragmatics, relegating it to an undescribed theory of performance (cf. Katz 1977: 16).

Katz champions Austin's distinction between 'assertives' (Austin's constatives) and performatives, which he construes as a difference in propositional type. He therefore distinguishes sharply between sentences with explicit performatives where the illocution is signaled in the semantics of the performative verb, for example, *I state you will go; I request that you tell me whether or not you will go; I order you to go,* and those without, for example, *You will go; Will you go? Go!* For Katz, the proposition is defined on the semantic content of the immediate constituents of sentence node in the lexically specified underlying phrase marker, and in particular the verb. In addition, Katz specifies certain conditions on the proposition to determine its illocutionary success. All types of proposition, 'assertive,' and performative must satisfy the denotation condition. This requires that each noun phrase must pick out the intended number of objects from the world spoken of, at the time spoken of; in other words, it requires that S should successfully refer with them. Satisfaction of the denotation condition guarantees the illocutionary success of an 'assertive' proposition and sets it up for truth-value assignment—its satisfaction condition.

The denotation condition is also a necessary, though not a sufficient, condition on the illocutionary success of performative propositions. It is, therefore, an essential part of the theory of propositional types. Yet it is incorrigibly pragmatic and can form no part of the sense of the proposition; it thus proves that Katz found it impossible to describe a theory of propositional types within the boundaries that he had set himself.

In Katz's view, performative propositions must satisfy an additional four illocutionary success conditions, and it is this which sets them apart from 'assertives.' These four, the performative branch condition, the speaker as agent condition, the present tense condition, and the punctual act condition, all identify necessary features of an explicit performative clause (see Sect. 6 above).

The illocutionary success conditions determine what kind of illocutionary act S performs. Katz also describes what he calls 'converted conditions' which identify the validity of the illocution in terms of its perlocutionary success or failure as an illocution of a particular kind (note that this is not the same concept as a perlocution of a particular utterance). 'Assertives' are subject to a truth condition; 'questions' to an answerhood condition; 'requestives' (which include imperatives) to a compliance condition; 'advisives' to a heeding condition; 'permissives' to a license condition (= license to authorize); 'obligatives' are subject to a fulfillment condition; 'expressives' to a compensation condition; 'expositives' (the making of declarations and claims) to an acknowledgment condition; and 'stipulatives' to a nomenative condition. Converted conditions are necessarily pragmatic since they involve decisions about the matching of what is said to the way the world is, or comes to be, etc.— that is, they are satisfaction conditions. For example, Katz states (1977: 234):

> The nomenative condition for a stipulative proposition *P* is that (a) there is a designatum of the recipient reading, (b) people identify the recipient by the name in *P* [...], and (c) people do so in part as a consequence of the communicative act in which the recipient becomes the bearer of the name.

Katz's theory of illocutionary type pretends to be a theory of sense, and the sense of *I'm sure the cat likes you pulling its tail* is compatible with it being an assertive proposition. This tends to confirm that Katz's theory of propositional type is perhaps what he claims it is, and to criticize it for *not* being a thoroughgoing theory of speech acts is to mistake its

nature. Unfortunately, however, the objection must still be made that Katz does not keep within the limits which he sets on his theory, because he defines all propositional types on satisfaction of the denotation condition—which corresponds to recognizing S's act of referring within the inferential theory of speech acts. This is not part of the sense of locution; it is a function of its use in U. On this point alone, Katz's theory falls short of its aims; and there are many points in the exposition of his theory where Katz necessarily strays into pragmatics (see Allan 1986 for a detailed critique). Katz's theory of propositional types purports to be a theory of speech acts; a theory of speech acts cannot be anything other than pragmatic because speech acts are, by definition, pragmatic events.

Searle and Vanderveken (1985: 7) remark the significant inadequacy of existing semantic theories because they merely assign propositions or truth conditions to sentences and cannot assign illocutionary forces to each sentence for each possible context of utterance. Searle and Vanderveken (1985) and Vanderveken (1990–91) offer the foundations for a formal theory of illocutionary forces in terms intended to extend intensional logics such as that of Montague (1974). According to Searle and Vanderveken (1985: 2):

> Just as propositional logic studies the properties of all truth functions (e.g., conjunction, material implication, negation) without worrying about the various ways that these are realized in the syntax of English ('and', 'but', and 'moreover', to mention just a few for conjunction), so illocutionary logic studies the properties of illocutionary forces (e.g., assertion, conjecture, promise) without worrying about the various ways that these are realized in the syntax of English ('assert', 'state', 'claim', and the indicative mood, to mention just a few for assertion) and without worrying whether these features translate into other languages. No matter whether and how an illocutionary act is performed, it has a certain logical form which determines its conditions of success and relates it to other speech acts.

Searle's five classes of illocutionary act (assertive, commissive, directive, declarative, expressive) are represented by the formula $i\Pi_F P$, to be read: S achieves illocutionary point F on a proposition P in context i. (By definition, Π_F is assertive for $F = 1$, commissive for $F = 2$, etc.) For example, the definition of 'assertive' (1985: 60) is:

$$\Pi_\vdash = \Pi_1 \,;\, \text{mode}(\vdash) = \Pi_1 \,;\, \text{degree}(\vdash) = \eta(\vdash) = 0;$$
$$\text{Prop}_\vdash(i) = \text{Prop}, \Sigma_\vdash(i, P) = [\{\rho a_i t_i P\}] \text{ and}$$
$$\Psi_\vdash(i, P) = [\{\text{Bel}(P)\}]$$

It is to be read: the illocutionary force of assertion is assertive. The mode of achievement of an assertion is via an assertive. The degree of strength of its illocutionary point is zero (though different assertives have different strengths; for example, *I insist* has a degree of $+1$, *I admit* of 0, and *I conjecture* of -1).

The propositional content is P uttered in context i given preparatory condition Σ—namely that P uttered by speaker a in context i at time t is true in world w_i. The sincerity condition Ψ on the assertion P uttered in context i is that a believes that P.

Overt performance of one illocution may commit S to another which is not overtly performed; for example, if S warns H that H is in danger, then S is also committed to the assertion that H is in danger: likewise if S successfully testifies, reports, or complains that p, s/he is committed to the assertion that p. Thus, according to Searle and Vanderveken, a complaint differs from an assertion in that there are additional clauses in its preparatory and sincerity conditions, respectively: $[\Sigma_{\vdash}(i, P) \cup \{$the state of affairs that P is bad, $P\}]$; and $[\Psi_{\vdash}(i, P) \cup \{$dissatisfaction $(P)\}]$ (1985: 191). It can clearly be seen from these that the illocution of assertion is properly included within the illocution of complaint. Their logic allows for many other properties of illocutionary forces to be formalized.

Here, it is only possible to glimpse a fragment of illocutionary logic. It is in the process of development, and is not yet integrated with theories of lexical and sentence meaning. Additionally, there is independent development of formal theories of communicative intentions within the field of artificial intelligence that go beyond single utterances (see Cohen, et al. 1990).

14. Speech Acts and Intercultural Pragmatics

Different cultural conventions and belief systems in different language communities result in different cooperative conventions. For example, there are different linguistic politeness strategies to reflect the culturally validated perceived roles of S and H, and whatever is being spoken of. Social interactive practices such as societal attitudes to the roles of men and women vary greatly across cultures; and, as a result, so do the language conventions which people use. Acts of complimenting and thanking are more frequent in Anglo communities than in, say, China or Africa. The Japanese and Chinese find refusing more offensive than Americans do, and so refuse off-record by using proverbs and impersonals. Preparatory conditions on illocutionary acts defined for one language cannot be expected to be universal. Intercultural miscommunication arises from the assumption that the language strategies appropriate to the delivery of the intended meaning in L_x can be used with equal efficacy in L_y. For instance, direct translation of the English *Would you like to go the cinema with me?* into Polish *Czy miałabyś ochotę pójść ze mną do kina?* will be interpreted as a direct question and not an invitation; the counterpart Polish invitation *Możebyśmy poszli do kina?* 'Perhaps we would go to the cinema?' will probably misfire in English as an intended invitation, because the off-record implication in Polish—'if I

asked you?'—is lost (cf. Wierzbicka 1991: 29. Other Polish speakers strongly disagree with Wierzbicka's intuitions claiming that *Czy miałabyś* . . . is a polite invitation and *Możebyśmy* . . . a suggestion).

All major speech act theorists have ignored cultural diversity, leaving it to empirical studies such as the Cross-Cultural Speech Act Realization Project (CCSARP) to investigate (cf. Blum-Kulka, et al. 1989). This project investigated and confirmed cultural differences in strategies for requesting and apologizing in German, Hebrew, Danish, Canadian French, Argentinian Spanish, British, American, and Australian English. For instance, both Americans and Hebrews generally prefer to use on-record H-oriented requests rather than off-record ones, but the second preferences differ: Hebrews prefer S-dominant direct requests, whereas Americans favor the off-record strategy. Interacting with familiars but not intimates, Slavs, Hebrews, and Germans use direct on-record requests mitigated with, for example, modal particles and diminutives (cf. Wierzbicka 1991); English lacks such devices and therefore uses fewer S-dominant strategies. There is much ongoing research into illocutions which touch on politeness concerns, because it is so very important to avoid inadvertently causing offense in social interaction, especially when H is from another culture.

15. Speech Acts and Discourse

Speech act theories have treated illocutionary acts as the product of single utterances based on a single sentence, thus becoming a pragmatic extension to sentence grammars. In real life, people do not use isolated utterances: U functions as part of a larger intention or plan. Attempts to break out of the sentence-grammar mold were made by Labov and Fanshel (1977) and Edmondson (1981), and then increasingly by researchers into cross-cultural spoken discourse (see Blum-Kulka, et al. 1989). The field of artificial intelligence has taken up speech acts in the context of modeling S's plans and intentions when uttering U (see Cohen, et al. 1990). Consider the following interchange in a pharmacy:

Customer:	Do you have any Actifed? [Seeks to establish preparatory condition for transaction and thereby implies the intention to buy on condition that Actifed is available.]
Server:	Tablets or linctus? [Establishes a preparatory condition for the transaction by offering a choice of product.]
Customer:	Packet of tablets, please. [Requests one of products offered, initiates transaction. Notice that in this context, even without the IFID 'please,' the noun phrase alone will function as a requestive]

465

Server:	That'll be $10. [On record statement of the payment required to execute the transaction; thereby making an off record request for payment to execute it]
Customer proffers money:	OK. [Agrees to contract of sale thereby fulfilling buyer's side of the bargain]
Server accepts money, hands over goods:	Have a nice day. [Fulfills seller's side of the bargain and concludes interaction with a conventional farewell]

As in most interactions, the interlocutors each have an agenda; and to carry out the plan, the illocutions within a discourse are ordered with respect to one another. The effect is to create coherent discourse in which S upholds his/her obligations to H. Future work on speech acts needs to account for the contribution of individual speech acts to a discourse or text; and that leads into the realm of conversational or discourse analysis.

Very little work has been done on the contribution of the illocutions within utterances/sentences to the development of understanding in written texts. (However, see Harrah (1994) for some interesting proposals.) Texts, whether spoken or written, display one or more of four perlocutionary functions, according to Brewer and Lichtenstein (1982). Social interaction predominates in what Malinowski called phatic communion (social chit-chat), informativeness predominates in academic texts, persuasiveness in election speeches, and entertainment in novels. But many texts combine some or all of these functions in varying degrees to achieve their communicative purpose; for instance, although an academic text is primarily informative, it also tries to persuade readers to reach a certain point of view; it needs to be entertaining enough to keep the reader's attention; and most academic texts try to get the reader on their side through social interactive techniques such as use of authorial 'we' to include the reader. The contribution of the illocutions of individual utterances to the understanding of topics and episodes (macrostructures) within texts is sorely in need of study.

Bibliography

Allan K 1986 *Linguistic Meaning,* vol. 2. Routledge and Kegan Paul, London
Allan K 1998 *Natural Language Semantics.* Blackwell, Oxford
Anderson S R 1971 *On the Linguistic Status of the Performative–Constative Distinction.* Indiana University Linguistics Club, Bloomington, IN
Austin J L 1962 *How to Do Things with Words.* Clarendon Press, Oxford
Austin J L 1963 Performative–constative. In: Caton C E (ed.) *Philosophy and Ordinary Language.* University of Illinois Press, Urbana, IL
Bach K, Harnish R M 1979 *Linguistic Communication and Speech Acts.* MIT Press, Cambridge, MA
Ballmer T, Brennenstuhl W 1981 *Speech Act Classification.* Springer-Verlag, Berlin
Blum-Kulka S, House J, Kasper G 1989 Investigating cross-cultural pragmatics: An introductory overview. In: Blum-Kulka S, House J, Kasper G (eds.) *Cross-Cultural Pragmatics. Requests and Apologies.* Ablex, Norwood, NJ
Brewer W, Lichtenstein E H 1982 Stories are to entertain: A structural-affect theory of stories. *JPrag* **6**: 473–86
Brown P, Levinson S 1987 *Politeness. Some Universals in Language Usage.* Cambridge University Press, Cambridge
Chomsky N 1965 *Aspects of the Theory of Syntax.* MIT Press, Cambridge, MA
Clark H H, Carlson T B 1982 Hearers and speech acts. *Lg* **58**: 332–73
Cohen P R, Morgan J, Pollack M E (eds.) 1990 *Intentions in Communication.* MIT Press, Cambridge, MA
Diogenes Laertius 1925 (trans. Hicks R D) *Lives of Eminent Philosophers,* vol. 2. Heinemann, London
Edmondson W 1981 *Spoken Discourse.* Longman, London
Fraser B 1974 An examination of the performative analysis. *Papers in Linguistics* **7**: 1–40
Gernsbacher M A 1990 *Language Comprehension as Structure Building.* Lawrence Erlbaum, Hillsdale, NJ
Goffman E 1981 *Forms of Talk.* University of Pennsylvania Press, Philadelphia, PA
Grice H P 1957 Meaning. *Philosophical Review* **66**: 377–88
Grice H P 1968 Utterer's meaning, sentence meaning, and word-meaning. *Foundations of Language* **4**: 225–42
Grice H P 1969 Utterer's meaning and intentions. *Philosophical Review* **78**: 147–77
Grice H P 1975 Logic and conversation. In: Cole P, Morgan J (eds.) *Syntax and Semantics. Vol. 3: Speech Acts.* Academic Press, New York
Grice H P 1989 *Studies in the Way of Words.* Harvard University Press, Cambridge, MA
Habermas J 1979 (trans. McCarthy T) *Communication and the Evolution of Society.* Beacon Press, Boston, MA
Hare R M 1971 *Practical Inferences.* Macmillan, London
Harnish R M 1975 The argument from *Lurk. LIn* **6**: 145–54
Harrah D 1994 On the vectoring of speech acts. In: Tsohatzidis S L (ed.) *Foundations of Speech Act Theory: Philosophical and Linguistic Perspectives.* Routledge, London
Karttunen L, Peters S 1979 Conventional implicature. In: Oh C-K, Dinneen D A (eds.) *Syntax and Semantics. Vol. 11: Presupposition.* Academic Press, New York
Katz J J 1972 *Semantic Theory.* Harper and Row, New York
Katz J J 1977 *Propositional Structure and Illocutionary Force.* Thomas Crowell, New York
Katz J J, Postal P M 1964 *An Integrated Theory of Linguistics Descriptions.* MIT Press, Cambridge, MA
Labov W, Fanshel D 1977 *Therapeutic Discourse.* Academic Press, New York
Lakoff G 1972 Linguistics and natural logic. In: Davidson D, Harman G (eds.) *Semantics of Natural Language.* Reidel, Dordrecht
Lakoff R 1968 *Abstract Syntax and Latin Complementation.* MIT Press, Cambridge, MA
Levinson S C 1983 *Pragmatics.* Cambridge University Press, Cambridge
Montague R 1974 *Formal Philosophy: Selected Papers of Richard Montague.* Yale University Press, New Haven, CT

Recanati F 1987 *Meaning and Force: The Pragmatics of Performative Utterances.* Cambridge University Press, Cambridge

Ross J R 1970 On declarative sentences. In: Jacobs R A, Rosenbaum P S (eds.) *Readings in English Transformational Grammar.* Ginn, Waltham, MA

Sadock J M 1974 *Toward a Linguistic Theory of Speech Acts.* Academic Press, New York

Searle J R 1969 *Speech Acts.* Cambridge University Press, Cambridge

Searle J R 1975a A taxonomy of illocutionary acts. In: Gunderson K (ed.) *Language, Mind, and Knowledge.* University of Minnesota Press, Minneapolis, MN

Searle J R 1975b Indirect speech acts. In: Cole P, Morgan J (eds.) *Syntax and Semantics. Vol. 3: Speech Acts.* Academic Press, New York

Searle J R 1979 *Expression and Meaning. Studies in the Theory of Speech Acts.* Cambridge University Press, Cambridge

Searle J R, Vanderveken D 1985 *Foundations of Illocutionary Logic.* Cambridge University Press, Cambridge

Seuren P A M 1985 *Discourse Semantics.* Basil Blackwell, Oxford

Vanderveken D 1990–91 *Meaning and Speech Acts,* vols. 1 and 2. Cambridge University Press, Cambridge

Vendler Z 1972 *Res Cogitans.* Cornell University Press, Ithaca, New York

Wierzbicka A 1987 *English Speech Act Verbs. A Semantic Dictionary.* Academic Press, Sydney

Wierzbicka A 1991 *Cross-Cultural Pragmatics. The Semantics of Human Interaction.* Mouton de Gruyter, Berlin

Wittgenstein L 1963 *Philosophical Investigations.* Blackwell, Oxford

Speech Acts and Grammar

K. Allan

A speech act is created when speaker S makes an utterance U to hearer H in context C with the reflexive-intention that H should recognize his/her message in the statement, request, promise, apology, command, etc. This entry deals first with the illocutionary effects of clauses within sentence structure, then with the representation of illocutionary force in grammar.

1. Clauses and Illocutionary Force

Suppose a herpetologist utters one of (1–4) to his or her spouse. (1–4) have a common propositional content: 'H's not ever handling the cobra'; the difference in meaning is indicated by the different moods or clause-types (S_n symbolizes 'speaker of (*n*)').

You never handle the cobra

> S_1 **makes a statement** using the declarative (1)

Do you never handle the cobra?

> S_2 **asks a question** using the interrogative (2)

Never handle the cobra!
> S_3 **issues an imperative** (3)

(a) Would that you never handle the cobra!
(b) If only you were never to handle the cobra . . .

> S_4 **expresses a wish** using the subjunctive (4)

Making a statement, asking a question, issuing an imperative, and expressing a wish are distinct illocutionary acts; i.e., S is doing something different in each of (1–4). Because the same proposition is used, the difference must be a function of the different mood

in each case. Hence, mood is the initial clue to determining the illocutionary point of the utterance (i.e., S's message). Thus mood has a role in speech act theory.

Grammarians in the western classical tradition have recognized a degree of coincidence between clause-type and illocutionary force at least since the time of Appollonius Dyscolus (100 AD, see Householder 1981: 12f) and probably since 300 BC (see Diogenes Laertius (1925) 'Life of Zeno' VII: 65–68). Lyons (1977) argues against the identification of mood with clause-type because in the western classical tradition both the declarative and the interrogative are indicative in mood. A different view is taken by Palmer (1986) who does distinguish the interrogative within the modality system. However, there is some justification for Lyon's conclusion because there are not only indicative interrogatives like (2) asking about the actual world, but also subjunctive interrogatives like (5) which ask questions about hypothetical worlds:

> Would you never handle the cobra? (5)

Sadock and Zwicky (1985) surveyed 35 languages representing a wide range of language families and linguistic areas: every one of them distinguishes a declarative to (among other things) make statements, an interrogative to ask things of people, and an imperative to get them to do things. These three moods are orthographically marked by '.,' '?,' and '!' respectively. Many languages have clause types with other functions—e.g., optative-subjunctive, expressive-exclamative, prohibitive, imprecative. English has not only the (optative-)subjunctive in (4) and (5), but also expressive(-exclamative) in mostly mono-lexical nonverb idioms of two kinds: those not necessarily addressed to anyone, e.g., *Goodness gracious! Shit! Wow!*, and those addressed to H: *Thanks. Please. Sorry. Pardon. Hi. Bye. Congratulations. Asshole!* (note that some are imprecatives). Some of the latter have idiomatic counterparts with verbs: *Thank you. How do you do? Screw you!* Often these expressives have similarly idiomatic counterparts in other languages. Imprecations of third persons appear to be expressives:

> X: Suzie found Tom in her own bed with another woman! (6)
>
> Y: Asshole!   ['Tom is an asshole']
>
> Fuck him!   [≠ 'You copulate with him']   (7)

But the following are imperative: *Apologize to him for me. Congratulate her. Thank him.*

Because the form of the utterance must be the starting point for H's interpretation of the utterance's meaning, it is reasonable to assume that mood identifies the primary illocution of a clause, providing the base from which H can determine the illocutionary point of the utterance in which that clause occurs. So we shall consider the five moods of English, which have close parallels in other languages.

The generalized form of the primary illocution of a declarative clause is as follows:

⟨form⟩ ⊢Φ, or simply Φ, an assertoric sentence (fragment) such as (1) or *Jack is bald. Frank loathes Harry.* [Q: Who called? A:] *Jack.*

indicates

⟨description⟩ S says that Φ. We refer to this as a statement.

indicates

⟨preparatory condition⟩ S has reason to believe that Φ.

indicates

⟨illocutionary intention⟩ S reflexively intends the utterance to be recognized as a reason for H to believe that S has reason to believe that Φ.

The generalized form of the primary illocution of an interrogative clause is:

⟨form⟩ ?Φ, e.g. (2), (5), or *Will you mail this? What's the time? Would you pass me the salt?* (the latter is also subjunctive, see below).

⟨description⟩ S asks H something. We refer to this as a request.

⟨preparatory condition⟩ S has reason to believe that H can or might be able to respond appropriately to what is asked in the utterance.

⟨illocutionary intention⟩ S reflexively intends the utterance to be taken as asking H something.

Bearing in mind that many imperative clauses are not at all imperious, cf. *Forgive me intruding. Excuse me. Let me help you with that. Have a beer. Take the first turning on your left and the third on the right. Have a good day!* the primary illocution of an imperative clause is:

⟨form⟩ !Φ, e.g. (3).

⟨description⟩ S proposes to H that H do A.

⟨preparatory condition⟩ S believes that H can do A.

⟨illocutionary intention⟩ S reflexively intends H to take the utterance as a reason to do A.

The primary illocution of an expressive is:

⟨form⟩ An expressive idiom.

⟨description⟩ S is reacting to Ω, i.e. something that has occurred.

⟨preparatory condition⟩ S believes it appropriate to express a reaction to Ω (showing some degree of feeling).

⟨illocutionary intention⟩ S (reflexively?) intends the utterance to be taken as expressing a particular (sometimes perfunctory, sometimes strongly felt) attitude toward Ω.

The primary illocution of a subjunctive is:

⟨form⟩ ¡Φ ('¡' is nonstandard, there is no standard symbol for the subjunctive), e.g., (4), or *I wish I were rich. I wish I was rich. Would that I were rich. If Harry should call*, tell him I'll be back this evening.

⟨description⟩ S imagines a world in which Φ.

⟨preparatory condition⟩ S has no reason to believe that it IS the case that Φ; indeed, S may know it is NOT the case that Φ.

⟨illocutionary intention⟩ S reflexively intends the utterance to be taken as a reason for H to believe that S does not believe that Φ and S reflexively intends H to consider the implications of Φ in a world in which it IS the case that Φ.

The subjunctive environment is the complement of a verb or wishing or wanting, invoking the hypothetical world. In *I wish I were rich* the past tense form 'were' is also the subjunctive form, but the past tense itself is used to make the subjunctive in *I wish I was rich*—the tense of all (subjunctive) examples given above is semantically nonpast. A past tense subjunctive would be *had been*. Conditional *if* marks a subjunctive clause when the proposition invokes a hypothetical world, so that *should* can be utilized in a paraphrase—e.g., *If Harry should call*, is a paraphrase of *If Harry calls*.

English interrogative subjunctives are restricted to requests with only four backshifted modals, cf. *Would you mail this for me? Could you do me a favour? Might he be there by now? Should I write to him?* They are all notably tentative which accounts for their use in polite contexts. They have the following properties:

⟨form⟩ ?[¡Φ]
⟨description⟩ S asks H about a hypothetical world in which Φ.
⟨preparatory condition⟩ S has reason to believe that H can or might be able to respond appropriately to what is asked in the utterance but wishes to appear tentative and not impositive.
⟨illocutionary intention⟩ S reflexively intends the utterance to be taken as asking H about Φ in some hypothetical world.

The primary illocutions fall into four classes corresponding to Searle's (1975a) notion 'direction of fit':

Declaratives show a *words-to-world* fit: the words match the way the world was or is or will be.

Requests and imperatives both show a *world-to-words* fit: things are to happen in the world to make it match the propositional content. They differ because S expressly gives H the option not to comply when using a request; whereas with imperatives, S expressly gives H no option but to comply.

For expressives, direction of *fit is irrelevant*.

Subjunctives fit the *words to a hypothetical world*.

Interrogative subjunctives *seek to fit the actual world to a hypothetical world*: things are to happen in the actual world to make it match the words that describe the hypothetical world.

The recognition of clause type identifies the primary (or initial) illocution in U, but not S's illocutionary point. For instance, depending on tone of voice and the context of utterance, (1) could have various illocutionary points: it could be a comment, a warning, scorn, a challenge, etc. *Can you open the window?* could be a question about the openability of the window, about H's ability to open the window, or a request to have the window opened. In order to determine which of these is meant, H will begin from the primary illocution and draw inferences from S's tone of voice and the context of utterance, knowledge of conversational conventions, and often general knowledge, until s/he is satisfied that S's message has been understood. An inferential process of this nature is described in Searle (1975b), Bach and Harnish (1977), and Allan (1986).

Many sentences contain more than one clause. Clauses that occur within the structure of noun phrases share the primary illocution of their governing clause and contribute nothing to the illocutionary force of U. Examples are the restrictive relative clauses underlined in (8), the NP complement in (9), and the adverbial adjunct clauses in (10):

The plums Joe bought got squashed on the journey home. (8a)

Here's the anthology in which Edith's poem is published. (8b)

It's a pity that Eric missed the early train. (9)

When he arrives, call me. (10a)

Will you go wherever he does? (10b)

He spends his money how he pleases. (10c)

It's better than we expected. (10d)

Although he was very tired Harry drove me home (10e)

fearing I'd be mugged.

Some adverbial clauses share but also modify the primary illocution of the main clause; for example, *To be frank/honest/serious I don't promise to come, but I'll try to do so*: here S is speaking frankly, honestly, or seriously and not 'notpromising' frankly, etc. Exclamatory codas like the tags in *So I'm a klutz, am I?!* or *The checkbook wasn't in your pocket, wasn't it?!* emphasize the irony but do not otherwise alter the nonliteral illocutionary intention. VP complement clauses also share the primary illocution of the main clause, but occasionally contribute to the illocutionary force of the utterance; for example, *I say I promise to visit tomorrow (you deaf old coot)* can be used to (re)make a promise.

Coordinate, conjoined, and appositive clauses of the same type share the primary illocution of the first clause in sequence: *I admit responsibility for the financial loss and hereby resign from the board* has the primary illocution of a statement and the compound illocutionary points of an admission and a resignation. *Come in but don't stay long* has the primary illocution of the imperative but compounds an invitation with a prohibition. *I forbid you to go to the pinball parlour; you can go to a movie, though* states first a prohibition and then permission. *Suzy, who loves cats, would never torture one* states information within a denial.

Alternatively, coordinate, conjoined, and appositive clauses may have different primary and indirect illocutions which will carry through to the compound or complex illocutionary point of U. In *If I were to take out a loan, how much interest will I have to pay?* or *How much interest will I have to pay if I take out a loan?* the subjunctive protasis identifies a hypothetical world in which S takes out a loan; but the main point of the utterance is the question in the apodosis. *Smoke, and you'll get cancer* uses an imperative telling H to smoke, conjoining it with a statement of the consequence of doing so—together they are intended to function as a warning not to smoke. *Be frank/Tell me frankly, what do you think?* presents an imperative invitation for H to be frank in responding to the request for information (the same effect is achieved when the clause sequence is reversed: *What do you think? Be frank*). In *I met Ted—Did you know he divorced Monica, by the way?—last night at the club ...*, the interrogative expressing a *yes-no* question is located as an appositive clause within the stating of a report.

A positive imperative may take a negative interrogative tag and together they mean 'S proposes to H that H do A unless H does not want to agree to do A'; e.g., *Sit dòwn,/wŏn't you₎* This is typically an

469

invitation because it has the H-oriented (fall-)rise on the tag. Compare the instructional imperative with a positive tag that has the S-dominant (rise-) fall tone: *Sīt dòwn,/wíll you* meaning 'S proposes to H that H do A and asks that H agree to do A.' Notice that H can more readily refuse the invitation than the instruction. Negative imperatives are used only with positive tags; for example, *Dòn't get lòst,/wíll yòu?* 'S proposes to H that H not get lost and asks that H agree not to get lost.' The reason why **Don't get lost, won't you* is not heard can be seen from the anomaly of 'S proposes to H that H not get lost unless H does not want to agree to not get lost' or, more simply, 'Don't get lost if you don't want to.'

When 'S says that *p*,' it implies satisfaction of the preparatory condition that 'S believes that *p*'; if S has any doubts, it is cooperative to express them, as in *Jack's in his room, I think*. Or S may venture that *p* but immediately check with H the truth of *p* (perhaps to flatter H) by using a tag question of opposite polarity to the declarative main clause: *Jack's in his ròom,/ĭsn't he? Jack ĭsn't in his ròom,/ĭs he?* Many clauses exist in English to express S's doubts about satisfaction of the preparatory conditions on an illocutionary act; others are *I promise to come if I can. If I've offended you, I apologize. Is Jack in his room, do you know? Can you tell me whether Jack's in today?*

S may signal uncertainty that H will believe him/her: *Would you believe that Joe and Edna have separated?* S's awareness of the potential violation of the cooperative maxim of quantity is signaled by the clause underlined in *Did you know that Max has a new job?* And if S wants to discourse on a topic whose introductory proposition is known to H, s/he will say *Max hates cats, as you know, but his new girlfriend has sixteen!* S may thank H for his/her trouble and/or explicitly seek H's cooperation, as in *I'd be grateful if you could show it to me if you don't mind*. The word *please* means more or less 'do A if it pleases you but don't if not' and thus appears to give H the option of refusing, although H cannot refuse without serious affront to S's face: *Two coffees, please. Please be advised your account is overdue*. S may excuse potentially impertinent questions with *may I ask* and impertinent statements with *if I may say so*. There are rhetorical requests for permission as in *May I say how happy I am to be here tonight*. S may try to deflect opprobrium by saying *I'm afraid I must ask you to leave immediately, sir. I regret that your application has been unsuccessful*. Alternatively, S is congratulatory in *I am delighted to inform you that your application has been successful*. In all such cases, and many additional ones, there is an illocutionary addition to the utterance whose primary function is to ease social interactive behavior.

Of course, S may cancel an illocution, too, replacing it with another; for example, *I'm sorry I called you an asshole, asshole* or *I advise you, or warn you rather, not to stroke the carpet viper*.

2. The Representation of Illocutionary Force in Grammar

It appears that no model of syntax incorporates a representation of illocutionary force; but that was not the case during the late 1960s and early 1970s in the heyday of 'performative analysis' in transformational grammar. Ross (1970: 261) claimed that 'every deep structure contains one and only one performative as its highest clause':

$$[_S[_{NP}I] \; [_{VP}\text{PERFORMATIVE VERB } (you)$$
$$[_S\text{NONPERFORMATIVE SENTENCE}_S]_{VP}]_S]$$

This was wrong, and so was the claim that a sentential phrase marker can contain one, and only one, performative. Ross (1970) presented 14 arguments based on almost unrelated bits of data in support of the hypothesis that the highest clause of every declarative sentence is a performative verb of stating. Every one of Ross's arguments has been assuredly refuted (along with additional ones in Lakoff 1972 and Sadock 1974) by Anderson (1971), Fraser (1974), Harnish (1975), and Allan (1986: 258ff.). Despite the overwhelming counterevidence, Ross's hypothesis was widely accepted for a decade.

Although Ross introduced the performative analysis within a syntactic framework, many of its champions (e.g., Lakoff and Sadock) discussed it within a kind of grammar known as 'generative semantics.' Generative semantics was named for the fact that its initial symbols represent semantic components set into structures based on a hybrid of predicate logic and natural language syntax; the structures were then rearranged in various ways by transformations before having lexicon items mapped onto them; after that, further transformational rules would rearrange or delete nodes to produce a final derived structure. Because it started from a semantic source, generative semantics could, in principle, represent illocutionary force—which is not a syntactic category, but a semantic, or more accurately, a pragmatic entity. Since the demise of generative semantics, the representation of illocutionary force in grammar has been ignored. The best hope is for someone to incorporate it into some kind of logico–semantic system such as model-theoretic truth-conditional semantics. The first steps in such a program have been undertaken by Searle and Vanderveken (1985) and Vanderveken (1990–91); but the development of illocutionary logic proceeds independently of the development of model-theoretic semantics.

Bibliography

Allan K 1986 *Linguistic Meaning*, vol. 2. Routledge and Kegan Paul, London

Anderson S R 1971 *On the Linguistic Status of the Performative–Constative Distinction*. Indiana University Linguistics Club, Bloomington, IN

Bach K, Harnish R M 1979 *Linguistic Communication and Speech Acts*. MIT Press, Cambridge, MA

Diogenes Laertius 1925 (trans. Hicks R D) *Lives of Eminent Philosophers*, vol.2. Loeb Classical Library, Heinemann, London

Fraser B 1974 An examination of the performative analysis. *Papers in Linguistics* **7**: 1–40

Harnish R M 1975 The argument from *Lurk*. *LIn* **6**: 145–54

Harnish R M 1994 Mood, meaning and speech acts. In: Tsohatzidis S (ed.) *Foundations of Speech Act Theory: Philosophical and Linguistic Perspectives*. Routledge, London

Householder F (ed. and trans.) 1981 *The Syntax of Apollonius Dyscolus*. John Benjamins, Amsterdam

Lakoff G 1972 Linguistics and natural logic. In: Davidson D, Harman G (eds.) *Semantics of Natural Language*. Reidel, Dordrecht

Lyons J 1977 *Semantics*, vol. 2. Cambridge University Press, Cambridge

Palmer F R 1986 *Mood and Modality*. Cambridge University Press, Cambridge

Ross J R 1970 On declarative sentences. In: Jacobs R A, Rosenbaum P S (eds.) *Readings in English Transformational Grammar*. Ginn, Waltham, MA

Sadock J M 1974 *Toward a Linguistic Theory of Speech Acts*. Academic Press, New York

Sadock J M, Zwicky A 1985 Speech act distinctions in syntax. In: Shopen T (ed.) *Language Typology and Syntactic Description. Vol. I: Clause Structure*. Cambridge University Press, Cambridge

Searle J R 1975a A taxonomy of illocutionary acts. In: Gunderson K (ed.) *Language, Mind, and Knowledge*. University of Minnesota Press, Minneapolis, MN (Reprinted in Searle (1979))

Searle J R 1975b Indirect speech acts. In: Cole P, Morgan J L (eds.) *Syntax and Semantics 3: Speech Acts*. Academic Press, New York (Reprinted in Searle (1979))

Searle J R 1979 *Expression and Meaning: Studies in the Theory of Speech Acts*. Cambridge University Press, Cambridge

Searle J R, Vanderveken D 1985 *Foundations of Illocutionary Logic*. Cambridge University Press, Cambridge

Vanderveken D 1990–91 *Meaning and Speech Acts*, vols. 1 and 2. Cambridge University Press, Cambridge

Speech Acts: Literal and Nonliteral

K. Allan

A speech act is created when speaker/writer S makes an utterance U to hearer/reader H in context C. To understand U, H constructs a mental model of the discourse world that s/he perceives S to be speaking of; in doing so, H uses not only knowledge of language, but knowledge of all kinds. When communicating, S relies on the fact that H's understanding is an active, not a passive process. This entry looks at the interpretation of nonliteral speech acts, and the conclusion is that nonliterally meant statements are interpreted in essentially the same way as literal ones.

Lakoff and Johnson (1980) made us aware that figurative language is not closeted in poetry, but pervades everyday speech. We use figures to be vivid, e.g., in animal descriptions of people as *dog, bitch, mouse;* exaggerations like *Your bedroom's a pigsty;* characterizing someone stupid as *two cans short of a six-pack;* describing a short person as *vertically challenged;* Barbara Bush describing Geraldine Ferraro as *something that rhymes with rich;* saying of something comic *It killed me.* Nonliteral language concretizes the abstract: saying *Language is a vehicle of communication;* describing wine or a piece of music as *lively.* We use nonliteral language to relate the unknown to a known, e.g., Saussure's (1974: 22, 88, 110) analogy between language and a game of chess.

When S says *It killed me* s/he cannot mean it literally, because dead people cannot make statements. H therefore infers that S is exaggerating and invoking the idiomatic sense 'I almost died laughing at it.' This account is feasible because every possible meaning is initially activated no matter how contextually absurd, but the context then suppresses all but the most likely interpretation (cf. Gernsbacher 1990).

Suppose, though, that Sue says and literally means *Maxine is a real dog;* using 'dog' as a dysphemism for a woman bone ugly despite overexpenditure of time and money on her appearance. Sue is exploiting the ambiguity of the word *dog* and being nonliteral at the lexical and therefore locutionary level; at the illocutionary level her statement of opinion is doubtless true (the same can be said of Barbara Bush vis-à-vis Geraldine Ferraro, cf. Allan 1992). How does H know that Sue does not mean 'Maxine is a canine animal?' One clue would be the intonation over 'real dog': a high-fall on 'real,' a possible disjuncture, and then low-fall on 'dog' would indicate 'canine animal'; on the other hand a level stress on 'real' and a high-fall on 'dog' implies the dysphemism. Furthermore, if H believes the referent Maxine is human not canine, then Sue is either deluded or using the dysphemism.

It is often assumed that in assigning meaning, H makes an initial presumption of literalness: If S utters

U to H in C, then H presumes that if S could be speaking literally, S probably is speaking literally (cf. Bach and Harnish 1979: 12). However, Sperber and Wilson (1986: 230) counter that there is 'no empirical evidence for a convention of literalness or anything of the sort.' They believe that S intends H to interpret both literal and nonliteral utterances by inference from the locution once its denotation/reference has been ascertained. Consider (1), whose illocutionary point is nonliteral and off-record, which makes it classically indirect:

I'm sure the cat likes you pulling its tail. (1)

In uttering (1), S is not normally taken to be commenting on the pleasures of a masochistic cat, but as asking H to desist from pulling the cat's tail. Just how one arrives at this conclusion can be seen in the following inference schema, derived from work of Bach and Harnish (1979) and Allan (1986); it is consistent with Sperber and Wilson's relevance theory with a few changes such as replacing 'cooperative principle' with 'relevance theory.'

In uttering (1) S intends H to reason that:	*Basis:*
1. S utters U in a context where H has been pulling the cat's tail (= C). [Recognition of the utterance act]	Hearing S utter U in C.
2. U consists of $<\pi,e>$ in English, and $<\pi,e>$ means 'S says I'm sure the cat likes you pulling its tail.' [Recognition of the locution]	1, cooperative principle, knowledge of English.
3. By 'I' S means 'S,' by 'the cat' S means 'the (contextually identified) cat,' by 'you' S means 'H', by 'its tail' S means 'the cat's tail'. S is using $<\pi,e>$ to mean 'S says that s/he is sure that the (contextually identified) cat likes H pulling its tail. [Recognition of reference]	2, semantic theory, context.
4. S reflexively-intends U to be taken as a reason for H to believe that S is sure that the cat likes H pulling its tail. [Recognition of the primary illocutionary intention]	3, definitions of illocutionary acts.
5. S is saying s/he is sure the cat likes H pulling its tail. [Recognition of the primary illocution]	4, definition of statements.
6. Animals do not generally like having their tails pulled, so S's statement is probably false, and S must know this; and s/he must know that H will know it, too. [Recognition that S blatantly violates the maxim of quality]	5, encyclopedic knowledge, cooperative principle.
7. People sometimes say the	5, 6, knowledge of
opposite of what they mean if they are being sarcastic. [Recognition of sarcasm]	language use.
8. If S is being sarcastic, S must reflexively-intend U to be a reason for H to believe that S is sure the cat does not like H pulling its tail. [Recognition of the secondary illocutionary intention]	5, 7, knowledge of language use, definitions of illocutionary acts.
9. S is saying that s/he is sure the cat does not like H pulling its tail. [Recognition of the secondary illocution]	8, definition of statements.
10. H has been pulling the cat's tail, and S has said s/he is sure the cat doesn't like it. In our society, it is unacceptable to do things to animals which they don't like unless there is good reason for doing it. And S has indirectly drawn this ethical principle to H's attention.	9, context, encyclopedic knowledge, cooperative principle.
11. S reflexively-intends U to be taken as a reason for H to desist from pulling the cat's tail or to inform S of the reason for not doing so. [Recognition of the tertiary illocutionary intention]	10, cooperative principle, definitions of illocutionary acts.
12. S is asking H not to pull the cat's tail or to inform S of the reason not to comply. [Recognition of the tertiary illocution]	11, definition of requests.
13. There is no reason to believe that any further illocutionary intention can be inferred, therefore S is asking H to desist from pulling the cat's tail or to explain why s/he should not. [Conclusion as to the illocutionary point of U]	3, 12, definitions of illocutionary acts, encyclopedic knowledge, context.

The speech act schema operates in the same way for a literal utterance such as *I'm sure the cat doesn't like you pulling its tail* for which steps 5–8 are omitted with the effect that step 9 of the schema above becomes step 5 (the secondary illocution of the schema above becomes the primary illocution of the new schema), 10 becomes 6, and so on, until the conclusion as to the illocutionary point is determined in step 9.

See also: Indirect Speech Acts; Speech Act Hierarchy.

Bibliography

Allan K 1986 *Linguistic Meaning*, vol. 2. Routledge and Kegan Paul, London
Allan K 1992 'Something that rhymes with rich.' In: Kittay E, Lehrer A (eds.) *Frames, Fields, and Contrasts*. Lawrence Erlbaum, Norwood, NJ

Bach K, Harnish R M 1979 *Linguistic Communication and Speech Acts*. MIT Press, Cambridge, MA

Gernsbacher M A 1990 *Language Comprehension as Structure Building*. Lawrence Erlbaum, Hillsdale, NJ

Lakoff G, Johnson M 1980 *Metaphors We Live By*. University of Chicago Press, Chicago, IL

Saussure F de 1974 (trans. Baskin W) *A Course in General Linguistics*. Fontana/Collins, Glasgow

Sperber B, Wilson D 1986 *Relevance: Communication and Cognition*. Blackwell, Oxford

SECTION IX
Key Figures

a) Pre-20th Century

Aristotle and the Stoics
F. W. Householder[†]

The period from about 350 BC to 150 BC was perhaps the most productive for Greek linguistics. In the case of Aristotle, there exists a substantial portion of his writings preserved in manuscript; for all the others, including the Academy, Epicurus, and the Stoics, as well as the various scholarly writers associated with Alexandria and Pergamon, there remain only fragments, summaries, and comments preserved in later writings (often in two or more steps: 'Sextus Empiricus quotes Chares quoting Crates,' for instance). But, fortunately, the fragments of the Stoics are sufficient to give an excellent idea of their linguistic teachings. And, like Aristotle, they approach language from a philosophical, logical perspective.

1. Aristotle

Aristotle's linguistic output falls into two parts, one represented especially by chapters 19–22 of the *Poetics* (1456a–1459a), but also four paragraphs elsewhere (*Rhetoric* III, 5, 1407b; *Prior Analytics* I, 36, 48b–49a; and *Sophistical Refutations* 14, 173b–174a and 32, 182a–b); the other by the *Categories* and the *de Interpretatione*. The former items seem to contain substantially the standard analysis presented in the *grammatikē* of the fifth and fourth centuries BC, much like what is seen in Plato, while the latter represent Aristotle's own original research.

In the *Poetics* are three of the recurring linguistic topics of antiquity: (a) sentence-types or illocutionary forces (question, command, statement, etc.); (b) parts of speech (Aristotle does not here use the expression *meros tou logou*, but lists *sundesmos, onoma, rhēma, arthron*); and (c) the four transformations (addition, deletion, substitution, and transposition—here used for the derivation of poetic words from ordinary ones). There is also a clear anticipation of the pattern of later *technai* (grammatical sketches like Dionysius Thrax's): first a list of some technical terms (providing a table of contents), then definitions, subclassification, and discussion of each in turn, then, in the *Poetics,* a

further subclassification of nouns and their inflections. The most interesting additions to Plato's treatment of phonology is the mention of voiced stops, shapes of the mouth, places (of articulation), and aspiration (a brief treatment, but basically better than in Dionysius Thrax). He treats tense, mood, case, and number in 1457a 17–22 (all called *ptōsis*), but gender in 1458a 8–17, since it is not an inflection (for nouns, at least), but an inherent property, partly signaled, in the nominative, by the final consonant or vowel. His only way of naming the cases is with the forms of *houtos* ('this'): *toutou* means 'genitive case,' *toutōi* 'dative,' etc. This usage recurs in *Prior Analytics* 4–9a 1–5 and *Soph. Refut.* 182a 32–b3 and 173b 26–37. It is interesting that Pāṇini sometimes uses the same device. Aristotle in some of these places uses it to indicate gender, though he knows the three Protagorean names also, and sometimes uses *metaxu* 'between' for the neuter.

The interesting addition in these last three passages and in the *Rhetoric* one (1407b) is what seems to be the standard fifth-century treatment of syntax. It is introduced under the heading of solecism (a word first attested in this sense in Herodotus 4.117.1). While there is only one word for correct Greek, 'hellenism,' there are two for errors: 'barbarism,' which includes all errors of pronunciation, spelling, inflectional morphology, and vocabulary choice, and 'solecism,' which means any error in syntax. In particular it refers to errors of agreement in gender, number (or case), of case government, and apparently certain instances of word-order and semantics (*Rhetoric* 1407b 6–7). The rules implied in these four passages are the following:

(a) correlative conjunctions (like *men* and *de*) should be made to correspond (and at a reasonable distance);

(b) each word should be placed so that its syntactical connection is unambiguous (remember the hyperbaton in Plato's *Protagoras* 343F);

(c) participles and adjectives must agree with the nouns they modify in case, gender, and number;

(d) the subject of a finite verb is in the nominative;

(e) the subject of an infinitive (unless identical with the subject of its governing verb) is in the accusative;

(f) the gender of a noun (as opposed to interrogative and sometimes relative and demonstrative pronouns) need not be the same as the sex or animacy of its referent;

(g) a relative pronoun must agree in gender and number with its antecedent;

(h) a predicate noun or adjective with a verb like *einai* 'to be' agrees in case with its subject;

(i) words like *isos* 'equal to' govern the dative;

(j) words like *diplasios* 'double' govern a genitive;

(k) transitive verbs (like *tuptō* 'hit' and *horō* 'see') govern the accusative.

All of these passages, except the one in *Rhetoric,* also include a technical term for 'nominative singular' (besides *houtos*) or, sometimes, 'nominative singular masculine,' or, perhaps, in one passage, 'the termination of the nominative singular,' *klēsis.* This is opposed, of course, to the *ptōseis,* which are all the other forms (case, number, and gender) of a noun, pronoun, or adjective (which are all *onoma* to Aristotle).

The reason why syntax is discussed in all these passages is the same, to show how some *soloikismoi* may either be used to deceive your interlocutor or audience, or else be analyzed to avoid being deceived or to refute an opponent. (Since the sixth century, when an educated man need only be able to discuss and analyze poems at a dinner party or drinking party, a new recreation had arisen in Athens, to which Plato's dialogs give literary life, the disputation on philosophical or technical points.)

To sum up, the grammar sketched in the *Poetics* and used in Aristotle's discussions of solecism may be said to summarize the linguistic achievements of the fifth century, and thus, in a sense, represent the earliest grammatical treatment of Greek that can be reconstructed.

The *Categories,* by contrast, contain a great deal that is new. In spite of the vague similarity of Plato's *onoma* and *rhēma* to 'subject' and 'predicate,' it is only in Aristotle that the notion of 'predicate' is really developed. And even he does not provide a perfect expression for 'subject': *hupokeimenon* is indeed the source of our term calqued into Latin—*hupo = sub, keimenon = jectum*—but none of the later grammarians made such use of it. For Apollonius Dyscolus it is almost as often used for the object as for the subject, and he often flounders around for lack of such a term. But after the rediscovery of Aristotle, the term does come into grammatical use. The *Categories* (the term means 'predicates' or 'predicate-types') does, however, provide the only elaborated classification of predicates outside of the Stoics. Essentially Aristotle

envisages a formula S = X + (is/are) + Predicate in which the 'is/are' may sometimes be swallowed up in the Predicate (see *De Interpretatione* 21b *badizei* 'walks' equals *badizōn esti* 'is walking') and lists 10 different types of Predicate, which he may or may not have meant to be an exhaustive list, based, apparently, on a mixture of semantic and formal (morphological or syntactic) criteria, but which certainly comes close to being exhaustive. The traditional names of these predicate-types can be matched up with grammatical classes as follows:

(a) Substance (including particulars, species, and genera) = noun phrases, including proper nouns and definite NPs as particulars, simple NPs as species and genera;

(b) Quantity (including size) = adjectival expressions of size and number (but excluding words like 'big' and 'little,' 'many' and 'few,' which are really *relative* terms (*pros ti*)), hence numbers and numerical phrases;

(c) Quality = nonquantitative, nonrelative (although Aristotle suggests that some adjectives are both qualitative and relative), adjectives, and adjective phrases;

(d) Relation (*pros ti*) = adjectives which may be compared (or modified by 'more,' 'very,' 'so,' etc.) and nouns which require or imply a dependent genitive (like *father,* inalienably possessed, or like *knowledge,* nominalizations of transitive verbs);

(e) Place = adverbs and prepositional phrases of place;

(f) Time = adverbs and phrases of time;

(g) Position (*keisthai*) seems to include stative verbs of sitting, standing, lying down, and the like, though it probably is not limited to human subjects;

(h) State (*echein*) appears to mean perfect passive verbs other than any included in Position;

(i) Action (*poiein*) seems to include both transitive and intransitive verbs (in the present or aorist especially);

(j) Affection (*paschein*) includes verbs in the passive voice plus other verbs of sensation or emotion.

Though a few of the same terms will be met later in Dionysius Thrax's lists of verb voices, noun types, and adverb types, most of these notions do not appear in later grammarians.

The *De Interpretatione* (*peri hermēneias*) starts out with some more precise definitions of terms seen before, like 'noun' and 'verb' and 'sentence,' plus some new ones like 'proposition.' The opening paragraph, however, contains an interesting refinement of the innateness assumption used by Psammetichus: 'What occurs in speech are symbols of feelings in the mind, and what is written are symbols of what is spoken.

Speech is not the same for all men, any more than writing is, but the mental feelings of which spoken words are signs, *are* the same for all, and likewise the things (*pragmata*) of which those feelings are symbols.' This defines four layers: 'things' in the outside world are symbolized by 'feelings' (*pathēmata*) in the mind (and both the things and the feelings are the same for all men), which are, in turn, symbolized by speech, spoken words (*phōnē*), which, in their turn, are represented by writing (*grammata*). This layer of *pathēmata*, then, constitutes a universal mental language common to all men. This view is, of course, more a matter of psychology than linguistics, but it seems to occur again in the Stoics, and to be presupposed by some modern linguistic and semantic theories.

Here again are met not all six of the illocutionary forces listed in the *Poetics* (command, wish/hope/ prayer, statement, threat, question, and answer), but at least one of them, statement or proposition (*apophansis*), which is the only one capable of truth or falsity (this must also include 'answer,' as he says in 17a, which does not really belong on the same list as the others). All through the *De Interpretatione* Aristotle emphasizes the arbitrariness of the sign (*kata sunthēkēn*), as in the initial paragraph quoted above.

The improved definitions of noun and verb include the notions of tense (verb is [+tense], noun is [−tense]) and minimality (no fully significant parts). The Greek negatives (*ouk/ou* and *mē*) are treated as prefixes, and negated nouns or verbs (remember adjectives are also nouns) are called indefinite (*aorista*) nouns and verbs. The name *ptōsis* is given to the oblique cases of nouns (genitive, dative, etc., is the order, though no names are used); subjecthood possibility is made the criterion for nouns in the strict sense (i.e., nominatives). The same name (*ptōsis*) applies to verbs for all tenses (he mentions past and future) except the present indicative; nothing is said here about subjunctives, optatives, infinitives, and participles. Unlike nouns and verbs, sentences (*logoi*) have meaningful parts, but not parts capable of being true or false (this clearly excludes complex and compound sentences, which he alludes to later). Incidentally, though this discussion of propositions or simple sentences makes much reference to subjects, neither *hupokeimenon* nor any other term for subject is used.

Numerous small references to linguistic matters (including phonetics) occur elsewhere in Aristotle, but these are the main passages of interest.

2. The Stoics

It is the work of the Stoics which clearly establishes most of the framework for later grammatical writing. Though Zeno (at least to some extent) and Chrysippus (see the numerous titles listed in Diogenes Laertius VII 191–92, and also for syntax, VII 63) did the basic work, much of our knowledge (for phonology and morphology) comes from Diogenes the Babylonian as quoted in Diogenes Laertius VII 55–60 (though there are many other sources). It is possible, of course, that if the complete works of Aristarchus had survived the Alexandrians might be assigned more importance than the Stoics. Diogenes of Babylon's treatise was not called 'Grammar' (*Technē grammatikē*) but *Peri Phōnēs*, which is hard to translate; *phōnē* is a very widely used word meaning, in grammarians, most often 'word' or 'phonological word,' but also 'voice' (of animals or man), 'speech,' 'utterance,' or even sometimes 'style' or 'sound' (though noises made by inanimate objects are sometimes excluded). Among the Stoics *phōnē* is sometimes restricted to the concrete *aisthēton* 'perceptible,' which is the *sēmainon* 'signifier' (as opposed to the *sēmainomenon* 'signified' which is *noēton* 'thinkable' or abstract), but Diogenes clearly includes more. Similar variation applies also in the case of other words for 'word,' e.g., *dialektos* (so used by Plato and Aristotle, though Diogenes narrows it down to 'other Greek dialect word') and *lexis*, 'significant word' or 'spellable word' for the Stoics, but often also 'speech,' 'expression,' 'style,' and, of course, *onoma* and *rhēma*, which may both be simply 'word' in Plato and Aristotle, though not in the Stoics. *Logos*, which always means 'sentence' or 'proposition' in grammar and logic, never means 'word,' though occasionally it means 'prose work' and, of course, 'reason' and related ideas.

Though the Stoics add only one new 'part of speech' (which should, of course, have been rendered 'part of the sentence' from Plato on) to Aristotle's list, the *prosēgoria* ('common noun,' *onoma* being now restricted to 'proper noun'), they give new definitions. This involves, in part, the incorporation of Aristotle's 'substance' into 'quality,' so that proper nouns signify an 'individual quality,' and the use of a feature [+incase] for verb, conjunction, and article (now apparently restricted to the definite article, though later the simple relative pronoun is also included). And, though Antipater's proposed adverb (*mesotēs*) does not catch on, a new term *morion* ('particle') does come into use, without being defined, entailing not a new part of speech, but a new classification of words, roughly into full words and empty words, to use modern terms. Examples are: Diogenes Laertius VII 64 referring to the preposition *hupo*, 70 referring to the negative *ou/ouk*, the negative prefix *a-/an-*, the indefinite pronoun *tis*—cf. Sextus Empiricus *Math.* 8.96—and the demonstrative *ekeinos*. It is often used for words which do not clearly come under any of the official parts of speech. Neither Plato nor Aristotle used the word in this way, nor does Dionysius Thrax, but Apollonius Dyscolus does. Schneider (in his index, *Grammatici Graeci* II, 3) thinks it is merely a synonym of *meros logou* or *lexis*, 'word,' but no two of these three are used in exactly the same way. Both *morion* and *lexis* (but not *meros logou*) may be used with adjectives like 'verbal,' 'pronominal,' but only *morion* occurs with a whole bunch of adjectives ('uninflected,' 'meaningless,' 'interrogative,' 'enclitic,' 'indefinite,' 'underlying,' etc.) and only *meros logou* is used with 'one,' 'two,' 'the same' and 'different' ('one m.l.' is a [compound] word, while 'two m.l.' is a phrase). Nouns and verbs are only rarely called *morion,* most of the examples being pronouns, small adverbs, interrogatives, indefinites, conjunctions, and prepositions. The Latin equivalent *particula* is used once by Priscian (*Inst.* XVII, IV, 29) for the Greek relative pronoun (here *infinita particula* 'indefinite particle'), though Portus in his translation of Apollonius uses it several times, with similar adjectives ('enclitic,' 'interrogative'), referring to various pronouns, conjunctions, interrogatives, articles, enclitics, and the comparative word 'more.' Aulus Gellius almost restricts his use to prepositions and verbal prefixes, but applies the word also to *saltem* ('at least') which is used like such Greek enclitic monosyllables as *ge,* a use which is almost the only one for modern grammarians. By Stoic definitions most of these 'particles' would be either adverbs or conjunctions.

Description of the major Stoic contributions to grammar, must start with the *lekta* ('sayables'), as expounded by Diocles Magnes (in Diogenes Laertius 7.66) and in Sextus Empiricus *Math.* 8.70. These are of two kinds, complete or sufficient (*autotelē*) and deficient or incomplete (*ellipē*). All *lekta* are said to be abstract (thoughts, in some sense, or meanings), though much that is said about them sounds us like talk about the *expression* of thoughts. A complete *lekton* is a *logos* ('sentence') and these may be of several kinds (illocutions, sentence-types), as follows:

(a) statement or assertion (*axiōma, apophantikon lekton*), which alone can be true or false (this follows Aristotle), e.g., 'Dion is walking';

(b) yes/no question (*erotēma*), e.g., 'Is Dion walking?';

(c) *wh*-question (*pusma*), e.g., 'where does Dion live?';

(d) command (*prostaktikon*), e.g., 'Come here,' requiring the imperative mood;

(e) address or vocative (*prosagoreutikon, klētikon*), e.g., 'O King Agamemnon';

(f) superassertion or exclamation (*pleion ē axiōma,* or *homoion axiōmati* or *thaumastikon*), e.g., 'How that boy resembles the princes!'—(*psektikon* apparently is a variant of this with derogatory content);

(g) rhetorical question (i.e., a question not requiring an answer—*epaporētikon*), e.g., 'I wonder if life and sadness are interrelated';

(h) wish/prayer/curse (*euktikon,* or, if bad, *aratikon*), e.g., 'Zeus give victory to Ajax' or 'May his brain spill like wine,' requiring the optative mood (unreal wishes are ignored);

(i) oath (*omotikon*), e.g., 'I swear by Zeus to do that!'; and, finally,

(j) hypothesis or assumption (*ekthetikon* and *hupothetikon,* treated as different by our source), e.g., 'Let X be the center of a circle' or 'Assume that the earth goes around the sun,' with verbs in the third person singular imperative.

Those of these ten which do not require specific morphology often allow special conjunctions or adverbs. These are all real types, all syntactically distinguished in Greek (as well as English), but not all possible types or all that are distinguished in Greek. The omissions are potential/unreal 'statements' and questions, as well as questions expecting an imperative reply ('Shall I go?'). But no modern grammarian has done any better. In the case of *axiōmata* (falsifiable sentences, i.e., those which are capable of being judged true or false), Chrysippus also allowed (in building a kind of logical calculus) for compound/complex sentences of five basic types, with three or more subtypes. Though the expressions themselves are more logical than grammatical, the conjunctions involved are assigned related names, which appear again in Dionysius Thrax and other grammarians. The types are:

(a.1) real, indicative condition (*sunēmmenon axiōma,* conjunction 'if' —*ei*—, *sunaptikos*);

(a.2) subtype inferential, 'since'-clause (*parasunēmme-non,* conjunction 'since' —*epei*—, *parasunaptikos*);

(b) compound sentence (*sumpeplēgmenon,* conjunction 'both–and' —*kai–kai*—, *sumplektikos*);

(c.1) disjunctive sentence (*diezeugmenon,* conjunction exclusive 'either–or' —*ētoi–ē*—, *diazeuktikos*);

(c.2) subtype nonexclusive disjunction (*paradiezeugmenon,* conjunction nonexclusive 'or' —*ē*—, *paradiazeuktikos*);

(d) causal sentence (*aitiōdes,* conjunction 'because' —*dihoti*—, *aitiōdēs, aitiologikos*);

(e) comparative sentence (*diasaphoun to mallon/hētton,* conjunction '(more/less...) than' —*ē, ēper*—, *diasaphētikos*).

All of these conjunctions appear on Dionysius Thrax's list and Apollonius Dyscolus' list; most appear in Latinized form in Priscian, who also uses some of the Greek names.

Before considering Stoic contributions to verb-classification and inflectional categories, first the modern view of the standard analysis of the Greek verb must be laid out. Greek verb forms are all assigned to one or another of four tense/aspect systems and three voices; this makes only 10, instead of 12 aspect–voice categories, because in two aspects (imperfective and stative/perfect) the forms for passive and middle are the same. The other two tense/aspects are the perfective (aorist) and the future, which is not really an aspect, and lacks two moods that all the others have: imperative and subjunctive. All 10 voice–aspect systems have an optative, an infinitive, a participle, and at least one indicative: the future has no forms with augment (i.e., a prefixed vowel) and past tense endings, the aorist (perfective) none without augment and with present endings, but the other two have both. Later grammarians (e.g., Dionysius Thrax and Apollonius Dyscolus) detached the participles entirely from the verb (because they satisfied both the [+tense] and the [+case] requirements which otherwise distinguish verbs from nouns). Two other forms are nowadays associated with verbs, the verbal adjectives or 'verbals' in *-tos, -tē, -ton* (like *lekton, aisthēton, noēton,* favorite Stoic terms) which more or less resemble adjectives in *-able* (*sayable, perceivable, thinkable*), and *-teos, -tea, -teon* (more or less like the Latin passive periphrastic, 'which must be said, perceived, thought'). All of the ancients, if they mention these at all, treat them as derivatives, not part of the conjugation. In each of the regular moods and tenses, most verbs have eight forms (first, second, and third person singular and plural, second, and third person dual), but imperatives lack a first person (for which the subjunctive is used). Some verbs are impersonal, and have only a third person singular (and it cannot have a nominative subject), meaning things like 'it is necessary,' 'it is best,' 'it is of interest,' etc.

Now can be considered which of these things the Stoics dealt with, and how. The treatment of predicates (*ellipē lekta,* 'incomplete sayables' or *katēgorēmata* (instead of *katēgoriai*) differs sharply from Aristotle's, most of whose predicates required a verb 'is,' in that they count verbs only, separated into four classes by the features [±__nom] and [±__oblique]. Verbs which are personal and intransitive (requiring no oblique case) are called *sumbama.* If they need an object of some kind, they are *hētton/elatton ē sumbama* (less than *sumbama*). If they are impersonal, i.e., do not allow a nominative case (i.e., subject) or more than one oblique case (usually dative), they are *parasumbama.* And if they occur with two obliques but no nominative, they are *elatton/hētton ē parasumbama* ('less than p'). But if they occur with two nominatives, but require no obliques (like 'is,' 'becomes,' etc.), the Stoics had no known name for them. These types continued to be distinguished, but new names were adopted for them.

The Stoics also introduced names for the voices: *sumbamata* in the active (governing accusative, dative, or genitive) are *ortha* (upright), a term which is sometimes mentioned by later grammarians, but is normally replaced (by *energētika* or *drastika* 'active'); the same verbs in the passive, capable of taking *hupo* (by) with a genitive ('of agent') are called *huptia* (prone), again normally replaced later by another word (*pathētika,* 'passive'); and verbs which take neither of those two constructions, being intransitive, whether active or middle in form, are called *oudetera* (neither).

Dionysius Thrax includes both *epoiēsamēn* (aorist middle for us) and *pepoitha* (second perfect active) in his category *mesotēs* (middleness), and Apollonius also treats second perfect actives as middle, but apparently no other intransitive actives are called that; so the later 'middle' is not the same as Stoic *oudetera.* Nor is it equal to the Stoic *antipeponthota* (reflexively influenced), which are middle verbs with some reference back to the subject, as *keiretai* 'he gets a haircut' (not 'he cut his own hair') from *keirei* 'he cuts (someone's hair).'

Turning to the treatment of tense by the Stoics, there is a curious passage in the Scholia to Dionysius Thrax (on a passage where Dionysius speaks of the three kinships—*sungeneiai*—present to imperfect [*paratatikos*], future to aorist, and perfect to pluperfect):

> The Stoics say the present should be called 'present imperfect' (*paratatikos,* 'extended' which in Dionysius and later means simply the imperfect tense) for when you say *poiō* 'I am doing,' you imply that you were doing it before and will be doing it after the moment of speaking; and the imperfect should be 'past imperfect' for similar reasons . . . And the perfect tense (*parakeimenos*) is called [sc. 'by the Stoics'?] 'present *suntelikon,*' and its past is the pluperfect.

But *suntelikon* cannot be translated here as 'perfect' (to give a neat match 'present perfect' and 'past perfect' corresponding to 'present imperfect' and 'past imperfect') because everywhere that *suntelikos* or *sunteleia* is used to refer to an aspect (four or five times, in all) it refers to the aorist, not the perfect (some of these are infinitives, others imperatives, and one, *hixon,* is indicative). A possible conclusion is that the perfect is 'present perfective,' the aorist is 'indefinite perfective' [*aoristos* means 'indefinite'] and the pluperfect is 'past perfective,' while *suntelikos* by itself includes all forms of the aorist system; but it is not known what the nonindicative forms of the perfect system were called by the Stoics. As for the generic term for aspect, it is clearly *diathesis* (which also serves for *mood* and *voice*). The effects of this analysis are evident in Apollonius Dyscolus as well as Quintilian and Varro (for Latin, which has no distinction like the Greek one between aorist and perfect).

It is difficult to summarize the contribution of the Stoics to linguistic theory, but it appears enormous, both in the way they raise new grammatical questions and in providing solutions for older ones.

Bibliography

Arens H 1984 *Aristotle's Theory of Language and its Tradition: Texts from 500 to 1750,* Studies in the History of Linguistics **29**. Benjamins, Amsterdam

Arnim H von 1902 *Stoicorum veterum fragmenta. Vol. II: Chrysippi fragmenta logica et physica.* Teubner, Leipzig. Repr. 1923

Ax W 1986 Quadripartita Ratio: Bemerkungen zur Geschichte eines aktuellen Kategoriensystems (*adiecto–detractio–transmutatio–immutatio*). *Historiographia Linguistica* **13**: 191–214

Baratin M 1978 Sur l'absence de l'expression des notions de sujet et de prédicat, etc. In: Collart J (ed.)

Baratin M, Desbordes F 1986 La 'Troisième partie' de *l'ars grammatica*. *Historiographia Linguistica* **13**: 215–40

Barwick K 1957 *Probleme der Stoischen Sprachlehre und Rhetorik*. ASAW **49**(3)

Collart J (ed.) 1978 *Varron, grammaire antique et stylistique latine*. Les Belles Lettres, Paris

De Mauro T 1965 Il nome del dativo e la teoria dei casi greci. *Atti della accademia nazionale dei lincei, serie ottava, rendiconti, classe di scienti morali, storiche e filologiche* **20**: 151–211

Desbordes F 1983 Le schéma 'addition, soustraction, mutation, métathèse' dans les textes anciens. *Histoire–Epistémologie–Langage* **5**: 23–30

Donnet D 1967 La place de la syntaxe dans les traités de grammaire grecque, des origines au XII siècle. *L'Antiquité Classique* **36**: 22–48

Egli U 1970 Zwei Aufsätze zum Vergleich der stoischen Sprachtheorie mit modernen Theorien. *Arbeitspapier* Nr. 2, Universität Bern, Institut für Sprachwissenschaft

Egli U 1986 Stoic syntax and semantics. *Historiographia Linguistica* **13**: 281–306

Frede M 1978 Principles of Stoic grammar. In: Rist J M (ed.)

Gentinetta P M 1961 *Zur Sprachbetrachtung bei den Sophisten und in der stoisch–hellenistischen Zeit*. P G Keller, Winterthur

Householder F W 1989 Review article on Taylor 1987. *Historiographia Linguistica* **16**: 131–48

Koller H 1958 Die Anfänge der griechischen Grammatik. *Glotta* **37**: 5–40

Pfeiffer R 1968 *History of Classical Scholarship*. Clarendon Press, Oxford

Pinborg J 1974 Classical antiquity: Greece. In: Sebeok T A (ed.) *Current Trends in Linguistics*, vol. 13. Mouton, The Hague

Pohlenz M 1939 Die Begründung der abendländischen Sprachlehre durch die Stoa. In: Pohlenz M 1965 *Kleine Schriften*, vol. 1. Olms, Hildesheim

Priscian (Priscianus) *Institutiones Grammaticae*, Hertz M (ed.) In: Keil H (ed.) 1859 *Grammatici Latini*, vol. III. Teubner, Leipzig

Rist J M (ed.) 1978 *The Stoics*. University of California Press, Berkeley, California

Robins R H 1990 *A Short History of Linguistics*, 3rd edn. Longman, London

Schenkeveld D M 1984 Studies in the history of Ancient Linguistics, II. *Mnemosyne* **37**: 291–353

Steinthal H 1890–91 *Geschichte der Sprachwissenschaft bei den Griechen und Römern*, 2nd edn. Dümmler, Berlin. Repr. 1961 Olms, Hildesheim

Swiggers P, Wouters A 1989a Langues, situations linguistiques et réflexion sur le langage dans l'Antiquité. In: Swiggers P, Wouters A 1989b

Swiggers P, Wouters A 1989b *Le langage dans l'antiquité, La pensée linguistique*, vol 3. Leuven University Press (Peeters), Leuven

Taylor D J 1986 Rethinking the history of language science in classical antiquity. *Historiographia Linguistica* **13**: 175–190

Taylor D J (ed.) 1987 *The History of Linguistics in the Classical Period*. Benjamins, Amsterdam

Telegdi Zs 1982 On the formation of the concept of 'linguistic sign' and on Stoic language doctrine. In: Kiefer F (ed.) *Hungarian General Linguistics*. Benjamins, Amsterdam

Descartes, René

J. Cottingham

Born near Tours and educated by the Jesuits at the College of La Flèche in Anjou, Descartes lived for most of his adult life in Holland. His first major work, the *Rules for the Direction of our Native Intelligence* (*Regulae ad directionem ingenii*, written in the late 1620s) outlines the plan for a universal science based on indubitable principles of the kind hitherto found only in mathematics. His early treatise on physics and cosmology, *Le Monde*, was cautiously withdrawn in 1633 following the condemnation of Galileo for defending the heliocentric hypothesis (which Descartes too advocated). His philosophical masterpieces were the *Discourse on the Method* (*Discours de la méthode*), written in 1637 as an introduction to a selection of scientific essays, and the *Meditations* (*Meditationes de prima philosophia*, 1641), which examine the foundations of knowledge, the existence of God, and the nature of the human mind. The *Principles of Philosophy* (*Principia philosophiae*), a comprehensive textbook of Cartesian metaphysics and science, appeared in 1644, and the *Passions of the Soul* (*Les Passions de l'akme*), dealing with physiology, psychology, and ethics, in 1649. Descartes died of pneumonia contracted during a visit to Stockholm at the invitation of Queen Christina of Sweden.

1. Descartes's Views on Language

Descartes attached great importance to language, which he regarded as 'the only sure sign indicating the presence of thought within.' He drew a sharp distinction between animal utterances, which he regarded as always elicited by a particular stimulus, and genuine linguistic performance, involving the ability to respond appropriately to an indefinite range of inputs. Thus a magpie can be 'taught to say good day to its mistress,' but this will merely be 'the expression of one of its passions, for example the hope of eating, if it has always been given a titbit when it says the word' (letter to Newcastle of November 23, 1646). Human language-users, by contrast, can 'give appropriately meaningful answers to whatever is said in their presence' (*Discourse on the Method*: part 5).

Because of his grasp of this crucial difference between human speech and animal utterance, Descartes has been seen as a precursor, or inspirer of the Chomskyan approach to linguistics. But Descartes's 'modernity' in this respect should not be exaggerated. For what Descartes himself takes his observations about human linguistic capacities to show is the truth of his metaphysical dualism—the thesis of the essentially incorporeal nature of the human mind. In general, Descartes's scientific program was robustly physicalist and reductionist; thus, all the capacities of animals were to be explained by reference to the purely mechanical operation of their internal organs. But a physical organ, Descartes argues, needs 'some particular disposition for each particular action'; so, bearing in mind the indefinite range of responses which a language-user can deploy, 'it is for all practical purposes impossible' for there to be a physical organ or set of organs responsible for language. The upshot is that language must depend on the activities of a 'rational soul' (*акте raisonnable*) which is 'not derived in any way from the potentiality of matter, but which must be specially created' (*Discourse*: part 5).

2. Cartesian Dualism and Its Consequences

Cartesian dualism involved an 'all or nothing' approach to consciousness: either something belongs in the special realm of *res cogitans*—it is a fully conscious 'thinking substance'—or else it is mere extended matter, and its operations are explicable simply on mechanical principles. This led Descartes to posit an unbridgeable gulf between mankind and all other species, which he regarded as mere mechanical automata. The doctrine of the *bête machine* (as it came to

be known after Descartes's death) is something which Descartes argues for very carefully and explicitly, on linguistic grounds. Predecessors of Descartes, such as Montaigne, had suggested that there was often more difference between one human and another than between a human being and an animal, but Descartes replies that 'it requires very little reason to be able to speak, and it would be incredible that a superior specimen of monkey or parrot should not be able to speak as well as the stupidest child if their souls were not completely different in nature from ours.' The upshot is that 'the beasts' do not merely have less reason than man, but 'have no reason at all' (*Discourse*, loc cit). Descartes is admirably clear that this difference has nothing to do with the presence or absence of organs of speech; for men born deaf and dumb lack speech organs, but can nonetheless invent signs (*signes*) which constitute a genuine language (*langue*).

It is impossible to say whether Descartes would have maintained his insistence that language-capacity could not be explained in physical terms had he known of the enormously complex electrochemistry of the brain as revealed by modern science. That issue aside, what gives his arguments an enduring interest for modern linguisticians and philosophers is his clear articulation of just how far genuine linguistic behavior diverges from the output of a machine (whether organic or artificial) programed with a set of finite responses. The label 'Cartesian linguistics' remains an apt one for any research program that takes seriously the problems posed by the seemingly infinite flexibility and creativity of human language.

See also: Chomsky, Noam.

Bibliography

Adam C, Tannery P (eds.) 1976 *Oeuvres de Descartes*, rev. edn. Vrin, Paris
Chomsky N 1966 *Cartesian Linguistics: A Chapter in the History of Rationalist Thought*. Harper and Row, New York
Descartes R 1991 (trans. Cottingham J, Stouthoff R, Murdoch D, Kenny A) *The Philosophical Writings of Descartes*, 3 vols. Cambridge University Press, Cambridge

Herder, Johann Gottfried

P. B. Salmon[†]

Herder, in his early adult years a leading figure in the German Storm and Stress movement of the 1770s, is known to linguists primarily for his essay on the origin

of language (*Abhandlung über den Ursprung der Sprache* 1772). His early writings include studies in folk literature and the advocacy of simple language based on the vernacular. Common to these and to later works, such as the *Ideen zur Philosophie der Geschichte der Menschheit* (1784–91), is an interest in continuity and development, which is accompanied throughout his writings by another in origins.

In the *Fragmente* (1766–68), a set of mainly literary essays, he suggests, much as Condillac had done, that language originated from a combination of gesture and natural reflex cries, which developed into irregular utterances, and thence into poetry. In social use language evolved further into oratory, before declining eventually into the dull regularity of 'philosophical' (i.e., scientific) language. His view of a language as a key to the national character of its speakers—also anticipated by Condillac—is often seen as a source of similar ideas expressed by Wilhelm von Humboldt.

The treatise on the origin of language, unlike other writings of the time, asserts unequivocally that language is not God-given, but man-made. However, instead of Condillac's scheme of development it suggests a specifically human quality of 'reflection' (*Besonnenheit*), nature's compensation for man's weak instinctual endowments, which enables man to identify an object by selecting one of the set of features which characterize it. For example, a lamb is identified by its bleat; the observer bleats mentally on seeing it again; this event alone is sufficient to constitute language, even without a listener. Speech is not a reflex sound; neither is it mere irrational imitation or 'aping' (*nachäffen*). Later passages speak of a gestural component in language, and of the mutual reinforcement of reason and language.

The recognition of an object by a distinguishing mark is also used as the initial stage of identification in the mental processes set up in the *Metacritique to the Critique of Pure Reason* (1799), an empiricist attack on Kant's *Critique*, paralleling the increasingly complex perceptions of identity, quality, and activity by the progressive introduction of nominals, adjectives, and verbs in grammar.

While Herder is best known to linguists for his views on the origin of language, the *Abhandlung* is perhaps more important for its vigor than its views; his most influential contribution may lie rather in his sense of the organic growth and decay of language, in his consciousness of the distinctive national quality of languages, and in his propagating the use of simple unaffected German.

Bibliography

Clark R T 1955 *Herder: His Life and Thought*. University of California Press, Berkeley, CA

Haym R 1958 [1st edn. 1877–85] *Herder*. Aufbau-Verlag, Berlin

Heintel E (ed.) 1964 *J G H Sprachphilosophische Schriften*, 2nd edn. Meiner, Hamburg

Herder J G 1877–1913 (ed. Suphan B) *Sämtliche Werke*. Weidmann, Berlin

Moran J H, Gode A (transl.) 1966 *On the Origin of Language: Jean-Jacques Rousseau, Essay on the Origin of Languages; Johann Gottfried Herder, Essay on the Origin of Language*. Ungar, New York

Stam J H 1976 *Inquiries into the Origin of Language. The Fate of a Question*. Harper and Row, New York

Humboldt, Wilhelm von

J. A. Kemp

Wilhelm von Humboldt, elder brother of the famous scientist and explorer Alexander von Humboldt, was born on June 22, 1767 in Potsdam, Prussia, and died in Tegel (now in Berlin) on April 8, 1835. Distinguished as a statesman and diplomat, he is generally regarded as one of the profoundest thinkers on linguistic matters, though the difficulty of his style often makes his meaning hard to interpret.

After private tuition at home Wilhelm attended Göttingen University (1788). Completing his legal studies, he traveled in Europe and pursued further studies in Greek language and civilization, which epitomized for him the versatile and harmonious way of life and remained a strong influence throughout his career.

His marriage into a wealthy family in 1791 meant that he was able to devote his time and energies to developing to the full the individuality and independence of mind which from an early age he had striven for. In Jena from 1794 he enjoyed a close and intellectually stimulating friendship with Schiller and Goethe. During a period in Paris he visited Spain, and contact with the Basque language was an early stimulus to the study of languages in general. In 1801 he reluctantly moved to Berlin and the next year to Rome, as Prussian ambassador to the Vatican from 1802 to 1808. State service claimed his full attention on his recall to Germany in 1808, and he was responsible for important educational reforms. It was not until 1819 that disagreements with other members of the Prussian government led him to retire from public life and to devote himself to his study of languages.

By temperament he was throughout his life reluctant to commit himself to writing, or to complete works he had begun, but he realized that his search for the nature of language, and its importance in the life of man, could only be based on a knowledge of a wide variety of languages. To his knowledge of Greek and Latin and other languages of Europe he added Sanskrit in 1821, which had a powerful influence on his view of language. In the same year he helped to secure the appointment of Franz Bopp, one of the great pioneers of comparative linguistics, to a professorship in Oriental and General Linguistics in Berlin. From grammars of the native languages of America, acquired by his brother, Wilhelm had extended his knowledge to the American continent; and Rémusat's work on Chinese led him to publish in this area also. Searching for a link between languages from different parts of the world he studied the Polynesian languages and the languages of Malaya. The search culminated in his great work, published posthumously, *On the Kawi Language on the Island of Java* (Humboldt 1836–39), with its lengthy introduction entitled 'On the Diversity of Human Language-Structure and its Influence on the Mental Development of Mankind.' What perhaps caused Humboldt to select the Kawi language for such close examination was not only the geographical position of Java, but the mixed nature of the Kawi language, combining a Sanskrit vocabulary with a Malayan structure. Although he believed that vocabulary and grammatical structure are inseparable and interdependent parts of language (except for the linguistic analyst), he thought the differences between languages to be most evident in their grammatical structure.

Greek and Sanskrit were for him the most perfect languages—at one extreme of a typological scale, exemplifying the supreme type of inflecting language. At the other extreme he placed Chinese, as an isolating language, lacking inflections or affixes. In between came the so-called 'agglutinating' languages, which he regarded as having an inferior variety of inflection, involving 'mechanical adding, not a truly organic accretion.' Similar classifications can be found earlier in Friedrich von Schlegel and his brother August Wilhelm von Schlegel. Humboldt, however, identified in the 'Mexican language' (Nahuatl) a new category of sentence form, called 'incorporating.' In this the main elements in the structure of the sentence are 'incorporated' into a single word. The superiority of languages such as Greek and Sanskrit for Humboldt lay in what he perceived as the organic nature of their grammatical structure, where inner modifications and inflections are welded into the root, which contains the crucial concept; but at the same time the unity of the word is maintained. Languages of very different types, such as Chinese and Mexican, clearly could also express the thoughts of their speakers, but are constrained by their structure to do this less perfectly.

The relationship of language with thought is crucial. Humboldt believed that all languages contain certain universal features, arising from the laws of thinking, shared by all men. But without language, he maintained, thinking is not possible, because only through expression in language is a concept given objectivity. Language, however, is not a fixed object or product (Humboldt uses the Greek word *ergon*) but involves constant creation, or activity (Greek *energeia*). This creativity of language is limited in particular languages by the structure or form they have developed. The creativity is constantly at work, but it can only act on what material is available to the speaker at a particular time. So particular languages acquire their individual character, which may be more or less imperfect, as a result of their being animated by 'a more or less fruitful principle of mental development.' Thus Humboldt ranks languages on a scale, at the top of which are those of the Sanskritic type (i.e., Indo-European). The form of Chinese is accepted as exhibiting perhaps more than any other language 'the power of pure thought,' but falls short in versatility and harmony. Humboldt proceeds to associate the particular national character of each language with a particular outlook of its speakers on the world—a thesis that was later to be developed by Edward Sapir and Benjamin Lee Whorf.

Among nineteenth-century writers, August Friedrich Pott acknowledges his debt to Humboldt, and Heymann Steinthal (see Di Cesare 1996) and Wilhelm Wundt were certainly influenced by him in developing the notion of 'national psychology' (*Völkerpsychologie*). However, Humboldt's influence on linguistics has been more apparent in the twentieth century than in the nineteenth, e.g., in so-called 'neo-Humboldtian' trends (see Basilius 1952), and in controversial claims as to the similarities between Humboldt's well-known, but variously interpreted, idea of the 'inner form of language' (*innere Sprachform*) and the rules of generative grammar (see Coseriu 1970). For the influence on Humboldt of earlier linguistic philosophers see Manchester (1985).

See also: Sapir–Whorf Hypothesis.

Bibliography

Basilius H A 1952 Neo-Humboldtian ethnolinguistics. *Word* **8**: 95–105 (repr. in Fishman J A (ed.) 1968 *Readings in the Sociology of Language*. Mouton, The Hague)

Coseriu E 1970 Semantik, innere Sprachform und Tiefenstruktur. *FoL* **4**: 53–63

Di Cesare D 1996 'Innere Sprachform': Humboldts Grenzbegriff, Steinthals Begriffgrenze. *HL* **23(3)**: 321–46

Humboldt W von 1836–39 *Über die Kawi Sprache auf der Insel Java, nebst einer Einleitung über die Verschiedenheit des menschlichen Sprachbaues und ihren Einfluss auf die geistige Entwickelung des Menschengeschlechts*. Königliche Akademie der Wissenschaften, Berlin. (The introduction is translated by P Heath as *On Language: the Diversity of Human Language Structure and its Influence* on the Mental Development of Mankind, with an introduction by H Aarsleff. Cambridge University Press, Cambridge, 1988)

Humboldt W von 1903–36 *Gesammelte Schriften*, 17 vols. Königlich Akademie der Wissenschaften, Berlin

Koerner E F K 1990 Wilhelm von Humboldt and North American ethnolinguistics: Boas (1894) to Hymes (1961). *HL* **17(1–2)**: 111–28

Manchester M L 1985 *The Philosophical Foundations of Humboldt's Linguistic Doctrines*. Benjamins, Amsterdam

Sweet P R 1978–80 *Wilhelm von Humboldt: A Biography*, 2 vols. Ohio State University Press, Columbus, OH

Kant, Immanuel

R. C. S. Walker

Immanuel Kant was born on April 22, 1724 in Königsberg, East Prussia (now Kaliningrad, Russia), where he spent his whole life, becoming Professor of Logic and Metaphysics in 1770 and eventually Rector of the University. In his lifetime he achieved a revolution in German philosophical thought, opening the way to the idealism of Fichte, Schelling, and Hegel. Elsewhere his influence was felt more slowly (though Coleridge was an early admirer), but its effect was again profound. He died on February 12, 1804.

1. Transcendental Idealism

The Critique of Pure Reason (1781) is concerned with how knowledge is possible. The rationalist tradition (then dominant in Germany) held that we possess certain concepts innately, and can recognize as self-evident certain truths from which can be deduced substantial knowledge about the world. The empiricists, in contrast, held that concepts and knowledge of the world could only be derived from experience, though Hume—the most consistent of them—argued that the only way of deriving from experience the concepts of cause and physical object showed them to be inherently confused. Kant believes they are not confused, and not derived from experience. He also holds that we have substantial knowledge which could not have been derived from experience: in his terminology, synthetic a priori knowledge. It includes mathematical truths, and truths like 'Every event has a cause.'

We can know these truths, Kant thinks, only because we ourselves make them true: i.e., read them into the world. Mathematics he takes to be about space and time, which however are not real independently of us, but forms which our mind imposes upon data it receives. Similarly concepts like those of cause and object are so read in by us as to guarantee they will apply within the world as we experience it, and in such a way that principles like 'Every event has a cause' will be true within that world. The world of 'appearances' or 'phenomena' is thus partly the product of our minds' activity. Yet truth in that world (the familiar world of space, time, and causality) is not just a matter of what we happen to believe. The concepts and principles which we ourselves supply provide standards for distinguishing true from false beliefs, and allow us to assign to physical objects a reality distinct from our perceptions of them. Because he treats objects in this way, and not (like Berkeley) as sets of perceptions, Kant calls himself an empirical realist; he calls himself also a transcendental idealist, because the phenomenal world as a whole is partly the product of our minds.

Kant does not simply postulate that our minds supply these elements to the world. He argues that they must, for experience would be impossible otherwise. Perhaps other beings could impose forms different from space and time, but some such forms are required for any experience of sensible particulars. Twelve fundamental concepts or 'categories' he argues to be indispensable, including that of cause, and he claims that principles like 'Every event has a cause' must hold for spatio-temporal experience to be possible. Arguments of this kind, that something must be so if experience is to be possible, are often called transcendental arguments.

The phenomenal world is only partly the product of our minds. Minds work on data supplied by things as they are in themselves (or 'noumena'). Things in themselves are wholly independent of us, and about them we can know nothing. We can know nothing about them empirically, since we do not experience them, nor a priori, for a priori knowledge is possible only in virtue of what we read into what is known. The failure to realize these limits to knowledge leads, Kant holds, to the errors of metaphysicians, and to natural mistakes in our thinking about the self, the world as a totality, and God—though the tendencies that lead to these natural mistakes have great heuristic value.

2. Judgment and Truth

Kant regards language as the expression of thought, though he also describes thinking as inner speech. Thought consists in making judgements, and he claims that logic, by revealing that there are twelve fundamental types of judgment, shows there are twelve ways in which the mind can act. It is because concepts also involve mental activity that he thinks there must correspondingly be twelve fundamental concepts, the categories.

Judgments may be either analytic or synthetic. Analytic judgments are those whose truth can be determined 'in accordance with the Principle of Contradiction,' or by means of logical laws and conceptual analysis: such as 'All unmarried men are unmarried,' or, equivalently, 'All bachelors are unmarried.' All other judgments are synthetic. Kant considers mathematical, as well as metaphysical, judgments to be synthetic, though also a priori.

Truth is correspondence: 'the agreement of knowledge with its object.' Judgments about things in themselves may be true, but there is no way for us to know they are. Judgments about the phenomenal world, however, can be shown to 'agree with their objects' by establishing their coherence with what is given to us empirically in sensation, in accordance with those forms and principles which our minds supply.

3. Aesthetics and Moral Philosophy

The appreciation of beauty is a matter of feeling, not reason, but in *The Critique of Judgment* (1790) Kant argues that it can be expected of everyone nonetheless. It arises whenever something appears well-adapted to our cognitive faculties, without our being able fully to capture why. The moral law, in contrast, is purely rational. In *Groundwork of the Metaphysic of Morals* (1785) and *Critique of Practical Reason* (1788), he argues it is an imperative which is 'categorical' in that it must be obeyed for its own sake, not for the sake of any further end to be achieved by it (like the promotion of happiness). Only actions performed out of respect for the moral law have genuine moral worth; actions which accord with the law, but are done for some other motive (e.g., because one feels generous), do not. Being purely rational, the categorical imperative must bind all rational beings universally. It can be formulated, 'Act only on those principles of action which you can rationally will as universal law.'

4. Kant Today

Kant's influence is pervasive, but one or two points may be specially noticed. In moral philosophy his conception of the law as a rational motive has often been dismissed, but recently there have been interesting attempts to give a greater place to rational motivation along roughly Kantian lines. Transcendental idealism also has its supporters, but since Kant's own day people have often been unconvinced by his retention of things in themselves. Many, also, have been unconvinced by the idealistic aspect—the conception of the phenomenal world as in part a product of our minds. The most trenchant of these has been Strawson, who nevertheless finds the key to metaphysics in Kantian transcendental arguments.

Bibliography

Allison H E 1983 *Kant's Transcendental Idealism.* Yale University Press, New Haven, CT
Guyer P (ed.) 1992 *The Cambridge Companion to Kant.* Cambridge University Press, Cambridge
Kant I 1929 (trans. Kemp Smith N) *The Critique of Pure Reason.* Macmillan, London
Kant I 1948 *Groundwork of the Metaphysic of Morals.* In: Paton H J (ed. and trans.) *The Moral Law.* Hutchinson, London
Kemp J 1968 *The Philosophy of Kant.* Oxford University Press, Oxford
Scruton R 1982 *Kant.* Oxford University Press, Oxford
Strawson P F 1966 *The Bounds of Sense.* Methuen, London
Sullivan R J 1994 *An Introduction to Kant's Ethics.* Cambridge University Press, Cambridge

Leibniz, Gottfried Wilhelm

R. C. de Vrijer

Gottfried Wilhelm Leibniz is most reputed as a philosopher, the designer of one of the great sytems of philosophy, and as a mathematician, co-inventor of the differential and integral calculus. He was, in fact, a universal genius, who made important contributions to almost every field of scientific investigation. Thus he was also alchemist, jurist, engineer, logician, historian, and linguist.

Leibniz was born in Leipzig, Germany, in 1646, the son of a professor of philosophy. At the age of 20, he obtained a doctorate in law and also wrote a dissertation in philosophy, *De Arte Combinatoria*, already showing some of his fascination with the idea of using mathematical methods for the design of a 'universal language' on the basis of an 'alphabet of human thought.' He did not succeed, in 1666, in obtaining a position at the University of Leipzig, whereupon, although being offered a chair in law in the nearby city of Altdorf, he left the university altogether.

For the rest of his life Leibniz was employed by members of the influential German nobility, first in Mainz, and from 1676 until his death by the dukes of Hanover. He served them as a legal and political adviser, as a diplomat, as an engineer, as a librarian, and as an historian, investigating the history of the House of Brunswick.

Next to these professional occupations he pursued his scientific interests, managing to communicate with leading European scientists through personal contacts during his diplomatic journeys and by writing letters. Relatively little of his work was published during his lifetime. The bulk of his writings consists of memoranda, unfinished manuscripts (including all his important papers on logic), and his tremendous correspondence. What is probably the most important source for Leibniz's philosophy of language, the New Essays on Human Understanding, appeared in print only in 1765, almost fifty years after his death in 1716. (And about 60 years after the death of Locke; thereby it somewhat missed its target, as it was a polemical writing, directed against Locke's *An Essay Concerning Human Understanding*.)

The lack of accessibility of Leibniz's own work contrasts with his continuous efforts, as a librarian, archivist, and encyclopedist, to make the vast but chaotic body of scientific knowledge of his time more tractable, by collecting, ordering, cataloguing, and so on. Leibniz aspired to be a science manager in quite a modern sense, writing enthusiastic (and often overoptimistic) research proposals in order to attract interest and raise funds for his projects. In general, he stimulated organization and institutionalization of academic life, one result of which was the foundation of the German Academy of Sciences in Berlin in 1700.

1. Historical Linguistics

Leibniz's inquiries into the origin and the development of languages were connected with his interest in the history of the peoples of Europe. For example, he established the kinship of Finnish and Hungarian, and concluded that an extended language area must have been split by intruding Slav peoples. Without coming to a definite conclusion on the tenability of a monogenetic theory of the origin of language, he held that an original language could anyway not be found among the languages that were known. Leibniz proposed etymological principles, in order that they should be used in historical linguistics, and criticized what he considered to be unsound etymological reasoning. (For further reading see Leibniz 1981; Arens 1969; Robins 1990.)

2. Universal Language

In Leibniz's time there existed several proposals (by Mersenne, Dalgamo, Wilkins, and others) for the construction of an artificial 'universal language,' that could be understood by people of all tongues, and which would allow all possible knowledge to be expressed unequivocally and in a systematic way. In this course Leibniz put forward his project for a *Characteristica Universalis*. Like the other proposals, its starting point was to be an analysis of concepts, backing up the nominal definitions of the signs of the language. What constituted an innovation was that the concepts would be coded as numbers. Reasoning could then be reduced to numerical calculation (*Calculus Ratiocinator*). Leibniz must have felt that reasoning could be performed on a mechanical calculator, like the one that he had designed himself and that he proudly demonstrated to the members of the Royal Society on his trip to London in 1673. In order to attain the high-pitched objectives of the universal language project, supporting results from many disciplines were needed. In fact much of Leibniz's work on logic and grammar should be situated within the project of the *Characteristica Universalis*. Moreover, he wanted a 'universal encyclopedia,' which was to provide the background material for the required concept analysis. Leibniz was always eager to recruit support for the immense task of designing such an encyclopedia. It never got very far. (In Leibniz 1969 one finds several writings of Leibniz on his *Characteristica Universalis*.)

3. Philosophy of Language

For Leibniz the function of language was twofold; for communication, and as an instrument in the process of thinking. The emphasis on the second, computational, aspect is especially characteristic for Leibniz. As pointed out, it played a central role in the *Characteristica Universalis* project.

Leibniz opposed the popular opinion (for example, held by Hobbes) that the meaning of words is completely arbitrary. In primitive languages there will always have been a natural correspondence between a word and its signification. Although Leibniz did not deny that conventional aspects may emerge when a language develops, he assumed that a causal link of the words with their source will always remain. As an exception to this rule Leibniz recognized, besides artificial languages, only Chinese.

According to Leibniz the structure of language, that is, its underlying logical form, mirrors the structure of the world. The concepts, being the elements of his ontology, are to be analyzed into their primitive constituents, and correspondingly the meaning of complex language expressions are to be derived from their primitive parts. This combination of doctrines makes Leibniz a precursor of the twentieth-century's logical atomism of Wittgenstein and of Russell (for a more thorough discussion see Ishiguro 1990).

Perhaps it should be stressed that Leibniz's philosophy of language is so intimately connected with his ontology, his theory of knowledge, and his logic, that it can only be properly understood as an integral part of his complete philosophical system. (Recommended reading is Leibniz 1981, Book III: *Of Words.*)

4. Logic

The first two millennia of formal logic can be summarized in terms of three giant steps and a tragedy. First, Aristotle created logic and introduced the syllogism. Then Leibniz turned the subject into mathematics. Finally, Frege invented the predicate calculus. The tragedy is that the second step remained unnoticed. This made it possible for Kant to remark in 1800 that the discipline of logic was apparently finished, as there had been no essential developments since Aristotle. Another consequence was that Boole, by redoing the second step, became recognized as the founder of mathematical logic.

In numerous unfinished and often fragmentary manuscripts Leibniz put down his attempts to develop a completely formalized system of logic. The algebraization of logic was a cornerstone of the project of the *Characteristica Universalis* and the *Calculus Ratiocinator*. The possibility of reducing reasoning to mere calculation rested on the premise that logical principles could be laid down in algebraic equations, thereby making them suitable for mathematical manipulation.

Adhering to the tradition of syllogistic logic, Leibniz attempted to render syllogistic reasoning as equational reasoning in an algebra of classes, much in the way George Boole would propose later. For Leibniz, the basic sentence form is: 'A is B,' where the term A is called the subject and B the predicate. Terms can be conjoined: if, e.g., A stands for 'red,' and B stands for 'flower,' then the term AB would stand for 'red flower.' The subject-predicate sentence 'A is B' will now be true, according to Leibniz, if the predicate is contained in the subject, that is, if for some term Y there is posited the equation $A = BY$. Leibniz uses one basic principle of proof; equal terms may be substituted for each other. A simple application is a derivation of 'A is C' from the premises 'A is B' and 'B is C': if $A = BY$ and $B = CZ$, then $A = CZY$. Note the conjoining is here assumed to be associative; Leibniz leaves this assumption implicit in his notation. In his manuscripts Leibniz has several tentative axiomatizations of his logical system, involving typical Boolean equations such as $AB = BA$ and $AA = A$. It is important to remark that Leibniz regards his terms as intensional, although he is aware of the possibility of an extensional reading of the same formalism as well.

A few other advances in logic deserve mention. Through the work of the German logician Jungius, Leibniz was aware of the fact that relations caused problems in logical analysis. Accordingly, Leibniz took pains to demonstrate that arguments involving relational expressions could always be reduced to arguments dealing only with sentences in subject-predicate form.

It is well-known that Leibniz introduced the concept of 'possible world' and argued that from the perfection of God it follows that humans must live in the best one. But he also used the notion of possible world in his analysis of necessary and contingent truths, the necessary ones being those holding in all possible worlds. He recognized the issue of cross-world identity, reducing it to similarity of individual concepts.

Finally a word on Leibniz's famous principle of the identity of indiscernables. According to Ishiguro (1990) it is often confused with another principle of Leibniz: that of 'substitutivity *salva veritate.*' The matter is rather subtle, but approximates to this. The first principle says that if what is true of *A* is true of *B* and vice versa, then *A* and *B* are the same. It offers a constraint on ontology. In contrast, substitutivity *salva veritate* acts as a metalogical principle: terms that can be substituted for each other in any proposition without affecting its truth value, are equal.

See also: Logic: Historical Survey; Possible Worlds.

Bibliography

Recommended further reading on Leibniz's logic: Leibniz 1966; Kneale and Kneale 1961; Ishiguro 1990.

Arens H 1969 *Sprachwissenschaft: der Gang ihrer Entwicklung von der Antike bis zur Gegenwart.* 2nd edn. Alber, Freiburg and Munich

Ishiguro H 1990 *Leibniz's Philosophy of Logic and Language*, 2nd edn. Cambridge University Press, Cambridge

Kneale W, Kneale M 1961 *The Development of Logic.* Oxford University Press, Oxford

Leibniz G W 1966 *Logical Papers.* Parkinson G H R (ed.) Oxford University Press, Oxford

Leibniz G W 1969 *Philosophical Papers and Letters.* 2nd edn. Loemker L E (ed.) Reidel, Dordrecht

Leibniz G W 1981 *New Essays on Human Understanding.* Remnant P, Bennett J (eds.) Cambridge University Press, Cambridge

Locke J 1975 *An Essay Concerning Human Understanding.* Nidditch P H (ed.) Clarendon Press, Oxford

MacDonald R G 1984 *Leibniz.* Oxford University Press, Oxford

Robins R H 1990 *A Short History of Linguistics*, 3rd edn. Longman, London

Locke, John
T. J. Taylor

Within the context of linguistic thought, John Locke is best known for proposing an empiricist, mentalist account of linguistic signification and for his skeptical conclusions regarding the efficacy of language as a vehicle of communicational understanding.

Locke was born on August 29, 1632, the eldest son of a liberal Puritan attorney who fought on the Parliamentary side in the English Civil War. Locke's two most important works—the *Two Treatises of Government* and the *Essay Concerning Human Understanding*—were written in self-imposed exile from the Britain of James II and published in 1689 and 1690 following his return to Britain upon the ascent to the throne of King William and Queen Mary. He died on October 28, 1704.

Locke's position in the history of linguistic thought is derived from his discussion of language in Book III of the *Essay Concerning Human Understanding*. Although the *Essay* is primarily an epistemological treatise on the foundations of human knowledge, Locke includes a long discussion of linguistic issues because he sees language as an imperfect vehicle for the communication of knowledge as well as a potentially dangerous obstacle to the acquisition of new knowledge. The whole of Book III (entitled 'Of Words') is devoted to an account of the nature of verbal communication and to an analysis of the characteristics of the words used in communicational acts. Communication is described as 'the Great Conduit' whereby speakers make their thoughts known to others. Thoughts are said to be composed of ideas, and it is by signifying, or 'standing for,' ideas that words have meaning and serve the ends of communication. Locke describes language and signification as voluntary acts performed by individual agents endowed with freedom of the will. That is, in communicating my ideas I voluntarily produce words as signs of those ideas. Which idea one such word signifies depends on my voluntary act of using that word to stand for an idea in my mind. Naturally, then, only I can ultimately know which of the 'private' ideas in my mind are signified by the words I use. Moreover, since the vast majority of my ideas are formed by similarly voluntary and private mental operations, there are no grounds for assuming that the ideas I have in my mind are the same as those in another person's mind. For instance, even though we (I and you, the reader) both use the word *justice* we cannot assume that the idea (in your mind) which you use that word to stand for is the same as the idea (in my mind) which I signify by the same word. Consequently, the conclusion of Locke's assessment of words and signification is that, while language may serve the 'vulgar' purposes of ordinary conversation well enough, it is not adequate to guarantee the true communication of thoughts.

The *Essay* is also known for Locke's identification of *sēmeiōtikē*, or 'the doctrine of signs,' as one of the three branches of science.

See also: Abstract Ideas; Meaning: Philosophical Theories; Natural Kinds.

Bibliography

Harris R, Taylor T 1997 *Landmarks in Linguistic Thought: The Western Tradition from Socrates to Saussure*, 2nd edn. Routledge, London

Kretzmann N 1977 The main thesis of Locke's semantic theory. In: Tipton I (ed.) 1977 *Locke on Human Understanding*. Oxford University Press, Oxford

Locke J 1690 *An Essay Concerning Human Understanding*. Printed 1979 for Thomas Basett, Clarendon Press, Oxford

Medieval Philosophy of Language
D. Perler

The origin and development of the philosophy of language in the Middle Ages—roughly speaking, in the period between Boethius (480–524) and John Mair (1467/69–1550)—was closely linked to the translation and interpretation of ancient texts. Most theories on the semantics of terms and propositions grew out of commentaries on such authoritative books. These theories relied on the basic assumption that language, thought, and reality were naturally related to each other. Like their ancient predecessors, the medievals considered language to be not only an instrument of communication, but also a system of signs representing the structure of mental and extramental reality. Thus, the analysis of the semantic function of language was supposed to provide a deeper understanding of reality itself.

1. Sources and Stages of Development

The most influential body of authoritative texts in the Middle Ages was Aristotle's Organon; its first treatise, the *Categories*, provided the basis for a theory of uncomplex linguistic signs, and its second treatise, *De interpretatione*, was the starting point for a theory of complex signs. These two works (translated into Latin with commentaries by Boethius), accompanied by Porphyry's *Isagoge* (an introduction to the *Categories*), were the main sources of the old logic (*logica vetus*), which was fully elaborated for the first time in the *Dialectica* of Garlandus Compotista (died before 1102) and culminated in the School of Chartres and in Peter Abelard (1079–1142/44) (see Tweedale 1988; Jacobi 1988). The new translations or retranslations of the four other works of the Organon (*Prior and Posterior Analytics*, *Topics*, *Sophistical Refutations*), which entered the Latin West in the twelfth century, constituted the textual basis of the *logica nova*, a logic that focused especially on the theory of linguistic fallacies. Together, the old and the new logics formed the *logica antiqua*, which was replaced by the *logica moderna* in the late twelfth century. Since the *logica moderna*, which reached its full-fledged stage in the works of William of Sherwood (1200/10–66/72), Peter of Spain (d.1277), and Lambert of Auxerre (fl.1250), was distinguished by detailed analysis of the properties of terms, it was also called 'terminism' (see Rijk 1967; Pinborg 1972: 13–18). Around 1300, the dominance of terminism was weakened by the Modistae, who introduced extensive grammatico–psychological analyses into semantic theory (Pinborg 1975; Marmo 1994).

An important transformation occurred in the early fourteenth century. On the basis of the ontological claim that only individual, really existing substances and accidents are beings in a strict sense, William of Ockham (1285–1347/49) elaborated a semantic theory which explained any linguistic reference as a reference to individual beings. This theory, labeled the *via moderna*, sparked a controversy that dominated university discussions of the fourteenth and fifteenth centuries (see Biard 1989: 203–88; Kaluza 1988). At the same time, humanist dialecticians, including Lorenzo Valla (1407–57) and Rudolphus Agricola (1443/44–1485), began emphasizing the rhetorical and pragmatic function of language, opposing the logico–semantic approach to language (see Jardine 1988: 173–76). However, the humanist approach did not simply supersede the logical approach characteristic of the Aristotelian tradition. A continuous scholastic tradition, especially active in Spain and Britain, transmitted medieval concepts to modern philosophers such as John Locke and G. W. Leibniz (see Ashworth 1988: 153–72).

Although the ideas of Aristotle exerted a strong influence on medieval thought, scholastic philosophy of language should not be identified with Aristotelianism. Its development was also markedly influenced by Augustine's theory of signs (developed in his *De doctrina christiana* and *De trinitate*), by later ancient grammar (especially Priscian's *Institutiones grammaticae*; see also *Roman ars grammatica*, including *Priscian*), and by a Neoplatonic tradition (transmitted by Boethius' theological treatises) which was particularly evident in the semantics of Gilbert of Poitiers (1085/90–1154) and William of Conches (ca.1085–after 1154). Scholastic philosophy of language, therefore, did not simply continue one tradition, but critically examined several interconnected traditions, thus bringing about the most innovative achievements in medieval linguistic theory.

2. The Properties of Terms

Following Priscian, medieval grammarians and logicians divided words into two main classes. First, any word that can be used as subject or predicate in a proposition and which has by itself a significative force is a categorematic term. (Strictly speaking, a term is one or the other end (*terminus*) of a subject–predicate proposition.) Included in this class are nouns, adjectives, verbs, and personal and demonstrative pronouns. Second, any word that can be used with a significative force only in connection with a subject–predicate pair is a syncategorematic word. Included in this class are prepositions, adverbs, conjunctions, etc. For example, the propositions 'Only Socrates is running' and 'Socrates is contingently running' each contain a syncategorematic word, since the quantifier 'only' and the modal functor 'contingently' cannot be used significantly unless they are attached to the subject term 'Socrates' in respect of the predicate term 'is running' (see Kretzmann 1982: 211–28).

A clear understanding of the logical function of syncategorematic words is particularly important in distinguishing names from pseudo-names, as Anselm of Canterbury's (1033–1109) analysis of the proposition 'Nothing taught me to fly' (*Nihil me docuit volare*) illustrates. 'Nothing' seems to be used as a name, so that one could be led to make the odd inference that something or somebody called 'Nothing' taught me to fly. But if one realizes that 'nothing' is a syncategorematic word which performs the office of propositional negation, one can avoid the logical mistake by reformulating the proposition as follows: *Non me docuit aliquid volare*—'It is not the case that something taught me to fly' (see Henry 1967: 211–218).

However, the list of syncategorematic words was not confined to logical operators. It also included expressions signifying the starting and ending points of a movement or action (e.g., 'begins,' 'ceases'). During the twelfth century, the reception of Aristotle's *Sophistical Refutations*, a treatise on fallacies, stimulated interest in such expressions, for fallacies arise when the logical relationships among all the words—

particularly the syncategorematic words—occurring in a syllogism are insufficiently analyzed. For instance, the *Fallacie Parvipontane* (an anonymous treatise from the late twelfth century) offers the following example of a fallacy of division: 'Those two men cease to be; if anyone ceases to be, he dies; therefore those two men die.' The fallacy consists in the fact that in the first premise the word 'cease' is said of the pair of men, but in the second of only one man, so that the conclusion fails in claiming that each of those men dies when only one of them dies (see Kretzmann 1976: 105–106).

In the thirteenth century, William of Sherwood, Nicholas of Paris (fl.1250) and others identified the semantics of syncategorematic words as a specific set of topics and discussed them in separate treatises. In the fourteenth century these discussions were absorbed into the sophismata-literature, which tried to explain paradoxes caused by the confusing use of syncategorematic words (see Read 1993). The strategies for dissolving the paradoxes may be recognized as an attempt to analyze by linguistic means problems associated not only with logic but also with metaphysics or natural philosophy. For instance, as regards the sophisma 'Socrates is infinitely whiter than Plato begins to be white'—an example discussed by Richard Kilvington (ca.1305–61)—an analysis of the syncategorematic words 'infinitely' and 'begins' was supposed to make understandable the comparison of a definite degree of a quality (white) in one substance (Socrates) with the state of another substance (Plato) considered at the instant at which its acquisition of that quality begins (see Kretzmann & Kretzmann 1990: 153–55).

The analysis of the use of syncategorematic words was linked to an investigation of the functions or properties of categorematic terms. In the *logica vetus* Anselm of Canterbury distinguished two main functions: the *appellatio* of a term is the actual indication or the naming of its referents, whereas the *significatio* conveys the understanding or concept (*intellectus*) expressed by the definition of the term. Thus, the term 'man' names (*appellat*) all individual human beings, but it signifies the concept of a rational, mortal animal. This important distinction was used by Peter Abelard in order to explain that a term can be used significantly even if there is no referent. In winter, Abelard writes, when there are no roses, the term 'rose' has no *appellatio* but it nevertheless preserves its *significatio*, since the understanding of the concept *rose* does not depend on the present existence of individual roses (see Rijk 1967: 190–99).

Gilbert of Poitiers also adopted the distinction between *appellatio* and *significatio*, but with respect to nouns—one kind of categorematic term—he claimed that two aspects of signification are to be taken into account: a noun conveys not only an understanding of a thing as such (*id quod est*) but also of the essential quality by virtue of which it is this particular thing (*id quo est*). Thus, 'man' signifies not only a particular human being, but also the humanity by virtue of which every man is a man, and 'stone' signifies not only a particular stone, but also the 'stone-ness' by virtue of which every stone is a stone (see Rijk 1987: 161). This claim is influenced by a Platonic ontology which posits universal beings with real, distinct existence in addition to particular beings.

The *logica moderna* provided a more detailed semantic theory avoiding such strong Platonic claims. This theory recognized four properties of terms (see Maierù 1972: 47–317; Spade 1982): (a) 'signification' is the capacity of a term to bring something to the mind, i.e., to establish an understanding of a thing. This property applies to all categorematic terms; (b) 'supposition' is the reference of a categorematic term or its 'standing for' (*stare pro*) something, applying only to subjects and predicates (many Continental logicians of the thirteenth century attributed it exclusively to substantives) and therefore determined by the actual use of a term in a syntactical context; (c) 'copulation' is the referential function of a dependent categorematic term (an adjective or a participle) linked with a substantive; and (d) 'appellation' is the reference of a categorematic term to an actually existing thing.

Obviously, one cannot attach the same importance to all four properties, since copulation and appellation are subordinate to supposition; copulation applies to a subclass of all suppositing terms, and appellation is a temporal restriction of supposition. For that reason, fourteenth-century authors focused almost exclusively on signification and supposition. These two properties provide the basis for a theory that is not purely logico–semantic, since signification—the establishment of an understanding—is an epistemologico–psychological property of a term.

Logicians in the thirteenth and fourteenth centuries distinguished three main sorts of supposition (for a schematic presentation, see Maierù 1972: 306–317). First, a subject or predicate term can stand for something of which it is truly predicable (in most instances an extramental thing), e.g., 'Socrates' in 'Socrates is a man.' The subject standing for an individual human being is said to have 'personal supposition.' Second, a subject or predicate term can also stand for a spoken or written expression, e.g., 'man' in 'Man is a monosyllable.' In this case, the subject is said to have 'material supposition.' And finally, a subject or predicate term can stand for a universal, e.g., 'man' in 'Man is a species,' where the subject is said to have 'simple supposition.' This third kind of supposition apparently presupposes the existence of universals and therefore has strong ontological commitments. It was redefined by nominalist authors of the fourteenth century, who claimed that the simple supposition of a term is confined to its reference to a concept (see Michon 1994: 213–44).

It is important to note that supposition was considered a propositional property of a term. The isolated noun 'man,' for instance, has no supposition at all. Thus medieval authors from the late twelfth century onwards distinguished themselves by a 'contextual approach' to supposition (see Rijk 1967: 113–117). They assigned a referential function not to single words but to the parts of a proposition. One exception to this general rule is the 'natural supposition' which was defined by Peter of Spain as the acceptance of a common substantival term for all those individuals which participate in the universal form signified by the term. So the term 'man' supposits naturally—i.e., by itself, without a propositional context—for all past, present, and future human beings participating in the universal *man*. Many fourteenth-century logicians however, including William of Ockham, Walter Burley (ca.1275–1344/45), Marsilius of Inghen (ca.1330–96), and Albert of Saxony (d.1390), rejected such nonpropositional supposition (see Rijk 1973: 45).

The principal threefold division of supposition was followed by a subdivision of personal supposition. This second part of supposition-theory was an attempt to 'descend' by logical inference from the referring term to its ultimate, singular referents (see Spade 1988). Only some terms (e.g., 'Socrates' in 'Socrates is running') have a 'discrete supposition' that is, a reference to one precise thing. Other terms have a 'common supposition' since they stand for a plurality of singular things. Such a common supposition is either determinate (*determinata*) or confused (*confusa*). In the proposition 'A man is running' the subject has a determinate common supposition, because there is no indication which man is running, so that the proposition can be verified by any single instance, and we can say 'This man or that man or some other man is running.' But in the proposition 'Man is an animal' the subject has a confused common supposition since every man is an animal, and we have to say 'This man and that man and that man, etc., is an animal,' i.e., we distribute the common term to singular referents.

Supposition-theory provided not only. a detailed theory of reference but also served as the basis for a theory of truth-conditions. According to Ockham, a singular, particular, or universal affirmative proposition is true if and only if the subject and the predicate terms supposit for the same thing (see Adams 1987: 385–96; Perler 1992: 109–25). 'Socrates is white,' for instance, is true if and only if 'Socrates' and 'white' stand for the same individual thing. It is clear, however, that 'white' does not stand exclusively for an individual thing but also indicates that this thing has a certain property. Ockham took account of this difference by introducing a distinction between absolute and connotative terms: 'Socrates,' an absolute term, supposits for Socrates and signifies the substance Socrates. But 'white,' a connotative term in this proposition, stands for Socrates and connotes (or signifies secondarily) the quality white; 'white' can be nominally defined as 'something having whiteness.' Thus 'white' stands for Socrates, but by virtue of its connotation it makes one think of the whiteness inhering in Socrates. This explanation is intended to avoid positing a universal for which 'white' would have to supposit.

In the middle of the fourteenth century, logicians paid special attention to the semantic function of verbs expressing an epistemic act ('to know,' 'to doubt,' 'to recognize,' etc.). John Buridan (1295/1300–58) claimed that these verbs always imply an *appellatio rationis* of the terms with which they are combined. But this *appellatio* applies differently to the terms preceding and following the verb. For example, in 'I recognize the approaching man' ('*Cognosco venientem*') the verb makes the postposited term name (*appellare*) only the *ratio* that someone is coming, whoever that person might be. In 'Regarding the approaching man, I recognize him' ('*Venientem cognosco*') instead the verb makes the preposited term name all the *rationes* of the approaching person. So the second proposition expresses not only that I recognize that someone is approaching, but also that I recognize this person as having certain features, for instance, as being my teacher or my father (see Nuchelmans 1988: 68–71). This is an attempt to explain how the word-order affects the semantic function of a particular class of terms. Such an analysis may thus be recognized as a transition from a theory of terms to a theory of propositions, since it establishes the properties of one term by analyzing the syntactic structure of the proposition in which the term is used.

3. The Semantics of Propositions

When the medievals analyzed a proposition (*propositio*) they were not speaking of the mere content of an indicative sentence (the standard twentieth-century philosophical use of 'proposition') but of a predicative composition of terms accompanied by an act of judging or asserting. After Abelard, two opposing theories were put forward in order to explain the function of the copula 'is' in 'S is P' (see Malcolm 1979). According to the inherence theory (defended by the majority of the thirteenth-century authors), the copula indicates that the referent of the predicate inheres in the referent of the subject; e.g., in 'Socrates is a man' the copula indicates that the species *man* is in the individual Socrates. The identity theory, on the other hand (held by most fourteenth-century authors), claims that the copula just points out that subject and predicate refer to the same object; in 'Socrates is a man' the copula makes plain that 'Socrates' and 'man' are both referring to Socrates who is an individual man. The two explanations of the semantic function of 'is' are obviously based on divergent ontological conceptions. Whereas the inherence theory posits a universal existing in an individual substance, the identity theory holds that an individual substance and an individual property are actually connected.

Like the terms (the integral parts of a proposition), every spoken or written proposition was said to have a mental counterpart, a *propositio mentalis*, composed of concepts. In addition to this traditional division, Walter Burley introduced another kind of proposition: the *propositio in re*, that is, extramental things insofar as they are thought of as being composed or divided by an affirming or denying predicative act (see Nuchelmans 1973: 219–25).

In accordance with Boethius, the medievals defined the proposition as an expression signifying what is true or false (*oratio verum falsumve significans*). This *oratio* was generally taken to be an instance of a proposition (in modern terminology: a sentence-token). The strict consequences of this thesis were explicitly formulated by Robert Holcot (ca.1290–1349), who claimed that a proposition cannot be said to be true or false unless it is actually thought, spoken, or written (see Perler 1992: 162–168). This claim raises the problem that even a proposition expressing a necessary truth, e.g., 'Man is an animal,' will be true only at the moment it is thought, spoken, or written by at least one person. Holcot's extreme claim was not widely accepted. Paul of Venice (1369–1429) later admitted not just sentence-tokens but also sentence-types as propositions by introducing a slight modification into the Boethian definition: a proposition is an expression *capable* of signifying what is true or false. From this point of view, it is not a thought, or a spoken, or a written instance of 'Man is an animal' that is said to be true, but rather the necessary predication of the genus *animal* of the species *man* expressed by the proposition, whether or not the proposition actually exists in thought, speech, or writing (see Nuchelmans 1973: 203–208 and 266–271).

In asserting that a proposition signifies, the medievals were confronted with the problem of explaining what its significate is (see Kretzmann 1970). In general, they assigned three functions to the significate: (a) in an assertoric proposition, it is that which is expressed as being true or false; (b) in a modal proposition, it is that which is expressed as being necessary, possible, contingent, or impossible; (c) in an affirmative proposition governed by an epistemic verb, it is that which is said to be known, doubted, believed, etc. In all three cases the significate is linguistically marked by a 'that'-clause (in Latin an *accusativus cum infinitivo*); e.g., in 'It is true (or: It is contingent, or: I know) that Socrates is running' the significate is 'that Socrates is running.'

Abelard had already noticed that the significate (which he called the *dictum* or *enuntiabile* of a proposition) is not a substance or a quality accessible to the senses, but that it nevertheless exists, since it can be grasped by reason (see Libera 1981). The anonymous author of the twelfth-century *Ars Meliduna* labeled

this peculiar being an extracategorical thing (*extra-praedicamentale*) belonging to a separate category of being not among the ten categories distinguished by Aristotle.

In the fourteenth century, philosophers again eagerly discussed the ontological status of the significate (see Nuchelmans 1973: 195–271; Perler 1994). According to the *res*-theory, held by Walter Chatton (1285–1344) and André Neufchâteau (fl.1360), that which is true or contingent or known is the thing signified by the terms of the proposition. Thus the significate of 'Socrates is running' is the running Socrates himself. This position succeeds in explaining propositions about actual, existing things but it can hardly explain propositions about fictive things or abstract states of affairs, for what thing could be the significate of the proposition 'The chimera is white' or 'The whole is equal to the sum of its parts'? The *complexum*-theory, held by Ockham, Robert Holcot, and John Buridan, tried to avoid this difficulty by claiming that the significate is nothing other than the composition of the terms—not simply the composition of spoken or written terms (in which case the significate would be a purely linguistic entity), but of mental terms signifying immediately and naturally extramental things. But this solution requires a potentially vast number of significates for one proposition, since every person thinking 'Socrates is running' forms his or her own mental terms and has therefore his or her own *complexum*. Adam Wodeham (ca.1298–1358) and Gregory of Rimini (ca.1300–58) rejected both theories and claimed that the total and adequate significate is something peculiar, a *complexe significabile*, which can be expressed only by a whole proposition. It is neither a being in a narrow sense (substance or quality) nor a nonbeing but rather a being of its own: something which positively or negatively is the case. Thus 'Socrates is running' signifies that-Socrates-is-running, a being which is neither the running Socrates the terms 'Socrates' and 'is running' stand for, nor the terms themselves. This explanation, which shows some similarity with Abelard's *dictum*-theory (although there is no textual evidence for a direct link between them), is apparently an attempt to establish an ontological category for states of affairs distinct from those for mental and extramental things.

4. Epistemological and Ontological Commitments

Taking their cue from Aristotle's *De interpretatione*, 1 (16a 3–8) and from Augustine's *De trinitate* XV, 10–11, most medieval authors held that the spoken and written terms which signify conventionally are correlated with mental terms (or concepts or intentions) which signify naturally. This correlation was taken to be a signification relation. The crucial question was whether the signification should be explained on the basis of an epistemological representationalism (i.e., conventional terms signify primarily mental terms and secondarily things insofar as they are represented by mental terms) or on the basis of a direct realism (i.e., conventional terms as well as mental terms directly signify things as they are in reality).

Following Boethius, many thirteenth-century commentators—among them Albert the Great (ca.1200–1280) and Thomas Aquinas (1225–74)—claimed that a conventional term signifies the corresponding mental term as its first, direct significate (*primum significatum*) and the thing as its ultimate, indirect significate (*ultimum significatum*). But there are some conventional terms, e.g., 'Caesar' or 'Antichrist,' that have no ultimate significate, since Caesar does not exist anymore and the Antichrist does not yet exist. Nevertheless, these terms do not lose their signification, since they have first significates, namely the mental terms *Caesar* and *Antichrist*.

Roger Bacon (ca.1214–92/94) sharply criticized this explanation, claiming instead that every conventional categorematic term signifies immediately and exclusively the thing itself. He denied that 'Caesar' or 'Antichrist' have a signification, because there is no actually existing significate (see Maloney 1983). John Duns Scotus (ca.1265–1308) also rejected the traditional interpretation, but without agreeing with Roger Bacon's strong extensionalistic thesis. He asserted that a categorematic term signifies the thing directly, however, not the thing insofar as it exists (*res ut existit*) but insofar as it is understood (*res ut intelligitur*). In contrast to the concept, this significate is not a psychic entity (*qualitas animae*) depending on a mental act; 'Caesar' signifies Caesar as he is understood even if no one actually thinks about Caesar. The significate is rather the nature of a thing expressed by its definition and distinct from the existing thing as well as from the concept (see Marmo 1989: 160–64; Libera 1991).

Ockham followed Duns Scotus in rejecting the representationalistic explanation offered by Boethius and his followers, but he insisted that there is no formal distinction between the individual existing thing and its nature. He claimed that a categorematic term signifies and refers to (*supponit*) a singular thing existing in reality. He granted that Caesar or a chimera can be signified, since one can have an understanding of a dead or fictive being. However, reference to such beings—technically speaking, *suppositio*—is impossible (see Biard 1989: 74–96).

Referring to Augustine's statement that concepts are words in the heart (*verba in corde*), Ockham held that mental terms have all the grammatical features which are necessary for signification, without synonymy and equivocation. Thus, there are mental substantives, mental verbs, mental adjectives, etc., forming a mental language that has a syntax similar to Latin syntax (see Panaccio 1992). This idea of a mental language was extensively discussed by sixteenth-century scholastic authors, including Fer-

nando de Enzinas (d.1523) and Domingo de Soto (1494–1560) (see Ashworth 1982).

William (or John, according to other sources) Crathorn (fl.1330) made a remarkable challenge to the whole tradition that assigned a natural signification to mental terms. He claimed that mental terms are not at all the most basic signs but only inner likenesses (*similitudines intrinsecae*) of spoken or written terms. According to this theory, when one utters the word 'man,' the mental term is nothing other than a quality in the mind following the spoken word (see Tachau 1987: 255–74).

At the end of the thirteenth and the beginning of the fourteenth century the ontological status of mental terms or concepts was the subject of a lively debate. Three main positions may be recognized (see Adams 1987: 73–107; Tachau 1987: 85–153). First, according to Duns Scotus and his followers, including William of Alnwick (fl.1315), a concept is a quality of the mind, having a subjective existence (*esse subiective*) since it exists in the soul as an accident exists in a subject. Second, Peter Aureol (ca.1280–1322), Hervaeus Natalis (1250/60–1323), and the early Ockham held that concepts are neither extramental nor purely mental entities but that they form a peculiar category of beings having an objective existence (*esse obiective*); they exist just in the way that they are objects of the mind. Finally, in the *Summa logicae* Ockham rejected his early view and claimed that concepts are nothing other than the acts of understanding (*actus intelligendi*) which exist just at the moment when the intellect is directed toward an object and apprehends it.

Since the medievals considered the predicative structure 'S is P' as a linguistic source of information regarding the structure of the things signified by the terms, their semantic analyses were closely linked with ontological theories. This link was particularly strong in the discussions of denominative terms. In accordance with Aristotle's *Categories*, 8 (10a 27ff.), a denominative term (or paronym) was defined as a term derived from a quality-term; e.g., 'grammatical' is derived from 'grammar,' and 'white' from 'whiteness.' But what does the denominative term signify: the quality or the subject in which the quality inheres? Both solutions seem to be unsatisfying. In the proposition 'Socrates is white,' for instance, 'white' signifies neither the quality whiteness absolutely (but precisely the whiteness inhering in Socrates) nor the subject Socrates absolutely (but precisely Socrates insofar as he is white). Anselm of Canterbury recognized this problem and discussed it extensively in his dialog *De grammatico*. He said that a satisfactory answer requires a distinction between two semantic functions: 'white' signifies being in possession of whiteness (*habens albedinem*) and at the same time names (*appellat*) something white, namely, Socrates himself. It is important to note that being in possession of whiteness is not something in possession of whiteness; 'white' signifies only the quality-category and the dependence structure of this quality, but it does not signify the subject-category on which the quality depends (see Henry 1967: 31–116).

The late thirteenth century witnessed a renewed interest in the semantics of denominative terms. Four theories were generally discussed (see Ebbesen 1988: 117–44). First, according to Avicenna, 'white' signifies the combination of subject and quality, but the subject primarily and the quality only secondarily. This appeal to an ontological priority of the subject was generally rejected in the thirteenth century with an argument stemming from Averroes: if 'white' signified primarily the subject, it could be replaced by 'white body' so that we could form the proposition 'Socrates is a white body.' But again, 'white,' signifying primarily the body, is replaceable so that we could say 'Socrates is a white body body,' and so on to infinity. Second, according to the modistic approach accepted by Boethius of Dacia (fl.1275) and Duns Scotus, 'white' signifies only the quality, but by its mode of signifying it makes one understand the subject in which the quality inheres. Obviously, this position presupposes that denominative terms have a peculiar mode of signifying distinct from the modes of other terms, and it claims that the quality can be signified in a distinct way. The latter claim relies on the assumption—criticized by opponents—that a quality has two ways of being, namely, in its pure essence (*essentia*) and in its existing essence (*esse essentiae*); being white in the first way is signified by 'whiteness,' in the second way by 'white.' Third, Siger of Brabant (ca.1240–84) and Siger of Courtrai (d.1341) held that 'white' signifies both subject and quality, each under its own *ratio*, but the quality primarily and the subject secondarily. Finally, Simon of Faversham (ca.1260–1306) and Radulphus Brito (d.1320) held that 'white' signifies both subject and quality and both under the *ratio* of the quality. The last two theories make the controversial claim that the *ratio* of a subject or quality, i.e., its nature expressed by the definition, is ontologically distinguishable from the subject or the quality itself.

The controversy on denominative terms illustrates that medieval philosophy of language was not confined to a purely semantical analysis of language. In examining the question of *how* such terms signify things, the medievals sought to reach an answer to the question of *what* these and other terms signify. An understanding of the structure and functions of language was not a goal in itself. It was rather supposed to give some insight into the structure of reality and into the linguistic representation of this structure. Therefore it is important to see medieval philosophy of language not as an isolated discipline, but as a philosophical field interrelated with others (above all ontology and epistemology), aiming at giving a comprehensive description of reality.

Bibliography

Adams M M 1987 *William Ockham*. Notre Dame University Press, Notre Dame, IN

Ashworth E J 1982 The structure of mental language: Some problems discussed by early sixteenth-century logicians. *Vivarium* **20**: 59–83

Ashworth E J 1988 Traditional logic. In: Schmitt C B (ed.) *The Cambridge History of Renaissance Philosophy*. Cambridge University Press, Cambridge

Biard J 1989 *Logique et théorie du signe au XIVe siècle*. Librairie Philosophique J Vrin, Paris

Ebbesen S 1988 Concrete accidental terms: Late thirteenth-century debates about problems relating to such terms as '*Album*'. In: Kretzmann N (ed.) *Meaning and Inference in Medieval Philosophy*. Kluwer, Dordrecht

Henry D P 1967 *The Logic of Saint Anselm*. Clarendon Press, Oxford

Jacobi K 1988 Logic: The later twelfth century. In: Dronke P (ed.) *A History of Twelfth-century Western Philosophy*. Cambridge University Press, Cambridge

Jardine L 1988 Humanistic logic. In: Schmitt C B (ed.) *The Cambridge History of Renaissance Philosophy*. Cambridge University Press, Cambridge

Kaluza Z 1988 *Querelles doctrinales à Paris. Nominalistes et réalistes aux confins du XIVe et du XVe siècle*. Lubrina, Bergamo

Kretzmann N 1970 Medieval logicians on the meaning of the *propositio*. *The Journal of Philosophy* **67**: 767–87

Kretzmann N 1976 Incipit/Desinit. In: Machamer P K, Turnbull R G (eds.) *Motion and Time, Space and Matter*. Ohio State University Press, Columbus, OH

Kretzmann N 1982 Syncategoremata, sophismata, exponibilia. In: Kretzmann N, Kenny A, Pinborg P (eds.) *The Cambridge History of Later Medieval Philosophy*. Cambridge University Press, Cambridge

Kretzmann N, Kretzmann B 1990 *The Sophismata of Richard Kilvington*. Cambridge University Press, Cambridge

Libera A de 1981 Abélard et le dictisme. *Cahiers de la Revue de théologie et de philosophie* **6**: 59–97

Libera A de 1991 *César et le Phénix. Distinctiones et sophismata parisiens du XIIIe siècle*. Scuola Normale Superiore, Pisa

Maierù A 1972 *Terminologia logica della tarda scolastica*. Edizioni dell'Ateneo, Rome

Malcolm J 1979 A reconsideration of the identity and inherence theories of the copula. *Journal of the History of Philosophy* **17**: 383–400

Maloney T S 1983 The semiotics of Roger Bacon. *Mediaeval Studies* **45**: 120–54

Marmo C 1989 Ontology and semantics in the logic of Duns Scotus. In: Eco U, Marmo C (eds.) *On the Medieval Theory of Signs*. Benjamins, Amsterdam

Marmo C 1994 *Semiotica e linguaggio nella scolastica: Parigi, Bologna, Erfurt 1270–1330. La semiotica dei Modisti*. Istituto storico italiano per il medio evo, Rome

Michon C 1994 *Nominalisme. La théorie de la signification d'Occam*. Vrin, Paris

Nuchelmans G 1973 *Theories of the Proposition: Ancient and Medieval Conceptions of the Bearers of Truth and Falsity*. North-Holland, Amsterdam

Nuchelmans G 1988 *Appellatio rationis* in Buridan, Sophismata, IV, 9–15. In: Pluta O (ed.) *Die Philosophie im 14. und 15. Jahrhundert*. Grüner, Amsterdam

Panaccio C 1992 *Les mots, les concepts et les choses. La*

sémantique de Guillaume d'Occam et le nominalisme d'aujourd'hui. Bellarmin, Montréal

Perler D 1992 *Der propositionale Wahrheitsbegriff im 14. Jahrhundert*. De Gruyter, Berlin

Perler D 1994 Late Medieval Ontologies of Facts. *The Monist* **77**: 149–69

Pinborg J 1972 *Logik und Semantik im Mittelalter: Ein Überblick*. Frommann-Holzboog, Stuttgart-Bad Cannstatt

Pinborg J 1975 Die Logik der Modistae. *Studia Mediewistyczne* **16**: 39–97

Read S (ed.) 1993 *Sophisms in Medieval Logic and Grammar*. Kluwer, Dordrecht

Rijk L M de 1967 *Logica modernorum. II (1): The Origin and Development of the Theory of Supposition*. Van Gorcum, Assen

Rijk L M de 1971–73 The development of *suppositio naturalis* in medieval logic. *Vivarium* **9**: 71–107; **11**: 43–79

Rijk L M de 1987 Gilbert de Poitiers: Ses vues sémantiques et métaphysiques. In: Jolivet J, Libera A de (eds.) *Gilbert de Poitiers et ses contemporains: Aux origines de la Logica modernorum*. Bibliopolis, Naples

Spade P V 1982 The semantics of terms. In: Kretzmann N, Kenny A, Pinborg P (eds.) *The Cambridge History of Later Medieval Philosophy*. Cambridge University Press, Cambridge

Spade P V 1988 The logic of the categorical: The medieval theory of descent and ascent. In: Kretzmann N (ed.) *Meaning and Inference in Medieval Philosophy: Studies in Memory of Jan Pinborg*. Kluwer, Dordrecht

Tachau K H 1987 *Vision and Certitude in the Age of Ockham*. Brill, Leiden

Tweedale M M 1988 Logic: From the late eleventh century to the time of Abelard. In: Dronke P (ed.) *A History of Twelfth Century Western Philosophy*. Cambridge University Press, Cambridge

Mill, John Stuart

V. Sánchez Valencia

In discussing the distinctions made by ordinary language and the operation of naming, John Stuart Mill 1806–73 arguably became the first modern thinker who developed a theory of meaning. Central to Mill's theory of meaning is the concept of name and the operation of naming. In Mill's view logic is concerned with the methods by which data are organized. The most fundamental of these methods is the operation of naming. Names, he holds, are names of things and clues to the things. In constructing a general logic one must start by recognizing the distinctions made by ordinary language.

1. Mill's Division of Names

Mill divides words into two classes: those which can stand by themselves as names of things, and those which are only parts of names. While *Heloise, whiteness, the wife of Abelard, logician* belong to the first class; *if, often, and* belong to the second one. Sometimes Mill defines a name as any expression which may occur as subject or predicate. Sometimes he defines a name as any expression which may occur as subject. According to the first definition, adjectives are names; according to the second they are not. Mill solves this conflict by assuming that adjectives are used elliptically. He holds that there is no difference in meaning between *round* and *round object*. Adjectives in their full form can appear as subject, although in their elliptical form they can appear only as predicates. Names are, subsequently, subdivided between abstract names and concrete names. A concrete name is a name which stands for a thing, an abstract name is the name of an attribute of things. *Heloise, the wife of Abelard, logician* are concrete names, *whiteness, consistency* are abstract names. For Mill, concrete names fall into two categories, general names and individual names. A general name is a name which can be applied in the same sense to an indefinite number of things. For instance, *woman* can be applied in the same sense to Heloise, Mary, etc. One applies these names to all these persons because they share some attributes and with this application it is asserted that they possess those attributes. An individual name is a name that can be applied in the same sense to only one person. *Heloise* can be applied in the same sense only to one person. Though there may be many persons who bear this name, it is not applied to them because they have some property in common. Mill, it will be observed, distinguishes between sorts of individual terms: proper names and many-worded names, in the language of later philosophers, 'descriptions.' Two of Mill's examples of a many-worded name are *the author of the Iliad* and *the present prime minister of England*. He points out that, though it is conceivable that more than one person might have written the *Iliad*, the use of the article *the* implies that this was not the case. With regard to the other example, he points out that the application of 'prime minister of England' being limited by the article and the adjective *present*, to such individuals as possess the attributes at one point of time, this name becomes applicable only to one object.

2. Mill's Fundamental Distinction

Mill considers the distinction between connotative and nonconnotative names as fundamental to the nature of language. A connotative name is defined as one which denotes a subject and implies an attribute. A denotative name is a name which only denotes a subject. According to Mill all general concrete names are connotative. The name *woman* denotes an indefinite number of individuals. It is applied to them because they possess and to express that they possess certain attributes. *Heloise* is called a woman because she possesses rationality, corporeity, animal life. If she missed one of these attributes, one would start questioning the application of the name *woman* to her. The use of a connotative name is dependent on the continuance of the attributes which the name connotes. By calling Heloise a woman, we entail that she possesses all those attributes at the point of reference—although she may lack some of them at the point of speech. By using a connotative name the information is conveyed that the object so named has the attributes connoted by the name. Mill recognizes that in some cases it is not easy to determine precisely the connotation of a name. Sometimes it is impossible to say precisely how much an individual must deviate from the beings called a woman, in order to refuse the name *woman* to it. In such cases the meaning of the name is unsettled and vague. But he finds relief in the idea that cases will appear in which the ends of language are better promoted by vagueness than by complete precision. Proper names, on the other hand, are denotative. *Heloise* denotes Heloise but fails to connote any attribute belonging to her. Proper names are marks attached to the objects to enable these objects to become subjects of discourse. They answer the purpose of fixing the thing being talked about, but they do not answer the purpose of telling something about that thing. On Mill's view the expression *Tully is Cicero* conveys that both names are marks for the same object. Mill asserts that there might have been a reason for calling Dartmouth *Dartmouth*, but once this name was given, the use of the name became independent of the reason. Suppose this town *Dartmouth* is called because it is situated at the mouth of the River Dart. If the course of the river were changed, one would not necessarily be inclined to change the name of the town. Mill holds that the use of proper names can be linked to information flow, but that is not something connected with the meaning of the name. Saying to someone *this is Heloise* does not convey to them any information about Heloise—except that *Heloise* is the name of the person we point at. By enabling them to pick out Heloise, they may connect her with information they might have. Thus, *this is Heloise* may elucidate the bit of information 'this is the wife of Abelard.' But the name does not imply this information. If the person one is talking to does not have the information *Heloise is the wife of Abelard* he will be unable to link *this is Heloise* to *this is the wife of Abelard*. But one shall not say that he does not know the meaning of *Heloise*, one shall rather say that he is not aware of a piece of intellectual history. Mill strongly links the meaning of a name with its connotation and not with its denotation. He holds that meaning resides not in what names denote but in what they connote. A person might know every individual to whom a name can be applied and yet could not be said to know the meaning of the name. A child knows the denotation of the name 'parents' long before it knows the meaning of this name. Mill's theory of meaning establishes that if the meaning of a general term were identical with the things it is applied to, no general name has fixed meaning except by accident. The only way in which a general name has a definite meaning is by being the name of an indefinite number of individuals which possess the attributes connoted by it. Proper names are the only names of objects which connote nothing and have, strictly speaking, no meaning. The other individual terms are connotative. The name *the father of Socrates*, as well as denoting Sophroniscus, connotes the attribute of having Socrates as a son. Mill concedes that two names denoting the same object may have a difference in meaning. For example, *the father of Socrates* and *Sophroniscus* denote the same individual. But they are not identical in meaning, since the proper name has no meaning at all. If denotation were meaning, then identity of denotation would imply identity of meaning.

3. Mill's View on Propositions

In Mill's view a proposition is a discourse in which something is affirmed or denied of something. A proposition is formed by putting two names together. Every proposition consists of three parts: the name denoting that which is affirmed or denied—the predicate; the name denoting the thing which something is affirmed or denied of—the subject; the word showing that there is an affirmation or denial—the copula. In the proposition *The earth is round*, the predicate is the word *round*, the subject is the word *the earth*, the copula is the word *is*. Mill observes that the copula is not the only means of showing that a name is predicate to another. In *fire burns*, the inflection of the verb *to burn* shows that this sentence can be used to predicate *burn* of *fire*. However, he considers that the copula is the most commonly used sign of predication. He warns the reader about the ambiguity of the verb *to be*. It has already been said that in an identity sentence the copula expresses that both individual names denote the same object. He also notices that in *Man is mortal* the copula signifies inclusion between classes while in *Socrates is a philosopher* the copula indicates that Socrates is a member of the class of philosophers. Moreover, the verb *to be* also means existence. Mill holds that when this verb is used as copula it does not imply the affirmation of existence.

Among propositions Mill distinguishes what he calls 'verbal propositions,' propositions which do not depend on nonlinguistic facts. An example of a verbal proposition is *every woman is rational*. Since rationality is part of the connotation of woman, as soon as we hear the name *woman*, we know that women are rational. A real proposition is a proposition in which we predicate of the subject an attribute which does not belong to its connotation. This predication can be wrong and can result in a false proposition. A real proposition can tell something new about the subject but it runs the risk of being false. A verbal proposition does not tell us anything about the subject, but it does not run the risk of being false. Verbal propositions are necessarily true. Furthermore, they are the only necessarily true propositions. Mathematical propositions are not, according to Mill, verbal propositions. This would mean that true mathematical propositions are not necessarily true: they are generalizations from experience, at permanent risk of being falsified by the facts.

4. Mill's View on Inference

Mill intends to show that syllogistic inference is not 'real' inference. Consider the syllogism, *All women are mortal, Heloise is a woman, so Heloise is mortal*. The premise *all women are mortal*, Mill says, already contains the conclusion. When we assert this sentence, we assert the mortality of *Heloise*—even if we have never heard of her. The universal premise is no evidence for the truth of the conclusion. The evidence for the truth of this sentence is that an unlimited number of individuals to which we apply the name of *woman* have died. The real inference takes place when we construct the universal sentence from the particular ones: *Mary died, Harriet died*, etc. In Mill's view a universal sentence does not properly give new information. It is, rather, a formula collecting our past experiences. These sentences are dispensable in ordinary reasoning. We usually reason from particular cases to particular cases. Mill often says that real inference consists in reasoning from particular cases to particular cases. But it is unclear if he means inferences of the type *Heloise is a woman, so Heloise is mortal*, or inferences of the type *Mary, Helena, etc., who are women, are mortal, so Heloise, who is a woman, is mortal*.

5. Concluding Remarks

Ryle (1957) assesses the historical importance of Mill's views on meaning. According to him Mill's theory of meaning set the questions and in large measure determined their answers for Brentano, Meinong, Husserl, Bradley, Jevons, Venn, Frege, Peirce, Moore, and Russell. Mill's attitude towards natural language is congenial to the attitude of the ordinary language philosophers. Kripke (1980) has developed a theory of proper names related to Mill's. Kripke, however, considers that Mill was wrong about general concrete terms: they are more like proper names than Mill thought: neither proper names nor general terms correspond to a conjunction of attributes. Mill's theory of propositions is criticized by Geach (1968) under the name 'the Two Terms Theory.' But it also has a small justification in the so-called generalized quantifier perspective of natural language quantification. Frege (1884) analyzed and rejected Mill's analysis of mathematical propositions. Kneale and Kneale (1962) devotes a few pages to a discussion of Mill's view on inference.

See also: Names and Descriptions.

Bibliography

Benthem J van 1986 *Essays in Logical Semantics*. Reidel, Dordrecht
Frege G 1884 *Die Grundlagen der Arithmetik*. Breslau. Published 1986 as *Foundations of Arithmetic*. Basil Blackwell, Oxford
Geach P 1968 *Reference and Generality*. Cornell University Press, Ithaca, NY
Kneale W, Kneale M 1962 *The Development of Logic*. Clarendon Press, Oxford
Kripke S 1980 *Naming and Necessity*. Blackwell, Oxford
Mill J S 1843 *System of Logic*. John W Parker, London
Ryle G 1957 The theory of meaning. In: Mace C A (ed.) *British Philosophy in Mid-Century*. Allen and Unwin, London

Peirce, Charles Sanders

C. J. Hookway

Charles Peirce (1839–1914) was an American philosopher and logician. The son of a distinguished Harvard professor of mathematics, he lectured at Harvard in the late 1860s and was subsequently appointed to teach logic at Johns Hopkins University. He was a vain, irascible, and intolerant man, and personal difficulties led to his removal from this post. His last 20 years were spent in poverty and isolation writing continuously on logic and philosophy. His friends, notably William James, arranged for him to give some lectures at Harvard during this period which developed his most famous doctrine, pragmatism. A systematic philosopher, much influenced by Kant, Peirce contributed to most areas of philosophy. Independently of Frege, he introduced quantifiers into logic in the 1880s; he made important contributions to the philosophy of science and metaphysics; he wrote on categories, on perception, on mathematics and, in later years, on the nature of religious experience. At the center of his work was a sophisticated and distinctive theory of language and representation: he once wrote that he could not approach any topic 'except as a study of semiotic' (the general theory of signs); and his other philosophical views all reflect his innovations in that area.

1. Semiotic: The Sign Relation

Peirce's theory of signs was present in his earliest lectures and publications, but his ideas became steadily more sophisticated over the ensuing 50 years. His correspondence with an Englishwoman, Victoria, Lady Welby, contains many later thoughts on the subject (Peirce 1977). Since he insisted that all thought and sensation involved signs, and he used his theory in developing an account of the nature of logical and mathematical notations as well as in defending a complex theory of language and meaning, it is easy to appreciate its importance for his philosophy. His fundamental claim was that the sign relation is irreducibly triadic: a sign can represent an object only by being interpreted in thought as standing for that object; an interpreting thought mediates between sign and object. Hence the focus of his work is the process of sign interpretation or 'semiosis.'

Interpretation need not involve merely judging that the sign has a distinctive object: inference can be involved, the sign being 'developed' through interpretation. If I already believe that Peter is either American or Canadian, I can interpret the announcement that he is not American by inferring that he is Canadian. My understanding is manifested by my drawing that inference. Or my interpretation of the claim that salt is soluble could be the acquisition of a tendency to be surprised if a sample of salt does not dissolve. Science can then be viewed as an attempt to arrive at ever richer and more stable interpretations of scientific assertions, adding information and removing error so that one arrives at a complete and accurate specification of the object of the sign.

2. Classifications of Signs

The core of Peirce's theory was a complex, somewhat baroque system of classifications of signs, objects, and interpretants, much of which depended on his theory

of categories. The most famous of these classifications concerns the connections between sign and object which enable the former to represent the latter: it distinguishes 'icon,' 'index,' and 'symbol.' An icon resembles its object: they share a property which either could possess even if the other did not exist. An index stands in a real 'existential' relation to its object: a weather vane is an index of wind direction, a pointing finger is an index of the object at which it points. A symbol represents its object only because there is a conventional practice of so using it: other 'replicas' or 'tokens' of the same 'type' have represented the same object in the past. Peirce is skeptical that there are any 'pure' icons and his discussion focuses on 'hypoicons': these are conventional signs, but the convention does not itself fix the sign's object but merely determines how the sign is to be used as an icon. Maps are thus hypoicons, as are systems of logical and mathematical notation. Analogously, expressions like 'that,' 'now,' 'here,' and 'I' are conventional signs, the conventions determining how they are to be interpreted as indices rather than fixing their objects unaided. So they are conventional indices rather than symbols.

From the 1880s, Peirce insisted that an adequate descriptive language must contain signs of all three kinds. Unless it contained symbols it would lack generality: if wisdom is a property that many can share, tokens of that type must be usable in different assertions; and reasoning involves using general standards, claiming that all tokens of certain inference or assertion types are correct. Moreover indices are required if one is to refer to external objects: ordinary proper names, demonstratives, and quantifiers are all (conventional) indices. Finally general terms or predicates are (hypo)icons. Since icons share properties with their objects, one can learn more about the object by examining the icon: for example, learn about the terrain by studying a map. The systematic relations between the predicates in the different sentences one accepts provides a kind of map of the relations between the corresponding properties in the world; so reasoning and reflection, experimenting on and observing icons, can increase knowledge of the objects of thought.

3. Pragmatism

Peirce's pragmatist principle was introduced in his 1877 paper 'How to make our ideas clear' as a device for clarifying the meanings of words, concepts, and sentences and for identifying those which lacked meaning:

> Consider what effects, which might conceivably have practical bearing, we conceive the object of our conception to have. Then, our conception of those effects is the whole of our conception of the object.
>
> (Peirce 1982–86: 266)

As his examples make clear, the claim that something

(*o*) falls under a concept (*F*) is clarified by listing conditionals of the form:

> If *o* is *F*, then, if we were to perform action *A*, experience *e* would result.

If salt is soluble, then if stirred vigorously in water, it would dissolve. Applying this rule to propositions of 'ontological metaphysics' reveals them to be empty. It is also proposed as fundamental to scientific methodology: its use clarifies how the experimental test is relevant to evaluating an hypothesis.

In 1905, Peirce renamed his doctrine 'pragmaticism' in order to distance his position from that of William James, and from the sort of position later expressed in the logical positivists' verification principle. Unlike these thinkers, he did not insist that the conditionals used to clarify a concept be analytic (true by virtue of meaning): they can reflect current scientific knowledge and thus grow and develop as science progresses. And he later grew emphatic that the principle required a realist account of subjunctive conditionals, or 'would bes': his own scientific metaphysics included an 'extreme' realism about universals and natural necessity. Much of his later work on semiotic was motivated by the desire to prove that no scientifically relevant aspect of meaning remains unclarified by the pragmatist principle.

The most famous application of the pragmatist principle is Peirce's theory of truth or reality. If a proposition is taken to be true, it is thought to be 'fated to be agreed upon by all who investigate' it: if anyone were to inquire long enough and well enough into whether that proposition was true, it is 'fated' or 'destined' that he will eventually arrive at a stable belief in it. As the examples above suggest, using the principle to clarify a proposition or concept relates it to a set of expectations, and this can present problems in connection with propositions about the past: they are transformed into propositions about future evidence.

4. Conclusion

Peirce's published writings and his extensive manuscripts contained detailed discussions of many issues about language. He explained the nature of assertion, linking this to a view of science as an institution based upon a practice of challenging and defending assertions (Brock 1974). He used this theory to sketch an approach to the semantics of quantifiers which is similar to Hintikka's recent game-theoretic semantics. There are explanations of the use of proper names and of the ability to refer to abstract objects, and many passages attempt to remedy the lack Peirce noted by remarking that 'logicians have been at fault in giving vagueness the go-by' (Peirce 1931–58, vol. 2: 293). Finally his writing on the semiotic of metaphor has influenced a number of authors working on the understanding of figurative language (e.g., Shapiro 1983).

Bibliography

Anderson D R 1995 *Strands of System: The Philosophy of Charles Peirce*. Purdue University Press, West Lafayette, IN

Brock J E 1974 Peirce's conception of semiotic. *Semiotica* **14**: 124–41

Hookway C J 1985 *Peirce*. Routledge and Kegan Paul, London

Liszka J J 1996 *A General Introduction to the Semeiotic of Charles S. Peirce*. Indiana University Press, Bloomington, IN

Peirce C S 1931–58 *Collected Papers of Charles S. Peirce*, 8 vols. Harvard University Press, Cambridge, MA

Peirce C S 1977 *Semiotic and Significs*. Indiana University Press, Bloomington, IN

Peirce C S 1982–86 *The Writings of Charles S. Peirce: A Chronological Edition*. Indiana University Press, Bloomington, IN

Ransdell J 1977 Some leading ideas of Peirce's semiotic. *Semiotica* **19**: 157–78

Shapiro M 1983 *The Sense of Grammar*. Indiana University Press, Bloomington, IN

Short T L 1981 Semiosis and intentionality. *Transactions of the Charles S. Peirce Society* **17**: 197–223

Skagestad P 1981 *The Road of Inquiry*. Columbia University Press, New York

Plato and His Predecessors

F. W. Householder[†]

The basic notion of grammar on which all later Greeks built was developed by various nameless people between Homer and Socrates. The few whose names are still known (other than mythical ones like Cadmus, the bringer of the Phoenician alphabet to Thebes) are all of the fifth century, some called 'sophists,' others 'philosophers,' and it is mainly from Plato that one learns of them.

1. The Beginnings

In the second book of the *Iliad*, at the beginning of the Trojan catalog (2.804), the goddess Iris offers a comment on the variety of languages spoken by the allies of the Trojans, and near the end (2.867) the poet mentions in particular the 'barbarity' (i.e., non-Greekness) of the speech of the Carians. But nowhere in the *Iliad* does a Greek warrior have any difficulty communicating with a Trojan (or Lycian or Carian, for that matter), nor are interpreters ever needed or mentioned. (The first Greek to mention them [ca. 430 BC] is Herodotus, 2.154, 4.24.) In the *Odyssey*, Odysseus sails all around the known world, and never meets anyone who speaks a language other than Greek (including Polyphemus, the Laestrygonians, Circe, and the Sirens). True, several words used by the gods are mentioned as distinct from human (i.e., Greek) words, but the difference is scarcely enough even to make divine speech a special dialect of Greek.

In the sixth book of the *Iliad* (6.119–236) Diomedes has a confrontation with the Lycian King Glaucus in which the latter traces his ancestry back to Bellerophon, a Greek from Argos who came to Lycia with some sort of message ('Kill the bearer' written in Linear B, perhaps) to the king. But the king, instead of killing him, puts him through a number of tests and then gives him his daughter's hand. This passage (6.169) is the only possible reference to writing in Homer, and even it is not unambiguous. Yet it cannot be doubted that some Greeks, namely those on Cyprus, could write at the time of Homer, since in Classical times (seventh to fourth centuries BC) they wrote in a syllabary closely related to Linear B, which was used by Greeks in Crete, Pylos, Mycenae, and Thebes (at least) around the thirteenth century BC. It cannot be doubted that some form of this syllabary was used continuously in the intervening centuries, though no specimens from those centuries survive, and hence there must have been teachers and schools throughout the period, apparently teaching both syllabary and alphabet by the fourth century BC.

The signs of the Cypriote syllabary are by no means all identical to corresponding signs of Linear B; 10 of them are, and another 20 are easily derived. Linear B was mainly written on wet clay (making curves easy); Cypriote on stones or metal (yielding a preference for straight lines), but, in addition, Cyprus dropped the separate set of *d* syllables (da, de, di, do, du), fusing them with *t*, but distinguished *l* syllables from *r* syllables. The first of these changes has occurred in other syllabaries (e.g., Cherokee, some Southeast Asian) and some alphabets, at least as an option (e.g., Gregg shorthand). It is not true that if a language once acquires a phonemically accurate script it never later drops any distinctions. But this particular case, in which voiced, voiceless, and aspirated stops are written alike, is very common in independently developed syllabaries all over the world: evidently the grouping of all labial stops is an easy piece of phonological analysis, and the Mycenaean and Cypriote Greeks certainly made it. The Semitic alphabet as

adopted by the Greeks implies a grouping of voiced stops in the alphabetic order (B, G, D) and also the nasals (M, N).

But the remarkable contribution of the Greeks, apparently unique in the history of writing systems, was the obligatory writing of vowels as letters of the same size and type as those used for consonants. This does not come naturally; syllabaries do. In the Greek alphabet the only grouping or nonwriting of a distinction appears in the case of vowel length, normally unmarked in Linear B, the Cypriote syllabary, most Greek alphabets, Italian alphabets, and their descendants. The Greeks did eventually have two long vowel characters (*eta* and *omega*) opposed to two short ones (*epsilon* and *omicron*), but vowel length was just as contrastive for A, I, U (*alpha, iota, upsilon*). No doubt the whole development was, in part, a fluke, but no other independent system did the same things. One other distinctive feature, which was not at first completely indicated by the Greek alphabet, was aspiration in stops, but *chi* and *phi* were soon provided.

As noted above, there is good reason to believe that schools existed in Mycenaean times, and that they continued right through into Classical times, with two possible modifications. It is likely that Linear B was used and maintained by a special class of scribes, and that the schools were scribal schools. And some authors hint that the Dorians were illiterate for a few centuries, though it is known that there were lyric poets in Sparta by 675 BC or so (Terpander). But certainly almost everywhere in the Greek world, by around 700 BC there were schools for boys, and quite often also schools for girls (Sappho ran one such school), in which the students spent much of the day from the age of 6 or 7 years to 16 or 17. Thucydides mentions (7.29) a school in a smallish town (Mycalessus) in Euboea, 'The largest one there.' The town must, then, have had at least three or four such schools, but it is hard to guess how many students there were, though the context does indicate that school started early in the morning, something that is also known from Aeschines (*Against Timarchus* 8–12), who cites a law of Solon forbidding (in essence) schools to open before sunrise or close after sunset. Summer vacation is not mentioned, but seems likely.

What the teachers and pupils did during a decade of schooling is not known. A year might conceivably be spent on elementary reading and writing; there is evidence of syllable sequences like ar, bar, gar, dar, er, ber, ger, der, etc., and beta, alpha, *ba*, beta, epsilon, *be*, beta, ēta, *bē*, etc. (see Callias' *Grammatical Tragedy* cited in Athenaeus 7.276A, 10.448B, 10.453C), but it seems unlikely that this went on 10 hours a day for more than a year. After the elementary lessons, all the evidence is that they read, studied, copied, memorized, recited, and sang (or chanted) the works of poets, principally lyric and epic, but also iambic and elegiac. Here it must be noted that none of these poets wrote in the Attic dialect or confined themselves to familiar Attic vocabulary. Aristotle (who probably provides the best evidence for the traditional lore of the schools in the *Poetics*, ch. 19–22: 1437a–59a) lists seven different kinds of poetic words, three of which involve the four 'transformations,' whose importance for Greek linguistics continues as one moves from Plato through to Apollonius Dyscolus. And as for dialects, all choral lyric poems were written in some form of Doric, solo lyrics in Aeolic, hexameter and elegiac poems in a kind of old Ionic with some Aeolic admixture. Choral lyric, in addition, often has a quite complex syntactic and metrical structure and unusual word order. It is improbable that the teachers have refrained for two or three hundred years from helping the students to understand the words and structures of these poems. Bear in mind what Protagoras says about education (Plato, *Prot*: 338e–39a) 'I think the greatest part of a man's education is to be expert on poetry, i.e., to be able to understand what is said by the poets, to tell whether or not it is properly written, and to know how to discriminate among poems and give an explanation when asked.' This is surely a fifth-century belief; and, as he says earlier, 'if you should advertize for a teacher of Greek (*hellēnizein*), not one would show up.' Of course, that is exactly what teachers did claim to teach in the days of Sextus Empiricus, six centuries later. But in the sixth, fifth, and fourth centuries, they taught what Protagoras wanted; when the students grew up, as gentlemen of leisure, they had to put up a good show of being experts on poets and poetry. Nevertheless, the two basic sins, *barbarizein* and *soloikizein*, are mentioned early, the latter in Herodotus 4.117.1, and both in Aristotle *Soph.El.* 165b2.

2. The Sophists

Besides the schools of the grammarians, the fifth century BC saw the rise of higher education, the schools of the sophists. What they taught was mainly what later became rhetoric, essentially the principles of writing good prose. While the Greek of the grammarians' schools was unlike their students' native dialect, that dealt with by most of the sophists was that very native dialect. But they rarely considered this from a grammatical or linguistic viewpoint. And, while the grammarians dealt with the rhythms of poetry, sophists might dispute about the appropriate rhythms for prose, especially at the ends of sentences (*clausulae*, to use the Latin name). In vocabulary they did not need to interpret rare or dialect words, but they did assign great importance to discriminating synonyms, and (in general) defining abstract words.

One sophist stands out above the rest for his interest in grammar, Protagoras, about whom tantalizing bits of information come from Plato and Aristotle, as well as Diogenes Laertius. He first distinguished four types of sentence—wish/prayer, question, answer, command (Diogenes Laertius 9.53; Quintilian, *Inst.* 3.4.10)—and reprehended Homer (Aristotle *Poetics* 1456b, 15–18) for using the imperative ('command') in prayer to a goddess instead of the optative ('prayer'). This criticism of course depends on the pre-existence of the name *euktikē* (from *euchomai*, 'I pray') for what one calls the 'optative mood.' In fact, Homer's use is the correct one: second-person prayers to divinities normally are in the imperative. And one can be reasonably sure that Protagoras used the four transformations (see Sect. 3), from Socrates' use of the term *hyperbaton* (transposition) in Plato's *Protagoras* (343F).

But the main contribution of Protagoras seems to have been in syntax, where a passage on solecism in Aristotle's *Rhetoric* (1407b) combined with one in his *Sophistic Refutations* (173b) seems to suggest that Protagoras discussed errors of agreement (solecisms) in gender, for which he used (possibly from the tradition of the *didaskaloi*) the names 'males,' 'females,' and 'things,' (in that order); and also in number (Aristotle says 'many and few and one,' probably for 'many and two and one').

3. Plato

It is primarily from Plato (especially the *Theatetus*, *Cratylus*, *Protagoras*, and *Sophist*) that an idea of fifth-century state-of-the-art grammatical science is gained (with additional evidence from Aristotle's *Poetics* and other works). There are several reasons for believing that Plato is not proposing innovative ideas and terms of his own, but merely avoiding anachronism in presenting the conversations of Socrates and his friends.

Clearly, several features of later grammatical art must have been introduced in the fifth century or before.

(a) the four *pathē* or transformations (addition—also known as pleonasm, redundancy, insertion, epenthesis, etc.; subtraction—deletion, ellipsis, elision, apheresis, etc.; substitution—enallage, hypallage, commutation, etc.; and permutation—transposition, metathesis, hyperbaton, anastrophe, etc.—in Plato *Cratylus* 394B, 414C–D, 426C, 432A, etc.) used for etymology, but also for morphology (in treating irregular inflexion) and syntax (as in *Protagoras* 343F).

(b) The terms '*onoma*' and '*rhēma*,' whether for 'noun' and 'verb' or 'subject' and 'predicate' (as often in Plato), and possibly '*arthron*' and '*sundesmos*' (later meaning 'article' and 'conjunction,' but at first including prepositions and some other function words).

(c) The word *ptōsis*, at first meaning any inflected form (as in Aristotle), but later 'case,' and some names for the cases—either the later *eutheia* for the nominative (or perhaps Aristotle's *klēsis*), *genikē* for the genitive, etc., or perhaps more likely the names used by Aristotle (*to toutou* 'the of-this,' i.e., 'genitive'; *to toutōi* 'the for-this,' i.e., 'dative,' etc.).

(d) The traditional order of the cases (nom, gen, dat, acc, voc) may have existed in the fifth century, though a clear example does not appear until Cleochares (ca. 300 BC), as quoted in pseudo-Herodian's *Peri schēmatōn*, produces an instance of *poluptōton*, the use of a particular noun or pronoun (in this case 'Demosthenes') in the same position in five successive phrases, in a different case each time, with the cases in the traditional order. The traditional order of genders (masc, fem, neut) appears already in Protagoras (quoted above) and several times in Aristotle, but the order of numbers (singular, dual, plural), though perhaps natural (since the *klēsis* or basic form is always nom, sing, masc) is not attested early.

(e) The notion of dual patterning (Hockett) or double articulation (Martinet), that, essentially, the rules for correctness of sequences of vowels and consonants are unrelated to those for sequences of nouns, verbs, etc., appears first in Democritus (565, as cited in Isidore's *Etym.* 13.2.4. 108) and then in Plato (*Theaet.* 202–04, *Cratylus* 424–25, 431–32), though until Apollonius Dyscolus (*Synt.* 1.1–2) it often appears as a merely hierarchical arrangement: letters make syllables, syllables make words, words make sentences, and (in Plato's *Cratylus* 432A–C) sentences make discourses. But Apollonius clearly makes letters and syllables concrete, perceptible entities (Stoic *aisthēta*), while words and sentences are abstract, thinkable entities (*noēta*), so the Stoics should be given credit for the correct form of 'dual patterning.'

The amount of phonology current in the fifth century BC is probably reflected in Plato, who (in *Crat.* 431–32) assigns the topic to the science of *grammatikē*, and in Aristotle's *Poetics* (ch. 20, 1456b 25–31). Here (and in Plato's *Theaet.*), the distinction between vowels and consonants is clear, and among consonants there is a distinction between *psophoi* (noises: presumably *s*, *ksi*, and *psi*) and *phōnai* (voices: *m*, *n*, *r*, *l*) and consonants which are *aphōna* (all the stops— *ptkbdg*, *phi*, *theta*, *chi*); Aristotle's *sumphōna* (latinized as 'consonants' but much narrower here) include both *s* and the liquids and nasals, i.e., our 'continuants.' Though words like 'labial' and 'dental' do not appear until much later, there is a curious inscription (*IG* II.5.4321) of about 350 BC which describes some sort of special notation (interpreted by some as shorthand) for just those two classes. There is no evidence of categories like 'aspirated,' 'voiced,' or 'voiceless' until much later, though the relation between [h] (for initial aspiration) and the aspirated stops must have been learned before students could spell correctly.

Another recurrent theme of Greek grammatical thought is the listing of sentence types, i.e., illocutionary forces (in the sense of John Austin) or (in a few instances) moods, which begins in Protagoras, as mentioned above, and culminates with the lists discussed in *Aristotle and the Stoics*.

Finally, the notion to which Saussure gave the name 'arbitrariness of the sign should be considered,' i.e., whether or not there is some rational basis for the association of any given phonological sequence (of a word or morpheme) with a particular meaning or function. As conceived by the Greeks, the question was this: is the sound–meaning relation of all or some Greek words inevitable and natural? This is the main topic of discussion in Plato's *Cratylus*, but Aristotle, the Stoics, and Epicurus all also discussed the question, generally agreeing that all words are now arbitrary, though some suggest that there was once a time when they were not. Democritus (as quoted in Proclus' commentary on the *Cratylus* 16) offered four arguments (with four specially coined names) in favor of arbitrariness: (a) 'homonymy' or 'polysemy,' i.e., the same sequence of phonemes may be associated with two or more unrelated meanings; (b) 'polyonymy' or 'isorrophy,' i.e., the existence of synonyms; (c) 'metonymy,' i.e., the fact that words and meanings change; (d) 'nonymy,' i.e., the nonexistence of single words for simple or familiar ideas. Elsewhere (in Diodorus Siculus 1.8.3) Democritus argues for the 'polygenesis' of language—in other words, that there was no single proto-human language.

But a stronger claim than that of nonarbitrariness is the one implied by the famous experiment of Psammetichus as narrated by Herodotus (2.1–2), not just that some Greek words have a natural origin, but that some existing language really is the single proto-human tongue. This entails monogenesis, of course, plus the notion that only some languages undergo linguistic change. Psammetichus arranged for a child to be raised in such a way that it never heard anyone speak. When, at last, the child spontaneously uttered a word, it was *bekos*, which Herodotus tells us is Phrygian for 'bread.' This belief in a single original language comes into later European thought from the biblical tale of the Tower of Babel.

Plato thus gives a good idea of what might be called 'normal linguistics,' the kind of grammar that every man knew who had been to school as a boy in the fifth and early fourth centuries BC. This information can be supplemented by what can be read in Aristotle's *Poetics*, and one or two other places.

See also: Aristotle and the Stoics.

Bibliography

Ax W 1986 Quadripartita ratio: Bemerkungen zur Geschichte eines aktuellen Kategoriensystems (adiecto—detractio—transmutio—immutatio). *HL* **13**: 191–214

Baratin M 1978 Sur l'absence de l'expression des notions de sujet et de prédicat etc. In: Collart J

Collart J 1978 *Varron, grammaire antique et stylistique latine*. Les Belles Lettres, Paris

De Mauro T 1965 Il nome del dativo e la teoria dei casi greci. *Atti della accademia nazionale dei lincei, serie ottava, rendiconti, classe di scienti morali, storiche e filologiche* **20**: 151–211

Desbordes F 1983 Le Schéma 'addition, soustraction, mutation, métathèse' dans les textes anciens. *Histoire—Epistémologie—Langage* **5**: 23–30

Donnet D 1967 La place de la syntaxe dans les traités de grammaire grecque, des origines au XII siècle. *L'antiquité classique* **36**: 22–48

Gentinetta P M 1961 *Zur Sprachbetrachtung bei den Sophisten und in der stoisch–hellenistischen Zeit*. Verlag P. G. Keller, Winterthur

Girard P 1889. *L'éducation anthénienne*. Hachette, Paris

Householder F W 1989 Review of Taylor 1987. *HL* **16**: 131–48

Koller H 1958. Die Anfänge der griechischen Grammatik. *Glotta* **37**: 5–40

Pfeiffer R 1968 *History of Classical Scholarship From the Beginnings to the End of the Hellenistic Age*. Clarendon Press, Oxford

Pinborg J 1974 Classical Antiquity: Greece. In: Sebeok T A (ed.) *Current Trends in Linguistics*, vol. 13. Mouton, The Hague

Robins R H 1967 *A Short History of Linguistics*. Longman, London

Steinthal H 1890–91 *Geschichte der Sprachwissenschsaft bei den Griechen und Römern*, 2nd edn. F Dümmlers Verlagsbuchhandlung, Berlin

Taylor D J 1986 Rethinking the history of language science in classical antiquity. *HL* **13**: 175–90

Taylor D J (ed.) 1987 *The History of Linguistics in the Classical Period*. Benjamins, Amsterdam

b) 20th Century

Austin, J. L.

P. V. Lamarque

John Langshaw Austin (1911–60) White's Professor of Moral Philosophy at Oxford from 1952–1960, was a prominent figure in what became known as Ordinary Language Philosophy and, through his hugely influential, posthumously published, William James Lectures *How To Do Things With Words*, the initiator of speech act theory in its modern form.

Austin's philosophical work, which ostensibly covered traditional problems such as free will, truth, other minds, knowledge, and meaning, was characterized by a close attention to the ordinary uses of words, those involved, for example, in offering excuses, or in judgments using 'ifs and cans' or centered on words like 'real' and 'see,' in the belief that such an examination would turn up important and neglected distinctions or connections. His paper 'A plea for excuses' (Austin 1961) explained the rationale for his methods and is perhaps the seminal work in Ordinary Language Philosophy. His posthumously published lectures, *Sense and Sensibilia*, an attack on the then fashionable sense-datum theory and logical empiricism, particularly of A. J. Ayer, is a sustained application of the 'ordinary language' method.

His work on speech acts, which culminated in *How To Do Things With Words*, began with an interest in what he called 'performative utterances,' that is, utterances of the kind 'I promise to do such-and-such,' or 'I name this ship the *Queen Elizabeth*' which he contrasted with statements or 'constatives.' His view was that performatives, unlike constatives, should not be assessed for their truth but for their 'felicity'; a range of different criteria, other than 'corresponding to the facts,' existed for judging the success or otherwise of performatives and this, Austin thought, was a salutary reminder to philosophers that truth is not the only aim of language. Significantly, when writing about truth itself, Austin defended a traditional 'correspondence' view (see 'Truth' in Austin 1961), though his followers, notably P. F. Strawson, sought to apply a performative analysis even to utterances like 'That statement is true'. Austin came to see that the performative/constative distinction was not as hard-and-fast as he first believed and that statements too could be judged for their 'felicity' as well as their truth. Thus was speech act theory born.

Austin now introduced a threefold distinction: between a locutionary act (the act *of* saying something, with a particular sense and reference), an illocutionary act (an act—such as promising, stating, asking a question, ordering—performed *in* saying something), and a perlocutionary act (an act—such as convincing or advising—performed *by* saying something). These are not exclusive categories; indeed many utterances will involve all three classes of acts. Austin held that an illocutionary act is essentially conventional, while a perlocutionary act is causal. Unfortunately, Austin left his theory largely unrefined, due to his early death, though he did attempt a rudimentary taxonomy for illocutionary acts. J. R. Searle, who had studied under Austin, developed the theory in his influential *Speech Acts* (1969), though he was critical of several aspects of Austin's pioneering work, particularly the distinction between locutionary and illocutionary acts. Since then speech act theory has become a central component not only in pragmatics but also in argumentation theory, in literary criticism, and many other disciplines.

See also: Ordinary Language Philosophy; Speech Act Theory: Overview.

Bibliography

Austin J L 1961 In: Urmson J O, Warnock G J (eds.) *Philosophical Papers*. Clarendon Press, Oxford
Austin J L 1962 *Sense and Sensibilia*. Clarendon Press, Oxford
Austin J L 1962 In: Urmson J O (ed.) *How To Do Things With Words*. Clarendon Press, Oxford
Fann K T (ed.) 1969 *Symposium on J L Austin*. Routledge and Kegan Paul, London
Searle J R 1969 *Speech Acts*. Cambridge University Press, Cambridge
Warnock G J 1989 *J L Austin*. Routledge and Kegan Paul, London

Carnap, Rudolf

D. Bell

For almost half a century Rudolf Carnap (1891–1970) was one of the dominant figures in analytic philosophy. He was a leading member of the Vienna Circle, and subsequently exercised a formative influence on the development of philosophy in the USA. His major contributions lie in such areas as logic, semantics, the foundations of mathematics, and the philosophy of science.

1. Carnap's Life

Carnap was born and grew up in the Barmen region of northwest Germany. Between 1910 and 1914 he studied mathematics, physics, and philosophy, first at the University of Freiburg, and then at Jena where he was taught mathematical logic by Gottlob Frege. In 1926 he moved to Vienna and joined the Vienna Circle. During this period the major influences on his thought were Gottlob Frege, Bertrand Russell, and Ludwig Wittgenstein. After five years in Vienna, Carnap moved to Prague on being appointed to the Chair of Natural Philosophy in the German University. Confronted by the rise of National Socialism, however, he left Europe for the USA, where he remained for the rest of his life. He held chairs of philosophy at Chicago (1936–52), Princeton (1952–54), and UCLA (1954–61), and by the time of his death in 1970 he had published over 20 books and 80 articles on philosophy.

2. Positivism

As a lifelong logical positivist, or logical empiricist, Carnap was committed to the view that every item of human knowledge falls into one of two mutually exclusive categories. Either the knowledge is substantive, in which case it can only originate in or be justified by observation and experience; or the knowledge is merely formal and is expressed in propositions that are 'tautological, that is, they hold necessarily in every possible case, and therefore do not say anything about the facts of the world.' This view allows that both synthetic propositions of natural science, and analytic propositions of logic and mathematics possess an intelligible cognitive content, but it denies that any such content can be possessed by the sentences of traditional metaphysics. The problems of metaphysics thus become pseudo-problems to which no solution is possible (Carnap 1932). Traditional philosophy, he announced, 'is to be replaced by the logic of science,' and this is 'nothing other than the logical syntax of the language of science' (Carnap 1934: Foreword).

3. Logical Syntax

During the period 1928–38 Carnap held the view that problems concerning the cognitive *content* of scientific sentences are a matter for the particular science in question: they will be substantive problems belonging to physics, botany, psychology, and the like. But as there is no cognitive content to sentences of metaphysics, the only task remaining to the philosopher is to investigate the pure *forms* of possible scientific sentences. These pure syntactic structures are, he believed, conventional: they are systems of rules governing permissible combinations or concatenations of signs, regardless of what those signs might mean. No language, syntactically defined, is intrinsically more accurate or more basic than any other. On the contrary one is free to invent notations and to use them as and how one sees fit. Carnap's Principle of Tolerance says that in philosophy: 'It is not our business to set up prohibitions, but to arrive at conventions' (Carnap 1934: 51). At this time Carnap believed that logic, mathematics, and (bona fide) philosophy were all essentially syntactical disciplines; all other (bona fide) disciplines belonged within the empirical sciences.

4. Semantics

By about 1939, under the influence of Gödel and Tarski, Carnap had come to see that not all the philosophically important properties of language can be given a purely syntactical interpretation: there are also semantic and pragmatic properties that need to be taken into account.

Carnap defines a semantical system as 'a system of rules [i.e., definitions], formulated within a metalanguage and referring to an object language, of such a kind that the rules determine a *truth-condition* for every sentence of the object language, i.e., a sufficient and necessary condition for its truth' (Carnap 1942: 22). A semantical system (a) assigns a denotation to appropriate subsentential expressions of a language, and (b) provides a recursive definition of *truth* for the sentences of that language. Typically the object languages studied by Carnap were formalized (not natural) languages, whereas the metalanguage he employed was usually a natural language like English, supplemented by special symbols and expressions wherever necessary.

In later works Carnap applied his semantic analyses to intentional and modal contexts (1956), and to inductive logic and the foundations of probability (1950).

See also: Linguistic Philosophy; Logical Positivism.

Bibliography

Carnap R 1928 *Der Logische Aufbau der Welt*. Weltkreis-Verlag, Berlin (1967 *The Logical Structure of the World and Pseudoproblems in Philosophy*. Routledge and Kegan Paul, London)

Carnap R 1932 Überwindung der Metaphysik durch logische Analyse der Sprache. *Erkenntnis* **2** (1959 The elimination of metaphysics through logical analysis of language. In: Ayer A J (ed.) *Logical Positivism*. Free Press, Glencoe, IL)

Carnap R 1934 *Logische Syntax der Sprache*. Springer, Vienna (1937 *The Logical Syntax of Language*. Kegan Paul, London)

Carnap R 1942 *Introduction to Semantics*. Harvard University Press, Cambridge, MA

Carnap R 1950 *The Logical Foundations of Probability*. University of Chicago Press, Chicago, IL

Carnap R 1956 *Meaning and Necessity: A Study in Semantics and Modal Logic*, 2nd edn. University of Chicago Press, Chicago, IL

Schilpp P A (ed.) 1963 *The Philosophy of Rudolf Carnap*. Open Court, La Salle, IL

Chomsky, Noam

F. J. Newmeyer

Given the central role that Noam Chomsky (b. 1928) has played in the linguistics of the past few decades, it is important to understand the philosophical system that underlies his ideas. This article traces the development of this system from Chomsky's earliest training to the present, pointing to its relevance to philosophy, psychology, and, most importantly, linguistic methodology.

1. Chomsky's Philosophical Training

Noam Chomsky was trained in the most rigidly empiricist linguistic tradition that has ever been practiced, namely that of 'post-Bloomfieldian structuralism.' Leonard Bloomfield, a central figure of American linguistics in the interwar period and the intellectual forefather of this tradition, had pioneered an approach to linguistic methodology that allowed only statements drawn from direct observation of the phenomena under investigation or generalizations that could be derived from observations by a set of mechanical procedures. As he put it, 'The only useful generalizations about language are inductive generalizations. Features which we think ought to be universal may be absent from the very next language that becomes accessible' (1933: 20). Such a view discouraged not only an inquiry into the universal properties of language, but the study of meaning as well, given the notorious difficulty of making explicit the precise meaning of an utterance.

The 'post-Bloomfieldians' consisted of those students of Bloomfield's, and their colleagues, who dominated American linguistics in the 1940s and 1950s. One of their most prominent members was Chomsky's teacher Zellig Harris. They set to work to devise a set of procedures in accord with Bloomfield's theoretical strictures, while avoiding what they saw as the pitfalls

in his actual analytical work, which was prone to make use of 'mentalistic' constructs and nonrigorous procedures. Their goal was explicitly to 'discover' a grammar by performing a set of operations on a corpus of data. Each successive operation was to be one step farther removed from the corpus. Since the physical record of the flow of speech itself was the only data considered objective enough to serve as a starting point, it followed that the levels of a grammatical description had to be arrived at in the following order: phonemics, morphemics, syntax, discourse.

The empiricism that dominated American linguistics from the 1930s to the 1950s was a simple reflection of the fact that this intellectual current dominated *all* the social and behavioral sciences in the USA at the time. Its wide appeal was in large part a function of the fact that there was no other period in American history in which there was greater respect for the methods and results of science. Contemporary philosophy of science (as well as naive common sense) informed linguists and others that what distinguishes science from other types of activity is the ability to generalize laws on the basis of precise measurement of observable data. Post-Bloomfieldian structuralism promised to bring linguistics in accord with what was seen as the practice in physics, chemistry, biology, and the other natural sciences.

Not surprisingly, the post-Bloomfieldians looked to behaviorist psychology for independent support for their approach to language. However, American psychology at this time, under the leadership of B. F. Skinner (1957) was under the grip of a form of empiricism that was so extreme that it would not even tolerate theoretical terms such as 'phoneme,' 'morpheme,' and so on, which could be derived by a set of mechanical operations. Hence, the marriage of structural linguistics and psychology did not take place until a less radical form of behaviorism was developed (Hull 1943) that gave these constructs the status of 'mediating responses,' that is, elements that, while not directly observable, could nevertheless (in principle) be linked deterministically to observable speech.

2. Chomsky's Break with Empiricism

Chomsky's training in the philosophical foundations of linguistics was strictly in this empiricist post-Bloomfieldian tradition—he even published a paper as a student which was designed to sharpen their analytical procedures. But as early as his undergraduate days, he had come to have doubts as to the philosophical worth of the enterprise. These doubts soon led him to rethink the philosophical foundations of the field and to set to work to develop an alternative conception of linguistic theory and practice. This approach was laid out in a 900-page manuscript entitled *The Logical Structure of Linguistic Theory*, written in 1955, but not published until 20 years later (Chomsky 1975a).

The central themes of this manuscript were condensed and published in Chomsky's (1957) book *Syntactic Structures*. This book's conceptual break with post-Bloomfieldianism was not over the question of whether linguistics could be a 'science'—Chomsky never questioned that it could be—but over the more fundamental issue of what a scientific theory is and how one might be constructed with respect to linguistic phenomena. Chomsky argued at length that no scientific theory had ever resulted from the scientist performing mechanical operations on the data. How the scientist happens to hit upon a particular theoretical notion, he pointed out, is simply irrelevant; all that counts is its adequacy in explaining the phenomena in its domain.

Chomsky's rejection of empiricist constraints on theory formation led him to propose a novel conception of what a linguistic theory is a theory *of*. Whereas to earlier structuralists, a theory was no more than a concise taxonomy of the elements extractable from a corpus of data, Chomsky redefined the goal of linguistic theory to that of providing a rigorous and formal characterization of a 'possible human language,' that is, to distinguishing as precisely as possible the class of grammatical processes that can occur in language from that which cannot. This characterization, which Chomsky later came to call 'universal grammar,' specifies the limits within which all languages function. In Chomsky's view, natural scientists set parallel tasks for themselves: the goal of physicists is to characterize the class of possible physical processes, that of biologists to characterize the class of possible biological processes, and so on.

Aside from his extended demolition of empiricist approaches to grammar construction (although the philosophy of 'empiricism' is never mentioned by name), there is little discussion in *Syntactic Structures* of philosophical issues, whether philosophy of language or philosophy of science. Indeed, the only philosophical works referred to in that book are by the arch-empiricists (and Chomsky's teachers) Willard Quine and Nelson Goodman, to whom Chomsky gave credit for his views on simplicity and the evaluation of formal systems.

Nevertheless, philosophers of science had, in the previous decade, been moving away from the empiricist constraints on theory construction and motivation that had generally been espoused earlier. For example, in two important papers (ultimately published in 1965) the philosopher Carl Hempel laid to rest any hope for an empiricist approach to theory formation. As he pointed out, even the more permissive empiricist approaches to this question fail to capture the essence of what it takes for a statement to be considered scientific. He illustrated at length that there is no direct connection between a scientific term or statement and the empirical confirmation of a theory containing that term or statement. Indeed, many fundamental scientific notions, such as 'gravitational potential,' 'absolute temperature,' and 'electric field,' have no operational definitions at all. Hempel concluded that science is more in the business of comparing *theories* than in evaluating *statements*. A theory is simply an axiomatized system which *as a whole* has an empirical interpretation.

Hempel's view, which had begun to gather currency by the late 1950s, signaled the demise of empiricism as a significant force in the philosophy of science. As its philosophical props gave way, post-Bloomfieldian structuralism found itself in a distinctly unstable posture. Not surprisingly, it was relatively simple for a theory that itself rattled these props to topple it completely.

3. Chomsky's Early Approach to Meaning

For all its ground-breaking work about theory construction in linguistics in general, there is nothing particularly innovative in the *Syntactic Structures* approach to meaning. On the one hand, in terms of the *analysis* of meaning, Chomsky adopted the post-Bloomfieldian view that grammar (i.e., syntax and phonology) are autonomous and independent of meaning, though he took pains to stress that this conclusion was based on an analysis of the data, not on some a priori stricture that demanded the exclusion of unobservable semantic phenomena from the domain of linguistic analysis.

As far as his views on the *nature* of meaning are concerned, he endorsed Goodman's (empiricist) attempt to extend the theory of reference to encompass much of meaning. The residue of meaning intractable to this approach was simply ascribed to language use, presumably based on the contemporary influence of the Oxford philosophers and their use theory of meaning.

Indeed, the terms 'meaning' and 'use' are used interchangeably so often throughout *Syntactic Structures* that Newmeyer (1986: 27) has argued that many of Chomsky's arguments in *Syntactic Structures* for the autonomy of syntax were in reality arguments for (what he would call a few years later) the competence–performance dichotomy. Many aspects of meaning, in his view at the time, were part of performance.

4. The Development of Chomsky's Theory of Mind

The decade following the publication of *Syntactic Structures* saw Chomsky's views mature into a philosophical system in which the boundaries between the fields of linguistics, psychology, and philosophy became ever less distinct.

Chomsky himself did not bring up the question of the psychological implications of transformational generative grammar in either *The Logical Structure of Linguistic Theory* or *Syntactic Structures*; as he wrote later, it would have been 'too audacious' for him to have done so (Chomsky 1975a: 35). But his student, Robert B. Lees, closed his review of *Syntactic Structures* with a frontal attack on inductivist learning theory, arguing that there could be no alternative but to conclude that the grammar the linguist constructed was 'in the head' of the speaker. But if that be the case, then how could these highly abstract principles possibly be learned inductively? 'It would seem,' he wrote, 'that our notions of human learning are due for some considerable sophistication' (1957: 408).

It was Chomsky's (1959) review of B. F. Skinner's *Verbal Behavior* in which he first stressed that his theory of language is a psychological model of an aspect of human knowledge. Chomsky's review represents, even after the passage of some 20 years, the basic refutation of behaviorist psychology. The review takes in turn each basic construct of behaviorism, and demonstrates that either it leads to false predictions or it is simply devoid of content. Chomsky went on to argue that this ability indicates that rather than being born 'blank slates,' children have a genetic predisposition to structure the acquisition of linguistic knowledge in a highly specific way.

By 1965, with the publication of his *Aspects of the Theory of Syntax*, Chomsky had come to characterize generative grammar explicitly as a 'rationalist' theory, in the sense that it posits innate principles that determine the form of acquired knowledge. As part of the theory's conceptual apparatus, Chomsky reintroduced two terms long out of fashion in academic discussion: 'innate ideas' and 'mind.' For Chomsky, innate ideas are simply those properties of the grammar that are inborn and constrain the acquisition of knowledge. So, for example, generativists believe, based on their abstractness, complexity, and limited amount of relevant information presented to the child,

that many grammatical constraints are 'prewired,' so to speak, into the child, rather than acquired by anything one might reasonably call 'learning.' Hence, these constraints are innate ideas.

Mind, for Chomsky, refers to the principles, both innate and acquired, that underlie actual behavior. Such principles, obviously, are not restricted to the realm of language. For example, as recent research has shown, many important aspects of the visual system are also prewired and need only a triggering experience from the environment to be set in motion. In Chomsky's terms, then, the theory of vision is a rationalist theory, and the structures underlying visual perception (innate ideas) form part of mind.

While mind may encompass more cognitive faculties than language, Chomsky believes that linguistic studies are the best suited of all to reveal the essence of mind. For one thing, language is the only cognitive faculty that is *uniquely* human. Not even the study of the communicative behavior of the lower animals sheds any light on it: the mental structures underlying animal communication seem to bear no evolutionary relation to those underlying human language. Also, language is the vehicle of rational thought—another uniquely human ability. And finally, more is known about language and how it functions than about other aspects of cognition. After all, more than two millennia of grammatical research have given us a more detailed picture of the structure of language than a bare century of research has clarified the nature of vision, memory, concept formation, and so on.

Chomsky is happy to refer to the faculty for language as an aspect of 'human nature.' The term 'human nature' for him has real content: it is characterized by the set of innately endowed capacities for language, other aspects of cognition, and whatever else, which, being innate, are immune to environmental influences. Chomsky sees such a conception in an entirely positive political light: our genetic inheritance—our human nature—prevents us from being plastic, infinitely malleable beings subjugable to the whims of outside forces.

Thus at a rather abstract level, there is a connection between Chomsky's philosophy of language and his renowned political anarchism. Just as our innate linguistic endowment shields our language from being shaped in its entirety by external forces, so it is also the case that no oppressive political system has the power to mold our minds entirely to its liking; we are, at root, free agents in this world.

Philosophical critiques of Chomsky's views on language and mind have been legion; while space limitations prevent even a sketchy outline of their content, a sampling may be found in Hook (1969), Harman (1974), and Kripke (1982). They have focused on those aspects of his overall theory that appear most vulnerable: his 'subjectivism,' which entails that a language 'has no existence apart from its mental representation' (Chomsky 1972: 95); his 'individualism,' which claims that the explanation of linguistic phenomena rests ultimately on the properties of individual human beings, rather than on their social interactions; his 'mentalism,' which posits that in some real sense speakers 'know' the grammars of their language; and his 'rationalism,' which claims that human language learning is mediated by innate mental schemata. Chomsky defends his views in various works (1972; 1975b; 1980; 1986); for a comprehensive defense of (the bulk of) Chomsky's system of ideas, see D'Agostino (1986).

5. The Further Development of Chomsky's Ideas about Meaning

Returning to more strictly linguistic themes, the decade after the publication of *Syntactic Structures* was also a time of various attempts to integrate a semantic theory into generative grammar. Chomsky, in a 1962 presentation, set the course for this development by raising the question: 'What are the substantive and formal constraints on systems of concepts that are constructed by humans on the basis of presented data?' (1964: 51–52).

Katz and Fodor (1963) attempted to answer Chomsky's question in the following way. First, they distinguished between two faculties involved in the interpretation of a sentence: that provided by a universal theory of meaning, whose primitive terms and principles form part of our strictly grammatical abilities; and that derived from extralinguistic beliefs about the world. The goal of semantic theory would be to explicate only the former faculty, a component of linguistic competence. Second, they developed an analogy between phonetics and semantics. Just as phonetic representations are based on a universal system of phonetic features, semantic representations would be built out of primitive conceptual elements. A reading for a sentence, then, would be determined by the syntactic structure of the sentence and the semantic features ('markers') in the lexical items that comprise it, similar to construction of the phonetic representation of a sentence on the basis of the phonological distinctive features characterizing each lexical item and the language's particular phonological rules.

Chomsky endorsed the Katz–Fodor approach in *Aspects of the Theory of Syntax*. Nevertheless, as time has passed he has become increasingly skeptical that there is a universal semantic system, parallel to a universal phonetic system. As he put it succinctly: 'I doubt that one can separate semantic representation from beliefs and knowledge about the world' (1979: 142).

6. The Generative Semantics Challenge to Chomsky's Philosophy

It seems to be the case that Chomsky believes that the danger of admitting a substantive theory of meaning

into generative grammar is a prescription for the ultimate abandonment of a rationalist theory of language in favor of a return of an empiricist one. He would surely point to generative semantics (McCawley 1976) as an object lesson illustrating this point. This approach to grammatical description flourished as a current within generative grammar in the late 1960s and early 1970s. In brief, it took the Katz–Fodor ideas about semantics seriously and attempted to push them to their logical conclusion. Given these ideas, and the related one that deep structure is the locus of semantic interpretation (the 'Katz–Postal Hypothesis'), generative semanticists came more and more to deny that any sensible boundary could be drawn between the syntactic and semantic components of grammar. They had many reasons for coming to this conclusion, but one of the central ones (and the most important for the present discussion) was that, given the existence of a universal semantic system, there exists an overlap between semantic constructs and those participating in what would appear to be strictly grammatical rules (e.g., constructs such as animacy, gender, and the common/proper distinction among nouns). Generative semanticists argued that the redundancy seemingly entailed by this overlap could be eliminated only by erasing the line between syntax and semantics (for detailed discussion of the steps that led them to this conclusion, see Newmeyer 1986).

As this model progressed, it came to challenge any dividing line between semantic and pragmatic facts as well. (Given Chomsky's hypothesis that no such dividing line exists, it would follow naturally that they would be led to this conclusion.) Thus by 1975 or so, the idea that a universal theory of semantic constructs exists had led the competence–performance dichotomy, the linchpin of linguistic rationalism, to be abandoned by generative semanticists.

7. Chomsky and Approaches to Meaning

Chomsky has been equally adamantly opposed to approaches to semantics with roots in the logical tradition, in which, by means of a model, an arbitrary sentence of a language is assigned a truth value with respect to a possible state of affairs. Such approaches began to gain currency among linguists in the mid-1970s and, in one version or another, continue to dominate linguistic semantics today (see Dowty, et al. 1981).

Chomsky argues that anyone who believes in possible world semantics is forced to make one of two choices about the status of the constructs that populate such models, and both of them are (in his opinion) unpalatable. On the one hand, they could be regarded in parallel to the way that constructs of syntax and phonology are regarded, namely, as elements of a theory of mind. But, Chomsky argues, it is not at all clear how possible worlds are mentally represented or how people can have access to calculations using possible worlds when they make their judgments. On the other hand, it would be possible to reject any psychological interpretation about possible worlds. But in that case, one would simply be doing some species of mathematics, devoid of linguistic interest. Hence, Chomsky concludes that model–theoretic possible world semantics must be rejected as a component of a linguistic theory.

8. Chomsky's Philosophy and Linguistic Methodology

In debates with his linguistic opponents over even the most seemingly minute aspects of linguistic structure, Chomsky has made it clear that there are philosophical issues at stake that transcend the particular analysis of the particular phenomenon under discussion. And invariably, Chomsky's position leads to the conclusion that the human mind must be more highly structured than had been heretofore believed. Consider again his debate with generative semantics. This framework took what it described as an 'abstract' view of syntax, in that it attempted to ground syntax in semantics. But Chomsky argued that generative semantics was at the root *anti*abstractionist, since the effect of its reductionist program was to derive unobservable syntactic structure from more accessible semantic structure. To this program, Chomsky counterposed and defended at length a view of syntax populated with null elements, abstract structural relations, and complex constraints, none of which have any direct semantic analogue. Since there is no way that the principles of syntax making use of these syntactic elements could have been learned from exposure to the environment (as, at least in principle, semantic constructs might be), the conclusion follows that the language faculty—i.e., the linguistic aspect of the human mind—must be innately endowed with a complex structure.

The more recent opposition to Chomsky's views of syntax have taken the (seemingly) opposite tack from that of generative semantics. Models such as 'generalized phrase structure grammar' and 'lexical functional grammar' have tended to downplay the need for abstract principles and constraints, arguing that syntactic generalizations can be stated to a much greater degree on surface structure than Chomsky has been wont to believe. Again, in combating the claims of these rival models, Chomsky makes it clear that more is at stake than the particular formulation of some particular principle. Rather, he sees these models as challenging the view of mind that he has developed over the last few decades.

Chomsky's methodology has always been to focus on the broad picture at the expense of working out fine analytic details. In one sense, this is no more than an exemplification of the 'hypothetico–deductive' method of scientific reasoning. As counterposed to the inductive method, which starts from an observed generalization and proceeds to a law, the hypothetico–deductive method begins with a law, derives conclusions from that law, and then matches those conclusions against observed reality. To give a concrete example, a hypothesized universal constraint, proposed on the basis of evidence from one language (or a small number of languages), might lead the investigator to make predictions about the syntactic behavior of some other language, which can then be tested empirically.

By 1980, Chomsky had begun to refer to his variant of the hypothetico–deductive method as the 'Galilean style' of theory construction, a style that carries this method one step farther in the domain of abstractness. Just as Galileo sought out broad principles governing nature, principles 'falsified' at every turn by a myriad of observable phenomena, Chomsky too has attempted to put forward sweeping generalizations about the structure of the language faculty, ignoring, or postponing the discussion of linguistic phenomena that seem to counterexemplify them. This has led Chomsky to receive many outraged attacks, ranging from mild charges of irresponsibility to the data to the more serious one of being an 'idealist,' rather than a responsible scientist.

Chomsky has dealt with these criticisms in a number of ways. First, he has replied that the 'modular' approach to grammar that he has increasingly espoused allows observed complexity to be derived from the interaction of the general systems that the Galilean style led him to posit. That is, he maintains that complex linguistic phenomena can be explained in terms of the interaction of the autonomous grammatical system with other systems involved in giving language its overall character, such as those based in physiology, cognition, and social interaction.

The modular conception of language, as Chomsky and others have noted, has received independent support from many diverse areas of investigation in recent years, in particular from studies of language acquisition, language–brain relationships, language processing, and language variation. For a summary of some of the most important evidence to that effect, see Newmeyer (1983).

The central principle of Chomsky's current approach to syntax (the 'principles and parameters' approach—see Chomsky 1981; 1995) is that the internal structure of the grammar is modular as well. That is, syntactic complexity results from the interaction of grammatical subsystems, each characterizable in terms of its own set of general principles. The central goal of syntactic theory thus becomes to identify such systems and characterize the degree to which they may vary from language to language (i.e., the extent to which they may be 'parametrized').

The modular approach to explanation, then, illustrates the internal logic of Chomsky's approach. From an approach to the methodology of science, he derives a linguistic methodology that focuses on broad generalizations at the expense of handling at the outset any number of detailed facts. These broad generalizations bolster his theory of mind, since they tend to be so abstract that they could not have been learned inductively. As a final step in the chain, the broad generalizations, in mutual interaction, do in fact account for a considerable portion of the empirical data.

In sum, Chomsky has moved to a position in which the study of the language faculty, the repository of what he has come to call 'I-language' (i.e., internalized language), has reached a depth of abstractness unprecedented in the development of the theory of generative grammar. But Chomsky considers himself first and foremost an empirical scientist, not (merely) a speculative philosopher. As he would be the first to acknowledge, the philosophical system upon which his approach to linguistic analysis is based will stand or fall depending on the depth of insight attained on the nature of the grammatical processes at work in the 5,000-odd languages of the world.

Bibliography

Bloomfield L 1933 *Language*. Holt, Rinehart, and Winston, New York
Chomsky N 1957 *Syntactic Structures*. Mouton, The Hague
Chomsky N 1959 Review of B F Skinner's *Verbal Behavior*. *Lg* **35(1)**: 26–58
Chomsky N 1964 *Current Issues in Linguistic Theory*. Mouton, The Hague
Chomsky N 1965 *Aspects of the Theory of Syntax*. MIT Press, Cambridge, MA
Chomsky N 1972 *Language and Mind*. Harcourt Brace Jovanovich, New York
Chomsky N 1975a *The Logical Structure of Linguistic Theory*. Plenum, New York
Chomsky N 1975b *Reflections on Language*. Pantheon, New York
Chomsky N 1979 *Language and Responsibility*. Harvester Press, Sussex
Chomsky N 1980 *Rules and Representations*. Blackwell, Oxford
Chomsky N 1981 *Lectures on Government and Binding*. Foris, Dordrecht
Chomsky N 1986 *Knowledge of Language*. Praeger, New York
Chomsky N 1995 *The Minimalist Program*. MIT Press, Cambridge, MA
D'Agostino F 1986 *Chomsky's System of Ideas*. Clarendon Press, Oxford
Dowty D R, Wall R E, Peters S 1981 *Introduction to Montague Semantics*. Reidel, Dordrecht
Harman G 1974 *On Noam Chomsky: Critical Essays*. Anchor Press, New York
Hempel C G 1965 *Aspects of Scientific Explanation*. Free Press, New York
Hook S (ed.) 1969 *Language and Philosophy*. New York University Press, New York
Hull C L 1943 *Principles of Behavior*. Appleton-Century-Crofts, New York
Katz J J, Fodor J A 1963 The structure of a semantic theory. *Lg* **39**: 170–210
Kripke S A 1982 *Wittgenstein on Rules and Private Language*. Blackwell, Oxford
Lees R B 1959 Review of N Chomsky, *Syntactic Structures*. *Lg* **33(14)**: 375–404
McCawley J D 1976 *Grammar and Meaning*. Academic Press, New York
Newmeyer F J 1983 *Grammatical Theory*. University of Chicago Press, Chicago, IL
Newmeyer F J 1986 *Linguistic Theory in America*. Academic Press, New York
Skinner B F 1957 *Verbal Behavior*. Appleton-Century-Crofts, New York

Davidson, Donald

E. M. Fricker

Donald Davidson (b. 1917) is a major figure in contemporary philosophy of the Anglo–American analytic school. From 1963 onwards he has published a series of seminal articles which have done much to shape the direction and development of philosophy within this tradition. In some cases what were originally bold new proposals by him have become a widely received view, although many of his doctrines remain provocative and controversial. Though he has written no single work of book length, his many articles are closely interconnected, and together form a distinctive and coherent philosophical system covering language, the mind, and metaphysics.

1. Philosophy of Language

In the late 1960s Davidson gave 'semantics' of natural languages a new form and direction by proposing that a 'theory of truth' for a natural language, similar to those devised by Tarski for formal languages, could constitute a 'theory of meaning' for that language, that is, a formal axiomatic theory which for any sentence of the language yields a theorem which specifies its meaning.

The proposal prompted a spate of work, by Davidson and others, which essayed theories of this form covering specific fragments of English. The first guiding constraint in this enterprise urged by Davidson is that each sentence's meaning be derivable in a finite axiomatic theory from axioms assigning semantic properties to component expressions discerned as semantic constituents. A second is that the structure imputed to a sentence must be such as to exhibit as valid the inferential relations between it and other sentences. Davidson's own contribution includes an account of the 'logical form' or semantic structure of action sentences, which he argues must be construed as involving an implicit quantification over events. He also proposed an ingenious new account of sentences giving reports of speech, such as 'Galileo said that the earth moved.' The 'that' is construed as being indeed a demonstrative, one which, on any occasion of utterance of the whole sentence, refers to the speaker's own utterance of the content clause 'the earth moved.' The whole utterance is thus paraphraseable as 'The earth moved. Some utterance of Galileo's and this last utterance of mine make us samesayers.' Davidson has also written about the relation between mood and force, which he argues cannot fully be explained in terms of convention. In a subtle article he argues that metaphor is a feature solely of the use of language, and is not to be ascribed to a sentence's meaning, which is confined to literal meaning. As to how one can tell when a given theory of meaning is the correct theory

of a given community of language users, Davidson approaches this issue in terms of the scenario of 'radical interpretation'.

2. Contribution to Other Areas of Philosophy

Davidson has made seminal contributions advancing the subject in philosophy of mind and action, metaphysics, and epistemology. He has argued, contra one tradition, that reasons for action are causes of the actions they rationalize. He was one of the first to suggest that the relation between mind and brain may be one of 'token identity' of mental with neural events, there being however no 'type identities,' between the two categories, due to the different nature and allegiances of mental and physical vocabularies. He has put forward an account of the nature of cause, and causal statements of English. Most recently he has turned explicitly to epistemology and metaphysics, developing a distinctive view of the nature of truth, which has implications for the coherence of global skepticism.

See also: Convention; Meaning: Philosophical Theories; Radical Interpretation.

Bibliography

Davidson D 1980 *Essays on Actions and Events*. Clarendon Press, Oxford
Davidson D 1984 *Inquiries into Truth and Interpretation*. Clarendon Press, Oxford
Davidson D 1990 The structure and content of truth. *The Journal of Philosophy* **87**(6): 279–328
LePore E (ed.) 1986 *Truth and Interpretation: Perspectives on the Philosophy of Donald Davidson*. Blackwell, Oxford

Dummett, Michael

D. E. B. Pollard

Michael Anthony Eardley Dummett (b. 1925), formerly Wykeham Professor of Logic at Oxford University, is a renowned authority on the work of the German philosopher and mathematician Gottlob Frege. He has made significant contributions to the philosophy of language. Of particular interest to linguistic theorists is the emphasis he has given to the theory of meaning, and his account of linguistic understanding.

1. Theoretical Context

Dummett's work is best understood in relation to a particular theoretical perspective. This position,

known as 'truth-conditional semantics,' involves the fundamental assumption that the meaning of a sentence in a language is given by stating the conditions under which it is true. The semantic properties of other expressions, e.g., nouns, verbs, etc., are then characterized in terms of the contribution they make to the truth-conditions of the sentences in which they appear. More complex expressions can be accounted for by recursion, i.e., they can be shown to be generated from simpler ones according to basic rules. It is crucial to this approach that truth is taken to be a more perspicuous and theoretically tractable notion than that of meaning. The provision of a theory of truth for a language should then enable anyone to understand any declarative sentence uttered by a native speaker of the language.

2. Dummett's Critique

Dummett's concern is with the knowledge in virtue of which anyone can speak and understand a language. He takes issue with what he sees as the fundamental assumptions behind the truth-conditional account. First, it is committed to realism, which not only entails the equation of meaning with truth-conditions, but is also committed to bivalence—the thesis that every sentence (more properly, statement or proposition) is determinately true or false whether or not it can be recognized as such. Second, this latter commitment has the effect of placing many of the sentences of natural language beyond the recognitional capacities of its speakers. Examples of such sentences include those about the past, other minds, and especially counterfactuals, e.g., 'If Hitler had conquered Britain, he would have executed Churchill.' Sentences of these kinds could be true without native speakers recognizing when their truth-conditions were fulfilled. By contrast, for Dummett, speakers' knowledge of meaning must be capable of being manifested in their linguistic practice. If knowledge of truth-conditions cannot be manifested because those truth-conditions exceed recognitional capacity, then knowledge of truth-conditions cannot amount to knowledge of meaning. Truth, then, realistically construed, is, according to Dummett, explanatorily idle. One can ascribe mastery of or competence in a language only to those who are capable of displaying it. This competence would be displayed in the use of sentences in circumstances in which their assertability was justified. Dummett is, therefore, appealing to some notion of 'verification'. A theory of meaning for a language will

thus be constructed on the recursive specification, not of truth-conditions but of 'verification' conditions.

3. Problems and Criticisms

Some of Dummett's own assumptions have attracted criticism. If the idea of verification is taken in the sense of conclusive verification, then it would appear too strong, since people frequently acquire linguistic understanding in conditions which are rarely evidentially conclusive. Additionally, there are cases in which use might mask differences of meaning, or even cases where sentences differing in meaning might nonetheless have identical evidential grounds. It suffices to note here that Dummett has identified serious problems for attempts to construct systematic theories of meaning.

See also: Formal Semantics; Holism; Meaning: Philosophical Theories; Realism.

Bibliography

Dummett M A E 1973 *Frege Philosophy of Language*. Duckworth, London
Dummett M A E 1975 What is a theory of meaning? In: Guttenplan S (ed.) *Mind and Language*. Oxford University Press, London
Dummett M A E 1976 What is a theory of meaning? Part II. In: Evans G, McDowell J (eds.) *Truth and Meaning: Essays in Semantics*. Clarendon Press, Oxford
Dummett M A E 1978 *Truth and Other Enigmas*. Duckworth, London
Dummett M A E 1981 *The Interpretation of Frege's Philosophy*. Duckworth, London
Dummett M A E 1982 Realism. *Synthese* **52**: 55–112
Dummett M A E 1996a *The Seas of Language*. Clarendon Press, Oxford
Dummett M A E 1996b *Frege and Other Philosophers*. Clarendon Press, Oxford
Wright C G 1986 *Realism, Meaning and Truth*. Blackwell, Oxford

Frege, Gottlob

D. Bell

Gottlob Frege (1848–1925) made massive, revolutionary, and lasting contributions to a variety of different philosophical fields. He is the founder of modern formal logic; he initiated the modern era in the philosophy of mathematics; his contributions to the understanding of how language relates both to the world of which it speaks, and to the thoughts which it expresses are second to none; and in philosophy as a whole, according to one authority, 'he achieved a revolution as overwhelming as that of Descartes,' by

formulating the methods, priorities, principles, and goals that were to become definitive of 'analytic' philosophy (see Dummett 1973: 665–66).

1. Life

Frege was born and spent his childhood in Wismar, in the Mecklenburg region of northern Germany. In 1869, at the age of 21, he entered the University of Jena as a student of mathematics. Two years later he moved to the University of Göttingen where in 1873 he was awarded the degree of Doctor of Philosophy for a dissertation in geometry. He returned to Jena almost immediately to take up the post of *Privatdozent* in the Faculty of Mathematics. As the post was unsalaried, Frege had to rely on his mother for financial support; during this period he also supplemented his means by keeping pigs. He remained in the mathematics faculty at Jena—receiving promotion to *außerordentlicher* Professor in 1879, and to Honorary Professor in 1896—until his retirement in 1918. He died in 1925 after a life in which the main adventures were, it seems, adventures of the mind.

2. The Fregean Program

Most of Frege's intellectual life was devoted to a single, narrowly circumscribed project: the reduction of arithmetic in its entirety to pure logic. He attempted to prove, that is, that there belong in arithmetic no concepts, objects, procedures, or truths which cannot be accounted for given only the resources of pure, deductive logic.

Clearly, however, the logic that Frege inherited was too weak for this purpose. So in his first publication, the *Begriffsschrift* of 1879, he set out to extend and strengthen it. To this end he invented a notation capable of expressing not only multiple generality, using quantifiers and bound variables, but also relations of any degree of complexity; he introduced a truth–functional account of the logical connectives, an anticipation of the theory of types, the beginnings of a categorial grammar, and a complete formalization of the first-order predicate calculus with identity. For logic, consequently, 1879 is now widely regarded as 'the most important date for the subject' (Kneale and Kneale 1962: 511).

Frege's next major publication, the *Grundlagen* (1884), contains an informal defense of the logicist program. In it Frege argues that an empirical ascription of number (e.g., *There are three people in the next room)* is an assertion about a concept, and that a proposition of arithmetic (e.g., $3+5=8$) is a logical truth, knowable a priori, concerning 'logical objects' called 'numbers.' Numbers, it turns out, are abstract objects, namely classes of equivalent classes.

In his two-volume magnum opus, *Grundgesetze der Arithmetik* (1893, 1903), Frege attempted nothing less than a formal proof of the logicist thesis, by providing a deductively valid derivation of the truths of number theory from just seven axioms or basic laws, each of which, he claimed, was itself a truth of logic. This formal proof is in fact invalid; for, as Bertrand Russell communicated to Frege in 1902, axiom V permits derivation of the logical contradiction that has since come to be known as Russell's Paradox.

3. The Linguistic Turn

If Frege's unprecedented additions to traditional logic were not to seem arbitrary or ad hoc, it was necessary to provide an informal, intuitively accessible defense of them. They had to be shown to be genuine 'laws of thought,' governing the significance, the truth or falsity, and the validity of our thoughts, judgments, and inferences. The attempt to provide such a defense led Frege to confront the *philosophical* problems that arise in connection with such notions as identity, existence, generality, logical form, truth, sense, reference, object, concept, function, assertion, thought, and judgment.

Logic studies and codifies certain formal, structural properties of thoughts, according to Frege. But 'this would be impossible,' he believed, 'were we unable to distinguish parts in the thought corresponding to parts of a sentence, so that the sentence serves as a model of the structure of the thought' (Frege 1923: 36). Within this perspective, the investigation of language becomes the most fundamental part of any philosophical enquiry into the nature of such diverse notions as those of, say, existence, object, truth, and thought.

4. Logical Syntax

Frege introduced a procedure of analysis, designed to isolate those components of an arbitrary sentence which are responsible for whatever logical powers the sentence possesses. The syntax that results is 'logical,' for 'only that which affects *possible inferences* is taken into account. Whatever is needed for valid inference is fully expressed.'

The procedure of analysis is functorial: it takes sentences and singular terms as complete expressions, and assigns all others to the category of incomplete or functional expressions. All syntactically complex expressions are construed as the values of component functional expressions for other component expressions as their arguments. Predicates, relational expressions, and propositional connectives are thus construed as first-order, and quantifiers as second-order, functional expressions.

5. Semantics

Frege's logical syntax is matched by a 'logical semantics,' which assigns extralinguistic entities of an appropriate kind to expressions of different syntactic categories: truth-values are assigned to sentences; objects to singular terms; truth functions to propositional connectives; second-order functions to quantifiers, and so on. The extralinguistic entity assigned to an expression Frege calls the reference (*Bedeutung*) of that expression; and expressions with the same reference can be intersubstituted anywhere *salva veritate*. Reference, then, is simply what an expression must possess if it is to participate in classically valid deductive inference.

In addition to the notion of reference, Frege's theory of meaning also assigns to expressions of every category a sense (*Sinn*), and to free-standing, unembedded sentences it ascribes a force (*Kraft*). The sense of an expression is both (a) that in virtue of which it has a reference, and (b) the cognitive value of the expression, that is, what is understood by it when one has grasped its meaning or content. The sense of a declarative sentence, for example, is its truth condition; the sense of a proper name is the identity condition of its bearer; and the sense of a predicate expression is its satisfaction condition. The force of a sentence, on the other hand, is what enables one to distinguish between, say, an assertoric, an imperative, and an interrogative occurrence of one and the same sentence type.

See also: Logic: Historical Survey; Names and Descriptions; Sense.

Bibliography

Bell D 1979 *Frege's Theory of Judgement*. Clarendon Press, Oxford

Currie G 1982 *Frege. An Introduction to his Philosophy*. Harvester Press, Sussex

Dummett M A E 1973 *Frege: Philosophy of Language*. Duckworth, London

Frege G 1879 *Begriffsschrift, eine der arithmetischen nachgebildete Formelsprache des reinen Denkens*. Nebert, Halle. Partial trans. in: Geach P T, Black M (eds.) 1970 *Translations from the Philosophical Writings of Gottlob Frege*. Blackwell, Oxford

Frege G 1884 *Die Grundlagen der Arithmetik*. Koebner, Breslau (1950 *The Foundations of Arithmetic*. Blackwell, Oxford)

Frege G 1892 Über Sinn und Bedeutung. *Zeitschrift für Philosophie und philosophische Kritik* **100**: 25–50. Trans. by Black M in: McGuinness B (ed.) 1984

Frege G 1893, 1903 *Grundgesetze der Arithmetik*, Vols. 1 and 2. Pohle, Jena. Partial trans. in: Furth M (ed.) 1964 *The Basic Laws of Arithmetic*. University of California Press, Berkeley, CA

Frege G 1923 Gedankengefüge. *Beiträge zur Philosophie des deutschen Idealismus* **3**: 36–51. Trans. by Geach P T, Stoothoff R H in: McGuinness B (ed.) 1984

Kneale W, Kneale M 1962 *The Development of Logic*. Oxford University Press, Oxford

McGuinness B (ed.) 1984 *Gottlob Frege: Collected Papers*. Blackwell, Oxford

Geach, Peter Thomas

J. van Eijck

Peter Thomas Geach (b. 1916) studied in Oxford and Cambridge and taught in Birmingham and Leeds. His main work is in philosophical logic, the theory of meaning, and the history of logic (Geach 1962, 1972a), but he has also written on logical problems in natural theology and metaphysics (Geach 1977). He has edited and translated the philosophical writings of Gottlob Frege.

Geach's method in logic is to trace back current logical questions to their Fregean, medieval, or even ancient origins. His essays on medieval logic make clear that scholastic logic went into decline not because it was misguided, but because it was too intellectually demanding. Traditional philosophical logic is concerned with arguments from metaphysics and natural theology that are expressed in natural language. Modern formal logic, on the other hand, is mainly inspired by mathematical reasoning. It is hardly surprising, then, that philosophical logic, as practiced by Geach, has at least as much relevance for the semantics of natural language as mathematical logic.

The discussion of 'donkey sentences' (Geach 1962) has provided the semantic community with enough food for thought for many years.

Every farmer who owns a donkey beats it. (1)

Some farmer who owns a donkey does not beat it. (2)

Example (1) is equivalent to the negation of (2). It follows that (1) involves wide scope universal quantification over farmers and donkeys. Thus, the indefinite noun phrase *a donkey* in (1) seems to acquire universal force from the context in which it appears. This poses a problem for a compositional analysis of natural language.

The 'program for syntax' (Geach 1972b)—a plea for polymorphic category to type assignment in categorial grammar—has proved to be prophetic in its prediction of the fruitfulness of a flexible approach to categorial grammar. Geach observes that since the rules of categorial grammar are semantically inspirated, syntacticians would do well to use the flexibility sanctioned by the intended semantics. For example, instead of combining a functor F with a constituent $G(H)$ consisting itself of a functor/argument combination, one may consider F as a functor which first combines with G to form a new functor which then takes argument H. To see that this semantically all right, assume that F, G, H are interpreted as f, g, h, respectively. The semantic effect of the syntax shift is the replacement of function f with a function f^* mapping g to $f \circ g$. In versions of flexible categorial grammar formalisms current in the early 1990s the rule $A/B \to (A/C)/(B/C)$, which reflects the category shift for F, is commonly referred to as the Geach rule.

See also: Categorial Grammar; Donkey Sentences.

Bibliography

Geach P T 1962 *Reference and Generality*. Cornell University Press, Ithaca, NY
Geach P T 1972a *Logic Matters*. Basil Blackwell, Oxford
Geach P T 1972b A program for syntax. In: Davidson D, Harman G (eds.) *Semantics of Natural Language*. Reidel, Dordrecht
Geach P T 1977 *Providence and Evil*. Cambridge University Press, Cambridge
Lewis H A (ed.) 1990 *Peter Geach: Philosophical Encounters*. Kluwer, Dordrecht

Grice, H. P.

P. V. Lamarque

Herbert Paul Grice (1913–1988) was a central figure in post-war Oxford philosophy, working alongside J. L. Austin and P. F. Strawson. In 1967 he moved from Oxford to the University of California, Berkeley, where he remained until his death in 1988. Despite a relatively small published output (his published work is collected in a single volume of essays, Grice 1989), his influence on the development of analytic philosophy of language has been incalculable. This influence resides in two distinct, though ultimately related, contributions: an analysis of 'nonnatural meaning' and a theory of 'conversational implicature.'

The analysis of nonnatural meaning first appeared in a famous paper of 1957 (Grice 1957) where Grice tentatively outlined an account of what became known as 'speaker's meaning.' First, he distinguished 'natural' from 'nonnatural' meaning, the former exemplified by 'Those spots mean measles,' the latter by 'Those three rings on the bell mean that the bus is full'; it was the latter kind he sought to analyze. His ambition was then to explain all cases of nonnatural meaning—including ('timeless') word and sentence meaning—on the basis of an analysis of what an utterer means on an occasion (an 'utterance' need not be linguistic but could encompass gestures, signals, movements, sounds, etc.). The hallmark of the analysis is a distinctive—now called 'Gricean'—reflexive intention. Thus the proposal in its original, most striking and simple, formulation, was this:

> "A meant$_{NN}$ [i.e. nonnaturally] something by x [i.e. some utterance on an occasion]" is (roughly) equivalent to "A intended the utterance of x to produce some effect in an audience by means of the recognition of this intention"
> (Grice 1989: 220)

On that base the derivative notions of 'x meant something' and 'x means$_{NN}$ (timeless) that so-and-so' could be defined. The ramifications of the program were far-reaching: meaning was to be explained in terms of human interaction (and communication) but not on a purely causal foundation; semantics was to be reduced ultimately to psychology; linguistic meaning was to be seen as only a more complex development of a wider species of rational behavior.

However, although the initial insight (the structure of 'Gricean intentions') was broadly welcomed by philosophers of language, a satisfactory working out of the details has proved elusive, both in the analysis of speaker's meaning and its relation to semantic meaning. Several deep-rooted problems had to be addressed, for example, how any but the simplest intentions could be recognized by a hearer without presupposing linguistic conventions (thereby threatening the account with circularity); David Lewis's work on conventions (Lewis 1969) went some way to alleviate this difficulty. There was also a problem in how to characterize the requisite 'effect' or 'response' involved in meaning. A series of putative counterexamples to the sufficiency of the 1957 analysis (Strawson 1964, Searle 1965, Schiffer 1972) led to increasingly recondite qualifications, culminating (in Grice's work) in a version which is worth quoting in full not only to illustrate the immense sophistication of Grice's thinking but also the distance traveled from the original simple intuition.

"*U* meant by uttering *x* that $*_\psi p$" is true iff $(\exists \phi)(\exists f)(\exists c)$:

I. *U* uttered *x* intending *x to be such that* anyone who has ϕ would think that
 (1) *x* has *f*
 (2) *f* is correlated in way *c* with ψ-ing that *p*
 (3) $(\exists \phi')$: *U* intends *x* to be such that anyone who has ϕ' would think, via thinking (1) and (2), that $U\psi$'s that *p*
 (4) in view of (3), $U\psi$'s that *p*;
and
II. (operative only for certain substituends for "$*_\psi$")
 U uttered *x* intending that, *should there actually be* anyone who has ϕ, he would via thinking (4), himself ψ that *p*;
and
III. It is not the case that, for some inference-element *E*, *U* intends *x* to be such that anyone who has ϕ will both
 (1′) rely on *E* in coming to ψ^+ that *p*

(2′) think that (∃φ′): U intends x to be such that anyone who has φ′ will come to ψ⁺ that p *without* relying on E.

(Grice 1989: 114)

Some philosophers have thought that the introduction of refinements of this complexity amounts to a *reductio ad absurdum* of the Gricean approach to meaning. For different reasons, an early prominent supporter of Grice has been led to abandon the program (Schiffer 1987).

Grice's second major contribution to philosophy of language is his theory of 'conversational implicature,' developed in his William James lectures at Harvard University in 1967 but not prepared for publication until several years later. Grice's starting point was a distinction between (i) *what is said*, determined by the semantic properties of the words uttered; (ii) *what is conventionally implicated*, including conventional but not strictly semantic implications; and (iii) *what is conversationally implicated*. Grice's account of this latter species of 'implicature,' which arises not from semantic or other conventions but from general features of discourse, has had enormous influence in pragmatics, speech act theory, and discourse analysis. The basic idea, in summary, is that conversations are governed by a general 'cooperative principle,' subsuming more specific 'conversational maxims,' which, in subtle ways (involving judgments about whether the maxims are being observed or flouted), enable hearers to draw inferences about what speakers intend (beyond what they literally said). A full account of the mechanisms of inference is given in the articles on *Cooperative Principle* and *Conversational Maxims*.

One important philosophical application of the theory of implicature concerns the meanings of *and*, *or*, *if … then*, *not* particularly in relation to the semantics of the logical particles (&, ∨, ⊃, ∼). Grice argued that the apparent divergence between ordinary usage and the truth-functional definitions in classical logic does not amount to a difference in meaning; the conventional or semantic meaning is the same in each case and the connotations of the ordinary language

expressions (e.g., the temporal connotation of *and* as *and then*) could be accommodated as conversational implicatures. This suggests one way in which a division between semantics and pragmatics might be drawn (the former based on austere truth-conditions, the latter drawing on broader principles of rational communication), although Grice's proposal has by no means met universal approval.

It is perhaps a mark of the influence and stature of Grice that the phenomena he characterized are as often as not identified, in theoretical writings, by the use of his name: e.g., 'Gricean intention,' 'Gricean implicature.' Above all, his work is distinctive not just as a body of ideas but as a style of philosophizing.

See also: Conversational Maxims; Cooperative Principle; Meaning: Philosophical Theories.

Bibliography

Grice H P 1957 Meaning. *Philosophical Review* **66**: 377–88

Grice H P 1968 Utterer's meaning and intentions. *Philosophical Review* **78**: 147–77

Grice H P 1969 Utterer's meaning, sentence-meaning and word-meaning. *Foundations of Language* **4**: 1–18

Grice H P 1975 Logic and conversation. In: Cole P, Morgan J L (eds.) *Syntax and Semantics Vol. 3: Speech Acts*. Academic Press, New York

Grice H P 1978 Further notes on logic and conversation. In: Cole P (ed.) *Syntax and Semantics*, vol. 9. Academic Press, New York

Grice H P 1981 Presupposition and conversational implicature. In: Cole P (ed.) *Radical Pragmatics*. Academic Press, New York

Grice H P 1989 *Studies in the Way of Words*. Harvard University Press, Cambridge, MA

Lewis D 1969 *Convention*. Harvard University Press, Cambridge, MA

Searle J R 1965 What is a Speech Act? In: Black M (ed.) *Philosophy in America*. Cornell University Press, Ithaca, NY

Schiffer S 1972 *Meaning*. Oxford University Press, Oxford

Schiffer S 1987 *The Remnants of Meaning*. MIT Press, Cambridge, MA

Strawson P F 1964 Intention and convention in speech acts. *Philosophical Review* **73**: 439–460

Travis C 1991 Annals of analysis. *Mind* **100**: 237–264

Husserl, Edmund

D. Bell

Edmund Husserl (1859–1938) made influential contributions to a wide variety of fields. He was responsible, along with Gottlob Frege, for the rejection of psychologism in logic and the philosophy of language; his investigation of semantic and syntactic categories influenced the development of categorial grammar; he founded the phenomenological movement in philosophy; and his last works exercised a formative influence on the subsequent history of existentialism.

1. Life and Thought

Husserl was born in what is now Prostějov, in the Czech Republic. He studied a variety of subjects at the Universities of Leipzig (1876–78), Berlin (1878–81), and Vienna (1881–83), eventually specializing in mathematics. In 1883 he was awarded a doctorate in mathematics at the University of Vienna. After 1884, however, he fell increasingly under the influence of Franz Brentano, who persuaded him to devote his life to philosophy. After studying with Carl Stumpf in Halle, Husserl completed his Habilitation in philosophy in 1887. Between 1901 and 1916 he taught philosophy at Göttingen University, and from 1916 until his retirement in 1929 he was Professor of Philosophy at Freiburg. He died in Freiburg in 1938.

There are three major phases in Husserl's intellectual development. First, between 1887 and 1907 he worked largely within the Brentanian discipline of descriptive psychology, on problems within logic, the philosophy of language, and the foundations of mathematics. Second, from 1907 until roughly 1930 he developed a phenomenological version of transcendental idealism. According to this theory, the most fundamental explanatory principles in philosophy are to be isolated by examining the essential structures in terms of which meaningful, intentional experience is possible. Finally, in the last years of his life Husserl came to believe that an appeal to individual, self-contained consciousness is incapable of explaining how objectivity is possible. He therefore began to develop a phenomenology that took as primitive, not the solipsistic consciousness of an individual considered in isolation, but rather the shared form of life, the *Lebenswelt,* that comprises the tacit background and foundation of all science, rationality, objectivity, and action.

2. Logic and Language

Husserl's first major, influential work was the *Logical Investigations* of 1900–01. It contains, amongst other things, a detailed and powerful refutation of psychologism in logic; a formal investigation of whole-part theory; a formulation of the principles of categorial grammar, based on an analysis of semantic categories; and a phenomenological theory of linguistic meaning. Within linguistics, Husserl's early work on syntactic categories formed the basis of subsequent developments by Leśniewski, Ajdukiewicz, Bar-Hillel, and others.

Husserl's early theory of meaning shares a number of elements with that of his contemporary, Gottlob Frege. Both, for example, distinguish between an expression, its sense or meaning, and its objective correlate or reference; and both construe the sense of an expression as an abstract entity. They differ, however, in three fundamental respects.

(a) For Husserl the object or reference of an expression is a merely 'intentional' object, rather than a genuine component of the real world. So, where Frege would deny that an expression can refer to a nonexistent object like Sherlock Holmes, Husserl maintains that the expression 'Sherlock Holmes' has both a content or sense, and an objective correlate or reference to which it is directed, namely, the intentional object Sherlock Holmes.

(b) While Frege construes the sense of an expression as an abstract object, that is, as an individual or particular entity, Husserl claims that a sense is a universal or 'species,' the instances of which are particular mental acts of meaning-intention.

(c) Frege's influential context principle, that 'a word only means something in the context of a sentence' is not one to which Husserl could subscribe. On the contrary, his analysis of intentionality—of the object-directedness of conscious mental acts and states—yields the conclusion that nominal acts are prior to, and independent of, propositional ones. Correspondingly, he maintains, isolated subsentential expressions such as singular terms express an intelligible meaning, and possess an objective correlate prior to, and independently of, their occurrence in any sentential context.

3. The Phenomenology of Meaning

Phenomenology, in Husserl's hands, is the study of the essen-tial structures of pure consciousness, as these are revealed directly within experience itself. Pure consciousness, in other words, comprises whatever is immediately given in experience, precisely *as* it is given. Within phenomenology, therefore, neither explicit reference to, nor tacit reliance on, any objects, facts, properties, or laws that in any way transcend consciousness is to be permitted; and the so-called transcendental phenomenological reduction is a device designed precisely to sever all naturalistic connections between pure consciousness, on the one hand, and the extramental world on the other. A phenomenological investigation of pure consciousness reveals, Husserl claims, that the single most important and problematic characteristic of experience is that it is meaningful. Accordingly, in the works of his middle period, and especially in *Ideas* (1913), Husserl's philosophical goal is the explanation of the origin and nature of meaning, of how anything can in principle come to be significant, possess a content, or refer to something beyond itself.

All meaning, he believes, can be traced back to the mind's synthetic activity; for it is only as a result of such activity that experience can be object-directed, that one experience can confirm or falsify another, and that perception and thought, rationality and objectivity are so much as even possible. The most basic structure of meaning he calls the 'noema' of an experience. He explicitly acknowledges, however, that 'the noema is nothing but a generalization of the idea of [linguistic] sense to the field of all acts.'

4. The *Lebenswelt*

In his last, unfinished work, *The Crisis* (1936), Husserl continued his investigations into the nature and origin of meaning. However, like Wittgenstein, who had simultaneously reached strikingly similar conclusions, Husserl came to see that many of the conditions and structures on which meaning depends are not discoverable within an individual consciousness. Rather, they comprise the inherited background of practices, criteria, assumptions, and customs that must be in place if such things as individual thoughts, judgments, perceptions, inferences, and expectations are to make sense. The holistic vision that finally emerges in Husserl's writings is this: not only the expressions of language, but also our intentional mental acts depend for their significance on the vast and hugely complex set of tacitly agreed practices and customs that characterize a given community, that is, on the *Lebenswelt* as a whole. The smallest unit of independent significance, one might say, is an entire form of life; it is with such a whole that any philosophical analysis of meaning must begin.

Bibliography

Bell D 1989 *Husserl*. Routledge, London

Hill C O 1991 *Word and Object in Husserl, Frege and Russell*. Ohio University Press, Athens, OH

Husserl E 1970 (trans. Findlay J N) *Logical Investigations*. Routledge and Kegan Paul, London; original publ. Husserl E 1900-01 *Logische Untersuchungen*. Niemeyer, Halle

Husserl E 1931 (trans. Boyce Gibson W R) *Ideas*. Allen & Unwin, London; original publ. Husserl E 1913 *Ideen zu einer reinen Phänomenologie und phänomenologische Philosophie. Erstes Buch: Allgemeine Einführung in die reine Phänomenologie*

Husserl E 1970 (trans. Carr D) *The Crisis of European Sciences and Transcendental Phenomenology*. Northwestern University Press, Evanston, IL; original publ. Husserl E 1936 *Die Krisis der europäischen Wissenschaften und die transzendentale Phänomenologie: Eine Einleitung in die phänomenologische Philosophie*

Smith D W, McIntyre R 1984 *Husserl and Intentionality*, 2nd edn. *A Study of Mind Meaning and Language*. Reidel, Dordrecht

Sokolowski R 1964 *The Formation of Husserl's Conception of Constitution*. Nijhoff, The Hague

Kripke, Saul

J. A. G. Groenendijk and M. J. B. Stokhof

The American philosopher and logician Saul Aaron Kripke (b. 1940) is considered to be one of the most influential figures in logic and philosophy of language since the 1960s. On a wide range of topics his publications have deeply influenced contemporary thinking in these areas.

Kripke's first contributions were to modal logic, especially to the semantics of modal systems ('Semantical Analysis of Modal Logic' 1963, reprinted in Linsky 1971). Along with that of Rudolf Carnap, Stig Kanger, and Jaakko Hintikka, Kripke's work forms the beginning of so-called 'possible worlds semantics.' The method of possible worlds semantics is one of the most important and fruitful developments in logic and philosophy, and in semantics. In logic, possible worlds semantics provided the necessary tool for a systematic semantic study of the confusing multitude of syntactic systems of modal logic that were developed since the pioneering work of C. S. Lewis in the 1920s. It also turned out to be a useful tool in the philosophy of mathematics (for example in the semantics of intuitionistic logic, and in the study of the notion of provability). Eventually, a whole new branch of logic, called 'intensional logic,' grew out of it, which studies the logical behavior of all kinds of intensional notions, not just modality, but also temporal, deontic, epistemic, and doxastic notions. In the study of the logical structure of these concepts also lies the basis of the philosophical applications of the method: it has been used in the philosophical study of time, existence, knowledge, and so on.

Another important area of research in which possible worlds semantics has been applied very fruitfully is that of semantics of natural language. Possible worlds semantics has been the primary tool of the enterprise of logical grammar since its inception in the work of Max Cresswell, David Lewis, and Richard Montague in the beginning of the 1970s. It forms the heart of the semantical part of Montague Grammar, and still is the most widely applied method in the semantic analysis of natural language in the logical tradition.

Besides his pioneering work in possible worlds semantics, Kripke has also made influential contributions to analytical philosophy, philosophy of language, and philosophy of logic.

In philosophy of logic, his work on truth and the analysis of the liar paradox ('Outline of a Theory of Truth' 1975, reprinted in Martin 1984) has spurred a renewed interest in logical and semantical paradoxes. In particular, attention has turned from the older techniques of neutralizing or avoiding the paradoxes (such as Russell's paradox, the liar paradox), to ways in which they can be incorporated in the semantics of a system as such. Kripke has also made important contributions to mathematical logic.

In analytical philosophy, the lectures which Kripke delivered in Princeton in 1970 (first published in a collection in 1972, in book form as *Naming and Necessity* in 1980), turned out to be nothing less than revolutionary. Overthrowing one of the cornerstones of analytical thinking, the sharp distinction between necessary and a posteriori truths, these lectures form one of the major turning points in the analytical tradition. Its main thesis, that of the rigid designation of names and natural kind terms, which was also explored independently by David Kaplan, Keith Donnellan, and Hilary Putnam, forms a sharp break with the Fregean analyses of these classes of expressions in terms of distinct meaning and reference. Its consequences are far-reaching, but the associated claim that the theory in itself would provide a signifi-cant class of necessary a posteriori truths did not stand up to closer scrutiny (see Salmon 1982).

In philosophy of language, Kripke's major contribution has been his interpretation of the work of the later Wittgenstein. His view is that the latter's *Philosophische Untersuchungen* have to be intepreted as a systematic skeptical attack on the notions of a rule and of rule following, and thereby on the notion of meaning, and that the celebrated argument against the possibility of a private language is simply a particular instance of this all-embracing radical skepticism. This view goes straight against the accepted traditional interpretation of the point and measure of Wittgenstein's later work. Interpretations resembling Kripke's have been proposed independently by other authors (Wright, Fogelin), but it was mainly through Kripke's forcefully argued presentation of this view (first published in a collection in 1980, in book form as *Wittgenstein on Rules and Private Language* in 1982) that it had the impact it had.

See also: Montague Grammar; Names and Descriptions; Natural Kinds; Necessity; Paradoxes, Semantic, Reference: Philosophical Issues.

Bibliography

Kripke S 1980 *Naming and Necessity*. Blackwell, Oxford
Kripke S 1982 *Wittgenstein on Rules and Private Language*. Blackwell, Oxford
Linsky L (ed.) 1971 *Reference and Modality*. Oxford University Press, Oxford
Martin R (ed.) 1984 *Recent Essays on Truth and the Liar Paradox*. Clarendon Press, Oxford
Salmon N U 1982 *Reference and Essence*. Blackwell, Oxford

Meinong, Alexius
D. E. B. Pollard

Alexius Meinong was an Austrian philosopher and psychologist. A pupil of the philosopher Franz Brentano, he is considered to have anticipated many of the concerns and preoccupations of the analytic movement in philosophy, especially in the fields of the philosophies of language and mind. His significance for linguistics resides principally in his systematic investigation of issues in syntax and semantics, and his theory of 'objects.'

1. Elements of the Theory

Meinong starts from the consideration that all thought appears to be directed at, or 'about' some-thing. This directedness has been taken as a constitutive feature of the mental and is standardly known as 'intentionality.' It is reasonable to say that if one thinks, there is (in some sense) something that one is thinking about. Additionally, there is the content of one's thought, what one thinks about the object. However, the objects of thought need not be concrete existing things like trees and tables. It is possible to think about all manner of things without thereby being committed to their existence. Meinong is concerned to explain how it is that we think about one thing rather than another, and this introduces questions of reference and truth. One person may be thinking about unicorns and another about dragons, and while neither of these animals exists, it nonetheless remains true that each person has distinct thoughts and is thinking about distinct things.

It is considerations such as these which motivate Meinong's introduction of a notion of 'object' which is neutral with regard to existence. In other words, on Meinong's account, it makes sense to say that some things exist and some things do not. Trees exist but dragons do not. But all objects have properties. Dragons do not exist, but they do have properties, e.g., breathing fire. There are also objects which do not exist in the sense that trees do, but which are nonetheless real. A paradigm instance would be mathematical objects like numbers: if one is thinking about the number seven that it is prime, then it seems true (a) that there is something being thought about, and (b) that what is being thought about it is true. In Meinong's own terminology, all objects have '*Sosein*' (character, properties) irrespective of whether they have '*Sein*' (being). This even applies to the case of impossible objects such as round squares, which are 'beyond being' (*Außersein*). One can think about the round square, and even in this extreme case, be correct in attributing it a shape.

Meinong distinguishes a further class of object which he calls an 'objective,' which most closely approximates what many philosophers call a 'proposition'—the sort of thing that can have a 'truth-value.' Objectives can be judged to be necessary, probable, or possible.

2. Developments and Ramifications

Almost all of the issues discussed by Meinong can be transposed into the arena of linguistic theory. There is a widely recognized analogy between the content of thoughts and the semantic content of linguistic expressions, and many of the same problems can be discerned in the theoretical debates about language.

Meinong's work is especially relevant to the analysis of what are called 'propositional attitude' constructions of the form 'X thinks (believes, hopes, fears) that . . .' and modal constructions, e.g., 'It is necessary that . . . ,' 'It is possible that . . . .' The analysis of existence and the notion of 'object' have implications for the treatment of quantification in natural language, i.e., of expressions such as 'All' and 'Some.'

Meinong, while showing great sensitivity to the subtleties of natural language, is to an extent prepared to take natural language and its constructions at face value. In this respect, his approach is at marked variance with some mainstream thinking in both philosophy and linguistics. Many philosophers of logic, influenced by the belief that natural language is messy and ill-adapted for the rigors of scientific or philosophical inquiry, have operated with a distinction between 'logical form' and 'grammatical form,' with the implication that the refined language of technical logic should replace ordinary idiom for such purposes. Interestingly, linguistic theorists, conspicuously those working within the paradigm of Transformational Generative Grammar have used the distinction between 'surface structure' and 'deep structure' to mark the discrepancy between the overt forms of natural language expressions and their 'real' structure and meaning. These two approaches led naturally to the equation of deep structure with logical form.

More recently, some logicians have developed new logics in a Meinongian vein which, it is claimed, do more justice to natural language, and are more adequate to deal with discourse about the nonexistent or the impossible.

See also: Fiction, Logic of; Intentionality; Ontology.

Bibliography

Jacquette D 1996 *Meinongian Logic: The Semantics of Existence and Nonexistence*. De Gruyter, Berlin

Meinong A 1960 The theory of objects. In: Chisholm R M (ed.) *Realism and The Background of Phenomenology*. Free Press, Glencoe, IL

Quine W V O 1953 On what there is. In: *From A Logical Point of View*. Harvard University Press, Cambridge, MA

Russell B A W 1905 On denoting. In: Marsh R C (ed.) 1956 *Logic and Knowledge*. Allen and Unwin, London

Parsons T 1980 *Nonexistent Objects*. Yale University Press, New Haven, CT

Putnam, Hilary

D. E. B. Pollard

Hilary Putnam (b. 1926) is a professor of mathematical logic at Harvard University. A pupil of Hans Reichenbach and W. V. O. Quine, he is best-known for his theory of functionalism in the philosophy of mind, and for his views on meaning and reference, although he has contributed widely to debates in the philosophy of science.

1. Language and Meaning

Not untypically for a philosopher, Putnam's views on

language have been heavily influenced by his stance on some major philosophical issues. Originally, he subscribed to what he himself has come to derogate as 'metaphysical realism,' the view which entails commitment to (a) the thesis that the world is determinately constituted and mind-independent, and (b) the thesis that there is one ultimate 'true' story of the world on which science is striving to converge.

One of the principal targets of attack has been the idea that meaning determines reference. More specifically, Putnam has argued that meaning is not a function of, or reducible to, psychological states and processes. Using the notorious fantasy of 'Twin Earth,' he imagines two worlds exactly alike but for the fact that one has water and the other an identical-seeming fluid of very different fundamental constitution. He further imagines two individuals (one for each planet) who are physical and psychological replicas. One speaks English, the other a language syntactically and phonetically identical with English. Each individual describes their experience of the respective fluids in the same way, uttering sentences of the form 'This is water.' But the term 'water' cannot have the same meaning in each case because it has a different reference from planet to planet. As Putnam wittily puts it, 'Either meaning ain't in the head, or meaning doesn't determine reference.' So the meaning of sentences is not to be characterized by procedures of verification but by states of the world. However, assigning truth-conditions to sentences does not uniquely determine what they refer to. Putnam is concerned to pin down how reference is secured, and this requires a shift from the level of sentences to that of terms (e.g., noun expressions). So the question becomes: how is the meaning of terms to be fixed? According to one analysis, ordinary proper names, e.g., 'Sappho,' 'Napoleon,' are abbreviations for 'clusters' of descriptions. Terms for kinds of things, e.g., 'gold,' are similarly accounted for.

Drawing on the work of Saul Kripke, Putnam classifies both sorts of terms as rigid designators, i.e., they pick out the same things in 'all possible worlds.' So, for instance, the term 'Napoleon' picks out the individual necessarily in a way in which the term 'The

Victor of Austerlitz' does not (Napoleon might never have entered upon a military career). For Putnam, what determines reference is a combination of deixis together with the structure of the world. Thus 'gold' rigidly picks out the metal whose nature is investigated by science. On the other hand, reference can be fixed by appeal to descriptions of a certain sort, e.g., for gold by 'yellow, malleable metal which does not dissolve in acid.' The appeal, therefore, is to stereotypes which are collections of ideas (inaccurate or imprecise) associated with the terms. Ultimately, for Putnam, meaning is interactional or social, a feature frequently ignored in most mentalistic accounts.

2. Developments

Putnam has come to reject his earlier realist assumptions, and has modified his views on language. His conclusion is that the theory of reference and the theory of language understanding are not as intimately related as many have thought. Plausibly enough, he argues that one can learn a language without having any sophisticated notion of truth, i.e., one does not need to know that there is a correspondence between words and reality. Rather, he has come to agree with Michael Dummett that understanding a sentence is not equivalent to knowing its truth-conditions, since it is then difficult to make sense of what that knowledge amounts to.

See also: Natural Kinds; Reference; Sense; Sortal Terms.

Bibliography
Putnam H 1978 *Meaning and the Moral Sciences*. Routledge & Kegan Paul, London
Putnam H 1981 *Reason, Truth and History*. Cambridge University Press, Cambridge
Putnam H 1983 *Realism and Reason*, vol. 3. Cambridge University Press, Cambridge
Putnam H 1987 *The Many Faces of Realism*. Open Court, La Salle, IL
Putnam H 1990 *Realism with a Human Face*. Harvard University Press, Cambridge, MA
Putnam H 1992 *Renewing Philosophy*. Harvard University Press, Cambridge, MA

Quine, Willard Van Orman

C. J. Hookway

Willard Van Orman Quine was born in 1908 in Akron, Ohio, and spent his academic career in the Philosophy Department at Harvard University. His earliest published work was in mathematical logic but he also produced many books and articles of the greatest importance for postwar American epistemology and philosophy of language. He was influenced by Rudolf Carnap and other logical positivists, his work sharing their commitments both to empiricism and to the view that the only genuine knowledge is scientific knowledge. However, most notably in the papers published in *From a Logical Point of View* (1953), he rejected the semantic doctrines most characteristic of positivism. From his 1960 book *Word and Object* onward, his work is identified with naturalism, the doctrine that philosophy should be pursued as part of natural science. *Pursuit of Truth* (1990) provides an elegant and concise statement of his overall philosophical position.

1. The Rejection of Analyticity and Intensionality

Quine's writings on language attempt to construct a naturalistic account of linguistic behavior and understanding. 'Two Dogmas of Empiricism,' published in the 1953 collection, attacks the positivist dogma that some statements are analytic, true by virtue of meaning: a plausible example is 'All bachelors are unmarried,' but the positivists extended the idea to include all of mathematics and much more. He claimed that the plausibility of this view rested on the empiricist idea that understanding a sentence involves knowing which experiences would confirm it and which refute it: analytic statements are then those which are confirmed by all observations. In contrast, Quine insisted upon the holistic character of evidence: background beliefs and general theoretical orientation are all implicated when we make predictions on the basis of hypotheses. All that a failed prediction shows is that there is error somewhere in our corpus of beliefs; there is considerable latitude in how we revise our beliefs in order to remove the conflict with experience. We cannot isolate certain implications as guaranteed by the meaning of a sentence.

This leads to a denial that talk of meanings and of intensional notions like property and proposition have any theoretical role in semantics or psychology. Chapter 3 of *From a Logical Point of View* introduces ideas about meaning which become more prominent in later work. Quine's skepticism about the concept surfaces in a consideration of synonymy. 'Synonymy of two forms is supposed vaguely to consist in an approximate likeness in the situation which evokes the two forms': but given the holistic character of the bearing of experience upon opinion, there are obstacles of principle to establishing whether the fact that two speakers produce a sentence in different circumstances is due to their associating different meanings with it or to differences lying elsewhere in their corpus of beliefs. This is the source of Quine's thesis

of the 'indeterminacy of translation,' which denies that there are any objective synonymy relations by claiming that when one tries to translate an unknown language, relying only upon evidence of the linguistic behavior of native speakers, one can construct alternative incompatible translation manuals, there being no fact of the matter which is correct.

2. Naturalism and Semantics

There being no analytic truths to uncover or meanings to analyze, Quine urges philosophers to forsake the search for a priori foundations for meaning and knowledge and be content with psychological explanations of our practices. His writings since 1960 have defended a naturalistic epistemology, sketching a psychological explanation of how theories are related to sensory input and, developing this theme, of our ability to refer to objects in our surroundings. Since he rejects notions like meaning and proposition he is unsympathetic to the kind of cognitive science which explains behavior by reference to inner representations: there is no room for a mentalistic or rationalistic psychology intermediate between the physiological study of the mind and a study of the mind which focuses on behavior. He insists now that in linguistics (but not in psychology) behaviorism is compulsory (Quine 1990: 37–38). This is because one learns language from experience of the extralinguistic world and the linguistic behavior of others; and one's understanding is adequate so long as one's linguistic behavior conforms to that of other speakers.

Quine's philosophical importance does not only lie in these areas. His explanations of the logical structure of the language of science have been influential; and the desire to combat his criticisms of intensionality, modal logic, and mentalistic psychology stimulated many of the developments within those areas since 1960.

See also: Analyticity; Indeterminacy of Translation; Occasion Sentences and Eternal Sentences; Ontological Commitment.

Bibliography

Quine W V O 1953 *From a Logical Point of View*. Harvard University Press, Cambridge, MA
Quine W V O 1960 *Word and Object*. MIT Press, Cambridge, MA
Quine W V O 1969 *Ontological Relativity and Other Essays*. Columbia University Press, New York
Quine W V O 1973 *The Roots of Reference*. Open Court, La Salle, IL
Quine W V O 1981 *Theories and Things*. Harvard University Press, Cambridge, MA
Quine W V O 1990 *The Pursuit of Truth*. Harvard University Press, Cambridge, MA

Russell, Bertrand

R. M. Sainsbury

Russell's most famous contributions to philosophy of language are his theories of names and definite descriptions, developed in the first decade of the twentieth century. Both theories exclude from the category of 'referring expressions' words that might naively have been taken as paradigms of the category, for example 'Bismarck' and 'the first man to walk on the moon.' In this early period, Russell also produced an account of propositional attitudes, which has been taken as a model in recent work. In his later philosophy, starting from the end of World War I, Russell sketched causal theories of meaning that are not dissimilar in approach to some accounts formulated over half a century later.

1. Life and Influence

Bertrand Russell (1872–1970), third Earl Russell, was a prolific writer not only on specialist topics in mathematical logic, epistemology, philosophy of mind, and philosophy of language, but also on a wide range of more popular social and political issues. He was awarded the Nobel Prize for Literature in 1950. His father, Viscount Amberley, was the son of Lord John Russell, the Whig politician who introduced the 1832 Reform Bill; his mother was the daughter of Lord Stanley of Alderley, his godfather John Stuart Mill. For many years, though by no means all his working life, he held a fellowship at Trinity College, Cambridge, where he worked closely with both G. E. Moore and Ludwig Wittgenstein. He collaborated with A. N. Whitehead in the monumental three-volume *Principia Mathematica* (1910–13), an attempted reduction of mathematics to logic, and like Gottlob Frege played a major role in the development and philosophical consolidation of first-order logic. He was the first modern philosopher to see the significance, and potential damage, of logical paradoxes, both in the foundations of mathematics and, more generally, for any systematic, logical theory of language. The main concerns here are his philosophy of language, in particular his accounts of reference, mental content, and meaning.

2. Reference

In his *Principles of Mathematics* (1903), his earliest discussion of semantic questions, Russell was simply unaware of a distinction between meaning and reference, and as a result had trouble with what he called 'denoting phrases' (e.g., 'a man,' 'all men,' 'the man'). Shortly afterwards, and certainly before he wrote the famous 'On Denoting' (1905), he became aware of Frege's distinction between *Sinn* ('sense') and *Bedeutung* ('reference' or 'meaning'), but argued that it was untenable. His agenda was thus to provide a semantic theory that did not make a Frege-like distinction, and yet which did not founder on the problem of denoting phrases.

To lack a distinction between sense and reference is to confront at least two conspicuous problems: there are apparently meaningful terms that do not refer; and there are coreferential but apparently non-synonymous expressions. In his 1903 work, Russell disposes of a range of apparent examples of the first problem by in effect denying that they do not refer. The fundamental semantic relation is that of indicating. Expressions indicate 'terms' (1903: 44), and a proposition is *about* its terms. The expression 'Vulcan' indicates the term Vulcan; there is such a thing (term) as Vulcan but, like many terms, it does not exist (1903: 45). There are more things to refer to than there are things that exist.

In this early work, there is no sign of awareness of the second problem. Rather, what mainly concerned Russell was the difficulty of accommodating denoting phrases within the framework based on the notion of indicating. For example, in the sentence 'I met a man,' the expression 'a man' ought to indicate a concept (a kind of term), but the sentence is not *about* the concept *a man* (1903: 53). A proper account of denoting is thus a crucial difficulty for Russell's aim of basing semantics upon the single notion of reference (indication).

2.1 The Theory of Descriptions

The key part of the solution to the problem is provided by the famous 'theory of descriptions.' Russell argues that denoting phrases are quantifier phrases, and are to be identified not by their actually denoting something, but by their form. In particular, 'the,' applied to a predicate in the singular, functions as a uniqueness quantifier, and sentences of the form 'The F is G' are equivalent to 'There is exactly one F and it is G.' The upshot is that denoting phrases like 'The present King of France' no longer need to refer to, denote, or indicate anything in order to have their proper semantic role. As Russell puts it, they are 'incomplete symbols' and 'have no meaning in isolation' (1905: 42). The last phrase may mislead, as it condenses two thoughts. One is that, whether in isolation or in context, these phrases do not have the semantic role of referring, so that a failure of reference is not a failure of semantic role. The other thought is that the right way to explain their semantic role is to say how they contribute to the meaning (not here equated with reference) of whole sentences in which they occur. His 'On Denoting' (1905) contains a rather creaking attempt to provide standard disquotational clauses for quantifiers.

Russell allows that some denoting phrases denote. For example, a definite description 'the F' denotes if and only if something is uniquely *F*. However, a phrase may be a denoting one without denoting: it is not an expression whose semantic role is to denote. If 'referring expression' means an expression whose semantic role is to refer, Russell's theory of descriptions places definite descriptions outside the category of referring expressions.

The theory is a major step towards permitting the identification of meaning and reference, subject to two restrictions: it is to apply only to genuinely semantically simple expressions, and it is not to apply to the logical constants. This provides solutions to the two problems mentioned earlier. Since the semantic complexity of definite descriptions ensures that they acquire their semantic role derivatively, they are not to be thought of as expressions whose role is to refer to or indicate entities, so there is no problem about meaningful but nonreferring descriptions. Moreover, since definite descriptions are no longer classifiable as referring expressions, there cannot be 'coreferential' definite descriptions, in the way that seemed to ensure synonymy. Of course, there can be codenoting descriptions, but their different semantic structure explains their nonsynonymy.

2.2 The Theory of Names

Both the original problems resurface in connection with apparently simple expressions. Some, like 'Vulcan,' are meaningful yet do not refer; and some pairs, like 'Hesperus' and 'Phosphorus,' are apparently coreferential while apparently nonsynonymous. Russell's solution is to deny that these expressions really are semantically simple. Rather, they are 'truncated' or 'abbreviated' definite descriptions, and the two problems disappear.

However, questions arise about what it could mean to say that a name like 'Vulcan' is 'really' complex and about how could it be settled, given the idiosyncratic nature of the information that people possess about individuals, which description a name abbreviates. Russell gives clear answers to these questions, answers which involve a modification of one standard interpretation of his views.

In his *Problems of Philosophy* (1912), his discussion of names is guided by the 'principle of acquaintance,' according to which one can understand an expression whose semantic role is to refer only if one is acquainted with its referent. Since he held that the only things with which we can be acquainted are sense data and

(perhaps) ourselves, this principle places severe limitations, derived from a source quite different from the two problems mentioned, upon which expressions can be counted as genuine names.

Russell takes the example of the name 'Bismarck,' which Bismarck himself can use as a genuinely semantically simple expression, but which his friends and anyone else cannot, since he is not a sense-datum. When people 'make a judgment about him, the description in our minds will probably be some more or less vague mass of historical knowledge... for the sake of illustration... "the first Chancellor of the German Empire."' The problem is that intuitively we want a stable role for 'Bismarck,' common to speakers and hearers in successful acts of communication, yet this cannot be provided by the idiosyncratic and variable descriptions we associate with a name. Russell's solution is to stress that the story about associated descriptions is intended only to give a correct account of what is in the mind of an individual speaker or hearer. In order to achieve a correct account of communication, one must see Bismarck himself as the common object of the judgments at which speakers are aiming:

> What enables us to communicate in spite of the varying descriptions we employ is that we know there is a true proposition concerning the actual Bismarck, and that however we may vary the description (so long as the description is correct) the proposition described is still the same.
>
> (1912: 31)

A major question in the philosophy of language is how to relate a notion of meaning appropriate to individuating units of communication (what is shared by a speaker and a hearer when they understand one another) and a notion of meaning appropriate to describing the states of mind of individuals when they think, speak, and understand. Russell's theory that many names are really truncated descriptions is clearly located by him as belonging to the latter enterprise and as unsuited to the former. So the many contemporary criticisms of Russell (e.g., Kripke 1980) which take him to hold that for each proper name there is a definite description that specifies the name's invariant contribution to communicative acts have not correctly identified their target. The most with which one could credit Russell is the view that on each occasion a proper name is used, there is a description that accurately represents what is going on in the mind of the user of the name on that occasion.

The difficulty with this weaker view is that it is unclear whether or not it speaks to the original problems of apparently meaningful yet bearerless names, and of apparently coreferential yet nonsynonymous ones. Perhaps the tendency to think of Russell's view as stronger than the texts justify is to be explained by the thought that only a stronger view could hope to resolve these problems.

3. Mental Content

If no distinction is made between meaning and reference, it is natural to see thoughts as involving direct or immediate relations to objects, mirroring the way that the words which can express thoughts relate directly to objects. Thus Russell (1912) analyzes the belief ascription 'Othello believes that Desdemona loves Cassio' as an extensional four-place relation (the belief relation), said to hold between Othello, Desdemona, love and Cassio. (It is necessary to pretend that Shakespeare's story is factual.) Russell insists that judging or believing does not involve ideas. In believing what he does, Othello is directly related to various particulars and universals in the world; the relation is not mediated by ideas, which are dangerous in that they lead to idealism. This explains why Russell was happy to equate meaning and reference: there is no room, in his philosophy at this time, for more than one way of thinking about a single thing. Thought involves an unmediated relation to its object. (This view led in turn to the restriction on the possible objects of thought to sense data.)

The account, which has been an inspiration to many contemporary philosophers (e.g., Salmon 1986; David Kaplan in Almog, et al. 1989), faces two main problems. First, it apparently runs foul of Frege's puzzle. As stated above, Russell would try to avoid this by saying that if the substitution of, for example, 'Phosphorus' for 'Hesperus' really fails to preserve truth value, then the substituted expressions must be descriptions, and not really names.

The other problem is that it is unclear how Russell's theory could be extended to sentences containing logical constants, and this is a problem that he did not address.

4. Later Views on Meaning

In *My Philosophical Development* (1959), Russell says that it was not until 1918 that he 'first became interested in the definition of "meaning" and in the relation of language to fact' (1959: 145). This raises questions, given that the problems of descriptions and names, to which he contributed so much before 1918, seem to be precisely such issues.

In the earlier period, he was content to identify the meaning of a genuinely simple name with its bearer, and leave the matter there. In *The Analysis of Mind* (1921), however, the question is 'not who is the individual meant, but what is the relation of the word to the individual which makes the one mean the other' (1921: 191). What he provides is an account of the conditions under which a speaker has internalized a name–object relation. An example of a sufficient condition for one to understand a word is that one be caused by the impact of that word to do what one would have been caused to do by the impact of what it stands for (1921: 199; 1940: 25). He is right to say that this is a topic, bringing as it does a causal element into meaning, to which he made no attempt to contribute before 1918.

The second way in which Russell's classification of his early work can be understood as not relating to linguistics is that in the early period he often writes as though what matters above all is what is going on in the mind of the thinker, rather than the words which may be used to express this. Hence his willingness to say that ordinary names are 'really' descriptions: as an account of language, thought of as a public vehicle of communication, this would be nonsensical, and, as seen above in connection with 'Bismarck,' Russell would not accept it. However, the view has a chance of being true if it is an account of nonlinguistic entities (Russell often speaks of 'propositions') which are the vehicles of thought.

See also: Names and Decriptions; Reference: Philosophical Issues.

Bibliography

Almog J, Perry J, Wettstein H (eds.) 1989 *Themes from Kaplan*. Oxford University Press, Oxford

Frege G 1892 Über Sinn und Bedeutung. *Zeitschrift für Philosophie und Philosophische Kritik* **100**: 25–50 (1952 On sense and reference. In: Geach P, Black M (eds.) *Translations from the Philosophical Writings of Gottlob Frege*. Basil Blackwell, Oxford)

Kripke S 1980 *Naming and Necessity*, rev edn. Basil Blackwell, Oxford

Russell B 1903 *Principles of Mathematics*. Allen and Unwin, London

Russell B 1905 On denoting. In: Marsh R C (ed.) 1956 *Logic and Knowledge*. Allen and Unwin, London

Russell B 1910 Knowledge by acquaintance and knowledge by description. In: Russell B 1963 *Mysticism and Logic*. Allen and Unwin, London

Russell B 1912 *Problems of Philosophy*. Oxford University Press, Oxford

Russell B 1921 *The Analysis of Mind*. Allen and Unwin, London

Russell B 1940 *An Inquiry into Meaning and Truth*. Allen and Unwin, London

Russell B 1959 *My Philosophical Development*. Allen and Unwin, London

Sainsbury R M 1993 Russell on names and communication. In: Irvine A, Wedekind G (eds.) *Russell and Analytic Philosophy*. University of British Columbia Press, Vancouver

Salmon N 1986 *Frege's Puzzle*. MIT Press, Cambridge, MA

Saussure, Ferdinand de

J. E. Joseph

The Swiss linguist Ferdinand de Saussure (1857–1913) established his reputation at an early age, with his 1878 monograph *Mémoire sur le système primitif des voyelles dans les langues indo-européennes* ('the original vowel system of the Indo-European languages'). The *Mémoire* posited the existence of two Proto-Indo-European 'sonant coefficients' which appeared in no attested forms of the daughter languages, but could account for certain vowel developments which had previously appeared irregular. (Fifty years later an *H* with exactly the distribution of Saussure's sonant coefficients was discovered in Hittite, confirming his hypothesis.) After his 1881 doctoral thesis on the absolute genitive in Sanskrit, Saussure published no more books, only articles on specific topics in historical linguistics.

But in 1907, 1908–09, and 1910–11, he gave at the University of Geneva three courses in general linguistics, a topic on which he never published anything. Soon after his death in 1913, his colleagues Charles Bally (1865–1947) and Albert Sechehaye (1870–1946), appreciating the extraordinary nature of the courses Saussure had given, began gathering what manuscript notes they could find, together with the careful and detailed notebooks of students who had taken one or more of the three courses, especially Albert Riedlinger (1883–1978). From these they fashioned the *Cours de linguistique générale*, published at Lausanne and Paris in 1916. It would become one of the most influential books of the twentieth century, not just for linguistics, but for virtually every realm of intellectual endeavor.

In order to trace the Saussurean agenda of twentieth-century linguistics, this article considers nine key elements of Saussure's view of language. For each a summary is given of the condition prior to Saussure, of Saussure's own view, and of how his view has shaped linguistic inquiry in the years since the publication of the *Cours*.

1. The Establishment of Synchronic Linguistics

At the time of Saussure's lectures, the study of language had been dominated for over 30 years by (a) historical work on the language of written texts (work which had only gradually come to be distinguished from 'philology,' inquiry aimed not at the language but at better understanding of the text itself); (b) dialectological work based on field investigation of local dialects; (c) phonetics, which demanded increasingly minute observation in strong adherence to the positivistic spirit; and (d) psychology, the principal domain of a global perspective on language, dominated by the ideas of Wilhelm von Humboldt (1767–

1835) and his followers, notably Heymann Steinthal (1823–99) and Wilhelm Wundt (1832–1920).

A fifth approach existed—the study of language as a general phenomenon independent of historical or psychological considerations—but it had made little progress since the death of the American scholar William Dwight Whitney (1827–94). Furthermore, the publication of a major study of language in 1900 by the Leipzig experimental psychologist Wundt appeared to signal that the new century would give the 'general' study of language over to psychology.

Saussure's problem was to delineate a study of language that would be neither historical nor ahistorical, neither psychological nor apsychological; yet more systematic than Whitneyan general linguistics, so as to be at least the equal in intellectual and methodological rigor to the historical, psychological, and phonetic approaches. His solution was to make a strong distinction between the study of language as a static system, which he called 'synchronic' linguistics, and the study of language change, which he called 'diachronic' linguistics (or, until 1908, 'evolutive'). Saussure's rejection of the traditional term 'historical' seems to have been based in part on a disdain for the reliance it suggested upon extralinguistic factors and written texts, and in part on a desire for terminological symmetry with 'synchronic.' Synchronic linguistics would henceforth designate the study of language systems in and of themselves, divorced from external considerations of a historical or psychological sort, or any factor having to do with actual speech production.

This is the most sweeping Saussurean change to the agenda of mainstream linguistics: for insofar as twentieth-century linguists have focused their efforts neither on simple description of languages, nor on their evolution, nor on their connection to 'national psychology,' they have realized Saussure's program of synchronic linguistics. Furthermore, historical linguistics has largely become the diachronic enterprise envisioned by Saussure (though the term 'historical' continues in general usage), and even the purely 'descriptive' approaches have been profoundly marked by the Saussurean concept of language as a system where *tout se tient* ('everything holds together'), a phrase often associated with Saussure, though there is no record of his using it in his Geneva lectures. However, it was used in a lecture delivered by Antoine Meillet in 1906 in reference to Saussure's *Mémoire* (see Meillet 1921: 16).

In establishing synchronic linguistics, Saussure was not engaging in an exercise of scholarly exactitude, but serving notice upon psychologists and others that the general study of language should fall to persons with historically based training in specific languages and language families, rather than to experts in the functioning of the mind. Many of Saussure's statements about language can best be understood in conjunction with this need for establishing the autonomy of linguistic inquiry from adjoining fields.

2. The Primacy of Spoken Language

The idea that speech is the original and primal form of language, and writing a secondary imitation of speech, runs counter to the general popular accordance of greater prestige to writing. Yet the primacy of spoken over written language became embedded in linguistics in the early nineteenth century, in connection with the Romantic belief that folk traditions embodied the national spirit more deeply than urban practices like writing, which were more subject to external influences. The trend continued over the course of the nineteenth century as linguistics moved away from philology and became increasingly concerned with the gathering of spoken forms from living dialects. By the turn of the twentieth century few linguists would have disputed that the best source for determining the original form of anything in any language was to reconstruct it from its living descendant dialects, and not from written records surviving from intermediate stages.

Saussure formalized the marginalization of written language as well as anyone, and it is particularly associated with him because he bore the brunt of the 1967 attack on this marginalization by Jacques Derrida (b.1930). For Saussure, writing is not language, but a separate entity whose only 'mission' is to represent real (spoken) language. The 'danger' of writing is that it creates the illusion of being more real and more stable than speech, and therefore gains ascendancy over speech in the popular mind. Derrida demonstrated the irrationality and internal inconsistency of this extreme phonocentrism; in his deconstructionist wordplay, all language is a kind of 'writing' (in a sense that is unique to Derrida).

But so deeply ingrained is this tradition in twentieth-century linguistics that few linguists saw the need to respond to Derrida, whose critique was summarily dismissed. Well over 10 years passed before linguists began to admit that the marginalization of writing had been carried to an irrational extreme; and despite some tentative steps toward a linguistics of writing in various quarters, this tradition of privileging spoken language—shared though not founded by Saussure—is in no danger of passing away.

3. The Object of Linguistics: *Langue* versus *Parole*

The role of the human will in language production has constituted a problem for linguistic thought at least since Plato's *Cratylus*: humans are constrained by the conventions of language, yet it is through language that will and individuality are shaped and realized. Modern science demands the elimination or at least the sublimation of the will from the object of inquiry; and so, human desire, action, and creation came to be excluded from the 'scientific' study of language. This has necessitated a considerable abstraction of language away from its role in human affairs, treating it as if it existed independently of speakers and speech acts. But here two problems arose: (a) the metaphor of language as organism became extremely attractive as a way of talking about language independently of speakers, and as Michel Bréal (1832–1915) complained in the introduction to his *Essai de sémantique* (1897), the metaphor was taken literally by many people, giving rise to gross misunderstandings; (b) Wundt's *Völkerpsychologie* ('national psychology') seemed to offer a more sophisticated way of dealing with linguistic phenomena: it eliminated the metaphysical abstraction of 'language,' but replaced it with still less satisfactory explanations based on the 'spirit of peoples,' which were untestable, and could not sustain any approach to language that was detailed or systematic.

Saussure's contribution was to dissect the total phenomenon of language (*langage*) into (a) actual speech production (*parole*), including the role of the individual will, and (b) the socially shared system of signs (*langue*) that makes production and comprehension possible. Although he spoke of a linguistics of *parole* that would cover the phonetic side of language and the products of individual will, Saussure made it clear that the linguistics of *langue* is the essential, real linguistics. *Langue* is beyond the direct reach of the individual will. Saussure's formulation is both a defense and a refinement of the procedures of traditional grammar and historical linguistics, yet at the same time it stakes out an autonomous realm for general linguistic inquiry.

Despite much debate among scholars as to just what Saussure meant by *langage*, *langue*, and *parole*, the distinction has held firm throughout twentieth-century linguistics. It has been suggested that certain work in stylistics (e.g., by Saussure's disciple Bally) and in discourse pragmatics constitutes an attempt at a linguistics of *parole*, but it is not yet clear how any aspect of language, once it is systematized, fails to enter the sphere of *langue*. The human will remains in exile from linguistics, and *langue* (naturally somewhat evolved from Saussure's original conception of it) continues to be the object of study of virtually every approach to which the name 'linguistics' is accorded.

4. *Langue* as a Social Fact

Saussure's insistence upon the social nature of *langue* grew during the years in which he lectured on general linguistics, largely at the expense of psychologically based considerations. Again, this may be tied in part to the need to establish synchronic linguistics independently of the dominant post-Humboldtian psychological establishment. The young science of sociology embodied the spirit of positivism, with which it shared the same recognized founder, Auguste Comte (1798–1857). Positivism was coming to be equated with scientificness in general thought, making classical psychology appear old-fashioned and metaphysical. For the sociologists, Wundt's *Völkerpsychologie*, based on non-empirical generalizations (and more akin to what today would pass as philosophy of mind) was already unacceptably passé.

Much ink has been spilled regarding the degree to which Saussure's conception of language was directly influenced by work in sociology, particularly by Emile Durkheim (1858–1917) and Gabriel Tarde (1843–1904). Saussure's former student and lifelong intimate Antoine Meillet (1866–1936) was closely allied with Durkheim and his journal *L'Année sociologique*; and there is often a close correspondence between Saussure's and Durkheim's use of terms like 'social fact' and 'collective consciousness.' But since Saussure never cites Durkheim or Tarde (he was after all teaching a course, not writing a book), support for any claim of direct influence is lacking.

In Saussure's view, *langue* is a 'treasury' or 'collection of impressions' that is 'deposited' in identical form in the brain of each member of a given speech community. He uses the metaphor of a dictionary, of which every individual possesses an identical copy. What the individual does with this socially-shared system falls entirely into the realm of *parole*. This distinction (which was not yet clear to Saussure at the time of his first course in general linguistics of 1907) differentiates Saussure's dichotomy from that between 'competence' and 'performance' established in the 1960s by Noam Chomsky (b.1928). Chomsky explicitly related competence with *langue* and performance with *parole*, though in actual fact the analogy was only partial: for Chomsky, competence (derived from innate universal grammar) is mental and individual, and performance the locus of its social actuation. Furthermore the considerable differences between Saussure's orientation toward language as a semiotic system and Chomsky's toward competence as a mental faculty make any such equations difficult.

Saussure's views on the social nature of language have had a great resonance in linguistics and many other fields. By the mid-1930s it was commonplace to equate 'synchronic linguistics' (indeed, 'scientific linguistics') with 'social linguistics,' and to include under this heading the work of Meillet and his many European disciples, including Alf Sommerfelt (1892–1965) and Joseph Vendryes (1875–1960); the American structuralists Leonard Bloomfield (1887–1949) and Edward Sapir (1884–1939); and even the 'social behaviorists' (or 'pragmatists') John Dewey (1859–1952) and George Herbert Mead (1863–1931). Bloomfield in particular exploited the power of the social as an antidote to the psychological (or 'mentalist')

approach at the time of his conversion from Wundtian social psychology to empirical behaviorism. Beginning in the 1940s dialect geographers such as Raven McDavid (1911–1984) began to realize the crucial importance of social factors in linguistic production; around the same time, the sociologist Paul Hanly Furfey (1896–1992) began training students jointly in the techniques of social class measurement and descriptive linguistics. By the early 1950s inquiry combining empirical sociological and linguistic techniques was underway, to be refined significantly by William Labov (b.1927) and others in the 1960s.

In terms of Saussurean traditions, sociolinguistics pursues the Saussurean view of the social nature of *langue*, while Chomskyan generative linguistics (to which sociolinguistics has stood in irreconcilable contrast for a generation) pursues the Saussurean view of the mental and abstract nature of *langue*. An eventual reconciliation of this split—to which a deeper understanding of Saussure's thought may provide a clue—would constitute a major breakthrough in the understanding of language.

5. *Langue* as a System of Signs: Semiology

The semiological conception of language as a collection of signs (a sign being understood as the collation of a signifying word and a signified concept) was anticipated in the philosophy of Aristotle (384–22 BC), elaborated by the Stoics, and reached its summit in the 'speculative grammar' of the twelfth century. But starting in the fourteenth century, the view of language as a sign system began to cede pride of place to that of language as a social institution, an approach more characteristic of Plato (ca. 429–347 BC), the diffusion of whose works defines the new era of humanism that led to the Renaissance. The semiological perspective was never entirely lost, and would resurface notably among the seventeenth-century British empiricists. But the 'conventional' perspective with which it coexisted periodically overshadowed it, and the early nineteenth century was one such period, when abstract systems disembodied from human activity ceased to be of central interest.

As noted in Sect. 3, abstraction and disembodiment would reemerge as part of the 'scientific' spirit of the later nineteenth century; and it is thus no great coincidence that the 'semeiotic' perspective on language was reopened independently by Charles Sanders Peirce (1839–1914) in the USA. Peirce's work in this area, like Saussure's, went unpublished during his lifetime, and was not seriously revived by philosophers until the 1930s. Only in the 1950s and 1960s were attempts made at unifying Saussurean 'semiology' (practiced mostly by European linguists) and Peircean 'semeiotics' (practiced mostly by American philosophers) into a single paradigm, under the organizational leadership of Thomas A. Sebeok (b.1920).

For Saussure, the network of linguistic signs which

constitute *langue* is made up of the conjunction of a *signifiant* ('signifier'), understood as a sound pattern deposited in the mind, and a *signifié* ('signified'), a concept that is also deposited in the mind. Saussure compares them to the front and back of a single sheet of paper. It is important to note that the signifier is wholly distinct from the actual uttered word, as is the signified from the actual physical thing conceived of (if one exists). Although the distinction between concept and object has existed since antiquity, that between sound pattern and actual sound is Saussure's own contribution, of which some have seen a foreshadowing in the hypothetical 'sonant coefficients' of his early *Mémoire*.

Saussure predicted that *sémiologie*—the study of signs both within and outside of language—would have linguistics as its 'pilot science' (a further challenge to psychology, for the semiological domain is precisely where language is most explicitly mental), and indeed this came to pass in the founding of modern semiotics discussed above. But while linguistics has furnished the paradigmatic model for semiotics, the impact of semiotic inquiry upon linguistics has been slow in coming. M. A. K. Halliday's (b.1925) view of language as 'social semiotic,' an attempt to combine two key elements of the Saussurean heritage, is together with its offshoots the one branch of linguistics in which a real impact is discernible.

Yet Saussure's sign theory has also profoundly affected linguistics through the nearly universal acceptance of his concept of the signifier as an abstract sound pattern. This view became the cornerstone of the concept of the phoneme as elaborated by Jan Baudouin de Courtenay (1846–1929) and Mikołaj Kruszewski (1851–87) in Russia, and subsequently by N. S. Trubetzkoy (1890–1938) in Vienna and Roman Jakobson (1896–1982) in Brno and Prague; Daniel Jones (1881–1967) in the United Kingdom; and Kenneth L. Pike (b.1912) in the USA, to name only the most prominent figures. It resulted in the marginalization of experimental phonetics in favor of more abstract phonology, based not upon physical differences of sound, but on the ability to distinguish between concepts (see Sect. 8). The distinction between a physical 'etic' level (from phon*etic*) and an abstract 'emic' level (from phon*emic*) would be extended to every level of linguistic structure, and would become a hallmark in particular of postwar American linguistics.

6. The Arbitrariness of Linguistic Signs

As with the semiological nature of language, the arbitrariness of language—the fact that a signifier like the series of sounds /p a i/ has no internal connection with the concept of a 'pie' which it signifies—reflects an ancient doctrine that had never fallen very far from the center of debate about the nature of language up through the end of the eighteenth century. Though not a direct concern for most of the historical linguists of the nineteenth century, the ancient debate between *physis* 'nature' and *nomos* 'convention' in the establishment and operation of language had been revived by Whitney and the Humboldtian psychologists, with Whitney's views of language positioned on the side of *nomos* and the Humboldtians' on the side of *physis*. Saussure, who at age 21 had met Whitney and greatly admired his work, doubtless encountered the debate there.

Saussure's precise formulation of the linguistic sign allows him to situate arbitrariness—which he called the 'first primary concept' of linguistics—precisely at the conjunction of signified and signifier, just as presented in the first sentence of the preceding paragraph. This represented an advance over most earlier formulations of arbitrariness, which (despite Aristotle) focused upon the relationship between the sign as a whole and the real-world objects conceptualized in the signified. Unfortunately, the *Cours* is not consistent in its presentation of arbitrariness, and quickly falls back into the older schema. Another problem with the presentation in the *Cours* is that the arbitrariness doctrine is first encountered in radical form in a very tense, strongly worded, and memorable section; then only later is this tempered with a section on relative arbitrariness which is often ignored, but without which Saussure's conception of language is inaccurately understood. Saussure's point in the later section is that while signifiers are always arbitrary relative to signifieds, they can be motivated relative to other signifiers. Thus, for example, the French numbers *dix-neuf* '19' and *vingt* '20' both show arbitrariness between signifier and signified, yet *dix-neuf* is motivated relative to the numerals *dix* '10' and *neuf* '9' which compose it, hence *dix-neuf* is relatively arbitrary while *vingt* is radically so. (This is connected to Saussure's distinction between syntagmatic and associative relations, discussed in Sect. 8.) Cases of onomatopoeia, where there seems to be a motivated relationship between signifier and real-world analogue, are dismissed as not really part of linguistic systems.

The fact that the *Cours* presents the radical version of arbitrariness first and most forcefully led to its assuming the status of dogma in twentieth-century linguistics (though undoubtedly it also appealed to something deeper in the Zeitgeist). It is one of the first views of language to which budding linguists are exposed in introductory courses and textbooks, often as one of the design features of language identified in 1958 by Charles Hockett (b.1916). Like most dogmas, the radical form of arbitrariness is counterintuitive and requires a certain faith beyond what reason can sustain. Also, it is not always observable in the practice of those who preach it, particularly because of the influence of Jakobson, who beginning in the early 1930s mounted a sustained attack on radical arbitrariness through his work on markedness, child language acquisition, and aphasia, which suggested that linguistic elements differ in naturalness. Jakobson was to have a significant impact upon Chomsky, Joseph Greenberg (b.1915), and many others, with the result that language is not treated as exhibiting anything like the radical arbitrariness of the dogma. Besides Jakobson, arbitrariness was problematized by Louis Hjelmslev (1899–1965), Emile Benveniste (1902–76), and numerous others in a series of attacks on and defenses of the Saussurean view (often poorly represented) appearing from 1939 to 1947.

7. The Linearity of Signifiers

After arbitrariness, the second primary principle of linguistics for Saussure is that linguistic signifiers are 'linear,' in the sense that, because they have a temporal existence, they represent a dimension that is measurable only as a line. This is one of the more mysterious of Saussure's ideas, in that he never made clear to what he was opposing it (he notes that it is obvious to everyone, but that its implications have not been appreciated). Linearity is part of what distinguishes spoken language as 'real' language, as opposed to writing, a secondary representation that is not necessarily linear (see Sect. 2); and it is what allows us to analyze connected discourse into meaningful units. One also detects a hedging on the inherent psychologism of the semiological view of language as consisting of perfectly juxtaposed signifiers and signifieds: Saussure here insists that signifiers exist in a completely separate dimension.

This principle, which is perhaps related to the theories of Condillac (1714–80) on how language organizes thought, has given rise to many interpretations. Jakobson formulated his doctrine of distinctive features in phonology—the idea that phonemesare not monoliths, but consist of bundles of features existing simultaneously—as part of a critique of the linearity of the signifier. Others have argued that Saussure's principle is not in disharmony with the concept of constituent features, but rather was intended (a) to deny the accumulation of signifiers, not their decomposition (a distinction which depends upon what one classifies as a signifier); (b) to insist that, however constituted, signifiers cannot be conceived apart from the dimension of time; and (c) to prepare the ground for the introduction of syntagmatic relations.

8. Syntagmatic and Paradigmatic Relations: *Langue* as Form, not Substance

Saussure distinguished between the 'syntagmatic' relations a linguistic element has with the elements preceding and following it in an utterance, and 'associative' (now usually called paradigmatic) relations it has to other elements with which it shares partial identity, but which do not occur in the particular utterance at hand. For example, in the sentence *Crime pays* the element *crime* has a syntagmatic relationship with *pays* that determines, among other things, their order relative to one another and the fact that *pays* has the inflectional -*s*. At the same time, *crime* has paradigmatic relations with countless other elements, including the inflectionally related *crimes*, the derivationally related *criminal*, the conceptually related *misdemeanor* (and the conceptually opposite *legality*), and the phonetically related *grime*. As the last example suggests, each sound of the word *crime* /kraim/ has paradigmatic and syntagmatic relations with at least the sounds around it: /k/ is paradigmatically related to the /g/ that could in principle replace it; and syntagmatically related to the following /r/, since in English the presence of /k/ as the initial element of the word immediately restricts the following sound to /l r w/ or a vowel.

Saussure notes that the two types of relations, which correspond to different types of mental activity, contribute in different ways to the 'value' of the sign. In particular, the paradigmatic relations generate a negative value: the identity of the /r/ in /kraim/ is essentially that it could be, but is not, /l w/ or a vowel. This is important because the actual sound that represents /r/ can differ dramatically from one English dialect to another (being rolled, flapped, retroflex, etc.); but the actual sound content does not matter, so long as /r/ is kept distinct from the other sounds to which it is associatively related. *Langue*, Saussure insisted, is form, not substance.

Before Saussure, the syntagmatic relations of morphemes within a given utterance were certainly recognized as a matter of linguistic concern, though relatively neglected. But there was little or no precedent for the idea suggested by the *Cours* that there exists a syntax not only of words, but of sounds, meanings, and the relations uniting them; or that every time a sound, word, or meaning is chosen, a vast network of related elements is summoned up in absentia. The latter concept in particular set the study of language on a new course of abstraction that did not rely on psychological theorizing, but remained internal to language.

In many ways, the Saussurean notion of paradigmatic and syntagmatic relations would become the hallmark of twentieth-century linguistics: first, because it proposed that a single principle of structure unites all the levels at which language functions— sound, forms, and meaning; second, because it suggested a way of analyzing language that would not depend on a simple listing of elements with their 'translation' into either another language or some sort of philosophical interpretation. Elements could henceforth be analyzed according to the relations they maintained with other elements, and the language could be understood as the vast system—not of these elements—but of these relations. This was the point of departure for structuralism.

To a large extent, the distributional method developed by Bloomfield is a working out of this Saussurean notion, with special emphasis on the paradigmatic relations. With the work of Bloomfield's follower Zellig S. Harris (1909–92) the syntagmatic relations assumed a status of equal importance, and with Harris's student Chomsky, overriding importance. (Regarding word order, Saussure's view is that the syntagmatic relations constitute that part of syntax which is predetermined—like the use of a 3rd person singular verb form after the singular subject *crime*—and so a part of *langue*; while the rest of syntax, being subject to free combination, is relegated to *parole*.)

9. The Systematicity of *Langue:* Structuralism

Certainly the most wide-reaching Saussurean intellectual tradition, both within and outside of linguistics, derived from Saussure's characterization of *langue* as a wholly self-contained network of relationships among elements which, as discussed above, have no positive content or value, but only the negative value generated by their differing from one another. Like most of his contemporaries, when Saussure thought of language he thought first of sounds and their combinations, and extrapolated outward from that level. The study of sounds had for several decades been a battleground between those who, later in the twentieth century, would be called the 'phoneticians,' proponents of a positivistic belief that the key to understanding language lay in ever more precise measurement of sound waves and vocal apertures; and those who would now be called 'phonologists,' who preferred to operate on a more abstract (and traditional) plane, dealing with classes of sounds rather than the minute differences within classes. But the phoneticians were steadily gaining prestige, since their positivistic approach had the characteristic look of modern science.

As noted in Sect. 4, Saussure was attracted to positivism, but within limits. If psychology represented the Scylla of hyperrationalism, experimental phonetics was the Charybdis of hyperempiricism. Perhaps excessive empiricism represented the greater danger to him, for whereas he never attempted a complete divorce of language from the domain of the mind, his characterization of *langue* as a network of pure relations, of form and not substance, succeeded in marginalizing phonetics to the point that within a few decades it would retreat to the position of an auxiliary discipline to linguistics. The term *phonème*, used by Saussure as early as 1878 (five years after its coinage by A. Dufriche-Desgenettes, 1804–79) to denote an abstract unit representing sound, but never actually defined by him, was taken up by Baudouin de Cour-

tenay and Kruszewski and joined to an essentially Saussurean conception: 'phoneme' became the name for Saussure's abstract mental sound pattern, identifiable as the minimal unit of sound capable of changing the meaning of a signifier in a language. It eventually became the basis for further, related new concepts: the morpheme (coined by Baudouin de Courtenay) or moneme (minimal unit of meaning), tagmeme (minimal meaningful unit of syntax), toneme, and so on.

The full implications of Saussure's view of *langue* were realized in Prague, principally by Trubetzkoy, who elaborated complete phonological schemata for a panoply of languages from all over the world; and Jakobson, who extended the implications of 'functional' phonology to other domains of linguistic (and literary) inquiry. But strikingly similar projects were underway in other quarters: in the USA with Bloomfield, who saw himself as at least partly under the influence of Saussure (in a 1945 letter he described his major work *Language* as showing Saussure's influence 'on every page'); in Denmark, with the overtly Saussurean glossematics of Hjelmslev; in France, where Meillet had transmitted the Saussurean perspective to a whole generation of students, including André Martinet (b.1908); Gustave Guillaume (1883–1960); and Benveniste. All the lines of affiliation among these 'schools' are not yet clear. But their work came to define the mainstream of linguistics in the twentieth century, and all of it assumes the conception of *langue* set out in the *Cours*.

The idea that language forms a self-contained system justified the autonomy of linguistic study not only vis-à-vis phonetics, but every other discipline as well, including psychology, anthropology, and sociology (the latter, again, was never deemed a threat). The only discipline under whose aegis it hypothetically fell was semiology, but even had semiology existed, the status of linguistics as its pilot science meant that it yielded its autonomy to no other field. The origins of 'structuralism' are generally traced to turn-of-the-century work by the Anglo-American psychologist E. B. Titchener (1867–1927). But by the period between the 1940s and the 1960s when most fields of human knowledge came under the domination of structuralism, it had come to be seen as the extrapolation out of linguistics of Saussure's concept of *langue* as a self-contained system of syntagmatic and paradigmatic relations among elements of negative content. Its most widely heralded application was in the field of anthropology, by Claude Lévi-Strauss (b.1908), who discovered Saussure in 1942 in a course taught by Jakobson. Other areas and their most prominent structuralist practitioners include, in biology, Ludwig von Bertalanffy (1901–72) and C. H. Waddington (1905–75); in literary theory, Roland Barthes (1915–1980); in Marxist theory, Louis Althusser (1918–90); in mathematics, 'Nicholas Bourbaki' (the pseudonym of a group of French mathematicians); in psychoanalysis, Jacques Lacan (1901–79); and in psychology (where Titchener's concept of structure had long since been replaced, for example by the concept of *Gestalt*), Jean Piaget (1896–1980). The rejection of structuralism by such figures as Jacques Derrida and, to a lesser degree, Michel Foucault (1926–84), became tied up with the French student revolts of 1968, launching the 'poststructuralist' era, whose very name indicates that the Saussurean tradition remains an active force even when shaping the direction of reactions against it. Meanwhile, the sociology of Pierre Bourdieu (b.1930) remains a powerful model with arguably as many structuralist as poststructuralist features.

Within linguistics, the effects of poststructuralist thought are only beginning to be felt; the field in which structuralism began is the last to let it go. Precisely at midcentury the great British linguist J. R. Firth (1890–1960) was able to state that 'Nowadays, professional linguists can almost be classified by using the name of de Saussure. There are various possible groupings: Saussureans, anti-Saussureans, post-Saussureans, or non-Saussureans.' As we approach the twentieth century's end, the only change one is tempted to make to Firth's statement is to remove 'non-Saussureans,' as it is doubtful that any survive. All work on or against language as an autonomous, self-contained system—and this includes work in generative grammar, universal–typological linguistics, discourse pragmatics,

and sociolinguistics—is pursuing some aspects of the Saussurean agenda.

Bibliography

Aarsleff H 1982 *From Locke to Saussure*. Athlone, London
Culler J 1986 *Ferdinand de Saussure*, 2nd edn. Cornell University Press, Ithaca, New York
Engler R 1968/1974 *Edition critique du Cours de linguistique générale de F. de Saussure*. Harrassowitz, Wiesbaden
Gadet F 1989 *Saussure and Contemporary Culture*. Hutchinson Radius, London
Harris R 1987 *Reading Saussure*. Duckworth, London
Holdcroft D 1991 *Saussure: Sign, Systems and Arbitrariness*. Cambridge University Press, Cambridge
Joseph J E 1988 Saussure's meeting with Whitney, Berlin, 1879. *Cahiers F. de Saussure* **42**: 205–13
Joseph J E 1998 Structuralist linguistics: Saussure. In: Glendinning S (ed.) *Edinburgh Encyclopedia of Philosophy*. Edinburgh University Press, Edinburgh
Koerner E F K 1973 *Ferdinand de Saussure: Origin and Development of his Linguistic Thought in Western Studies of Language*. Vieweg, Braunschweig
Koerner E F K 1988 *Saussurean Studies/Etudes saussuriennes*. Slatkine, Geneva
Meillet A 1921 *Linguistique historique et linguistique générale*. Champion, Paris
Saussure F de 1916 *Cours de linguistique générale*. Payot, Lausanne
Saussure F de 1922 *Recueil de publications scientifiques*. Sonor, Geneva
Saussure F de 1983 (trans. Harris R) *Course in General Linguistics*. Duckworth, London

Strawson, Peter Frederick

D. E. B. Pollard

Sir Peter Frederick Strawson (b. 1919) was Waynflete Professor of Metaphysical Philosophy at Oxford from 1968 to 1990. Although associated with what has come to be known as 'linguistic philosophy,' he has done much to stimulate interest in traditional problems, not least through his work on Kant. Nonetheless, it is his contributions to the philosophy of language that are outlined here.

1. Background and Orientation

On the issue of meaning, Strawson discerns two basic types of approach: (a) that of formal semantics, and (b) that of theorists of 'communication-intention.' In seeing meaning as arising from what we do with language, he identifies with the second of these

approaches, evincing a longstanding skepticism about the capacity of logical formalisms to capture the nuances of informal reasoning and natural language generally. However, he has shared many of the preoccupations of the formal semanticists, especially those to do with truth and reference.

2. Reference and Truth

In an early paper (Strawson 1950), Strawson criticized Bertrand Russell's theory of descriptions and its underlying semantics. Russell assumed singularly referring expressions as a fundamental category. But given that there are instances of proper names in ordinary language which lack reference, he was committed to a strategy of dispensing with such problematic expressions using the formal apparatus of quantification. For Strawson, Russell's error was the conflation of the use of an expression to make unique reference with the assertion that there is just one object possessing certain characteristics. The meaning of an expression cannot be identified with its purported referent. Additionally, Russell overlooked the fact that it was not sentences, properly speaking, which are true or false, but rather the assertion or proposition they are used to state. In his later criticism of Quine, Strawson reiterated his doubts about the eliminability of singular terms, since they played a vital role in identifying the topic of discourse for the purposes of communicating facts about it. A condition of successful reference is that it is presupposed that there is some known description under which the identified object falls. This view contrasts with causal theories, where successful reference may obtain without such knowledge.

Interestingly, it was in opposition to a fellow Oxonian, John Austin, that Strawson ventured his own account of truth. Austin had sought to rehabilitate the correspondence theory in terms of conventions linking words to the world. Strawson maintained that saying that a statement was true was tantamount to endorsing it, i.e., expressing agreement. In taking this stance, Strawson once again showed his preoccupation with the question of how expressions are used, and of the presuppositions behind that use.

3. Problems and Ramifications

Strawson introduced a notion of presupposition according to which a statement A presupposes a statement B, if, and only if, A is neither true nor false unless B is true. To take the example from the critique of Russell: if there is no King of France, the statement 'The present King of France is bald' has no truth-value, and the question of its truth 'does not arise.' There has been a sizable literature in linguistics on the subject of presupposition, and some doubt over whether it is either well-defined or distinct from logical entailment. Moreover, there has been much debate since the time of Frege over whether sentences with nonreferring subject terms make statements which lack truth-value, or else fail strictly to make statements at all.

See also: Presupposition; Presupposition, Pragmatic; Reference: Philosophical Issues; Truth.

Bibliography

Strawson P F 1950 On referring. *Mind* **59**; repr. in Flew A (ed.) 1956 *Essays in Conceptual Analysis*. Macmillan, London
Strawson P F 1952 *Introduction To Logical Theory*. Methuen, London
Strawson P F 1959 *Individuals*. Methuen, London
Strawson P F 1971 *Logico–Linguistic Papers*. Methuen, London

Tarski, Alfred

F. Veltman

Alfred Tarski, one of the greatest logicians of the twentieth century, was born in Warsaw, Poland, on January 14, 1902. His family name was Tajtelbaum. Tarski studied mathematics, biology, philosophy, and linguistics at Warsaw University. In 1924 he received his PhD under the guidance of Lesniewski. He was appointed docent at the University of Warsaw in 1926 and adjunct professor shortly afterwards.

In 1939, while Tarski was on a lecture tour of the United States, World War II broke out and as a consequence he decided not to return to Poland. For a time he taught at Harvard University, then at the City College of New York. Later he became a member of the Institute for Advanced Study in Princeton. In 1942 he was appointed lecturer at The University of California at Berkeley, where he became a Full Professor

in 1946. He stayed in California until his death on October 27, 1983.

1. Mathematics

From the beginning of his career, Tarski enjoyed great fame. At first his reputation was due mainly to his work on mathematics and its foundations. Throughout his lifetime mathematics would remain his main interest. He wrote on general algebra, set theory, (un)decidability, algebraic logic, pure and applied model theory, and geometry. An exhaustive survey of his work can be found in *The Journal of Symbolic Logic*, vol. 51. In most of his writings Tarski explored areas not investigated before.

Tarski published his first paper on problems connected to the axiomatization of the well-ordered sets (1921). Throughout the 1920s set theory remained the main subject of his publications. His work on the foundations of mathematics, however, involved him in the study of metalogical notions like 'true sentence,' 'logical consequence,' and 'undefined concept.' As a result he embarked on a new series of papers of which the most important was the one published in 1933 under the title *Pojęcie prawdy w językach nauk dedukcyjnych*.

2. Truth

In this monograph Tarski seeks to provide a concept of truth suitable for scientific and mathematical purposes, that is, a concept of truth which, unlike its everyday counterpart, is free of inconsistencies. His analysis of 'truth' sets out with the following example:

'It is snowing' is true if and only if it is snowing.   (1)

A distinction is made between a language L, the one containing 'It is snowing,' and a language L', which contains sentence (1). It is supposed that the latter can be used to talk about L. In particular this means that L' is assumed to be rich enough to express the truth and falsity of sentences of L. A possible definition in L' of a true sentence of L can be called *adequate* if all of the (possibly infinitely many) sentences of L' having the same form as (1) are provable in L'. Given this, the question can now be asked in a rigorous fashion whether or not an adequate definition of truth for sentences of L in L' can be given .

Tarski gives two answers to this question. Assume, to begin with, that L and L' are identical. That is, suppose a language is capable of expressing its own truth predicate, as is natural language. Then, for any proposed definition of truth, there is a sentence of the form of (1) that can be disproved in L. Hence, no adequate definition of truth can be given in L.

Second, suppose L' includes second-order logic over L and Peano–Arithmetic. Then an adequate definition of a 'true sentence' in L *can* be given in L'. To prove this, Tarski first tackled the more general problem of defining satisfaction. Using satisfaction, other semantic notions like 'definable relation' and 'logical consequence' are then easily defined.

3. Paradox

Tarski's first result pertains to a semantic paradox that had distressed philosophers of language as well as scientists for quite some time. Consider the following famous sentence, known as the liar sentence:

This sentence is false.   (2)

In the languages of deductive sciences such sentences are really dangerous, because of the possibility of proving anything from a single contradiction. Tarski's solution is based on the clear distinction between the language to be described, the object language, and the language of description, the metalanguage. It is obvious that a sentence is true or false only as a sentence of a language. One can eliminate the paradox above by observing that whatever language L the reference of the expression 'this sentence' belongs to, the sentence that 'this is not a true sentence of L' does not belong to L but to its metalanguage, say L'.

An important appendix was added to the German translation of this monograph (entitled *Der Wahrheitsbergiff in den formalisierten Sprachen*) in which Tarski showed how to extend his method to languages not respecting the basic principle of the Lesniewski–Ajdukiewicz theory of semantic categories, especially to the language of the Zermelo–Fraenkel set theory.

4. Influence

Tarski's writings have had—and still have—a tremendous influence on various areas of fundamental research. His method of defining metalogical concepts, as well as the model–theoretical techniques he developed, are among the foundations of contemporary logic. Tarski's famous book *Logice matematycznej i metodzie dedukcyjnej* (1936) has been the basic textbook of logic for decades all over the world. It is translated into a dozen languages. The English translation appeared in 1941 under the title *Introduction to Logic and to the Methodology of Deductive Sciences*.

The importance of Tarski's work for what is, in the 1990s, known as formal semantics is also hard to overestimate. Contemporary research into truth-conditional semantics, and model-theoretic semantics, as well as investigations into the analysis of truth and semantic paradox can be traced back directly to Tarski's work on metalogical concepts, especially his theory of truth.

See also: Formal Semantics; Paradoxes, Semantic; Truth.

Bibliography

Givant S R, McKenzie R N (eds.) 1981 *The Collected Works of Alfred Tarski*, vols. i–iv. University of California, Berkeley, CA
Tarski A 1956 *Logic, Semantics, Metamathematics*. Clarendon Press, Oxford

Wittgenstein, Ludwig

C. Travis

Ludwig Wittgenstein, arguably the most original and influential philosopher of the twentieth century, took up philosophy as a vocation in 1911, having first studied engineering. His choice was prompted by interest in the philosophy of mathematics, a subject on which he lectured and wrote extensively until the end of his life. He also wrote extensively, over long periods, on philosophy of mind, epistemology, and other areas. This article concentrates on his philosophy of language. No area in Wittgenstein's philosophy can be called the foundation, or core, of all the rest. There are many mutual dependencies. His philosophy of language, for example, cannot get started without the proper epistemology—one that can only be understood completely in the light of the resultant view of language. But in Wittgenstein's treatment of language there are keys to much of the rest.

1. The Influence of Frege and Russell on Wittgenstein's Early Work

In his first years in philosophy, Wittgenstein was greatly influenced by ideas of Gottlob Frege and Bertrand Russell, changing earlier Schopenhauer-inspired views. (On choosing philosophy, he visited Frege, who directed him to Cambridge to study with Russell.) Two leading ideas of Frege and Russell were fundamental to Wittgenstein's early views, as epitomized in *Tractatus Logico–Philosophicus* (completed in 1918), although they also remained important in his later work: the idea of 'logical form' and the idea of an 'ideal' language.

1.1 Logical Form

The idea of 'logical form,' and relatedly 'logical analysis,' is roughly this: for each meaningful proposition (one that actually says something in particular to be so), or thought (one that is actually of things being in some definite way), or any proper component of these, there is a unique true logical form which it really has—a way that is constructed out of some unique stock of constituents, where the rules by which it is thus constructed show the contribution each constituent makes to what the whole says, and to what it requires for truth. Logical form may be discovered by thoroughgoing logical analysis which involves, for each bit of an expression, examining the systematic effect of its presence or absence on the conditions of which the whole would be true. Wittgenstein extended these ideas by arguing that a fully analyzed, simple proposition, if it is meaningful, will picture a possible state of affairs with which it shares a form, and also

that all complex meaningful propositions are truth–functions of simple 'atomic' propositions. The paradigm for a successful search for logical form was taken to be Russell's analysis of sentences containing definite descriptions (in Russell 1905), which became a sort of oblique manifesto for those who thought discovering such form to be the main business of philosophy.

1.2 An Ideal Language

The other leading idea, strongly promoted by Frege, was that of an ideal language 'suitable for scientific purposes.' Such a language would, first, be totally without ambiguity. So it would never call for disambiguation. What this seems to mean is: the question whether some bit of it is to be understood in this way or that could never arise as a question to be resolved by some fact outside of the language itself. Any such question would be decided uniquely and effectively by the properties already conferred on the language's bits in setting it up, or in specifying which language it is; all this while for any bit, since it has a semantics, there is such a thing as 'the way in which it *is* to be understood.' (One might see in this Frege's fondness for *tertium non datur* elevated to a creed.)

So an ideal language is a sort of self-propelled linguistic perpetual motion machine: everything it does, it does quite independently of outside help, or of any surroundings in which it might occur. If P is one of its predicates, and V an arbitrary item, then P is true of V or it is not, with no thanks to us, or to anyone; and quite apart from anyone's reactions to P. That is the sort of meaning conferred on P by its place in the ideal language; and it is what having a proper meaning would look like.

One might regard such an ideal language as a 'language of thought(s),' provided one understands that in an appropriately Fregean, nonpsychologistic way. The point is not that the language is realized in the brain, though in fact Frege sometimes seems committed to that too (see Frege 1918: 26). The point is this: consider the maximally expressive ideal language that it is humanly possible to construct, or to grasp. Then each thought that we can think, each thing that we can state, will be said by exactly one item in that language, which, conversely, will say nothing *but* that. (Thoughts here are logical, not psychological, objects; individuated by the situations of which they would be true.) Since an ideal language is completely perspicuous, the item will reveal what the structure and essence of that thought really is.

Natural language, being defective, may fail to be univocal: there may fail to be any one thing fixed by the ideal language which is correctly said to be the thought some natural sentence expresses. Still, Frege insists, we may understand such a sentence in one way or another, as saying this or that. Any of us, on hearing it, may take it to state thus and so, even if, strictly speaking, it does not univocally do that. The maximal ideal language reveals what we do in doing that: it exhibits all the understandings it is possible to have, the ways in which words may be understood, in taking them to say something in particular. To take them to say something specific to be so is always to associate them with an item in that language. That is the sense in which it is a language of thought, or better, of thoughts.

Wittgenstein's early interest centered on the question of what an ideal language would be like, leading him to another early and abiding interest: the bounds of sense, or the distinction between sense and nonsense. Both ideas are prominent in the *Tractatus*. Within the picture just sketched, a sentence of one of our defective natural languages expresses nonsense just in case there is nothing in the maximal ideal language which says what it does, if anything. In that case, there is nothing which it says, or says to be so. To express nonsense is to express, and say, exactly nothing. The interesting sort of nonsense is that where, so to speak, 'syntax outstrips semantics'; we produce words which seem grammatically in order, but they lack the semantic properties they must actually have if they are to say something. That notion is central in Wittgenstein's later, as well as in his early, philosophy. But in the later philosophy he has very different ideas as to the specific causes of such failure.

In 1914, Wittgenstein entered the Austrian army. In 1918 he became a prisoner of war in Italy. Between 1919 and 1929, he remained quasi-retired from the philosophical arena. He returned to Cambridge in 1929 with a new view of philosophy and of language; with ideas in terms of which the old leading ideas may be seen as false ideals. (It is important to keep in mind that, like any philosopher, Wittgenstein had to struggle with, and thereby develop, the new ideas. He did not always see clearly what they were, and certainly did not see the *same* thing in them from 1929 on. Nor did he always have the words, or the uses of them, to state those ideas perspicuously, whether to himself or to others. To think otherwise would be idolatry.)

2. Wittgenstein's Later Work on Language

The old leading ideas remained central to Wittgenstein's later philosophy, though his new concern was to exhibit in detail what is wrong with them. Thus, for example, he aims to show exactly why it is wrong 'to think that if anyone utters a sentence and means or understands it he is operating a calculus according to

definite rules' (*Philosophical Investigations*, Sect. 81). Or why it is not 'as if our usual forms of expression were, essentially unanalyzed, as if there were something hidden in them that had to be brought to light ... as if we were moving towards a particular state, a state of complete exactness; and as if this were the real goal of our investigation' (Sect. 91). Or exactly what the mistake is in the following:

> '*The essence is hidden from us*': this is the form our problem now assumes. We ask: '*What is* language?,' '*What is* a proposition?' And the answer to these questions is to be given once and for all; and independent of any future experience.'
>
> (Sect. 92)

Wittgenstein was also guided continuously during his later period by another thought, which G. E. Moore reports as follows:

> One chief view about propositions to which he was opposed was ... that a proposition is a sort of 'shadow' intermediate between the expression ... and the fact ... he said ... [this view] was an attempt to make a distinction between a proposition and a sentence .... it regarded the supposed 'shadow' as something 'similar' to the fact in question; and he said that, even if there were such a 'shadow' it would not 'bring us any nearer to the fact,' since 'it would be susceptible of different interpretations ...'... 'No interpolation between a sign and its fulfillment does away with a sign.' He said ... 'the expression of an expectation contains a description of the fact that would fulfill it,' pointing out that if I expect *to see a red patch* my expectation is fulfilled if and only if I do *see a red patch* ....
>
> (Moore 1959: 260–61) (Compare Sects. 95, 429)

Wittgenstein's rule was thus: do not try to solve a problem by drawing technical distinctions between different types of items that might bear semantic properties, as between 'proposition' and sentence, or between concepts and predicates. He had various reasons for the rule. The one that matters here is that the same sorts of problems which arose for the original items (words, for example, which may bear various understandings) are bound to arise for the newly introduced items as well; fresh items are not the means for solving problems. That rule, combined with his insights about the false Fregean/Russellian ideals just discussed, yielded a truly radical approach to semantics, and to understandings.

2.1 Naming and Meaning

To see what the new view is, we should look at the beginning of the *Philosophical Investigations*. Here Wittgenstein's first concern is, ostensibly, with the relation between naming and meaning. (Meaning thus and so is what words of a language do. Though Wittgenstein sometimes uses 'meaning,' or a word that so translates, to apply to words as used on a particular occasion, here he does not.) Take the English word 'blue.' We might say that that names a certain color, namely, blue. What is the relation between its doing that and its meaning what it does? Perhaps, for it to do that just *is* for it to mean what it does; in saying that it names the color blue, one states exactly what it means. (What extra fact should one mention? What fact not determined by that one is determined by what 'blue' means?)

But if that is so, as it seems to be, then Wittgenstein's next question arises. What has all that—either what it means or what it names—got to do with the standards for its correct use or, inter alia, with what it would be true of? Here Wittgenstein uses his notion of a language game to make the point. (A language game is defined by its rules. By contrast with actual words, it is thus explicit which rules set its standards of correctness for words and responses that are moves in it.) A language game is an object of comparison: we may sometimes view some properties of our words as modeled in one or another such game. There is no such thing as 'the language game we are playing' in speaking given words (see Sects. 81, 130). That a word, e.g., 'blue,' names what it does is compatible with its figuring in an indefinite variety of language games, with indefinitely many different, and sometimes conflicting, standards of correctness. So its naming what it does does not settle what it could truly apply to.

Now all of these remarks about what naming does not do apply intact to meaning. That 'blue' means what it does does not fix what it would be true of. Take the sky. Is it blue? If you said so, in the wrong surroundings, someone might be very disappointed when he looked at it for the first time from close up, in an airplane. Sometimes it counts as blue—in some surroundings, for some purposes—and it is then true to say that it is blue. Sometimes it does not so count, and it is false to say so. What changes from one case to another is not what 'blue' names, nor what it means. Throughout it speaks of the color blue, and does so by and in meaning what it does.

By now, the above point has been widely taken, even by those who, not long ago, still thought that meanings of words could be stated by specifying what they were true of. The most usual way of assimilating the point is to echo J. L. Austin in saying that an English sentence is precisely not what can be true or false (it doesn't say anything), then positing some other item (a thought, a proposition) that may be. The point then becomes: an English sentence expresses different thoughts on different speakings, an English predicate different concepts, etc. But a thought has just the sort of truth condition a sentence was originally supposed to.

2.2 Semantic Properties and Occasion-sensitivity

It is just here that Wittgenstein's second guiding idea—the avoidance of 'shadows' between us and the world—leads to major innovations. The principle is: do not try to solve the problem (accounting for vari-

ation in what words with fixed meaning say) by postulating new bearers of semantics, since the same problem will arise for them. They, too, will be governed by different standards of correctness in different surroundings. (We cannot cancel out the sign.) If we are debarred from this solution, what solution remains? The answer is to treat semantic properties as normal properties, on a par with ground-level ones. Consider the property of being blue. Having it, we have just seen, is, or may be, an occasion-sensitive affair. Sometimes the sky counts as having it, sometimes it does not. Now shift to the property of being true, or true of the sky. If that behaves normally, then having it is an occasion-sensitive affair too. Whatever the semantic item—say, a sentence—if that item may ever count as having that property, then the basic state of affairs is: in some circumstances it would, in others it would not. More generally, the having of a semantics (some set of semantic properties) is an occasion-sensitive affair: which semantics an item counts as having varies with the occasions for counting it as having, or lacking, any.

If an item may count, in different surroundings, as having different semantics, then something more than just the item's occasion-independent nature is required for fixing which semantics it counts as having in any given surroundings. The surroundings must help, of course. But, Wittgenstein points out, there being a result depends also on there being such a thing as the reasonable way of understanding the item, or assigning it a semantics, in those surroundings. Facts as to what is reasonable depend, in some way, on facts about us, beginning with the simple fact that we are very often capable of seeing what is reasonable. Without the right background of facts about users, or treaters, or evaluators, of an item, there would also be no facts as to the semantics it counted, in given surroundings, as having.

If the above sort of sensitivity to occasions or surroundings is intrinsic to semantic properties, thus a feature of any item that has a semantics, then the Fregean ideal language is ruled out. Any language would be, necessarily, dependent on the reactions of us, or its users, for the semantic facts about it, particularly those about its applications, being what they are. Languages cannot, in principle, be self-propelled, as they would be on Frege's view.

Wittgenstein argues for the pervasiveness of semantic occasion-sensitivity in two ways: first in his discussion of rules and what they require (see especially Sects. 84–7); and second in the private language discussion (roughly Sects. 243–72). The first is a direct argument, relying on facts as to the conceivable ways of specifying which rule a given rule is. Any specification leaves at least conceivable doubts as to whether in this case, this, or perhaps rather that, would be in compliance with the rule. ('Can't we imagine a rule determining the application of a rule, and a doubt which *it* removes—and so on?' (Sect. 84).) The private language discussion proceeds by stripping away the background of a user's reactions (except for a degenerate and futile case: the lone private linguist), and examining what happens. The upshot is that a language that got along entirely on its own steam would be no genuine language at all. No intelligible language could, in principle, conform to Frege's ideal.

3. More General Issues

With this outline of a new view, some questions that run persistently through all of Wittgenstein's philosophy will now be addressed. First, perspicuity. Wittgenstein remarks in a different connection: 'It is so difficult to find the beginning, Or better: it is difficult to begin at the beginning. And not try to go further back' (*On Certainty*, Sect. 471). We may always make fresh demands for further perspicuity, pushing the identification of an understanding farther back. But if we do so indefinitely, we will never arrive at anything. We are not en route to the Fregean ideal. So:

> It is not our aim to refine, or complete, the system of rules for the use of our words in unheard-of ways.
>
> For the clarity that we are aiming at is indeed *complete* clarity. But this simply means that the philosophical problems should *completely* disappear.
>
> (Sect. 133)

Within or without philosophy:

> an explanation serves to remove or avert a mis-understanding—one, that is, that would occur but for the explanation; not every one that I can imagine.
>
> (Sect. 87)

Complete perspicuity is achieved by our ordinary explanations (inter alia of meaning or content) when they achieve their goal; that is, when they leave no real or live doubt as to whether what was said/meant is this or that. Perspicuity so conceived is, of course, an occasion-sensitive affair.

Finally, nonsense. Nonsense, on this view, comes in many varieties. The most significant one is this. The view is that words depend on their surroundings, or the facts of their speaking, for bearing the sort of semantics words would bear where they said this or that to be so. Their mere semantics (meaning) as words of such and such language (say, English) is not enough for them to do this. The English sentence, 'The sky is blue,' viewed merely as an English sentence, in total abstraction from surroundings, says nothing in particular to be so. There could be no such thing as isolating those states of affairs which would be: things being as that sentence, so viewed, says things to be. For though 'is blue' speaks of being blue, there are various 'sometimes-correct' ways of counting such things as the sky as being, or failing to be, that. Meaning alone does not show which of these ways to rely on in evaluating the truth of those words. We must rely on surroundings to show this—typically those of a speaking—or the project of evaluation cannot begin.

There is, then, a substantive burden on the surroundings in which words are used. Since it is a substantive one, some surroundings may fail to provide what is needed from them (see Sects. 117, 501, 514, 515). Words spoken in such surroundings may be fully grammatical and meaningful. Their semantics may be perfectly coherent. They will still have said nothing to be so, or at least nothing could count either as their being true or as their being false. This is a new conception of a way in which syntax may outstrip semantics: not by outrunning it entirely, nor by getting words paired with an incoherent or internally contradictory semantics (the English sentence is not incoherent), but rather by outrunning the situations in which words would have an adequate semantics—notably, adequate for evaluating them as to truth. This sort of nonsense is what one produces by ignoring the contribution surroundings must make, or by failing to foresee how surroundings may fail to do so. Since philosophers tend to overlook the ways in which their words depend for their semantics on surroundings, assuming that a meaningful sentence, used any old time, will say something, this is one typical sort of philosophical nonsense. It is epitomized not by patently opaque and turgid metaphysical prose, but rather by a philosopher who, clutching his nose says, 'I know I have a nose,' or, pointing at the ground, 'I am here,' or who, for no reason, remarks, 'Hamburger is red'—or who, for no reason, says of Jones, whose accomplishments he has briefly sketched, 'Jones understands the words "Aardvarks live in Africa".'

The profound implications of Wittgenstein's views on language and meaning have been felt in nearly all areas of philosophy from, for example, philosophy of science to ethics and aesthetics. A ceaseless outpouring of commentary and debate followed his death in 1951 and not only his ideas but many of his illustrative terms—'picture' from his early work or later 'game,' 'form of life,' 'family resemblance'—have become common currency in discussions of language.

See also: Family Resemblance; Language Game; Logical Form; Names and Descriptions; Picture Theory of Meaning; Private Language.

Bibliography

Cavell S 1979 *The Claim of Reason*. Oxford University Press, Oxford

Kenny A 1973 *Wittgenstein*. Harvard University Press, Cambridge, MA

McGuinness B (ed.) 1967 *Ludwig Wittgenstein und der Wiener Kreis*. Blackwell, Oxford

Pears D 1988 *The False Prison*. Oxford University Press, Oxford

Rhees R (ed.) 1981 *Recollections of Wittgenstein*. Oxford University Press, Oxford

Travis C 1989 *The Uses of Sense*. Oxford University Press, Oxford

Wittgenstein L 1956 (trans. Anscombe G E M) *Remarks on the Foundations of Mathematics*. Blackwell, Oxford

Wittgenstein L 1958 *The Blue and Brown Books*. Blackwell, Oxford

Wittgenstein L 1961 (trans. Pears D, McGuinness B) *Tractatus Logico–Philosophicus*. Routledge and Kegan Paul, London

Wittgenstein L 1967 (trans. Anscombe G E M) *Philosophical Investigations*, 2nd edn. Blackwell, Oxford

Wittgenstein L 1969 (trans. Paul D, Anscombe G E M) *On Certainty*. Blackwell, Oxford

Wittgenstein L 1974 (trans. Kenny A) *Philosophical Grammar*. Blackwell, Oxford

Wright von G H *Wittgenstein*. University of Minnesota Press, Minneapolis, MN

List of Articles

Titles are listed in alphabetical order along with their author(s) and corresponding page number.

List of Contributors

Contributors are listed in alphabetical order together with their affiliations. Titles of articles which they have written follow in alphabetical order, along with respective page numbers. Co-authorship is indicated by *.

DEKKER, P.J.E.* (Amsterdam University, Amsterdam, The Netherlands)
Situation Semantics: 376

D'AGOSTINO, F. (University of New England, Armidale, NSW, Australia)
Foundations of Linguistics: 23

FISHER, A. (University of East Anglia, Norwich, UK)
Natural Deduction: 281; *Reasoning*: 294

FLETCHER, P. (University of Reading, Reading, UK)
Language Acquisition in the Child: 64

FORBES, G. (Tulane University, New Orleans, LA, USA)
De Dicto/De Re: 316; *Necessity*: 284

FRICKER, E.M. (University of Oxford, Oxford, UK)
Davidson, Donald: 512; *Radical Interpretation*: 168

GARNHAM, A. (University of Sussex, Brighton, UK)
Representation, Mental: 74

GROENENDIJK, J.A.G.* (Amsterdam University, Amsterdam, The Netherlands)
Kripke, Saul: 520

GUNDEL, J.K. (University of Minnesota, Minneapolis, MN, USA)
Shared Knowledge: 84

GUTTENPLAN, S.D. (University of London, London, UK)
Logic, Historical Survey: 269

HAACK, S. (University of Miami, Coral Gables, FL, USA)
Deviant Logics: 256

HENDRICKS, H.L.W.* (Amsterdam University, Amsterdam, The Netherlands)
Categories and Types: 313; *Situation Semantics*: 376

HOOKWAY, C.J. (University of Sheffield, Sheffield, UK)
Indeterminacy of Translation: 119; *Occasion Sentences and Eternal Sentences*: 286; *Ontological Commitment*: 33; *Peirce, Charles Sanders*: 497; *Quine, Willard Van Orman*: 523

HORWICH, P.G. (University College London, London, UK)
Truth: 198

HOUSEHOLDER, F.W.† (Indiana University, Bloomington, IN, USA)
Aristotle and the Stoics: 475; *Plato and his Predecessors*: 499

ITKONEN, E. (Helsinki, Finland)
Hermeneutics: 116

JANSSEN, T.M.V. (Amsterdam University, Amsterdam, The Netherlands)
Compositionality of Meaning: 102; *Meaning Postulate*: 150; *Montague Grammar*: 344

JOSEPH, J.E. (University of Maryland, College Park, MD, USA)
Saussure, Ferdinand de: 528

KEMP, J.A. (University of Edinburgh, Edinburgh, UK)
Humboldt, Wilhelm von: 482

KEMPSON, R.M. (University of London, London, UK)
Semantics versus Syntax: Shifting Perspectives on Natural Language Content: 370

ROWE, M.W. (University of York, York, UK)
Language Game: 126

SAGE, V.R.L. (University of East Anglia, Norwich, UK)
Metaphor in Literature: 156

SAINSBURY, R.M. (University of London, London, UK)
Russell, Bertrand: 525

SALMON, P.B.† (University of Edinburgh, Edinburgh, UK)
Herder, Johann Gottfried: 481

SANCHEZ VALENCIA V. (Amsterdam University, Amsterdam, The Netherlands)
Aristotle and Logic: 250; *Mill, John Stuart*: 495

SELLS, P.* (Stanford University, Stanford, CA, USA)
Anaphora: 207

SEUREN, P.A.M. (University of Nijmegen, Nijmegen, The Netherlands)
Donkey Sentences: 220; *Presupposition*: 359; *Sign*: 244

SHALKOWSKI, S. (University of Leeds, Leeds, UK)
Truth Conditions: 203; *Verificationism*: 44

SMITH, P.T. (University of Reading, Reading, UK)
Thought and Language: 85

STAAL, F. (University of California, Berkeley, CA, USA)
Indian Theories of Meaning: 120

STEEDMAN, M. (University of Pennsylvania, Philadelphia, PA, USA)
Categorial Grammar: 301

STEINHART, E.* (State University of New York, Stony Brook, NY, USA)
Metaphor: 151

STERELNY, K. (Victoria University of Wellington, Wellington, New Zealand)
Reference: Philosophical Issues: 234

STOKHOF, M.J.B.* (Amsterdam University, Amsterdam, The Netherlands)
Kripke, Saul: 520

TALBOT, M.M. (Preston, UK)
Relevance: 445

TAYLOR, T.J. (College of William and Mary, Williamsburg, VA, USA)
Locke, John: 488

THOMAS, J. (University of Wales, Bangor, UK)
Conversational Maxims: 388; *Cooperative Principle*: 393

THREADGOLD, T. (University of Sydney, Sydney, NSW, Australia)
Literary Structuralism and Semiotics: 129

TRAVIS, C. (Univerity of Stirling, Stirling, UK)
Family Resemblance: 113; *Innate Ideas* 52; *Private Language*: 70; *Wittgenstein, Ludwig*: 537

VAN DER DOES, J. (Amsterdam, The Netherlands)
Intension: 329; *Intensionality*: 332; *Possible Worlds*: 355

554

Name Index

Subject Index

569